Encyclopedia of
AFRICAN HISTORY AND CULTURE

Encyclopedia of
AFRICAN HISTORY
AND CULTURE

VOLUME V

INDEPENDENT AFRICA

(1960 TO PRESENT)

R. Hunt Davis, Jr., Editor

A Learning Source Book

☑®
Facts On File, Inc.

Encyclopedia of African History and Culture,
Volume 5: Independent Africa (1960 to Present)

Copyright © 2005 by The Learning Source, Ltd.

A Learning Source Book
Editorial: Brian Ableman, Christopher Roberts,
Bodine Schwerin, Ismail Soyugenc

Facts On File, Inc.
132 West 31st Street
New York NY 10001

Library of Congress Cataloging-in-Publication Data

Page, Willie F., 1929–
  Encyclopedia of African history and culture / edited by Willie F. Page; revised edition edited by
R. Hunt Davis, Jr.—Rev. ed.
    p. cm.
  "A Learning Source Book."
  Includes bibliographical references and index.
  ISBN 0-8160-5199-2 ((set ISBN) hardcover)
  ISBN 0-8160-5269-7 (vol. I)–ISBN 0-8160-5270-0 (vol. II)–
  ISBN 0-8160-5271-9 (vol. III)–ISBN 0-8160-5200-X (vol. IV)–
  ISBN 0-8160-5201-8 (vol. V)

  1. Africa—Encyclopedias. I. Davis, R. Hunt. II. Title.
  DT3.P27 2005
  960'.03—dc22
                          2004022929

For my students who have gone on to teach
about the African past and present

CONTRIBUTORS

General Editor

R. Hunt Davis, Jr., Ph.D., is professor emeritus of history and African studies at the University of Florida. He received a Ph.D. in African studies from the University of Wisconsin, Madison. Dr. Davis is an expert on the history of South Africa, African agricultural history, and the history of education in Africa. His published works include *Mandela, Tambo, and the African National Congress* (1991) and *Apartheid Unravels* (1991), along with numerous articles and book chapters. He served as director at the University of Florida Center for African Studies and is also a past editor of the *African Studies Review*.

Senior Authors

Agnes Ngoma Leslie, Ph.D., outreach director, Center for African Studies, University of Florida

Richard R. Marcus, Ph.D., assistant professor, Department of Political Science, University of Alabama, Huntsville

James Meier, Ph.D., adjunct assistant professor of history, University of Florida

Dianne White Oyler, Ph.D., associate professor of history, Fayetteville State University

Leah A. J. Cohen, M.A., graduate student in geography, University of Florida

Other contributors

Mohammad Alpha Bah, Ph.D., professor of history, College of Charleston; Brian Hollingsworth, doctoral student in African history, University of Florida; Bo Schwerin, M.A., creative writing, Johns Hopkins University

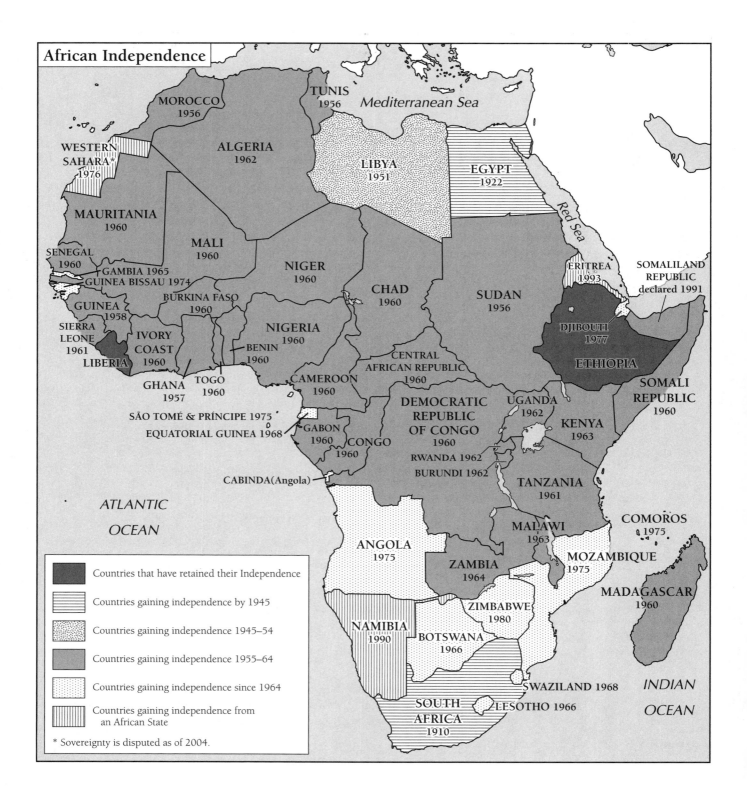

African Independence

MOROCCO 1956

TUNIS 1956

Mediterranean Sea

WESTERN SAHARA* 1976

ALGERIA 1962

LIBYA 1951

EGYPT 1922

Red Sea

MAURITANIA 1960

SENEGAL 1960

GAMBIA 1965

GUINEA BISSAU 1974

MALI 1960

NIGER 1960

CHAD 1960

SUDAN 1956

ERITREA 1993

SOMALILAND REPUBLIC declared 1991

BURKINA FASO 1960

GUINEA 1958

SIERRA LEONE 1961

LIBERIA

IVORY COAST 1960

BENIN 1960

NIGERIA 1960

CENTRAL AFRICAN REPUBLIC 1960

DJIBOUTI 1977

ETHIOPIA

SOMALI REPUBLIC 1960

GHANA 1957

TOGO 1960

CAMEROON 1960

SÃO TOMÉ & PRÍNCIPE 1975

EQUATORIAL GUINEA 1968

GABON 1960

CONGO 1960

DEMOCRATIC REPUBLIC OF CONGO 1960

UGANDA 1962

RWANDA 1962

BURUNDI 1962

KENYA 1963

CABINDA(Angola)

TANZANIA 1961

ATLANTIC OCEAN

ANGOLA 1975

ZAMBIA 1964

MALAWI 1963

MOZAMBIQUE 1975

COMOROS 1975

MADAGASCAR 1960

NAMIBIA 1990

ZIMBABWE 1980

BOTSWANA 1966

SWAZILAND 1968

SOUTH AFRICA 1910

LESOTHO 1966

INDIAN OCEAN

Countries that have retained their Independence

Countries gaining independence by 1945

Countries gaining independence 1945–54

Countries gaining independence 1955–64

Countries gaining independence since 1964

Countries gaining independence from an African State

* Sovereignty is disputed as of 2004.

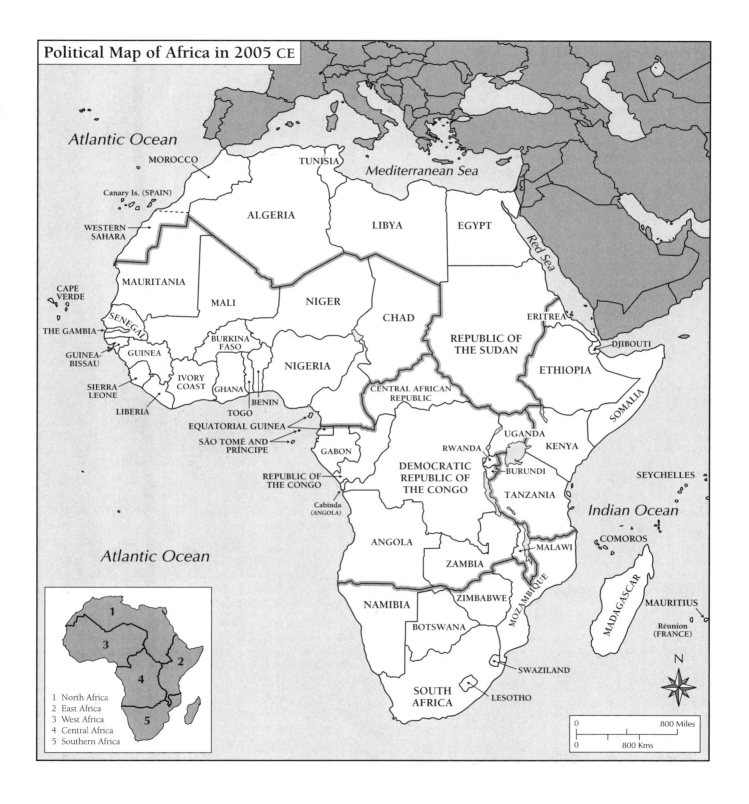

Political Map of Africa in 2005 CE

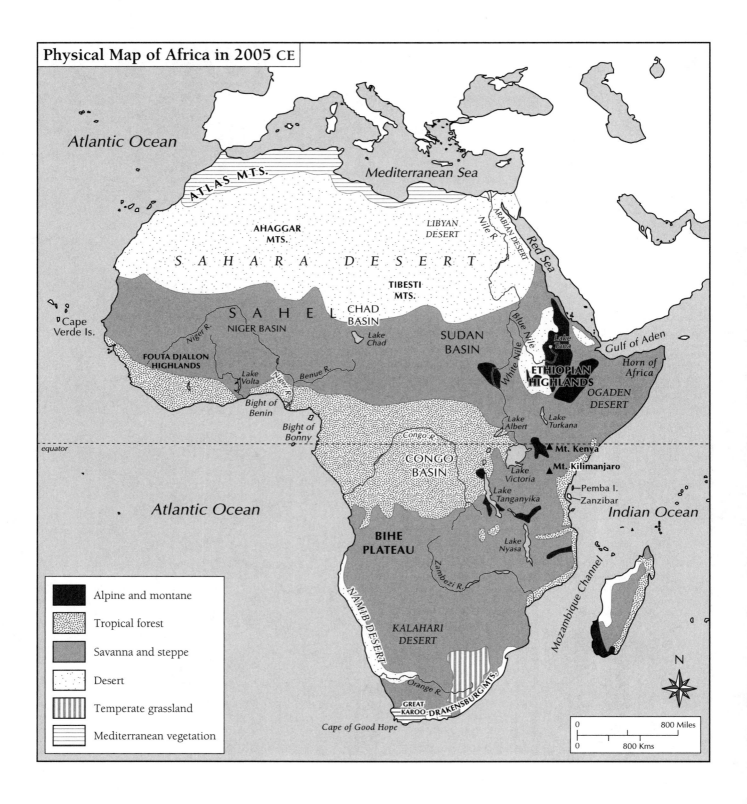

Physical Map of Africa in 2005 CE

Atlantic Ocean

Mediterranean Sea

ATLAS MTS.

AHAGGAR MTS.

LIBYAN DESERT

Nile R.

ARABIAN DESERT

Red Sea

S A H A R A   D E S E R T

TIBESTI MTS.

Cape Verde Is.

S A H E L

CHAD BASIN

NIGER BASIN

Niger R.

Lake Chad

SUDAN BASIN

Blue Nile

Lake Tana

Gulf of Aden

FOUTA DJALLON HIGHLANDS

Lake Volta

Niger R.

Benue R.

White Nile

ETHIOPIAN HIGHLANDS

Horn of Africa

OGADEN DESERT

Bight of Benin

Bight of Bonny

Congo R.

Lake Albert

Lake Turkana

equator

CONGO BASIN

▲ Mt. Kenya

Lake Victoria

▲ Mt. Kilimanjaro

Atlantic Ocean

Lake Tanganyika

Pemba I.

Zanzibar

Indian Ocean

BIHE PLATEAU

Lake Nyasa

Zambezi R.

Mozambique Channel

NAMIB DESERT

KALAHARI DESERT

Orange R.

GREAT KAROO

DRAKENSBURG MTS.

Cape of Good Hope

N

Legend

■	Alpine and montane
▦	Tropical forest
▓	Savanna and steppe
░	Desert
▥	Temperate grassland
▤	Mediterranean vegetation

0				800 Miles
0				800 Kms

CONTENTS

LIST OF ENTRIES

HOW TO USE THIS ENCYCLOPEDIA

This encyclopedia is organized chronologically, dividing the African past into five major eras. This division serves to make it easier to study the vastness and complexity of African history and culture. It also allows students and general readers to go directly to the volume or volumes they wish to consult.

Volume I, *Ancient Africa,* deals with Africa up to approximately 500 CE (roughly, in terms of classical European history, to the Fall of the Roman Empire and the dissolution of the Ancient World on the eve of the emergence of Islam). The volume also includes articles on the continent's key geographical features and major language families. In addition you will find articles that deal with certain basic aspects of African life that, in essential ways, remain relatively constant throughout time. For example, rites of passage, funeral customs, the payment of bride-wealth, and rituals related to spirit possession are features common to many African societies. Although these features can evolve in different cultures in radically different ways, their basic purpose remains constant. Accordingly, rather than try to cover the evolution of these cultural features in each volume, we offer a more general explanation in Volume I, with the understanding that the details of these cultural touchstones can vary widely from people to people and change over time.

On the other hand there are entries related to key cultural and social dimensions whose changes are easier to observe over time. Such entries appear in each of the volumes and include architecture, art, clothing and dress, economics, family, music, religion, warfare, and the role of women.

Volume II, *African Kingdoms,* focuses on what may be loosely termed "medieval Africa," from the sixth century to the beginning of the 16th century. This is the period that witnessed the rise and spread of Islam and, to a lesser degree, Arab expansion throughout much of the northern and eastern regions of the continent. It also saw the flowering of some of Africa's greatest indigenous kingdoms and empires. Other Africans, such as the Maasai and Kikuyu living in and around present-day Kenya, did not live in powerful states during this time yet developed their own dynamic cultures.

Volume III, *From Conquest to Colonization,* continues Africa's story from roughly 1500 to 1850. During this era Africa became increasingly involved with the Atlantic world due to European maritime exploration and subsequent interaction through trade and cultural exchanges. This period also included the rise of the transatlantic slave trade, which in turn created the African Diaspora, and the beginnings of European colonization. As a result, it marks a period when the dynamics shaping African culture and society began to shift.

Volume IV, *The Colonial Era,* covers Africa during the years 1850–1960. This historical period begins with Europe's conquest of the continent, leading to the era of colonial rule. Political control enabled Europe to extend its economic control as well, turning Africa into a vast supply depot of raw materials. Volume IV also covers the rise of nationalist movements and the great struggle Africans undertook to regain their independence.

Volume V, *Independent Africa,* deals with the continent since 1960, when Africans began regaining their independence and started to once again live in sovereign states. (This process, of course, took longer in the southern portion of the continent than in other parts.) In common with the rest of the world's people, however, Africans have faced a host of new and challenging problems, some of which are specific to Africa, while others are of a more global nature.

In addition to the aforementioned cultural entries that appear in all five volumes, there are entries for each of the present-day countries of the continent as identified on the Political Map found at the front of each volume. Readers can thus learn about the key developments in a given country within a given time period or across the entire span of African history. There are also articles on individual ethnic groups of Africa in each of the volumes. Since there are more than a thousand identifiable groups, it has been necessary to limit coverage to the major or key groups within a given period. Thus, a group that might be historically important in one period may not be sufficiently important, or may not even have existed, in a period covered by one or more other volumes. Likewise, there are entries on the major cities of the continent for given time periods, including, in Volume V, all the present national capitals. Another key set of entries common to all volumes concerns historically important persons. In general, historians are more readily able to identify these individuals for recent periods than for earlier times. As a result the latter volumes contain more individual biographical entries. An exception here is the case of Ancient Egypt, where historical records have enabled us to learn about the roles of prominent individuals.

In preparing these volumes, every attempt has been made to make this encyclopedia as accessible and easy to use as possible. At the front of each volume, readers will find an introduction and a timeline specific to the historical era covered in the volume. There are also three full-page maps, two of which appear in all five volumes (the current political map and a physical map), and one that is specific to the volume's time period. In addition the front of each volume contains a volume-specific list of the photographs, illustrations, and maps found therein. The List of Entries at the front of each volume is the same in all volumes and enables the reader to quickly get an overview of the entries within the individual volumes, as well as for the five-volume set. Entries are arranged alphabetically, letter-by-letter within each volume.

Entry headwords use the most commonly found spelling or representation of that spelling, with other frequently used spellings in parentheses. The question of spelling, of course, is always a major issue when dealing with languages utilizing an alphabet or a script different than that used for English. Changes in orthography and the challenges of transliteration can produce several variants of a word. Where there are important variants in spelling, this encyclopedia presents as many as possible, but only within the entries themselves. For easy access to variant and alternate spelling, readers should consult the index at the end of each volume, which lists and cross-references the alternate spellings that appear in the text.

Each volume contains an index that has references to subjects in the specific volume, and the cumulative index at the end of Volume V provides easy access across the volumes. A cumulative glossary appears in each volume and provides additional assistance.

The entries serve to provide the reader with basic rather than exhaustive information regarding the subject at hand. To help those who wish to read further, each entry is linked with other entries in that volume via cross-references indicated by SMALL CAPITALS. In addition the majority of entries are followed by a **See also** section, which provides cross-references to relevant entries in the other four volumes. The reader may find it useful to begin with one of the general articles—such as the ones dealing with archaeology, dance, oral traditions, or women—or to start with an entry on a specific country or an historically important state and follow the cross-references to discover more detailed information. Readers should be aware that cross-references, both those embedded in the text and those in the **See also** section, use only entry headword spellings and not variant spellings. For those readers who wish to research a topic beyond the material provided in individual and cross-referenced entries, there is also a **Further reading** section at the end of many entries. Bibliographical references listed here guide readers to more in-depth resources in a particular area.

Finally, readers can consult the **Suggested Readings** in the back of each volume. These volume-specific bibliographies contain general studies—such as atlases, histories of the continent, and broad works on culture, society, and people—as well as specialized studies that typically cover specific topics or regions. For the most part, these two bibliographic aids contain those recently published works that are most likely to be available in libraries, especially well-stocked city and college libraries. Readers should also be aware that a growing number of sources are available online in the form of e-books and other formats. The World Wide Web is also a good place to look for current events and developments that have occurred since the publication of this encyclopedia.

LIST OF IMAGES AND MAPS IN THIS VOLUME

Photographs and Illustrations

Maps

INTRODUCTION TO THIS VOLUME

This volume covers the independence and postcolonial era in Africa. The year 1960 was called "the year of Africa" because of the wave of independence that swept over the continent. It would take more than three decades, however, for the entire continent to achieve independence. The process included several lengthy wars of liberation, especially against Portuguese colonial rule and the white minority government of Rhodesia. The last step did not come until 1994, when South Africa's first democratic elections ended the long era of apartheid and led Nelson Mandela to the presidency.

The political history of the independent African states has in many instances been a turbulent one. A series of both human-made and natural disasters have plagued the continent over the past four decades. These include abusive and oppressive dictatorships and the Sahelian drought of the 1970s. Yet it would be as erroneous to place too much emphasis on the negative as it would be to ignore it altogether. The continent contains dynamic societies, innovative peoples, and vibrant cultures. Increasingly Africans have become part of a more global society, contributing significantly to it and in turn being significantly affected by it in all spheres of life.

The entries in this volume seek to capture the broad range of developments that have occurred in Africa since 1960 and the key individuals who were at the heart of these developments. Extensive scholarly research on this period provides the information contained in these entries. Hence, there are entries on African studies, anthropology and Africa, archaeology, and historical scholarship on Africa. There are also articles on some of the key scholars, such as Kenneth O. Dike, Cheikh Anta Diop, Mary and Richard Leakey, and Walter Rodney. The "Further reading" sections of individual articles and the "Selected Readings" at the end of the volume provide a guide to many of the key publications resulting from this recent scholarship.

Particularly important are those entries that cover the main threads of developments within what are now the national boundaries of the present-day states of Africa. Readers of this volume can thus continue to pursue the history and culture of contemporary African nations, following up on related entries in the earlier volumes of the *Encyclopedia*. The length of the entries is determined by the size and relative importance of the individual countries. In a few cases, such as Nigeria and South Africa, the developments are so extensive and complex, and the countries so important for the continent as a whole, that they receive extended treatment. Not all of the states were in existence as of 1960, and in some cases, such as Eritrea and Western Sahara, the process of the emergence of states continued deep into the period covered by this volume. There are also entries on the capital cities for each country as well as other major contemporary African cities. Entries also exist for the heads of state at the time this encyclopedia was published. Many of the ruling political parties—and in some instances the major opposition parties—are also the subjects of entries.

As sovereign nations, the countries of Africa still maintain relationships with former colonial rulers—England, France, Portugal, Italy, and Spain. There are international relations, too, with the United States and countries throughout North and South America, the Middle East, and Asia. International organizations, both global and intra-African entities, play important roles. Africa's involvement in the global arena also means that significant global issues impinge on the continent.

Political developments, and hence political leaders, play a prominent role in this volume. Some entries are for individuals, such as Nnamdi Azikiwe of Nigeria, who were important in developing the nationalist movements that led to independence and are covered in Volume IV as well. Other leaders, such as Abdou Diouf of Senegal, emerged to prominence after 1960. Some figures, such as Nigeria's Sani Abacha and Jean-Bedel Bokassa of the Central African Republic, are less-than-admirable individuals, and they often came to power through coups d'état, but they play significant roles that warrant entries.

A particularly important political development was the continuation of liberation struggles, especially in southern Africa. In South Africa there was the protracted effort to rid the country of apartheid, while more than a decade of fighting was needed to remake Rhodesia into the country of Zimbabwe. A common goal of ending white rule did not necessarily mean a united nationalist movement, as the competing nationalist movements in Angola demonstrated. Indeed, these divisions undermined the liberation struggle against Portugal and led to a protracted post-independence civil war. Cuba was to become deeply engaged in Angola, as was the United States, though more covertly. Such national struggles were not confined to efforts against European or European-settler governments, however, as demonstrated by the efforts of Polisario to create a state independent of Morocco and the revolt and war against Ethiopia that led to an independent Eritrea in 1991.

Many independent African countries witnessed military takeovers of civilian governments, sometimes resulting in civil war. A particularly fierce and seemingly unending civil war has pitted the non-Arab, non-Muslim south against the Arabic-speaking Islamic north in the Republic of the Sudan. The entire Horn of Africa has been the scene of destructive warfare and unstable governments. Some civil wars result, in part at least, from ethnic conflict. Entries on many of the continent's major ethnic groups illuminate issues of ethnicity and identity that continue to shape how many of the continent's people view both themselves and those of different backgrounds. Political developments in certain countries receive extended attention, within the country entries and with separate entries.

The creative arts have flourished in Africa since independence. The importance of the African authors profiled here extends far beyond literary circles, since so much of their writing deals with everyday conditions that people face. Music also reveals much about modern African life, for songs often directly address common problems while the instrumental music catches the pulse and diversity of life on the continent. Entries on groups and individual musicians such as Salif Keita and Miriam Makeba enable the reader to go into greater depth on this critical and very prominent dimension of African culture. Much of this musical efflorescence has taken place in the context of urban life and culture. Radio and television, theater, and the cinema have interacted with literature and music. For example, the Senegalese writer Ousmane Sembène has moved into cinema, and South Africa's Abdullah Ibrahim has written musical scores for films. Another cultural dimension that has continued to grow in importance is sports, both professional and amateur. Sports has become linked with politics, and team success in international venues, such as the Olympics, and intra-African competition, such as the All-Africa Games, has served to enhance national pride. Individual African athletes, too, have become increasingly prominent internationally.

Religion is also significant to African culture, with the two so-called universal religions of Christianity and Islam gaining more and more converts, generally at the expense of those adhering to traditional religions. Religion needs to be examined in terms of belief and spirituality, but it can also play an important political role. Church leaders such as Desmond Tutu and Allan Boesak were in the forefront of the anti-apartheid movement, while Omar Hasan Ahmad al-Bashir heads a fundamentalist Islamic government in the Sudan. Northern Nigerian provinces that have adopted Islamic law, or *sharia*, into their legal systems on religious grounds have caused further strife between Christians and Muslims.

Education witnessed a great expansion at the elementary, secondary, and tertiary levels in the early independence eras. Large universities such as Makerere, in Uganda, gained international reputations.

A wide variety of reasons, including some of the political ones noted above and others such as government and business corruption, help account for the growing inability of many African states to meet the needs of their citizens. But there are also important economic reasons. Africa has to a large extent not witnessed significant development since independence and has remained in a situation of dependency. Neocolonialism has certainly contributed to economic failure. Agriculture has been unable to keep pace with population growth, in part because of environmental issues and problems, but also due to a general lack of economic resources across the continent. African cash crops often face increasing competition on the world market, thus dimishing the income derived from exports.

Mining has also seen a contraction, often due to decline in world demand for many of Africa's minerals and metals. Oil is one resource for which demand has continued to grow, but oil prices fluctuate widely, thereby destabilizing the African national economies that rely on petroleum exports. Industrialization has continued to lag, and infrastructure such as transportation and telecommunications is often lacking. Labor in Africa is often uncertain in terms of the returns that can be expected, whether in the informal or the formal sectors. Africans are increasingly working in the global economy, in trade and commerce, and as migrant workers. Tourism creates jobs for many Africans, but it too has boom-and-bust dimensions, though Africa's national parks and wildlife remain great tourist attractions. This in turn has helped promote conservation in Africa, as there are clear economic benefits.

At the beginning of the new century, the political map of Africa remains largely what it was in 1960. However, the dramatic cultural, social, and economic changes taking place mean that today's Africans lead lives that have changed significantly from those of the independence generation.

TIME LINE (1956–2004)

1956 — Morocco, Tunisia, and Sudan achieve independence

1957 — Ghana achieves independence

1958 — Guinea declares independence

1959 — Led by Robert Sobukwe, the Pan-Africanist Congress splits from the African National Congress in South Africa

1960 — On March 21, 69 Africans are shot dead by South African police at a protest in Sharpeville

South African ANC President Albert Lutuli becomes first person from outside Europe and North America to win the Nobel Peace Prize

Benin, Cameroon, Central African Republic, Chad, Republic of Congo,Dahomey, Democratic Republic of Congo, Ivory Coast, Gabon, Madagascar, Mali, Mauritania, Niger, Nigeria, Senegal, Somalia, Togo, and Upper Volta all achieve independence

Running the entire course barefoot, Ethiopian Abebe Bikila wins the Olympic marathon in Rome, Italy

1960–1965 — Congo crisis and civil war; Joseph Mobutu assumes control following a coup

1961 — Tanganyika, Sierra Leone achieve independence

Umkhonto we Sizwe, the guerilla wing of the African National Congress, begins its armed insurgency against the South African government

War of liberation against Portuguese rule begins in Angola

1962 — Algeria, Burundi, Rwanda, and Uganda achieve independence

Ethiopia claims Eritrea as a province, setting off prolonged war of liberation

1963 — Kenya achieves independence

Founding of the Organization of African Unity in Addis Ababa, Ethiopia

War of liberation against Portuguese rule begins in Guinea-Bissau

1964 — Malawi and Zambia achieve independence

Zanzibar joins with mainland Tanganyika to create the United Republic of Tanzania

FRELIMO launches war of liberation in Mozambique

1965	In Southern Rhodesia, Ian Smith issues a unilateral declaration of independence from the British Commonwealth
1966	Abubakar Tafawa Balewa and Ahmadu Bello assassinated in Nigeria
	Military coup overthrows Ghana's founding president, Kwame Nkrumah
	Former Basutoland gains independence as Lesotho, and Bechuanaland becomes independent as Botswana
	Flora Nwapa's *Efuru* becomes the first novel published by a Nigerian woman
1966–1979	Zimbabwean guerillas wage liberation war known as Chimurenga
1967	Omar Bongo becomes president of Gabon following the death of Leon Mba, thus initiating the continent's longest presidency
	Egyptian Air Force destroyed by Israel during the Arab-Israeli "Six-Day War"
	South African surgeon Christiaan Barnard performs first successful heart transplant surgery in Cape Town
1967–1970	Nigerian civil war rages with eastern region of Biafra attempting, unsuccessfully, to secede from the Nigerian federation
1968	Equatorial Guinea achieves independence from Spanish colonial rule
	Kingdom of Swaziland achieves full independence

1969	1969 Pope Paul VI visits Uganda, venerating the young late-nineteenth-century Buganda martyrs and consecrating 12 African bishops
	FRELIMO President Eduardo Mondlane assassinated
	Kenyan leader Tom Mboya assassinated
	Muammar Qaddafi takes power in Egypt after overthrowing King Idris
1970	1970 Homelands Citizenship Act passed by white-minority government in South Africa, creating ethnically divided Bantustans, or "tribal homelands," for the county's black African population
	Aswan High Dam is operational
	President Gamal Abdel Nasser of Egypt dies
1971	Mobutu Sese Seko—formerly General Joseph Mobutu—changes name of the Republic of the Congo to Zaïre
	Idi Amin takes power in Uganda following a military coup d'état
	1971 Walter Rodney publishes influential book, *How the West Underdeveloped Africa*
1972–1974	Severe drought devastates Sahel from Senegal to the Horn of Africa
1973	Guinea-Bissau declares independence
	Polisario founded in Western Sahara to secure independence of the indigenous Saharawi people from Spanish colonialism

1974	Portugal's pro-colonial government overthrown in revolution

Coup led by Mengistu Haile Mariam overthrows long-serving Emperor Haile Selassie in Ethiopia

1975   Mozambique, Angola, Cape Verde, and São Tomé and Príncipe achieve independence from Portuguese colonial rule

Comoros declares independence from France

Following Marxist coup led by Mathieu Kérékou, the former Dahomey becomes the People's Republic of Benin

1976   Spain officially ends colonial occupation in Western Sahara

Senegalese intellectual Cheikh Anta Diop publishes influential treatise, *The African Origin of Civilization*

Police repression in Soweto, South Africa, sparks violent reprisals from Africans in the Johannesburg area

1977   Popular South African activist Steve Biko murdered while in police custody

French Territory of Afars and Issas becomes independent Djibouti

1977–1978   War breaks out between Somalia and Ethiopia in disputed Ogaden territory

Late 1970s   Beginning of AIDS epidemic that kills more than 17 million Africans by the end of the century

1978   Daniel arap Moi begins his 24-year tenure as president of Kenya

1979   Junior military officer Jerry Rawlings seizes power in Ghana

Egypt signs Camp David peace agreement with Israel

1980   Kenya becomes the first of 29 African countries to adopt World Bank structural adjustment policies in order to secure international loans

African heads of state adopt the Lagos Plan of Action for economic development

African majority in Rhodesia declares independence, renaming the country Zimbabwe

1981   Islamic extremists assassinate Egypt's Anwar as-Sadat for making peace with Israel; Hosni Mubarak assumes the presidency

Libya invades and occupies mineral-rich region of northern Chad

Jerry Rawlings stages second coup and begins his 20-year rule of Ghana

1982   The World Bank publishes its influential "Accelerated Development in Sub-Saharan Africa" (the "Berg Report")

1982–1989   Senegal and The Gambia form the short-lived Senegambia Confederation

1983   Civil war re-erupts in the Republic of the Sudan

1984   Upper Volta renamed Burkina Faso

Archbishop Desmond Tutu awarded Nobel Peace Prize for efforts to end the racist apartheid policies in South Africa

1984   Severe famine begins in the Horn of Africa

In Kenya, Richard Leakey's archaeological team discovers "Turkana Boy," a nearly complete fossilized *Homo habilis* skeleton

Long-time Guinean president Ahmed Sekou Touré dies

1985   Julius K. Nyerere voluntarily steps down from the presidency in Tanzania, a position he held since Tanzanian independence in 1962

1986   United States bombs military installations in Libya

Nigerian Wole Soyinka becomes first African to win the Nobel Prize in Literature

1987   Habib Bourguiba, Tunisia's president since independence, is deposed because of failing mental health

1988   Egyptian author Naguib Mahfouz wins the Nobel Prize for Literature

1989   Muammar Qaddafi of Libya organizes Maghrib Arab Union of Libya, Algeria, Mauritania, Morocco, and Tunisia

1990   South West Africa wins its independence from South Africa, becoming Namibia

South African ANC leader, Nelson Mandela, released after 26 years in prison

1990–1995   Tuareg people rebel against the government in northern Niger

1991   Soviet Union collapses, easing Cold War tensions throughout Africa and the world

1991   Nadine Gordimer of South Africa wins Nobel Prize in Literature

1992   Election results in Algeria are voided; civil war ensues

United Nations brokers cease-fire in Mozambique, ending long civil war

1992–1993   United Nations imposes sanctions on Libya for that country's role in the bombing of a Pan-Am Airlines plane over Lockerbie, Scotland

1993   Eritrea wins independence from Ethiopia after long war of independence

Felix Houphouët-Boigny, president of Ivory Coast since independence, dies

South Africans Nelson Mandela and F. W. de Klerk share Nobel Peace Prize

Loss of helicopters and soldiers in Mogadishu street battle leads United States to withdraw forces from peace-keeping operation in Somalia

1993–2002   Jonas Savimbi heads UNITA rebels in Angolan civil war

1994   National elections in South Africa bring Nelson Mandela and the African National Congress to power

As many as 1 million are killed in Hutu-led genocide in Rwanda, Burundi, and Zaïre (present-day Democratic Republic of the Congo)

1994–1995   Nigerian-born basketball star Hakeem Olajuwon leads the Houston Rockets to back-to-back national championships in the United States

1995	Outbreak of Ebola virus kills up to 250 people in Kikwit, Zaïre (present-day Democratic Republic of Congo)
	Ogoni activist Ken Saro-Wiwa executed by the Nigerian government
	Truth and Reconciliation Commission established in South Africa
1996	Huge oil reserves found off coast of Equatorial Guinea
1997	Laurent Kabila assumes power in Zaïre, country is renamed the Democratic Republic of the Congo
	Kofi Annan, from Ghana, elected the United Nations Secretary General
	Full-scale civil war breaks out in Republic of Congo
1998	Despite provisions of the Houston Accord, elections in Western Sahara are postponed
	U.S. embassies bombed in Kenya and Tanzania
1999	Former military leader Olusegun Obasanjo elected as a civilian to lead Nigeria
	Morocco's King Hassan II dies after 38-year reign; successor is Mohammad VI
1999	African heads of state form the African Union to replace the Organization of African Unity
2000	Cameroon wins Olympic gold medal in soccer in Atlanta, Georgia, U.S.A.
	Election of John Kufuor as president marks Ghana's ongoing transition to democracy

2000	Mugabe government supports occupation of white farms, leading to an ongoing political crisis in Zimbabwe
2001	Presidential elections in Zambia end 10-year presidency of Frederick Chiluba
	Rebel forces in Sierra Leone disarm as British and UN troops restore civil order
2002	Overloaded ferry capsizes in Senegal; 1,000 passengers die
	Hostilities end in Angola following the death of UNITA leader Jonas Savimbi
	Severe drought hits Malawi; thousands perish
	United States and France recognize Marc Ravalomanana as legitimate leader of Madagascar after disputed 2001 election
	Mwai Kibaki's election ends Daniel arap Moi's 24-year rule over Kenya
2002	Ivory Coast engulfed in civil war
2003	J. M. Coetzee of South Africa wins Nobel Prize in Literature
	United States assists with forcing Liberia's Charles Taylor into exile to end country's civil war
2004	Ongoing civil war in the Darfur region of the Republic of the Sudan; hundreds of thousands of African villagers flee to refugee centers in Chad
	President Qaddafi of Libya accepts responsibility for 1988 bombing of Pan-Am flight; economic sanctions against Libya end

Abacha, Sani (1943–1998) *Nigerian army officer who came to power in 1993*

A career military officer, Sani Abacha was born in KANO, in the HAUSA-dominated, predominantly Muslim Northern Region of NIGERIA. Educated in Kano, Abacha entered the military at the age of 18, rising steadily in rank during the 1970s and 1980s. He first came to prominence in 1983, when he announced on Nigerian radio a COUP D'ÉTAT that toppled Nigeria's Second Republic. Abacha continued to gain political influence during the 1980s, maintaining a steady level of power through several successive military governments.

Throughout this period, however, he was outspoken in his opposition to the army's continued political role in Nigeria, advocating, in public at least, a rapid return to civilian government. Abacha apparently reversed his views on civilian rule and surprised many people when he supported the voiding of the 1993 elections by military strongman Ibrahim BABANGIDA (1941–). However, Abacha was instrumental in convincing Babangida to leave office later that year and turn power over to the quasi-civilian government of Ernest Shonekan (1936–).

Abacha was serving as minister of defense in Shonekan's government when he initiated another coup in November 1993. Under Abacha's rule Nigeria continued to struggle under the pressure of economic, political, and ethnic crises. Confronting economic woes ranging from rampant inflation to chronic fuel shortages to CORRUPTION, he seemed unable to improve conditions in Nigeria. Nor was Abacha able to do anything to alleviate Nigeria's ethnic hostilities.

Although he consistently asserted that he was determined to move Nigeria toward civilian rule, Abacha took only token steps in that direction, maintaining an iron-fisted authority over the country. Never hesitating to use whatever means he had in order to silence criticism or opposition, he even had the distinguished, Nobel Prize-winning author Wole SOYINKA (1934–) charged with treason.

> In the early years of his regime, Abacha faced acute criticism from the OGONI activist, playwright Ken SARO-WIWA (1941–1995). Saro-Wiwa ultimately was arrested on charges of treason, and, despite an international outcry, was executed in 1994 along with eight other Ogoni activists.

Abacha's sudden death in 1998 was greeted in many parts of Nigeria—particularly in the YORUBA-dominated southwest and the IGBO-dominated east—with jubilation and renewed calls for a civilian government. However, his immediate successor, Maj. Gen. Abdulsalami Abubakar (1943–), was another northerner and long-time member of Nigeria's military establishment.

See also: ETHNIC CONFLICT IN AFRICA (Vol. V).

Abdikassim Salad Hassan (1941–) *President of Somalia*

Abdikassim Salad Hassan was born to the Hawiye clan in the Galgaduud region of SOMALIA in 1941. He studied in EGYPT and later in the Soviet Union, obtaining a master's degree from Moscow State University in 1965. He returned home to work for the ministry of agriculture, where his meteoric rise in politics began. Instrumental in transforming local agricultural methods, he went on to hold a series of other ministerial posts in the government of Mohammed Siad BARRE (c. 1919–1996), who ruled Somalia from 1969 until his fall from power in 1991. In 1989 Abdikassim became Barre's deputy prime minister and interior minister. As a government official, Abdikassim played a fundamental role in building Somalia's ties to the United States.

The disorder and chaos following Barre's ouster led to UN forces entering Somalia in 1992. Abdikassim was a prominent member of a peace committee of Somali elders. He criticized both the militancy of faction leader General Mohamed F. AIDEED (1934–1996) and the use of force by the United Nations to impose order. Abdikassim later served as a mediator between Aideed and the UN special envoy to Somalia in a failed attempt to resolve the conflict between the warring factions.

In the mid-1990s Abdikassim became a leading voice for national reconciliation and a united Somalia, opposing the secession of the northern Somali states of Somaliland and Puntland. In August 2000 Somalia's moderate leaders met in Arta, DJIBOUTI, to negotiate a cease-fire and lay the foundation for a new Somali central government. Abdikassim vocally rallied popular support for what was to be the first such government since Barre was deposed in 1991. Later that month Somalia's transitional National Assembly elected Abdikassim president of Somalia. In the years that followed, he continued to fight for a united Somalia, garnering support from the United States and staving off threats from Somali warlords.

See also: SOVIET UNION AND AFRICA (Vols. IV, V); UNITED NATIONS AND AFRICA (Vol. V); UNITED STATES AND AFRICA (Vol. V).

Abdullahi Yussuf Ahmed (unknown–) *Somali political leader*

Abdullahi Yussuf Ahmed was cofounder of the Somali Salvation Democratic Front (SSDF), which helped to oust the repressive regime of President Mohammed Siad BARRE (1910–1995) from power in SOMALIA in 1991. A former commander in chief of the army, Barre had been dictator of Somalia for more than 20 years. He came to power in 1969 in a military coup that overthrew the democratically elected government of President Abdi Rashid Ali Shermarke (r. 1967–1969).

Abdullahi Yussuf Ahmed was a minor leader in the Mejertein clan and a colonel in the military. Growing discontent with Barre's authoritarian regime led Abdullahi and other dissident Somalis to establish a number of opposition movements. Because unauthorized political activity was illegal, these movements generally operated

from outside the country. Yussuf Ahmed helped to form the Somali Salvation Front, headquartered in ETHIOPIA, which attempted to overthrow President Barre by force in 1978. After the coup failed, Colonel Abdullahi helped form the Somalia Salvation Democratic Front (SSDF), which claimed to command a guerilla force numbering in the thousands. Politically adept, Abdullahi forged bonds at home and abroad, notably with the leader of LIBYA, Muammar QADDAFI (1942–). Both Libya and Ethiopia supplied the SSDF with arms.

After a bloody rebellion that began in 1988, Siad Barre fell from power in 1991. At the time, Abdullahi was imprisoned in the Somali city of MOGADISHU. After his release, he led an independence movement in the northeastern region of Somalia called Puntland, staving off challenges in 1994 from competing SSDF leaders.

In June 1998 Abdullahi proclaimed himself president of Puntland, but his government was not formally recognized by the international community, which was determined to see a united Somalia. After a brief period of calm, he faced opposition from a faction led by JAMA ALI JAMA. Jama ultimately unseated Abdullahi shortly after he was sworn in for a second term in 2001. In May 2002, however, Abdullahi returned to power.

Abidjan

Former capital city of IVORY COAST. By 1960, when Ivory Coast became independent, its coastal capital city of Abidjan was already well established. It boasted new port facilities, served as the hub of the national road system and the terminus of the Abidjan-Niger Railway, and was a leading communications center. Over the next two decades, the city's population underwent explosive growth, increasing from 180,000 at independence to more than 1.4 million in 1980. By century's end it exceeded 2.8 million people. While many of the newcomers came from within the Ivory Coast, nearly 40 percent came from elsewhere in West Africa.

Several factors account for the dramatic increase in Abidjan's population. As a commercial center, the city provides regional import-export businesses with access to port facilities for ocean-going vessels and a rail system into the interior. As an industrial center, Abidjan is a manufacturing center for electronics, textiles, metal products, and clothing. As the financial center of French-speaking West Africa, Abidjan has continued to support a large number of French expatriates (approximately 20,000), who work as civil servants or as managers in private enterprise. The significant French presence has given the city a French flavor, which in turn has been a factor in the growing importance of TOURISM to the city's economy.

Abidjan is also a center of EDUCATION and the arts. In addition to the national university (founded in 1958), the city also features a national library and institutes for agricultural and scientific research. Abidjan is home to a museum of traditional Ivory Coast ART. The city's largest traditional market is in the neighborhood called Teichville.

In 1983 YAMOUSSOUKRO, the home city of long-time President Félix HOUPHOUËT-BOIGNY (1905–1993), became the new administrative capital of the Ivory Coast. Abidjan, however, remained the capital in all but name, retaining most government offices and foreign embassies. The French also maintain a marine infantry brigade at Abidjan. The presence of these troops enabled the French to intervene militarily during the civil disturbances of 2002–03 and attempt to mediate between the rebel and government forces.

See also: ABIDJAN (Vol. IV); FRANCE AND AFRICA (Vol. V); FRENCH WEST AFRICA (Vol. IV); POPULATION GROWTH (Vol. V).

Abiola, Mashood (1937–1998) *Nigerian opposition leader*

Mashood Abiola was born to a poor family in Abeokuta, southwestern NIGERIA. That he belonged to the YORUBA ethnic group, came from the south, and followed Islam was critical to the formation of his identity, his success, and, ultimately, his death. An exceptional student, Abiola attended Baptist Boys School in his hometown and earned a scholarship to the University of Glasgow, Scotland. Upon his return to Africa, he took a post as chief accountant of Pfizer Nigeria, a part of the multinational pharmaceutical conglomerate. Abiola went on to work for International Telephone and Telegraph (ITT) Nigeria, becoming chairman of the branch in 1969.

Mashood Abiola became one of Nigeria's wealthiest businessmen during the country's OIL boom in the 1970s. His diversified holdings came to include Concord Airlines and Concord Press, a chain of newspapers admired in business circles for their sophistication. He also founded Africa Ocean Lines, Abiola Bookshop, and Abiola Farms.

Abiola's connections in the business sector allowed him to forge formidable political alliances, and, beginning in 1979, he enjoyed success as a popular political figure. In 1993 Nigeria's self-proclaimed president and military leader, General Ibrahim BABANGIDA (1941–   ), called for general elections, and Abiola became the presidential candidate of the center-left Social Democratic Party. Judging by Abiola's popularity, it appeared that he would triumph over his main opponent, Bashir Tofa (1947–   ). Before a winner was officially announced, however, Babangida annulled the results. While his reasoning was

unclear, many speculate that Babangida, a Nigerian from the HAUSA territory in the north, feared the rule of Abiola, who was a Yoruba from southern Nigeria. Abiola vocally asserted that the election was stolen from him and proclaimed himself the rightful president of Nigeria. His persistent questioning of the results eventually led to his imprisonment in 1994.

About the same time, Babangida was deposed by General Sani ABACHA (1943–1998). Despite internal dissension and international condemnation, Abacha chose to let Abiola languish in prison. During Abiola's incarceration, his senior wife Kudirat (1951–1996) tirelessly lobbied for her husband's release. In 1996, in the city of LAGOS, she was killed when unknown gunmen opened fire on her as she sat in her car.

After Abacha's death in 1998, his close colleague, Maj. Gen. Abdulsalami Abubakar (1943–   ), assumed the presidency and continued to keep Abiola in prison. In July of that year, an American delegation visited Abiola in prison and pressed Abubakar for his release. Abiola died during the visit. Although Abiola's supporters believed that he was poisoned, the official cause of death according to the state autopsy report was a heart attack.

Abuja

Capital city and federal capital territory of NIGERIA, centrally located in the Chukuku Hills. Abuja became Nigeria's first planned city and capital in December 1991. Planning began in 1976, after it was decided that the overcrowded city of LAGOS was no longer a suitable capital. The Department of Architecture at Ahmadu Bello University in Zaria undertook the planning and design. The site for the new capital offered a central location, low population density, a cooler climate, and ample land for expansion. Equally important, the new capital was developed in a neutral territory, away from the heartlands of the major ethnic groups in the country, the HAUSA, YORUBA, and IGBO. This latter factor was particularly important in the aftermath of Nigeria's Civil War (1966–70), which divided the country along ethnic lines. The city plan included two basic zones, one for the numerous government-related institutions and one for residential and commercial facilities.

Abuja is connected to other major cities in the country by a network of expressways and by an international airport that also serves domestic locations. In 1988 the University of Abuja was founded. Spreading over about 3,080 square miles (8,000 sq km), Abuja was home to approximately 340,000 people in 1995. Today, more than 1 million people live there.

See also: URBANIZATION (Vols. IV, V).

Abuja Accords

Agreements signed in the Nigerian city of ABUJA, part of the peace process within LIBERIA.

During the 1970s and 1980s the government of Liberia was hampered by constant instability. The situation worsened in December 1989, when Charles TAYLOR (1948–) led his National Patriotic Front of Liberia (NPFL) in an invasion of the country. Entering from the IVORY COAST, the NPFL sparked a full-scale civil war, as multiple warlords gathered armies in emulation of Taylor. Despite these new armed factions, the NPFL soon held most of Liberia, with President Samuel K. DOE (c. 1952–1990) controlling only the capital city of MONROVIA. In August 1990 ECOMOG, the peacekeeping force of the ECONOMIC COMMUNITY FOR WEST AFRICAN STATES (ECOWAS), entered Liberia to stabilize the situation. Doe was soon captured and killed by an offshoot of the NPFL led by Prince Yomie Johnson.

Despite Doe's death, ECOWAS brokered the Bamako Cease-fire, which was followed by the Yamoussoukro Accords I–IV. These agreements were intended to secure the peace in Liberia and allow elections to take place. They failed, however, as none of the warring factions followed the agreements.

In July 1993, following another failed NPFL siege on Monrovia, ECOWAS brokered the Cotonou Accord. This agreement formed the Liberian National Transitional Government and stated that leaders from the different warring factions would be included in a new coalition government. The political situation in Liberia remained in disarray, however, as the different factions fought over government appointments.

In 1994 Jerry RAWLINGS (1947–) took over chairmanship of ECOWAS. His presence infused the peace process with new energy, culminating with the signing of the Abuja Accord on August 19, 1995. This created the Council of State, a ruling political body that was to include the warlords of every faction capable of disturbing the peace process. More importantly to Taylor, the Abuja Accord secured his involvement in Liberia's new government. In an oversight the Council of State did not include the leader of the ULIMO-J faction, Roosevelt Johnson, who promptly violated the Abuja Accord. In early 1996 the Council of State brought murder charges against Johnson, but an attempt to arrest him sparked violent protests that weakened the authority of the accord.

Later in 1996 the Abuja Accord Supplement was signed. This new agreement scheduled elections for the following year and paved the way for a new Council of State. In July 1997, aided greatly by his perceived ability to bring together Liberia's disparate factions, Taylor was elected president of Liberia.

Another political arrangement also bears the name "Abuja Accord." This second Abuja Accord was an agreement between ZIMBABWE and Britain. Signed by Zimbabwe president Robert MUGABE (1924–) in 2001, the agreement called for Britain to provide financial reimbursement to white farmers displaced by Zimbabwe's land reforms. The Zimbabwe-Britain Abuja Accord called for the land reclamation process to be carried out under the rule of law and in a civil manner. As of late 2004, however, the process was still marked by violence and accusations of illegal land seizures by the Zimbabwe government.

See also: CIVIL WARS (Vol. V).

Accra Capital of present-day GHANA, located on the Gulf of Guinea. Accra was the capital of Gold Coast, a former British colony, and remained the capital of Ghana after the country's independence in 1957. At that time it had a population exceeding 350,000. During the colonial era, the city had developed into a major port and trading city, but in 1962 port services were transferred to the town of Tema, 17 miles (27 km) to the east.

Accra remains the administrative, economic, educational, and cultural center of Ghana. It hosts the principal offices of major banks and trading companies, and is a central hub for rail and road TRANSPORTATION, with reliable INFRASTRUCTURE linking it to the major towns of Tema on the coast and KUMASI in the interior. Major industries in Accra include oil refining, food processing—including brewing, distilling, and fruit canning—and the production of textiles, shoes, lumber, pharmaceuticals, and plastic products. The city is also home to large open markets. Its rich and diverse nightlife, from which highlife emerged to become the dominant form of popular music in the 1960s, attracts a growing number of tourists. Accra exhibits diverse ARCHITECTURE including modern, colonial, and precolonial styles; visitors are often struck by the proximity of gleaming skyscrapers to ramshackle shantytowns.

Points of interest in the city include the national museum, a national academy of arts and sciences, and Christianborg Castle, a former slave depot built by the Danes in the 17th century. Several advanced educational, research, and technical institutions are located in Accra, and the University of Ghana is situated in the nearby town of Legon.

The Accra metropolitan area has grown rapidly, with the population surging from around 985,000 in 1988 to more than 1,780,000 in 1995. At the beginning of the 21st century there were nearly 3 million people in the greater Accra area. Such rapid POPULATION GROWTH has a common feature of URBANIZATION within Africa.

See also: ACCRA (Vols. II, III, IV); DENMARK AND AFRICA (Vol. III); GA-DANGME (Vols. II, III); GOLD COAST (Vols. III, IV); HIGHLIFE (Vol. IV); URBAN LIFE AND CULTURE (Vols. IV, V).

Further reading: John Parker, *Making the Town: Ga State and Society in Early Colonial Accra* (Portsmouth, N.H.: Heinemann, 2000).

Achebe, Chinua (1930–) *Nigerian writer*

Perhaps Nigeria's most popular author, Achebe began his career as a journalist at the Nigerian Broadcasting Corporation. There he developed the character Okonkwo, the central figure of his first and most successful novel, *Things Fall Apart* (1958). The book follows the story of Okonkwo as he struggles against the changes colonialism has exacted on his traditional IGBO culture. The novel garnered tremendous international acclaim and has been translated into 45 languages, becoming one of the most widely read novels by an African writer and establishing Achebe as Africa's leading literary figure.

Achebe followed the success of *Things Fall Apart* with three novels that trace the history of the Igbo through colonialism and up to 1966, when a bloody military coup led to the fall of Nigeria's First Republic. These novels, *No Longer at Ease* (1961), *Man of the People* (1966), and *Arrow of God* (1967), cemented Achebe's reputation as a chronicler of Nigeria's troubled colonial past and uncertain future as an independent nation.

The same year as the publication of *Arrow of God*, ethnic and political tensions exploded into the Nigerian Civil War (1967–70). Achebe's Igbo people seceded from Nigeria, declaring the independent Republic of BIAFRA in 1967, prompting a bloody conflict that badly destabilized the country. Achebe served as the Biafran minister of information during the war, living in the new Biafran capital of Enugu until it fell late in 1967.

Afterward Achebe traveled throughout the world, attempting to draw attention to the Biafran cause and the atrocities committed against them by Nigerian troops. His experiences during the war led to the poetry collection *Christmas in Biafra and Other Poems* (1973), for which he was awarded the British Commonwealth Poetry Prize. The war, however, discouraged Achebe greatly, and more than a decade passed before he could write another novel.

After the war ended in 1970, Achebe became director of publishing companies in Enugu and IBADAN. He also taught extensively at the University of Nigeria and at a number of universities in the United States. In 1987 he published *Anthills of the Savannah,* a novel in which, contrary to his previous works, he expresses hope for Nigeria's future. Achebe has also published a number of children's books as well as essay and short story collections. His body of work has established him as one of the finest writers of the 20th century.

See also: ACHEBE, CHINUA (Vol. IV); LITERATURE IN COLONIAL AFRICA (Vol. IV); LITERATURE IN MODERN AFRICA (Vol. V); *THINGS FALL APART* (Vol. IV).

Further reading: Ezenwa-Ohaeto, *Chinua Achebe: A Biography* (Bloomington, Ind.: Indiana University Press, 1997); Ode Ogede, *Achebe and the Politics of Representation: Form against Itself, from Colonial Conquest and Occupation to Post-independence Disillusionment* (Trenton, N.J.: Africa World Press, 2001).

Action Front for Renewal and Development (Front d'action pour le rénouveau et le développement, FARD)

Prominent political party in the Republic of BENIN. The Action Front for Renewal and Development (FARD) was formed at the meeting of its first constituent assembly held in Parakou, Benin, in April 1994. Its purpose was to bring together many small opposition political parties to unseat then President Nicephore Soglo (1935–). The first electoral victory for FARD came in March 1995, when it won 14 seats in Benin's legislative elections. Its principal success, however, came in providing a vehicle for Matthieu KEREKOU (1933–) to defeat Soglo in the presidential election of 1996. Kerekou, a Marxist-Leninist, had been dictator of Benin from his successful military coup of 1972 until 1991, when he lost to Soglo. He thus became the first incumbent African strongman ousted at the polls to subsequently win an election and return to office.

Addis Ababa

Capital and largest city in ETHIOPIA, located in the geographic center of the country on a plateau near the foot of Mount Entoto. Soon after its founding by Emperor Menelik II (1844–1913) in 1887, Addis Ababa became the capital of Ethiopia. The completion of a railway to the port city of DJIBOUTI in 1917 established Addis Ababa as Ethiopia's political and economic center. Italian forces occupied the city from 1936 to 1941, causing massive social disruption but also leaving behind much improved housing and TRANSPORTATION networks.

When Allied forces drove the Italians out of Addis Ababa the during World War II (1939–45), Emperor HAILE SELASSIE (1892–1975) returned to power, after having previously fled from the Italian invaders. Ethiopia had been one of only two African members of the League of Nations and thus was represented at the founding of the United Nations (UN). Because of this, Addis Ababa hosted the continent's principal international organizations. In 1958 the UN Economic Commission for Africa set up its headquarters in Addis Ababa and built Africa Hall, which is noteworthy for its beautiful stained glass windows. In 1963 a meeting of African heads of state held in Addis Ababa led to the founding of the ORGANIZATION OF AFRICAN UNITY (OAU). The OAU then set up its secretariat and administration in the city. Its successor organization, the AFRICAN UNION, founded in 2002, also established its administrative offices there.

In 1967 the city began to see a boom in population, fueled by immigration from rural areas. By 1970 the population had reached 683,500. In 1974 poor economic conditions led to uprisings among students and laborers, and a military COUP D'ETAT removed Haile Selassie from power. Addis Ababa then became the seat of power for the socialist government of MENGISTU HAILE MARIAM (c. 1937–). Despite desperate economic circumstances arising from

Mengistu's Marxist policies, Addis Ababa's population underwent a second wave of growth during the period 1975–87. This wave was augmented by large numbers of peasants fleeing to Addis Ababa from war-torn regions in northern Ethiopia, where rebels from ERITREA battled for that country's independence from Ethiopian rule. By 1990 the city's population was 1.6 million. In 1991 Eritrean rebel forces ousted Mengistu, and Addis Ababa became the capital of a new, often troubled, democratic government.

Addis Ababa is a unique city in terms of its layout and ethnic makeup. Physically, the city is demarcated by elevation, with the old section, featuring St. George's Cathedral, the old Arada market, and Addis Ababa University, on a hill in the north of the city. The commercial area of Lower Addis Ababa lies to the south on lower ground. Addis Ketema, or the "new town," was constructed by Italians during the occupation and features the Merkato Indigino, or African market. A majority of southern Ethiopia's agricultural EXPORTS pass through the Merkato, including Addis Ababa's prime export, coffee.

Ethnically, the city is populated mostly by people of Amharan extraction, with Amharic being the prominent language. A diverse number of other peoples also call the city home. Much of the residential layout of Addis Ababa is dictated by the development of ethnic neighborhoods, or *safars*. Due to the international organizations that remain headquartered there, the city is Africa's premier diplomatic hub.

See also: ADDIS ABABA (Vol. IV); AMHARIC (Vols. I, II); COFFEE (Vol. IV); ITALY AND AFRICA (Vol. IV); URBANIZATION (Vols. IV, V); POPULATION GROWTH (Vol. V); URBAN LIFE AND CULTURE (Vols. IV, V).

Ade, King Sunny (Sunday Anthony Ishola Adeniyi Adegeye) (1946–) *Nigerian musician and bandleader*

King Sunny Ade was born in 1946 in present-day Ondo State, NIGERIA. His father was a Methodist minister and his mother a member of the church choir. Against the wishes of his parents, who wanted him to become a lawyer, he left school at age 17 to pursue a career as a musician. He became a percussionist and guitarist in a local band in LAGOS, Nigeria's capital at the time. Two years later, in 1965, he formed his own group, the High Society Band, renamed the Green Spots in 1966, that went on to make 12 recordings. In 1974, King Sunny Ade founded his own record company and changed the band's name to the African Beats.

The African Beats is normally made up of between 20 and 30 musicians. Their multi-layered percussion and synchronized vocal harmonies, combined with synthesizers, electric keyboards, and electric and pedal steel guitars, represent a unique modern adaptation of the genre

of MUSIC known as *juju*. King Sunny Ade has been the style's most popular performer, and he is often called the King of Juju. Originally considered poor people's music, juju is based on traditional YORUBA rhythms and incorporates the two-headed, hourglass-shaped "talking drum" once used to communicate between villages. Ade is also called the Chairman for his many business investments, which include MINING, OIL, film and video production, and public relations.

King Sunny Ade and the African Beats are popular in Nigeria, where they have 100 albums to their credit. They have released 14 albums in North America, beginning with the release of the album *Juju* in 1982. To a certain extent, the interest King Sunny Ade generated in the West during the early 1980s has waned. Nevertheless, he remains widely popular in his homeland, where he is constantly in demand, particularly for concerts commemorating important functions of state and private celebrations.

African National Congress (ANC) South African political organization that led the resistance movement against APARTHEID and became the ruling party in 1994. Founded in 1912, during the first 50 years of its existence the African National Congress (ANC) achieved only modest success at best in bettering the lives of black South Africans. In fact, by the mid-1960s, increased government repression had left the ANC struggling to remain a viable resistance organization. Because of the state's crackdown on the ANC, the PAN-AFRICANIST CONGRESS (PAC), and other opposition groups in the early 1960s, the ANC had to operate underground in SOUTH AFRICA and in exile abroad.

Beginning in 1961 the ANC forswore its commitment to nonviolence and established a militant wing, UMKHONTO WE SIZWE (Spear of the Nation, also known simply as MK), which carried out acts of sabotage against the white-supremacist regime. In 1962 Nelson MANDELA (1918–), head of MK, was captured after returning from a trip abroad. The following year other key ANC leaders such as Walter SISULU (1912–2003) and Govan MBEKI (1910–2001) were seized in a raid on their secret hideout outside JOHANNESBURG. In 1964 Mandela, Sisulu, and Mbeki were sentenced to life in prison on ROBBEN ISLAND. Oliver TAMBO (1917–1993), who headed the external ANC, became president once Mandela could no longer serve in that capacity.

Over the next decades ANC headquarters-in-exile were variously based in LUSAKA, ZAMBIA and DAR ES SALAAM, TANZANIA, as well as in London, England. ANC operations were based in the countries that bordered South Africa, often involving alliances with anticolonial resistance movements, most notably the ZIMBABWE AFRICAN PEOPLE'S UNION in ZIMBABWE and SOUTH WEST AFRICAN

PEOPLE'S ORGANIZATION in SOUTH WEST AFRICA (today's NAMIBIA). Even outside of South Africa, however, ANC operatives faced threats from an extensive network of spies employed by the South African police and intelligence services. The government's repressive measures created logistical difficulties that limited the effectiveness of ANC activities until the latter half of the 1970s.

Beginning in the mid-1970s the ANC drew upon the mounting anger of African youth, causing the organization's prestige in South Africa to grow. In part the radicalization of young blacks was fueled by the impact of the BLACK CONSCIOUSNESS MOVEMENT, spearheaded by Steve BIKO (1946–1977). In 1976 this increasing militancy among young South Africans spilled over in the uprising in SOWETO, a black residential township of Johannesburg. The event triggered an upsurge in black protest. This rendered black urban townships ungovernable during much of the 1970s and 1980s, despite ongoing attempts by both the South African police and army to impose order.

Many young black activists joined the ranks of MK in neighboring countries, where they were exposed to military training, organizational discipline, and ideological indoctrination. At about the same time, the ANC benefited from the support of the newly independent nations of MOZAMBIQUE and ANGOLA, which had won hard-fought battles for autonomy from Portugal in 1975 and 1976, respectively. After 1980 Zimbabwe (formerly RHODESIA), which had gained its independence from the white settler-led UNILATERAL DECLARATION OF INDEPENDENCE government, also offered a haven to MK cadres. These countries permitted the ANC to set up bases close to the South African border, from which it could launch guerilla attacks against the state. In addition, the legalization of South African trade unions that occurred during the late 1970s gave the ANC an opportunity to forge closer ties to organized labor.

Increasingly during the 1980s, African protesters rallied around readily recognizable ANC symbols. These included people, such as its imprisoned leader, Nelson Mandela, as well as its unique raised-fist salute and handshake, and its distinctive black, green, and gold flag. At the funerals of prominent black activists, protestors utilized these symbols and sang ANC songs to register their solidarity, transforming funerals into antiapartheid political rallies. In 1983 the leaders of South African trade unions, civic organizations, and church groups joined together to form the UNITED DEMOCRATIC FRONT. It adopted the Freedom Charter (the political blueprint for change in South Africa authored in 1955 by the ANC and sympathetic opposition organizations) as the basis of its core principles, formed close ties with the exiled ANC, and effectively functioned as the ANC's legalized front in South Africa.

By the mid-1980s white business leaders initiated meetings with the ANC leadership in Lusaka, laying plans for a future day when the ANC would play an important role in shaping South African political life. Internationally, as world opinion hardened against apartheid practices, economic and diplomatic sanctions intensified against South Africa. The South African government increasingly came to be regarded as an illegitimate, pariah regime because of its racist laws and the violence that its enforcement agencies perpetrated against the country's majority black population. Many outside observers saw the ANC as the country's legitimate potential government that alone could speak for the oppressed masses.

Recognizing the necessity of negotiating with the ANC to secure public tranquility and appease world opinion, President P. W. BOTHA (1916–) initiated halfhearted attempts with Mandela in the mid-1980s. Years later, his successor, F. W. DE KLERK (1936–), continued these discussions in earnest. In February 1990, for example, he lifted the ban on extra-parliamentary opposition groups. This led to the rapid emergence of the ANC as the leading political party to challenge the ruling National Party. Also in 1990 the government released all political prisoners, including Mandela, who assumed the presidency of the organization the following year. In response to these steps, the ANC suspended its armed struggle against the government and rapidly evolved from a resistance group to a political party. Most of the power-sharing discussions that the government conducted with opposition groups focused on winning the approval of the ANC.

In the period leading up to the 1994 national elections in which black South Africans could freely vote for the first time, violence threatened to undermine the process. The most significant clashes erupted between supporters of the ANC and the INKATHA FREEDOM PARTY, an organization made up mostly of ZULU South Africans that was led by Mangosuthu Gatsha BUTHELEZI (1928–). To shore up its support, the ANC entered into an alliance with the Congress of South African Trade Unions (COSATU) and the South African Communist Party (SACP). In the elections of May 1994 the ANC won approximately 63 percent of the national vote. Except for the Western Cape and Kwa Zulu/Natal provinces, the ANC gained control of the country's seven other provincial legislatures.

Mandela served a single term as president, from 1994 to 1999. At that time Thabo MBEKI (1942–), Mandela's handpicked successor as ANC president, assumed leadership of the ANC. Under Mbeki the ANC again won the national election of 1999. However, fractures within the party weakened it. Specifically, because of the conservative fiscal policies the ANC government has pursued, its alliance with COSATU and SACP has suffered. Regardless, through 2003 the ANC remained an unchallenged force among South Africa's electorate.

Further reading: Saul Dubow, *The African National Congress* (Stroud, U.K.: Sutton Publishing, 2000); Dale T. McKinley, *The ANC and the Liberation Struggle: A Critical Political Biography* (Chicago: Pluto Press, 1997).

African Party for the Independence of Guinea and Cape Verde (Partido Africano da Independência da Guiné e Cabo Verde, PAIGC) African nationalist political organization founded by Amílcar CABRAL (1924–1973). The PAIGC resistance group had its roots in the Movement for the National Independence of Portuguese Guiné, a clandestine, BISSAU-based organization made up of workers and civil servants from CAPE VERDE and GUINEA-BISSAU. When that organization failed to garner broad support it evolved into the PAIGC in 1956. Led by Cabral, a former civil servant in the Portuguese colonial agricultural service, the PAIGC became the major nationalist party in the struggle to liberate both Guinea-Bissau and Cape Verde from Portuguese colonial rule.

The main objectives of PAIGC included the immediate granting of independence and the establishment of social and economic stability. PAIGC followed a Marxist-Leninist ideology that relied on fomenting revolution among the masses. However, since the majority of the PAIGC members were from Guinea-Bissau's educated, urban elite, they had difficulty attracting working-class members. Ultimately the original PAIGC program failed, and the leadership then decided to focus on organizing the peasant masses living in the countryside.

By 1962 various independent African nations as well as the communist Soviet Union strongly supported PAIGC. By 1967 the organization controlled more than half of Guinea-Bissau. During these years Portuguese resistance stiffened, but so did African resolve. In 1973 Portuguese secret police assassinated Amílcar Cabral, and the leadership of PAIGC passed to Aristides Maria PEREIRA (1923–). Later in 1973 Pereira declared Guinea-Bissau's independence from Portugal. The following year, despite Pereira's leading the party, Luis Cabral (1931–), Amílcar's half-brother, became the first president of the newly independent state.

In 1980 a new Cape Verdean constitution made provisions for the country to be united as a single state with Guinea-Bissau. Before the unification could take place, however, Cabral was ousted in a COUP D'ÉTAT led by army general João Bernardo Vieira (1939–), also a member of PAIGC. Vieira nullified the 1980 constitution and directed the drafting of a new one, which separated Cape Verde from Guinea-Bissau. The coup led to tensions between the Guinea-Bissau and Cape Verde wings of the PAIGC, eventually splitting the party in 1981. At that time the Cape Verde PAIGC reorganized as the African Party for the Independence of Cape Verde.

In 1990 a group of 350 PAIGC representatives met to discuss the plan for advancing political reform and DEMOCRATIZATION in Guinea-Bissau, and the following year the country's national assembly chose to abandon single-party rule. Following multiparty elections held in 1994, Vieira and the PAIGC remained in control. By 1999, however, civil war and dissatisfaction with Vieira's rule forced him to flee the country. In the 2000 elections Koumba YALA (c. 1953–), leader of the Social Renewal Party, was elected president. As an indication of how far the PAIGC leadership had fallen out of favor, in the 1999 legislative elections the PAIGC received less than one-quarter of the 102 seats in the National Assembly.

See also: COLD WAR AND AFRICA (Vols. IV, V); COLONIAL RULE (Vol. IV); INDEPENDENCE MOVEMENTS (Vol. V); NATIONALISM AND INDEPENDENCE MOVEMENTS (Vol. IV); POLITICAL PARTIES AND ORGANIZATIONS (Vol. V); PORTUGAL AND AFRICA (Vols. III, IV, V).

African studies Academic discipline encompassing the study of Africa, its peoples, and its societies. Initially African studies centered on anthropology, archaeology, history, political science, and the study of languages. More recently it has broadened to include AGRICULTURE, EDUCATION, ENVIRONMENTAL ISSUES, public health, and other more technical and applied disciplines. Organized African studies programs are for the most part located outside the continent, mainly in the United States and to a lesser degree in Great Britain, France, the Netherlands, Canada, and the Nordic countries.

> The historian and educator William Leo Hansberry (1894–1965) was one of the pioneering African American scholars in African studies. As a freshman at Atlanta University, he became curious about Kush and ETHIOPIA, which were mentioned in the Bible but about which he could find little additional information. Later, as a professor at Howard University he devoted his career to providing such information, conducting research on Ethiopian history and on the classical writers' views of Africa and Africans.

African studies emerged as a field of academic endeavor in the United States in the late 1950s and early 1960s. There were essentially three sources of origin. One was the long-standing interest of African Americans regarding the continent of their ancestry. One of the earliest scholarly books in this tradition was *The Negro*, by the famed black intellectual W. E. B. Du Bois (1868–1963), which appeared in 1915. Howard University was at the forefront of African American scholarship on Africa, and in 1953 it established a Department of African Studies that offered an M.A. degree. It later became the first American university to offer a Ph.D. in African studies. These developments reflected a heightened African American awareness about Africa as a result of intensifying nationalism and INDEPENDENCE MOVEMENTS on the continent and the civil rights struggle at home.

The second source of African studies was the growing general American interest in the world as a result of World War II (1939–45). One of the lessons learned from the war was that the isolationism of the inter-war period had given Americans a false sense of security. They now needed to be more aware of other parts of the world, including Africa. Foundations such as the Carnegie Corporation and the Ford Foundation began to support area studies, including study of Africa, which led the distinguished anthropologist Melville J. Herskovits (1895–1963) to found the country's first African studies research program at Northwestern University in 1949.

The movement toward independence, beginning with GHANA in 1957, further fueled academic interest in Africa. The U.S. government also showed a greater interest in Africa and, in 1958, established the position of assistant secretary of state for Africa within the Department of State. That same year Congress passed the National Defense Education Act (NDEA), which funded area studies in general. Over the next decade a number of universities established major African studies centers and programs, which in turn encouraged other colleges and universities to set up smaller programs on their own campuses. By 1981 there were approximately 70 such programs nationwide, and by the mid-1990s there were nearly 90 programs. Today the African Studies Association—which was founded in 1957 by a small group of 36 scholars, foundation leaders, and government officials—has a membership well in excess of 2,000.

Related to but separate from the general growth of American academic interest in Africa was the emergence of the Cold War rivalry between the United States and the former Soviet Union. The Cold War prompted President John F. Kennedy (1917–1963) to establish the Peace Corps, which in turn led many returned Peace Corps volunteers to pursue graduate degrees related to the African countries in which they served.

The United States has been well served by the convergence of these three sources, which has produced a vibrant and diverse field of highly knowledgeable scholars who are in turn training students who are well informed about the continent and its peoples. Today, those teaching and conducting research about Africa at American universities and colleges include not only individuals born in the United States but also scholars from Europe and, increasingly, Africa itself. Indeed, the addition of the latter group as permanent rather than visiting faculty members is a relatively recent phenomenon. Many of these scholars received their graduate degrees in the United States, Canada, or Europe and returned to their home countries to teach. However, the political instability and economic woes of many African countries has greatly weakened their universities and has led members of their faculties to seek positions outside the continent. While this has impoverished African universities, it has enriched the field of African studies in the United States by providing more of an African perspective to teaching and research.

See also: ANTHROPOLOGY AND AFRICA (Vols. IV, V); ARCHAEOLOGY IN AFRICA (Vols. IV, V); COLD WAR AND AFRICA (Vols. IV, V); DU BOIS, W. E. B. (Vol. IV); HISTORICAL SCHOLARSHIP ON AFRICA (Vols. IV, V); UNITED STATES AND AFRICA (Vols. IV, V).

African Union (AU) Continental body bringing together the leadership of all African countries to work toward common goals. The African Union replaced the ORGANIZATION OF AFRICAN UNITY (OAU) as the continentwide constituent assembly. The purpose of the OAU was to remove the vestiges of the colonial period and to promote African unity and cooperation during the early nationalist period. At inception, in 1963, the mission of the OAU clearly reflected Africa's needs. By the 1990s, however, its mission no longer seemed suited to meeting the shifting requirements of the community of African states. Specifically, African leaders saw the need for the organization to be more focused on economic advancement and less concerned with erasing the remaining traces of the colonial era.

Growing out of an OAU summit meeting held in Sirte, LIBYA, the African Union was established by the Sirte Declaration on September 9, 1999. All 53 African heads of state played a part. Looking at present needs and future challenges, they stated their goals as promoting economic and political integration, promoting and defending African positions in the global sphere, and fostering democracy and good governance on the continent.

In the years following the Sirte Declaration, several additional AU conventions helped define its purpose. The Lome Summit, in 2000, adopted the Constitutive Act of the Union. The Lusaka Summit, in 2001, created a plan to implement the AU. And the Durban Summit, in 2002, served as the inaugural assembly of the heads of states of the African Union. Amara Essy (1944–), president of the IVORY COAST and the first chairman of the AU, was charged with heading the institutional transition. Joaquim Alberto CHISSANO (1939–), president of MOZAMBIQUE, took over Essy's role two years later.

The AU is made up of nine primary organs that distribute power among different branches and institutions. These include offices that coordinate projects regarding peace and security, the economy, cultural and social affairs, justice, and monetary and financial affairs. The AU supports three banks: the African Central Bank, African Monetary Fund, and African Investment Bank. Other AU offices deal with human resources, industry, science and technology, energy, NATURAL RESOURCES, and TOURISM.

The creation and continued role of the African Union has not been free from contention. Symbolic of the long road that lay ahead of the AU, its early efforts to assert its authority revealed as much divisiveness—especially among the old-guard leaders—as it did cooperative and innovative progress toward the future. At the outset, the international community fully supported the idea of the AU but objected to the significant role afforded controversial Libyan president Muammar QADDAFI (1942–) in its creation. Also, the AU has been cautious about many of its mandates and whether they will challenge those of existing international organizations.

Further reading: Henning Melber, *The New African Initiative and the African Union* (Somerset, N.J.: Transaction Publishers, 2002).

Afrikaans An official language of SOUTH AFRICA that developed from a dialect of Netherlandic (Dutch-Flemish) in the late 18th century. During the APARTHEID period (1948–90) Afrikaans was the language of white privilege. Along with English it was one of the two official languages of South Africa. The National Party government institutionalized Afrikaans as the language of government and EDUCATION. Consequently, Afrikaans is the first language of 60 percent of white South Africans. It is also the first language of more than 90 percent of those categorized as Coloured and is a second language of many black South Africans.

Because it was the tool of Afrikaner cultural imperialism, Afrikaans became a symbolic target of rebellion. In 1976, for example, schoolchildren in SOWETO demonstrated against having their subjects taught in Afrikaans.

In 1994 the Constitutional Assembly of the newly democratic South African Republic chose the following 11 languages as official languages of the nation: Afrikaans, English, isiNdebele, Sesotho sa Leboa, Sesotho, isiSwai, Xitsonga, Setswana, Tshivenda, isiXhosa, and isiZulu.

Although three other South African languages are more widely spoken, English was selected by the post-apartheid government as the official international language for commercial and diplomatic exchanges. Similar to some other African countries, the South African government chose an outsider language to avoid favoring one of its indigenous languages over the others. Following this policy the government removed Afrikaans as the language of public offices, courts, and the education system. It now allows Afrikaans to be visible only on signs that present it in conjunction with the country's other 10 official languages. Aware of the contempt held for the history of Afrikaans and in light of the expected changes concerning its use, many AFRIKANERS now educate their children in English.

See also: AFRIKAANS (Vols. III, IV); BOERS (Vols. III, IV); LANGUAGE USAGE IN MODERN AFRICA (Vol. V); LITERATURE IN COLONIAL AFRICA (Vol. IV), LITERATURE IN MODERN AFRICA (Vol. V).

Further reading: Rajend Mesthrie, ed., *Language in South Africa* (New York: Cambridge University Press, 2002).

Afrikaners White South Africans predominantly of Dutch or Huguenot Calvinist ancestry who speak the language of AFRIKAANS. With the victory of the National Party (NP) in the 1948 parliamentary elections, and the rise of D. F. Malan (1874–1959) to the position of prime minister, the South African government evolved to serve the goals of Afrikaner nationalism. The tenets of Afrikaner nationalism promoted the improvement of the financial and political position of Afrikaners and the protection of Afrikaner culture from the influence of British, English-speaking South Africans.

Many of these concerns, however, dissipated as the 20th century progressed. By the 1960s Afrikaner POVERTY was nearly nonexistent, with South Africa's white population reaping the economic benefits granted to them by the racist APARTHEID system. Powerful Afrikaners were probably members of the BROEDERBOND, an all-male secret society that worked as a proving ground for the Afrikaner political elite. Furthermore, as Afrikaners increasingly dominated South African politics—every president of SOUTH AFRICA was an Afrikaner from 1948 to 1994—the political threat from English-speakers waned. With the diminution of power of English speakers, the Afrikaner political apparatus placed an increased importance on maintaining the legislated inequalities between whites and non-whites. Ignoring a historically acrimonious relationship, the NP even reached out to English-speakers with the hope that, as fellow whites, they would forget any past hostilities in favor of maintaining their preferential status over blacks.

This courting of English speakers in large part resulted from the changing dynamic of the Afrikaner population, which failed to keep pace with the growth rate of South Africa's black populace. At the same time, an ideological split within Afrikaner society began to threaten the paradigm of apartheid. Many Afrikaners began to question the racist system, especially those who held commercial interests dependent upon the LABOR and latent purchasing power of black South Africans. In 1982 this division culminated with many members of the NP defecting to form the Conservative Party, which was dedicated to defending the apartheid system without any concessions or changes.

The two opposing factions within the Afrikaner community were dubbed the *verkramptes* and the *verligtes*. The *verkramptes* held traditional Afrikaner values and wanted apartheid to continue as it had, while the *verligtes* were less conservative and rejected the rigidity of apartheid, wishing to "modernize" it instead.

Though the defection of the NP members may have prolonged the transition of South Africa to a multiracial, representative government, the ascension of the black majority was inescapable. The transition to a representative government was completed in 1994 under the leadership of Prime Minister F. W. DE KLERK (1936–). That year Nelson MANDELA (1918–) and the previously banned AFRICAN NATIONAL CONGRESS carried the first free, multiracial elections in the country's history. Having lost their hold on power and now in the political as well as demographic minority, the Afrikaners are attempting to find their place within post-apartheid South Africa. The political unity of a half-century earlier has disappeared, but there remains a deep sense of a shared history and common language to build on.

See also: AFRIKANERS (Vol. IV); BOERS (Vols. III, IV); ETHNICITY AND IDENTITY (Vol. I); MALAN, D. F. (Vol. IV).

Further reading: Hermann Giliomee, *The Afrikaners: Biography of a People* (London: C. Hurst, 2003); Dan O'Meara, *Forty Lost Years: The Apartheid State and the Politics of the National Party, 1948–1994* (Athens, Ohio: Ohio University Press, 1997).

Afro-Shirazi Party (ASP) Political party of ZANZIBAR that was active from 1957 to 1977. In the 1950s, as Zanzibar moved toward independence, an Arab minority controlled the government under the umbrella of the Zanzibar National Party (ZNP). In 1957 Abeid Amani KARUME (1905–1972), with the assistance of Julius NYERERE (1922–1999), the president of Tanganyika, founded the Afro-Shirazi Party (ASP) to organize the African majority of the country.

After gaining independence from Britain in 1963, Zanzibar held elections to determine the makeup of its National Assembly. The results solidified ZNP control of the government despite its members' minority status. In 1964 the ASP sparked a bloody revolution against the government. In the chaos that ensued, thousands died and thousands more fled the island. Once in control, the ASP named Karume president of Zanzibar.

In 1964 Zanzibar joined in political union with Tanganyika, but retained its own electoral system and continued to exercise considerable local autonomy. The union resulted in the creation of the country of TANZANIA, with Nyerere remaining president and Karume becoming vice president. Karume was assassinated in 1972. In 1977 Nyerere combined the ASP with his own TANZANIAN AFRICAN NATIONAL UNION to form the PARTY OF THE REVOLUTION (Chama Cha Mapinduzi, CCM). The CCM then was made the only legal political party of Tanzania.

See also: JUMBE, ABOUD (Vol. V); POLITICAL PARTIES AND ORGANIZATIONS (Vol. V); SHIRAZI ARABS (Vol. II); SHIRAZI DYNASTY (Vol. III); TANGANYIKA (Vol. IV).

agriculture Between 1850 and 1960 Africa's agriculture underwent a tremendous transformation in terms of both its structure and its food production capabilities. Instead of producing FOOD CROPS for local consumption, African agriculture had become increasingly focused on exporting CASH CROPS to overseas markets. This fundamental change in agriculture was accompanied by growing URBANIZATION, which meant that fewer Africans were able to grow their own food. But with the emphasis on export production, African farmers had not developed agricultural production geared to feeding Africa's growing cities. POPULATION GROWTH surged after 1950, from an annual rate of approximately 1.2 percent over the previous 50 years to a dramatic 3.3 percent rate in the 1980s. This surge put additional stress on Africa's already challenged food production capabilities. As African countries launched into the new era of independence, therefore, they found themselves saddled with a colonial inheritance of agricultural systems ill prepared to meet their needs.

Beyond the deeply rooted problem of cash crop exportation, food production was further affected by the fact that the economies of many countries depended on the production of a single crop. Such mono-crop economies were highly susceptible to the fluctuations in world commodity prices. As a result many African nations were increasingly dependent on external markets and economic forces that were beyond their control.

In light of the situation, Africa's leaders at independence were not in a position to depart radically from the economic strategies of the colonial era. Therefore they continued to promote the production of cash crops in order to earn the foreign exchange needed for their efforts at modernization. In the 1960s modernization meant INDUSTRIALIZATION and urbanization. Furthermore, leaders strongly influenced by Marxist ideology and the example of the Soviet Union viewed the state—rather than the private sector—as the central engine for DEVELOPMENT. Many countries thus continued the colonial practice of marketing boards, or state-run agencies through which all farmers had to sell their crops. At the expense of agricultural development in the rural areas, these marketing boards kept producer prices low in order to divert earnings from export sales to the modernization enterprise. The boards also enabled governments to keep food prices low for the urban areas. Lacking price incentives to increase their output, Africa's peasant farmers cut back on their production. White commercial farmers, on the other hand, faced their own challenges. After independence the numbers of white farmers declined as European settlers emigrated or had their farms expropriated. Those who remained continued to produce largely for export, as did the large industrial plantations.

Where the government did invest in agriculture, it was usually in the form of collectivization and state farms. In TANZANIA, for example, President Julius NYERERE (1922–1999) implemented *UJAMAA*, an economic and social policy that envisaged collective, grassroots development through the rural population in villages. The irony was that in one of the few instances in which an African government sought to infuse resources into the rural sector, agricultural production fell sharply. An increase in management demands, inadequate INFRASTRUCTURE, and the disruption of long-standing farming practices led most farmers to retreat into subsistence production. The marketing of foodstuffs to the urban areas declined, forcing a country in which more than 75 percent of the labor force was employed in agriculture to import food to feed its coastal cities. Ultimately the Tanzanian government had to admit to the failure of *ujamaa*.

In 1960 African agriculture was still meeting food consumption needs in most parts of the continent. Over the next few decades, however, per-capita food production declined at an average rate of about 1 percent per year. While government policies exacerbated the decline, they were not its root cause. Rather, the growing scarcity of arable land meant that farmers in certain regions were not able to bring new land into production to expand output. The affected areas included ETHIOPIA, parts of North Africa, parts of West Africa, including the densely populated HAUSA region of northern NIGERIA, and the well-watered upland areas of eastern and southern Africa. In other cases farmers brought into production land that did not yield good crops or was quickly degraded. Africa's crisis, simply put, was the inability of African farmers to produce sufficient quantities of food for the growing population.

One of the confounding aspects of Africa's agricultural decline was the fact that, up to that point, Africa's farmers had largely been able to meet their various challenges. For many centuries they had successfully adapted

to produce crops and raise livestock in difficult environments. With some exceptions in areas with highly fertile soils, such as the Nile River Valley and RWANDA, the continent's soils were not conducive to high agricultural productivity. Many regions also had highly variable rainfall patterns that limited productivity. LABOR constraints, which were only becoming more severe with the migration of younger people to the cities, placed further limitations on the output of African farmers. In the face of such difficulties African farmers had long been successful in crop and livestock production through strategies such as intercropping (growing multiple crops in a single field at one time), slash-and-burn agriculture coupled with long fallow periods, and seasonal migration of herds. These techniques, however, developed a low-productivity form of agriculture that was not readily changed.

Between 1968 and 1985 a particularly severe and prolonged drought in the Sahel, the zone to the south of the Sahara Desert, led to terrible crop failures. During that period local food needs were met largely through relief supplies, but many farmers lost their livelihoods as their crops and livestock disappeared.

By the 1980s the dimensions of Africa's agricultural problems were beginning to attract attention. Unfortunately the continent's relatively low productivity was not open to the type of "fixes" that worked in other areas, including India and Southeast Asia. In these and other regions, crop shortages were addressed by rapidly increasing yields of grain crops such as wheat and rice. This approach was so successful that it ushered in the so-called Green Revolution, a time of great gains in agricultural output. Unfortunately, neither wheat nor rice is a significant crop for much of Africa. Moreover, native African grain crops such as sorghum and millet have never received the same intense agricultural research that has benefited the cultivation of grain crops in the Northern Hemisphere. Other factors that hinder a transformation of African agriculture include inadequate infrastructure and TRANSPORTATION as well as instability in the region's MARKETS. POVERTY, which is more prevalent in rural than in urban areas, further reduces efforts to improve the productivity of Africa's farmers.

The food production crisis is perhaps the single most important of all the crises facing the continent at the present time. But given the enormous ecological diversity of the continent and the great variety of agricultural systems and crops, not to mention the enormous other social, economic, and political differences that exist across the continent, there is no simple answer.

See also: AGRICULTURE (Vols. I, II, III, IV); COLONIALISM, INFLUENCE OF (Vol. IV); DROUGHT AND DESERTIFICATION (Vol. V); ENVIRONMENTAL ISSUES (Vol. V); FAMINE AND HUNGER (Vol. V); MONO-CROP ECONOMIES (Vol. IV); NATURAL RESOURCES (Vol. V) NEOCOLONIALISM AND UNDERDEVELOPMENT (Vol. V).

Further reading: T. S. Jayne, I. J. Minde, and Gem Argwings-Kodhek, eds., *Perspectives on Agricultural Transformation: A View from Africa* (New York: Nova Science, 2002).

Ahidjo, Ahmadou (1924–1989) *President of Cameroon*

The son of a Fulani chief, Ahidjo was born in the river port city of Garoua, on the Benue River in then French-ruled northern CAMEROON. At the time, the former German colony was divided between Great Britain and France under the terms of a League of Nations mandate. Ahidjo received a secondary school education in YAOUNDÉ.

Ahidjo initially became active in politics in 1947, when he was elected first as a territorial deputy and then in 1953 to the Assembly of the French Union. Though a Muslim, Ahidjo joined the Catholic-based Démocrates party in 1956, helping the party gain support in the mainly Muslim north of the French Cameroons.

In 1957 Ahidjo became vice premier and interior minister under Premier André Marie Mbida. The following year, however, he split from Mbida to form a new party, the Cameroon Union (Union Camerounaise, UC). Mbida resigned, and Ahidjo assumed the position of premier. When the independent Cameroon Republic was established in 1960, Ahidjo was elected president.

Ahidjo and the UC began what became a long-term domination of Cameroon politics. Supporting strong connections with both France and other African nations, in 1961 Ahidjo convinced the leaders of the British Southern Cameroons to unite with the Cameroon Republic to form the Federal Republic of Cameroon. In the meantime, the UC gradually subsumed its opposition, with Ahidjo occasionally jailing political rivals. Eventually the UC became the sole political entity in Cameroon. After Ahidjo was reelected in 1965, the UC became the Cameroon National Union (Union Nationale Camerounaise, UNC).

Ahidjo won reelection in 1970, 1975, and once again in 1980. During this time, he established a new constitution, forming the United Republic of Cameroon over protests against a unitary government. In 1982, after 22 years in office, Ahidjo voluntarily resigned, and Prime Minister Paul BIYA (1933–) became president. Ahidjo remained head of the UNC, however, and differences between Ahidjo and Biya escalated. Ultimately, Ahidjo was accused of plotting a COUP D'ÉTAT against Biya, and in 1983 he was forcibly exiled to France. The Cameroon government tried him in absentia and sentenced him to death. Ahidjo remained an exile until his death of a heart attack in 1989, in DAKAR, SENEGAL.

Aideed, Mohamed F. (Farah) (1934–1996) *Somalian military leader*

Aideed was born to Fatuma Salah and Farah Hassan, a minor clan chief of the Habar Gedir, a sub-clan of the Hawiye, the largest of the Somali clans. At a young age, he traveled to Ogaden, ETHIOPIA, to study the Quran. Aideed joined the Somali Youth League and later enlisted in the colonial Italian Gendarmeria. In 1954 he was selected to receive training at the NATO Infantry School at Cesano in Rome. When Aideed completed his training, the Italian government assigned him to head the Bakool indigenous police force in the Upper Juba Division. He received more training in the Soviet Union and returned home to be a Somali nationalist leader. When SOMALIA achieved independence in 1960, the United Nations (UN) looked to Aideed to help build the new country. In the 1980s Aideed and his Somali National Alliance fought against the Somali strongman Mohammed Siad BARRE (1910–1995), ultimately driving the latter from the country to pave the way for Aideed's rise to power.

Aideed will be remembered for embarrassing UN forces and driving them from Somalia in 1993. When the United States, under the auspices of the UN, entered Somalia for what it proclaimed were humanitarian purposes, Aideed took this as a threat both to Somali sovereignty and to his own position of power. In October 1993, in a conflict that resulted in as many as 1,000 Somali casualties, Aideed's forces shot down an American army helicopter, killing 18 soldiers. They later dragged the bodies of the dead soldiers through the streets of MOGADISHU, an event broadcast on international television. After that disturbing scene, Aideed became an international pariah. In 1995 he declared himself president of Somalia, though no sovereign state recognized his authority. Aideed was killed August 2, 1996 by rival Somali warlord Ali Mahdi Muhammad.

> The shooting-down of an American UH-60 Blackhawk helicopter by Somali forces was an event that seriously damaged America's sense of military invulnerability. The phrase "Black Hawk Down" was popularized by a book detailing the incident (1999) and later by Ridley Scott's movie adaptation (2001), both of the same name.

See also: SOVIET UNION AND AFRICA (Vols. IV, V); UNITED NATIONS AND AFRICA (Vol. V).

Aidoo, Ama Ata (1942–) *Ghanaian writer*

Ama Ata Aidoo was born in 1942 at Abeadze Kyiakor, near Dominase in the Fante-speaking region of what was then Gold Coast Colony (present-day GHANA). The daughter of a chief, Aidoo received an early education that emphasized the importance of African oral tradition and ritual and the techniques of storytelling. She later attended Wesley Girls' High School in Ghana, and then the University of Ghana, Legon, where she earned an honors degree in English in 1964.

From 1964 to 1966 Aidoo was a junior research fellow at the university's Institute of AFRICAN STUDIES. She began her literary career by attending writers' workshops at the School of Drama, where she produced her first two plays. She then attended the creative writing program at Stanford University, in the United States. In addition to her writing, Aidoo taught at the University of Ghana and at other universities in Africa and in the United States, including the University of Florida.

During the 1970s Ghana's military governments and the associated political oppression of the country's academic community forced her to stop publishing. After army Lieutenant Jerry RAWLINGS (1947–   ) led a successful coup of young military officers and became president of Ghana, Aidoo served as minister for education in 1983–84. She ultimately resigned because of political differences and went into self-exile in ZIMBABWE, where she worked as a freelance writer. She currently lives in the United States, where she writes and lectures.

Aidoo's writing has been influenced by both her formal and informal education, the influence of PAN-AFRICAN-ISM, and her experiences in Ghana during the nationalist push for independence. Her themes focus on colonial history and the legacy of slavery that helped shape the character of her beloved Ghana.

Aidoo's first play was first performed in 1964 and then published in 1965. Entitled *The Dilemma of a Ghost,* it focuses on the cultural conflict and sense of alienation felt by a young African woman who returns home after receiving an American education. The story illustrates the competition between Western individualism and African communal values that exposure to the colonial world has engendered. This theme reappears in her semi-autobiographical novel, *Our Sister Killjoy: Or, Reflections from a Black-Eyed Squint* (1977).

Many of Aidoo's works also deal with the role and place of women in African society. Examples include her *No Sweetness Here* (1970), a collection of 11 short stories, and her second novel *Changes: A Love Story* (1991), which received the 1993 British Commonwealth Writers Prize.

See also: LITERATURE IN MODERN AFRICA (Vol. V).

Akosombo Dam   Built in 1966 in the Akwamu Highlands of GHANA, the Akosombo Dam harnesses the Volta River to generate up to 768,000-kilowatts of hydroelectric power. In addition to generating electricity, the dam was also intended to improve WATER TRANS-PORTATION and to store water for agricultural, industrial, and recreational use.

The government of the then Gold Coast Colony began planning a dam as early as 1949, when it commissioned engineers to conduct a feasibility study. In 1959 the Kaiser Company of the United States recommended that the dam be built at Akosombo Gorge and that a grid of electrical transmission lines be created to supply electricity to the southern region of the country. An aluminum smelter at Temna was later added to the plan. In 1962 Ghana's Parliament approved the master agreement with Valco (the Volta Aluminum Company), a subsidiary of Kaiser. An Italian engineering consortium received the contract to build the dam for the government's Volta River Authority. By 1966 construction was set to start.

The town of Akosombo, built to house the construction workers for the Volta dam, became a major port on VOLTA LAKE, which formed behind the new dam. Akosombo is today the starting point for ships and ferries to ports further north, such as Buipe and Yapei near Tamale. Covering an area of 3,275 square miles (8,482 sq km), Volta Lake is the largest artificial lake in the world.

Foes of President Kwame NKRUMAH (1909–1972) felt that the dam was an overly ambitious project that benefited the Kaiser Industries Corporation more than Ghana. The Akosombo Dam and similar prestige projects were factors in the overthrow of President Nkrumah in 1966.

See also: GOLD COAST (Vols. III, IV) VOLTA RIVER (Vol. II), VOLTA BASIN (Vol. III).

Algeria   North African country along the Mediterranean Sea measuring about 919,600 square miles (2,381,800 sq km) Algeria shares borders with TUNISIA and LIBYA, to the east, with NIGER, MALI, and MAURITANIA, to the south, and with MOROCCO, to the west.

An OIL-rich country of more than 30 million people, Algeria struggles with deep economic divides that are exacerbated by its French, Islamic, and military identities. The country's population is made up mostly of Malekite Sunni Muslims, complemented by other Muslim groups as well as Chenoua, Berber-speaking Kabyles, and Tuareg speakers. Algeria is a member of the Arab League, the ORGANIZATION OF PETROLEUM EXPORTING COUNTRIES (OPEC), the Organization of Arab Petroleum Exporting Countries, and the Arab Monetary Fund. These alliances give Algeria close ties to much of the Islamic world, and the Saudi peninsula in particular.

Algeria at Independence Algeria has long been at the center of regional trade and imperialism. In the 16th century the capital, ALGIERS, was the North African base for the ruling Ottoman Turks. In 1830 France took control of the region, formally annexing Algeria in 1842. This led to a fundamental shift in Algerian society that included a large French settler population in Algeria and a large Algerian population within France that currently numbers about 1 million.

Algeria's struggle for independence culminated in a war that began in 1954 and that resulted in more than 1 million deaths. The war, which did not end until July 5, 1962, propelled the NATIONAL LIBERATION FRONT (Front de Libération Nationale, FLN) to the forefront of Algerian political life. Its leader, Ahmed BEN BELLA (1916–), became the president of the new country. Yet while he was a gifted nationalist leader, he proved to be a poor head of government, and his policies led to economic ruin and intra-governmental factionalism. The result was continued social upheaval, militancy among the Berber-speaking Kabyle, and an eventual COUP D'ETAT led by Colonel Houari BOUMEDIENNE (1927–1978), creator and head of the armed forces.

Military and Political Instability Boumedienne was not a gifted leader, but he did put down much of the insurgency. He also promoted centralized agrarian reforms and rapid INDUSTRIALIZATION to improve the economy. When Boumedienne died in 1978, Colonel Chadli Bendjedid (1929–) took over as president.

Bendjedid worked to decentralize power and privatize many of the failing public companies. In 1984 he was elected to a second five-year term. However, the resulting economic growth benefited only a small segment of the population, and following his reelection, Bendjedid faced increasing public discontent. By October 1988 intra-party class warfare plagued the nation; as the FLN leadership prospered, the masses went without jobs and opportunities for EDUCATION. Abroad, Algerian-led demonstrations in Paris caused anxiety throughout Western Europe, as memories of the violent independence struggle of the 1950s came surging to the fore.

1988–1992: The Rise of Islamic Insurgency In 1990 Algeria declared that it would be a multiparty democracy. Nascent political groups, notably those of Islamic and Kabylian origin, were organized and began expressing political will. Yet it appeared that the opening of political competition did little to open up the nexus of power within the Algerian state. The real power, it turned out, lay in the presidency and in the military, which remained in the control of the FLN.

Algeria's first multiparty elections, held on June 12, 1990, were for local government positions. The new Kabyle Movement for Culture and Democracy made significant strides against the FLN. However, it was the success of the Islamic Salvation Front (Front Islamique

du Salud, FIS) that made the FLN, and the world, take notice. By the time the country held its first plural legislative elections, in December 1991, the new FIS had successfully built a base of support from among the majority population of Muslims disenchanted with FLN leadership. Despite the earlier arrest of FIS leaders Abassi Madani and Ali Belhaj, the party won an estimated 188 of the 231 seats in the first round of legislative elections. When it appeared that the FIS was headed for a victory in the scheduled second elections, the military stepped in to depose Bendjedid and annul the first elections. The FIS was immediately banned, and its leadership was forced into exile. In taking these steps, the military leadership undermined the process of DEMOCRATIZATION in favor of political liberalization. Its actions only increased popular dissent.

The 1990s and the Increase of Algerian Dissension In light of the annulled elections, the military leadership rapidly sought legitimization. In January 1994 it appointed a retired general, Liamine Zeroual (1941–), as president. The following year Zeroual was elected to the office after winning a presidential election from which all significant opposition parties were barred. Legislative elections held in 1997 were widely criticized by opponents as fraudulent.

Despite the disbanding of the FIS and the subsequent constitutional revisions that banned Algeria's Islamic parties, Islam has not left the country's political scene. The FIS continues to garner great support in the streets of Paris as well as in Algiers. Immediately following the 1992 elections the FIS was divided between the so-called *jazairists,* who pledged to respect the new government, and the *salafists,* who saw a turn to violence as the only viable alternative. The latter group quickly garnered support from Iranian-backed Hezbollah guerillas in Lebanon and began a bombing campaign. Fearing the rise of Islam, France kept silent on the issue of the 1992 coup and called for new elections. The United States, for its part, called the coup and the subsequent annulment of the elections "constitutional."

In addition to the FIS, another, more militant Islamist group has risen since 1992—the Armed Islamic Group (Groupe Islamique Armee, GIA). Although some Western countries consider the GIA to be a threat to regional stability, it is well organized and has solid support among segments of Algerian society. The GIA also enjoys support from other states in the Muslim world. Other Algerian groups that have support from local bases include the Armed Islamic Movement, the Movement for an Islamic State, and the Armed Islamic Front.

Algerian Politics Today Following the attacks on the United States on September 11, 2001, Islamic groups called tens of thousands of demonstrators to the streets to show support for Osama bin Laden (1957–) and Iraq's former president, Saddam Hussein (1937–). As a result of the public display of contempt for Western power there is a tendency to consider Algerian politics today as a microcosmic clash of civilizations—the struggle of democracy against radical Islam. This would, however, be an oversimplification.

From one perspective, the challenges to pluralism of the early 1990s and the rise of a Muslim alternative might be viewed as a positive, democratic progression. From another perspective, the violence that has gripped Algeria since 1989 is regressive. The shift to pluralism forced leaders to vest power in institutions other than political parties, resulting in a more powerful military and a revival of regionalized, precolonial institutions. From a third perspective, radical Islam can be viewed not as an effort to purge secular or Christian elements from Algerian society but, rather, as an attempt at finding a viable alternative to decades of political domination by the country's elite FLN leadership.

Liamine Zeroual resigned in 1999, and elections held in April of that year brought Abdelaziz BOUTEFLIKA (1937–) to the presidency. This went a long way toward bringing international legitimacy to Algerian governance after the 1992 coup. At home, though, the elections lacked legitimacy since all of the other candidates pulled out the day before the election. The rise of Bouteflika can be seen as a further entrenchment of the *ancien regime*. For example, Bouteflika had been foreign minister in 1963, and he was involved in the 1965 coup that brought Boumedienne to power. Even so, he has a reputation of spurning the constraints placed on him by the FLN.

Serious issues continue to divide Algeria's people. As late as 2004, the country was threatened by divisions between moderate and radical Islam, elite leadership and marginalized society, military and civilian rule, inward-looking and outward-looking governance, and socialist and capitalist economic plans. Further, since 1988, POVERTY has risen to engulf nearly one-fourth of the Algerian population. Despite regular economic growth, unemployment con-tinues to rise, and public services have decayed.

See also: ALGERIA (Vols. I, II, III, IV); FRANCE AND AFRICA (Vols. III, IV, V); INDEPENDENCE MOVEMENTS (Vol. V); ISLAM, INFLUENCE OF (Vols. II, III, IV, V).

Further reading: William B. Quandt, *Between Ballots and Bullets: Algeria's Transition from Authoritarianism* (Washington D.C.: Brookings Institution Press, 1998); Michael Willis, *The Islamist Challenge in Algeria: A Political History* (Reading, N.Y.: Ithaca Press, 1996).

Algiers Capital and port city located on the northern coast of ALGERIA. In the months before Algeria finally won its independence in 1962, bombings by the European Algerians, the *pieds-noirs*, had damaged industrial and communications facilities in Algiers. In spite of this, the new government rushed to make Algiers its base. Like CAIRO, EGYPT, Algiers is divided into two parts. The newer, French-built sector is similar to French cities in terms of urban planning and architectural style. The original Muslim quarter, in contrast, has narrower streets and numerous mosques. Since independence, Algiers's suburbs have expanded southward.

The Algerian government made use of many of the palaces built during Ottoman rule, renovating them to house museums, such as the National Museum of Antiques and the Museum of Popular Arts and Traditions. The History Museum, too, is located in a former palace. Algiers also has an observatory and Algeria's national library. The influence of European ARCHITECTURE can be seen in the opera house and Catholic churches, including the Basilica of Notre Dame and the Cathedral of Sacre Coeur, which was designed by the noted Swiss-born modernist architect Le Corbusier (1887–1965).

In 1981 Algiers introduced plans for a metro underground system that would run on three rail lines. However, in 1986, the collapse of global OIL prices caused planners to put the project on hold. By 1999 interest in the project had picked up again, and the government eventually made funding arrangements with the World Bank. The first rail line is expected to be operational in 2008.

See also: ALGIERS (Vols. III, IV).

Further reading: Zeynep Celik, *Urban Forms and Colonial Confrontations: Algiers under French Rule* (Berkeley, Calif.: University of Calif. Press, 1997).

All-Africa Games See SPORTS AND ATHLETICS (Vol. V).

Alliance for Patriotic Reorientation and Construction (APRC) Ruling party of The GAMBIA since 1994. On July 22, 1994, the Alliance for Patriotic Reorientation and Construction (APRC) came to power when Captain Yahya A. J. J. JAMMEH (1965–) led a bloodless coup against President Dawda Kairaba JAWARA (1924–). Jawara had been The Gambia's president since the country became a republic in 1970, but his government was seen as increasingly corrupt and autocratic.

Jammeh quickly suspended the country's constitution and officially banned all political action by opposition parties. He maintained control of the Gambian military by purging the ranks of dissidents, and further tightened his grip on the country by imposing government censorship and harsh restrictions on the press.

Bowing to international pressure, Jammeh resigned from the army for the presidential elections in 1996, which he won handily. At the same time, the APRC assumed control of both the Gambian house and legislature, but many condemned the elections as fixed in light of Jammeh's harsh government restrictions.

Following Algerian independence in 1962, Algiers became increasingly urbanized, with modern, European-style architecture dominating the city. This photo shows a section of the Algerian capital in 1967. © *United Nations*

Although many of the restrictions were lifted in time for the presidential elections in 2001, the polling was boycotted by all major parties, most notably the United Democratic Party. This paved the way for Jammeh's re-election to a second five-year term. In 2002 legislative elections also were heavily boycotted by opposition parties, allowing the APRC to win 45 of the National Assembly's 53 seats. Though closely related, the APRC is distinct from the Armed Forces Provisional Ruling Council (AFPRC), which was the name of the military junta led by Jammeh at the time of the coup.

Amhara National Democratic Movement Leading Ethiopian political party, instrumental in ousting President MENGISTU HAILE MARIAM (c. 1937–) and closely tied to the current prime minister, MELES ZENAWI (1955–).

The Amhara National Democratic Movement (ANDM) was founded in 1989 as the Ethiopian People's Democratic Movement (EPDM). Its purpose was to draw the Amhara people, long Ethiopia's dominant ethnic and political community, into the effort of the Tigray People's Liberation Front (TPLF) to oust President Mengistu from

power. Mengistu had taken control of ETHIOPIA in 1977 through a military coup. His Soviet-backed socialist government battled both Tigray and Eritrean separatist movements, deepening the ethnic dividing lines in the country just as it also faced a devastating famine. The rebel coalition, under the name of the ETHIOPIAN PEOPLE'S REVOLUTIONARY DEMOCRATIC FRONT (EPRDF), took control of the capital ADDIS ABABA in 1991, and Mengistu was exiled to ZIMBABWE. The EPRDF leader, Meles Zenawi, was elected to head the transitional government, and he later assumed the role of prime minister.

After the success of the coalition, the EPDM became a political party, changing its name to the Amhara National Democratic Movement, in January 1994. As such it became influential on the regional level, particularly among Ethiopia's northeast constituencies, as well as nationally.

See also: AMHARA (Vols. I, III, IV).

Amin, Idi (Idi Amin Dada) (c. 1925–2003) *Former Ugandan dictator*

Perhaps the most notorious of Africa's many brutal dictators of the postcolonial era, Amin was born in

Koboko in northwestern UGANDA. A member of the minority Kakwa ethnic group, Amin enlisted with the King's African Rifles, a British colonial army regiment, while still in his teens. He fought in Burma during World War II (1939–45) and then against the Mau Mau rebels in KENYA. Amin eventually rose to the rank of lieutenant, one of only two Ugandans to achieve that distinction before independence. Tall and athletic, Amin was also the heavyweight boxing champion of Uganda from 1951 to 1960.

Upon Uganda's independence, in 1963, President Milton OBOTE (1925–2000) overlooked Amin's record of brutality, which had greatly concerned the British colonial authorities, and eventually promoted him to general. The murder of one of Amin's rival officers and the disappearance of a large amount of military funds, however, led Obote to become suspicious of the young general. Sensing the threat, Amin launched a COUP D'ÉTAT in 1971, taking control of the government while Obote was out of the country.

Seeking to eliminate any opposition to his control, Amin immediately began his reign of terror. Supporters of Obote were murdered en masse, including nearly half of the armed forces personnel. His extermination squads created a state of fear throughout Uganda.

In 1972 Amin ordered the expulsion of all non-citizen Asians (primarily Indians) with the ostensible purpose of Africanizing the economy. Though initially applauded by Ugandans who were tired of the Asian dominance of trade, the mass expulsion had a profoundly negative impact. The Asian expulsion, coupled with Amin's increased spending on the military (from 20 percent of the national budget to 60 percent), essentially destroyed Uganda's economy.

Also in 1972, Amin abruptly converted to Islam and declared his intent to make Uganda a Muslim nation. This was in direct conflict with the previous Ugandan alliance with Western powers and Israel. Amin began support of the Palestine Liberation Movement (PLO) and garnered funds from LIBYA for the purposes of spreading Islam in Uganda. It remained in question, however, as to whether these funds were put to this use.

In 1976 PLO terrorists hijacked an Air France jet and forced it to land in Uganda's major airport in the city of ENTEBBE. Though Amin's involvement in the hijacking has not been verified, Ugandan troops aided in guarding the hostages. A daring raid by Israeli special forces ended the standoff with minimal casualties, but Amin, outraged by the result, executed 200 members of his government and military.

By 1976 Amin's rule had fully demolished any semblance of a functioning state in Uganda. Retaliating against growing internal and international pressure, he engaged in further large-scale massacres, mainly targeting certain ethnic groups, such as the Acholi and Langi. As divisions emerged within the military, Amin attempted diversionary tactics to avoid losing power. Using the pretext of an invasion from TANZANIA, Amin attacked Tanzania's northwestern province of Kagera. This proved his undoing, for the Tanzanians, supported by exiled Ugandan troops, pushed into Uganda, and, in 1979, captured the capital city of KAMPALA. Amin fled to Libya before relocating to Saudi Arabia—where he received sanctuary as a Muslim—along with a number of his wives and several of his 43 children. All told, Amin's eight-year regime resulted in the deaths of 300,000 to 500,000 Ugandans. Amin died in Saudi Arabia in August 2003, from complications related to a kidney ailment.

See also: ARMIES, COLONIAL (Vol. IV) ISLAM, INFLUENCE OF (Vol. V); MAU MAU (Vol. IV); OBOTE, MILTON (Vol. IV).

Amnesty International and Africa   The world's leading HUMAN RIGHTS organization, Amnesty International has played an influential role in pushing for the transparency of African regimes. Founded in the United Kingdom in 1961, Amnesty International promotes internationally recognized human rights worldwide. The organization has campaigned in virtually every African country. Its first action in Africa occurred in 1962, when the organization fought for the release of Ghanaian "prisoners of conscience," or people who were jailed solely for expressing their political views. The same year, the organization sent a representative to SOUTH AFRICA to observe the trial of Nelson MANDELA (1918–), who was acquitted of treason. Later, in 1965, Amnesty International supported the cause of South Africa's political prisoners who challenged the government's policies of APARTHEID, or racial segregation.

As the South African political structure changed in the 1990s, Amnesty International was on hand to document the treatment of former political prisoners and to uncover the crimes of government-sponsored "death squads," groups that systematically murdered political opponents during the apartheid era. In NIGERIA Amnesty International has recorded the human rights transgressions of myriad military leaders, including General Sani ABACHA (1943–1998), who ruled the country in the 1990s. The organization even criticized the democratically elected government of Nigerian president Olusegun OBASANJO (c. 1937–), demonstrating that it is willing to speak out on human rights abuses by all governments, not only those that may be perceived by the international community as despotic. With the rise of democracy in Africa in the 1990s, Amnesty International has expanded its role to become a force for the continued expansion of civil liberties and government accountability.

Amnesty International's stated mission is "to undertake research and action focused on preventing and ending grave abuses of the rights to physical and mental integrity, freedom of conscience and expression, and freedom from discrimination, within the context of our work to promote all human rights."

ANC See AFRICAN NATIONAL CONGRESS.

Angola Southwest African country, about 476,200 square miles (1,233,400 sq km) in area, bordered by the Democratic Republic of the CONGO, ZAMBIA, NAMIBIA, and the Atlantic Ocean. Also part of Angola is CABINDA, a northern province that is separate from the main part of the country. From 1960 to the present, Angola has undergone the transition from Portuguese colonial rule to independence to civil war and, finally, to a rocky road toward DEMOCRATIZATION.

In the late 1950s the Angolan people joined with the people of other African nations in calling for their liberation from colonial rule. However, Portugal, the colonial power in Angola, proved resistant to independence. Angolan liberation movements exploded onto the scene in the early 1960s, with the country's major ethnic groups represented by different parties and organizations. The militaristic NATIONAL FRONT FOR THE LIBERATION OF ANGOLA (Frente Nacional de Libertação de Angola, FNLA), a group representing the Kongo people, was led by Holden ROBERTO (1923–   ). Also taking arms against the colonial system was the Marxist POPULAR MOVEMENT FOR THE LIBERATION OF ANGOLA (Movimento Popular de Libertação de Angola, MPLA), led by Agostinho NETO (1922–1979), a group that represented the country's large Mbundu population.

By 1966 the FNLA leadership came to an impasse, and Jonas SAVIMBI (1934–2002) split from the group to found the NATIONAL UNION FOR THE TOTAL INDEPENDENCE OF ANGOLA (União Nacional para a Independência Total de Angola, UNITA). Made up mostly of ethnic Ovimbundu and Chokwe soldiers, UNITA immediately became a major force in the independence struggle. The three rebel groups were united in the aim of independence from Portugal, but ethnic and ideological differences had them all facing off against each other by the end of the 1960s.

In 1974 the government of Portugal was overthrown. An administration was installed that was willing to relinquish control of its overseas possessions, and it became clear that Angolan independence was not far off. In January 1975 the three competing Angolan liberation movements, the MPLA, FNLA, and UNITA, met in KENYA to discuss the future of their nation. Under the auspices of Kenyan president Jomo KENYATTA (c. 1891–1978), the Angolan representatives forged a trilateral agreement that called for each of the three organizations to recognize officially the right of the others to exist. It also formalized their mutual desire for a transitional government whenever independence from Portugal finally came.

On November 11, 1975, the MPLA declared Angolan independence. However, the FNLA and UNITA parties refused to acknowledge MPLA legitimacy and held separate independence ceremonies of their own. Because there was no clear successor to the Portuguese colonial government, Portugal, too, refused to acknowledge exclusive MPLA rule. As it proceeded to act as the official Angolan government, the MPLA found that independence did not necessarily improve the domestic situation, which was still rife with internal conflicts and ethnic aggression.

MPLA forces had control of the capital, LUANDA, and were supported by personnel and military hardware from both Cuba and the former Soviet Union. The FNLA and UNITA both received assistance from various, often conflicting sources, including the United States, China, Portugal, and SOUTH AFRICA. Both groups used outside assistance to continue waging their guerrilla campaigns, now against their own countrymen in the MPLA. Soon, however, the FNLA pulled out of what was by then a full-blown civil war, and its former members joined the ranks of the MPLA and UNITA.

A striking part of the Angolan civil war was the widespread abuse of children on both sides of the conflict. Young boys of all ethnicities were abducted and trained to fight on the front lines or perform other dangerous tasks, such as clearing minefields. It was not uncommon for these abducted children to be forced to murder their own parents and burn their villages in order to eliminate the possibility of returning to their native home. Girls, too, were abducted from villages and made to cook and perform sexual favors for the rank-and-file members of the warring factions.

By the end of the 1970s the Angolan conflict had been drawn into the vortex of the Cold War, with the United States and the former Soviet Union supporting opposing sides in the conflict, often through third party "proxy" forces, including South Africa and Cuba, respectively. In this way, both sides in the conflict greatly improved their military technology and their ability to kill the other. As a result massive casualties—more than 500,000 in all—piled up on both sides.

In 1988 the bloody Battle of Cuito Cuanavale led to the withdrawal of South African and Cuban troops from southern Angola. Over the next three years, hostilities abated enough for the MPLA and UNITA to agree to plan an end to the war. The Bicesse Accords, signed in 1991, paved the way for elections to be held in 1992. The closely observed and generally fair elections confirmed the MPLA as the legitimate government in Angola. Savimbi, however, deemed the elections fraudulent, re-igniting the UNITA guerrilla campaign and once again turning Angola into a bloodbath.

The Angolan military conflict was costly not only in human lives lost but also monetarily. By 1990, when the end of the Cold War had caused the foreign powers to lose interest in the Angolan conflict, the warring sides were forced to look elsewhere for financial resources. Before long the two sides found that they could fund their campaigns with Angola's rich NATURAL RESOURCES. The MPLA used OIL revenues, which account for 80 to 90 percent of Angola's state income, to build up its war chest. UNITA, for its part, turned to the diamond market. Ignoring the de Beers cartel, which controls the international diamond trade, Savimbi and UNITA raised hundreds of millions of dollars by selling unofficial "conflict diamonds" outside of the regulated business channels. In this way both sides maintained their ability to wage war until 2002. That year government troops of MPLA President José Eduardo DOS SANTOS (1942–) assassinated Savimbi, removing UNITA's only real leader and thereby terminating the organization's ability to continue fighting.

Angola is now a republic divided into 18 provinces. It has a constitution and a National Assembly. The president, appointed by the victorious party in multiparty elections, enjoys a strong position in government. Currently, the Angolan government is headed by dos Santos, an MPLA official who has held his post since Agostinho Neto died in 1979.

In 1974 a coup d'état in Portugal led the country to relinquish its African colonies. On the eve of Angolan independence in 1975, two happy soldiers, one Portuguese and one Angolan, celebrated the pending withdrawal of Portuguese troops. © *United Nations/J. P. Laffont*

Immediate challenges facing Angola include poor ED-UCATION and lacking health facilities, especially concerning HIV/AIDS, which has devastated certain regions. Also, after nearly three decades of civil war, the Angolan economy is in shambles. Numerous other war-related problems exist as well, including sporadic resurfacing of hostilities and millions of unexploded land mines and ordnance throughout the countryside. On the positive side, Angola could have one of the world's fastest growing economies if oil production reaches its potential. Further, the reintegration of former UNITA soldiers into positions in the Angolan military and government is proving successful, and former child combatants are returning to their homes in peace.

Angola has vast amounts of natural resources, including oil, diamonds, iron, phosphates, copper, and uranium. Angola's agricultural EXPORTS include bananas, sugar cane, coffee, corn, cotton, manioc, and tobacco. The country also exports livestock and fish.

See also: ANGOLA (Vols. I, II, III, V); CIVIL WARS (Vol. V); COLONIAL RULE (Vol. IV); ETHNIC CONFLICT IN AFRICA (Vol. V); ETHNIC GROUP (Vol. I); ETHNICITY AND IDENTITY (Vol. I); HIV/AIDS IN AFRICA (Vol. V); INDEPENDENCE MOVEMENTS (Vol. V); NATIONALISM AND INDEPENDENCE MOVEMENTS (Vol. IV); OVIMBUNDU (Vol. IV); PORTUGAL AND AFRICA (Vols. III, IV, V); SOVIET UNION AND AFRICA (Vols. IV); UNITED STATES AND AFRICA (Vol. IV).

Further reading: James Ciment, *Angola and Mozambique: Postcolonial Wars in Southern Africa* (New York: Facts on File, 1997); Linda Heywood, *Contested Power in Angola, 1840s to the Present* (Rochester, N.Y.: University of Rochester Press, 2000); Keith Somerville, *Angola: Politics, Economics, and Society* (Boulder, Colo.: Lynne Rienner Publishers, 1986).

Anjouan   Island of the COMOROS archipelago. A separatist movement begun on the island in 1997 brought about a period of instability and resulted in a new Comorian constitution granting each island greater autonomy. Since Comorian independence in 1975, the people of Anjouan (also called Nzwani) and the neighboring island of Moheli (Mwali) asserted that they did not receive enough support from the central government on the main island of Grand Comoros (Ngazidja). Complaints centered around a lack of opportunity and low standard of living.

As a result of this general dissatisfaction on Anjouan, in August 1997 Abdallah Ibrahim and his Anjouanais Popular Movement began attempts to secede from the Comoros union; Moheli soon joined the movement. Their initial proposal was to return the two islands to the status of a French territory, but when France refused this arrangement, they sought outright independence.

To make the secession movement legitimate, in October 1997 Abdallah Ibrahim called for a referendum, which revealed nearly unanimous support for self-determination. The referendum also marked the beginning of Anjouan's five years of armed conflict with the Comorian central government. Four months later a second referendum in Anjouan called for a new constitution for the Comoros. Abdallah Ibrahim briefly claimed a new presidency and formed an Anjouan government, but he soon turned power over to Col. Said Abeid Abderemane. In August 1999 an Anjouan National Assembly was voted in. In August 2001 Abeid was removed from power in a COUP D'ÉTAT led by soldiers loyal to Col. Mohamed Bacar (1962–   ).

The following year, in a pivotal action, the people of the Comoros as a whole approved by referendum a new constitution. This innovative document codified a confederation that would allow for highly independent island governments to function within a Comorian union. The AFRICAN UNION had to step in to sponsor negotiations thereafter, but the new arrangement marked a first step toward peace and reconciliation in the Comoros.

See also: FRANCE AND AFRICA (Vols. III, IV, V).

Annan, Kofi (1938–   ) *Secretary-general of the United Nations*

Kofi Atta Annan was born to Fante parents in KUMASI, in what was then the British Gold Coast colony (present-day GHANA). After studying in Kumasi, he won a scholarship in 1959 to study at Macalester College in St. Paul, Minnesota, where he earned a degree in economics. While a student, Annan witnessed the American civil rights movement, which he related to the struggle for Ghana's independence. Annan then studied in Switzerland before taking a position with the World Health Organization, a division of the United Nations (UN). This served as a launching point for Annan's UN career, and he went on to various positions in cities such as CAIRO and ADDIS ABABA before being promoted to the UN headquarters in New York City. From 1990 to 1996, Annan headed successful UN activities in Iraq and Bosnia-Herzegovina. In 1993 he achieved promotion to under-secretary-general, and in 1996 Annan was elected secretary-general, becoming the first black African to assume the position, as well as the first to be appointed from within UN ranks.

As secretary-general, Annan has faced a number of pressing issues in relation to Africa, most immediately the refugee situations arising from CIVIL WARS in countries such as RWANDA and the Democratic Republic of the

CONGO. In 1998 Annan launched a UN mission to help establish civilian rule in NIGERIA, and in 1999 he brokered an agreement with the North African country of LIBYA regarding the surrender of the perpetrators of the 1988 airline bombing over Lockerbie, Scotland. Annan's efforts, both in Africa and in the tumultuous Middle East, earned him and the United Nations the Nobel Peace Prize in 2001.

Annan was in charge of UN peacekeeping efforts in 1994, when ethnic violence between the HUTU and TUTSI populations in Rwanda resulted in the deaths of as many as one million people. When Annan visited Rwanda as secretary-general, in 1998, many in the government boycotted his appearances out of anger for the United Nations' failure to intervene in the massacres. Annan admitted that the United Nations failed in this instance due to the absence of "political will" among its members.

Fluent in English, French, and a number of African languages, Annan has promoted the United Nations' involvement in several issues of special importance to Africa, particularly DEVELOPMENT, POVERTY, HUMAN RIGHTS, ENVIRONMENTAL ISSUES, and HIV/AIDS, which Annan has called his "personal priority." In 2001 Annan was appointed to a second term as Secretary-General, a testament to his popularity in the organization.

See also: HIV/AIDS AND AFRICA (Vol. V); REFUGEES (Vol. V); UNITED NATIONS AND AFRICA (Vols. IV, V).

Antananarivo (Tananarive) Capital city of MADAGASCAR, located in the island's central highlands. Founded in 1625 among rocky ridges that rise 4,700 feet (1,433 m) above sea level, Antananarivo served as the capital of the Merina as their monarchy grew to dominate the island in the 19th century. Antananarivo then served as the capital of Madagascar throughout the French colonial period (1896–1960), and remained so at independence in 1960.

Antananarivo remains the country's center for economic, cultural, and administrative activities. Major industries include tobacco farming, food processing, and manufacturing of leather goods and textiles. The city is home to the University of Antananarivo (founded in 1961), an astronomical observatory, the French Residency, and several Anglican and Roman Catholic cathedrals. Antananarivo is connected by good roads to Toamasina, the island's main east coast port, the cities of Antsirabe, Fianarantsoa, and Mahajanga, and the rice-producing region

of Lake Alaotra. In addition, an international airport is located in nearby Ivato.

Antananarivo was originally organized following feudal caste divisions, with the royal family (Atinandriana) at the highest elevation, and the seven noble castes (Andriambaventy) descending in order. Free people (Hova) lived in the commercial area below the nobles, and slaves (Andevo), lived in their quarters below them. Under the French the city remained divided into sectors by location on the hills, with the Royal Estate at the highest elevation, the banks and administrative buildings below it, and the commercial district occupying the lowest areas of the city.

Present-day Antananarivo is a city of contrasts. It has a rich history as a center of Malagasy culture, and its rolling hills and unique architectural influences make it a city of beauty and drama. Boutiques selling precious stones and fine French clothing line the streets of the Haute Ville; banks and industries abound.

At the same time, Antananarivo has a homeless population that the United Nations estimates at more than 10,000; up to 6,000 street children eke out an existence by begging. Narrow streets are continuously overwhelmed by high traffic, and air and water quality are among the worst in the world. Although the number of doctors has increased, most people are too poor to afford their services, and MEDICINE is poorly distributed. Public EDUCATION is wanting, and, in some places, shantytowns and substandard houses dominate the landscape. As URBANIZATION continues, the city's limited number of industrial and civil servant jobs will fail to provide enough work for a population that, by 1999, had already grown to more than 2 million.

See also: ANDRIANAMPOINIMERINA (Vol. III); FRANCE AND AFRICA (Vols. III, IV, V); MERINA (Vols. III, IV); URBAN LIFE AND CULTURE (Vols. IV, V).

anthropology and Africa Anthropology is a social-science discipline concerned with the study of humans and their societies in all their dimensions. Of particular concern to anthropology as it developed as a field of study was understanding how human societies and their cultures have evolved. Also, during the colonial era anthropological studies provided important information about African societies for colonial administrators. By 1960 anthropologists had produced a substantial body of works on Africa's peoples. But these studies were virtually all by outsiders, mostly British, who were based in European universities and research institutes as well as in the few universities on the continent. With the passing of colonial rule and the coming of independence, the discipline underwent tremendous change.

Independence for Africa brought tremendous intellectual change as well. A whole new field of academic inquiry, AFRICAN STUDIES, opened up. HISTORICAL SCHOLARSHIP ON AFRICA entered an entirely new phase, one that could properly be called the beginning of major historical writing about Africa. Anthropology in Africa also underwent a fundamental transformation. While in contrast to history there was already a major body of published studies, continuing along established paths of inquiry increasingly out of step with overall thinking about Africa. Thus while the classical earlier studies of African societies focused on small communities that were viewed as closed systems, anthropologists now had to show the interaction of local communities with the larger world. Also, American scholars began to enter the field in large numbers and Africans also began to take their place in the ranks of anthropologists.

One of the major shifts in the 1960s was to focus on the economy, leading to the sub-field of economic anthropology. For example, the British scholar Polly Hill (1914–) produced a pioneering study of migrant cocoa farmers in GHANA and did subsequent work on economic transformations among the HAUSA of northern NIGERIA. Given the importance of AGRICULTURE in African economies and the role of both FOOD CROPS and CASH CROPS in Africa's DEVELOPMENT, the interest in economic anthropology led some anthropologists into development anthropology. Some of the early studies in this context reflected back to colonial anthropology in that they sought to explain the workings of African societies and economies to various international and national officials engaged in implementing development projects. This approach has come under increasing criticism, however, as in James Ferguson's (1959–) 1990 critique from an anthropological perspective of the conceptual underpinnings of the development community.

Economic issues stretch well beyond agricultural communities and workers. One important area of focus has been on MARKETS. A recent book by Karen Tranberg Hansen, for example, examines the market for second-hand clothing in ZAMBIA. The clothing comes from Europe and the United States and makes up a multibillion-dollar business. The book's title, *Salaula*, which literally means "to rummage through a pile," captures the local view of the buying and selling of these clothes. Other studies are looking at the role of transnational African traders both within Africa and outside the continent. They are to be found in major cities such as Paris, London, and New York, and studies on them have increasingly contributed to our knowledge of a new African diaspora.

The study of African URBAN LIFE AND CULTURE has constituted another new direction for the anthropological study of Africa. Except for a few pioneering scholars such as J. Clyde Mitchell (1918–), who examined life on Zambia's Copperbelt, there were few anthropological studies of urban life prior to 1960. Also contributing to this is James Ferguson, who has provided an important ethnography of urban lives on the present-day Copperbelt. Another dimension of urban culture is the role of women. A 1996 study by Kathleen Sheldon (1952–) examined the place of women in terms of "courtyards, markets, [and] city streets." Women are also intricantly involved in the process of URBANIZATION, which has often involved migration of women from the rural areas to the cities. There women often play an important role in feeding the people of African cities. Indeed, as Jane Guyer noted in a 1987 study, women provide much of the basic LABOR in farming and as well as the effort in marketing much of the produce of the fields.

Anthropologists have also begun to study how earlier anthropological knowledge came into being. This can be through writing about the lives of other anthropologists, such as the biography of Colin Turnbull (1924–1994) written by Roy Grinker (1961–) in 2000. It can also take the form of an examination of a colonial African research institute, such as Lyn Schumaker's study of the Rhodes-Livingstone Institute in colonial Zambia. Another example is Johannes Fabian, a Dutch scholar who examined the psychological state of the 19th-century explorers and ethnographers in his book, *Out of Our Minds* (2000). Fabian argued that explorers' descriptions of their encounters with African societies—descriptions on which later scholarship relied—were clouded by drugs, illness, alcohol, fatigue, and violence.

See also: ANTHROPOLOGY AND AFRICA (Vol. IV); COPPERBELT (Vol. IV); WOMEN IN MODERN AFRICA (Vol. V).

Further reading: Jack Goody, *The Expansive Moment: The Rise of Social Anthropology in Britain and Africa, 1918–1970* (New York: Cambridge University Press, 1995); Sally Falk Moore, *Anthropology and Africa: Changing Perspectives on a Changing Scene* (Charlottesville, Va.: Univ. Press of Virginia, 1994); Lyn Schumaker, *Africanizing Anthropology: Fieldwork, Networks, and the Making of Cultural Knowledge in Central Africa* (Durham, N.C.: Duke University Press, 2001).

apartheid Legalized system of racial segregation that characterized the state of SOUTH AFRICA from 1948 to 1991. The word means, literally, "aparthood," or separateness, in AFRIKAANS. The history of strict racial segregation in South Africa dated back to the founding of the Union of South Africa, in 1910. After that time the country's all-white parliament successfully pushed legislation that limited blacks' participation in society, politics, and business and industry. After World War II (1939–45), when most other African countries were beginning the push toward independence, South Africa began the process of completely segregating its society by race. When the conservative National Party was elected to power by an all-white electorate in 1948, legalized racial segregation, called apartheid, was institutionalized.

In the early 1950s the National Party government, led by Prime Minister Hendrik VERWOERD (1901–1966), enacted laws that prevented blacks from getting good jobs or living or working in certain areas reserved for whites. Additional laws banned interracial sexual relations and marriage, while other legislation provided a framework for the implementation of BANTU EDUCATION, a system that fostered racial segregation. Among the most controversial apartheid laws were the pass laws, which required black South Africans to carry identification papers with them at all times. Taken as a whole, the laws isolated blacks from white society and discriminated against them in all facets of social organization. Once apartheid laws were in place, the South African government used them to silence opposition with brutal and systematic efficiency. In 1960 it declared the AFRICAN NATIONAL CONGRESS (ANC), the PAN-AFRICANIST CONGRESS (PAC), and other opposition organizations illegal, thus driving them underground. The result was a sharply segregated society in which only whites enjoyed basic HUMAN RIGHTS.

Under apartheid, blacks were forced to relocate to nominally independent BANTUSTANS, or "tribal homelands," which the government had set aside for black settlement. In general, these areas were too small or lacked sufficient NATURAL RESOURCES to sustain the populations that the government consigned to them. Moreover, they lacked a viable economic base capable of encouraging DEVELOPMENT. The ultimate aim of the Bantustan system was to give blacks the status of "foreigners" in the rest of South Africa, thereby stripping them of any civil protections as soon as they left their territories. Urban Africans consistently objected to moving onto the overcrowded, barren Bantustans. Even so, the state forcibly relocated 3.5 million Africans between 1963 and 1985.

With the beginnings of the BLACK CONSCIOUSNESS MOVEMENT in the late 1960s, South Africans exhibited a heightened race consciousness and a fierce determination to end racial discrimination. The government's repressive tactics aimed at crushing the growing opposition were, by and large, successful for the duration of the 1960s and into the early 1970s. However, they transformed South Africa into a police state in which basic civil liberties were routinely abridged or violated.

As the white-minority government stubbornly insisted on clinging to apartheid, South Africa's standing in the international community progressively eroded. In 1973 the UN General Assembly went so far as to declare apartheid "a crime against humanity." Four years later the UN Security Council authorized an arms embargo against the country.

One of the most effective means by which the South African government repressed its opposition was through "banning." An entire political or social group might be banned, making future meetings illegal and marking its members for special surveillance. An individual might be banned, as well, meaning that that person was prohibited from attending social, political, or educational gatherings and was required to remain within certain boundaries. A banned person was also prohibited from preparing any document for publication and could be arrested for communicating with other banned individuals. Although most of the people banned were black, whites who joined the Communist Party also frequently received banning orders.

The struggle against apartheid acquired a new sense of urgency on June 16, 1976, with the shooting of teenage African students who were protesting against mandatory school instruction in Afrikaans, which in their view was the language of the oppressor. In response to the shooting, a protest occurred in SOWETO, a black township southwest of JOHANNESBURG. Soon, however, riots and protests spread to other urban centers across the country, as black youth rose rebellion.

The government responded by declaring a state of emergency and violently repressing all forms of anti-government agitation. The harsh government response catapulted South Africa into the international spotlight, where it became the target of intense condemnation. As neighboring countries gained their independence, power transferred to Africans, who found South Africa's white-minority government repugnant. Several Western governments cut off trade with South Africa and otherwise imposed restrictions on investment. The South African economy, which had thrived in the 1960s, began to stall.

Responding to this crisis, in the latter half of the 1970s Prime Minister P. W. BOTHA (1916–) embarked on a series of reforms, with the goal of reinforcing apartheid by rationalizing it and easing some of its restrictions. Over the next several years Botha dismantled many features of "petty apartheid," those facets of apartheid that kept the races apart in the public sphere. As a result blacks and whites were once again allowed to marry, and many beaches, parks, and other public amenities were desegregated. The process Botha initiated also brought about the eventual legal recognition of black LABOR UNIONS.

By 1973, apartheid touched on all aspects of life in South Africa, even everyday actions like sitting on a public park bench. © *UPI*

Africans became legally entitled to occupy skilled industrial positions for the first time since the 1920s. The hated pass system, which profoundly limited the mobility of Africans, was eliminated in 1985. In an especially controversial move, Botha introduced a three-chamber parliament, one that gave representation to Coloured and Indian South Africans, but significantly, excluded the country's majority population group—black Africans.

In 1983 the multiracial UNITED DEMOCRATIC FRONT (UDF) was established to fight this development. The UDF represented more than 500 organizations, among them trade unions, civic associations, and various philanthropic groups dedicated to ending the inequities of apartheid. Anti-apartheid demonstrations became increasingly militant and often violent. Public protests, although illegal, were frequently held, often at the funerals of slain anti-apartheid activists. These strikes, boycotts, and marches collectively demonstrated the strength and determination of the liberation movement.

For his efforts, Botha was criticized on all fronts. The country's anti-apartheid activists felt his reforms were not aggressive enough. Afrikaner hard-liners, on the other hand, opposed all concessions to the nation's black majority. Within the Afrikaner community, the relative unity it once enjoyed broke down at more than just the political level. Several key Afrikaner business leaders opened talks with the exiled leaders of the African National Congress, recognizing the inevitability of soon having to negotiate with the black majority.

Other developments also gave indication of the government's inability to stem the rising tide of opposition. In 1984 a renewed wave of anti-government protests and violence swept over the country, causing the government to declare another repressive state of emergency. International condemnation mounted in the wake of this new South African crackdown. The awarding of the 1984 Noble Peace Prize to Desmond TUTU (1931–), the Anglican archbishop outspoken in his opposition to South

Africa's racial policies, was intended to send an unambiguous political message. The U.S. Congress passed the Comprehensive Anti-Apartheid Act, overriding the veto of President Ronald Reagan (1911–2004). It imposed restrictions on American capital investment, the importation of South African goods, and direct airline access between the two countries. Both the Reagan administration and the conservative government of Great Britain generally pursued a conciliatory diplomatic approach toward South Africa—a policy called CONSTRUCTIVE ENGAGEMENT—and opted to promote progress in racial relations through positive incentives instead of public criticism. The approach, however, yielded little in the way of tangible results. International pressure mounted, resulting in further economic and diplomatic sanctions that severely undermined the already struggling South African economy.

In 1988 Botha suffered a stroke, precipitating a rapid and unprecedented sequence of events. Within months F. W. DE KLERK (1936–) assumed the presidency. In response to the growing crisis the apartheid state faced, de Klerk began implementing the integration of black South Africans into mainstream political life. Although he sought to preserve white privilege in his targeted reforms of apartheid, de Klerk also demonstrated a willingness to extend much more significant concessions to black South Africans. For example, he entered into negotiations with Nelson MANDELA (1918–), the former and future leader of the ANC who had been imprisoned since 1963, to discuss a future political arrangement that would include the black population. On December 2, 1990, de Klerk announced that Mandela and other political prisoners would be unconditionally released from prison.

Within two years de Klerk and Mandela began the process of rescinding the apartheid laws that had separated South Africans for so long. For their efforts toward a peaceful transition to a new, more inclusive South African state, de Klerk and Mandela were jointly awarded the Nobel Peace Prize in 1994. In April of that year South Africa held the first national elections in which all South Africans of age could freely vote. When the ANC won the elections Mandela became South Africa's first black president, and his long-held dream of an apartheid-free South Africa was that much closer to becoming a reality.

See also: BAASKAAP (Vol. IV); ETHNIC CONFLICT IN AFRICA (Vol. V); ETHNICITY AND IDENTITY (Vol. I); RACISM AND RACE RELATIONS (Vol. IV).

Further reading: R. Hunt Davis, Jr., ed., *Apartheid Unravels* (Gainesville, Fla.: University of Florida Press, 1991); Heather Deegan, *The Politics of the New South Africa: Apartheid and After* (New York: Longman, 2001).

Arab world and Africa The Arab world inextricably overlaps Africa in language, culture, economy, RELIGION, and geopolitical concerns. There is a long history of interaction between the Arabian peninsula and the African continent, some of it going back to ancient times. As Islam rose in the seventh century CE it spread throughout the north of the continent into modern day LIBYA, TUNISIA, ALGERIA, and MOROCCO, and the northern portions of the states running along the Sahelian belt south of the Sahara. It then continued down Africa's east coast. Religion joined trade in bringing together hitherto disparate civilizations. The result has been cultural and linguistic blending. The Arab world and Africa are thus not separate. The Arab world covers an area of 5.4 million square miles (14.2 million sq km), much of it overlapping the African continent.

The uneasy relationship between North and sub-Saharan Africa has been instrumental in guiding the relationship between the continent and the Arabian peninsula. Battleground states such as NIGERIA, the Republic of the SUDAN, and CHAD, in the north, and KENYA and TANZANIA, in the east, have seen tumultuous civil conflicts between Muslim and non-Muslim regions of the country. In each of these cases African Muslims have turned to support from other corners of the Arab world to gain a foothold within their own countries. In turn, Arab countries benefited from increases in pan-Arab nationalism associated with conflicts with and within non-Arab states.

Geopolitics also guides Arab-African relations. The Arab League was formed in 1945 in an effort to create a single Arab state. Nine of its 22 member countries are in Africa: DJIBOUTI, Algeria, Tunisia, Sudan, SOMALIA, The COMOROS, EGYPT, Morocco, and MAURITANIA. The Arab League has never garnered the power necessary to achieve its original objective, but it has been influential in creating a political interest bloc.

The most obvious arena for observing Arab solidarity was during the ARAB-ISRAELI WARS. As early as the Bandung Afro-Asian Conference (1955), nascent African countries signed a resolution condemning Israeli occupation of Arab lands. With independence in the 1960s, new African countries could join and vote in the United Nations, where they were quick to vote with the Arab bloc. Further, when the ORGANIZATION OF AFRICAN UNITY was formed in 1963, it immediately had a close relationship with the Arab League, since it shared many constituencies. At a critical stage in 1973 Algerian President Houari BOUMEDIENNE (1927–1978) became chairman of the non-aligned movement. The movement passed resolutions supporting Egypt, Syria, and Jordan against Israel's occupation. Leaders in the African countries of TOGO and ZAÏRE (present-day Democratic Republic of the CONGO) rapidly severed ties with Israel, and nearly every country on the continent followed suit. As argued by Zaïre's president at the time, MOBUTU SESE SEKO (1930–1997), there was an African dimension to the Arab-Israeli conflict. Two decades passed before the majority of African countries once again had reestablished ties with Israel.

Nationalist goals have guided African policies towards Middle Eastern Arab countries. Israel was a long-time supporter of ETHIOPIA in its effort to block the formation of an independent state of ERITREA. The Jewish state funded insurgency movements against the governments in Algeria, Nigeria, MOZAMBIQUE, and elsewhere. As a result, governments have turned to Arab counterparts to seek assistance with training and funding.

The Arab-Israeli conflict has played out in the African Arab world in other ways. Israel was a supporter of the APARTHEID regime in SOUTH AFRICA. It maintained economic, political, and military ties long after South Africa was marginalized by the rest of the world. FRONTLINE STATES, such as BOTSWANA and Mozambique, were thus quick to lend support to the Arab cause not out of cultural or religious solidarity but out of political agreement.

France has also played a unique role in shaping the Arab world relationship with Africa. President Charles de Gaulle (1890–1970) introduced the France Arab Policy in 1967, following the Six-Day War in which Israel gained territory from Jordan, Egypt, and Syria. De Gaulle saw presidential politics as being enhanced by "strongman" leadership. He used this position to encourage the rise of African strongmen such as President Félix HOUPHOUËT-BOIGNY (1905–1993) of IVORY COAST, who supported French efforts to nurture relations with Arab states while providing French trading opportunities. France's role as a mediator has seen a resurgence under President Jacques Chirac (1932–   ), who had strong ties to Arab countries dating back to his early presidential ambitions in the mid-1970s. In particular, he maintained close ties to President Muammar QADDAFI (1942–   ) of Libya and, more auspiciously, he strongly supported President Henri Konan Bédié (1934–   ), Houphouët-Boigny's protege.

A fourth way in which the Arab world and Africa have come together geopolitically and economically is in OIL production. For example, Nigeria is a member of the ORGANIZATION OF PETROLEUM EXPORTING COUNTRIES (OPEC). This effectively means that oil proceeds, the backbone of the Nigerian economy, are governed by limitations placed by an international organization dominated by Arab member states. Other oil-producing countries in sub-Saharan Africa, such as ANGOLA, Chad, and GABON, are not presently OPEC members, but the organization dominates the price of the resource, significantly influencing those countries' economies.

Qaddafi has been a tremendous individual force in linking the Arab world and Africa. He long sought influence in the Arab League and held sway over other leaders in the Arab world. Then, in 1999, he turned over to international authorities two Libyan men suspected of bombing a Pan Am flight over Lockerbie, Scotland. This greatly improved his diplomatic position in Europe, where Libyan trade rapidly increased. It also made great strides toward rebuilding Libya's relationship with the United States. However, Qaddafi's move eroded his support in the Arab world and dashed his hopes of becoming the preeminent pan-Arab leader. He then focused on pan-African leadership, becoming a pivotal force in the establishment of the AFRICAN UNION. His unique combination of Arab and African leadership has made him a lynchpin between the two worlds.

Today's global political climate, and in particular the U.S.-led war on TERRORISM, has led to a divide within the African Arab world. In particular, the United States has invested significantly in East Africa and the Horn of Africa, mandating cooperation from countries such as Somalia, Djibouti, and Kenya, all of which had strong historical ties with the Arabian peninsula. When these countries agreed to join the United States in the war on terrorism, it challenged some of the established relationships between Arab and African partners.

Compounding newly strained relations between the sub-continent and Middle Eastern Arab countries has been the precipitous drop in foreign ECONOMIC ASSISTANCE. Arab aid to Africa peaked in 1976 and then fell 44 percent by 1982. In the 1990s aid from Arab countries became more institutionalized and project-oriented. The Arab Bank for Economic Development in Africa, headquartered in KHARTOUM, Sudan, paid out only $675 million in its fourth Five-Year Plan (2000–04), most of it in the form of technical assistance. Thus, Arab influence through development aid is minor compared to the $15.2 billion in commitments that the Western-dominated World Bank has on the continent.

See also: BANDUNG AFRO-ASIAN CONFERENCE (Vol. IV); DE GAULLE, CHARLES (Vol. IV); FRANCE AND AFRICA (Vols. IV, V); NON-ALIGNED MOVEMENT AND AFRICA (Vol. V); ISLAM, INFLUENCE OF (Vols. II, III, IV, V); UNITED NATIONS AND AFRICA (Vol. V); UNITED STATES AND AFRICA (Vols. IV, V).

Further reading: David Westerlund and Ingvar Svanberg, *Islam Outside the Arab World* (Richmond, U.K.: Curzon, 1999).

Arab-Israeli Wars Series of violent confrontations that began in 1948–49 and continued in 1956, 1967, 1973, and 1982. Since the early years of the 20th century relations between Arabs and Jews in Palestine were marked by tension over the establishment of a Jewish state. On May 14, 1948, with the support of Britain and the United States, the state of Israel became an independent nation. The first Arab-Israeli War (1948) was declared that same day. It ended in an armistice that established Israel's borders.

The second Arab-Israeli War (1956–57) was part of a secret plan between Britain, France, and Israel to regain control of the SUEZ CANAL, which Egyptian president Gamal Abdel NASSER (1918–1970) had nationalized. As part of the agreement ending the war, Israel gave back its territorial gains in Sinai.

The third Arab-Israeli War (1967) is sometimes called the Six-Day War. Clashes between Israel and Syria led EGYPT to join with Jordan, Syria, and Iraq to mobilize their forces in preparation for an attack on Israel. ALGERIA, Kuwait, and Saudi Arabia supported the Arab nations' plans. However, on June 5, 1967, Israeli warplanes made a preemptive strike against the Egyptian air force, destroying it before any plane could leave the ground. With air superiority guaranteed, Israeli troops repelled invading Arab ground forces in six days. As a result of the Six-Day War Israel occupied additional territory, including the Golan Heights, the West Bank, the Gaza Strip, and the Sinai Peninsula, that had once belonged to Egypt, Syria, and Jordan.

Israel's decision to take possession of this new land led the Arab world to view Israel as imperialistic. Consequently, on October 6, 1973, Egypt and Syria attacked Israel once again. This fourth Arab-Israeli War is sometimes called the Yom Kippur War because the initial attacks—by Egypt across the Suez Canal and by Syria across the Golan Heights—took place on the Jewish holiday of that name. Israeli forces once again made immediate advances. Israel's success on the battlefield motivated the government of the former Soviet Union to airlift military equipment and supplies to Egypt and Syria. A day later the United States (U.S.) intervened by airlifting supplies to Israel. By the time U.S. Secretary of State Henry Kissinger (1923–   ) negotiated a cease fire 18 days later, 8,500 Arab soldiers and 6,000 Israeli soldiers had been killed or severely wounded.

The territorial gains that Israel made as a result of the Yom Kippur War led to further condemnation of Israel as racist and imperialistic. At its 1972 meeting the pan-African ORGANIZATION OF AFRICAN UNITY (OAU) also joined in the chorus of voices against Israeli imperialism and condemned Portugal and SOUTH AFRICA for the same reasons. The OAU censure of Israel led CHAD, ZAÏRE (present-day Democratic Republic of the CONGO), and NIGER to join UGANDA in severing ties with Israel by the end of 1973. The majority of African countries soon followed suit. Ironically, in 1979, when Egypt signed the Camp David Peace Accords that formally ended the 30-year state of war between Egypt and Israel, 18 African countries severed ties with Egypt. In 1982 Egypt, no longer at war with Israel, was not involved in the Sixth Arab-Israeli War, which was fought entirely inside Lebanon. Israeli forces finally withdrew from Lebanon in 1985.

In 1982, President MOBUTU SESE SEKO (1930–1997) of Zaïre restored ties with Israel in exchange for economic support. By 1990 most of Africa had normalized relations.

However, the region is still characterized by political unrest and instability, and African sentiments remain subject to change. Because they share a common religion, many Muslim states in Africa perceive the Arab-Israeli conflict as a war against Islam. As a result, when U.S. president George W. Bush (1946–   ) turned to African countries to support Operation Iraqi Freedom (2003) against Iraq, he found only ERITREA and ETHIOPIA at his side.

See also: ARAB-ISRAELI WARS (Vol. IV); ARAB WORLD AND AFRICA (Vol. V); SUEZ CANAL (Vol. V).

Further reading: Samuel Decalo, *Israel and Africa: Forty Years, 1956–1996* (Gainesville, Fla.: Florida Academic Press, 1998); Chaim Herzog, *The Arab-Israeli Wars* (New York: Random House, 1982); Arye Oded, *Africa and the Middle East Conflict* (Boulder, Colo.: Lynne Rienner, 1987).

archaeology Archaeology, which involves the systematic recovery and study of material culture representing past human life and activities, made vast strides as an academic discipline after 1960 in its contribution to our understanding of the African past. Until 1960 the practice of archaeology in Africa had two distinct trends. One was what might be called monumental archaeology, which was especially prominent in EGYPT and the northern part of the continent. The second trend was a focus on both human origins and early human material culture. While both of these traditions continued with important new advances, the advent of political independence led to a broadening of archaeological research and to attempts to learn more about African history and prehistory. The focus of this new trend was on the development of modern African societies, and it paid particular attention to recent millennia. Accompanying this third trend was a shift away from explaining developments in Africa primarily as a result of external influences. Instead, there was an effort to explain what happened within Africa in terms of internal, African sources.

Advances in scientific techniques facilitated these new directions in archaeological research. Particularly important in this regard was the advent of C-14, or radiocarbon, dating. By the 1950s this became an effective tool for determining the age of artifacts found at an archaeological site.

Archaeological research in the monumental vein has continued to make valuable contributions to our knowledge of the African past. For example, during the 1990s Hafed Walda, a scholar from the University of London, conducted excavations of the UNESCO World Heritage site at the Roman city of Lepcis Magna. Located in the Tripolitania area of LIBYA, the remains of this ancient city are particularly well-preserved and offer exciting opportunities for learning more about the Roman era in North Africa. Equally exciting discoveries have been made about the kingdom of Kush, which stretched along the Nile River in the present-day Republic of the SUDAN. There, important archaeological excavations of its capital city of Meroë took place from 1965 to 1972 and again in the 1990s.

The Carbon-14 (C-14) atom, also termed *radiocarbon*, is present in all organisms and is constantly replenished while organisms are alive. When an organism dies, however, the C-14 in it begins to decay. This decay takes place at such a constant rate that scientists have determined that C-14's half-life—meaning the time it takes for half the atoms in a radioactive substance to disintegrate—is 5,730 years (plus or minus 40 years). Scientists can measure the amount of C-14 in bones, dried seeds, wood, and so forth, compare it with the original amount of C-14 that would have been present, and then determine when those things ceased to be part of living organisms. Thus, if archaeologists find a site containing cattle bones, they can determine, fairly accurately, when the cattle died.

While important advances were made in our understanding about human origins in Africa prior to 1960, the decades since then have provided even more critical knowledge. Louis Leakey (1903–1972) and his wife Mary LEAKEY (1913–1996) continued their important research in the Olduvai Gorge area of TANZANIA. Then, in the 1970s, their son, Richard LEAKEY (1944–), found hominid remains in the Lake Turkana region of northern KENYA. These dated back 2.5 million years. Our understanding of the beginnings of human origins was pushed further back in time later in the 1970s, when Donald Johanson (1943–) discovered a fossil female skeleton in northeastern ETHIOPIA. Named "Lucy," the fossil was nearly 3.2 million years old. Continuing research has pushed human origins back to nearly seven million years ago with the 2002 discovery of a skull, named *Toumai* (meaning "hope of life" in the local Goran language), in northern CHAD. It combined the features of both chimpanzees and humans.

Another focal point for the study of human origins concerns the question of when anatomically modern human beings emerged. Here the fossil evidence is rather scanty. However, the DNA evidence suggests that at some point—generally believed to have been between 150,000 and 100,000 years ago—the first anatomically human creatures emerged from one of these earlier African hominids. Early humans then moved out from Africa to the rest of the Afro-Euro-Asian landmass. An important dis-

covery in this regard was made in 2001 by archaeologists in SOUTH AFRICA. At Blombos Cave, some 200 miles (322 km) east of CAPE TOWN, they found evidence that 70,000 years ago there were human beings in the area making artifacts revealing both abstract and creative thought. The present evidence thus suggests that not only did modern humans first emerge on the African continent but also that modern human behavior appeared earlier in Africa than elsewhere.

This period also saw significant developments in the third trend in archaeology in Africa, which was the focus on human and material culture over the past 10,000 or so years. One of the most important developments in this regard was the founding, in 1959, of the British Institute of History and Archaeology in East Africa (BIHAEA) and its journal, *Azania*, in 1966. This led to important research on such topics as the origins of the kingdoms in the lakes area of the interior, the salt trade, and the linkages between the Swahili Coast and the interior. In addition, the BIHAEA also worked with African museums to promote EDUCATION about the East African past. This in turn helped open the profession of archaeology to African researchers.

A particular focus of this research during recent years was on Iron Age sites. Initially this research was done at sites that were linked with the spread of iron and of AGRICULTURE in sub-Saharan Africa over the past two millennia. Later there was research on Iron Age sites elsewhere on the continent.

These Iron Age sites were associated with the spread of crops that had originated earlier in Africa. Aided by additional botanical evidence, archaeologists have now shown that Sudanic Africa was one of the world's three earliest centers for the development of agriculture between 9500 and 8000 BCE. Between 8000 and 5000 BCE three additional African centers of agricultural innovation emerged, two in the Horn of Africa and a third in the West African woodlands. While farmers in North Africa grew crops and raised animals that had originated in the Middle East, crops and domesticated animals dispersed throughout sub-Saharan Africa from these African centers of origin.

Archaeological discoveries are often a matter of chance. In 2000, for example, a team of paleontologists researching dinosaur fossils in the Agadez region of NIGER happened on a large Neolithic site that is at least 5,000 years old. Evidence from the site suggests that people once lived in an area that for several millennia has been desert. The area's inhabitants herded cattle, goats, and sheep and harvested wild grains but did not grow their own crops.

See also: ARCHAEOLOGY (Vols. I, II, III, IV); KUSH (Vol. I); LEAKEYS, THE (Vol. I); MEROË (Vol. I); ROME (Vol. I); SWAHILI COAST (Vols. II, III, IV); TRIPOLITANIA (Vol. I).

Further reading: Graham Connah, *African Civilizations: An Archaeological Perspective,* 2d ed. (New York: Cambridge Univ. Press, 2001); David W. Phillipson, *African Archaeology* (New York: Cambridge Univ. Press, 1993); Thurstan Shaw, ed., *The Archaeology of Africa: Foods, Metals, and Towns* (New York: Routledge, 1993).

architecture Throughout Africa the architecture found in European-styled cities established during the colonial era became the model for cities, towns, and villages built during the independence period. With increasing URBANIZATION Western styles of construction have come to replace traditional home-building techniques, eventually being used in even the most remote areas. Across the continent modern methods of construction have been seen as supposedly civilized and a reflection of wealth. On the other hand, traditional materials—such as mud bricks and clay stucco—have been thought to indicate substandard or "primitive" housing. As a result, the use of indigenous, or "vernacular," techniques and materials has become more rare.

In some African countries cultural guardians worry that the knowledge of traditional vernacular architecture may disappear within a few generations. In ZAMBIA, however, a group of architects is working against this trend by constructing large, beautiful buildings using only local materials. The finished products demonstrate that traditional building materials can be used to make houses as strong, comfortable, and attractive as houses built using modern, Western materials.

Challenges of Urban Architecture Even in colonial times cities were filled with indigenous architectural elements. In the post-independence period, however, increasing numbers of urban Africans have come to occupy planned cities, living and working in buildings constructed with imported materials and designed by European or European-trained architects. In the 1960s designers following in the footsteps of modern European masters like Le Corbusier (1887–1965) strove for architectural and urban standardization. This ethos competed with existing African aesthetics and environmental realities to produce a hybrid urban construction style.

The use of modern, standardized building materials in Africa began during the colonial period and continues to this day. However, the cost of acquiring foreign-made, prefabricated building materials has contributed to the African dependence on imports from industrialized countries. In general, without a healthy import-export economy, African countries do not have the financial resources to continue imitating European design and construction.

In some areas of North, East, and West Africa city planning and construction appear to be similar despite varying environments. This often can be attributed to the involvement of Islamic architects and civic planners. The cities of CAIRO, EGYPT; KANO, NIGERIA; and Fez, MOROCCO, for example, are laid out in an east–west orientation with a center city square. Radiating out from the square, usually in irregular patterns, are neighborhoods with narrow streets over which the buildings cast protective shadows. Buildings are typically uniform in height, with their monotony often broken by the towers of palaces and large civic buildings or the minarets of mosques.

In some Islamic countries, such as LIBYA, elements of indigenous architecture were generally ignored in the construction of European-style, urban high-rise buildings. However, outside influences from regions other than Europe are increasingly involved in construction in both urban and rural areas. In Wa, GHANA, Pakistani Muslims funded the construction of a new central mosque. Also, Islamic organizations from Saudi Arabia have financed the construction of mosques in CHAD, SUDAN, and NIGERIA.

Within the living quarters in these cities are compounds arranged according to the lineage of the occupants. To keep with traditional Islamic social customs, compounds often have interior courtyards that allow women to go out of doors while remaining secluded from public view.

In capital cities established by Europeans, including LAGOS, Nigeria; NAIROBI, KENYA; and CONAKRY, GUINEA, European planners did not make accommodations for local, lower-income workers. As a result, rapidly growing shantytowns on the cities' outskirts have become problematic. Housing is one of the most pressing needs in African urban areas. Cities that are already densely populated continue to receive new arrivals daily. In the rural-to-urban migration, many people come to the cities to find jobs and to enjoy urban amenities—such as electricity and running water—that are unavailable in the rural

During the era of independence, structures built using traditional architecture became increasingly rare sights, as western influences spread even to Africa's rural areas. These traditional Dogon homes in Mali were photographed in 1976. © *National Archives*

areas. However, many immigrants arrive in the city without an education or marketable skills. Consequently, they fail to find paying jobs and end up as squatters in substandard housing on the edge of town. This leaves them without access to the INFRASTRUCTURE that attracted them to the city in the first place.

For decades Egyptian architect Hassan "Bey" Fathi (1900–1989) was one of the world's most respected architects. His book, *Architecture of the Poor* (1976), was translated into 22 languages and is used as a textbook in architecture classes around the world. In 1977 the International Federation of Architects named Fathi the "World's Best Architect."

In precolonial indigenous cities the exteriors of family compounds tended to look the same. Wealth was demonstrated through access to prestige goods and by maintaining servants. However, changes during the colonial period emphasized housing construction and neighborhoods that divided people on the basis of class and lifestyle.

In South Africa a volunteer project called Architecture for Humanity has been designing mobile HIV/AIDS health clinics that can be flown into remote areas to serve African people all over the continent. The renowned Canadian-born architect Frank Gehry is an adviser for the project. Other advisers include humanitarian architects and designers from Kenya, ZIMBABWE, and South Africa.

In SOUTH AFRICA the urban areas reflect European ideas of construction with little Islamic influence. Cities like PRETORIA, capital of the Republic of South Africa, were planned around the needs of its white citizens.

Similarly architectural styles in major South African cities like CAPE TOWN, DURBAN, and JOHANNESBURG reflect European styles. In these cities the government's public works programs acted as the training ground for the first generation of white South African-born architects. These people, mostly men, built Victorian and Edwardian structures that today stand in the shadows of modern high-rises such as the IBM building in Johannesburg.

Despite the overwhelming movement toward modernization and standardization, it is possible that the face of African architecture may be changing. With progress, DEVELOPMENT, and increasing levels of education, African architects are beginning to design and construct modern buildings using materials and stylistic elements borrowed from the rich traditions of African design.

See also: ARCHITECTURE (Vols. I, II, III, IV); TOWNS AND CITIES (Vols. I, II, III, IV, V); URBAN LIFE AND CULTURE (Vols. IV, V).

Further reading: Nnamdi Elleh, *Architecture and Power in Africa* (Westport, Conn.: Praeger, 2002); Nnamdi Elleh, *African Architecture: Evolution and Transformation* (New York: McGraw-Hill, 1997); Udo Kultermann, *New Directions in African Architecture*, John Maass, trans. (New York: G. Braziller, 1969).

AREMA See PILLAR AND STRUCTURE FOR THE SALVATION OF MADAGASCAR.

Armah, Ayi Kwei (1939–) *Ghanaian author*

Ayi Kwei Armah was born into a Fante-speaking family in Sekondi-Takoradi, the coastal capital of the western region of present-day GHANA. He was educated at the prestigious Achimota College and then went to the United States to continue his education. He earned a bachelor's degree in sociology from Harvard University, worked in ALGERIA, Ghana, and France, and then returned to the United States to get an MFA in creative writing from Columbia University.

Armah has worked throughout Africa and has also taught at universities in the United States. He is the author of six novels in addition to many essays, poems, and short stories. He currently lives in DAKAR, SENEGAL, where he continues to write and teach.

Armah's writing focuses on Africa's need to retrieve its authentic past and for Africans to reinvent themselves and create a united, pan-African community. In this he echoes the stance of Ghana's founding president, Kwame NKRUMAH (1909–1972), who called for a United States of Africa. Armah's works, such as his first novel, *The Beautyful Ones Are Not Yet Born* (1968), which satirized the corruption of Ghana's postcolonial elite, often have a polemical tone. This has made him a controversial figure in African literature, for he openly addresses the key issues of identity and lack of economic and political progress that have plagued the continent since independence.

See also: AKAN (Vols. III, IV, V); LITERATURE IN MODERN AFRICA (Vol. V).

Further reading: Ode Ogede, *Ayi Kwei Armah, Radical Iconoclast: Pitting Imaginary Worlds Against the Actual* (Athens, Ohio: Ohio University Press, 2000).

art Contemporary African artists have applied new techniques and new materials in adapting to the rapidly changing structure of African society. While some artists have been studio-trained either in Europe or Africa, others are self-taught. Because Africa is such a large continent and its artists are so widely dispersed, there have been no continent-wide art movements. Thus, artists generally do not know one another or share their techniques. There are few art galleries, and even fewer art critics.

Indigenous Arts Most Africans living in rural settings produce indigenous art. These arts are divided by gender within each ethnic group. In many societies, for example, women are potters and men are blacksmiths. Depending upon the ethnic group, the women or the men may be weavers. Regions may be known for specific artistic styles. Art in North Africa, for example, is defined by an Islamic aesthetic that insists upon abstraction, geometrical decoration, and embellished Arabic script.

In East Africa personal adornment, including scarification, tattooing, and body painting, remains dominant. From ETHIOPIA to TANZANIA, for example, there is a rich tradition of using henna for body painting, including the decorative painting of a bride's hands and feet in preparation for the wedding ceremony. In northern ZAMBIA and the neighboring Democratic Republic of the CONGO, various ethnic groups practice body adornment by creating raised scars, called *cicatrices*.

Regardless of region, however, African art generally serves a function in society. Evidence of this is seen in the way many artists in western and Central Africa decorate objects used in religious rituals or items used as tools of everyday life. At many levels, African societies change to reflect new influences. So, as Christianity and Islam have spread, artistically decorated ritual objects have changed in appearance. Old art forms that expressed indigenous religious practices are abandoned in favor of new forms. As a result masks, statues, and ceremonial adornments sometimes become commodities to be sold to museums, art dealers, or professional collectors. Without an accompanying explanation of the object's function in society, museums and art patrons often do not understand the original meaning of the object. Other misunderstandings stem from incorrect classification. Many art objects in museums are identified by the "tribe" from which the object is thought to come. This is an inappropriate system because art styles crosscut ethnic lines or differ within the boundaries of a single ethnic group.

Tourist Arts Especially after the end of colonialism, indigenous artists began producing objects for sale as souvenirs for foreign travelers. At first, these items were made for a small market of Europeans. African art students and craft shops produced replicas of popular styles for sale in urban MARKETS in and around major hotels and at airports. As demand for African art increased, indigenous producers of African textiles, woodcarvings, and metal castings moved to the urban areas and began teaching others their crafts. In this way, art provided jobs for some of the urban unemployed.

Niké of Oshogbo, NIGERIA, created an artists' cooperative where she taught women how to tie-dye fabric using indigo, and how to create batik textiles for sale in the tourist market. She used indigenous methods and indigenous themes in the production of these textiles.

In BENIN CITY, Nigeria, craftsmen made bronze castings using the same lost-wax process that was utilized by the city's famed sculptors for hundreds of years. Tourists bought most of these statues. Similarly, Makonde artisans in DAR ES SALAAM, Tanzania, became well known for their wood carvings in the 1960s. Even today they sell their work through dealers who export it around the world. In EGYPT imitation Pharaonic items, as well as papyrus copies, can be found in the tourist markets.

Tourist art has become a big entrepreneurial business. West African producers and sellers, many from SENEGAL, peddle items in an expanding African tourist-arts market in the United States. Millions of dollars worth of art objects from KENYA, Tanzania, and Zambia are imported into the United States each year. Another important market for tourist art is the African urban middle class, which, like middle classes around the world, has a great appreciation for art.

Popular Art After independence, the changing lives of Africans was reflected in their art forms. A new school of African artists began producing pop art sculptures that portrayed new technology, such as planes and cars, but that also retained old themes, such as the Shona bird sculptures that have become the new symbol of ZIMBABWE. New technology was used by artists in CAMEROON as well, where aluminum became a medium for casting objects. In GHANA, IVORY COAST, Nigeria, and the Congo region, artists created Christian cemetery sculptures with the relatively new religious emblems of crosses and female angels.

Painting was a genre of African art as early as the 1930s. Since then pictures of rural life were sold to tourists and also became valued by urban elites and the middle class. In SOUTH AFRICA and Zimbabwe, MISSIONARIES introduced mural painting to Ndebele women, who then used the techniques they learned to decorate local ARCHITECTURE.

Academic Arts Influences of the international art community have contributed to the development of academic arts in Africa. Even during colonial times European artists set up schools, and Africans trained in Europe. Following a European model, Africans trained in local academic institutions. For example, in 1927 the Margaret Trowell School of Fine Arts was established at MAKERERE UNIVERSITY in KAMPALA, UGANDA. By 1957 Ethiopia had the Fine Arts School of Addis Ababa. One of the early teachers at that academy was Alexander "Skunder" Boghossian (1937–2003), Ethiopia's well-known painter. In his art, he blended Western philosophy and cultural movements with indigenous African cultural traditions.

Influenced by a school of Mexican mural painting, Valente Malangatana (1936–   ) of MOZAMBIQUE introduced a new art style for liberation movements in southern Africa. Sculptor Sobari Douglas Camp, from Calabar, Nigeria, studied in London and created popular sculptures using welded metal and battery power to create movement. Contemporary governments used the arts for prestige by giving patronage to high-profile artists such as Kofi Antubam (1922–   ) of Ghana, Ben Enwonwu (1921–1994) of Nigeria, and Liyolo of the Democratic Republic of the Congo. In the 21st century the field of African art continues to be dynamic in its merger of indigenous themes with international styles.

See also: ART (Vols. I, II, III, IV); ETHNIC GROUP (Vol. IV); GENDER IN COLONIAL AFRICA (Vol. IV); NDEBELE (Vol. IV); OSHOGBO (Vol. III); SHONA (Vol. I); TEXTILES (Vol. IV).

Further reading: Karin Ådahl and Berit Sahlström, eds., *Islamic Art and Culture in sub-Saharan Africa* (Uppsala, Sweden: Acta Universitatis Upsaliensis, 1995); Katy Deepwell, ed., *Art Criticism and Africa* (London: Saffron Books, 1998); Tobias Döring, ed., *African Cultures, Visual Arts, and the Museum: Sights/Sites of Creativity and Conflict* (New York: Rodopi, 2002).

Arusha Declaration Statement of principles by which Tanzanian president Julius NYERERE (1922–1999) hoped to guide the economic and social DEVELOPMENT of his nation. Issued on February 5, 1967, the Arusha Declaration was more a philosophical statement than a step-by-step program. It rejected as "stupid" the previous reliance that TANZANIA had had on foreign aid. It also rejected the notion that INDUSTRIALIZATION could be immediately brought to developing nations like Tanzania, since the economies of these nations were primarily agricultural and their people were rural. Instead, Nyerere argued, equitable and long-lasting development would come only via a community-based policy that grew out of the roots of Tanzania's own land and people.

According to this strategy, money for economic development—and eventual industrialization—would come primarily by expanding Tanzania's agricultural resources. To accomplish this the declaration urged the people to work harder and longer, to share knowledge of farming techniques, and to dedicate themselves to the notion of community. "From now on," the declaration asserted, "we shall stand upright and walk forward on our feet rather than look at this problem upside down. Industries will come and money will come, but their foundation is *the people* and their *hard work*, especially in *agriculture*. This is the meaning of self-reliance…"

See also: AFRICAN SOCIALISM (Vol. IV); NYERERE, JULIUS (Vol. IV); SOCIAL CAPITAL (Vol. V); *UJAMAA* (Vol. V).

Asian communities

Asian communities The principal Asian communities in modern Africa are from South Asia and are located in the former British colonies of East and southern Africa and the Indian Ocean islands. Because Britain ruled what is today India, Bangladesh, and Pakistan as part of its empire, it drew LABOR from the Indian sub-continent for use in African colonies. These workers built railroads in East Africa and provided the labor force for the sugar plantations of both the island of MAURITIUS and Natal. Some from then British-ruled India also emigrated to Africa as merchants.

The largest South Asian community in terms of percentage lives on the island of Mauritius, where it constitutes about 40 percent of the population. Many of the island's Creoles have Indian ancestry as well. Another 2 percent or so originate from China. About one-half of the Mauritian Asians are Hindu and about one-sixth are Muslim. Many still work in the agricultural sector, but others are part of the expanding technologically driven business community. The South African Indian community, as the South Asians are known there, makes up less than 3 percent of the country's population, but that still amounts to more than one million people. They are concentrated in KwaZulu/Natal Province, especially in DURBAN and its surrounding urban area. Indeed, they outnumber the city's white population, though they, in turn, are far outnumbered by the area's African residents.

The Asian communities of former British East Africa and central Africa, while still significant, are far smaller. Many emigrated from KENYA after its independence in 1963 so that today they account for less than 1 percent of the population there. Hindu, Muslim, and Sikh in terms of RELIGION, these people reside principally in the urban centers of Kisumu, MOMBASA, and NAIROBI. In TANZANIA the South Asian community, which expanded during the colonial period, has declined since independence. Much of the retail sector in DAR ES SALAAM and other towns, however, continues to be in the hands of Indian businesspeople.

In his 1979 novel, *A Bend in the River*, V. S. Naipaul (1932–), the Trinidadian writer, captures the experience of much of the Asian community in Africa in the years following independence. The book's narrator, Salim, is a Muslim Indian merchant who operates a store in a town located on the banks of the fictionalized Congo River. He describes the events and deteriorating conditions as political CORRUPTION takes hold of a country, freed from colonial rule, seeking a new identity in the modern world.

The transition from living under colonial rule to living under independent African governments was difficult for the Asian communities, as attested by their declining numbers due to emigration in Kenya and Tanzania. Nowhere, however, did they face such difficulties as in UGANDA. When Idi AMIN (c. 1925–2003) seized power in 1971 he capitalized on the general unpopularity of Asians among the African population to gain more political support for his reign. In 1972 he expelled all the estimated 50,000 non-citizen Asians (few had become citizens at independence in 1962) and confiscated their businesses and possessions, which he redistributed to Africans. This was a popular move, but it proved disastrous to the Ugandan economy and also undermined the Amin government's international standing. As part of the efforts in the early 1990s to rebuild the economy, President Yoweri MUSEVENI (1944–) invited the former Asian residents to return to Uganda and restored much of their property. Thousands did so, resuming their vital role in the business sector.

See also: ASIAN COMMUNITIES (Vol. IV); ENGLAND AND AFRICA (Vols. IV, V).

Further reading: Yasmin Alibhai-Brown, *No Place Like Home* (London: Virago Press, 1997); Bill Freund, *Insiders and Outsiders: The Indian Working Class of Durban, 1910–1990* (Portsmouth, N.H.: Heinemann, 1995).

Asmara (Asmera)

Asmara (Asmera) Capital and largest city of ERITREA, located near the Red Sea in the Eritrean highlands. Asmara, which was originally a minor TIGRAY village, was the capital of the Italian colony of Eritrea from 1889 until 1941, after which it was the capital for British-administered Eritrea. With the 1952 United Nations resolution that aligned Eritrea with ETHIOPIA, Asmara became a provincial capital.

Starting in 1961 Eritrea gradually became engulfed in warfare. At that time, an armed nationalist movement, the ERITREAN PEOPLE'S LIBERATION FRONT, began fighting a prolonged war against the Ethiopian government in an attempt to secure the country's independence. Asmara itself did not suffer much from the direct effects of the war, though indirect effects included a disrupted economy and a deterioration of the city's INFRASTRUCTURE. It remained a provincial capital until Eritrean independence in 1993, at which time it became the new country's capital.

Due to the continued Italian presence in Asmara, a holdover from the colonial era, the city, in the words of one observer, has "a string of boutiques, coffee-shops, and restaurants reminiscent of southern Italy."

Today Asmara is a city of more than 400,000 inhabitants, with approximately equal numbers of Muslims and Ethiopian Orthodox Christians. There is also still a significant Italian population. The city is accessible by the Eritrean Railway, an international airport, and the nearby Red Sea port of Massawa, located about 40 miles (65 km) away. Major industries in Asmara include textiles, footwear, soft drinks, and leather tanning, and the city also supports a robust agricultural market. As the capital, the city is home to the national University of Asmara, which was founded in 1954 as a Roman Catholic institution.

See also: ASMARA (Vols. II, IV); NATIONALISM AND INDEPENDENCE MOVEMENTS (Vol. IV); ITALY AND AFRICA (Vol. IV); UNITED NATIONS AND AFRICA (Vols. IV, V).

ASP See AFRO-SHIRAZI PARTY.

Assoumani, Azali (1959–) *President of the Union of Comoros*

Azali Assoumani was born in 1959 on Grande Comore, the principal island of the COMOROS. He rapidly moved up the military ranks, becoming army chief of staff when President Mohamed Said Djohar (1918–) came to power by military coup in 1989. In 1992 Azali was wounded in a failed rebel coup attempt, but he remained head of the Comoran military throughout the 1990s, under both President Mohamed Taki Abdoulkarim (1936–1998) and interim president Tajiddine Ben Said Massounde (1933–).

In 1997 INDEPENDENCE MOVEMENTS on the other large Comoran islands of ANJOUAN and Moheli took a vio-

lent turn, and Azali became the chief facilitator of the peace negotiations. When representatives from the three islands refused to approve a new peace plan in April 1999, Azali mounted a successful, bloodless coup of his own. Upon deposing Massounde, Assoumani dissolved the existing constitution and government and promised to replace his military regime with a civilian government. In 2002 each of the three islands—Grande Comore, Anjouan, and Moheli—elected its own civilian president, and Assoumani retired from the army in order to assume the overall presidency of the reunited Union of Comoros. In this role Assoumani controls the defense, finance, and security apparatus of the union.

Aswan Dam Either of two dams across the Nile River near Aswan, EGYPT. The Aswan "Low" Dam was completed in 1902. It was supplanted in the 1960s by the much larger Aswan "High" Dam. In 1898 British engineers began construction of a massive dam near the city of Aswan, Egypt, designed to control the Nile's annual flooding and help provide a stable source of water for crops. The Aswan "Low" Dam was completed in 1902 but it quickly became apparent that the dam was incapable of handling the Nile's more extreme floods. In 1952 planning began for a second dam, the Aswan "High" Dam, four miles upriver from the Low Dam.

To help finance the dam Egypt played on Cold War tensions between the United States and the Soviet Union. The United States initially agreed to help fund the project, but it then withdrew, presumably over the conflicts between Egypt and Israel. Egypt then turned to the Soviet Union, which provided funding, along with military advisers and workers.

Egypt and the Republic of the SUDAN signed the Nile Water Agreement in 1959, and construction began the following year. Even before the High Dam was completed, complications arose, however. The dam's reservoir would submerge much of Lower Nubia, the area stretching along the Nile from Aswan past the ancient town of Wadi Halfa, in the northern Sudan. With a rich history intertwined with that of Egypt, the region was home to many ancient monuments, temples, and archaeological sites of great value. In order to help save these cultural treasures, the United Nations Educational, Scientific, and Cultural Organization (UNESCO) began an extensive rescue operation in 1960, relocating as many as twenty monuments in Egypt and another four in the Sudan. The most recognizable of these is the temple of Abu Simel, which was relocated in its entirety. Despite these efforts countless other monuments and artifacts were lost when the reservoir was created. No less traumatic was the displacement of over 90,000 Nubians who lived in the reservoir area. Those in the Sudan were moved as far as 370 miles from their previous homes.

In 1970 the dam was completed. Two miles long, the High Dam created Lake Nasser; named after Egyptian president Gamal Abdel NASSER (1918–1970), the reservoir is approximately 300 miles (483 km) long. The new dam succeeded in controlling the Nile and produced a 30 percent increase in arable land in Egypt. The dam's hydroelectric capabilities doubled Egypt's power supply.

Despite its benefits, the dam caused significant ecological problems. Downstream areas of the Nile, once fertilized by sediments left after the seasonal floods, now had to be artificially fertilized by farmers. The fertile Nile Delta began to shrink, also due to lack of sediment deposits. Even the Mediterranean shrimping industry was adversely affected by the change in the Nile's flow.

See also: ASWAN (Vol. I); ASWAN DAM (Vol. IV); COLD WAR AND AFRICA (Vol. IV); EGYPTOLOGY (Vols. IV, V); KUSH (Vol. I); MEDITERRANEAN SEA (Vols. I, II); NILE DELTA (Vol. I); NILE RIVER (Vol. I); NILE VALLEY (Vol. I); SUDAN, THE (Vol. II); WATER RESOURCES (Vol. V).

atmospheric change Shifts in Africa's climate—the result of natural occurrences and, in recent years, exacerbated by INDUSTRIALIZATION, URBANIZATION, and increased levels of AGRICULTURE—have led to important changes in temperature, rainfall, and air quality. With an area of 11,700,000 square miles (30,303,000 sq km), continental Africa has a widely varying climate characterized by low rainfall in the north, high rainfall near the equator, and temperate conditions with low rainfall in the south. Over the centuries variations have been caused by everything from El Niño to long-term climatic events that have affected the entire planet. Changes in the African climate, however, have increased exponentially over the past half-century. Rainfall, for example, has generally decreased, and at least 16 African countries are expected to suffer from a scarcity of WATER RESOURCES by the year 2050. Unlike situations in the past, however, this contemporary scarcity of rain has not been caused by natural events. Rather it is the result of human actions, primarily the cutting of FORESTS and a marked increase in greenhouse gases.

Another atmospheric change has been a rise in temperature, perhaps as much as half a degree Celsius (0.9 degrees Fahrenheit) during the past century. In Africa's mountains, this has led to a melting of snow caps and a decrease in the amount of water stored in snow packs. It has also led to an increase in soil erosion and flooding, which can create environments in which diseases such as malaria and cholera spread easily.

Although several forces are involved in this temperature rise, the central cause is an increase in the amount of greenhouse gases, primarily carbon dioxide. Indeed, although the emission of carbon dioxide and other greenhouse gases is a problem worldwide, Africa has been hit harder than most other parts of the world. The vast majority of these gases come from industrial and automotive emissions in Europe and North America. However, an increasing number are now coming from Africa itself, where many countries have been slow to enact clean air legislation. As a result, some of Africa's cities—including CAPETOWN, SOUTH AFRICA; ANTANANARIVO, MADAGASCAR; NAIROBI, KENYA; ACCRA, GHANA; and LAGOS, NIGERIA—have some of the worst air quality in the world. In spite of the risks to both health and the overall climate, though, change has not come readily. Too often, clean fuels, low-emission factories and vehicles, and technological innovations are all too costly for most African nations.

How does cutting trees lead to a loss of rainfall? The answer lies in the fact that forests are an important part of the water cycle. Trees not only control soil erosion, but they also store rainwater. When forests are cut on a large scale, less water is returned to the atmosphere, so there is less water available to produce rain. In Africa, this has led to an unfortunate cycle. Hunger and POVERTY drive people to attempt to grow more crops. But as people clear forests in order to create farmland, the loss of trees leads to a decrease in the rain that is needed to grow crops.

Fortunately, however, some important steps are now being taken to monitor atmospheric change. The more substantive changes that are needed require action not only from African countries themselves, but also from those foreign nations whose activities make them the greatest contributors to atmospheric change.

See also: POPULATION GROWTH (Vol. V); ECOLOGY AND ECOLOGICAL CHANGE (Vol. V); ECONOMIC ASSISTANCE (Vol. V); ENVIRONMENTAL ISSUES (Vol. V); FAMINE AND HUNGER (Vol. V).

Awolowo, Obafemi (1909–1987) *Yoruba national leader from Nigeria*

Obafemi Awolowo was born in a small town in the Protectorate of Southern NIGERIA. Politically active as a young man, he was educated locally and worked as a teacher, journalist, and trade-union organizer before going to London to study law. Living in London from 1944 to 1947, he organized a YORUBA cultural society called *Egbe Omo Oduduwa* (Society of the Descendants of Oduduwa) after the legendary founder of the Yoruba people. In 1950–51 the political arm of Egbe Omo Oduduwa became the Action Group, a political party, with Awolowo as its president. He then became active in the politics of the Yoruba-dominated Western Region of the protectorate, serving from 1954 to 1959 as its regional prime minister. In 1959 he was elected to the Federal House of Representatives and became active in national politics.

At the time of independence in 1960, Nigeria was divided into regions dominated by competing ethnic groups: the Yoruba in the west, the IGBO in the east, and the HAUSA in the north. In 1963 Awolowo was imprisoned after a failed coup by the Action Group against Nigeria's Hausa prime minister, Abubakar Tafawa BALEWA (1912–1966). Awolowo was released in 1966 following a successful military coup against Balewa. The new military government banned all political parties.

In 1967 the Igbo-dominated Eastern Region attempted to secede from Nigeria and form the state of BI-AFRA. This resulted in the Nigerian Civil War of 1967–70. Awolowo eventually took the federal government's side and opposed Biafran succession. From 1966 to 1971, the year after the war, Awolowo served as federal finance minister and also as vice chairman of the Federal Executive Council. In 1971 he resigned his federal government positions and returned to his private law practice.

In 1978 the ban on political parties was lifted and Awolowo, with the help of friends from the old Action Group, formed the United Party of Nigeria. He was defeated in the presidential elections of 1979 and 1982. The latter, according to his friends and supporters, was one of the worst cases of electoral tampering in Nigeria's history. In 1983, following another military coup, the United Party was banned, and Awolowo disappeared from the political scene. He lived a private but active life until his death on May 9, 1987, at the age of 78.

Obafemi Awolowo's death and funeral for once brought Nigerians together. Government officials, members of the Nigerian Bar Association, traditional rulers, and ordinary people gathered in Ikene, the town of his birth, to witness his burial. To this day, Obafemi Awolowo remains one of West Africa's most admired politicians.

See also: AWOLOWO, OBAFEMI (Vol. IV).

Further reading: Olasope O. Oyelaran et al., eds., *Obafemi Awolowo, the End of an Era?* (Ile-Ife, Nigeria: Obafemi Awolowo University Press, 1988).

Awoonor, Kofi (George Awoonor-Williams)

(1935–) *Ghanaian author writing in English*

Kofi Nyedevu Awoonor was born in Wheta in the former Gold Coast Colony (present-day GHANA) in 1935. Informally educated by his Ewe grandmother, who was a singer of funeral dirges, he learned from her about the oral poetry and performance arts of his people. Much of his early poetry is modeled on Ewe dirges.

Awoonor was educated at Achimota College. In 1963 he received a bachelor's degree, with honors, in English

from the University of Ghana, Legon. He then worked as a research fellow at the Institute of African Studies, Legon. He completed his studies only six years after Ghana became independent (1957) and was indebted to the national cultural movement, sponsored by Ghana's president, Kwame NKRUMAH (1909–1972), that supported artists like himself. Awoonor became so closely associated with Nkrumah that he left Ghana shortly after the 1966 coup in which Nkrumah was overthrown.

In 1967 Awoonor left for Britain to do graduate studies in English at the University of London. A year later, in 1968, he went to the United States to attend the State University of New York at Stony Brook, where, in 1972, he received a PhD. in English and comparative literature. He subsequently served as chair of the comparative literature program at Stony Brook and as a visiting professor at several American universities before returning to Ghana in 1975. Shortly after his return, he was arrested and charged with aiding a Ewe political fugitive. In 1979 his sentence was commuted to time served. His experience in prison, including the two months he spent in solitary confinement, became the basis for the collection of poems, *The House by the Sea,* which was published in 1978.

Awoonor's time abroad in the late 1960s and early 1970s was his most productive in terms of literary output. His first volume of poetry, *Rediscovery,* published under his former name, George Awoonor-Williams, appeared in 1964. His second volume of poetry, *Night of My Blood* (1971), is considered his most compelling. A subsequent collection of poems, *Until the Morning After* (1987), earned him the 1988 Commonwealth Poetry Prize for Africa. As a poet Awoonor often denounced European presumptions of superiority and criticized the imposition of European culture and values on Africa.

Beyond this, he earned a reputation as a leading Afri-can literary critic. Among his best-known critical works is his revised doctoral dissertation, which was published in 1975 under the title *The Breast of the Earth: A Critical Survey of Africa's Literature, Culture, and History.* He is also known for his 1971 novel, *This Earth, My Brother . . . .*

As Awoonor grew older his writing took second place to his political activities. In the early 1990s he served as Ghana's ambassador to the United Nations. At the end of the decade, he was an aide to President Jerry RAWLINGS (1947–) until Rawlings stepped down from office in 2002 after his party lost the presidential elections.

See also: LITERATURE IN MODERN AFRICA (Vol. V).

Azikiwe, Nnamdi (Benjamin Nnamdi Azikiwe)

(1904–1996) *First president of independent Nigeria*

Azikiwe's anticolonial activism, expressed primarily through the newspapers he headed first in the Gold Coast (present-day GHANA) and then in his homeland of NIGE-RIA, won him great fame and popularity. In 1944 he founded the National Council for Nigeria and the Cameroons (NCNC), a pan-Nigeria political organization. In 1948 he was elected president of the IGBO Union, a position which put him in competition with rival ethnic political parties, particularly the HAUSA-Fulani NORTHERN PEOPLE'S CONGRESS (NPC), led by Alhaji Sir Ahmadu BELLO (1910–1966), and the YORUBA Action Group, led by Obafemi AWOLOWO (1909–1987).

When, in 1961, the Northern Cameroons joined with Nigeria and the Southern Cameroons united with the Republic of CAMEROON, the NCNC changed its name to the National Convention of Nigerian Citizens.

As Nigeria prepared for independence from Britain, a new federal legislature was formed, and, in 1960, Azikiwe became president of the Senate. The NPC, the majority party in the legislature, formed a coalition government with Azikiwe's NCNC. Under these auspices, also in 1960, Azikiwe became the governor-general of Nigeria, which was now a sovereign state.

Ethnic and political strife began to boil during the first three years of Nigeria's independence. The coalition of the NPC and NCNC was strained, with the NPC being Muslim, upper class, and regional in its interests, and the NCNC, Christian, non-aristocratic, and nationalistic. The relationship was maintained essentially because of the NPC's majority power, to which the NCNC wanted to remain close. In addition census results, which determined representation in the legislature, were hotly contested in 1962–63, with the NCNC accusing the NPC of altering the results to their benefit.

Meanwhile, in 1962, dissension within the opposition Action Group spilled over into mass riots in the Western Region. The violence entered the legislature as well, which was then dissolved under a declaration of a state of emergency. It was in the aftermath of these circumstances that Azikiwe became president of Nigeria, when the country became a republic in 1963.

The creation of a Midwestern Region in 1963 heralded a shifting of political alliances and further turmoil, as the NPC–NCNC coalition fell apart. From 1964–65, election disputes spawned more violence and general disorder, and Azikiwe and Prime Minister Abubakar Tafawa BALEWA (1912–1966) were deeply at odds.

In 1966, while Azikiwe was in London for medical treatment, Igbo army officers led by General Johnson Aguiyi-Ironsi (1924–1966) rose up in a COUP D'ÉTAT, killing Balewa and other government leaders and forcing Azikiwe from the presidency. This was followed by another coup that same year, this time led by Hausa-Fulani officers. Ethnic clashes followed, with many Igbo living in the Northern Region massacred by the Hausa-Fulani majority. The Igbo in Azikiwe's Eastern Region responded by seceding from the nation in 1967, declaring the independent Republic of BIAFRA. Azikiwe's attempts to prevent the secession failed, and the country erupted in what came to be known as the Biafran War. Azikiwe served as an advisor for the Biafrans for a time but switched to the federal side after the Biafran cause became hopeless, an action that earned him the ire of his native Igbo. The war ended in 1970 with the defeat of the Biafrans.

In 1978 civilian rule was again established, and Azikiwe became the head of the Nigerian People's Party (NPP). He ran for the presidency in 1979 and 1983, losing each time to Alhaji Shehu Shagari (1925–   ), leader of the National Party for Nigeria (NPN). Azikiwe retired from politics in 1983, having regained the support of his native Igbo people.

See also: AZIKIWE, NNAMDI (Vol. IV); ETHNIC CONFLICT IN AFRICA (Vol. V); FULANI (Vols. II, III).

B

Bâ, Amadou Hampâté (1901–1991) *Islamic scholar and writer of African folklore and oral tradition*

Born into a well-to-do Peul-speaking, Fulani Muslim family in Bandiagara, MALI, Bâ received his primary education at a French colonial school in Jenne before moving on to study in the Malian capital of BAMAKO and in Gorée, SENEGAL. About the same time, Bâ became a pupil of the Sufi mystic Tierno Bokar (1875–1940). Bâ worked for a time in the French colonial service in UPPER VOLTA before joining the French Institute for Black Africa, where he began research in African history and ethnography. In 1958 he founded the Malian Institute for Research in Human Sciences. He also became an ambassador to the United Nations Educational, Scientific and Cultural Organization (UNESCO).

The Peul (Pulaar) language is widely used in West Africa. In its various dialects, it is spoken by roughly 14 million people of Fulani background from Fouta Jallon (modern GUINEA) through NIGER, Mali, NIGERIA, and CAMEROON. Fulani traders and merchants can be found in almost every major city in West Africa.

As a Muslim scholar, Bâ was an unlikely champion for the preservation of African folklore and oral traditions. Bâ strongly believed that oral traditions held a wealth of essential cultural information, once saying, "In Africa, when an old person dies, it is a library that burns down." However, it was his desire and ability to bridge cultural gaps that became the foundation of his educational legacy. After his retirement, in 1970, Bâ moved to ABIDJAN, IVORY COAST, where he taught until his death in 1991.

Bâ produced a number of scholarly works during his lifetime, as well as stories and one novel, *L'Etrange destin de Wangrin* (*The fortunes of Wangrin,* 1973). It tells of an African man caught between European culture and African traditions. He also produced an autobiography, *Amkoullel, l'enfant peul* (*Amkoullel, the Fulani child,* 1991).

See also: BÂ, AMADOU HAMPÂTÉ (Vol. IV); HISTORICAL SCHOLARSHIP ON AFRICA (Vols. IV, V); ISLAM, INFLUENCE OF (Vols. II, III, IV, V); JENNE (Vols. II, III); LITERATURE IN MODERN AFRICA (Vol. V); ORAL TRADITION (Vols. I, IV); SUFISM (Vol. IV).

Ba, Miriama (1929–1981) *Writer and educator from Senegal*

Miriama Ba was born into a prominent Muslim family in DAKAR, the capital of SENEGAL. Miriama was sent to live with her maternal grandparents at a young age after her mother's death and was raised in a traditional Muslim environment, in which the formal EDUCATION of women was not a high priority. Even so, she stayed in touch with her father, a progressive government official, who encouraged her to develop her natural intellectual brilliance. (Ba's father would become Senegal's first health minister when the country achieved independence in 1960.)

Ba won a scholarship to the École Normale, a Western-style secondary school in Dakar, where she learned the French language in which she wrote. After graduating she started teaching and married Obeye Diop, a member of the

Senegalese Parliament. Although they eventually divorced, Ba and Diop had nine children together. With a large family to look after, and with her health in a delicate state, Ba gave up teaching and began writing essays and giving lectures on subjects such as women's rights, West African education, and traditional social customs.

Ba published her first novel, *Une si longue lettre* (published in English as *So Long a Letter*), in 1980, at the age of 51. Widely lauded by critics, the short novel examines the pernicious double standards of traditional patriarchal societies. *So Long a Letter* won the first Noma Award for publishing in Africa and became a cause célèbre for West African women and feminists around the world.

The Noma Award is an annual prize that recognizes outstanding African writers. The award, first given in 1980, comes with a $10,000 prize.

Ba wrote one other novel, *Un chant éclarate* (*Scarlet song*), but died before its publication in 1981.

See also: ISLAM, INFLUENCE OF (Vols. II, III, IV, V); LITERATURE IN MODERN AFRICA (Vol. V); WOMEN IN COLONIAL AFRICA (Vol. IV); WOMEN IN MODERN AFRICA (Vol. V).

Babangida, Ibrahim (Ibrahim Badamosi Babangida) (1941–) *Nigerian military head of state*

Originally from Niger State, Babangida was born into an ethnic Gwari family, outside of the traditional Nigerian aristocracy. This, combined with an outgoing personality and a willingness to accept other points of view, made him a popular officer and helped him rise steadily in the Nigerian army. Beginning in 1976 he played a larger role in the various military regimes that governed NIGERIA, eventually serving as the army's chief of staff under General Muhammadu Buhari (1942–). Growing increasingly dissatisfied with Buhari's rule, Babangida helped initiate a COUP D'ÉTAT in 1985 that brought himself and the Armed Forces Ruling Council to power.

Publicly committed to transferring power to civilian rule, Babangida took steps to improve the political situation in Nigeria, including releasing political prisoners. Yet he also stifled dissent, issuing temporary bans of journals critical of his actions and even forbidding former office holders from having positions in the new government. He continued, however, to confront severe economic crises, primarily brought on by the sharp downturn in OIL prices that crippled the Nigerian economy during the 1980s and 1990s. In 1993 Babangida promised free, democratic elections. When it became appar-

ent, however, that the 1993 election was going to be won by the YORUBA financier Mashood ABIOLA (1937– 1998), Babangida declared the election invalid before the final results could be announced.

Criticized both at home and abroad, Babangida's actions set off a period of unrest punctuated by strikes and protests. Eventually, Sani ABACHA (1943–1998), a career military officer and part of many Nigerian governments, pushed Babangida into resigning and turning power over to the civilian business leader Earnest Shonekan (1936–) and his interim national government. Following Shonekan's brief tenure as chief of state (82 days), Abacha took control of the government, restoring power to the military.

See also: ETHNIC CONFLICT IN AFRICA (Vol. V).

Balewa, Abubakar Tafawa (Sir; Alhaji; Malam Abubakar) (1912–1966) *First prime minister of independent Nigeria*

Balewa, a Muslim and former teacher from northern NIGERIA, began his political career in 1947, when he was elected to the Northern Region's House of Assembly in colonial Nigeria. When the British replaced the House of Assembly with a federal House of Representatives in 1951, the popular Balewa continued to represent his native Northern Region. He also held the post of minister of the Department of Works and Transport.

In the early 1950s the Nigerian federation became self-governing and pushed for even greater independence from Britain. In preparation for the coming independence, Balewa, along with Ahmadu BELLO (1910–1966), founded the conservative NORTHERN PEOPLE'S CONGRESS (NPC). His party's members were mostly HAUSA and Fulani northerners, and Balewa believed for a while that Nigeria should be partitioned into two countries, one for the Muslim majority in the north and the other for the non-Muslim southern groups, including the IGBO and YORUBA. Balewa's NPC party vied for votes with other key regional political parties, including the National Council for Nigeria and Cameroons, led by eastern Nigerians Dr. Nnamdi AZIKIWE (1904–1996) and Herbert Macaulay (1864–1946), and the western-based Action Group opposition party, led by Yoruba chief Obafemi AWOLOWO (1909–1987).

In 1957 Balewa was appointed prime minister of the Nigerian federation and Azikiwe was named governor general. The NPC then won the 1959 election, so Balewa remained prime minister at independence in 1960. That same year Queen Elizabeth II (1926–) knighted Balewa for his strong leadership. That Balewa accepted this honor, reminiscent of the colonial era, angered younger and more militant African nationalists. In 1963 Nigeria became a republic, although it remained within the British Commonwealth. As the prime minister of a parliamentary system,

Balewa exercised broad executive and legislative power; Azikiwe's new presidential post, on the other hand, was mostly ceremonial. Balewa, now leading a multiparty government, toned down his argument for a divided Nigeria and put his faith in the Nigerian coalition.

Balewa soon found himself leading a country in disarray, reeling from regional and ethnic disputes, unable to agree on whether to pursue Western-style capitalism or socialism, and unable or unwilling to enforce its constitutional laws. The 1964 elections were marred by violence and boycotted, and in 1965 Balewa's party was accused of rigging the election process, especially in the Igbo region. Typical of the political maneuvering that went on, Azikiwe, as president, attempted but failed to dismiss Bello as prime minister. In general Balewa's personal integrity was unquestioned, but his government was increasingly seen as corrupt, with individuals having political ties becoming rich while much of the country suffered from POVERTY and starvation. In 1966 Balewa was assassinated in a military COUP D'ÉTAT led by officers from the Igbo ethnic group of southern Nigeria. Major General Johnson Aguiyi-Ironsi (1924–1966), an Igbo army commander, emerged as Nigeria's new leader and dismantled the civilian government, replacing it with a military regime. Widespread anti-Igbo violence followed in the wake of the coup, and Aguiyi-Ironsi was assassinated within months in a second coup that brought army chief of staff Yakubu GOWON (1934–) to power. In 1967 the eastern region seceded, declaring itself the independent state of BIAFRA, and Nigeria's civil war (1967–70) had begun.

See also: BALEWA, ABUBAKAR (Vol, IV); NATIONALISM AND INDEPENDENCE MOVEMENTS (Vol. IV).

Further reading: Trevor Clark, *A Right Honourable Gentleman: Abubakar from the Black Rock: A Narrative Chronicle of the Life and Times of Nigeria's Alhaji Sir Abubakar Tafawa Balewa* (London: Edward Arnold, 1991).

Bamako Capital city of Republic of MALI, located in the southwestern part of the country, on the Niger River. Bamako was the French colonial capital from 1883 until independence in 1960, at which point it became the federal capital of Mali. The administrative, commercial, financial, manufacturing, and TRANSPORTATION center for the country, Bamako is the base of industries including textiles, ceramics, pharmaceuticals, and the generation of electricity. Motor vehicles, farm equipment, processed food, and building supplies are also produced. Cement and petroleum products from SENEGAL arrive at Bamako's river-port facilities via rail for further shipment inland. In the other direction, rice and groundnuts (peanuts) from the interior are sent upstream for transfer to the rail system at Bamako. The city has an international airport, several research institutes and colleges, a large market, and a vibrant URBAN LIFE AND CULTURE.

Some of the greatest modern African musicians come from Mali, honing their performance skills in Bamako before going on to the wider world stage. In 1970 the government sponsored the Super Rail Band, which went on to become famous and still performs today. The internationally known Afro-pop star Salif KEITA (1949–) played with the band from 1970 to 1973.

Bamako grew from a collection of villages in the early 1880s to a city of approximately 880,000 people today. About 10 percent of Mali's total population lives in the city. It experienced a particularly rapid period of growth between 1960 and 1970, when migration from the rural areas more than tripled its population during a period of DROUGHT AND DESERTIFICATION. Today, Bamako straddles both sides of the Niger River.

See also: BAMAKO (Vols. II, III, IV); NIGER RIVER (Vols. I, III); POPULATION GROWTH (Vol. V); URBANIZATION (Vols. IV, V).

Banda, Hastings Kamuzu (Ngwazi Hastings Kamuzu Banda) (c. 1898–1997) *President of Malawi from 1966 to 1994*

Born in the British protectorate of Nyasaland, Banda became a successful doctor in England, using his money and position to become a figure of influence within the Nyasaland African Congress, a Nyasaland nationalist organization. In 1957 Banda went to Nyasaland as the leader of a protest against British plans to assimilate Nyasaland, Northern Rhodesia, and Southern Rhodesia (these territories already linked as the Central African Federation) into a single state. Violent demonstrations, which Banda helped foment with his impassioned public speaking, led to a British backlash, and Banda was imprisoned. He was released in 1961 and named president for life of the Malawi Congress party, which was formed while he was in prison. He led the party to sweep the elections that same year. In 1962 Banda led the African side of a temporary, joint white and black government. In 1963 he became Nyasaland's first prime minister. Nyasaland became the fully independent MALAWI in 1964, and in 1966 Banda was established as the president of the Republic of Malawi.

In 1967 Banda established diplomatic relations with SOUTH AFRICA. In doing so, he was alone among the African heads of state, for the ORGANIZATION OF AFRICAN UNITY had a policy of boycotting South Africa because of its APARTHEID policies. Banda, however, received major economic benefits from South Africa in the form of investments and trade.

A highly authoritarian leader, Banda quickly established himself as the country's sole decision maker, purging the government of any possible opposition and imposing a policy of "guided democracy." By assuming the title of president for life of Malawi in 1971, clearly Banda intended to guide the democracy himself. Banda exerted control over all of Malawi's media, as well as the Congress party's Press Holdings company, whose profits mostly went to Banda's personal fortune. Using intimidation tactics that he enforced with the Malawi Young Pioneers, a loyalist group he founded, Banda seized money for his treasury and drove his opposition into exile. In the 1980s these exiles faced assassination and kidnapping at the hands of Malawi secret police.

However, there were also some positive sides to Banda's rule, especially in the area of AGRICULTURE. His efforts to improve the rural areas meant that, in contrast to much of the rest of the continent, Malawi did not witness uncontrolled URBANIZATION.

Banda's control over Malawi was near total. Short skirts and pants were banned from the female wardrobe, as was long hair for men. He used money from the nation's treasury to fund construction of seven presidential palaces, and relocated the national capital from Zomba to LILONGWE, in the lands of his Chewa heritage. He also sought to impose chiChewa as the national language but encountered great resistance from speakers of other languages. He even forced those who came near him to do so on their knees.

Despite his efforts, by the 1990s Banda's rule buckled under opposition both at home and abroad. In 1993 Banda underwent brain surgery in JOHANNESBURG, but managed to maintain his power until 1994, when he gave in to calls for multiparty elections. Banda and his followers were crushed in the elections, and Bakili MULUZI (1943–), of the UNITED DEMOCRATIC FRONT, became president. Banda's treatment of his opposition while in office continued to haunt him, and he was charged with murder in 1995, though he was acquitted. He died of pneumonia in 1997 in Johannesburg, where he had been seeking medical treatment.

See also: BANDA, HASTINGS KAMUZU (Vol. IV).

Bangui Capital city of the CENTRAL AFRICAN REPUBLIC. A sprawling city of more than 700,000 residents, Bangui traces its roots back to its establishment as a French colonial military outpost in 1889. When the Central African Republic (CAR) achieved independence from France in 1960, Bangui, already a thriving administrative and commercial center, was named the capital. Today the city is home to CAR's government, judicial courts, banking centers, cultural archives, and major media outlets.

Between periods of relative calm, the history of Bangui has been marked by civil unrest, labor riots, ethnic clashes, and armed insurrections. In 1966 Colonel Jean-Bedel BOKASSA (1921–1996) replaced CAR's first president, David DACKO (1930–), and began dismantling the republic, eventually declaring himself emperor in 1977. As a result violent riots and political protests filled the streets of Bangui. By 1979 the situation was so grave that the French military intervened on Dacko's behalf, toppling Bokassa's regime and returning the country to a republic. In 1981, however, a COUP D'ÉTAT led by General André Kolingba removed Dacko from power once again.

In the 1990s the parliament of the Central African Republic ushered in reforms that sparked more violence between security forces and groups pushing for democracy. In 1993 Ange-Félix PATASSÉ (1937–) won the presidency in the country's first multiparty elections, but his victory was disputed by various opposition groups, throwing Bangui into upheaval once again. Early in 1997 French troops returned to the city to establish peace, and in 1999 these troops were replaced by an all-African peacekeeping force.

See also: BANGUI (Vol. IV); FRANCE AND AFRICA (Vols. IV, V).

Banjul Capital city and seaport of The GAMBIA, located at the mouth of the Gambia River. Founded as a British military post in 1816, and given the name of Bathurst, the city was an important commercial center because of its strategic TRANSPORTATION location at the mouth of the highly navigable Gambia River. The principal commodity that flowed through its waterfront, beginning in the 1840s and continuing through the colonial period, was groundnuts (peanuts). From 1889 until The Gambia's independence in 1965, it was also the administrative capital of the British Protectorate and Colony. It became the national capital upon The Gambia's independence in 1965. The country became a republic in 1970, and in 1973 the city's name was changed to Banjul, which was the original name of the island on which it is located.

Banjul is the largest city in the smallest country in size on the mainland continent, with one of the smallest economies. Major improvements in Banjul's port facilities during the 1970s increased its capacity to serve as the commercial and transportation center of the country. The economy is based mostly on agricultural products, with groundnut products and palm kernel as the principal EXPORTS and rice as a major domestic crop. Recently the

TOURISM industry has been growing, which has led to the development of a substantial handicraft market.

Groundnuts were originally introduced by the Portuguese in the 15th century. Later the British promoted cultivation of groundnuts as an economic activity after the prohibition of slavery. Investment in the groundnut industry was increased again in the 1950s in order to make the area more self-sufficient. Today groundnuts are a chief crop for export. Oil made from the crushed nuts is exported to Europe.

Banjul is accessible from the mainland by both a three-mile (5 km) ferry and the Banjul-Serekunda highway. The international airport lies in Yundum, 18 miles (30 km) distant to the southwest. The main ethnic groups are the Wolof, Fulbe, and Mandinka, some of whom come from neighboring SENEGAL, which borders The Gambia to the south, north, and east. The population of Banjul was estimated at 35,000 in 2003.

See also: ENGLAND AND AFRICA (Vols. III, IV, V); FULANI (Vols. I, II, III, IV) FULFULDE (Vol. I); GAMBIA RIVER (Vol. II); GROUNDNUTS (Vol. III, IV); MANDINKA (Vol. II, IV); PORTUGAL AND AFRICA (Vols. III, IV, V); SENEGAMBIA REGION (Vols. III, IV); SLAVE TRADE (Vol. IV) SLAVERY (Vols. I, II, III, V) WOLOF (Vol. II, IV).

Bantu education   SOUTH AFRICAN system of EDUCATION for Africans under APARTHEID. The Bantu Education system was an attempt to reinforce the white minority's political control of the country by reinforcing Africans' sense of ethnicity and identity in contrast to a national South African identity.

The 1953 Bantu Education Act was one of the legislative cornerstones of apartheid. It took the control of African schooling out of the hands of MISSIONARIES and placed it with mostly Afrikaner government officials to devise and implement an education that defined rural life along ethnic lines. The language of instruction at the elementary level was to be one of the Bantu African languages. South Africa's official languages, AFRIKAANS and English, were gradually introduced as the languages of instruction only at the junior secondary and secondary school levels. However, few African children managed to enter high school, let alone attend a tertiary institution such as FORT HARE COLLEGE. Bantu Education also reinforced the social organization of the BANTUSTANS, with their emphasis on ethnicity and their physical location in rural areas.

Politically aware Africans and their organizations, such as the AFRICAN NATIONAL CONGRESS, bitterly opposed Bantu Education as inferior education, or, in the words of one outspoken critic, "education for barbarism." The SOWETO Rebellion of 1976–77 erupted over language issues linked to Bantu Education. While the number of African children attending school, especially at the elementary level, increased sharply under Bantu Education, the students were taught in overcrowded classrooms, without adequate books and supplies, and generally by poorly prepared teachers. The legacy of Bantu Education for post-apartheid South Africa is an adult African population that, by and large, lacks adequate education and thus is less able to obtain training to develop job skills.

Further reading: Peter Kallaway, ed., *The History of Education Under Apartheid, 1948–1994: The Doors of Learning and Culture Shall Be Opened* (New York: Peter Lang, 2002).

Bantustans (Black Homelands)   Ten mostly fragmented territories established by the racist APARTHEID government of SOUTH AFRICA to serve as "homelands" for the country's various black African peoples. The systematic policy of racial segregation and discrimination known as apartheid (AFRIKAANS for "separateness") was not officially instated in South Africa until the National Party came to power in 1948. However, segregation had been a government goal for some time, with land acts in 1913 and 1936 establishing a system of "native reserves" for black Africans well before apartheid became state policy. After many years of expanding and redefining the boundaries of reserves, in 1959 plans for black African self-government within the reserves were put into action. Each reserve was designated as a "homeland" for a specific ethnic group. In 1970 the Homelands Citizenship Act revoked South African citizenship (and any of the few appertaining rights) from all black Africans in South Africa, making them legal citizens of their appropriate homelands.

Transkei was the first official Bantustan, as the reserves came to be known, and was designated as a homeland for the XHOSA people. Nine others were also established, including Ciskei (for the Xhosa), Bophuthatswana (Tswana), Gazankulu (Tsonga-Shangaan), KwaNdebele (Ndebele), KaNgwane (Swazi), KwaZulu (ZULU), Lebowa (Pedi), Qwaqwa (Sotho), and Venda (Venda). Of these, only Ciskei and Qwaqwa were contiguous territories; the other Bantustans were largely fragmented into between two and 30 parcels of land that were often widely scattered. All told the Bantustans, which were intended to accommodate all of South Africa's black African majority, only accounted for 13 percent of the country's land. In addition to their insufficient size, the Bantustans had irregular boundaries that confused even the government officials who had drawn them up. For example, the South African embassy to Bophuthatswana had to be relocated once it was determined it had been mistakenly built in South African territory.

> Though each Bantustan was intended for a specific ethnic group, this was often not the case. The Bophuthatswana Bantustan, for example, was established as the homeland for the Tswana people. However, nearly half of the Tswana lived outside Bophuthatswana, while a full third of the Bantustan's population was made up of other African peoples.

The Bantustans were exclusively rural, and their inhabitants survived only by subsistence farming, by providing LABOR in the cities, mines, and on white-owned farms, and by utilizing financial aid provided by the South African government. Each Bantustan was somewhat self-governing, managing to some degree its own schools, health care, road maintenance, and police. With the goal of eventually rendering all black Africans in South Africa as "foreigners," the South African government declared four Bantustans to be fully "independent" states. These black states, Transkei (1976), Bophuthatswana (1977), Venda (1979), and Ciskei (1981), were never recognized by the international community. By the late 1980s the South African government gave up on the plan to make the remaining six Bantustans independent as well. With the fall of apartheid in 1994, the 10 Bantustans were dissolved, and their inhabitants were reinstated as full South African citizens.

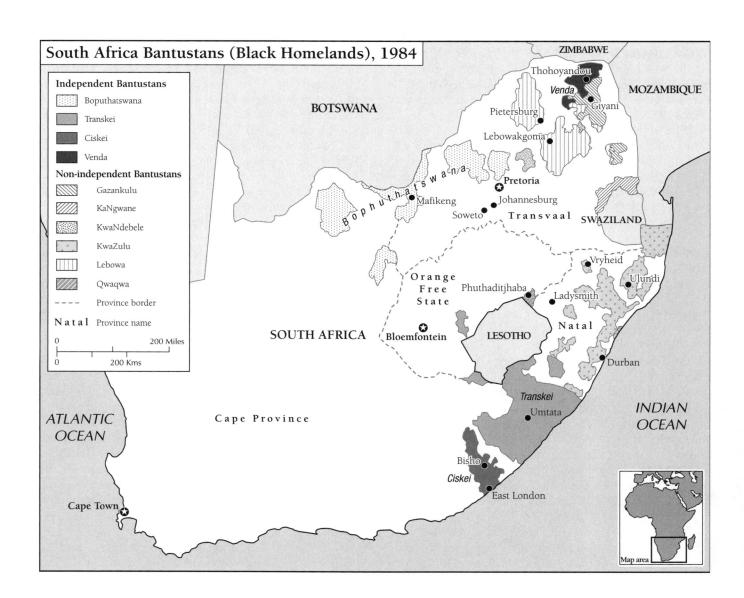

South Africa Bantustans (Black Homelands), 1984

Independent Bantustans
- Boputhatswana
- Transkei
- Ciskei
- Venda

Non-independent Bantustans
- Gazankulu
- KaNgwane
- KwaNdebele
- KwaZulu
- Lebowa
- Qwaqwa
- ---- Province border
- **Natal** Province name

0 — 200 Miles
0 — 200 Kms

See also: ETHNIC GROUP (Vol. IV); ETHNICITY AND IDENTITY (Vol. I); RACE AND RACISM (Vol. IV).

Further reading: Anne Kelk Mager, *Gender and the Making of a South African Bantustan: A Social History of the Ciskei, 1945–1959* (Portsmouth, N.H.: Heinemann, 1999).

Barnard, Christiaan (1922–2001) *South African heart transplant pioneer*

Christiaan Neethling Barnard was born in the small South African town of Beaufort West and grew up in humble circumstances. Excelling in his studies, he graduated from the University of Cape Town in 1946, and then earned his MD in 1953. A grant then enabled him to study under heart surgery expert Dr. C. Walton Lillehei (1918–1999) at the University of Minnesota in 1956. Barnard returned to CAPE TOWN in 1958 and, at Groote Schuur Hospital, established what became one of the world's premier heart surgery units.

After performing a successful human kidney transplant and a number of experimental heart transplants in dogs, Barnard attempted the world's first human-to-human heart transplant in 1967. The operation itself was a success, but the patient died of pneumonia after 18 days, a result of the immunosuppressant drugs designed to prevent the patient's body from rejecting the transplanted heart. Undaunted, Barnard performed a second transplant shortly the first one. This time, the patient survived for 19 months. Though Barnard was pioneering a largely unexplored field of surgery, his success was ultimately remarkable, with his fifth and sixth patients both living for more than 10 years after their transplants.

Barnard's first patient, a 55-year-old man named Louis Washkansky (d. 1967), suffered from incurable heart disease. After the operation, which replaced Washkansky's heart with that of a young woman who had died in a car accident, Washkansky reportedly said, "I am the new Frankenstein."

Barnard continued to push the envelope in the field of heart transplant surgery, performing the first "piggyback" heart transplant, in 1974, the first animal-to-human transplant, in 1977, and the first heart and lung transplant, in 1981. His initial operations launched similar efforts worldwide, though it was not until the advent of improved immunosuppressants that heart transplants became more viable. Barnard's accomplishments also touched off extensive ethical and moral debates about the practice of organ donation.

"Piggyback" refers to a transplant operation where a second heart is implanted in a patient to assist the original failing heart or to aid it while it heals. Barnard's animal-to-human transplants were performed as piggyback operations as well.

Barnard retired from MEDICINE in 1983. He wrote a number of books over his career, including various novels and his autobiography, *One Life* (1969). Since his landmark operation in 1967, more than 100,000 heart transplant surgeries have been performed worldwide.

See also: HEALTH AND HEALING IN MODERN AFRICA (Vol. V).

Barre, Mohammed Siad (1910–1995) *Somali dictator*

Born in Italian Somaliland, Barre became an orphan at age 10 and made a meager living as a shepherd. He later joined the colonial police and began a successful military career. In 1960 Italian Somaliland joined with British Somaliland and became the independent country of SOMALIA. Barre became vice commander of the Somali army and then was promoted to the rank of commander-in-chief.

In 1969 Somali president Abdi Rashid Ali Shermarke (1919–1969) was assassinated, and Barre led a military COUP D'ÉTAT to assume control of the country. Barre immediately began to install a socialist regime. He suspended the Somali constitution, outlawed political parties, and disbanded the National Assembly. In 1976 Barre founded the Somali Revolutionary Socialist Party (SRSP). By 1979 a new constitution established Somalia as a one-party socialist state, dominated by Barre and the SRSP and backed by the Soviet Union.

Operating under a nationalistic impulse and the notion of a "Greater Somalia," Barre began armed support of ethnic Somali rebels in the Ogaden Plain of ETHIOPIA. In 1974, after the overthrow of Ethiopian emperor HAILE SELASSIE (1892–1975), Barre's Soviet allies switched their support to Ethiopia. Playing on Cold War tensions, Barre turned to the United States for military and financial aid and invaded the Ogaden Plain in July 1977. Despite American backing, by 1978 the Somalis were driven from Ethiopia, though guerrilla fighting in Ogaden continued until 1988.

In Somalia Barre faced increasing resistance to his regime. In 1978 a military coup failed to unseat Barre, and violent battles between rebels and Barre's forces resulted in massive casualties. In 1991, in spite of Barre's brutal reprisals, rebels led by the United Somali Congress (USC) captured the Somali capital of MOGADISHU. Barre was forced to flee to LAGOS, NIGERIA, where he remained until his death. Somalia thereafter descended into constant civil war between factions struggling to assume power.

See also: COLD WAR AND AFRICA (Vol. V); SOVIET UNION AND AFRICA (Vols. IV, V); UNITED STATES AND AFRICA (Vols. IV, V).

al-Bashir, Omar Hasan Ahmad (1945–   ) *President of the Republic of the Sudan*

Omar Hasan Ahmad al-Bashir rose to prominence in the Republic of the SUDAN in the 1980s as an army colonel fighting against the Sudan People's Liberation Army (SPLA), a Christian rebel group in southern Sudan. In 1989 he led the "June 30 National Salvation Revolution," installing himself as "head of state, prime minister, defense minister and commander in chief of the army." In a fundamental reform, al-Bashir's 15-man military junta universally replaced the Sudanese government and system of laws, based on English common law, with Islamic law, or *SHARIA*.

Battles with the SPLA intensified throughout the 1990s, killing an estimated 2 million Christians and Muslims. In 1999 the legislature moved to decrease presidential authority and hold a multiparty election. In reaction al-Bashir dissolved parliament and declared a three-month state of emergency.

Al-Bashir's support from the Islamic Front, with which he had allied himself at the start of his presidency, began to show strains. Relations worsened in 2001 when al-Bashir had the leader of the National Islamic Front, Hassan Abd Allah al-TURABI (1932–   ), imprisoned for opposing him. However, with every threat, al-Bashir has reacted by further consolidating his power. His authoritarian tendencies have led to discontent within his government, while his support for other Islamic regimes, including LIBYA and Iran, made the Sudan an outcast among Western governments.

Al-Bashir's control of the government, however, has not led to either peace or tranquility in Sudan. For almost 19 years, civil strife raged between the northern and southern parts of the country, with al-Bashir's troops frequently being accused of human rights violations that included rape, torture, and the murder of women and children.

International pressure, which began to intensify in 2001, eventually forced al-Bashir to find a peaceful solution to the conflict, and in 2004 he granted limited autonomy to the southern part of the country and promised a full referendum on southern independence at the end of six years.

This did not mark the end of civil strife in Sudan, however, as rebels began actively revolting in the western region of DARFUR. To aid in combatting the rebels al-Bashir provided government money and support to independent militias, commonly known as *Janjaweed*. In the years since the revolt began, in 2003, reports of atrocities, ethnic cleansing, and starvation have steadily increased, and international pressure for a solution has become intensified.

See also: ISLAM, INFLUENCE OF (Vol. V).

Bayi, Filbert (1953–   ) *Tanzanian middle-distance runner*

Born in Karratu, TANZANIA, Bayi first appeared on the international track stage at the 1972 Olympics in Munich, Germany. His first notable victory was at the 1973 African Games, where he won the 1,500-meter race over Kip KEINO (1940–   ), the reigning Olympic gold medalist in the event.

Bayi is best remembered for his world-record performance in the 1,500-meter race at the 1974 Commonwealth Games, in New Zealand. In a contest that many track aficionados regard as the greatest 1,500-meter race ever, he broke the world record with a time of 3 minutes 32.16 seconds. In the same race, the host country's John Walker (1952–   ) also broke the world record, only to lose to Bayi by 0.3 seconds. In 1980 Bayi was the Olympic silver medalist in the 3,000-meter steeplechase.

See also: BIKILA, ABEBE (Vol. V); SPORTS AND ATHLETICS (Vol. V).

Bebey, Francis (1929–2001) *Cameroonian musician and writer*

Francis Bebey was born in DOUALA, the main port city of CAMEROON, where he received his early education. In the mid-1950s he studied at the Sorbonne University in Paris, followed by a stint at New York University, in the United States. After earning his degree in broadcasting, he worked in Paris as a radio producer and journalist, beginning in 1957. Four years later, still in Paris, Bebey began studying and documenting indigenous African MUSIC for UNESCO, the United Nations cultural and educational organization. Based on his research, Bebey published two works, *La radiodiffusion en Afrique noire* (Broadcasting in black Africa) in 1963 and, in 1969 *Musique de l'Afrique* (translated and published as *African Music: A People's Art*, in 1975). The UNESCO project occupied him until 1974.

Beyond his scholarly musical interests, Bebey was also an accomplished instrumentalist and singer. As a teenager he had played guitar in a band in Douala, and he continued to perform throughout his life, with his last recordings made in the late 1990s.

Acclaimed as a musician, Bebey was equally well known as a novelist. In 1968 he won the Grand Prix Littérraire de l'Afrique Noire—a prestigious award for African French writers—for his novel, *Le Fils d'Agatha Moudio* (The son of Agatha Moudio), which tells the story of a young Cameroonian from a coastal fishing village who is unlucky in marriage. The book appeared in English, German, Italian, and Dutch translations. In his distinguished literary career, Bebey published several other novels, poems, and works on African music, and even wrote a screenplay. Throughout his works as both musician and writer, Bebey consistently attempted to present African cultural values and performance arts in a positive light, thus opposing racism.

See also: LITERATURE IN MODERN AFRICA (Vol. V).

Bello, Ahmadu (Alhaji Sir Ahmadu Bello)
(1910–1966) *Political leader from Northern Nigeria*

Bello, head of the HAUSA-Fulani NORTHERN PEOPLE'S CONGRESS (NPC), retained his position as premier of the Northern Region when NIGERIA achieved independence in 1960. With fellow NPC member Abubakar Tafawa BALEWA (1912–1966) as the country's prime minister, Bello and the NPC held great political sway.

Nigeria, however, faced increasing discord during the early years of its independence. Shifting political alliances and tensions among Nigeria's main ethnic groups, the Hausa-Fulani in the north, the IGBO in the east, and the YORUBA in the west, contributed to national instability. Western Nigeria, in particular, fell into chaos, as riots occurred over a split in the Action Group, the Yoruba political party led by Obafemi AWOLOWO (1909–1987). Controversy over the 1962–63 census, which many in the rest of the country felt was manipulated to favor the north politically, stoked animosity toward Igbo living in the north. This helped fuel the "Igbo-must-go" campaign, a movement to rid the northern region of the Igbo minority. Leading the movement was the Sardauna Brigade, a paramilitary group Bello formed as his private army.

Ethnic tensions in Nigeria during the first few years of independence were not limited to the three major ethnicities. In 1964 the Tiv, a large ethnic minority located in the Benue State, in north central Nigeria, conducted a series of attacks on the NPC. The Nigerian army quickly quelled the uprising.

In 1964 Bello led a political alliance between the NPC and the Nigerian National Democratic Party (NNDP), which had splintered off from the Yoruba-led Action Group. The alliance, called the Nigerian National Alliance (NNA), won that year's elections. The following year, the NNDP declared victory in a controversial regional election in Western Nigeria. Once again chaos erupted. The political and ethnic divisions boiled over in 1966, when a group of mostly Igbo army officers staged a COUP D'ÉTAT and seized control of the federal government. Bello was assassinated, as were prime minister Tafawa Balewa and a number of other high-ranking officials. Major General Johnson Aguiyi-Ironsi (1924–1966) briefly assumed control of Nigeria until he, too, was killed in a coup later that year. The stage was then set for the attempted secession of BIAFRA, a crisis that led to the Nigerian civil war of 1967–70.

See also: BELLO, AHMADU (Vol. IV); CIVIL WARS (Vol. V); ETHNIC CONFLICT IN AFRICA (Vol. V); ETHNIC GROUP (Vol. I).

Further reading: John N. Paden, *Ahmadu Bello Sardauna of Sokoto: Values and Leadership in Nigeria* (London: Hodder and Stoughton, 1986).

Ben Bella, Ahmed (1916–) *First president of Algeria*

Prior to the independence of ALGERIA in 1962, Ahmed Ben Bella was an Algerian freedom fighter and a founding member of the NATIONAL LIBERATION FRONT (Front de Liberation Nationale, FLN), the key organization in the Algerians' armed revolt against French rule. In 1956 French authorities arrested him for revolutionary activities, and he remained in prison until 1962. Upon his release Ben Bella was appointed prime minister of Algeria. Like many North African leaders, Ben Bella ascribed to pan-Arabism, a cultural-political movement that encouraged the unity of Arab people from across North Africa and the Middle East. Accordingly, he followed a foreign policy of nonalignment during the Cold War, and his domestic policy applied a pro-Arab socialist agenda to the economy and to EDUCATION.

Ben Bella initially was supported by the Algerian army, which was led by his friend and former FLN ally, Defense Minister Houari BOUMÉDIENNE (1927–1978). However, Ben Bella's persistent meddling in the affairs of the other government ministers alienated Boumédienne, who deposed Ben Bella in 1965, placing him under house arrest.

Following his release in 1980, Ben Bella lived in Switzerland for 10 years. From there he tried to instigate a rebellion in Algeria that would return him to power. Eventually he founded the Movement for Algerian Democracy and returned to Algiers in 1990. Ben Bella made a bid for the Algerian presidency that same year, but his long absence from the local political scene made him an unpopular candidate, and he was soundly defeated.

See also: BEN BELLA, AHMED (Vol. IV); NONALIGNED MOVEMENT AND AFRICA (Vol. V).

Further reading: Merle, Robert, *Ahmed Ben Bella* (New York: Walker, 1967).

Benin, Republic of West African country located on the Gulf of Guinea, bordered by TOGO to the west, BURKINA FASO and NIGER to the north, and NIGERIA to the east. The Republic of Benin covers approximately 43,500 square miles (112,700 sq km) and has an Atlantic Ocean coastline measuring about 75 miles (121 km). The legal capital of Benin is Porto-Novo, but the de facto capital is COTONOU, located on the coast.

Benin at Independence Until 1975 today's Republic of Benin was known as DAHOMEY. It was a French colony prior to 1958, at which time it joined the French Community as an autonomous republic. Dahomey achieved independence from France two years later, with Hubert Maga (1916–2000) serving as the country's first president.

From 1960 to 1972 the country was marred by governmental instability and a succession of military coups d'état. In all, there were 12 changes in leadership during this time. All of these, however, occurred with very little violence, and none of the deposed leaders was killed. Although Dahomey had achieved independence from its colonizers, it remained very much under French control, both politically and economically. French expatriates worked within Dahomey's government as technical advisers to facilitate decision making and policy. In addition, France provided ECONOMIC ASSISTANCE for DEVELOPMENT and also covered the nation's deficit. These measures ensured firm French control over its interests in the former colony.

Marxist Revolution In the 1970s a strong Marxist movement emerged among Dahomey's students and civil service trade unionists. In light of this popular sentiment, in 1972 army major Mathieu KÉRÉKOU (1933–), touting a socialist agenda, staged a COUP D'ETAT and assumed the presidency. In 1974 Kérékou officially announced that Dahomey was a Marxist country. The following year, he changed the name of the country to the People's Republic of Benin, and he set about nationalizing segments of Benin's economy, including banks, insurance companies, AGRICULTURE, and utilities. He also made concerted efforts to rid the country of foreign—especially French—influence.

During the early 1980s the economic policies instituted by Kérékou and his ruling Revolutionary Peoples Party of Benin were reaping benefits. Within a few short years, however, the country was on the brink of economic disaster. Unemployment rose uncontrollably, state-owned banks collapsed, and government workers were paid only sporadically, leading to widespread popular discontent. Government crackdowns led to accusations of HUMAN RIGHTS abuses. Exacerbating the situation, turmoil in neighboring Nigeria caused that country to expel thousands of Benin nationals and subsequently close the border to any more immigration from Benin.

In the 1970s Benin saw the escalation of generational conflict involving both politics and RELIGION. Younger activists wanted to replace village elders with people more inclined to support Kérékou's revolutionary government. These people felt that the older generation had been irredeemably influenced by both outdated religious practices, such as *vodun*, or voodoo, and by colonial ways of thinking. Labeling these elders "enemies of the revolution" and accusing them of sorcery, leaders of the movement came to employ torture and even execution as punishment.

By 1988 Benin was threatening to default on several of its loans, and the international community stepped in to force Kérékou into making economic reforms. Bowing to the pressure, he privatized some state industries and cut government expenditures by doing away with a number of social services. In 1989 as Benin society reeled and the communist framework was collapsing worldwide, Kérékou finally agreed that the Marxist path had failed Benin, and he began negotiations for a new democratic constitution.

Democracy and Liberalization in Benin In 1990 the People's Republic of Benin was renamed once again, this time as the Republic of Benin. The following year, Benin held its first free, multiparty elections. Nicéphore Soglo (1934–), a long-time political figure in Benin, won election to the office of president. Immediately after his election, Soglo enjoyed widespread popularity. However, in order to continue receiving monetary aid from the INTERNATIONAL MONETARY FUND and the WORLD BANK, Soglo's government had to adopt harsh budgetary restrictions as part of free-market STRUCTURAL ADJUSTMENT. Further, the nation's currency was devalued, and import prices increased.

By 1996 Soglo had fallen out of favor. He was defeated in elections held that year, and Mathieu Kérékou reclaimed the presidency. Kérékou won election again in 2001. Although Benin is mired in POVERTY, its improving economy and its political stability have made it one of the rare African countries to have success with DEMOCRATIZATION.

See also: BENIN, REPUBLIC OF (Vols. I, II, III, IV); FRANCE AND AFRICA (Vols. IV, V); MAGA, HUBERT (Vol. IV).

Further reading: Mathurin C. Houngnikpo, *Determinants of Democratization in Africa: A Comparative Study of Benin and Togo* (Lanham, Md.: University Press of America, 2001).

Benin City Urban center located on the Benin River in southern NIGERIA; unrelated to present-day Republic of BENIN. Benin City was the center of the ancient kingdom of Edo, which was invaded and ransacked in 1897 by British troops. The British deposed and exiled the *oba* (king), but restored the office in 1914. Today the *oba* still serves in an advisory and ceremonial role for Edo State.

Benin City was known for its bronze, ivory, and wood artistry. Much of the artwork was stolen during the British invasion and auctioned off by the British to defray military costs. Therefore, fine examples of Benin's ART can be found throughout the world. An important collection has been preserved, however, in the museums of Benin City. Many of the city's artisans still practice the ancient methods, including the lost-wax process, to make their ART.

Today the city is an important trade center, linked to LAGOS and other major Nigerian cities by highways, the Benin River, and air transport. Benin City is considered the center of Nigeria's rubber industry; wood products, palm oil, and palm kernels are also important EXPORTS. The city is also home to the University of Benin, founded in 1970. The inhabitants of Benin City, most of whom are from the Edo, or Bini, ethnic group, numbered about 230,000 in 1996.

See also: BENIN CITY (Vols. III, IV); BRONZE (Vol. II); EDO (Vols. I, II); ENGLAND AND AFRICA (Vols. III, IV, V); (Vols. III, IV) LOST-WAX PROCESS (Vol. II); PALM OIL (Vol. III, IV).

Berbers Indigenous people of North Africa. With a current population of between 20 and 30 million, Berbers have played a major role in the histories of several North African countries. Nearly 40 percent of the population of MOROCCO is Berber, as is 30 percent of ALGERIA. Berbers also make up lesser but still significant parts of the populations of LIBYA, TUNISIA, EGYPT, NIGER, and MALI.

In recent times, like many other indigenous peoples around the world, Berbers are struggling to establish their political and social power as well as their cultural and linguistic identity. As a result of this pressure, the Moroccan government has decided to teach Tamazight, the Berber language, alongside Arabic in all schools. Mali and Niger also recognize Tamazight as an official language. The situation in Algeria, where the government is also under intense pressure from Islamic fundamentalists, has been problematic. After much pressure and even civil unrest, the Algerian government recognized Tamazight as

a "national language." However, it has stopped short of acquiescing to Berber demands that Tamazight be treated as an official language equal to the Arabic language. The tension within Algeria began not long after the country's independence, in 1962. At that time, Berbers, many of them from the Kabylia region east of ALGIERS, confronted the government over cultural, linguistic, and political issues. By 1963, the situation had deteriorated to the point that Hocine Ait Ahmed (1919–   ), a Berber and one of the founding figures and major heroes of the Algerian independence movement, founded the Socialist Forces Front in a Berber rebellion against the Algerian government. Ahmed remained a key figure in the Berber struggle for many years.

In March 1980 the tense situation boiled over when police prevented Berber writer Mouloud Mammeri (1917–1989) from giving a lecture on ancient Berber poetry. This touched off student protests and riots throughout the Kabylia region and culminated in repressive police actions. Known as "Berber Spring," the events have become a focal point and a rallying cry for Berber discontent. A major school boycott took place in Kabylia in 1994–95. In the spring of 2001, the death of a Berber student in police custody touched off major rioting leading to up to 120 deaths. Berbers subsequently formed the activist Citizens Movement, demanding, among other things, full recognition of the Tamazight language.

One of the leading figures in the Berber cultural insurgency was Matoub Lounes (1956–1998), a singer and an activist for Berber causes. Matoub Lounes became a prominent agitator for Berber rights and an internationally recognized talent. With songs openly challenging both the Algerian government and fundamentalist Islamists, he asserted the linguistic and cultural rights of the Berbers of Kabylia. Ultimately, in 1998, Matoub Lounes was assassinated by unknown individuals in a roadside ambush.

The TUAREGS, a distinct Berber subgroup, have also faced grave difficulties. Beginning in 1990 they launched repeated uprisings in both Niger and Mali, and thousands of Tuareg refugees left those countries. Many of these refugees settled in MAURITANIA, Libya, BURKINA FASO, and even Algeria, where their presence aggravated already tense situations. Peace talks took place in Mali in 1994 and in Niger in 1995. Agreements were reached to provide the Tuaregs greater autonomy in both countries, but violence has continued to break out in the years since.

See also: ALMOHADS (Vol. II); ALMORAVIDS (Vol. II); BERBERS (Vols. I, II, III, IV); COLONIAL CONQUEST (Vol. IV); FRANCE AND AFRICA (Vols. III, IV, V).

Further reading: Fadhma A. M. Amrouche and Dorothy Blair, *My Life Story: Autobiography of a Berber Woman* (New Brunswick, New Jersey: Rutgers University Press, 1981); Michael Brett and Elizabeth Fentress, *The Berbers* (London: Blackwell, 1997).

Beta Israel Ethiopian people of the Jewish faith. In the 1970s through the 1990s the Beta Israel began an Israeli-assisted mass exodus from ETHIOPIA. Though an ancient people, the Beta Israel ("House of Israel") were essentially a forgotten people outside of Ethiopia until the mid-1800s and were fully accepted as Jews much later in 1973. That year the Beta Israel were officially recognized by Israel as one of the Ten Lost Tribes of Israel, and thus authentic Jews. In 1975, one year after a military COUP D'ETAT brought Colonel MENGISTU HAILE MARIAM (c. 1937–) to power in Ethiopia, an Israeli law was signed granting all Ethiopian Jews full citizenship in Israel and the right to immigrate to Israel under the Israeli Law of Return.

Long persecuted in predominantly Christian Ethiopia, the Beta Israel saw their situation become increasingly dire due to the political upheaval and devastating famine that wracked Ethiopia in the 1970s and 1980s. Mengistu's Marxist agrarian reform programs took a major toll on the country, and the Beta Israel, part of the landless peasantry, suffered tremendously. Beginning in the late 1970s small groups of Beta Israel emigrated on foot from Ethiopia to neighboring Republic of the SUDAN, from where they hoped to gain passage to Jerusalem. Such attempts were extremely dangerous, and by 1976 only about 250 Beta Israel had successfully made their way to Israel. With secret Israeli help, another 8,000 Ethiopian Jews were spirited out of the Sudan to Israel between 1977 and 1983. In 1984 a wave of 10,000 Beta Israel attempted to cross into the Sudan, but many perished during the journey or the subsequent stay in Sudanese refugee camps, where they lived in squalor and were forced to hide their religious affinities.

That same year the Israelis undertook Operation Moses, a large-scale airlift designed to ferry all of the Beta Israel out of Sudan. Intended to be a secret operation, word of the airlift leaked out and the operation was cut short, leaving many Beta Israel stranded. Israel continued to improve relations with the Mengistu regime, offering military aid in return for securing further Beta Israel emigration from Ethiopia. Following Operation Moses, thousands of Beta Israel flooded into ADDIS ABABA with the hope of emigrating, where they lived in compounds under terrible conditions. In 1991, with Eritrean rebels on the verge of removing Mengistu from power, Operation

Solomon airlifted more than 14,000 Beta Israel in two days time. After this action, nearly all of the Beta Israel had been relocated to Israel.

Two groups of the Beta Israel actually remained in Ethiopia following Operation Solomon. One group, located in remote Quara, was airlifted to Israel in 1999. The other group consisted of Beta Israel who, because of their partial assimilation into Christian society, were not recognized by Israel as Jews, though many had relatives who had already emigrated. Called the Falasha Mura, or fake Falasha, these Beta Israel continue to claim the right to Israeli citizenship, but as of 2003, they had yet to receive that right. Instead, they live in extreme POVERTY in Addis Ababa and the Gondar region.

The arrival of the Ethiopian Jews in Israel did not mark the end to their troubles, however. Numbering about 60,000, the Beta Israel had an extremely difficult time assimilating into Israeli culture. Coming from a background of subsistence farming, many Beta Israel lacked job skills and had difficulty finding work. Culture shock, housing problems, racial discrimination, and dissension within their own ranks all contributed to making the Beta Israel transition to their new homeland a difficult one. The Israeli military is one group into which the Beta Israel have fit successfully, with a growing number of males joining the armed forces.

See also: BETA ISRAEL (Vols. I, II, III, IV); CHRISTIANITY, INFLUENCE OF (Vols. II, III, IV, V); RELIGION (Vols. III, IV, V).

Beti, Mongo (pseudonym of Alexandre Biyidi-Awala) (1932–2001) *Cameroonian author writing in French*

Mongo Beti was born Alexandre Biyidi-Awala, in Akométan, CAMEROON. He was educated at Catholic mission schools and then attended Leclerc Lycée in YAOUNDÉ, the capital of Cameroon. As with many budding African intellectuals of his era, he subsequently traveled to the European country that ruled his homeland, in this case, France. He studied first at the University of Aixen-Provence and then at the prestigious Sorbonne University.

Beti's work falls into two periods: before and after Cameroon's independence in 1960. In the 1950s he began to publish his first novels, which took up the themes of injustice and violence in the colonial system. His earliest work, written under the pen name Eza Boto, includes the short story, "Sans haine, sans amour" (Without hatred, without love), which appeared in *Présence*

Africaine in 1952. This was followed by the 1954 novel *Ville cruelle* (Cruel city). Then, writing as Mongo Beti, he published his best known works in 1956 and 1957: *Le Pauvre Christ de Bomba* (The poor Christ of Bomba) and *Mission terminée,* which later appeared in English, in 1964, as *Mission to Kala.*

Despite the end of French colonial rule in 1960, the living conditions for ordinary Cameroonians did not improve much, and Beti soon became an outspoken critic of Cameroon's government. He lived in self-imposed exile in France from 1966 until 1996, earning his livelihood teaching in Rouen, France.

While in France, he kept up with the politics of his home country and continued to speak out on issues. In 1972, for example, he published a pamphlet entitled "Main Basse sur le Cameroun" (Rape of Cameroon) that sharply criticized Cameroon's one-party political system and its relationship with French MULTINATIONAL CORPORATIONS. The French government immediately seized the pamphlet and banned it for five years, causing Beti to return to fiction as a platform for his criticism. A series of novels in the 1970s focused on the CORRUPTION of the postcolonial state and the despair it caused. After retiring from public life in 1996, Beti returned to Cameroon where he owned a book-store. His last novel, *L'Histoire du fou* (The history of a madman), which appeared in 1994, told the story of an unjustly imprisoned hero, revealing the continuing pessimism Beti felt about Cameroon's corruption and deceit.

See also: LITERATURE IN COLONIAL AFRICA (Vol. IV), LITERATURE IN MODERN AFRICA (Vol. V), *PRÉSENCE AFRICAINE* (Vol. IV).

Further reading: Kandioura Dramé, *The Novel as Transformation Myth: A Study of the Novels of Mongo Beti and Ngugi Wa Thiong'o* (Syracuse, N.Y.: Syracuse University Press, 1990).

Biafra Southeastern region of NIGERIA that in 1967 declared itself an independent republic. Named after the Bight of Biafra, the body of water that its coastline bordered, Biafra is mainly inhabited by the IGBO ethnic group.

In 1967 Igbo leaders formally seceded from what was then the Federal Republic of Nigeria. This declaration of secession caused the immediate outbreak of the Nigerian civil war, otherwise known as the Biafran War. The causes of the civil war lay in the vastness of Nigeria, its ethnic complexity—more than 400 ethnic and tribal groups—the differences in RELIGION, particularly Islam and

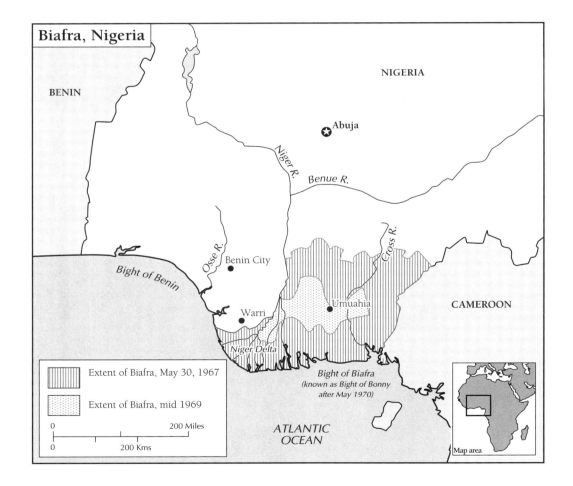

Christianity, and the historical mood of the times in relation to the Cold War.

Nigeria was Africa's most populous country at the time, as it still is today, with 130,000,000 people. During the colonial era this vast land was divided into three main regions. The north was inhabited mostly by the Muslim HAUSA-Fulani alliance, the southeast had an Igbo majority, and the southwest was mainly inhabited by the YORUBA people. Before Nigerian independence (1960), each of these three main regions was autonomous, organized and governed differently. The only thing common to all three was British colonial rule. Suddenly, on the eve of independence Britain decided to unite the three regions as provinces within the single federal state of Nigeria. The Queen of England appointed a nominal head of state, the governor-general. However, the de facto head of government was an elected prime minister, who was the leader of the party with the majority in Parliament.

The Queen appointed Dr. Nnamdi AZIKIWE (1904–1996), an Igbo from eastern Nigeria, as governor-general. As a famous pan-Africanist, Azikiwe was intended to sym-

In Nigeria, civil war spilled over into the streets when Biafra seceded from the Nigerian union, in 1967. Federal troops, such as those shown here in 1968, finally won the war after three years of bloodshed.
© *AP/Wide World Photos*

bolize a united Nigeria. The prime minister was a northern Hausa-Fulani named Sir Abubakar Tafewa BALEWA (1912–1966). The majority of the officers in the Nigerian Federal Army came from the eastern, Igbo-dominated region, while the bulk of the rank and file were northerners. In January 1966 an elite group of Igbo officers—including Major Emmanuel Ifeajuna, Major David Ejoor, and Captain Nwobosi—led a COUP D'ÉTAT against the Balewa government. The violence that ensued killed a large number of government leaders, mostly from the Northern Region, including Balewa and Ahmadu BELLO (1910–1966), the prime minister of the Northern Region. Johnson Aguiyi-Ironsi (1924–1966), an army colonel from the Eastern Region, became the leader of the new military government. His policies led to further anger in the north, and the desire for revenge quickly brought about another coup, in July 1966, overthrowing Ironsi and his ruling council. This coup also brought unprecedented atrocities against Igbos in northern Nigeria. General Yakubu GOWON (1934–), a non-Muslim northerner, became the new leader of the federal military government.

Despite attempts to reunify the government, acute disagreements ensued between General Gowon and military leaders from the Eastern Region. In 1967 the federal government announced plans to divide the Eastern Region in such a way that the Igbo-dominated territories would be left landlocked and without access to Nigeria's rich OIL reserves. As a consequence Lieutenant Colonel Chukwuemeka Odumegwu Ojukwu (1933–) led the Eastern Region to secede from the federation and declare the sovereign state of Biafra, with its capital at Enugu. Federal Nigerian troops advanced into the country, forcing the transfer of the Biafran capital from Enugu to Aba. Under continued pressure from the federal troops, Biafrans moved their capital twice more, to Umuahia and finally to Owerri.

The consequences of the Biafran secession brought about untold sufferings for the inhabitants of the Eastern Region. The war also led to a tremendous waste of monetary resources. As the violence and oppression increased, Biafra was determined to stay independent from the rest of Nigeria. At the same time, however, the federal government was determined to bring Biafra back into the fold.

The Nigerian civil war not only divided the people of Nigeria but also played into the hands of the major parties in the Cold War. It drew so much international attention that it was referred to as "world war in microcosm." While Britain supported the federal government led by Gowon, France sided with the Biafrans. Israel supported Biafra to show its opposition to EGYPT, which supported the federal government. SOUTH AFRICA, led by its APARTHEID government, threw its support behind Biafra to spite the ORGANIZATION OF AFRICAN UNITY (OAU). The former Soviet Union, for its part, supported the federal government, which drove the Chinese to the Biafran side. The United States sympathized with the Biafrans but remained formally neutral. As could be expected, the global involvement prolonged the conflict and helped accelerate it into a full-fledged war. However, the odds were against Biafra, which ultimately submitted to defeat in 1970. An estimated 1 million people died from the violence and the resulting food shortages that ravaged the Eastern Region.

See also: COLD WAR AND AFRICA (Vols. IV, V); ENGLAND AND AFRICA (Vols. III, IV, V); NIGERIA (Vols. I, II, III, IV); SOVIET UNION AND AFRICA (Vol. V).

Bikila, Abebe (1932–1973) *Ethiopian marathon runner*

Born to a peasant family in ETHIOPIA, Bikila joined the army at age 17, becoming a member of the Imperial Guard and bodyguard to Emperor HAILE SELASSIE (1892–1975). The Imperial Guard was well known for its members' distance running skills, and Bikila trained at a special camp under the tutelage of Swedish trainer Onni Niskanen, who recognized his rare talent.

Bikila won his first marathon, held in ADDIS ABABA, in 1960. That same year, he entered the Olympic Games, held in Rome, Italy. An unknown, Bikila won the marathon competition with a then-record time of 2:15.16. Just as remarkable as his record time was the fact that he ran the entire race barefoot. He was the first athlete from sub-Saharan Africa to win an Olympic gold medal.

Italy and Ethiopia had long been antagonists, fighting repeatedly during Italy's attempts to establish a colonial empire. The day after Bikila's stunning victory, newspapers proclaimed that the entire Italian army was needed to conquer Ethiopia, but only one Ethiopian soldier was needed to conquer Rome.

In 1964 Bikila entered the Olympic Games in Tokyo, Japan. Despite having undergone surgery for appendicitis only six weeks before, Bikila again won gold, shattering his own world record with a new time of 2:12.11 and becoming the first person to win two Olympic marathons. He participated in the 1968 Olympics in Mexico City as well, but was forced to withdraw due to a foot injury. A fellow member of the Ethiopian Imperial Guard, Degaga "Mamo" Wolde (1932–2002), won the gold that year.

In all, Bikila ran in 15 marathons in his lifetime, winning 12 of them. His remarkable success made him a national hero in Ethiopia, and Haile Selassie promoted him to captain. In 1969, however, Bikila was severely injured in a car accident that left him a paraplegic, and he died four years later. Haile Selassie established the day as a national day of mourning, and as many as 65,000 people took part in the funeral.

Bikila's exploits have inspired a generation of Ethiopian distance runners, both male and female. In the 1996 Olympics, in Barcelona, Spain, an Ethiopian woman, Fatuma Roba (1973–), won the gold in the marathon. In 2000, at the Olympics in Sydney, Australia, Gezaghne Abera (1978–), was the men's marathon gold medalist.

See also: BAYI, FILBERT (Vol. V); KEINO, KIP (Vol. V); SPORTS AND ATHLETICS (Vol. V).

Biko, Steve (Stephen Bantu Biko) (1946–1977)
Leader of the Black Consciousness Movement in South Africa

Along with Nelson MANDELA (1918–), Biko best personified the valiant struggle of Africans against APARTHEID in SOUTH AFRICA. For many outside of Africa, the 1987 film, *Cry Freedom*, which highlighted Biko's plight, provided a vivid glimpse into the nature of the apartheid system. While pursuing medical studies at the University of Natal in 1969, Biko helped found the SOUTH AFRICAN STUDENTS ORGANIZATION. The organization's membership was exclusively black, unlike the white-dominated National Union of South African Students with which Biko had become disenchanted. He sought to counter white racism with an ideology of black pride, which drew on the civil rights and black power movements in the United States. He brought together people not only in the African community, but also those among the Cape coloured and Indian populations of South Africa. In 1972 various organizations among these supporters coalesced into the Black People's Convention. Biko became the most recognizable activist within the BLACK CONSCIOUSNESS MOVEMENT.

Because of his activism, the apartheid state subjected Biko to constant harassment. In 1973 he was restricted to King William's Town, in the eastern Cape Province, and was not allowed to meet with more than one person at a time or to be quoted in the media. He was arrested in August 1977 and died in police detention the following month as a result of torture and a lack of medical attention. The minister of justice's official statement that Biko died owing to a hunger strike contrasted with the brutal circumstances of his death, which were finally revealed in 1997, during testimony offered before the TRUTH AND RECONCILIATION COMMISSION. His death inspired a wave of outrage both in South Africa and abroad and served to provide momentum to the anti-apartheid struggle.

See also: ETHNIC CONFLICT IN AFRICA (Vol. V); RACE AND RACISM (Vol. IV).

In 1977 the funeral procession for anti-apartheid activist Steve Biko attracted a huge throng of his supporters in Ginsberg Location, South Africa. © *Press Images Inc.*

Further reading: Aelred Stubbs, ed., *I write what I like / Steve Biko; a selection of his writings* (San Francisco: Harper & Row, 1986); Donald Woods, *Biko* (New York: H. Holt, 1987).

biodiversity Variety of plant and animal species in a particular area. In Africa biodiversity helps guard against the detrimental effects of ATMOSPHERIC CHANGE, ensures the productivity of FORESTS for fuel and other needs, purifies and maintains WATER RESOURCES, and helps provide medicinal plants and food for African populations. From the sands of the Saharan desert to the cape of SOUTH AFRICA, the African continent is home to a wealth of plants and animals found nowhere else. In the Sahara, for example, scientists estimate that there are approximately 500 different plant species. Of these, 162 are believed to be found only in that region. Also in the Sahara, which people have traditionally seen as a barren wasteland, there are some 70 species of mammals, 90 species of birds, and more than a hundred species of reptiles.

South Africa's Cape Floristic Region is one of the richest plant kingdoms in the world; two-thirds of the country's plant species are found only in this one location. Africa's tropical rainforests are even richer in biodiversity. For example, the Guinean forest, which runs through West Africa, has the highest level of mammalian diversity in the world: 1,150 different species. The small island of MADAGASCAR, isolated in the Indian Ocean, is equally remarkable. It is believed to be home to some 700 species of vertebrates alone.

As important and diverse as the continent's biological life is, at the same time it suffers from a great number of threats. There are five large "biodiversity hotspots" in Africa, areas high in biodiversity but under significant threat. These include Madagascar and the Indian Ocean Islands, the Eastern Arc Mountains and Coastal Forests of TANZANIA and KENYA, the Guinean Forests of West Africa, the Cape Floristic Region, and the Succulent Karoo of western South Africa and NAMIBIA.

Hotspots are areas of unusually high biodiversity (generally more than 1,500 plant species) that are particularly threatened (meaning that they have lost up to 70 percent of their original area). Generally, hotspots can develop where an ecosystem has evolved in isolation over a long period of time. For example, Africa's remote Eastern Arc Mountains, which have an average altitude of 2,000 feet, developed over a period of 30 million years or more. Only 2,200 square miles (5,698 sq km) of its original 11,500 square-mile area still remain intact, less than 800 of which remain pristine. This is primarily the result of human activities, which degrade the region at a rate of approximately 2 percent each year.

The primary threats to biodiversity are natural habitat loss, species loss, invasion by alien species, and ignorance of indigenous knowledge. All of these are closely tied to human activities and, in particular, to the decision to exploit resources for short-term needs. For example, cutting down forests—even if it is for such seemingly beneficial activities as farming, hunting, MEDICINE production, or national and international trade—contributes to the degradation of fragile ecosystems.

The economic impact of species loss is dramatic. In Madagascar, for example, some 90 percent of the forests have been destroyed, leading to the loss of great numbers of plant and animal species. At the same time that the destruction of these forests has taken away wood needed for heating, cooking, and construction, it also has removed the homes of animals that were once hunted for food, along with the plant life that protected

the soil from erosion. As a consequence the majority of Madagascar's rural population lives in POVERTY. Under such conditions, there is a direct connection between the loss of biodiversity and backsliding in the struggle for economic DEVELOPMENT. In Africa today, protection against the loss of biodiversity takes two predominant forms: SUSTAINABLE DEVELOPMENT and CONSERVATION. Sustainable development focuses on local populations meeting their needs while ensuring that NATURAL RESOURCES will remain for future generations. It requires significant scientific input to estimate what those future needs are, as well as to manage the interactions of humans and the ecosystem.

By a conservative estimate, 247 plant and animal species are known to have gone extinct in Africa, and another 3,789 are currently threatened. This, however, may represent only a small percentage of what has actually been lost. Almost 98 percent of the earth's mammal and bird species have been identified, but only a tiny fraction of the other species have been categorized. For instance, barely one million of an estimated eight million insects, and 275,000 of an estimated 1.8 million marine species, have been identified. The same is true of fungi and bacteria. Because of this, many scientists believe that the actual species loss in Africa might be significantly higher than what is currently known.

The other main form of protection, conservation, has most often come in the form of NATIONAL PARKS and other protected areas. As of 1999 there were 1,050 national parks and protected areas in Africa, and an additional 197 internationally protected areas. These amount to a total of approximately 7 percent of Africa's land and COASTAL AND MARINE ECOSYSTEMS.

Although sustainable development and conservation represent the best-known preventions to the loss of biodiversity, they are not without problems. Sustainable development has been criticized for being "too little, too late," while the creation of protected areas often leads to conflicts with people's need to survive.

What is clear is that biological diversity presents a difficult and, for now, perhaps unsolvable problem. On the one hand, maintaining biodiversity is crucial to the survival of both individual ecosystems and humankind as a whole. But, on the other hand, the costs of protecting Africa's biodiversity are often beyond what the African people can tolerate when they consider all of the human, economic, and political consequences.

See also: LAND USE (Vol. V); ECOLOGY AND ECOLOGICAL CHANGE (Vol. V); ENVIRONMENTAL ISSUES (Vol. V).

Further reading: United Nations Environment Programme, *Africa Environmental Outlook: Past, Present and Future Perspectives* (Nairobi, Kenya: UNEP, 2002); United Nations Environment Programme, *Cultural and Spiritual Values of Biodiversity—A Complementary Contribution to the Global Biodiversity Assessment* (Nairobi, Kenya: UNEP, 2000).

Bissau Capital, principal city, and major port of GUINEA-BISSAU, located on the Atlantic coast at the entrance to the estuary of the Geba River. Once a part of the Mali Empire, Bissau was first visited by the Portuguese, in 1687, and developed into a center for the slave trade. The area did not become an official Portuguese colony, however, until 1879, when the other European powers recognized the Portuguese claim to the region. In 1941 the city became the colony's capital, which had previously been located at Bolama, on the south side of the the Geba River.

During their tenure the Portuguese regarded Bissau as a resource for slaves, palm oil, and groundnuts (peanuts), and they did not invest in the development of the area beyond the bare minimum necessary for the successful extraction of its resources. When the end of World War II (1939–45) did not see any improvement in the poor living conditions for Bissau's African residents, they began to organize politically, founding, in 1956, the AFRICAN PARTY FOR THE INDEPENDENCE OF GUINEA AND CAPE VERDE (Partido Africano da Independência do Guiné e Cabo Verde, PAIGC). Urban unrest led to a dock strike, in 1959, in which 50 strikers died at the hands of the Portuguese colonial authorities.

By 1963 the area saw the beginning of an armed insurrection, led by the PAIGC president Amílcar CABRAL (1924–1973), against the colonial government. The ensuing guerrilla war, which lasted from 1963 to 1974, gradually stifled the commercial life of Bissau, since the city depended on the export of agricultural commodities from rural areas that increasingly fell under PAIGC control. When the war ended and Guinea-Bissau gained independence in 1974, Bissau was in a state of economic depression.

The city began to recover by the late 1980s, as major improvements to the port boosted the trade of rice as well as nuts, fish, wax, and hides. Bissau's economic development faced a sharp setback, though, in June 1988, when an army rebellion ignited fighting in the capital. Several thousand deaths and major destruction resulted. Ultimately, however, a peace accord was signed, and the country's first democratic elections took place in 1994.

Today, Bissau, with its ethnically mixed population approaching 300,000, remains the only significant urban center in the country. The economic base for the city, unfortunately, still remains largely agricultural, just as the country remains one of the world's poorest.

See also: GEBA RIVER (Vol. II); MALI EMPIRE (Vol. II); GROUNDNUTS (Vols. III, IV); PALM OIL (Vols. III, IV); PORTUGAL AND AFRICA (Vols. III, IV, V); SLAVERY (Vols. I, II, III, IV); SLAVE TRADE (Vols. III, IV).

Biya, Paul (1933–) *Second president of Cameroon*

Biya was born in the southern Cameroonian village of Mvomeko. As a youth he attended a Catholic mission school and later studied at Eda and Akono Junior Seminaries and the Lycee Leclerc, French Cameroon's most prestigious high school. His strong academic performance permitted Biya to enroll at the University of Paris, where he earned his law degree in 1960. Biya remained in Paris for further legal studies at the Institute of Overseas Studies, returning to Cameroon in 1962.

Upon his return Biya joined the government of President Ahmadou AHIDJO (1924–1989) and was placed in charge of the Department of Foreign Development Aid. Serving in multiple government positions, Biya formed a close relationship with President Ahidjo. In 1975 Ahidjo chose Biya as prime minister, making Biya successor to the presidency.

On November 6, 1982, Ahidjo resigned as president and Biya succeeded him. Ahidjo, however, remained as chairman of Cameroon's only legal party—the Cameroon National Party (CNP). Believing that the chairmanship of the CNP was a more powerful position than the presidency, Ahidjo probably thought that he would effectively retain control of the country. Soon after, however, Biya began to replace Ahidjo's government appointees and aides with people more loyal to him. In 1983 Ahidjo was implicated in an attempted COUP D'ÉTAT, resulting in his forced resignation from the CNP chairmanship as well as his exile from Cameroon. In 1984 there was another coup attempt against Biya. Again, the coup was put down and Ahidjo was implicated once again. This time he was sentenced to death in absentia. Biya, meanwhile, consolidated his hold on power. He had been elected chairman of the CNP in 1983, but abolished the party and formed the CAMEROON PEOPLE'S DEMOCRATIC MOVEMENT.

Though President Biya met with some initial successes, including the expansion of freedom of speech and press, his presidency became burdened by a poor economy. By the late 1980s the country was mired in recession, and Biya agreed to accept loans from the International Monetary Fund and the ensuing STRUCTURAL ADJUSTMENT required by the organization. The changes did little to stem the decline of Cameroon's economy.

By the late 1980s the continent-wide movement for DEMOCRATIZATION reached Cameroon, forcing Biya, in 1990, to call for multiparty elections. In 1992 Cameroon held its first multiparty presidential elections, with Biya declared the winner. The results, however, were widely disputed and massive demonstrations took place to protest the outcome. In response Biya declared a state of emergency and violently repressed the opposition. The presidential elections of 1997 were similarly tainted, as Biya refused independent oversight of the results. In response the three major opposition leaders refused to partake in the elections, which Biya won easily.

See also: FRANCE AND AFRICA (Vol. IV); INTERNATIONAL MONETARY FUND AND AFRICA (Vol. V).

Further reading: Joseph Takougang and Milton Krieger, *African State and Society in the 1990s: Cameroon's Political Crossroads* (Boulder, Colo.: Westview Press, 1998).

Biyidi-Awala, Alexandre See BETI, MONGO.

Black Consciousness Movement (BCM)

South African political and social action associated with anti-APARTHEID and pro-nationalism groups. Although the ideology of Black Consciousness has existed since the early 20th century, the founding of the Black Consciousness Movement (BCM) is usually attributed to Steve BIKO (1946–1977), the South African militant who had formed the SOUTH AFRICAN STUDENTS' ORGANIZATION (SASO). The BCM, however, was not the province of a single organization, nor did it ascribe to a single doctrine. It was, rather, a rallying point for the promotion of black pride, dignity, self-awareness, and self-determination. While the black power movement in the United States and the example of Malcolm X (1925–1965) helped inspire BCM, the principal wellspring was internal to SOUTH AFRICA.

In addition to SASO, the BCM attracted and fostered the development of many other black South African anti-apartheid groups, including the Black Peoples Convention, the South African Students' Movement, and the Black Allied Workers Union. These organizations provided the opportunity for blacks to set the tone of the anti-apartheid debate. Also, with the AFRICAN NATIONAL CONGRESS and PAN-AFRICANIST CONGRESS outlawed by the South African government, the BCM offered a legal outlet for anti-apartheid activity.

The positive legal status of BCM organizations, however, did not last long. The South African government began to arrest the leaders of the BCM, and, in 1977, South African police murdered Biko while he was in their custody. That same year the government banned all groups associated with the BCM. The BCM did not die, but was reorganized under the name Azanian People's Organization (AZAPO). In 1980 AZAPO formed the Black Consciousness Movement of Azania (BCMA). With its headquarters in London, England, the BCMA

provided an organizational structure for exiled members of the banned BCM groups. In 1990 the South African government lifted the ban on all nationalist organizations, including those of the BCM. In 1984 all the BCM organizations joined together under the AZAPO name. BCM declined with the collapse of the apartheid system in the early 1990s. Africans were now in the political majority and thus able to elect the government. The notion of black consciousness as a way to unify people of color against white political oppression thus lost its central rationale.

See also: BANTUSTANS (Vol. V) RESISTANCE AND REBELLION (Vol. IV).

Further reading: George M. Fredrickson, *Black Liberation: A Comparative History of Black Ideologies in the United States and South Africa* (New York: Oxford University Press, 1995).

Black Sash

Women's organization founded in 1955 to protest the treatment of blacks under APARTHEID in SOUTH AFRICA. Officially called the Women's Defense of the Constitution League, the Black Sash was begun by progressive, white, middle-class women. To register their opposition to apartheid and repression, Black Sash members maintained peaceful vigils and participated in marches, clad in a distinctive black belt, or sash, a symbol of mourning for violations of the country's constitution. Their silent vigils were normally held in places frequented by members of the white parliament. At its height, membership exceeded 10,000, testifying to the fact that a significant portion of South Africa's white population opposed apartheid.

The original purpose of the Black Sash was to prevent the government from withdrawing voting rights from South Africa's Cape coloured population. Although it failed to achieve that goal, the organization persevered, taking on the broader task of defending Africans against various civil rights abuses, especially the oppressive "pass laws" that required Africans to carry passes at all times or face arrest and possible imprisonment.

Nelson MANDELA (1918–), the first black president of post-apartheid South Africa, once referred to the Black Sash as "the conscience of white South Africa."

The Black Sash also maintained advice offices, which assisted Africans who had legal problems or who were being unjustly treated with respect to housing and employment. In 1983 the organization took an active role in the formation of the End Conscription Campaign, which was designed to bring an end to compulsory conscription of white men into the South African Defense Forces. Since the collapse of apartheid in the early 1990s, the organization has been dedicated to helping the poor.

See also: CAPE COLOURED PEOPLE (Vol. IV); WOMEN IN COLONIAL AFRICA (Vol. IV); WOMEN IN INDEPENDENT AFRICA (Vol. V).

Boesak, Allan (1945–) *Anti-apartheid activist in South Africa*

Allan Aubrey Boesak was born into an AFRIKAANS-speaking Cape Cape coloured family in the small town of Kakamas, Northern Cape Province, SOUTH AFRICA. His father was a schoolteacher. After his father's death in 1953, his mother moved the family to Somerset West, a distant suburb of CAPE TOWN, where she supported her children by working as a seamstress. Boesak attended the Bellville Theological Seminary, which trained clergy for the Cape coloured branch of the segregated Dutch Reformed Church. Ordained in 1968, he spent three years as a parish minister before going to Europe for further studies. In 1976 he earned a doctorate in theology from the Kampen Theological Institute, in the Netherlands.

In 1976, upon his return to South Africa, Boesak served as a parish minister in the Dutch Reformed Mission Church, which was established for South Africa's Cape coloured population. He became politically active in the campaign to end APARTHEID and soon emerged as one of the leading figures in the black opposition, mobilizing both the Christian community and the Cape coloured community against that policy. In 1982, as president of the World Alliance of Reformed Churches (WARC), he succeeded in having the WARC adopt a proposal to declare apartheid a heresy and suspend the white South African churches from the Alliance.

In 1983 white South African voters were asked to approve a new constitution, which, among other provisions, would establish a new tricameral parliament, with separate houses for whites, Coloureds, and Indians. This constitution represented the attempt of President P. W. BOTHA (1916–) to give the appearance of sharing power with the country's nonwhite population without granting them any real authority. In response, Boesak helped found the UNITED DEMOCRATIC FRONT, an umbrella organization coordinating some 700 opposition groups. He accused the government of trying to subvert Coloureds and Indians into supporting the apartheid system that oppressed them. Furthermore, he encouraged a boycott of the subsequent parliamentary elections that followed the adoption of the new constitution. The boycott was successful, as only 20 percent of the Coloureds and Indians went to vote. Boesak was arrested several times for taking part in demonstrations, and the government attempted to silence him.

During the mid-1980s, as the tempo of popular protest and state repression increased, Boesak became more active and traveled widely abroad. His moral authority, however, was undermined by revelations of extramarital affairs with white women, first in 1985 and again in 1990. In South Africa's racially segregated society, these affairs brought him considerable notoriety. After news of the second scandal broke, Boesak resigned from Dutch Reformed Mission Church and from the World Alliance of Reformed Churches, which he then headed. He later divorced his wife and married Elna Botha (1960–)—no relation to P. W. Botha—a television producer.

In 1998 Boesak again became embroiled in controversy when he was found guilty of stealing a large sum of money that had been donated to his Foundation for Peace and Justice. He was imprisoned in May 2000 and sentenced to a three-year term. He was released on parole in 2001.

See also: CAPE CAPE COLOURED PEOPLE (Vol. IV).

Bokassa, Jean-Bedel (1921–1996) *President of the Central African Republic from 1966 to 1979*

Bokassa grew up an orphan, his mother having having been a suicide and his father, a murder victim. Raised by MISSIONARIES in the French colony of Oubangui-Chari (present-day CENTRAL AFRICAN REPUBLIC), he received his education at mission schools until he joined the French army in 1939. Bokassa saw action with the Free French in World War II (1939–45) and later in French Indochina, rising to the rank of captain in 1961. In 1964 Bokassa's cousin David DACKO (1930–), the president of the newly independent Central African Republic, asked for Bokassa to become commander in chief of the armed forces. With the country in economic shambles, Bokassa launched a COUP D'ÉTAT in 1966, overthrowing Dacko and taking the titles of president and prime minister. Three days later he abolished the constitution and claimed dictatorial control.

Bokassa's 13-year regime as head of the Central African Republic was marked by incredible brutality and excess. Under constant threat of coups (attempted in 1969 and 1974) and assassination (attempted in 1976), Bokassa moved to consolidate his power and suppress his opponents through imprisonment and murder. In 1972 he declared himself president for life and ruled as such until 1976, when Bokassa anointed himself Emperor Bokassa I and renamed the country Central African Empire. Bokassa held a ceremony designed to mimic the coronation of his hero, Napoleon Bonaparte (1769–1821), who had crowned himself emperor of France in 1804.

Under Bokassa's increasingly unstable and autocratic rule, the Central African Empire fell into further decline, as Bokassa exploited the country's mineral wealth for his personal purposes, including frequent gifts of diamonds to French president Valéry Giscard d'Estaing (1926–).

In 1979 riots in the capital city of BANGUI led to violent reprisals on citizens, and, in April of that year, Bokassa had 100 schoolchildren arrested and executed for protesting the cost of school uniforms that featured Bokassa's portrait. After that incident, the French government, which despite Bokassa's excesses had supported his regime, ceased backing the dictator. In September while Bokassa was visiting Libya, French paratroopers stormed Bangui and reinstated David Dacko as president. Bokassa was forced into exile in the IVORY COAST and later France.

Bokassa converted to Islam after a meeting with Muammar QADDAFI (1942–) of LIBYA and then changed his name to Salah Eddine Ahmed Bokassa in 1976. He quickly resumed Christianity, however, when he proclaimed himself emperor later that year. He then named his Muslim alter-ego as the imperial prime minister.

In 1980 Bokassa was sentenced to death in absentia for the crimes of treason, embezzlement, murder, and cannibalism. However, in 1986 Bokassa attempted to return to the Central African Republic and was arrested. The ensuing trial was filled with graphic claims against Bokassa, including statements that he personally participated in the beating deaths of the schoolchildren and later cannibalized the bodies. He was sentenced to death the following year, but that sentence was commuted and eventually reduced to 20 years imprisonment. Bokassa was released in 1993 and died three years later of a heart attack. Though his reign as dictator was indisputably oppressive, many in the Central African Republic still hold mixed feelings, and even some measure of admiration, for Bokassa.

Bokassa and French president Valéry Giscard d'Estaing maintained a particularly cordial relationship. Bokassa took the president on hunting excursions and exported uranium for use in France's nuclear arms program. In return, the French president backed the dictator financially and militarily, even footing the bill for Bokassa's $20 million coronation ceremony. The revelation of d'Estaing's acceptance of gifts of diamonds from Bokassa led to his eventual defeat in France's 1981 presidential elections.

See also: ARMIES, COLONIAL (Vol. IV); FRANCE AND AFRICA (Vols. III, IV, V); FRENCH EQUATORIAL AFRICA (Vol. IV); OUBANGUI-CHARI (Vol. IV).

Bongo, Omar (Albert Bernard Bongo) (1935–)
President of Gabon

Born Albert Bernard Bongo, Bongo received his education in BRAZZAVILLE, Republic of the CONGO. After serving as a conscript in the French military, he found employment in the civil service. After GABON secured its independence in 1960, he held several cabinet positions before President Leon M'Ba (1902–1967) selected him in 1967 as his vice-presidential running mate. Within a few months of winning reelection, M'Ba died, and Bongo assumed the presidency, which he has maintained since. Bongo changed his given name to Omar in 1979, following his conversion to Islam.

In 1968 Bongo moved to centralize Gabon's government, disbanding all political parties save his Parti Democratique Gabonais (PDG), and assuming a number of cabinet-level responsibilities himself. He essentially refined the government into a one-man–one-party system. Applying the same notions of singularity to the rest of the country, Bongo opposed ethnic and regional differences and encouraged intermarriage as a way of promoting Gabonese nationality. Trade unions were merged into a single entity and linked to Bongo's PDG. Bongo consolidated his power to such a degree that, in the 36 years he has been president, he has rarely faced serious challenges to his administration.

In 1993, however, Bongo came close to losing his control after winning only 50.7 percent of the vote. He was able to soothe protests by participating in talks with opposition groups and agreeing to an independent electoral commission, which he later rendered politically ineffectual. By the 1998 elections, Bongo once again had a firm grasp on the presidency, winning handily and without much popular protest.

Bongo's extravagance is such that one French publication noted that the Gabonese leader owns more real estate in Paris than any other foreign head of state.

Bongo's repeated electoral success cannot be attributed to Gabon's national well-being, however. Economic failures in the country's OIL and lumber industries have led to financial uncertainty, and the threat of an almost $4 billion national debt has become prominent. Bongo himself, however, uses his state-derived wealth flagrantly, having spent $300 million U.S. dollars on a presidential palace, among other luxuries. In the meantime, his country has yet to develop adequate roads, EDUCATION, or health services. Despite the failing economy and accusations of CORRUPTION, there seems to be little challenge to Bongo's continued reign as Gabon's central political figure.

See also: FRANCE AND AFRICA (Vols. III, IV, V).

book publishing Although the spread of Islam in Africa beginning in the seventh century led to the appearance and trade of books, these were in handwritten script. The contemporary form of publishing in Africa with printing presses is associated with Christian MISSIONARIES, which, in the 19th century, introduced printing presses. Missionary publications continued to be published during the period of colonialism and even after the African countries had gained independence. During colonialism, governments established publishing houses that produced their own publications, including textbooks used in schools. Even when they wrote the materials locally they employed only their own writers, resulting in stereotypical portrayals of Africans.

Indigenous African book publishing sprang up in the 1960s, after most African countries became independent. Despite numerous challenges African book publishing developed rapidly in the following three decades. One of the major issues faced by African governments at independence was the lack of appropriate schoolbooks, including textbooks and literature, since the colonial governments had in many cases used books with no relevance for the local people. As a result most governments were compelled to set up publishing houses to meet the educational needs of their countries. The need for books written by Africans expressing their own views and experiences encouraged the establishment of independent publishing houses. Numerous books were published that were written in English, French, Portuguese, Arabic, Kiswahili, as well as in many indigenous African languages.

By the 1970s most African countries had firmly established publishing houses. In 1973 the International Conference on Publishing and Book Development in Africa was held at the University of Ife, NIGERIA. It was a landmark event that underlined the importance of book publishing in Africa. In order to recognize meritorious authors and publishers, African countries established awards including the Noma Award, which was created in 1979 as an annual prize for an outstanding book from Africa. Other prizes include the Nigerian Book Foundation Award, Ghana Publisher of the Year Award, and the Caine Prize for African Writing.

In 2002 Africa celebrated the best 100 books on Africa written in the 20th century. The top 12 on the list included *Things Fall Apart* (1958), by Chinua ACHEBE (1930–),

Sosu's Call (1999), by Meshack Asare (1945–), *So Long a Letter* (1979), by Mariama BÂ (1929–1981), *Terra Sonambula* (1992), by Mia Couto (1955–), *Nervous Conditions* (1988), by Tsitsi DANGAREMBGA (1959–), *The African Origins of Civilization: Myth or Reality* (1955), by Cheikh Anta DIOP (1923–1986), *La'Amour, La fantasia* (1985), by Assia Djebar (1936–), *The Cairo Trilogy* (1945), by Naguib MAHFOUZ (1911–), *Chaka* (1925), by Thomas Mofolo (c. 1875–1948), *Ake: The Years of Childhood* (1981), by Wole SOYINKA (1934–), *A Grain of Wheat* (1967), by NGUGI WA THIONG'O (1938–), and *Oeuvre Poétique* (1961), by Léopold SENGHOR (1906–2001). Both Mahfouz, in 1988, and Soyinka, in 1986, received the Nobel Prize for Literature.

After an optimistic period of expansion in the 1970s African publishers faced a host of challenges that have led to the industry's present stagnation. These include distribution problems and insufficient marketing, worsening economic conditions, high illiteracy, poor TRANSPORTATION and communications, and lack of training and expertise. What have not been lacking, however, are authors. Publishers are responding to these challenges at the national and regional levels. At the national level this has led to the autonomy of publishing houses and the promotion of mass marketing of popular books. At regional levels publishers are seeking collective approaches. In 1992 African publishers formed the African Publishers' Network (APNET), based in HARARE, ZIMBABWE, in order to strengthen indigenous publishing in Africa and to promote intra-African trade in books. APNET aims to give a unified voice to publishers, promote joint ventures, assist in training publishing personnel, and help establish licensing agreements between publishers. In addition, the Zimbabwe International Book Fair, a non-profit organization, operates as Africa's largest and most diverse information and publishing showcase which exhibits the largest and most diverse collection of books, magazines, journals, CD-ROM and publishing and printing technology and services in sub-Saharan Africa. The ongoing political and economic crisis in Zimbabwe, however, threatens the fair's future. Despite the challenges privately owned public houses are emerging and publishing a wide range of high-quality books.

See also: LITERACY (Vols. IV, V); LITERATURE IN COLONIAL AFRICA (Vol. IV); LITERATURE IN MODERN AFRICA (Vol. V); *THINGS FALL APART* (Vol. IV).

Further reading: Hans M. Zell, *The African Publishing Companion: A Resource Guide* (Lochcarron, Scotland: Hans Zell Pub., 2002).

Botha, P. W. (Pieter Willem Botha) (1916–)
South African prime minister from 1978 to 1989

Often simply referred to as P. W., Botha was born into a Boer, or Afrikaner, family in Free State Province, SOUTH

AFRICA. The Bothas counted themselves among the most fiercely nationalistic Boer families in the province. His father had fought against the British in the Anglo-Boer War of 1899–1902, the unsuccessful Afrikaner effort to preserve the independence of the two Boer Republics, the Orange Free State and the Transvaal. His mother had been among those the British interned in concentration camps, where 28,000 Boer civilians, mostly women and children, died of disease and malnutrition.

Botha entered the University of the Orange Free State to study law, but in 1935 dropped out to become an organizer for the National Party (NP). In 1948 he entered Parliament in the so-called APARTHEID election that swept the National Party into power. He held a number of ministerial posts, serving, most importantly, from 1966 to 1980 as minister of defense. In 1978, upon the resignation of B. J. Vorster (1915–1983), he became the prime minister of South Africa.

In his first years in office, Botha initiated a series of "adapt or die" reformist measures that promised a more progressive approach to the country's black population. Among other measures, he legalized African LABOR UNIONS and abolished the pass law system, which had limited the mobility and residency rights of Africans within South Africa. In actuality, many of his changes were instituted only for appearance's sake. Botha's true intent was to strengthen apartheid by making it appear less repressive while maintaining its core policies.

In 1983 Botha called a whites-only referendum to endorse a new constitution. The proposed constitution allowed for limited power sharing by the Cape coloured and Indian populations of South Africa; however, it ignored the black-African majority. The constitution also transformed the structure of government, changing it from a parliamentary system with a prime minister to a presidential system with a strong executive branch. There was also to be a new tricameral parliament, with separate houses for whites, Coloureds, and Indians. White voters endorsed Botha's constitution, and it became law. Botha became South Africa's first state president. However, in the subsequent parliamentary elections under the new constitution, 80 percent of the newly enfranchised Cape coloured and Indian voters boycotted the polls and refused to vote.

The new constitution, with its limited empowerment of nonwhites, precipitated a split in Afrikaner politics, as the right wing of the National Party broke away and formed the Conservative Party. To calm the mounting internal dissent, Botha adopted what he referred to as "total strategy," which gave broad powers to the country's military and internal security agencies. South Africa increasingly became an authoritarian state, with power concentrated within Botha's inner circle of military advisors.

Botha also pursued a defiant and aggressive foreign policy. He launched periodic raids on neighboring countries that harbored members of the banned AFRICAN NATIONAL CONGRESS and refused to withdraw South Africa's forces from NAMIBIA. In 1984 black anger and discontent spilled over, triggered by the violence that erupted in SOWETO and other urban townships. In 1985 Botha responded by declaring a state of emergency. Initially acknowledged in only select areas, the state of emergency was expanded the next year to span across the entire country.

International condemnation and economic sanctions intensified, weakening South Africa's economy and isolating it diplomatically. After suffering a stroke in January 1989, Botha relinquished his position as head of the National Party and was subsequently forced out as president by F. W. DE KLERK (1936–).

See also: AFRIKANER REPUBLICS (Vol. IV); ANGLO-BOER WAR (Vols. III, IV).

Botswana Located in southern Africa with a total area of 231,800 square miles (600,400 sq km), Botswana is bordered by NAMIBIA to the west and north, ZIMBABWE to the northeast, SOUTH AFRICA to the south and east, and ZAMBIA to the north. Botswana is and arid land, with the Kalahari Desert covering much of the western portion of the country. Most of the population of 1.5 million lives in the eastern part of the country. Its capital and largest city is GABORONE. Botswana is Africa's longest and only uninterrupted liberal democracy. It also is one of the continent's most stable countries and is relatively free of CORRUPTION.

Botswana at Independence By 1960 a new generation in Botswana organized movements to take over the leadership from the British colonial administration of what was then still known as Bechuanaland. The first mass-based political party, the Bechuanaland People's Party (BPP) was formed in December 1960. However, the party failed to attract significant support in most of the rural areas. It was also weakened by internal struggles. The Bechuanaland Democratic Party (BDP, later known as the Botswana Democratic Party) emerged in 1962 as a coalition of educated local notables including Sir Seretse KHAMA (1921–1980) and Ketumile MASIRE (1925–). In 1965 the BDP won a landslide victory in the country's first "one man, one vote" election. The country became independent in 1966 with Seretse Khama as its first president. At independence Botswana was a poor, rural country. It was not until 1967, one year after its independence, that diamonds were discovered, which has led to the country becoming one of the most prosperous in Africa.

Botswana has been described as Africa's premier democracy. The country's economic development has tended to facilitate democracy. In the four decades since independence, Botswana's economy has grown rapidly. At independence it was one of the world's poorest countries with an annual per-capita GDP of $474. By 2001 Botswana had transformed itself to a middle-income country

Exotic wildlife, such as these ostriches running in the Kalahari Desert, is Botswana's major tourist attraction. © *Corbis*

with an annual per-capita GDP of $7,800. Its currency, the Pula, is among the strongest in developing countries. As a result of Botswana's economic status Western aid has declined sharply since the 1990s, but Botswana is sufficiently developed to sustain its economic growth. The government has provided extensive social services in urban, rural, and even remote villages. These include health clinics, clean water, free public EDUCATION, and numerous types of agricultural extension, food relief in times of drought, and good roads and TRANSPORTATION systems.

The basis for Botswana's economy is the diamond MINING that accounts for one-third of its total GDP and three-fourths of its export earnings. The country also EXPORTS copper, nickel, soda ash, and beef. Subsistence AGRICULTURE and TOURISM are two other key sectors.

Upon gaining independence Botswana continued the colonial tradition of having the highly educated and politically sophisticated bureaucratic elite set the policy directions. The government has been effective in managing the DEVELOPMENT process with a minimum of corruption.

Coupled with its diamond wealth, Botswana is one of the few African countries to follow systematically a democratic political process. Most commentators attribute the country's successful democracy to a precolonial culture based on the Tswana *kgotla* institution. The *kgotla* is a community gathering for people to consider issues raised by the chief or headmen. Historically, women, young adults, and minorities could be present at the *kgotla* but did not take part in the discussions unless they were asked in matters pertaining to their group. Much later women were allowed to attend, although *kgotla* meetings were dominated by men. Chiefs set the agenda, but the *kgotla* was a place where people could debate issues and take part in making decisions for their community. After independence the state continued to seek public support for major programs. In terms of major projects affecting the nation, national forums are held and people discuss the intended project before implementation. As a result the general public has been part of the political process.

However, since independence only one party has been in power: the Botswana Democratic Party (BDP). The other major parties include the Botswana National Front, the Botswana People's Party and the Botswana Independence Party. Although the BDP's domination over the other parties has decreased, the other parties have not been strong enough to gain control of the government. The first president, Khama, ruled the country from 1966 until his death in 1980. After his death, Ketumile Masire, who was known as a highly competent technocrat, was chosen as the next president. He successfully ruled the country and retired as president in 1998 after being elected to the position twice. Festus MOGAE (1939–) took over the presidency on April 1, 1998, and he was elected for a five-year term in 1999.

While Botswana's progression toward democracy has been good, its progress in dealing with women's rights was slow. Beginning in 1986, women's groups, including EMANG BASADI, pressured the government to change discriminatory laws, finally succeeding in the 1990s. The government provides funding to promote women's education related to health, relevant laws, and employment. The government has also been taken to task in its dealing with minority groups including the Basarwa and the Kalanga. Faced with strong criticism the government and the opposition parties are beginning to articulate minority interests and cultural diversity.

Given its political and economic status Botswana has started to play a significant role in the region's economy and political affairs. The country is an active member of the SOUTHERN AFRICA DEVELOPMENT COMMUNITY whose headquarters are located in the capital city of Gaborone. It is a member of the Southern African Customs Union as well. Botswana has also played an effective role in helping countries in conflict attain peace. In the conflict in the Democratic Republic of the CONGO, former Botswana president Masire has played a leading role as a United Nation's envoy, acting as a facilitator of the peace process.

On the negative side many of Botswana's people have been affected by the HIV/AIDS crisis, and infection rates are the highest in the world. (Approximately 38.5 percent of the adult population is infected.) The government has initiated antiretroviral therapy, while prevention remains the cornerstone of its national HIV/AIDS strategy. In this regard Botswana has become the first African country to provide antiretroviral (ARV) therapy to its citizens on a national scale to address the HIV/AIDS emergency.

See also: BECHUANALAND (Vol. IV); BOTSWANA (Vols. I, II, III, IV); COLONIAL RULE (Vol. IV); ENGLAND AND AFRICA (Vols. IV, V).

Further reading: Olufemi Vaughan, *Chiefs, Power, and Social Change: Chiefship and Modern Politics in Botswana, 1880s–1990s* (Trenton, N.J.: Africa World Press, 2003).

Boumedienne, Houari (Mohammed Ben Brahim Bankharouba) (1927–1978) *Algerian leader from 1965 to 1978*

Known for his commitment to giving ALGERIA control over its own economy and NATURAL RESOURCES, as well as for policies designed to improve the living standards of his nation's people, Houari Boumedienne became a leading figure in the Arab world. Throughout his career, Boumedienne remained committed to both a moderate socialism and to Islamic tenets, making him a key figure in the political movements sweeping Arab states in the 1960s and 1970s.

Born in a small town in eastern Algeria, Mohammed Ben Brahim Bankharouba, as he was named at birth, was educated in French and Islamic schools. In 1952 he fled to TUNISIA and EGYPT to avoid serving in the French military. While in Egypt, he joined the Algerian independence movement led by Ahmed BEN BELLA (1916–). After adopting the name Houari Boumedienne he joined the NATIONAL LIBERATION FRONT (Front de Liberation National, FLN) and received military training. A natural soldier and leader, he rose quickly in the revolutionary army, and by 1960 he was head of its general staff.

Quiet and reserved, and as loyal to his troops as they were to him, Boumedienne steered a careful course through the political intrigues of the various factions of the independence movement. By the time Algerian elections were held in September 1962, FLN troops had gained control of most of the country. With Ben Bella's victory in the elections, Boumedienne became the minister of defense in the government of the newly independent Algeria. For the next several years the two men led Algeria together, although there was constant tension between the reserved Boumedienne and the outgoing Ben Bella.

Although he favored Ben Bella's pragmatic form of socialism as the best course for Algeria, Boumedienne found himself unable to support Ben Bella's authoritarian tendencies. Nor did he share Ben Bella's vision of a secular, non-Islamist Algeria. After several attempts by Ben Bella to undermine his authority, Boumedienne seized control of the government in a bloodless COUP D'ÉTAT on June 19, 1965, appointing himself president and minister of defense and suspending the National Assembly.

Once in power, Boumedienne launched domestic programs aimed at improving the living standards for all Algerians rather than just a handful of the elite. In addition to instituting agricultural reforms and INDUSTRIALIZATION programs, he nationalized the country's OIL industry in 1971, giving him control of one of Algeria's key resources and an important source of income.

With Egypt's decline in influence among the Arab states following the 1967 Arab-Israeli War, many in the Islamic world began to look to Boumedienne for leadership. It was a position he seemed willing to take, and he soon became a spokesperson for Arab—and African—causes. Firmly committed to the principle of nonalignment, he kept the former Soviet Union from playing major, direct roles in Algeria, in spite of his own moderate socialism. He urged similar policies for other newly independent and developing nations, and he eventually assumed a significant role in the Nonaligned Movement, becoming its chairperson in 1973. Equally committed to liberation from colonial powers, he continued to support revolutionary movements in other parts of Africa, such as WESTERN SAHARA, even at the expense of maintaining friendly relations with neighbors like MOROCCO. Boumedienne died of natural causes on December 27, 1978.

See also: ARAB-ISRAELI WARS (Vols. IV, V); COMMUNISM AND SOCIALISM (Vol. IV); FRANCE AND AFRICA (Vols. IV, V); NON-ALIGNED MOVEMENT AND AFRICA (Vol. V); SOVIET UNION AND AFRICA (Vol. V).

Further readings: David Ottaway and Marina Ottaway, *Algeria: Politics of a Socialist Revolution* (Berkeley, Calif.: University of California Press, 1970).

Bourguiba, Habib (Habib ben Ali Bourgiba)
(1903–2000) *First president of Tunisia*

After leading TUNISIA to independence from France in 1956, Bourguiba was elected president the following year. Once in control, he guided the nation's assembly in drafting a new constitution and made his Destour Socialist Party (Parti Socialiste Destourien, PSD) the only officially recognized Tunisian political party. Bourgiba then set about modernizing the Tunisian economy, developing its OIL industry, inviting FOREIGN INVESTMENT, and encouraging TOURISM.

Despite his early successes, by the early 1970s Bourguiba's government was hampered by numerous conflicts within the PSD, with major problems largely the result of the rift between the party's liberals and Islamic conservatives. However, in contrast to the disarray in Tunisian domestic affairs, Bourguiba's foreign policies at this time were mostly successful. Tunisia enjoyed a long period of favorable relations with France, especially since Bourguiba represented a moderating influence in the increasingly anti-Western Arab world.

Bourguiba was known to be wary of aligning Tunisia with other Arab unions, but in 1974 he acted without consultation from his advisors and signed a treaty of union with Muammar QADDAFI (1942–) in neighboring LIBYA. The proposed merger would have brought together the governments, parliaments, and armies of the two nations. Within two days, however, Bourguiba annulled the treaty, creating strained diplomatic relations between the two countries that would last for years.

Bourguiba began to show signs of mental deterioration in the 1970s, as his memory failed and his behavior became erratic. In spite of this, however, in 1975 the Constituent Assembly appointed Bourguiba president for life. In 1980

Bourguiba authorized the legal formation of opposition political parties, and within a few years Tunisia became the scene of widespread popular unrest. By the mid-1980s the Tunisian economy was depressed, and Bourguiba's weak leadership had cost him his popular support. Finally, in 1987 doctors confirmed that Bourguiba's health left him unfit to rule, and by a provision of the constitution, the president for life was replaced by his prime minister ZINE EL ABIDINE BEN ALI (1936–). In the 1990s arteriosclerosis gradually destroyed Bourguiba's health; he died at home early in 2000.

See also: BOURGUIBA, HABIB (Vol. IV), DESTOUR PARTY (Vol. IV).

Further reading: Derek Hopwood, *Habib Bourguiba of Tunisia: The Tragedy of Longevity* (New York: St. Martin's Press, 1992); Pierre Rossi, *Bourguiba's Tunisia* (Tunis, Tunisia: Editions Kahia, 1967); Norma Salem, *Habib Bourguiba, Islam, and the Creation of Tunisia* (London: Croom Helm, 1984).

Bouteflika, Abdelaziz (1937–) *President of Algeria*

Born in Oujda, MOROCCO, near the border with ALGERIA, Bouteflika became involved in the Algerian independence movement in 1956. Following the end of colonial rule Bouteflika took a position in the government of President Ahmed BEN BELLA (1916–) and later became foreign minister. When Ben Bella was removed from office during a COUP D'ÉTAT, Bouteflika continued to serve as foreign minister under Colonel Houari BOUMEDIENNE (1927–1978).

Bouteflika nearly assumed the presidency following Boumedienne's death in 1978, but Colonel Chadli Benjedid (1929–) took power instead and, in 1980, dismissed Bouteflika. After being accused of embezzlement, Bouteflika went into exile in Switzerland.

In 1999 a cadre of Algerian military and civilian leaders asked Bouteflika to run in the presidential elections, viewing him as a "consensus candidate" who could possibly bridge the differences between the various factions in Algeria that had been at odds since independence. At the time the country was in economic shambles, with its military fighting radical Islamist groups and opposition parties. Bouteflika won a controversial election and became Algeria's first civilian president since 1965. Many in Algeria welcomed his election, even though Bouteflika actually won the presidency by default. His six opponents withdrew from the race, complaining of irregular electoral practices, leaving Bouteflika as the only remaining candidate.

Bouteflika faced the immense task of resurrecting Algeria's economy while also establishing a lasting peace in a country long under martial rule. Further complicating the situation was the military's determination to prevent Islamic fundamentalists from gaining power. The ensuing civil war has led to more than 100,000 deaths in the past dozen years. The new president sought to create dialogues between the various opposition groups and eased ethnic tensions in the Kabylie region, where Berbers violently refused to give up their native tongue in favor of Arabic, the official state language. However, as of 2003, while announcing his plans to run for reelection, Bouteflika was still hindered by the military's influence in the government.

See also: CIVIL WARS (Vol. V); ISLAM, INFLUENCE OF (Vols. III, IV, V).

Further reading: Luis Martínez, *The Algerian Civil War, 1990–1998* (New York: Columbia University Press, 2000); William B. Quandt, *Between Ballots and Bullets: Algeria's Transition from Authoritarianism* (Washington, D.C.: Brookings Institution Press, 1998).

Bozizé, François See CENTRAL AFRICAN REPUBLIC.

Brazzaville Major port and capital city of the Republic of the CONGO, located in the southeast. Originating as a small African village, the town of Brazzaville was founded by explorer Pierre Savorgnan de Brazza (1852–1905). Due to its strategic location on the Congo River, it became a center for administration, serving as the capital of French Equatorial Africa from 1910 to 1958, and as the center of the Free French administration during World War II (1939–45). It became the capital of the Republic of the Congo in 1960 and today functions as the administrative, communications, and economic center. Major industries include beverage processing, textiles, and construction supplies. Growth of the city took off after 1945, and the population in 1995 was estimated at more than 1 million.

Brazzaville is located on the north bank of the Congo River near Malebo Pool, which serves as a deep-water river port. Goods are shipped to and from many central African countries via the Congo-Oubangi waterway and transferred to the Congo-Ocean Railway to reach the Atlantic port city of Pointe-Noire, located just north of the Angolan city of CABINDA.

In its role as the country's administrative and commercial center, Brazzaville has been the site of a great deal of political unrest. In 1960, on the eve of independence, there were violent urban riots as various ethnic groups staked their claims for prime positions in the future government.

In 1992 civil war erupted again when Brazzaville became the scene of "ethnic cleansing," with rival factions struggling for control of the city. A fragile peace was restored in 1994, but by 1997 renewed fighting led to an exodus of several hundred thousand REFUGEES from the city. Unfortunately, the violence in Brazzaville was symptomatic of the chaos and civil strife that gripped the entire country toward the end of the 20th and the beginning of the 21st centuries.

Despite the recurring violence, Brazzaville has developed into a center for learning and research. It is host to the World Health Organization and the Pan-African Union of Science and Technology headquarters. It is also home to the Poto-Poto School of African Art, and to Marien-Ngouabi University, which started out as a teacher's college in 1961 and now admits students from all over Central Africa.

See also: BRAZZAVILLE (Vol. IV); CONGO (Vol. III); CONGO RIVER (Vol. I); FRANCE AND AFRICA (Vols. III, IV, V); FRENCH EQUATORIAL AFRICA (Vol. IV); LUMUMBA, PATRICE (Vols. IV, V); WORLD WAR II (Vol. IV); URBANIZATION (Vols. IV, V); URBAN LIFE AND CULTURE (Vols. IV, V).

Brink, Andre (1935–) *South African novelist*

Born into an Afrikaner family in the Orange Free State, SOUTH AFRICA, Andre Philippus Brink earned both bachelor's and master's degrees in literature from the conservative AFRIKAANS-medium Potchefstroom University. In 1959 he traveled to Paris, France, where he studied at the Sorbonne and had his first experiences interacting with blacks on equal terms. This led him to develop a sharp awareness of the political and social oppression under APARTHEID in his homeland. News of the SHARPEVILLE massacre, in 1960, shocked him.

In the early 1960s Brink published his first two novels, *Lobola vir die lewe* (The price of living) (1962) and *Die Ambassadeur* (The ambassador) (1963), which were relatively nonpolitical. After witnessing the student riots in Paris in 1968, however, Brink returned to South Africa to challenge that country's policies through his writing.

Positioning himself as an internal critic of the apartheid government and Afrikaner society, Brink became a leader of a group of young Afrikaner writers and poets named the Sestigers, or the Sixty-ers, referring to the writers' rise to prominence in the 1960s. Brink and his fellow Sestigers blatantly flaunted the traditional, conservative standards of Afrikaner writing, directly addressing sexual and moral themes and criticizing apartheid. Brink himself revolutionized the Afrikaans literary style, introducing prose elements from European writers such as Albert Camus (1913–1960) and Jean-Paul Sartre (1905–1980).

> The Sestigers were founded by the controversial South African writer, Jan Rabie (1920–2001). Their goal was to "broaden the rather too parochial limits of Afrikaner fiction." Claiming Ingrid Jonker (1933–1965), Breyten Breytenbach (1939–), and others as members, the Sestigers are credited with introducing modernism into Afrikaner literature.

In 1973 Brink published *Kennis van die aand* (*Looking on darkness*), which was one of the first Afrikaner books to be banned by the South African government. It told the story of an interracial relationship between a black actor and a white woman. His next novel, *'N Droë wit seisoen* (*A dry white season*) (1979), was also banned. He also published *Houd-den-bek* (*A chain of voices*), in 1982. Along with the publicity he achieved from the censorship of his books, Brink won critical claim abroad. He is a three-time nominee for the Nobel Prize in Literature, and in 1982 he was awarded the Legion of Honor by the French government. In South Africa, however, most of his fellow AFRIKANERS decried his work as perverse and amoral.

With the end of apartheid in 1994, and the election of Nelson MANDELA (1918–   ) as South Africa's first black president, Brink became one of his country's most publicly celebrated authors. He remains a controversial figure in Afrikaner literary circles, however, which is why he presently holds a chair in English literature at the English-medium University of Cape Town rather than teaching at an Afrikaans-medium university. Furthermore, he has written his more recent works, including *States of Emergency* (1988), *An Act of Terror* (1991), and, most recently, *An Act of Silence* (2002), in English rather than Afrikaans.

See also: LITERATURE IN MODERN AFRICA (Vol. V).

Further reading: Rosemary Jane Jolly, *Colonization, Violence, and Narration in White South African Writing: André Brink, Breyten Breytenbach, and J. M. Coetzee* (Athens, Ohio: Ohio University Press, 1996).

Broederbond South African secret society dedicated to Afrikaner nationalism. Initially founded in 1918, the Afrikaner Broederbond was for almost 70 years a secret society made up of white males seeking to gain economic, social, and political power for South Africa's AFRIKANERS. By the late 1940s, when the Reunited Nationalist Party took control of the nation, the Broederbond exerted enormous power within SOUTH AFRICA. Indeed, the majority of the nation's leaders were Broederbond members, including most members of Parliament and, it has been surmised, every prime minister and president serving from 1948 to 1994

As anti-apartheid feeling grew during the 1960s and 1970s, and as the extent of the power of the secret Broederbond was exposed, the organization gradually lost support. Still, as late as the 1990s, the Broederbond was believed to have between 10,000 and 15,000 members in more than 1,200 branches. This gave the organization enough power for the government to use it as a sounding board to test public opinion as it began to lessen the strictures of APARTHEID.

In 1993 the organization adopted a new constitution that radically transformed what was once a whites-only,

males-only bastion of Afrikaner nationalism. The organization then lifted its veil of secrecy and became public, officially changing its name to the Afrikanerbond. At that time membership became open to both women and members of other races or ethnic groups. Still, new members required the approval of current members. They also had to be fluent in the Afrikaner language, AFRIKAANS, and be willing to follow the group's new constitution.

See also: BROEDERBOND (Vol. IV).

Further reading: V. February, *The Afrikaners of South Africa* (London: Kegan Paul, 1991).

Buganda Historic African kingdom in UGANDA. After independence, Buganda sought to maintain the autonomy it had preserved under colonial rule. At the time of Uganda's independence, in 1962, Buganda was, to a significant degree, an autonomous kingdom. Unlike many similar pre-colonial African states, it had managed to retain its political and territorial identity within the framework of a larger colonial state. In recognition of Buganda's special status, its *kabaka* (king), Mutesa II (r. 1939–1969), was named the country's new president. This was a largely ceremonial post, however, for control of the government lay with Prime Minister Milton OBOTE (1924–2000). As a northerner, Obote was unsympathetic with Buganda's claims for special status. Soon after independence, Buganda's efforts to continue its autonomy clashed with Obote's intent to develop a more fully integrated national state. As early as 1962 he had used force to suppress separatist efforts elsewhere in the country. In 1964 the prime minister signed legislation that removed two counties from Buganda that it had received under the terms of the Buganda Agreement it had negotiated with Britain in 1900. Obote rightly felt that Buganda opinion had turned against him, and he sent police to put down any opposition. In this tense atmosphere, a minor incident led to the deaths of six people in Buganda, shot by Obote's police in what was later determined to be an unprovoked attack.

> **The 1964 police shootings in Buganda killed four adults and two children. Three of the shootings occurred at point-blank range inside the victims' houses. This was all conducted under the pretense of putting down a riot that apparently never happened.**

By 1966 Obote had assumed full dictatorship over Uganda. In May of that year, Buganda's Lukiiko protested Obote's rule and demanded all Ugandan government presence be removed from Buganda. Obote countered by assaulting the kingdom and burning down the royal palace. Mutesa barely escaped and Buganda fell. One year later, Obote abolished all kingdoms in Uganda.

Uganda was thereafter subject to the brutal regimes of General Idi AMIN (c. 1925–2003) and later Obote again, until 1986, when Obote was permanently overthrown. The new president Yoweri MUSEVENI (1944–   ) reinstated the kingdom of Buganda, in 1993, and Mutebi II (1955–   ) became *kabaka*. Museveni realized that unless he, too, were to assume dictatorial powers, the central government had to accommodate itself to the historical political and cultural identities that Buganda and the other kingdoms within the country's borders represented.

See also: BUGANDA (Vols. II, III, IV); COLONIAL RULE (Vol. IV); COLONIALISM, INFLUENCE OF (Vol. IV); ETHNICITY AND IDENTITY (Vol. I).

Bujumbura Capital city of BURUNDI. Bujumbura is the economic as well as administrative center of Burundian life. Its location on the northern shore of Lake Tanganyika makes it the country's principal port, shipping EXPORTS of cotton, tin ore, and coffee to the neighboring Democratic Republic of the CONGO and TANZANIA.

The region has long been densely populated by farmers and herders. Known as Usumbura until Burundi's independence in 1962, Bujumbura was only a village when the German colonial government created a military outpost there in 1899. After Germany lost its African colonies in the aftermath of World War I (1914–18), Bujumbura became the seat of government for Ruanda-Urundi, a Belgian mandate under the League of Nations. At that time it became home to a sizable European population.

In the 1930s the city's African population increased dramatically. The Belgian colonial government responded by setting up a court system in the city, which ultimately came to be a center for adjudication throughout the area. Combined with its administrative capacity, this assured Bujumbura's political centrality. By 1993 the city's population reached 300,000.

Since Burundi's independence Bujumbura has become the site of ongoing conflict between rival HUTU and TUTSI ethnic factions and has seen the violent overthrow of successive governing regimes. One such case occurred in 1996, when the city's Tutsi mayor staged a successful coup against the country's elected Hutu president.

See also: RUANDA-URUNDI (Vol. IV).

Burkina Faso Landlocked West African country about 105,900 square miles (274,300 sq km) in size, located south of the Sahara Desert. Burkina Faso is bordered by MALI to the west and north, by NIGER to the east, and by BENIN, TOGO, GHANA, and IVORY COAST to the south. Called UPPER VOLTA during the period of French colonial rule, the country retained that name for the first 23 years of its independence.

Upper Volta at Independence Upper Volta was granted full independence from France on August 5, 1960, under the dictatorial rule of Maurice Yaméogo (1921–1993). In the years leading up to independence Yaméogo was active in the African Democratic Assembly (Rassemblement Démocratique Africain, RDA), a multicountry political organization of French West Africa. When he assumed leadership of the country, he succeeded in silencing most of his political opponents by banning the leading opposition party. Under Burkina Faso's newly drafted constitution, the powers of the president were strengthened and a unicameral legislature was created. Yaméogo moved his country in a decidedly pro-Western direction. In 1965 he was reelected with an overwhelming majority of the vote. However, by 1966 Yaméogo's economic austerity measures were sparking LABOR strikes. Amid popular unrest the military staged a COUP D'ETAT, overthrowing Yaméogo.

The army chief of staff, Colonel Sangoulé Lamizana (1916–   ), took control of the country as the new president. Military rule prevailed for four years. Then, in 1969, following the drafting of a new constitution, political parties were once again allowed to exist. Upper Volta's Second Republic emerged in 1970. The RDA swept the legislative elections, and Gerard Kango Ouedraogo (1925–   ) was elected prime minister. Four years later Ouedraogo refused to step down after losing elections, and Lamizana stepped in and established military control once again. In 1976 Lamizana appointed a primarily civilian government, which then led to the establishment of the Third Republic, in November 1977. The state drafted yet another constitution.

Continuing Political Instability and Marxist Revolution In 1978 Lamizana was reelected president, and Joseph Conombo (1917–   ) was elected prime minister. Within a few years, the government was once again plagued by striking trade unionists, violence, and civil unrest. The instability resulted in another military coup in 1980, this one led by Colonel Saye Zerbo (1932–   ). In 1982 the government changed yet again when a radical military faction toppled Zerbo. The new administration created the Council for the People's Salvation (CSP), and Seargent-Major Jean-Baptiste Ouedraogo (1942–   ) took control as president. Army Captain Thomas Sankara (1949–1987) served as his prime minister.

Early in 1983 Sankara shifted Upper Volta's course, taking an anti-Western stance that favored relationships with countries such as LIBYA, Cuba, and North Korea. Later that year, however, CSP conservatives imprisoned Sankara, leading Captain Blaise COMPAORÉ (1951–   ) to organize a coup to bring down the CSP. Compaoré reinstalled Sankara, who formed the Marxist-Leninist National Revolutionary Council to rule the country. At first, Sankara enjoyed widespread support. He preached women's equality and implemented state-sponsored programs intended to relieve the nation's persistent food shortages. To mark the revolutionary changes, in 1984 Sankara changed the name of the country from Upper Volta to Burkina Faso.

Sankara's popularity did not last, however, and in 1987 Compaoré led yet another coup. Sankara was deposed and killed. During the two-year period that followed, Compaoré tried to right the struggling country. Eventually, though, he came to suspect that two of his former allies, the military leaders Henri Songo (d. 1989) and Jean-Baptiste Boukary Lengani (d. 1989), were planning to oust him. Compaoré had the two men executed, leaving him in full control as the president. Despite condemnation of the executions, both at home and abroad, Compaoré moved forward, setting about "correcting" the socialist development programs that Sankara had instituted.

After reorganizing the government and naming himself minister of defense and security, Compaoré easily won Burkina Faso's 1991 presidential election. Despite the autocratic nature of his leadership, the 1991 election led to greater DEMOCRATIZATION, since it galvanized opposition among key elements in the governing party, the Popular Front (PF). The election also served to bring international pressure to bear from more liberal donor countries and agencies. Compaoré's PF party soon adopted a new constitution, abandoned its Marxist-Leninist programs, and encouraged FOREIGN INVESTMENT. In 1992 the PF won the majority of the contested legislative seats. In 1998 Compaoré was reelected in a landslide victory.

Although he assumed the mantle of a democrat and introduced an era of rare political stability, Compaoré failed to improve his country's economy. In the 1990s prolonged periods of drought did much to undermine Burkina Faso's AGRICULTURE, making life difficult for the nearly 80 percent of the population living in rural areas. Burkina Faso thus remains one of the world's poorest nations. Continuing POVERTY led to growing opposition from trade unions, which long exercised considerable political and social clout.

Compaoré came under heavy criticism for supporting several unpopular African leaders, including Charles TAYLOR (1948–) of LIBERIA, who was deposed in 2003. Compaoré also allegedly supplied the Angolan rebel leader Jonas SAVIMBI (1934–2002) with arms and fuel in exchange for illegally mined diamonds, thereby making the peace process in ANGOLA more difficult.

See also: BURKINA FASO (Vols. I, II, III, IV); FRANCE AND AFRICA (Vols. IV, V).

Further reading: Lars Engberg-Pedersen, *Endangering Development: Politics, Projects, and Environment in Burkina Faso* (Westport, Conn.: Praeger, 2003); Pierre Englebert, *Burkina Faso: Unsteady Statehood in West Africa* (Boulder, Colo.: Westview Press, 1996).

Burundi Country located in the highlands of east-central Africa. Measuring approximately 10,700 square miles (27,700 sq km) in area, Burundi shares borders with RWANDA to the north, TANZANIA to the east and south, and the Democratic Republic of the CONGO to the west. Lake Tanganyika forms the country's southwest border. Its turbulent history since independence has hindered the development of the high agricultural potential of its rich volcanic soils and has left it one of the world's poorest countries.

Burundi at Independence After the end of World War I (1914–18) Burundi was made part of the Belgian trust territory known as Ruanda-Urundi. In 1961, with Burundi prepared for independence, elections brought the moderate TUTSI Prince Louis Rwagasore (1932–1961) to power as prime minister. The Tutsi-dominated Union for National Progress (Union Pour le Progrès National, UPRONA) became the dominant political party. A hint at Burundi's tumultuous political future came a month later, however, when members of the rival Christian Democratic Party assassinated Rwagasore. In 1962 Mwami, or King, Mwambutsa IV (r. 1915–1966) stepped into the power vacuum created by Rwagasore's death and Burundi became fully independent as a monarchy.

Like that of neighboring Rwanda, the post-independence history of Burundi is very much tied to the relationship between its two major ethnic groups, the HUTU and the Tutsi. Though the struggle between the two groups was largely divided along ethnic lines, the issues at stake were more related to class differences exacerbated during colonial rule. Within their system of indirect rule, Belgian colonial authorities favored the Tutsi minority, placing them in positions of power over Burundi's Hutu majority. The fighting that erupted between the two groups at independence continued into the 21st century.

In 1965 the situation became dire when the elected Hutu prime minister, Pierre Ngendandumwe (1930–1965), was assassinated by Tutsi agents. Despite a Hutu victory in the election that followed Ngendandumwe's murder, the Tutsi king nullified the results and appointed Leopold Biha, a Tutsi, as the new prime minister. This political underhandedness prompted the Hutu to attempt a COUP D'ÉTAT to overthrow Mwambutsa. The attempt failed, leading to brutal reprisals against Hutu military personnel, police, and politicians, many of whom were killed.

Out of the events of 1965, Michel Micombero (1940–1983), a Tutsi, emerged as prime minister. In 1966, when Mwambutsa's son, Ntare V (1947–1972), was overthrown, Micombero became president of the newly proclaimed Republic of Burundi. Under Micombero the violence in Burundi reached unprecedented heights. Hutu uprisings against Micombero in 1972 were met with brutal repression. As many as 200,000 Hutu died in the ensuing rash of violence.

Priests and MISSIONARIES of the Roman Catholic Church were viewed by the Tutsi government as supporting the Hutu. Many members of the religious community were thus driven from Burundi in 1985, as the government attempted to take control of the country's Catholic Church.

1970s and 1980s: Ethnic and Class Violence

The extent of the anti-Hutu violence ultimately upset moderate Tutsis in the government. In 1976 Micombero was ousted in a military coup that brought the Tutsi Lieutenant Colonel Jean-Baptiste Bagaza (1946–) to power as the head of a military council. Bagaza was officially elected to the presidency in 1984, after which he made Buganda a one-party state. In 1987, however, Bagaza was removed from office in a coup led by Major Pierre BUYOYA (1949–).

Buyoya's coup sparked revolts by the Hutu and set off a new wave of mass repression that resulted in an estimated 20,000 more deaths. Buyoya, however, made moves to reconcile the Hutu-Tutsi conflict that had ravaged the country. Ultimately a new constitution was enacted, and multiparty elections were scheduled for 1993. That year Melchior Ndadaye (1953–1993) of the FRONT FOR DEMOCRACY IN BURUNDI (FRODEBU) won the presidency, finally giving power to the Hutu majority.

Ndadaye attempted to form an ethnically balanced government, but he was assassinated in yet another coup attempt, in 1993. This time, retributions were carried out by Hutu, resulting in 150,000 Tutsi casualties. FRODEBU and the Hutu retained power, and Cyprien NTARYAMIRA (1955–1994) became president. Ntaryamira's brief presidency ended with his death in a plane crash that also killed Rwanda's President Juvenal HABYARIMANA (1937–1994), in 1994. The crash, believed to be the result of a missile attack, occurred as the two men were returning from peace talks aimed at ending the Hutu-Tutsi conflict. The two groups continued to attack each other throughout the subsequent presidency of Sylvestre Ntibantunganya (1956–). His term ended in 1996, when Pierre Buyoya again seized power.

Moderately successful peace talks were initiated in 1995 by former Tanzanian president Julius NYERERE (1922–1999) and were continued by the former president of BOTSWANA, Sir Ketumile MASIRE (1925–) following Nyerere's death. In 2000 negotiations led by former South African president Nelson MANDELA (1918–) finally produced an agreement, completed the following year as the Arusha Accords. The accords created a tense peace in Burundi, giving Buyoya an 18-month presidency, to be followed by a similar presidential term for the current

Hutu vice president, Domitien Ndayizeye (1953–). Elections would follow Ndayizeye's term.

See also: BURUNDI (Vols. I, II, III, IV); ETHNIC CONFLICT IN AFRICA (Vol. V); RUANDA-URUNDI (Vol. IV).

Further reading: René Lemarchand, *Burundi: Ethnic Conflict and Genocide* (New York: Cambridge University Press, 1996).

Busia, Kofi (Kofi Abrefa Busia) (1913–1978)
Ghanaian scholar and political leader

Busia, who held a doctorate from Oxford University, began his political career in 1951 as an Ashanti representative to the Gold Coast (now GHANA) Legislative Council. He became the head of the Ghana Congress Party in 1952 and became one of the leaders of the United Party in 1957, following Ghana's independence from Britain. As a member of the United Party, Busia opposed Prime Minister Kwame NKRUMAH (1909–1972), and this opposition forced Busia into exile in 1959.

When he went into exile, Busia taught in the Netherlands and then took up an academic post at Oxford. His reputation as an outstanding intellectual dates from this period. He wrote several important books dealing with issues of African development and democracy, among them, *The Challenge of Africa*; *Purposeful Education for Africa*; and *Africa in Search of Democracy*.

After Nkrumah was overthrown in a COUP D'ÉTAT in 1966, Busia returned to Ghana. There he faced political opposition from Komla Gbedemah (1912–) and the ruling National Liberation Council (NLC). His Ashanti heritage, however, earned Busia the support of the sizeable Ashanti vote, and in 1969 he was elected prime minister as the candidate for the Progress Party (PP), which he had helped form in 1968.

Busia's short term as prime minister was marked most notably by the Alien Compliance Order of 1971, an ill-fated attempt to improve Ghana's economy by forcing as many as a half million immigrant workers, mostly Nigerians, from the country.

Despite its unpopularity, the Alien Compliance Act was sustained through future Ghanaian administrations. Similar policies also appeared in NIGERIA to a more terrible degree, where in the early 1980s hundreds of Ghanaians living in Nigeria were burned alive by those wishing to cleanse Nigeria of "aliens."

What many viewed as Busia's political ineptness, coupled with the declining economy, led to another coup d'état. This one overthrew Busia's government while

Busia was in England for medical treatment. Lieutenant Colonel Ignatius Kutu Acheampong (1931–1979) assumed control of the country, and Busia remained in exile in England. He died there in 1978.

See also: ASHANTI (Vol. II); ASHANTI EMPIRE (Vols. III, IV); BUSIA, KOFI (Vol. IV).

Further reading: Kofi Busia, *The Challenge of Africa* (New York: Praeger, 1962); *Purposeful Education for Africa* (The Hague: Mouton, 1964); and *Africa in Search of Democracy* (London: Routledge and Kegan Paul, 1967).

Buthelezi, Mangosuthu Gatsha (1928–) *Zulu leader*

Buthelezi was born in Mahlabatini, a village in what is now KwaZulu-Natal, SOUTH AFRICA. Of ZULU nobility, he claimed that he descended from such notable Zulu kings as Shaka (1787–1828), Cetshwayo (1826–1884), and Dingane (1795–1840). Buthelezi was raised in a traditional Zulu manner, tending cattle as a herdboy in his youth. He was educated at Adams College and FORT HARE COLLEGE, although he was expelled from the latter for his political activities. While at Fort Hare College Buthelezi joined the Youth League of the AFRICAN NATIONAL CONGRESS (ANC) and became acquainted with future African leaders such as Robert Mangaliso SOBUKWE (1924–1978) and Robert MUGABE (1924–).

Buthelezi spent a couple of years working as a clerk in the Department of Bantu Administration and in a law firm in DURBAN. Then in 1953 he returned to Mahlabatini to become chief of the Buthelezi clan. By 1970 he had risen to chief executive officer of the KwaZulu Territorial Authority, and two years later, he was chief executive councilor of the KwaZulu Legislative Assembly. By the mid-1970s Buthelezi cemented his position as the preeminent Zulu political figure by becoming chief minister of KwaZulu and founding Inkatha yeNkululeko yeSizwe (Freedom of the Nation), later renamed the INKATHA FREEDOM PARTY (IFP).

Both a cultural and a liberation organization, the IFP drew its support predominately from Zulus, particularly in rural areas. As his personal power base grew, Buthelezi's ties with the ANC became strained, and in the mid-1970s he broke from the organization. Because of the complexity of Zulu history, Buthelezi steered an independent course with respect to both the mainstream anti-APARTHEID movement and the white-minority government. In 1982 he successfully defeated the attempt to transfer the Ingwavuma region from KwaZulu Natal to SWAZILAND. The following year he also energetically opposed the government's new constitutional arrangement, which supposedly introduced power sharing with South Africa's Cape coloured and Asian populations.

Unlike most anti-apartheid leaders, Buthelezi opposed the sanctions that were imposed on South Africa by the international community during the 1970s and 1980s. His stance in part allowed many white South Africans to regard him as a moderate, and he therefore had backing in white business circles. Clashes between IFP and ANC supporters frequently turned violent during the 1980s, resulting in considerable loss of life and a significant fragmenting of the black opposition movement. Violence intensified in the years leading up to the first fully democratic elections held in South Africa during 1994.

Nationally, under Buthelezi's leadership, the IFP finished third, with approximately 10 percent of the general vote. Locally, however, the party won political control of KwaZulu/Natal. Buthelezi became minister of home affairs in the new ANC government under President Nelson MANDELA (1918–), and he maintained that position under Mandela's successor, Thabo MBEKI (1942–).

See also: CAPE CAPE COLOURED PEOPLE (Vol. IV); CETSHWAYO (Vol. IV); NATAL (Vol. IV); POLITICAL PARTIES AND ORGANIZATIONS (Vols. IV, V); SHAKA (Vol. IV).

Buyoya, Pierre (1949–) *Two-time president of Burundi*

Born into a modest family of TUTSI ethnic origin, Pierre Buyoya went to school in his home town of Rutovu, BURUNDI, before completing his university degree in social and military science in Belgium. Upon his return to Burundi in 1975, he commenced his military career as a squadron commander, receiving further military training first in France in 1976, and then in Germany from 1980 to 1982. His military rank rose steadily until 1984, when he became Burundi's state commander in charge of military instruction and operations. During this period he also became a member of the central committee of the Union for National Progress party (UPRONA).

Dissatisfied with the direction of Burundi's government, Buyoya styled himself as a reformer and launched a COUP D'ÉTAT on September 3, 1987, overthrowing President Jean Baptiste Bagaza (1946–), who himself had come to power through a coup. Buyoya acted on behalf of the Tutsi-led Military Committee for National Redemption (MCNR), the 30-member military junta that appointed him president a week later. In 1991 the UPRONA central committee replaced the MCNR and reelected Buyoya.

As the desire for democracy increased in Africa during the 1990s, international pressure led Buyoya to hold multiparty elections in June 1993. A HUTU, Melchior Ndadaye (1953–1993), defeated Buyoya, a Tutsi, in what was widely viewed as an ethnically charged election. Ndadaye was assassinated four months later and a succession of Hutu leaders followed. In June 1996 Buyoya launched another coup, this time ousting Sylvestre Ntibantunganya (1956–), to retake the presidency.

See also: ETHNIC CONFLICT IN AFRICA (Vol. V); ETHNICITY AND IDENTITY (Vol. I).

C

Cabinda Angolan province north of the Congo River and separated from the main country by a narrow strip of the Democratic Republic of the CONGO. The Cabinda area was under the domain of the Kongo kingdom before it became a Portuguese protectorate, in 1885. At that time, it was separated from what would become the main part of ANGOLA when the Congo Free State (today's Democratic Republic of the Congo) acquired the land bordering the Congo River. Later, in 1956, Portugal joined Cabinda with Angola.

With the outbreak of the national war for liberation in 1961, Cabindan INDEPENDENCE MOVEMENTS sprang up. In 1963 various movements joined together to fight as the Front of Liberation of the State of Cabinda. In the early 1970s the Spinoza government of Portugal appeared to support independence for Cabinda. This support, however, was an effort to keep the region from becoming part of Angola, which was on the verge of declaring independence from Portugal and would most likely block access to Cabinda's rich NATURAL RESOURCES, which included gold, diamonds, timber, and OIL. However, when the Spinoza government fell in 1974, Angolan forces took the opportunity to occupy Cabinda. By the end of the following year Angola had gained its independence and claimed Cabinda as a province.

Cabinda, which covers about 2,800 square miles (7,252 sq km), has a dense tropical forest cover that produces timber, cacao, coffee, and palm products. However, the exploitation of the province's oil reserves has produced an economic dependence on petroleum products. In fact, oil earnings were essential to financing the fight for Angolan independence and subsequently became a source of contention in the civil war that beset the country shortly after independence. Cabinda's economic significance to Angola stems from the fact that oil accounts for the majority of the country's income coming from foreign sources.

> It has been difficult to calculate Cabinda's population due to its long-term political instability, but estimates have ranged anywhere from 100,000 to 200,000 in the late 1990s. There are perhaps as many as 400,000 more Cabindans who have fled the country because of colonial and Angolan occupations, and many others live in refugee camps.

See also: CIVIL WARS (Vol. V); COLONIALISM, INFLUENCE OF (Vol. IV); CONGO RIVER (Vol. I); KONGO KINGDOM (Vols. II, III); MBUNDU (Vols. II, III); PORTUGAL AND AFRICA (Vols. III, IV, V); PROTECTORATE (Vol. IV).

Further reading: Robin Cohen (ed.), *African Islands and Enclaves* (Beverly Hills, Calif.: Sage Publications, 1983).

Cabral, Amílcar (Amílcar Lopes Cabral)
(1924–1973) *Political leader in Guinea-Bissau and the Cape Verde Islands*

Amílcar Lopes Cabral was a founding member of the AFRICAN PARTY FOR THE INDEPENDENCE OF GUINEA AND CAPE VERDE (Partido Africano da Independência da Guiné e Cabo Verde, PAIGC), a nationalist movement in the Portuguese colonies of GUINEA-BISSAU and the CAPE VERDE

ISLANDS. Initially, he led peaceful protests against Portuguese colonial rule but, when this proved ineffective, Cabral and the PAIGC began a guerrilla war campaign in 1962. By 1969 the PAIGC had won control of more than two-thirds of Guinea-Bissau. The organization's success was based on the military training members received in other countries, as well as Cabral's extensive connections among the rural population, which he had established during his tenure with the Department of Agriculture and Forestry Services. Cabral's knowledge of peasant needs and desires proved essential in mobilizing support for the PAIGC. In addition to liberation efforts, Cabral's organization developed schools and medical facilities, as well as judicial systems and commercial enterprises, all in preparation for independence.

Despite Portugal's superior military, by 1972 Cabral and the PAIGC had essentially defeated the colonialists. In 1973, however, Cabral was assassinated by Portuguese secret police while in CONAKRY, GUINEA. The PAIGC survived the loss of its leader and, in 1973, declared Guinea-Bissau's independence (though Portugal did not acknowledge defeat until the following year). After independence, Cabral's half-brother, Luis Cabral (1931–), became Guinea-Bissau's first president. Cape Verde became independent in 1975.

Amílcar Cabral is also well known for his writings on colonialism, which include *Revolution in Guinea* (1969), *Return to the Sources* (1973), and *Unity and Struggle* (1980).

See also: CABRAL, AMÍLCAR LOPES (Vol. IV); COLONIALISM, INFLUENCE OF (Vol. IV); COLONIAL RULE (Vol. IV); PORTUGAL AND AFRICA (Vols. III, IV, V).

Further reading: Patrick Chabal, *Amílcar Cabral: Revolutionary Leadership and People's War* (New York: Cambridge University Press, 1983).

Cahora Bassa Dam (Cabora Bassa)

The largest dam in southern Africa, located on the Zambezi River in northern MOZAMBIQUE. Begun in the late 1960s the Cahora Bassa Dam project was a joint effort between SOUTH AFRICA and Portugal, which, at the time, still administered Mozambique as a colony. After construction was completed in late 1974, the basin area was flooded, creating a huge reservoir. By the middle of 1975 the level of the reservoir had come to within 40 feet (12 m) of the top of the 558-foot (170-m) concrete dam structure. About the same time, a civil war began in Mozambique—one of the last African countries to achieve independence—and the full potential of the dam's electric generators went unrealized.

Finally, in 1992 peace agreements were signed, and the Portuguese hydroelectric company that controls the dam began repairing the lines and structures that had been destroyed by sabotage during the war. By 1997 the dam was able to produce power at full capacity, and it now produces far more electricity, in excess of 3,000 megawatts, than any other dam in Africa.

Although Portugal owns 80 percent of the Cahora Bassa Dam and Mozambique owns 20 percent, nearly all of the electricity it produces goes to South Africa.

The remote location of Cahora Bassa combined with Mozambican civil war left the reservoir's fish population largely untouched. There was some small-scale fishing, however, and daily catches supplied MARKETS in local lakeside towns, including Songo, which came into existence along with the dam. Since 1992 larger South African commercial fishing companies have begun taking a larger catch from the reservoir, and several fisheries are now operational. Especially plentiful in Cahora Bassa's waters are the sardine-like kapenta and the fierce, razor-toothed tigerfish, which can grow to more than 22 pounds (10 kg). Recently a recreational sportfishing lodge that caters to tourists, mostly South Africans, has begun to operate on the reservoir, and more DEVELOPMENT is planned. It remains to be seen what will be the long-term effects of the increased use of Cahora Bassa's resources.

See also: INFRASTRUCTURE (Vol. V); PORTUGAL AND AFRICA (Vols. III, IV, V); ZAMBEZI RIVER (Vol. I).

Cairo

Capital of EGYPT and largest city in Africa. After the coup in 1952 that brought Gamal Abdel NASSER (1918–1970) to power, Cairo grew so fast that urban planners could not keep up with the city's staggering increase in both physical size and population density. The city sprawled across onto the west bank of the Nile, and new middle-class suburbs sprung up where once only the Giza pyramids had stood. The city also expanded northward.

The city's expansion resulted in high levels of overcrowding, with several families often sharing one living unit. Low-income housing was in short supply, and, since it was easier and cheaper to build up than to find land available to construct a new building, government officials turned a blind eye to the construction of additional floors above existing apartment buildings. Unfortunately, many deaths resulted when these modified buildings collapsed inadequate structural support.

The Nasser government tried to reduce overcrowding by finding foreign money to create new commercial and residential space in the city. Following a foreign policy of non-alignment that Nasser called Positive Neutralism, Egypt was willing to accept aid from the Western nations

Cairo, Egypt—Africa's largest city—straddles the Nile River. Since the 1960s new construction has boomed, and, as this recent photo shows, Cairo is today a thoroughly modern metropolis. © *Corbis*

or the Soviet Union, as long as Egypt could benefit. For example, in 1955 the 614-foot (187-m) Cairo Tower, complete with a revolving restaurant, was built with alleged bribe money from the U.S. Central Intelligence Agency that Nasser, taunting the United States, rechanneled for a public purpose. The massive ASWAN DAM, completed in 1970, was also built with foreign help—this time British and Soviet. This dam helped regulate the flow of the Nile River, on which Cairo is located.

In the 1960s the face of the city changed under the direction of Nasser's Ministry of Construction. A state office tower (headquarters of the Arab League), a Hilton hotel, and a building housing Nasser's Arab Socialist Union were built on the site of the demolished British barracks. The land around the British Embassy, from which British consuls once ran Egypt's affairs, became part of a highway that alleviated traffic congestion. Bridges were built, and the Salah Salem highway was built from Old Cairo to the Cairo airport. In 1970 the Opera House burned down and was replaced with a parking garage.

Upon Nasser's unexpected death in 1970, the government of Anwar as-SADAT (1918–1981) returned construc-

tion to the private sector. Construction boomed, and the return to capitalism created a surge in land speculation, sharply driving up property prices in Cairo. New chains of hotels rose along the Nile. Old villas were torn down and replaced by high-rise apartment buildings, and new shops and international department stores opened their doors. Western forms of advertising appeared everywhere. Cairo became an important center of the entertainment industry, and MUSIC and CINEMA thrived.

However, as the city grew, public services were unable to cope with the additional population. Sewage seeped onto the streets, buses were overloaded, apartments often had no water pressure, and electricians made extra money by unofficially connecting apartments to electric service. Telephone service was sporadic at best. Schools operated on double and triple sessions, and the average class size reached 80 students. Underpaid teachers supplemented their salaries by giving private lessons outside of regular school hours. Government hospitals lacked necessary supplies and equipment.

After Sadat's assassination in 1981, Hosni MUBARAK (1928–   ), the new president, had to deal with the problems that rapid growth had brought to the city. By 1986 the population had reached 8.6 million, and by the end of the decade Cairo had become a megacity (defined as a city with at least 10 million inhabitants), complete with smog and skyscrapers that extended out to the perimeter of the Great Pyramids and the Sphinx. Cairo suffered from overcrowding, collapsing INFRASTRUCTURE, a widening POVERTY gap, unemployment, and health-endangering pollution. Despite a French-built subway system, a million cars clogged the streets.

Mubarak opened the economy by accepting massive transfusions of foreign aid that he applied to Cairo's infrastructure. Under his direction, 45 bridges and roads with viaducts and overpasses were completed between 1982 and 1988. While fewer than half of Cairo's households had running water in 1980, 75 percent were connected to city WATER by 1990. Owners of high-rise buildings were made to install pumps to get the water to their tenants. The percentage of households connected to the official electric grid rose from 33 to 84 percent. However, in 1990 at least a hundred neighborhoods had yet to be connected to the sewer system.

Other changes were made to improve the quality of life. Tree-planting campaigns helped to reverse effects of desertification, and new residential projects were built. Japan built a grand opera house to replace the old one that had burned in 1970, and mainland China contributed the world-class Cairo International Conference Center.

Urban DEVELOPMENT in Egypt was not driven mainly by INDUSTRIALIZATION. Instead, regular agrarian problems caused exoduses from the countryside. Consequently, unemployment has remained very high in Cairo. The government is a major employer, with twice as many jobs existing in the civil sector as in the industrial sector. About one-quarter of Cairenes are officially classified as poor.

See also: CAIRO (Vols. I, II, III, IV).

Further reading: André Raymond, *Cairo* (Cambridge, Mass: Harvard University Press, 2000); Max Rodenbeck, *Cairo: The City Victorious* (New York: Vintage Departures, 1998).

Camara Laye (1928–1980) *Guinean novelist and government minister*

Hailing from the Upper Guinea region of present-day GUINEA, Camara Laye attended a technical school and an arts conservatory in Paris, France. He worked as an auto mechanic in a suburb of Paris before taking up writing in the 1950s, and by the time he and his wife returned to Africa in 1956, he had already solidified his status as a major African writer. His reputation was based on *L'enfant noir* (The dark child, 1953), which drew from warm memories of his Guinea childhood, and *Le regard du roi* (The radiance of the king, 1954), an evocative allegory of the colonial relationship between Europe and Africa.

Camara Laye's family was Camara (sometimes spelled Kamara), a Malinke clan that traces its lineage to the 13th century. The author preferred to invert his family and given names, writing all his novels as Camara Laye.

Camara Laye first went to DAHOMEY (present-day Republic of BENIN) and then onto GHANA, where he taught French. In 1958, when Guinea became independent, Laye was appointed the nation's ambassador to Ghana. He later held other government positions; however, as Guinea's political situation became progressively unstable under president Ahmed Sékou TOURÉ (1922–1984), Laye became a vocal critic of Touré's policies. In 1965 he was forced to leave Guinea for SENEGAL.

Although he continued writing, Laye had a difficult life in exile. Residing with his family in DAKAR, Senegal's capital, he compiled research for a collection of Malinke myths and folktales at the Institut Fondamental du Afrique Noire (IFAN). In 1966 he published *Dramouss* (published two years later in English as *A Dream of Africa*), a continuation of the autobiography he began in *L'enfant noir* that was at the same time a severe critique of Guinea's leadership.

In 1970 Laye's wife, Marie, was arrested when she returned to Guinea to visit her ailing father, and since Laye was left to raise their children without their mother, he took a second wife. (Marie would later divorce Laye after she was released in 1977.) In 1971 Laye began writing *Le Maître de la parole* (The guardian of the word), which would prove to be his final major work. Borrowing heavily from the research that Laye did at IFAN, the book, published in 1978, is a rendering of the great epic of Sundiata, the founder of the ancient Mali Empire.

During the last years of his life, Laye suffered from a kidney ailment that required him to travel to Paris, a trip he could afford only through the contributions of admirers, most prominent of whom was Félix HOUPHÔUET-BOIGNY (1905–1993), the first president of IVORY COAST. Camara Laye died in 1980 in Dakar.

See also: FRANCE AND AFRICA (Vols. III, IV, V); LITERATURE IN COLONIAL AFRICA (Vol. IV); LITERATURE IN MODERN AFRICA (Vol. V).

Further reading: Adele King, *Rereading Camara Laye* (Lincoln, Neb.: University of Nebraska Press, 2003).

Cameroon Southern West African country measuring about 183,600 square miles (475,500 sq km) in size. Cameroon is bordered by NIGERIA to the north and west, CHAD to the northeast, the CENTRAL AFRICAN REPUBLIC to the east, the Republic of the CONGO to the southeast, and GABON to the south. It also has a western coast, measuring about 240 miles (386 km), on the Gulf of Guinea. YAOUNDÉ is the capital.

Cameroon at Independence   Following World War I (1914–18) the German colony of Kamerun was divided into the French Cameroons and the British Cameroons. This remained the case until 1960, when the French Cameroons won its independence. Ahmadou AHIDJO (1924–1989), head of the Cameroon Union (Union Camerounaise, UC) political party, was elected president. Ahidjo immediately began pushing to reunite the British and French Cameroons. However, in 1961 a referendum in the British Cameroons led the northern part of the territory to join with NIGERIA. The southern region elected to join the French Cameroons, and in 1961 the Federal Republic of Cameroon was formed, with the former British and French territories each represented by a prime minister and Ahidjo as president.

Ahidjo and the UC gradually increased their control over Cameroon. In 1972 the country adopted a new constitution forming a union instead of a federation, creating the United Republic of Cameroon. This move resulted in a one-party state dominated entirely by Ahidjo and the UC, which was known as the Cameroon National Union (Union National Camerounaise, UNC) from 1965 to 1985, when it became known as the CAMEROON PEOPLE'S DEMOCRATIC MOVEMENT. Under Ahidjo's heavy hand, civil rights in Cameroon suffered greatly. Ahidjo did initiate agricultural plans, including the 1973 Green Revolution that, along with the discovery of large OIL reserves, helped transform Cameroon's economy into one of the most most stable in Africa. However, along with this relative prosperity came pervasive CORRUPTION in both government and business.

At the end of the 1990s Cameroon was named "the most corrupt country in the world," as determined by Transparency International, a top NON-GOVERN-MENTAL ORGANIZATION dedicated to combating government corruption worldwide.

Ahidjo continued his political dominance until 1982, when, in a surprise move, he resigned from the presidency and turned his full attention to leading the UNC. Ahidjo felt the UNC presidency was a more influential position than the national presidency, but his successor, Prime Minister Paul BIYA (1933–   ), soon proved Ahidjo wrong.

Biya began to remove Ahidjo loyalists from government positions, limiting the former president's power. He also moved toward DEMOCRATIZATION, allowing the press greater freedom of speech and opening elections for the National Assembly and the UNC.

This changed in 1983 when Biya accused Ahidjo of taking part in a failed COUP D'ÉTAT. Ahidjo was forced to resign from the UNC and flee to France. The following year an armed uprising by the country's Republican Guard in Yaoundé threatened to overthrow Biya. One thousand people died before the insurrection was put down. Once again Ahidjo was accused of masterminding the coup attempt, and this time he was sentenced to death in absentia. Ahidjo remained in France until his death in 1989.

Cameroon under Biya   In response to the coup attempts Biya continued his presidency, becoming more and more like his autocratic predecessor. Quick to put down any threat to his power, he won the 1994 and 1998 presidential elections by being the only candidate, a result of his suppression of the opposition. In 1990 Biya allowed for multiparty elections but then stopped short when he felt threatened by burgeoning opposition influence. In July 1991 an extraordinary, nationwide strike named Operation Ghost Town essentially shut down all of Cameroon for nearly five months, all for the purpose of forcing multiparty elections. In November the strike ended with an agreement to release all political prisoners and to allow registered opposition parties. In 1992 Biya won the open elections. The results were widely disputed and violent protests erupted, forcing Biya once again to abandon the multiparty system and declare a state of emergency in order to restore peace. HUMAN RIGHTS groups protested the brutal quelling of the protests, which resulted in many arrests, deaths, and claims of torture.

Beyond internal strife Biya faced a growing economic crisis, especially with the decline of the oil industry in the 1980s. Loans from the International Monetary Fund and attempts at STRUCTURAL ADJUSTMENT failed to produce significant results. Though still relatively strong by post-independence standards, Cameroon's economy has remained too dependent on international MARKETS to support sustained growth.

In 1986 an unusual ecological disaster occurred at Lake Nyos, in northwestern Cameroon. Naturally forming carbon dioxide at the bottom of the lake suddenly burst through the water's surface in a process called a *limnic eruption.* This dispersed a toxic cloud of carbon dioxide that suffocated virtually every human and animal in a 16-mile (25-km) radius. Nearly 2,000 people died. A similar event had occurred two years earlier at nearby Lake Monoun, killing 37 people. Today degassing projects on both lakes are in effect to prevent another catastrophe.

Tension developed in the early 1990s between Cameroon and neighboring Nigeria over the rights to the oil-rich Bakassa Peninsula. By 1996 the hostilities had escalated into a military conflict. In 2002 the International Court of Justice ruled that the territory belonged to Cameroon, but Nigeria has since contested the decision and refused to remove its troops from the peninsula.

At the start of a new century Cameroon is still led by the largely authoritarian Biya and faces rampant corruption and rising crime rates. Plans for an oil pipeline from Cameroon to Chad promise a solid boost for the economy, though environmental groups have strongly denounced the project as ecologically disastrous.

See also: CAMEROON (Vols. I, II, III, IV); DEVELOPMENT (Vol. V); ENVIRONMENTAL ISSUES (Vol. V).

Further reading: Joseph Takougang and Milton Krieger, *African State and Society in the 1990s: Cameroon's Political Crossroads* (Boulder, Colo.: Westview Press, 1998).

Cameroon People's Democratic Movement (Rassemblement Démocratique du Peuple Camerounais, RDPC) Ruling party of CAMEROON since 1960, formerly known as the Cameroon Union (1958–65) and the Cameroon National Union (1965–85). In 1958 Ahmadou AHIDJO (1924–1989) founded the Union Camerounaise (UC), a political party that promoted Cameroon's independence from France. The UC's support mostly came from the Beti ethnic group, Muslims who lived in the northern region. As the country moved closer to independence the UC secured a majority within the country's new legislative assembly and gained the upper hand on its rival, the Cameroon Peoples Union (Union des Populations du Cameroun, UPC). The latter group received most of its support from the Bamileke people of southern Cameroon. In 1960, when Cameroon became an independent republic, the UC assumed control of the government, and Ahidjo became president. Soon after, some southern Bamileke rose up in protest, but the UC put down the insurgency with the help of French military support.

In 1965 Ahidjo was reelected president, and a year later he orchestrated the merger of most of Cameroon's political organizations into one party—the Cameroon National Union (Union Nationale Camerounaise, UNC). A few opposition parties remained, but they were generally dismantled by 1971. In 1972 Cameroon abolished its federal system and established a unitary state, eliminating regional control of governance. Ahidjo remained president through the 1970s, preserving his power by intimidating the opposition and censoring the media. In 1982, however, citing health concerns, Ahidjo suddenly resigned from the presidency. The country's prime minister, Paul BIYA (1933–   ), then became Cameroon's president. Ahidjo remained chairman of the UNC, believing that this position actually afforded him more power than the presidency. He was mistaken, however, and Biya gradually usurped Ahidjo's authority, becoming UNC's chairman in 1983. Biya, in direct opposition to Ahidjo, believed that the state was more important than the party.

In 1985, after a couple of Ahidjo-orchestrated COUP D'ÉTAT attempts, Biya changed the name of the UNC to the Cameroon People's Democratic Union (Rassemblement Démocratique du Peuple Camerounais, RDPC). Abandoning his initial movement toward liberalization, Biya gradually strengthened his control of the government by eliminating the position of prime minister, violently oppressing the opposition, and surrounding himself with allies who shared his Beti ethnic background.

As the 1980s came to a close Cameroon's political and economic situation worsened. By the early 1990s the push for eliminating the single-party state increased, and Biya was eventually forced to allow the return of a multiparty system. The new system did not end the RDPC's political dominance, however. Biya won reelection in 1992 and 1997, and the party retained its control of the National Assembly. After the 1997 elections Biya attempted to make the RDPC more inclusive, forming a coalition with other political parties and appointing people from different regions and ethnic groups to important government positions.

See also: INDEPENDENCE MOVEMENTS (Vol. V); NATIONALISM AND INDEPENDENCE MOVEMENTS (Vol. IV); POLITICAL PARTIES AND ORGANIZATIONS (Vols. IV, V).

Cape Town Modern port city and location of the first European settlement in SOUTH AFRICA, it is also the country's present-day legislative capital. Founded by the Dutch in 1652, Cape Town became part of the British Cape Colony 150 years later. In the late 19th century, with the economic boom associated with the Mineral Revolution, Cape Town became an important transshipment center for goods and people destined for the MINING centers of Kimberley and JOHANNESBURG. Its port is still an important contributor to the economy. Over the past century, however, the industrial sector also has developed significantly, and, today, it includes OIL refining, shipbuilding, diamond cutting, food processing, printing, and cement, fertilizer, and chemical manufacturing. In addition, the post-APARTHEID political climate has encouraged world travelers to visit the city to enjoy Cape Town's vibrant nightlife, arts, spectacular scenery, and outdoor activities.

The population, currently estimated at about 2,733,000 (and at 4 million for the greater metropolitan area), is diverse. The largest single group is Cape Coloured people, who for the most part speak AFRIKAANS. There is also a large segment of the population that is of British and Afrikaner ancestry, a majority of whom also speak Afrikaans. In all more than 60 percent of the Western Cape Province population, of which Cape Town is the provincial capital, speak Afrikaans as their first language. English is second, and third is XHOSA, which reflects the rapidly growing African population of Cape Town. There is also a sizeable population originating from India, some of whom, along with a minority of the Cape Coloured people, are Muslims.

The presence of two of the world's top-rated hotels, the Cape Grace Hotel and the Table Bay Hotel, testify to the post-apartheid significance of Cape Town as an international TOURISM destination as well as its role as an international conference venue.

Between 1948 and the early 1990s the system of apartheid led to a highly segregated urban geography, which in turn created tension and violence among the different population groups. Cape Town's apartheid government instituted a city plan that reserved the comfortable suburbs for whites only and reassigned Africans and, to a somewhat lesser degree, Coloured people and Asians, to rigidly segregated townships far from both the city center and the comfortable white suburbs. This system of discrimination resulted in housing shortages and increased POVERTY for Africans, Cape Coloured people, and Asians alike. As in other parts of South Africa, in Cape Town only whites were exempted from the requirement to carry pass cards labeling each person's race, a practice that promoted almost daily harassment and discrimination at the hands of the mostly Afrikaner police. During the mid- and late 20th century the city was the site of frequent antiapartheid protests, which often ended in violence and a resulting crackdown on the limited freedoms of black residents.

Although organized protest groups, boycotts, and marches were common in Cape Town, the social divisions that apartheid promoted made it difficult to unite the oppressed groups across racial lines, decreasing the

With a metropolitan population exceeding 4 million, Cape Town is the largest city in western South Africa. As this recent photo shows, its ports bustle with commercial activity. © Corbis

chances of forcing changes in the system. Yet, despite the government's efforts to sharply limit the city's African population, the system largely failed to do so. This was mainly due to the growing industrial and commercial sectors, where the need for laborers was so great that employers often were willing to overlook the official race restrictions. As a result the number of Africans in Cape Town continued to grow, increasing from 70,000 in 1960 to 160,000 in 1974. (These are figures for "legal" residents; there was a high influx of "illegal" residents as well, making the actual percentage of African residents much higher.)

The beginning of the end of apartheid in Cape Town was marked by the successful and peaceful march of more than 30,000 people in September 1989. Today the political climate has changed dramatically, and Cape Town is known for its more tolerant social atmosphere. However, there are still housing shortages, which leave poor residents living in shantytowns scattered around the periphery of the city. In addition, crime continues to be a problem, as the decades of active resistance to discriminatory laws have left some residents with little respect for the law.

See also: AFRIKANERS (Vols. IV, V); ASIAN COMMUNITIES (Vols. IV, V); CAPE COLONY (Vols. III, IV); CAPE COLOURED PEOPLE (Vol. IV); CAPE TOWN (Vol. IV); ENGLAND AND AFRICA (Vols. III, IV, V); URBAN LIFE AND CULTURE (Vols. IV, V); URBANIZATION (Vol. IV, V).

Further readings: Zimitri Erasmus, ed., *Coloured by History, Shaped by Place: New Perspectives on Coloured Identities in Cape Town* (Colorado Springs, Colo.: International Academic Publishers, 2001).

Cape Verde, Republic of

Small, impoverished island nation off the coast of West Africa. Cape Verde is an archipelago of 10 islands and five islets located 360 miles (579 km) off the coast of West Africa. With few NATURAL RESOURCES, the islands have historically relied on their strategic position in the Atlantic Ocean to become a trading depot for goods traveling between Africa, Europe, and the Americas. The islands were a colonial possession of Portugal from 1462 until 1975.

Although anticolonial resistance had begun as early as the late 19th century, a sustained, armed insurrection did not emerge until the early 1960s. At that time, Amílcar CABRAL (1924–1973) and the AFRICAN PARTY FOR THE INDEPENDENCE OF GUINEA AND CAPE VERDE (Partido Africano da Independência da Guiné e Cabo Verde, PAIGC) spearheaded the nationalist movement.

Finally, on July 5, 1975, after more than 500 years of colonial control, Cape Verde became independent. The country adopted a republican form of government, with PAIGC leader Aristides Maria PEREIRA (1923–) as president. For a few years the PAIGC continued as a united

political party, but actions related to a 1980 Guinea-Bissau coup led the Cape Verde branch of the organization to split and form the African Party for the Independence of Cape Verde (Partido Africano da Independência de Cabo Verde, PAICV).

> The PAIGC sought to achieve independence jointly for Cape Verde and GUINEA-BISSAU, another West African Portuguese colony that had been historically linked to the islands. However, the two nations declared independence separately.

Its POVERTY notwithstanding, Cape Verde has been a success story of African DEMOCRATIZATION. After devolving into a one-party state under Pereira during the 1980s Cape Verde held its first multiparty elections in 1991. Antonio Macarenhas Monteiro (1944–) led the opposition party, the Movement for Democracy, to electoral victory then, and again in the 1995 elections. However, in 2001 the PAICV returned to power, with Pereira's former prime minister, Pedro PIRES (1934–), becoming the new president.

Economically the country has foundered, due primarily to the long period of Portuguese colonial neglect and lack of DEVELOPMENT. Only 10 percent of Cape Verde's land is arable, and the islands have struggled throughout their history to provide adequate food for their inhabitants. Cape Verde claims the dubious distinction of receiving the highest amount of international aid per capita of any country. Its poverty explains in large part why so many Cape Verdeans live outside the country. In 2000 Cape Verde's population was estimated at 448,000, but there are more than 500,000 people of Cape Verdean origin living in the United States alone, mainly in the New England area. Other significant Cape Verdean communities are found in Portugal and SENEGAL.

Because of its centuries-old role as an Atlantic Ocean trading center, Cape Verde bears the cultural imprint of not only Portugal and West Africa, but of many other regions of the globe. Its MUSIC, which in recent years has become increasingly popular internationally, reflects these cultural crosscurrents. Portuguese is the official language, but Crioulo, a Creole based on Portuguese, is commonly spoken. Roman Catholicism is the dominant RELIGION, although traditional African religions are not uncommon. The majority of Cape Verdeans are of mixed African and European descent.

See also: CAPE VERDE, REPUBLIC OF (Vols. I, II, III, IV); INDEPENDENCE MOVEMENTS (Vol. V); PORTUGAL AND AFRICA (Vols. III, IV, V).

Casablanca group (Casablanca bloc) From 1960 to 1963, a collection of independent African countries united by a desire for the establishment of a continental "United States of Africa." With many African states gaining independence, especially in the early 1960s, several attempts were made to establish pan-African organizations that could operate on a continental scale. One such group met in CASABLANCA, MOROCCO, in December 1960, under the auspices of Morocco's King Mohammed V (1909–1961). Kwame NKRUMAH (1909–1972), the president of GHANA, and Gamal Abdel NASSER (1918–1970), the president of EGYPT, were the de facto leaders of the conference. Other participants included leaders from GUINEA, MALI, Morocco, ALGERIA, and LIBYA, as well as Ghana and Egypt.

The Casablanca group or bloc, as these countries came to be called, advocated an immediate union of the African continent. They felt that broad economic, social, military, and cultural cooperation would be the most effective way to combat the lingering negative effects of Western colonialism.

Before long the group was able to define itself in opposition to the MONROVIA GROUP, a bloc of countries that met the following year in the capital of LIBERIA. At first the Monrovia group, led by Abubakar Tafawa BALEWA (1912–1966) and William TUBMAN (1895–1971), included Liberia, NIGERIA, TOGO, and CAMEROON. In time, however, the group came to include 24 countries. Leaders from the Monrovia group desired the gradual establishment of regional alliances before trying to unite the entire continent in a single federation. The more radical and "progressive" Casablanca group thought of the Monrovia group as "lackeys of imperialism."

The divisions that separated the Casablanca and Monrovia blocs became more acute when the former Belgian Congo (today's Democratic Republic of the CONGO) descended into chaos following its independence in 1961. Ongoing border disputes across the continent also divided the groups along ideological lines.

During the early 1960s each bloc tried to convince newly independent African states to join its alliance. Ultimately, on May 25, 1963, the leaders of what were then Africa's 32 independent states met in ADDIS ABABA, ETHIOPIA. (Under HAILE SELASSIE [1892–1975], Ethiopia was loosely aligned with the Monrovia group.) At the summit the leaders adopted a pan-African unity charter, which was subsequently ratified by the governments of the participating states. Thus, the ORGANIZATION OF AFRICAN UNITY (OAU) was established. Following the founding of the OAU the alignment of countries in the Casablanca group and the Monrovia group was no longer necessary, and the two groups were dissolved.

See also: PAN-AFRICANISM (Vols. IV, V).

cash crops Crops grown specifically to be sold on the market; in contrast, farmers grow FOOD CROPS primarily for domestic household consumption. Farmers use the income from cash crops to purchase goods and services, pay taxes and fees, purchase fertilizer, seeds, farm implements, and so forth. The market is thus a necessary mechanism. For Africa, the market lies primarily outside the continent.

Cash crop production increased tremendously in Africa under colonial rule, as colonial administrators promoted TRADE AND COMMERCE in agricultural commodities and minerals in order to stimulate economic activity. The climate and soils of Africa were well suited for growing tropical and sub-tropical crops such as cocoa, coffee, cotton, groundnuts (peanuts), palm oil, rubber, and tea. Because of the increasing demand for these products in Europe and North America, colonial administrations encouraged and promoted their production primarily for export. Individual colonies usually specialized in growing only one or two crops and thus developed mono-crop economies.

As a consequence of colonial practices, African countries, upon becoming independent, inherited export-oriented economies. Needing the income generated from export earnings for their economic DEVELOPMENT, the newly independent governments continued to promote cash crops over food crops when planning agricultural policies. Furthermore, the international community encouraged this trend in terms of the advice and ECONOMIC ASSISTANCE they offered African countries. The WORLD BANK played a particularly important role in this regard. In 1981, for example, its influential and controversial *Accelerated Development in Sub-Saharan Africa: An Agenda for Action* (commonly known as the Berg Report after its author Eliot Berg), emphasized continuing export-oriented AGRICULTURE over seeking food self-sufficiency. This emphasis also served to highlight the fact that cash-crop production takes land away from the production of food crops. This became an even more important issue in the face of Africa's rapid POPULATION GROWTH.

The IVORY COAST provides a useful case study for the limitations of an economy based on cash-crop agriculture. Under the leadership of President Félix HOUPHOUËT-BOIGNY (1905–1993), who was himself a coffee planter, the country had one of the world's highest rates of economic growth in the 1970s and 1980s. This expansion was largely the result of an aggressive expansion of the commercial agriculture sector. During this period Ivory

Coast displaced neighboring GHANA as the world's leading cocoa producer. It also became the world's third-leading coffee producer, behind Brazil and Colombia. Nearly 70 percent of the population was engaged in agriculture, with 2.5 million people engaged in coffee production alone.

Despite being perceived as a major "success story," the Ivory Coast economy was being determined by forces that were largely beyond its control. The consumption of its two major EXPORTS, cocoa and coffee, depended largely on the tastes of Western consumers. Also, with growing demand, new producers entered the coffee market, and others expanded their production. This worldwide expansion in coffee production in turn enabled the four multinationals (Nestlé, Kraft, Sara Lee, and Proctor & Gamble) that control the coffee market to cut producer prices, which plunged to their lowest point in 30 years. Ivorian cocoa production fared better than coffee, with the country's more than 900,000 cocoa farmers producing more than 40 percent of the world's total. However they, too, faced fluctuating prices. In 1977 the price of cocoa exceeded $3,000 per ton. In the early 1990s the figure sank to one-third that amount. By 2003 the price had recovered and settled at greater than $1,500 per ton.

Coffee, which was first domesticated as a crop in ETHIOPIA, is that country's principal export crop. Although Ethiopia exported only about 2.6 percent of the world total, between 1988 and 1999 coffee accounted on average for 56.7 percent of its total exports. A sharp plunge in world coffee prices since 1997 created an enormous crisis for the one million Ethiopia coffee growers as well as for the country's overall economy. When producer coffee prices were high, many farmers planted coffee on land formerly dedicated to food production. Now they no longer earn enough from the sale of their coffee to cover their production costs, let alone meet their other income needs, including money to purchase food.

Falling coffee and cocoa prices, combined with population growth, led to a general economic decline in Ivory Coast. The per-capita gross national product (the value of goods and services provided by an individual on an annual basis) declined from US $727 in 1996, to $669 in 2003. This drop-off led to a decline in demand for agricultural LABOR, much of which was supplied by low-wage workers from Ivory Coast's neighbor, BURKINA FASO. A major cause of the country's current political crisis is the large-scale unemployment and bitter competition for jobs in the agricultural sector that have resulted from the

steady decline in cash-crop prices. There has also been an ecological dimension to cash-crop agriculture. The steady expansion of land under production for cocoa and coffee, along with the export of tropical hardwoods, has resulted in the destruction of large areas of tropical rainforest.

Cotton was the preeminent cash crop of the colonial era, with colonial governments in every part of the continent encouraging and, in some instances, compelling its production. This is why 23 of the world's 68 cotton-producing countries are in Africa. In contrast to cocoa and coffee, African cotton production is not as significant on a global scale. In 2003, for example, African countries produced a mere 6 percent of the world total. However, that year African cotton made up nearly 20 percent of the world total of cotton export sales. This disparity between production numbers and export earnings reflects the comparative lack of INDUSTRIALIZATION in Africa. While all the major producers export some of their cotton, they also turn much of their raw cotton into domestically produced, finished textiles.

EGYPT was long the continent's leading cotton grower, producing in the range of 551,150 tons (500,000 metric tons) during the 1960s. Its cotton production was of the high-value, long staple variety. The area planted in cotton, however, began to decline after the mid-1960s. As a result, by the end of the century, land dedicated to cotton cultivation was only about 40 percent of what it was during the earlier era. Yields, on the other hand, increased, so that the total production was about 60 percent of the 1960s level. Egypt today produces about 40 percent of the world's long staple cotton. Cotton thus remains an important cash crop for the estimated one-third of the Egyptian population engaged in agriculture. However, in contrast to most African countries, local textile manufacturers utilize some of the cotton to produce domestic cotton goods.

Cotton producers in Mali and other West African countries can produce cotton at about half the cost per bale as North American producers. However, the United States, the European Union, and China have paid steadily increasing subsidies to their cotton growers, who in turn have expanded their production. This led to a glut on the world market and a sharp decline in prices. African cotton growers sell their product for less than it costs to produce it.

In recent years MALI has surpassed Egypt as Africa's leading cotton producer, and in 2003, it ranked ninth in the world in overall production. While cotton was an important colonial crop for Mali, production has grown tremendously over the past two decades, up some 300 percent from previous levels. Today more than 200,000 farm households, which constitute about 30 percent of the country's population, are engaged in producing cotton, virtually all of which is exported. Cotton is Mali's principal export, making Mali—one of the world's poorest countries—highly vulnerable to changes in the world cotton markets. From the mid-1980s through the late 1990s, cotton prices were steadily climbing. They plunged in 2000–01, however, falling to a 30-year low. Mali's farm families found their incomes halved, and the government export earnings similarly dropped.

See also: CASH CROPS (Vol. IV); COCOA (Vol. IV); COFFEE (Vols. II, IV); COLONIALISM, INFLUENCE OF (Vol. IV); COLONIAL RULE (Vol. IV); COTTON (Vols. I, II, III, IV); GROUNDNUTS (Vol. IV); MONO-CROP ECONOMIES (Vol. IV); PALM OIL (Vols. III, IV).

CCM   See REVOLUTIONARY PARTY OF TANZANIA.

Central African Customs and Economic Union (Union Douaniere et Economique de L'Afrique Centrale, UDEAC)   Regional economic community among the central African states that was created by the Brazzaville Treaty in 1964. Its founding members included CAMEROON, GABON, the CENTRAL AFRICAN REPUBLIC (CAR), the Republic of the CONGO, CHAD, and EQUATORIAL GUINEA. UDEAC was founded with the purpose of fostering the economic integration of former French Equatorial Africa plus the former Spanish colony of Equatorial Guinea. The goal was to create a broad market and to coordinate sectors such as TOURISM, TRANSPORTATION, TELECOMMUNICATIONS, and DEVELOPMENT among member states. As an economic union, the organization also sought common policy in areas such as AGRICULTURE, industry, and investment. The central currency for UDEAC has always been the CFA Franc, which facilitates the free transfer of capital.

Governed by a Head of States Council, UDEAC joined another, broader economic community in 1983. This organization, called the Economic Community of Central African States (ECCAS), added ANGOLA, BURUNDI, the Democratic Republic of the CONGO, RWANDA and SÃO TOMÉ AND PRÍNCIPE to the original six UDEAC members. The leaders hoped that a more inclusive body would lead to greater regional INDUSTRIALIZATION as well as reducing their dependence on France. The ECCAS began operations in 1985 but it has remained largely inactive since the early 1990s. At the beginning of 21st century, ongoing CIVIL WARS in the two Congos, Rwanda, and Burundi—along with the associated economic disruption and increase in the amount of REFUGEES—dashed the region's hopes for economic progress.

See also: FRANCE AND AFRICA (Vols. III, IV, V); FRENCH EQUATORIAL AFRICA (Vol. IV).

Further reading: Patrick Manning, *Francophone sub-Saharan Africa, 1880–1995,* 2nd ed. (New York: Cambridge University Press, 1998).

Central African Republic (CAR)   Country in the heart of Africa measuring about 240,300 square miles (622,400 sq km). It is bordered by (clockwise from north to west) CHAD, the Republic of the SUDAN, the Democratic Republic of the CONGO, the Republic of the CONGO, and CAMEROON. The capital is BANGUI. Independence brought great political turmoil and oppressive autocratic rule to the Central African Republic.

The Central African Republic at Independence In 1958 the former French colony of Oubangui-Chari won autonomy within the French Community, becoming the Central African Republic (CAR). The country was headed by Barthélémy Boganda (1910–1959), a leading nationalist and founder of the Socialist Evolution Movement of Black Africa (Mouvement d'Evolution Sociale en Afrique Noire, MESAN). Boganda served as the country's prime minister until the ratification of a national constitution in 1959, at which point he became president. Boganda's presidency was cut short, however, when he died in a plane crash that same year. In 1960 the CAR became fully independent, with Boganda's cousin, David DACKO (1930–   ), as president.

In 1962 MESAN became the only legal political party in the CAR as Dacko tried to secure his power. He won the next presidential elections two years later by default, as he had no opponents. Dacko's second term as president began with the collapse of the economy. As financial disaster loomed, opposition to Dacko grew, and in 1966 the military's commander-in-chief, Jean-Bedel BOKASSA (1921-1996), overthrew Dacko in a COUP D'ÉTAT. Moving quickly and decisively, Bokassa abolished both the constitution and the National Assembly and assumed complete control. This began a 13-year reign of terror during which Bokassa used excessive violence and brutality to maintain power. In 1976 he declared himself Emperor Bokassa I and changed the country's name to the Central African Empire.

Unstable and egotistical to the extreme, Bokassa drove the CAR into economic devastation, as he sold the country's mineral rights for his own personal enrichment. In addition to his own iron-fisted repression of any and all opposition to his rule, Bokassa was further supported by France, which wanted to maintain interests in the country's diamond and uranium mines. By 1979, however, Bokassa's regime became untenable, and in September of that year French forces captured the capital while Bokassa was in LIBYA. David Dacko was reinstated as president.

In 1981, after continuous strikes and outbreaks of violence, General André Kolingba (1935–) overthrew Dacko. The authoritarian military government that followed lasted until 1985, when Kolingba installed a new civilian government. The unrest and violence continued, and in 1991 Kolingba instituted a series of new constitutions that led to gradual DEMOCRATIZATION. Multiparty elections held in 1993 brought Ange-Felix PATASSÉ (1937–) to the presidency.

By this time years of economic neglect had nearly bankrupted the nation. Patassé faced great unrest as government workers and military personnel demanded their salaries, which had gone unpaid for months. In 1996-97 a series of military-led coup attempts in Bangui were quelled by French troops. The destruction and looting that occurred during these uprisings further damaged the CAR's economy.

Following the attempted coups in 1996–97, special police forces in Bangui formed the Squad for the Repression of Banditry. Anyone unfortunate enough to be arrested by the squad often faced torture and a quick execution, sometimes without trial.

In 1997 Patassé gathered opposition groups to sign the Bangui Accords in an attempt at reconciliation. The accords had little effect, however, as violence continued. Late that year French troops were replaced by United Nations' peacekeepers, who remained in the CAR until 2000.

In 2003 General François Bozizé (1946–) assumed the presidency of the troubled country, ousting Patassé in a coup while the president was at a meeting in Niger. The years of political turmoil and instability have led the government into ever deeper debt. Furthermore, political CORRUPTION has imposed an even greater burden on the economy, as high government officials have lined their own pockets from the illegal exploitation of NATURAL RESOURCES rather than developing them for the national good.

See also: CENTRAL AFRICAN REPUBLIC (Vols. I, II, III, IV); FRANCE AND AFRICA (Vols. III, IV, V); UNITED NATIONS AND AFRICA (Vols. IV, V).

Chad Country of north-central Africa, bordered by LIBYA to the north, the Republic of the SUDAN to the east, the CENTRAL AFRICAN REPUBLIC and CAMEROON to the south, and NIGERIA and NIGER to the west. Approximately 496,000 square miles (1,284,600 sq km) in size, Chad straddles the Sahel, with its north a desert and its south a tropical region. Its capital is NDJAMENA.

Chad at Independence In 1959 Chad appeared to be headed toward independence under Gabriel Lissette (1919–2001), leader of the Chadian Progressive Party (Parti Progressiste Tchadien, PPT). However, regional tensions undermined Lissette's coalition government, made up of both northern Muslims and southern black African Christians. During the instability LABOR UNION leader François-Ngarta TOMBALBAYE (1918–1975) stepped in to assume control of the PPT. Just prior to Chad's independence in 1960, Tombalbaye solidified his power by revoking Lissette's citizenship while he was abroad and denying him reentry into the country. Under Tombalbaye the PPT became a southern party, and in 1960 it became independent Chad's dominant political entity. Tombalbaye became the country's first president.

Immediately establishing an autocracy, Tombalbaye initiated a regime that exacerbated Chad's ethnic and regional tensions and eventually led the country into civil war. In 1962 he banned all political parties save the PPT and imprisoned real and perceived political opponents. A campaign of Africanization replaced a majority of French government officials with untrained and inexperienced African counterparts, and CORRUPTION began to pervade the government. High taxes led to increasingly hostile protests.

Unconcerned with Chad's northern population, Tombalbaye gradually alienated a large portion of the country. Muslim riots that erupted in N'Djamena in 1963 were brutally repressed. In 1965 anti-tax riots broke out and rapidly spread. Rebel groups began to form in northern Chad, among the more prominent being the National Liberation Front of Chad (Front de Libération Nationale du Tchad, FROLINAT), founded in 1966. The country descended into a civil war that threatened to overwhelm Tombalbaye's government forces. This division between a Muslim north and non-Muslim south fit into a pattern of CIVIL WARS such as those that also occurred in Nigeria and the Sudan. The president was forced to call in French troops to secure a peace.

The French pressured Tombalbaye into reforming his government. Tombalbaye took a number of conciliatory measures, releasing hundreds of political prisoners and including more Muslim and northern representatives in the government.

However, in 1971 Tombalbaye used a supposed Libyan-sponsored coup attempt to revert to his authoritarian ways. Over the next four years Tombalbaye managed to alienate both the south and the military, and his government fell apart. In 1975 a military uprising killed Tombalbaye and put the government in the hands of Colonel Felix Malloum (1932–).

Ongoing Conflict Malloum headed a Supreme Military Council (Conseil Supérieur Militaire, CSM), which did little to improve the beleaguered country. Faced with the burgeoning power of a number of liberation armies, including FROLINAT and the Armed Forces of the North

(Forces Armeés du Nord, FAN), led by Hissène HABRÉ (1942–), the CSM attempted to negotiate an alliance, installing Habré as prime minister under President Malloum in 1978. The alliance collapsed a year later, however, and Habré's rival, Goukouni Oueddei (1944–), led his Libyan-supported rebel troops to seize N'Djamena and overthrow Malloum.

A series of conferences attempted to resolve the political confusion and rampant violence to little avail. Finally, in 1979, the Lagos Accord was signed, establishing a transitional government. Goukouni became president, and Habré became minister of defense. The agreement quickly disintegrated in the face of Goukouni's and Habré's rivalry, however, and the resulting conflict drew in Libyan troops and forced Habré into exile in the Sudan.

In 1981 Chad and Libya moved toward possible unification, though this was met with great opposition. Conflict between the two countries eventually nullified this possibility, and Libyan troops left Chad at the end of 1981. This opened the door for Habré and FAN to launch a new incursion into Chad. By 1982 FAN had captured the capital and ousted Goukouni.

Under Habré war continued to be the status quo for Chad. Highly autocratic and faced with armed resistance to his government, Habré was exacting in his repression of all who opposed him. Ultimately, after eight years of conflict during which about 40,000 Chadians were killed, Habré was driven from power by the Patriotic Salvation Movement, led by one of Habré's former military leaders, Idriss DÉBY (1952–). In 1991 Déby became president.

Chad under Déby With Déby as president, Chad finally made some moves toward DEMOCRATIZATION. Multiple political parties were allowed in 1991, and in 1996 Déby won the country's first elections. Déby also made efforts to include opposition members in the government.

However, Chad still faces both political and economic crises. The country remains highly militarized, with an oversized army whose oppressive power and ethnic skew towards Déby's Zaghawa people is indicative of Chad's overall problems with violence and ethnic and regional strife. The north and the south remain polarized, and rebel groups still pose threats to stability despite Déby's attempts at negotiation. Meanwhile, Chad's economy has been thoroughly devastated by years of warfare. The country remains among the most impoverished in Africa. The promise of a lucrative, WORLD BANK-funded OIL pipeline from southern Chad to Cameroon, initiated in 2000, offers hope for a massive boost to Chad's economy. Despite assurances from the government, however, only time will tell if the money is used for DEVELOPMENT of INFRASTRUCTURE and not the continued prosecution of warfare. Déby's use of $4 million from the initial oil profits to buy advanced weaponry was not a promising sign.

See also: CHAD (Vols. I, II, III, IV); FRANCE AND AFRICA (Vols. III, IV, V).

Further reading: Mario J. Azevedo and Emmanuel U. Nnadozie, *Chad: A Nation in Search of its Future* (Boulder, Colo: Westview Press, 1997); J. Millard Burr and Robert O. Collins. *Africa's Thirty Years War: Libya, Chad, and the Sudan, 1963–1993* (Boulder, Colo.: Westview Press, 1999).

Chama Cha Mapinduzi See PARTY OF THE REVOLUTIONARY

Chikamoneka, Julia (Mary Nsofwa Mulenga Lombwe, Mama Julia Chikamoneka, Mama UNIP) (1904–1986) *Zambian anticolonial activist*

Mary Nsofwa Mulenga Lombwe was born in Kasama, in the northern part of Northern Rhodesia (present-day ZAMBIA). She was the daughter of Mutale Mpungwa and Mulenga Lombe, the son of Chief Chitimukulu-Ponde of the Bemba ethnic group. In 1936 she was baptized in the Catholic Church and given the name Julia. She later took on the name Chikamoneka (meaning "victory will be seen") for her fearless attitude in Northern Rhodesia's independence struggle.

After working as a housemaid for high-ranking white people, in 1951 she decided to go into business for herself, starting a restaurant in Kabwata, LUSAKA. It was at this time that she got into politics, attending rallies, planning protest marches, and organizing boycotts of shops that discriminated based on race. Chikamoneka had no formal education, but that did not prevent her from being a leader in the independence struggle. She was known for her effective fundraising in addition to leading protest marches. She also provided food and shelter for soldiers fighting the Zambian independence war and risked arrest by opening her house for political meetings.

During the independence process in the early 1960s the colonial government and the UNITED NATIONAL INDEPENDENCE PARTY (UNIP), Northern Rhodesia's leading nationalist group, could not reach a settlement regarding a new constitution. Britain sent colonial secretary Ian Macleod to Lusaka to discuss the impasse. When Macleod arrived at the airport, he was shocked and embarrassed to be surrounded by women led by Chikamoneka, with bared breasts and loin cloths around their waists, weeping and demanding immediate independence. Traditionally, this was the strongest way of expressing anger. The white press, however, uncomprehendingly referred to her as the "mad African girl."

Throughout the early 1960s Chikamoneka and other leaders of the independence movement organized marches to disrupt functions held by the colonialists and urged them to grant independence to Africans. Ultimately, at the end of this period known as Cha-Cha-Cha, the colonialists gave in to the people's demands.

Affectionately called "Mama UNIP" for her contributions to the party that led Zambia to independence, Chikamoneka inspired all women to join in the struggle. Her contribution was publicly acknowledged, in 1969, when President Kenneth KAUNDA (1924–) bestowed her with the Order of Distinguished Service. When she died in 1986 she was accorded a state funeral and buried with full military honors.

See also: INDEPENDENCE MOVEMENTS (Vol. IV, V); WOMEN IN INDEPENDENT AFRICA (Vol. V).

Further reading: Mbuyu Nalumango and Monde Sifuniso, eds., *Woman Power in Politics* (Lusaka, Zambia: Zambia Women Writer's Association, 1998).

Chiluba, Frederick (Frederick Jacob Titus Chiluba) (1943–) *Zambia's president from 1991 to 2001*

Chiluba went to school at Kawambwa Secondary School in northern ZAMBIA but was suspended for student activities. He later completed his education via correspondence. He worked as a personnel clerk and accounts assistant at Atlas Copco, an industrial corporation working in the Copperbelt region. There he joined the National Union of Building, Engineering, and General Workers. He gradually rose through the ranks of the organization, eventually becoming chairman. Chiluba gained even greater recognition in the 1970s, when, as leader of the Zambia Congress of Trade Unions, he effectively negotiated for large increases in salaries for the general workers in Zambia.

In the early 1990s Chiluba was one of the founding members of the MOVEMENT FOR MULTIPARTY DEMOCRACY (MMD), an opposition group that accused President Kenneth KAUNDA (1924–) of CORRUPTION and ineffectiveness. Kaunda and his ruling party, the UNITED NATIONAL INDEPENDENCE PARTY (UNIP), had controlled Zambia since independence in 1964. In the 1991 elections Chiluba led the MMD to victory over UNIP. As the chairperson of the organization, Chiluba then replaced Kaunda as Zambia's president. In 1996 he was reelected to a second five-year term. In 2001 Chiluba attempted to change the constitution so that he could run for a third term but failed and stepped down. Chiluba was replaced by his former vice president, Levy MWANAWASA (1948–).

During his second term, Chiluba promised to revamp the economy and encourage foreign investments. He privatized a number of state-owned companies, leaving many people unemployed. At the end of the Chiluba presidency, Zambia was among the world's poorest countries. His administration was charged with corruption, abuse of office, and embezzling public funds. Chiluba became the first African statesman to be taken to court after leaving office. The Zambian Parliament voted to lift his immunity, and he is presently being tried for misappropriating and embezzling millions of dollars in public funds.

It is not clear where Chiluba was born. He claimed he was born in Zambia on April 30, 1943, to parents Jacob Titus Chiluba Nkonde and Diana Kaimba. However, his birthplace and parentage were subjects of controversy when Chiluba ran for the second term of office in 1996. Some publications and candidates claimed he was born in the Democratic Republic of the CONGO. If proven true, that claim would have disqualified Chiluba from standing for Zambia's presidency.

See also: COPPERBELT (Vol. IV).

Chimurenga

Shona word meaning *fight* or *struggle*. It came to signify a struggle for political and social rights and was applied by Africans trying to liberate themselves from British colonial rule in Southern Rhodesia (today's ZIMBABWE). The first Chimurenga, or Chimurenga Chekutanga, was fought on and off during 1896–97 by Shona and Ndebele forces rebelling against the colonial British South Africa Company, administered by Cecil Rhodes (1853–1902). The British won convincingly, executing a number of rebel leaders, including the Shona prophetess, Mbuya Nehanda (d. 1898).

Nearly 100 years later, the second Chimurenga, or Chimurenga Chechipiri, erupted in 1966. It was largely a guerrilla war, led by the ZIMBABWE AFRICAN NATIONAL UNION (ZANU) and the ZIMBABWE AFRICAN PEOPLE'S UNION (ZAPU). The rebels, aided by other independent African nations as well as China and the Soviet Union, won independence in 1979, forming the state of Zimbabwe in 1980.

Today Chimurenga lives on as a musical genre. Thomas Mapfumo (1945–) coined the term *Chimurenga music* as a way of describing his politically motivated, revolutionary MUSIC that combined traditional mbira music with electric guitars, drums, and horns. Influenced by artists as diverse as Miriam MAKEBA (1932–), Hugh MASEKELA (1931–), Frank Sinatra (1915–1998), and Elvis Presley (1935–1977), Mapfumo was exceedingly popular in Southern Rhodesia during the second

Chimurenga. His popularity and outspoken lyrics led to imprisonment in 1977 by the white-settler government of RHODESIA. Known as the "Lion of Zimbabwe," Mapfumo continues to tour with his band, Blacks Unlimited, producing music with contemporary sociopolitical messages.

See also: BRITISH SOUTH AFRICA COMPANY (Vol. IV); INDEPENDENCE MOVEMENTS (Vol. V); NATIONALISM AND INDEPENDENCE MOVEMENTS (Vol. IV); RHODES, CECIL JOHN (Vol. IV); SHONA (Vol. I); SHONA KINGDOMS (Vol. III); SOUTHERN RHODESIA (Vol. IV).

China and Africa Long positioning itself as an alternative to either Soviet or United States influences, China has built a reputation in Africa as a beneficent donor even while it has used these relationships to buoy its own international standing. From the 17th to the 19th centuries European countries brought Chinese laborers to Africa believing that they were better workers. They were subject to treacherous conditions that reverberated in Sino-British and Sino-French relations. As countries gained their independence, China was eager to help shape their polities, conspiring with revolutionaries in ZAÏRE (present-day Democratic Republic of the CONGO), KENYA, and BURUNDI.

China's foray into postcolonial Africa was born out of the Bandung Conference. Held in Indonesia in 1955, this conference was the first Asian-African summit of its kind, leading to the establishment of diplomatic relations between China and African countries. The next year EGYPT was the first African country to establish diplomatic relations with China; the number increased steadily until today some 45 African countries have such ties. In the midst of the Cold War between the United States and the Soviet Union, China resolved to recognize new African countries as being independent of Soviet or Western influence. This often meant that China established ties with any fledgling government, regardless of its regime type.

At the same time China saw itself as having suffered from European expansionism and thus suggested that it was offering an alternative path to DEVELOPMENT. The LABOR-intensive models it adopted in the 1960s were viewed by many African leaders as taking place in a climate free of significant aid conditionalities or political commitments. China shifted from revolutionary support to supporting the PAN-AFRICANISM of Kwame Nkrumah (1909–1972) and even the new government of MOBUTU SESE SEKO (1930–1997), in Zaïre. In offering ECONOMIC ASSISTANCE for little in return, China was also promoting one of its largest geopolitical goals: to have the large group of emerging countries—all with votes in the United Nations—recognize China as holding sovereign control over its "renegade province" of Taiwan.

China invested significantly in such countries as GUINEA, SIERRA LEONE, The GAMBIA, and MADAGASCAR. Its greatest African partner was TANZANIA. Tanzanian president Julius NYERERE (1922–1999) sought the social equity of socialism but wished to eschew a Cold War alignment with the Soviet Union. He invited Chinese labor to work on INFRASTRUCTURE development and, through his UJAMAA policies, grew a communal farming model based on the Chinese collective farming model. China thus focused its aid on turnkey projects. It would send workers by the thousands to build projects in their entirety before giving them over to the Tanzanians. In this way China gained a reputation for letting countries do what they want. Unfortunately, ujamaa policies failed and the collective village model in Tanzania collapsed. The myriad projects built by Chinese workers rapidly fell into decay. The poorest of society, whom Nyerere hoped to protect from an emerging class of African capitalists, were instead oppressed by economic stagnation.

By 1978 Chinese foreign policy began to change, espousing economic modernization programs. It continued to provide an alternative to the Cold War-entrenched Soviet Union and United States, in fact increasing its levels of investment in reaction to its failures. By the early 1980s there were some 150,000 Chinese technicians in Africa working on more than 500 projects.

The pervasive belief was that there was a choice between the communism of the East and the capitalism of the West. It was in fact just the opposite. China's largesse in Africa had as much to do with its differences with the Soviet Union as with its differences with the United States. In the mid-1980s there was a Sino-Soviet rapprochement and relations improved. The Cold War began to thaw and China was inwardly focused on its own reforms. These reforms, promulgated by Deng Xiaoping (1905–1997), were based on maximizing markets. Africa was not seen as a priority market region compared to Western economic monoliths. As a result, Chinese aid declined. But with the geopolitical shifts of 1989 China saw a critical moment in which it must garner sympathy and support. The Chinese crackdown in Tiananmen Square, on June 4, 1989, certainly had an impact. Global accusations of HUMAN RIGHTS abuse rapidly made China a pariah. It began courting favor through increased foreign aid. Whereas in 1988 Chinese aid commitments were $60.4 million to 13 African countries, by 1992 it leapt to $345 million in 44 African countries.

The increase in aid in the 1990s also reflected China's shifting needs for influence in the world sphere. Under Chinese tutelage, many African leaders came to link increasing Western aid conditions requiring human rights to be respected to an effort to undermine China's growth into a new superpower. As such, they increasingly challenged U.S. notions with barely cloaked accusations that the United States sought to undermine African attempts at development through the regulatory process. China continued to project an image as the one benefactor with few demands, while seeking to expand its influence outside of East Asia.

For their part, African leaders accepted this image of Chinese beneficence. Strong-armed leaders such as Daniel arap MOI (1924–) of KENYA and Robert MUGABE (1924–) of ZIMBABWE feared the threat to their position from pressures to democratize. There was concurrent rising resentment in Africa toward what many in the post-Cold War climate saw as neocolonial influence in domestic affairs. Further, new Chinese aid was carefully tied to its post-reform trade policies. China thus opened trade ties with African countries. By 1995 African trade only accounted for 1.4 percent of Beijing's total trade. But trade rose 431 percent between 1989 and 1997, to the great benefit of African economies.

Today China continues to expand its market-oriented approach to African aid. As if to contrast the conditions of trade in the U.S. African Growth and Opportunity Act, it has granted duty-free market access to many commodities coming from African countries without mandates. Instead of focusing on the turnkey projects of the past, aid is focused on training and human resources development to expand trade.

To date SOUTH AFRICA has been the greatest benefactor of China's foreign aid shift. Between 50,000 and 100,000 Chinese live in South Africa. There are also large industrial corporations providing FOREIGN INVESTMENT. As these Sino-African relations expand other countries in sub-Saharan Africa hope to benefit from the increased financial interaction.

See also: BANDUNG AFRO-ASIAN CONFERENCE (Vol. IV); CHINA AND AFRICA (Vol. IV); COLD WAR AND AFRICA (Vols. IV, V); COMMUNISM AND SOCIALISM (Vol. V); SOVIET UNION AND AFRICA (Vols. IV, V); UNITED STATES AND AFRICA (Vols. IV, V).

Further reading: Goran Hyden and Rwekaza Mukandala, eds., *Agencies in Foreign Aid: Comparing China, Sweden, and the United States in Tanzania* (New York: St. Martin's Press, 1999); Deborah Brautigam, *Chinese Aid and African Development: Exporting the Green Revolution* (New York: St. Martin's Press, 1998).

Chissano, Joaquím Alberto (1939–) *President of Mozambique*

The son of a Methodist minister, Joachim Alberto Chissano was born in the southern Gaza province of MOZAMBIQUE. Despite a childhood in relative POVERTY, he finished primary and secondary school and furthered his education in MEDICINE in Portugal. Chissano eventually dropped his medical studies, went to France, and returned to Mozambique to become a leader in the country's struggle for liberation.

> The fact that Chissano received any education was in itself quite remarkable in Mozambique under Portuguese colonial rule. As of the mid-1950s, for example, official statistics showed only some 26,000 African students enrolled in primary schools for the colony as a whole.

Chissano was instrumental in the armed resistance against Portuguese rule. He was one of the founding members of the MOZAMBICAN LIBERATION FRONT (Frente de Libertação de Mozambique, FRELIMO), becoming a member of the organization's central executive committee in 1963. Chissano headed educational training for the party and later became its secretary under Eduardo MONDLANE (1920–1969), FRELIMO's first leader.

When Mozambique's liberation war ended in 1974 Chissano became the prime minister in the transitional government. In 1975 he became the country's first foreign minister under President Samora MACHEL (1933–1986). In November of 1986, following the untimely death of Machel, Chissano was elected president of Mozambique. Working slowly toward democracy Chissano continued Machel's policies of openness toward the West. His government put an official end to Mozambique's Marxist-Leninist political programs and adopted a more moderate form of socialism. In light of a worldwide wave of DEMOCRATIZATION in 1990, Chissano's government introduced a multiparty democracy.

Chissano is described as a quiet and spiritual man, and he is especially known for his abilities in behind-the-scenes negotiations. His leadership skills were instrumental in ending the civil war between his FRELIMO forces and the rebel MOZAMBICAN NATIONAL RESISTANCE (Resistencia Nacional Mocambicana, RENAMO), which sought control of Mozambique. To bring about peace he sought the support of the Church and the government of neighboring MALAWI, which had been supporting the RENAMO rebels, eventually bringing all parties to the table for negotiations. Chissano's leadership—along with the help of the United Nations—brought an end to the civil war (1992–94) and paved the way for elections in 1994. Numerous cease-fire violations delayed the process, but the country remained largely at peace under Chissano's leadership.

Due to his country's importance in southern Africa, Chissano became a major figure in regional organizations such as the SOUTHERN AFRICA DEVELOPMENT COMMUNITY and the Common Market for Eastern and Southern Africa.

See also: COMMUNISM AND SOCIALISM (Vol. V); INDEPENDENCE MOVEMENTS (Vol. V); NATIONALISM AND INDEPENDENCE MOVEMENTS (Vol. IV); PORTUGAL AND AFRICA (Vols. III, IV, V).

Chona, Mathias (Mathias Mainza Chona)
(1930–2001) *Zambia's first prime minister*

The son of a local chief, Mathias Chona was born at Nampeyo, Monze, in the southern region of Northern Rhodesia (modern-day ZAMBIA). As a youth, he attended a Catholic mission school before going to LUSAKA for secondary school. He then studied law at Gray's Inn, London, where he was called to the bar in 1958, becoming the first Zambian to qualify as a lawyer.

Upon his return home he became active in Northern Rhodesia's struggle for independence. In 1959 Chona joined Kenneth KAUNDA (1924–) and others in leaving the Northern Rhodesia African National Congress, which was led by Harry Mwaanga NKUMBULA (1916–1983), to form the Zambia African National Congress (ZANC). However, the British colonial government banned the ZANC later that year and imprisoned Kaunda. Chona maintained the organization and ideology of the ZANC by forming the UNITED NATIONAL INDEPENDENCE PARTY (UNIP), but he made it clear that the party's presidency was Kaunda's upon his release from jail. Chona was briefly UNIP's deputy president, but for the most part he served as its national secretary both before and after the country's independence. Chona later held other government positions, including minister of justice and ambassador to the United States.

Chona became Zambia's vice president in 1972 and chaired the commission that drew up the constitutional amendment bill that made Zambia a one-party state. Using his position as vice president, he later steered the passage of the act through the National Assembly.

In the legislative debate leading up to enactment of the One-Party State Act, Chona summed up the justification for the legislation. According to him, it was a very simple bill, but a historic one. "The bill is designed to introduce national unity in the country," Chona said, "so that all our people are assured of a peaceful and happy future."

Although he always appeared jovial and entertaining, with an engaging manner of speech, Chona was a shrewd politician. He continued to assume important political positions, becoming the country's first prime minister in 1973. His last government posts were as ambassador to France and later China. In 1991, however, when Zambia reverted to multiparty politics and the MOVEMENT FOR MULTIPARTY DEMOCRACY assumed power, Chona was forced to resign his ambassadorship. He remained loyal to UNIP and to his political ideals up until his death, frequently appearing in court to argue constitutional issues.

See also: INDEPENDENCE MOVEMENTS (Vol. IV); NATIONALISM AND INDEPENDENCE MOVEMENTS (Vol. V); NORTHERN RHODESIA (Vol. IV); POLITICAL PARTIES AND ORGANIZATIONS (Vols. IV, V).

Further reading: Eugenia W. Herbert, *Twilight on the Zambezi: Late Colonialism in Central Africa* (New York: Palgrave Macmillan, 2002).

Christianity, influence of
During the 20th century Catholic and Protestant MISSIONARIES brought their specific forms of Christianity to the peoples of Africa, changing the religious lives of many indigenous Africans. At the same time the religions they spread were, in turn, changed by Africans to reflect indigenous beliefs.

The World Church Many of independent Africa's new political leaders received their education from mission schools. Because of these affiliations many missionaries were secure in their leadership positions under the new governments. Autonomy was largely the result of exterior funding. As fledgling governments struggled with the challenges of single-party states, authoritarian leaders, and civil rights abuses, the church remained steadfast, providing social services in the areas of education and healthcare. The Church preached the values of democratic ideals, such as freedom of speech and the rights to free association and assembly. In southern Africa it supported liberation theology.

The influence of Christianity has manifested itself in both positive and negative ways throughout Africa. In TANZANIA, for example, Julius NYERERE (1922–1999) developed an African socialism that had some success blending typically Christian values and indigenous communalism. In GHANA, Kwame NKRUMAH (1909–1972) was hailed as the "deliverer," a word equated with God in the local Methodist church.

In NIGERIA, however, an increasingly polarized population of Christians and Muslims descended into catastrophic conflict regarding the adoption of a state RELIGION. In UGANDA, Idi AMIN (c. 1925–2003), a Kwaku Muslim, persecuted that country's Christian population. Since 1955 the Muslim-dominated northern region of the Republic of the SUDAN has been embroiled in a civil war against the southern regions, which are approximately 27 percent Christian. (Practitioners of African traditional religions, also persecuted by the northerners, make up 70 percent of the southern population.) In 1983 the Muslim-dominated government officially made the Sudan a Muslim state, thereby intensifying the war.

White Catholic and Protestant missionaries brought Christianity to Africa, preaching their own understanding of the gospel and its place in the particular African culture to which they were assigned. In ETHIOPIA, where the state religion is the ETHIOPIAN ORTHODOX CHURCH, Roman Catholic and Protestant missionaries eventually gained a toe-hold and proliferated. It was difficult for the missionaries to separate their own cultural orientations from their instruction and even harder for them to understand the African culture in which they lived. Because many missionaries believed theirs was a "civilizing" mission, they generally did not promote independence, and the changes brought about by independence made many churches rethink their capital and human investments in Africa. Large numbers of white missionaries were recalled, with Africans stepping into their places. In 1968 the Roman Catholic Vatican Council II approved the translation of the liturgy into vernacular languages. By promoting African male leadership in both preaching and teaching positions, the Church accelerated the development of African clergy. In 1970 the Church appointed its second black bishop from west-central Africa. (The first had been Henrique from the Kongo kingdom, in the 16th century.)

At the same time, however, the Church diminished much of its ritual character, which contained the elements

Following his ordination in 1962, the Reverend Raphael S. Ndingi, the first Catholic priest from the Kamba ethnic group of Kenya, blessed his mother. His father observed the ceremony. *© British Information Services*

that spoke most directly to African worshipers. Some issues that were culturally foreign, such as monogamy and the celibacy of the clergy, also presented challenges to the African Church. Further, in light of the obvious wealth of the European Church, clergy questioned the validity of the scriptural demand for poverty. Other problem issues included the rejection of women as officiants, especially since it was most often they who filled the pews.

In IVORY COAST, where a mere one-tenth of the population was Catholic, Félix HOUPHOUËT-BOIGNY (1905–1993) built Basilique de Notre Dame de la Paix, a cathedral with a seating capacity of 300,000. Opened in 1990 by Pope John Paul II, the cathedral was modeled on St. Peter's Basilica in Rome.

Some countries nationalized their mission schools after independence, and both the Catholic and Protestant churches lost important links in their ability to indoctrinate new indigenous leadership. In recent decades world churches are in decline in Africa, having lost financial support and much of their personnel.

African Independent Churches As national independence spread, it brought with it the development of fully African Christian churches, tended to by African administrators and clergy and attended by black members. African Independent Churches, also known as African Initiated Churches (AICs), included both Ethiopian Independent churches and Zionist Independent Churches. These churches were led by charismatic leaders who claimed to have direct communication with God and who saw themselves as Christian reformers. Taking into consideration indigenous beliefs and values, they emphasized the parishioner's direct communication with God through prayers, dreams, and possession by the Holy Spirit. Generally they also allowed women to play a more active role in church leadership. However, some independent governments have not been tolerant of the AICs. In ZAMBIA, for example, The Lumpa Church, founded in 1955 by Alice LENSHINA (1924–1978), came into conflict with the UNITED NATIONAL INDEPENDENCE PARTY led by Kenneth KAUNDA (1924–). Many of the Lumpa members went into self-imposed exile. Alice and her husband died in detention, and her church was burned.

Where prophetic movements such as Lenshina's emerged, Africans saw religion as a way to combat the injustices visited upon them by white settlers and colonial governments. Elements of a prophetic movement could be identified in the speeches and sermons of Bishop Desmond TUTU (1931–), a Nobel laureate and one of the most prominent anti-APARTHEID crusaders in SOUTH AFRICA.

Membership in Pentecostal churches has risen since the 1970s. Many evangelical AIC groups converted Christians and others to the Gospel of Prosperity, which teaches that God gives material rewards to, and promises economic miracles for, those who give to the church.

See also: CHRISTIANITY (Vols. I, II); CHRISTIANITY, INFLUENCE OF (Vol. IV); PROPHETS AND PROPHETIC MOVEMENTS (Vol. IV, V).

Further reading: James L. Cox and Gerrie ter Haar, eds., *Uniquely African?: African Christian Identity from Cultural and Historical Perspectives* (Trenton, N.J.: Africa World Press, 2003); Elizabeth Isichei, *A History of Christianity in Africa: From Antiquity to the Present* (Grand Rapids, Mich.: W. B. Eerdmans Pub. Co., 1995); Isaac Phiri, *Proclaiming Political Pluralism: Churches and Political Transitions in Africa* (Westport, Conn.: Praeger, 2001); Bengt Sundkler and Christopher Steed, *A History of the Church in Africa* (New York: Cambridge University Press, 2000).

cinema In the years since independence, African filmmakers have focused on establishing a cinematic tradition that leaves behind Eurocentric approaches to film. In their efforts, they have produced films recognized by international audiences. However, in broad terms, Africa has yet to develop a viable film industry to rival those on other continents.

> Worldwide analysis of African films tends to perpetuate the "outsider" perspective of African cinema. By focusing too much on either content or the educational value, critics fail to acknowledge that African films are infused with culturally relevant aesthetic elements. This Eurocentric or neocolonialist attitude is evident in the way critics lump together films by the language spoken in them—English, French, Portuguese, or Arabic—regardless of the nation of origin or cultural tradition from which the film comes.

Cinema in West Africa After independence, GHANA and NIGERIA attempted to incorporate film into their cultural policy. In 1957 President Kwame NKRUMAH (1909–1972) of Ghana nationalized his country's film production and distribution. However, because previous colonial policy reserved the most important filmmaking positions for whites, Ghana's film industry had to import foreign directors to make its educational and dramatic feature films. In 1969 the Ghanaian government appointed Sam Aryeetey (1927–) director of the Ghana Film Corporation. A 1949 graduate of the Accra Film Training School, Aryeetey sought foreign distribution for Ghanaian films. Although this brought broader awareness of Ghana's film industry, it also limited it by turning over some control to outsiders.

At independence Nigeria was one of the few African countries with both a television industry and established movie theaters. Segun Olusola, the director of the Nigerian television network, produced teleplays by European and African authors. Together with Lebanese business partners, Olusola founded Fedfilms Limited to produce Nigerian films. The Nigerian filmmaker Francis Oladele founded Calpenny Limited, a production company financed by investors from the United States. Regarded as Nigeria's preeminent filmmaker, Oladele has produced movie adaptations of works by Wole SOYINKA (1934–) and Chinua ACHEBE (1930–). Nigeria's most prolific director is Ola Balogun (1945–), who has produced at least one film per year since 1977.

While film production in Nigeria is done largely by Nigerians, film distribution remains in the hands of foreigners. This, along with poor funding and state censorship, has hurt the development of Nigerian cinema. Also, the popularity and availability of television retards the growth of the industry by reducing receipts at the box office.

Cinema in Southern Africa In APARTHEID-era South Africa, AFRIKANERS continued producing films subsidized by the Afrikaner-dominated government. These films often attempted to legitimize white minority rule in SOUTH AFRICA and neighboring RHODESIA (today's ZIMBABWE). Although some anti-apartheid films were produced in South Africa, most outsider productions were banned from the country. Films made by whites for a black audience tended to be patronizing and exploitative. However, even these films maintained a degree of cultural authenticity to hold the attention of viewers.

In 1976 Gibson Kente (1932–) wrote *How Long (must we suffer)*, a protest play that became the first black-financed and black-directed feature film to criticize apartheid. Apartheid censors misunderstood the multilingual script of a later film, *Mapantsula* (1988), and allowed the production of that anti-apartheid film. In the 1980s anti-apartheid films were also produced in neighboring countries. *A Dry White Season* (1989), for example, was produced in Zimbabwe. Two of the more successful anti-apartheid films are *Sarafina* (1993), by Anant Singh, a South African of Indian descent, and the remake of Alan Paton's *Cry the Beloved Country* (1995).

Today, South Africa's business structure, including filmmaking and distribution, is fully integrated into the global economy. With the collapse of apartheid and the strict film censorship that was part of that system, South African audiences now eagerly consume foreign films, especially those from the United States. Indeed, the country is among the top 10 international markets for Hollywood films. South Africa also acts as the central distribution point for films—and other products—throughout southern Africa.

Filmmaking in the Congo In post-independence Democratic Republic of the CONGO (known from 1971 to 1997 as ZAÏRE), there was a conspicuous absence of Congolese film directors. Despite having a film and photo bureau, the Zaïrian government did not create a national cinema. Instead, it was left to a private group, Saint-Paul Audiovisual Editions (EPA), to replace the Catholic MISSIONARIES who had produced educational films during the colonial period. Since 1975 the EPA has financed and distributed religious programming produced and directed by Congolese. The government of MOBUTU SESE SEKO (1930–1997) authorized a National Film Center to tax foreign films and use the money to promote Zaïre's national cinema.

Cinema in the Former French Colonies After independence, the French Minister of Coopération provided both financial and technical support for the film industry in post-independence nations. As a result, Coopération became the biggest film producer of African cinema. In 1962 France created the Consortium Audiovisuel International (CAI) to help the newly independent African states develop communications. Film was then used as a tool for educating illiterate citizens. Each year between 1961 and 1975, more than 400 newsreels and documentaries were made, with partial production taking place in the African capitals and post-production in Paris.

In 1963 Coopération established the Bureau du Cinema to provide funding to help independent African filmmakers. For some films, the Coopération took on the role as film producer, providing the director with financial and technical support. For others, it waited for the African producer to make the film and then paid for the cost of production in return for the rights to film distribution.

In 1979 the French government of Valéry Giscard d'Estang (1926–) stopped funding African films because some African heads of state were concerned that the political nature of the films being produced could lead to unrest. In 1980 François Mitterrand (1916–1996) inaugurated a new policy of sending aid to an inter-African organization, Organization Commune Africaine et Mauritienne (OCAM). By promoting the inter-African organization, France de-emphasized aid to independent directors. Instead, it made more funds and equipment available to OCAM-sponsored film schools, such as the Institute Africain d'Education Cinematographique in OUAGADOUGOU, the capital of BURKINA FASO.

In addition to promoting African films in educational and film festival venues, Coopération began distributing them to commercial cinemas and airing them

on French television. Now 80 percent of all African films are produced and directed by Africans in the former French colonies.

Africa's best known filmmakers include OUSMANE SEMBÈNE (1923–) and Safi FAYE (1943–), from SENEGAL; Oumarou Ganda (1932–1981), from NIGER; Dikongue Pipa (1940–), from CAMEROON; Med Hondo (1936–), from MAURITANIA; and Souleymane Cissé (1940–), from MALI. They have won awards at African film festivals in Ouagadougou and Carthage, as well as at the prestigious European festivals at Cannes, Paris, Rome, and Moscow.

Cinema in North Africa In post-independence North Africa, the film industry has become a powerful cultural force for the Arabic-speaking world. During the colonial era people in the MAGHRIB region of North Africa—ALGERIA, TUNISIA, and MOROCCO—watched foreign films censored by the French authorities. Since independence, however, the region has developed its own strong film industry that produces a wide range of films in both Arabic and French. Such films have garnered international praise, but they still face stiff competition from foreign films in their home markets.

Algeria's film industry developed during its war of independence from France. Within a few years of independence in 1962, the country's film industry was a modernized, state-owned monopoly, although it has since been privatized. Since the 1990s political turmoil and civil unrest has caused the Algerian film industry to collapse due to lack of stability and lack of funding. Also, the marketing of Arabic-language Algerian films to the Middle East has become problematic. Since the Algerian form of vernacular Arabic is sometimes considered slang, conservative Arabic-speaking countries do not want to promote what they see as an impure form of the language.

Since 1976 the Egyptian film industry, which advertises itself as the "Hollywood of the Middle East," has sponsored the influential Cairo International Film festival.

In the present day African film is suffering from the gradual loss of both foreign and domestic funding for production. There were few African-owned and operated film processing laboratories, editing facilities, and film distribution companies. Consequently, artists in ANGOLA, KENYA, NAMIBIA, and many other African countries have no opportunity to express themselves through film.

See also: CINEMA (Vol. IV); ENGLAND AND AFRICA (Vols. IV, V); FRANCE AND AFRICA (Vols. IV, V).

Further reading: Françoise Pfaff, *Twenty-five Black African Filmmakers: A Critical Study, with Filmography and Bio-bibliography* (New York: Greenwood Press, 1988); Françoise Pfaff, *The Cinema of Ousmane Sembène, a Pioneer of African Film* (Westport, Conn.: Greenwood Press, 1994); Nancy J. Schmidt, *Sub-Saharan African Films and Filmmakers: An Annotated Bibliography.* (London: Hans Zell, 1988); Keyan G. Tomaselli, *The Cinema of Apartheid: Race and Class in South African Films* (New York: Smyrna/Lakeview Press, 1988); Nwachukwu Frank Ukadike, *Black African Cinema* (Berkeley, Calif.: University of California Press, 1994).

civil society Groups of citizens voluntarily organized into large social constituencies. An effective civil society at once challenges the state while deepening its ability to serve the needs and desires of its people.

Civil society marks the border at which the state and societal spheres meet. The concept of "the state," although commonly used interchangeably with "the government," is actually a political community defined by its population and territorial boundaries. The state alone retains the legitimate right to use force. Society, on the other hand, is the sum of the interactions and associations of people who live within a particular state. Where a government is a democracy, leaders of the state are supposed to be accountable to the people. One mechanism for establishing that accountability is through elections. Yet elections alone don't make a democracy. Additional mechanisms are needed to allow the people to communicate their needs and desires to their leadership, and to hold them accountable. This is where civil society becomes important.

In a functioning, democratic civil society, church groups, LABOR UNIONS, student associations, and the like bring people together into a collective voice. Where this voice is loud, leaders must listen and respond or face electoral difficulties and social upheaval. In fact, new leaders often come from the ranks of powerful civil society groups.

Political scholars and historians disagree on what, exactly, defines civil society and its relationship with the state. An analysis of the differences shows that there are two broad schools of thought. The first one sees civil society as a bulwark against the state. According to this liberal view, a society of individuals uses the organs of civil society to protect itself from the excesses of a state and to ensure that state leaders do not become dictators. The second school of thought sees the role of civil society as inextricably intertwined with the state. This latter view holds that the respective functions of civil society and the state overlap, compete with, and complement each another.

Some scholars argue that the history of colonialism in Africa proves that the second concept of civil society is more valid. With the histories of Europe and Africa so deeply intertwined, they argue, the institutions must also be intertwined. However, the first view is probably more prevalent today. A civil society that becomes *too* intertwined with the state will be unable to build the trust necessary to protect democracy. It is easier to encourage fledgling democracies with an active, independent civil society. Thus, all people who desire democracy at both the national and international level have a stake in investing in a strong civil society.

Only with an independent civil society in place is it possible to protect against the excessive power mongering that has characterized the regimes of such leaders as MOBUTU SESE SEKO (1930–1997) of the Democratic Republic of the CONGO (what was then called ZAÏRE), Charles TAYLOR (1948–) of LIBERIA, and Jean-Bédel BOKASSA (1921–1996) of the CENTRAL AFRICAN REPUBLIC. With their authority unchecked, these men dominated all facets of the state. In UGANDA, on the other hand, a relatively strong civil society is often credited with protecting the Ugandan people against the potential profiteering of President Yoweri MUSEVENI (1944–). Museveni made Uganda a one-party state, but most of the country's civil society organizations are NON-GOVERNMENT ORGANIZATIONS that receive foreign funding. Therefore, although they are not very strong voices in government, their ability to be heard has increasingly forced Museveni to open up roles for them in the policy process. In this way they play important roles in such activities as overseeing the transparency of elections as well as in the planning of economic policy to overcome POVERTY in rural areas.

In addition to helping democracy protect against excessive state power, civil society also helps develop a middle class that can exercise political influence while providing a proving ground for new leaders. While widespread poverty in many African countries limits the voluntarism necessary for civic associations to flourish, large African organizations do require effective leaders with administrative skills and an ability to function in political spheres. Perhaps the greatest example of this in Africa is Nelson MANDELA (1918–), the former president of SOUTH AFRICA. Mandela was elected to the National Executive Committee of the AFRICAN NATIONAL CONGRESS (ANC) in 1950. At that time the ANC was a young civic organization struggling against the severe racist laws of the nation's APARTHEID government. Mandela soon became deputy president of the ANC and used his authority to fight for legal rights and fairer LABOR policies for blacks. He also voiced the objections of South Africa's non-white citizens regarding relocations in the western provinces as well as the government's unfair BANTU EDUCATION schemes. Mandela also helped write the Freedom Charter.

In 1961 at the All-in African Conference in Pietermaritzburg, he gave a speech in favor of democracy that the nation—and the world—still hasn't forgotten. Arrested soon thereafter, Mandela was imprisoned until

1990. In 1991 he became ANC president and, later, president of the new South Africa and winner of the Nobel Peace Prize. Mandela is now an icon for democratic change the world over.

Unfortunately, civil society is not always so positive. Some critics argue that it is a "neocolonial" perpetuation of Western ideals poorly situated in an African context. Others point out that associations often take on tasks they are ill-prepared to perform, creating crises of governance. In the worst cases, these critics argue, the goals of a civic association might be inconsistent with those of a democratic polity. A terrorist organization, for instance, could claim to be part of civil society.

In some cases, the associations that make up civil society have proven to be poor proving grounds for leaders. For example, Frederick CHILUBA (1943–) of ZAMBIA rose to the presidency in 1991, pushing the former president, Kenneth KAUNDA (1924–), from office. As Chiluba rose through the ranks of the labor unions, both Zambians and the West hailed him as one of Africa's great new democrats. As a labor leader he regularly cited scripture, winning him a hero's status among the Zambian church groups in civil society.

A prodigal son of Zambia's new leadership class, Chiluba challenged Kaunda's state and, for a time, seemed to be the exception for those concerned that Africa lacked strong ties between political parties and civic organizations. Yet, when he rose to the presidency, he soon became enamored with centralized policies. He created a de jure one-party state and perpetuated the inefficient political norms that had brought about the end of his predecessor. Chiluba was criticized by HUMAN RIGHTS organizations as CORRUPTION in Zambia rose to new levels. By the end of the 1990s he had lost the support of key civil society groups, such as the Catholic Commission for Justice and Peace. After being thrown out of office following the 2001 elections, Chiluba was brought up on no less than 150 different criminal charges.

Civil society remains an elusive concept with controversial applications. Yet, the other option is a state left unchecked by its citizenry, free to assert power in excess as has been done in so many African autocracies. Democracy by election can bring about a measure of accountability, but an active, engaged civil society is still necessary to ensure rule by the people.

See also: DEMOCRATIZATION (Vol. V), POLITICAL PARTIES (Vol. V), POLITICAL SYSTEMS (Vol. V).

Further reading: John L Comaroff and Jean Comaroff, *Civil Society and the Political Imagination in Africa: Critical Perspectives* (Chicago: University of Chicago

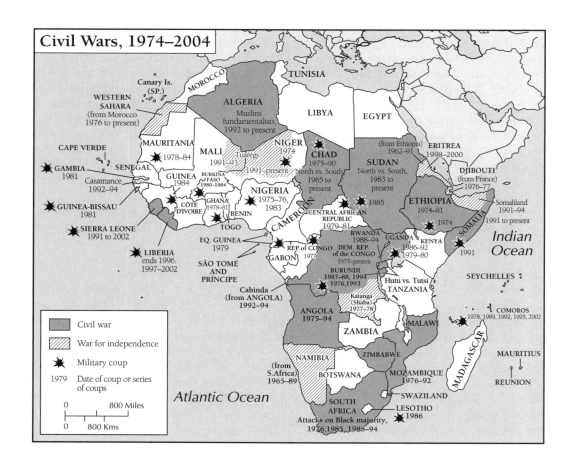

Press, 1999); Nelson Kasfir, *Civil Society and the State in Africa* (Portland, Ore., Frank Cass Publishers, 1998); Stephen Ndegwa, *The Two Faces of Civil Society: NGOs and Politics in Africa* (West Hartford, Conn.: Kumarian Press, 1996); Naomi Chazan, John Harbeson, and Donald Rothchild, *Civil Society and the State in Africa* (Boulder, Colo.: Lynne Rienner Publishers, 1994); Jean-Francois Bayart, *The State in Africa: the Politics of the Belly* (New York: Longman, 1993); Adam B. Seligman. *The Idea of Civil Society* (New York: The Free Press/Maxwell Macmillan, 1992); Robert Fatton, *Predatory Rule: State and Civil Society in Africa* (Boulder, Colo.: Lynne Rienner Publishers, 1992).

civil wars Conflicts that take place within the borders of a state or community. Civil wars are reasons for great concern in Africa, since recent ones have increased in complexity and grown in scope, frequency, and level of violence. In Africa civil wars often involve several countries and hold multiple root causes. At the beginning of the post-independence period a great number of African countries were embroiled in open conflict. By the mid-1960s combatants in ANGOLA and the Congo region, for example, were fighting regional wars as part of a greater struggle for independence from colonial rule. These local conflicts became more complex when the United States, the former Soviet Union, and their allies began assuming support roles in order to protect their own Cold War interests. Civil war in MOZAMBIQUE—which, like Angola, was a Portuguese colony—was largely a result of threats to the regional strategic interests of SOUTH AFRICA, which at the time was seeking to defend APARTHEID both domestically and internationally.

By the end of the 1990s the Cold War was over and South Africa's government had made the transition to majority rule, but civil strife still raged throughout Africa. Eventually, local conflicts merged into three large regional conflagrations that involved a quarter of the continent's countries. One zone of conflict included the Horn of Africa, ETHIOPIA, ERITREA, and the Republic of the SUDAN. A second zone involved the Democratic Republic of the CONGO, the Republic of the CONGO, ZIMBABWE, and Angola. And a third zone included the West African countries of SENEGAL, SIERRA LEONE, GUINEA, and LIBERIA.

One of the factors that separates African nations from countries in other parts of the world is the crisis of the so-called soft state. Where states are weak, it is possible for groups or individuals to challenge the supremacy of its leadership through military engagement. Greed and CORRUPTION are often cited as reasons for individuals to launch such a challenge.

The control of a region's mines, oilfields, FORESTS, or other valuable NATURAL RESOURCES can be another cause of civil wars. Countries such as Angola, Liberia, Sierra Leone, and the Democratic Republic of the Congo are rich in dia-

Liberation movements sometimes fought against each other as well as against the colonial armies in Portuguese territories. In 1972, these FRELIMO soldiers underwent weapons training during the civil war in Mozambique. © *United Nations/N. Basom*

monds and other minerals. Since these natural resources are considered part of a state's wealth, the control of the state brings with it the ability to profit from the resources.

A number of 20th-century African leaders have been accused of starting civil wars for their own personal enrichment. These include Jonas SAVIMBI of Angola, Foday SANKOH of Sierra Leone, Charles TAYLOR of Liberia, Laurent KABILA of the Democratic Republic of the Congo, Paul KAGAME of RWANDA, and Alfonso Dhlakama of Mozambique.

Generally, the cause most often cited as the reason for the increase in civil wars in Africa is religious, ethnic, or racial identity. For example, the war begun in the Republic of the Sudan in the 1950s had its roots in religious and territorial conflicts dating to the 19th century. At that time Mahdist forces imposed Islam on the population in the mostly Christian and animist southern parts of the country. An estimated 2 million people have died in Sudan's civil war, which continues today amid charges of "ethnic cleansing" and even genocide. From the 1960s into the 1990s CHAD, too, went through similar conflicts. The civil war begun in ALGERIA in 1992 is often attributed to the rise of extremist Muslims who disagree with the country's historically secular mode of governance.

While identity is a key part to each of these conflicts, looking at civil war solely as a clash of identities obscures the larger issues. For example, the 1994 civil war in Rwanda certainly was the result of a longstanding ethnic conflict between HUTU and TUTSI groups. However, it also involved political and economic disagreements that are not directly associated with ethnic differences.

See also: COLD WAR AND AFRICA (Vols. IV, V); ETHNICITY AND ETHNIC CONFLICT IN AFRICA (Vol. V); ISLAM, INFLUENCE OF (Vols. IV, V); MINERALS AND METALS (Vols. IV, V); SOVIET UNION AND AFRICA (Vols. IV, V); UNITED STATES AND AFRICA (Vols. IV, V).

Further reading: Stephen Ellis, *The Mask of Anarchy: The Destruction of Liberia and the Religious Dimension of an African Civil War* (New York: New York University Press, 2001); Donald L. Horowitz, *The Deadly Ethnic Riot* (Berkeley, Calif.: University of California Press, 2003).

coastal and marine ecosystems Biological communities in areas where land and sea meet. In Africa these important environmental zones and their resources are threatened on a number of fronts. Coastal ecosystems are found in all coastal areas where land and sea come together. Rich in BIODIVERSITY, these areas make up only 8 percent of the world's surface. Yet 26 percent of the earth's biodiversity is contained in their tide pools, floodplains, marshes, tide-flats, beaches, dunes, and coral reefs.

In all, nearly 25,000 miles (40,234 km) of Africa's coast falls into the category of coastal and marine ecosystems. In countries such as GUINEA-BISSAU, the coastal system is the most complex of all of its environments, supporting hundreds of plant and animal species found nowhere else in the world. Similarly, the coastal regions of SÃO TOMÉ AND PRINCIPÉ are home to 26 unique bird species.

Coastal and marine ecosystems are as important to Africa's economies as they are to the continent's ecology, however. Fishing is particularly critical in this regard. In MAURITIUS, for example, fishing accounts for 36,000 jobs and 10 percent of the gross domestic product. It also ac-counts for one of the country's fastest-growing export economies, with large amounts of fish currently being sent to the European Union.

Mangrove trees are a key element of Africa's coastal ecosystems. With roots that stick out from the mud and water in order to take in oxygen, these trees are unusually well adapted to survival in both salt and fresh water. Home to many plants and animals, they also play an important role in local AGRICULTURE by helping to stabilize riverbanks and coastlines.

International TOURISM is another area in which coastal systems contribute to national economies. Approximately 10,000 tourists visit the SEYCHELLES islands each year to enjoy the beautiful beaches and snorkel along their spectacular coral reefs. This makes tourism the largest sector of the Seychelles economy, employing one-third of the country's 80,000 people. With both fishing and tourism becoming increasingly important each year, coastal systems have come to play a major role even in larger economies, such as those of GHANA, SOUTH AFRICA, IVORY COAST, and TANZANIA.

These valuable coastal areas are under dramatic threat, however. The coast of Guinea-Bissau, for example, like that of so many other countries, has been significantly degraded by pollution from URBANIZATION and industry. ATMOSPHERIC CHANGE plays a part in this as well, for as climates change, sea levels rise and more and more pressure on is put on the coastal zones. As a result erosion increases, populations are displaced, and freshwater resources are contaminated. In addition, WATER temperatures increase, changing the nature of the habitat and making it no longer suitable for many species, both plant and animal.

Other threats come from economic and social forces. In the Seychelles, for instance, the commercial FISHING industry has been expanding so rapidly that many areas are being over-fished. This reduces not only the number of fish and fish species but also decreases the number of birds that eat the fish. But attempts to limit the catch have led to illegal fishing, which, on islands such as Cousine and Aride, has become the major threat to the economy.

Other nations share this ecological crisis. Both COMOROS and MADAGASCAR have quadrupled their fish catch in the past 20 years; Mauritius and NAMIBIA have tripled theirs; MOROCCO has doubled its fish catch over that same period. Even in East Africa, where fishing is not nearly as productive as in other parts of the continent, fishing remains the single greatest threat to coral reefs and the coastal ecosystem.

In the Seychelles the threat to sea birds is particularly deadly. Not only is their population endangered by the decrease in the number of fish for them to eat, but there has been an increase in demand for sea bird eggs. This has led to extensive poaching of these eggs, which, in turn, has resulted in a dramatic decrease in the number of sea bird hatchlings born each year.

For thousands of years Africa's coastal and marine areas have supported some of the most remarkable and diverse ecosystems on the planet. They also have provided the people of Africa with economic survival. But precisely how or even if those environments—and their economic and social benefits—will be preserved for future generations is still unknown.

See also: ECOLOGY AND ECOLOGICAL CHANGE (Vol. V); ENVIRONMENTAL ISSUES (Vol. V).

Further reading: United Nations Environment Programme, *Africa Environmental Outlook: Past, Present and Future Perspectives* (Nairobi, Kenya: UNEP, 2002).

Coetzee, J. M. (John Maxwell Coetzee) (1940–)
South African novelist

Born to Afrikaner parents in CAPE TOWN, SOUTH AFRICA, Coetzee attended an English school and thus spoke English as his first language, as opposed to AFRIKAANS. He continued his education at the University of Cape Town before traveling to the United States, earning master's and doctorate degrees at the University of Texas. He taught at the State University of New York at Buffalo until 1971, when he returned to South Africa. In 1972 Coetzee accepted a professorship at the University of Cape Town, which he has maintained throughout his career.

In 1974 Coetzee published his first work, a pair of novellas under the joint title of *Dusklands*. The novellas, *The Vietnam Project* and *The Narrative of Jacobus Coetzee*, compare the American experience in wartime Vietnam with that of Boer settlers in southern Africa. It was proclaimed South Africa's first modern fictional work and established the nature and effects of oppressive regimes as one of Coetzee's main themes.

Dusklands was followed, in 1977, by *In the Heart of the Country*, and by Coetzee's breakout novel, the allegorical *Waiting for the Barbarians* (1980). The novel, which won South Africa's most prestigious literary prize, the CNA Award, focuses on the imperialistic mentality

that caused so much damage to Africa since the scramble for colonies began near the end of the 19th century. Coetzee's subsequent novel, *The Life and Times of Michael K.* (1983), continued to build on his international reputation, earning him the Booker Prize, Britain's highest literary award.

Foe (1986), *Age of Iron* (1990), and *Disgrace* (1999), for which Coetzee won an unprecedented second Booker Prize, continued to examine with varying degrees of directness the ravages of APARTHEID on the author's native country. By the turn of the century Coetzee had developed an impressive body of essays, criticism, and translations. The essay collection *White Writing: On the Culture of Letters in South Africa* (1988) examined the dilemma of white writers in South Africa, who write from a position of being not European, but not fully African either.

One of the major concerns addressed in Coetzee's writing is the attempt to determine what right, if any, white writers have to speak for the oppressed black African population. Other white South African writers, such as Nadine GORDIMER (1923–), have expressed similar apprehension.

Coetzee also accumulated awards ranging from the Jerusalem Prize to the Prix Femina Étranger. In 2003 he was awarded the Nobel Prize for Literature, becoming Africa's fourth Nobel laureate, joining Nigerian Wole SOYINKA (1934–), Egyptian Naguib MAHFOUZ (1911–), and Gordimer.

See also: LITERATURE IN MODERN AFRICA (Vol. V).

Cold War and Africa
The Cold War was a period of international tension and rivalry between the United States (U.S.) and the Soviet Union (USSR) lasting from the end of World War II (1939–45) through the early 1990s. Prior to the late 1950s, when Africa was the site of emerging INDEPENDENCE MOVEMENTS, the Cold War's effect on African countries was limited. From 1960 onward, however, the Cold War took on a greater significance. This included superpower support for certain independence movements as well as the expansion of regional conflicts into protracted wars influenced by international politics.

One of the earliest consequences of the Cold War for Africa was its effect on the DECOLONIZATION. Egypt's nationalization of the SUEZ CANAL in 1956, and the subsequent Suez War between EGYPT and an English-French-Israeli alliance, was played out under the threat of Soviet involvement, to which the United States was staunchly opposed. As a result, the United States intervened on the side of Egypt, strengthening that country's sovereignty and weakening English and French influence over Africa. With the power of the two colonial powers lessened, the stage was set for other African countries to gain their independence.

The events of the Suez War illustrate how the existence of the USSR as an alternative to Western colonial and capitalist ambitions affected 1960s Africa. In an effort to lessen the ability of the USSR to gain allies among the newly independent African nations, the United States likely supported African independence movements more than it might have otherwise. Concerned about the advance of communism, however, the United States was careful to support only individuals who were perceived to be anti-Communist and pro-Western, such as Kenya's Tom MBOYA (1930–1969). Meanwhile, the USSR also offered aid to African independence movements in the form of financial and military support. The competing interests of the two superpowers created an environment in which nascent African nations could gain a foothold in international politics that otherwise may not have existed.

On the negative side, the Cold War contributed to the formation of authoritarian regimes within Africa, most maintaining their hold on power with the help of foreign support. A good example of this is reflected by the CONGO CRISIS, in which the military dictator MOBUTU SESE SEKO (1930–1997) arose to power after the assassination of the pro-Marxist and anticolonial Patrice LUMUMBA (1925–1961) in 1961. Furthermore, these African authoritarian regimes often appropriated foreign aid marked for social improvements to finance their own activities.

The environment of the Cold War also exacerbated regional conflicts into large-scale military conflicts, many of which were actually proxy wars between the United States and USSR. Most of these conflicts resulted in a stalemate, with neither side able to achieve a clear and decisive victory. This was certainly the case in the civil war that erupted in ANGOLA following the country's independence in 1975. The government, formed by the POPULAR MOVEMENT FOR THE LIBERATION OF ANGOLA (Movimento Popular de Libertação de Angola, MPLA) had the backing of the Soviet Union, which supported Cuban troops and technicians to assist the government. Meanwhile, MPLA's rivals, the Union for Total Independence of Angola (UNITA) and the NATIONAL FRONT FOR THE LIBERATION OF ANGOLA (Frente Nacional de Libertação de Angola, FNLA), received backing from the United States, which in turn covertly supported the presence of military forces from SOUTH AFRICA to assist UNITA's troops. Once the Cold War ended, the external actors withdrew from Angola, which in turn led to internal talks and some measure of reconciliation.

The Cold War also affected southern Africa. Internal warfare took place in MOZAMBIQUE along lines similar to those in Angola. In South Africa the AFRICAN NATIONAL CONGRESS received considerable Soviet backing for its efforts to overthrow the APARTHEID government. In another example, independence for NAMIBIA was delayed due to Cold War maneuverings by the superpowers and related actions by the South African government.

The Horn of Africa was yet another major theater of the Cold War. The United States strongly supported ETHIOPIA while HAILE SELASSIE (1892–1975) was emperor. During this time, the United States maintained satellite-tracking facilities and other military installations within the country. Meanwhile, the USSR backed the government of neighboring SOMALIA, which was at odds with Ethiopia over control of the Ogaden region. The superpower constructed naval port facilities at the Somalian city of Berbera, on the Gulf of Aden, which allowed access to the Red Sea. When, in 1974, the Ethiopian revolution overthrew Haile Selassie, the USSR soon moved in to establish ties with the country's new Marxist-oriented government. With Ethiopia now in the Soviet camp, Somalia switched its allegiance to the United States. This move was propelled by the 1977–78 war over the Ogaden, in which the intervention of Cuban troops and other Soviet-bloc personnel on the side of Ethiopia proved decisive. Ultimately, the United States and Somalia signed a 10-year pact that gave the United States access to military facilities at Berbera.

After the collapse of the Soviet Union in 1991, DEMOCRATIZATION gained momentum in Africa, and African leaders often lost the support they received from siding with one of the superpowers. This created a power vacuum in many African states. As authoritarian regimes lost the support that allowed them to maintain their hold on power, formerly suppressed political groups now had the opportunity to gain strength and rise to positions of influence.

See also: COLD WAR AND AFRICA (Vol. IV); COLONIAL RULE (Vol. IV); COLONIALISM, INFLUENCE OF (Vol. IV); INDEPENDENCE MOVEMENTS (Vol. V); NATIONALISM AND INDEPENDENCE MOVEMENTS (Vol. IV); SOVIET UNION AND AFRICA (Vols. IV, V); UNITED STATES AND AFRICA (Vols. IV, V).

Further reading: S. Akrinade, *Africa in the Post-Cold War International System* (London: Frances Pinter, 1998).

communism and socialism Political, economic, and social paradigms that refute the value of corporate ownership of the means of production. The implied equity, along with promises from the communist Soviet Union and China, made them popular ideals for many new African states in the 1960s.

Karl Marx (1818–1883) was a German political journalist who worked for the Communist League in Paris and Brussels. With his colleague Friedrich Engels

(1820–1895), Marx wrote the *Communist Manifesto* in 1848. In this famous work the authors acknowledged that capitalism produced remarkable industrial advances, but they also saw that its social costs were dear. New production, they argued, led to a few people becoming rich and powerful and the majority becoming poorer and more dependent on the few rich. Marx found it unjust that the workers bore the weight of market crises through decreasing wages and layoffs. What Marx envisioned instead was a world in which the workers, not the capitalists, ultimately would own the means of production. Cooperatively, workers would build the products and make the profits. In this way, Marx and Engels argued, the public good would replace the narrow benefits of private ownership, and specialization would be replaced with a communal work ethic.

As Marx explained in the *Communist Manifesto* and elaborated in *Das Kapital* (Capital, 1867), this great society could not be achieved all at once. First, the capitalist repression had to lead to such strong class divisions as to cause workers to unite in revolutionary fervor. Then, once the bourgeoisie was ousted from the factories and positions of power, the state would need to take control of the means of production. This, they argued, was the ideal of socialism. Once maximum efficiency was achieved, the need for the state would fall away, and the citizenry would work in collaboration for the communal good. This was the ideal of communism.

African Socialism   In the 1950s and 1960s African nationalist leaders made a conceptual link between colonial governments and the capitalist oppressors Marx described. To many leaders, there was a natural connection between Marx's workers and the African people, who also had been oppressed. They saw African societies as historically egalitarian, not capitalist. A doctrine that would focus on sharing common economic resources would thus be consistent with the precolonial social structure.

Léopold SENGHOR (1906–2001), the first president of SENEGAL, was one of the most eloquent supporters of African socialism. He argued that African societies and African culture emphasized communal values and orientation and that, as a result, a communal independent Africa could develop rapidly. Thus, he was advocating a socialism that emerged and evolved out of African experience and perceptions.

The most significant attempt at instituting African socialism occurred in TANZANIA, where President Julius NYERERE (1922–1999) instituted the collective farming policy known as UJAMAA. In this famed doctrine Nyerere wrote, "All land now belongs to the nation . . . communal ownership of land is traditional in our country—it was the concept of freehold which had been foreign to [Africans]. In tribal tradition an individual or family secured rights in land for as long as they were using it."

Leaders as diverse as Ahmed Sékou TOURÉ (1922–1984) of GUINEA, Kenneth KAUNDA (1924–   ) of ZAMBIA, Modibo KEITA (1915–1977) of MALI, Patrice LUMUMBA (1925–1961) of the Democratic Republic of the CONGO, King Idris (1890–1983) of LIBYA, Felix Moumié (d. 1960) of CAMEROON, and Ahmed BEN BELLA (1916–   ) of ALGERIA all sought African socialist paths focused loosely on Marxist principles.

Similar to African nationalism, African socialism challenged the status quo but failed to provide viable alternatives. Kwame NKRUMAH (1909–1972), first president of GHANA and a key leader of PAN-AFRICANISM, was often considered an African socialist, and he did emphasize collective action and equity. However, he also stated that "[t]o suppose that there are tribal, national, or racial socialisms is to abandon objectivity in favor of chauvinism." Nkrumah, like many others, questioned that there was a necessary link between African ways of life and socialism and even if there was an African way at all. As nationalism lost its luster, so did African socialism. In the 1970s and 1980s the concept developed into more of a tool for dictators to seize state power than an ideology. To a great degree, African socialism died in the 1990s with the rise of African democracy, even if the collective ideal is still often discussed.

Among the key works on the concept of African socialism are Nkrumah's *Neo-Colonialism: the Last Stage of Imperialism*, Nyerere's *Socialism and Rural Development*, and Senghor's *On African Socialism*.

As various African countries achieved independence in the early 1960s they had to choose a path of economic DEVELOPMENT. In general, they could choose between socialism, emphasizing equity of resource distribution among the citizenry, or capitalism, emphasizing individual rewards for individual work. For years Africans had suffered economic exploitation at the hands of colonial regimes and their associated corporations. French colonial administrations sometimes even ceded administrative power to concessionaire companies, as they did in what is now the Republic of the Congo. Socialism was thus very attractive in many countries, but how socialism was manifested varied markedly.

Some regimes (in ETHIOPIA, ANGOLA, for example) took on the revolutionary traits associated with communism. Others (in Tanzania, Zambia, SOMALIA, Ghana, MALI, Senegal, Guinea and ultimately MADAGASCAR and ZIMBABWE) believed that capitalism should not be abolished but rather its businesses should be reappropriated to the control of the state for the good of all citizens. These countries formed the nexus of African socialism, which grew "scientific" socialist or communitarian principles. There are two common threads in African socialist thinking. The first is that socialism is more consistent with longstanding communal structures prevalent in African societies. The second is that capitalism is not a good choice for poor countries, since it necessarily leads to unequal development and social discord. In a capitalist system, private companies generate capital to the benefit of the elite social classes, but in socialism, the state is responsible for distributing profits equally to all workers based on their efforts, not on their function. As Marx famously remarked, socialism is "from each according to his ability, to each according to his needs." With the Cold War fueling Soviet and American foreign aid, African countries that chose a socialist path generally did so with the backing of the Soviet Union, China, or both. Indeed, at the Bandung Afro-Asian Conference in 1955, the premier of communist China, Zhou Enlai (1898–1976), was influential in promoting nonalignment, thereby encouraging African socialism. The somewhat unique case of Tanzania even saw the creation of *ujamaa* villages, loosely based on a Chinese communal farming model. Nevertheless, few African socialist states actually managed to attain even Tanzania's modest degree of non-alignment, tending instead to become Soviet tributary states.

In theory, African socialism is consistent with democracy. Whereas socialism should provide economic justice, democracy should provide political justice. In practice, however, most African socialist leaders used social equity as a tool for maintaining their own oppressive, autocratic rule.

African socialism thrived from the 1960s to the 1980s, yet it ultimately succumbed to its two major flaws: it was poor at creating work incentives, and it never represented the more "African" way that its leaders professed. As a result, the early 1980s saw catastrophic economic failures throughout African socialist states, often followed by political and social disarray. The fall of the Soviet Union and the scaling back of Chinese aid led to a near extinction of African socialist paradigms by the 1990s.

African Communism African socialism has yet to reflect Marx's ideal, but African communism has never even been attempted in earnest, despite the specious invocation of its name. Much like the Soviet, Chinese, Cuban, and North Korean models, communism in Africa became synonymous with a process by which revolutionary fervor led to the emergence of a strong-armed leader from ranks of the movement. In some cases, as in Angola, communism took root as part of a nationalist movement toward independence. Political parties, such as the NATIONAL FRONT FOR THE LIBERATION OF ANGOLA of Holden ROBERTO (1923–) and the POPULAR MOVEMENT FOR THE LIBERATION OF ANGOLA of Agostinho NETO (1922–1979),

sought links with Congolese, Mozambican, and Zambian revolutionary forces to liberate the African people from European tyranny. A push for Ethiopian communism began on September 12, 1974, when Colonel MENGISTU HAILE MARIAM (c. 1937–) deposed Emperor HAILE SELASSIE (1892–1975) in the name of the Revolutionary Armed Forces. Using persuasive communist rhetoric, Mengistu called himself the chairman of the Provisional Military Administrative Council and the chairman of the Commission to Organize the Party of the Working People, and claimed that he would hold the reigns of power in the name of the people. In the end, this proved to be a ploy that he used as a tool of social stratification, and an attempt to forge national alliances. The Ethiopian revolution never produced the fundamental change in rule that the French and even Russian revolutions did. When, in 1978, Ethiopia moved towards villagization, the government claimed, as Marx did, that humans are social animals. Their natural tendency is toward village settlements, the first step toward a non-exploitative agrarian society. It also claimed, following Russian communist leader Vladimir Lenin (1870–1924), that revolutionary restructuring required strong political control at first. Mengistu worked for that strong local control, but didn't release his iron fist until it was forced open by myriad rebel armies, including the Tigrayan People's Liberation Front, ERITREAN PEOPLE'S LIBERATION FRONT, and the ETHIOPIAN PEOPLE'S REVOLUTIONARY DEMOCRATIC FRONT. Mengistu fled to Zimbabwe in 1991 and Ethiopia's communist experiment was over.

In the end African communism became more of a tool for fighting international proxy wars than for achieving social justice. Cuba, for example, sent troops to Angola in 1976 and Ethiopia in 1977 on behalf of the Soviet Union. While this may have helped prop up the Mengistu regime and the MPLA in Angola, it did little to feed the masses, stimulate class equity, or bring about the economic development African populations yearned for.

See also: CHINA AND AFRICA (Vol. V); COLONIAL RULE (Vol. IV); COLONIALISM, INFLUENCE OF (Vol. IV); NATIONALISM AND INDEPENDENCE MOVEMENTS (Vol. IV); NONALIGNED MOVEMENT AND AFRICA (Vol. V); SOVIET UNION AND AFRICA (Vols. IV, V).

Further reading: Joel D. Barkan, *Beyond Capitalism vs. Socialism in Kenya and Tanzania* (Boulder, Colo.: Lynne Rienner, 1994); Robert C. Tucker, ed. *The Marx-Engels Reader* (New York: Norton and Company, 1977).

Comoros (Comoro Islands) Island nation off the coast of East Africa. Comoros is an Indian Ocean archipelago of four islands and several islets located between MADAGASCAR and northern MOZAMBIQUE. Collectively, the four islands of Maore (called Mayotte by the French), Mwali (Mohéli), Njazidja (Grande Comore), and Nzwani (ANJOUAN) cover only 838 square miles (2,170 sq km). MORONI, on the island of Njazidja, serves as the nation's capital. Comoros had an estimated population of 614,000 in 2002, although an additional 150,000 Comorans live abroad, with approximately 60,000 of the latter residing in France. Comorans speak three main languages, Shikomoro (a Kiswahili dialect), Malagasy (the principal language of Madagascar), and French. The overwhelming majority of Comorans—an estimated 98 percent—are Sunni Muslims.

Approximately 80 percent of the population is engaged in AGRICULTURE, even though the islands' land is generally of poor quality. The Comoros are the world's second leading exporter of vanilla; other export items include bananas, cloves, and copra, which is dried coconut meat suitable for extracting coconut oil. International trade, however, has been inhibited, until recently, by a lack of a deepwater port. As a result Comoros is an extremely poor nation and relies heavily on foreign aid.

Comoros is the world's foremost producer of *ylang-ylang*—a flower that yields an essential oil similar in aroma to jasmine—which is used in the production of perfumes.

French possessions since 1886, the Comoro islands were given internal autonomy in 1961 and full independence in 1975. At independence they became the Federal Islamic Republic of the Comoros, but in 2002, along with the introduction of a new constitution, their official name changed to Union of the Comoros. At independence the island of Maore (Mayotte) remained under French control and, despite diplomatic initiatives to align it politically with the other Comoran islands, it still is a French possession. France maintains a naval facility and foreign legion post on the island.

Since 1975 political stability in Comoros has been nonexistent, with as many as 19 coups being attempted, many successful. The islands also have suffered an ongoing series of secessionist movements. In 1997 Mwali and Nzwani declared their independence, further destabilizing the country's fragile political unity.

See also: COMOROS (Vols. I, II, III, IV); FRANCE AND AFRICA (Vols. III, IV, V); KISWAHILI (Vols. III, IV).

Compaore, Blaise (1951–) *President of Burkina Faso*

Compaore was born to an elite military family near OUAGADOUGOU, the capital of UPPER VOLTA (now BURKINA FASO). After military training in France, CAMEROON, and MOROCCO, he rose to the rank of captain and returned to Upper Volta. In 1983 Compaore led a COUP D'ÉTAT to bring charismatic socialist Thomas Sankara (1949–1987) to power. Despite his relatively young age of 33, Compaore was named Sankara's minister of state and was later named minister of justice, as well.

Sankara's rule did not stabilize the country's volatile political scene, however, and in 1987 Compaore led another successful coup in which Sankara was deposed and killed. Despite condemnation of the coup both at home and abroad, Compaore named himself president and set about "correcting" the socialist DEVELOPMENT programs that Sankara had instituted. With its increasingly autocratic nature, however, Compaore's leadership ultimately proved unpopular with key elements in his party, the Popular Front (PF). As a result, in 1989, following a trip overseas, Compaore learned of a supposed plot to overthrow him. In reaction he summarily executed two former party allies, Henri Songo (d. 1989) and Jean-Baptiste Boukary Lengani (d. 1989).

After reorganizing the government and assuming the post of minister of defense and security, Compaore easily won Burkina Faso's 1991 presidential election. His PF party soon adopted a new constitution, abandoned its Marxist-Leninist programs, and encouraged FOREIGN INVESTMENT. In 1992 the PF won the majority of the contested legislative seats, and in 1998 Compaore was reelected in a landslide victory.

Compaore's wife, Chantal, is the daughter of former president of the IVORY COAST, Félix HOUPHOUËT-BOIGNY (1905–1993).

Although it does not seem to have affected his popularity, Compaore has failed to improve the economy of Burkina Faso, which remains one of the most impoverished nations in the world. Compaore himself has come under heavy criticism for supposedly ordering the torture and arrest of political opponents. He also has been implicated in supporting several unpopular regimes throughout Africa, including that of recently deposed Charles TAYLOR (1948–), in LIBERIA. Further, Compaore has been identified as one of the African leaders who supplied Angolan rebel leader Jonas SAVIMBI (1934–2002) with arms and fuel in exchange for illegally mined diamonds, thereby making the peace process in ANGOLA more difficult.

Conakry (Konakry) Capital and principal port city of the Republic of GUINEA, on the West African coast. The area of present-day Conakry was part of the western Mali

Empire from the 13th through the 15th centuries. The French first settled the city of Conakry, located on the offshore island of Tombo, in 1887. From 1891 to 1893, the city served as the capital of a French protectorate, and then, from 1893 to 1958, it was the capital of French Guinea, a dependency in French West Africa. When Ahmed Sékou TOURÉ (1922–1984) led French Guinea to independence in 1958, Conakry was made the capital of the new republic.

After independence Guinea struggled to sustain itself under Touré's socialist economic policies. The economic, administrative, and communications center of the nation, Conakry was home to an estimated 1,100,000 people in 1996. While its INFRASTRUCTURE and amenities have improved since Touré's time, this prosperity is relative. The main EXPORTS of the port are bauxite and iron ore, which are shipped to the port by rail. Fruit, coffee, and fish are among the other leading exports. In addition, there are industrial plants nearby that process textiles, tobacco, matches, furniture, bricks, and MINING explosives. The city is host to several educational institutions, including the University of Conakry. It is also the site of Guinea's only international airport.

See also: FRANCE AND AFRICA (Vols. III, IV, V); FRENCH WEST AFRICA (Vol. IV); MALI EMPIRE (Vol. II); URBANIZATION (Vols. IV, V); URBAN LIFE AND CULTURE (Vols. IV, V).

Congo Crisis Period of political and military instability that immediately followed Congolese independence, in 1960. Commentators also refer to the ethnic violence and civil war that developed in the late 1990s as a second Congo Crisis.

Ill-prepared by its Belgian colonial rulers, the Congo plunged into a crisis within days of celebrating its independence from Belgium on June 30, 1960. By July 5 the Congolese army mutinied over a lack of pay. During the same time Prime Minister Patrice LUMUMBA (1925–1961) gave an incendiary, anticolonialist Independence Day speech that resulted in riots, looting, and attacks on Belgian civilians.

The Belgian government promptly dispatched paratroopers, insisting that the troops were to protect Belgian citizens and their property. Many Congolese, however, feared that Belgium was attempting to reassert its authority in the country.

The Secession of Katanga In the midst of this crisis, mineral-rich KATANGA province, under Moïse TSHOMBE (1919–1969), seceded from the new country. Katanga's declaration of independence, on July 11, immediately received the tacit endorsement of the Belgian government. More importantly, Belgium quickly dispatched military and technical assistance, leading Lumumba to charge that Belgium was behind the entire secessionist movement

and that it was seeking to re-establish control of the valuable MINING interests in Katanga.

On July 12 both Lumumba and Congo's president Joseph KASAVUBU (c. 1913–1969) appealed to the United Nations (UN) for help. The UN peacekeeping forces eventually arrived, but their initial mandate did not authorize them to interfere in the Congo's internal affairs. Thus, although they could attempt to halt actual bloodshed, they lacked authority to help put down the Katangan rebellion. Realizing that his own army was unable to deal with the Katangan forces—strengthened as they were with the arrival of Belgian officers, advisors, and materiél—Lumumba urged the United Nations to join the fight. Kasavubu, however, was firmly opposed.

When the United Nations failed to negotiate a settlement, Lumumba appealed to the former Soviet Union for technical and logistical assistance to end Katanga's rebellion. (While trying to negotiate a peace agreement, Dag Hammarskjöld (1905–1961), the UN secretary-general, was killed in a plane crash in the Congo.) Lumumba's request not only angered the United States and its allies, but also drew the Congo Crisis into the East-West divisions of the Cold War.

All of this also served to reignite the tensions between Lumumba and the Congo's president, Joseph Kasavubu. Their relations broke down almost completely in September, with Kasavubu suspending Lumumba's authority and Lumumba, in turn, dismissing Kasavubu.

Although both had been leaders in the Congolese independence movement, Lumumba and Kasavubu had long been opponents. The more radical Lumumba, who in some ways considered himself a staunch anticolonialist and a Marxist, favored a strong, centralized Congo government. Kasavubu, on the other hand, had risen to power as the leader of the Bakongo Tribal Association, and he favored a loose, "federal" government that would grant the majority of power to the Congo's individual ethnic groups and regions. Lumumba also charged that his rival favored a more accommodating relationship with Belgium.

Continued Instability In the face of the dissolution of central authority and the continued rebellion of Tshombe's Katanga, the Congo began to break into regional fragments and was nearing complete collapse by the end of the summer. On September 14, 1960, Lumumba's army chief of staff, Joseph Mobutu (1930–1997), who would later become MOBUTU SESE SEKO, seized power in the name of the military. While Kasavubu sup-

The Congo quickly descended into crisis following independence in 1960. Here, a man protesting the government of Prime Minister Patrice Lumumba is hauled away by armed policeman in Leopoldville (present-day Kinshasa). © AP/Wide World Photos

ported Mobutu, Lumumba refused to acquiesce to Mobutu. He managed to escape from Leopoldville, and continued to attempt a return to power. Lumumba's struggle ended in February 1961, when Mobutu's soldiers in Katanga captured and murdered him. In August 1961, when Mobutu returned power to a civilian administration, Kasavubu became president of the new Congolese government. Two years later a combination of Congolese troops and UN peacekeepers forced Tshombe to admit defeat and go into exile, ending Katanga's secession.

Although Katanga's surrender and the return of a civilian government marked an easing of the crisis, it by no means ended it. Dissatisfaction with Kasavubu and his prime minister, Cyrille Adoula (1921–1978), grew steadily. When Adoula dissolved the legislature, in 1963, ethnic rebellions broke out all around the country.

Kasavubu dismissed Adoula in July 1964, and brought his one-time enemy, Tshombe, back from exile to become prime minister. Employing European mercenaries and ruthless measures, Tshombe was able to put down most of the rebellions and then declared his intentions of running for the presidency. Kasavubu immediately dismissed Tshombe, triggering a new governmental crisis that was resolved only after Mobutu once again seized control, in November 1965, in a military coup that ultimately kept him in power for 32 years.

A Second Congo Crisis A second major crisis developed in the 1990s, as ethnic hostilities spread into the Congo from neighboring RWANDA and UGANDA. There, conflict between HUTU and TUTSI ethnic groups had led to increasing levels of violence, eventually leading more than a million Hutu to seek refuge in ZAÏRE, as the Congo was then called. By 1996 the Hutu had accumulated so much power in the eastern part of the country that local Tutsi were threatened with expulsion from their own homeland. They rebelled, forming alliances with Rwanda's Tutsi government and its main ally, UGANDA. Amid widespread violence, Congolese rebel leader Laurent KABILA (c. 1939–2001), who was a long-time Mobutu opponent, established a Tutsi-based military force. Eventually Kabila and his allies were able to defeat Mobutu's troops and oust the long-time dictator. Ethnic violence and civil war continued, however, even after the assassination of Laurent Kabila and the coming to power of his son, Joseph KABILA (1971–). Today various peacekeeping forces maintain a fragile truce in the area.

When it gained independence in 1960, the Congo was officially named the Republic of the Congo. In August 1964, when Moïse Tshombe was prime minister, it became the Democratic Republic of the Congo. In 1971, as part of his Africanization policy, Mobutu changed the name of the country once again, this time to Zaïre. The name was changed back to the Democratic Republic of the Congo after Mobutu was ousted in 1997.

See also: BELGIAN CONGO (Vol. IV); BELGIUM AND AFRICA (Vol. IV); CIVIL WARS (Vol. V); COLD WAR AND AFRICA (Vols. IV, V); ETHNIC CONFLICT IN AFRICA (Vol. V); SOVIET UNION AND AFRICA (Vol. IV, V); UNITED STATES AND AFRICA (Vol. V); UNITED NATIONS AND AFRICA (Vol. V).

Further reading: Crawford Young, *The Rise and Decline of the Zairian State* (Madison, Wisc.: University of Wisconsin Press, 1985); Alan P. Merriam, *Congo: Background of Conflict* (Evanston, Ill.: Northwestern University Press, 1961).

Congo, Democratic Republic of the (Congo-Kinshasa; formerly Zaïre)

Largest country in Africa, measuring approximately 905,400 square miles (2,345,000 sq km). The Democratic Republic of the Congo (DRC) is located in southern central Africa, south of the Congo River, and has a short Atlantic Ocean coastline. The DRC borders the CENTRAL AFRICAN REPUBLIC to the north, the Republic of the SUDAN to the northeast, UGANDA, RWANDA, BURUNDI, and the Republic of TANZANIA to the east, ZAMBIA and ANGOLA to the south, and the Republic of the CONGO to the west. The DRC is home to approximately 57 million people, who together speak more than 200 languages. The country

has been plagued since independence with conflicting interests vying for political power and access to its great mineral wealth.

Crisis in the Congo At independence on June 30, 1960, the former Belgian Congo immediately became one of the world's most politically fractious countries. The creation of the country came about not through a unified nationalist movement, as was the case in SENEGAL or KENYA, but through a convergence of highly polarized political organizations. These included the Alliance of the Kongo People (ABAKO) and the Confederation of Katanga Associations, which had pushed for independence beginning in 1956. The socialist Congolese National Movement (Mouvement National Congolais, MNC), formed in 1958, had split into both a moderate faction and a more radical faction led by Patrice LUMUMBA (1925–1961).

Municipal elections held in 1957 brought ABAKO and its leader, Joseph KASAVUBU (c. 1913–1969), to the national fore. However, legislative elections in 1960 led to a victory for Lumumba's MNC. The departing Belgian authorities attempted to maintain order by appointing Lumumba prime minister and naming Kasavubu president. However, this approach failed, and violence erupted within days of independence, leading to what became known as the CONGO CRISIS. The Belgians remained in the country in an effort to restore order, but the severity of the crisis eventually required the intervention of the United Nations (UN) Security Council, which authorized the deployment of 20,000 peacekeeping troops.

Soon the Belgian army was gone and UN troops were on the ground. Meanwhile, another nationalist leader, Joseph Mobutu (1930–1997), who would later be known as MOBUTU SESE SEKO, attempted to overthrow Lumumba by military COUP D'ÉTAT. Although the attempt failed, Mobutu increased his power base and immediately assumed a more significant role in the political crisis. He quickly became head of the military and created a powerful alliance with Kasavubu.

Complicating the power-play were underlying ideological differences. Kasavubu and Mobutu were self-serving but had Western leanings. Lumumba, on the other hand, had a socialist vision, and he turned to the communist Soviet Union for support. Both the UN and France appeared eager to protect Lumumba and the power-sharing arrangement. Yet by September 1960 Lumumba was forced to seek protection in KATANGA, where the UN presence was strongest. Despite UN protection, Mobutu's agents captured Lumumba and assassinated him on or around January 17, 1961. Although the details are not clear, it is likely that the assassination was accomplished with the aid of agents from the U.S. Central Intelligence Agency (CIA).

Following four more years of instability, in November 1965 Mobutu ousted his former ally, Kasavubu, and set up a pro-capitalist dictatorship. The treachery involved in the Congo's founding set the stage for the challenges that have confronted it ever since.

Mobutu Sese Seko and the Cold War The country Mobutu controlled was critical because of its central location on the African sub-continent. Therefore, as a political ally, Mobutu was instrumental to U.S. Cold War interests throughout the 1960s and 1970s. The United States and other pro-capitalist countries sent massive amounts of aid in order to keep him in power. In return he allowed the United States to use military bases in his country to launch its own (ultimately unsuccessful) CIA paramilitary attacks in ANGOLA. At the time Angola was the site of a proxy war between the Soviet-backed POPULAR MOVEMENT FOR THE LIBERATION OF ANGOLA and the U.S.-backed NATIONAL UNION FOR THE TOTAL INDEPENDENCE OF ANGOLA.

In 1965 Mobutu's coup was generally welcomed by a Congolese population tired of conflict. However, when he dissolved the legislature and centralized his power, the people began to see his true colors. His economic policies failed, CORRUPTION became rampant, prices skyrocketed, and popular dissatisfaction was met with state-sanctioned violence. Even as Mobutu's legitimacy dissipated, however, he managed to further his own power and generate the wealth necessary to buy the loyalty of the military and a close group of advisors. Ethnic uprisings were dealt with harshly; the Katanga secessionist movement was suppressed with military threats.

In the late 1960s and early 1970s Mobutu launched an "African authenticity" campaign, changing place names that recalled the country's colonial past. The capital, Leopoldville, for example, became KINSHASA; Elizabethville was renamed LUBUMBASHI; Stanleyville became KISANGANI. In 1971 the country itself was renamed ZAÏRE by Mobutu's decree. Mobutu also forced people to abandon their Christian names in favor of more African-sounding names.

Mobutu began amassing incredible personal wealth during this period. The country, in general, is rich in diamonds, copper, and zinc. In particular, the soil in Katanga Province—renamed Shaba Province—is especially rich in valuable minerals. Mobutu secured the mines in the name of the Zairian people and then sold MINING rights to DeBeers and other large international companies. Rather than use the proceeds for the DEVELOPMENT of the country, he used it to enlarge his personal bank account as well as the accounts of those who remained close to him. Meanwhile, Zaïre remained a country with one of the lowest quality-of-life ratings in the world.

By 1975 the political situation in Shaba province and neighboring Angola had become critical. Soviet forces airlifted Cuban soldiers to Angola from ETHIOPIA, and secessionist Katangan rebels were amassing along the Angolan border, poised to overthrow Mobutu. With Cuban assistance the Katanga rebels attacked Mobutu's forces, only to be repelled by a contingent of 1,500 specialized troops from MOROCCO who had been airlifted in by France. Similarly aligned international action helped Mobutu survive another attack in 1977–79. U.S. and French intervention, like UN intervention in 1960, most likely had as much to do with the fear of Soviet influence as with a genuine concern for Zaïre. It is unlikely that Mobutu could have remained in power for as long as he did without the significant military assistance he received from the United States. As recently as 1990, President George H. W. Bush (1924–) negotiated favorable terms of trade to support Mobutu Yet with the demise of the Soviet Union in the early 1990s the United States began changing its global spending policies, particularly in Africa. When the United States began promoting DEMOCRATIZATION in an effort to bring about economic prosperity and peace, Mobutu lost his most important ally.

Crisis in Rwanda and the Fall of Mobutu In 1994 conflict erupted between HUTU and TUTSI in Rwanda, ultimately exacerbating the ethnic and regional tensions in Mobutu's Zaïre. In the wake of the Rwandan genocide in 1994, waves of ethnic Hutu flooded Zaïre. Mobutu, in a bid to shore up his own power, effectively gave them sanctuary. The U.S., for its part, had since given up on Mobutu and was now interested in fostering the rise of any leadership that could stabilize the region. France supported both Mobutu's flagging regime and Rwanda's ousted Hutu regime on the grounds that the Hutu are Rwanda's majority ethnic group.

By mid-1996 the Rwandan state, led by President Paul KAGAME (1957–), an ethnic Tutsi, supported an uprising of Banyamulenge, ethnic Tutsi of Rwandan origin who were living in the Congo. Also supporting the Tutsi agenda were Uganda president, Yoweri MUSEVENI (1944–), an ethnic Bahima closely related to the Tutsi, and Burundi president Pierre BUYOYA (1949–), also an ethnic Tutsi. Thus, an alliance was formed between Banyamulenge, Tutsi in Rwanda, Uganda, and Burundi, and former Lumumbaists, who still opposed Mobutu for his part in Lumumba's murder back in 1961. In the Congo this anti-Mobutu Tutsi alliance backed rising rebel leader Laurent KABILA (c. 1939–2001), who also sought Mobutu's ouster.

In March 1997 Kabila and his forces took control of Zaïre's eastern city of Kisangani. His troops then steadily worked their way westward, eventually threatening the capital at Kinshasa. After a series of U.S.- and UN-brokered peace talks failed, in May, Kabila finally removed the ailing Mobutu from power. Suffering from prostate cancer, Mobutu died in exile on September 7, 1997.

To symbolize the passing of the Mobutu regime, Kabila quickly renamed the country the Democratic Republic of the Congo. After Mobutu's demise, who Laurent Kabila was and how he assumed power seemed of less concern to the people of the DRC and the international community than the fact that he represented the possibility of a new beginning. Ultimately, however, Kabila proved in many ways to be as unsavory a character as Mobutu.

Kabila took control of the country's diamond mines, leaving agreements in place to keep MULTINATIONAL CORPORATIONS appeased. Since wealthy corporations in ZIMBABWE, NAMIBIA, and Angola all had diamond interests in the Congo, as soon as Kabila took control the governments of these countries, too, turned to support him. Because of his ethnic connections and the international community's desire for regional peace, Kabila received support and praise from Uganda, Rwanda, the United States, Zimbabwe, NAMIBIA, and Angola. Also, when Denis SASSOU-NGUESSO (1943–) took control of the Republic of the CONGO in 1997, Kabila had yet another regional supporter. Coincidentally, Sassou-Nguesso had substantial diamond interests in the DRC. These backers were necessary for Kabila to defend himself from the growing number of Congolese rebel groups that sought his removal.

Regional Civil War   Over the next year relations between Kabila and his Rwandan, Ugandan, and Republic of the Congo backers became strained. In July 1998 Kabila ordered all foreign armies out of the country. Rwanda and Uganda refused, and the DRC slipped into civil war. Rwanda began backing the Rally for Congolese Democracy, a rebel faction, and Uganda began backing the Movement for the Liberation of the Congo (MLC), another rebel faction. Together these groups established control of one-third of the country. The conflict escalated as troops from Zimbabwe, Namibia, Angola, and CHAD all continued to support Kabila against the foreign-backed rebel organizations.

In July 1999 the various warring factions reached a peace agreement in LUSAKA, Zambia. Provisions of the agreement, called the Lusaka Accords, included a cease-fire, the withdrawal of foreign troops, a dialogue among the different Congolese factions, a transitional government, and the deployment of a UN peacekeeping force until there could be elections.

The Lusaka Accords were already failing when in June 2000 Rwandan and Ugandan troops launched into a bloody battle. The location of the conflict, Kisangani, suggests that the conflict revolved around control of diamond mines. More than a thousand Congolese civilians died in the crossfire. The Red Cross estimates that at least 2 million people have died either directly or indirectly from the civil war in the DCR.

Death of Laurent Kabila and the Rise of his Son
On January 17, 2001, Laurent Kabila was assassinated by one of his bodyguards. In the aftermath of his sudden demise, the military government quickly installed Laurent's 29-year-old son, Major General Joseph KABILA (1971–). The plan worked, insofar as it kept the country together. In an effort to win support for his regime abroad, Joseph Kabila went on state visits to countries as varied as LIBYA and the United States, where his advocacy of the Lusaka Accords won him favor. At home, however, gaining popular support in the toxic political climate he inherited proved more difficult. He nonetheless moved forward to consolidate power and start the inter-Congolese dialogue described in the Lusaka Accords. He also encouraged a small deployment UN peacekeepers.

In December 2002 SOUTH AFRICA brokered new negotiations, leading to a tenuous peace. Foreign troops officially began to leave the country, culminating with the exit of Ugandan troops in 2003. However, the exploitation of Congolese mineral wealth did not abate, nor did Kabila's use of that wealth to maintain his power base. It was agreed that Kabila would remain head of state until new elections could be held within 30 months. The planned interim government would include four vice presidents named from the government, the two primary rebel groups, and the political opposition. Since all the major political players signed the agreement, most international observers viewed this agreement as a landmark moment in Congolese history. Yet the complexity of the groups' inter-relationships is indisputably the hallmark of postcolonial history in Africa's largest country.

See also: BELGIUM AND AFRICA (Vol. IV); CONGO, DEMOCRATIC REPUBLIC OF (Vols. I, II, III, IV), CONGO FREE STATE (Vol. IV); CUBA AND AFRICA (Vol. V); LEOPOLD II (Vol. IV); SOVIET UNION AND AFRICA (Vols. IV, V); UNION MINIÈRE (Vol. IV); UNITED NATIONS AND AFRICA (Vol. V), UNITED STATES AND AFRICA (Vol. V).

Further reading: Georges Nzongola-Ntalaja, *The Congo from Leopold to Kabila: a People's History* (New York: Zed Books and Palgrave, 2002); Michael G. Schatzberg, *The Dialectics of Oppression in Zaire* (Bloomington, Ind.: Indiana University Press, 1988); Christian P. Scherrer, *Genocide and Crisis in Central Africa: Conflict Roots, Mass Violence, and Regional War* (Westport, Conn.: Praeger, 2002); Crawford Young and Thomas Turner, *The Rise and Decline of the Zairian State* (Madison, Wisc.: University of Wisconsin Press, 1985); *Crawford Young, Politics in the Congo: Decolonization and Independence* (Princeton, N.J. : Princeton University Press, 1965).

Congo, Republic of the (Congo-Brazzaville)

Country located in west-central Africa, north of the Congo River, and measuring approximately 131,900 square miles (341,600 sq km). The Republic of the Congo has a short Atlantic Ocean coastline and borders GABON, CAMEROON, the CENTRAL AFRICAN REPUBLIC, the Democratic Republic of the CONGO, and the Angolan enclave of CABINDA. Most of the inland comprises tropical rain forest drained by tributaries of the Congo River. Congo's capital is BRAZZAVILLE.

Congo at Independence Formerly a part of the colony of French Equatorial Africa, the Republic of the Congo gained its independence in 1960. At that time Congo's National Assembly elected the first president, a Roman Catholic priest named Fulbert Youlou (1917–1972). After three years, however, LABOR UNIONS and the other political parties combined to oust him. The Congolese military took charge of the country briefly and installed a civilian provisional government headed by Alphonese Massamba-Debat (c. 1921–1977). Although Massamba-Debat was elected president for a five-year term under the new 1963 constitution, he was ousted by another military COUP D'ÉTAT in 1968, led by Capitan Marien Ngouabi (1938–1977). Ngouabi assumed the presidency and proclaimed the People's Republic of the Congo, a one-party state. Ngouabi held the country together until 1977, when he was assassinated. A Marxist military figure, Colonel Denis SASSOU-NGUESSO (1943–), became president in 1979.

With the collapse of the Soviet Union the Congo gradually shifted its economic and political views so that, by 1992, it had become a multiparty democracy. In 1992 Sassou-Nguesso was defeated at the polls, and Pascal Lissouba (1931–), a university professor, was elected president. The contest between the two political rivals escalated into a violent conflict. By 1997 the democratic process had dissolved, the INFRASTRUCTURE in the southern part of the country was severely damaged, and the capital city of Brazzaville was all but destroyed. Ultimately, Sassou-Nguesso was able to declare himself president. His government decided upon the new constitution and the elections, but it met with fierce opposition. The dispute was briefly settled in 1999 through agreements with the representatives of the rebel groups, mediated by the president of Gabon, Omar BONGO (1935–). Fighting broke out again between the military and rebel groups in March of 2002, but the military quickly put down this latest flare-up. A cease-fire was signed in March of 2003.

Sassou-Nguesso was elected president in 2002 and began a seven-year term. Since that time civil war at home and in the neighboring Democratic Republic of the Congo has exacerbated Congo's political and economic instability.

See also: CONGO (Vol. III); CONGO, REPUBLIC OF THE (Vols. I. II, III, IV); FRANCE AND AFRICA (Vols. IV, V); FRENCH EQUATORIAL AFRICA (Vol. IV).

Further reading: Amnesty International, *Republic of Congo: An Old Generation of Leaders in New Carnage* (New York: Amnesty International USA, 1999); Mbow M.

Amphas, *Political Transformations of the Congo* (Durham, N.C.: Pentland Press, 2000); G. Nguyen [et al.], *Agriculture and Rural Development in the People's Republic of the Congo* (Boulder, Colo.: Westview Press, 1987).

Congolese National Movement (Mouvement National Congolais, MNC) See CONGO, DEMOCRATIC REPUBLIC OF THE (Vols. IV, V); LUMUMBA, PATRICE (Vols. IV, V).

conservation Sustainable use of NATURAL RESOURCES and the protection of WILDLIFE, plant species, soil, habitats, and WATER RESOURCES. African conservation is inevitably linked with the fates of the continent's unique wildlife populations. Indeed, to a great extent, it is the charismatic nature of Africa's "big five"—lions, leopards, rhinos, buffaloes, and elephants—that has drawn global attention to conservation issues on the continent. Ironically, much of this attention comes from outsiders, the very ones who, during the colonial period, severely diminished the populations of many of these animals through sport hunting.

In many parts of Africa conservation of wildlife and natural areas has been promoted primarily by designating large tracts of land as preserves or NATIONAL PARKS. Countries such as SOUTH AFRICA, BOTSWANA, NAMIBIA, KENYA, TANZANIA, and ZIMBABWE are notable in this regard, all of them having devoted many natural areas to conservation.

One of the main reasons that this has proved successful in these countries is that they have been able to capitalize on conservation by developing TOURISM. This has led to a substantial income from ecotourists who come to Africa to view wildlife in its natural environments. As a result, many African countries are actively seeking to increase their protected lands. South Africa, for example, which already has 21 national parks, has recently announced a goal of increasing the area of its protected lands from 5 to 8 percent and of protected marine coastline from 17 percent to 30 percent.

Governments are not the only parties actively involved in conservation efforts. Private individuals also have made a mark on conservation, especially in South Africa. Thousands of acres of former ranchland have been converted to private game parks with high-end lodges and resorts for ecotourists. These have transformed the big-game hunting industry at the same time that it has preserved large tracts of land from DEVELOPMENT.

International bodies are another factor. Especially effective in this are several conventions, as well as the establishment of endangered and threatened species lists. A worldwide ivory ban, for example, was implemented by the Convention on Trade and Endangered Species in

1990. This has decreased the market for internationally traded ivory, which previously had led to the slaughter of countless elephants. In another area the Producers Group for West and Central Africa, formed in 2002 by the World Wildlife Federation, has promoted sustainable use of timber resources. This effort, which has the support of many logging companies, has had some success in limiting illegal logging activities. Elsewhere the World Summit on Sustainable Development had a hand in setting goals for water conservation and sustainable use, while increasing the number of people with access to safe water.

MADAGASCAR received pledges of financial support from several international bodies, including the World Bank and the U.S. Agency for International Development, for its National Environmental Action Plan. This plan is intended to increase the amount of land under protection in an area that is renowned for its large number of endemic plant and animal species.

Wildlife conservation in southern Africa sometimes results in unusual roadside signs. This one in a national park in South Africa warns drivers of the possibility of "elephant crossing." © Corel

In addition to wildlife conservation, soil conservation is of vital importance in Africa, particularly because so many people in Africa depend, either partially or completely, on subsistence AGRICULTURE. Numerous international agencies and governmental bodies are currently conducting research in Africa on soil erosion and conservation. One result of this research has been strategies for protecting against both soil erosion and nutrient leaching. Among the most prominent strategies is agroforestry, which encourages farmers to intersperse trees and bushes with FOOD CROPS. This stabilizes the soil and replenishes it with nitrogen, making farmers' fields more productive.

Scientific research has also been useful in exploring the possibility of breeding and reintroducing endangered or threatened animals into the wild in order to increase their populations. South Africa has a research center that has begun to reintroduce wild dogs that have been raised in captivity. In addition, this research center raises cheetahs for use in zoos so that fewer cheetahs will be taken from the wild. Centers like these also provide educational services, something that has proved to be of great importance, especially with regard to wildlife conservation. When farmers and ranchers know the importance of preserving local wildlife they are more likely to call for endangered animals to be picked up rather than killing them on sight.

Despite the gains that have been made in many areas of natural resource conservation, there is still much work to be done with regard to conservation in Africa. Increasing populations have put added pressure on wildlife and habitats, as well as on water and soil resources. Land scarcity has resulted in squatters cutting down FORESTS for cultivation. Population increases have led rural people to cut down trees for use as cooking firewood. National and international agencies have started to address these issues, developing conservation strategies that are realistic for rural Africans. For example, fuel-efficient cook stoves have been introduced to reduce the amount of wood needed by each household. In addition, the planting of eucalyptus trees has been encouraged because these trees grow quickly and can be cut repeatedly for use as firewood.

Another area in need of continuous monitoring in Africa is poaching. Persistent POVERTY has resulted in the need for people to make a living however they can. Killing animals for meat—as well as for body parts that are in high demand on the international market—are commonplace for some Africans. Many governments have established anti-poaching squads whose job is to protect the wildlife from this danger.

Interfacing conservation efforts with the local population has become an essential part of protecting natural resources. Educational extension programs have emerged all over Africa to provide information on specific animal species and to enlist the help of local people in protecting these animals. Strategies have been developed, for example, for keeping elephants out of maize fields as well as keeping cheetahs and lions away from cattle and other livestock. In this way, these programs are making strides toward the protection of important wildlife species.

See also: ENVIRONMENTAL ISSUES (Vol. V); WORLD BANK AND AFRICA (Vol. V).

Further readings: Bruce Aylward and Ernst Lutz, eds., *Nature Tourism, Conservation, and Development in KwaZulu-Natal, South Africa* (Washington, D.C.: International Band for Reconstruction and Development/The World Bank, 2003); Ted T. Cable, *Commitments of the Heart: Odysseys in West African Conservation* (Champaign, Ill.: Sagamore Publishing, 2002); C. M. Hill, F. V. Osborn, and A. J. Plumptre, *Human-Wildlife Conflict: Identifying the Problem and Possible Solutions* (Bronx, N.Y.: Wildlife Conservation Society, 2002); Thomas P. Ofcansky, *Paradise Lost: A History of Game Preservation in East Africa* (Morgantown, W.Va.: West Virginia University Press, 2002).

constructive engagement   Controversial international diplomatic policy. A government that opts for constructive engagement eschews radical change in favor of maintaining the status quo and encouraging incremental change. The policy was a subject of debate in the 1980s, as countries—including Great Britain and the United States—chose a path of constructive engagement in diplomatic relations with the APARTHEID government of SOUTH AFRICA. Though the term is usually associated with the policy toward South Africa, debate continues today about this approach as Western countries maintain trading and diplomatic relations with other African states run by undemocratic or repressive governments. The heart of the debate is whether governments pursuing such a policy are genuinely supportive of DEMOCRATIZATION or whether it is an excuse for conducting "business as usual."

Early in the 1980s the United States began its constructive engagement policy under President Ronald Reagan (1911–2004). Rejecting more direct action against South Africa, Reagan and his administration claimed that the processes of free market capitalism would naturally create an environment in which South Africa's racist apartheid policies could no longer survive. Reagan's administration encouraged American companies operating in South Africa to serve as models for fair hiring and racial equality in the workplace. Reagan himself also made regular statements calling for democratic change in the country.

Those who supported constructive engagement conceded that certain features of the South African government were contrary to American values of democracy and equality. However, they also stated that non-confrontational diplomacy was the best way to effect peaceful, lasting change in South Africa. Critics of constructive engagement argued that a path of quiet diplomacy with the white-minority government was a tacit endorsement of apartheid.

One of the key testing grounds of the policy was in the area of arms sales. Throughout the 1970s, the South African government had been locked in armed struggles against insurgents at home. The country also supplied weapons and military expertise to its allies in such war-torn countries as MOZAMBIQUE, SOUTH WEST AFRICA (today's NAMIBIA), southern ANGOLA, and ZIMBABWE. Because of this, the United States had refrained from large-scale arms sales to South Africa. Indeed, in 1979 the United States had approved the sale of only $25,000 worth of military equipment to South Africa. Significant changes followed the constructive engagement policy, however. From 1981 to 1984 the U.S. government led by Ronald Reagan approved the sale of more than $28 billion dollars worth of military equipment to the country. Claiming that constructive engagement valued business profits over democracy and HUMAN RIGHTS, opponents labeled the American policy "morally suspect" and called for immediate trade sanctions and disinvestment from South Africa.

Ultimately, in 1986 the U.S. Congress passed the Comprehensive Anti-Apartheid Act, which approved limited sanctions on the sale of American arms and goods to South Africa. The sanctions, along with growing anti-apartheid sentiment worldwide, helped to finally bring about change in South Africa. In 1994, less than a decade after the end of American constructive engagement, South Africa held its first free and democratic elections.

Further reading: Elliott P. Skinner, ed., *Beyond Constructive Engagement: United States Foreign Policy Toward Africa* (New York: Paragon House, 1986).

Conté, Lansana (1934–) *President of Guinea*

Born in Dubreka, GUINEA, Conté had an underprivileged upbringing and little formal education. A colonel in the military, he served as a bodyguard and close confidante of dictator Ahmed Sékou TOURÉ (1922–1984) until Touré unexpectedly died during heart surgery in the United States. Conté and the military stepped in, suspending the national constitution, banning Touré's ruling political party, and establishing the Military Committee for National Recovery (Comité militaire de redressement national, CMRN) to guide the creation of a new government. Conté assumed the presidency.

The CMRN was greeted with enthusiasm by Guineans, who were relieved to be rid of Touré's oppressive leadership, and, initially, the CMRN took action to remove the lasting effects of Touré's rule. However, a split between Conté and his prime minister, Colonel Diarra Traoré (1936–1985), eventually led to an attempted COUP D'ÉTAT by Traoré in 1985. The attempted coup resulted in violent reprisals against Traoré's Maninka-speaking people by Guineans who recalled the torments they suffered under Sékou Touré, also a Maninka speaker. Conté, a member of the smaller Susu population, approved of the reprisals, setting the stage for increased ethnic tensions, though the tensions were among those who spoke one or another of the Mande languages.

After the failed coup, Conté reorganized the government, establishing a Council of Ministers and giving civilians a majority presence in the government for the first time. However, he came under fire for attempting to strengthen his personal power by appointing a disproportionate number of his fellow Susu to government positions. In 1990 a new constitution was established, and in 1993 Conté was officially elected president as a member of the Party for Unity and Progress (PUP). He was re-elected in both 1998 and 2001. Conté and the PUP then amended the constitution to allow Conté to run again, drawing criticism and raising fears of another authoritarian regime.

In spite of the positive economic reforms and general movement toward continued DEMOCRATIZATION that he oversaw, Conté has yet to fully exploit the financial potential of his mineral-rich country. Unrest among the Maninka-speaking population, who claim unfair treatment under Conté's largely Susu government, has been increasing. Conté also faces problems arising from Guinea's huge numbers of incoming REFUGEES fleeing CIVIL WARS in neighboring LIBERIA and SIERRA LEONE. He has been accused of aiding Liberian rebels in their attempts to overthrow the government of Charles TAYLOR (1948–), since ousting him, it was hoped, would end the refugee crisis.

See also: ETHNIC CONFLICT IN AFRICA (Vol. V); ETHNICITY AND IDENTITY (Vol. I); SUSU (Vols. II, III).

corruption Illegal acts by officials that come at the expense of their constituency or the state. Most commonly, corruption takes the form of bribes, which necessarily undermine the fidelity of leadership. Corruption threatens democracy, stability, and economic DEVELOPMENT. Rooting out corruption is of particular concern in Africa. According to Transparency International, a leading nongovernment organization, eight of the world's most corrupt countries are African.

The African states of NIGERIA, ANGOLA, IVORY COAST, CAMEROON, UGANDA, KENYA, and the Democratic Republic of the CONGO have all suffered from rampant misdeeds of leadership. With regard to corruption, there is often a close relationship between large, rich businesses trying to cut through bureaucratic red tape and the officials who are in place to apply laws to preserve the public good. Industries that work with a country's NATURAL RESOURCES, particularly OIL, tend to generate high levels of corruption. The profit margins are high and state officials often centralize control of the resources in the name of the people.

In extreme cases, corruption transcends the national level and becomes a part of daily life. Even the most basic of official tasks—getting a driver's license or national identity card, going to the post office, purchasing property, even voting—can require an extra cash payment to the local bureaucrat in charge. As a consequence of corruption, people become disenfranchised, trust in leaders diminishes, and democratic rule is threatened. State employees, from ministers to clerks, find that their salaries often go unpaid for long periods of time. Corrupt officials say they are collecting "fees for services" not "bribes." Many international businesses cannot function in such a climate and invest elsewhere.

There is debate about the origin and nature of what Western observers call *corruption* in Africa. To some, it is a feature of traditional life that has not disappeared over time. To others, corruption was inherited from unethical European colonial regimes along with the poor state of economic affairs. Still others point to exploitative trading practices and corporate mismanagement to show that corruption in developed countries is even more deeply seated than in Africa.

Regardless of where corruption originates and the form it takes, legislative controls and an independent judiciary are the greatest protections against it. The former promotes transparency while the latter offers disincentives from running afoul of the law. An active and independent CIVIL SOCIETY also helps by monitoring public expenditures on private goods and private payments for public services.

See also: DEMOCRATIZATION (Vol. V), COLONIAL RULE (Vol. IV).

Further reading: Jean-Francois Bayart, *The State in Africa: The Politics of the Belly* (New York: Longman, 1993); Robert I. Rotberg, *Africa's Discontent: Coping With Human and Natural Disasters* (Cambridge, Mass.: World Peace Foundation, 2003); William Reno, *Corruption and State Politics in Sierra Leone* (Cambridge, U.K.: Cambridge University Press, 1995).

Cotonou Largest city and principal port of the Republic of BENIN (formerly DAHOMEY), located between the Gulf of Guinea and Lake Nodoué. Cotonou fell under the rule of the kingdom of Dahomey in the 18th century. In 1851, the French were allowed to establish a trading post there, and 32 years later they occupied the city to prevent British domination of the area. They then used Cotonou as a base to expand their control in the region. The country gained independence in 1960. Although Porto Novo is the official national capital, many government offices are in Cotonou, and most international diplomats remain based there.

With a port facility that was improved to allow for sea-faring vessels in 1965, the city is the TRANSPORTATION hub of Benin. It also has a terminal for the Benin-Niger Railway, and an international airport. Various CASH CROPS and commodities such as groundnuts (peanuts), palm products, coffee, cacao, and cotton, along with petroleum products, bauxite, and iron, all make their way through the city. Export goods are shipped out of the city's port or transported to the interior by rail and then by road until they reach the navigable portion of the Niger River, which is located to the northeast. There is also a small manufacturing sector in Cotonou that produces motor vehicles and bicycles, textiles, cement, beer, and timber products.

While the city's main importance is as a transportation and communications center, Cotonou also houses the National University of Benin (founded in 1970) and several research institutes for AGRICULTURE, geology, and textiles. In 2000 Cotonou was the site of the signing of the Cotonou Agreement, which specified trade relations between the African, Caribbean, and Pacific states and the European Union. In 2003 the city's population was estimated at 734,600.

coup d'état   Sudden change in government, usually referring to the violent overthrow of an existing government by a small group. Literally meaning *a stroke of state* in French, the coup d'état has been a regular feature of African politics since the beginning of the independence period. Why they have become so common in Africa is a subject of debate, but the political, economic, and social conditions, as well as the often negative repercussions, are clear.

Usually carried out by factions within a country's military, coups have proven to be among the most common, and destructive, forms of regime transition in Africa. Between 1960 and 2004 there were 75 coups in Africa and close to 300 coup attempts. The COMOROS alone has been the site of 19 coups or coup attempts, more than any other country in Africa. Coups have superceded elections, revolution, and heredity as the primary means of governmental change. The causes of coups are manifold, but they are generally functions of both weak social organization and individual military ambition.

Throughout Africa, rivalries, often based on ethnic differences, lead to significant social, political, and economic disruption. These disuprtions often a lead to a coup d'état. Furthermore, coups d'états are more common than revolutions when military leaders make up a nation's elite class. Examples of coup engineers who came from a military elite include Major-General Ibrahim BABANGIDA (1941–) in NIGERIA, General Francois Bozize (1952–) in the CENTRAL AFRICAN REPUBLIC, and Denis SASSOU-NGUESSO (1943–) in the Republic of the CONGO. In contrast, the military in the Comoros is weak, and elites have hired mercenaries, most notably Robert DENARD (1929–), to stage coups.

Commonly, once a military leader assumes power in a coup, the military itself becomes the surrogate for social or political institutions that may have been weak during the rule of corrupt or ineffective civilian leaders. Coup leaders of this ilk include Idi AMIN (c. 1925–2003), in UGANDA, MOBUTU SESE SEKO (1930–1997), in former ZAÏRE, and MENGISTU HAILE MARIAM (c. 1937–), in ETHIOPIA. In their cases, after the coup, coercion by the military became very common.

What follows a coup d'état is commonly problematic, for it is all too rare that military leaders also have political expertise. When General Robert GUÉÏ (1941–2002) took over the IVORY COAST in 2000, for instance, the economy came to a grinding halt. The regime of Mobutu Sese Seko was so corrupt that the word *kleptocracy,* meaning *rule by thieves,* was coined to describe it. A coup d'état is an opportunistic action, so if a post-coup leader does not make certain changes to the system, he can expect that it is just a matter of time before another coup is attempted. Coups in contemporary Africa are likely to diminish not because the opportunities are fewer but because alternate ways for elites to gain power, including electoral democracy, are becoming more viable.

Further reading: A. B. Assensoh and Yvette M. Alex-Assensoh, *African Military History and Politics: Coups and Ideological Incursions, 1900–Present* (New York: Palgrave Macmillan, 2002).

Cuba and Africa   When Fidel Castro (1926–) came to power in Cuba in 1959, his nation's diplomatic relations with the African continent consisted of only one diplomat in EGYPT. Beginning in the early 1960s, though, the interaction between Castro's Cuba and nations throughout Africa increased rapidly.

Although it is located a mere 90 miles (145 km) off the coast of Florida, the island nation of Cuba under Castro was politically aligned with the communist Soviet Union. After World War II (1939–45), communist regimes challenged democratic nations around the world, and Africa, with many of its newly independent countries in search of foreign support, became a hotly contested region in the political and ideological battles known as the Cold War.

Soon after Castro came to power, Cuba became involved in ALGERIA, supporting the socialist NATIONAL LIBERATION FRONT as it fought for independence from French colonialism. Cuba's support for African INDEPENDENCE MOVEMENTS included not only overt and covert military operations, but also humanitarian aid. Non-military aid ranged from medical missions supplying desperately needed doctors to the training of teachers in the fight against illiteracy.

In 1965 Cuba's famed military leader Che Guevara (1928–1967) traveled with a contingent of Cuban officers to the Congo (now the Democratic Republic of the CONGO). There, they spent six months trying to train fighters for the "Simba Rebellion," a movement begun by members loyal to assassinated Congolese prime minister Patrice LUMUMBA (1925–1961). The movement sought to overthrow President Moïse TSHOMBE (1919–1969), whom the rebels considered a puppet for Western MINING interests. Within six months, however, Guevara became disillusioned by the lack of commitment exhibited by both the rebel soldiers and their leaders, which included future Congolese president Laurent KABILA (c. 1939–2001). Sensing that the rebellion was doomed to failure, Guevara fled east across the border to TANZANIA, then returned to Cuba.

With Cuba's involvement in the Congo, Castro soon became familiar with the battles that were being waged against the Portuguese colonial government in nearby ANGOLA. By 1966 Cuban soldiers were training and fighting side-by-side with the forces of the pro-communist POPULAR MOVEMENT FOR THE LIBERATION OF ANGOLA (Movimento Popular de Libertação de Angola, MPLA). The conflict in Angola pitted the MPLA against the NATIONAL FRONT FOR THE LIBERATION OF ANGOLA (Frente Nacional de Libertação de Angola, FNLA) and the NATIONAL UNION FOR THE TOTAL INDEPENDENCE OF ANGOLA (União Nacional para a Independência Total de Angola, UNITA), both of which were anti-communist.

Cuban aid in Angola continued through the 1970s and even increased in November 1975, when the MPLA declared Angolan independence from Portugal. Despite independence, Angola remained unstable, and the volatility of the political situation eventually drew the Soviet Union and the United States—enemy superpowers—into the fray. The Soviet Union began supporting the MPLA-Cuban faction with military advisors and weapons. The United States, for its part, helped the FNLA and UNITA, covertly funneling support through SOUTH AFRICA, which also sided with the two anti-communist factions.

Throughout the 1970s both the United States and the Soviet Union took an increasing interest in the outcome of the independence struggles in Angola. As each nation sent its cutting-edge military weaponry to be used in the conflict, the fighting became increasingly deadly. Because of this, some observers referred to Angola as a "Cold War killing field."

Cuban military action in Angola culminated in the Battle of Cuito Cuanavale (1988), a bloody conflict in the southeastern part of the country that led to the eventual withdrawal of South African forces from southern Angola into the northern part of neighboring NAMIBIA.

As civil war raged in Angola, Cuba also became involved in the Ogaden War (1976–78) between ETHIOPIA and SOMALIA, in northeast Africa. Originally, Cuba (and the Soviet Union) supported the Somali government. However, when Somalia persisted in rejecting diplomatic means to ending the war, Cuba became more sympathetic with the Ethiopian side. By 1978 as many as 15,000 Cuban soldiers—some of whom had previously fought in Angola—were fighting alongside Ethiopian troops, quickly turning the tide in favor of Ethiopia. When Ethiopia and Somalia finally signed a peace agreement in 1988, the last of the Cuban troops, numbering about 3,000, withdrew from the region.

Since 1990, when Namibia, Angola's neighbor to the south, finally achieved independence, Cuba's involvement in Africa has been limited mostly to humanitarian aid, such as medical missions in South Africa.

See also: CIVIL WARS (Vol. V); COLD WAR AND AFRICA (Vol. IV); NATIONALISM AND INDEPENDENCE MOVEMENTS (Vol. IV); PORTUGAL AND AFRICA (Vols. III, IV, V); SOVIET UNION AND AFRICA (Vols. IV, V); UNITED STATES AND AFRICA (Vols. IV, V).

Further reading: Gleijeses, Piero, *Conflicting Missions: Havana, Washington, and Africa, 1959–1976* (Chapel Hill, N.C.: University of North Carolina Press, 2002).

Cummings-John, Constance (Constance Horton Cummings-John) (1918–2000) *Sierra Leonean educator and politician*

Cummings-John was born into the Krio (Creole) elite of FREETOWN, SIERRA LEONE. Active politically from age 20, she held municipal office for much of the 1940s, 1950s, and 1960s. As one of the country's leading educators, in 1952 she founded both a school for girls and the Sierra Leone Women's Movement (SLWM). Her administrative career culminated in 1966 with her election as mayor of Freetown, a first for an African woman.

When Sierra Leone gained its independence from Britain in 1961, Cummings-John was perhaps the leading female political figure in the SIERRA LEONE PEOPLE'S PARTY (SLPP). In 1962, however, a split within the SLPP cost her election to parliament. She then focused her efforts on her school, the Sierra Leone Women's Movement, and Freetown's municipal government.

While Cummings-John was in England in 1967, a military COUP D'ÉTAT led to the abolition of Freetown's city council. She remained abroad until 1976, at which time she returned to Sierra Leone to work for the women's movement. The political situation again deteriorated under the increasingly despotic government of President Siaka Stevens (1905– 1988), so Cummings-John returned to London, where she remained. In her 1995 autobiography, *Memoirs of a Krio Leader,* she re-flected back on her career with pride in her accomplishments on behalf of EDUCATION and women.

See also: CUMMINGS-JOHN, CONSTANCE (Vol. IV).

D

Dacko, David (1930–) *Two-time president of the Central African Republic*

Born in Bouchia in what was then the French colony of Oubangui-Chari, Dacko had familial ties to the leading figures in the colony's movement toward independence. He was the cousin of Barthélémy Boganda (d. 1959), the leader of the Movement for Social Development in Black Africa (Mouvement pour l'Evolution Sociale de l'Afrique Noire, MESAN) and the first president of the CENTRAL AFRICAN REPUBLIC (CAR) under its 1959 constitution. He was also the cousin of Jean-Bedel BOKASSA (1921–1996), who would later overthrow Dacko in a COUP D'ÉTAT.

In 1959 Boganda died in a plane crash, and, in 1960, the CAR became fully independent from the French Union with Dacko as president. Dacko revised the constitution, making himself the center of power and making MESAN the only legal political party. A new constitution was adopted in 1964 but did not last long, as Dacko was overthrown the following year by Bokassa, who was then the commander-in-chief of the military. Bokassa's brutal 13-year dictatorship came to an end when French paratroopers stormed the CAR's capital city of BANGUI in 1979, reinstating Dacko as president. In 1981 Dacko and his new party, the Central African Democratic Union, won the presidential elections. Later that year, however, Dacko was overthrown again, this time by General André Kolingba (1936–).

See also: FRANCE AND AFRICA (Vols. III, IV, V); OUBANGUI-CHARI (Vol. IV).

Dahomey
Former name of the Republic of BENIN during French colonial rule and for the first 15 years of independence. In 1975 Dahomey was renamed in honor of the great Edo kingdom of Benin, which once flourished in the region of present-day NIGERIA, to the east of the Republic of Benin.

See also: BENIN, KINGDOM OF (Vols. II, III, IV); DAHOMEY (Vols. III, IV).

Dakar
Port city and capital of modern SENEGAL located on the Cap-Vert Peninsula, the westernmost point of the African continent. Strategically located between Europe and southern Africa—and also a logical launching point for ships sailing from Africa to the Americas—Dakar has a long history as an important commercial port. Because of this Dakar was constantly undergoing improvements to its INFRASTRUCTURE. By the time of Senegal's independence in 1960, the city was connected by rail, air, and road to most major cities in West Africa. Its status as a leading commercial port continues today, with trade items including groundnuts (peanuts), peanut oil, petroleum, and phosphates. More recently, tuna fishing has become important. Major industries in the city include the production of sugar, peanut oil, flour, beverages, textiles, soap, and fish.

International TOURISM has also become important. There are excellent African ART and anthropology museums in Dakar proper, and thousands of tourists also visit the Slave Museum on nearby Gorée Island, which was one of the most heavily trafficked West African ports during the time of the transatlantic slave trade.

See also: DAKAR (Vol. IV); FRANCE AND AFRICA (Vols. III, IV, V); GORÉE ISLAND (Vol. III); SLAVE TRADE (Vol. IV); WOLOF (Vols. II, IV).

Dangarembga, Tsitsi (1959–) *Zimbabwean author, filmmaker, and playwright*

Tsitsi Dangarembga was born in Mutoko, ZIMBABWE. She attended primary and secondary school in Zimbabwe before going on to study MEDICINE at Cambridge University, in England. Before completing her degree in 1980, she returned home. She then attended the University of Zimbabwe, where she received a degree in psychology. While at the university she wrote plays and participated in the production of two of them. In 1983 she became an active member of a theater group known as Zambuko, which performed some of her plays.

Dangarembga is best known for her first novel, *Nervous Conditions* (1988), which dealt with the life of a young African woman living in colonial RHODESIA during the 1960s. It was the first novel to be published in English by a black Zimbabwean woman. Now translated into a number of languages, the novel won the 1989 Commonwealth Writers Prize in the Africa section. Later, in 1992, Dangarembga wrote the story for *Neria*, which was adapted into the highest-grossing film in Zimbabwean history. Produced by Zimbabwe's Media for Development Trust, *Neria* deals with a woman's fight for her rights and property.

The well-known Zimbabwean musician Oliver Mtukudzi (1952–) recorded the soundtrack for *Neria* and also played the role of Neria's brother in the film. Mtukudzi won the 1992 Best Soundtrack award from M-Net, a popular South African satellite network.

In 1996 Dangarembga directed *Everyone's Child*, which deals with the issue of HIV/AIDS IN AFRICA. The film, which is the first feature to be directed by a black Zimbabwean woman, has garnered praise at film festivals worldwide.

See also: CINEMA (Vols. IV, V); LITERATURE IN MODERN AFRICA (Vol. V); WOMEN IN MODERN AFRICA (Vol. V).

Dar es Salaam (Dar al-Salam) Port, acting capital, and largest city of TANZANIA.

The city's name means "haven of peace" in Arabic. After the German East Africa Company set up a trading center at the port's location in 1888, Dar es Salaam became the capital of German East Africa (1891–1916). The city later served as the capital of Tanganyika (1961–1964) and the capital of TANZANIA, the nation created when Tanganyika and ZANZIBAR united in 1964. In 1974 the government of Tanzania decided to relocate its capital to DODOMA because of its more central loca-

tion. Relocation planning began in earnest in the early 1980s, and it was supposed to be completed by 1990. The executive branch of the government, however, remains in Dar es Salaam, though the National Assembly now meets in Dodoma.

Improvements to the INFRASTRUCTURE, completed by the British in the years after 1916, put Dar es Salaam on its path to becoming a major trade and commercial center. The railroad, which the Germans started building in 1905, linked the port with the interior. Further improvements have been made to the rail system since independence in 1961, which have enhanced Dar es Salaam's capacity as a port. As a result Dar es Salaam is now connected to Lake Tanganyika, Lake VICTORIA, ZAMBIA, and to a tributary of the Congo River, which allows shipments to travel to and from many places in eastern Africa. Equally important was the construction of the Tanzam Railway, built with the assistance of the Chinese People's Republic between 1970 and 1976. Its completion allowed Zambia to ship its copper through Tanzania, bypassing port facilities in SOUTH AFRICA with its much-hated system of APARTHEID.

In addition to copper, the major EXPORTS include coffee, sisal, cotton, and other CASH CROPS. Major industries that have developed in the city to take advantage of its commercial and TRANSPORTATION facilities are food products, textiles, clothing, shoes, OIL, cigarettes, and metal products.

Dar es Salaam is home to one of the most important discoveries of modern archaeology. On July 17, 1959, archaeologist Mary LEAKEY (1913–1996) found an *Australopithecus boisei* cranium in the Olduvai Gorge, in the Serengeti Plains of northern TANZANIA. Named for its massive teeth, "Nutcracker Man," which dates from 2.3 to 1.4 million years ago, is now housed in Dar es Salaam's National Museum.

In 1964 Julius NYERERE (1922–1999), who had been premier of independent Tanganyika, became the first president of Tanzania. He moved the country in the direction of African socialism, which in Tanzania was known as *UJAMAA*. During this period the focus of government policy was on the rural areas—where the vast majority of Tanzanians lived—which caused the urban infrastructure to suffer from neglect. At the same time, the government's emphasis on greater social equity led to a major downturn in the economy, putting great pressure on Dar es Salaam. As the economy began to recover in the 1990s, the city underwent a period of growth. As a result roads were improved and the service industry was expanded.

Today Dar es Salaam features many modern buildings that contribute to the mix of Swahili, German, Asian, and British ARCHITECTURE in the urban landscape. There is a major medical institution as well as several other educational facilities, including the University of Dar es Salaam (founded in 1961), a national museum, and nearby botanical gardens. By 2000 the population of Dar es Salaam was hovering near 2 million.

See also: DAR ES SALAAM (Vols. III, IV); GERMAN EAST AFRICA (Vol. IV); OLDUVAI GORGE (Vol. I); SWAHILI COAST (Vols. II, III, IV); TANGANYIKA (Vol. IV); URBANIZATION (Vols. IV, V); URBAN LIFE AND CULTURE (Vols. IV, V).

Darfur Region in western Republic of the SUDAN. Bordered by the CENTRAL AFRICAN REPUBLIC and CHAD, Darfur is mostly dry plateaus, with mountains rising in the central region. It covers about 75,900 square miles (196,555 sq km) and is home to almost 6,000,000 people, who are largely divided between African agriculturalists and nomadic Arab pastoralists.

In the spring of 2003 a revolt broke out in western Sudan in the wake of a final resolution to the civil war in the southern Sudan. That conflict, during the 1990s, had cost almost 2 million lives, and its temporary resolution required the peace-making efforts of many nations. The rebellion in Darfur was spearheaded by the Sudanese Liberation Army, a mostly Christian group. Their grievances were in part the result of the way in which the central government, focused for so long on the war in the south, had ignored the problems of the drought-stricken western part of the country. But it was also an outgrowth of many Darfurians' resentment of the way in which the central Sudanese government consistently favored the Muslim Arab population when it came to carrying out public works projects and dispensing jobs. Demanding a new style of government that would be more inclusive of the Sudan's various religious and ethnic groups, the rebels carried out a series of daring raids that humiliated the government in KHARTOUM.

After a brief period of trying to ignore the rebellion, the government finally decided to take steps to put it down. Not trusting its own army, which contained a high percentage of soldiers from Darfur, the government turned to Arab tribal leaders to deal with the revolt. Using their own forces, called *janjaweed* by the Sudanese, these tribal leaders began, with government assistance, a campaign that rapidly turned into bandit-style raids, terror, and murder. Amid charges of "ethnic cleansing" and even genocide, thousands of Darfurians left their homes, often driven out by violent raids by the *janjaweed*. The displaced people ultimately made their way into hastily arranged refugee camps in Chad and other parts of Sudan. By the summer of 2004, between 50,000 and 80,000 people had died, and more than a million people were left homeless.

Although it took many months for the world to take notice, the depths of the humanitarian crisis eventually became clear. Thousands of Darfurians had been the victims of rape, pillage, and murder, and thousands more were homeless, weakened by disease, and on the verge of starvation. With the Sudanese government continuing to deny responsibility for the situation, international pressure mounted as the possibility of many more deaths became increasingly probable.

See also: ARAB WORLD AND AFRICA (Vol. V); CIVIL WARS (Vol. V); DARFUR (Vols. II, III, IV); ETHNICITY AND IDENTITY (Vol. I); ISLAM, INFLUENCE OF (Vol. V); REFUGEES (Vol. V).

debt, foreign Money owed as a result of loans from the governments of foreign countries or from private lending institutions based in foreign countries. Escalating 25-fold since independence, foreign debt levels in Africa are now well beyond the ability of many countries to repay them. According to the World Bank, as of 1998 25 of the 30 countries categorized as "severely indebted, low-income countries" were in sub-Saharan Africa. A major problem is that the value of goods and services produced by poor African countries rarely balances out the amount of debt they carry. For instance, in 1998 the Democratic Republic of the CONGO owed more than $15 billion to foreign investors. This figure was 40 percent greater than the value of goods and services produced by the country in the same year. High debt keeps nations from sustaining a healthy economy and makes economic DEVELOPMENT nearly impossible.

The southern African country of ZAMBIA is one of the world's poorest, as measured by the 2002 United Nations Human Development Index. Out of a total of 173 nations, Zambia ranked 153. Its per-capita foreign debt is approximately $1,000, while its per-capita income is $870.

Although rooted in colonialism, Africa's recent economic woes started at independence, in the 1960s. Most new African countries had limited capital and suffered from disadvantageous trade agreements, fragile political institutions, and limited industry. In order to develop everything from AGRICULTURE to industry to INFRASTRUCTURE, they needed capital—which could only come from foreign lenders. Originally their loans were borrowed from developed countries under reasonable terms. However, the general economic situation quickly grew worse, and various competing views emerged on to explain how development economics led to the economic deterioration. One view, held by the World Bank, claimed that weak political institutions and rapidly growing populations led to economic instability. African states saw their EXPORTS deteriorate throughout the 1960s and 1970s. And without surging exports, a balance-of-payment crisis emerged and economies stagnated.

Another view argued that private markets were the *problem,* not the solution. Africa's poor infrastructure and unstable socio-political organization led to a dependence on wealthy countries. Thus, when there have been significant global economic disturbances—for instance, the OIL crises of 1973–74 and 1978–79 or the occasional collapse of commodity markets, such as coffee—vulnerable African economies were hit disproportionately hard.

Yet another view saw lending to African countries as an extension of neocolonialist policies, similar to the imperialist policies of the past. As the global system broke down into crisis, dependent African countries were forced to borrow more even as they produced less. Under this model, wealthy lender countries could thrive only if poor countries such as those in Africa were kept poor. In other words, willful *underdevelopment* was related to the expansion of wealth in rich countries. Whether or not this was the case, the debt grew worse, and, by 1971, sub-Saharan African countries owed $8.8 billion. By 1980 this figure had risen to $60.8 billion.

As the economic situation became worse, international lending policies began to change. Multilateral donors, such as the World Bank and International Monetary Fund, insisted that poor countries enter into STRUCTURAL ADJUSTMENT programs. These were based on the principal that if poor countries could build economic infrastructures and create a more sensible monetary policy, they could attract investment from businesses in the world's private markets. This, in turn, would increase production of exports. However, in order for structural adjustment to work, it was necessary to balance capital accounts, deflate currencies, and change economic conditions. Of course these changes required investment in the institutions needed to carry them out, so new loan programs were added to structural adjustment programs. As these programs were put in place throughout the continent, debt levels surged once again, to $107 billion, in 1985, and $235 billion, in 1995.

The creditors' rationale was that structural adjustment lending was an investment that would lead to economic growth. If and when that growth happened, the debt would become a comparatively small part of the economy, making debt service manageable. Unfortunately, economies remained stagnant. Domestic investment capital shrank through the 1980s and much of the 1990s, with many countries suffering from a declining quality of life for the average citizen. Where there was growth, the impact was commonly felt by only a small, well-placed part of the population, thereby aggravating already significant divides between the rich and the poor. Without an industrial engine of growth or an augmented tax base, debt burdens increased beyond any capacity to manage them.

In the early 1990s attempts were made to relieve some countries of their debt burdens. Some donors sought to swap debt for assurances that the African countries would fully pay off existing debt. Countries with fragile ecosystems of great global importance, such as KENYA and MADAGASCAR, instituted programs that allowed them to swap debt for the preservation of NATURAL RESOURCES. Under these programs, international CONSERVATION agencies bought up debt in return for government promises of environmental protection. All of these efforts were minor in scale, however.

By 1996 the World Bank recognized that debts had reached staggering proportions and that existing debt-rescheduling mechanisms were insufficient. It therefore embarked on an ambitious debt reduction program called the Highly Indebted Poor Countries Initiative (HIPC). The HIPC was launched as a comprehensive effort to reduce debt in the world's poorest countries to manageable levels. To qualify, a country had to be eligible for assistance from World Bank and the International Monetary Fund's Poverty Reduction and Growth Facility. The World Bank did a "debt sustainability analysis" and then compared existing debt to current export levels. With a few exceptions, if debt was 150 percent of exports or lower, then it was considered sustainable, and the country did not qualify. Those countries that had higher debt levels could apply for a reduction. In order to do so the applicant country had to meet certain demands. In 1999 this program expanded dramatically, and, by 2002, 36 African countries had qualified for HIPC.

Some critics have argued that the African debt was created through the erroneous policies of lenders. It should therefore be cancelled universally by these same lenders without any conditions or requirements. The Jubilee 2000, a global movement of CIVIL SOCIETY organizations set up in 1997 to campaign for debt relief, most broadly elaborates upon this idea. Rather than ensuring recipient-country transparency in fiscal policies, the movement's leaders argue that debt forgiveness should be accompanied by more transparent and innovative practices by lending agencies in order to avoid a repeat of the grave social and economic consequences felt under lending programs to date.

Some countries, including UGANDA and BURKINA FASO, benefited greatly from the HIPC. Nonetheless, critics have assailed the program for failing to make a difference in the

African countries that qualified for debt reduction. Other critics contend that the program essentially created the same conditions as the failed structural adjustment programs of the 1980s, thereby increasing the debt burden rather than helping to alleviate it.

See also: ECONOMIC ASSISTANCE (Vol. V); FOREIGN INVESTMENT (Vol. V); INDUSTRIALIZATION (Vol. V); TRADE AND COMMERCE (Vol. V).

Further reading: Omar Kabbaj, *The Challenge of African Development* (Oxford, U.K.: Oxford University Press, 2003); E. Wayne Nafziger, *The Debt Crisis in Africa* (Baltimore, N.J.: Johns Hopkins University Press, 1993); John Serieux and Yiagadeesen Samy, *Debt Relief for the Poorest Countries* (New Brunswick, N.J.: Transaction Publishers, 2003).

Déby, Idriss (1952–) *Military president of Chad*

A member of the Zaghawa people, Déby was born in the village of Fada in French Equatorial Africa, in the region that, in 1960, became independent CHAD. Déby entered the army, and, in 1982, he participated in a COUP D'ÉTAT that placed Hissène HABRÉ (1942–) in power and Déby at the head of the army. Déby gained popularity by repelling invading Libyan forces. Envious of Déby's successes, Habré sent him to France for military training and then named Déby's cousin, Hassan Djamous, to command the army.

> Déby's skills in desert warfare earned him the nickname "cowboy of the desert" from French troops who were stationed in Chad.

Déby returned to find Chadians chafing under Habré's regime. Named as co-conspirators in an attempted coup, Déby and Djamous escaped to the Republic of the SUDAN, where they rallied an army of mostly Zaghawa and Sudanese soldiers, forming the Patriotic Salvation Movement (Mouvement Patriotique du Salut, MPS). Receiving aid from France and LIBYA, in 1990 the MPS invaded Chad and conquered the capital of N'DJAMENA. Habré fled with a large portion of the country's treasury.

When he assumed the presidency, Déby moved toward DEMOCRATIZATION. He allowed for the establishment of political parties in 1991 and formed a commission on HUMAN RIGHTS to investigate violations perpetrated by Habré's administration. In 1996 a constitution was established, and, that same year, Déby and the MPS won Chad's first elections. He won a second term in 2001.

Déby has accumulated both praise and criticism as president. Though he has made efforts to incorporate opposition members into his government and has negotiated with rebel groups, Habré loyalists still raid the Lake Chad region, and the nation is showing a political polarization between the north and south of the country. Despite reforms enacted in 1991, Chad's military remains oversized, oppressive, and ethnically imbalanced, favoring Déby's Zaghawa over other groups.

> The World Bank demanded that Chad use its oil profits only for non-military development purposes. However, Déby used $4 million from the initial payments to purchase weaponry, reasoning, "It is patently obvious that without security, there can be no development programs."

Déby's main problem, however, is the Chadian economy, which has been one of the worst in Africa. In 2000 Déby signed a deal with the World Bank to fund an OIL pipeline from southern Chad to CAMEROON. The pipeline, which would exploit Chad's newly discovered oil supply and bring billions of dollars in revenue to the impoverished nation, is generally seen as the key to Chad's DEVELOPMENT and Déby's ultimate legacy.

See also: WORLD BANK AND AFRICA (Vol. V); ZAGHAWA (Vol. III).

de Klerk, F. W. (Frederik Willem) (1936–) *South African president from 1989 to 1994*

Very little in de Klerk's political career prior to 1989 gave indication that he would boldly initiate a significant reform of APARTHEID that ultimately culminated in its abolition. He and his politically prominent Afrikaner family were widely perceived as staunch supporters of the apartheid regime. Following a career in law, de Klerk formally entered politics, in 1972, as a member of Parliament for the ruling National Party. Six years later he became a cabinet minister holding several portfolios. De Klerk also served as the leader of the Transvaal wing of the National Party. After P. W. BOTHA (1916–) suffered a heart attack, de Klerk replaced him as head of the National Party in February 1989. Later that year he became president of SOUTH AFRICA.

In an unanticipated move, de Klerk began meaningful negotiations with imprisoned and exiled members of the anti-apartheid movement, most notably Nelson MANDELA (1918–). Then, on February 2, 1989, he opened Parliament by announcing the unbanning of black opposition political groups—such as the AFRICAN NATIONAL CONGRESS (ANC), PAN-AFRICANIST CONGRESS, and the South African Communist Party—and the release of

Although he hailed from a prominent conservative Afrikaner family, F. W. de Klerk (seen here, center, in 1994) helped reform South Africa's government so that the country's black majority could participate more fully in the political process. © AP/Wide World Photos

many political prisoners. He undertook this radical course of action despite opposition within his own party and with the understanding that these actions would eventually result in the end of both National Party political dominance and white-minority rule. Although negotiations with the ANC and other political parties toward a new power-sharing arrangement progressed fitfully over the next four years, these meetings succeeded in establishing a provisional constitution. They also laid the groundwork for South Africa's first fully democratic elections.

The National Party emerged from the historic 1994 elections as the second-largest party within the new Government of National Unity (GNU), and de Klerk occupied the position of second deputy president. To register his discontent with the ruling ANC government, however, in 1996 de Klerk withdrew his party from the GNU to assume the position of the official opposition. De Klerk stepped down as party leader the following year and quit political life.

In 1993 de Klerk and Mandela were jointly awarded the Nobel Peace Prize for their extraordinary efforts to end more than 45 years of apartheid rule in a remarkably peaceful fashion.

Further reading: Willem de Klerk, *The Last Trek— A New Beginning: The Autobiography* (Basingstoke, South Africa: Macmillan, 1998).

de Menezes, Fradique (1942–　) *President of São Tomé and Príncipe*

De Menezes was born to a São Toméan mother and Portuguese father and grew up as a Portuguese citizen in a Portuguese colony. After receiving his education in Portugal, with further study in Belgium, de Menezes entered business in SÃO TOMÉ AND PRINCIPE and soon rose to prominence exporting cocoa and importing cement. In addition to making him wealthy, his business dealings made him a prominent figure in his own country as well as throughout the west-central African region, and his status helped him become his country's minister of foreign affairs (1986–87) and an ambassador in Europe.

In 2001 de Menezes ran for president as the candidate of the Party for Democratic Convergence-Group Reflection

(PDC-GR). In spite of his relative inexperience, he won the election. He achieved his victory in part because the incumbent party had instituted strict economic reforms. But his popularity was also due to his campaign promise to see that the potential wealth from recently discovered offshore OIL deposits would be fairly distributed among a populace that had been, up to that point, relatively poor.

Until 2002 the majority Liberation Movement of São Tomé and Príncipe-Social Democratic Party controlled the country's parliament, sharing power with the PDC-GR and other minority parties. In the 2002 parliamentary election, however, no party won a majority, and de Menezes committed himself to governing by consultation.

In July 2003 de Menezes was in NIGERIA when a small group from São Tomé's army took advantage of his absence to stage a bloodless COUP D'ÉTAT. The action, most likely motivated by the wealth that will flow into government coffers from oil, threw the political future of São Tomé and Príncipe into question.

democratization Process of making a political system democratic. At the end of the 20th century, most countries south of the Sahara Desert embarked on a political path to bring about popular rule with free MARKETS and economic growth. Democratization was sometimes an integral part of the reform efforts.

Democracy means "rule by the people." In ancient Greece, where democracy has its roots, the community, not the government or state, had the authority.

Democracy as an ideal of governance has enjoyed unparalleled success. The challenge has been how to make it work in societies with large, diverse populations and complex bureaucracies. Since it was impractical to expect that all citizens could participate in governing decisions at all times, the original Greek model of direct democracy was untenable under certain conditions. In response to this problem, the Greek philosopher Aristotle (384–322 BCE) spoke of the systemization of politics. From this grew the idea of a "representative" democracy, in which leaders are elected by the people to represent their view within a governing body. In the 2,300 years that have followed, statesmen have tried to figure out democratic systems that are direct enough to ensure that the voice of the people is heard but is sufficiently representative that the system continues to function.

In the 18th century, European and American democracies grew organically out of crumbling monarchal sys-

tems. Along with this form of democracy came the basic liberal notions of personal freedom and equality. Compromises between direct and representative democracy resulted in hybrids like the common parliament. Under such a democratic system representatives are elected, but constitutional and other important changes must be put to the people in the form of a popular vote, or referendum.

As these views were popularized in the 20th century, the challenge became figuring out how to institutionalize and translate democratic ideals. In the process, the modern concept of democracy came to include government transparency, accountability of leadership, the viability of a CIVIL SOCIETY, and the DEVELOPMENT of an economic middle class that could support democratic values.

At independence African countries had a choice between dictatorship and democracy, although the choice was not all that straightforward. The economic freedoms associated with democracy, it was thought, would lead to a widening of the gap between rich and poor, which, in Africa, was already large. Other critics of unbridled economic freedom warned about the domination of some groups in society over others and the inability of the postcolonial state to bring about development. As a result many African countries opted for "developmental dictatorships" or other systems that significantly limited popular participation in the political process.

Some countries that chose the other, democratic path at independence saw political instability that led to democratic failure. Most notably, the first republic in NIGERIA struggled from 1960 until 1966, at which point a military COUP D'ÉTAT ended the democratic experiment. In fact, there is only one African case of a continued success with democracy: BOTSWANA. When Botswana gained its independence from Great Britain on September 30, 1966, it was a single-party, authoritarian state. However, since it held its first multiparty elections in 1969, it has seen only a broadening and deepening of its democratic institutions. Botswana's success with democracy is generally attributed to two things. First, the Bechuanaland Democratic Party, which was born of an elite nationalist movement headed by Sir Seretse KHAMA (1921–1980), was forced early on to employ democratic practices in building ruling coalitions. This helped mend existing social and economic rifts while simultaneously minimizing government graft and CORRUPTION. Second, the various ethnic groups of Bechuanaland gained power early and created a society that tended toward decentralized leadership. By 1989 there were only five functioning democracies in Africa—Botswana, SENEGAL, MAURITIUS, The GAMBIA, and ZIMBABWE. However, not one of these is an example of a democracy that survived from the early 1960s.

African Democracy and the End of the Cold War
With the collapse of the former Soviet Union in 1990–91,

autocratic African leaders such as MENGISTU HAILE MARIAM (c. 1937–) of ETHIOPIA could no longer look to communist countries to prop up their regimes. And as the influence of communism subsided, the United States, too, began to withdraw its support from some of the African leaders it had backed during the height of the Cold War. Congolese strongman MOBUTU SESE SEKO (1930–1997) is one such example. As the 1990s unfolded, the United States came to offer support for democratic transitions rather than for democracy-minded dictators. Within a two-year period, 40 of the 47 countries in sub-Saharan Africa launched into ambitious democratic reform programs. There were immediate concerns about whether democracy could work in Africa. However, it soon became clear that there was significant awareness of, and support for, political reform that could give African countries a democratic indigenous political base.

The challenge that emerged was that a popular African political base did not always keep with the type of democracy that the West wanted. For example, in the late 1980s ALGERIA began to move away from a one-party authoritarian state based on socialist principles toward a more politically pluralistic society. This led, in 1989, to elections in which other parties were allowed to compete with the NATIONAL LIBERATION FRONT (*Front de Libération Nationale,* FLN), which had been the sole legal political party until that point. The sitting FLN president, Chadli Bendjedid (1929–), won reelection, and the stage was set for elections for the National Assembly. In those elections, held in 1991, the fundamentalist Islamic Salvation Front won the first stage of a two-part election, at which point the army stepped in and suspended further voting. This step ushered in an era of violence that produced an estimated 100,000 deaths by the end of the decade. The present government of Abdelaziz BOUTEFLIKA (1937–), who was elected president with 74 percent of the vote in 1999, has stated its continuing commitment to further opening up the country's political processes and has scheduled new presidential elections for April 2004. The Islamic Salvation Front, however, remains outlawed and ineligible to participate in the electoral process.

Thus, such variables as the type of constitution, the relationship between different interest groups, and the challenges of development have combined to present powerful obstacles to democracy. As a result the United States and other donors have begun backing more simplified versions of democracy that focus on democratic procedures rather than democratic values. In other words, the United States might recognize a country as sufficiently democratic if it simply held free and fair elections in which multiple parties competed. In the case of UGANDA, even the idea of no parties was found acceptable. The hope is that a "procedural" democracy would be a good first step. Further, the elections themselves might serve as a deterrent to conflict, since it has been observed that

democracies rarely go to war with one another. According to the model of a procedural democracy, the freedom of the citizenry, the equality of the society, and the establishment of a civil society remain important but secondary.

Following the original round of elections, the champions of democratization in Africa quickly became focused on follow-up elections. The thinking was that if a country could repeat democratic elections, then it was deepening its democratic roots. Unfortunately, while most countries did in fact hold second elections, the quality of those elections was often questionable. Elected leaders found that, by manipulating the system, they could legitimize their rule at the ballot box and achieve solid control of the country while simultaneously evading real tests of legitimacy and escaping accountability to the people.

At the beginning of the new millennium countries such as Mauritius, Botswana, MALI, and GHANA stood as exceptions to the assertion that African democracy was thin in rewards for the people. In other countries, however, economic inequality has led to instability, and a lack of individual freedoms has detracted from economic growth. When economic development trumps all other factors in a democratic decision-making process, its failure invariably undermines the efficacy of rule by the people.

See also: POLITICAL SYSTEMS (Vol. V).

Further reading: Michael Bratton and Nicolas Van de Walle, *Democratic Experiments in Africa: Regime Transitions in Comparative Perspective* (New York: Cambridge University Press, 1997); Larry Diamond, *Consolidating the Third Wave Democracies* (Baltimore, Md.: Johns Hopkins University Press, 1997); Larry Diamond and Marc F. Platter, *The Global Divergence of Democracies* (Baltimore, Md.: Johns Hopkins University Press, 2001); Samuel P. Huntington, *Third Wave: Democratization in the Late Twentieth Century* (Norman, Okla.: University of Oklahoma Press, 1991).

Denard, Robert (1929–) *French mercenary*

Born in France in 1929, the young Denard served with the French navy in Indochina and with the French colonial police in MOROCCO. In 1961 he went to sub-Saharan Africa as a mercenary, seeing service in KATANGA during its war of secession at the onset of the CONGO CRISIS. After this he was "employed" in a number of African conflicts and coups, eventually gaining renown as one of the soldiers of fortune known as *les affreux* (the terrible ones) in the Congo of the mid- to late 1960s.

Denard reached the pinnacle of his notoriety in 1978, when he led a force of approximately 50 other mercenaries in an invasion of the COMOROS. Arresting President Alih Solih (1937–1978), Denard and his forces seized power and installed Ahmed Abdallah (1918–1989) as president. Solih died during the COUP D'ÉTAT, shot while supposedly attempting to escape from the mercenaries.

Following the coup Denard remained in Comoros, becoming head of the presidential security detail and assigning various posts to other mercenaries. He thwarted several attempted coups, until, in 1989, yet another coup toppled and killed Abdallah.

Fearing that Abdallah's ouster would lead to further instability in Comoros, French authorities sent a military force to restore order. Denard was then forced into exile in SOUTH AFRICA, where he remained until 1993. At that time he returned to France—in spite of the fact that the French authorities still wanted to seize him for his involvement in a coup in the West African nation of BENIN nearly 20 years earlier. Successfully arguing that his activities there were, in effect, sponsored by various agencies of the French government, Denard was given a suspended sentence and set free.

In 1995 Denard led yet another coup in the Comoros, though the action was reversed by French troops.

See also: ARMIES, COLONIAL (Vol. IV); FRANCE AND AFRICA (Vols. III, IV, V).

Further reading: Samantha Weinberg, *Last of the Pirates: The Search for Bob Denard* (New York: Pantheon, 1995).

development Improvement of the material well-being of a population along with the growth of political, social, and INFRASTRUCTURE capacity offered at the state level. Development is at once a reaction to POVERTY and the promotion of a belief that those countries lacking the basic structures, services, and quality of life of wealthy countries can and should move toward attaining those goals. Economic advancement and the material well-being of people is the central tenet of the concept of development. Implied is an improvement in political and social institutions to deliver such change. Development is a perpetual process in the sense that a country is not "developed" unless it intends to stagnate at its current level.

Socialist vs. Capitalist Development In the 1940s development was a marginal concept in colonial Africa, where the goal was economic stability. In the decades that followed, however, the thinking about development shifted, and governments began to consider ways in which new countries could achieve the goals of development: attaining electricity, running WATER, INFRASTRUCTURE, markets, and the like.

Modernization comes from the idea of "modernity" based on rational, scientific principles rather than RELIGION or mythology. In the 1960s emerging independent African nations were given a choice between achieving modernity through an economic model based on socialism, with an emphasis on equity in resource distribution, or on capitalism, with an emphasis on individual rewards for individual work. Some regimes, including those in TANZANIA, SOMALIA, GHANA, MALI, SENEGAL, ZAMBIA, and eventually MADAGASCAR and ZIMBABWE, chose the socialist path. Taking into consideration the longstanding communal structures already in place in African society, the leadership in these countries tried to adapt their economic realities to socialist theories. Eventually, however, African socialism proved largely unsuccessful. By the early 1980s those countries that had chosen African socialism were experiencing catastrophic economic collapses. In 1991 the fall of the former Soviet Union, which supported some of the socialist regimes, further contributed to the downfall of the African socialist experiment.

Elsewhere in Africa new nations chose to follow a model loosely based on Western Europe and North America. This model emphasized the development of a market economy and the establishment of democracy. It implies that the modernized countries—the United Kingdom, France, and the United States, in particular—have formed an economic model to which all other countries could aspire. According to this thinking, increased investment in developing countries will lead to increased incomes and, therefore, a tax base to draw from to finance infrastructure and institutions. Ideally, following this model, lifestyles and cultures can be transformed from the traditional to the modern.

Frameworks for assessing the path to modernization emerged in the 1960s. Notably, *evolutionary* and *functionalist* conceptions tried to make sense of development goals. Both theories required a certain amount of social change as well as economic and institutional change. Evolutionary theories, on one hand, considered that the fate of human evolution is predetermined, and humankind must move inexorably from a traditional lifestyle to a modern lifestyle. In so doing, humans will give up personal, emotional social structures in favor of neutral social structures guided by a rational drive to create more efficient product markets.

Functionalist theories, on the other hand, thought of human society as a biological organism, with different social institutions corresponding to different parts that make up a healthy organism. Each institution performs specific functions, including adaptation to the environment, goal attainment, integration, and latency (maintaining social and cultural values across generations). Society would then reduce the role of the family in such issues as reproduction, emotional support, and EDUCATION to allow the state to control these parts of life. In this way once society made the necessary investments in "human capital," economic development could take off.

Dependency Unfortunately for the developing countries of Africa, there never was "take-off." Neither developing countries nor their citizenry saw significant changes in either the quality of life or economic improvement in the 1960s and 1970s. In the backlash that followed, first in Latin America and then in Africa, leaders and scholars began considering that the investment that comes from modernization keeps poor countries dependent on the graces and production of wealthy countries. The scathing *How Europe Underdeveloped Africa* (1974), written by West Indian Africanist and scholar Walter RODNEY (1942–1980), is perhaps the most widely-read of such critiques.

Proponents of this "underdevelopment" view often come from a Marxist tradition, where class is the primary framework for explaining social relations. They argue that the relationship of the small core of wealthy, "developed" countries to the large periphery of poor countries is similar to the relationship of the small core of wealthy people to the large periphery of poor people found in most countries. In their model those who form the small, wealthy core in a poor country have more in common with the wealthy in a rich country than they have with others in their own country. For this reason, they argue, FOREIGN INVESTMENT is the wrong approach for Africa, since it benefits the wealthy few but does nothing for the poor majority.

ZAMBIA provides an interesting case study in this. The Zambian economy is dependent on copper MINING for the majority of its export earnings. In the 1960s Zambia was one of the world's largest sources of copper. Modernization, it was thought, would come rapidly through extracting this resource, selling it on the international market, and building domestic revenue. However, starting in the early 1970s the market began to change. OIL price increases damaged economies worldwide and copper prices began to collapse. As a result the economy contracted an average of 5 percent annually between 1974 and 1990. Dependency theorists would argue that if there were more of a focus on development as a state enterprise for the good of all, then regional trading would stimulate local markets, making the nation less dependent on developing a marginal commodity. As it was, the foreign investment in copper benefited only a small handful of investors in Zambia, creating low-paying, unskilled jobs, and detracting from domestic growth potential.

There were other reactions to the failures of modernization. Some countries continued down a capitalist path but with modifications. Following a liberal economic model, they encouraged investment, international business, and export-led growth. Yet at the same time they protected nascent domestic industries and pushed to substitute imported goods with domestic goods, creating new domestic markets. High tariffs and complex import procedures thus became commonplace in an effort to encourage the purchase of domestic goods.

For instance, in 1986 President Daniel arap MOI (1924–) of KENYA decided that his country should build its own make of car. Critics argued that Kenya did not have a large enough market to make car production profitable, but the project continued. While he lowered tariffs in general, arap Moi kept import tariffs on foreign cars high to give the Nyayo Pioneer Car a chance to enter into production. The selective import tariff contradicted the economic liberalization called for by modernization, and, ultimately, the Nyayo project failed.

Structural Adjustment By 1982 the problems related to severing foreign investment and implementing import substitution were compounded by the already high debt that was owed to wealthy countries. It was proving impossible for African economies to grow autonomously apart from a rapidly growing world economic system. Most importantly, many argued, the reforms were breaking the fundamental rules of economics that maintained that markets, not states, are the primary engines for economic growth and change.

> The Bretton Woods Institutions are the World Bank and the International Monetary Fund (IMF). They were set up in July 1944, when 43 countries met in Bretton Woods, New Hampshire. The institutions were designed to help rebuild the postwar economy and to promote international economic cooperation.

In the 1970s, shifts in the missions of the World Bank and the International Monetary Fund rapidly made them the world's largest and arguably most influential multilateral donors. In this context, a major break in development thinking came with the World Bank's publication of *Accelerated Development in Sub-Saharan Africa—An Agenda for Action* (1982). The Berg Report, as it came to be known after its author Elliot Berg, highlighted the major problems plaguing the African economies: underdeveloped human resources, political fragility, climate and geography, rapid POPULATION GROWTH, the persistence of constraints such as malaria, and high transport costs. The best way to address these shortcomings, it was proposed, was through a comprehensive program of STRUCTURAL ADJUSTMENT.

The goals of structural adjustment included the basic tenets of modernization but brought in new safeguards and refinements. Specifically, they included removing restrictions to foreign investments, making exports more competitive, privatizing all state enterprises, deregulating sectors of the economy to enhance competition, and reducing LABOR protections.

Few countries in Africa signed on at first. However, with debt mounting and economies stalled, the Bretton Woods Institutions became increasingly unwilling to lend money outside of structural adjustment loans. African leaders saw few other options, and by the end of the decade nearly all of sub-Saharan Africa had entered into a

Structural Adjustment Program or Enhanced Structural Adjustment Facility.

Structural Adjustment Programs increased the debt burden dramatically in most African countries, in many cases to more than 100 percent of total earnings. Yet few countries benefited. According to a study by the United Nations Children's Fund, one of many on the subject, economic growth actually slowed down under structural adjustment in the majority of the countries they looked at. In 11 of those countries exports increased, but not to a level that compensated for the economic loss to increased imports. In 13 countries, exports simply decreased.

Critics have argued that the World Bank misdiagnosed the problem as a lack of African integration into the world economy and its inability to attract investment. The real problem, they countered, was African nations' inability to recover from the economic impacts of the global oil crises of the 1970s and 1980s and the heavy debt burden that resulted. For its part, the World Bank and its supporters have argued that poor leadership, government CORRUPTION, and inept implementation of economic changes caused the failure of structural adjustment programs. Indeed, there is ample evidence that corruption in Africa has caused tremendous setbacks. According to Transparency International, a leading organization measuring government corruption, five of the 10 most corrupt countries in the world are in Africa, with NIGERIA frequently being identified as the most corrupt.

Poverty Reduction The 1990s brought about a change once again in the approach African countries took to development. Recognizing that development is about more than adjustment and fiscal management, the World Bank began promoting the empowerment of people—especially women and children—and the establishment of protective laws. To this end it set up a development framework focusing on good governance and a greater focus on education and healthcare. It also continued to extol the virtues of the regulatory and institutional fundamentals necessary for a market economy to flourish. Development efforts now pay more attention to public services and infrastructure objectives to ensure environmental and human sustainability. These new norms were codified in Poverty Reduction Facilities throughout the continent.

Development in Africa Today The World Bank's poverty reduction goals are consistent with other global development goals, including SUSTAINABLE DEVELOPMENT and URBANIZATION. As defined by the World Commission on Environment and Development, sustainable development is "development that meets the needs of the present without compromising the ability of future generations to meet their own needs." This can take many institutional forms and does not necessarily negate any of the ideas and approaches espoused by the World Bank. It does, however, bring environmental concerns to the forefront of the development agenda. That is because this view pre-sumes that environmental degradation and resource exploitation will necessarily undermine development efforts. If, for instance, a subsistence farmer in MADAGASCAR degrades the land under rice cultivation to such a degree that it is no longer usable for agricultural purposes, then it increases land pressures elsewhere while it drags down development potential.

Urbanization also plays a role in the trend toward sustainable development. Both theories and empirical evidence suggest that urban countries more readily take advantage of markets and services that drive development. BOTSWANA, for example, with more than 60 percent of its population being urban, has grown more rapidly than other African countries.

The greatest efforts to shift the approach to development at the dawn of a new century are summed up by the UN Millennium Development Goals. Supported by 150 countries, including the United States, these goals aim to develop human potential and not settling for mere economic development. They include: eradicating extreme poverty and hunger in the world, achieving universal education by 2015, improving gender equality and women's empowerment, reducing child mortality rates, improving maternal health care, halting the spread of HIV/AIDS and malaria, ensuring environmental integrity through sustainable development, and establishing a global partnership for development.

Unfortunately it appears that, with the exception of Kenya and, perhaps, a small handful of others, sub-Saharan African countries will not achieve the Millennium Development Goals. Major differences between rich and poor African countries quickly showed the program to be more of an opportunity for attractive rhetoric than for determined action.

In the rapidly shrinking modern world the failures of the past and the grim forecasts for future development in Africa are of concern to countries around the globe. Economic growth and poverty are inextricably linked. Where there is high poverty, there are structural impediments to development. In reverse, structural barriers such as poor economic governance, limits on health care and education, and limited market access increase poverty and hamper the potential for countries to meet the development goals. Many scholars argue that the greatest obstacle to economic development is not poverty but the absence of real individual rights throughout much of the continent. Their argument holds that where people living in poverty have basic civil and political rights, they have more opportunities for creating social and economic opportunities consistent with the Millennium Declaration.

Critics of the Millennium Declaration argue that its greater emphasis on community, or the creation of social capital, and on popular participation simply represents an effort to reduce wealthy countries' responsibility to contribute economically to the reduction of poverty and the augmentation of development infrastructure. These critics cite the low contribution of Organization for Economic Co-operation and Development (OECD) countries to overseas development aid. The United Nations has argued that with an average contribution of .7 of one percent of Gross National Product given in foreign aid to development, the world's poorest countries will have the investment necessary to move forward. Few OECD countries meet this threshold, with the United States ranking on the bottom of the list at .11 of one percent of Gross National Product given to foreign development aid. Instead, the United States argues, the principle of the Millennium Declaration focusing on trade instead of aid should be emphasized.

If the new turn in development cannot deliver as promised, then there is no doubt that another approach will be attempted. Yet the cost of failure will be high. With each passing year the infant mortality rate in AN-GOLA will rise above its current level of 139 deaths for every 1,000 births. The number of children under five who die in NIGER will rise above its current rate of 284 for every 1,000 children. The number of countries in Africa suffering from extreme failures in water resources will increase beyond the 27 now on the list. Most importantly, the opportunities individuals have to increase their economic well-being will continue to evaporate.

See also: COLD WAR AND AFRICA (Vol. IV); COLONIALISM, INFLUENCE OF (Vol. IV); COMMUNISM AND SOCIALISM (Vol. V); DEBT, FOREIGN (Vol. V); EUROPE AND AFRICA (Vols. IV, V); NEOCOLONIALISM AND UNDERDEVELOPMENT (Vol. V); SOVIET UNION AND AFRICA (Vols. IV, V); UNITED NATIONS AND AFRICA (Vols. IV, V); UNITED STATES AND AFRICA (Vols. IV, V).

Further reading: Amartya Sen, *Development as Freedom* (New York: First Anchor Books, 2000); Jan Knippers Black, *Development in Theory and Practice: Bridging the Gap* (Boulder, Colo.: Westview Press, 1991); Gro Harlem Brundtland, *Our Common Future* (Oxford, U.K.: World Commission on Environment and Development and Oxford University Press, 1987); Immanuel Wallerstein, *The Capitalist World-Economy* (New York: Cambridge University Press, 1979).

Dike, Kenneth O. (Kenneth Onwuke Dike)
(1917–1983) *Nigerian historian and author*

A widely respected historian and academic administrator, Dike was a leader in many fields. As an educator, he taught at Nigeria's University College, in IBADAN, and served as its vice chancellor when it became the University of Ibadan. He also founded Nigeria's National Archives, serving as its director from 1951 to 1964, and was one of the key spokespersons for the secessionist republic of BIAFRA during its brief period of independence (1967–70).

It is as a Nigerian historian of NIGERIA, however, that Dike is best remembered. For many years the study of African history belonged to non-Africans, primarily to scholars in Europe and North America. Dike, however, helped revolutionize the study of Africa's past. He was educated in Nigeria as well as at Achimota College, in GHANA, and at Fourah Bay College, in SIERRA LEONE, before going on to earn his BS and PhD degrees in Great Britain. He then returned to Africa to teach and continue his research. Writing of African history from an African point of view, he helped transform HISTORICAL SCHOLARSHIP ON AFRICA. In works like *Trade and Politics in the Niger Delta, 1830–1860* and *A Hundred Years of British Rule in Nigeria*, both of which appeared in the 1950s, he revealed, from the African point of view, the process by which indigenous states were transformed into colonial territories.

By the 1960s, as a noted scholar and university administrator, Dike had accumulated both status and power. But as ethnic tensions mounted between the IGBO-dominated eastern part of Nigeria and the YORUBA-dominated west, Dike—an Igbo man—found his position in a Western Nigerian environment to be untenable. No longer able to hold onto his posts at Ibadan or as director of the national archives, he returned to eastern Nigeria in 1967. There he helped establish a university at Port Harcourt and later became a roving ambassador, working to win support for the Biafran independence cause.

After the defeat of Biafra in 1970, Dike went into exile, teaching at Harvard University, in the United States, where he eventually became the first Mellon Professor of African History. He returned to Nigeria in 1978, becoming president of Anambra State University, not far from his birthplace in northeastern Nigeria. He died in 1983, at the age of 65.

See also: ACHIMOTA COLLEGE (Vol. IV); FOURAH BAY COLLEGE (Vol. IV); IBADAN, UNIVERSITY OF (Vol. V).

Further reading: E. J. Alagoa, ed., *Dike Remembered: African Reflections on History, Dike Memorial Lectures 1985–1995* (Port Harcourt, Nigeria: University of Port Harcourt Press for Historical Society of Nigeria, 1998).

Diop, Cheikh Anta (1923–1986) *Senegalese historian, physicist, and writer*

Born to a prominent Muslim family in Diourbel, SENEGAL, Diop was a precocious student, earning degrees in philosophy and mathematics by the time he was 23 years old. He continued his studies in France, at the University of Paris and the Sorbonne, taking classes in philosophy, chemistry, nuclear physics, and linguistics. He also became a political activist, founding two African student groups. Diop earned a doctor of letters degree in 1960, with a controversial dissertation that, in contrast to the prevailing view, offered evidence showing that ancient Egyptian civilization was black, rather than Caucasoid.

In 1960 Diop returned to Senegal to direct the radio-carbon lab at the Fundamental Institute of Black Africa (IFAN), a leading West African research center located in DAKAR. The lab's radiocarbon dating of various archaeological artifacts from the African continent further solidified many of Diop's claims about the nature of the ancient African past. Diop also continued his political activism, founding an opposition party, the Bloc des Masses Senegalaises, in 1961. The government of Léopold SENGHOR (1906–2001) arrested and then freed Diop without charging him. Considering Diop's party a threat to national order, Senghor declared the group illegal, and ordered it to disband. In 1963 Diop founded another opposition party, the National Front of Senegal, which Senghor's government also dissolved.

In 1976 Diop founded yet another political party, the National Democratic Rally, which was once again declared illegal by Senghor. Four years later Senghor retired from politics, and his successor, Abdou DIOUF (1935–), allowed opposition parties. Disillusioned by what he saw as a fraudulent democratic process, however, Diop refused to re-establish his party.

It was as an intellectual and writer, therefore, and not as a politician, that Diop achieved prominence. Throughout the 1960s Diop continued to extol African civilization, writing numerous academic papers and books that insisted on the importance of an image of African greatness in world history. When the first Black Arts Festival took place in Dakar under Senghor's sponsorship in 1966, Diop was honored, along with W. E. B. Du Bois (1868–1963), as one of the 20th century's most influential black writers.

In 1967 Diop published one of his most popular works, *Antériorité des civilisations nègres: mythe ou vérité historique* (published in English, in 1974, as *The African Origins of Civilization: Myth or Reality)*, in which he made available to the general public the argument developed in his doctoral dissertation.

In light of Diop's thorough knowledge of African civilization, in 1970 the United Nations' cultural organization, UNESCO, asked him to help write their authoritative *General History of Africa*. In the decade that followed, he served as an expert spokesman on various international committees in Africa and around the world.

In 1981 Diop published the influential *Civilisation ou Barbarie* (translated in 1991 as *Civilization or Barbarism*),

culminating a lifetime of wide-ranging research. Following his death in 1986, the University of Senegal established University Cheikh Anta Diop to honor the man who had done so much to promote African culture and civilization.

See also: ANTHROPOLOGICAL SCHOLARSHIP ON AFRICA (Vol. V); DIOP, CHEIKH ANTA (Vol. IV); DUBOIS, W.E.B. (Vol. IV); HISTORICAL SCHOLARSHIP ON AFRICA (Vols. IV, V); *NÉGRITUDE* (Vol. IV); POLITICAL PARTIES (Vol. V); SCIENCE (Vol. V).

Diori, Hamani (1916–1989) *First president of Niger*

Hamani Diori was born outside NIAMEY, the capital of present-day NIGER, which at the time was part of French West Africa (L'Afrique Occidentale Française, AOF). He graduated from the prestigious École William Ponty (William Ponty School) in DAKAR, SENEGAL, before returning to Niger in 1936 to become a teacher. After World War II (1939–45) he became involved in nationalist politics and was closely associated with Félix HOUPHOUËT-BOIGNY (1905–1993) from the IVORY COAST, who sought an autonomous AOF within the French community rather than independence for the nations. However, that vision was not fulfilled, and by 1960 all eight colonies of the AOF had become independent nations.

Diori was Niger's leading political figure and became its first president at independence in 1960. During the early years of his government, Diori faced considerable political instability and survived an assassination attempt. But by the late 1960s he had shored up his political base and had also emerged on the continental stage as one of Africa's leading statesmen.

A strong national rival of Diori's was Djibo Bakary (1922–1998), who had served as prime minister of the pre-independence government. After Diori won the 1958 election and banned Bakary's Sawaba political party, Bakary went into exile.

Niger's economic problems, however, were beyond his government's ability to solve, for it was among Africa's poorest countries. The Sahelian drought of the early 1970s resulted in widespread FAMINE AND HUNGER and led to renewed political unrest. The army staged a successful COUP D'ÉTAT in 1974, and the new military leadership imprisoned Diori until 1980. He was then kept under house arrest until 1987.

See also: ÉCOLE WILLIAM PONTY (Vol. IV); FRANCE AND AFRICA (Vols. III, IV, V); FRENCH WEST AFRICA (Vol. IV); INDEPENDENCE MOVEMENTS (Vol. V); NATIONALISM AND INDEPENDENCE MOVEMENTS (Vol. IV).

Diouf, Abdou (1935–) *President of Senegal from 1981 to 2000*

Senegal's second president, Abdou Diouf was born in Louga, near DAKAR. He was raised and educated by his grandmother and aunt, in the former colonial capital of St. Louis. After attending Quranic and secular schools, he went to law school, first in Dakar and then in France. After returning to newly independent SENEGAL, in 1960 he began a career as a public administrator. At the age of 26 he became a regional governor and steadily climbed through a series of government positions until, in 1970, Senegal's long-time president, Léopold SENGHOR (1906–2001), named him prime minister. Diouf served as prime minister for more than a decade, gradually assuming more and more of the duties of the aging president. In 1981 he was chosen by the retiring Senghor to succeed him as president.

A firm believer in self-determination, Diouf liberalized many of Senegal's laws, lifting restrictions on political parties and even repealing some travel and other restrictions on the country's citizens. He also attempted to maintain peaceful relations with neighboring countries.

In the mid-1980s, however, Diouf was confronted with a severe national crisis, brought on, in part, by an extended drought. As a result falling farm production and rising unemployment led to dismal economic conditions. Faced with increasing demands for governmental reform, he was frequently charged with allowing election irregularities that kept Senegal's leading political party, the Senegalese Socialist Party (Parti Socialiste, PS), in power. In 1990, in an attempt to retain control of the government for himself and his party, Diouf began a program of shrinking the civil service and broadening the base of his cabinet. The latter was accomplished by restoring the post of prime minister—a position he had eliminated in 1983 in order to strengthen his own position as head of state. He also appointed his leading critic, Abdoulaye WADE (1926–), to the post of minister of state. Diouf managed to be reelected several more times, but Wade finally defeated him in the elections of 2000. Many saw this event, which brought the 40-year dominance of the PS to an end, as a landmark victory for DEMOCRATIZATION in Africa.

disease in modern Africa From the 1960s to the present, disease and the treatment of disease in Africa have undergone radical changes. At the beginning of this period many African nations achieved independence from colonial rule, a shift that had a substantial impact on health care. Also, more recently, the international community has expanded its efforts to alleviate disease and human suffering in Africa. Perhaps most significant, however, has been the introduction and rapid spread of the HIV/AIDS virus, which has caused an increase in the spread of other diseases while also devastating public health care and slowing economic progress throughout the continent.

Impact of Decolonization on Health Care
Beginning in the 1950s Africa's population began increasing rapidly. As the population grew, population density increased, resulting in overcrowding in both urban and rural settings. This overcrowding caused widespread sanitation problems and malnutrition that have increased the spread of communicable diseases in Africa.

The 1960s and 1970s were a time of great celebration as African nations fought for and gained their independence. However, as fledgling nations, the systems of production and commerce, governance, TRANSPORTATION and INFRASTRUCTURE, and social services had to be reorganized and managed with a new focus. As part of the decolonization process, African governments had to take over management of many Western-style hospitals and biomedical facilities that had come into existence under the colonial governments (though not generally to the advantage of the broader population). For many countries this adjustment period meant a decline in services that resulted in an increased burden of disease on the population.

By the 1970s and 1980s many international aid agencies and organizations began to focus their attention on alleviating human suffering in the developing world. Consequently, African countries received substantial financial and logistical support from the World Health Organization (WHO), the United States Agency for International Development (USAID), the Red Cross, and the United Nations (UN), among others. These international bodies have set up programs such as the Measles Initiative, the Southern Africa Youth Initiative, and the Integrated Management of Childhood Illnesses. These initiatives, along with the UN declaration of the 1980s as the International Drinking Water Supply and Sanitation Decade, greatly contributed to decreasing the spread of some diseases on the continent.

Current Challenges The diseases that have become the biggest public health problems today include malaria and diarrheal diseases, including cholera, dysentery, and typhoid. Respiratory infections, including tuberculosis, pneumonia, and bronchitis are also very common. The HIV/AIDS virus, which attacks victims' immune systems, will be a health care issue for decades to come, especially in sub-Saharan Africa.

A *vector* is an organism, usually a parasite or insect, that transmits a disease-causing agent, also known as a *pathogen*.

In Africa malaria is spread by the Anopheles mosquito and is endemic, or constantly present, in many places on the continent. People who live in endemic zones build up a resistance to the disease after repeated exposure to the parasite. However, this means that malaria is a major cause of death for children under five years old, who have not yet built up this immunity.

The continuing spread of malaria, a longtime African public health problem, is made worse by people living in an ideal habitat for the Anopheles mosquito vector or by alterations in the landscape that create this habitat. As populations expand and land becomes scarce, humans increasingly come to inhabit these mosquito habitats. Moreover, irrigation schemes for AGRICULTURE actually create habitat for the mosquito vector, thereby contributing to the spread of the disease.

Numerous diarrheal diseases are contracted by drinking, cooking with, or washing in unsanitary WATER. Many people in Africa, in both rural and urban settings, do not have access to clean water. In undeveloped rural areas, people commonly use open, communal water sources that are easily contaminated when rain causes flooding. In urban areas, overpopulation has led to extensive slums and shantytowns that often do not have clean water or proper waste disposal. When water sources become contaminated, many people suffer from diarrhea, which, along with the dehydration that accompanies it, is a major cause of death for children in Africa. Diarrhea can ravage adult populations as well.

Respiratory infections are also a major cause of death in both children and adults in Africa. These infections spread easily in overpopulated areas. Tuberculosis, in particular, has spread to epidemic proportions since the early 1900s.

HIV/AIDS The Human Immunodeficiency Virus (HIV) that causes AIDS was first recognized in Africa in the 1980s. Since then prevalence rates have reached unprecedented levels across southern Africa, especially in ZIMBABWE, BOTSWANA, LESOTHO, and SWAZILAND. The Joint United Nations Program on HIV/AIDS (UNAIDS) has determined that Africa is the world region suffering the worst from this disease. In Africa, HIV/AIDS is spread predominantly through sexual contact, so it has been associated with other sexually transmitted diseases, such as gonorrhea and syphilis; it also has been identified as a complicating factor in the spread of non-sexually transmitted diseases, such as tuberculosis. The economic and social burdens of this disease are unprecedented, and many countries are now trying to manage health EDUCATION strategies to address them. Despite some positive trends, it is estimated that the worst effects of HIV/AIDS are still yet to come for the continent as a whole.

Common Diseases in Contemporary Africa There are numerous other diseases that negatively affect the health of African people and their livelihoods. Leishmaniasis is a disease that produces lesions and sores on the bodies and faces of humans. Since it is spread by sand flies that feed on the cave-dwelling hyrax, it is

prevalent in areas where people seek shelter near caves. Intestinal worms of several different kinds infect children and adults and have serious consequences for nutrient uptake. Lassa fever is spread to humans by the multimammate rat, which lives in the thatched roofs of West African huts. Schistosomiasis was discovered in EGYPT in 1851, and is transmitted to humans from drinking or bathing water that has been inhabited by a snail that is infected with parasites called schistosomes. Similar to malaria, schistosomiasis is linked to the creation of vector habitats through agricultural irrigation.

Yellow fever, spread by the Aedes mosquito, which breeds in water containers, was once a rare disease but has become more common with URBANIZATION and the destruction of forest. Today, yellow fever epidemics regularly occur in the Republic of the SUDAN and ETHIOPIA, even though a vaccine is common and highly effective. Measles is still a major cause of morbidity and mortality for children in rural areas of Africa; however, an effective measles vaccine has reduced its threat to those who have access to health care. While rheumatic heart disease and lung cancer were not previously widespread public health concerns, they are becoming more common today. Cervical cancer and Burkitt's tumor, a form of lymphoma, have long been problems and remain widespread forms of cancer in Africa.

Winning the Battle Against Disease In the last several decades, health care in Africa has not been dominated entirely by expanding disease, and some very important advances have been made for disease eradication and control. For example, in the 1980s, river blindness (onchocerciasis) was brought under control using a two-pronged attack: distributing effective drugs to the masses and reducing the number of black flies, which is the vector species, by dumping insecticides into rivers where the black fly breeds. Although this practice has its own public health concerns, river blindness was eliminated in KENYA and Uganda and greatly reduced near KINSHASA, which is located on the Congo River, in the Democratic Republic of the CONGO. Meningitis has been brought under control through the use of antibiotics, although outbreaks still occur in impoverished areas where population densities are high. Another success story is the eradication of yaws—a disease that was found in humid coastal regions in West Africa. The eradication was largely attributed to the WHO- and UN-implemented campaign of the 1950s that distributed penicillin to infected people with yaws-related lesions and bone inflammation.

Beyond the direct focus on the treatment and control of diseases, there have been gains in the prevention of some of the more common diseases, as well. Despite the lack of clean water in rural areas and slums, public health campaigns to improve water quality for many citizens have made great strides. Governmental agencies and NON-

GOVERNMENTAL ORGANIZATIONS have worked together in this effort, as well as in the construction of latrines, which has reduced the prevalence of diarrheal diseases in some areas. Through ongoing modernization, attempts are being made to build better relationships between Africa's extensive network of traditional health care practitioners and biomedical practitioners in order to provide health care to more people.

See also: DISEASE IN ANCIENT AFRICA (Vol. I); DISEASE IN COLONIAL AFRICA (Vol. IV); DISEASE IN MEDIEVAL AFRICA (Vol. II); DISEASE IN PRECOLONIAL AFRICA (Vol. III); HIV/AIDS AND AFRICA (Vol. V); UNITED NATIONS AND AFRICA (Vol. V).

Further reading: Rais Akhtar, ed., *Health and Disease in Tropical Africa: Geographical and Medical Viewpoints* (New York: Harwood Academic Publishers, 1987); Richard G. Feachem and Dean T. Jamison, eds., *Disease and Mortality in Sub-Saharan Africa* (New York: Oxford University Press, 1991); Julia Kemp, *Women and Sexually Transmitted Diseases in West Africa* (Norwich, U.K.: School of Development Studies, University of East Anglia, 1993).

Djibouti   Northeastern African country bordered by ETHIOPIA, SOMALIA, ERITREA, and the Gulf of Aden. Despite its small size (approximately 9,000 square miles [23,300 sq km]) and lack of NATURAL RESOURCES, the Republic of Djibouti is an important part of the Horn of Africa. Its capital, DJIBOUTI (CITY), functions as the main commercial transit center for Ethiopia because of its deepwater port facilities and modern INFRASTRUCTURE. In 2000 the country's population stood at approximately 454,000, two-thirds of whom resided in the city of Djibouti. The country claims sub-Saharan Africa's most urbanized population, with four-fifths of its inhabitants living in urban areas. Djibouti's population is made up primarily of Afar and Issa peoples, although others of Somali, Yemeni, and French origins are found there as well. The country has two official languages, French and Arabic, but Issa is the most widely spoken. As much as 94 percent of the population is Muslim.

Djibouti's Long Road to Independence   From 1888 to 1977 Djibouti was either a colony or formal territory of France. In a 1967 referendum, a majority of the inhabitants of French Somaliland—as the country was

In 1967 the people of Djibouti (then called French Somaliland) voted on a referendum for independence from France. With the vote date approaching, writing on this wall exhorted the people to vote "no" on continued French control. © *AP/Wide World Photos*

known from 1888 to 1967—opted to remain a French territory, with most Afars choosing continued French status and most Issas in favor of severing ties with France. Also in 1967 the country's name was changed to the FRENCH TERRITORY OF THE AFARS AND ISSAS. Since that time a series of events occurring within and beyond Djibouti's borders have hindered its stability and prosperity.

The closure of the SUEZ CANAL from 1967 to 1975 devastated the territory's economy, since it relied heavily on its role as a trans-shipment center for the region's goods to the Indian Ocean and the Mediterranean Sea via the Red Sea and the Suez Canal. The civil war raging in neighboring Ethiopia during the late 1970s led to further economic decline, largely because of sabotage of the railroad from Djibouti to ADDIS ABABA. The REFUGEES who migrated from Ethiopia and Somalia during the 1980s and 1990s also eroded the ability of the Djibouti state to provide services for its inhabitants.

The territory gained its independence on June 27, 1977, assuming its new name, Djibouti. Hassan GOULED APTIDON (1916–), an Issa, became Djibouti's first president. In 1981 Gouled Aptidon transformed Djibouti into a one-party state, thereby consolidating control under the rule of his own political party, Popular Rally for Progress (Rassemblement Populaire pour le progrès, RPP). An Afar rebellion erupted in 1991, partly as a result of events occurring in Ethiopia and Somalia and partly because of the favoritism that the Issa-controlled government showed its Issa population. In 1999 Gouled Aptidon was succeeded as president by Ismail Omar GUELLEH (1947–), and a complete cease-fire between the government and Afar rebel groups was finally reached in 2000.

See also: AFAR (Vols. I, II, III); DJIBOUTI (Vols. I, II, III, IV); FRANCE AND AFRICA (Vols. III, IV, V); FRENCH SOMAILILAND (Vol. IV); RED SEA TRADE (Vol. II).

Djibouti (city) Strategic port city in the Horn of Africa. Djibouti is the capital and only city of substantial size in the Republic of DJIBOUTI. It has a modern, deepwater harbor situated on the Gulf of Tadjoura, an inlet of the Gulf of Aden. Djibouti's economic importance derives from its strategic position between the Indian Ocean and the SUEZ CANAL. More precisely, it benefits from its role as a regional transit trade center, especially in linking ADDIS ABABA, the capital of ETHIOPIA, to the sea. The city is at the head of a railroad line to Addis Ababa and also hosts a French naval base.

Petroleum products, hides, and salt are traded through Djibouti but, other than trade, Djibouti's only industry of significance is the extraction of salt from the sea. At the beginning of the 21st century, more than 400,000 people lived in the capital.

See also: ADEN, GULF OF (Vol. II); DJIBOUTI (Vols. I, II, III, IV); FRANCE AND AFRICA (Vols. III, IV, V); TRANSPORTATION (Vol. V).

Dodoma City in central TANZANIA, located 300 miles (483 km) west of the Indian Ocean coast. In 1974 it was chosen to be the new federal capital of Tanzania, the nation created when the former Tanganyika was united with the island of ZANZIBAR. Today Dodoma is home to an estimated 190,000 people.

Dodoma was founded in 1907, during the German colonial period, as the administration was constructing the railroad from DAR ES SALAAM to Lake Tanganyika. The town served as the district and provincial headquarters of colonial Tanganyika under the British from 1914 until 1918, and then served the same purposes for independent Tanganyika. In 1974 the decision was made to move the capital from Dar es Salaam to more centrally located Dodoma. Although the surrounding area was dry and sparsely populated, the road and railroad connections to other parts of the country made Dodoma a good choice for the new capital.

Through the 1960s Dodoma was a small town, but once the National Assembly was relocated there in 1974, it began to grow rapidly. It has not yet become a true national capital city, however, because funds have not been available to complete many of the proposed administrative buildings. As a result many of Tanzania's government bodies have remained in Dar es Salaam. Today Dodoma serves as a marketplace for regional agricultural products, which include groundnuts (peanuts), coffee, tea, tobacco, maize, beans, rice, sorghum, and cattle. The limited industrial sector focuses on food processing and furniture making.

See also: ENGLAND AND AFRICA (Vols. III, IV, V); GERMAN EAST AFRICA (Vol. IV); GERMANY AND AFRICA (Vol. IV); TANGANYIKA (Vol. IV); TANGANYIKA, LAKE (Vols. I, II); URBANIZATION (Vols. IV, V).

Doe, Samuel (Samuel K. Doe) (c. 1952–1990) *Liberian military dictator*

Born outside of Liberia's long-ruling Americo-Liberian elite, Doe dropped out of high school, joining the army in 1969. He steadily rose through the noncommissioned ranks, eventually becoming a master sergeant in 1979. During the 1980s opposition to the administration of President William TOLBERT (1913–1980) and his True Whig party grew, culminating in widespread rioting in the wake of Tolbert's decision to radically raise the price of rice, a Liberian food staple. On April 12, 1980, Doe led a group of soldiers from the Liberian national guard in executing a violent COUP D'ÉTAT. In the coup, Tolbert was assassinated, and a "People's Redemption Council" dominated by military figures seized power.

For the next 10 years Doe ruled LIBERIA with an iron fist, despite promises to return the country to civilian rule. By 1989, with his regime assailed on all sides by charges of brutality and CORRUPTION and unable to deal with increasing political and economic chaos, Doe faced rebellion from an armed force of the Patriotic Front of Liberia, led by Charles TAYLOR (1948–). Doe eventually was confronted by several rebel groups, all vying against his forces and each other. In the resulting battles and ethnic conflicts that these groups carried on over the next two years, tens of thousands of Liberians were killed, and nearly three-quarters of a million people fled the country. Eventually, in July 1990, Doe was captured and killed by a rebel force led by Prince Yomie Johnson (c. 1959–). Doe's death, however, did not lead to the restoration of peace or order in the country, which has been plagued with violence and instability through the beginning of the 21st century.

See also: ETHNIC CONFLICT IN AFRICA (Vol. V).

dos Santos, José Eduardo (1942–) *President of Angola since 1979*

José Eduardo dos Santos was born on August 28, 1942, to a poor family in LUANDA, the capital of ANGOLA. In 1961 he joined the POPULAR MOVEMENT FOR THE LIBERATION OF ANGOLA (Movimento Popular de Libertação de Angola MPLA) in his desire to work toward Angola's independence from Portugal. Chosen by the MPLA to study in the Soviet Union, dos Santos was trained as an engineer with a focus on the OIL industry, which was developing into an important aspect of the Angolan national economy.

After returning to Angola, in 1970 dos Santos served successfully with the MPLA's military front in CABINDA, the country's oil rich northern province. When the MPLA declared independence from Portugal in 1975, dos Santos was made Angola's first prime minister. The new MPLA government was not universally recognized as Angola's legitimate government, however, and the country became mired in a civil war. Over the next two decades, MPLA forces fought against insurgents from the NATIONAL UNION FOR THE TOTAL INDEPENDENCE OF ANGOLA (União Nacional para a Independência Total de Angola, UNITA) and, to a lesser extent, the NATIONAL FRONT FOR THE LIBERATION OF ANGOLA.

In 1978 dos Santos was named minister of planning. The following year Angola's first president, Agostinho NETO (1922–1979), died, and dos Santos took control of the MPLA government. Once in control, he began gearing Angola's existing Marxist-Leninist political stance to one that was friendlier and more palatable to the non-communist West, whose support he would need in order to establish legitimacy. This pragmatic course of action led to closer relations with the United States, which finally recognized the MPLA government.

In the early 1990s the dos Santos government abandoned its Marxist-Leninist philosophy and ordered the withdrawal of Cuban troops, which had been operating in the country since the 1970s. This, however, did not stop UNITA's rebels, led by Jonas SAVIMBI (1934–2002), from continuing their insurrectionist campaign.

In 1991 dos Santos forged a peace agreement with UNITA. However, the following year, the MPLA defeated UNITA in national elections, and UNITA returned to waging its guerrilla war. Because of the nation's instability, elections planned for 1997 were postponed. When Savimbi died in 2002, UNITA finally ceased its armed rebellion, leaving dos Santos as Angola's president.

See also: CIVIL WARS (Vol. V); COLD WAR AND AFRICA (Vols. IV, V); COLONIAL RULE (Vol. IV); CUBA AND AFRICA (Vol. V); INDEPENDENCE MOVEMENTS (Vol. V); NATIONALISM AND INDEPENDENCE MOVEMENTS (Vol. IV); PORTUGAL AND AFRICA (Vols. III, IV, V).

Douala Principal port of CAMEROON, located at the mouth of the Wouri River on the Gulf of Guinea. Germany, which took control of the region in 1884, officially named the city Douala in 1907. It served as the colonial capital from 1901 until 1916. France gained control after World War I (1914–18), and Douala again served as the capital from 1940 until 1946.

Germany and France both developed the local INFRASTRUCTURE to facilitate the export of raw materials. Douala has a deepwater port, which is only 15 miles (24 km) from the sea, and railroads into the interior. These and the country's international airport have made Douala a major commercial center. The main manufactured goods are beer, textiles, palm oil, soap, processed foods, building materials, aluminum products, plastic products, glass, paper, and timber products. In addition, there are ship repair and railway manufacturing facilities. The deepwater port is responsible for most of the country's export and import trade, exporting mostly cocoa and coffee. In addition, a large portion of the trade traffic for CHAD passes through the port at Douala.

Aside from being the nation's main port and one of its principal commercial centers, Douala is the site of several EDUCATION and research institutes. It also has a museum and a handicraft center for Cameroonian ART. Although the climate is humid and hot, visitors are attracted to Douala by the vibrant nightlife and bustling city streets. The population was estimated at 1,500,000 in 2003.

See also: CASH CROPS (Vols. IV, V); DOUALA (Vol. IV); FRANCE AND AFRICA (Vols. III, IV, V); GERMANY AND AFRICA (Vol. IV); URBAN LIFE AND CULTURE (Vols. IV, V); URBANIZATION (Vols. IV, V).

Dow, Unity (1959–) *Botswana's first female high court judge*

Born in Mochudi, in southern BOTSWANA, Unity Dow grew up in a village environment. After studying law, she became an activist and helped found the Metlhaetsile

Women's Information Center, an advocacy group that ran a legal-aid clinic for women. She also was a founder of the Women and Law in Southern Africa Research Project.

> Unity Dow's novel, *Juggling Truths*, examines the impact of AIDS on the people of Botswana. She says, "I really could not have written a contemporary novel on Botswana without devoting a major part of it to AIDS. I can't imagine a five-minute conversation about anything not somehow veering towards AIDS. If I invite guests to dinner, I can expect at least one to cancel at short notice because of a funeral or illness to attend to."

In 1990 Dow challenged the constitutionality of the Citizenship (Amendment) Act of 1984, which denied women the possibility of passing their Botswana citizenship to their children if the father was not a citizen of Botswana. Dow had a vested interest in the challenge, since she herself was in such a situation. In 1992, after a long, protracted court case, the Botswana courts found in favor of Dow, say-ing that the law violated the provisions of the Botswana constitution. The case is celebrated in Botswana as a landmark for women's rights. In January 1998 Dow was appointed high court judge. She is also the author of three novels: *Far and Beyon'* (2000), *The Screaming of the Innocent* (2002), and *Juggling Truths* (2003).

See also: EMANG BASADI (Vol. V); HIV/AIDS IN AFRICA (Vol. V); LITERATURE IN MODERN AFRICA (Vol. V); WOMEN IN MODERN AFRICA (Vol. V).

drought and desertification   The United Nations defines desertification as "land degradation in arid, semi-arid, or dry sub-humid areas resulting from climatic conditions and human activities." Drought, on the other hand, is solely a natural climatic process that is defined by below-average rainfall for long periods of time. The two processes, however, are often related.

Numerous environmental changes are associated with desertification. Ecological diversity, a sign of a healthy environment, is lost when plant species cannot survive, a typical occurrence as conditions degrade. More importantly, human livelihoods are made more difficult in regions where surface WATER and ground water are depleted and where soil nutrients are eroded. This is critical as

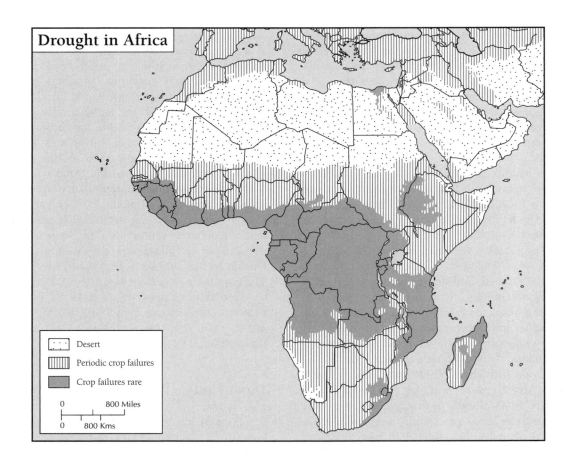

Drought in Africa

Desert
Periodic crop failures
Crop failures rare

0 ___ 800 Miles
0 ___ 800 Kms

During the 1980s drought and famine were harsh realities for many Africans. These people from the Karal Region of Chad, photographed in 1984, traveled with all of their belongings in search of water. © *United Nations/J. Isaac*

Africa's urban population grows, which requires increased agricultural production in surrounding rural areas. In recent decades land degradation has been a major factor in the widespread FAMINE AND HUNGER that have swept Africa, and it has also caused massive population movements across the continent.

The human activities that are most commonly cited as contributing to desertification include overgrazing of livestock, overcultivation, high water use, and deforestation. These activities are more prevalent in areas of widespread POVERTY, as people attempt to make a living by whatever means possible, regardless of long-term environmental impact. Economic conditions, therefore, play a role in the overuse of NATURAL RESOURCES.

Human activities, however, provide only a partial explanation for desertification. Although the mechanisms involved are still being studied, climatic variations that lead to extended periods of below-average rainfall levels have also been considered causes of desertification. In the past, areas such as the Sahel, in sub-Saharan northern Africa, recovered more easily after periods of drought.

However, increasing populations have led to more intensive use of land and water resources, increasing the likelihood of degradation and desertification. Many people associate the expansion of the southern edge of the Sahara desert to the droughts of 1968–73 and 1983–85 in the Sahel. Although some observers point out that fluctuations in the border of the Sahara desert are part of a natural cycle, the rapid rate of recent desertification has alarmed the international community.

In 1996 the United Nations implemented the Convention to Combat Desertification, which 178 countries had ratified by 2002. Today many African nations have national action programs designed to address the problems of land degradation and desertification.

See also: ENVIRONMENTAL ISSUES (Vol. V); INTERNATIONAL MONETARY FUND AND AFRICA (Vol. V); POPULATION GROWTH (Vol. V); SAHARA DESERT (Vol. I, II); SAHEL (Vol. I); SUSTAINABLE DEVELOPMENT (Vol. V).

Further reading: Charlotte Benson and Edward J. Clay, *The Impact of Drought on sub-Saharan African Economies* (Washington, D.C.: World Bank, 1998); Michael

Mortimore, *Roots in the African Dust: Sustaining the Sub-Saharan Drylands* (New York: Cambridge University Press, 1998).

Durban Major port city on the Indian Ocean, located in eastern SOUTH AFRICA in the province of KwaZulu-Natal. Durban is the world's second-fastest growing city, trailing only Mexico City. Its current population is estimated at 2,400,000.

Soon after the discovery of gold in the 1880s, Durban, which was the closest South African port to the booming Witwatersrand region, developed into one of sub-Saharan Africa's major port cities. Since then, it has continued to provide port services for Witwatersrand industries. Dealing in raw materials, industrial equipment, and capital goods, the main EXPORTS passing through it are minerals, coal, and grains. Sugar, too, has become a major economic activity, and Durban is presently considered the headquarters of South Africa's sugar industry.

During the 1930s and 1940s Durban further developed as a major industrial city, with INDUSTRIALIZATION progressing even more rapidly since the 1960s. Major industries now include OIL refining, machinery manufacturing, and railroad repairing, as well as soap, paint, and fertilizer production.

As Durban's economic growth attracted migrants from the surrounding rural areas, shantytowns developed around the city. In the 1960s the South African government responded by creating planned communities, known as townships, in areas surrounding the city. Under the APARTHEID system, most Africans were forced to live in these outlying townships. The Indian and Muslim communities also were forced out of more centrally located parts of the city, leaving the choicest neighborhoods to whites. Highly segregated by South Africa's apartheid laws

until the 1990s, Durban still struggles to integrate its three major ethnic groups—ZULUS, British settlers, and Indians, both Muslim and Hindu.

During the early 1970s Durban was the scene of important episodes in the struggle against apartheid. For example, between 1973 and 1976, Durban's African industrial workers organized a series of industry-paralyzing strikes. Ultimately, the workers gained the right to organize LABOR UNIONS that could bargain with employers on their behalf. In the 1980s the struggle became more political in nature, as pro-apartheid forces successfully drove wedges between the two major pro-African, anti-apartheid political groups, the AFRICAN NATIONAL CONGRESS and the INKATHA FREEDOM PARTY. The strife and resulting violence intensified in late 1993 and early 1994, as the nation's first universal elections approached. Following the elections, however, the two parties were able reach a political truce.

Today Durban is a modern city with a tall skyline and a booming economy. Known as a vacation spot for both South Africans and foreign tourists, its major attractions are its plentiful parks, beaches, nightclubs, theaters, and resorts, and its proximity to exotic game reserves. In addition to the successful business, industrial, and TRANSPORTATION sectors, Durban also has several educational facilities including the University of KwaZulu-Natal.

See also: DURBAN (Vol. IV); ENGLAND AND AFRICA (Vols. III, IV, V); URBAN LIFE AND CULTURE (Vols. IV, V); URBANIZATION (Vols. IV, V); WITWATERSRAND (Vol. IV).

Furhter reading: Bill Freund, *Insiders and Outsiders: The Indian Working Class of Durban, 1910–1990* (Portsmouth, N.H. Heinemann, 1995); Paul Maylam and Iain Edwards, eds., *The People's City: African Life in Twentieth-Century Durban* (Portsmouth, N.H. Heinemann, 1995).

E

East African Community (EAC)

East African Community (EAC) Regional intergovernmental organization to promote political, economic, and social cooperation among its three member states of KENYA, UGANDA, and TANZANIA, which share English and Swahili as major languages. Its headquarters are in Arusha, Tanzania.

The origins of the EAC lie with the East African Common Services Organization (EACSO), which the British government established in the 1950s to promote greater economic cooperation among its colonies in Kenya, Tanganyika (now Tanzania), and Uganda. This effort paralleled Britain's development of the Central African Federation in the same period. Among the common services were the railway system, the postal system, East African Airways, TELECOMMUNICATIONS systems, and a common currency. The EACSO also permitted the free movement of people, goods, and services across national borders.

The member states transformed the EACSO into the EAC in 1967 to more effectively promote the management of their common resources and to encourage closer economic and political integration. However, political and ideological differences arose among the three respective states leaders, Jomo KENYATTA (c. 1891–1978), Julius NYERERE (1922–1999), and Idi AMIN (c. 1925–2003). By 1977 the differences caused the collapse of the EAC and ultimately the division of its assets and liabilities under the East African Mediation Agreement of 1984.

The underlying rationale of regional economic and political unity among the three states remained a sound one, however, and worldwide regional organizations were gaining in importance. By the 1990s a new generation of national leaders were in place in the three countries, and they initiated steps toward reviving the EAC. In 1993 they set up a Permanent Tripartite Commission to establish a regional common market and currency zone. Then, on November 30, 1999, the heads of the three states signed the Treaty for the Establishment of the East African Community. A secretariat served as the EAC's executive organ, and an East African Legislative Assembly and East African Court of Justice were established.

With its three member states all bordering Lake VICTORIA, in 2001 the EAC established the Lake Victoria Development Program. Its goal is to promote the SUSTAINABLE DEVELOPMENT of the lake and its adjacent land areas through a coordinated, regional approach to the CONSERVATION of its NATURAL RESOURCES and careful management of economic DEVELOPMENT activities in the area.

See also: CENTRAL AFRICAN FEDERATION (Vol. IV); ENGLAND AND AFRICA (Vols. III, IV, V).

Ebola

Ebola Viral hemorrhagic fever that infects human and non-human primates. Ebola is named after the river in the Democratic Republic of the CONGO where it was first recognized in 1976. From the time of its discovery until the beginning of 2000 sporadic outbreaks resulted in a total of 1,500 victims and 1,000 deaths. Since 2001 there have been five additional outbreaks in Congo and GABON.

Ebola is considered an extreme biohazard because there is no known cure or vaccine. It is highly contagious and the natural host is unknown. In addition, its fatality rate ranges from 50 percent to 90 percent, depending on the subspecies of the virus. Because so little is known about it, the only prevention strategies are early detection and the quarantining of infected people. In Africa, the virus commonly infects the caretakers of those who become ill. It also affects health-care workers who do not identify it early enough and fail to use protective barrier methods, such as masks and latex gloves.

Ebola is transmitted through contact with bodily fluids or organs. Symptoms, which appear within days, include the sudden onset of fever, body aches, headaches, and sore throat. Because these symptoms are common to many ailments, early detection is difficult. Vomiting and diarrhea follow, and rashes, red eyes, hiccups, and internal and external bleeding are observed in some victims.

There are very few laboratories in the world that can test blood for the Ebola virus. Therefore, detection is still a major concern in early identification of outbreaks. When an outbreak is reported, many national and international bodies respond by providing staff, doctors, and scientists. Research is ongoing to develop an understanding of Ebola's history and ecology.

See also: DISEASE IN MODERN AFRICA (Vol. V); HEALTH AND HEALING IN MODERN AFRICA (Vol. V).

ecology and ecological change The African environment is ever-changing. As human beings and other life forms interact with the world around them, the land, sea, and air all change with them. The great diversity of Africa's ecosystems makes ecological shift all the more dynamic—and potentially perilous.

Ecology is the study of the interrelationships between plants and animals and their biological and physical environment. This broad concept includes atmospheric composition, soil composition, WATER, and all living things. Thus ecological change looks at the relationships between plants and animals in the face of ATMOSPHERIC CHANGE, land development, and water quality and quantity variations. Ecology is different from environment in that it looks at the interactions between humans and the entire ecosystem. In this sense, ecology is more a human construct to conceptualize nature than it is nature itself.

Africa is an ecologically diverse continent. In fact, five of the world's 25 biological "hotspots"—places where high levels of BIODIVERSITY are matched by significant threats from human interaction—are located in Africa. As a result of its diversity, African ecology is complex.

Ecologists study the interactions of species in areas that have their own unique characteristics, such as the grasslands of ZIMBABWE and the tropical rain FORESTS of

GUINEA, CAMEROON, and the Republic of the CONGO. They think about where a particular rice variety might grow best or where it will cause irreparable damage to the ecosystem. They identify ways to improve NATIONAL PARKS and protected areas, which makes ecologists crucial in responsible land use planning. They consider, for example, how MAASAI livestock herders in TANZANIA impact the Ngorongoro Conservation Area. They examine how an increase in a particular bird species in SOUTH AFRICA might impact farming and vice versa, or they look at the impact of drought on flora and fauna, including the effects on human populations, in ERITREA.

Colonialism in Africa brought important historic considerations of ecological change. Beyond the apparent impact of colonial land policy on ecology, other factors—including declines in nutrition, constraints on animal husbandry, fluctuating cultural patterns, and increased POVERTY—combined to cause ecological imbalances that were beyond the concerns of colonial officials. Some of these ecological changes persist today and may well continue to challenge human development.

Awareness of the importance of ecological change in Africa has increased in recent years. While environmental CONSERVATION efforts once focused primarily on large mammals, today the interest is just as intense in protecting forests, rivers, grasslands, and deserts. The broader interactions between life forms and their environments have become a central component of both conservation and DEVELOPMENT policymaking.

See also: COLONIALISM, INFLUENCE OF (Vol. IV), PASTORALISM (Vol. IV).

Further reading: William Beinart William and Peter Coates, *Environment and History* (New York: Routledge, 1995); David Anderson and Richard Grove, eds. *Conservation in Africa: People, Policies and Practice* (Cambridge, U.K.: Cambridge University Press, 1987).

economic assistance Sometimes referred to as DEVELOPMENT assistance or foreign aid. During the 1960s, as many African nations gained independence, the former colonial powers and other developed countries such as the United States began to offer economic aid. Communist countries, such as the former Soviet Union and China, also offered economic assistance. Often this type of aid was a way to maintain or gain influence over political affairs during the Cold War era. At other times this aid was the result of former colonizers recognizing the debilitating role they had played in the severe lack of development in many of the newly independent countries. As a result, they wanted to promote development and improve living conditions for people in Africa. Also, economic aid to Africa was—and still is—seen as a way to forge ties that will eventually lead to economic gain for donor countries. For example, many donor countries see great potential in developing Africa as a market for their consumer products.

The African Growth and Opportunity Act (AGOA), which the U.S. Congress passed in 2000, is an example of economic assistance that does not rely on the distribution of money. According to the AGOA web site, "The Act offers tangible incentives for African countries to continue their efforts to open their economies and build free markets." The apparel provisions of the Act are an example of the incentives it provides. Eligible countries can export—free of import duties and quotas—unlimited amounts of manufactured apparel, as long as it is made of fabric, yarn, and thread produced in the United States. Critics believe, however, that programs like AGOA undercut the potential for manufacturing on the continent, making it more difficult to cultivate indigenous industrial production and maintaining Africa's dependence on imported goods.

Today, Africa receives money from many countries in the world. France, the United States, Germany, Japan, England, and the Netherlands are major providers of economic assistance. In 1994 alone France provided $3.1 billion in economic aid to countries south of the Sahara. This was three times the amount offered by the United States, which was the second-highest contributor of foreign aid to Africa. In addition to governmental funds, economic assistance is provided by NON-GOVERNMENTAL ORGANIZATIONS.

Economic assistance comes in many forms including loans that are often earmarked for specific activities and projects, food aid for famine victims, and donations that support development agencies and organizations in Africa. There are numerous development programs, such as U.S. Agency for International Development's Initiative to End Hunger in Africa, the African Education Initiative, and the Mother and Child HIV Prevention Initiative. Other examples of economic aid programs include the granting of preferential trade partnerships through instruments such as the LOMÉ CONVENTION, the construction of INFRASTRUCTURE to promote the marketing of goods and services, and EDUCATION programs designed to train public workers, including teachers and health-care workers.

Much of the economic aid that is given to African nations comes with conditions. For example, since the 1980s the WORLD BANK and the INTERNATIONAL MONETARY FUND have required the implementation of belt-tightening STRUCTURAL ADJUSTMENT programs as a condition for receiving development loans. Also, advancing the DEMOCRATIZATION of political systems is often a stipulation for economic aid.

Over the past 50 years Africa has received hundreds of billions of dollars in aid. There have been many success stories, such as the family-planning programs that have reduced fertility rates in KENYA and the eradication of river blindness in West Africa. However, despite these and other successes, many critiques of the system of economic assistance say that development in Africa has not improved substantially. The causes of Africa's slow economic development are hotly debated. Some argue that donors have not enforced the conditions of democracy and transparency, which has led to CORRUPTION and the misuse of donor funds. Others argue that economic assistance programs have been donor-led, which creates resentment and resistance among Africans and results in the failure of many projects. Recently there has been a push to promote African-led development projects.

See also: CHINA AND AFRICA (Vol. V); COLD WAR AND AFRICA (Vols. IV, V); EUROPE AND AFRICA (Vol. V); FAMINE AND HUNGER (Vol. V); SOVIET UNION AND AFRICA (Vol. V); TRADE AND COMMERCE (Vol. V); UNITED STATES AND AFRICA (Vol. V).

Further reading: Leslie O. Omoruyi, *Contending Theories on Development Aid: Post-Cold War Evidence from Africa* (Aldershot, U.K.: Ashgate, 2001); Humphrey Orjiako, *Killing sub-Saharan Africa With Aid* (Huntington, N.Y.: Nova Science Publishers, 2001).

Economic Community of West African States (ECOWAS)

Regional community of West African countries seeking economic integration, political and social cooperation, self-reliance, and stability. The Economic Community of West African States, also known as ECOWAS, was established in 1975 to promote regional trade and economic DEVELOPMENT. Its members include the Republic of BENIN, BURKINA FASO, The Republic of CAPE VERDE, The GAMBIA, GHANA, GUINEA, GUINEA-BISSAU, IVORY COAST, LIBERIA, MALI, MAURITANIA, NIGER, NIGERIA, SENEGAL, SIERRA LEONE, and TOGO. Since it accounts for approximately half of West Africa's population and economic activity, Nigeria is the member with the most influence within ECOWAS.

The governing structure of ECOWAS includes several central bodies headed by The Conference of Heads of State, which meets annually and is made up of the presidents—or heads of state—of each of the member nations. The chairperson of ECOWAS is chosen from this commission, and the position is rotated among state leaders. It is, however, the Council of Ministers that actually runs the economic community. The council, which meets semi-annually, is made up of two representatives from each member country.

Within ECOWAS, there are also specialized commissions, each with its own specific agenda. These commissions work together toward eliminating trade barriers and encouraging travel rights among the community's citizens. For example, the Social Programs Commission recognizes the importance of social and cultural activities in promoting regionalism and supports organizations such as the West African Football Union and the West African Women's Association.

ECOWAS has made notable contributions to regional security and stability. It established the ECOWAS Monitoring Group, or ECOMOG, a body that focuses on peacekeeping and peace enforcement. ECOMOG peacekeeping forces are military units and technical experts from member states. In recent years ECOMOG troops have intervened in Ivory Coast, Liberia, Guinea-Bissau, and Sierra Leone.

In July 2003 Human Rights Watch (HRW) expressed concern about the mixed history of ECOWAS peacekeeping operations. HRW recognized that ECOMOG has had notable success, but also expressed concerns regarding accusations of serious HUMAN RIGHTS abuses and an overall lack of accountability. These concerns came to the fore in 1999 when ECOMOG troops confronted an armed offensive by the REVOLUTIONARY UNITED FRONT (RUF) in Sierra Leone. Four years later, when ECOMOG troops were sent to Liberia to stabilize the country after Charles TAYLOR (1948–) was forced to depart, HRW carefully watched ECOMOG activities to ensure that peacekeepers adhered to the human rights provisions of international law.

See also: CIVIL WARS (Vol. V); RAWLINGS, JERRY (Vol. V).
Further reading: Adekeye Adebajo, *Building Peace in West Africa: Liberia, Sierra Leone, and Guinea-Bissau* (Boulder, Colo.: Lynne Rienner Publishers, 2002).

economy   The African economy changed greatly under colonial rule. This transformation has accelerated over the decades since independence. Increasingly, the key features of the African economy have moved away from its historical subsistence basis centered on AGRICULTURE to an economy that is linked to the GLOBAL ECONOMY. More and more, the African FAMILY is unable to meet its economic needs by producing its own FOOD and using the surplus of its food production to obtain tools, cooking oil, salt, and other items in the local market. Instead, rural families must engage in producing CASH CROPS for consumption in

distant locations or engage in some form of wage LABOR to generate the cash needed to purchase necessities that often include food. Families in the urban areas are almost wholly dependent on earning a cash income to meet their needs.

The African economy is still mainly producing raw materials for export in order to import manufactured goods. Across the continent, the MINING industry produces MINERALS AND METALS for export to go along with the cash crops and other commodities such as lumber. Since the 1960s, OIL has joined the list of export commodities. INDUSTRIALIZATION remains relatively limited except in a few countries such as SOUTH AFRICA and EGYPT. Likewise, a modern INFRASTRUCTURE, whether in terms of TRANSPORTATION, the electricity grid, or TELECOMMUNICATIONS also remains limited outside of a few more favored countries. There are some areas of the economy that are prospering. The continent's WILDLIFE and natural beauty have led to a steady growth in TOURISM from the West and also from countries such as Japan, as has the heritage dimension of African history, particularly for African-Americans. In addition to generating employment in the hotel and transport sectors, tourism has generated a growing market for African ART and crafts from tourists wishing to bring home remembrances of their trips.

At present, much of Africa is in dire economic straits. In some countries, this is the result of political upheavals that have led to numerous CIVIL WARS, while in other countries DROUGHT AND DESERTIFICATION and other ENVIRONMENTAL ISSUES have had severe economic consequences. Mostly, though, the current economic problems have their origins in the disruption of the indigenous economy that began with the transatlantic slave trade and continued during the period of colonial rule. In recent decades various attempts at ECONOMIC ASSISTANCE by the INTERNATIONAL MONETARY FUND, the WORLD BANK, the United States and other western development agencies, and from CHINA and the SOVIET UNION sought to mitigate the continent's economic underdevelopment. By and large, however, solutions to the weaknesses of the African economy have eluded the development experts. The problems are deeply structural in nature and thus extremely difficult, both politically and technically, to address.

See also: COLONIAL RULE (Vol. IV); COLONIALISM, INFLUENCE OF (Vol. IV); ECONOMY (Vols. I, II, III, IV); TRANS-ATLANTIC SLAVE TRADE (Vol. III).
Further reading: Ralph A. Austen, *African Economic History* (Portsmouth, N.H.: Heinemann, 1987).

ECOWAS   See ECONOMIC COMMUNITY OF WEST AFRICAN STATES.

education   In Africa, since the outmoded educational systems of the colonial era were overhauled in the 1960s, students have faced numerous challenges in preparing themselves for a rapidly changing world. In 1961 the United Nations Economic, Social and Cultural Organization convened in ADDIS ABABA, ETHIOPIA, to discuss the two most pressing issues facing African education: expansion of enrollment in public schools at all levels and the development of an educational system to meet the needs of African society. The following year another conference discussed the same issues in regards to higher education.

In the 1960s many African nations employed a European university model to cultivate an elite cadre of leaders for government, business, and various professions. Outside of these elite, university students, however, school enrollment remained very low. The convention at Addis Ababa proposed to increase the enrollment of elementary students to 100 percent with compulsory and free primary education. It also proposed to raise the enrollment of secondary students to 30 percent and elevate higher education enrollment to 20 percent. Despite claiming to invest between 25–35 percent of government expenditures on education, a majority of African states proved unable to reach the stated goals. This failure was blamed on an overall lack of economic resources, a dearth of qualified teachers, and, in many cases, on governmental instability and discontinuity.

By 1980 only about one-fourth of Africa's states had come close to achieving the goal of compulsory and free primary education. It is estimated that, on average, only about two-thirds of the school-age population was enrolled at the primary level. In recent decades African governments have continued to fund programs to improve enrollment levels—especially the enrollment of women in secondary and higher education—and to increase LITERACY at all levels.

Since independence, public schools have been the point for disseminating a country's official language, often the language of the former colonial power. However, because independence governments have been unable to fund adequately their education programs, the processes of language acquisition and literacy have been slow and uneven at best. At times the choice of a language of instruction in schools became a highly politicized issue. For example, in 1976 the APARTHEID government of SOUTH

In the 1960s the United Nations helped devise a plan to develop primary education in Africa. Here, in 1971, a trainee is working with young students at the UN-funded Primary Teacher Training Center in Bangui, Central African Republic. © United Nations

AFRICA insisted that AFRIKAANS be used for teaching key subjects to African high school students. In addition to being viewed as the language associated with the repressive government, Afrikaans was not familiar enough to many teachers and students to be readily used in their classrooms. The government's decision prompted student demonstrations that led to the SOWETO rebellion.

One of the greatest challenges facing African states in their quest to raise student enrollment is the under-representation of females. This is especially crucial regarding secondary education in Muslim communities, where girls are encouraged to marry early. It has been shown that investing in the education of females has a high social return. An educated woman who becomes a mother is more likely to have literate children and will be more likely to have the resources to pay for uniforms, books, and school fees. In addition, a literate woman has a better chance of contributing to a household income, thus reducing POVERTY.

Although education has remained the most powerful factor of upward social mobility, African teaching curriculums generally remain inadequate to satisfy the needs of present-day Africans. An education that provides the tools for obtaining a white-collar job is only a part of the picture. Not everyone can work for the government, so nations need vocational education to develop a more complete work force. Because most workers in African nations are farmers, it is also important to consider agricultural courses at all levels of education. Qualified workers in research and in regional agribusiness could help African nations to become more self-sufficient in food production.

Today the concerns of African educators also include developing the skills and knowledge needed for an individual to participate in a strong, civil, democratic society. However, this lofty goal is too often derailed by the lack of textbooks, educational materials, and facilities, as well as the lack of qualified and committed teachers.

See also: CHRISTIANITY, INFLUENCE OF (Vols. IV, V); EDUCATION (Vol. IV); ISLAM, INFLUENCE OF (Vols. IV, V).

Further reading: Birgit Brock-Utne, *Language, Democracy and Education in Africa* (London: Global, 2002).

Egypt   African country about 386,700 square miles (1,001,600 sq km) in size, centered on the Nile River Valley in the northeastern part of the African continent. It shares borders with the modern-day states of LIBYA and the Republic of the SUDAN.

In 1923 Egypt became nominally independent from Britain. However, its former colonial ruler continued to exercise considerable control and maintained a military force in Egypt. The 1952 military coup that brought Gamal Abdel NASSER (1918–1970) to power also brought full independence. This independence was complete in 1956, when international pressure forced Britain to cede full control of the SUEZ CANAL to Egypt.

The United Arab Republic   In 1958, under Nasser, Egypt's name was changed to the United Arab Republic, abbreviated as UAR, when it united with neighboring Syria in an attempt to create a unified pan-Arab socialist state in the Middle East. Nasser had hoped that the unification of Egypt and Syria would attract other Arabic-speaking states to join this federation, with Nasser as the leader. Domestic issues however, kept Iraq from joining, and a COUP D'ÉTAT in Syria in 1961 led to the disintegration of the union after only three years. Although Nasser kept the UAR name for Egypt alone as a symbol of his initiative, the name was dropped after Nasser's death.

Popular enthusiasm for Arab unity reached its peak in 1963. Under Nasser Egypt became a great leader in the Arab world. During the 1960s, as a sign of Egypt's prominence, half of the liberation organizations in developing Arab countries, including the Palestine Liberation Organization, or PLO, had set up offices in CAIRO.

Arab Socialism   On the home front Nasser announced a social revolution. In addition to nationalizing heavy industry, in 1962 he nationalized the press, the CINEMA, THEATER, and BOOK PUBLISHING. Various national ministries oversaw industries as well as the public expression of ideas. Nasser even nationalized Cairo's al-Azhar University, an important center of Islamic thought. This act infuriated many Muslims, especially members of the Muslim Brotherhood. They resented and feared the growing secularization of the government, which was increasingly guided, they feared, by socialist principles rather than Islamic law.

Strong popular support, however, encouraged Nasser to maintain his socialist course. Under his policy of African Socialism, the state was to became the engine that would make Egypt prosperous. The other Arab states generally followed Nasser's example. As a result, by 1970 most Arabs lived under a form of socialism or totalitarian rule.

Conflict with Israel   The existence of the state of Israel, established in 1948, continued to cause unrest in the region. Already having been involved in two ARAB-ISRAELI WARS, one in 1948 and a second war in 1956, Israel was again under threat of attack from its Arab neighbors. In 1967 a third Arab-Israeli War commenced. Pressuring Israel, Nasser closed the Suez Canal to Israeli ships and expelled the UN peacekeeping force from the Gaza Strip. Egypt's navy blockaded the Gulf of Aqaba so that ships could not reach Israel's Red Sea port of Eliat. Israel retaliated, destroying Egypt's idle air force on the first day of fighting. Israel then launched a surprise ground attack that lasted several days.

As a result of this conflict, which came to be known as the Six-Day War, Egypt lost the Gaza Strip and the Sinai Peninsula, where the country's richest OIL fields were located. Egyptians refused to accept Nasser's resignation, however, and he remained popular. Nevertheless, at this time, many Egyptians emigrated to the United States and other countries, critically draining Egypt of some of its best and brightest citizens.

Egypt under Sadat Upon Nasser's death in 1970, Vice President Anwar as-SADAT (1918–1981) became Egypt's next leader. Like Nasser before him, he had been an original member of the Free Officers Movement that deposed King Faruk (1920–1965) and made Egypt a republic. In 1971 Sadat consolidated his power through a governmental purge known as the "corrective revolution," thus removing any future competition from among Nasser's followers. Although Sadat outwardly ascribed to Nasser's socialist principles, he began immediately making changes. Sadat dismantled Nasser's internal security apparatus and gave amnesty to political prisoners. He also lifted censorship of the press, reduced governmental secularism, invited Egyptians and foreign capitalists to invest in local enterprises, and changed the country's name to the Arab Republic of Egypt.

In foreign policy, Sadat was unsure of his approach to Israel. On one hand, he was afraid that any mediation with Israel would risk isolating Egypt from the rest of the Arab world, and he did not want to antagonize the oil-exporting nations, which could devastate Egypt's economy. On the other hand, Sadat wanted the Sinai Peninsula and the Gaza Strip returned to Egyptian control.

In 1972 Sadat actively solicited armaments from the Soviet Union, but when he could not get the weapons he wanted, Sadat expelled most of Egypt's Soviet advisers and technicians. Although the United States had tried to mediate an Arab-Israeli settlement, Sadat resisted diplomacy. In 1973 Egypt joined other Arab nations in a surprise attack on Israel known as the Yom Kippur War.

The war began with a massive Egyptian air and artillery assault on Israel east of the Suez Canal. Thousands of Egyptian soldiers had moved across the canal but their advance stalled on the other side. When the Israelis recovered from the surprise attack, they defeated the Egyptians on the eastern bank of the canal, trapping Egypt's Third Army behind enemy lines.

U.S. secretary of state Henry Kissinger's (1923–) so-called shuttle diplomacy concluded a separation of forces agreement in 1974. Israel's troops withdrew to the east side of the canal, and in 1975 Sadat reopened the Suez Canal, allowing passage to ships with Israeli cargoes. Under the terms of the Sinai Accords of 1974 and 1975, Israel returned the Sinai oil fields, and Egypt renounced war as a means of resolving the Middle East conflict.

In 1977 at the invitation of Israeli prime minister Menachem Begin (1913–1992), Sadat went before Israel's legislative body, the Knesset, to argue for peace. Continuing to assert itself as the leader of the Arab world, Egypt offered peace if Israel would recognize a Palestinian state and withdraw from all the territory it had occupied in the 1967 war. While Israel was willing to make peace with Egypt, Sadat wanted a comprehensive settlement that returned lands to Syria, Jordan, and the Palestinians. Unfortunately, the other Arab states ignored Sadat's call for a general peace conference. Sadat, however, saw that peace with Israel was the first step to economic recovery.

The 1978 summit meeting at Camp David, organized by American president Jimmy Carter (1924–), led to the 1979 Israeli-Egyptian Peace Accord. In 1982 under the provisions of this accord, Israel returned the Sinai Peninsula to Egypt. The United States expanded economic and military aid to Egypt, but the Egyptian economy remained stagnant. Sadat's popularity declined in the Arab world and at home. In 1981 Islamic extremists assassinated Sadat for making peace with Israel.

Egypt under Mubarak Vice President Hosni MUBARAK (1929–), Sadat's hand-picked successor, was elected president in 1981. His most pressing concern was economic reform, and he instituted an open-door economic policy that encouraged the world community to invest in Egypt. However, economic growth remained slow, and rapid POPULATION GROWTH continued to limit economic gains. In the 1990s alone, for example, the population of Egypt increased by 10 million, reaching 68 million in 2000.

Mubarak also loosened the restraints on political liberties, allowing freedom of the press and the formation of new political parties. In 1984 five parties, including the formerly outlawed Muslim Brotherhood, participated in the national elections. Using milder measures to curb Muslim militants, however, has not dissuaded the Muslim fundamentalist opposition groups. In 1995, on a visit to Ethiopia, Mubarak survived an assassination attempt at the hands of a religious extremist. Mubarak's government has accused the Muslim opposition groups of sponsoring the terrorist attacks on tourists like the 1996 incident in Cairo, which left 18 dead.

In his foreign policy, Mubarak tried to remain neutral during the last years of the Cold War (1947–91) between the United States and the Soviet Union. He tried also to improve relations with the other Arab states, including by acting as advisor to the Palestinians at peace conferences. In 1990 Mubarak supported the UN sanctions against the regime of Iraqi president Saddam Hussein (1937–) resulting from Iraq's invasion of Kuwait. In 1991, with other members of the Arab League, Egypt fought in the

Gulf War on the side of the coalition forces allied against Iraq, sending the third-largest contingent of troops after the United States and Britain. Egypt also played a leading role in the 1991 Madrid peace conference that tried to try to stabilize the region. As a reward for its participation in the Gulf War, the United States forgave $7 billion in military debt owed by Egypt.

Although Mubarak was reelected repeatedly, he faced strong opposition for economic and demographic reasons. In 2000, of 173 countries, Egypt ranked 115 in terms of its gross national product. At the beginning of the 21st century Egypt experienced a 20 percent rate of unemployment, a situation caused by a high annual rate of population growth (almost 2 percent) and a weak economy with a high annual rate of inflation. These elements continued to keep Egypt relatively poor among the world's nations. Amid heightened political tensions in the Middle East, Mubarak's ties with Israel and, increasingly, with the United States reinforced domestic economic-based tensions.

See also: COLD WAR AND AFRICA (Vol. V); EGYPT (Vols. II, III, IV); SOVIET UNION AND AFRICA (Vols. IV, V); UNITED STATES AND AFRICA (Vols. IV, V).

Further reading: M. W. Daly, ed., *The Cambridge History of Egypt*, Vol. 2, *Modern Egypt from 1517 to the End of the Twentieth Century* (New York: Cambridge University Press 1998), Arthur Goldschmidt, *Modern Egypt: the Formation of a Nation-State* (Boulder, Colo.: Westview Press, 2002); James Jankowski, *Egypt: A Short History* (Oxford, U.K.: Oneworld, 2000); Caryle Murphy, *Passion for Islam: Shaping the Modern Middle East: the Egyptian Experience* (New York: Scribner, 2002).

Egyptology Study of Ancient EGYPT of the Pharaonic era (3000 BCE–30 CE), utilizing disciplines such as archaeology, art history, and history. Egyptology, as a field of study, had its beginning with the French invasion of Egypt in 1798 and the massive array of antiquities that subsequently reached Europe. The methods used by the earliest Egyptologists were generally haphazard and unsystematic. Digging was uncontrolled, and archaeologists were more interested in amassing than cataloging artifacts. By the late 1800s, however, Egyptology became an academic discipline, employing scientific methods to collect, record, and analyze data gathered at excavations. Today departments of Egyptology at major universities around the world incorporate the insights of archaeology, ART, art history, history, ancient languages, and other disciplines to increase understanding of ancient Egyptian life and culture and the relationship of Egypt to other parts of Africa.

Ancient Egyptian civilization fascinates archaeologists to this day. In 1990 Egyptologists excavated the burial sites of the laborers who built the pyramids at Giza, shown here in a recent photo. © *Corbis*

Modern Egyptologists also use the tools of 21st century science to expand their knowledge of sites and artifacts. Researchers use satellite data and infrared imaging devices to locate ancient sites lost deep in the sand. They also employ sophisticated carbon-dating techniques to accurately determine the age of artifacts already unearthed. Performing chemical analyses of DNA fragments taken from preserved teeth, bones, and hard tissue, other researchers are attempting to establish an exact chronology of Egyptian rulers. Still other researchers have used computers to analyze and translate hieroglyphic texts. As scientific inquiry becomes more precise, new archaeological cross-specializations, such as zoo-archaeology and botanical-archaeology, have emerged to offer insights into ancient Egyptian life. With these additional capabilities, Egyptologists can re-examine the work of earlier generations of researchers to substantiate or revise their conclusions.

Much of the cultural heritage of Egypt is in foreign hands, on display at major museums in Britain, France, and the United States. However, an extensive collection of some 120,000 objects is housed in the Egyptian Museum in CAIRO, Egypt. In addition, local museums have been opened at Luxor, Aswan, Alexandria, and other sites in the country. Strict controls have now been placed on removing artifacts from Egypt, and all antiquities unearthed at archaeological sites now belong to the nation.

In the second half of the 20th century major finds were made, particularly in Alexandria and at Bawit, in the Bahariya Oasis south of Cairo. In 1987 archaeologists excavated the tomb of the sons of Ramesses II (r. c. 1279–1212 BCE) and, in 1990, the tombs of the pyramid builders at Giza. In 1994 the French archaeologist Jean-Yves Empereur (1952–   ) found at an underwater site the remains of what may be the Tower of Pharos, a great lighthouse built on the island of Pharos, at Alexandria, during the reign of Ptolemy Philadelphus, 285 BCE. Another significant discovery was made in 1996, when Egyptian-born archaeologist Zahi Hawass (1947–   ), undersecretary of state for the Giza Monuments, unearthed a cemetery in Bawit—now called Valley of the Golden Mummies—containing approximately 10,000 Greco-Roman mummies.

See also: ARCHAEOLOGY AND AFRICA (Vols. IV, V); EGYPTOLOGY (Vol. IV); RAMESSES II (Vol. I).

Further reading: Angela McDonald and Christina Riggs, eds., *Current Research in Egyptology 2000* (Oxford, U.K.: Archaeopress, 2000).

Ekwensi, Cyprian (Cyprian Odiatu Duaka Ekwensi) (1921–   ) *Nigerian author*

The IGBO writer Ekwensi, a man of many professions ranging from forestry to teaching to pharmacy, published his first book, a collection of short stories and Igbo folk-tales, in 1947. Though his earliest long fiction contained some elements of URBAN LIFE AND CULTURE, it was *People of the City* (1954) that truly established Ekwensi's subject and style. Unlike the authors Chinua ACHEBE (1930–   ) and Onuora Nzekwu (1928–   ), both famous Nigerian writers whose work Ekwensi's preceded, Ekwensi shifted his focus away from the colonial past. Instead, he focused on Nigeria's present, in which newly won independence from Britain and rampant URBANIZATION had produced a highly unstable environment. His less formal, journalistic writing style and themes appealed to a largely urban-based readership over the succeeding decades and made him a highly popular author within NIGERIA.

In 1961 Ekwensi published *Jagua Nana*, his most celebrated and perhaps most controversial novel. The story of a prostitute in LAGOS, the novel addresses themes of materialism and political CORRUPTION, among others. Upon its publication *Jagua Nana* became the focus of harsh criticism from conservative factions and women's organizations on the grounds of the book being "obscene" and "pornographic." Critics also labeled Ekwensi's work as "amateurish" and the stuff of pulp fiction. Nevertheless, Ekwensi's supporters were as numerous as his detractors, and his realistic portrayal of urban conditions in Nigeria could not be easily dismissed.

Serving as an indicator of the effects of urbanization and growing materialism in Nigeria, the titular character of *Jagua Nana* derives her name (pronounced Jag-wa) from the English luxury car Jaguar.

Outside of his writing, Ekwensi was very active in the media industry, working at the Nigerian Broadcasting Corporation from 1957 to 1961. He served as the chair of the Bureau of External Publicity, as well as director of the independent BIAFRA radio station during the Nigerian civil war (1967–70), traveling to the United States and Europe to raise money for the rebel cause. He has also directed a number of publishing companies and served as consultant for various newspapers and print media.

Ekwensi's other works include *Burning Grass* (1962), *Beautiful Feathers* (1963), and *Iska* (1981). He has also authored a number of children's books, for which he is well known and liked in Nigeria. However, it is Ekwensi's urban novels that have garnered the greatest acclaim and produced the largest impact, earning him the title of "Father of the Nigerian Novel."

See also: EKWENSI, CYPRIAN (Vol. IV); LITERATURE IN COLONIAL AFRICA (Vol. IV); LITERATURE IN MODERN AFRICA (Vol. V).

Emang Basadi Women's group formed in Botswana to fight against the country's discriminatory laws. Emang Basadi means "Stand Up Women" in Tswana, a principal language spoken in BOTSWANA. The organization was created in 1986 as a protest movement to demand women's rights. The group's founders, which included lawyers, businesswomen, and university women, were inspired by the 1985 United Nations International Conference on Women held in NAIROBI, KENYA.

At the time of the organization's creation, 25 statutes in Botswana discriminated against women. The most controversial of these was the Citizenship (Amendment) Act, which denied the right of citizenship to children born to Botswana women and foreign men. Emang Basadi led legal awareness and political campaigns to advocate the removal of this and all other discriminatory laws. It also led political campaigns to encourage more participation of women in leadership positions.

In 1994, and again in 1999, Emang Basadi published strategic documents called the Manifestos of Botswana Women, which summarized the major issues concerning women and listed their demands for change. They deliberately produced the manifestos in election years so that the political parties could address the women's demands in their campaigns. As a result of the women's strategies, many of the offending laws were changed by the year 2000. Emang Basadi continued to lobby the government on women's issues and provide counsel and training for women's empowerment.

See also: LAW IN MODERN AFRICA (Vol. V); WOMEN IN MODERN AFRICA (Vol. V).

Emecheta, Buchi (Florence Onye Buchi Emecheta) (1944–) *Igbo novelist from Nigeria*

Over the course of 11 novels and other works, Buchi Emecheta established a literary career that garnered her international acclaim. Writing in English, as opposed to her native IGBO, in order to reach a wider audience, Emecheta addresses the obstacles faced by women in modern Africa, as well as the changes levied upon African traditions through the influence of Western culture.

Born in the village of Yaba on the outskirts of LAGOS, NIGERIA, Emecheta was raised by a foster family after her parents died while she was still very young. She attended the Methodist Girls High School in Lagos until age 16. She married in 1960 and two years later, after bearing two children, Emecheta moved to London to be with her husband while he studied there. Within a few years Emecheta had borne five children in all. During this time Emecheta began to write, selling segments of her diary to the British publication *The New Statesman*. Her abusive husband attempted to suppress Emecheta's writing aspirations, and even burned an early manuscript of her first novel. This led to divorce in 1969, after which time Emecheta was forced to support her children through her writing.

In the Ditch, the book version of Emecheta's publications in *The New Statesman*, was published in 1972. In 1974 Emecheta earned a degree in sociology from the University of London. That same year her first novel, *Second Class Citizen*, appeared. A largely autobiographical story, the novel follows a young Nigerian woman named Adah who moves to London and struggles to balance education, writing, and motherhood while living in an alien, and not always accommodating culture.

Her second novel, *The Bride Price* (1976), continued Emecheta's examination of African womanhood, critiquing the Igbo traditions that she perceived as detrimental to women. *The Slave Girl* (1977) and *The Joys of Motherhood* (1979), widely considered Emecheta's best novel, also featured African women facing antagonistic societal constraints.

Emecheta's focus was not limited to issues concerning only African women, however. Her novel *Destination Biafra* (1982) expanded her studies of the African female experience beyond tradition and family into politics and nationalism, following a young woman who becomes involved in the upheaval of the Nigerian civil war in BIAFRA (1967–70). *The Rape of Shavi* (1983) strayed even further from her initial focus, presenting the tale of an imaginary African country that falls victim to Western colonialism.

Emecheta stressed that her novels contain universal subjects that apply not only in Africa but to the general conflict between traditional and modern cultures, and to the overall situation of women in a largely patriarchal world. Her novels won her an appreciative international audience and gained her teaching positions at the University of Calabar, in Nigeria, at Yale University, in the United States, and at the University of London. She also wrote for television, published a number of children's books, and produced an autobiography, *Head above Water*, published in 1986.

See also: LITERATURE IN MODERN AFRICA (Vol. V); WOMEN IN INDEPENDENT AFRICA (Vol. V).

England and Africa Starting in the 1950s England relinquished its formal control of its colonial holdings and established new relations based on economic and educational links with its former colonies. Beginning with GHANA (formerly the Gold Coast) in 1957, most of England's former African colonies achieved independence in the decade that followed. With the process of decolonization well underway, England's diplomatic efforts were focused on facilitating the smooth and peaceful transfer of power to local national elites. For the most part this transition proved orderly and amicable, particularly in West Africa, where indigenous leaders had been granted a measure of self-rule in anticipation of independence. The greatest complications arose in southern and central Africa, where England ruled colonies with large white-settler populations. The brutally suppressed Mau Mau movement of the 1950s in KENYA offered an ominous indication that considerable strife would be involved in the transition to democratic majority rule in RHODESIA (today known as ZIMBABWE) and SOUTH AFRICA, two other countries with large white-settler communities.

England gave clear signals that it would be unwilling to tolerate white-dominated governments in Africa that withheld political rights from their African populations. In February 1960 the British prime minister, Harold Macmillan (1894–1986), spoke before the South African Parliament in CAPE TOWN, warning that "the winds of change," as represented by the emergence of triumphant African nationalist movements, were sweeping across the African continent. Defiantly, South Africa transformed itself into a republic the following year and subsequently left the British Commonwealth rather than subject itself to ongoing criticism from Commonwealth members for its legally entrenched system of racial discrimination known as APARTHEID. In Rhodesia, too, England's Labour government called on the white settler community to make meaningful moves toward extending political rights to the country's African majority. In 1965 this led Rhodesian prime minister Ian SMITH (1919–) and his party, the Rhodesia Front, to break off ties with England and issue a UNILATERAL DECLARATION OF INDEPENDENCE. Despite applying diplomatic pressure and economic sanctions, England was unable to force Smith to back down. Ultimately Rhodesia negotiated a settlement only in 1978, after a long civil war with the country's insurgent forces led by Robert MUGABE (1924–) and Joshua NKOMO (1917–1999).

Despite misgivings concerning many political developments in Africa in the years following independence, England has rarely intervened directly in the internal affairs of its former colonies. The British government maintained its distance even during the destructive civil war that enveloped NIGERIA from 1967 to 1970, as well as during the brutal reign of Idi AMIN (c. 1925–2003) in UGANDA during the 1970s. In those instances in which England became involved—such as deploying troops to squash army mutinies in TANZANIA and Uganda in 1964, or attempting to restore order to SIERRA LEONE—its goals were limited and its actions were ostensibly prompted by humanitarian concerns.

By 1968, with the independence of SWAZILAND, England had divested itself of all its African holdings. In most instances England retained close ties to those countries it had once colonized, linked to them by organizations and programs promoting trade and diplomatic relations, cultural and educational exchange, and affiliations related to churches and professional societies.

See also: COLONIAL RULE (Vol. IV); ENGLAND AND AFRICA (Vols. III, IV); GOLD COAST (Vols. III, IV); MAU MAU MOVEMENT (Vol. IV); NATIONALISM AND INDEPENDENCE MOVEMENTS (Vol. IV).

Entebbe City in south-central UGANDA on the shores of Lake VICTORIA. Entebbe was the British administrative center of UGANDA from 1894 until 1953. It was passed up as the federal capital of Uganda upon independence in 1962 in favor of the city of KAMPALA, which is located 21 miles (34 km) to the north. Entebbe's elevation—3,760 feet (1,146 m) above sea level—gives it a pleasant climate, and the city has become popular as a residential community for many of Uganda's civil servants, including the president. As of 2000 the estimated population was about 50,000.

On June 27, 1976, armed terrorists from the Popular Front for the Liberation of Palestine forced an Air France plane to land at the airport at Entebbe. Once on the tarmac, they released the crew and the non-Jewish passengers, demanded the release of Palestinian prisoners in Israel, and threatened to begin executing the remaining passengers if their demands weren't met.

During the week that followed, Israeli soldiers planned a daring raid on the plane involving dozens of heavily armed Israeli commandos. In the end, all eight terrorists were killed in the rescue. The operation's commander and two hostages also died in the gunfight that ensued.

Industry in the city is not extensive, although it is well connected to KENYA and TANZANIA because of its position on a peninsula in Lake Victoria. It also has the main international airport for Uganda and several tourist hotels. Aside from servicing the tourists who visit the nearby game sanctuary and Lake Victoria, Entebbe's people make their livings by farming, fishing, and producing consumer goods.

See also: TOURISM (Vol. V).

environmental issues Africa's geographical and geological complexity makes for diverse environmental challenges. However, many countries share environmental concerns, since the type of ecosystem determines the particular environmental issues faced by a region.

Water Use Issues People living in Africa's arid areas have regularly dealt with WATER shortages. In northern

Africa, for instance, much of the available water is used for irrigating agricultural fields. Therefore, patterns of personal water consumption conform to fit availability. In the years since independence, however, the URBANIZATION of the region and rapid POPULATION GROWTH have combined to put unrealistic demands on water supplies. To meet the needs of urban dwellers, piped water and sewage treatment have become more common. One of the past solutions for the water crisis was the construction of the ASWAN DAM on the upper Egyptian Nile. However, damming rivers solves one problem while introducing a different set of environmental problems, such as upstream flooding and silt build-up in reservoirs. In addition, dams prevent crucial silt from reaching deltas downstream where they used to replenish nutrients that make for productive AGRICULTURE. Changing the flow of silt to deltas also alters ecosystems and affects fisheries.

Water sources are also being compromised by commercial agriculture, which uses chemical fertilizers and pesticides that run off into drinking water sources. Environmentalists and public officials in countries like SOUTH AFRICA are calling for the protection of water catchment areas in order to alleviate water shortage and pollution issues.

Deforestation One of the ways that water sources are naturally protected from pollutants is through a buffer of FORESTS or wetlands, which serve to filter pollutants before they reach the open water. However, since the end of the colonial era, many smaller wetlands in Africa have been filled in for settlement or destroyed for rice-planting schemes. This type of land use inhibits the environment's natural protective function and also decreases its ability to slow runoff and prevent soil erosion.

Much of Africa's denser forest environments have suffered as population pressure has led to increased deforestation. In rural areas, people must cut down trees to use as fuel for cooking. In areas where land is scarce, farmers clear forests in order to cultivate crops. Also, lumber companies, both foreign and domestic, continuously harvest trees, sometimes illegally. Many African nations recognized the importance of ecological BIODIVERSITY and the protective effects of forests and wetlands. They have, therefore, established laws that prohibit deforestation. However, enforcement continues to be a problem for these nations. Without strategies to deal with the needs of an increasing population, deforestation will remain a serious obstacle. Countries such as TANZANIA have only "national guidelines for environmental protection," which do not provide a means to punish those who cut protected forests. Recent efforts, however, have sought to convert these guidelines into laws that will allow for prosecution of offenders.

Declining Soil Fertility Agricultural production depends on plentiful nutrients in the soil. Africa has a wide range of different soils. Some are very old and have low fertility because of the leaching of nutrients over time. Other soils, such as those produced by volcanic activity, are relatively new and are very fertile. As people repeatedly use land to grow crops, soil fertility declines. When this occurs, crop output also declines, and humans must then add nutrients if they hope to maintain or increase production. However, most African farmers do not have the resources to purchase commercially produced fertilizers to replenish the soil nutrients. Historically, farmers rotated their crops in order to allow fields to lie fallow, or rest in an overgrown state, in order to replenish nutrients. But population pressure and land scarcity result in continuous farming, which does not allow the soil to recover between plantings. African governments and international aid organizations have responded to this problem by researching and implementing strategies that can help struggling farmers. One such strategy, agroforestry, has been employed successfully to increase soil nutrients in some tropical areas. However, it does not work for all areas.

Agroforestry **is the practice of growing crops and trees together. In theory, the organic matter produced by trees replenishes nutrients in earth that has been used repeatedly to grow crops. When it is effective, agroforestry helps restore soil fertility and improves agricultural productivity.**

Desertification Another issue that has recently been cause for concern is desertification, or the conversion of non-desert land into deserts. There is much debate regarding desertification, which is a natural, unavoidable long-term ecological process. Some models, however, point to human activity as a contributing factor in the process. Human land-use practices, such as increased water use and increased livestock grazing, are identified as causes for increased desertification. Other possible causes include increased greenhouse gases, long-term climatic change, and short-term climatic variability. Regarding desertification, the area of most concern to climatologists and environmentalists is the Sahel, which is the band of dry grassland on the southern edge of the Sahara.

Shrinking Wildlife Habitat One pressing environmental problem that is generally associated with increasing populations and continued widespread POVERTY in Africa is the loss of habitat for WILDLIFE. When people encroach on protected forests and grasslands in search of a better livelihood, habitat for Africa's spectacular array of wildlife is diminished. Many protected areas were created for the purpose of preserving this valuable natural resource. As habitats shrink, Africa is in danger of losing its biodiversity. In some countries, national and international bodies are working to implement policies that encourage protection of wildlife habitat by the general population as well as the government. These strategies might include employing rural people in wildlife preserves, thereby giving them a way to make a living other than using the protected areas to farm or graze livestock. It is increasingly common for environmental protection policies to include a component that addresses the needs of the local population.

For example, farmers on the fringes of wildlife preserves in KENYA and MOZAMBIQUE have lost crops to elephants. These gigantic animals like to eat mature maize and can destroy most of a farmer's field in a single night. As a consequence, farmers commonly kill these beasts, seeing them as little more than mammoth pests. However, animal rights groups and government agencies are working with farmers on alternative solutions to prevent elephants from destroying crops.

In some countries, such as Kenya and BOTSWANA, NATIONAL PARKS have employed rural peoples to guard against poachers. Poaching, or the illegal taking of game, has been common in Africa since colonial times, when certain wild animals—or their parts—became highly prized for both medicinal and aesthetic reasons. For instance, elephants and rhinos are often killed solely for their tusks and horns, and their carcasses are left to rot wherever the animal was killed. The ivory ban, established in 1990, is an example of the international community responding to the plummeting elephant populations. However, even though laws may prohibit poaching, the money that can be earned by trading in African skins or animal parts can be a powerful enticement to conduct illegal activity.

Since Africa's wildlife attracts millions of tourist dollars every year, governments and citizens alike recognize the importance of protecting wildlife populations from poaching. In some countries, such as SOUTH AFRICA, elephant populations have rebounded and elephant overpopulation is now a problem.

Africa's increasing human population has brought with it overharvesting of resources, such as fish stocks in coastal areas. In SENEGAL, for example, overfishing has drastically depleted fish populations. In response, Senegal's government has recently made commitments to establish its first marine preserve to protect its COASTAL AND MARINE ECOSYSTEMS and allow for sustainable harvesting of fish and other marine products.

Because some African nations lack the resources to address their myriad environmental issues, international environmental and animal rights bodies are becoming involved. These agencies, including the World Wildlife Federation, the International Tree Foundation, and the United Nations Environmental Protection Agency, are contributing to the research and policy-making that are ongoing to address effectively the human and environmental concerns of each region.

See also: CONSERVATION (Vol. V); DROUGHT AND DESERTIFICATION (Vol. V); ECOLOGY AND ECOLOGICAL CHANGE (Vol. V); NILE RIVER (Vols. I, III); SAHARA (Vols. I, II); SAHEL (Vol. I); SUSTAINABLE DEVELOPMENT (Vol. V); TOURISM (Vol. V); UNITED NATIONS AND AFRICA (Vol. V).

Further readings: Michael Darkoh and Apollo Rwomire, eds., *Human Impact on Environment and Sustainable Development in Africa* (Burlington, Vt.: Ashgate, 2003); Paul Richards, *African Environment, Problems and Perspectives* (London: International African Institute, 1975); United Nations Environment Programme Staff, *Environmental Problems of the East African Region* (Geneva, Switzerland: United Nations Publications, 2003).

Equatorial Guinea Country located in west-central Africa. It is made up of Río Muni, a rectangular continental region, the large island of Bioko, and four smaller islands named Elobey Grande, Elobey Chico, Corisco, and Annobón. All told, the country measures about 10,800 square miles (28,000 sq km). Río Muni is bordered by CAMEROON, to the northeast, and GABON, to the southeast. Equatorial Guinea is the sole country in Africa with Spanish as an official language.

Equatorial Guinea at Independence In 1963 Spain granted its colony of Spanish Guinea limited self-rule and changed its name to Equatorial Guinea. Five years later the fully independent Republic of Equatorial Guinea was established, with nationalist leader Francisco Macías Nguema (1922–1979) winning the presidential elections. At the time the country was in relatively good shape, with high levels of LITERACY and health care. It also had one of Africa's highest per-capita incomes, due mostly to cocoa plantations on Fernando Po (now Bioko) island that were farmed primarily by migrant workers from NIGERIA.

Under Nguema things changed quickly. In 1970 he began what would become one of Africa's most brutal dictatorial regimes by merging all political parties into the United National Party, with himself as the head. In 1972 Nguema declared himself president for life. The following year Río Muni and Fernando Po, which were then partially autonomous, were joined fully under Nguema's central government.

Seeking to consolidate and secure his power, Nguema ceased virtually all government activities other than security. The country collapsed as all of its basic services, from electricity to water to TRANSPORTATION, were abandoned. Schools closed in 1975, and, in an attempt to eliminate all Spanish influence in the country, Nguema banned the Catholic Church and shut down all churches in 1978. He also launched an Africanization campaign to fully eradicate colonial influence. Santa Isabel, the country's capital, was renamed MALABO. A clear indication of his megalomania, Nguema renamed the island of Fernando Po after himself. All Equatoguineans were also instructed to change their Spanish names to African ones. Nguema changed his own name frequently. By the end of his presidency he was known as Masie Nguema Biyogo Ñegue Ndong.

Nguema maintained his power through sheer brutality. It is estimated that his regime killed between 25,000 and 80,000 Equatoguineans. In 1976 the country's huge population of Nigerian migrant workers, numbering some 60,000, left in a mass exodus, crippling Equatorial Guinea's economy. These same workers had faced violent repression when they protested poor wages.

Finally, in 1979, Nguema was overthrown and executed as a result of a military COUP D'ÉTAT led by his cousin, Lieutenant Colonel Teodoro OBIANG (1942–). When Obiang assumed the presidency, he was confronted by a decidedly bleak situation. The country was in complete ruins, the government bankrupt, and two-thirds of the population had either been killed or had fled into exile.

Obiang acted to heal the country, lifting the ban on RELIGION, reaching out to the numerous REFUGEES in Cameroon and Gabon, and releasing many prisoners. Foreign ECONOMIC ASSISTANCE was used to begin rebuilding the nation's shattered INFRASTRUCTURE. In a symbolic move to rid the remnants of Nguema's regime, Masie Nguema Biyogo island was renamed Bioko.

Equatorial Guinea's national capital, Malabo, is on Bioko island, which lies off the coast of Cameroon. Río Muni's administrative capital is Bata.

However, despite creating a new, more democratic constitution (1982) and allowing for multiparty elections (1992), Obiang has remained only somewhat less autocratic than his predecessor. Obiang and his Democratic Party for Equatorial Guinea (Partido Democrático de Guinea Ecuatorial, PDGE) easily won elections in 1993 and 1996. These victories, however, came amid accusations of political repression against opposition parties. Legislative elections in 1999 and 2000 saw the PDGE gain political dominance.

In the late 1990s the discovery of large deposits of OIL of its coast led to an economic boom in Equatorial Guinea. However, little of this substantial income has been toward rebuilding the country. Instead, much of the money obtained from the oil industry has gone into Obiang's personal accounts. With 100,000 Equatoguineans still in exile at the turn of the century, and with only minor improve-

ments in government, Equatorial Guinea faces a slow process of economic and political rehabilitation.

See also: CORRUPTION (Vol. V); EQUATORIAL GUINEA (Vols. I, II, III, IV); SPAIN AND AFRICA (Vols. IV).

Eritrea   Country located in northeastern Africa that achieved independence in 1993 following a long war with ETHIOPIA. A country of some 46,800 square miles (121,200 sq km), Eritrea is bordered by the Red Sea, to the east, Ethiopia, to the south, and the Republic of the SUDAN, to the west. The country's dry coastal plain rises gradually to less arid highlands in the interior.

An area whose history goes back to the first millennium BCE, Eritrea has been controlled by Aksum, EGYPT, the Ottoman Empire, Britain, Italy, and, after World War II (1939–45), by Ethiopia. By 1960, however, Eritrean nationalists had begun an armed independence effort, led initially by the Eritrean Liberation Front (ELF). Using this rebellion as a justification, Ethiopia announced a complete annexation of the territory, going beyond the federated system intended by the United Nations when it gave Ethiopia jurisdiction over the region in 1952.

Eritrean resistance grew during the 1960s, becoming more effective as the Ethiopian emperor, HAILE SELASSIE (1892–1975), began to lose control over the day-to-day affairs of his own country. The ELF was soon joined in the field by a second military force, the ERITREAN PEOPLE'S LIBERATION FRONT (EPLF), and, by the mid-1970s, the two movements had almost 20,000 troops in action. By that time, too, they had made sufficient progress that they were beginning to gain control of many rural areas of the country, where they began to establish their own schools, hospitals, and factories.

In 1980 the EPLF split with the ELF, eventually becoming the single fighting force against Ethiopia. By this time, Haile Selassie had fallen, replaced by the brutal regime of MENGISTU HAILE MARIAM (c. 1937–), which, assisted by massive infusions of aid from the Soviet Union, was able to keep up the war against the Eritrean rebels for many years. By 1990, however, the EPLF had control of almost 90 percent of the country and had effectively won. Under the supervision of the United Nations, a referendum was held in April 1993, and independence was overwhelmingly approved.

A transitional National Assembly was formed following the April 1993 referendum. It was composed entirely of members of the EPLF (which changed its name to the People's Front for Democracy and Justice, or PFDJ, in February 1994). The PFDJ led the writing of a new constitution and the transitional assembly elected ISAIAS AFEWERKI (c. 1945–) the new president. Independence was declared on May 24, 1993.

The challenges facing Isaias Afewerki and the PFDJ have been tremendous. The president is chief of state,

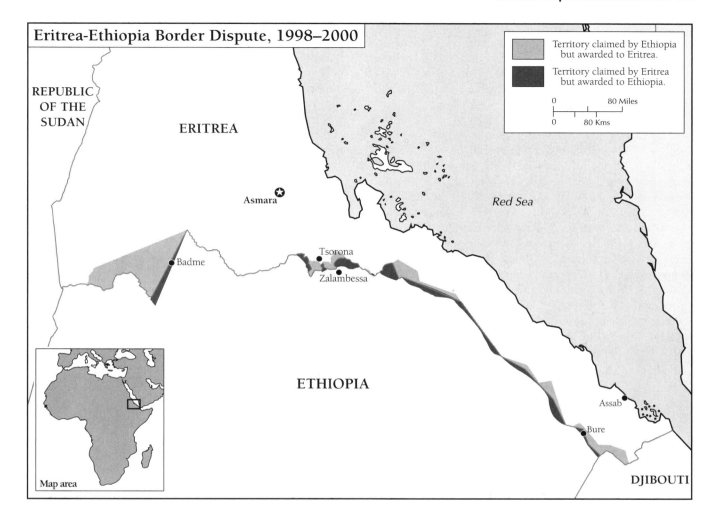

Eritrea-Ethiopia Border Dispute, 1998–2000

Territory claimed by Ethiopia but awarded to Eritrea.

Territory claimed by Eritrea but awarded to Ethiopia.

REPUBLIC OF THE SUDAN

ERITREA

Asmara

Red Sea

Badme

Tsorona

Zalambessa

ETHIOPIA

Assab

Bure

Map area

DJIBOUTI

head of government, head of the state council, and head of the National Assembly, thereby limiting political opposition and ensuring that Isaias's transitional government will continue to govern well into its second decade. It confronts both secular and religious opposition including the ELF and the Eritrean Liberation Front-Revolutionary Council, among others. Also opposing the PFDJ is the allegedly Sudan-backed Eritrean Islamic Jihad, an extremist Islamic organization that has claimed responsibility for numerous bombings of civilian populations on the Eritrean-Sudanese and Eritrean-Ethiopian borders.

Eritrea is a desperately poor country in which 80 percent of the 3.5 million people rely on subsistence AGRICULTURE; it ranks 157 out of 173 countries on the United Nations Development Program's Human Development Index. Unemployment and illiteracy plague an economic situation aggravated by ongoing conflict with Ethiopia. From 1998 to 2000, Ethiopia and Eritrea engaged in one of the continent's fiercest border wars, crashing the economy. Even with the cessation of violence, the damage to the economy caused by limited trade with Ethiopia—in partic-

ular, the loss of rents formerly collected from Ethiopian businesses using the Eritrean port—continues to limit economic growth.

See also: ERITREA (Vols. I, II, III, IV); ITALY AND AFRICA (Vol. IV).

Further reading: Lionel Cliffe and Basil Davidson, *The Long Struggle of Eritrea for Independence and Constructive Peace* (New Jersey: Red Sea Press, 1988).

Eritrean People's Liberation Front (EPLF) Leading group in the struggle for an independent ERITREA. After independence in 1993, it changed its name to the People's Front for Democracy and Justice (PFDJ) and became the state party.

Eritrea, which had been an Italian colony, came under British control in 1941 when Italy was defeated in World War II (1939–45). In 1952 the United Nations Security Council made Eritrea a semiautonomous state within ETHIOPIA. However, in 1962, Ethiopian emperor HAILE SELASSIE (1892–1975) unilaterally dissolved Eritrea's special status in favor of a united Ethiopia. The Eritrean reaction was dramatic, and the Eritrean Liberation Front (ELF), formed in 1958, began what would become a 30-year armed struggle to create an independent Eritrea. In 1970 a more militarily inclined faction of the ELF broke away and formed the Eritrean People's Liberation Front (EPLF), eventually supplanting the ELF in the fight for Eritrean independence.

The EPLF maintained its war even during the momentous political shifts in the 1970s that saw the overthrow of Haile Selassie and the establishment of the Marxist government of MENGISTU HAILE MARIAM (c. 1937–   ) in 1974. As Mengistu's regime began to weaken in the mid-1980s, the EPLF captured strategic Eritrean towns. It also joined with the Tigray People's Liberation Front and other Ethiopian opposition elements to oust Mengistu in 1991. That same year the EPLF captured AS-MARA, the Eritrean capital, and established itself as the provisional government of Eritrea. The new Ethiopian government then supported Eritrea's independence vote in 1993. The EPLF became the ruling party, and its leader, ISAIAS AFEWERKI (1945–   ), became president. In February 1994 the EPLF changed its name to the People's Front for Democracy and Justice (PFDJ). The PFDJ became Eritrea's only legal party. Since Eritrea's independence it has governed in an increasingly authoritarian manner, with no elections to challenge its dominance.

Further reading: Dan Connell, *Against All Odds: A Chronicle of the Eritrean Revolution* (Trenton, N.J.: Red Sea Press, 1997).

Ethiopia Land-locked country, about 435,100 square miles (1,126,900 sq km) in size, located in the Horn of Africa. Ethiopia borders the modern states of DJIBOUTI, ERITREA, KENYA, SOMALIA, and the Republic of the SUDAN. One of Africa's oldest and most influential states, Ethiopia continues to try to rectify the ethnic conflicts of its past while facing the economic and leadership challenges of its future.

Haile Selassie in the Independence Era The history of the modern Ethiopian nation-state began in 1941, when Emperor HAILE SELASSIE (1892–1975) returned from exile in England. He immediately began attempts to expand Ethiopia to include Eritrea, its northern neighbor with a long Red Sea coast, and Italian Somaliland (part of present-day Somalia). The movement to "reunite" with Eritrea took the form of the Society for the Love and Land of Eritrea (later to be known as the Unionist Party). Its members believed that the Italians had stolen Eritrea from Ethiopia.

Haile Selassie garnered an international reputation as an anticolonialist and nationalist leader. The United Nations (UN), at first a supporter of independent Eritrean and Somali states, began to question the will of the majority in these locations. It set up a UN Commission of Inquiry for Eritrea, ultimately refusing to advocate either independence or a broad Ethiopian Union. By the time the ORGANIZATION OF AFRICAN UNITY (OAU) was established in May 1963, Haile Selassie was viewed as one of the most important elements of pan-African policy. As a result of his and Ethiopia's prestige, the OAU set up its headquarters in Ethiopia's capital, ADDIS ABABA.

While Haile Selassie was seen as a great reformer throughout the continent and overseas, at home, criticism was already mounting against him as early as the 1950s. During the 1960s the Ethiopian state itself showed significant progress in modernizing. Increasingly, however, wealthy Christian nobles lived privileged existences on the backs of the impoverished peasantry. Urban INDUSTRIALIZATION increased and FOREIGN INVESTMENT flowed into the country, but urban wages were exceedingly low. Among the military ranks, junior officers were critical of corrupt seniors, who reappropriated portions of the state military budget for their personal gain. Also at the root of the tensions was the fact that the principal beneficiaries of the new state were primarily Coptic Christians of Amharic ethnicity. This stirred great resentment in the Eritrean, Somali, Tigrayan, and OROMO populations.

The turning point in Haile Selassie's rule came with the great famine of 1972. By 1974 some 200,000 people had died in the northern provinces. In the TIGRAY region, where anti-government sentiments ran high, Haile Selassie mishandled the relief efforts so badly that he was accused of allowing the famine to continue in the hopes that it would weaken the resistance against him.

Mengistu Haile Mariam and Ethiopian Marxism Haile Selassie was overthrown in 1974 by a COUP D'ÉTAT led by junior military officers of the Dergue (meaning *committee* in Amharic). Originally, Ethiopians saw the officers as Marxist leaders heading a populist movement. Before long, however, Dergue leaders quickly went from revolutionaries to oppressors. The new president, Colonel MENGISTU HAILE MARIAM (c. 1937–   ), launched a bloody campaign of political intimidation and consolidated power in the hands of a small, loyal group of followers.

The Dergue coup plunged Ethiopia into civil war. The peasantry, for its part, was unhappy that the status quo put in place by Haile Selassie was not satisfactorily uprooted. Mengistu did work to diminish the dominance of the Coptic Amharan people in the countryside. Yet his efforts to foment a revolution from above failed to appease the masses below. In a well-known move, he executed 57 Amharan officials of the deposed monarchy and began a full-scale attack on separatists. Tigrayan, Eritrean, and Somali nationalist movements became more fervent. By 1977 it appeared likely that Mengistu might be overthrown. His military rule had proved unable to garner widespread legitimacy and his government failed to maintain stability or bring about DEVELOPMENT.

However, Mengistu's positioning in the Cold War was strong. The former Soviet Union began supporting his quasi-Marxist rule, making Ethiopia one of the Soviet Union's most important allies in Africa. Some 17,000 Cuban troops were sent to Ethiopia at Soviet expense to help support the Mengistu regime. The Ethiopian army grew to 300,000 and military expenditures increased to half of the total national budget—a percentage it held throughout the 1980s.

Unable to appease the myriad demands of the disparate Ethiopian peoples, Mengistu chose to rule by oppression. He attempted to maintain a greater Ethiopia through military victories over the ERITREAN PEOPLE'S LIBERATION FRONT (EPLF), the Oromo Liberation Front (OLF), the Tigray People's Liberation Front (TPLF) and other ethnically and regionally based nationalist movements. He created collective associations called *kebeles*, nationalizing lands and companies, and organizing workers under state rule. In 1984 he announced that Ethiopia was a one-party state led by the Workers Union. This, however, proved to be a ruse for his own aggrandizement.

The famines of the mid-1980s threatened Mengistu in much the same way that the famine of 1972 brought down Haile Selassie. A large international movement to mitigate the impact of the famine through aid was largely blocked by a regime intent on controlling every aspect of Ethiopian society. Mengistu's position would have been entirely untenable if not for massive Soviet aid. As the Soviet Union headed toward its own collapse in the late 1980s, Mengistu found himself with little support in a sharply divided state filled with factions eager to see him overthrown. In 1989, Mengistu's forces achieved one last, great victory against Eritrean, Tigray, Oromo, and Somali rebels before the final removal of Soviet aid and Cuban troops. In 1991 the TPLF, with the help of the ETHIOPIAN PEOPLE'S REVOLUTIONARY DEMOCRATIC FRONT (EPRDF), successfully took control of Addis Ababa. Mengistu fled to sanctuary in ZIMBABWE.

The Rise of Meles Zenawi and the New Ethiopian State Following Mengistu's downfall in May 1991, EPRDF leader MELES ZENAWI (1955–) seized power to lead the transitional government. Despite significant political infighting, Meles pushed through an ethnically based

In 1974 Col. Mengistu Haile Mariam led a Marxist revolution in Ethiopia. In 1980 these soldiers marched in Addis Ababa to show support for Mengistu on the sixth anniversary of the coup that brought him to power. (Note the Ethiopic script on the placard.) © AP/Wide World Photos

federal constitution, in December 1994. Under this constitution, the president has a mostly ceremonial role, and executive powers are vested primarily in the office of the prime minister. By 1995 Meles' EPRDF rebel movement had been reconstituted as a political party, and it won a majority of seats in the elections that year. Five years later, in a controversial vote, Meles and his EPRDF dominated national and regional elections to secure him a second term. He was still in power at the end of 2003.

Meles has attempted to create a new Ethiopian state with greater accountability between the state and society. He has rooted out some CORRUPTION and has tried to develop policies that would allow a free market to drive economic prosperity. Stability, rather than the deepening of DEMOCRATIZATION, has been the refrain.

Nationalist movements based on ethnicity have continued to pose the most important political challenges throughout Meles' time in office. The OLF came to blows with its former rebel partner, the EPRDF, in 1991, and it subsequently boycotted the June 1992 local government elections. In December 1993 the OLF joined with the Council of Alternative Forces for Peace and Democracy, which then boycotted the 1995 national election. Similarly, the Ogadeni National Liberation Front (ONLF) of Somali Ethiopians also has fought with the EPRDF, though it has participated, with moderate success, in local elections.

The Politics of Ethnicity Ethnic-based and regional conflict has been a blow to the federal system that Meles has backed. The arrangement of 12 ethnic states and two independent cities set up under the new constitution was intended to give enough autonomy to quell secessionist tendencies. However, this approach to governance in a large, divided, multiethnic, multi-religion society has led to unequal growth among states. Centrally located states continue to receive a disproportionately large share of the national wealth. Nevertheless, this model of the Ethiopian national state has remained viable for more than a decade.

By 2001, however, it appeared Ethiopia might again be threatened by a secessionist Tigray state led by the TPLF. In response, Meles purged the TPLF leadership from his government. Parallel trends continue in Oromo areas with increasing violence and unrest. Further complicating the situation is a concern with the promotion of international TERRORISM in the region.

Ethiopia and Eritrea In 1993, with the assistance of the United Nations, Eritrea gained independence under the leadership of President ISAIAS AFEWERKI (c. 1945–). Fearing that Tigray and Oromo would quickly follow suit, Meles attempted to bring Eritrea back into the Ethiopian fold. From May 1998 to December 2000 Ethiopia and Eritrea fought one of Africa's most devastating wars. The immediate reason for the clash was the placement of the border between the two states, but the origins of the conflict predate World War II (1939–45). Between 1941 and 1952 Eritrea was administered by Britain under a UN agreement. At that time, with British support, Eritrea was considered an autonomous unit within Ethiopia. However, in 1962 Haile Selassie ignored protests and annexed Eritrea, making it an integral part of the Ethiopian state and sparking a long period of hostility.

When Eritrea voted for independence in 1993, it left landlocked Ethiopia dependent on access to Eritrean Red Sea ports. In return, the Eritrean economy needed Ethiopia's markets. Each side played its advantage over the other, furthering existing tensions.

In December 2000 the peace treaty signed by the two states led to the creation of an independent Ethiopia-Eritrea Boundary Commission (EEBC). However, the EEBC proved to be controversial, with the Ethiopian government accusing it of favoring Eritrea. Continuing attempts at demarcating the Ethiopian-Eritrean border made governing Ethiopia more complex.

The Ethiopian Economy Further challenging Meles, and any possible successor, is a lack of economic growth. Ethiopia remains one of the world's poorest countries. In addition to its size and difficult terrain, the nation's ethnic diversity challenges economic growth. Moreover, with an overwhelming majority of its nearly 60 million people living in rural areas, the country is highly dependent on rainfall for the sufficient production of FOOD CROPS to feed its population. As a result the naturally caused fa-mine that brought down Haile Selassie and threatened Mengistu Haile Mariam also threatens Meles's government. Depending on rainfall and climatic conditions, the production of coffee, Ethiopia's most important commodity, can fluctuate up to 100 percent from year to year. Compounding the problem, consumer prices inflate to unmanageably high levels in times of scarcity. In all, this makes Ethiopian economic change far more volatile than that in sub-Saharan Africa as a whole.

Ethiopia has worked with the International Monetary Fund to try to stabilize fiscal policy and economic patterns. However, it continues to suffer from high levels of debt, an undeveloped industrial sector, and insufficient INFRASTRUCTURE.

See also: ADOWA, BATTLE OF (Vol. IV); AMHARA (Vols. I, III, IV); COFFEE (Vols. II, IV); COLD WAR AND AFRICA (Vols. IV, V); COMMUNISM AND SOCIALISM (Vol. V); CUBA AND AFRICA (Vol. V); ETHNIC CONFLICT IN AFRICA (Vol. V); ETHNICITY AND IDENTITY (Vol. V); ETHIOPIA (Vols. I, II, III, IV); ITALO-ETHIOPIAN WAR (Vol. IV); ITALY AND AFRICA (Vol. IV); NATIONALISM AND INDEPENDENCE MOVEMENTS (Vol. IV); SOVIET UNION AND AFRICA (Vol. V).

Further reading: Edmond J. Keller. *Revolutionary Ethiopia: From Empire to People's Republic* (Bloomington, Ind.: Indiana University Press 1988); Harold G. Marcus, *History of Ethiopia* (Berkeley, Calif.: University of California Press, 1994); Peter J. Schraeder, *African Politics and*

Society: A Mosaic in Transformation (New York: Bedford/St. Martin's, 2000).

Ethiopian Orthodox Church Long-time state church of ETHIOPIA, theologically and organizationally distinct from Western Christian churches. Because of tumultuous events in its recent history, although it is currently enjoying a revival of independence, the worldwide Ethiopian Orthodox Church is undergoing a crisis over just who is its legitimate leader.

Movement toward Independence Although it is of Coptic origin, the Ethiopian Orthodox Church is distinctive because of ancient roots that purportedly connect the Queen of Sheba with King Solomon of Israel. Historically, however, the Ethiopian church was long dominated by Egyptian Copts, a situation opposed by the Ethiopian church, which resented outside hegemony and sought to appoint Ethiopian-born clerics.

In 1929 four Ethiopian-born bishops were ordained to assist the Coptic-appointed patriarch of Ethiopia, as the head of the church was known. The movement toward Ethiopian control was furthered by the Emperor HAILE SELASSIE (1892–1975). As head of the Ethiopian church and state, Haile Selassie negotiated an agreement with the Egyptian Coptic leadership for the local election of an indigenous patriarch. This leadership of the Ethiopian Orthodox Church went into effect, in 1951, with the election of Baslios to the position of patriarch. The Egyptian Copts eventually confirmed this election in 1959.

After Baslios's death in 1971, Tewophilos was installed as head of the church, becoming the first patriarch to be installed within Ethiopia. Under his supervision, the St. Paul Theological College was opened in ADDIS ABABA in 1974.

According to the canon law of the Ethiopian church, the appointment to the position of patriarch is for life.

Aftermath of Revolution In 1974, when Haile Selassie was overthrown by a Marxist-oriented revolution, Colonel MENGISTU HAILE MARIAM (c. 1937–) assumed control of Ethiopia. This opened a new chapter in the history of the Ethiopian church as the Marxists separated church and state and nationalized church land. As part of this, the Mengistu government sought to diminish and even destroy the church by attacking its leadership. They imprisoned Patriarch Tewophilos in 1977 and appointed a hermit monk, Abba Melaku, as the new patri-

arch. Because this violated religious canon law, the Coptic Orthodox Church of EGYPT severed its relationship with the Ethiopian Orthodox Church.

In spite of this, Abba Melaku was installed as patriarch, taking the name Tekle Haimanot, a name with regal associations in Ethiopian history. In 1979 the government executed Tewophilos. Over the next few years, Patriarch Tekle Haimanot proved to be not as easy to manipulate as the new government had thought. However, he did maintain a general silence against governmental injustices, probably because he was afraid to provoke a violent backlash against the church.

Upon Tekle Haimanot's death in 1988, a new patriarch, Merkorios, was installed. However, another governmental change occurred in 1991, and the Mengistu government fell from power. Freed from the control of the Marxist regime, the church removed Merkorios on the grounds that he had been elected under direction of the Communists. In 1992 Merkorios resigned, and a new election was held. Paulos, who had been ordained a bishop by Tewophilos in 1975 and who had been imprisoned by the Marxists and exiled in the United States, was selected as the new patriarch of Ethiopia. Merkorios left Ethiopia and went to KENYA where he challenged the new election as invalid.

The 1990s witnessed a revival of the Ethiopian Orthodox Church, with the establishment of six clergy training centers throughout Ethiopia. This period also saw the revival of parish Sunday school programs and the founding of church social programs for REFUGEES, famine relief, and orphans.

See also: COPTIC (Vol. I); COPTS (Vol. I); COPTIC CHRISTIANITY (Vol. II); COPTIC CHURCH (Vol. IV); ETHIOPIAN ORTHODOX CHURCH (Vol. IV).

Ethiopian People's Revolutionary Democratic Front (EPRDF) Ruling party in ETHIOPIA founded in the late 1980s. The current president of Ethiopia, MELES ZENAWI (1955–), is the founder and chairman of the Ethiopian People's Revolutionary Democratic Front (EPRDF). The party grew out of a largely TIGRAY-based movement and emerged as an umbrella organization that fought to liberate ETHIOPIA from the repressive Provisional Military Administrative Council (PMAC), also known as the Dergue, which administered the country under the rule of MENGISTU HAILE MARIAM (c. 1937–). One of the organization's central objectives was to broaden its base of support; consequently, the EPRDF partnered with the largely Amhara Ethiopian People's Democratic Movement (EPDM). Rebels from the EPRDF eventually ousted Mengistu's Marxist dictatorship, in 1991, and came to power as a democratic regime.

Once in power the EPRDF created a radical constitution that gave each ethnic group the right to self-determination, including its right to secede from Ethiopia. Critics viewed Ethiopia's transformation into a multiethnic federation of 14 self-governing regions as a threat to national unity. The most fervent critics came from among the Amhara, who had dominated Ethiopia's politics and government throughout the modern era.

As an umbrella group the EPRDF also created other organizations, such as the Oromo Peoples Democratic Organization (OPDO), after the Oromo Liberation Front (OLF) refused to join EPRDF. This led the country's president, NEGASSO GIDADA (1943–), who was an OROMO, to break with the EPRDF, though he refused to relinquish the presidency. The EPRDF also faced resistance from other ethnically and regionally based parties such as the Ogadeni National Liberation Front (ONLF). Other groups, such as the Ethiopian Teachers Association (ETA), also opposed the EPRDF because of the EPRDF's regional linguistic education policy, which, they argued, threatened the status of Amharic as the national language. Despite these divisions, and in spite of controversial elections in 1994–95, the EPRDF remains the dominant political group and maintains popular support.

See also: AMHARA (Vols. I, III, IV); ETHNIC CONFLICT IN AFRICA (Vol. V); ETHNICITY AND IDENTITY (Vol. V); POLITICAL PARTIES AND ORGANIZATIONS (Vols. IV, V).

ethnic conflict in Africa People who share a common group identity may clash with others because of long-rooted animosities, differences in a neighboring country, fear of state instability, or because of manipulation carried out by elite groups of leaders. The trend toward ethnic violence, however, has been escalating in recent years, especially in Africa.

An ethnic group is one in which people share a common inherited culture, racial similarity, RELIGION, and belief in common history and ancestry. While the forging of ethnic identities is a primary building block in virtually any society, the creation of "sameness" often leads to a sentiment of difference. Neighbors who share a common citizenship, religion, or even work pattern identify with their cultural heritage rather than these other factors. The result can be ethnic conflict.

There are a number of reasons why ethnic conflict may arise. Some people point to ancient hatred between peoples that rises under certain political circumstances. Conflicts between Kosovars and Serbs in Yugoslavia, like that between TUTSI and HUTU in RWANDA and BURUNDI, have often been described as such. In recent years, however, this view of deep primordial differences has been challenged.

Another reason why ethnic conflict may arise is that a state presses the allegiance of a group within its neighbor's borders in an effort to propel its own interests. In reverse, ethnic manifestation in one country can lead to

ethnic insurgence in a neighboring country. For example, ethnic Diola insurgency in the Casamance region of SENEGAL spread violence to GUINEA-BISSAU and The GAMBIA, just as the rise of Somali identity in SOMALIA bled into neighboring ETHIOPIA.

A third reason for the rise of ethnic conflict is the fear of state collapse. Where central authority begins to crumble, inter-group competition increases. This competition is often on ethnic lines, galvanizing differences between ethnic identities. Also, ruling elites and regimes that have used ethnic identities as a tool for their own advantage can begin to fail or fragment. Other times the state is not threatened but elites continue to manipulate ethnic identities. Where this is the case we sometimes see African states that can successfully manage ethnic differences. Low-level conflict becomes a regularized pattern of state-society relations. Other times states are unable to handle this exchange, and it leads to intervention from outside states or organizations such as the AFRICAN UNION or the United Nations. Situations like this have arisen in ANGOLA, SOUTH AFRICA, and the Republic of the SUDAN. While in these cases ethno-political conflict continues, it is managed with external state support.

In West Africa, NIGERIA stood as a case in which DEMOCRATIZATION heightened political competition and exacerbated regional, ethnic, and religious conflict. In 1999 violence was the direct result. The federal system was intended to manage these cleavages, but the pervasiveness of ethnic favoritism in Nigeria's federal system allowed certain elites to win more power and economic benefits than others.

See also: ETHNIC GROUPS (Vol. IV); ETHNICITY AND IDENTITY (Vol. I); STATE, ROLE OF (Vol. V).

Further reading: Donald Rothchild, *Managing Ethnic Conflict in Africa: Pressures and Incentives for Cooperation* (Washington D.C.: Brookings Institution Press, 1997); Rotime T. Suberu, *Federalism and Ethnic Conflict in Nigeria* (Washington D.C.: United States Institute of Peace Press, 2001).

Europe and Africa At independence the relationships between African countries and their European counterparts were paradoxical. On one hand, years of colonial rule followed by nationalism and INDEPENDENCE MOVEMENTS had strained both institutional and interpersonal ties. On the other hand, African countries tended to maintain their former colonial powers as their largest trading partners. For much of the 1960s African countries suffered from continued power imbalances, which exacerbated postcolonial tensions and undermined DEVELOPMENT.

The LOMÉ CONVENTION, signed in 1975, was an attempt to rectify this problem. At its core it was intended to address the African development debacle. It offered

European trade concessions to new and struggling economies as well as financial, industrial, and technological assistance. Unfortunately, the Lomé Convention failed to achieve its goals. Three subsequent Lomé Convention charters increased the number of member states in the agreement. However, these also resulted in deteriorating terms of trade and a decline in development indicators.

Europe-Africa relations substantively changed toward the end of the 20th century. In 1957, Europe had begun a long process of economic unification and cooperation with the founding of the European Economic Community. This largely economic governing body grew into today's European Union (EU), which continued to accept new member states into the 21st century. Similarly, Africa embarked on an ambitious plan to create a pan-African parliament and increase regional solidarity through trade and institutional development. Ultimately, in July 2002 African states joined to create the AFRICAN UNION (AU), which replaced the outdated ORGANIZATION OF AFRICAN UNITY.

In anticipation of the pending launch of the AU, African and European leaders met in CAIRO, EGYPT, in April 2000. All heads of state present at the summit subscribed to the Cairo Declaration and the Cairo Plan of Action. The result was the NEW PARTNERSHIP FOR AFRICA'S DEVELOPMENT (NEPAD), which became the functional economic overlap between the European Union and the new African Union. It was a first step in rectifying earlier trade imbalances and normalizing European-African relations.

NEPAD replaced the Lomé Conventions. Through the partnership of the European and African Unions, NEPAD seeks to reduce POVERTY, promote SUSTAINABLE DEVELOPMENT, and reverse the marginalization of Africa in the globalization process.

The timing of NEPAD also reflected a greater global dynamic. Both Europe and the United States have exerted influence over the African continent, and both have fought for supremacy in setting global trade terms. Recently Europe began navigating a middle course between African economic efforts to protect nascent industries and American-style liberal market reform. Already the largest donors to Africa, the EU member states even increased funding. In all, they provide more than $9.5 billion to Africa annually, with more than $3 billion coming from the European Commission's Overseas Development Aid program.

See also: COLONIAL RULE (Vol. IV); COLONIALISM, INFLUENCE OF (Vol. IV); EUROPE AND AFRICA (Vol. IV); NATIONALISM AND INDEPENDENCE MOVEMENTS (Vol. IV) NEO-COLONIALISM, AND UNDERDEVELOPMENT (Vol. V).

Further reading: William Brown, *The European Union and Africa: the Restructuring of North–South Relations* (New York: I. B. Tauris, 2002).

Evora, Cesaria (1941–) *Cape Verdean singer*

At age 16, Evora began performing in local bars of her hometown, Mindelo, on the Cape Verdean Island of São Vicente. In 1975, after 18 years, she gave up her singing career, but then resumed it in earnest in 1985.

She launched her international career in France, where she went to record and perform in the late 1980s. With the release of her fourth album, *Miss Perfumado* (1992), Evora established her credentials as a legitimate star. Her rich, expressive voice and the haunting, melancholy nature of her deeply personal songs caught the attention of many listeners in Europe. By the mid-1990s her reputation had spread to the United States and other parts of the world.

Evora's songs are normally in the *morna* genre: mournful songs that usually chronicle lost love, nostalgia, and separation. Some of her music, however, takes the form of *coladeras*, which are faster-paced and less melancholy. Evora is often referred to as the Queen of Morna, and just as often the Barefoot Diva (owing to her habit of performing on stage without shoes or socks). She normally sings in Cape Verdean Creole, derived from Portuguese and West African languages.

Evora has recorded several albums, some of which have been nominated for Grammy awards. Despite her fame, wealth, and often hectic worldwide touring schedule, Evora still resides in Cape Verde. In recognition of her role as an informal cultural ambassador for her homeland, the Cape Verdean government has issued her a diplomatic passport.

exports Products traded on foreign markets. With historically weak domestic markets, most African countries embarked on a DEVELOPMENT strategy that relies on on export-led growth. At independence most African states traded predominantly with the European countries that had colonized them. This trade, which invariably worked to the advantage of European markets, tended to be export-driven and focused on a single crop or minerals. Exports included such items as coffee, tea, cocoa, cotton, groundnuts (peanuts), lumber, sorghum, sugar, livestock, and palm products. Countries with mineral wealth, such as ZAMBIA, Botswana, SOUTH AFRICA, the Democratic Republic of the CONGO, and GHANA, were mined predominantly by European industries to the benefit of a small number of European and African entrepreneurs. Some countries, such as ZIMBABWE, Ghana, BOTSWANA, and MAURITIUS, developed textiles or other industries to export basic commodity goods. However, ownership was usually foreign, and the opportunities to benefit from the industries were generally realized by only a select few.

Since that time, African product markets have diversified, and industries have grown throughout the continent. Still, there has been little basic change in the export focus. Most countries continue to have the strongest trade ties with the European powers that once colonized them. Raw goods and limited basic industrial items still account for the majority of African exports. More recently, the high demand for OIL in the West has dwarfed the demand for other extractable resources.

By 1973 the narrow export markets of most non-oil-producing African countries led to significant deficits. Oil-producing countries fared slightly better, but not enough to make up for their economic shortfalls. For example, although NIGERIA, ANGOLA, GABON, EQUATORIAL GUINEA, and CAMEROON all profited from the export of oil, none succeeded in converting the resulting export funds into significant Development initiatives. Indeed, in some cases, such as Angola and Nigeria, oil riches have proven to be a curse, since proceeds supported the warlords, insurgent groups, and narrow government coalitions that waged decades-long conflicts.

Throughout the 1970s most African countries, whether following a capitalist or socialist model of development, worked to diversify their industrial bases. Governments in countries from KENYA to IVORY COAST imposed high import tariffs in order to protect nascent industries and control foreign exchange rates. The results were disastrous. Exports dropped precipitously, as capital accounts and foreign exchange holdings fell along with them.

In the early 1980s many African countries turned to the INTERNATIONAL MONETARY FUND and the WORLD BANK for support. These organizations determined that the main cause of rising deficits and shortages of foreign exchange was the slow growth of exports. To support its assessment the World Bank noted that, in the 1970s, export growth declined in 24 of the 29 countries it examined. TANZANIA, Ghana, and others were cited for a bias against agricultural exports. The solution, African finance ministers were told, was to identify the product for which the country held a comparative advantage and then export that product to the fullest extent.

A decade later the World Bank measured the impact of the new approach only to find that not one of the countries measured performed adequately. RWANDA, for example, focused on exporting coffee. Although its coffee export proceeds rose by more than 70 percent, by the late 1980s the overall performance of the country's economy remained poor. Some historians argued that, when global coffee prices collapsed in 1989, Rwanda's overdependence on coffee exports led to instability that contributed to the Rwandan genocide in 1994.

Despite the failures the World Bank and other donors continued to believe that export-led growth was the key to linking Africa to the global economy. However, they began asking countries to diversify their export bases—in other words, to find multiple products in which the country has a comparative advantage. Commonly, these were extractive goods, such as MINERALS AND METALS, which feed markets first developed during the colonial era. The key difference was that the benefactors in Africa were a nascent business class, not the colonial government.

Formed in 1995, the World Trade Organization began efforts to secure free and fair trade between all countries. With this organization, African countries gained a new forum for improving terms of trade and for expanding their export markets. At the dawn of the 21st century, African states are still working toward export-led growth. However, with the exception of Mauritius and a few other countries, exports of African countries are still raw goods that cannot generate earnings to compete with technology, manufactured goods, and services produced by advanced industrialized countries.

See also: EXPORTS (Vol. IV).

Further reading: Peter Uvin, *Aiding Violence: The Development Enterprise in Rwanda* (West Hartford, Conn.: Kumarian Press, 1998); Elliot Berg, *Accelerated Development in Sub-Saharan Africa: An Agenda for Action* (Washington D.C.: The World Bank, 1981).

Eyadema, Gnassingbe (Étienne Eyadema)
(1935–2005) *President of Togo from 1967 to 2005*

Étienne Eyadema was born to peasant parents living in Pya, in northern TOGO. He was a member of the Kabye people, a Togolese minority. With a limited formal education, at age 16 he quit school to join the French colonial army. Fighting for the French in Indochina and ALGERIA, he rose to the rank of sergeant. When the French colonial army was demobilized, the soldiers demanded to be integrated into the Togolese army. However, when their demands went unmet, Eyadema helped organize a military COUP D'ÉTAT to topple the government of President Sylvanus Olympio (1902–1963).

After the coup Eyadema installed Nicolas Grunitzkey (1913–1969), Togo's former prime minister, to head the government. Within four years, however, Eyadema, by then a self-promoted army general, deposed Grunitzkey and assumed the leadership of the country. Once in power he established the Togolese People's Rally and made Togo a one-party state.

In 1974 Eyadema began rejecting foreign influence and expelling foreign corporations from the country. He even cast off his French name, Étienne, and assumed a more Togolese name, Gnassingbe. Eyadema ruled with an iron fist. At times he threatened to suspend the constitution and dissolve the National Assembly in order to ensure that the political situation in Togo conformed to his will. To maintain his authority, Eyadema was known to imprison, torture, and even execute members of the political opposition. During his tenure thousands of Togolese citizens fled the country to escape his oppression. Although Togo held free elections, Eyadema reportedly used his military might to intimidate opposition candidates and voters, thereby ensuring poor voter turnout. He was also accused of fixing results in elections he feared losing. During the last decade of his presidency, his government faced fierce riots and massive popular dissent, with domestic groups and Togolese diaspora from around the world calling for multiparty elections and new leadership. In February 2005 Eyadema died in his home village of Pya, while in transit for emergency medical treatment in Paris. Following an emergency parliamentary session, Eyadema's son, Faure Eyadema, was chosen to succeed his father as Togo's president.

See also: ARMIES, COLONIAL (Vol. IV); FRANCE AND AFRICA (Vols. IV, V); OLYMPIO, SYLVANUS (Vol. IV).

Further reading: A. A. Curkeet, *Togo: Portrait of a West African Francophone Republic in the 1980s* (Jefferson, N.C.: McFarland & Co., 1993)

F

family Many of the values and structures of modern African families, which vary considerably from region to region and culture to culture, have continued to be rooted in the traditions and values of the precolonial past. The sense of family remains strong, as does the value placed on children and respect for age and seniority. Yet, as in so many other parts of the world, the family in Africa is under great pressure. Some of this pressure comes from economic forces, such as wages and migrant LABOR, that had their origin in the colonial era. Also, while the colonial era witnessed growing URBANIZATION, urban development exploded once African countries became independent. In countries such as EGYPT and CAMEROON, for example, nearly all of the population growth in recent decades has been in the cities. The urban area of CAIRO, for instance, has a population of nearly 16 million, making it the largest in Africa and the tenth-largest urban area in the world.

URBAN LIFE AND CULTURE forced Africans to adapt their family structures to a new setting from the rural life had had been the norm for the vast majority of Africans until the 20th century. Not only did new social forces come into play, but new economic forces arose too, as families were increasingly dependent on sources of income external to the family for their existence. Even in the rural areas, the dependence on cash income instead of subsistence AGRICULTURE became increasingly important. Some rural people worked for wages on plantations, such as those growing tea in MALAWI. Individual African farmers also increasingly engaged in growing CASH CROPS, whether it be cut flowers in KENYA, cotton in MALI, or coffee in RWANDA. In both rural or urban areas, African families are thus increasingly dependent on the vagaries of the global MARKET for their economic needs. Such dependence has introduced a comparatively new phenomenon, that of POVERTY, into Africa, which in turn has had negative repercussions for the family, affecting the availability of such necessities as EDUCATION and health care.

See also: FAMILY (Vols. I, II, III, IV).

Further reading: Mario Azevedo, "The African Family," in Mario Azevedo, ed., *Africana Studies: A Survey of Africa and the African Diaspora* (3rd ed.; Durham, N.C.: Carolina Academic Press, 2004).

famine and hunger Although technological advances in AGRICULTURE have helped lessen the problem of mass starvation in most of the world, food crises remain frequent in much of Africa. Famine is generally defined as starvation so intense that it causes the loss of human life. The causes of famine are many. The most common is a food shortage resulting from drought, climatic or ATMOSPHERIC CHANGE, or changes in the condition or use of the land. However, these natural conditions are often combined with other factors. Indeed, famine can sometimes occur when there is no food shortage at all. Changes in prices and market conditions, political decisions, civil war, disease, and shifts in agricultural policies all can lead to a reduction in the amount of food available for a population.

Famine is not a new phenomenon. The Bible refers to Abraham's journey to EGYPT as a response to famine (Genesis 12:10). The Irish Potato Famine (1845–49), which is thought to have been responsible for the deaths of more than a million people, set off one of the largest mass migrations in European history. More recently, Josef

Stalin (1879–1953) starved 7 million or more Ukrainians in 1932–33, in an effort to force a policy of collective AGRICULTURE. In the late 1970s the policies of Cambodia's Khmer Rouge government led to an estimated 1 million deaths from starvation. The Ethiopian famine of 1988–89 was perhaps the worst ever seen in Africa.

In recent years what was once a global crisis has become a particularly African one. The primary reason is that the so-called Green Revolution, which had dramatic effects elsewhere in the world but has not been fully felt in Africa. Indeed, Africa has been relatively isolated from those gains, primarily through a combination of POVERTY, a lack of agricultural technologies, political strife, and crises in DEVELOPMENT and social policy.

The Green Revolution, in which agriculture was transformed from a purely "farming" concern to a scientific one, ended agriculture's reliance on nature alone. The Green Revolution took its first leap forward with Fritz Haber (1868–1934), the winner of the first Nobel Prize in chemistry (1918), who demonstrated the synthesis of ammonia. This ultimately led to the creation of chemical fertilizers. Combined with modern irrigation techniques, the availability of these fertilizers helped farmers grow crops on lands that were once considered marginal or even barren. Agricultural productivity skyrocketed, making it possible, for the time being at least, to contradict the famed prediction of economist Thomas Malthus (1766–1834) that the starvation of the human species was imminent.

As the Green Revolution progressed, strategies also were developed for mitigating the natural disasters that once were the primary causes of famine. As a result the human population has grown from approximately 950 million, in Malthus's time, to more than 6 billion today.

Nature, of course, is one of the primary causes of hunger in Africa. One area that consistently faces drought from turns of nature is the Sahel, which encompasses large parts of SENEGAL, MAURITANIA, MALI, BURKINA FASO, NIGER, and CHAD. All too often, the 50 million people who live in this area deal with weather conditions that can produce dramatic shortages of food. Droughts in 1973–74 and 1984, for example, were particularly costly in terms of both economics and human life. The cause of this lies in the fact that approximately 80 percent of the region's need for cereal foods must be met by local production. Unfortunately the local growing conditions are poor, with low rainfall, inferior soil, and underdeveloped markets. As a result the populations are vulnerable to the shock of drought or other natural factors.

Food production in the Sahel actually increased by 70 percent between 1961 and 1996. But this increase in food production did not keep pace with the increase in population. As a result, in spite of the gains in total food production, net food production *per person* actually declined 30 percent during this period.

Famine, especially today, does not start and stop suddenly with rain or other natural causes. Rather, it is closely tied to economic and political processes. In the most famine-prone areas of Africa—the Horn of Africa and other parts of East Africa, the Sahel, and Southern Africa (ZIMBABWE, ZAMBIA, and MALAWI in particular)—volatile market conditions that ultimately lead to hunger are a regular way of life. Indeed, in the Horn of Africa, famine seems to be merely a period in which the normal food insecurity becomes more intense.

In this sense, famine in Africa is closely tied to poverty. Not only is there insufficient rain and poor soil conditions, there also is a lack of money to properly irrigate or fertilize farmlands. Farmers do not invest in materials that could increase productivity because they are too costly and because market conditions are too risky. Instead, farmers try to meet their food needs by bringing new, often marginal land into cultivation. This response reduces the farmers' market risk, but it increases their vulnerability to natural occurrences. It also can have devastating ecological effects and can lead to great environmental problems.

Further, markets respond to purchasing power. Where poverty is great or inflation is high, markets can be full of food while the population starves. When this happens, producers either have to find other markets—usually abroad—or watch the market collapse. This can happen both locally and on a regional scale. For instance, in 1994 the common currency of the African Financial Community, a group of 16 African countries with financial cooperation arrangements, was devalued, leading to price increases for food staples and the inability of many people, particularly in Mali, to feed themselves.

Politics also are a frequent element of famine in Africa. Political causes of famine in Africa date back to the colonial era. In one of the most extreme cases, millions died because Belgium's King Leopold II (1835–1909) treated the farmlands of the Congo Free State as his own private resource. Elsewhere, in 1896 the British colonial authority in RHODESIA (now Zimbabwe) destroyed the crops of ethnic Ndebele people in order to starve them to the point that they would be unable to rebel.

At the global level, market failures cause other problems with the availability of food. One of the most striking of these is the situation in highly developed agricultural countries in which there is such a surplus of food commodities that crops must be destroyed.

The end of colonialism, unfortunately, did not bring an end to politically caused starvation. The severe 1984 famine in Ethiopia, for example, was initially caused by drought. The situation was worsened, however, by the civil war involving TIGRAY and ERITREA. To compound matters, the Ethiopian ruler, MENGISTU HAILE MARIAM (c. 1937–   ), blacked out news of the famine, which delayed foreign assistance. Then, he and his Dergue military committee used the famine as an excuse to forcibly relocate hundreds of thousands of people from the north of the country to the south. Although the relocations were called an attempt at agricultural collectivism, in reality they were the removal of potential combatants from regions opposed to the Mengistu regime. Finally, when record amounts of foreign aid did manage to get to Ethiopia—largely as a result of Live Aid support from musicians in the United States and Europe—Mengistu withheld the aid from his people in order to further his political strength. This multitude of factors caused an estimated 800,000 deaths. Unfortunately the situation in Ethiopia represents an extreme, but not unfamiliar, example.

It has been difficult to take steps to avoid the political causes of famine. Consequently, many other countries—including ANGOLA, LIBERIA, SIERRA LEONE, SOMALIA, the Republic of the SUDAN, and the Democratic Republic of the CONGO—have experienced similar periods of famine exacerbated by politics and conflict. One positive note, however, is that it increasingly has become possible to confront some of the causes of famine that arise from nature or policy decisions.

Monitoring the problem of famine has become the first step. One leader in this is the Famine Early Warning System (FEWS), which is part of the U.S. Agency for International Development. Created to supply information to decision makers, the agency's primary goal is to reduce vulnerability to famine by creating more effective response networks. To accomplish this, it tracks famines and their causes, assessing an area's vulnerability to famine each season, monitoring rainfall, providing alerts and warnings, and assisting with emergency planning. In this way, FEWS accumulates information that can help determine what can be done to reduce the impact of a famine.

Equally important in the battle against famine have been organizations that provide information about weather and climate, such as the Drought Monitoring Centers for eastern and southern Africa. Organizations like these monitor droughts and their impact on agriculture; they also provide recommendations for how to avoid or reduce the severity of droughts.

Monitoring and policy-making efforts like these can play an important role in understanding the problem of hunger and famine. However, they are not a cure in and of themselves. Instead, long-term changes in the situation would seem to lie in understanding that food security—which is the ultimate protection against hunger and famine—lies in integrated rural development.

See also: ECOLOGY AND ECOLOGICAL CHANGE (Vol. V); ECONOMIC ASSISTANCE (Vol. V); ENVIRONMENTAL ISSUES (Vol. V); LAND USE (Vol. V); SAHEL (Vol. I).

Further reading: Famine Early Warning System (http://www.fews.org; http://www.fews.net); Stephen Devereux and Simon Maxwell, *Food Security in Sub-Saharan Africa* (London: Institute for Development Studies, 2001); Alex de Waal, *Famine Crimes: Politics & the Disaster Relief Industry in Africa* (Bloomington, Ind.: Indiana University Press, 1998).

Faye, Safi (1943–   ) *Filmmaker from Senegal*

Born in Fad Jal, a Senegalese village south of DAKAR, Faye studied at the École Normal in the Dakar suburb of Rufisque, where she obtained her teaching certificate. In 1966 Faye met Jean Rouch (1917–   ), the famous French ethnographic filmmaker and one of the originators of cinema verité, at the World Black and African Festival of Arts and Cultures. Rouch introduced Faye to the world of filmmaking, casting her in his film *Petit à Petit*.

Following Rauch's advice, Faye went to France to study filmmaking and ethnology. She earned her degree from the University of Paris in 1977 and received her doctorate in ethnology two years later. She later studied at the Louis Lumière Film School, also in Paris.

In 1973 Faye made her first film, *Revanche (Revenge)*, in collaboration with other students in Paris. Faye's most acclaimed work is the ethnographic film *Kaddu Beykat*, which garnered her numerous awards, including the Georges Sadoul Prize, a French movie award given for the best film by a new director.

Faye's distinction as an ethnographic filmmaker is tied to her position as a member of the society that she has documented. Able to engage her surroundings in a familiar way, instead of as an observer, Faye understands her subject matter in a way that outsiders may not. Among the many examples of Faye's uncommon perspective is the documentary *Selbé: One Among Others* (1982), which offered a vivid look at the struggles of daily life for rural Senegalese women.

See also: CINEMA (Vols. IV, V); WOMEN IN INDEPENDENT AFRICA (Vol. V).

Fela (Fela Anikulapo-Kuti) (1938–1997) *Nigerian singer, composer, and musician*

More than merely a popular singer, Fela was also a political activist who was critical of politics in NIGERIA and of Western big business practices in Africa. Born into a prominent family, Fela went abroad, in 1959, to study music in London, where he formed a band called Koola Lobitos. He returned to Nigeria, in 1963, and established himself as a major force in the nightclub scene of LAGOS, Nigeria's capital. In 1969 Fela took his band on a 10-month tour of the United States, where he was exposed to the pro-African ideology of the Black Panthers and Malcolm X (1925–1965). He subsequently became an impassioned advocate of PAN-AFRICANISM. By this time he had developed a musical style that he termed Afro-Beat, which fused elements of American jazz with West African rhythms. Fela's subsequent bands, Africa 70 and Egypt 80, featured large numbers of back-up singers, dancers, and musicians, and were notable for their high-energy, driving rhythms.

Upon his return to Nigeria, Fela opened a popular Lagos nightclub, the Shrine, and became something of a national celebrity. Commercial success outside Nigeria, however, was hindered by the nature of his MUSIC and lyrics, which were delivered in a mixture of pidgin English, his native YORUBA language, and other Nigerian languages. His songs were often long (sometimes exceeding an hour) and Fela was opposed to performing songs live once he had recorded them. Over the course of his career, he became an accomplished musician on the saxophone, trumpet, and keyboards.

Fela's forays into politics were almost as notable as his musical accomplishments. In public speeches and in the lyrics of his provocative songs, he frequently denounced government CORRUPTION and incompetence, as well as military rule. His overtly political messages made him the target of repeated arrest, harassment, and imprisonment, especially when Nigeria was under military rule. In 1974 he erected an electric fence around his compound in Lagos and declared it an independent state, the Kalakuta Republic. Eventually the police invaded the compound, attacked the occupants of Fela's home, and burned it to the ground. His mother, a noted activist for women's rights in Nigeria, was thrown from a second-story window and later died of her injuries. Fela responded by forming his own political party, Movement of the People. Representing his party, he unsuccessfully stood as a presidential candidate in 1979 and again in 1983. In 1984 he was found guilty of "false currency" charges and served 20 months of a 10-year sentence.

Fela's unique politics and personality appealed to millions of politically disaffected, unemployed, and oppressed Nigerians. He flouted convention in his personal life, as well. In 1978 he married 27 women in a collective ceremony. His advocacy of sexual promiscuity, polygyny, and marijuana use drew much attention. Fela died of AIDS-related complications in 1997, and his public funeral attracted more than 100,000 mourners. His son, Femi Kuti (1962–), also a saxophonist and bandleader, has achieved commercial success in recent years.

See also: HIV/AIDS AND AFRICA (Vol. V).

Further reading: Michael E. Veal, *Fela: The Life and Times of an African Musical Icon* (Philadelphia: Temple University Press, 2000).

fishing, commercial

Africa's commercial fishing sector encompasses a wide span of businesses, from multinational joint ventures that send out numerous vessels to small-scale operations using canoes and selling solely to markets within a local community. Commercial fishing in Africa reached its economic peak in the mid-1960s, soon after most African countries achieved independence from European colonizers. However, the industry began declining shortly thereafter, primarily due to the decrease and even disappearance of certain types of marine resources. Since then, governments have placed restrictions on both local and national fishing operations, but overfishing still remains the greatest challenge to Africa's commercial fishing industry.

Strong fishing industries are found in many parts of the continent, particularly in southern Africa. In SOUTH AFRICA, for example, the fishing industry employs more than 22,000 people, and the Department of Environment Affairs licenses more than 4,500 commercial fishing vessels. Along the coastline, from MOZAMBIQUE to NAMIBIA, these boats bring in anchovies, pilchard, herring, and lobsters; deep-sea vessels bring in hake, barracuda, mackerel, monkfish, sole, and squid.

The island nation of MADAGASCAR, located in the Indian Ocean, also has a strong fishing industry working over a vast area. With numerous rivers and lakes as well as an extensive coastline, the country has a wide range of fish, including prawn, crayfish, tuna, squid, and octopus. The combination of both a saltwater and freshwater catch makes fishing Madagascar's second-largest export industry.

In West Africa, NIGERIA has a strong fishing sector, with Atlantic Ocean coastal waters in the south, Lake Chad in the northeast, and rivers in the northwest. Crabs, croakers, moonfish, sharks, and thread fin make up the bulk of the Nigerian industry. The island nation of CAPE VERDE, off the coast of West Africa, also has a major export fishing industry.

Small-scale fisheries, also referred to as artisanal fisheries, are difficult to clearly define, as their role changes throughout the African countries. Usually, they are worked by individuals or extended family households instead of corporate fleets, and their fishing does not reach far from shore. However, pure subsistence fisheries are probably rare, as the artisinal fish catch is generally sold or exchanged for goods. Some of these smaller, localized fishing industries can be found in the villages surrounding Lake Tanganyika, in the Great Rift Valley of east Africa.

See also: COASTAL AND MARINE ECOSYSTEMS (Vol. V); FISHING (Vol. I); NATURAL RESOURCES (Vol. V).

FLN See NATIONAL LIBERATION FRONT.

Foccart, Jacques (1913–1997) *French administrator*

From 1958 to 1974 Foccart served as the France's secretary-general for African affairs. Even while French colonial rule in Africa was on the decline, Foccart was instrumental in shaping the relationship between FRANCE AND AFRICA for the independence era. Born into a wealthy French family from Mayenne, France, Jacques Foccart was raised in Guadeloupe, French West Indies. By 1935 he had set up a successful import-export business. Early in World War II (1939–45), Foccart joined the French resistance, proving to be a masterful tactician with a secretive nature. He became a close ally of General Charles de Gaulle (1890–1970), leader of the anti-Nazi Free French forces. Later, in 1958, Foccart played a key role in de Gaulle's return to the French government during the crisis over Algerian independence.

As de Gaulle's secretary-general for African affairs, Foccart set up the CFA franc, a common currency for French-speaking, African countries. Using his many political connections, Foccart also promoted French business interests in Africa. Behind the scenes he was a "kingmaker," using his influence to orchestrate the rise to power of African leaders who would be sympathetic with the French. Among these were Omar BONGO (1935–), of GABON; Jean-Bedel BOKASSA (1921–1996), of the CENTRAL AFRICAN REPUBLIC; and David DACKO (1930–), whom Foccart chose to replace Bokassa.

As a rule, Foccart acted with France's best interest in mind, sometimes to the detriment of Africans. To protect French businesses in ZAÏRE (present-day Republic of the CONGO), he backed MOBUTU SESE SEKO (1930–1997), who came to be known as one of Africa's most vicious and despotic dictators. After Foccart left his post in 1974, he maintained an office in the Elysée Palace in Paris, helping to orchestrate France's Africa policy until his death in 1997.

See also: COLONIAL RULE (Vol. IV).

Foley, Maurice (Anthony Maurice Foley) (1925–2002) *Leading figure in Africa-Europe postcolonial relations*

Born in Durham, England to working-class Irish parents, Foley was a leader first in the Electrical Trades Union and then the Transport and General Workers' unions. Elected to Parliament as a Labor Party representative in 1963, he quickly moved into senior posts. He served in different positions within the Department of Economic Affairs, the Home Office, and the Navy Office. He became the Foreign Office minister for Africa in 1969, at a time when Britain was rapidly granting independence to its African colonies.

Foley was pro-European at a time when many in Britain preferred to remain isolated from European affairs. As a result of his pro-European stance he worked to unite British, German, and French interests in postcolonial Africa. This became the foundation of European DEVELOPMENT policy, which was finally written into the Maastricht Treaty, also known as the Treaty on European Union. In 1973 Foley became the European Commission's deputy director-general for development.

Foley retired in 1987. For his outstanding service, Queen Elizabeth II (1926–) made him a Companion of the Most Distinguished Order of St. Michael and St. George.

See also: ENGLAND AND AFRICA (Vols. III, IV, V); EUROPE AND AFRICA (Vol. V).

food The modern era has seen an acceleration of the changes that began taking place in the patterns of African food consumption during the colonial era. Certainly, long-standing food preferences continue to hold sway, but there are also major changes taking place.

Some of the ongoing food-pattern changes have been related to crops that Africans have consumed for a number of centuries. In particular, cassava, a food that was part of the American food complex that entered Africa after 1500, has steadily grown in importance as a food staple. It is a root crop, heavy in carbohydrates, but its leaves are also edible, providing those who eat them with protein, vitamins, and minerals. It is easy to grow and is suitable for virtually every climate zone. Originally considered a famine food, it is now widely marketed in urban areas.

In addition, with transportation and communication becoming increasingly easier and more economical, food preferences from one particular region are spreading elsewhere on the continent. For example, due to the geographical position and early agricultural history of ETHIOPIA, the country possesses a unique cuisine. At its center is *injera*, a large, circular, spongy flatbread made from flour that comes from *teff*. Rather than using utensils, Ethiopians use the bread to scoop up cooked meats and vegetables that are served with it. Ethiopian restaurants are increasingly popular in African cities such as NAIROBI, DAR ES SALAAM, and JOHANNESBURG, and they have become an increasingly familiar sight outside Africa. London, which in the late 1990s had six Ethiopian restaurants, now has more than 20. In the United States, Washington, D.C., with a regional population of perhaps 50,000 Ethiopians, has the largest concentration of such restaurants outside Ethiopia itself.

Foodstuffs from outside the continent have continued to grow in importance over recent decades. Sometimes this has been in the nature of efforts to relieve FAMINE AND HUNGER in times of natural disasters and CIVIL WARS. The United States has contributed large quantities of grain, especially corn and wheat, for such efforts. The importation of food from abroad for commercial purposes has also steadily increased. For example, much of the rice that is at the center of the Gambian diet comes from Taiwan. Shops throughout the continent also stock items such as Coca-Cola and other soft drinks, along with imported canned meat, fish, tomatoes, and the like. While these goods are found in limited quantities in rural areas, modern supermarkets in the large cities are fully stocked with these items, catering to both expatriate westerners and the local African elite. As the pace of URBANIZATION and globalization increases, Africa's food preferences and consumption patterns continue to evolve.

See also: AGRICULTURE (Vol. V); CASH CROPS (Vol. V); FOOD (Vols. I, II, III, IV); FOOD CROPS (Vol. V); FISHING, COMMERCIAL (Vol. V).

food crops Crops that farmers grow principally for their own consumption. In contrast, CASH CROPS are grown for the market. Some major crops, such as palm oil and groundnuts, are grown as both food and cash crops.

Many of modern Africa's food crops, such as millet, sorghum, and yams, originated on the continent thousands of years ago. Some, such as bananas, cassava, and maize (corn), have been present in Africa for many centuries, brought there by trade. Others, such as wheat in sub-Saharan Africa, were introduced along with a number of cash crops during the colonial era. As a result, at independence African countries inherited an AGRICULTURE that was substantially different from what it was a century earlier. This was due in large part to the colonial emphasis on cash crop production for export. Consequently both land and LABOR were diverted away from growing food for local consumption. This shift in agricultural production accompanied rapid POPULATION GROWTH, beginning about 1960. By the end of the century the population was growing at nearly 3 percent annually in much of the continent. Paralleling this population growth was a much slower growth in agricultural production, so that the food crops grown by Africans now fail to meet the continent's consumption needs. The pressure caused by Africa's rapid, if uneven, process of URBANIZATION further compounded the situation. While in most of the continent rural people have grown enough food to feed themselves, they have not been growing sufficient additional food along with their cash crops to feed Africa's growing cities. Hence, African populations have increasingly come to rely on imported foods.

A pressing issue that took precedence in the 1980s was whether or not Africa could feed itself. In part, the question emerged because of the FAMINE AND HUNGER that resulted from natural disasters like the droughts of 1968–73 and 1983–85 in the Sahel. The production of food crops was also negatively affected by the CIVIL WARS and other political upheavals that gripped countries such as the Republic of the SUDAN and ANGOLA. As the gap between food production and food needs widened, it seemed that a continent that was still primarily rural should be able to meet its own food needs. However, some people, Africans among them, asked whether or not the continent *should* seek to feed itself. Instead, in agreement with a 1981 report put out by the WORLD BANK, they suggested that Africa should expand its export agricultural production and then meet any food deficits through imports. The choice, then, seemed to be either cash crops or food crops.

An alternative has emerged in the food crop/cash crop debate, one that suggests that rather than being in opposition, the two forms of agriculture can be complementary. Through the 19th century African farmers had sufficient land to allow some of it to lie fallow for a long period of time, giving the soil an opportunity to replenish its nutrients. Increasing pressures on farmlands over the course of the 20th century, however, have meant shorter fallow periods and subsequent soil depletion. Fertilizers can restore and preserve soil fertility, but they cost money, which food crops do not generate. Cash crops, too, require fertilizers. However, especially when prices are good, cash crops themselves provide the income to purchase fertilizer. When cash crops are combined with food crops in the use of fertilizer, food crop production also rises. The problem with this approach, though, is that it does not work if international commodity prices plunge, as they have recently for both coffee and cotton.

The 1970 Nobel Peace Prize winner Norman Borlaug (1914–) commented that "You can double, triple and quadruple yield—so the potential is there. But you can't eat potential. You've got to have reality—grain, food to eat to relieve human misery."

Given the market limitations of the combined cash crop/food crop option, another approach is for the emphasis to shift to those food crops that originated on the continent thousands of years ago. These are much more suited to African climatic conditions than are the crops that accompanied colonial rule. Thus, they pose fewer ENVIRONMENTAL ISSUES. Research focusing on improving the yields of such crops—and also finding new uses for them—may be the best way for Africans to achieve food security, which in turn could provide a more reliable base for DEVELOPMENT than now exists in many countries.

See also: BANANA (Vol. II); CASSAVA (Vol. II); FOOD CROPS (Vol. IV); GROUNDNUTS (Vol. IV); MILLET (Vol. I); PALM OIL (Vols. III, IV); SAHEL (Vol. I); SORGHUM (Vol. I); YAMS (Vol. I).

Further reading: Jane I. Guyer, ed, *Feeding African Cities* (Bloomington: Indiana University Press, 1987); Art Hansen and Della E. McMillan, eds., *Food in Sub-Saharan Africa* (Boulder, Colo.: Lynne Rienner Publishers, 1986).

foreign investment For countries lacking capital to promote their own DEVELOPMENT, it is critical to attract foreign investment to bring jobs and money. Over the past two decades African countries have struggled to attract sufficient foreign investment.

> **Investment is that part of current output that is used to produce future output. For private companies this generally means that a percentage of earnings is spent on building INFRASTRUCTURE, conducting research and development, or shoring up the capital base necessary for future success. For governments, the goals are similar, but they also include social development as well as economic development.**

A problem in many African countries—UGANDA, for instance—is that there are relatively few domestic, private businesses and a large percentage of the population lives in POVERTY. Because of this, governments cannot generate the tax revenue necessary for investment. However, countries with a LABOR glut and low salaries can provide prime opportunities for investment by foreign corporations. When they build factories in such countries, foreign companies produce their products more cheaply, making them more competitive for trade in the international marketplace. In return, the host countries see an increase in jobs created. When jobs are created, the competition for jobs decreases, driving wages higher to benefit workers. Higher wages mean higher tax revenue for the state. Other benefits for

the state include moneys generated by taxes and export tariffs paid by the foreign corporations. These mechanisms build government revenue and increase the potential for governments to invest in social improvements. Often, a private company and the government forge an agreement that requires the company to provide direct infrastructure investments. In exchange, the company is given favorable terms of operation, including reduced taxes.

Foreign investment is widely viewed as a shortcut to development, and governments go to great lengths to attract outside companies. There were some notable successes during the 1990s. NIGERIA, for example, received an average of more than $1.5 billion per year in foreign investment. SOUTH AFRICA ($755 million), ANGOLA ($254 million), and Uganda ($112 million) also attracted large amounts of foreign investment. Other countries experiencing some foreign investment success include BOTSWANA, EQUATORIAL GUINEA, GHANA, MOZAMBIQUE, and NAMIBIA. In addition, some of these countries have been able to diversify the type of investment to include manufacturing, services, and technology in addition to natural resource extraction. In the 1990s the rate of investor return in Africa averaged 29 percent, higher than any other region in the world.

Unfortunately, the majority of African countries have not had much success in attracting foreign investment. With the exception of South Africa, most foreign capital in Africa is still concentrated in the exploitation of NATURAL RESOURCES, particularly OIL. The dominant view of global economists is that Africa has to be made more attractive to potential foreign investors. To this end, wealthy countries can help by reducing the debt burden, increasing technical assistance, making it easier for African products to be marketed in their countries, and disseminating information on African investment opportunities.

See also: EXPORTS (Vol. V); MINING (Vol. V); TRADE AND COMMERCE (Vol. V).

Further reading: Nicolas van de Walle, *African Economies and the Politics of Permanent Crisis 1979–1999* (Cambridge, U.K.: Cambridge University Press, 2001); George B. N. Ayittey, *Africa in Chaos* (New York: St. Martin's Press, 1999).

forests Forests cover 22 percent of Africa's land area. They are diverse in forest cover type, rich in flora and fauna species, and rapidly being depleted. Forests cover 650 million acres of the African continent. They are highly diverse, from the lowland evergreen rain forests of the CENTRAL AFRICAN REPUBLIC and the Congo to the montane forests of UGANDA and ANGOLA to the dry, deciduous forests of ZIMBABWE, BOTSWANA, and MOZAMBIQUE—14 forest types in all.

African peoples have long relied on the resources of forested areas for survival. This way of life is threatened, however, because the resources in all forest types are vulnerable. Fuel is the most common use of forest wood, and it accounts for more than 60 percent of total energy use within the continent. Other uses for wood include building, fencing, irrigation, craft materials, and the production of medicines. In addition to local consumption, forests are depleted through commercial logging and the creation of agricultural land. Both activities are closely tied to the challenges of DEVELOPMENT and POVERTY.

Governments have worked with the private sector to increase Africa's benefits from the global trade in African timber. This sort of resource harvesting is a quick fix for heavily cash-strapped national economies, but it is also one of the greatest contributors to ecological change.

The needs of Africa's burgeoning populations have put a critical strain on forest resources. The current average rate of land cover decrease—0.8 percent per year—means that Africa's forests could disappear in little more than a century. This threat has led to a broad global movement to establish NATIONAL PARKS and protected areas, which can both ensure the survival of key pockets of forest and produce much-needed revenue from TOURISM. Economists point out that the long-term economic value of forests—as estimated by the ecological benefits they provide—is commonly greater when forests are left standing. However, to a hungry population needing to fill short-term needs for survival, this argument is often unconvincing.

The ecological benefits of Africa's forests are numerous. Humid forests alone support an estimated 1.5 million species. These species support local economies, but, where they are found nowhere else, they also provide needed BIODIVERSITY. Diverse flora and fauna serve critical functions, such as producing oxygen, filtering out carbon dioxide, regenerating soils, producing organic matter, and absorbing and storing rainwater. . In central Africa, for instance, some scientists believe that as much as 75 percent of all rainwater comes from evapotransporation—the evaporation of water from vegetation and the underlying soil. The clearing of forests is thus closely associated with ATMOSPHERIC CHANGE.

The preservation of African forests helps mitigate the impacts of climate change just as their felling exacerbates them. And since scientists know little about what ecosystems high in biodiversity provide, they can't say what the effects of destroying them will be on future generations.

See also: ECOLOGY AND ECOLOGICAL CHANGE (Vol. V); ENVIRONMENTAL ISSUES (Vol. V); FAMINE AND HUNGER (Vol. V); DROUGHT AND DESERTIFICATION (Vol. V); POPULATION GROWTH (Vol. V).

Further reading: Tamara Giles-Vernick, *Cutting the Vines of the Past: Environmental Histories of the Central African Rainforest* (Charlottesville, Va.: University of Virginia Press, 2002); William Weber, et al., eds., *African Rainforest Ecology and Conservation: An Interdisciplinary Perspective* (New Haven, Conn.: Yale University Press, 2001).

Fort Hare College Leading institution of higher EDUCATION in SOUTH AFRICA and rallying ground for the anti-APARTHEID political opposition. Established in 1916 as a missionary teaching college, Fort Hare evolved into an institution at which black South Africans could acquire a comprehensive liberal arts education. In 1959, however, Fort Hare came under the administrative control of the Department of Native Affairs, and its academic integrity was severely undermined. The curriculum was altered to conform to the requirements of BANTU EDUCATION and, consistent with the government's apartheid policy of divide and conquer, only XHOSA-speaking Africans could register as students. Faculty and students who expressed anti-government sentiments were expelled, as the government sought to suppress its political opponents.

Despite these repressive measures, protests continued. In fact, in the late 1960s Fort Hare became a hotbed of anti-government political activity. The BLACK CONSCIOUSNESS MOVEMENT took root at the college, primarily through the auspices of the SOUTH AFRICAN STUDENTS ORGANIZATION (SASO), and the college became central to the development of a number of Africa's most influential black politicians, doctors, writers, and artists. Counted among Fort Hare's alumni are Oliver TAMBO (1917–1993), Robert SOBUKWE (1924–1978), Robert MUGABE (1924–), Stanlake SAMKANGE (1922–1988), and Nelson MANDELA (1918–), South Africa's first African president.

In recognition of its role in educating many future political leaders, Fort Hare houses the papers of the AFRICAN NATIONAL CONGRESS and those of other opposition groups who fought against apartheid.

Since the collapse of apartheid and the white-minority government in 1994, however, Fort Hare has been beset by serious problems. Many students have refused to pay tuition and have accumulated student debts, jeopardizing the school's financial viability. In addition, African students today can attend any of South Africa's universities, many of which were once reserved almost exclusively for white students. Most of these universities still command superior resources and now attract the best African students, who previously had little choice other than to attend Fort Hare. Fort Hare also suffers from its remote rural setting, which lacks the appeal of the major urban areas where many of the former whites-only universities are located.

See also: FORT HARE COLLEGE (Vol. IV).

France and Africa Most of France's former African colonies had been granted independence by 1960. However, during the post-independence era, France has institutionalized its political, economic, and cultural dominance over its former African dependencies.

The French Community and African Independence In 1958 all but one of France's sub-Saharan African former colonies, now territories, voted for membership in the proposed French Community. (Only GUINEA voted "no" to this union and thus remained outside the Franco-African Community until about 1978.) The spokesperson for the Franco-African Community was Félix HOUPHOUËT-BOIGNY (1905–1993) of the IVORY COAST.

In 1956 France had passed the *Loi Cadre* (Overseas Reform Act), which provided the basic administrative hierarchy for the new governments. And although increased independence changed the administrative relationship between France and its colonies, France continued to control the African states economically, through financial aid. Most of the newly constituted African nations had a small, well-educated elite, some of whom had political experience, but the next level of administration lacked sufficient numbers of experienced workers; those who were available were poorly trained for the task at hand. Consequently, even after independence, former French colonial civil servants stayed on as advisers. In 1960, when members of the French Union formally became independent, only SENEGAL, Ivory Coast, and Guinea could claim to be prepared for the occasion.

Although independent in many respects, some of the 12 member states of the French Community still relied on France to stimulate their economies. As a result, France's buying power allowed it to maintain a monopoly on African EXPORTS. In addition, the landlocked, impoverished countries of NIGER, UPPER VOLTA (now BURKINA FASO), French Soudan (now MALI), CHAD, and Oubangui-Chari (now the CENTRAL AFRICAN REPUBLIC) were left few options but to buy French imports. The revenue derived from markets in these countries helped to stabilize France's economy after the World War II (1939–45).

Two dominant groups emerged within the African states of the French Community: those who favored federation and those who did not. In 1958 Senegal and French Soudan formed the Mali Federation within the Community and looked to work closely with France's President Charles de Gaulle (1890–1970). The following year, de Gaulle agreed that the two African states could become independent and retain their status as partners in the French Community. De Gaulle's decision was greatly influenced by his fear that rejecting French Soudan would antagonize its new government into supporting ALGERIA in that country's bloody war for independence from France.

Further, de Gaulle did not want the other members of the French Community to follow Guinea's lead and push for independence outside of the community. For its part, the Mali Federation insisted that it wanted to remain within the community and was therefore able to avoid the punitive measures that France took against Guinea.

By 1959 France was spending more on ECONOMIC ASSISTANCE to Africa, per capita, than any other industrialized country. To ensure that France would remain the dominant power in the region, de Gaulle negotiated defense agreements and bilateral treaties that included all types of economic and technical assistance. These agreements also guaranteed France access to strategic raw materials.

De Gaulle's policy of maintaining close interpersonal relationships with African heads of state helped France maintain its privileged position. In 1960 de Gaulle chose Jacques FOCCART (1913–1997) to be the first secretary-general of the French Community. Foccart would later carry out de Gaulle's African policies from 1969 to 1981 under French presidents Georges Pompidou (1911– 1974) and Valéry Giscard d'Estaing (1926–   ). Because of his position and longevity, Jacques Foccart was second only to de Gaulle in influencing France's relationship with French-speaking Africa. In 1978 d'Estaing brought Guinea back into the French economic sphere at the "unity summit," which was held in MONROVIA, LIBERIA. Other than the change regarding Guinea, however, during this time only minor adjustments were made to the Gaul-list policy.

In 1981 François Mitterrand (1916–1996) became France's new president, representing the Socialist Party. Believing that France's relationship with Africa was a form of neocolonialism, Mitterrand tried to reduce the personal privilege of the African presidents while increasing financial spending on poor nations worldwide. However, the weight of colonial history—and the economic recession of 1981—eventually forced Mitterrand to abandon his policy changes. In 1986 Mitterrand's prime minister, Jacques Chirac (1932–   ), appointed Jacques Foccart to be his adviser on African affairs. With Foccart's guidance, the Ministry of Coöperation produced a new African policy guide that reflected a continuation of the Gaullist approach to Africa.

In 1990 Mitterrand declared that France's domestic economic decline precluded his country from bailing out

Africa on its own and called for a worldwide effort to help the continent. He called for the establishment of a special international fund to help the African countries and committed French funds to help the world's 35 poorest nations, including 22 in sub-Saharan Africa. Also, France promised a new debt-forgiveness program for countries that had shown progress toward democracy and reduced the interest rate on French loans to four African countries (CAMEROON, Congo, GABON, and Ivory Coast).

The result of French neocolonialism has been that the French-speaking African states have failed to replace or to eliminate colonial institutions, thereby keeping those states politically, economically, and, to a certain extent, culturally dependent on France.

See also: DE GAULLE, CHARLES (Vol. IV); FRANCE AND AFRICA (Vols. III, IV).

Further reading: Anton Andereggen, *France's Relationship with Subsaharan Africa* (Westport, Conn.: Praeger, 1994); Charles O. Chikeka, *Britain, France, and The New African States: A study of Post-independence Relationships, 1960–1985*, (Lewiston, N.Y.: E. Mellen Press, 1990); John Chipman, *French Power in Africa* (Malden, Mass.: Basil Blackwell, 1989); Frederick Cooper, *Colonization and African Society: The Labor Question in French and British Africa* (New York: Cambridge University Press, 1996); David Fieldhouse, *Black Africa, 1945–1980: Economic Decolonization & Arrested Development* (Boston: Allen & Unwin, 1986); John Kent, *The Internationalization of Colonialism: Britain, France, and Black Africa, 1939–1956* (Oxford, U.K.: Clarendon Press; New York : Oxford University Press, 1992).

Freetown Capital, principal port, and largest city of SIERRA LEONE, located on Africa's Atlantic coast at the mouth of the Sierra Leone River. Freetown was founded by British abolitionists, in 1878, as a haven for freed and recaptive slaves from throughout western Africa. Hence, the city developed a population that included both indigenous peoples and Krios, the descendants of North American slaves who speak an English-based language. When Sierra Leone became independent in 1961—with Freetown as the capital—the city's population of about 130,000 was still very much dominated by the Krio element.

Once it became a national capital rather than a colonial administrative center, however, Freetown started to diversify. Substantial numbers of Mende and Temne peoples from the interior migrated there, and, by 1975, the population reached approximately 300,000 people. By 2000, that number had climbed to nearly 1 million.

Freetown is the home of many educational institutions, including sub-Saharan Africa's oldest university, Fourah Bay College. In addition, it is the site of the Anglican Saint George's Cathedral (1852), a botanical garden that dates from the 19th century, and Sierra Leone's National Museum, which is housed in the old railway station. The colonial-era ARCHITECTURE of central Freetown gives it an appearance reminiscent of English-speaking Caribbean islands.

Major EXPORTS from Freetown's port include agricultural commodities, such as palm oil and kernels, sugar, cacao, tobacco, coffee, and ginger, and the output of the bauxite and iron mines in the country's interior. Manufacturing and industrial exports include processed foods, paint, and shoes.

The diamond-MINING industry of Sierra Leone, which began with a discovery of the gems in the 1930s, peaked by 1970. Even so, illicit diamond trading helped fuel the political instability that wreaked havoc on Sierra Leone throughout the 1990s. In 1997 troops associated with REVOLUTIONARY UNITED FRONT (RUF) staged a COUP D'ÉTAT and seized control of the capital. Then, between 1998 and 2000, intense fighting between the RUF and peacekeeping forces of the ECONOMIC COMMUNITY FOR WEST AFRICAN STATES devastated the city and left thousands of its residents dead or injured. In 2002 combined British troops and UN peacekeeping forces finally brought a tentative peace to Freetown.

See also: ENGLAND AND AFRICA (Vols. III, IV, V); MENDE (Vol. III); MINERALS AND METALS (Vols. IV, V); PALM OIL (Vols. III, IV); RECAPTIVES (Vol. IV); SLAVE TRADE (Vols. III, IV); URBAN LIFE AND CULTURE (Vols. IV, V); URBANIZATION (Vols. IV, V).

Further reading: Sorious Samara, *Cry Freetown* [videorecording] (London: Insight New Television, 2000).

FRELIMO See MOZAMBICAN LIBERATION FRONT.

French Territory of the Afars and Issas Former name of the northeast African country of DJIBOUTI.

See also: FRENCH SOMALILAND (Vol. IV); SOMALIA (Vols. I, II, III, IV).

Front for Democracy in Burundi (FRODEBU) HUTU-backed ruling party of BURUNDI during the country's brief democratic period, from 1993 to 1996. Under mounting international pressure, President Pierre BUYOYA (1949–), an ethnic TUTSI, held Burundi's first multiparty elections in May 1993. Melchior Ndadaye (1953–1999) of the Front for Democracy in Burundi (FRODEBU) won the presidency with 65 percent of the vote to Buyoya's 32 percent. The following month, FRODEBU won 71 percent of the vote for positions in the legislature.

Although Buyoya's government had prohibited political parties before the 1993 elections, FRODEBU emerged as a cohesive organization with a national campaign and strong leadership. As expected, Burundi's Hutu majority almost unanimously supported the party. Surprisingly, however, the party also fared well in some non-Hutu regions where the Tutsi-dominated Buyoya regime had instigated ethnic violence.

President Ndadaye was assassinated only months after the 1993 elections, but FRODEBU demonstrated the strength of its legislative leadership, appointing Cyprien NTARYAMIRA (1955–1994) to succeed him. The party showed its resiliency again, in April of 1994, when Sylvestre Ntibantunganya (1956–   ) became president after Ntaryamira was killed in a plane crash. In 1996

Ntibantunganya was ousted in a military COUP D'ÉTAT led by the former president, Buyoya, but FRODEBU remains an influential political entity in Burundi.

Frontline States Alliance of southern African countries that joined forces to help black South Africans fight APARTHEID in their country. In the 1980s the governments of six southern African countries—ANGOLA, BOTSWANA, MOZAMBIQUE, TANZANIA, ZAMBIA, and ZIMBABWE—began coordinating efforts to combat the apartheid regime of

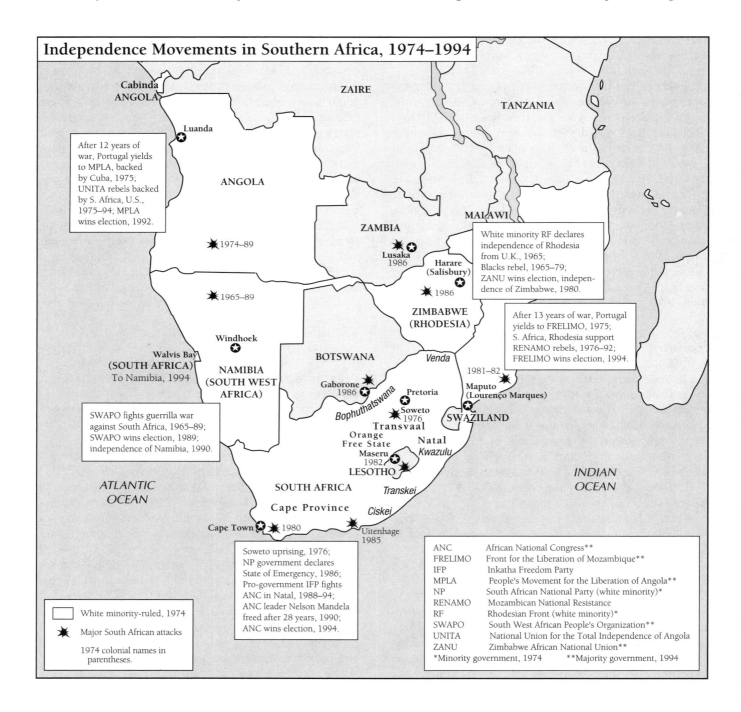

Independence Movements in Southern Africa, 1974–1994

Cabinda
ANGOLA

ZAIRE

TANZANIA

Luanda

After 12 years of war, Portugal yields to MPLA, backed by Cuba, 1975; UNITA rebels backed by S. Africa, U.S., 1975–94; MPLA wins election, 1992.

ANGOLA

1974–89

MALAWI

ZAMBIA

Lusaka
1986

White minority RF declares independence of Rhodesia from U.K., 1965; Blacks rebel, 1965–79; ZANU wins election, independence of Zimbabwe, 1980.

Harare
(Salisbury)

1965–89

1986

ZIMBABWE
(RHODESIA)

After 13 years of war, Portugal yields to FRELIMO, 1975; S. Africa, Rhodesia support RENAMO rebels, 1976–92; FRELIMO wins election, 1994.

Windhoek

Walvis Bay
(SOUTH AFRICA)
To Namibia, 1994

NAMIBIA
(SOUTH WEST
AFRICA)

BOTSWANA

Venda

1981–82

Maputo
(Lourenço Marques)

Gaborone
1986

Bophuthatswana

Pretoria

SWAPO fights guerrilla war against South Africa, 1965–89; SWAPO wins election, 1989; independence of Namibia, 1990.

Soweto
1976

SWAZILAND

Transvaal

Natal

Orange
Free State

Kwazulu

Maseru
1982

LESOTHO

INDIAN
OCEAN

ATLANTIC
OCEAN

SOUTH AFRICA

Transkei

Cape Province

Ciskei

Cape Town   1980

Uitenhage
1985

Soweto uprising, 1976; NP government declares State of Emergency, 1986; Pro-government IFP fights ANC in Natal, 1988–94; ANC leader Nelson Mandela freed after 28 years, 1990; ANC wins election, 1994.

☐ White minority-ruled, 1974

✴ Major South African attacks

1974 colonial names in parentheses.

ANC	African National Congress**
FRELIMO	Front for the Liberation of Mozambique**
IFP	Inkatha Freedom Party
MPLA	People's Movement for the Liberation of Angola**
NP	South African National Party (white minority)*
RENAMO	Mozambican National Resistance
RF	Rhodesian Front (white minority)*
SWAPO	South West African People's Organization**
UNITA	National Union for the Total Independence of Angola
ZANU	Zimbabwe African National Union**

*Minority government, 1974   **Majority government, 1994

SOUTH AFRICA. Known collectively as the Frontline States, these countries played different roles in supporting the right to vote for blacks in South Africa. For example, Angola, Tanzania, and Zambia provided military bases for the AFRICAN NATIONAL CONGRESS of South Africa. All the countries received South African REFUGEES. Tanzanians and Zimbabweans also helped defend Mozambique, the most vulnerable of South Africa's neighbors. Zimbabwe and also MALAWI accepted hundreds of thousands of Mozambican refugees.

In retaliation against the Frontline States, the South African government occasionally sent armed strike teams to destroy what it thought were bases for guerrillas planning to infiltrate its borders. As a result of their stand to assist black South Africans, the Frontline States suffered great structural, economic, and human losses. Combined, the countries lost an estimated $90 billion and more than 2 million people from the attacks.

In 1990 NAMIBIA joined the Frontline States after achieving its independence. The Frontline States, plus LESOTHO, SWAZILAND, and Malawi made up the SOUTHERN AFRICAN DEVELOPMENT COMMUNITY (SADC). This alliance, originally set up in 1980, collaborated on plans to increase economic independence in the region. In August 1994, following the fall of its apartheid government, South Africa became the eleventh member of SADC. With its original purpose of freedom from white-minority rule achieved, the Frontline States joined with other SADC members in a new Association of Southern African States. This group now complements SADC's economic programs with a new focus on conflict prevention and conflict management.

See also: UNITED DEMOCRATIC FRONT (Vol. V).

Fugard, Athol (Harold Athol Lannigan Fugard)

(1932–) *South African dramatist*

Born in Middleburg, SOUTH AFRICA, Fugard was the son of an English father and an Afrikaner mother. Though his father was racist in his views, Fugard's mother encouraged her son to cultivate an open mind. An accomplished student, Fugard attended Port Elizabeth Technical College and later the University of Cape Town before dropping out, convinced that the institutions were limiting his freedom of thought.

In 1953 Fugard traveled extensively throughout eastern Africa. Upon his return home, Fugard worked for the South African Broadcasting Corporation and then clerked at the Fordsburg Native Commissioner Court, where cases involving pass laws were tried. The contrast of Fugard's experiences while traveling and then while working for the APARTHEID government opened his eyes to the rampant racial discrimination that was present in South Africa.

After marrying an actress, Fugard became involved in the THEATER, and turned his interest in writing to the pro-

duction of plays. He studied drama with his wife in England until 1960, when he received news of the SHARPEVILLE massacre, the notorious incident during which South African police fired into a crowd of Africans demonstrating against the pass laws. Fugard then returned to South Africa, where he began work on his groundbreaking play, *The Blood Knot*.

The Blood Knot, first performed in JOHANNESBURG in 1961, portrayed the story of two brothers of mixed parentage, one of whom has skin light enough to pass as white. Fugard himself played the role of the light-skinned brother. *The Blood Knot*'s racially integrated cast and its performance in front of a mixed-race audience, caused an instant uproar in South Africa and established Fugard as a central, if controversial, figure in the fight against apartheid. The South African government subsequently banned *The Blood Knot*, and Fugard's passport was revoked, restricting him to South Africa under the threat of permanent exile. Fugard was undaunted, writing and producing plays until his passport was returned four years later.

To perform his plays, Fugard organized the Serpent Players, a theater group made up of both black and white actors. Acting, directing, and often writing plays in cooperation with his actors, Fugard continued to produce theater that overtly challenged apartheid policies. *Boesman and Lena* (1969), *Orestes* (1971), and the plays of *The Statements Trilogy* (1972) won Fugard notice in Britain and in the United States as well. The autobiographical *"Master Harold" . . . and the Boys* (1982) earned Fugard a significant American audience, who encountered the theme of apartheid in a dramatic production for the first time through Fugard's play.

Fugard and the Serpent Players, who derived their name from the former snake pit of a local zoo where they first performed, were consistently harassed by South African police. For the plays *Sizwe is Dead* and *The Island*, both part of the Statements Trilogy, the actors memorized their scripts and then destroyed them, preventing the government from seizing any hard evidence of their activities.

Fugard's play *"Master Harold" . . . and the Boys* was revived as a Broadway production in 2003. It starred Danny Glover (1947–), who also was an actor in the play's previous Broadway run, 21 years earlier.

Though Fugard's anti-apartheid stance was clear, he often found himself in a crossfire of criticism between Africans who would not support a privileged white as a spokesman for their issues, and the radical white liberals who felt Fugard was not aggressive enough in his efforts. Fugard himself denied any intentional political motivations behind his work, claiming that any subject related to South Africa naturally included such elements.

After the fall of apartheid, in 1994, Fugard came to be recognized not only for his struggle against the racist South African government, but also for innovations that had an impact on theater worldwide. He has been recognized with many awards in England and the United States.

His other works include *A Lesson from Aloes* (1978), *The Road to Mecca* (1984), *My Children! My Africa!* (1990), and *Valley Song* (1996). He has also authored one novel, *Tsotsi* (1980).

See also: AFRIKANERS (Vols. IV, V); LITERATURE IN MODERN AFRICA (Vol. V).

G

Gabon Country covering about 103,300 square miles (267,500 sq km) located on the west-central coast of Africa, with a narrow coastal plain giving way to a high and forested, interior plateau with wooded grasslands in the east and south.

More than 80 percent of Gabon's relatively small population of less than 1.5 million live in the capital city of LIBREVILLE and other urban areas. The country has vast OIL and other mineral resources and has a comparatively high per-capita income by African standards, though the income is very unevenly distributed and many Gabonese remain poor. Thanks to its low population density and wealth, Gabon has been able to maintain much of its tropical FORESTS with their rich BIODIVERSITY.

Gabon at Independence As a former French colony, Gabon was part of French Equatorial Africa. The country gained its independence from France in 1960, with Leon M'ba (1902–1967) as its first president. The French, however, retained a considerable political and cultural influence, and a significant number of French have continued to live in Gabon since independence. In fact, M'ba's presidency rested on the French presence. Upon assuming the presidency M'ba acted in an authoritarian manner, which provoked a military COUP D'ÉTAT in 1964, but French troops quickly intervened, inflicted a crushing defeat on the Gabonese army, and restored M'ba to office. When he died, in 1967, a trusted lieutenant, Omar BONGO (1935–), became president. The next year he declared Gabon a one-party state with the Gabonese Democratic Party as the sole legal party. This kept Bongo in power into the early 21st century.

Under Bongo, Gabon's economy shifted away from its reliance on such CASH CROPS as cocoa, coffee, and palm oil and the export of forest products. The key event was the discovery of significant offshore OIL reserves in the early 1970s. In 1975 Gabon became the fourth African member state of the ORGANIZATION OF PETROLEUM EXPORTING COUNTRIES, although it withdrew from membership in 1994 over a dispute about the amount of oil it could market. The resulting oil-boom economy led to growing URBANIZATION, so that today it is essentially an urban country. Oil production reached its peak in 1997. Unfortunately Gabon did not make good use of its oil bonanza by planning for the day when it disappeared. The country now faces a major FOREIGN DEBT problem and is under significant pressure from the International Monetary Fund as a result.

In 1974 Gabon began construction of the Transgabonais Railway, which now stretches from Libreville and its Atlantic Ocean port of Owendo 400 miles (660 km) to Franceville deep in the interior. This important addition to the country's TRANSPORTATION system has been one of modern Africa's most significant construction projects. It has greatly facilitated the export of manganese and forest products.

The decline of the oil economy had heightened Gabon's economic disparities and has led to renewed political unrest. In 1990 there were two failed coup attempts, reflecting growing discontent on the part of

LABOR and students. Serious rioting broke out in the country's second city, Port-Gentil, and France again intervened militarily to support the government. Bongo claimed a disputed victory in the 1993 presidential elections and had a landslide victory in the subsequent 1998 election. The PDG, which is no longer the sole legal political party, continued its control of Parliament. Bongo also effectively co-opted many of his political opponents, and he continued to count on support from France.

See also: FRANCE AND AFRICA (Vols. III, IV, V); FRENCH EQUATORIAL AFRICA (Vol. IV); GABON (Vols. I, II, III, IV) INTERNATIONAL MONETARY FUND AND AFRICA (Vol. V).

Further reading: Michael C. Reed and James F. Barnes, eds. *Culture, Ecology, and Politics in Gabon's Rainforest* (Lewiston, N.Y.: E. Mellen Press, 2003).

Gaborone (Gaberones)

Capital of BOTSWANA, located in the less arid southeastern portion of the country. In the 1890s the British South Africa Company founded Gaborone as a white settlement along the Cape-Zimbabwe railway. It was named after King Gaborone Matlapin of the Tlokwa people. It remained a small town until 1965, when the capital of Botswana, then known as Bechuanaland, was moved there from Mafeking, which was actually located in SOUTH AFRICA. The country became independent one year later, but Gaborone grew slowly at first, not obtaining official city status until 1986.

Today the city is the center of national government. It is also the headquarters for the SOUTH AFRICAN DEVELOPMENT COMMUNITY. Due to its capital status and a strong national economy propelled by diamonds, the city has a prosperous appearance. In addition, there is a small industrial sector, which focuses on metal and wood products and brewing beer. Gaborone is home to the University of Botswana, a museum, and an ART gallery. With about 159,300 people, the city is home to about 10 percent of Botswana's total population.

See also: BECHUANALAND (Vol. IV); BRITISH SOUTH AFRICA COMPANY (Vol. IV); URBAN LIFE AND CULTURE (Vols. IV, V); URBANIZATION (Vols. IV, V).

Gambia, The

Long, narrow West African country of some 4,360 square miles (11,290 sq km) in size that, except for its western coastline along the Pacific Ocean, is surrounded by SENEGAL. The Gambia's borders extend about 6 miles (9.7 km) on either side of the Gambia River and reach about 200 miles (322 km) inland from the river's mouth.

Like many other African nations, The Gambia's independence movement gained momentum during the mid-20th century. Sir Dauda Kairaba JAWARA (1924–) emerged as a leader of the Progressive People's Party and, in 1962, became the country's first prime minister.

Although The Gambia was granted independence from the United Kingdom on February 18, 1965, it remained within the British Commonwealth until 1970. That year Gambians used a referendum to decide that the country should become a fully independent republic.

> **Both during the colonial era and after independence, The Gambia's economy relied almost exclusively on the export of groundnuts (peanuts), which are still found there in abundance.**

In July 1981, while Jawara was in England, the Senegalese military helped put down an attempted COUP D'ÉTAT within The Gambia. Senegal's intervention brought the two countries closer, and, in February 1982, The Gambia and Senegal united to form the SENEGAMBIA CONFEDERATION. However, after a prolonged military presence by the Senegalese, Gambians ultimately called for their withdrawal. After failing to achieve its original goal of strengthening the economic and military positions of its two members, in 1989 the Senegambia Confederation dissolved.

President Jawara served as president of The Gambia for more than two decades. During that time, the country became one of Africa's most successful liberal democracies as well as an important advocate of HUMAN RIGHTS. Still, Jawara's rule was unstable, and, in 1994, The Gambia's military leadership, the Armed Forces Provisional Ruling Council (AFPRC), led a coup against Jawara, forcing him to leave the country. Yahya A.J.J. JAMMEH (1965–), chairman of the AFPRC, became head of state. Soon after, he dissolved the old regime, suspended the constitution, and prohibited all political parties and their activities. In August 1996 the country adopted a new, pro-military constitution, causing many industrialized nations from the West to stop supporting Jammeh's government. As a result The Gambia turned to the governments of NIGERIA, LIBYA, Iran, EGYPT, and Cuba for assistance. Meanwhile opposition to the Jammeh regime gradually increased. It came to a head in April 2000 when a student-led protest in BANJUL ended in 14 deaths and many injuries.

In 2001 Jammeh was elected to a second term, leading opposition parties to boycott legislative elections held in 2002. Continuing political unrest caused the devaluation of The Gambia's currency, exacerbating the country's steadily declining economy.

See also: ENGLAND AND AFRICA (Vol. IV); GAMBIA, THE (Vols. I, II, III, IV); SENEGAMBIA (Vol. III); SENEGAMBIA REGION (Vol. IV); TOURISM (Vol. V).

Further reading: Andy Gravette, *The Gambia* (Derbyshire, Eng.: Landmark Publishing Ltd., 1999).

Gbagbo, Laurent (1945–) *President of Ivory Coast*

Born in his mother's village of Gagnoa, IVORY COAST, Laurent Gbagbo excelled as a student and graduated with a degree in history from the University of Abidjan in 1969. In 1970 he became a professor at the Lycée Classique d'Abidjan, where he joined a secret organization seeking to oust President Félix HOUPHOUËT-BOIGNY (1905–1993). Active in trade union politics, Gbagbo was arrested, in 1971, for "subversive teaching" and remained in prison for two years.

After his release he earned a doctorate in history from the University of Paris, and, in 1979, he began teaching at the University of Abidjan. The following year he became the director of the Institute of African History, Art, and Archaeology at the university. In 1982 he joined with several colleagues to create the IVORIAN PEOPLE'S FRONT (Front Populaire Ivoirienne, FPI). This political activity made him a target of the government and caused him to flee to Paris, where he remained until 1988.

In 1990 multiparty elections were allowed, and Gbagbo ran against Houphouët-Boigny, losing what was widely viewed as a rigged vote. From 1990 to 1995 Gbagbo was the FPI's opposition leader in Parliament. In 1992, however, he spent six months in jail for leading demonstrations protesting the army's handling of student riots. In 1995, because of electoral irregularities, he and his party boycotted the national election. Henri Konan Bédié (1934–), Houphouët-Boigny's hand picked-successor, became president.

In 1999 a military COUP D'ÉTAT led by General Robert GUÉÏ (1941–2002) overthrew President Bédié. Gbagbo and the FPI joined other opposition parties to form Guéï's transitional government. Soon, however, all but the FPI dropped out. Subsequently, Gbagbo ousted General Guéï and, in October 2000, was elected president.

gender in modern Africa

Men and women in Africa today still have clearly defined realms of influence, although opportunities for women have increased since colonial times. Women today are usually involved in many activities including subsistence farming, ART and craft production, small business, child rearing, and social groups. In addition women in urban areas are more frequently occupying wage LABOR positions. Men today are also often involved in several activities, such as wage labor, cash-crop production, and livestock rearing. It is not uncommon for a rural household to have one or more male members working in town at a wage labor job, a pattern that began with colonialism and has only increased with the rising population density and land scarcity that characterize some areas.

Generally men have more say than women over household finances; however, women who earn their own money can often decide how it will be spent. The phenomenon of urban wage labor has created households in which women are acting decision-makers in the rural areas while men live and work in town. Often there is an exchange of resources between the couples; men may return home to assist in land clearing for cultivation, women may send food to the city with men, and men may send cash home in the form of remittances. While rural and poor women and men usually have separate incomes, women tend to be more dependent on their male partner's salary in the urban middle-class setting. This is a new phenomenon for women in Africa, and could cause new strains on relationships.

One of the major reasons behind the improvements in women's access to opportunities is the Western-based gender movement and the many scholars and scientists who have made gender analysis an important topic. One of the results of this movement is the ratification by a number of African nations of an international convention prohibiting discrimination based on gender. However, while some court cases settled across the continent have made important strides against male dominance in land tenure or other rights, they are few and many more will have to be heard and settled before equality is widespread.

Another result of the gender movement is that various agencies and organizations are responding by including gender analysis in studies and extension programs. Because it is generally true that women are responsible for most of subsistence AGRICULTURE, agricultural agencies realized that to implement changes in production women had to become more of a focus of agricultural policy and extension projects. Agricultural divisions of African governments and NON-GOVERNMENTAL ORGANIZATIONS have made an effort to target women in their efforts to spread new technologies and improve agricultural production. That said, many women are still underrepresented and have less access to land rights, credit, and other resources than men do.

See also: COLONIALISM, INFLUENCE OF (Vol. IV); GENDER IN COLONIAL AFRICA (Vol. IV); WOMEN IN INDEPENDENT AFRICA (Vol. V).

Ghana

Present-day country of West Africa covering approximately 92,100 square miles (238,500 sq km) and bordered by BURKINA FASO to the north, TOGO to the east, the Atlantic Ocean to the south, and IVORY COAST to the west. The national capital is ACCRA. Once the center of PAN-AFRICANISM, Ghana fell under autocratic rule and then suffered from political instability brought on by a series of coups.

Ghana at Independence Ghana officially won its independence in 1957, with Convention People's Party (CCP) leader Kwame NKRUMAH (1909-1972) as prime minister of a parliamentary government. A leader of the pan-Africanist movement, Nkrumah hosted the first pan-

By March of 1966, Ghana's first president, Kwame Nkrumah, had been run out of office amid charges of corruption. Here, the people of Accra, Ghana's capital, demonstrate to show their support for the National Liberation Council, which replaced Nkrumah. © *Washington Star*

African convention on African soil in Ghana in 1956 with hope of making his country a continental leader. Nkrumah focused on INDUSTRIALIZATION and the DEVELOPMENT of INFRASTRUCTURE and an educated workforce as the means for distancing Ghana from colonialism and allowing it to take a lead role in Africa.

Unfortunately Nkrumah carried out his plans in a highly authoritarian way. Insisting on total control to make his vision a reality, Nkrumah forced through legislation allowing the deportation and detention of opposition party members. In 1960 Ghana became a constitutional republic with Nkrumah as president, and four years later Nkrumah banned all political parties except the CCP and named himself president for life.

Ghana's economy is based largely on EXPORTS, such as cocoa and GOLD, that have historically volatile market prices. Because of this, the country's economy is greatly affected by downturns in those markets. In the early

1960s the fall of cocoa prices led Nkrumah to implement austerity measures and raise taxes, moves that were met with much popular protest. Nkrumah imprisoned hundreds in response, but by 1966 he was no longer able to hold on to power. That year, while the president was abroad, the military National Liberation Council (NLC) seized power, banning the CCP.

The NLC promised a return to civilian government, and in 1970 Edward Akufo-Addo (1906–1979) became president, with Kofi BUSIA (1913–1978) as prime minister. Like a number of future Ghanian governments, Busia's administration was unable to solve the problems with the economy. In 1972 another military coup, led by Colonel I. K. Acheampong (1931–1979), took place.

By 1975 the Supreme Military Council headed by Acheampong was in control of Ghana and already in the throes of economic mismanagement and CORRUPTION. He attempted to implement a no-party political system, an idea met with strong opposition in the form of strikes and protests in 1977-78. In 1978 Acheampong was replaced by Lieutenant General Frederick Akuffo (1937–1979). Akuffo also fell victim to a poor economy and corrupt government. In 1979 the Armed Forces Revolutionary Council again seized power, and Lieutenant Jerry RAWLINGS (1947–   ) took charge of the country.

Ghana under Rawlings Rawlings allowed for elections to create a civilian government the next month, resulting in Hilla Limann (1934-1998) assuming the presidency. Rawlings kept a close eye on the new government, however, and when it became apparent that Limann could not improve Ghana's situation, he overthrew Limann and took control again.

This time Rawlings remained in power longer, suspending the constitution and ridding himself of Parliament and all political parties. Ruling as head of the Provisional National Defense Council, Rawlings set out on an anticorruption campaign and made plans to decentralize power from Accra to regional governments. Eventually, however, Rawlings gave in to calls for DEMOCRATIZATION. In 1992 a new constitution was established and multiparty elections were allowed. In 1993 Rawlings won election and became president. He was reelected in 1996.

In 2001 the Rawlings era ended with the election of John Agyekum KUFUOR (1938–   ) to the presidency. The turn of the century brought no relief for Ghana's economic problems, however, as unstable cocoa and gold prices continued to cause significant problems.

See also: AKOSOMBO DAM (Vol. V); COUP D'ÉTAT (Vol. V); GHANA (Vols. I, II, III, IV).

global economy, Africa and the
Regional and local markets continue to be a central force in African societies, even though most African countries cannot compete globally in the buying and selling of goods. Markets are created when one person wants to buy a product and another person wants to sell the product. The buyer creates a demand for the product and the seller has a supply. While there are any number of tools for the bartering of goods, usually the exchange is made through purchase using a commonly agreed upon currency. All told, the total value of world goods and services is estimated at about $37 trillion (2000), with a $6.3 trillion global market for exported goods. At $3.5 trillion (2000), TOURISM is the world's largest market sector, followed closely by OIL.

The fact that the world's two largest industries are tourism and oil underscores Africa's difficulties in entering global markets. Regarding tourism, the lack of offerings—and, in some cases, security—has meant that the continent captures a mere 4.4 percent of the global market. Together, SOUTH AFRICA, MOROCCO, and TUNISIA account for more than half of Africa's share. Widespread POVERTY

means that the priorities for African consumers are oriented more toward securing basic goods than toward tourism and the consumption of oil. It is therefore the goal of most African countries to lure FOREIGN INVESTMENT by offering goods and services of interest not to local markets but to global markets. Yet Africa attracts only $6.8 billion (2001), or 3 percent, of the world's investment. In return, African export models have developed only marginally from the colonial model of extracting NATURAL RESOURCES. To some, this is an advantage. The WORLD BANK, for instance, maintains that "extractive" industries—oil, gas and MINING—represent major opportunities for developing countries. While there are opportunities for investment in agro-processing, textiles, and a handful of other industries, the greatest share of export earnings in Africa is from oil in countries such as LIBYA, NIGERIA, and ANGOLA. Thus, extractive markets are seen as having the greatest potential to both engage the global marketplace and create jobs at home. Some critics, however, say that the low prices of raw commodities as compared to manufacturing, technologies, and services, ensures that African markets will continue to stagnate, limiting the growth of African economies.

There are numerous reasons cited for Africa's inability to engage the global market. Some people, Africans among them, have referred to the way in which markets are peripheral to African livelihoods in comparison to Western livelihoods. Others refer to a lack of industrial growth, inadequate resources for investment, a dearth of intellectual capital, high poverty, low levels of EDUCATION, state intervention in the market, CORRUPTION, regional instability, and insufficient market experience to name a few. Still others note the comparative size of African economies. The average African economy is $2 to $3 billion per year. This is a very small market when one considers that markets in the United States move more than $10 trillion annually and the world's five largest companies alone are worth a combined $1.9 trillion.

Market analysts in developing countries commonly point to tremendous efforts by wealthy countries to block African trade to protect their own markets. For instance, the wealthy member states of the Organization for Economic Co-operation and Development provide $300 billion in subsidies for their own agriculture. Since this is nearly as much as Africa's $319 billion net worth, it is clear that African governments cannot afford to prop up their agricultural producers with similar levels of subsidies. Their products, therefore, must sell for more money. Higher prices, of course, make products less enticing for buyers. Add to this imbalanced tariff structures between wealthy and poor countries and it is easy to see why some economists argue that Africa's markets suffer from "planned underdevelopment."

As a result of this failure to successfully engage the global market, some observers say that the situation in

Africa is hopeless. While it is true that African markets do not compete well globally, such positions fail to note the dynamism in African markets at the regional, state, and sub-state level. Looking from within, it becomes clear that markets are central to African livelihoods. English economic anthropologist Dr. Polly Hill (1914–), for instance, has shown how the distribution of specific commodities, market strategies, social relations, and cultural concepts must be considered when analyzing the "success" of a particular market. Under her model the African economic sphere is seen as a complex layering of markets and market types built over a long history of market exchanges. In Hill's example, small-scale farmers in GHANA actually created the market for cocoa, now the country's largest export. The government's role in her model was creating a marketing board to ensure that prices would not fluctuate dramatically.

Since the 1990s Africa's trading networks have undergone a transformation. In contrast to Dr. Hill's Ghanaian cocoa example, states are now playing less of a role. Stock markets have flourished in BOTSWANA, IVORY COAST, Ghana, KENYA, MAURITIUS, Nigeria, South Africa, and ZIMBABWE. Economic liberalization has not generated the high export earnings many have sought, but it has resulted in the emergence of new trading networks. Moreover, there is evidence that this sort of trade is helping to transform African societies in ways that may well help them overcome their lack of market history, which is often cited as a barrier to global trade.

See also: COLONIALISM, INFLUENCE OF (Vol. IV); NEOCOLONIALISM AND UNDERDEVELOPMENT (Vol. V).

Further reading: Robert H. Bates, *Markets and States in Tropical Africa: the Political Basis of Agricultural Policies* (Berkeley, Calif.: University of California Press, 1981); Brenda Chalfin, *Shea Butter Republic: State Power, Global Markets, and the Making of an Indigenous Commodity* (New York: Routledge, 2004); Polly Hill, *Development Economics on Trial: the Anthropological Case for a Prosecution* (Cambridge, U.K.: Cambridge University Press, 1986); Todd Moss, *Adventure Capitalism: Globalization and the Political Economy of Stock Markets in Africa* (Basingstoke: Palgrave Macmillan, 2003).

gold   The modern gold-MINING industry in Africa dates to the 1880s, when British companies began extracting rich ore deposits found on the Witwatersrand of SOUTH AFRICA. The industry continued to grow through the decades that followed, and today South Africa is the world's largest producer of gold. It contains an estimated 40 percent of world gold reserves, with substantial deposits located outside the original core area of the Witwatersrand.

Large-scale transnational corporations using mechanized extraction methods dominate the gold mining industry. They are still expanding their investments in

Africa, hoping to locate some of the continent's numerous undiscovered reserves. South Africa has four recent gold mine investments worth more than $1.6 billion. In 2000, two companies, Gold Fields of Ghana and Anglogold, announced plans to increase mining activities at Geita Gold Mine in TANZANIA, which is the richest gold mine in East Africa.

By 2001 falling gold prices and the high cost of mining deep below the earth's surface led to South Africa's lowest production since 1956. However, world economic uncertainties since then have led to a rebound in prices. In 2004 the price of gold fluctuated around $400 an ounce.

The Samira Hill Gold Project, in NIGER, should be completed by 2004. While this mining project is not nearly as large as those of the major producers on the international market, the income that it is expected to generate might substantially transform the economy of Niger. With improved geological knowledge and continued worldwide demand, gold and gold mining will continue to play a substantial role in the economies of African countries.

See also: ANGLO-AMERICAN CORPORATION (Vol. IV); GOLD (Vols. I, II, IV); MINERALS AND METALS (Vols. IV, V); WITWATERSRAND (Vol. IV).

Gordimer, Nadine (1923–) *South African novelist*
By the late 1950s, with her short stories and her novels—including *The Lying Days* (1953) and *A World of Strangers* (1958)—Nadine Gordimer had already launched a career that would place her at the forefront of the literary anti-APARTHEID movement both in SOUTH AFRICA and throughout the world.

The year 1960, however, marked the first time apartheid directly affected Gordimer's life, with the arrest of her close friend, the Afrikaner trade union leader Bettie du Toit (c. 1911–2002). That same year the SHARPEVILLE massacre convinced Nelson MANDELA (1918–) and the AFRICAN NATIONAL CONGRESS (ANC) that nonviolent protests against apartheid were ineffective. Mandela's subsequent underground activities against the apartheid government led to his arrest and trials, in 1962 and 1964, the latter ending in his imprisonment on ROBBEN ISLAND. Gordimer spent a great deal of time observing the trials and became friends with Mandela's lead counsel, Bram Fischer (1908–1975), and his family, who would become the basis for her novel *Burger's Daughter* (1979).

Gordimer became deeply involved with the ANC, defying South African law to become a member. Her writing career, in the meantime, blossomed, in spite of the censorship of the South African government, which banned a number of her books, including *The Late Bourgeois World* (1966) and *Burger's Daughter.* In 1970 she published what is widely considered her best novel, *A Guest of Honour,* and, in 1974, *The Conservationist,* which won the Booker Prize, the highest literary award in the British Commonwealth.

As apartheid grew more oppressive through the 1970s and into the 1980s, Gordimer continued her political activism. Her position as a member of the white minority afforded her freedoms her African counterparts, many of whom were imprisoned or forced into exile, did not have. On a number of occasions Gordimer housed fugitive ANC members at her residence, and she visited frequently with African leader Steve BIKO (1946–1977), who was murdered by South African police in 1977. She spoke out against apartheid both publicly and through her writing, which earned her a worldwide audience and did much to expose the terrible realities of African life under the racist regime. In spite of her unabashed position, Gordimer managed to avoid the prison sentences levied on some of her fellow white, anti-apartheid writers, such as Breyton Breytonbach (1939–) and Jeremy Cronin (1949–).

Gordimer anticipated the end of apartheid in her novels of the 1970s and 1980s, including *July's People* (1981), which drew from the SOWETO uprising of 1976 and considered the future of whites in South Africa. In 1987 she helped found the Congress of South African Writers to promote the literary dimension of the struggle against apartheid, which had grown increasingly repressive as the state sought to quell the rising tide of revolt against it. Her testimony at the 1987 treason trial of leaders of the UNITED DEMOCRATIC FRONT helped save the defendants' lives. Gordimer's commitment and efforts were such that, when Nelson Mandela was finally released from prison, in 1990, she was among the first he requested to see. In 1991 Gordimer was awarded the Nobel Prize in literature, becoming only the third person from Africa to receive the honor, after Egypt's Naguib MAHFOUZ (1911–) and Nigeria's Wole SOYINKA (1934–).

Apartheid officially ended in 1994, with Mandela and the ANC assuming control of the government through decisive electoral victories. Since then, Gordimer has continued to write about post-apartheid South Africa, publishing *The House Gun* (1998) and *The Pickup* (2001). She also continues to downplay her role in the struggle against apartheid and as an international voice for the African population in South Africa, agreeing with African critics of her work that her position as a privileged white places her in a far different situation from those she championed. Nevertheless, Gordimer's literary efforts and political activism undoubtedly played an important role

in the downfall of one of the most oppressive governments of the modern era.

See also: GORDIMER, NADINE (Vol. IV); LITERATURE IN MODERN AFRICA (Vol. V).

Gouled Aptidon, Hassan (1916–) *First president of independent Republic of Djibouti*

Born in Zeila, SOMALIA, Hassan Gouled Aptidon was a long-time figure in the political scene of the Republic of DJIBOUTI. From 1952 to 1958 he served as a representative in Paris for French Somaliland, as Djibouti was called during the colonial era. Then, from 1959 to 1962, he served as French Somaliland's deputy in the French National Assembly.

Belonging to Djibouti's majority Issa ethnic group, Gouled defended Issa interests when, in 1967, France allowed French Somaliland to become semi-autonomous as the FRENCH TERRITORY OF THE AFARS AND ISSAS. Ten years later Gouled led the country to independence as the Republic of Djibouti.

In 1979 Gouled formed the PEOPLE'S RALLY FOR PROGRESS (Rassemblement Populaire Pour le Progres, RPP), which claimed to represent both Issas and Afars. Before long, however, it became clear that the Issa contingent dominated the RPP government. Two years later Gouled declared a one-party state, much to the chagrin of the Afar community, which had enjoyed considerable power when the country was under French control. The popular unrest among the disenfranchised Afars—fueled by simultaneous ethnic conflicts in neighboring ETHIOPIA, ERITREA, and SOMALIA—erupted in civil war in 1991. With the war raging, Gouled bowed to international pressure and allowed multiparty elections in 1992. However, Gouled barred the Afar candidates of the Front for the Restoration of Unity and Democracy (FRUD), the party of the rebels waging the civil war.

As a result Gouled's RPP swept the elections and fighting continued. In 1994 Gouled struck a power-sharing agreement that brought the main, unarmed faction of FRUD into a coalition government, but still the fighting continued. In 1999 an aging Gouled decided to step down. His nephew, Ismail Omar GUELLEH (1947–), representing a coalition of parties that included the RPP, won election to become the second president of Djibouti. Guelleh's government and the Afar rebels signed a ceasefire agreement in 2000.

See also: CIVIL WARS (Vol. V); ETHNIC CONFLICT IN AFRICA (Vol. V); FRANCE AND AFRICA (Vols. IV, V).

government, systems of
The end of colonial rule and the emergence of independent African states reintroduced greater diversity in the continent's systems of government. In a few instances, such as with SWAZILAND and

its monarchy, older forms of African government resurfaced. Also, African communities at the local level recovered some of their former autonomy. However, there remained a central uniformity in that virtually all of Africa's leaders subscribed to the concept of the modern nation state. They viewed the role of the STATE as the focal point of power. While the government of individual countries could take democratic, military, or authoritarian forms, there was an underlying agreement as to the centrality of the state itself.

States have not fared equally well throughout the continent over recent decades, however. This has given rise to a new diversity in African systems of government at the outset of the 21st century. Some states, such as SOUTH AFRICA and ALGERIA, have emerged out from the shadow of highly authoritarian systems to become functioning democracies with strong central institutions. Others, such as NIGERIA, have survived CIVIL WARS—and the centrifugal forces that accompany them—to remain intact, although the central institutions of these governments often have found their authority circumscribed. In other cases, such as LIBERIA, the Democratic Republic of the CONGO, and SOMALIA, the states authority has virtually collapsed in the face of civil wars and other problems. This has led to a revival of older forms of government at the local and even regional level, as people draw on indigenous political systems to provide the governmental structures they need. The revival of older systems of government has also occurred in states that, while remaining intact, lack sufficient governmental resources to assert fully the authority of central institutions over the entire country.

See also: GOVERNMENT, SYSTEMS OF (Vols. I, II, III, IV); POLITICAL SYSTEMS (Vol. V).

Gowon, Yakubu (1934–) *Military head of state in Nigeria*

An ethnic Tiv from Nigeria's Middle Belt, Yakubu Gowon joined the army in 1954. After attending various training programs at home and abroad, he served with UN peacekeeping forces in the Congo during the 1960s. Only a lieutenant colonel at the time, Gowon was named army chief of staff when a group of young IGBO officers overthrew Nigeria's civilian government in a January 1966 COUP D'ÉTAT. A counter-coup by rival northern officers took power, however, in July. Gowon, as a member of none of the major Nigerian ethnic groups, seemed a viable choice for leadership, and he was made head of state and supreme military commander.

Although Gowon made major efforts to restore Igbo confidence in the central government, the Igbo eventually declared independence for Eastern Nigeria in May 1967, establishing the independent nation of BIAFRA. In the bloody civil war that followed, Gowon's federal government—supported by both Britain and the former Soviet Union—eventually defeated the new Biafran state, which had France as its only substantial ally. By 1969 the federal army had effectively won the war, in which anywhere from 1 to 2 million Biafrans lost their lives, primarily due to starvation. The United States remained officially neutral during the Biafran Civil War, although private American humanitarian organizations sent aid to the beleaguered Biafran people.

> Throughout the history of independent NIGERIA, rivalries and outright violence between the major ethnic groups have been commonplace. The traditionally Muslim HAUSA are the dominant ethnic group in the northern part of the country; in the southwest, the YORUBA are dominant; in the southeast and delta region, the Igbo are the major ethnic group. There are, however, dozens of minority groups, all of whom vie for political and economic power, making Nigerian politics very complex.

Following the end of the civil war, Gowon attempted to restore unity to the nation. Despite numerous reforms, Regaining Igbo confidence in the government was difficult. Unable to restore stability to either the military or the nation as a whole, Gowon was overthrown by yet another coup in July 1975. Settling in England, he eventually earned a PhD in political science from the University of Warwick, in 1984.

See also: CIVIL WARS (Vol. V); ETHNIC CONFLICT IN AFRICA (Vol. V); TIV (Vol. IV).

Further reading: John D. Clarke, *Yakubu Gowon: Faith in a United Nigeria* (London: Frank Cass, 1987).

Guéï, Robert (1941–2002) *Former president of Ivory Coast*

Born in Kabacouma, IVORY COAST, Robert Guéï came to power in 1999 by a military COUP D'ÉTAT. An army general, he was educated at a military academy in OUAGADOUGOU, UPPER VOLTA (today's BURKINA FASO) and, later, at France's military academy, Saint Cyr. In 1965 he returned to the Ivory Coast as a second lieutenant and, during the presidency of Félix HOUPHOUËT-BOIGNY (1905–1993), quickly rose through the ranks of the army.

From 1971 to 1975 Guéï worked as military training officer, ultimately becoming commander of Ivory Coast's military academy. In 1978 he returned to France for further study. Promoted to colonel on his return, he was, from 1980 to 1985, commander of military firefighters. In addition to other postings, Guéï briefly served in Korhogo as commander of the Fourth Military Region before becoming a brigadier general and head of the armed forces in 1990.

A popular military leader, Guéï was a Houphouët-Boigny loyalist. In 1995, under Ivory Coast's new president, Henri Konan Bédié (1934–), Guéï was relieved from command of the military. Remaining in government service, he became minister of civil service and then minister of sports. Guéï considered Bédié's government corrupt and xenophobic, and on December 24, 1999 he led a military coup to unseat the president.

While Guéï purported to support a democratic transition, he did not accept the victory of Laurent GBAGBO (1945–) in the October 2000 elections until he was forced to by popular protest. Guéï died in October 2002 during a rebellion against President Gbagbo.

Guelleh, Ismail Omar (1947–) *President of Djibouti*

Born in 1947 in pre-independence Djibouti, Guelleh was a member of a politically active family. Beginning in 1977, when his uncle, nationalist leader Hassan GOULED APTIDON (1916–), became Djibouti's first president, Guelleh served as chief of cabinet and chief of internal and external security. While Aptidon was in office, Guelleh was instrumental in navigating Djibouti's relations with Somalia's president, Mohammed Siad BARRE (1910–1995), and maintaining strong ties with France.

In 1999, at the age of 83, Gouled Aptidon decided to step down. Elections for his replacement were held in April of that year. To strengthen his position, Guelleh formed a four-party alliance called the Union for the Presidential Majority (UMP), which included Guelleh's party, the PEOPLE'S RALLY FOR PROGRESS, and the unarmed faction of the former rebel group Front for Reestablishment of Unity and Democracy (FRUD). The UMP provided enough support for Guelleh, and he beat his only challenger, Moussa Ahmed Idriss, to become the country's second president.

However, the legitimacy of Guelleh's electoral victory was widely challenged. Idriss, who was also publisher of the newspaper *Le Temps*, was arrested in September 1999 because the government did not approve of a story his paper had reported. Meanwhile, the FRUD's armed, radical wing, which never reconciled with the government, continued its insurgence. In 2001, however, this faction of FRUD also came to terms with Guelleh's government, and signed a peace agreement to end the hostilities that had plagued Djibouti for almost a decade.

Guinea

West African country on the Atlantic coast, some 95,000 square miles (246,100 sq km) in size, that takes its name from the term used to describe the coast of West Africa south of the WESTERN SAHARA. It borders on GUINEA-BISSAU, SENEGAL, and MALI to the north, Mali and the IVORY COAST to the east, and LIBERIA and SIERRA LEONE to the south. Its capital is CONAKRY.

When Guinea achieved its independence from France in 1958 it was a highly centralized one party-state led by President Ahmed Sékou TOURÉ (1922–1984) and his Democratic Party of Guinea (Parti Démocratique de Guinée, PDG). Touré's approach to both domestic and foreign policies was similar to that of other African presidents who had led their nations along the road of independence. Domestically, he adopted African Socialism as his policy, while internationally, wishing to avoid being drawn into the Cold War, he assumed a stance of "positive neutralism." In both spheres he was following the lead of the acknowledged leader of the third world at the time, Gamal Abdel-NASSER (1918–1970) of EGYPT.

After independence France withdrew the financial aid to Guinea that had made the territory the second richest of the eight territories comprising the colonial federation of French West Africa. While Guinea had achieved its political independence, it was not completely independent because its economy had been too intricately integrated into that of France which had purchased 65 to 75 percent of Guinea's EXPORTS, provided 70 percent of Guinea's imports, and given $75 million in DEVELOPMENT aid. Although Guinea had substantial mineral wealth, it remained poor because it did not have the means to develop its potential.

Because of France's retaliatory actions, Guinea was isolated from its major trading partner, and its economy grew too slowly. Guinea received financial support from its newly independent African neighbors such as GHANA, which gave Guinea a loan of $28 million. Guinea's neighbors, however, lacked large economic reserves, too, and they did not offer trading opportunities since they also had commodity export economies. Although Sékou Touré rejected capitalism, he did accept no-strings-attached loans and gifts from the United States and western European nations. However, Guinea was locked out of substantial trade with the Western capitalist nations and overly impressed by Soviet and Chinese Communist claims of rapid economic development. Thus, Guinea began trading with the Communist bloc nations and suffered from this trade relationship because the Communist bloc nations paid Guinea using a barter system in which they traded factory-made products such as buses or tanks in return for Guinea's raw materials that they then sold on the world market for dollars. However, by 1978 Sékou Touré reestablished trade relations with the capitalist West.

In the social arena the reforms of the 1940s, 1950s, and 1960s emerged in 1968 as Sékou Touré's Socialist Cultural Revolution. As a part of this cultural revolution, Touré instituted the Maternal Language Program. This program turned its back on the colonial language as the only language of EDUCATION. Touré believed that students would learn all subject matter more quickly and easily in their maternal languages. Students learned school subjects in one of the country's eight major indigenous languages with one course per year in the French language through the elementary level. When students passed the ordinary examination that allowed them to go on to high school, they would then learn school subjects in French.

There were many attempts to overthrow Sékou Touré, as Guineans objected to socialism and because political opposition was not allowed. Touré's opponents went into self-imposed exile, were imprisoned with an uncertain future in the infamous Camp Boiro, or were killed. Touré broke off diplomatic relations with France amid accusations of a French-backed COUP D'ÉTAT, and the Portuguese-supported invasion of Guinean exiles in 1970 caused Touré to purge the political, administrative elites. By the mid 1980s Sékou Touré's regime had become so repressive that mutual fear and mistrust kept various anti-Touré factions from working together. In 1984 Sékou Touré died during emergency heart surgery in the United States.

At first the PDG appeared to be strong, appointing Prime Minister Lansana Béavogui (1923–1984) interim president until they could select a new leader. However, when Touré's brother Ismael (1926–1985) returned to Guinea to challenge the leadership, the army seized power. On April 13, 1984, the army deposed and arrested the Maninka-speaking members of government and established a military council. The power behind the takeover was Colonel Diarra Traoré (1936–1985) who became prime minister while Colonel Lansana CONTÉ (1934–) became president. The Military Committee of National Recovery suspended the constitution and the single-party system, freed political prisoners, encouraged exiles to return to Guinea, and established the Second Republic. In 1985 Traoré attempted an unsuccessful coup d'état against the Susu-speaking Lansana Conté that prompted a further purge of suspected Sékou Touré supporters and an attack on the Maninka-speaking population.

In 1990 Conté ordered a new constitution, paving the way for civilian government, and in 1993 Guinea participated in its first multiparty elections. Although there were several political parties, the only candidate to successfully compete against Conté and his Party of Unity and Progress was another Maninka speaker, Alpha Condé, who represented the Guinean Democratic Party. According to the international observers, the election was fair with Conté designated as the first civilian president of the Second Republic. In 1996 Guinea's armed forces mutinied over low pay and poor conditions resulting in the destruction of the presidential palace in Conakry.

From 1989 through 2003 the CIVIL WARS in Liberia and Sierra Leone have driven REFUGEES into Guinea, many of whom now live with their extended families. By the end of 2000 Guinea was home to about half a million refugees, increasing the strain on the economy and generating ethnic tension. In the summer of 2000 rebels from Liberia and Sierra Leone attacked Guinea at their shared borders, trying to destabilize Guinea to gain access to its diamonds.

The Second Republic has been faced with many challenges in the areas of economic development and the establishment of a viable form of governance. Persistent ethnic tensions and the social unrest caused by the economic reforms under the STRUCTURAL ADJUSTMENT demanded by the INTERNATIONAL MONETARY FUND, such as the devaluation of the Guinean currency, have hurt the economy. However, President Conté's government has enjoyed Western backing as a bulwark against instability in the region.

See also: CASH CROPS (Vol. V); CHINA AND AFRICA (Vol. V); COLD WAR AND AFRICA (Vols. IV, V); FRANCE AND AFRICA (Vols. III, IV, V); FRENCH WEST AFRICA (Vol. IV); GUINEA (Vols. I, II, III, IV); SOVIET UNION AND AFRICA (Vols. IV, V).

Further reading: 'Ladipo Adamolekun, *Sékou Touré's Guinea: An Experiment in Nation Building* (London: Methuen, 1976); Human Rights Watch, *Guinea: Refugees still at risk: Continuing refugee protection concerns in Guinea* (New York: Human Rights Watch, 2001); Aguibou Y. Yansané, *Decolonization in West African States, with French Colonial Legacy: Comparison and Contrast: Development in Guinea, the Ivory Coast, and Senegal, 1945–1980,* (Cambridge, Mass.: Schenkman Pub. Co., 1984).

Guinea-Bissau Country in coastal West Africa with an area of 14,100 square miles (36,500 sq km) and bordered by SENEGAL to the north and GUINEA to both the south and east. One of the world's poorest countries, Guinea-Bissau has an economy based almost exclusively on AGRICULTURE, exporting CASH CROPS such as groundnuts (peanuts), cashews, palm kernels, timber, and other commodities. Since the 1960s the political history of Guinea-Bissau has been closely intertwined with that of the Republic of CAPE VERDE.

Ethnically, the people of Guinea-Bissau are closely related to the Fula and Mandinka peoples in neighboring Senegal and Guinea. In the interior, the Maninka language and Islam are unifying forces. Christianity and traditional religions are widely practiced along the coast and in the southern regions.

Portugal Forestalls Guinea-Bissau's Independence The origins of Guinea-Bissau's ills lay in the harsh imposition of colonial rule in Portuguese Guinea, as the country was called from 1879 to 1973. In 1952 Portugal changed the status of its colonies to "overseas provinces" in an attempt to derail the various independence movements that began calling for African self-government after World War II (1939–45).

In Guinea-Bissau, the opposition was quick to mobilize. By 1956 Amílcar CABRAL (1924–1973) and other political leaders had formed the AFRICAN PARTY FOR THE INDEPENDENCE OF GUINEA AND CAPE VERDE (Partido Africano da Indepêndencia da Guiné e Cabo Verde, PAIGC). With Marxist-Leninist leanings and plans for an inclusive government, Cabral's PAIGC was especially popular in Guinea-Bissau's rural areas.

Unlike most other European nations with African colonies, Portugal violently suppressed INDEPENDENCE MOVEMENTS from their inception. As a result, in 1961 PAIGC rebels began launching counterattacks from their headquarters in CONAKRY, the capital of Guinea. Following a series of small-scale raids on Portuguese government installations, in 1963, open warfare erupted. Portugal eventually sent more than 35,000 troops to Guinea-Bissau in its attempts to defeat the PAIGC guerrillas, whom they outnumbered by more than three-to-one. Despite Portugal's superior numbers, however, by 1968 the PAIGC controlled most of the country outside of the coastal urban centers.

In 1972 the PAIGC established a national people's assembly based on elections held in the liberated parts of the country, and the war for independence seemed to be coming to an end. Before the hostilities ended, however, Portuguese agents infiltrated the PAIGC ranks in Conakry and assassinated Cabral. Secretary General Aristides Maria PEREIRA (1923–), a Cape Verdean and cofounder of the PAIGC, assumed leadership of the party. On September 24, 1973, the PAIGC declared the end of Portuguese Guinea and the beginning of the independent Republic of Guinea-Bissau. The following year Luis Cabral (1931–), half-brother of Amílcar Cabral and also a cofounder of the PAIGC, became the first president of the newly independent republic.

Despite its name, the PAIGC was not very active in Cape Verde until 1973, when Guinea-Bissau declared independence. Two years later Cape Verde declared independence with Aristides Pereira as president.

Guinea-Bissau Since Independence Many countries around the world immediately accepted the PAIGC as the legitimate government of Guinea-Bissau. Portugal, however, did not officially recognize the new nation-state until 1974, after a COUP D'ÉTAT established a new Portuguese government in Lisbon.

From the start Luis Cabral's one-party government was beset by political and economic problems. Cabral tended to govern in an authoritarian manner, which caused widespread dissatisfaction. One of the most divisive issues that threatened the PAIGC was the political domination of Guinea-Bissau by Cape Verdeans such as the Cabrals. As a consequence, in 1980, João Bernardo Vieira (1939–), an army general, led a successful coup to overthrow Luis Cabral while the latter was in Cape Verde for meetings to discuss the unification of Cape Verde and Guinea-Bissau. Following the coup, the Cape Verdean leadership of the PAIGC abandoned plans to unify with Guinea-Bissau. Instead, they split, creating the African Party for the Independence of Cape Verde. Vieira would hold power in Guinea-Bissau for more than a quarter century.

In 1984 Vieira was officially elected president in closely watched elections. Over the next few years of his term, he led the country away from its Marxist path, privatizing whole sectors of the Guinea-Bissau economy. Before long, however, Vieira was accused of CORRUPTION, and his government had to fend off repeated attempts to overthrow it in the 1980s and 1990s. Despite his waning popularity, in 1994 Vieira won the country's first multiparty elections, which came about through political reforms that began in 1990.

Vieira's election did little to mend the political rifts in Guinea-Bissau. The infighting came to a head in 1998, when civil war erupted following Vieira's dismissal of army general Asumane Mane. By the middle of 1999 Mane's army had forced Vieira into exile in Portugal, and the PAIGC's Malam Balai Sanhá was then chosen to preside over an interim government. Although peace was restored after only a few years of fighting, an estimated 2,000 civilians were killed and hundreds of thousands more were displaced during the war.

Guinea-Bissau has plans to develop its hitherto untapped offshore OIL deposits in the coming years. It is hoped that the exploitation of this natural resource will give the people of Guinea-Bissau a reprieve from the grinding POVERTY that has hindered their DEVELOPMENT.

In 2000 the interim government handed over power to Koumba YALA (c. 1953–) of the Social Renewal Party. However, yet another coup took place in mid-September 2003, resulting in Yala's exit. Control of the country then passed into the hands of General Verissimo Correia Seabre (1947–), who promised to restore civilian democratic rule and promptly named Henrique

Pereira Rosa (c. 1946–   ), a business leader, as interim president. Presidential elections were set for March, 2005. Unlike Yala and most of Guinea-Bissau's armed forces, Rosa does not belong to the Balanta ethnic group.

See also: CIVIL WARS (Vol. V); COLD WAR AND AFRICA (Vols. IV, V); COLONIAL RULE (Vol. IV); GUINEA-BISSAU (Vols. I, II, III, IV); NATIONALISM AND INDEPENDENCE MOVEMENTS (Vol. IV); PORTUGAL AND AFRICA (Vols. III, IV, V); PORTUGUESE GUINEA (Vol. IV).

Further reading: Malyn Newitt, *Portugal in Africa: The Last Hundred Years* (Harlow, U.K.: Longman, 1981); Richard Gibson *African Liberation Movements: Contemporary Struggles Against White Minority Rule* (London: Oxford University Press, 1972).

H

Habré, Hissène (Habre Hissein) (1942–)
President of Chad from 1982 to 1990

Born to a family of herders in Northern CHAD, Habré was educated in local schools before going on to study and earn a law degree in Paris, France. Upon his return home in 1971, he initially worked in the foreign affairs ministry, but he became increasingly active as a leader of the National Liberation Front of Chad (Front de Libération Nationale du Tchad, FROLINAT). This movement, which had its origins among the Muslim herders and peasants of the north, launched a rebellion against the government of President Felix Malloum (1932–), who represented the interests of the mostly Christian south. Malloum himself had assumed the presidency in 1975 after leading a successful coup against President François-Ngarta TOMBALBAYE (1918– 1975). Habré gained international recognition for the rebellion he was leading when he kidnapped French archeologist Françoise Claustre in 1975. France refused to comply with ransom demands, and Claustre was not released until January 1977.

By February 1978 FROLINAT controlled nearly 80 percent of the country. Six months later, Habré was named prime minister in a vain bid to restore national unity. FROLINAT splintered, with new rebel leader Goukouni Oueddei (1944–), who ousted President Malloum, receiving support from president Muammar QADDAFI (1942–), of LIBYA. In January 1981 Qaddafi and Ouaddei proposed a merger of the two countries. Fear of the expansion of Libyan influence led to covert U.S. support for Habré. His forces took the capital, NDJA-MENA, in June 1982. The United States continued to give Habré significant military aid throughout his rule.

Habré was ousted by his own commander-in-chief, Idriss DÉBY (1952–), in December 1990. A 1992 truth commission estimated that 40,000 Chadians died during Habré's ruthless eight-year rule. This legacy led to him being nicknamed as "the African Pinochet" because of the similarities with the reign of the Chilean dictator, Augusto Pinochet (1915–). Upon his ouster, Habré fled to SENEGAL. Chad waived its legal protections and Habré was tried in absentia by a Belgian court. He was convicted of crimes against humanity in 2000, and President Abdoulaye WADE (1926–) of Senegal agreed to hold him in house arrest until he could be extradited. Since then the case has been mired in disputes over which country and court does not have jurisdiction over the case.

Habyarimana, Juvenal (1937–1994) *President of Rwanda from 1973 to 1994*

Habyarimana was born into an aristocratic HUTU family in Gaziza, northern RWANDA. He completed his secondary education and began studies in MEDICINE in ZAÏRE (present-day Democratic Republic of the CONGO) before returning to the Rwandan capital of KIGALI, where he attended the military academy. Upon completion of his course of studies he rose through the ranks to become army chief of staff, in 1963. Two years later, he became minister for Rwanda's armed forces and police, and he subsequently established close ties with President Gregoire KAYIBANDA (1924–1976), a fellow Hutu.

Citing increased ethnic strife, in July 1973 Major General Habyarimana launched a successful COUP D'ÉTAT, taking over the presidency. Given his power-base in the

Hutu elite, Habyarimana's rule led to many years of economic growth. But it was also marked by regular TUTSI insurgency from bases in UGANDA. In 1975 Habyarimana created the governing National Revolutionary Movement for Development party, winning the single-party popular elections three times. He also gained significant French support.

In 1992 Habyarimana held Rwanda's first multiparty elections, and he won a fourth term. Yet, within the year, the fall of the economy—associated with declines in international coffee prices—brought simmering ethnic tensions to the fore. Under the leadership of Paul KAGAME (1957–), the Tutsi RWANDA PATRIOTIC FRONT (RPF) took over much of northern Rwanda. Habyarimana was forced into peace talks. In April 1994 the plane carrying both him and Cyprien NTARYAMIRA (1956–1994), president of BURUNDI, crashed, probably shot down by RPF agents. The deaths of the two presidents sparked a brutal three-month genocide directed against Rwanda's Tutsi population. When the Tutsi recovered, they invaded Rwanda, driving several hundred thousand Hutu into refugee camps in the eastern Democratic Republic of the CONGO and elsewhere.

Haile Selassie, Emperor (Tafari Makonnen)
(1892–1975) *Ethiopian emperor from 1930 to 1974*

Hailing from the dominant Amhara ethnic group of ETHIOPIA, Haile Selassie was a long-time symbol of independence and African rule. Admired early on in his political career for abolishing slavery in Ethiopia, he also created a national constitution, improved the country's educational system, and led the resistance against the 1935 Italian invasion of his homeland. However, Haile Selassie failed to modernize throughout the 1960s and 1970s and became more authoritarian as a leader, moving away from the European style of governance that he once wanted to emulate.

Called Ras (Prince) Tafari Makonnen prior to becoming emperor, Haile Selassie inspired RASTAFARI-ANISM, a political-religious movement named in his honor. Founded in Jamaica in the 1950s, Rastafarianism held that Selassie was a living god. However, as a member of the Christian ETHIOPIAN ORTHODOX CHURCH, Haile Selassie never made such claims for himself and, in fact, he generally dismissed the movement as frivolous.

On the strength of his proud Ethiopian nationalism, Selassie became a world leader and an international statesman. He was one of the original founders of the OR-GANIZATION OF AFRICAN UNITY (OAU), which was chartered in 1963. As a leader of PAN-AFRICANISM, he believed that Africans should unite to deal with their common problems. His leadership in forming the group resulted in the OAU headquarters being stationed in Ethiopia's capital, ADDIS ABABA.

As emperor, Haile Selassie traveled extensively and was well received abroad. Beginning in the early 1960s, however, he faced a number of domestic crises. The most pressing of these problems involved territorial disputes in both ERITREA, Ethiopia's neighbor to the north, and the Ogaden region of southeast Ethiopia.

In the years prior to World War II (1939–45) Eritrea was an Italian colony. In 1952, in the wake of Italy's defeat and the loss of its overseas territories, Haile Selassie successfully lobbied the United Nations to designate Eritrea an autonomous, federated province of his country. Such an arrangement was strategically important to Ethiopia, for it guaranteed access to crucial Red Sea ports. However, many Eritreans rejected the plan, since they were separated from Ethiopians not only by history but also by their Islamic faith. Ethiopia's outright annexation of Eritrea, in 1962, marked the beginning of a protracted war for independence.

In the Cold War environment of the times, Eritrean rebels garnered support from communist countries, including the former Soviet Union and China, and also from co-religionists in Islamic states. The conflict lasted more than three decades, ending only with Eritrean independence in 1993.

Meanwhile, in southeastern Ethiopia, the emperor was facing a different kind of territorial dispute. Known as Ogaden, the vast region had long been considered by Ethiopia to be an integral part of its territory. In the early 1960s, however, with backing from the Soviet Union, SOMALIA was making claims to the territory. The United States, for its part, supported Ethiopia, and armed conflict erupted in 1964. Haile Selassie's subsequent efforts proved unsuccessful in negotiating a settlement of the contested areas.

In the early 1970s, aging and deteriorating mentally, the emperor was unable to lead Ethiopia through challenging times. The violent disputes in Eritrea and Ogaden continued, and new domestic problems, including inflation, increasing government corruption, and a disastrous famine required strong and able leadership. Ultimately, in September 1974 a military coup d'état forced Haile Selassie from power. Colonel MENGISTU HAILE MARIAM (c. 1937–) took over, placing Haile Selassie under house arrest. Within a year, in August 1975, the former emperor died under mysterious circumstances. In 1991, when the regime of Mengistu Haile Mariam was overthrown, Haile Selassie's body was finally found. Apparently, it had been buried directly under Mengistu's desk in the imperial palace grounds.

See also: COLD WAR AND AFRICA (Vols. IV, V); HAILE SELASSIE (Vol. IV); ERITREA (Vol. IV); FAMINE AND HUNGER (Vol. V); UNITED NATIONS AND AFRICA (Vol. V).

Further readings: Ryszard Kapuscinski, *The Emperor: Downfall of an Autocrat* (New York: Vintage, 1989); John H. Spencer, *Ethiopia at Bay: A Personal Account of the Haile Selassie Years* (Algonac, Mich.: Reference Publications, 1984).

Hani, Chris (Martin Thembisile Hani)
(1942–1993) *Prominent South African anti-apartheid activist*

At the time of his assassination in 1993, Chris Hani was one of the foremost contenders for the leadership of the AFRICAN NATIONAL CONGRESS (ANC) in the wake of the dismantling of APARTHEID. In 1957 Hani committed himself to the liberation struggle when he joined the ANC Youth League. In 1962 he was arrested for anti-government activities. The following year, while out on bail, he fled SOUTH AFRICA and took up residence in LESOTHO, an independent country completely surrounded by South Africa.

For most of the next three decades, Hani lived in exile, assuming various positions of authority within UMKHONTO WE SIZWE, the military wing of the ANC known commonly as MK. He went to the Soviet Union for training and, on his return in 1967, he was active in MK operations in ZIMBABWE, Lesotho, ANGOLA, and ZAMBIA. His military and political activities won him recognition, and in 1987 he became the MK chief of staff. In 1990 Hani became a member of the Politburo (leadership committee) of the South African Communist Party (SACP).

After the ANC, MK, and SACP were legalized in 1991, Hani returned to South Africa, flouting social custom by taking up residence in a neighborhood traditionally inhabited by white South Africans. At this time, Hani was one of the most prominent young ANC leader to emerge among the new generation of anti-apartheid activists. On April 10, 1993, he was assassinated outside his home by a Polish immigrant. Afterwards, a mass outpouring of anger among Africans led to violent uprisings throughout South Africa. If it had not been for the call for calm from Nelson MANDELA (1918–), the president of the ANC and South Africa's future president, the peaceful transition to democracy might have been derailed.

harambee Kiswahili word translated as "let's work together." In KENYA the leaders of farming cooperatives, school groups, and even the government have invoked *harambee* to pull people together in order to achieve a common goal.

Indentured workers from India brought the word *harambee* into Kiswahili during the building of colonial rail systems in East Africa. Foremen for construction teams chanted the word to inspire dedication and good will as they completed their difficult task.

Indicative of the importance of the *harambee* ethic, the Kenyan national soccer team is named the Harambee Stars.

Harare Capital of ZIMBABWE, located in the northeastern part of the country. Founded in 1890 with the name of Salisbury, Harare was very much a colonial city through the mid-19th century, serving as the capital of both the British colony of Southern Rhodesia and the breakaway state of RHODESIA, led by Ian SMITH (1919–). With its rigid residential segregation and socially and culturally dominant white population, Salisbury reflected the region's political structure. In fact, as late as 1960, whites made up approximately 30 percent of the city's population.

As part of the short-lived Central African Federation (1953–63), the city added an industrial sector to its commercial, government, and service sectors. After Smith's UNILATERAL DECLARATION OF INDEPENDENCE in 1965, the industrial sector continued to grow despite the international sanctions imposed on Smith's racist government.

In 1980, after independence, the city's name was changed to Harare, which was the name of one of the main segregated African residential areas. By this time the city, with its population of some 630,000, was much more African in makeup, with whites making up only 15 percent of its residents. Today the city is the commercial, governmental, and industrial center for the country. It is the site of the University of Zimbabwe, as well as the National Gallery of Zimbabwe, which houses some of the internationally acclaimed Chapungu stone sculptures.

Harare's economy has faltered in recent years in connection with the political crisis that gripped the country as a result of the efforts of President Robert MUGABE (1924–) to hold onto the reins of power. As foreign exchange has dwindled and the value of the Zimbabwean dollar has plummeted, many of the city's factories have been forced to lay off workers or close completely. The city's shops also have fewer goods, and OIL shortages hamper the TRANSPORTATION system. TOURISM, which recently seemed to be a promising sector of the economy, has also dwindled. The city has lost much of its prosperous appearance, and the future for Harare's approximately 1 million residents is now uncertain.

Chapungu stone sculpture originated with the Shona ethnic group, who have lived in the region of present-day Zimbabwe for centuries. Shona farmers carve stones into forms that they perceive as representing the spirits of the stones. They use hammers, chisels, and files to sculpt the basic shape, and then they use a series of progressively finer sheets of sandpaper to smooth it. Finally a wax coating is applied and polished to protect the hard stone. Frank McEwen, the curator of the National Museum of Harare, has been able to bring international exposure to the sculptures, which were already well known locally. Today the Shona artists are considered among the best stone sculptors in the world, and their work has been displayed in numerous countries.

See also: CENTRAL AFRICAN FEDERATION (Vol. IV); ENGLAND AND AFRICA (Vols. III, IV, V); SHONA (Vol. I); SHONA KINGDOMS (Vols. III, IV); SOUTHERN RHODESIA (Vol. IV); URBAN LIFE AND CULTURE (Vols. IV, V); URBANIZATION (Vols. IV, V).

Further readings: Terri Barnes and Everjoyce Win, *To Live a Better Life: An Oral History of Women in the City of Harare, 1930–1970* (Harare, Zimbabwe: Baobab Books, 1992); Carl Fredrik Hallencreutz, *Religion and Politics in Harare: 1890–1980* (Uppsala, Sweden: Swedish Institute of Missionary Research, 1998).

Hassan II, King (1929–1999) *King of Morocco*

Born Prince Moulay Hassan, the son of Mohammed V (1927–1961) received a Quranic education and then attended universities in RABAT, MOROCCO, and Bordeaux, France, where he received a master's degree in public law. In 1954 Prince Hassan was exiled to the island nation of MADAGASCAR, along with his father and the rest of the

Shown here in the 1990s, the King Hassan II Mosque in Casablanca is the largest Islamic monument outside of Mecca. It can accommodate up to 25,000 worshipers inside, with room for another 80,000 outside. © *Corbis*

Moroccan royal family. Late in 1955 they returned from exile. As both crown prince and chief of staff, Hassan advised his father and acted as a partner in the transition from French colonial state to independence. At independence, in 1957, Hassan became Morocco's prime minister. When he ascended the throne, in 1961, he was both king and prime minister.

Very much a product of the colonial period, Hassan II was an autocrat, similar to his father when Morocco was a French protectorate. Hassan II used his position as "Commander of the Faithful" to control Morocco's Muslim majority, and he also utilized his secular power to control the rural and urban elite as well as the army. Despite ruling with an iron fist, Hassan II struggled to implement his father's plan for a constitutional monarchy. In his attempts to do so, Hassan II used his police force to stifle opposition in Parliament and the community, and he intimidated voters to shape the outcome of elections. This repression of his opponents brought about public protests and several failed attempts to overthrow his government.

In the 1970s, to redeem his reputation at home, Hassan II attempted to "liberate" neighboring WESTERN SAHARA from Spanish colonial rule. Ultimately, he assembled an estimated 350,000 unarmed Moroccan civilians to march south and occupy parts of the region. This massive demonstration of Moroccan solidarity, called the Green March, resulted in the return of parts of the region to Moroccan control. However, it also conflicted with the aims of the indigenous SAHARAWI people, whose armed rebels, called the POLISARIO Front, embarked on a campaign to establish a truly independent Western Sahara. Hassan II spent the 1980s and early 1990s trying to regain the trust of the Moroccan people, finally implementing a new constitution in 1996.

In foreign policy, Hassan II promoted Arab nationalism. As a member of the Arab League, Morocco supported the cause of the Arab states against Israel. At the same time, Hassan II used the relatively large Moroccan Jewish community to help broker a settlement of the crisis in the Middle East. While Hassan II never sat at the table during negotiations, his low-key mediation helped deliver a 1979 treaty between Israel and EGYPT.

When Hassan II died in 1999, his son, Mohammed Ben al-Hassan, ascended the throne as King MOHAMMED VI (1963–).

See also: MOHAMMED V (Vol. IV); POLITICAL SYSTEMS (Vol. V).

Further reading: Stephen O. Hughes, *Morocco under King Hassan,* (Reading, U.K.: Ithaca Press, 2001); Richard Gillespie and Richard Youngs, eds., *The European Union and Democracy Promotion: the Case of North Africa* (Portland, Ore.: Frank Cass Publishers, 2002); C. R. Pennell, *Morocco since 1830: A History* (New York: New York University Press, 2000).

Hausa Ethnic group populating the region known as Hausaland, located in present-day NIGERIA. The nation of Nigeria that became independent in 1960 was ostensibly a federal republic with three major regions: the Hausa-Fulani-dominated north, a Western Region that was predominantly IGBO in makeup, and the YORUBA-dominated Eastern Region.

In the months following independence the Hausa increasingly allied themselves with the Muslim north, and this allowed the north to dominate the federal government during Nigeria's First Republic. Unrest and protests followed, mostly instigated by Igbo and Yoruba but attended by individuals from Nigeria's hundreds of other ethnic groups, as well. By January 1966 Igbo army officers, led by Major General Johnson Aguiyi-Ironsi (1924–1966), instigated a COUP D'ÉTAT, setting off even more violent ethnic dissension. Anti-Igbo sentiment increased in the north, and in July General Yakubu GOWON (1934–), a northern Hausa, led yet another military coup. In short order, Gowon assassinated Aguiyi-Ironsi and swept the Igbo from power. In the months that followed, northern troops attacked Igbo soldiers with whom they were stationed, mobs attacked Igbo speakers living in northern cities, and, in the end, tens of thousands of Igbos were killed. All of this eventually culminated in the rise of Igbo nationalism and, in 1966, the proclamation of an Ibgo state, which was named BIAFRA. During a bloody civil war the Hausa- and Muslim-dominated central government fought to put down the rebel state. The repression of Biafra ultimately succeeded but at a cost of hundreds of thousands—perhaps even millions—of lives. In addition to cost in lives, Nigeria was left with a heightened legacy of ethnic animosity that has continued to this day.

During the 1990s democracy eventually was restored after a series of brutal military regimes. Still, to many Nigerians, control of the government never truly left the hands of the northern Hausa and Muslims. This sense has been exacerbated during the 21st century by Muslim attempts to make the Islamic law of SHARIA the official legal system of various Nigerian states. As a result, conflict between Muslims, Christians, and practitioners of traditional African religions—as well as between members of the Hausa, Igbo, and Yoruba ethnic groups—remains intense.

See also: BALEWA, ABUBAKAR TAFAWA (Vols. IV, V); BELLO, AHMADU (Vols. IV, V); CHRISTIANITY, INFLUENCE OF (Vols. IV, V); ETHNICITY AND IDENTITY (Vol. V); HAUSA (I, II, IV), HAUSA STATES (II, III); ISLAM, INFLUENCE OF (Vols. IV, V); NORTHERN PEOPLE'S CONGRESS (Vol. V).

Further reading: Philip Koslow, *Hausaland: The Fortress Kingdoms* (New York: Chelsea House Publishers, 1995); Paul Staudinger, *In the Heart of the Hausa States* (Athens, Ohio: Ohio University Center for International Studies, 1990).

Head, Bessie (1937–1986) *South African writer*

Bessie Head's childhood was a traumatic one. Her parents were a wealthy white Scottish woman and a black stableman who worked on her mother's estate. Such liaisons were illegal under South Africa's Immorality Act, and Head's mother was subsequently committed to a mental institution, where Head was born in 1937. The child was then cared for by a Coloured, or mixed-race, family in Pietermaritzburg, under conditions of extreme POVERTY. In 1951 she was placed in the care of St. Monica's mission school, where she had been enrolled a year earlier.

In 1956 Head graduated and briefly worked as a teacher before moving to CAPE TOWN, where she worked as a journalist for the *Golden City Post* and later for *Drum* magazine. In Cape Town, Head joined the PAN-AFRICANIST CONGRESS and became involved in the political struggle against APARTHEID. South African authorities imprisoned her briefly, leading Head to a failed suicide attempt. In 1961 she married political activist Harold Head and relocated to District Six, the Coloured-only ghetto in Cape Town. In 1964 personal troubles drove Head to leave her husband and move with her son to Bechuanaland (present-day BOTSWANA), where she settled in the small town of Serowe. There, Head lived in abject poverty and began the writing career that would carry her to prominence.

When Botswana became independent in 1966, Head was able to live off of refugee funds from the United Nations and the advance money for her first novel. She moved to Francistown, and in 1969 *When Rain Clouds Gather* was published to strong critical reviews. About the same time, Head began to display symptoms of mental illness that would plague her throughout her life.

Head's second novel, *Maru* (1971), centered on the Tswana people of Botswana, but it was the mostly autobiographical *A Question of Power* (1973) that is considered her best. The story of a young South African Coloured woman who moves to Botswana and suffers a nervous breakdown, the novel gives a harrowing account of a life that mirrors Head's own.

Head gradually gained international recognition for her work. Granted citizenship in Botswana in 1979, she traveled to writers' workshops around the world. However, Head was afflicted with alcoholism, and her mental health steadily deteriorated. She died in 1986 from hepatitis. Several of Head's works were published posthumously, including *The Cardinals* (1993), a novella she wrote while still in South Africa.

See also: BECHUANALAND (Vol. IV); DRUM (Vol. IV); LITERATURE IN MODERN AFRICA (Vol. V); WOMEN IN INDEPENDENT AFRICA (Vol. V).

health and healing in modern Africa

In contemporary Africa there are several different categories of healing systems that are used to fight illness. These include the traditional healing systems, western biomedical care, RELIGION-based healing systems, and self-care. Within these categories there exist numerous ideologies on health and illness. At the same time, these different systems can often influence each other, making it difficult to distinguish boundaries. There are also high rates of pluralism in treating illnesses, meaning that many people in Africa use treatments from more than one healing system to treat a particular condition.

Traditional Healing   Indigenous MEDICINE is diverse and dynamic. It includes healing systems that are not considered Western biomedicine. These healing systems have been a part of life in Africa for centuries and have continually evolved as environmental and social forces have changed over the years. Although there are many different types of traditional healing, most hold to the general theme of equating physical health with the maintenance of an equilibrium throughout all areas of a patient's life.

During the colonial period traditional healing was labeled as pagan and unscientific by colonial authorities, and its practitioners were often persecuted. This caused many traditional healers to practice in secret, and with the introduction of Western biomedicine the use of traditional healing declined. This decline continued even after many nations achieved independence. The decrease in the use of traditional healing was sharpest between the 1960s and 1980s, when many newly independent African states attempted to model themselves after western European countries. Extending this emulation into the field of health care, these nations turned against traditional healing and, instead, fought to follow the precepts of Western medicine.

Toward the end of the 20th century, however, there was a national and international movement, led by the World Health Organization, to gain official legitimacy for traditional healing. The governments of many African nations set up programs within their health-care facilities to provide collaboration and training for traditional healers. There was a new recognition of the knowledge held by these healers, accompanied by a fear that it may have been lost if it were not embraced by official medical institutions. In addition, the resurgence of traditional healing was seen as a way to provide affordable health care in an economic environment characterized by social-service cutbacks. As a result, by the end of the 20th century more than half of all Africans used some type of traditional healing.

Western Medicine   In addition to the many traditional healing systems available, an extensive network of Western health-care facilities and programs are present throughout Africa. Western health care originally was introduced in Africa during the colonial period in an attempt to protect the health of European colonists and the indigenous LABOR force. Today Western biomedical facilities provide the foundation for government-provided health care throughout Africa. Recent attempts to improve health conditions for rural populations have focused on decentralizing control of health care away from the urban areas. In addition, there has been a push to incorporate preventative health care, rather than simply to cure ailments, which was the prevalent practice during the colonial period.

The economic downturn facing many African governments in the 1980s resulted in the implementation of strict STRUCTURAL ADJUSTMENT programs. These programs reduced spending on many social services, including health care. This has left existing health-care facilities with insufficient funds to serve the needs of the growing population, resulting in under-staffing, overcrowding, and medication shortages. Private hospitals have ameliorated these deficiencies, but the majority of Africans cannot afford to go to a private hospital. Many international NON-GOVERNMENTAL ORGANIZATIONS have attempted to fill the resulting gaps in health care by implementing research and outreach programs such as the Global Malaria Control Strategy and the Expanded Program on Immunization.

Although recent decades have witnessed the emergence of new and severe diseases, most notably HIV/AIDS, the spread of Western biomedical care has improved certain aspects of health in Africa. For example, average life expectancy has increased from 43 years, in 1960, to 51 years, in 1994. These positive results, however, are not equally dispersed in all locations and countries.

Religion-based Health Care   The third general category of healing systems centers on religious individuals and institutions directly involved in healing. Their practices often overlap with the tenets of traditional healing systems, incorporating the intervention of God or deities for the purpose of healing physical ailments. The Independent African Churches, which are multiplying rapidly in urban areas, are known for their assistance with healing. Some churches have specific chambers designated for healing. Also, it is the duty of some church officials to visit the sick and perform healing rituals. Although orthodox Christians and Muslims generally do not endorse the melding of traditional and western medical practices, the mixing of secular and religion-based health care does occur often in less orthodox churches and mosques throughout the continent.

Self-Healing   One of the most widespread healing systems is that of self-healing. Due to limited income and frequent illness, many poorer households rely on self-diagnosis and self-medication when someone is sick. Africans frequently use herbs, roots, or over-the-counter medication to treat illnesses at home. Popular drugs have been mass-produced and are available at both registered pharmacies and informal street vendors. Due to the widespread availability of these drugs and long lines at government health-care facilities, purchasing drugs for self-healing is often the fastest treatment available. One of the problems with this approach is that improper or in-complete self-medication can give rise to drug-resistant strains of disease.

See also: COLONIALISM, INFLUENCE OF (Vol. IV); DISEASE IN MODERN AFRICA (Vol. V); HEALTH AND HEALING IN COLONIAL AFRICA (Vol. IV); HIV/AIDS IN AFRICA (Vol. V); MEDICINE MEN (Vol. I); RELIGION (Vol. V).

Further reading: Gerald Bloom, H. Lucas, A. Edun, *Health and Poverty in Sub-Saharan Africa* (Brighton, U.K.: Institute of Development Studies, 2000); Kimbwandende Kia Bunseki Fu-Kiau, *Self-healing Power and Therapy: Old Teachings from Africa* (New York: Vantage Press, 1991); Emmanuel Lartey, Daisy Nwachuku, Kasonga Wa Kasonga, eds., *The Church and Healing: Echoes from Africa* (New York: Peter Lang, 1994).

Herero   Ethnic group of NAMIBIA, western BOTSWANA, and southern ANGOLA. The greater Herero group is made up of various sub-groups, including the Himba, Tijimba, and Mbanderu peoples. In the 1950s the Herero paramount chief, Hosea Kutako (1870–1970), sent Mburumba Kerina to petition the United Nations for support in achieving self-rule. Although Namibian independence was granted only in 1990, the early diplomatic efforts of the Herero brought attention to the repression and HUMAN RIGHTS abuses perpetrated by the South African authorities in SOUTH WEST AFRICA (as Namibia was known at the time).

See also: HERERO (Vols. II, III, IV).

historical scholarship on Africa   Writing about African history emerged as an important field of scholarship in the late 1950s and early 1960s. The achievement of independence by a majority of African countries during this period was the principal motivating force for establishing African history as a major research and teaching area within the discipline of history.

Africa had few universities prior to independence. Beginning in the 1960s, however, each country developed its own national university or, in the case of populous countries such as NIGERIA, several universities. Each of these universities had a department of history that was staffed by professionally trained African scholars who focused to a large extent on the national pasts of their respective countries. This led to publications such as *Milestones in Nigerian History* (1962), by J. F. Ade Ajayi (1929–   ), *Kenya before 1900* (1976), by Bethwell A. Ogot (1929–   ), and *A History of the Maghreb* (1971), by Jamil M. Abun-Nasr. The first generation of these historians was trained at universities in the European countries that were former colonial powers or in the United States. Over the first decades of independence, however, African universities trained more and more of the continent's historians.

The imperatives of African independence also demanded that history departments at universities in the former colonial countries and North America also teach African history. A milestone in this development was the founding of the *Journal of African History* (JAH) by two English historians, Roland Oliver (1923–   ) and John D. Fage (1921–   ). The JAH rapidly became the field's leading journal. The development of AFRICAN STUDIES in the United States led to the establishment of African history at its universities. The University of Wisconsin-Madison, under the leadership of Philip D. Curtin (1922–   ) and Jan Vansina (1929–   ), was at the forefront of this effort and trained many of the senior historians of Africa now at American universities.

John Fage's career exemplified that of many of the first generation of Western and especially British scholars of Africa. As a member of the Royal Air Force, he was in both the African and Asian theaters of World War II (1939–45). In 1949 he went to GHANA, at the time still the British colony of the Gold Coast, to help develop the history department at its new university. His tenure in Ghana led to the publication of *Ghana: An Historical Interpretation* (1959). He then was a visiting professor at the University of Wisconsin before returning to England, where he ultimately became the head of the Centre of West African Studies and professor of African history at the University of Birmingham. In 1962 he co-authored with Roland Oliver the first modern general history of the continent, *A Short History of Africa*, which subsequently appeared in six editions, the last coming in 1988.

The study of the African past has gone through a number of distinct phases over the past half-century or so. The first was to establish that Africa had a history, a fact that had been undermined by decades of colonial rule and countless assertions of African inferiority. The noted Cambridge University historian of Europe, Hugh Trevor-Roper (1914–2003), captured this sentiment when he wrote, in 1963, that the African past consists of nothing more than "the unrewarding gyrations of barbarous tribes in picturesque but irrelevant corners of the globe." The focus of this first phase of historical scholarship, then, was to counter this negative image and to assert that Africa indeed possessed a historical past worthy of study. The emphasis was primarily on trade and states during the precolonial era, leading to books such as *Kingdoms of the Savanna* (1966), by Vansina, and *Trade and Politics in the Niger Delta, 1830–1860,* by Kenneth DIKE (1917–1983). The title

of *Africans and Their History* (1972), by Joseph E. Harris (1929–   ), captures the heart of this approach. Much of our present knowledge of the early African states and empires and trade routes dates from this period.

The second phase of historical scholarship on Africa emerged from the disillusionment with the results of African independence. Scholars of Africa had been optimistic that Ghana's pioneering Kwame NKRUMAH (1909–1972) was right with his dictum of "Seek ye first the political kingdom and all else will come." But by the 1970s many perceptive observers saw that rather than DEVELOPMENT African countries faced NEOCOLONIALISM AND UNDERDEVELOPMENT. Nor was this limited to Africa, for scholars from Latin American, the Middle East, and parts of Asia also were concerned with the continued global dominance of the Western world. The Egyptian economist Samir Amin (1931–   ), who in 1971 published *L'Afrique de l'Ouest Bloquee: L'Economie Politique de la Colonisation, 1880–1970* (translated and published in 1973 as *Neo-Colonialism in West Africa*), was one such key figure. The leading historian of Africa to take this approach was the French Guyana-born historian Walter RODNEY (1942–1980), who taught at the University of Dar es Salaam in TANZANIA. In 1972 he published *How Europe Under-developed Africa*, which became perhaps the most influential study of African history for an entire generation of students educated at African universities. Numerous studies along these lines subsequently appeared from scholars based both within and outside the continent.

Historical studies centered around concepts of neocolonialism, underdevelopment, and dependency helped explain Africa's growing POVERTY by revealing how Africa had been victimized by forces beyond its control. This view, however, denied Africans a role as communities or individuals in making their own history. This proved to be unsatisfactory to many scholars both inside and outside the continent. Thus, in the 1984 edition of *Topics in West African History,* which originally appeared in 1964, the Ghanaian historian A. Adu Boahen reiterated that the history of Africa, "like that of most regions or countries of the world, is the result of internal and external factors." Furthermore, "the internal or local factors [which consist of the people and their resources] . . . are usually more fundamental and far more important."

Most of the studies that sought to place Africans as central actors in shaping the continent's history have focused on the 19th and, especially, 20th centuries. The availability of historical documentation provided sufficient information for examining the lives and actions of individual Africans and their communities in a way not possible in earlier centuries. The scope of studies also broadened well beyond the earlier political and economic history. Studies such as Frederick Cooper's (1947–   ) investigation of colonial MOMBASA (*On the African Waterfront,* 1987) contributed to better historical understanding of urban

African LABOR, while Elias Mandala's study of colonial MALAWI, *Work and Control in a Peasant Economy* (1990), provided insight into rural labor in the agricultural sector. Anne Kelk Mager examined the social history of the Ciskei BANTUSTAN in *Gender and the Making of a South African Bantustan* (1999), while Jean Allman's *The Quills of the Porcupine* (1993) delved into the social conflicts underlying and fueling the politics leading to Ghana's independence.

During the 1980s another approach to the study of the African past, known as Afrocentrism, emerged among a group of African American scholars. Molefi Asante (1942–), a specialist in intercultural communication and a professor at Temple University, first popularized the term Afrocentrism and the related terms Afrocology and Afrocentricity in his 1987 book *The Afrocentric Idea*. Part of the inspiration for the concept of Afrocentrism stems from PAN-AFRICANISM and the scholarship of individuals such as W. E. B. Du Bois (1868–1963). One of his lasting legacies was the *Encyclopaedia Africana: Dictionary of African Biography* project. Initiated in Ghana in 1962, after Asante became a citizen of that country, the project will ultimately have 20 volumes (only three have appeared to date).

A more direct intellectual precursor of Afrocentrism was Cheikh Anta DIOP (1923–1986), the Senegalese scholar. Diop's *Antériorité des civilisations nègres: mythe ou vérité historique,* which was published in 1967, appeared in 1974 in English as *The African Origins of Civilization: Myth or Reality.* Its carefully argued thesis that ancient Egyptian civilization was black rather than Caucasoid thus became accessible to the African American community in general. The prestige and historical significance of ancient EGYPT was such that Diop's argument had wide appeal to those who sought to counter white racism and its views of black inferiority. This has given a major boost to their argument that people of African descent should take pride in their ancestral African civilizations as a starting point for articulating their own Afrocentric history and their own Afrocentric system of values.

By the turn of the century historical scholarship on Africa was continuing to explore new avenues for understanding the African past in ways that were appropriate for the African present. Just as the emergence of social history a couple of decades earlier had opened up new vistas beyond those provided by the conceptual approach of the development of underdevelopment, so in recent years a cultural approach has enabled historians to ask new questions about the past. For example, Emmanuel Akyeampong explored the changing social role of alcohol in Ghana over two centuries in his *Drink, Power, and Cultural Change* (1996). Laura Fair examined in *Pastimes and Politics* (2001) how the emancipated slave population of ZANZIBAR utilized musical performance, soccer, manners

of dress, Islamic ritual, and ethnicity to fashion a new identity that was in keeping with their new social status. Likewise, Heather Sharkey's 2003 study, *Living with Colonialism,* examines culture in the Anglo-Egyptian Sudan in terms of such topics as colonial EDUCATION, privilege, and national identity and life under the colonial regime.

See also: DUBOIS, W.E.B. (Vol. IV); HISTORICAL SCHOLARSHIP ON AFRICA (Vol. IV).

Further reading: Toyin Falola, ed., *Tradition and Change in Africa: The Essays of J. F. Ade Ajayi* (Trenton, N.J.: Africa World Press, 2000); E.S. Atieno Odhiambo, ed., *African Historians and African Voices: Essays Presented to Professor Bethwell Allan Ogot on his Seventieth Birthday* (Basel, Switzerland: P. Schlettwein, 2001); Roland Oliver, *In the Realms of Gold: Pioneering in African History* (Madison, Wisc.: University of Wisconsin Press, 1997); Jan Vansina, *Living with Africa* (Madison: University of Wisconsin Press, 1994).

HIV/AIDS and Africa   Human Immunodeficiency Virus/Acquired Immunodeficiency Syndrome (HIV/AIDS) was first recognized in Africa in the 1980s. Although the disease is making a mark on every country worldwide, Africa bears more than its share of the burden. Today, the alarming scope of the pandemic in Africa is attracting the attention of both national and international bodies.

> The Joint United Nations Program on HIV/AIDS (UNAIDS) reported that of the estimated 5 million people worldwide who contracted the HIV virus in 2002, 3.5 million live in sub-Saharan Africa. For the same year, nearly 90 percent of the HIV/AIDS-related deaths worldwide occurred in sub-Saharan Africa.

Recent Developments in Combating HIV/AIDS

In recent years most African nations have initiated research and EDUCATION programs to decrease the risk of contracting HIV/AIDS among their populations. In 2003 UNAIDS reported that 19 nations have national HIV/AIDS councils, and 40 countries have developed strategic HIV/AIDS plans. In some countries, including UGANDA, KENYA, and SOUTH AFRICA, most DEVELOPMENT programs include an HIV/AIDS component. One such program is the Southern Africa Youth Initiative, which makes education, support networks, and health care available to adolescent girls in an attempt to prevent the spread of HIV/AIDS. In BOTSWANA, the government has promised to provide antiretrovirals—medicines to combat the HIV virus—to all its citizens who need them.

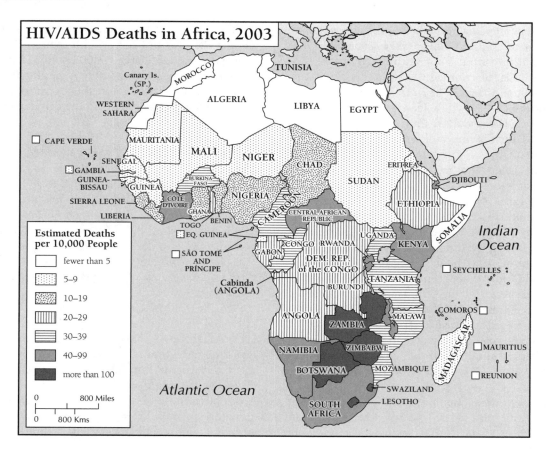

HIV/AIDS Deaths in Africa, 2003

Estimated Deaths per 10,000 People
- fewer than 5
- 5–9
- 10–19
- 20–29
- 30–39
- 40–99
- more than 100

0   800 Miles
0   800 Kms

Despite the alarming HIV/AIDS infection rates and projections for increases in the future, positive trends have been reported in some areas in Africa. For example in 1998, after the implementation of an aggressive public health campaign, Uganda became the first African country to report a decrease in HIV rates. The decline has been steady among pregnant women 15 to 19 years old, and condom use by single women in the same age group reportedly has doubled since 1995. In South Africa the reported HIV/AIDS rates for pregnant women under 20 dropped from an alarming 21 percent, in 1998, to 15 percent, in 2001. Declines were also reported for young women in the city center of ADDIS ABABA, ETHIOPIA. Although it is expected that the worst is yet to come for Africa, particularly for parts of West Africa, where rates are still low relative to eastern and southern Africa, these positive trends indicate that well-planned public health campaigns may prove successful in decreasing the rates of infection.

Poverty and the Spread of HIV/AIDS in Africa

There are numerous factors, many of which differ from those of developed nations, contributing to the spread of HIV/AIDS in Africa. Transmission has been characterized differently in Africa than in other regions, since the majority of infections occur through heterosexual contact. The rest are attributed to exposure to the virus through contaminated blood transfusions and to mother-to-child transmission during pregnancy or breast-feeding.

In general, HIV/AIDS in Africa infects an equal number of men and women, although a higher percentage of young women (ages 15 to 24) are infected than men in the same age group. This pattern has been attributed to discrimination against women and girls regarding access to education, financial resources, health care, and employment. Limited access to these resources puts women and girls in a position that often necessitates relations with men who have adequate financial resources. These men, because of their age, are more likely to be infected with HIV/AIDS.

A major contributing factor to the spread of HIV/AIDS is that widespread POVERTY throughout Africa has led to an increase in migration. People traveling in search of employment often end up in cities, causing overpopulation that overburdens the INFRASTRUCTURE and causes unemployment. As a result, migrants often live in shantytowns or slum areas that usually do not have clean running water, waste disposal, or electricity. These living conditions promote the spread of disease, in general. Sexually transmitted diseases (STDs), in particular, are common in these areas, since many women and girls are forced by their circumstances to sell sex. The sex-for-money cycle is related to HIV/AIDS as well as other sexually transmitted diseases, such as gonorrhea, syphilis, and chancroid. The genital ulceration caused by some sexually transmitted diseases facilitates the transmission of HIV/AIDS. Limited use of health-care facilities for the treatment of STDs—due to both the lack of access as well as to the social stigma associated with STDs—also plays a role.

Many African governments responded to the economic crisis of the 1980s and to the STRUCTURAL ADJUSTMENT programs imposed by the WORLD BANK and the INTERNATIONAL MONETARY FUND with cuts in social programs, including health care. This has led to overcrowding at the few available facilities and has necessitated the introduction of user fees, which are prohibitive for the poor.

Other Factors An additional factor associated with the spread of HIV/AIDS in Africa is military conflict, which has resulted in the looting and destruction of health-care facilities in many war-torn areas, further limiting access to treatment and health education. Conflicts have also contributed to widespread poverty through the destruction of farmland and infrastructure.

Certain culture-specific practices may also contribute to Africa's high HIV/AIDS transmission rates. Scientists have reported an association between uncircumcised men and the spread of STDs, including HIV/AIDS. Also, researchers are exploring links between sexual practices and the spread of HIV/AIDS. For example, intercourse is sometimes performed after applying drying agents to the female genitals, increasing the chances of tearing and, therefore, transmission of HIV/AIDS.

The Impact of HIV/AIDS-related Mortality Extensive research projects are examining the destructive impact of HIV/AIDS on African society. The disease has led to the loss of adults in the prime of life, plunging families into economic hardship. Too often, when a household loses a source of income, children and teens must quit school in order to work. This results in a lack of education, which has been associated with increased poverty and the further spread of HIV/AIDS. In this way the loss of a family member can create a vicious cycle of poverty and exposure to HIV/AIDS.

Hardship increases dramatically when both parents die, a situation that occurs often due to the nature of HIV/AIDS. Orphans then become the heads of households, join other households, or attempt to survive on the streets, and these options do not bode well for an improved quality of life. Even before death occurs, HIV/AIDS is an economic burden on a family or a village because of medical bills and the loss of productivity due to a reduction in the LABOR force. Because of its far-reaching implications, HIV/AIDS in Africa will continue to be an area of research for decades to come.

See also: DISEASE IN MODERN AFRICA (Vol. V); HEALTH AND HEALING IN MODERN AFRICA (Vol. V); UNITED NATIONS AND AFRICA (Vols. IV, V).

Further readings: Max Essex, ed., *AIDS in Africa* (New York: Kluwer Academic/Plenum Publishers, 2002); Ronald Hope Kempe, ed., *AIDS and Development in Africa: A Social Science Perspective* (New York: Haworth Press, 1999); Douglas Webb, *HIV and AIDS in Africa* (Chicago: Pluto Press, 1997).

Houphouët-Boigny, Felix (1905–1993) *First president of independent Ivory Coast*

Houphouët-Boigny began his political career, in 1945, as leader of a farmers' union called the African Agricultural Union. The following year, he was elected a deputy of the French National Assembly. Later that same year, he helped found the African Democratic Assembly (Rassemblement Démocratique Africaine, RDA), an inclusive political party that served the whole of French West Africa. After IVORY COAST achieved independence in 1960, Houphouët-Boigny became president, and his political party, the Democratic Party of Ivory Coast (Parti Démocratique de la Côte d'Ivoire, PDCI) dominated the country's legislature.

During the initial years of Houphouët-Boigny's administration, Ivory Coast prospered under a highly centralized, one-party government. Houphouët-Boigny strategically denied the development of a multiparty political system, believing it would create an unhealthy divisiveness in a country trying to establish itself. Economically, Houphouët-Boigny cooperated extensively with other states in Africa, supporting the ORGANIZATION OF AFRICAN UNITY (OAU), as well as with France, deeming that independence had little significance if Ivory Coast could not develop its economy. Despite criticism leveled at Houphouët-Boigny's cooperation policy by the likes of Kwame NKRUMAH (1909–1972) of GHANA and Sékou TOURÉ (1922–1984) of GUINEA, Ivory Coast's economy, called the "Ivorian miracle," developed remarkably well into the late 1970s. The country became the world's top cocoa producer and third in terms of coffee production. Houphouët-Boigny used his financial gains freely. He built an entirely new national capital in his home city of YAMOUSSOUKRO, which was completed in 1983.

Debt and a collapsing cocoa market soon undercut Ivory Coast's booming economy, however, and political opposition began to emerge against Houphouët-Boigny's government. He had many of his opponents arrested or exiled, but was forced by an international outcry to proclaim a short-lived amnesty in 1988. Declining economic conditions and the threat of a pay cut led to protests by government workers in 1990. In response Houphouët-Boigny called for more arrests, but ultimately he was forced to allow for presidential elections. He won the presidency again, though the elections were widely thought to be rigged.

Conditions in Ivory Coast continued to worsen for the remainder of Houphouët-Boigny's presidency. He died of prostate cancer, in 1993, and was buried in a basilica in Yamoussoukro. This extravagant building, constructed of imported materials entirely along the lines of a European church, cost some $200 million in state funds. It came to represent the excesses of what had become a highly idiosyncratic rule.

See also: AFRICAN DEMOCRATIC ASSEMBLY (Vol. IV); HOUPHOUËT-BOIGNY, FÉLIX (Vol. IV).

human rights In Africa the guarantee of human rights is a prominent feature of the legal protections in most states. However, the common occurrence of armed conflicts and CIVIL WARS and the despotic nature of certain regimes have resulted in frequent human rights violations. The phrase "universal human rights" typically refers to the rights described by the General Assembly of the United Nations in its Universal Declaration of Human Rights (1948). The Declaration states that people's civil, legal, political, economic, social, and cultural rights are guaranteed against discrimination based on race, ethnic group, color, sex, RELIGION, political or any other opinion, national and social origin, fortune, birth, or other status.

In light of the widespread human rights abuses visited on the people of Africa during the colonial era, independent African states were conscious of making provisions to

ensure the human rights of their citizens. To that end, numerous articles of the charter of the ORGANIZATION OF AFRICAN UNITY (OAU) stipulate that freedom, equality, justice, and dignity are essential objectives for the achievement of the legitimate aspirations of the African peoples. From its inception the OAU called for all African member states to have due regard for the Charter of the United Nations and the Universal Declaration of Human Rights.

> The OAU charter stipulates that member states shall eliminate discrimination against women, but this can present challenges, especially with regard to cultures that traditionally extend different rights to men and women. In NIGERIA, for example, northern Muslims have been calling for the greater implementation of Islamic law, or SHARIA, which treats women differently from men. Nigerians living in the more secular southern regions appeal to the OAU charter, which can result in drastically different interpretations of what are the inalienable "human rights" to be guaranteed to an individual.

According to the OAU charter, no one may be arbitrarily arrested or detained or otherwise deprived of the right to life and the integrity of his or her person.

Shown here in a photograph from 1972, Felix Houphouët-Boigny was the president of Ivory Coast for 33 years. © AP/Wide World Photos

Slavery, torture, and cruel or unusual punishment are thus naturally prohibited. The charter also covers worker rights, legal rights, freedom of speech and religion, and freedom of association, movement, and residence within the borders of a state. It also protects against gender inequality and preserves the rights of children and the elderly. The OAU attempted to enforce these aspects of its charter through the African Commission on Human and People's Rights.

The often unstable political, economic, and ethnic circumstances left in the wake of colonialism produced environments in which human rights are constantly under threat. As newly independent African countries attempted to establish stable economies and resolve differences between vying political parties and ethnic groups, many nations fell under the power of autocratic rulers who suppressed many basic human rights in an effort to maintain their power. In countries such as GHANA, KENYA, and MALAWI nationalist leaders evolved into dictators of one-party states with control over the national media and no allowances for political opposition. In EQUATORIAL GUINEA, UGANDA, and the CENTRAL AFRICAN REPUBLIC, brutal dictatorships ruled through violent oppression and abolished any semblance of human rights. The government of SOUTH AFRICA represented perhaps the most blatant and long-term disregard for human rights with the establishment of its racist APARTHEID regime, which lasted until 1994.

Another aspect of the independence era that has made the preservation of human rights difficult has been the frequent outbreak of violence and civil war. These conflicts, typically fueled by either political disagreement or ethnic motivations, interfere with the rights of citizens caught in the crossfire of the warring sides. Atrocities committed during civil wars in Nigeria, MOZAMBIQUE, the Republic of the CONGO, and the Democratic Republic of the CONGO were in gross violation of human rights, as were genocidal campaigns conducted in BURUNDI and RWANDA. Devastating conflicts such as these also forced millions to become REFUGEES. The OAU charter made provisions for protecting refugees.

The constant threat to human rights in many African nations has led to the involvement of a number of NONGOVERNMENTAL ORGANIZATIONS that work to protect human rights and bring violations of those rights to the attention of the international community. Groups such as Amnesty International, which first became involved in Africa in 1962, the U.S.-based Human Rights Watch, and the UN Human Rights Committee are among those which champion human rights in Africa. Though the situation may be bleak in a number of African nations, others—BOTSWANA stands out as a prime example—have strong human rights records and represent the hope that human rights violations will soon be the exception, not the norm, in Africa.

See also: AMNESTY INTERNATIONAL AND AFRICA (Vol. V); ETHNIC CONFLICT IN AFRICA (Vol. V); RACE AND RACISM (Vol. IV); UNITED NATIONS AND AFRICA (Vol. V).

Hutu Majority ethnic group of both RWANDA and BURUNDI. The second half of the 20th century has been a period of devastating conflict between the Hutu and their rivals, the TUTSI. The Hutu, who make up approximately 85 percent of the population in both Rwanda and Burundi, have for many years been subject to the rule of minority Tutsi monarchs. Belgian favoritism toward the lighter-skinned Tutsi during the period of colonial rule only exacerbated tensions.

Following independence for both Rwanda and Burundi in 1962 the struggle between the two groups often erupted in violent confrontations. In the mid-1990s the violence in Rwanda turned genocidal following the death of the country's Hutu president, Juvenal HABYARIMANA (1937–1994). He was killed when his plane was brought down by what many Hutu claimed was a Tutsi-launched missile. The crash also took the life of Burundi's Hutu president, Cyprien NTARYAMIRA (1956–1994). Hutu anger over the deaths of the two presidents erupted into bloodshed, with civilian Hutu death squads—known as the Interahamwe—systematically killing between 800,000 and 1 million people, mostly Tutsi.

> For all of their differences, the Hutu share many aspects of Tutsi culture, and vice versa. Centuries ago the Tutsi adopted the Hutu language, a Bantu tongue. The Hutu, in turn, took on the Tutsi kinship system. The Hutu also largely share the same Christian and animist religious beliefs as the Tutsi.

Later in 1994 the Tutsi-dominated RWANDA PATRIOTIC FRONT, led by Paul KAGAME (1957–), invaded from neighboring UGANDA and took control of Rwanda. A large portion of the Hutu population fled west, into the Democratic Republic of the CONGO, where they were given refuge by Congolese president Robert MUGABE (1924–). Kagame set up a joint Hutu-Tutsi government, but in time it became clear that the Tutsi had once again become the dominant political force in Rwanda.

In Burundi conflict between the Hutu and Tutsi existed from independence, with the government suffering through a series of coups. In 1972 Hutu uprisings against the Tutsi government led by Michel Micombero (1940–1983) resulted in government reprisals in which as many as 150,000 Hutu lost their lives. In 1988 an estimated

20,000 Hutu were killed in a similar genocidal wave of violence after Tutsi Pierre BUYOYA (1949–) came to power following a COUP D'ÉTAT.

After the assassination of Hutu president Melchior Ndadaye (1953–1993) in 1993, the Hutu launched reprisals against the Tutsi, killing an estimated 150,000. The plane crash in 1994 that killed Ntaryamira did not produce the same horrific reaction in Burundi as it did in Rwanda, although fighting continued. Peace talks initiated in 1995 began to ease the crisis.

See also: ETHNIC CONFLICT IN AFRICA (Vol. V); HUTU (Vols. I, II, III, IV).

Further reading: René Lemarchand, *Burundi: Ethnic Conflict and Genocide* (New York: Cambridge University Press, 1996); Aimable Twagilimana, *Hutu and Tutsi* (New York: Rosen Publishing Group, 1998).

I

Ibadan Capital of Oyo State in NIGERIA, located in the southwestern YORUBA-speaking portion of the country. In the early 20th century Ibadan became a major colonial commercial center under British administration. The city and surrounding area have a long history of producing agricultural products for the market, and many of its residents still cultivate their land in a part-time basis.

Ibadan's markets flourish, with vendors on every street corner. Numerous stalls and shops sell items as varied as beads, indigenous cloth, cotton, timber, rubber, palm oil, furniture, soap, and leather goods. Dugbe, a huge traditional marketplace, is located at Ibadan's TRANSPORTATION hub. Ibadan also has its own highly popular amusement park, Transwonderland, which is Nigeria's answer to Disneyland.

Industry in the city is limited, but there are many hotels as well as businesses specializing in printing, photography, and car repair. In 2000 the city's population was estimated at more than 1.5 million.

See also: IBADAN (Vol. IV); URBAN LIFE AND CULTURE (Vols. IV, V); URBANIZATION (Vols. IV, V).

Ibadan, University of Government-supported university located in NIGERIA. It was founded in the second half of the 19th century as the Yaba Higher College and, in association with London University, it awarded higher education degrees to students pursuing professional training. In 1948 the school changed its name to the University College, Ibadan. It was Nigeria's first university and one of the earliest universities in sub-Saharan Africa. In the 1948–49 academic year, the University College supported three schools: Arts, Sciences, and MEDICINE.

From its inception, the university adapted its classes to suit local needs. In 1962 it moved out from under the aegis of London University and became autonomous. The school's first chancellor was Abubakar Tafawa BALEWA (1912–1966), independent Nigeria's first prime minister. From 1960 to 1967 Dr. Kenneth O. DIKE (1917–1983) was the university's principal and vice chancellor. He led the efforts to establish a postgraduate school at Ibadan. In the 1970s the university expanded, opening new campuses at Jos and Ilorin. Although it is government-supported, the University of Ibadan has also received funds from many non-governmental contributors.

Today the University of Ibadan supports academic programs in medicine, arts, science, agriculture and forestry, the social sciences, EDUCATION, veterinary medicine, technology, law, public health, and dentistry. It also has the largest library in Nigeria.

See also: ILORIN (Vol. IV).

Further reading: Paul Beckett and James O'Connell, *Education and Power in Nigeria* (New York: Africana Publishing Co., 1978); Pierre L. van den Berghe, *Power and Privilege at an African University* (Cambridge, Mass.: Schenkman Publishing Co., 1973).

Ibrahim, Abdullah (Adolphe "Dollar" Brand) (1934–) *South African jazz pianist and composer*

Born Adolphe Brand in CAPE TOWN in 1934, Abdullah Ibrahim converted to Islam and changed his name in the late 1960s. Ibrahim grew up in an environment in which he regularly heard traditional African songs, religious MUSIC, and American jazz. Jazz soon became his vocation, and it led to his nickname, "Dollar," for the dollars he used to purchase the current jazz recordings from the sailors on American ships that put in at Cape Town's busy docks. Going by the name "Dollar" Brand, Ibrahim, along with two other future jazz greats, Hugh MASEKELA (1931–) and Kippie Moeketsi (1925–1983), formed the Jazz Epistles in 1959. The group quickly rose to prominence in the lively JOHANNESBURG jazz scene.

Although greatly influenced by his close collaboration with American jazz musicians, Ibrahim's compositions and performance remain firmly rooted in the South African popular music tradition. As he once said, he writes his music "as songs, as if meant to be sung."

In 1963, having recently married the jazz vocalist Sathima Bea Benjamin (1936–), Ibrahim began a tour of Europe with his trio, during which he met legendary American musician and composer Duke Ellington (1899–1974). Recognizing the South African's talent and skill, Ellington became Ibrahim's mentor and sponsored an American tour for the young musician. Over the next decade Ibrahim worked closely with Ellington, Thelonious Monk (1918–1982), and other American jazz musicians and continued to tour with his band. He returned to South Africa and, in 1976, recorded the all-time South African jazz hit, "Manenberg." The oppressiveness of APARTHEID led him to leave South Africa again, however, and he did not return until 1990. After that time he lived and worked in his home country as well as continuing to record and tour internationally. He also devoted extensive time to the music education of young people.

Ibrahim became a composer of feature-length film scores. His CINEMA credits include the scores for *Chocolat* (1988) and *S'en Fout La Mort* (No Fear, No Die, 1992), both by the French director Claire Denis (1948–). Ibrahim also composed the score for *Tilai*, which was directed by the BURKINA FASO filmmaker Idrissa Ouedraogo (c. 1954–) and which won the 1990 Grand Prix Award at the Cannes Film Festival.

Igbo (Ibo) People living chiefly in southeastern NIGERIA who speak Igbo, a language of the Kwa branch of the Niger-Congo family. Independence, which came in 1960,

did little to smooth the path for the country that British colonial powers had pieced together from hundreds of ethnic and religious groups and called Nigeria. The country's First Republic, led by the British-installed prime minister, Sir Abubakar Tafawa BALEWA (1912–1966), was ostensibly a federal republic. It included three large regions, a Northern Region dominated by the HAUSA-Fulani, who were primarily Muslims, a Western Region dominated by the YORUBA, and an Eastern Region that was primarily Igbo in makeup. Beyond this, there were more than 400 other ethnic groups, as well as major religious divisions between Muslims, Christians, and followers of traditional African religions. Control, however, was firmly in the hands of northerners, primarily Muslim Hausa, despite the fact that a large part of Nigeria's civil service and military personnel were either Igbo or Yoruba.

Wrangling among the three dominant ethnic groups intensified in the months following independence, with sharp conflicts between ethnic-based political groups and intense disagreements over boundaries between the nation's regions. The question of whether to establish another region, one in the middle of the country, became a topic of passionate debate. By 1966 a series of coups resulted, with power ultimately falling into the hands of General Yakubu GOWON (1934–), a Hausa from the Northern Region. Bloody ethnic violence ensued, with tens of thousands of Igbos killed and thousands more forced to leave their homes in the north. Igbo nationalism grew, and, eventually, the governor of the Eastern Region, Chukwuemeka Odumegwu Ojukwu (1933–), began calling for secession and the establishment of an Igbo state. Rejecting attempts from Gowon's government to forge a compromise, in May 1967 Ojukwu declared an Igbo-led independent state of BIAFRA. A devastating civil war ensued as the central government, which was dominated by northerners, sought to put down the breakaway Igbo state. By the time hostilities ceased as many as 100,000 Biafran soldiers and between 500,000 and 2 million civilians had perished.

The conclusion of the civil war brought an end to armed conflict but not to Nigeria's difficulties. Although the central government seemed to make attempts to peacefully reintegrate ethnic Igbo back into the nation, such efforts were not completely successful. In the 21st century the conflict between Muslims and practitioners of either Christianity or traditional religions has become particularly bitter, with the question of the establishment of the Islamic law of SHARIA being a principal issue.

See also: CHRISTIANITY, INFLUENCE OF (Vols. IV, V); ETHNICITY AND IDENTITY (Vol. I); IGBO (Vols. I, II, III, IV); ISLAM, INFLUENCE OF (Vols. IV, V).

IMF See INTERNATIONAL MONETARY FUND.

independence movements   African independence movements of the 1960s were rooted in the African nationalism and independence movements of the colonial era. For most countries the DECOLONIZATION process proceeded without interruption, so that by the end of the 1960s, only eight countries remained under European colonial rule.

Aside from SOUTH AFRICA, which gained independence with the formation of the Union of South Africa in 1910, EGYPT, which regained its independence in 1922, and ETHIOPIA, which was independent except for a short-lived Italian occupation from 1936 until 1941; the 1950s witnessed the first successes of the independence movements. Except for ALGERIA, where the NATIONAL LIBERATION FRONT was conducting a bloody war to end French rule, the remaining North African countries were independent by 1956. The next year, GHANA became independent, followed by GUINEA in 1958. The "Year of African Independence" was 1960, when 17 countries, including 13 members of the French Union, achieved their independence. Over the remainder of the decade independence movements succeeded in ending colonial rule in most of the remaining colonies—including Algeria in 1962.

It was only in the southern portion of the continent and in Portuguese West Africa that political independence movements faltered. Portugal was determined to hang onto its colonial empire in the face of liberation struggles that began in the early 1960s. In 1973 the AFRICAN PARTY FOR THE INDEPENDENCE OF GUINEA AND CAPE VERDE finally gained independence for GUINEA-BISSAU and CAPE VERDE, and two years later Portugal capitulated in ANGOLA and MOZAMBIQUE. The loss of its protected eastern border with Mozambique ultimately undercut the efforts of the government of RHODESIA to maintain white-minority rule. By 1979 the guerrilla forces spearheading the independence movement were proving too successful, and Rhodesia's government agreed to end its "rebellion" against the British crown. The next year, the country became independent with the name ZIMBABWE.

On February 3, 1960, British Prime Minister Harold Macmillan (1894–1986) addressed South Africa's Parliament. In discussing the progress of African nationalism and INDEPENDENCE MOVEMENTS to the north, he stated that "the wind of change" was blowing throughout the continent, heralding the end of colonial rule. His government was not going to stand in its path. Macmillan's comments created great resentment and apprehension among white South Africans. In 1961 South African voters opted to become a republic and the country withdrew from the British Commonwealth.

With Zimbabwe's independence, South Africa was now isolated. As long as the Cold War continued, however, it had sufficient support among conservative Western governments, particularly those of the United States and England, to continue its efforts to retain control over SOUTH WEST AFRICA (soon to become independent NAMIBIA) and persevere its own APARTHEID system. South Africa had been independent since 1910 and had its own colony in South West Africa, so, technically, organizations such as the AFRICAN NATIONAL CONGRESS and the PAN-AFRICANIST CONGRESS were not seeking independence from colonial rule. Rather, their goal was to end what amounted to domestic colonial rule. By the late 1980s a series of internal and external forces led first to Namibia's independence, in 1990, and then the 1994 election that brought Nelson MANDELA (1918–   ) to the presidency.

Mandela's election signaled the final victory of African nationalism and independence movements over the forces of European colonialism. In the meantime, however, a new type of independence movement had emerged on the continent. In some instances, political competition within independent African countries led to domestic independence movements. These were organized along both ethnic and regional lines. The two most prominent examples were those of ERITREA and the WESTERN SAHARA. In 1973 the ERITREAN PEOPLE'S LIBERATION FRONT emerged to lead the struggle, which had begun in 1961, for Eritrea's independence from Ethiopia. Twenty years later it succeeded. The independence movement for an independent Western Sahara emerged from Spain's withdrawal, in 1976, from its colony of Río de Oro and its agreement that it be partitioned between MAURITANIA and MOROCCO. The SAHARAWI population of the area supported the POLISARIO independence movement seeking an independent country. Polisario guerrillas forced Mauritania to renounce its claims in 1978, but Morocco then claimed the entire area. While the Polisario governing structure has been accorded some international recognition, Western Sahara has yet to receive full international recognition as an independent country.

See also: COLONIAL RULE (Vol. IV); ENGLAND AND AFRICA (Vols. III, IV, V); FRANCE AND AFRICA (Vols. IV, V); FRENCH UNION (Vol. IV); NATIONALISM AND INDEPENDENCE MOVEMENTS (Vol. IV); PORTUGAL AND AFRICA (Vols. IV, V); SETTLERS, EUROPEAN (Vol. IV).

industrialization   Development of manufacturing industries and associated INFRASTRUCTURE. Initially Africa's industries revolved around the urban centers that developed as a result of the MINING industry. In these cities light industries were started to meet the demands of the growing populations, which needed processed foods and manufactured products such as housewares and furniture. Toward the middle of the 20th century industries such as textile production, OIL refining, cement manufacturing, and chemical and coal production had emerged in some African countries.

After 1950 worldwide industrialization accelerated rapidly. In most African countries, however, industrialization lagged. This was partly due to colonial economic policies that created trade imbalances. Even today many African countries import more than they export, which has led to economic stagnation. In addition, DEVELOPMENT has been hampered by the lack of good roads, railroads, and electrical power grids.

Despite the overall lack of industrialization across Africa, SOUTH AFRICA, having been liberated from the shackles of APARTHEID, has managed to develop even further an already exceptionally strong industrial sector. With a gross national product of more than $427 billion, South Africa is the largest economy in Africa and the twenty-second largest economy in the world. South Africa accounts for nearly half of industrial output for the entire continent.

After independence, Africa's industrialization required an increase in the production of construction materials. In 1960 the Nigerian Cement Company, Ltd. provided the country with about 20 percent of the country's needs. © Eastern Nigeria Information Service

Services make up the biggest sector in the South African economy, but the diversified industrial sector is also vast, including mining (the world leader in platinum, GOLD, and chromium production), automobile assembly, metalworking, machinery, textiles, iron and steel, chemicals, fertilizer, and foodstuffs.

South Africa, with manufacturing and sales of 366,900 units (in 2000), has the world's 18th-largest automotive market. It accounts for less than 1 percent of the world market, however. Sales of domestically produced cars amounted to 296,000, with an additional 78,500 exported (21 percent of the total), while imports accounted for 70,400 units. The automotive industry, which contributes about 7 percent of the national GDP, employs about 250,000 people.

EGYPT, with the continent's second-largest gross domestic product at $289 billion, and ALGERIA, with the continent's third-largest gross domestic product at $173.8 billion, also have accelerated industrial development. Egypt's industrial sector, which accounts for 34 percent of the country's gross domestic product and 22 percent of its employment, is dominated by textiles, food processing, chemicals, hydrocarbons (it has growing natural gas exports), construction, cement, and metals. Algeria's industrial sector, which contributes 60 percent of the gross domestic product and employs 11 percent of the LABOR force, rests on the hydrocarbon sector (petroleum, natural gas, and petrochemicals). Indeed, hydrocarbons account for 30 percent of the gross domestic product (half of the industrial sector's total) and 95 percent of the country's EXPORTS. In addition, there are light industries, electrical manufacturing, and food processing.

Countries such as EQUATORIAL GUINEA and NIGER, on the other hand, have been very slow to develop industries. An oppressive, corrupt, and tyrannical government in Equatorial Guinea undermined that county's moderately successful cash-crop-agricultural sector, which was inherited at independence in 1968. For a number of years, sawmills and fishing were Equatorial Guinea's major industries, but recent discoveries of significant oil and natural gas reserves have already begun to expand the country's $1.27 billion gross domestic product. Niger's economy, with a gross domestic product of $8.7 billion, centers largely on subsistence AGRICULTURE, which employs 90 percent of the labor force while contributing 39 percent of the gross domestic product. Uranium mining is declining in importance due to falling world demand. Other industries in Niger include brick making, textiles, food processing, chemicals, and slaughterhouses. Altogether industry and commerce account for a paltry 6 percent of total employment.

The situation in NIGERIA is a good example of the difficulties many African countries face in the industrialization process. Significant industrialization began to take place there only during the mid-20th century, just prior to independence. Early INDUSTRIALIZATION efforts required Nigeria to import machinery, equipment, and semi-processed raw materials. As a result domestically produced raw materials were neglected, and trade deficits began to grow. Despite some advances in Nigeria's port towns and in a few northern urban centers, the situation never turned around. By the mid-1990s less than 10 percent of Nigeria's gross domestic product came from the manufacturing sector. Oil production and the extraction of MINERALS AND METALS accounted for less than 15 percent of the gross domestic product. Agriculture, on the other hand, still contributed nearly 40 percent of the gross domestic product. With three times the population of South Africa, Nigeria has an overall gross domestic product that is approximately one-third that of South Africa.

Since the 1990s the industrialization of Africa has become a high priority for the international community. For example, the United Nations named November 20 African Industrialization Day, with the aim of "promoting greater international commitment to the development of industry across the continent."

See also: DEVELOPMENT (Vol. V); INDUSTRIALIZATION (Vol. IV); MINERALS AND METALS (Vols. IV, V); MINING (Vol. IV); TRADE AND COMMERCE (Vol. V); UNITED NATIONS AND AFRICA (Vol. V); URBANIZATION (Vols. IV, V).

Further readings: Makonnen Alemayehu, *Industrializing Africa: Development Options and Challenges for the 21st Century* (Trenton, N.J.: Africa World Press, 2000); Jeffrey James, *The State, Technology and Industrialization in Africa* (New York: St. Martin's Press, 1995); Samuel M. Wangwe, ed., *Exporting Africa: Technology, Trade and Industrialization in Sub-Saharan Africa* (New York: Routledge, 1995).

infrastructure The collective aspects of a country's service systems, including WATER and sanitation, electricity, TRANSPORTATION, TELECOMMUNICATIONS, and so forth. The lack of sufficient infrastructure in Africa is considered one of the greatest roadblocks to DEVELOPMENT.

The demands of infrastructure DEVELOPMENT are interconnected. For example, improvements to water systems may increase agricultural output, but if there are no adequate roads, produce cannot make it to market. Communication between producers, buyers, and distributors in fledgling industries is thwarted by a lack of telephones. The lack of electricity limits the development of technologies that save time and increase efficiency. Continent-wide there are only 14 telephone lines per 1000 people, compared to 41 lines per 1000 people in East Asia and the Pacific, and 102 lines per 1000 people in Latin America. Less than 50 percent of the continent's people have access to safe drinking water, compared to 84 percent in East Asia and 73 percent in Latin America. Roads are scarce, and the ones that do exist are generally in poor condition. Perhaps the most distressing aspect of this lack of infrastructure is the fact that sub-Saharan Africa is the only region of the world where these problems are steadily getting worse.

The severity of the infrastructure problem in Africa has made it difficult to assess. The United Nations Global Urban Indicators Program shows that the top infrastructure priority is the water supply, followed by electricity, sewage, sanitation, and telecommunications. Despite identifying and prioritizing the challenges, however, few advances have been made to rectifying shortages, mostly because of the tremendous cost. For instance, South Africa estimates that, between 2002 and 2012, it will need $14.5 billion in infrastructure investment. But many South African municipalities lack institutional and financial capacity and don't have the economic strength to borrow funds. With a total national gross domestic product of approximately $104 billion, it seems that even sub-Saharan Africa's richest, most economically diverse, and most globally connected country faces an insurmountable challenge.

Africa's underdeveloped infrastructure suffers from uneven distribution among countries. Take, for example, the availability of telephones. In SOUTH AFRICA more than 5 million telephone lines result in a ratio of about 1 per every 8 people. The ratio in EGYPT is about 1 to 22. In MALAWI, on the other hand, the ratio is closer to 1 to 289, and in NIGER, the ratio is about 1 to 550. In recent years improvements in cell phone technology have augmented the existing systems. However, this growth, too, occurs disproportionately in those countries with the strongest existing telephone systems.

With limited resources, African countries have begun to shift their view of infrastructure development. Whereas this was once considered a government mandate, today it is thought that communities and the private sector also share equal responsibility. The WORLD BANK has been instrumental in helping countries find private companies to work with public water companies. For instance, JIRAMA, the state water and electricity company of MADAGASCAR, is responsible for providing services to municipal users throughout the country. In 2002 JIRAMA began looking to establish public-private partnerships that would allow for greater private investment in its services. The World Bank helped design the plan and vet potential suitors. Through this process the Malagasy government, like the governments of South Africa, KENYA, and UGANDA, has placed more responsibility on municipal-level governance.

While the processes of privatization and decentralization are common themes throughout the continent, they face the challenge of public perception. They do bring increased funding, but many people hold a negative perception of the private sector, and they find it objectionable to have private corporations responsible for public services.

Other international organizations besides the World Bank have worked to find a private solution to this public problem. A group called the Private Infrastructure Development Group, made up of British, Swedish, Dutch, and Swiss development agencies, has invested more than $300 million in private corporate funds to assist in African infrastructure development. Similarly, the International Finance Corporation set up a $500 million fund to pool private interest and equity.

While it remains to be seen whether or not private funding will lead to improved access to water, electricity, transportation, and sewage, it has already shown signs of success in telecommunications. In BOTSWANA, for example, the private consumer-driven telecom sector is one of the most successful in Africa. There are only 82 telephones per 1000 people, but there are 170 cellular phones per 1000 people. Also, there are 11 Internet service providers and 21 Internet users per 1000 people. These figures are higher than those of any other sub-Saharan country outside of South Africa. Other countries developing telecommunications systems with help from private international companies include GHANA, NIGERIA, ANGOLA, and ZIMBABWE.

See also: ECONOMIC ASSISTANCE (Vol. V); STATE, ROLE OF (Vol. V).

Further reading: Augustin Fosu, Mwangi Kimenyi, and Njuguna Ndung'u, *Economic Reforms and Restructuring in Sub-Saharan Africa: the Financial Sector and Regulation/Deregulation of Infrastructure* (Oxford, U.K.: Oxford University Press, 2003).

Inkatha Freedom Party (IFP) Political party in SOUTH AFRICA that claims a large following among the ZULU. The Inkatha Freedom Party (IFP) was created in 1990 by Mangosuthu Gatsha BUTHELEZI (1928–), the prominent Zulu politician. Buthelezi had founded the IFP's precursor, Inkatha, in 1975. That organization drew upon a Zulu cultural movement—also named Inkatha—that was established by Buthelezi's grandfather in 1924. From 1975 to 1990 Buthelezi's original Inkatha organization functioned as both a cultural and a political organization, dedicated to mobilizing the Zulu populations residing in KwaZulu-Natal Province and the greater JOHANNESBURG area.

In general, both Inkatha and the IFP operated as vehicles for Buthelezi's political goals. Inkatha membership has always been overwhelmingly made up of Zulu, although technically it is open to South Africans of other ethnic backgrounds. In the struggle to end APARTHEID, Inkatha often stood apart from other important opposition groups on account of its exclusionist appeal to Zulu ethnic pride. It was also different in that its leaders were more willing to discuss power-sharing agreements with and failed to support economic sanctions against South Africa's white-minority government.

The IFP's breach with the UNITED DEMOCRATIC FRONT and the AFRICAN NATIONAL CONGRESS (ANC) significantly widened during the late 1980s and early 1990s. Violence between ANC supporters and IFP members often translated into conflict between Zulus and Africans of other ethnicities, or sometimes between rural Zulu migrant workers and more permanently urbanized non-Zulus. This resulted in thousands of deaths and threatened a peaceful transition to a non-racial, democratic rule.

Revelations came to light in the early 1990s that the apartheid state had provided financial assistance and training to the IFP in order to strengthen it, and, in the process, destabilize the black opposition front. Even so, President F. W. DE KLERK (1936–) and Nelson MANDELA (1918–) offered important concessions to the IFP in order to encourage its participation in the process that culminated in a transfer of power and South Africa's first free election, in 1994. The IFP was registered just a week before the elections and went on to win approximately 10 percent of the general vote, in addition to winning control of the KwaZulu-Natal provincial government. After 1994 the IFP continued to play an important role in South African politics, although it has been limited by its inability to attract non-Zulu supporters.

See also: ETHNICITY AND IDENTITY (Vol. I); POLITICAL PARTIES AND ORGANIZATIONS (Vol. IV, V).

International Monetary Fund (IMF) The International Monetary Fund is a private lending corporation, located in Washington, D.C., that is charged with promoting economic growth through economic liberalization. Created in 1945 to "help promote the health of the world economy," the International Monetary Fund, known informally as the IMF, has been a major lender to

African countries. The concern of the 45 initiating states was to avoid the sort of global depression that had taken place during the 1930s. Today the 184 member countries of the IMF empower it to "promote international monetary cooperation, exchange stability, and orderly exchange arrangements; to foster economic growth and high levels of employment; and to provide temporary financial assistance to countries to help ease balance of payments adjustment."

At its inception the IMF, along with its sister organization, the WORLD BANK, were specialized units within the United Nations. However, the highly disparate voting systems have made them functionally separate institutions. Except the UN Security Council, the United Nations maintains a "one country, one vote" system. In contrast, the IMF and the World Bank have a weighted voting system in which the more money a country puts in, the heavier the vote. This amounts to a system that means essentially "one dollar, one vote." The contribution to the IMF and World Bank is directly proportionate to the gross domestic product (GDP) of the country, that is the total value of goods and services produced in a year. Thus while the system generally used by the United Nations empowers poor countries by awarding them equal status, the IMF and World Bank systems empower wealthy countries.

Of the $45 billion in IMF lending in 2003, only $1.1 billion (2.6 percent) went to Africa. With a continental GDP of $319 billion, this figure alone is not of great influence. However, the IMF serves as an approving agency to certify that a country is on a viable economic path. Without IMF approval a country will not receive its share of the World Bank's $334 billion (2003) in lending. More important, many MULTINATIONAL CORPORATIONS follow the IMF guidelines, and thus FOREIGN INVESTMENT is contingent on government compliance. The IMF therefore has tremendous influence over the economies of African countries. Some scholars even argue that since Western countries control the IMF, Western countries effectively dominate economic policymaking in African countries. This is particularly true of the United States, which holds approximately 20 percent of the vote in the IMF. Under IMF voting rules, certain special decisions require approval by a "supermajority" of 85 percent. As a result, the United States can effectively veto a number of decisions.

The most apparent national economic policy shifts in Africa that came as a result of IMF (and World Bank) action have been STRUCTURAL ADJUSTMENT programs (SAPs). These were formed during the early 1980s in response to World Bank calls for improved national macro-policies. Ultimately, SAPs became a series of conditional demands placed on loans by the IMF and the World Bank. The demands were for structural changes in national economies, changes that would encourage the removal of government controls on economic structures. They also encouraged the reduction of government spending on social services, and

the expansion of the private sector. Along with these changes came currency devaluation, public-sector job reduction, more open MARKETS, greater financial disclosure, and reduced import tariffs. There also was a focus on building EXPORTS.

Although structural adjustment programs were tremendously unpopular in African countries, they were almost universally adopted. While perhaps mandated for the best of reasons, SAPs have largely resulted in increased POVERTY without economic expansion. Over the past decade there have been significant reforms in policies governing lending by the IMF. However, the basic liberal economic tenets remain in place, largely unpopular in much of Africa, and under great controversy.

See also: DEBT, FOREIGN (Vol. V); DEVELOPMENT (Vol. V); ECONOMIC ASSISTANCE (Vol. V); HIV/AIDS IN AFRICA (Vol. V).

international organizations   See AFRICAN UNION (Vol. V); CASABLANCA GROUP (Vol. V); CENTRAL AFRICAN CUSTOMS AND ECONOMIC UNION (Vol. V); EAST AFRICAN COMMUNITY (Vol. V); ECONOMIC COMMUNITY OF WEST AFRICAN STATES (Vol. V); FRONTLINE STATES (Vol. V); INTERNATIONAL MONETARY FUND (Vol. V); LOME CONVENTION (Vol. V); MONROVIA GROUP (Vol. V); NEW PARTNERSHIP FOR AFRICA'S DEVELOPMENT (Vol. V); NONALIGNED MOVEMENT AND AFRICA (Vol. V); ORGANIZATION OF AFRICAN UNITY (Vol. V); ORGANIZATION OF PETROLEUM EXPORTING COUNTRIES (Vol. V); SENEGAMBIA CONFEDERATION (Vol. V); SOUTHERN AFRICA DEVELOPMENT COMMUNITY (Vol. V); UNITED NATIONS AND AFRICA (Vols. IV, V).

Internet and Africa   See TELECOMMUNICATIONS.

Isaias Afewerki (1945–   ) *President of Eritrea*

The second of seven children, Isaias Afewerki was born in 1945, when ERITREA was semi-independent and under the oversight of the United Nations. In 1952, however, ETHIOPIA annexed Eritrea. Eritrean resistance eventually turned into armed rebellion when, in 1962, Ethiopian Emperor HAILE SELASSIE (1892–1975) tried to integrate Eritrea into Ethiopia.

After almost a decade of conflict, a new, more radical rebel group, the ERITREAN PEOPLE'S LIBERATION FRONT (EPLF), split off from the long-standing Eritrean Liberation Front (ELF). Isaias joined the EPLF in the early 1970s, and, after training in military tactics for a time in communist China, he returned to Eritrea as an EPLF division commander. Battling the Ethiopians and, at the same time, competing against the rival ELP, Isaias steadily rose in the EPLF hierarchy. When the ELF and EPLF merged into a single force, in 1977, he became the de facto rebel leader. Isaias eventually was elected secretary general of the EPLF, in 1987.

The Eritrean rebellion began when Ethiopia was still ruled by its long-term emperor, Haile Selassie. In 1974, however, Haile Selassie was overthrown by MENGISTU HAILE MARIAM (1937–   ), who set up a Marxist government. Despite the change in leadership and ideology Ethiopia continued its attempts to hold on to Eritrea by military force.

Eritrea finally gained its independence from Ethiopia in April 1993. The EPLF leadership transformed into the National Assembly of the new transitional government, with Isaias as the nation's president. Since then, he has consolidated his power and ensured his continuation in office by assuming the roles of chief of state, head of government, head of the state council, and head of the National Assembly. His strong leadership style has been seen as both a boon and a burden as Eritrea warred, once again, with Ethiopia (1998–2000) and continued to battle both severe POVERTY and mounting economic crises.

Adding to Isaias's difficulties is his attempt to build ties with Israel. In the forefront of African leaders seeking to accomplish this, he has received personal medical attention in Israel while also allowing Israel to establish a military and intelligence base in Eritrea. This has led to increasing diplomatic tension with the states of the Persian Gulf and the Palestinian Authority as well as with the domestic Eritrean Islamic Jihad.

See also: INDEPENDENCE MOVEMENTS (Vol. V); NATIONALISM AND INDEPENDENCE MOVEMENTS (Vol. V); UNITED NATIONS AND AFRICA (Vols. IV, V).

Islam, influence of   The history of Islam in Africa since independence is a continuation of the spread of Islam to all corners of the continent. In the 21st century Islamic communities are now found in virtually all of Africa, from the Muslim-dominated north—in countries such as EGYPT, LIBYA, MOROCCO, and ALGERIA—to nations in central and southern Africa, where there are significant Muslim communities everywhere from MALAWI, ZIMBABWE, and BOTSWANA to SOUTH AFRICA, TANZANIA, and ZAMBIA.

In Africa Muslims are particularly noticeable in business and trade, and Muslim traders and businesspeople have become influential in shaping the modern African economy. Today Muslims run many businesses, especially in West Africa, where African Muslim businesspeople have a dominant role in the retail trade in European manufactured goods. Muslims also have an important role in both local and interstate TRANSPORTATION in West Africa, especially in SENEGAL, GUINEA, SIERRA LEONE, LIBERIA, The GAMBIA, and MALI. In western and central Africa, Muslims are particularly active in the diamond trade.

This economic power has led to political influence, especially in countries such as Sierra Leone, Guinea, and Liberia, where Muslim businesspeople make large-scale contributions to political causes. These efforts have given Muslims significant roles in politics, leading to the rise of Ahmad Tejan KABBAH (1932–   ), in Sierra Leone, and Lansana CONTÉ (1934–   ), in Guinea.

Apart from North Africa, where there is a clear Muslim majority, independence came to most African countries under the leadership of non-Muslims. Indeed, the new independent nations of Africa were modeled primarily on the western European concept of the state. Since, in Western views, most African Muslims were less educated than other citizens, this left them less intimately involved with politics and national affairs. In addition, during the colonial era most of the African colonial bureaucrats received a Christian mission-school EDUCATION. This reinforced the relative political estrangement of Muslims from political leadership during the end of the colonial era and the dawn of independence. Only a handful of Muslim political leaders succeeded in gaining independence for their countries, most notably Sir Abubakar Tafawa BALEWA (1912–1966), a Muslim from the north who led Nigeria to independence in 1960, and Ahmed Sékou TOURÉ (1922–1984), who led French Guinea to independence, in 1958. In The Gambia, Sir Dawda Kairaba JAWARA (1924–   ), also a Muslim, led the country to independence, and Ahmadou AHIDJO (1924–1989) led Cameroon to independence, in 1960.

In general religion did not prove central to the political agendas of newly independent African countries. Instead, economic DEVELOPMENT and political stability were of paramount importance. This was true in countries with Muslim leaders as well as those led by non-Muslims.

Regardless of whether the leaders of African nations are Muslim or not, relations between Muslim Arab leaders and African leaders have, on the whole, been cordial. Beyond this African Muslim leaders have enjoyed particularly good relations with Arab countries and heads of state, and African nations with Muslim leaders have particularly benefited from ECONOMIC ASSISTANCE coming from Arab countries. Saudi Arabia and Kuwait in particular have helped build central mosques and schools in many African capitals. African countries also have had medical facilities renovated, such as Donka Hospital in CONAKRY, Guinea. Similar aid has been given in the economic sphere. Indeed the Islamic Bank was established in the 1960s to help finance development projects in African Muslim states. In addition, many Muslim African

Since independence, Islam has continued to gain converts throughout Africa. Prayer lines, like this one shown outside a mosque at Jenne, Mali, in the 1960s, became an increasingly common sight throughout West Africa. © *AP/Wide World Photos*

states have become members of the Organization of Islamic Countries (OIC) over the last decade.

Over the past 20 years the number of Muslim heads of state in Africa has increased. This has been a cause for concern among many non-Muslim citizens of these states, especially in light of the rise of Islamic fundamentalism in various parts of the world. To these non-Muslims, the potential for religious radicalism—such as has been seen recently in Nigeria and other areas—is real and dangerous.

For the most part, however, these fears have not been realized, and civil conflict has not been the result of conflict between Muslims and non-Muslims. Indeed today, as in the past, most of the civil unrest in Africa is the result of economic, political, and social problems rather than religious ones.

Further reading: Mervyn Hiskett, *The Course of Islam in Africa* (Edinburgh, U.K.: University of Edinburgh Press, 1994); Nehemia Levtzion and Randall L. Pouwels, eds., *The History of Islam in Africa* (Athens, Ohio: Ohio University Press, 2000); Lamin Sanneh, *The Crown and the Turban: Muslims and West African Pluralism* (Boulder, Colo.: Westview Press, 1997).

Ivorian People's Front (Front Populaire Ivorien, FPI)

Party of IVORY COAST president Laurent GBAGBO (1945–) and the ruling political party in that country since 2001. Gbagbo and his associates founded the Ivorian People's Front in 1982 as a clandestine political organization. The group pushed to reform the one-party government of former president Félix HOUPHOUËT-BOIGNY (1905–1993), who had led Ivory Coast since independence in 1960. In 1988 the FPI was reorganized as a legitimate political party.

In 1990 popular sentiment forced Houphouët-Boigny to allow other political parties. In April of that year, the democratic-socialist FPI gained official recognition as a political party. It called for multiparty elections and the replacement of the aging president. Nonetheless, Houphouët-Boigny was elected to his seventh consecutive five-year term.

Houphouët-Boigny died in 1993, whereupon his hand-picked successor, Henri Konan Bédié (1934–), became Ivory Coast's second president. He immediately restricted the activities of the FPI. Bédié was reelected to a second term in 1995, although the election was boycotted by all the major parties, including the FPI.

In 1999 General Robert GUÉÏ (1941–2002) led a successful military COUP D'ETAT against Bédié's government. The FPI and other key political parties refused to join Guéï's transitional government, and clashes with government forces ensued.

When Gbagbo won the presidential election of October 2000, the Guéï government suspended the elections. However, after a period of popular protests Guéï fled the country, and Gbagbo was declared the winner. Subsequently, in the January 2001 legislative elections, the FPI won a majority of seats. Although the party secured its hold on power, ongoing popular rebellion left that hold increasingly tenuous.

Ivory Coast (Côte d'Ivoire)

West African country approximately 124,500 square miles (322,400 sq km) in size that is bordered to the north by MALI and BURKINA FASO, to the east by GHANA, to the south by the Gulf of Guinea, and to the west by LIBERIA and GUINEA. In 1983 the capital, which had been ABIDJAN, was moved to YAMOUSSOUKRO.

Ivory Coast at Independence The Ivory Coast gained its independence from France on August 7, 1960, under the direction of Félix HOUPHOUËT-BOIGNY (1905–1993). As the leader of the victorious Democratic Party of

the Ivory Coast, Houphouët-Boigny became president, a position he held until his death more than 30 years later. His years in office were marked by regimented, political stability and reasonable prosperity based on the cultivation of CASH CROPS.

Ivory Coast began offshore OIL drilling in the early 1980s, but this yielded very few profits. The government also pushed to mine diamonds, GOLD, and iron in order to steer the nation away from economic dependence on the exportation of cocoa and coffee. This, too, met with little success.

In 1981 Ivory Coast adopted STRUCTURAL ADJUSTMENT reforms recommended by the WORLD BANK and the INTERNATIONAL MONETARY FUND. Over the ensuing decades the country came to be considered a structural adjustment success story, yielding budget surpluses and real economic growth.

Ivory Coast after Houphouët-Boigny Upon Houphouët-Boigny's death, Henri Konan Bédié (1934–) assumed the presidency, then won the presidential election held in 1995. He adopted a policy of "regulated openness" in which opposition was allowed, but Bédié's power was never seriously threatened.

In 1998 Bédié increased the powers of the presidency. He also initiated new requirements for Ivorian citizenship that stipulated only Ivorians born in Ivory Coast of parents born in Ivory Coast proper could be citizens. This definition limited the number of people who could claim citizenship and aspire to political leadership. This new law also eliminated many Ivorians and their children from leadership, since as many as 40 percent of the country's people were born outside of Ivory Coast. Alassane Dramane Ouattara (1942–), an economist and former prime minister under Houphouët-Boigny, was one popular figure whose political future was affected by the new law. Despite his claims to the contrary, Ouattara was declared unable to run for office because, his opponents claimed, his mother was born in Burkina Faso.

In 1999 Ouattara assumed the leadership of the political party, Rally of the Republic. Fearful of the strengthening opposition, Bédié arrested thousands of its leaders. Later in 1999, Ivory Coast witnessed its first COUP D'ÉTAT, as General Robert GUÉÏ (1941–2002) overthrew President Bédié. General Guéï suspended the constitution and called for a constitutional convention to be held in July 2000. New elections were to follow later that year. Once again, however, Ouattara was denied a run for office, this time by the Supreme Court. Many Ivorians protested Ouattara's exclusion from elections, and riots erupted as the opposition showed their displeasure with the newly elected president, Laurent GBAGBO (1945–   ). In protest, the opposition boycotted the ensuing parliamentary elections. As a result Gbagbo's Ivorian Popular Front gained control of Ivory Coast's legislature.

Ethnic Tensions and Civil War At the beginning of the 21st century riots remained a common occurrence within Ivory Coast. The violence gradually took on a religious spin. Believing that Ouattara had been excluded from the elections because he was a Muslim from the north, Ouattara supporters began targeting Christian buildings. Hoping to alleviate the roiling ethnic tensions, Gbagbo and Ouattara issued joint broadcasts on national television and radio appealing for calm.

In 2002 Muslims within the military struck out against Christians in the central area of Baouké. By the end of 2002 Ivory Coast was fully enveloped in civil war, with rebels controlling the north and the government the south. Guéï died in the violence. Beyond the loss of life and political instability it caused, the war also accelerated the economic downturn that undermined the country's once-strong economy. Finally, in January 2003, the warring sides reached a peace accord.

Though the conflict was officially over, fighting likely would have continued without the presence of French military forces. In early 2004 peace within Ivory Coast remained tenuous, as the country prepared for the presidential election scheduled in 2005.

See also: AMNESTY INTERNATIONAL AND AFRICA (Vol. V); ETHNIC CONFLICTS IN AFRICA (Vol. V); ETHNIC GROUP (Vol. I); FRANCE AND AFRICA (Vols. IV, V); IVORY COAST (Vols. I, II, III, IV).

Further reading: John Rapley, *Ivoirien Capitalism: African Entrepreneurs in Côte d'Ivoire* (Boulder, Colo.: L. Rienner Publishers, 1993); I. William Zartman and Christopher Delgado, eds., *The Political Economy of Ivory Coast* (New York: Praeger, 1984).

J

Jama Ali Jama (dates unknown) *Rebel leader from Puntland state, in Somalia*

A military leader turned political figure, Jama Ali Jama spent 13 years in solitary confinement as a result of his vocal criticism of Mohammed Siad BARRE (1910–1995), the former president of SOMALIA. When he was released, in 1990, Jama became a self-styled dissident and worked to oust Barre. In the aftermath of Barre's fall in 1991, Somalia's centralized government crumbled. Jama rose as a spokesperson for the independence-minded Somalis living in the country's northeastern region, the area which would become the Puntland state. Simultaneously, other factions were seeking to establish independence for the neighboring area of Somaliland, which prior to the creation of Somalia in 1960 had been a British colonial protectorate.

In 1998, when clan leaders formed an independent Puntland government, Jama's rival, ABDULLAHI YUSSUF AHMED, emerged as president. Jama's influence grew with the support of the militant Al-Ittihad Al-Islami, and, later, his breakaway group, the Total Liberation Tigers. When Yussuf's mandate was up, in 2001, the clan elders elected Jama president—a ruling that Yussuf rejected, claiming to have another three years to rule. In November 2001 clan leaders met and refuted Yussuf's claim, swearing-in Jama.

Jama's rise to power touched off more than a year of heavy fighting between Jama's "government forces" and Yussuf's rebels. Jama accused Yussuf of sabotaging independence efforts by establishing strong ties with ETHIOPIA. Yussuf, in turn, accused Jama of having ties to radical Islamic organizations, including Al-Ittihad Al-Islam, which the U.S. government placed on its terrorist list. Despite receiving arms shipments from both LIBYA and the Somali government, Jama was deposed in 2002. The crisis of independence in Puntland state is ongoing.

Jammeh, Yahya A. J. J. (1965–) *President of The Gambia*

Born in Kanilai Village, The GAMBIA, Jammeh finished high school and, in 1984, joined the Gambia National Gendarmerie, the nation's police force. He transferred to the National Army and, in 1989, was commissioned an officer. In 1993 he was stationed in the United States and was trained as a military police officer at Fort McClellen in Alabama. The following year he returned to The Gambia.

On July 22, 1994, the Armed Forces Provisional Ruling Council (AFPRC) carried out a bloodless COUP D'ÉTAT, seizing power from The Gambia's five-term president, Dawda Kairaba JAWARA (1924–). Shortly thereafter, the AFPRC named its chairman, Captain Jammeh, president of The Gambia.

Jammeh, 29 years old in 1994, was little known in The Gambia or abroad. His leadership was immediately put to the test when a bloody coup attempt four months later nearly unseated him. In the months that followed, military leaders, civil servants, journalists, and even cabinet members were arrested and imprisoned until Jammeh consolidated his power. Internationally, the United States, Britain, and other major Western powers refused to recognize Jammeh's government.

In 1996 Jammeh resigned from the military and conducted multiparty elections. He claimed victory, although the opposition leader, Ousainou Darboe (c. 1950–) of the United Democratic Party, was widely thought to have received more votes. The years that followed were marked with accusations of CORRUPTION and heavy-handed rule, culminating, in 2000, with the slaying of 14 protesters, mostly students.

In October 2001 Jammeh won reelection, having banned all Dawda-era politicians from running. He has publicly supported rule by *SHARIA* (Islamic law) in The Gambia, and it is believed by some that his political thinking is strongly influenced by Libya's president Muammar QADDAFI (1942–   ).

Jawara, Dauda Kairaba (Sir David Jawara)
(1924–   ) *Leading political figure in The Gambia from 1962 to 1994*

Born in Barjaly, on Macarthy Island, Jawara attended a Methodist boys' school before studying to become a veterinarian. After earning a veterinary degree in Scotland, he returned to Gambia and took a government post as a veterinary officer. In 1959 he joined the People's Progressive Party (PPP), a multiethnic nationalist movement, and was elected to Parliament. In 1960 he was appointed Gam-

bia's minister of EDUCATION, serving in that capacity until 1961. The following year the PPP won elections, and Jawara became the colony's prime minister. The Gambia achieved its independence from Britain in 1965, although it remained a member state of the British Commonwealth. With independence Jawara became the leader of the smallest independent African state. In 1965 Jawara, who had converted to Christianity in 1955, converted back to Islam.

In 1970 Gambia formally adopted a new constitution and became a fully independent republic, now named *The* Gambia. Jawara served as its first president. He proved to be popular, leading the PPP to victory four times between 1972 and 1987. However, throughout his presidency he struggled to diversify the Gambian economy, which continued to rely too heavily on the export of groundnuts (peanuts). In the 1980s, as unemployment rose and the economy continued to falter, he had to quell political dissent.

Jawara's greatest threat came in 1981 when Islamic radicals led by Kukoi Samba Sanyang attempted a COUP D'ÉTAT. Jawara was able to survive the coup with the sup-

Seen here in an undated photo, Sir Dauda Jawara (left, standing) traveled throughout the countryside to appeal to local leaders during an electoral campaign in The Gambia. © *United Nations*

port of troops sent by President Abdou DIOUF (1935–   ) of SENEGAL. The following year the two presidents forged the SENEGAMBIA CONFEDERATION, which aimed for mutual protection and economic cooperation between the two nations. By 1989, however, the confederation had become a political nuisance and it was dissolved.

In 1994 Jawara was deposed in a bloodless military coup led by a young lieutenant, Yahya A. J. J. JAMMEH (1965–   ). Although Jammeh exiled him to Senegal after the coup in 2002, Jawara was allowed to return to The GAMBIA as a private citizen.

See also: ENGLAND AND AFRICA (Vols. III, IV, V); SENEGAMBIA REGION (Vol. IV).

Further reading: Andrew Burke and David Else, *The Gambia & Senegal* (Oakland, Calif.: Lonely Planet Publications, 2002); Andy Gravette, *The Gambia* (Derbyshire, U.K.: Landmark Publishing Ltd., 1999).

Joachim, Paulin (1931–   ) *Poet from Benin*

Born in Cotonou, DAHOMEY (modern-day Republic of BENIN), Joachim studied in Dahomey and GABON and later attended law school in Lyon, France. His EDUCATION was put on hold for a time because of financial difficulties, but he ultimately was able to earn a degree in journalism in Paris. During his hiatus from school Joachim found employment as secretary to the surrealist French poet Phillipe Soupault (1897–1990), who would become Joachim's mentor.

Joachim's education led him, in 1960, to positions as political editor of *France Noir*, editor-in-chief of *Bingo*, and, in 1971, as manager of *Décennie 2*, an illustrated journal that focused on Africa. Before he turned 40, Joachim published two volumes of poetry, *Un nègre raconte* (1954) and *Anti-grâce* (1967). However, it was his essays and poems in the journal PRÉSENCE AFRICAINE that gained him the greatest attention in French-speaking African and African-diaspora literary circles.

While Soupault left a clear impression, Joachim's work was also influenced by other African literary figures such as Léopold SENGHOR (1906–2001) and particularly David Diop (1927–1960), to whom Joachim wrote a poetic homage. However, Joachim diverged from the rebellious tone of his contemporaries and tapped instead into the emotional core of poetry, using the human soul as his subject and a romantic sensibility as his vehicle of exploration.

See also: FRANCE AND AFRICA (Vols. IV, V); LITERATURE IN MODERN AFRICA (Vol. V); *PRÉSENCE AFRICAINE* (Vol. IV).

Johannesburg Major city and the financial and commercial center of SOUTH AFRICA. The city of Johannesburg—called "Jo'burg" by many locals and known as *eGoli*

(the place of gold) among Africans for its history of GOLD mining—quickly emerged as one of the continent's principal cities. While today only two out of the 14 original gold mines are still in production, the city's role as a major financial and industrial center has continued to provide a strong economic base for its population. Johannesburg boasts its own stock exchange, and many leading businesses and organizations have their principal or regional headquarters there.

As a result of its importance, Johannesburg includes of the country's principal international airport, an extensive and well-maintained road network that includes a freeway system, highways and rail connections to areas throughout the country, and modern shops, restaurants, galleries, and museums. It is also home to the University of the Witwatersrand, South Africa's leading university, and to several other educational institutions and research institutes.

Johannesburg's history has been marred by racial segregation from its origins during the mining era of the late 19th century. Racial strife intensified during the APARTHEID era (1948–94), leaving Johannesburg a city of contrasts, with sprawling shantytowns and abject POVERTY alongside towering skyscrapers and the bustle of international business. The city's northern suburbs have long been enclaves of white privilege and wealth, and, with the end of apartheid, many of the core city's white residents and businesses moved to this area. While segregation is no longer legally enforced, Johannesburg is still a city significantly divided along racial lines. For example, the 1,240,000 people living in SOWETO, a conglomerate of townships from the apartheid era, are almost all black Africans. Despite the relative wealth of both the city and Gauteng Province, in which it is located, poverty and crime constitute significant social issues.

Gauteng Province—which contains both Johannesburg, the provincial capital, and PRETORIA, the national administrative capital—is both the smallest and the richest of South Africa's nine provinces. Nearly all of its population is urban, and it accounts for almost 40 percent of the country's gross domestic product (GDP). Given the size of the South African economy, this means that Gauteng Province generates 20 percent of the GDP for the continent as a whole.

With a steady influx of South Africans to Johannesburg, it is difficult to determine accurately its population. The official count for the entire metropolitan area, which includes Soweto, is approximately 4.9 million, but some observers think this figure is low. The Johannesburg area ranks behind CAIRO and LAGOS as Africa's third-largest urban agglomeration, and its growth trajectory is likely to place it among the world's 10 largest cities by 2010. Covering an area of 965 square miles (2,500 sq km), Johannesburg is the world's largest inland city. With its wealth, geographic area, and population, it is one of the world's most significant urban centers.

See also: JOHANNESBURG (Vol. IV); URBAN LIFE AND CULTURE (Vols. IV, V); URBANIZATION (Vols. IV, V).

Further reading: Nigel Mandy, *A City Divided: Johannesburg and Soweto* (New York: St. Martin's Press, 1984).

Jonathan, Leabua   (1914–1987) *First prime minister of Lesotho*

Founder of the Basutoland National Party, Jonathan worked to secure the independence of Basutoland, then a crown colony of Britain, while also keeping the small country out of the Union of South Africa. Seeing the obvious importance of SOUTH AFRICA to his country and its economy (Basutoland lay entirely within South African borders), Jonathan also tried to normalize relations with the South Africans despite their government's policy of APARTHEID. In 1962 he helped write a new constitution for Basutoland, and in 1965 Basutoland held the first elections under the new constitution. Though Jonathan was not elected, the BNP claimed the majority. Through political sleight-of-hand, Jonathan once again secured a legislative seat and stepped into the positions of prime minister and minister of external affairs. When Basutoland became the independent Kingdom of LESOTHO, in 1966, Jonathan assumed the role of the country's first prime minister.

Jonathan's term as prime minister was shaky at best. In 1970, facing a possible electoral loss, Jonathan immediately acted to protect his power, suspending the constitution and declaring a national state of emergency. He had opposition members arrested and sent the king, Mshweshwe II (1938–1996), into exile. Riots broke out, resulting in more than 150 deaths. Order was restored when Jonathan assembled a national coalition to write a new constitution, a process that Jonathan made sure involved little input from the opposition.

The outcry against Jonathan rose again when, in 1982, he permitted the opening of embassies by the Communist states of the Soviet Union, China, and North Korea. Moreover, in 1986 Jonathan's policy of maintaining good relations with both South Africa and its opposition collapsed. The South African government accused Lesotho of harboring rebel guerrillas of the AFRICAN NATIONAL CONGRESS (ANC) and imposed an economic embargo. Two weeks later Jonathan's government was ousted in a COUP D'ETAT. Jonathan died a year later, while under house arrest.

See also: BASUTOLAND (Vol. IV); ENGLAND AND AFRICA (Vol. III, IV, V); JONATHAN, CHIEF JOSEPH LEABUA (Vol. IV); UNION OF SOUTH AFRICA (Vol. IV).

Jugnauth, Anerood (Sir)   (1930–   ) *Political leader in Mauritius*

Born to a family of modest means, Jugnauth was educated at the Palma Church of England School before studying at Lincoln's Inn in England and becoming a barrister, or lawyer. After returning to MAURITIUS, Jugnauth began his career as a teacher, in 1948, but became a civil servant a year later. Jugnauth was a Hindu in a country where ETHNICITY AND IDENTITY played a large role in politics, with Hindus having an advantage. He entered Parliament in 1963, when Mauritius was still a British colony. From 1967 to 1969, the period during which Mauritius attained self-government, Jugnauth was a district magistrate. He later held positions in the national cabinet, including minister of labor and minister of state development for Prime Minister Sir Seewoosagur Ramgoolam (1900–1985), and was named senior crown counsel in 1971.

Following civil unrest, Jugnauth resigned from his office and joined the Militant Movement of Mauritius (MMM). Heading the MMM, Jugnauth became Mauritius's prime minister, in 1982, but the following year he broke with the MMM to head the Militant Socialist Movement (MSM). Joining with two other parties, Jugnauth created the Alliance Party, which won a majority of parliamentary seats in the 1983 elections, allowing him to remain prime minister.

Jugnauth presided over Mauritius's economic expansion in the early 1990s, and he was instrumental in the country's becoming a fully independent republic in 1992. His party lost the 1995 elections to one-time MMM members Navin Ramgoolam (1947–   ), a Hindu, and Paul Berenger (1945–   ), a Creole. In 2000, however, the MSM swept back into power. Jugnauth returned as prime minister, although in 2003 he relinquished the prime ministership and became president. Jugnauth, a married father of two, was knighted in 1988.

Jumbe, Shiekh Aboud (Abou Jumbe)   (1920–   ) *Former president of Zanzibar*

During the early 1960s Aboud Jumbe was active within the AFRO-SHIRAZI PARTY (ASP), the ruling party in his native ZANZIBAR. In 1965 Julius NYERERE (1922–1999) of Tanganyika led the drive to unite Zanzibar, nearby Pemba Island, and mainland Tanganyika to form TANZANIA. Under the unification agreement, Zanzibar retained most of its autonomy and President Abeid Amani KARUME (1905–1972), the ASP leader, continued to run the island's government. In April 1972, however, Karume was assassinated, and Jumbe assumed leadership of the ASP, thereby becoming Zanzibar's new president. As the Zanzibari president, he also became vice president of Tanzania, under Nyerere. Jumbe encouraged close relations with the mainland.

In 1977 Jumbe approved of the merger of the ASP with Tanganyika's ruling party, the Tanganyika Africa National Union (TANU), to create the new PARTY OF THE REVOLUTION (Chama Cha Mapinduzi, CCM). Led by Nyerere, the CCM came under criticism from its Zanzibari members for favoring mainland Tanzania over Zanzibar. Jumbe continued to support Nyerere, however, thinking that his loyalty would result in his being chosen Nyerere's successor as president of the United Republic of Tanzania.

However, when Nyerere began favoring a mainlander for the position, Jumbe changed his position regarding the union government, taking a stance that encouraged Zanzibari nationalism. The union stayed together, but Jumbe distanced his government from Nyerere's by paving the way for the first post-revolution Constitution of Zanzibar, which became law in 1979. Five years later

Zanzibar adopted yet another constitution, this one with provisions for the creation of both a bill of rights and a house of representatives. As these changes took effect, however, anti-union sentiment in Zanzibar led to Jumbe's resignation and to a reshuffling of the government. Ali Hassan MWINYI (1925–) became Zanzibar's next president and, the following year, he succeeded Nyerere as president of the Tanzanian union.

Jumbe remained in the spotlight as a writer and defender of Zanzibar's sovereignty. A devout Muslim, he decried the marginalization of Tanzania's Muslims in a series of controversial articles printed in *Mwananchi,* a weekly newspaper. He also published *The Partnership* (1994), a book in which he accused mainland Christians of dominating Zanzibar's underprivileged Muslims. In his writing, which provoked strong reaction from local churches, Jumbe called for research to investigate the nature and scale of discrimination based on religion in Tanzania.

See also: TANGANYIKA (Vol. IV).

K

Kabbah, Ahmad Tejan (1932–) *President of Sierra Leone*

Born in Pendembu, in the Eastern Province of SIERRA LEONE, Kabbah attended secondary school in his home country before traveling to Wales, U.K., where he earned a Bachelor's degree in economics. Upon his return to Sierra Leone Kabbah served as a district commissioner under the British colonial government. He continued to work in government following independence in 1961.

Because of his experience as a public servant he was appointed permanent secretary of several ministries, including Trade and Industry, and Social Welfare and EDUCATION. After earning his law degree in 1969 he maintained a private law practice for a few years before going on to work for the United Nations (UN) Development Program. Initially serving at the UN headquarters in New York City, he later served as a UN representative for the African countries of LESOTHO, TANZANIA, and UGANDA before retiring in 1992.

In 1992, following the military COUP D'ETAT that brought Valentine STRASSER (1966–) to power, Kabbah was asked to chair an advisory council responsible for bringing political stability to Sierra Leone. In this position he helped draft a new constitution that brought about a multiparty system. Pushed by his supporters to represent the SIERRA LEONE PEOPLE'S PARTY, Kabbah ended up winning the 1996 presidential election, taking office in March. He quickly appointed a broad-based coalition government that brought hope of stability to Sierra Leone. By the end of the year he also traveled to ABIDJAN, the capital of IVORY COAST, to sign a peace accord with Foday SANKOH (1937–2003), the leader of the rebellious REVOLUTIONARY UNITED FRONT. This agreement brought an end to years of civil strife.

The peace was short-lived. In May 1997 a coup d'état led by Johnny Paul Koroma (1960–) forced Kabbah into exile in neighboring GUINEA. Within a year, however, with the help of military intervention from the ECONOMIC COMMUNITY OF WEST AFRICAN STATES, Kabbah was restored to power. In July 1999 Kabbah and Sankoh signed another accord, the Lomé Peace Agreement. Despite ongoing hostilities, the Lomé agreement allowed for a dialogue that eventually brought a formal conclusion to the worst of the conflict. Kabbah officially declared the war over on January 18, 2002, at a ceremony that marked the successful disarmament and demobilization of ex-combatants under the auspices of the United Nations Mission in Sierra Leone.

Kabila, Joseph (1971–) *President of the Democratic Republic of the Congo*

The son of the late Congolese dictator Laurent KABILA (c. 1939–2001), Joseph Kabila became president of the Democratic Republic of the CONGO upon his father's assassination, in January 2001. Joseph was born in TANZANIA during his father's days of self-imposed exile from eastern Congo.

Trained by his father as a military tactician, Joseph led his father's forces as they laid siege to KINSHASA and, in 1997, overthrew President MOBUTU SESE SEKO (1930–1997). Mobutu died in exile shortly after being forced out of office.

When Joseph Kabila took over the presidency, few thought that he could fill the power vacuum left by his father. He proved them wrong, maintaining the support of Robert MUGABE (1924–), the president of ZIMBABWE, and winning the support of the United States and French governments. While his detractors consider his methods heavy-handed and doubt his commitment to democracy, Kabila has been instrumental in working with President Thabo MBEKI (1942–) of SOUTH AFRICA, President Benjamin MKAPA (1938–) of Tanzania, President Paul KAGAME (1957–) of RWANDA, and President Yoweri MUSEVENI (1944–) of UGANDA to forge a viable peace process for the region. This objective, however, remains somewhat elusive.

Joseph Kabila grew up speaking Kiswahili and English. While Kiswahili is a language common in eastern Congo, upon his return to the Congo, in the late 1990s, he had to study Lingala, the common national language, and French, the nation's official language.

See also: KISWAHILI (Vol. IV), LINGALA (Vol. IV).

Further reading: Georges Nzongola-Ntalaja, *The Congo from Leopold to Kabila: a People's History* (Manchester, U.K.: Manchester University Press, 2002).

Kabila, Laurent (Laurent Désiré Kabila) (c. 1939–2001) *Military president of the Democratic Republic of the Congo*

Laurent Kabila was born in northern KATANGA and educated at mission schools in what is now the Democratic Republic of the CONGO. He went on to university studies in France and DAR ES SALAAM prior to returning to the Congo before independence. In 1960 he allied himself politically with Patrice LUMUMBA (1925–1961), and, declaring himself a Marxist, became a member of the North Katangan assembly.

Early independence was a time of crisis for the Congo, and after the 1961 COUP D'ÉTAT, led by Joseph Mobutu (soon to be MOBUTU SESE SEKO [1930–1997]), Kabila organized a rebel force that fought for the secession of Katanga province from the fledgling country. By the mid-1960s, however, he had been forced to acknowledge defeat and took what remained of his rebel force into the forest.

Little is known of Kabila's activities during the next two decades. However, during this time, his People's Revolutionary Party seized control of a part of the Congo, and, as a result, he was extensively involved in regional coffee, GOLD, and ivory trades.

Kabila resurfaced in 1988, emerging as a pro-TUTSI leader during the HUTU-Tutsi conflict in RWANDA and UGANDA. Eventually he organized a Tutsi rebel force that operated within and outside ZAÏRE, as the Democratic Republic of the Congo was then called. By 1997 Kabila's forces posed a serious challenge to Mobutu's army on the battlefields, and, ultimately, Kabila forced Mobutu to flee the country. Kabila then seized the government, installing himself as head of state in May 1997.

Given the widespread antipathy to Mobutu's rule, there was great hope—both within the Congo and in the international community—for the Kabila regime. Those hopes, however, were quickly dashed. After restoring the country's pre-Mobutu name of the Democratic Republic of the Congo, Kabila immediately abolished the post of prime minister and concentrated power in the presidency that he claimed for himself. He banned political parties and excluded opposition leaders from his new government. Then, despite promises of a new constitution and the quick re-institution of democracy, he proceeded to rule by decree, harshly putting down protests and using his Rwandan and Ugandan allies to keep himself in power.

During his brief regime, Kabila announced several economic policy changes that pointed toward a more open and democratic direction for the country. For example, his attempt at creating a free-market economy led to the dismissal of many Mobutu cronies who had taken control of key commercial enterprises. The attempt also encouraged foreign investment. Unfortunately, however, little actual benefit was received and few inroads were made in the other problems facing the nation. As a result Kabila's government was forced to rely, unsuccessfully, on foreign aid and currency devaluation as a way to combat inflation. Ultimately the lack of viable money caused problems ranging from chronic fuel shortages to an inability to meet government or private payrolls.

As the 1990s drew to a close discontent with Kabila's regime became intermingled with ethnic conflict and the continuing Rwanda-Uganda conflict. Ultimately, as Kabila turned on his various allies, hostilities broke out between Kabila's Congolese government and these two other powers; various Congolese ethnic and rebel groups also became involved. Despite a short-lived peace accord in July 1999, hostilities continued off and on even after Kabila was assassinated, apparently by one of his own guards, on January 16, 2001. Ten days later his son Joseph (1971–), who previously had been the leader of Kabila's military forces, assumed the presidency.

See also: BELGIAN CONGO (Vol. IV); CIVIL WARS (Vol. V); CONGO CRISIS (Vol. V); ETHNIC CONFLICT IN AFRICA (Vol. V); KABILA, JOSEPH (Vol. V).

Further reading: Georges Nzongola-Ntalaja, *The Congo from Leopold to Kabila: a People's History* (Manchester, U.K.: Manchester University Press, 2002); Crawford Young and Thomas Turner, *The Rise and Fall of the Zairian State* (Madison: University of Wisconsin Press, 1995).

Kagame, Paul (1957–) *President of Rwanda*

Born in the Gitarama Prefecture of Rwanda, Kagame's wealthy family, along with many other ethnic TUTSI, fled to UGANDA in 1960. There he fought for the Ugandan National Liberation Army in the attempt to overthrow the country's dictator, Idi AMIN (c. 1925–2003), in 1979. A year later Kagame fought alongside Yoweri MUSEVENI (1944–) to overthrow the government of Milton OBOTE (1924–2000), who had been elected president after Amin fled the country for Saudi Arabia. When Museveni became president of Uganda in 1986, he made Kagame his Chief of Military Intelligence.

Kagame attended a staff and command course at Fort Leavenworth Military School in Kansas, United States, returning to Africa to take over the leadership of the rebel Tutsi RWANDA PATRIOTIC FRONT (RPF). Drawing its members from the Tutsi exile community in Uganda, the RPF began launching incursions into Rwanda, in 1990, attempting to unseat the ethnic HUTU government. Thousands of civilians were allegedly massacred in these incursions. By February 1994 Kagame's troops were within 30 miles of Rwanda's capital, KIGALI.

In 1994 the plane of Rwanda's Hutu president, Juvenal HABYARIMANA (1937–1994), was shot down as he returned from peace talks. Kagame's RPF was one of several groups accused of plotting the assassination. The Hutu-led genocide that ensued left nearly 800,000 Rwandans, mostly Tutsi, dead. In spite of this, the RPF captured Kigali in July 1994. The RPF asked Faustin Twagiramungu (1945–), a Hutu, to form a new government. Kagame became vice president and minister of defense, running the country with Prime Minister Twagiramungu and, later, President Pasteur Bizimungu (1950–). In March 2000 Bizimungu resigned, and Kagame became president.

Kagame earned a reputation as a stern disciplinarian, gaining the admiration of many Rwandans and Ugandans alike for his low-key but strong leadership. In 1989 he married Jeannette Nyiramongi, a school administrator, with whom he fathered four children.

Kampala Capital of UGANDA, located in the southern part of the country on Lake VICTORIA, near the site of the previous BUGANDA capital of Mengo. The city site dates from the mid-19th century, when it was the center of the Buganda state. In 1890 the British built a fort atop Old Kampala Hill, and Kampala was then the capital of the British Uganda Protectorate until the capital was moved to nearby ENTEBBE, in 1905. Under colonial rule the city continued to grow and remained the principal urban center in the country. At independence, in 1962, Kampala became the national capital.

Today, the city—home to an estimated 1,244,000 people—is spread out over several hills, with the main city center located on Nakasero Hill. At the higher elevations are the international embassies, government offices, and upscale homes and services. The wide, tree-lined streets and numerous parks in this sector give Kampala its reputation as one of the greenest cities in Africa. At lower elevations one finds smaller shops, inexpensive restaurants, and crowded markets and streets. The wide variety of foods and consumer items available in the city markets is indicative of Kampala's diverse ethnic population.

In addition to being a government and commercial center, Kampala is also a manufacturing center, producing metal goods, furniture, textiles, cigarettes, cement, and heavy equipment. There are also factories for milling, tanning hides, and processing foods. Kampala's coffee, cotton, tea, tobacco, and sugar are exported to the other countries in East Africa through Port Bell, located 6 miles (10 km) to the southeast, on Lake Victoria.

In the last decade, under the leadership of Yoweri MUSEVENI (1944–), the city has been recovering from the damage, both physical and social, that it sustained during the years of civil unrest following the overthrow of Ugandan dictator Idi AMIN (c. 1925–2003), in 1979. At the beginning of the twentieth century, Kampala underwent a period of reconstruction of infrastructure, including the building of new roads and the lighting of city streets.

Cultural and educational attractions are numerous in Kampala and include Uganda's National Theater, a museum, which houses an excellent collection of musical instruments, MAKERERE UNIVERSITY (founded in 1922), Uganda Technical College (1954), and several impressive Christian, Hindu, and Muslim places of worship. The city also offers nightclubs and casinos for visitors and residents looking to enjoy the lively nightlife.

See also: BRITISH EAST AFRICA (Vol. IV); ENGLAND AND AFRICA (Vols. III, IV, V); KAMPALA (Vol. IV);); URBANIZATION (Vols. IV, V); URBAN LIFE AND CULTURE (Vols. IV, V).

Kankan Mande town in present-day GUINEA, located along the banks of the Milo River, a tributary of the Niger River. Kankan is the capital of the Upper Guinea region. With an airport and a network of paved roads, it is a regional and international center for trade. Although it is the country's second-largest city by population, Kankan resembles an extended village with Islamic architectural influence. Most of the population is Maninka-speaking and Muslim.

See also: KANKAN (Vol. IV); MANDE (Vol. IV); URBANIZATION (Vols. IV, V); URBAN LIFE AND CULTURE (Vols. IV, V).

Kano (Kano City) Major HAUSA city in northwestern NIGERIA, located on the Jakara River. Kano's importance dates to 1095 CE, when it served as the capital of the Hausa city-state of the same name. By the early 1800s Kano had become part of the Sokoto Caliphate and had developed into the region's major commercial center. This continued after the British conquest of northern NIGERIA, in 1903, when subsequent improvements to the infrastructure—including rail links to LAGOS—expanded the city's ties to other places in western and central Africa.

Kano today is a commercial and industrial center with more than 600,000 people. Its major industries include dyeing and the production of leather, pottery, metal goods, textiles, building supplies, processed foods, automobiles, and printed materials. It engages in extensive trade in agricultural products such as peanuts (groundnuts) and livestock. The city also hosts numerous educational institutions including the Bayero University (founded in 1977), the Kano State Institute for Higher Education (1934), and many teaching and research schools.

A city wall, built in the 15th century, which was typical for Hausa cities of the time, still surrounds the historic sector. The imposing wall stretches more than 12 miles (20 km) and is 40 feet (12 m) wide at the base and 30 to 50 feet high.

Kano is divided into several different sectors, one of which is the industrial sector and another the historic sector, which includes the Emir's Palace. In addition, the city has the largest mosque in Nigeria, which was built in 1951. There is also the Sabon Gari, the area for outsiders to reside. With the urban growth of Kano, southern non-Muslim and non-Hausa-Fulani Nigerians have moved into Kano. This has led to outbursts of rioting along regional, ethnic, and religious lines reflecting the wider tensions and divisions in Nigeria. The first serious riots occurred in 1953, triggered by north-south political rivalries. The death toll, officially put at 36, was minor in comparison to later violence in 1966, 1981, 1999, and 2001. The 2001 outbreak was supposedly in protest against the American invasion of Afghanistan and saw Muslims and Christians battling each other, leaving as many as 200 people dead.

See also: FULANI (Vols. I, II, II); ISLAM, INFLUENCE OF (Vols. II, III, IV, V); KANO (Vols. II, III, IV); TRANS-SAHARAN TRADE ROUTES (Vol. II); URBANIZATION (Vols. IV, V); URBAN LIFE AND CULTURE (Vols. IV, V).

Kano, Aminu (Alhaji Aminu Kano, Mallam Aminu Kano) (1926–1983) *Nigerian political leader and activist*

Born into the Muslim HAUSA-Fulani aristocracy, Kano turned his back on his roots to become a champion of northern Nigeria's poor, uneducated masses. A scholar and teacher before entering the political fray, Aminu Kano led various progressive, left-leaning parties throughout his career. These included the Northern Elements Progressive Union, the United Progressive Grand Alliance, and the People's Redemption Party.

Widely respected for his humility, austere lifestyle, and a sharply honed sense of justice, Kano fought tirelessly for the empowerment of the *Talakawas*, as the poor masses are called in Kano State, Northern Nigeria. His supporters faced violent retribution from the northern elites for calling attention to government CORRUPTION and for demanding their civil and HUMAN RIGHTS. Kano was one of the few northern Nigerians to openly support women's rights.

See also: ISLAM, INFLUENCE OF (Vols. IV, V); POVERTY (Vol. V).

Kanté, Souleymane (1922–1987) *Guinean creator of the indigenous N'ko alphabet*

During the 1950s Souleymane Kanté perfected the N'ko alphabet, which was his personal invention for writing his Maninka language, and other Mande languages, in an indigenous script. In 1959 President Ahmed Sékou TOURÉ (1922–1984) of GUINEA awarded Kanté a substantial cash prize for his intellectual achievement and invited him to return from the IVORY COAST, where he had been living. At the time Touré was busy instituting his Maternal Language Education policy, which promoted education in eight of Guinea's 20 indigenous languages. Touré did not, however, accept Kanté's N'ko alphabet as the national alphabet, but rather intended to adapt the Roman alphabet for writing these languages. Kanté had sought to adapt the Roman alphabet to writing Maninka before deciding it was inadequate for his purpose.

Called upon by educators in KANKAN, Kanté assisted with the standardization of Maninka, despite his disapproval of Touré's National Language Program and its dependence upon a foreign alphabet and constructions. Kanté soon began his own LITERACY program in which he and others working with him taught informally in the marketplace and people's homes. His policy was for each person who became literate in N'ko to teach his or her family members plus seven other people. Many in the N'ko teaching force donated time and resources to Kanté's literacy campaign. While much of N'ko education took place in homes, more formal schools were gradually established.

As Ahmed Sékou Touré became dictatorial in his rule, he came to see Souleymane Kanté's literacy campaign as a threat to his own national literacy program. During the 1960s Touré tried to isolate Kanté's work by accepting him in the National Language Program. In 1973 Touré nominated Kanté to the National Islamic Council, but Kanté declined the appointment, claiming to bo too busy with N'ko translations and transcriptions.

Kante's N'ko program provided literacy to those without access to the public school system. Adults and children used the alphabet for correspondence and record keeping, and were also able to read the increasingly available translations of religious, historical, and scientific texts.

Fearing arrest or worse, Kanté went into self-imposed exile, living in various neighboring countries with large Mande-speaking populations. Wherever he stayed, he continued preparing materials to share with other readers of the N'ko alphabet. He also compiled indigenous knowledge of the Mande healing arts that was being lost as students focused on modern MEDICINE.

After Sékou Touré's death, in 1984, Kanté returned to Guinea. In 1986 Kanté established a NON-GOVERNMENT ORGANIZATION for the promotion of literacy in N'ko. Called ICRA-N'KO, the organization was officially sanctioned by the government in 1991. ICRA-N'KO continues to promote his pioneering literacy efforts with great effect in Guinea and the nine other West African countries that are using N'ko for communication in their own indigenous languages. Until his death, in 1987, Kanté lived in CONAKRY teaching his alphabet.

See also: EDUCATION (Vols. IV, V); KANTÉ, SOULEYMANE (Vol. IV); MANDE (Vol. II, III, IV); MANDINKA (Vols. II, IV).

Further reading: Dianne White Oyler, *The History of the N'ko Alphabet and its Role in Mande Transnational Identity: Words as Weapons* (Cherry Hill, N.J.: Africana Homestead Legacy Press, 2003).

KANU See KENYAN AFRICAN NATIONAL UNION.

Karume, Abeid Amani (1905–1972) *First president of Zanzibar*

Karume was born to a woman captive in the then German colony of Ruanda-Urundi. During his youth the two moved to ZANZIBAR. Karume occasionally attended school before becoming a seaman in his late teens. He later ran a motorboat taxi service, carrying passengers to shore from ships harbored at ZANZIBAR CITY.

Karume gained his first political leadership position in the early 1950s, becoming president of the Zanzibar African Association, a labor union of black migrant workers. In 1957 the Zanzibar African Association joined the Shirazi Association to form the AFRO-SHIRAZI PARTY (ASP); Karume was named the party's president.

As Zanzibar moved towards independence from Great Britain, the ASP was in a bitter struggle for command of the country's government with the Arab-dominated Zanzibar National Party (ZNP), which supported the rule of the Busaidi Sultanate. The ZNP initially gained the upper hand, ascending to power upon Zanzibar's independence in 1963. Within a year, however, a COUP D'ETAT overthrew the sultan and brought the ASP to power. The revolution unleashed a wave of violence that targeted those of Arab and Indian ancestry, who were perceived as members of an oppressive, ruling elite. Thousands died and thousands more fled. Karume became president of the People's Republic of Zanzibar.

Soon after Karume assumed leadership he struck a deal with the president of Tanganyika, Julius NYERERE (1922–1999), who was Karume's long-time political ally and co-founder of the ASP. The agreement called for the two countries to unite and form a new country—TANZANIA. Under the agreement, Nyerere became president, with Karume as vice president. In addition, Zanzibar retained a large amount of independence from the mainland.

Over the next decade the political situation in Zanzibar deteriorated, with the government arbitrarily arresting opposition members and refusing to hold elections. In April 1972 members of Zanzibar's military assassinated Karume. Sheikh Aboud JUMBE (1920–   ) then became the head of Zanzibar's government and vice president of Tanzania.

See also: BUSAIDI (Vol. IV); REVOLUTIONARY STATE PARTY (Vol. V); ZANZIBAR (Vols. II, III, IV); ZANZIBAR CITY (Vol. IV).

Kasavubu, Joseph (c. 1913–1969) *First president of the Republic of the Congo*

A one-time seminary student, Joseph Kasavubu was a teacher until 1942, when he became a bookkeeper. He entered local politics while in his thirties, eventually becoming president of the Bakongo Tribal Association (ABAKO), in 1954. Even though actual political parties were banned at this time by the Belgian colonial authorities, Kasavubu developed the ethnically based ABAKO into an effective organization. When political activity was legalized, in 1956, ABAKO was able to win the first city elections held in Léopoldville (present-day KINSHASA).

By 1959, as the ABAKO leader, Kasavubu was playing a substantial role in the process of decolonization as Belgium hastily attempted to set up an independent Congo. ABAKO, with its emphasis only on the concerns of the Kongo people, or Bakongo, alienated many people throughout the Congo. Still, when it came time for national elections, in 1960, the other major figure in the drive for independence, Patrice LUMUMBA

During the Congo Crisis in the first half of the 1960s, President Joseph Kasavubu (walking, on the left) maintained a tenuous hold on his power. Here he is seen reviewing Congolese troops. © AP/Wide World Photos

(1925–1961), chose to endorse Kasavubu as a compromise candidate for president. (Lumumba preferred to become prime minister, which he saw as a more powerful position.)

During the early, tumultuous days of Congolese independence, Kasavubu, as president, and Lumumba, as prime minister, managed to cooperate through civil unrest, army mutinies, and the secession of mineral-rich KATANGA Province. But, on September 5, 1960, Kasavubu utilized a clause in the Congo constitution and dismissed Lumumba from his post. This set off an escalation in the CONGO CRISIS that, in September 1960, led to a COUP D'ETAT by Joseph Mobutu, who was later known as MOBUTU SESE SEKO (1930–1997). Compromising with and even endorsing Mobutu and his regime, Kasavubu held onto tokens of power until the military leader eventually returned power to a civilian government, in 1961.

For the next few years, Kasavubu maintained his tenuous hold on power, supporting the government of Prime Minister Cyrille Adoula (1921–1978) until dismissing Adoula in favor of the one-time Katangan leader Moïse TSHOMBE (1919–1969), in 1964. Then, when Tshombe declared his candidacy for the presidency in the next election, Kasavubu attempted to dismiss Tshombe just as he had "fired" Lumumba and Adoula. Tshombe balked,

however, and the Congolese legislature refused to ratify Kasavubu's handpicked candidate, Evariste Kimba (1926–1966). In the resulting crisis, Mobutu once again seized power, dismissing Kasavubu in November 1965, and installing himself as chief of state. Never breaking completely with the Congo's new military ruler, Kasavubu helped to legitimize the regime until he retired to a farm, where he eventually died, in March 1969.

Among the many questions raised about Kasavubu's actions is one concerning his exact involvement in the death of Patrice Lumumba. Although the precise details may never be known, it is suspected that he played at least some part in handing the one-time prime minister over to authorities in secessionist Katanga, where Lumumba apparently was beaten to death.

See also: KONGO (Vols. II, III, IV); BELGIAN CONGO (Vol. IV); COLONIAL RULE (Vol. IV); DECOLONIZATION (Vol. IV); NATIONALISM AND INDEPENDENCE MOVEMENTS (Vol IV).

Katanga (Shaba) Province in southeastern Democratic Republic of the CONGO (DRC). Covering approximately 200,000 square miles (518,000 sq km), Katanga is endowed with vast mineral resources, making it a key player in the political crises that have plagued the DRC since independence. Today about 7.5 million people live in Katanga, with about 3 million residing in LUBUMBASHI, the provincial capital.

In 1960 the Belgian government gave independence to the former Belgian Congo and quickly exited the country. Immediately the lack of coherent leadership led to uncontrollable violence. In light of the instability, Moïse TSHOMBE (1919–1969), Katanga's provincial governor, declared Katanga an independent republic.

Independence for Katanga was viable largely because Belgium had developed the INFRASTRUCTURE of the region in its efforts to facilitate mineral extraction and TRANSPORTATION. However, the Congolese government led by Joseph KASAVUBU (c. 1913–1969) and Patrice LUMUMBA (1925–1961) refused to recognize an independent Katanga. At Lumumba's request, UN peacekeeping forces arrived to help the central government maintain control over Katanga. Belgium, for its part, supported the idea of an independent Katanga and sent troops to help the Kantangan rebels. The region's main copper MINING operations belonged to Union Miniere de Haut Katanga, a Belgian corporation.

By 1963 Tshombe was forced to concede that the Katangan secession had failed, and he fled the country. However, at Kasavubu's invitation, Tshombe returned to Katanga. His return sparked a new round of political infighting, and in the chaos that followed, MOBUTU SESE SEKO (1930–1997) seized control of the DRC in a military COUP D'ETAT. Again Tshombe was forced into exile.

In 1966 Mobutu nationalized the Congolese mining operations and changed the Union Miniere de Haut Katanga into Générale des Carrières et des Mines (Gécamines). Unfortunately for the Congolese people, however, Mobutu diverted huge amounts of Gécamines profits into his own personal accounts.

In 1971, as part of his African "authentication" program, Mobutu changed the name of the Congo to ZAÏRE. About the same time, Katanga was renamed Shaba. In 1997, however, Laurent KABILA (c. 1939–2001), a Katanga native, overthrew Mobutu and restored the province's original name.

By the 1980s Mobutu's mismanagement of Gécamines left the company unable to afford proper maintenance, and the machinery fell into disrepair. Although Gécamines still operated, mining profits represented a fraction of what they had been under Belgian colonial rule. When Mobutu was overthrown in 1997, his successor, Laurent Kabila, also squandered the province's riches, using mining profits to buy military hardware and to pay mercenaries during his costly war against Ugandan and Rwandan rebels. Despite Katanga's massive amounts of valuable MINERALS AND METALS, unending crisis in the DRC has left the majority of Katangans in abject POVERTY.

See also: CONGO CRISIS (Vol. V); COPPER (Vols. I, II, IV); COPPERBELT (Vol. IV); UNION MINIERE DU HAUT KATANGA (Vol. IV); UNITED NATIONS AND AFRICA (Vol. V).

Further reading: Georges Nzongola-Ntalaja, *The Congo from Leopold to Kabila: A People's History* (Manchester, U.K.: Manchester University Press, 2002).

Kaunda, Kenneth (Kenneth David Kaunda)
(1924–) *First president of Zambia*

Active in the anticolonial movement within Northern Rhodesia in 1950s, Kaunda was imprisoned in 1959 for his involvement in a meeting of the banned Zambia African National Congress. Released in 1960, Kaunda was soon elected president of the UNITED NATIONAL INDEPENDENCE PARTY (UNIP). He continued to press Britain for Northern Rhodesia's independence, leading a country-wide protest campaign that eventually led to the dissolution of the beleaguered British colonial alliance, the Central African Federation. In the 1962 parliamentary elections UNIP and the Northern Rhodesian African National Congress (NRANC), which was led by Harry NKUMBULA (1916–), won two-thirds of the votes and formed a coalition government. The 1964 election saw UNIP winning 55 parliamentary seats. The ANC won 10 seats. UNIP's majority of seats ended the necessity of a coalition government, and the party took control of the country upon independence, with Kaunda becoming Zambia's prime minister.

Kaunda's rallying slogan was the national motto "One Zambia, One Nation," which he emphasized throughout his rule. He wrote and advocated the philosophy of "Humanism," which he explained as similar to the person-centered, classless society that had existed before colonialism. In 1967 he declared Humanism a national ideology. However, very few other Zambian leaders understood or believed in the ideology, making it difficult to implement. Kaunda later attempted to introduce socialist ideals into the EDUCATION curriculum, but the move was dropped after many religious leaders labeled the ideology as antireligious.

Early in his presidency Kaunda fostered a mixed economy in which both the government and private sectors were involved in major industries. Government control over industry became more pronounced in 1969, however, after Kaunda initiated a number of economic reforms.

During his tenure Kaunda attempted to ease the tensions between Zambia's ethnic groups by having people of different ethnic backgrounds hold key government positions. However, Kaunda still faced political opposition in his early presidency. Just after independence the Lumpa Church, led by Alice LENSHINA (1924–1978), challenged the state rule, leading to violent confrontation that resulted in 700 deaths and the imprisonment of Lenshina.

In 1968 Simon Kapwepwe (1922–1980) formed the United Progressive Party (UPP) and alleged that people from his ethnic group, the Bemba, were not being treated fairly. Kaunda banned the UPP on charges of subversion. Meanwhile the activities of NRANC, which had a strong following in the southern and western provinces of the country, threatened to divide the country along ethnic lines. Fearing a civil war Kaunda declared Zambia a one-party state in 1972 and made it illegal for other political parties to exist. In 1978, after rejoining UNIP, Nkumbula and Kapwepwe attempted to run for president of the party. Their efforts failed, however, and they were later barred from running when the party changed the requirements for its presidential candidates.

Within Africa Kaunda played a key role in supporting different liberation movements, especially those in ZIMBABWE, MOZAMBIQUE, ANGOLA, NAMIBIA, and SOUTH AFRICA. He worked hard to help other countries gain their independence, acting for a time as president of the Pan-African Freedom movement for East, Central and Southern Africa. Under his leadership Zambia welcomed REFUGEES from countries in turmoil. Kaunda also hosted numerous regional and international conferences related to Africa's liberation. He was recognized internationally as a leading African statesman. He served as chair of the ORGANIZATION OF AFRICAN UNITY (OAU) in 1970–71 and 1987–88. He also played key roles in the mitigation of territorial disputes between KENYA and SOMALIA. His trademark was a white handkerchief, which he always wore on one hand as a symbol for peace.

While his positive reputation on the international scene grew, Kaunda's popularity at home began to wane. In the 1970s the country's economy suffered, largely due to the drop in world copper prices. In addition, LABOR UNIONS and other business groups began to criticize UNIP for the handling of the economy.

In 1984 Zambia suffered a severe drought, resulting in a food shortage. At the same time the government announced a price increase of 70 percent on basic foodstuffs as part of an INTERNATIONAL MONETARY FUND (IMF) adjustment program. This led to strikes in various parts of the country in 1985. In 1990 Kaunda was compelled to introduce more harsh economic changes, leading to more protests and an attempted COUP D'ETAT. In addition to domestic instability the international community began pressuring Kaunda's government to introduce a multi-party political system. Kaunda eventually acquiesced, reintroducing multiparty politics and amending the constitution in the same year.

Kaunda wrote several books, including *Black Government,* (with C. M. Morris, 1960), the autobiographical *Zambia Shall Be Free* (1962), and *Humanism in Africa and a Guide to Its Implementation* (1967).

In 1991 the newly formed MOVEMENT FOR MULTI-PARTY DEMOCRACY, led by Frederick CHILUBA (1943–   ), campaigned for a change in political leadership and privatization of major industries. Chiluba stood for election against Kaunda and won. Kaunda conceded defeat and allowed for the peaceful transition of power. Kaunda, who had ruled the country for 27 years, attempted to return to politics and run for the presidency in 1996. However, Chiluba, whose popularity quickly waned, feared that the charismatic Kaunda might regain the presidency. Chiluba blocked Kaunda by amending the constitution.

Kaunda, who in 1996 lost a son to HIV/AIDS, retired from politics and campaigned nationally and internationally to fight the disease. He continued to enjoy popularity at home and abroad. He received several awards while in office but what is remarkable are the several awards he received after his tenure. In 2002 Kaunda became the first Balfour African President-in-Residence at Boston University's African Presidential Archives and Research Center. In the same year, the South African president, Thabo MBEKI (1942–   ), recognized Kaunda's contribution in the fight against APARTHEID by bestowing on him a national award. In 2003, in a rare occurrence of a current African president honoring a former president, Zambia's president, Levy MWANAWASA (1948–   ), presented Kaunda with the Grand Order of the Eagle of Zambia for his selfless contribution to humanity in general and Zambia in particular.

See also: CENTRAL AFRICAN FEDERATION (Vol. IV); KAUNDA, KENNETH (Vol. IV).

Further reading: Stephen Chan and Craig Clancy, ed., *Zambia and the Decline of Kaunda, 1984–1998* (Lewiston, N.Y.: Edwin Mellen Press, 2000).

Kawawa, Rashidi Mfaume (1929–   ) *Tanzanian independence activist*

Kawawa, the eldest of eight children, was born in the Songea district of Tanganyika, the colonial name of mainland TANZANIA. He attended primary school in DAR ES SALAAM and later the Tabora Government Secondary

School. Soon after graduation, Kawawa joined the Public Works Department as an accountant. He later became a social worker, organizing and implementing a government adult LITERACY program.

In the early 1950s Kawawa was involved in LABOR organization and helped found the Tanganyika Federation of Labor. Although Tanganyika's independence movement had emerged, Kawawa's government job limited his political involvement. In 1956, however, he resigned from his position to dedicate his time to political organizing. He joined the Tanganyika African National Union (later TANZANIAN AFRICAN NATIONAL UNION [TANU]), becoming a central committee member, in 1957, and its vice president, in 1960. During this time he formed a close relationship with Julius NYERERE (1922–1999), who became prime minister of the newly independent Tanganyika, in 1961.

A year later Nyerere briefly resigned his position as prime minister and appointed Kawawa to replace him and take on the task of reforming the government. Kawawa used his position and his extensive experience in organizing to consolidate TANU's power. He rewarded party militants and removed opponents from positions of influence. Kawawa later introduced a republican constitution. Soon after, Nyerere returned from his hiatus to win the presidency and named Kawawa his vice president.

In 1964 Tanganyika joined the neighboring island-nation of ZANZIBAR to form the country of Tanzania. Under this new union, Kawawa became the country's second vice-president. He remained a close aid to Nyerere and was an important proponent of the president's UJA-MAA programs, which formed the Tanzanian variant of African socialism. Kawawa resigned from government service in 1985, the same year as Nyerere.

See also: INDEPENDENCE MOVEMENTS (Vol. V); LABOR UNIONS (Vols. IV, V); TANGANYIKA (Vol. IV).

Kayibanda, Gregoire (1924–1976) *First president of Rwanda*

Kayibanda was born in then Belgian-ruled southern Ruandi-Urundi (now RWANDA and BURUNDI) and was educated in Roman Catholic school. He became a teacher and then, in the 1950s, a journalist. Entering the political realm, Kayibanda wrote the "Hutu Manifesto," which outlined demands for the transfer of political power in Rwanda to the HUTU majority. That same year Kayibanda founded the Hutu Social Movement.

In 1959, with encouragement and guidance from the Catholic Church, Kayibanda founded the Party for Hutu Emancipation (Parti du Mouvement de l'Emancipation du Peuple Hutu, PARMEHUTU), a political organization that was openly anti-TUTSI. Later in 1959 PARMEHUTU led a small peasant revolt that evolved into a full-fledged revolution. The party dominated communal elections in

A teacher and journalist before entering politics, Gregoire Kayibanda became the first elected president of Rwanda in 1962, the year this photo was taken. © United Nations

1960. That same year Kayibanda became prime minister of the newly formed provisional government.

In 1962 Rwanda was declared a republic, and Kayibanda became its president. His rule was unstable, however, and under the constant threat of revolt. In 1963 Tutsis from neighboring Burundi led an uprising against Kayibanda's government, reaching the gates of Rwanda's capital, KIGALI. The insurgence was put down, however, leading the government to kill more than 20,000 Tutsi. In an attempt to consolidate his power, Kayibanda created a one-party state in 1965, declaring his PARMEHUTU the only legal party. Despite his authoritative rule, Kayibanda's hold on power was tenuous. In 1973 a bloodless, military COUP D'ETAT led by General Juvenal HABYARIMANA (1937–1994) overthrew Kayibanda. Habyarimana jailed Kayibanda, who, after being denied needed medical attention, died while under house arrest.

See also: BELGIUM AND AFRICA (Vol. IV); NATIONALISM AND INDEPENDENCE MOVEMENTS (Vol. IV); RUANDI-URUNDI (Vol. IV).

Keino, Kipchoge (Kip Keino, Hezekiah Keino)
(1940–) *Kenyan distance runner*

A member of the Kenyan police force at age 18, Keino won his first race, the Kenyan three-mile championship, in 1962. That same year he set Kenya's three-mile record, finishing in 13:46.8. In 1965 Keino set a world record of 7:39.6 in the 3,000-meter race.

Keino ran extensively in the mountains of western KENYA, and was a pioneer in high-altitude training for athletes. Acclimated to running at elevations more than 9,000 feet (2,743 m) above sea level, Keino was well prepared for the thin air of Mexico City, where he competed in the 1968 Olympic Games. Despite a painful gallbladder infection, Keino won the silver medal in the 5,000-meter race and the gold medal at the 1,500-meter distance. In the 1972 Munich Olympics, Keino again dominated in the middle-distance races, winning silver in the 1,500-meter race and gold in the 3,000-meter steeplechase.

At the 1968 Olympics, doctors recommended Keino withdraw from competition because of a severe gallbladder infection. Keino ran the 10,000-meter race anyway, leading most of the way before collapsing in pain near the end. He then competed in the 5,000-meter race and won silver. Intending to withdraw from the 1,500-meter race, Keino changed his mind at the last minute, but was caught in traffic trying to get to the stadium. He jogged more than a mile to the track, then proceeded to win the gold, beating American Jim Ryun (1947–), who until that point had not lost a race of 1,500 meters or more since 1965.

In 1974 Keino retired and founded a home for abandoned children in Eldoret, Kenya. An inspiration for future Kenyan athletes, who have become a dominant force in the middle- and long-distance events, Keino was awarded with the Order of the Burning Spear, Kenya's highest civilian honor.

See also: SPORTS AND ATHLETICS (Vol. V).

Keita, Modibo (1915–1977) *First president of the Mali Republic*

Born in BAMAKO, MALI, Keita was educated in SENEGAL and served as a teacher upon his return to Mali in 1936. In the mid-1940s he became politically active, joining the African Democratic Assembly (Rassemblement Democratique Africain, RDA), a political party that was closely associated with the French Communist Party. In 1947 Keita was elected secretary general of the RDA branch in the French Soudan (the colonial name of the state that later became Mali). Over the next decade Keita served in various political positions both at home and in France, where he represented French Soudan in the National Assembly.

In 1958 French Soudan became a self-governing republic within the French Community and was renamed the Sudanese Republic. In 1959 the Sudanese Republic joined with Senegal, UPPER VOLTA (present-day BURKINA FASO), and DAHOMEY (present-day Republic of BENIN) to form the Mali Federation, with Keita as its president. The federation was short-lived, however. In 1960, following Senegal's withdrawal and the dissolution of the Mali Federation, Keita emerged as the president of the newly formed, independent Mali Republic.

Throughout his presidency Keita played the dangerous game of Cold War politics by maintaining relations with France as well as the Communist Soviet Union and China. In fact, in 1963 the Soviet Union recognized Keita's efforts at cultivating socialist ideology in Mali by awarding him the Lenin Peace Prize.

Before long Keita's nation began failing economically and faced the growing financial burdens of his socialist policies. Ultimately, in 1968 Keita was removed in a military COUP D'ETAT led by Moussa Traoré (1936–). Fearing reprisals Traoré placed Keita in military detention, where he remained until his death in 1977.

See also: AFRICAN DEMOCRATIC ASSEMBLY (Vol. IV); COLD WAR AND AFRICA (Vols. IV, V); FRANCE AND AFRICA (Vols. III, IV, V); FRENCH SOUDAN (Vol. IV); FRENCH WEST AFRICA (Vol. IV); FRENCH UNION (Vol. IV).

Further reading: R. James Bingen, David Robinson, and John M. Staatz, eds., *Democracy and Development in Mali* (East Lansing, Mich.: Michigan State University Press, 2000).

Keita, Salif (1949–) *Singer and songwriter from Mali*

Born in Djaliba, MALI, Salif Keita is one of the best-known contemporary African singers. However, he did not achieve his musical success without a struggle. In traditional Malian society singers belong to a low social caste, so when his father learned that Keita sang for tips in the markets of BAMAKO, Mali's capital, he refused to speak to his son for six years. In Bamako, however, Salif rose to prominence as a featured vocalist, first with the government-sponsored group, Rail Band (1970–73) and then with a dance band called Les Ambassadeurs (1973–80). Because of political violence in Mali, Keita moved to ABIDJAN in IVORY COAST in the mid-1970s, and his band was renamed Les Ambassadeurs Internationales.

In 1984 Keita began a solo career in Paris, where he found himself surrounded by other artists and writers from throughout the former French colonial world.

Known as the Golden Voice of Mali, Keita achieved widespread popular and critical success for his albums and emotionally charged live performances. He was the first African to be nominated for a Grammy Award (for the album *Amen*).

Salif Keita was born into a family that claimed direct descent from Sundiata Keita (d. 1225), the 13th-century founder of the great Mali Empire. Like the physically challenged Sundiata, the future pop star also had to overcome great odds in order to succeed. Because he was born an albino, Salif faced harassment and hostility in his rural hometown, Djaliba, where albinos are traditionally seen as omens of bad luck. Fortunately for Salif, his remarkable singing talents won over most of his listeners, bringing him fame and prosperity.

Critics note that Keita's MUSIC is a unique blend of traditional West African styles and instruments, rock 'n' roll and jazz styles from the West, Latin rhythms from Cuba, and Islamic musical forms from North Africa and the Middle East.

See also: SUNDIATA (Vol. II); URBAN LIFE AND CULTURE (Vols. IV, V).

Kenya East African country approximately 224,900 square miles (582,491 sq km) in size, bordered by ETHIOPIA and the Republic of the SUDAN to the north, SOMALIA and the Indian Ocean to the east, TANZANIA to the south, and UGANDA to the west. The capital is NAIROBI, in the fertile central highlands.

Kenya at Independence The road to Kenya's independence involved the violent upheaval of the Mau Mau crisis of the 1950s, which left at least 13,000 Africans dead, 80,000 detained, and more than 1 million people forcibly relocated. While British security forces ultimately were able to suppress Mau Mau, the British government decided that the only viable long-term solution was to grant independence to the colony. The development of political parties that this decision in part produced led to the formation of the KENYAN AFRICAN NATIONAL UNION (KANU) and the Kenyan African Democratic Union (KADU). KANU, a political coalition between Kenya's two most influential ethnic groups, the KIKUYU and the LUO, became dominant at independence in 1963. The party was led by Jomo KENYATTA (c. 1891–1978), whom the British had imprisoned for his alleged involvement with Mau Mau. He became the leading figure of the independence movement and a national hero. The prime min-

ister at independence, Kenyatta became the nation's first president when Kenya became a republic in 1964.

When KADU was assimilated into KANU, Kenyatta became the leader of a de facto single-party state. Following a capitalist program, he established a stable economy, but ethnic tensions ultimately disrupted his program. Espousing the ideal of HARAMBEE, or "coming together," Kenyatta, a member of the Kikuyu majority, established policies that seemed to favor his own people over Kenya's minority ethnic groups. One such policy was Kenyatta's program of "Kenyanization," which focused on buying back land from willing European settlers and redistributing it to Kenyans. The majority of the redistributed land ended up in Kikuyu hands, creating a Kikuyu hegemony in both politics and economics. Such policies created conflict between Kenyatta and powerful members of the Luo community, including Vice President Oginga ODINGA (1912–1994). Odinga believed Kenyatta's economic plans overlooked the nation's poor, and in 1966 he split from KANU to form the Kenya People's Union (KPU). Through KANU's legislative manipulation, however, the KPU was rendered politically ineffective.

While there is no majority ethnic group in Kenya, the Kikuyu, with about 22 percent of the total population, form the largest group. The Luhya, Luo, Kalenjin, and Kamba are also large, each having between 11 and 14 percent of the population. The remaining 28 percent is made up of some 64 other African ethnic groups as well as smaller European and Asian communities.

The repression of the KPU and the 1969 assassination of economic minister and KANU co-founder, Tom MBOYA (1930–1969), a Luo, led many among the Luo to suspect a Kikuyu conspiracy. That same year the KPU was officially banned, and Odinga and a number of KPU officials were imprisoned. In 1971 Kenyatta granted extensive tracts of land to a number of wealthy Kikuyu, and the Luo became fully convinced that ethnic favoritism was at play in the government. An attempted COUP D'ETAT that same year signaled growing popular discontent in Kenya. Although Kenyatta made moves to placate the opposition, KANU remained firmly in control of the nation's political arena. Kenyatta gradually became more and more autocratic as criticism of his government grew.

In 1978, after serving three terms in office, President Kenyatta died and was replaced by Daniel arap MOI (1924–), a member of the Kalenjin ethnic group. Democracy in Kenya deteriorated under Moi, who maneuvered to keep threats to his power out of the government.

Using censorship and imprisonment, Moi centralized all power in the presidency and officially declared KANU the sole legal political party of Kenya. He displayed open favoritism to his Kalenjin people, raising the ire of the Kikuyu and Luo. As a result, in 1982 a group of Luo military officers attempted to unseat the president, but they were quickly defeated. One year later Moi was reelected.

Opposition to Moi gradually increased, particularly among university students. In the face of increasing hostility and a declining economy, Moi continued to strengthen his control. In 1988 he was reelected in a hotly disputed contest, and riots erupted. Moi responded by amending the constitution to further increase his essentially dictatorial powers.

Ultimately, however, the opposition became too powerful for Moi to control. In 1990 Oginga Odinga resurfaced to found the Forum for Restoration of Democracy (FORD), a new party that gained widespread support. Further destabilizing Moi's regime, many sources of international ECONOMIC ASSISTANCE withdrew their support in protest against Moi's authoritarianism. Ultimately, in 1992 Moi allowed multiparty elections. Amid ethnic clashes that left thousands dead—events that Moi's government blamed on the polarizing effect of the multiparty system—Moi was reelected again. His victory was aided by dissent within FORD, which was unable to challenge Moi and KANU. Moi won the presidency once again, in 1997, setting off widespread protests and rioting.

In 1990 Kenya's Luo foreign minister, Dr. Robert Ouko (d. 1990), spoke out against government CORRUPTION and declared his intent to expose corrupt officials. His subsequent assassination led many foreign nations to cease providing economic assistance to Kenya.

Moi's final term in office was marked by continued civil unrest and ethnic strife, underscored by a bombing that destroyed the United States Embassy in Nairobi in 1998. In 2002 Moi was forced to step down by constitutional term limits, and he could only stand by as the opposition, led by Mwai KIBAKI (1931–), finally ended KANU's stranglehold on Kenyan politics. The new government presented Kenya with hope for a stable, democratic future. This, it is hoped, will lead to a renewal of economic growth. Nairobi is already the major industrial and commercial hub for East Africa, and a more settled political climate will serve to enhance its position.

See also: DEMOCRATIZATION (Vol. V); ENGLAND AND AFRICA (Vols. III, IV, V); ETHNICITY AND IDENTITY (Vol. I); KENYA (Vols. I, II, III, IV); MAU MAU (Vol. IV).

Further reading: Angelique Haugerud, *The Culture of Politics in Modern Kenya* (New York: Cambridge University Press, 1995); Norman Miller and Rodger Yaeger, *Kenya: The Quest for Prosperity*, 2nd ed. (Boulder, Colo.: Westview Press, 1994); B. A. Ogot & W. R. Ochieng', eds., *Decolonization and Independence in Kenya* (Athens, Ohio: Ohio University Press, 1995).

Kenyan National African Union (KANU)

Political party founded by Tom MBOYA (1930–1969) and Jomo KENYATTA (c. 1891–1978) that controlled Kenya's government for almost 40 years. Founded in 1960 in the midst of Kenya's advance toward independence, KANU initially was a union of the KIKUYU and LUO peoples' political interests, which were rooted in the desire for a strong, centralized government. That same year a coalition of smaller African groups formed the Kenyan African Democratic Union (KADU), a rival political party that promoted a federal form of government to offset the Kikuyu's numeric strength. In 1962 the two parties formed a coalition government. It dissolved, however, after the elections of 1963, which KANU carried convincingly. In 1964 Kenya became a republic, with Kenyatta, a Kikuyu, as president, and Oginga ODINGA (1912–1994), a Luo, as vice president.

In 1960 an attempted military COUP D'ETAT had been put down, but only with British intervention. In light of the failed insurgency, Kenyatta had convinced many of KADU's leaders, including Ronald Ngala (1923–1972) and Daniel arap MOI (1924–), to join KANU for the sake of stabilizing the country's government. This newfound unity did not last long, however, as Odinga had a falling out with Kenyatta. Resigning from the vice presidency, Odinga formed the Kenya People's Union (KPU), in 1966. In 1969 KANU's co-founder, Tom Mboya was assassinated. Because Mboya was a Luo, many Luo came to believe that Kenyatta was leading an anti-Luo movement. Later in 1969 this belief was bolstered when the government banned the KPU and arrested Odinga and other KPU leaders.

Despite the suggested favoritism towards the Kikuyu, in 1967 Kenyatta chose Moi—a member of the Kalenjin ethnic minority—to be his vice president. In the mid-1970s Kenyatta's health began to fail, and many Kikuyu, wanting to ensure a Kikuyu successor, planned to undermine Moi's claim to the presidency. This plan was thwarted, however, by Charles Njonjo and Mwai KIBAKI (1931–), two Kikuyu with great influence within KANU. Njonjo, Kenya's attorney general, and Kibaki, the minister of finance, backed Moi's vice-presidential claim to the presidency upon Kenyatta's death, in August 1978. Later that year, Moi was elected head of KANU, affirming his hold on power.

Initially Moi's presidency cultivated a vibrant, free society, and Moi appointed people from many different ethnic groups to government positions. Coming from the Kalenjin minority, however, made Moi's position tenuous, and he gradually began to increase the number of Kalenjin appointed to the government. Meanwhile, KANU gained political strength. In 1982 the KANU-controlled National Assembly amended the constitution to make Kenya a one-party state. Later that year the army put down a coup attempt led by Luo air force officers. After this attempted coup, Moi consolidated his power by removing many Kikuyu and Luo officers from the military, replacing them with Kalenjin or other minority groups. During this time KANU, with the help of its youth wing, greatly expanded its membership base and further entrenched the party into Kenyan society. KANU gained a reputation for brutal repression of democratic activities, with its paramilitary police force, the General Services Unit, enforcing the ban on opposition parties.

In 1983 Moi further consolidated his power, turning on a former KANU ally. Wanting to further rid the party of Kikuyu influence, he orchestrated the fall of Njonjo, who was branded a traitor and forced to resign from his cabinet position as well as from the National Assembly. Despite this internal disharmony, KANU remained the sole political power in Kenya through the rest of the 1980s. Calls for democratic reforms, however, increased in the early 1990s, and the National Assembly repealed the ban on opposition parties. Despite the renewed political competition, KANU carried the elections of 1992 and 1998, as Moi retained the presidency through the end of the century. The party, however, began to feel the strain of member defections to other parties. In the 2002 elections one of these defectors and Moi's former ally, Mwai Kibaki, defeated the KANU presidential candidate, Uhuru Kenyatta (1960–   ). Kibaki's party, the National Rainbow Coalition, also carried the parliamentary elections, ending KANU's nearly 40-year rule.

See also: DEMOCRATIZATION (Vol. V); ETHNIC CONFLICT IN AFRICA (Vol. V); INDEPENDENCE MOVEMENTS (Vol. V); MAU MAU MOVEMENT (Vol. IV); POLITICAL PARTIES AND ORGANIZATIONS (Vols. IV, V).

Further reading: Angelique Haugerud, *The Culture of Politics in Modern Kenya* (New York: Cambridge University Press, 1995).

Kenyatta, Jomo (Johnstone Kamau, Kamau Ngengi, Kamau wa Ngengi) (c. 1891–1978) *First prime minister and later president of Kenya*

Born Kamau wa Ngengi in Kikuyuland, KENYA, Jomo Kenyatta began his political career in the 1920s. He rose quickly through the ranks of Kenya's activists, until 1931, when he went to Europe to live and study. He returned to Kenya in 1946. By then he had become a symbol of both the independence movement and Africans' resentment over the white takeover of land in Kenya.

An imposing figure fond of appearing in traditional dress—complete with feathered or animal-skin headwear—Kenyatta often was addressed as "Savior" and "Great Elder," a sign not only of Kenyans' affection but also of the role which the people saw for him in the country's political life.

Jailed in the wake of the violence brought on by the Mau Mau movement, Kenyatta, in spite of his denials of any involvement with the Mau Mau, spent from 1953 to 1959 in prison, and then endured another two years under house arrest. With the British decision to grant Kenya its independence, however, Kenyatta moved once again into the forefront of Kenyan politics, having become president of the KENYAN AFRICAN NATIONAL UNION (KANU) while still under house arrest. Released, he was elected to the Kenyan legislature in 1962, ultimately serving in the multiracial transition government that guided the country during the immediate pre-independence years. With the victory of KANU in the 1963 legislative elections, Kenyatta became prime minister and then, upon independence in 1964, he became president.

After taking office, the historically radical Kenyatta took pains to adopt a moderate, or gradualist, approach on many issues. Rather than push for immediate redistribution of white-owned land to Africans, for example, he reassured Europeans that they would have a role in post-independence Kenya. Similarly, although he willingly accepted foreign assistance from the former Soviet Union and other Communist-bloc countries, he rejected the program known as African socialism favored by many other leaders of the time. Instead, he fostered a capitalistic system that, he believed, would increase economic opportunity for his developing country.

His policies, however, ultimately may have done more for the KIKUYU people—and, in particular, his own family and close associates—than they did for the mass of Kenyans, and charges of CORRUPTION began to surface quite early in his administration. At the same time, he became increasingly autocratic in his rule, favoring centralization of authority and the abolition of all political parties save KANU. Ultimately this led to defections by many of his former allies and, in response, to his government's repressive tactics against any possible opposition.

Throughout the 1970s Kenyatta was the undisputed primary politician not only in Kenya but in all of East Africa. His power, however, began to erode as the charges of corruption mounted and his government began using increasingly harsh methods to silence criticism and eliminate opposition. Still, his economic policies and his ability to halt the flight of whites from the country, helped

Once seen as the savior of the Kenyan people, Jomo Kenyatta was soon accused of corruption and criticized for his excesses. Here he is pictured in 1975 with his fourth wife, Mama Ngina.
© *New York Times*

turn Kenya into the showcase of 1970s Africa. Kenyatta's death, in 1978, marked the passing of an era, as Kenya entered a new and more-troubled phase.

See also: BRITISH EAST AFRICA (Vol. IV); COLD WAR AND AFRICA (Vols. IV, V); ENGLAND AND AFRICA (Vols. IV, V); INDEPENDENCE MOVEMENTS (Vol. V); KENYATTA, JOMO (Vol. IV); MAU MAU MOVEMENT (Vol. IV); NATIONALISM AND INDEPENDENCE MOVEMENTS (Vol. IV).

Further reading: *Jomo Kenyatta: Harambee! The Prime Minister of Kenya's Speeches, 1963–1964* (New York:

Oxford University Press, 1964); Jeremy Murray-Brown, *Kenyatta* (London: Allen & Unwin, 1979).

Kerekou, Mathieu (Mathieu Ahmed Kérékou)
(1933–) *Two-time president of the Republic of Benin*

Kerekou was born into a military family in Koufra, Natitingou, DAHOMEY (present-day Republic of BENIN). He was educated in schools for children of soldiers in MALI and SENEGAL and then attended officer's school in

France, which was the colonial power in Dahomey. He served in the French army until 1961, after which he joined the national army's fight for an independent Dahomey. In the early 1960s Kerekou served as a military aide to Dahomey's first president, Hubert Maga (1916–2000). Over the next 10 years Kerekou watched the tumultuous political scene, serving as military attaché. He also furthered his EDUCATION in France and began forging his own political ambitions.

In 1972, following a violent military COUP D'ÉTAT that he organized, Kerekou came to power and assumed the positions of president, prime minister, and minister of defense. Using anti-imperialist rhetoric he steered his nation according to a Marxist-Leninist ideology, and in 1975 he renamed his country the People's Republic of Benin. After nationalizing banks, schools, OIL distribution, and insurance, Kerekou had to survive several attempted coups by pro-capitalist forces. One such coup attempt was led by Dahomean exiles aided by French mercenaries. Although the centralization of the government led to some positive changes in industry and AGRICULTURE, a bleak economic outlook in the 1980s caused more coup attempts.

In 1980 Kerekou converted to Islam and changed his name to Ahmed. However, it was rumored that he subsequently became a "born-again" Christian. Later in the 1980s Kerekou shifted his economic policy from Marxism to socialism, but the financial burdens of the nation were overwhelming. Responding to the demands of the people, Kerekou began moving toward a more representative government in the late 1980s. In 1990 he called for a conference to rewrite Benin's constitution. In free elections held the following year, Nicephore Soglo (1934–), a former president, defeated Kerekou, who stepped down peacefully and retired from politics. In 1995, however, Kerekou came out of retirement and won the presidential election. He won again in 2001, although the results of that election were disputed. Since returning to office Kerekou has managed to bring some stability to the economy, and many people now regard Benin as a rare example of a successful African democracy.

See also: FRANCE AND AFRICA (Vols. IV, V); MAGA, HUBERT (Vol. IV).

Khama, Sir Seretse (1921–1980) *First president of Botswana*

From the age of four, Seretse Khama was recognized as the *kgosi,* or king, of the Bangwato people of the British protectorate of Bechuanaland, in central southern Africa. He was sent abroad, to England, where he studied law and married a white Englishwoman named Ruth Williams. Upon his return to Bechuanaland, the popular Khama was considered a potential threat to the British colonial administration and, in 1951, was sent into exile in London. By

1956, however, the international community had begun calling for the dismantling of the racist APARTHEID political system in southern Africa, and Khama, suffering from diabetes, was welcomed back to Bechuanaland.

In 1965, once again healthy and inspired by the optimistic outlook of African nationalist politics, Khama led his Bechuanaland Democratic Party to victory over pan-Africanist and socialist rivals in the country's first universal franchise elections, becoming prime minister. Then, in September of 1966, he was elected the first president of the new Republic of BOTSWANA. Botswana celebrates Sir Seretse Khama Day as a public holiday on July 1, Khama's birthday.

When Khama became president, the Republic of Botswana was widely regarded as one of the poorest countries in Africa, plagued by colonial mismanagement and continually indebted to Britain. But, under Khama's liberal-democratic leadership, Botswana quickly developed a thriving economy based on the export of its agricultural and MINING resources, especially to SOUTH AFRICA. Khama centralized his own power, controlled the influence of local traditional chiefs, and successfully devised a citizen-led administration that was neither too bureaucratized nor reliant on military backing.

During Khama's presidency (1966–80), the Republic of Botswana was the fastest-growing economy in the world. The general prosperity of the country was reflected in improvements to the country's INFRASTRUC-TURE, and also in the development of its educational and health systems in both urban and rural areas.

Throughout the 1970s Khama's poor health drained his energy but, nevertheless, he managed to uphold his reputation as a strong, intelligent leader with great personal integrity. Toward the end of his life Khama was an active negotiator in the independence movements of ZIMBABWE and NAMIBIA as he worked to realize his vision of a southern Africa that was peaceful, democratic, and prosperous. Khama died in July, 1980, and Ketumile MASIRE (1925–) succeeded him as Botswana's president.

See also: BECHUANALAND (Vol. IV); COLONIAL RULE (Vol. IV); KHAMA, SIR SERETSE (Vol. IV).

Further reading: Willie Henderson, Neil Parsons, and Thomas Tlou, *Seretse Khama, 1921–1980.* (Braamfontein, South Africa: Macmillan, 1995)

Khartoum

Capital city of the Republic of the SUDAN, located near the confluence of the White and Blue Nile rivers in north central Sudan. Once a colonial government and trading center, in 1956 Khartoum became the capital of the independent Republic of the Sudan. The city is connected by bridges to the cities of Khartoum North, an industrial center, and Omdurman, an Islamic center. Shipping on the White and Blue Nile Rivers, as well as Sudan's rail and road networks, bring goods from other parts of the country, making Khartoum the nation's chief TRANSPORTATION hub. The city's major industries include food processing, textiles, printed materials, gums, and glass manufacturing. A pipeline, completed in 1977, brings OIL from the country's main Red Sea port.

Khartoum hosts the University of Khartoum (founded in 1902), Nilayn University (1955), and the Sudan University of Science and Technology (1950), as well as other technical educational institutions.

With its history as a crossroads for traders and having a continuous influx of immigrants from all over Africa, Khartoum has maintained a diverse atmosphere. Most of its 930,000 inhabitants (1993 estimate) speak Arabic. During the 1990s an ongoing war in southern Sudan brought shortages and hardship to the city, and Sudan remains one of the continent's poorest and least politically stable countries.

See also: ARABIC (Vols. I, II); BLUE NILE (Vol. I); ENGLAND AND AFRICA (Vols. III, IV, V); ISLAM (Vol. II); ISLAM, CENTERS OF LEARNING (Vol. II); KHARTOUM (Vols. I, III, IV); WHITE NILE (Vol. I).

Kibaki, Mwai (Emilio Mwai Kibaki) (1931–   )
President of Kenya

Kibaki, the youngest of eight children, was born in the village of Gatuyaini in the Central Province of KENYA. There he attended primary and high school and learned carpentry as well as AGRICULTURE. Later Kibaki went to MAKERERE UNIVERSITY, in neighboring UGANDA, earning a degree in economics in 1955. That same year he gained a postgraduate scholarship to study in England, eventually choosing to attend the London School of Economics, where he earned his master's degree in public finance. In 1958 Kibaki returned to Makerere University to teach economics.

In 1960 Kibaki helped found the KENYAN AFRICAN NATIONAL UNION (KANU). Later that year he resigned from his teaching position and returned to Kenya to take a job as an executive with KANU. Three years later Kibaki, running on the KANU ticket, was elected a member of Parliament. That same year Kenya's president Jomo KENYATTA (c.1891–1978) appointed him parliamentary secretary to the minister of finance. Kibaki became minister of finance in 1969.

Upon Kenyatta's death Daniel arap MOI (1924–   ) ascended to the country's presidency and appointed Kibaki his vice president. In 1983 Kibaki moved from the ministry of finance to become the minister of home affairs. In 1988 he fell out of favor with arap Moi and was replaced as vice president. Kibaki then became the minister of health.

Kibaki remained active in KANU, but left the party when Kenya restored the multiparty political system in 1991. He formed the Democratic Party, which later became the National Alliance Party of Kenya (NAK). Making successive bids for Kenya's presidency, Kibaki finished third in the 1992 elections and then second in 1997. In an effort to change his fortunes, Kibaki united the NAK with the Liberal Democratic Party and formed the National Rainbow Coalition (NARC). The maneuver paid off, as the NARC thoroughly defeated KANU in the 2002 elections. Kibaki, who garnered 63 percent of the vote, became president.

See also: DEMOCRATIZATION (Vol. V).

Kigali
Capital of RWANDA, located in the highlands in the center of the country, on the Ruganwa River, just south of the equator. Kigali was part of German East Africa from 1899 until 1916. After World War I (1914–18) it came under Belgian control, from 1919 until 1962, as part of the Ruanda-Urundi territory. In 1962 the Ruanda-Urundi territory was divided into the countries of Rwanda and BURUNDI, and Kigali was made the capital of independent Rwanda.

Kigali has an international airport and a technical college. Major industries include textiles, radio, paint and varnish manufacturing, tanning, and cassiterite (tin) MINING. It also trades coffee and cattle. However, the economy has been severely damaged by the civil war that started, in 1994, with the assassination of President Juvenal HABYARIMANA (1937–1994). Instability and genocidal killings between the country's HUTU and TUTSI ethnic groups have made it impossible to estimate the current population of the city, although it had perhaps 250,000 inhabitants in the early 1990s.

Two of the major political groups, the Hutu Coalition of the Defense of the Republic and the RWANDA PATRIOTIC FRONT (RPF), a Tutsi organization, fought for control of Kigali and left the city nearly depopulated. A tenuous peace that was restored by the turn of the century is giving Rwandans hopes for recovery.

See also: BELGIUM AND AFRICA (Vol. IV); GERMAN EAST AFRICA (Vol. IV); GERMANY AND AFRICA (Vol. IV); KIGALI (Vol. II); RUANDA-URUNDI (Vol. IV); WORLD WAR I (Vol. IV).

Kikuyu (Gikuyu)
Largest ethnic group in KENYA. At the forefront of the struggle for independence, the Kikuyu were politically and economically dominant in the postcolonial years. A largely agricultural people whose homeland centers on Mount Kenya, the Kikuyu emerged from British colonial rule as Kenya's most influ-

ential ethnic group. Together with the LUO ethnic group, the Kikuyu established the KENYAN AFRICAN NATIONAL UNION (KANU), in 1960, to lead the country to independence. Upon Kenya's full autonomy, in 1963, KANU became the nation's chief political entity. Kikuyu nationalist leader Jomo KENYATTA (c. 1891–1978), became Kenya's first president.

Conditions during Kenyatta's administration favored the Kikuyu, causing much tension between the group and its primary rivals, the Luo. Kenyatta's Africanization plan, which bought back parcels of land from departing European settlers, primarily benefited the Kikuyu, who gradually established economic superiority. Politically,

the Kikuyu became even more influential as high-ranking Luo members of the government were either maneuvered out of power or assassinated. The Kikuyu also constituted a majority of the population of Kenya's capital city of NAIROBI and thus had access to the economic and social opportunities provided by its rapid commercial and industrial growth after independence.

However, when Kenyatta died in 1978 Daniel arap MOI (1924–   ), a member of the Kalenjin people, rose to the presidency, and the Kikuyu found themselves in opposition to the government instead of in control of it. The autocratic Moi consolidated his power by replacing many Kikuyu officials with Kalenjin counterparts. Despite upset-

In 1964, when this photo was taken, the Kikuyu were the most influential ethnic group in Kenya. Dressed in traditional garb, these Kikuyu women appeared at a rally in Nairobi to support President Jomo Kenyatta, also a Kikuyu.
© AP Wirephoto

ting many in the Kikuyu majority Moi stayed in power until 2002. In elections held that year Kikuyu-dominated KANU was defeated for the first time by opposition parties. However, Mwai KIBAKI (1931–), the leader of the opposition, was also a Kikuyu. Thus the Kikuyu once again returned to political prominence in Kenya.

The Kikuyu are also known as the Gikuyu, after the name of their traditional founder. According to Kikuyu lore, Gikuyu was led to the top of Mount Kenya (known to the Kikuyu as Kirinyaga) by the divine spirit, Ngai. There he was given a wife and had nine daughters who founded the nine Kikuyu clans.

See also: ETHNIC CONFLICT IN AFRICA (Vol. V); ETHNICITY AND IDENTITY (Vol. I); KIKUYU (Vols. I, II, III, IV).

Further reading: Claire C. Robertson, *Trouble Showed the Way: Women, Men, and Trade in the Nairobi Area, 1890–1990* (Bloomington, Ind.: Indiana University Press, 1997).

Kinshasa (formerly Leopoldville) Capital and principal city of the Democratic Republic of the CONGO. Kinshasa originated, in 1881, as a European colonial trading station. Named Leopoldville in honor of King Leopold II (1835–1909) of Belgium, it occupied a strategic geographical location as the terminus for navigation on the Congo River. The city served as the capital of the Belgian Congo from 1923 onward and then at independence, in 1960, became the capital of the new republic. Shortly after MOBUTU SESE SEKO (1930–1997) overthrew the government of President Joseph KASAVUBU (c. 1913–1969), he further erased the colonial legacy by renaming the city *Kinshasa*.

As the administrative, commercial, and communications center of the country, and the home of the major educational, cultural, and medical facilities, continued growth of the city was to be expected. However, the process of URBANIZATION far outstripped expectations. Already a sizeable city of 400,000, in 1960, Kinshasa became a mega-city over the decades following independence. A 1984 census placed its population at 2,664,000, while the most recent estimates show that it now has more than 5 million inhabitants. This would make it second only to LAGOS, NIGERIA in size among the cities of contemporary sub-Saharan Africa.

As its population grew, so did its physical size. In 1960 it occupied about 21 square miles (55 sq km). However, in 1984, the last year for which there are reliable statistics, the city had grown to cover 82 square miles (212 sq km), and by century's end it was even larger. By then, approximately 10 percent of the country's population lived in the capital.

Much of Kinshasa's POPULATION GROWTH was fueled by the warfare and violence that has frequently wracked the country since independence, beginning with the civil war of 1960–65. Indeed, for many thousands of Congolese, the city, despite the overcrowding, crime, and dearth of jobs, seemed safer than the countryside. As the city grew, unemployment and underemployment did as well, since the modern economic sector is modest in comparison to the city's size. Today, many of its people survive by participating in the informal economy. In the 1990s the violence that pervaded so much of the Congo swept into the city, and President Mobutu had to call on Belgian and French troops to put down urban unrest. More recently, in 1997, the insurgent forces of Laurent KABILA (c. 1939–2001) fought their way to the city's edge before Mobutu fled into exile.

See also: BELGIAN CONGO (Vol. IV); BELGIUM AND AFRICA (Vol. IV); LEOPOLDVILLE (Vol. IV); URBAN LIFE AND CULTURE (Vol. V).

Kisangani (formerly Stanleyville) Major port city of the Democratic Republic of the CONGO (DRC), located on the Congo River. Founded in 1882 by Anglo-American explorer and adventurer Sir Henry Morton Stanley (1841–1904), Kisangani is strategically located at the bottom of Boyoma (formerly Stanley) Falls, which is the terminus of the navigable stretch of the Congo River from KINSHASA, 770 miles (1,239 km) to the southwest. The city offers a port to offload shipments and a rail link around the falls to the port of Ubundu. Aside from its role as a transshipment location, the city has a small manufacturing sector in brewing, printing, furniture, metal products, clothing, and food processing.

Kisangani was a city of strategic importance during conflicts in the DRC. In the 1950s the city was a stronghold of Congolese prime minister Patrice LUMUMBA (1925–1961), the charismatic former postal clerk whose leadership of the opposition to the Belgian colonial government eventually lead to national independence in 1960. Not long after gaining independence, however, Lumumba retreated back to Kisangani as opposition to his government rose. After Lumumba was seized by his political opponents and executed in 1961, Antoine Gizenga (1925–) chose Kisangani as the seat of government for his separatist Republic of Congo state. The central government in Léopoldville (now KINSHASA), however, ended his attempted rebellion in 1967, forcing the city and surrounding region back into the greater Congolese state.

In 2000 the city was the site of fighting among the Uganda Patriotic Defense Forces, the RWANDA PATRIOTIC ARMY FRONT, and the Congolese Rally for Democracy

During the crisis in Rwanda in the 1990s, many refugees fled west into neighboring Democratic Republic of the Congo. Along with 80,000 others, this woman and her child lived in extremely difficult conditions in a camp in Kisangani. © *United Nations*

(RCD). By 2003 the RCD had gained control of the city. At the beginning of the 21st century, the city was home to an estimated 846,000 inhabitants.

See also: BELGIAN CONGO (Vol. IV); BELGIUM AND AFRICA (Vol. IV); CIVIL WARS (Vol. V); CONGO RIVER (Vol. I); STANLEY, HENRY MORTON (Vol. IV); URBAN LIFE AND CULTURE (Vols. IV, V); URBANIZATION (Vols. IV, V).

Konaré, Alpha Oumar (1946–   ) *President of Mali from 1992 to 2002*

Born in Kayes, MALI, Konaré received his EDUCATION at the École Normale Superieure in BAMAKO. He then went on to earn a doctorate in archaeology from University of Varsovie, in Poland, completing his studies in 1975. Back home in Mali he was an active member of several international organizations, including the United Nations Economic, Social, and Cultural Organization. In 1978 Konaré was appointed Mali's minister of youth, sports, arts, and culture. He served only two years in this position, however, before resigning in protest of the corrupt regime of Moussa TRAORÉ (1936–   ).

In 1986 Konaré helped create the National Democratic and Popular Front, which participated in covert opposition activities against Traoré's military dictatorship. To further his political agenda, several years later, he also began publishing *Les Echos,* an independent weekly newspaper. In 1991 military leader Amadou Toumani TOURÉ (1948–   ) led the effort to depose Traoré and then called for a new multiparty political system in Mali. Konaré co-founded the Alliance for Democracy in Mali and then led the party to victory in the 1992 elections, winning nearly 70 percent of the vote. As Mali's president Konaré promoted the DEMOCRATIZATION process and proved to be a popular leader. He was reelected in 1997 but the new Malian constitution barred Konaré from seeking a third term. In 2002 the office passed to the duly elected Amadou Toumani Touré.

See also: POLITICAL PARTIES AND ORGANIZATIONS (Vol. V).

Further reading: R. James Bingen, David Robinson, and John M. Staatz, eds., *Democracy and Development in Mali* (East Lansing, Mich.: Michigan State University Press, 2000).

Kourouma, Ahmadou (1927–) *Novelist from Ivory Coast*

Born in IVORY COAST in 1927, Ahmadou Kourouma attended secondary school in BAMAKO, MALI. After being expelled for leading a student strike he joined the Tirailleurs Senegalais, the colonial army of French West Africa, in 1945. While stationed in Ivory Coast, he refused to participate in suppressing a mutiny. As a result the army transferred him to French Indo-China (1951–54), where a bitter war was raging. He became a broadcaster for the French military radio network. After leaving the army he studied accounting in Lyon, France, graduating in 1959. He then returned to the Ivory Coast and worked as a banker and accountant. In the early 1960s his outspoken criticism of the country's president, Félix HOUPHOUËT-BOIGNY (1905–1993), forced him to go into exile in ALGERIA. He did not return until after Houhphouët-Boigny's death. Kourouma spent the 1970s working in CAMEROON as the head of the African Insurance School in YAOUNDÉ. In the 1980s he became the head of the Reinsurance Company of the Franc Zone.

Kourouma's career as a novelist began in the 1960s when he began to write about the post-independence political events of West Africa. He had a difficult time finding a publisher for his first novel, *Les Soleils des independences* (Suns of independence), in part because of the way he wrote, in an Africanized French. This, along with his openly critical analysis of Ivory Coast's neo-colonial politics and society, caused French publishers in 1964 to reject his manuscript. It was only in 1968 that he found a publisher in Montreal, Canada. The book won international critical acclaim and sold 100,000 copies, leading to its publication in France in 1970. His other novels include *Monnè, outrages et défis* (1990), *En attendat le vote des bêtes sauvages* (Waiting on the vote of the savages, 1998), which was based on his observation of tyranny in TOGO, and *Allah n'est pas obligé* (*God is Not Obliged*; 2000). Although not numerous, Kourouma's works have established him as one of contemporary Africa's most significant writers.

See also: LITERATURE IN MODERN AFRICA (Vol. V).

Kufuor, John Agyekum (1938–) *President of Ghana since 2001*

A member of the Ashanti royal family, Kufuor was born in KUMASI, the traditional Ashanti capital in present-day GHANA (called Gold Coast Colony at the time). There he attended Prempeh College before studying law at Lincoln's Inn, in London. In 1961 Kufuor was admitted to the bar and then attended the University of Oxford, earning a master's degree in economics, philosophy, and political science.

In 1967, after returning to Ghana, Kufuor became chief legal officer and town clerk for his hometown of Kumasi. Elected in 1969 to serve as a member of parliament, he was also appointed deputy foreign minister by Kofi BUSIA (1913–1978) that same year. Busia's government was overthrown, however, in 1972, and Kufuor left government to try his hand in the business world. Kufuor returned to politics in 1979, helping to draft a new constitution. Following this he was once again elected to Ghana's parliament. In 1981 a military officer named Jerry RAWLINGS (1947–) led a COUP D'ETAT, again changing Ghana's government. This time Kufuor remained in public service, becoming Rawlings's secretary for local government in January 1982. Kufuor, however, never found a common ground with Rawlings and his authoritative regime and resigned from his position seven months later.

For the next decade Kufuor worked mostly in the private sector. In the early 1990s, as Ghana moved towards a more democratic political system, Kufuor helped found the New Patriotic Party (NPP) in opposition to Rawlings's government. In 1996 Kufuor was the NPP's presidential candidate but lost to Rawlings. He ran again in 2000, this time winning the presidency with a platform that called for economic reform and an improved educational system.

See also: ASHANTI (Vol. II); ASHANTI EMPIRE (Vols. III, IV); DEMOCRATIZATION (Vol. V); GHANA (Vols. III, IV); GOLD COAST COLONY (Vol. IV).

Kumasi (Coomassie)

Large market city and capital of the former Ashanti Empire, located in the dense forests of central GHANA. Kumasi, as the Ashanti capital city, grew into a major commercial center in the 17th century. Later, toward the end of the 19th century, it became part of the British Gold Coast colony. Good TRANSPORTATION facilities built by the British linked Kumasi to coastal ports, and the city's economic activities centered around the production and exportation of cocoa.

Today, Kumasi is one of the largest urban centers in Ghana, with a population that was estimated at 630,000, in 2002. It boasts one of the largest markets in all of western Africa. Principal traditional products sold at the market include woven *kente* cloth, wood carvings, and bronze castings. The city is still a center for cocoa production and has a substantial food processing industry, as well.

Kumasi's old British fort, built in 1897, is now the home of the Ghana Regiment Museum. The city also hosts the University of Science and Technology, founded in 1951, and has several other educational and research institutes, as well as numerous parks and an airport.

The Ashanti political and cultural legacy continues to this day. In 1999 Barima Kwaku Dua (1950–   ), a popular member of the Ashanti royal line, became the sixteenth *asantehene,* or Ashanti king. He took the title Otumfuo Osei Tutu II.

See also: ASHANTI (Vol. II); ASHANTI EMPIRE (Vols. III, IV); COCOA (Vol. IV); ENGLAND AND AFRICA (Vols. III, IV, V); GOLD COAST (Vols. III, IV); KUMASI (Vols. III, V); URBANIZATION (Vols. IV, V), URBAN LIFE AND CULTURE (Vols. IV, V).

Kuomboka Ceremony   Spectacular African cultural ceremony practiced for centuries by the Lozi ethnic group in ZAMBIA. The ceremony is an annual event in the country's Western Province. Usually taking place in late March or early April, the Kuomboka Ceremony marks the movement of the Lozi *lutunga,* or king, from his summer capital of Lealui to his winter capital in Limulunga.

Kuomboka literally means "to get out of water" and refers to the annual flooding of the Zambezi River that necessitates the *lutunga's* migration. The flooding turns the farmlands of the Barotse plains into a huge lake, forcing the people to move to higher ground. For years the Lozi ethnic group has turned this annual exodus into a huge ceremonial procession that includes small boats and dugout canoes led by the massive royal barge of the *lutunga.* The royal barge is named the Nalikwanda, which means "for the people," and is painted in huge white and black stripes that signify spirituality and black people. The Nalikwanda transports the *lutunga,* his attendants, and royal musicians. It is powered by the rowing of more than 100 people, who all wear traditional outfits. The queen's barge and a flotilla of smaller canoes follow the Nalikwanda.

The journey from Lealui to Limulunga takes about six hours. Throughout the trip the royal musicians play Lozi xylophones, called *salimbas,* and three huge royal war drums, called *maoma* drums. The drums are more than 3 feet (1 m) wide and are believed to be at least 170 years old. The music calls on the people to follow their king to higher, drier land. A huge celebration lasting at least three days follows the end of the *lutunga's* journey to Limulunga. The return trip marking the end of the floods, usually in July or August, is less celebrated.

The Kuomboka ceremony has become a national event that includes the participation of the country's president as well as foreign dignitaries. It is the continuation of a long-standing cultural ceremony, but lacks the political importance of the past, when the Lozi were an independent state. Still, it continues to have an important cultural meaning and has become a major tourist attraction.

See also: LOZI (Vols. III, IV); TOURISM (Vol. V).

L

Laayoune (El Aaiun) Former colonial capital of Spanish Sahara (present-day WESTERN SAHARA). Now the political center of the disputed territory, Laayoune is located in the northern part of the region, on the Atlantic coast.

The Spanish laid claim to the region that is now Western Sahara in 1884. Laayoune was established as the administrative headquarters for the colony, which was officially granted to Spain during the Berlin Conference of 1884–85. In 1963 the discovery of massive phosphate deposits in nearby Boukra led to the construction of a conveyor belt to transport the phosphate to a pier 18 miles (29 km) southwest of Laayoune proper. Phosphate has since become Laayoune's primary export. The city also has a significant fishing industry.

In the early 1970s the indigenous SAHARAWI people, who had clashed with the Spanish for much of the 20th century, organized the POLISARIO, a resistance group that launched a guerrilla campaign aimed at securing independence. By 1976 Spanish troops had withdrawn from Laayoune, and MOROCCO claimed control of the city and the northern half of the former Spanish territory. The Polisario continued to fight, now against the Moroccans, and established a government-in-exile for the Saharawi Arab Democratic Republic, which has since been recognized by seventy countries.

During the fighting much of Laayoune's population fled to refugee camps in ALGERIA. A cease-fire was signed in 1991, but a UN referendum on the status of Western Sahara was repeatedly postponed, and Morocco made clear its intent to maintain its claims to the region. As of 2003 Laayoune remained a city in limbo. Due to the contentious status of Laayoune and difficulties with gathering legitimate census numbers, Laayoune's population is not well established, though 2003 estimates indicate roughly 300,000 people inhabit the city.

See also: INDEPENDENCE MOVEMENTS (Vol. V); SPAIN AND AFRICA (Vols. III, IV); UNITED NATIONS AND AFRICA (Vols. IV, V); URBAN LIFE AND CULTURE (Vols. IV, V); URBANIZATION (Vols. IV, V).

labor Africa entered the era of political independence with labor systems that were vastly changed from what had existed prior to colonial rule. The process of diversification of labor that began during the colonial period accelerated greatly after 1960. The increasingly rapid URBANIZATION of much of the continent contributed significantly to the diversification of labor, as did the continued growth in using MONEY AND CURRENCY for economic transactions. While AGRICULTURE continued to occupy much of Africa's labor force, the MINING industry as well as the government also were major employers.

It is difficult to generalize about labor practices for Africa as a whole, since regional differences are important. For example, there are major contrasts between North Africa and sub-Saharan Africa. North Africa is the most urbanized region of the continent, with an average of 54 percent of the population living in urban areas. In LIBYA the figure is about 86 percent of the population, while in EGYPT the figure is about 45 percent. (However, Egypt's relatively low urbanization rate belies the fact that CAIRO, the Egyptian capital, is the largest city in all of Africa). The country with the next-highest urban percentage is GABON, a small, lightly populated country in west-central Africa where the development of rich OIL deposits has resulted in large-scale rural-to-urban migration. Africa's most *industrialized* country is SOUTH AFRICA, but 50 percent of its population still lives in rural areas.

Another major difference between North Africa and sub-Saharan Africa involves gender relations. North Africa, due to the influence of Islam, has a far smaller percentage of women workers. Only 8 percent of the women there were economically active in 1970, but that number rose to 21 percent by 1990. On the other hand, a little less than 40 percent of sub-Saharan African women were economically active in 1970, a figure that barely changed by 1990. The republics of BENIN and BURUNDI, MOZAMBIQUE, and TANZANIA have the highest percentage of women in the overall economically active population (47 percent). Libya, with 10 percent, has the continent's lowest representation of women in the overall labor pool. In neither North Africa nor sub-Saharan Africa, however, does involvement in the economically active population take into account women's domestic labor. The 1990 statistics also show a major disparity in terms of children under age 15 in the work force. In North Africa only 4 percent of girls and 7 percent of boys age 10–14 were economically active, but in sub-Saharan Africa 21 percent of the girls and 33 percent of the boys were active.

Gauging gender dimensions by economic sector also brings out regional differences. Sub-Saharan African women overwhelmingly work in agriculture, as do men, but by a larger percentage (75 percent to 61 percent) than in North Africa. In North Africa a large percentage of economically active women—46 percent—are in the service sector, as are 40 percent of the men. Also, across all main professional groups, sub-Saharan African women participated more fully than did those in North Africa. The greatest disparity was in the sales industry, where women made up 52 percent of the labor force in sub-Saharan Africa but only 10 percent in North Africa.

Such a distribution of labor suggests not only how labor is utilized in Africa, but also provides insights into the economic DEVELOPMENT of the various countries. As noted, the agricultural sector is the largest employer in sub-Saharan Africa but much less so in North Africa. Only Egypt, with its large rural population, has a major concentration of labor in the agricultural sector, 42 percent of the male labor force and 8 percent of the female force. Much of Egyptian agriculture is oriented toward providing foodstuffs for the urban markets as well as producing cotton for export. Much of sub-Saharan African agriculture, on the other hand, is aimed at producing FOOD CROPS for domestic consumption. This is especially true for Sahelian countries such as NIGER (92 percent of the women and 84 percent of the men) and BURKINA FASO (85 percent of both men and women) as well as Burundi (98 percent of women and 87 percent of men) and RWANDA, with similar percentages. Countries producing a significant amount of CASH CROPS often have a smaller percentage of their labor force in agriculture than do sub-

sistence-oriented economies. GHANA, for example, has 50 percent of its female labor and 55 percent of its male labor in agriculture, while the respective figures for the IVORY COAST are 62 percent and 50 percent. Countries in which large numbers of men participate in migrant labor reflect this in the high gender imbalance in the agricultural labor force. Leading examples of this phenomenon are Mozambique, with 97 percent of the women but only 68 percent of the men, and MALAWI (women, 92 percent, and men, 63 percent).

On the whole Africa is the least industrial of the six inhabited continents, but there are pockets of industrialization. South Africa is the leader in this respect, with 48 percent of its male labor and 17 percent of its female labor working in the industrial sector as of 1994. Also, many of the 40 percent of the male workers and of the 70 percent of the women workers in the service sector were in areas supportive of the industrial sector. These figures have changed somewhat over the past decade, with perhaps the biggest change being a jump in the unemployment rate from 31 percent to 40 percent over this time span. Many of the formally unemployed, however, survive through work in the informal economy. They hawk goods and foodstuffs, work at odd jobs, and also engage in activities that are extra-legal.

Egypt also has a well-developed industrial sector (20 percent the female labor and 25 percent of the male labor) and service sector (71 percent of the female and 33 percent of the male labor) in its economy. Considering that Egypt's population is nearly 70 million and that its economy is second only to that of South Africa, it is clear that the health of the country's industrial and service sectors is crucial to millions of people. As in South Africa, TOURISM constitutes a growing component of the services sector. MAURITIUS is the country that is most rapidly developing its service sector by emphasizing information and communications technology. By 1999 nearly 61 percent of the total labor force of Mauritius was working in this sector.

The type of work that Africans do thus varies greatly depending upon whether they are rural or urban, in which part of the continent they live, the state of the economy in the countries in which they live, and whether they are men or women. Labor patterns in Africa have steadily evolved as the economies of the continent change, but they also can be greatly disrupted by events such as CIVIL WARS, natural disasters, and world economic factors.

See also: COLONIALISM, INFLUENCE OF (Vol. IV); GENDER IN MODERN AFRICA (Vol. V); LABOR (Vols. I, IV); WOMEN IN MODERN AFRICA (Vol. V).

Further reading: Owen Crankshaw, *Race, Class, and the Changing Division of Labour under Apartheid* (New York: Routledge, 1997); Bill Freund, *The Making of Contemporary Africa: The Development of African Society since 1800,* 2nd ed. (Boulder, Colo.: Lynne Rienner, 1998).

labor unions (trade unions) Organizations that bring together workers in the interest of improving wages, working conditions, and benefits. A labor union's concerns can draw members into the political arena in order to secure or force government support for the issues they deem beneficial to them.

African labor unions were strong supporters of African nationalism and the INDEPENDENCE MOVEMENTS that ended colonial rule in Africa. Labor leaders often became political leaders and, in a few instances, presidents of a newly independent country. Ahmed Sékou TOURÉ (1922–1984) of GUINEA was a prime example of this. In general, the alliance between labor unions and the nationalist political parties in the struggle for independence did not survive long after the struggle achieved its goals. As with other potential rivals to their newly found political power, African heads of state often tried to co-opt or silence the labor movement. Indeed, Touré acted in this manner, all the while claiming to be establishing a people's democracy based on the principals of African Socialism. One-party states became the norm for much of Africa, a development that was reinforced when one COUP D'ÉTAT after another installed military officers in the presidential palaces of newly independent African countries. In SOUTH AFRICA the APARTHEID government worked diligently to prevent the emergence of any labor movement in its black LABOR force, though white workers were free to unionize and had considerable political influence.

The political realm was not the only challenge to labor unions in the postcolonial era. As Africa increasingly faced an economic crisis in the 1970s, the economic base for successful trade unions also eroded. INDUSTRIALIZATION had been slow to take hold in most countries, despite the efforts of leaders such as Kwame NKRUMAH (1909–1972) of GHANA, who had sought to develop an industrial base for his country with such projects as the massive AKOSOMBO DAM. A strong industrial base was important for the emergence of labor unions. Mineworkers were an important source of union membership, but in countries such as ZAMBIA the decline of the copper MINING industry reduced the power of unions. Also, as growing URBANIZATION outpaced job creation, large armies of the unemployed were available to break any strike by unionized workers. This significantly undercut their ability to wield the strike as a weapon in their efforts to improve their situation.

Somewhat surprisingly, given the repressive and harsh reality of life under apartheid, it was in South Africa that the labor movement had unprecedented success. African trade unions, although not illegal, lacked the legal right to engage in collective bargaining or to strike, and where they did exist they were under great pressure from government authorities. In 1973, however, a wave of strikes that the government found itself unable to suppress broke out in the heavily industrialized port city of DURBAN. The strikes essentially led to a rebirth of the union movement. Under labor leaders such as Cyril RAMAPHOSA (1952–), the movement became increasingly energized, eventually leading to the formation of the Congress of South African Trade Unions (COSATU) in 1985. COSATU in turn was a major force within the UNITED DEMOCRATIC FRONT, the organization that was leading the internal political opposition to apartheid. After the AFRICAN NATIONAL CONGRESS (ANC) and other political parties were no longer banned, in 1990 COSATU entered into an electoral alliance with the ANC and the Communist Party to win the elections. The labor movement has been sufficiently strong in South Africa to continue as a viable force in the country's government. More recently labor unions have also challenged the government policies of Thabo MBEKI (1942–). In 1999, for example, 1 million workers staged a massive one-day strike to protest his plans to institute changes that could potentially send South African jobs abroad.

The same forces of DEMOCRATIZATION that have been at work in South Africa over the past 15 years have also strengthened labor unions elsewhere on the continent. Economic issues often crystallized the situation and led to increased labor-union activities. For example, in 1994 the purchasing power of workers was struck a heavy blow when the CFA—the contemporary currency of the former French colonies—was devalued by 50 percent. Unions in a number of West African countries waged a series of strikes seeking wage increases that would counter the CFA's diminished value. In Zambia Frederick CHILUBA (1943–), a former shop steward and the head of the 300,000-member Zambian Congress of Trades Unions, won 75 percent of the vote in the 1991 presidential elections. He then privatized Zambia's copper mines to help revive the moribund mining industry and improve the fortunes of the mineworkers. In neighboring ZIMBABWE the Zimbabwe Congress of Trade Unions, under the leadership of Morgan TSVANGIRAI (1952–), has been at the core of the electoral challenges to the long rule of Robert MUGABE (1924–). This political challenge has come at a great cost, however, with the government charging Tsvangirai with plotting to murder Mugabe.

Labor unions have survived through difficult times in much of Africa since the early 1960s. Though they remain weak in many parts of the continent, there is a persistence to their existence and their struggle to better the lives of their members and, in many instances, society in general.

See also: COLONIAL RULE (Vol. IV); LABOR UNIONS (Vol. IV); NATIONALISM AND INDEPENDENCE MOVEMENTS (Vol. IV).

Further reading: Frederick Cooper, *Decolonization and African Society: The Labor Question in French and British Africa* (New York: Cambridge University Press, 1996); Gay W. Seidman, *Manufacturing Militance: Work-*

In South Africa the Nationalist government resorted to lethal violence to suppress the protests of black laborers. When labor-related violence did break out, headlines like the one shown in this 1973 photo served to galvanize the black labor movements. © *UPI*

ers' *Movements in Brazil and South Africa, 1970–1985* (Berkeley, Calif.: University of California Press, 1994).

Ladysmith Black Mambazo   South African vocal group. Ladysmith Black Mambazo was founded by Joseph Shabalala (1940–   ) and named in tribute to the group's hometown of Ladysmith, KwaZulu-Natal, SOUTH AFRICA. Black Mambazo literally means "Black Axe." Shabalala, the group's founder, lead vocalist, and chief songwriter, is the unquestioned leader. Usually having about 10 members at any time, the group is made up of Shabalala's brothers, cousins, and family friends.

Ladysmith Black Mambazo first achieved success in South Africa in the early 1970s, but it was in the mid-1980s when they gained international prominence. The group benefited greatly from their involvement in American musician Paul Simon's (1941–   ) *Graceland* album, in 1986, and the subsequent tour, allowing the group to perform to great acclaim all over the world.

Their first album released in the United States, entitled *Shaka Zulu,* won the Grammy award for Best Traditional Folk Album of 1987.

Ladysmith Black Mambazo has become synonymous with the ZULU male a capella choral music known as *isicathamiya*. This style evolved among Zulu mine workers who participated in singing competitions for leisure. *Isicathamiya* means "to step on one's toes lightly," probably referring to the nimble dance steps that the miners choreographed so as not to bother sleeping security guards.

Since then, Ladysmith Black Mambazo has been nominated for six additional Grammy awards. The group has recorded and toured with many of the world's leading musical artists and has performed for numerous state functions both in South Africa and abroad. Their distinctive harmonizing has appeared on the soundtracks of numerous full-length motion pictures, including *Coming To America*; *Cry, The Beloved Country*; *A Dry White Season*; *Moonwalker*; and *Let's Do It A Capella*. Appearances on *Sesame Street* and commercials for Heinz, Lifesavers, 7-UP, and IBM have further enhanced the group's stature. Since the mid-1980s Ladysmith Black Mambazo has increasingly integrated Western popular and gospel music into its distinctive Zulu style.

Lagos Major port city and former capital of NIGERIA, located on the Bight of Benin, a series of lagoons and islands in the Atlantic Ocean. By the latter half of the 19th century Lagos was West Africa's leading port. Part of the Colony and Protectorate of Nigeria of the early 20th century, in 1914 it was named the capital. When Nigeria achieved independence in 1960, Lagos became the federal capital.

In the decade prior to independence Nigeria's economy had begun to turn away from the cash-crop production that the British had promoted. In its place OIL production became the country's crucial industry. As one of Nigeria's leading centers of petroleum processing, Lagos grew tremendously during the oil boom of the early 1970s, eventually boasting a population of nearly 1 million. The growth outpaced the expansion of the city's INFRASTRUCTURE and services, however, and Lagos became cramped, its atmosphere polluted by industry. Movement through the city became a major problem, with traffic often at a standstill on the bridges that connected the four main islands on which the 115-square-mile (300 sq km) city rests. By 1975 the problem had become so severe that officials decided to move the capital to ABUJA, in central Nigeria. Although the seat of government officially moved to Abuja, in 1991, many government offices still operated out of Lagos.

In 1981 a worldwide recession and a drop in oil prices greatly affected the Lagos economy, forcing officials to make cuts in social services. Nevertheless, a constant inflow of migrants from other parts of Nigeria and western Africa arrived at the city, resulting in a diverse urban population. Lagos's island topography restricted its expansion, resulting in high population densities (in 1995, the population was estimated at 1,480,000), which put an extra burden on the city's resources. Urban renewal projects are currently underway to improve the inadequate WATER, sewage, electricity, and health-care services. Lagos is projected to be one of the world's five largest cities by the early part of the 21st century.

Lagos still has a strong industrial sector centered on food processing, metal products, automobile and radio assembly, textiles, cosmetics, pharmaceuticals, paint, soap, and fishing. It also hosts the Nigerian National Museum (founded in 1957) and the University of Lagos (1962).

See also: BIGHT OF BENIN (Vol. III); ENGLAND AND AFRICA (Vols. III, IV, V); LAGOS (Vols. III, IV); URBAN LIFE AND CULTURE (Vols. IV, V); URBANIZATION (Vols. IV, V).

Further reading: Margaret Peil, *Lagos: The City is the People* (London: Belhaven, 1991).

La Guma, Alex (Justin Alexander La Guma)
(1925–1985) *South African novelist*

Born to a Cape Coloured family, La Guma spent his youth in the inner urban area of CAPE TOWN known as District Six. He received both a high school and technical college EDUCATION and then worked in clerical and factory jobs. He also married, in 1954, and had two sons. In 1947, following in the footsteps of his political activist father, La Guma joined the Young Communist League. The following year, he officially joined the Communist Party, marking the beginning of his political activities.

La Guma's father, James (Jimmy) La Guma (1894–1961), was a Cape Town activist and a member of the Communist Party until it was banned in 1950. He was deeply involved in many ANTI-APARTHEID and labor organizations, such as the National Liberation League and the Industrial and Commercial Workers Union. Like his son, he was also imprisoned for heading a strike, in this case among garment workers in the Cape region.

La Guma joined the AFRICAN NATIONAL CONGRESS (ANC), in 1955, and the South African Coloured People's Organization (SACPO), which he helped lead through the 1950s and 1960s. In connection with these memberships, La Guma participated, in 1956, in the Congress of the People, which led to the Freedom Charter, a statement of rights for Africans in SOUTH AFRICA. His participation subsequently led to his being named a defendant in the infamous Treason Trial, which began that same year. In all, 156 defendants were tried, and though the trial lasted five years, ultimately there were no convictions.

La Guma began work as a journalist for the activist newspaper, *New Age*, in 1955. The following year he also began his career in fiction, publishing a short story in the magazine *Fighting Talk*, which continued to be a forum for La Guma as his activism intensified.

In 1961, however, one year after the SHARPEVILLE massacre and the imposition of the ban on the ANC, La Guma was arrested for his involvement in organizing a strike and was sentenced, without trial, to five years under house arrest. During that time La Guma wrote a number of short stories and the novel *And a Threefold Cord* (1964). After the end of his sentence La Guma went into exile in England, where he published *The Stone Country* (1966) and *In the Fog of the Season's End* (1972), which is generally considered his finest work. Incorporating autobiographical elements, La Guma's novels expose the brutality and hopelessness of apartheid-era South Africa and feature characters struggling to gain their basic human rights.

The butcherbird feeds on ticks that in turn feast on the blood of livestock such as cattle. Because it removes the ticks, which often carry disease, the butcherbird is seen as a sign of good luck and health. La Guma's *The Time of the Butcherbird* concerns a racist landowner who is eventually killed by an African, an act symbolized by the butcherbird killing the tick, removing the cause of South Africa's apartheid disease.

In 1979 La Guma moved to Cuba and published his final novel, *Time of the Butcherbird*. He served as the ANC's official representative to Cuba until his death, in 1985, a decade before the fall of apartheid.

See also: COMMUNISM AND SOCIALISM (Vol. V); FREEDOM CHARTER (Vol. IV); LITERATURE IN MODERN AFRICA (Vol. V); *NEW AGE* (Vol. IV); NEWSPAPERS (Vol. IV); NEWSPAPERS AND PRINT MEDIA (Vol. V).

land use In Africa, land use has often engendered conflict over the small percentage of land that is suitable for farming. At 11.44 million square miles (29.62 million sq km), the African continent accounts for 20 percent of the world's land surface. With some 18 land-cover types, it is also highly diverse. Yet competing human needs and changing political norms present a dramatic challenge to establishing sustainable land use patterns.

African Land Given a population of approximately 820 million, it would seem that 11.44 million square miles would leave ample territory to suit all human and ecological needs. Compared to the United States, where 270 million people live on only 3.5 million square miles, population density in Africa is similar. Yet this masks the fundamental diversity of African land area and its ecological and political challenges.

Two-thirds of the continent is classified as desert, a highly challenging, inhospitable environment for humans. Dense, humid FORESTS cover much of central Africa as well as the island-nation of MADAGASCAR, but—while the

biomass that accumulates on the forest floor is integral to the incredible levels of African BIODIVERSITY—tropical soils do not lend themselves to sustainable agricultural practices. Approximately 21 percent of the African continent can be used for farming—this on a continent where about 61 percent of the population engages in agricultural activity. Limited infrastructure and the unavailability of irrigation, fertilizer, pesticides, and technologies all ensure that family farms remain small and that competition for land rights associated with the 2.4 million arable square miles (6.21 million sq km) remains fierce.

Agricultural Use Where AGRICULTURE is a large part of daily life and the largest economic sector, it invariably is closely linked to DEVELOPMENT. The WORLD BANK has estimated that for every 1 percent increase in agricultural production there is a 1.5 percent increase in economic growth due to the rise of associated industries and sectors.

As a result, in the 1980s and 1990s many African nations focused on dedicating increasing amounts of agricultural land to nine primary commodities: bananas, cocoa, coffee, cotton, groundnuts (peanuts), rubber, sugar, tea, and tobacco. While some countries benefited from such a strategy, major problems have resulted from this policy. First, global agricultural markets are notoriously volatile, with many of these key products undergoing rapid, unforeseeable decreases in value. Second, it is often difficult to move from agricultural production to increased production in other sectors. Since crops are generally low-cost goods with low profit margins, it is unwise to view agriculture as a panacea for economic development ills. Third, the impact of agriculture on ECOLOGY AND ECOLOGICAL CHANGE can be tremendous.

Land Quality Degradation Because of the wide range of land types, the quality of the land in Africa is extremely varied. Higher-quality land suffers from overexploitation, and many areas of lower-quality land have been forced into the service of food production. Increased population, inappropriate policies and management practices, and climate change all contribute to degrading the land. This degradation can be hyrdrological, chemical, physical, or biological.

Where there is hydrological degradation, WATER supplies are insufficient or become unusable because of high levels of dissolved salts or minerals. Chemical degradation is most commonly caused by irrigation runoff. Most critical in the short term, however, is physical degradation leading to soil loss. Where forests are cleared for agricultural purposes, soils erode rapidly. Compounding the problem is the tendency of tropical soils to hold their primary nutrients in the biomass closer to the surface, meaning that valuable nutrients are depleted quickly as the first layers of soil runoff. What is left of the former forest floor is marginal land with slow regenerative capacities and little agricultural potential. Further, the biodiversity of the land decreases, as do the ecological functions that biodiversity provides.

Perhaps even more troubling than land degradation caused by agriculture in Africa is land degradation caused by livestock grazing. Indeed, grazing accounts for nearly half of all land loss in Africa. In total about 66 percent of Africa's land area has been either moderately or significantly degraded already. Some regions, such as southeast NIGERIA, have felt the impact of this more than others.

Land degradation necessarily reduces the amount of land available for agriculture. This, in turn, significantly affects a country's ability to feed itself. Land quality is thus closely linked to food security. For instance, in Turkana District, northern KENYA, overgrazing, agricultural practices, and climate change all have contributed to land degradation. As a result, livestock mortality has increased, and food security, income, and economic assets have decreased. In years of drought and famine, the region has required as much as 600,000 tons of food aid to forestall mass starvation. Kenya's neighbor ETHIOPIA has faced even greater challenges, with persistent food shortages leaving up to 50 percent of the population undernourished. As a result of this food security debacle, land-conservation policy is as closely tied to politics as it is to land-tenure policy, or the conditions under which land is held.

Land-Tenure Policies Although rooted in the colonial era, Africa's land tenure dilemmas have been perpetuated by the unsuccessful practices of modern governments. At the turn of the century, French and British authorities set "vacant land" policies as a way of acquiring land for the state, and land thus became a tool to control the masses. As land rights became based on race, African lands were viewed as collective and European lands were viewed as private. In addition there was poor documenting of, or accounting for, indigenous land-tenure systems.

In many cases both the techniques used to cultivate the land as well as the crops grown were adapted to satisfy European tastes. In the 1920s and 1930s there was further "re-imagining" of land tenure, with colonial governments criticizing what they perceived as inefficient traditional farming methods, leading them to take more control of agricultural management

At independence many new African elites inherited the existing land-tenure and agricultural management policies and adopted them for their own gain. European private-land holdings became commercial farms for emerging African business classes while the majority poor remained on "communal" lands (if there were no state-recognized land-tenure systems). How these lands were appropriated was often closely linked to the ideological goals of the new leadership, touching off firestorms of divisive land struggles throughout the continent just as African economies faced their greatest challenges.

Privatization vs. Public Land It was in this context that the World Bank began encouraging land priva-

tization and the reassessment of land-tenure systems in the 1980s and 1990s. The challenge was to do something about so-called collective lands while recognizing "traditional" land claims. This meant that local land users had to "modernize" their land claims. In practice, many failed to do so, and well-placed domestic elites were able to grab lands and increase their holdings. Thus, while this process of privatizing lands may have been introduced with the best of intentions, in practice it has disproportionately benefited the rich at the expense of the poor.

Perhaps no more contentious case of this inequality exists than in ZIMBABWE, where land policies have been closely tied to the ability of president Robert MUGABE (1924–) to hold onto office. His state patronage system has benefited only commercial farmers and those of the land-holding classes who align themselves with his government. Further complicating the crisis is the fact that the Lancaster Agreement, which established Zimbabwe's independence from Great Britain in 1980, did not address adequately the role of white farmers of British descent still living in the country. Hence, land productivity in Zimbabwe decreased markedly between 1980 and 1995.

Land conflicts such as those found in Zimbabwe are increasingly common in Africa, even if the causes vary. They can be demographic, ecological, economic, or social. Specifically, population increases, environmental degradation, slow economic growth, continued dependence on small-scale farms, land scarcity, and social inequalities all contribute to the rise in land-use conflicts.

Further exacerbating these tensions are global environmental policies geared toward increasing the amount of state lands dedicated to NATIONAL PARKS and protected areas. Although conservation-driven land plans affect a relatively small percentage of the total land area (currently about 7 percent of the continent), local communities often see them as extensions of colonial policies that marginalize existing community-based land rights. The challenge in the coming years will be to find ways of decreasing these tensions while integrating local and national land-tenure policies in an equitable fashion. MOZAMBIQUE, TANZANIA, UGANDA, and other countries have tried to confront this situation in recent years through land acts and associated legislation.

Land Use Reform There have been increasing efforts to rectify land use inefficiencies and improve land quality and productivity in Africa. Between the years 2000 and 2002, for example, the United Nations Convention to Combat Desertification has helped 24 African countries adopt national action plans to manage soils, reduce land degradation, fight desert encroachment, and improve land governance. Other international organizations, such as the Food and Agriculture Organization of the United Nations and the Consultative Group on International Agriculture Research have joined with

African governments to try to improve land use while ameliorating the effects of less-than-ideal land-use and tenure policies.

See also: CASH CROPS (Vol. V).

Further reading: Kathleen M. Baker, *Indigenous Land Management in West Africa: An Environmental Balancing Act* (Oxford, U.K.: Oxford University Press, 2000).

language usage in modern Africa As a rule, Africans are multilingual, speaking a maternal language as a first language and one or more other languages for specific purposes in society. Today there are more than 2,000 African languages spoken on the continent, plus the European languages that are holdovers from the colonial era.

During the colonial period European language and governmental systems supplanted or limited those of the indigenous Africans. As a result European languages, the language of the colonizers, became the official languages of most modern-day African countries. North Africa was an exception, however. Arabic, with its long tradition of LITERACY and its intimate association with Islam, persisted through the colonial period to become the official language at independence. Even in the north, however, fluency in European languages was widespread. In EGYPT, for example, English was—and still is—widely spoken.

As the colonies approached independence, they wrestled with the question of a national identity associated with the formation of a nation-state. Central to this question is the concept of a national language. Two issues emerged in the choice of an official language. The language needed to be politically neutral, and it needed to be one that could help the new nation participate in global commerce. Each new country needed to choose one language for its official language. Given that almost every African country featured numerous languages, often spoken by competing ethnic groups, many of the former colonies chose the European colonizers' language as a "neutral" official language. This was one way to reduce the potential for ethnic conflict that could emerge by offending any one group as a result of giving preference to a single indigenous language within the country.

While there are 410 languages in NIGERIA, for example, there are three regional lingua francae, or languages used for inter-group communication. These include IGBO, HAUSA, and YORUBA, as well as the official language, English. For Nigeria to have selected any of the three linguae francae as official languages could have had disastrous results in a country already plagued by divisive issues of ETHNICITY AND IDENTITY. In fact, even without a debate regarding Nigeria's official language, the country descended into a brutal civil war (1966–70) because of long-standing ethnic differences.

If a nation chose an African language as its national language, it would limit its interaction within the global community. One example of this limitation is South Africa's appointment of a monolingual, AFRIKAANS-speaking ambassador to the United States, in 1948. He required an interpreter to communicate in the English-speaking milieu of the United States.

Today many Africans speak an indigenous African language as a first language, a local lingua franca as a second language, and a European tongue as a third language. Kenyans, for example, speak an indigenous tongue, the national language, Kiswahili, and the official language, English.

Because children learn faster and more easily in their first language(s), primary school instruction is conducted in the maternal language or, in some instances, a lingua franca. Secondary schools and schools of higher EDUCATION almost universally utilize European languages for purposes of instruction. Even in Egypt, technical subjects such as the engineering sciences are taught in English at the university level. Outside North Africa the official business of the government and the economy are generally conducted using European languages.

A language problem occurs when students are unable for one reason or another to complete their education, e.g., failure of the exit exam or passing the exam but unable to pay for books and uniforms. Because they have not been able to compete in the secondary classroom in the European language, these "school leavers," as they are called, may be unable to compete for higher paying jobs in the economy due to a language barrier. Many of those students living in rural settings have not completed their education, precluding them from participating in political or economic discourses. Language deficiency creates a two-tiered system in competition between the rural and urban areas and within the urban areas among those competing for jobs in the formal economy. In this and other ways, then, patterns of language acquisition and usage are central to many of the challenges that Africans face today, including problems related to DEVELOPMENT, POVERTY, and education.

See also: LANGUAGE IN COLONIAL AFRICA (Vol. IV); LANGUAGES, MAJOR (Vol. I); COLONIALISM, INFLUENCE OF (Vol. IV).

Further reading: Ali and Alamin M. Mazrui, *The Power of Babel: Language & Governance in the African Experience* (Chicago: University of Chicago Press, 1998); Zaline Makini Roy-Campbell, *Empowerment through Language: The African Experience—Tanzania and Beyond* (Trenton, N.J.: Africa World Press, 2001).

law and justice Legal systems in Africa are generally made up of some combination of statutory law, customary law, court decisions, and common law. The legislature or the executive branch of government writes *statutory law.* *Customary laws* are based on patterns of social behavior and customs developed over time. They are commonly ethnic or local in root. *Court decisions* interpret laws and guide their application. And *common law* is based on the British system of laws in which tradition, custom, and precedent are used to shape statutes or codes.

Perhaps the greatest challenge facing governments is finding a way to bring together these different systems of law. This is especially important in countries going through DEMOCRATIZATION or constitutional transitions. For them, new statutory or common laws at the state level must work hand-in-hand with customary laws that can vary dramatically from region to region. And this must be done while supporting courts that can effectively interpret and uphold the various laws.

In SOUTH AFRICA, for example, the legal code is based on a combination of Roman-Dutch and common law. It has been used to codify both the separation of powers and the participation of the public in a way that might ensure the growth of their young democracy. However, the constitution guarantees that customary law will be followed where it exists, as long as it does not go against the Bill of Rights. In fact, the state courts are obliged to recognize traditional leadership and apply customary laws.

While South Africa has one of Africa's more successful legal designs, there are still challenges. First, courts are fairly strong but cannot change policy. Second, the courts are sometimes reluctant to challenge the executive arm of the government, especially in a case that involves the poor or politically marginal. This is a sign that there is a weakness in the rule of law compared to the strength of executive leaders. Third, there is an ongoing question about the strength of customary law. For instance, land rights generally fall under customary law, but they are not always consistent with land registration related to common law. As a result the question of who holds rights to the land often becomes as issue. Recently this situation has arisen with increasing frequency when governments claim common law rights over property set aside for conservation and the "public good." Their claims often conflict with individuals or groups who already claim customary rights to the land for agricultural or other purposes.

An example of one of the greatest challenges in integrating types of law can be seen presently in NIGERIA. There, the constitution guarantees that customary law is honored by states. This customary law, however, is often the system of Islamic law called *SHARIA*, which sometimes contradicts other legal elements that are central to Nigerian democracy. Overcoming this deep-rooted divide in types of law will be crucial to promoting DEVELOPMENT and the success of the government in reflecting the will of the people.

See also: LAW AND JUSTICE (Vols. I, II, III, IV); SHARIA (Vol. II).

Further reading: Thomas V. McClendon, *Genders and Generations Apart: Labor Tenants and Customary Law in Segregation-Era South Africa, 1920s to 1940s* (Boulder, Colo.: Greenwood Publishing Group, 2002); A. A. Kolajo, *Customary Law in Nigeria Through the Cases* (Bloomsburg, Pa.: Spectrum Publishers, 2000); George Ayittey, *Indigenous African Institutions* (Ardsley N.Y.: Transnational Publishers, 1991).

Leakey, Mary (1913–1996) *Archaeologist, anthropologist, and paleontologist*

Born in 1913 and raised in England, Italy, and France, Mary Douglas Nicol Leakey was excited by prehistory even as a child. This sense of excitement remained with her throughout her life. As she was to write in her 1984 autobiography, *Disclosing the Past,* throughout her career she had been "impelled by curiosity." In 1933 she married the well-known paleoarchaeologist Louis Leakey (1903–1972), thus launching what was to become a formidable archaeological team that was to be responsible for some of the most important discoveries about early hominids. Her son, Richard LEAKEY (1944–), and his wife Maeve Leakey (1942–) continue the Leakey paleontological tradition of research on human origins, as does their daughter, Louise Leakey (1972–).

Mary Leakey and her husband Louis early on became known for their work at Olduvai Gorge in northern TANZANIA, where, in 1959, she discovered the famous 1.75-million-year-old *Zinjanthropus* skull. Then, in 1960, she came across an even older hominid, *Homo habilis,* who was perhaps the first to make stone tools. The late 1960s found Mary increasingly on her own, continuing to work after her husband's death in 1972. She now began to receive full recognition for the enormously important work she was undertaking. In the mid-1970s she began excavation at Laetoli, located some 30 miles to the south of Olduvai Gorge. The hominid materials she began to uncover dated from as early as 2.4 million years ago and were thus far older than the remains found at Olduvai. The most important discovery of all was of a parallel set of hominid footprints that proved to be 3.6 million years old and was the earliest evidence of bipedalism (walking upright). As with so many such discoveries, the prints were found serendipitously, when Paul Abell, a visitor to the site, came across the prints. Leakey thought that the creatures that left these footprints belonged to the genus *Homo,* but Donald Johanson (1943–) and other prominent scientists argued for a different genus, *Australopithecus.* The debate over who left these footprints is illustrative of the difficulties of interpreting the scientific evidence related to the early hominids.

During the 1980s Mary Leakey continued her excavations, but her most important discoveries were behind her. She received honorary doctorates from some of the world's leading universities, including Chicago, Oxford, and Yale, as well as other major honors. Even a blood clot that led to blindness in her left eye did not seem to slow her down. She continued writing and directing excavations until close to her death in 1996. She was one of the 20th century's leading scholars on human origins.

See also: ARCHAEOLOGY (Vols. I, II, III, IV, V); ARCHAEOLOGICAL SCHOLARSHIP ON AFRICA (Vols. IV, V); AUSTRALOPITHECUS (Vol. I); HOMO ERECTUS (Vol. I); HOMO HABILIS (Vol. I); LEAKEY, MARY (Vol. IV); LEAKEYS, THE (Vol. I); OLDUVAI GORGE (Vol. I); ZINJANTHROPUS (Vol. I).

Further reading: Mary Leakey, Disclosing the Past (Garden City: Doubleday, 1984); Virginia Morrell, Ancestral Passions: The Leakey Family and the Quest for Humankind's Beginnings (New York: Touchstone Books, 1996); Barbara Williams, Breakthrough: Women in Archeology (New York: Walker, 1981).

Leakey, Richard (1944–) Kenyan paleoanthropologist and politician

The son of famous paleoanthropologists Mary LEAKEY (1913–1996) and Louis Leakey (1903–1972), Richard Leakey was born on December 19, in NAIROBI, KENYA. As a child, Richard frequently joined his parents on their anthropological digs. He had little interest, however, in following in their footsteps and dropped out of high school to become a safari guide. But he soon grew bored with the work, and when he found a lower jawbone of an Australopithecus in 1963, Leakey decided that anthropology was indeed his calling.

In 1967 Leakey, while on an expedition in southern ETHIOPIA, noticed a stretch of land that looked like a potential excavation site. The site was later named Koobi Fora, and over the next decade it offered up a large number of fossils—more than 400, representing approximately 200 individuals. In terms of human fossils, Koobi Fora is the richest excavation site in history.

Leakey's interpretations of the fossils were controversial. He theorized that, about 3 million years ago, at least three kinds of humanlike species coexisted with each other. Leakey's findings pushed him to the forefront of the anthropological field, and his status only increased as his theory was supported by further finds at Koobi Fora, including a reconstructed Homo habilis skull named "1470," after its initial identification number.

In 1968 Leakey was appointed to direct the National Museum of Kenya, a position he held for 20 years. During the 1970s and 1980s Leakey continued his fossil hunting. In 1984 his team made a monumental discovery—an almost complete skeleton of a Homo erectus boy catalogued as "WT 15000," nicknamed "Turkana Boy."

Leakey's involvement in paleoanthropology diminished in the late 1980s, as he turned his efforts towards conservation. In 1989 he became director of the Wildlife Conservation and Management Department, which later became Kenya Wildlife Services (KWS). As director, Leakey worked to reduce CORRUPTION within the department and developed programs to eliminate elephant and rhinoceros poaching. During this time he angered a number of politicians, many of whom wanted to use KWS land for commercial purposes. In 1993 a plane Leakey was flying malfunctioned and crashed. Leakey lost both of his legs below the knee, necessitating his use of prosthetics to walk. After recovering, in 1994 Leakey resigned from the KWS, citing differences with Kenyan president Daniel arap MOI (1924–). That same year Leakey formed Safini, an opposition political party named after the Swahili word for Noah's ark.

Richard's wife, Maeve (1942–), and his daughter, Louise (1972–), have continued the Leakey family tradition of making important discoveries about human origins. Working in the Lake Turkana region of western Kenya in the late 1990s, they came across a hominid skull they named *Kenyanthropus platyops* (flat-faced Kenya man). Some 3.5 million years old, *K. platyops* represents a new genus that was possibly a direct ancestor of modern humans.

In 1997 Leakey won election to Kenya's Parliament. He is a staunch proponent of democratic reforms and racial unity, and some believe that he may become Kenya's first white president. However, the recent 2002 election of Mwai KIBAKI (1931–) as president may have diminished this possibility.

See also: ANTHROPOLOGY AND AFRICA (Vols. I, II, II, IV, V); ARCHAEOLOGY IN AFRICA (Vols. I, II, III, IV, V); AUSTRALOPITHECUS (Vol. I); DEMOCRATIZATION (Vol. V); HOMO ERECTUS (Vol. I); HOMO HABILIS (Vol. I); HOMO SAPIENS (Vol. I); KENYA (Vols. I, II, III, IV); LEAKEY, LOUIS (Vol. IV); LEAKEYS, THE (Vol. I).

Lenshina, Alice (Mulenga Mubisha) (1924–1978) Bemba prophetess from Zambia (former Northern Rhodesia)

In the mid-1950s Alice Mulenga Mubisha split from the Presbyterian Church in Lubwa, Northern Rhodesia (present day ZAMBIA), following a quarrel with church MISSIONARIES. She subsequently founded the Lumpa Church, and took the name Lenshina, meaning "queen."

Based on her supposed mystical visions, Lenshina's Lumpa Church attracted many followers and, indeed, by the late 1950s, it had emerged as a powerful religious and political force among the rural population. Her organization essentially rejected all earthly authority, whether it be in the form of the colonial administration of Northern Rhodesia, the village chiefs, or, after 1964, the newly independent Zambian government.

When Zambia became independent, in 1964, the new UNITED NATIONAL INDEPENDENCE PARTY (UNIP) government saw the Lumpa Church as a challenge to its authority, since Lenshina had ordered her followers to burn UNIP membership cards, issuing them church membership cards instead. A cycle of retribution and violence ensued, with UNIP members burning the homes of church members and destroying buildings belonging to the Lumpa Church. Church members responded by attacking and killing several UNIP members, causing the government to intervene with force. Subsequent clashes resulted in the deaths of about 700 of Lenshina's followers. Lenshina, for her part, was arrested, and her church was banned. Released in 1975, Lenshina defied the ban by holding church services. She was arrested again, in 1977, and restricted to the LUSAKA area, where she died in 1978.

See also: BEMBA (Vol. III); CHRISTIANITY, INFLUENCE OF (Vols. IV, V); INDEPENDENCE MOVEMENTS (Vol. V); LENSHINA, ALICE (Vol. IV); LUMPA CHURCH (Vol. IV); NATIONALISM AND INDEPENDENCE MOVEMENTS (Vol. IV); PROPHETS AND PROPHETIC MOVEMENTS (Vols. IV, V); RELIGION (Vols. IV, V); WITCHCRAFT (Vol. I).

Further reading: Andrew Roberts, "The Lumpa Church of Alice Lenshina," in *Protest and Power in Black Africa,* Robert Rotberg and Ali Mazuri, eds. (New York: Oxford University Press, 1970).

Lesotho Impoverished, mountainous country, 11,700 square miles (30,300 sq km) in area, that is wholly surrounded by SOUTH AFRICA.

Lesotho at Independence Lesotho, formerly known as Basutoland, was a British High Commission Territory from 1884 to 1966. It achieved its independence on October 4, 1966, when it officially became the Kingdom of Lesotho, a constitutional monarchy complete with a Senate and a National Assembly. Arguably, its existence as an independent nation is improbable, given its small size and geographical constraints, since the country is landlocked and extremely mountainous, with more than 80 percent of its surface area at more than 1 mile (1.6 km) above sea level. It possesses little arable land or other NATURAL RESOURCES. Its 2002 population was about 2,208,000. The capital, MASERU, is located on the border with SOUTH AFRICA, which surrounds Lesotho, and has historically dominated it economically, culturally, and politically.

British colonial rule in Basutoland had allowed for Sotho chieftains to maintain a significant amount of power, and independent Lesotho's political system evolved around the issue of chieftain power. By the time of independence three prominent political parties had formed: the Basutoland Congress Party (BCP), the Basutoland National Party (BNP), and the Marema-Tlou Freedom Party. The 1965 pre-independence elections brought the BNP to power, with Mshweshwe II (1938–1996) as king and BNP leader Chief Joseph Leabua JONATHAN (1914–1987) as prime minister.

The first post-independence elections did not go as smoothly, however. The BCP won the majority, but Jonathan immediately moved to retain his power, suspending the constitution, arresting opposition members and sending Mshweshwe into exile. Though the BCP resisted and attempted a COUP D'ÉTAT in 1974, Jonathan remained in control of the country.

During this period Lesotho struggled to remain free of South Africa's APARTHEID influences while at the same time being economically dependent on the much larger country. Lesotho's resistance to apartheid raised its profile internationally but brought it into conflict with South Africa. Attempting to undermine the Sotho government, South Africa supported the BCP and other opposition groups, including the Lesotho Liberation Army. In 1982, based on claims that Lesotho was harboring guerrilla fighters of the AFRICAN NATIONAL CONGRESS, South African troops attacked Maseru, killing about 40 Sotho citizens. Tensions heightened until South Africa blockaded its border with Lesotho in 1986, isolating the country and placing it in an economic stranglehold.

The blockade had its desired results, as a pro–South African military faction overthrew Jonathan that same year. The blockade was lifted, and relations between the countries improved. Economic conditions in Lesotho continued to decline, however, due to a drop in the MINING of GOLD and a general recession in South Africa.

In 1990 King Mshweshwe II, who had returned to the throne following the 1986 coup, was once again ousted as a result of political intrigue. His son, Mohato (1963–), became King Letsie III, and the following year the military regime gave way. In 1993 elections were held that finally brought the BCP to power.

King Letsie III abdicated in January 1995 when his father returned to Lesotho and was restored to the throne. Mshweshwe II was killed in an automobile accident in January 1996, however, and Letsie III again became king.

Led by Ntsu Mokhehle, the BCP governed Lesotho through continued instability. After the fall of apartheid in South Africa, in the mid-1990s, Lesotho's economy actually declined further as foreign countries lifted sanctions against South Africa. Unemployed and underpaid workers rioted and scared off any potential foreign investments.

In 1997 Mokhehle split from the BCP and formed the Lesotho Congress of Democrats (LCD), which won the elections held the following year. Pakalitha MOSISILI (1945–) became prime minister amid claims of voter fraud. Demonstrations ensued, and the government was forced to appeal to the SOUTH AFRICAN DEVELOPMENT COMMUNITY for military support from South Africa and BOTSWANA. Order was restored after extensive destruction in and around Maseru. The LCD was forced to allow for the formation of an interim government that included opposition party involvement.

See also: BASOTHO (Vol. III); BASUTOLAND (Vol. IV); LESOTHO (Vol. IV); SOTHO (Vol. III).

Further reading: Colin Murray, *Families Divided: The Impact of Migrant Labour in Lesotho* (New York: Cambridge University Press, 1981).

Lessing, Doris (1919–) *British novelist*

After the failure of her marriage to communist-activist Gottfried Lessing, Doris Lessing left her home in Salisbury (present-day HARARE) in Southern Rhodesia (now ZIMBABWE) and traveled to London with the couple's son. There she published her first novel, *The Grass is Singing* (1950). Lessing then produced a string of novels, short story collections, and poetry that used autobiographical material to depict the racial rivalries existing in southern Africa. Her vocal anticolonialism and criticism of the racist regimes in southern Africa led to her being declared a "prohibited alien" and effectively exiled by the Rhodesian government of Ian SMITH (1919–).

Disenchanted with the Communist ideals she had found appealing while living in Africa, Lessing turned to the radical psychological theories of R. D. Laing (1927–1989). These ideas played a major role in her groundbreaking novel, *The Golden Notebook* (1962), which uses multiple narratives to chronicle the character Anna Wulf's fragmentary experience. Wulf's struggles resonated with many women and firmly established Lessing as a feminist figure.

In 1965 Lessing published *African Stories,* a collection of new and previously published works that captures the immense scope of the African landscape, as well as Lessing's intense feelings against the white-settler society in her native land. In 1980, after years of white political dominance, Rhodesia became the independent nation of Zimbabwe, and Lessing was finally allowed to return to her former home. She visited there regularly over the next decade, chronicling her impressions in *African Laughter: Four Visits to Zimbabwe* (1992). The book approaches Zimbabwe through an outsider's perspective, yet one with an intimate knowledge of what the country once was and what it had to overcome. Covering every aspect from ECOLOGY AND ECOLOGICAL CHANGE and political CORRUPTION to the impact of AIDS, *African Laughter* thoroughly examines the young nation still seeking to establish itself after its long struggle for independence. It also portrays Lessing's increasing disillusionment with the status of Zimbabwe's DEVELOPMENT as an independent nation.

In 1964 Lessing discovered Sufism, the ancient, mystical religion tied to Islam. Sufis maintain that Sufism contains the central tenets of all religions, and Lessing readily embraced Sufism's universal scope. Lessing's interest in Sufism led to her anomalous science-fiction series, *Canopus in Argos: Archives* (1979–83), which tells the history of humanity from the perspectives of extraterrestrial beings. Lessing's critics have marked her foray into science fiction as the reason why she has not yet won the Nobel Prize.

With books such as the critically acclaimed first volume of her autobiography, *Under My Skin* (1994), Lessing further cemented her position as one of southern Africa's, and the world's, exceptional writers and social commentators. Recently a harsh critic of Zimbabwe president Robert MUGABE's (1924–) oppressive regime, in 2001, Lessing received the Prince of Asturias Prize in literature, one of Spain's most prestigious awards, for her literary defense of freedom and her activism.

See also: LESSING, DORIS (Vol. IV); LITERATURE IN MODERN AFRICA (Vol. V); SETTLERS, EUROPEAN (Vol. IV); SOUTHERN RHODESIA (Vol. IV); SUFISM (Vol. IV); WOMEN IN MODERN AFRICA (Vol. V).

Liberia Country located on the Atlantic coast of West Africa, some 38,300 square miles (99,200 sq km) in size, bordered by SIERRA LEONE, IVORY COAST, and the Republic of GUINEA. Elected in 1944, William TUBMAN (1895–1971) remained president of Liberia for nearly 30 years. Throughout his presidency Tubman continued his national policy of establishing unity between the minority population of Americo-Liberians and the indigenous population. He also encouraged international investment. Serving for seven consecutive terms, Tubman supported the United Nations, and the ORGANIZATION OF AFRICAN UNITY, and sided with the United States during the Cold War. He also supported INDEPENDENCE MOVEMENTS in other African nations. Within Liberia, however, Tubman censored the press and used clandestine operations to spy on his political rivals, impeding the development of a

truly democratic state. Two months after his reelection in 1971 Tubman died and was succeeded by his vice president, William R. TOLBERT (1913–1980). The last president of what is known as Liberia's First Republic, Tolbert emulated many of Tubman's policies, but he failed to reinvigorate a tepid economy. Tolbert, a rice importer by trade, was suspected of price manipulation when the cost of Liberia's staple food increased by 50 percent. As a result there were massive riots.

In April 1980 Master Sergeant Samuel DOE (c. 1952–1990), from the Krahn ethnic group, led a military COUP D'ÉTAT. After executing Tolbert and his top leaders, Doe and the People's Redemption Council suspended the constitution and took over the leadership of the country. Doe promised a return to civilian rule and invited the input of respected Liberians, such as civic leader Amos Sawyer (1945–), to lend legitimacy to the creation of a new constitution.

The elections of 1985 were based on the provisions of the new constitution, which included at least two points subverted by Doe's candidacy. First, a candidate had to be at least 35 years old, so Doe had his birth certificate altered. Second, the candidate could not be a member of the military, but Doe maintained his rank until he was sure of an electoral victory.

Amid accusations of ballot-box fraud and voter intimidation Doe won the 1985 elections, initiating Liberia's Second Republic. Soon after, General Thomas Quiwonkpa, a Gio from Nimba County, initiated a failed coup attempt. Consequently Doe became paranoid about future coups. He placed members of his Krahn ethnic group into positions of power, attacked the Gio and related Mano ethnic groups, and intimidated the press and political opposition.

At the time Liberia's economy was rapidly deteriorating, but the Doe administration's CORRUPTION and HUMAN RIGHTS abuses forced Liberia's major benefactor, the United States, to suspend aid to the country. Doe's deputy minister of commerce, Charles TAYLOR (1948–), exemplified the extensive government corruption, funneling millions of dollars in government funds into his own bank accounts. Taylor's impropriety resulted in his arrest and imprisonment in the United States, where he had fled from Liberia to avoid embezzlement charges. Taylor escaped from prison in the United States, however, and returned to Liberia. There, he organized the National Patriotic Front of Liberia (NPFL), a rebel group made up of anti-Doe sympathizers and partially supported by Libya's Muammar QADDAFI (1942–).

In 1989, from his base in the Ivory Coast, Taylor led the NPFL in an invasion of Liberia. A year later, troops from the armed wing of the ECONOMIC COMMUNITY OF WEST AFRICAN STATES (ECOWAS) were sent to Liberia as a peacekeeping force. Doe was captured, tortured, and executed by a splinter group of Taylor's NPFL. This did not end the conflict, however. The civil war lasted from 1989 to 1996, with new, armed factions organizing to join the fighting. The warring sides engaged in massive violence, murdering thousands. More than a million Liberians fled the bloodshed, becoming REFUGEES in neighboring countries that could ill-afford to provide help for them. A multitude of broken cease-fire agreements, interim governments, and peace agreements constantly gave and banished hope for an end to the civil war. As the death toll mounted, many of Liberia's warlords put guns in the hands of children, initiating a new generation into Liberia's cycle of violence.

In 1995 ECOWAS helped negotiate the first of the ABUJA ACCORDS, which called for a cease-fire and set the date for multiparty elections. Violence erupted again in 1996, when the ruling council attempted to arrest a popular warlord, Roosevelt Johnson. Despite the renewed violence, elections were set for July 1997. Liberians voted for Taylor and his new political organization, the National Patriotic Party, hoping that it could put an end to the country's endless warfare,. The fighting continued, however, as the opposition parties coalesced into the Liberians United for Reconciliation and Democracy. Although Liberia's economy and INFRASTRUCTURE were all but destroyed and Liberia was more than $2 billion in debt, Taylor still involved himself in the affairs of Liberia's neighbors. Toward the end of the century, Taylor and Liberia were accused of supporting rebels in Sierra Leone in return for diamonds. At the same time Taylor accused GHANA of supporting Liberian rebels.

In 2000 Liberia fired across Guinea's border into the towns of Macenta and Guekedougou. The next year violence again erupted between rebels and Taylor's troops. In 2003, amid pressure exerted by international governments and internal insurgents, a UN-brokered cease-fire was established and Taylor left Liberia for self-imposed exile. Upon Taylor's departure Gyude Bryant (1949–), of the Grebo ethnic group and a member of the Liberia Action Party, was chosen to head the Liberian transitional government. Bryant, who was given the offices of chief of state and head of government in October 2003, was to remain in interim control until presidential elections scheduled for 2005.

See also: AMNESTY INTERNATIONAL AND AFRICA (Vol. V); CIVIL WARS (Vol. V); COLD WAR AND AFRICA (Vol. IV, V); ETHNIC CONFLICT IN AFRICA (Vol. V); ETHNICITY AND IDENTITY (Vol. V); LIBERIA (Vols. I, II, III, IV); UNITED NATIONS AND AFRICA (Vol. IV, V); UNITED STATES OF AMERICA AND AFRICA (Vol. IV, V).

Further reading: Adekeye Adebajo, *Liberia's Civil War: Nigeria, ECOMOG, and Regional Security in West Africa* (Boulder, Colo.: Lynne Rienner Publishers, 2002); James Marten, ed., *Liberia: Back to the Brink: War Crimes by Liberian Government and Rebels* (New York: Human Rights Watch, 2002).

Libreville Capital city and secondary port of GABON, located on the estuary where the Gabon River enters the Gulf of Guinea. The Mpongwe people had settled around the site of modern-day Libreville as early as the 16th century. Fang people also had settled in the area prior to the colonial era.

The modern history of Libreville dates from 1843, when the French established a mission at the site. In 1849 the town became a refuge for freed slaves and was named Libreville (French for "free town"). During the colonial era, it developed a French character somewhat along the lines of DAKAR and the three other towns that made up the Quatre Communes of SENEGAL. The town's wide boulevards and paved roads continue to reflect this French colonial heritage and stand in sharp contrast to the towns of Gabon's interior.

Libreville is the nation's seat of government as well as its educational and industrial center; it shares port activities with Port-Gentil, to the south. Industries include timber processing, textiles, fishing, food and palm oil processing, brewing, and shipbuilding.

Investments made in Libreville's industrial sector in the 1960s resulted in a doubling of the city's population, which, by 2003, stood at about 660,000.

The main EXPORTS of Libreville and the nearby deepwater port of Owendo, which was opened in 1964, include tropical wood products, cocoa, rubber, and palm products. OIL and manganese—Gabon holds 25 percent of the world's known manganese reserves—are also important exports. In 1974 the 400-mile (646-km) Trans-Gabonese Railway was completed, linking Owendo with the interior and thus increasing the city's level of economic activity.

See also: FANG (Vol. II); FRANCE AND AFRICA (Vols. III, IV, V); MPONGWE (Vol. III); QUATRE COMMUNES (Vol. IV); SLAVE TRADE (Vols. III, IV); URBAN LIFE AND CULTURE (Vols. IV, V); URBANIZATION (Vols. IV, V).

Libya North African country, some 680,000 square miles (1,761,200 sq km) in size, situated on the Mediterranean coast with a dry, desert interior. Libya is bordered by EGYPT, the Republic of the SUDAN, CHAD, NIGER, ALGERIA, and TUNISIA.

Libya at Independence After receiving its independence in 1951, Libya was governed under a constitutional monarchy with a bicameral legislature and a prime minister. The United Nations (UN) appointed the conservative King Idris (1889–1983), the head of the Islamic Sanusiyya Brotherhood, as Libya's first leader. With nearly all his support coming from the Brotherhood itself, Idris generated little enthusiasm or loyalty from other Libyans, who saw him as a leader imposed by outsiders rather than chosen by them. Until OIL was discovered, in 1958, Libya was a poor country, dependent upon loans and handouts from the industrialized nations. oil revenues, initially at least, did nothing to change this, as the overwhelming majority of oil profits went to international corporations headquartered in foreign nations.

Qaddafi's Rise to Power and Pan-Arabism In 1969 the political discontent in Libya manifested itself in a COUP D'ÉTAT led by small group of army officers under Captain Muammar QADDAFI (1942–). The monarch was then replaced by a 12-member Revolutionary Command Council (RCC), with Qaddafi as the prime minister. The new government soon expelled a great number of foreigners, including former Italian colonists and the British and American troops who had occupied military bases near TRIPOLI since World War II (1939–45).

Like many of its North African counterparts, Qaddafi's regime supported a domestic policy based on a loose concept of socialism, which led the state to reinvest oil profits in the nation's INFRASTRUCTURE, such as roads, schools, hospitals, agricultural programs, and housing. During the 1970s the regime eventually launched a social revolution that declared Libya to be a Jamahiriya—a state run by the masses—a concept Qaddafi had articulated in a work entitled *The Green Book*. The government dismantled the government imposed by the United Nations, replacing it with a socialist one that supposedly placed decision making in the hands of people's committees. This gave the appearance of broad-based communities of local people making governmental decisions that would be either ratified or vetoed by the national government. In practice, however, Libya remained a strict, military dictatorship.

The ensuing 1973 cultural revolution combined African socialism with Islamic principles. However, as the president of the RCC (which became the seat of dictatorial power), Qaddafi generated political discontent that resulted in several attempts to overthrow him. This, in turn, led to the assassinations of Libyan dissidents both at home and in their self-imposed exile in Europe.

Meanwhile, world economic events had their effect on Libya's domestic situation. Dependent, as it was, on oil revenues, Libya was particularly vulnerable to price fluctuations in the petroleum market. During the 1970s, when the ORGANIZATION OF PETROLEUM EXPORTING COUN-TRIES was firmly in control of oil prices, Libya's profits were able to pay for its internal and external programs. However, conservation measures taken by the industrial nations precipitated a drop in oil prices in the 1980s, thereby reducing profits and making the Libyan government susceptible to rising discontent over the economy.

In the 1970s Libya's foreign policy sought to foster a practical pan-Arabism and to wage war against Israel and its allies. Furthering the ideals of Gamal Abdel NASSER (1918–1970), Libya attempted to implement a pan-Arab state by joining with Egypt and Syria in the Federation of Arab Republics. The union fell apart, however, when Egypt sued for a separate peace with Israel, in 1978, and Libya and Syria alienated other Arab states by backing Iran in the Iran–Iraq War (1980–88). After this, Libya unsuccessfully attempted a union with Algeria and Tunisia, its neighbors to the west, and, following this failure, it sought to create a Saharan Islamic state with its southern neighbors Chad and Sudan.

Similar to the way in which PAN-AFRICANISM seeks to unite black Africans across ethnic and geographic divisions, Pan-Arabism encourages unity among various Arab groups in North Africa and the Middle East.

Unable to join with other states, in 1973 Libya invaded Chad and occupied the mineral-rich Aouzou Strip, on the Chadian side of a disputed, common border. (In 1994, however, Qaddafi was forced to end the occupation when an international court of justice rejected Libya's claim to the land.) Also in 1973, Libya supported the Arab side during the Arab-Israeli War, sending troops and materials to the conflict. It used its position in OPEC to advocate a reduction of oil sales and to raise oil prices to those countries that supported Israel.

On a more peaceful note, in 1989 Libya organized the Arab Maghreb Union, a North African common market. Made up of Algeria, Libya, MAURITANIA, MOROCCO, and Tunisia, this organization was crafted by Qaddafi to promote economic cooperation among its members.

Libya, Freedom Fighters, and Terrorism Since it came to power, the Qaddafi government has built a reputation as a staunch anti-Western, anti-imperialist regime, supporting liberation movements throughout the world. It reportedly has provided a safe haven, financial support, and military training for anti-imperialist or anti-Israeli groups that call themselves "freedom fighters" (and that the United States and its allies often label "terrorists").

Over the years, some 30 organizations—including Hamas, the Palestine Islamic Jihad, and the Popular Front for the Liberation of Palestine-General Command—supposedly have benefited from Libyan backing. Libya also is reputed to have provided financial support for the Palestine Liberation Organization, the Sandinistas in Nicaragua, and the Irish Republican Army in the United Kingdom.

In the early 1980s, as a perceived "terrorist threat" intensified, the U.S. government tried to intimidate Libya by having its Sixth Fleet conduct training maneuvers in the Gulf of Sidra, off of Libya's northern Mediterranean coast. In 1981 tensions escalated as the United States shot down Libyan jets that had engaged American aircraft over the gulf. A year later the United States applied further pressure by placing a ban on Libyan oil imports, a political move that shored up anti-American sentiment in Libya. The situation continued to deteriorate, and in 1986 U.S. President Ronald Reagan (1911–2004) ordered a bombing of Libyan government and military installations in the coastal cities of Benghazi and TRIPOLI.

Following the bombing of Pan-Am Flight 103 in 1988, an investigation produced evidence of Libyan involvement in the affair. The Libyan government refused to turn over the suspects in the bombing for trial, a refusal that resulted in UN sanctions. In 1998 the Libyan government agreed that the men could be tried under Scottish law at the International Court of Justice at The Hague, in the Netherlands. The following year the men were detained at a UN-monitored jail in Scotland, and the United Nations then lifted its sanctions after Libya accepted responsibility, paid compensation, disclosed intelligence, and renounced TERRORISM. The suspects' trial, in 2001, led to the conviction of one defendant but not the other.

Since the beginning of the 21st century Libya, with Qaddafi still it's leader, has managed to improve relations with neighboring North African countries. Furthermore, in late 2003 Libya announced plans to abandon its chemical and nuclear weapons programs, an action that was welcomed by U.S. president George W. Bush (1946–   ) and British prime minister Tony Blair (1953–   ).

See also: ARAB-ISRAELI WARS (Vols. IV, V); ARAB WORLD AND AFRICA (Vol. V); LIBYA (Vols. I, II, III, IV); MAGHREB (Vols. IV, V); UNITED NATIONS AND AFRICA (Vols. IV, V); UNITED STATES AND AFRICA (Vols. IV, V).

Further reading: Brian L. Davis, *Qaddafi, Terrorism, and the Origins of the U. S. Attack on Libya* (New York: Praeger, 1990); G. L. Simons, *Libya: The Struggle for Survival* (New York: St. Martin's Press, 1993); Ronald Bruce

St. John, *Historical Dictionary of Libya* (Metuchen, N.J.: Scarecrow Press, 1991).

Lilongwe   Capital city of MALAWI, located on the Lilongwe River in the country's fertile central plains. Lilongwe was founded in 1947 as an agricultural commercial center. In 1965 President Hastings Kamuzu BANDA (c. 1898–1997) made the city a center for economic expansion for the central and northern regions of the country. Subse-quent development included the improvement and construction of TRANSPORTATION networks, including a new airport and a rail line linking the city with the eastern and western parts of Malawi. At the start of 1975 Lilongwe was designated the new federal capital, and a new section of the town was built 3 miles (5 km) from the old town. This new area now houses government offices and businesses, some of which moved from the former capital, Zomba.

Markets located in the old sector of town focus mainly on selling the region's groundnuts (peanuts) and tobacco. Visitors to the markets can also find a myriad of South Asian spice and textile shops.

The tobacco trade is an important part of Lilongwe's economy. A lively auction house moves approximately 15,000 bales every day. Lilongwe offers several well-maintained parks and a 370-acre (1.5 sq km) nature sanctuary containing numerous birds, mammals, and reptiles. The city's population was estimated at 500,000, in 2003.

See also: URBAN LIFE AND CULTURE (Vols. IV, V); URBANIZATION (Vols. IV, V).

literacy   In general African people are literate in the European language that had been the colonial language for their country. After independence public schoolrooms became the point of dissemination for the official language and, hence, for the acquisition of literacy. However, because the newly independent governments were largely unable to adequately fund their EDUCATION programs, the process of inculcating students in the official language was slow and uneven.

Unencumbered by some of the agricultural chores required of their rural counterparts, urban students tend to have more educational opportunities to pursue literacy. Also, generally speaking, males are more likely than females to have access to education. Levels of literacy have remained low because education is often made too expensive by the cost of textbooks and school uniforms. Many students are denied an education because the community lacks the required INFRASTRUCTURE or has facilities only for primary schooling. In some African countries the uneven acquisition of literacy creates a two-tier society in which those who can read and write have great advantages over those who cannot.

For students in North Africa, Arabic is the language of instruction. Many students are functionally literate in Arabic early on, learning first at Quranic schools, then at the *madrasas,* or theological schools, and later at Islamic universities such as al-Azhar in EGYPT. In the MAGHRIB, students may also gain literacy in the languages of former colonizers—English, French, or Italian. For students in East and West Africa, an Arabic education is acquired much the same as it is in North Africa.

Public schools in East Africa may require literacy in Kiswahili and English, the two official languages in the region. In West Africa public schools require literacy in either French or English, depending on whether France or England was the former colonial power.

> Students who attend Quranic schools for strictly religious purposes often achieve what is called level-two literacy in the Arabic language. This means that they can read Arabic only after memorizing the text.

Many West African ethnic groups choose either Arabic or Roman script to write their indigenous languages. Fulbe speakers in GUINEA, for example, write the Fulbe language using Arabic script.

In the 1960s the issue of maternal languages and literacy was discussed by leaders in the ORGANIZATION OF AFRICAN UNITY. Guinea's Ahmed Sékou TOURÉ (1922–1984) was one of the few who chose to institute a national language program. From 1968 until his death in 1884 the dominant regional languages were chosen as the languages of instruction. In Upper Guinea, for instance, elementary students were taught in Maninka, since that was the regional lingua franca. They also learned French, the official national language, since classes at the high school level were taught in French. Those students who did not move on to high school would be literate only in the indigenous language, thus limiting their ability to secure certain government or civil-service jobs.

In SOUTH AFRICA Dutch-based AFRIKAANS developed as an indigenous language, but by 1915 it had been standardized for academic and official use. From 1948 to 1990 the Afrikaner-dominated government promoted literacy in Afrikaans and English. Afrikaans was the first language of 60 percent of white South Africans and more than 90 percent of those categorized as "Coloured." It was also the second language of many black Africans. In the new, democratized South Africa, Afrikaans is merely one of the 11 national languages. The government now encourages literacy in English for use in international trade and global communication.

Widespread illiteracy at the end of the 1960s led the United Nations Educational Scientific and Cultural Organization (UNESCO) to organize adult literacy classes like this one near Bamako, Mali. © *United Nations*

Many West Africans are literate in indigenous writing systems that were created specifically to express indigenous languages. For example, the Vai of Liberia and SIERRA LEONE use the Vai syllabary, which was invented in the 19th century for correspondence and record keeping. The Vai syllabary lists characters that represent syllables in the spoken language. Other groups in the region, including the Mende, Loma, Kpelle, and Bassa base their indigenous scripts on the Vai syllabary.

The N'ko alphabet was invented in 1949 by Souleyman KANTÉ (1922–1987), a Muslim scholar from KANKAN, Guinea. He standardized a blend of the four linguae francae used for trade—Bamana, Dyula, Maninka, and Mandenko—to create the N'ko alphabet. By doing this, Kanté made it possible for West Africa's various Mande-speaking people to communicate over long distances in writing. For instance, using the N'ko alphabet, a Soninke speaker in MAURITANIA who knows the Bamana language can communicate in writing with a Nigerian Busa speaker who knows the Dyula language. While they are unable to speak to one another in their first languages, they are able to communicate across great distances by using a lingua franca written in the N'ko alphabet.

See also: KISWAHILI (Vols. II, III, IV); LANGUAGE (Vol. IV); LITERACY (Vol. IV).

literature in modern Africa   As African nations emerged from colonial rule, many writers continued to explore the theme of the imposition of Western values on the African people first explored novelistically in *Things Fall Apart* (1958), by Chinua ACHEBE (1930–   ), of NIGERIA. They also adopted new themes related to the conflicts accompanying independence, including political problems and cultural conflicts over indigenous lifestyle and practices.

African authors after Achebe faced challenges unique to the African situation. Immediately after independence, questions arose about which language an African author should use to write literature. At the Makerere Conference in 1963 a group of authors including NGUGI WA THIONG'O (1938–   ) took a stand, saying that literature should be written in indigenous languages and not in European, colonial languages, even if those languages were now the official languages of the country. Ngugi continued writing novels and plays but used his mother tongue, KIKUYU, to communicate his ideas to his countrymen, whom he considered his primary audience. Others, including Achebe, disagreed. These authors continued to write in the official, European language of their respective countries.

Some African writers focused on producing a body of literature acceptable to the mainstream literary community. Those who excelled at this received recognition from the Western literary establishment. African winners of the prestigious Nobel Prize in literature include Wole SOYINKA (1934–), in 1986, Naguib MAHFOUZ (1911–), in 1988, Nadine GORDIMER (1923–), in 1991, and J. M. COETZEE (1940–), in 2003.

For reasons of politics as well as economics, African authors have had to seek out publishing houses in Europe and North America in order to expose their work to large audiences. With the exception of French-language publishers such as the Centre de Literature Evangelique, in YAOUNDÉ, CAMEROON, and Nouvelles Editions Africaines du Senegal, in DAKAR, most African novels in French of the 1990s were published in France. Similarly, most African novels in English were published in the United Kingdom or in North America.

North African Literature Considered by many to be the greatest contemporary Egyptian novelist, Nagib Mahfouz was deeply concerned about European exploitation, focusing his work on the life of the urban poor. Westernization is also a theme in Tawfik al-Hakim's modern novel, *The Bird from the East*. In North Africa, the languages of the literature of the Maghrib—ALGERIA, TUNISIA, and MOROCCO—are Arabic and French.

West African Literature In West Africa, literature written in English developed more rapidly than literature in French. Nigerians led the literary way, with Achebe following up the success of *Things Fall Apart* with *No Longer at Ease* (1960) and *Arrow of God* (1964). Often, the themes of Nigerian literature tend toward the negative aspects of post-independence Nigerian society, including governmental CORRUPTION, civil war, and the frequent military coups d'état that have plagued the country. The Nigerian author and activist Ken SARO-WIWA (1941–1995) wrote essays about the damage caused by government-sponsored OIL refining in the NIGER DELTA. These essays contributed to the government's decision to repress Saro-Wiwa, who was ultimately executed for his activism.

In GHANA, Ayi Kwei ARMAH (1939–) is recognized for his novel *The Beautyful Ones Are Not Yet Born* (1968). Fellow Ghanaian Kofi AWOONOR (1935–) is widely praised for his poetry. Gambian poet and novelist Lenrie Peters (1932–) gained recognition for *Second Round* (1965), a novel that describes the homecoming of an African man after studying abroad. In SIERRA LEONE, the genre of choice is poetry rather than fiction, written on the same themes as those found in West African novels and drama.

Women writers emerged, expressing their own ideas in their own voices centering on themes important to that largely underrepresented segment of the community. For instance, Nigerian author Flora NWAPA (1931–1993), Africa's first woman novelist, wrote *Efuru* (1966), which described the life of precolonial, rural women as they coped with the "tyranny of tradition." Other Nigerian women writers such as Buchi EMECHETA (1944–), Ifeoma Okoye, and Zaynab Alkali (1950–) provided an authentic women's perspective on Nigerian society and its changes. Other prominent women writing in English include, from Ghana, Ama Ata AIDOO (1942–) who wrote among other things *Changes: A Love Story* (1993), and from SENEGAL, Mariama BÂ (1929–1981) who wrote the celebrated *So Long A Letter* (1981). Similar to authors writing in English, the authors writing in French continued to produce anticolonial novels. However, they also developed new themes centering on the use and abuse of power. In *Le bel immonde*, written in 1976, Valentine Y Mudimbe (1941–) described the imbalance of power and the general disappointment of unfulfilled high hopes for independence. French African literature in various sub-genres—such as mysteries, science fiction, and political fiction—have proliferated recently.

East African Literature In SOMALIA, the leading novelist, Nuruddin Farah (1945–), wrote a trilogy against military tyranny. Somali literature often portrays the realities of rural life without nostalgia or idealization. Many East African novelists from KENYA and TANZANIA chose the city and its relations to the Mau Mau guerrilla warfare of the 1950s as the setting for their exploration of the trials of contemporary life. Four novels in English by Ngugi wa Thiong'o focus on the doubts and dreams of his heroes. The condition of modern women in Kenya was depicted in such books as *Kenyan Women Heroes and their Mystical Power* (1984), by Rebeka Njau (1932–), and in novels such as *The Graduate* (1980), by Grace Ogot (1930–).

East African poets include Okot P'BITEK (1931–1982), who started the tradition of using blank verse in Ugandan song poetry. Shaaban Robert, from Tanzania, used disciplined rhymes to write poetry in Kiswahili based upon Islamic and African traditions. Fellow Tanzanian Euphrase Kezilahabi experimented with blank verse. Kenya's best known poet, Jared Angira (1947–) wrote affectingly about the self-delusions of political leaders in *Tides of Time: Selected Poems* (1996).

Literature in Southern Africa In SOUTH AFRICA, novelists including André BRINK (1935–), Nadine Gordimer (1923–), J. M. Coetzee (1940–), and Athol FUGARD (1932–), penned the literary deconstruction of the nationalist apartheid government. Because books critical of APARTHEID were banned in South Africa, they had to be published overseas. However, books like *A Walk in the Night* (1962), by Alex LA GUMA (1925–1985), and the poetry of Dennis Brutus (1924–   ) evaded the censors and brought the message home to the townships. Many authors writing in AFRIKAANS, the language of the ruling National Party, expressed their dissatisfaction with apartheid and the society created under Afrikaner rule. Among these writers, Étienne Leroux (1922–   ), Brink, and the poet Breyten Breytenbach (1939–   ) stand out. Afrikaans poets of note since the 1960s have been mostly women, such as Wilma Stockenström (1933–   ), Sheila Cussons (1922–   ), and Antjie Krog (1952–   ). Exiles such as the poets Dennis Brutus, Keoraptse Kgositsile, Mazisi Kunene (1930–   ), and Daniel P. Junene published from abroad and epitomized the literary aspects of the BLACK CONSCIOUSNESS MOVEMENT of the 1970s. These poets invoked a cultural revolution in literary magazines and through monographs published by small publishing houses run by whites. By the 1980s the literary movement became a political one, with writers such as J. M. Coetzee and Nadine Gordimer writing eloquently about the personal and social destruction caused by the apartheid system, even as it crumbled around them.

The most poignant aspect of the literature of independence is the lack of indigenous publishing to advance the works of African authors and critics. This seems a necessary step in challenging the misperceptions of the international literary world.

See also: LITERATURE IN COLONIAL AFRICA (Vol. IV).

Further reading: Derek Attridge and Rosemary Jolly, eds., *Writing South Africa: Literature, Apartheid, and Democracy 1970–1995* (New York: Cambridge University Press, 1998); Edmund L. Epstein and Robert Kole, eds, *The Language of African Literature* (Trenton, N.J.: Africa World Press, 1998); David I. Ker, *The African Novel and the Modernist Tradition* (New York: P. Lang, 1997); Stephanie Newell, ed., *Readings in African Popular Fiction* (Bloomington, Ind.: Indiana University Press, 2002); Pamela Smith, J. Olubunmi, and Daniel P. Kunene, eds., *Tongue and Mother Tongue: African Literature and the Perpetual Quest for Identity* (Trenton, N.J.: Africa World Press, 2002).

Lomé Capital and chief port of TOGO, located in the southwestern corner of the country on the Gulf of Guinea, in West Africa. Within a few years of its founding in 1884, Lomé had become the administrative center of German Togoland. Germany developed much of the city's INFRASTRUCTURE, including a pier, which facilitated the export of raw materials and, later, CASH CROPS. In addition they built rail lines to link the town with other commercial centers in Togo, including Anecho, Palime, and Sokode, in the north.

Lomé came under Anglo-French control as a result of World War I (1914–18), and then French control from 1922 until 1960, at which time Togo gained its independence. After independence, in 1968, Lomé's port facilities were improved, leading to an increase in exports, which include cocoa, coffee, copra (dried coconut meat), cotton, and palm nuts. The port of Kpeme, near Lomé, became Togo's principal exporter of phosphates, which are shipped to Lomé by rail. Industries in the city include textile manufacturing and food processing. In 1978 a new OIL refinery began production.

In addition to serving as the administrative, commercial, and TRANSPORTATION center for the country, Lomé is the site of the University of Benin (founded in 1970) and has a 3,000-seat international conference hall. The conference hall was the site of the diplomatic meeting that resulted in the LOMÉ CONVENTION, an agreement signed in 1975 that outlined trade relations between developing countries and the nations of industrialized Europe.

Although the population of Lomé grew rapidly before the 1970s, an economic crisis in the 1980s resulted in stricter economic policies known as STRUCTURAL ADJUSTMENT policies. This, in turn, led to civil unrest and migration from the city to neighboring GHANA. In 2002 Lomé's population was estimated at 658,000.

See also: FRANCE AND AFRICA (Vols. III, IV, V); GERMANY AND AFRICA (Vol. IV); URBAN LIFE AND CULTURE (Vols. IV, V); URBANIZATION (Vols. IV, V); WORLD WAR I AND AFRICA (Vol. IV).

Lomé Convention Series of trade agreements aimed at increasing the economic support given by wealthy countries of the European Economic Community (EEC) to poorer countries in Africa, the Caribbean, and the Pacific (sometimes called the ACP states). Signed February 28, 1975, in LOMÉ, TOGO, the Lomé Convention was intended to help stabilize earnings from African EXPORTS. To achieve this the Convention outlined a system of trade concessions, and financial, industrial, and technological aid. It was hoped that $3.6 billion spent over five years would improve the strained relations between developed countries and 46 former colonies that continued to suffer from the legacy of past exploitation.

The results of the original agreement hardly lived up to expectations. By the time the Convention was implemented, in 1976, there was already significant dissatisfaction with the distribution of aid for both national and regional projects. Efforts to improve cross-regional industrial cooperation were insignificant, and trade continued to be viewed by many recipient countries as a neocolonial tool that enabled Europe to extract valuable NATURAL RESOURCES inexpensively. In addition, disagreements erupted over the addition of other member states.

A second Lomé Convention was signed in November 1979, enlarging the number of ACP states to 58 and the terms of trade to $7.5 billion. A third Lomé Convention, signed in December 1984, enlarged the group once again, this time to 66, and settled on a $6.3 billion package.

All along there had been disagreement over the amount of aid, but the greatest threat to the Lomé Convention was the fundamental nature of the agreement itself: it did not serve its primary function of founding contractual relationships between institutions of rich and poor countries. The developed EEC countries continued to be seen as the dominant partners of the Convention, while the gap between rich and poor countries grew.

A fourth Lomé Convention was signed in December 1989. At that time a proposed single European Union market was set to launch in three years, raising fears that it would be even more difficult for poor countries to find open markets to the north. Amid growing suspicion that Lomé—already in violation of shifting international trade law—was destined to fail. the Cotonou Agreement replaced the Lomé Convention, in June 2000. While Cotonou maintained many of Lomé's basic precepts, it shifted the open-market laws to bring the agreement in compliance with World Trade Organization regulations by 2007. The new Cotonou Agreement increased the focus on CIVIL SOCIETY rather than governments, and membership increased to 71.

See also: COLONIALISM, INFLUENCE OF (Vol. IV); ECONOMIC ASSISTANCE (Vol. V); EUROPE AND AFRICA (Vols. IV, V); NEOCOLONIALISM AND UNDERDEVELOPMENT (Vol. V); TRADE AND COMMERCE (Vols. IV, V).

Further reading: John Ravenhill, *Collective Clientelism* (New York: Columbia University Press, 1985).

Luanda Capital city and major port of ANGOLA, located on the Atlantic coast in the northern part of the country. Founded by the Portuguese in 1576, Luanda was a major center for the slave trade well into the 19th century. Its economic focus then switched to exporting CASH CROPS—coffee, cotton, palm oil, and other commodities, including copal (a resin used in making varnish), leather, and cassava flour.

During the 1950s the city's population grew as a result of massive economic expansion brought on by favorable international coffee prices and government incentives for industries. Luanda attracted a number of Portuguese immigrants, and vibrant African communities developed within city limits. Although many of the Portuguese settlers left Luanda when Angola declared independence, the city's population still increased as REFUGEES moved there to escape the civil war that broke out in the Angolan interior. Between 1975 and 2003 the population of Luanda quadrupled to 2,700,000.

In response to the war-induced collapse in the urban economy, an informal market sector flourished, providing income to many of Luanda's residents. Roque Santeiro, one of the largest markets in Africa, is located in the city. Today,

many buildings are being constructed as Luanda recovers slowly from the war. However, basic INFRASTRUCTURE and social services, designed for a Portuguese colonial city of 30,000, are inadequate for the current population.

See also: CIVIL WARS (Vol. V); LUANDA (Vols. III, IV); NATIONALISM AND INDEPENDENCE MOVEMENTS (Vol. IV); POPULATION GROWTH (Vol. V); PORTUGAL AND AFRICA (Vols. III, IV, V); SLAVE TRADE (Vols. III, IV); URBAN LIFE AND CULTURE (Vols. IV, V); URBANIZATION (Vols. IV, V).

Lubumbashi (formerly Elisabethville) Capital and center of the MINING industry for the Democratic Republic of the CONGO, located near the border with ZAMBIA. With an advantageous location in the Copper-belt, the town of Elizabethville was founded by Belgian colonists as a mining camp in 1910. The town prospered after a transcontinental railroad was built, linking Elizabethville with the city of LUANDA, on the Atlantic coast, and with the port of Beira, MOZAMBIQUE, on the Indian Ocean. These ports, as well as river transport, conveyed the region's plentiful NATURAL RESOURCES to overseas markets. Elizabethville was said to be the "boomtown of the Congo" during the colonial period.

Immediately after the nation gained independence in 1960, the state of KATANGA declared itself an independent nation with Elizabethville as the capital. After a three-year civil war that eventually involved UN peacekeeping forces, Katanga agreed to rejoin the country. In 1966, in an attempt to purge the colonial legacy, the name of the capital was changed to Lubumbashi, after a local river.

Today the city is still the center of the mining activities for the region, prospering from the productive Copperbelt and processing zinc, cobalt, cadmium, germanium, tin, manganese, and coal as well. The government oversees a large portion of the processing, but some foreign mining companies also operate in Lubumbashi. The manufacturing of printed materials, flour, cigarettes, bricks, soap, textiles, metal products, and processed foods also contribute to the economy.

The city is also the site of the Lubumbashi campus of the University of Kinshasa (founded in 1955) and a museum, which holds a substantial collection of African ART. The population in 2003 was estimated at 1,206,000.

See also: BELGIAN CONGO (Vols. IV); BELGIUM AND AFRICA (Vol. IV); CIVIL WARS (Vol. V); COPPER (Vols. I, II, IV); COPPERBELT (Vol. IV); ELIZABETHVILLE (Vol. IV); UNITED NATIONS AND AFRICA (Vols. IV, V); URBAN LIFE AND CULTURE (Vols. IV, V); URBANIZATION (Vols. IV, V).

Lumumba, Patrice (1925–1961) *First prime minister of independent Democratic Republic of the Congo*

Patrice Lumumba became prime minister of the Republic of the Congo (now the Democratic Republic of the CONGO) as a result of the 1960 elections that set the stage for his country's independence from Belgium. He inherited a very unstable situation, however, for Belgium had planned for the decolonization process less than other colonial powers.

Furthermore, there existed no unity of purpose among the Congolese. Lumumba's own political party, the Congolese National Movement (Mouvement National Congolais, MNC), de-emphasized ethnicity and stood for a unified, centralized, and racially equal Congo. Many of the rival political parties, such the ABAKO party, under Joseph KASAVUBU (c. 1913–1969), and CONAKAT, headed by Moïse TSHOMBE (1919–1969), were ethnically based and stood for considerable provincial autonomy. Kasavubu was the country's president at independence.

During his Independence Day speech June 30, 1960, Lumumba recalled the brutality of the former Belgian rule, inflaming an already tense situation and, whether intitionally or not, causing widespread riots. In the following week the army mutinied against its white, Belgian officers, and many of the country's white population began to flee the country. The CONGO CRISIS had begun.

Next came the secession of the Katanga province, with its rich mineral resources. When Moïse Tshombe, the Katanga leader, invited the Belgian military to return, Lumumba responded by appealing to both the United Nations (UN) and the Soviet Union to send soldiers as well. Given the Cold War tensions of the time, this move alienated the United States, which backed the defense minister, Joseph Mobutu (soon to be MOBUTU SESE SEKO [1930–1997]), who then ousted both Lumumba and Kasavubu from their positions.

Lumumba retreated to his official residence in Léopoldville (now KINSHASA), where a standoff ensued between Mobutu's soldiers, who had placed him under house arrest, and UN troops, who were sent to protect him. Mobutu and Kasavubu then secretly agreed to an interim government that would exclude Lumumba. Fearing for his life, Lumumba fled but was seized by Mobutu's soldiers before he reached the safety of Stanleyville (today's KISANGANI). Mobutu had Lumumba flown to Elizabethville (modern LUBUMBASHI) and handed over to Tshombe's Katanga government. Within days, Lumumba was murdered under mysterious circumstances.

News of Lumumba's death became public days later, spurring international condemnation of the violence in Congo. He was a victim of the Cold War as much as of Congo's internal rivalry. The Soviet Union named a university in his honor, while the United States and its NATO allies denounced him as a Communist.

See also: CIVIL WARS (Vol. V); COLD WAR AND AFRICA (Vols IV, V); DECOLONIZATION (Vol. IV); ETHNIC CONFLICT (Vol. V); LUMUMBA, PATRICE (Vol. IV); SOVIET UNION AND AFRICA (Vols. IV, V); UNITED NATIONS AND AFRICA (Vols. IV, V); UNITED STATES AND AFRICA (Vols. IV, V).

Further reading: Thomas Kanza, *Conflict in the Congo: The Rise and Fall of Lumumba* (Harmondsworth, U.K.: Penguin, 1972).

Luo (Kavirondo) Nilotic-speaking ethnic group located mostly along the shores of Lake VICTORIA in KENYA. Making up about 13 percent of the population, the Luo were influential in Kenyan politics in the years following independence.

Also known as the Kavirondo, the estimated 3 million Luo in Kenya form that country's third-largest ethnic group, after the KIKUYU and the Luhya. Traditionally, they sustained themselves through fishing and AGRICULTURE. In the early postcolonial era, the Luo were second only to the Kikuyu in terms of their contributions to the Kenyan political scene.

Members of the Luo group became high-ranking officials in the administration of Jomo KENYATTA (c. 1891–1978), the first president of independent Kenya. Among them were Oginga ODINGA (1912–1994) and Tom MBOYA (1930–1969). Odinga and Mboya were cofounders of the KENYAN AFRICAN NATIONAL UNION, the driving political force behind the Kenyan independence movement and the party that dominated Kenyan politics until 2002. Both Luo leaders, however, eventually came into conflict with Kenyatta. Mboya's assassination in 1969 led many Luo to suspect Kenyatta, a Kikuyu, of leading a campaign against their people. With the rise of Daniel arap MOI (1924–   ), a member of the minority Kalenjin people, to the presidency, the Luo became less prominent in the government. In 1982 a group of Luo military officers attempted unsuccessfully to oust Moi in a COUP D'ÉTAT.

The Luo contributed significantly to Kenya's popular culture with the introduction of *benga* MUSIC during the 1970s. With guitar and bass heavily influenced by the traditional Luo *nyatiti* harp and lyrics sung in Luod, *benga* became Kenya's national signature sound. The pioneering *benga* musician was D. O. Misiani, who sang in Luo accompanied by his band Shirati Jazz. The Victoria Kings, named because they came from the Lake Victoria region, were another of the pioneering groups.

See also: ETHNICITY AND IDENTITY (Vol. V); LUO (Vols. II, III, IV).

Lusaka Capital of ZAMBIA, located in the south of the country on a plateau that rises 4,200 feet (1,280 m) above sea level. Founded in the 1890s by the British South Africa Company, Lusaka grew slowly as the capital of the British protectorate of Northern Rhodesia. However, after the town became the capital of the independent nation of ZAMBIA in 1964, the population grew rapidly, with people from around the countryside attracted by the temperate climate and the opportunities they believed the capital city would offer.

Although the town had been neglected during the colonial era, the Zambians who moved to the capital city began playing major roles in its DEVELOPMENT, buying property in previously segregated areas. The government, for its part, took over the formerly private schools and hospitals, enforcing racial integration. As the city developed, the middle-class residents migrated out to the suburbs, leaving the city center to poor and working-class Zambians. The city still displays distinct sectors, including the modern government center and the old downtown area.

Although Lusaka's economy still relies heavily on AGRICULTURE, other industries have developed, including food processing, and the manufacturing of textiles, electronics, shoes, and cement. Railroad links to Livingstone and the Copperbelt, to the west, and the city's location on major thoroughfares to TANZANIA and MALAWI, to the east, have encouraged economic diversification and POPULATION GROWTH. (By 1995 the population had grown to about 1,300,000.) In addition to being an economic, TRANSPORTATION, and population center, Lusaka, with its numerous ART galleries and museums, also has become an excellent location for local artists to show their work.

Because of its centrality, Lusaka quickly became a "melting pot" of the country's ethnic groups. Similar to the situation in the Copperbelt, people from all over the country come to Lusaka and coexist. It is common to find children who speak various languages playing together and communicating easily in one or two languages. Chinyanja is widely spoken among the people in Lusaka, while English is the official language.

Politically, Lusaka has played a major role in regional and continental affairs. From the 1960s it served as a base for liberation movements from ZIMBABWE, SOUTH AFRICA, and NAMIBIA, and in the 1980s Lusaka began hosting major continental and international conferences.

See also: BRITISH SOUTH AFRICA COMPANY (Vol. IV); COPPERBELT (Vol. IV); ENGLAND AND AFRICA (Vols. III, IV, V); LUSAKA (Vol. IV): NORTHERN RHODESIA (Vol. IV); URBAN LIFE AND CULTURE (Vols. IV, V); URBANIZATION (Vols. IV, V).

Further reading: Karen T. Hansen, *Keeping House in Lusaka* (New York: Columbia University Press, 1996).

Maasai Ethnic group of southern KENYA and northern TANZANIA. The largely pastoralist Maasai, whose Maa language belongs to the Nilo-Saharan language family, number an estimated 500,000. Once among the most powerful and feared warrior peoples of East Africa, the Maasai had declined dramatically by the end of colonialism. Already devastated by disease and British colonial practices, the Maasai suffered further under the independent Kenyan government led by Jomo KENYATTA (c. 1891–1978), who was an ethnic KIKUYU. Land redistribution and the creation of the Maasai Mara Game Reserve under Kenyatta led to extensive loss of land for the Maasai, who required large expanses to graze the cattle that are essential to their livelihood and culture.

Beginning in the 1980s, the Maasai received somewhat better treatment from Kenyan president Daniel arap MOI (1924–), a member of the linguistically related Kalenjin ethnic group. Many came to view the warrior-like Maasai as the muscle behind Moi in his power struggle with the Kikuyu people, a traditional Kalenjin rival.

Regardless of the country's leadership, the Maasai in both Kenya and Tanzania have been subject to repeated attempts to undermine their traditional ways of life. Their cattle-centered, pastoral culture has slowly failed in the face of imposed agricultural reforms and private land ownership. Long-held Maasai traditions—including female circumcision and other initiation rites—have been subject to intense criticism and repression from outsiders. The practice of sending young Maasai males, or *morans*, into the bush for the development of their warrior skills has also been threatened by various restrictions, including the outlawing of lion hunting, once an essential activity for *morans* to prove their manhood.

Today, the gradual loss of their traditional culture has forced the Maasai to move into other areas of economic DEVELOPMENT. One of the most easily recognized of African peoples, the Maasai play a large role in TOURISM. Facing greater and greater difficulty in maintaining their herds, some Maasai have also branched out into ostrich farming and beekeeping. Other Maasai have found work in the nature reserves that took over their ancestral lands. However, most Maasai continue to cling to traditional life in spite of the ongoing difficulties.

See also: ETHNICITY AND IDENTITY (Vol. I); MAASAI (Vols. I, II, III, IV); NATIONAL PARKS (Vol. V).

Further reading: Thomas Spear and Richard Waller, eds., *Being Maasai: Ethnicity and Identity in East Africa* (Athens, Ohio: Ohio University Press, 1993).

Machel, Graça (1945–) *Mozambican nationalist*

The youngest of six children, Graça Simbine was born in a rural village in MOZAMBIQUE. Her father, a Methodist minister, died three weeks before her birth. Before he died, though, he made provisions to assure that his daughter would receive a high school EDUCATION—at the time, a rare commodity for someone living in rural Mozambique. After high school, in 1968, Graça Simbine earned a scholarship to attend Lisbon University, in Portugal. There she studied romance languages and associated with other students that were from Portuguese colonies in Africa, frequently engaging in antigovernment discussions. The Portuguese secret police uncovered the group in 1972, and Simbine, fearful of a prison term if she returned to Mozambique, fled to Switzerland.

In 1973, while still in Europe, she joined the MOZAMBICAN LIBERATION FRONT (Frente de Libertação de Mozambique, FRELIMO), a nationalist movement that was on the verge of fulfilling its goal of Mozambican independence. Later in 1973 Simbine traveled to TANZANIA, Mozambique's neighbor to the north and staging ground for the FRELIMO offensive against the Portuguese. There she underwent military training, participated in insurgent activities, and met her future husband, Samora MACHEL (1933–1986). In 1974 Mozambique gained its independence, with Samora Machel as president.

While married to the president, Graça Machel saw her life change dramatically. Not only was she the first lady of Mozambique but she also cared for her husband's five children from a previous marriage. In addition, Graça Machel was named minister of education, an assignment she took on in earnest. During the following 12 years Graça Machel succeeded in decreasing Mozambique's staggering illiteracy rate. In 1986, however, Samora Machel died when his plane crashed in SOUTH AFRICA, near the Mozambican border. Devastated, Graça resigned her position as minister of education.

In 1990 Graça Machel reentered public service, helping to establish the Foundation for Community Development, an organization set up to improve local schools and health clinics. Later in the decade, she worked with the United Nations to begin the process of rehabilitating the numerous children affected by Mozambique's prolonged civil war. During this time she formed a close relationship with South Africa's president, Nelson MANDELA (1918–). In 1998, after years of courtship, the two married at Mandela's JOHANNESBURG home.

See also: INDEPENDENCE MOVEMENTS (Vol. V); PORTUGAL AND AFRICA (Vols. III, IV, V); WOMEN IN INDEPENDENT AFRICA (Vol. V).

Machel, Samora (1933–1986) *First president of Mozambique*

The son of an indigenous farmer, Machel was born in the village of Chilembe, located in the Gaza Province of MOZAMBIQUE. He attended a Catholic mission school in the town of Souguene as a youth but left school in his late teens to become a nurse in the capital city of Lourenço Marques (now MAPUTO). While working as a nurse, Machel was disturbed by the poor treatment given to black patients. Spurred by this and other social inequalities resulting from colonialism, Machel joined the Nucleus of Mozambican Students, a nationalist political organization. His membership brought him to the attention of the Portuguese government's secret police, known as PIDE. Fearing arrest, Machel fled to DAR ES SALAAM, the capital of TANZANIA, where he encountered a burgeoning Mozambican nationalist movement.

In 1963 Machel joined the nationalist MOZAMBICAN LIBERATION FRONT (Frente de Libertacão de Mozambique, FRELIMO) and soon after went to ALGERIA for military training. Machel returned to Tanzania in 1964, taking charge of FRELIMO's nascent military training camp. In 1966 Machel became commander of FRELIMO's Defense Department. He quickly streamlined the department, allowing FRELIMO to offer services such as agricultural assistance and LITERACY classes.

During this time FRELIMO greatly increased its membership. However, this expansion led to an ideological split within the organization. Machel was loyal to a faction that supported the power of the common citizenry, opposing the FRELIMO faction that called for a leadership run by the educated elite. The two sides briefly fought over control of FRELIMO, with Machel and his faction emerging victorious.

In 1969 FRELIMO's president, Eduardo MONDLANE (1920–1969), was assassinated, and the following year Machel assumed the organization's presidency. Also in 1970 the Portuguese colonial government of Mozambique staged a military offensive against FRELIMO. During the next four years Machel led FRELIMO to a decisive victory over Portuguese forces. It was also during this time that he met his wife, Graça Simbine, who became known as Graça MACHEL (1945–).

In 1974 a military COUP D'ÉTAT in Portugal changed the dynamic of that country's presence in Africa. Later that year Machel signed the Lusaka Agreement, which paved the way for Mozambican independence under a FRELIMO-controlled government. This led to Mozambique's independence in 1975, with Machel as the first president. He instituted a one-party, Marxist government, nationalizing all Mozambican land and providing free EDUCATION and health care to all Mozambicans. Machel's efforts, however, were burdened by a failing economy and, later, by attacks from the MOZAMBICAN NATIONAL RESISTANCE (Resistencia Nacional Mozambicana, RENAMO), a guerilla group based in RHODESIA and later SOUTH AFRICA.

RENAMO's activities made it difficult for Machel to improve Mozambique's economy—at the height of the conflict, more than 40 percent of the country's budget was spent combating the group. In 1984 Machel and the South African president, P. W. BOTHA (1916–), signed the Nkomati Accord, which called for the end of South Africa's support for RENAMO. Botha, however, never honored the agreement, and fighting continued. In the midst of his effort to end the conflict with RENAMO Machel died when his plane crashed into the Lebombo Mountains, in South Africa. Although South African involvement was strongly suspected, the cause of the accident was never determined.

See also: COMMUNISM AND SOCIALISM (Vol. V); INDEPENDENCE MOVEMENTS (Vol. V); PORTUGAL AND AFRICA (Vols. III, IV, V).

Madagascar (Malagasy Republic)

Large island, some 226,700 square miles (587,200 sq km) in size, located in the Indian Ocean about 242 miles (390 km) off the coast of MOZAMBIQUE on the southern coast of East Africa. Madagascar is a lightly industrialized nation, and less than one-third of the country's people live in urban areas. Major EXPORTS, mostly to European nations, include vanilla, coffee, and sugar. Most of Madagascar's population (totaling nearly 16 million in 1999) practices either a traditional, animistic religion or Christianity. A small minority is Muslim. Official languages are Malagasy and French.

Politics in Independent Madagascar

Madagascar was a monarchy prior to French colonization. The island began its transition from colony to independent democracy in 1956. The country's two significant political parties at the time were the Democratic Social Party of Mada-gascar (Parti Social Démocrate de Madagascar, PSD), led by Philibert TSIRANANA (c. 1912–1978), and the Congress Party for the Independence of Madagascar (Antokon'ny Kongresy Fanafahana an'i Madagasikara, AKFM), led by Richard Andriamanjato (1930–). The differences between the two parties presaged the fundamental rifts in Madagascar politics during the four decades that followed.

In the precolonial period the people of Madagascar fell into two groups, the Merina and the *cotier* (or "coastals"). The Merina were the long-dominant Asian ethnic group from the interior highlands. The *cotier*, on the other hand, was made up of people from the various African, Arabic, and Afro-Arabic ethnic groups along the coasts.

The PSD's Tsirinana came from the Tsimhety ethnic group of the *cotier*. He sought open trade along with continued close ties to France. On the other hand, Andriamanjato and the Merina-dominated AKFM sought a clean break from France. They desired a protectionist economy, and they promoted a movement to root out the vestiges of French influence and values among the Malagasy-speaking population. Andriamanjato himself was a Merina from the capital region of ANTANANARIVO, having served as the city's mayor from 1959 to 1977. Because of this, much of his support came from the urban population.

Called the Malagasy Republic, Madagascar gained independence from France on June 26, 1960, with Tsirinana as president. For much of the 1960s Tsirinana's First Republic benefited from cross-ethnic and cross-regional support for its pro-Western nationalist agenda of reconciliation. The country's French settlers, however, found the island's environment oppressive, and many departed the island, taking their businesses and money with them.

Continuing economic deterioration in the late 1960s eroded the support for Tsirinana. Under heavy pressure, he effectively turned the country over to the head of the military, a Merina general named Gabriel Ramanantsoa (1906–1979). This move gave rise to *cotier* discontent. Failing to bring the peace, Ramanantsoa turned power over to the more conciliatory Colonel Richard Ratsimandrava (1931–1975), on February 5, 1975. When Ratsimandrava was assassinated five days later, marshal law was declared.

On June 15, 1975, the military directorate appointed Lieutenant Commander Didier RATSIRAKA (1936–) as the country's new president. He enjoyed strong *cotier* support, especially in his home province of Toamasina, on the east coast. Ratsiraka nationalized banks and industries and adopted a Marxist charter for a Second Malagasy Republic. He also pushed Madagascar toward federation, handing significant political and economic power to regional and community governments. This turn was seen by some as an attempt to bring power to the people but was seen by others as an attempt to wrest power from the Merina-controlled capital.

In March 1976 Ratsiraka founded the Vanguard of the Malagasy Revolution (Antokin'ny Revolisiona Malagasy, AREMA), which became the lead party in a six-party governing coalition. Before long, the country's economy worsened and it became clear that the nation's socialist economic principals were failing. Nevertheless, Ratsiraka continued to ally his country with Communist countries, including China, North Korea, and the former Soviet Union. Popular dissatisfaction with Ratsiraka began in 1977, eventually leading to a series of government crackdowns the following year. By 1980 the socialist experiment had given way to a more authoritarian style of leadership that would characterize Ratsiraka's rule over the decade that followed. Economically, however, he turned to the WORLD BANK and the INTERNATIONAL MONETARY FUND to help him liberalize the nation's beleaguered economy.

Despite growing unpopularity, Ratsiraka won reelection in 1982 and again, in a disputed election, in 1989. By 1991, though, the loss of support from the dissolved Soviet Union made Ratsiraka's government increasingly vulnerable. Finally, opposition to Ratsiraka's leadership led to a civil servants' strike that brought the capital to a halt. When Ratsiraka appeared unable to control the situation, Dr. Albert Zafy (1927–) led the Hery Velona ("Active Forces" in Malagasy) coalition in setting up a parallel government. In October 1991, Zafy's success led to the signing of the Panorama Convention, a power-sharing arrangement that prepared for a transition to democracy. A new constitution was popularly ratified in August 1992, and Zafy was elected president in February

1993. The Hery Velona parties won a landslide legislative victory in June 1993.

Despite his ability to mobilize the opposition, Zafy proved to be a poor leader. He was identified with the *cotier*, but he relied heavily on the Merina base to centralize political power in the capital. In 1995, following a referendum, Ratsiraka reinvested the presidency with unprecedented authority, raising some eyebrows in the capital. By August 1996 he was convicted of CORRUPTION and impeached. In December 1996, following an election marked by poor voter turnout, Didier Ratsiraka came back to power and AREMA soon took control of the legislature.

Recent Political Developments Ratsiraka's second term was fraught with controversy. In July 2001 it appeared that Ratsiraka would win the December 2001 election. However, in August 2001 Marc RAVALOMANANA (1949–   ), Antananarivo's popular mayor and founder of the Tiko milk products company, declared his candidacy. Although Ravalomanana was of Merina descent, he had wide support among the general population. Despite dubious changes in the electoral rules called for by Ratsiraka, Ravalomanana won the election. Ratsiraka contested the vote count and the AREMA-controlled National Electoral Commission determined that Ravalomanana failed to win at least 50 percent of the vote. The commission then called for a run-off election. On the other hand, Ravalomanana and the independent National Committee of Election Observers claimed he won more than the necessary 50 percent.

Both Ratsiraka and Ravalomanana refused to budge, and when Ravalomanana declared himself president in February 2002, the country became divided. Ratsiraka was ousted from Antananarivo and went with his forces to Toamasina. After four months of military conflict and failed negotiations, Ratsiraka fled to Paris. Ravalomanana was sworn in—again—in May 2002. Shortly thereafter he oversaw the formation of Tiako-i-Madagasikara (I Love Madagascar), a political party that won commanding control of the Madagascar legislature in December 2002.

See also: FRANCE AND AFRICA (Vols. III, IV, V); MADAGASCAR (Vols. I, II, III, IV); MERINA (Vols. III, IV).

Further reading: Mervyn Brown, *A History of Madagascar* (Princeton, N.J.: Markus Wiener Publishers, 2000).

Maghrib (Maghreb)

Maghrib (Maghreb) Muslim region of northwest Africa along the Mediterranean Sea, extending eastward from the Atlas Mountains, in MOROCCO, to the coasts of ALGERIA, TUNISIA, and LIBYA. The countries of the Maghrib have shared similar historical and cultural experiences, as three of them—Algeria, Tunisia, and Libya—were under the Ottoman Empire, and all of them fell under European colonial rule. After obtaining their independence, the North African countries that comprise

the Maghrib charted their individual courses as sovereign nation-states. The individual character of society and governance of each kept them divided politically. In the 1980s, however, a united northern Africa became possible as these countries entertained the idea of forming a North Africa common market known as the Arab Maghrib Union, which is sometimes referred to as the Maghrib Economic Space. Discussed by Arab nationalists first in the 1920s and again in the mid-1960s, the union was formalized in 1989. It promotes the region's common economic interests and commercial exchanges, but pledges non-interference in the domestic affairs of its member states. Member nations include Morocco, Algeria, Tunisia, Libya, MAURITANIA, and WESTERN SAHARA.

See also: COLONIAL RULE (Vol. IV); MAGHRIB (Vols. I, III, IV); OTTOMAN EMPIRE AND AFRICA (Vol. IV).

Mahfouz, Naguib

Mahfouz, Naguib (1911–   ) *Egyptian writer and Nobel laureate*

Regarded as the leading figure in Egyptian and Arabic literature, Mahfouz was born in one of the oldest quarters of CAIRO in 1911. He was 17 when he began writing, but it was not until 1939 that his first novel, *Hams al-junun*, was published. This work was followed by 10 more. The first three concerned ancient EGYPT. Thereafter Mahfouz shifted his focus to modern Egypt, a move that helped revolutionize Egyptian and Arabic fiction by establishing the novel as a legitimate genre within Arabic literature. His crowning achievement of this period, and perhaps of his career, was the Cairo Trilogy, published in 1956–57. These three books, *Bayn al-qasrayn* (1956), *Qasr al-shawq* (1957), and *Al Sukkariya* (1957) (published in English as *Palace Walk, Palace of Desire,* and *Sugar Street* respectively), made up an epic story of three generations within a middle-class Cairo family in the period between the two world wars.

Mahfouz's first work to be translated into English was *Midaq Alley* (1947) in 1966. However, it was not until after he won the Nobel Prize in 1988 that Mahfouz garnered widespread Western attention and had a significant portion of his literary corpus translated into English.

In 1952 King Faruk (1920–1965) of Egypt was overthrown in a COUP D'ÉTAT carried out by a group of army officers. Shortly thereafter Colonel Gamal Abdel NASSER (1918–1970) assumed the presidency and instituted a socialist regime. Mahfouz initially supported the fall of the monarchy, and, until 1972, served in various governmental positions. However, the writer became increasingly disgusted and frustrated with Nasser's administration. For seven years following the coup Mahfouz produced no new works, though his previous novels gained dramatic new popularity in Egypt.

In 1959 Mahfouz's frustrations finally boiled over into a new novel, serialized as *Awlad haratina* (published in English as *Children of Gebelawi*). The novel's narrative mirrored that of a religious quest and lashed out at the social injustice Mahfouz perceived in socialist Egypt.

The book raised the ire of Islamic fundamentalists, who issued a fatwa, essentially a death sentence, on Mahfouz. Fundamentalist displeasure with Mahfouz's works later led to an assassination attempt in 1994. The author survived the stabbing, and the perpetrators were captured and executed.

Children of Gebelawi began a string of novels and short stories that used symbolism and allegory to thinly cover Mahfouz's critique of Nasser's government. In 1967 Mahfouz published the novel *Miramar,* which was his final address against Nasser and the socialist revolution. Mahfouz's later works became more experimental in nature, often in the form of lengthy fables. The author's new direction earned mixed reviews, but nevertheless he has remained very popular in Egypt, where each new Mahfouz publication marks an important cultural event.

In 1988 Mahfouz became the first Arab and, two years after Wole SOYINKA (1934–) won, the second writer from Africa to receive the Nobel Prize for Literature. As of 2003 he has published more than 30 novels and numerous short stories and articles.

In the address he gave while accepting the Nobel Prize, Mahfouz said, "I am the son of two civilizations that at a certain age in history have formed a happy marriage. The first of these, 7,000 years old, is the Pharaonic civilization; the second, 1,400 years old, is the Islamic civilization."

See also: FARUK, KING (Vol. IV); LITERATURE IN COLONIAL AFRICA (Vol. IV); LITERATURE IN MODERN AFRICA (Vol. V).

Makeba, Miriam (1932–) *South African singer*

Widely known as "Mama Africa," Miriam Makeba has been the most recognizable female ambassador of African MUSIC over the last four decades. From humble origins in SOUTH AFRICA, Makeba gained fame during the 1950s as a talented vocalist through her appearances with local South African bands. She soon became an international star.

Shortly after a cameo appearance in the 1957 anti-APARTHEID film, *Come Back, Africa,* Makeba met Harry Belafonte (1927–), the famous African-American singer. Belafonte became her mentor and was instrumental in introducing her to American audiences, where her concert performances and record sales met with great success. Her music popularizes the songs of Africa, as well as those of other cultures. She is best known for such standards as "Pata, Pata" and "The Click Song," which utilize the click sounds of her XHOSA mother tongue.

Makeba's political and private lives have also been noteworthy. In 1960 the South African government prevented her, on political grounds, from returning to her own country. In 1964 she married South African trumpeter Hugh MASEKELA (1931–), who was also a political exile from South Africa, but they divorced two years later. In 1968 Makeba married African-American civil rights activist Stokely Carmichael (1941–1998), later known as Kwame Ture, one of the most influential leaders of the civil rights and black liberation movements of the 1960s in the United States and, later, a leader of the Black Panther Party. Her marriage to Carmichael resulted in a music industry boycott and constant surveillance by the United States Federal Bureau of Investigation.

Stokely Carmichael changed his name to Kwame Ture when he and Makeba moved to GUINEA. He chose the name in honor of President Kwame NKRUMAH (1909–1972) of GHANA and President Ahmed Sékou TOURÉ (1922–1984) of Guinea, two leaders of the Pan-African movement. Kwame Ture became active in African nationalist causes.

As a result she and Carmichael left the United States in 1969 and took up residence in Guinea. Makeba continued to tour widely, mainly in Europe and Africa. In 1975 she represented Guinea in the United Nations, where she proved to be an outspoken critic of APARTHEID. In recognition of her activism, she was awarded the Dag Hammarskjöld Peace Prize in 1986. Her career in the United States was revived in 1987, when she performed in the new nation of ZIMBABWE with American folk-rock singer Paul Simon (1941–) on his *Graceland* tour. In the late 1980s, after a 30-year exile, Makeba returned to South Africa, where she has continued to take an active role in her homeland's cultural life.

See also: UNITED NATIONS AND AFRICA (Vols. IV, V).

Makerere University Institute of higher EDUCATION located in KAMPALA, UGANDA. Founded in 1922 as Makerere College, Makerere University began as a technical school that taught carpentry, construction, and mechanics. Later it became an inter-territorial institution for British East Africa, preparing students from KENYA, Uganda, Tanganyika, and ZANZIBAR for professions in AGRICULTURE, education, MEDICINE, and governmental administration in the colonies. In 1937 the College began its program in higher education and later formed a partnership with the College of London, from which students received general university degrees. Makerere was the only institution of higher education in East Africa during the colonial period.

In 1963, a year after Ugandan independence, Makerere College joined the universities of Kenya and Tanzania to form the University of East Africa (UEA). Offering its own degree program, the UEA produced the next generation of African leaders in government and business. In 1970, with a solid reputation in academic research and teaching, Makerere became the University of the Republic of Uganda.

However, political events during the 1970s and 1980s destroyed the INFRASTRUCTURE of the University. While Uganda was under the control of first Idi AMIN (c. 1925–2003) and then Milton OBOTE (1925–2000), Makerere lost much of its funding. As a result it was unable to keep up with revolutionary changes in informational technology. Because of government CORRUPTION and a general lack of attention to social concerns, faculty members were the last civil servants to be paid. (Army staff, on the other hand, were the first to be paid.) Low faculty salaries caused many teachers to leave.

To compound Makerere's problems, at the same time that faculty were leaving and university resources were diminishing, the school's student population was increasing. This was a logical result of the fact that independent Uganda's students were moving through the country's free educational system from primary school through secondary school to the university.

By the 1990s the university was beginning to benefit from changes in governmental organization that removed it from state control. No longer dependent on the government for its revenues, Makerere began instituting alternative methods of funding, including charging student fees. As a result, the university has regained its status within Uganda as a solution to the challenges of DEVELOPMENT.

Malabo Primary port and capital city of EQUATORIAL GUINEA, located at the northern end of Bioko Island (formerly called both Fernando Po and Santa Isabel) on the Gulf of Guinea. The British founded the city in 1827, having leased the island from Spain in order to suppress the slave trade. As a result many freed slaves ended up settling there. Spain regained full control in 1900, renaming the city Santa Isabel and making it the capital of Spanish Guinea. The two periods of Spanish rule are clearly reflected in the city's ARCHITECTURE. In 1968 Santa Isabel remained the capital when Spanish Guinea became the independent nation known as Equatorial Guinea. Five years later the city's name was changed to Malabo.

Malabo has been in decline since independence. In 1969 the country's president, Macías Nguema Biyogo (1924–1979), encouraged rioting against the European residents of the island, mostly Spanish, which caused many people to flee the country. The population declined further in the 1970s, when numerous contract workers returned home to NIGERIA. In addition, local people left the city and the country due to Biyogo's brutal rule, which oppressed the island's Bubi ethnic minority in favor of his own Fang people.

Today Malabo has a relatively small population of 93,000. Even so, it remains the commercial and economic center of the country. The city's main industry is fish processing and, along with fish, Malabo's EXPORTS include coffee, cotton, cocoa, and timber. The recent development of offshore OIL fields holds the potential for an economic revival, but Malabo's citizens have not yet realized any great benefits.

See also: ENGLAND AND AFRICA (Vols. III, IV, V); FANG (Vol. II); FERNANDO PO (Vol. III); SLAVE TRADE (Vols. III, IV); SPAIN AND AFRICA (Vols. III, IV).

malaria Human parasitic disease common throughout the tropical areas in Africa. Malaria probably originated in Africa and infected prehistoric man. The transmission mechanism was known as early as 1898, and the life cycle of the disease was confirmed by 1948. Today malaria is considered one of the major health problems in Africa.

The African continent, where malaria causes more child deaths than any other disease, has approximately 80 to 90 percent of the world's malaria cases. In places where malaria is endemic, adults often develop immunity to the disease. However, this immunity is compromised during pregnancy or during prolonged periods of non-exposure. Also, many places in Africa have seasonal or sporadic malaria outbreaks that do not allow for immunity in adult populations.

While there are four species of malaria worldwide, only three are important in Africa. One of these, *Plasmodium falciparum,* is blamed for most of the infections on the continent. *Anopheles* mosquitoes in Africa are responsible for transferring the disease to humans. The three main types of *Anopheles* mosquitoes, *A. gambiae, A. funestus,* and *A. arabiensis,* inhabit different areas depending on climate, water sources, and vegetation. The female mosquito transmits the malaria parasite through its bite.

Malaria infects an estimated 300–500 million people worldwide each year, killing 2 million of them. The massive scale of the human suffering malaria produces attracted the attention of the world's richest couple, Bill and Melinda Gates. Through their William H. Gates Foundation, in 2003, they awarded $50 million to support a Malaria Vaccine Initiative. To date, no vaccine has been discovered. Most malaria research takes place in developed countries, which are generally located in temperate regions. Since malaria is a disease of the tropics, there has been limited interest and little incentive to commit significant resources to fighting malaria.

The World Health Organization initiated the Global Eradication of Malaria Program in the 1950s. This effort was primarily based on the use of DDT, an insecticide, to eliminate the mosquito vector. However, by 1972, after it became apparent that eradication was impossible, the program officially ended. The failure of the initiative was blamed on several factors, including the ineffectiveness of DDT to kill all mosquito vectors and the frequent misdiagnosis or ineffective treatment of the infection. The organization also found that the overuse of malaria medication had accidentally helped develop malaria strains that were resistant to treatment.

Current malaria programs focus on educating the population to recognize symptoms and seek early treatment. Other preventive measures include using mosquito nets and insecticide and destroying potential breeding places, such as pots with water, bushy areas, and puddles. Africa Malaria Day, April 25, was established in 2000 to commemorate the commitment made by 44 African leaders to work toward reducing malaria infection rates.

See also: DISEASE IN MODERN AFRICA (Vol. V); DISEASE IN COLONIAL AFRICA (Vol. IV); HEALTH AND HEALING IN MODERN AFRICA (Vol. V); MEDICINE (Vols. IV, V).

Beginning in the 1950s a concerted effort was made to end the frequent malaria outbreaks that plagued tropical Africa. Shown in 1963, a World Health Organization worker is spraying DDT, an insecticide, to kill the mosquitoes that carry malaria. © *United Nations*

Malawi Country located in southeastern Africa and bordered by TANZANIA to the north, MOZAMBIQUE to the east and south, and ZAMBIA to the west. About 45,700 square miles (118,400 sq km) in size, Malawi is land-locked, though its borders do include the massive Lake Nyasa, which covers some 8,900 square miles (23,051 sq km).

Malawi at Independence Ruled as the British colony of Nyasaland after 1907, by 1960 the drive for independence was in full force behind the Malawi Congress Party (MCP) and its leader, Dr. Hastings Kamuzu BANDA (c. 1898–1997). Demonstrations instigated by Banda and the MCP forced the British to declare a state of emergency, in 1959–60. In 1963 the Central African Federation, a colonial entity of which Nyasaland was a part, was dissolved. One year later Nyasaland became independent Malawi.

Banda served as prime minister until 1966, when the Republic of Malawi was formed and Banda became the country's first president. He put into place a government that was called a "guided democracy," but in practice was a one-party dictatorship, dominated by the MCP. Using a loyalist faction of the MCP called the Malawi Young Pioneers as his muscle, Banda took control over every aspect of Malawian society, from the media to the national treasury to the way citizens were allowed to dress. He imposed his Chewa heritage on the entire nation, attempting to make chiChewa the national language and moving the capital from Zomba to LILONGWE, in Chewa lands. Political opponents were driven into exile or assassinated by the feared secret police.

At the time of Banda's rule, Malawi was one of the poorest nations in Africa. Little progress was made toward DEVELOPMENT under Banda, who used much of the country's funding for his own personal benefit. In 1967 Banda's highly controversial decision to form diplomatic relations with the racist APARTHEID government of SOUTH AFRICA was made with the intent of benefiting economically from the larger country. Ultimately, however, it was not its relationship with South Africa but large amounts of foreign ECONOMIC ASSISTANCE that boosted Malawi's economy during the 1970s.

In 1971 Banda seemingly extinguished all possibility for the DEMOCRATIZATION of Malawi by declaring himself president for life. He ruled the country as such until the early 1990s. By 1992, in the midst of a terrible drought, Banda was no longer able to ignore pressure to reform the government. A letter by the Catholic church criticizing the dictator's regime was read in churches throughout Malawi, sparking mass demonstrations against Banda. In addition, foreign economic assistance was withdrawn. With little choice Banda, who was in ill health, acquiesced and was stripped of his president-for-life title in 1993. The following year multiparty elections resulted in a victory for the United Democratic Front (UDF) and its leader, Bakili MULUZI (1943–), a former official in Banda's government.

Malawi under Muluzi Muluzi became president of a nation with a 65 percent POVERTY rate and drastic food shortages. Health care had become a serious issue as HIV/AIDS began to ravage the population. In addition Malawi had to adjust to a democratic system and avoid the kind of political infighting that could lead to governmental instability. Muluzi moved to aid this adjustment by forming a coalition government with the other major opposition party, the Alliance for Democracy (AFORD). However, the political regionalism that has emerged under the multiparty system, with the UDF dominating the south, the MCP the central region, and AFORD in the north, has made for a tense situation.

In 1995 Muluzi had former president Banda arrested on four counts of murder committed during Banda's rule. Banda, along with six of his cohorts, was acquitted of the crimes. Muluzi himself faced claims by opponents that he should be held accountable for any transgressions by the Banda regime, considering that Muluzi was a high-ranking official in the MCP.

In 1999 Muluzi was reelected amid accusations of electoral fraud. In 2004, however, he had to step down because Malawi's constitution does not allow for a third presidential term. Muluzi put his support behind Bingu wa Mutharika (1934–), a WORLD BANK economist and former Muluzi rival in the UDF party. Mutharika won the elections amid more accusations of fraud.

Malawi still remains highly dependent on foreign aid to support its economy. Privatization programs are being employed to encourage investments, though the economy is largely based on AGRICULTURE and Malawi is subject to the recurring droughts and floods. Life expectancy among Malawians is very low (37 years), and by 2003, 15 percent of the population was thought to be infected with the HIV virus. Government CORRUPTION is also a growing concern, leading some nations to withhold foreign assistance.

See also: HIV/AIDS AND AFRICA (Vol. V); MALAWI (Vols. I, II, III, IV).

Mali Landlocked central West African country 478,800 square miles (1,240,100 sq km) in size stretching north into the Sahara Desert, where it shares borders with MAURITANIA and ALGERIA; other countries bordering Mali include NIGER, BURKINA FASO, IVORY COAST, GUINEA, and SENEGAL. The population is concentrated in the southern half of the country in the watershed of the Niger River. Mali is the largest country in West Africa.

Mali at Independence Mali is noted for being the geographical center of several powerful empires, including the Soninke empire of Ghana (c. 900–1250), the Muslim Almoravid empire (c. 1050–1146), the Mandinka empire (1235–1368) of Mali—the country's namesake—and the Songhai Empire (c. 1375–1591). The country received its independence from France in 1960. Modibo KEITA (1915–1977) was the country's first president within a one-party system. Under Keita, Mali endured a difficult economic environment as well as the festering of a violent opposition movement. Popular discontent with Keita's rule steadily grew through the 1960s, culminating in a COUP D'ÉTAT led by Lieutenant Moussa Traoré (1936–) in 1968. Over the next decade Traoré ruled Mali under a military monarchy.

In 1974 a new constitution was adopted that allowed for popular elections. However, Mali remained a one-party state, ensuring the continuing reelections of Traoré. During the 1970s and 1980s Mali suffered from a series of crises, including severe droughts, which had a devastating impact on the already weakened economy. In 1990 the country's situation grew worse, with disaffected Tuaregs staging an unsuccessful rebellion. Soon after, in March 1991 lieutenant colonel Amadou Toumani TOURÉ (1948–) led a military coup that ousted Traoré.

Mali Today In early 1992 Mali held multiparty elections that resulted in 10 parties winning seats in the new 129-member legislature; the leader of the Alliance for Democracy in Mali, Alpha Oumar KONARÉ (1946–), won the presidency. Konaré's term was marked by instability and political tensions punctuated by periodic violent protests. At the same time, however, Mali moved toward a more democratic society while encouraging a free press. This process of DEMOCRATIZATION succeeded in attracting FOREIGN INVESTMENT, which in turn sparked economic growth and stabilized the country's politics.

With his days as president winding down, in 2002 Konaré pardoned Traoré and his wife, releasing them from the death sentences they received for misappropriation of Mali's funds and for Traoré's role in the deaths of pro-democracy demonstrators in the days leading up to the coup that ousted him from power. The death sentences were subsequently commuted to life imprisonment.

Mali's progress toward a democratic and stable political system got a further boost from the 2002 elections. That year, Konaré relinquished the office of president, submitting to the two-term limit mandated by the constitution. In the ensuing election, Amadou Toumani Touré, who had reentered Malian political life, ran on a popular anticorruption platform and handily won the presidency. Touré committed his government to ensuring domestic peace and alleviating the country's POVERTY.

See also: ALMORAVIDS (Vol. II); FRANCE AND AFRICA (Vols. IV, V); GHANA (Vol. III); MALI (Vols. I, II, III, IV); MALI EMPIRE (Vol. II); MANDE (Vols. I, II, IV); SONGHAI (Vols. II, III); SONINKE (Vols. IV).

Further reading: R. James Bingen, David Robinson, and John M. Staatz, eds, *Democracy and Development in Mali* (East Lansing, Mich.: Michigan State University Press, 2000); Rhéal Drisdelle, *Mali: A Prospect of Peace?* (Oxford, U.K.: Oxfam UK, 1997).

Mancham, James (c. 1939–) *First president of Seychelles*

In the 1960s the development of a professional urban middle class caused a political shift in the SEYCHELLES and led to the formation of two major political parties. James Mancham led the Seychelles Democratic Party (SDP), in opposition to the Seychelles People's United Party (SPUP), led by Mancham's political nemesis, France-Albert RENÉ (1935–). With Britain slowly preparing the islands for independence, Mancham favored continuing ties with Britain, a position he reversed once Britain's lack of interest in the Seychelles became obvious. In 1974 Mancham and the SDP won control of the country in what was largely decried as a rigged election. Mancham overcame the controversy and formed a coalition government with the SPUP, and in 1976 Mancham became the president of the Republic of the Seychelles, with René as his vice president.

Mancham's presidency was short-lived, however. In 1977, while Mancham was in London, a group of SPUP members staged a COUP D'ÉTAT, supposedly without René's knowledge, and installed René as president. René quickly moved the government in a socialist direction and banned all political parties save his own, now renamed the Seychelles People's Progressive Front (SPPF). Exiled, Mancham agitated against René's government to no avail.

In 1991 pressure from Britain and France forced René to allow for multiparty elections. The following year, Mancham returned to the Seychelles as a hero. Now leading the Democratic Party, Mancham promised to win the 1993 elections. However, René and the SPPF easily dominated, a feat they repeated in 1998 and 2001, keeping Mancham's political influence to a minimum.

Mandela, Nelson (Nelson Rolihlalah Mandela) (1918–) *South Africa's first black African president*

Rising from modest beginnings to become a leading activist in the struggle against APARTHEID in SOUTH

AFRICA, Nelson Mandela faced even greater challenges in the second half of the 20th century, when the conflict between the country's ruling white minority and the oppressed black majority reached its highest levels.

In 1960 the South African government banned the AFRICAN NATIONAL CONGRESS (ANC), the highly active anti-apartheid organization of which Mandela was a leader. The banning forced Mandela to take the resistance underground. It also forced the rebels to reconsider their nonviolent stance. In 1961 Mandela and other influential ANC leaders such as Walter SISULU (1912–2003) decided violence was the only answer to the ruthless tactics of the apartheid government. That same year they formed the UMKHONTO WE SIZWE (meaning "Spear of the Nation" and known as the MK), a guerilla military group that Mandela commanded. In 1962 Mandela secretly left South Africa to travel to ETHIOPIA, TANZANIA, England, and ALGERIA to rally support for the MK and to undergo military training.

However, not long after his return to South Africa Mandela was arrested and sentenced to five years in prison on charges of encouraging strikes and leaving the country without permission. Then a raid by South African police on MK headquarters at a Rivonia farm to the north of JOHANNESBURG produced strong evidence of Mandela's involvement in the MK sabotage campaign. During the following 1964 trial, which became known as the Rivonia Trial, Mandela—a lawyer by trade—gave a rousing defense, staunchly maintaining his opposition to apartheid and openly criticizing the racist regime. Ultimately, however, Mandela and six of his fellow MK members were sentenced to life in prison.

During his defense, Mandela declared, "I have cherished the ideal of a democratic and free society in which all persons live together in harmony and with equal opportunities. It is an ideal which I hope to live for and to achieve. But if needs be, it is an ideal for which I am prepared to die."

Even while imprisoned on ROBBEN ISLAND Mandela was recognized as the central figure of the fight against the tyranny of apartheid, serving as an inspirational leader to those who carried on the movement for equality and majority rule. Throughout the 27 years he remained behind bars, Mandela never ceased to support his cause and prepare himself for the time when apartheid would fall, teaching himself AFRIKAANS and becoming a leader among his fellow inmates.

The End of Apartheid At the end of the 1980s the racial conflict in Africa was reaching a fever pitch. By this time Mandela had been twice offered a conditional re-

lease from prison, which he refused in each instance. However, in 1986, he began negotiations with President P. W. BOTHA (1916–) and, later, with F. W. DE KLERK (1936–), who had promised upon his election to make provisions for multiracial elections. Finally, in 1990, the ANC ban was rescinded, and Mandela was released.

The end of apartheid did not come quickly, however. Mandela and de Klerk negotiated for four years, through periods of renewed protests and violence. De Klerk wanted a guarantee of continued white influence through a power-sharing system, while Mandela uncompromisingly demanded a fully democratic system where the vote of the majority determined those who would form the government. In 1993 both Mandela and de Klerk were awarded the Nobel Peace Prize for their efforts to end racial conflict in South Africa. Ultimately, in 1994 the first multiracial national elections ever in South Africa were held. Mandela was elected president, with the ANC capturing nearly two-thirds of the votes. Apartheid had been dealt its deathblow.

Mandela as President Though Mandela had accomplished the once seemingly impossible task of overcoming apartheid rule, he found himself in the unenviable position of leading a nation shattered by violence and still seething with racial hatred. He had to balance a number of volatile factors. As head of a government still largely staffed by white officials, Mandela had not only to head off further racial conflict in South Africa but he also had to ease ethnic tensions within the black majority. The ANC and the ZULU people, represented by the INKATHA FREEDOM PARTY, had long been at odds. The remnants of apartheid still lingered, as well, in the form of white extremist groups like the Afrikaner Resistance Movement.

Ultimately, it was Mandela's open lack of bitterness toward his former antagonists that set the tone for South Africa's healing process. In 1995 Mandela formed the TRUTH AND RECONCILIATION COMMISSION, headed by Desmond TUTU (1931–), an anti-apartheid leader and the Anglican Church's Archbishop of CAPE TOWN. The commission gathered testimony from both perpetrators and victims of the apartheid era. It offered amnesty to those who confessed to racial crimes, so long as they could prove their motives were purely political in nature. Though criticized by some as too lax, the commission allowed the events of South Africa's past to come to light. Their findings helped place the blame on the appropriate people and made provisions for those people to be forgiven in the eyes of the new government. In order to prevent divisive political disputes, Mandela also encouraged the participation of black ANC opponents in his new government.

In addition to having to overcome South Africa's past, Mandela faced the equally daunting task of rescuing a nation in economic disarray, particularly among the long-oppressed black population, which was badly underemployed. To combat the situation, Mandela launched the Reconstruction and Development Plan, which set various economic goals to encourage DEVELOPMENT. The return of FOREIGN INVESTMENT and the lifting of economic and political embargoes on the country helped make those goals more realistic. International admiration for Mandela also helped the president raise millions for charity causes in South Africa.

In 1996 Mandela divorced Winnie Nomzamo MANDELA (1936–) after she became an open critic of his government and was indicted on kidnapping charges. Nelson Mandela later married Graça MACHEL (1945–), the widow of the late president of MOZAMBIQUE, Samora MACHEL (1933–1986).

Mandela Steps Down In 1999, in a move rarely seen in Africa, Mandela voluntarily stepped down from the presidency after serving only one term. His successor, Thabo MBEKI (1942–), had been groomed to take his place, and Mbeki continued the process of healing and rebuilding the nation.

Among Mandela's many causes is the HIV/AIDS epidemic in Africa. In 2003 Mandela launched the 46664 initiative, named after his prisoner number while he was on Robben Island. The initiative seeks to raise awareness of AIDS through MUSIC. The 2003 Nelson Mandela Concert brought musicians from around the world to CAPE TOWN to raise money and attract attention to the crisis.

This was by no means a retirement for Mandela. The former president became deeply involved in resolving other devastating conflicts in Africa, most notably the ethnic conflict between the HUTU and the TUTSI peoples in BURUNDI. Mandela's continued efforts to promote peace have earned him many accolades, including an honorary degree from Harvard University and a lifetime achievement award from the Congress of South African Trade Unions. Through 2003 Mandela remained perhaps Africa's best-known and internationally respected statesman. He has since returned to his humble beginnings, building his retirement home in his former hometown of Qunu, in the Transkei region of the Eastern Cape Province.

See also: ETHNIC CONFLICT IN AFRICA (Vol. IV); HIV/AIDS AND AFRICA (Vol. V); MANDELA, NELSON (Vol. IV); RACE AND RACISM (Vol. IV).

Further reading: C. R. D. Halisi, *Black Political Thought in the Making of South African Democracy* (Bloomington, Ind.: Indiana University Press, 1999); *Nelson Mandela, Long Walk to Freedom: The Autobiography of Nelson Mandela* (Boston: Little, Brown, 1994); Anthony Sampson, *Mandela: The Authorized Biography* (New York: Knopf, 1999).

Mandela, Winnie (Nomzamo Winifred Madikizela) (1936–) *Anti-apartheid activist and ex-wife of former South African president Nelson Mandela (1918–)*

Known by a number of nicknames ranging from "mother of the nation" to "mugger of the nation," Winnie Madikizela-Mandela is both adored and despised by factions within the population of SOUTH AFRICA. Born Nomzamo Winifred Madikizela in Pondoland, South Africa, Mandela trained as a social worker in JOHANNESBURG, subsequently becoming South Africa's first black medical social worker.

While in Johannesburg Madikizela became involved in the anti-APARTHEID activities of the AFRICAN NATIONAL CONGRESS (ANC). She established ties with a number of ANC figures, including Adelaide Tsukudu (1929–), the wife of Oliver TAMBO (1917–1993), a prominent activist. In 1957 Madikizela met ANC leader Nelson MANDELA, marrying him the following year.

Madikizela's marriage to Nelson Mandela began a deep involvement in the struggle to overthrow South Africa's racist apartheid government. She became a leader of both the Federation of South African Women and the ANC Women's League. In September 1958 she was arrested during demonstrations against the pass laws, the much-hated laws that required black South Africans to carry official identification booklets at all times.

In 1962 Madikizela-Mandela's activism led to her being banned by the government, meaning she was essentially under house arrest with limitations on visitation and communication with the outside world. Two years later the already extremely difficult life for Madikizela-Mandela became even more so, when her husband was sentenced to life imprisonment for planning to sabotage installations of the white government. Madikizela-Man-dela was left with two children and no livelihood.

Madikizela-Mandela remained banned for almost all of the next 11 years. However, she consistently ignored the restrictions placed upon her, and so suffered numerous periods of incarceration and solitary confinement. Nevertheless, she continued to defy the authority of the apartheid government, which resulted in increasingly stringent government restrictions. In 1976 the government forced her from her home in Orlando, near Johannesburg, and relocated her to remote Phatakahale, in the Orange Free State.

While in Phatakahale she worked tirelessly to help improve the surrounding black neighborhoods. In 1985 her home was bombed, most likely by the government. Unfazed, Madikizela-Mandela continued to defy banning orders until, in 1986, the government essentially gave up and lifted the restrictions.

Madikizela-Mandela's new freedom, however, led to a period of troubles for her. She moved to SOWETO, where controversy soon began to swirl around her and her group of bodyguards, known as the Mandela United Football Club. Members of the neighborhood often complained about the bodyguards, accusing them of crimes from theft to murder. In 1988 charges were brought accusing Madikizela-Mandela and her bodyguards of kidnapping four local youths and murdering one of them, the 14-year-old leader of a local "children's army" that had fought back against the Football Club. The following year, the Congress of South African Trade Unions and the UNITED DEMOCRATIC FRONT both publicly distanced themselves from Madikizela-Mandela. In 1990 Nelson Mandela was finally freed from prison, but this joyous occasion was overshadowed for Madikizela-Mandela by her conviction in the kidnapping case the following year. The six-year prison sentence was reduced to a fine during the subsequent appeal.

This conviction marked the beginning of a downward spiral for Madikizela-Mandela. Nelson Mandela separated from her in 1992, as the long years of separation and negative publicity took a toll on their marriage. Madikizela-Mandela was then forced to resign as head of the ANC's social welfare department, leaving the position amid rumors of $130,000 dollars in missing funds. She became a vocal opponent of the ANC and her husband during the negotiations that eventually led to the fall of apartheid in 1994. Nelson Mandela became the country's first black president following multiracial elections held that year.

Madikizela-Mandela was appointed minister for arts, culture, science, and technology in her husband's government. However, in 1995, seeking evidence of financial scams run by one of Madikizela-Mandela's charities, Soweto police searched her home. The negative publicity that this event sparked led Nelson Mandela to fire Madikizela-Mandela from her government position. The couple divorced the following year.

In 1997 she became a candidate for the deputy presidency of the ANC, in spite of her open criticism of her ex-husband and Thabo MBEKI (1942–), Mandela's chosen successor. Once again, however, Madikizela-Mandela's questionable past interfered, as she was called before the TRUTH AND RECONCILIATION COMMISSION to testify about the crimes committed in the 1980s by the Mandela United Football Club.

Demonstrating the resiliency that earned her the nickname "Teflon Queen of Africa," Madikizela-Mandela has remained immensely popular with many South Africans, despite her legal troubles. Her strongest supporters are among the nation's poor and oppressed, who see Madikizela-Mandela as a champion for the lower classes. Though there is little doubt that Madikizela-Mandela's reputation has suffered greatly, her uncompro-

mising struggle against apartheid and her role as a symbol of strength during her former husband's lengthy imprisonment still mark her as one of South Africa's most influential figures.

In 2001 Madikizela-Mandela was charged with 85 counts of fraud and theft linked to bank loans she approved for impoverished people who did not qualify. The judge in the case called Madikizela-Mandela a "modern-day Robin Hood," but this comparison has done little to help her avoid further disgrace. She was found guilty in April 2003 and sentenced to five years imprisonment with one year suspended. She was subsequently freed on bail while she appealed her sentence. In July 2004 an appeals court judge overturned her convictions for theft and suspended her sentence for fraud. This left Madikizela-Mandela free, for the time being.

See also: WOMEN IN INDEPENDENT AFRICA (Vol. V).

Further reading: Emma Gilbey, *The Lady: The Life and Times of Winnie Mandela* (London: Vintage, 1994); Winnie Mandela, as edited by Anne Benjamin and adapted by Mary Benson, *Part of My Soul Went with Him* (New York: Norton, 1985).

Mao Zedong (1893–1976) *Revolutionary Chinese leader*

Born in Hunan Province, China, Mao helped form the Chinese Communist Party (CCP) and became the organization's general secretary for Hunan. In 1946 his communist forces emerged victorious from China's civil war, with Mao declaring the People's Republic of China on October 1, 1949.

A heavy-handed leader, Mao initiated what he termed the "Great Leap Forward," an attempt to utilize peasant unity to industrialize China in a single decade. By 1959, Mao had driven most of China's population into organized, self-governing communes. This attempt at quickly industrializing China failed, however, and the period of 1958–66 proved a time of terrible famine.

Regardless of his experiment's failure, however, Mao's communistic ideals made a lasting impression on several African leaders, including Kwame NKRUMAH (1909–1972), Patrice LUMUMBA (1925–1961), and Amílcar CABRAL (1924–1973), all of whom had organized ideological, anti-imperialist movements on their own. Most notable among the Africans was the Tanzanian revolutionary leader Julius NYERERE (1922–1999), who studied both Mao's peasant revolution of the 1940s and his revisionist ideas of peaceful coexistence in the 1950s.

Nyerere saw the policies of the Great Leap Forward as an attempt to revitalize ideas and assumptions about how best to manage a society. The by-product of this ideological expansiveness—communes—became a centerpiece of Nyerere's revolutionary movement. In the form of UJAMAA villages, communes were to be one of the cores of his early policy initiatives as Tanzania's first president

See also: CHINA AND AFRICA (Vol. V); COMMUNISM AND SOCIALISM (Vol. V).

Further reading: David E. Albright, ed.. *Communism in Africa* (Bloomington, Ind.: Indiana University Press, 1980); Bernhard Nett, et al., *Agricultural Transformation and Social Change in Africa* (New York: Peter Lang Publishing, 1993); Jonathan Spence, *Mao Zedong* (New York: Penguin, 1999).

Maputo   Major port city and capital of MOZAMBIQUE, located in the southeastern part of the country on Delagoa Bay. Maputo was called Lourenço Marques, after an early Portuguese explorer, until the country's independence in 1975. (As part of the decolonization process, African place names replaced many of the names given during the colonial era.) It had become the capital of Portuguese East Africa in 1907, and it remained the capital of Mozambique after 1975.

The city's port facilities first became important with the discovery of GOLD in the Transvaal in the late 1800s. Today the city remains an important port for the landlocked countries of ZAMBIA and ZIMBABWE as well as for the interior portions of SOUTH AFRICA. Goods passing through the port include cotton, coal, sugar, sisal, minerals, and processed foods. The city also has an industrial sector that includes petroleum refining, brewing, shipbuilding, iron working, manufacturing of textiles, shoes, and cement, and food processing.

Before independence Lourenço Marques was a popular tourist spot for whites from South Africa and the former Southern Rhodesia (now Zimbabwe). Maputo's TOURISM declined dramatically, however, as the quality of city life worsened during the warfare of the 1970s and 1980s. Now tourism is beginning to rebound as the city is portrayed as a destination of world rather than regional tourism, attracting visitors to its beaches, temperate climate, and the nearby Maputo Elephant Reserve.

In addition to being the country's main administrative center, Maputo is also home to the Eduardo Mondlane University (founded in 1962) and the Museum of Natural History. The population of Maputo was estimated at 1,115,000 in 2003.

See also: DELAGOA BAY (Vol. IV); LOURENÇO MARQUES (Vol. IV); MAPUTO (Vol. III); URBAN LIFE AND CULTURE (Vols. IV, V); URBANIZATION (Vols. IV, V).

Marrakech (Marrakesh)   Major urban center in west-central MOROCCO, located at the foot of the Atlas Mountains. This ancient city was founded in the 11th century and developed into an important Saharan trade center before falling under French control in 1912. The city is divided into two distinct sectors: the ancient Moorish sector, known as Medina, and the French-built modern sector known as Gueliz.

Today the city is still an important commercial center and is linked by road and rail with the port cities of Safi and Casablanca on the Atlantic coast. The city produces fruit, vegetables, hides, wool, flour, building materials, carpets, and crafts. It also has several mineral mines nearby. The palm groves that dot the landscape, along with the many famous parks, add to the ancient beauty that attracts tourists.

Marrakech's famed Medina, the area that makes up the ancient Moorish quarter, is surrounded by a wall that was built in the 12th century. The narrow pedestrian streets form a maze among urban dwellings. These urban dwellings, known as *riads*, are constructed in an ancient Moroccan design with a simple exterior, a comfortable and decorative interior, and an inner courtyard. Numerous specialized markets scattered throughout the sector sell products such as dyed fabrics, leather products, jewelry, spices, and carpets.

The city promotes itself, with its unique Berber culture, as "the other Morocco," reflecting an earlier era. Visitors also come to enjoy skiing in the Atlas Mountains during the winter months. The population of the Marrakech urban area was estimated at 755,000 in 2003.

See also: ATLAS MOUNTAINS (Vol. I); BERBERS (Vols. I, II, III, IV, V); FRANCE AND AFRICA (Vols. III, IV, V); MARRAKECH (Vols. II, III, IV); SAHARA (Vols. I, II); URBAN LIFE AND CULTURE (Vols. IV, V); URBANIZATION (Vols. IV, V).

Masekela, Hugh (1931–   ) *South African jazz musician*

Over four decades Masekela gained worldwide recognition as a talented jazz musician, prolific recording artist, and an inveterate opponent of APARTHEID. As a teenager, he was encouraged to play by Father Trevor Huddleston (1913–1998), a British-born Anglican priest (and later, archbishop). Renowned in SOUTH AFRICA for his anti-apartheid views, Huddleston taught Masekela at St. Peter's School in JOHANNESBURG.

During the late 1950s Masekela became one of the leading young jazz musicians of South Africa. He eventually joined notable South African jazz pianist Abdullah IBRAHIM (1934–), then known as "Dollar" Brand, in a group called the Jazz Epistles. In 1959 this became the first African jazz band to record an album.

Masekela left South Africa in the early 1960s to study MUSIC, first at the Guildhall School of Music in London and then at the Manhattan School of Music in New York City. In 1960 he released his first solo album, and in 1968 he released "Grazin' in the Grass," one of the few instrumentals to reach the top of the pop charts. Further adding to his stature, from 1964 to 1966 he was married to Africa's preeminent female vocalist, Miriam MAKEBA (1932–), also an anti-apartheid activist, whom he began dating in the 1950s. The couple fled South Africa in the early 1960s because of apartheid.

During the 1970s Masekela infused his bebop jazz more and more with different African genres of music to create a sound all his own. His association with Nigerian bandleader FELA (1938–1997) increased his exposure to West African music and helped add a rich texture to his sound.

In 1983 he returned to Africa, taking up residence in BOTSWANA. In the late 1980s Masekela's career received a boost from his collaboration with American musician Paul Simon (1941–), with whom Masekela toured in 1987–88 to support Simon's *Graceland* album. Masekela also garnered acclaim for cowriting the music for the 1987 hit musical, *Sarafina!*

In the early 1990s Masekela ended a 30-year, self-imposed exile and returned to South Africa. He continued to play an active role on the South African and international music scene, regularly recording albums such as *Sixty*, in 1999, to celebrate his sixtieth birthday and *Tsepothola—A New Dawn* in 2002. This latter recording provides a musical tribute to South Africa's new dawn after the long night of apartheid.

Maseru (Masero) Capital of LESOTHO and the country's only sizeable city, located in the western part, near the border with SOUTH AFRICA. In 1869 the Sotho king, Mshweshwe I (1786–1870), moved his capital from Thaba Bosiu to Maseru. When the British annexed Basutoland (as Lesotho was called at the time), Maseru became the colonial capital. The town remained a backwater during the colonial era and did not even have a paved street until 1947. When Basutoland gained its independence and became Lesotho in 1966, Maseru achieved a new status as the capital city of a sovereign state. In addition to the executive, legislative, and judicial offices of the country, the city also hosts numerous foreign embassies and international agencies engaged in providing ECONOMIC ASSISTANCE for DEVELOPMENT.

Today Maseru remains an active trading center, with road, rail, and air links to South Africa and roads to many parts of Lesotho. Major EXPORTS include livestock, hides, wood, and grains. The principal manufactured products are candles, carpets, and textiles. In addition to providing transport for agricultural products and manufactured goods, Maseru's rail system also transports laborers to South Africa, where the majority of Lesotho's LABOR force works. The city's population was estimated at 174,000 in 2003.

See also: SOTHO (Vol. III, IV); BASUTOLAND (Vol. IV); MSHWESHWE (Vol. III); THABA BOSIU (Vol. III); URBANIZATION (Vols. IV, V).

Mashinini, Emma (1929–) *South African trade union organizer and author*

Mashinini was born in JOHANNESBURG, SOUTH AFRICA, and raised in an environment of POVERTY and insecurity that was the direct result of the rigors of APARTHEID. Twice the apartheid state forcibly relocated her family. Following her parents' breakup she left school at age 14 to work as a nanny. Three years later she married and went on to bear six children, although three died shortly after birth. Her marriage failed owing to her husband's physical abuse and Mashinini's keen resentment of the gender inequalities in their relationship. To support herself and her children she became a machinist in a textile factory manufacturing uniforms. Her job led to her involvement with LABOR UNIONS.

Mashinini's remarkable career as a trade unionist began when her coworkers elected her as a shop steward of the Garment Workers' Union. She remarried in 1967 to Tom Mashinini, a fellow trade union organizer. Through her tireless efforts she helped build the Commercial, Catering and Allied Workers Union of South Africa into a powerful organization. As a result of her activism the state subjected her to harassment and eventually imprisonment. In 1981 Mashinini was charged under the draconian provisions of the Terrorism Act and held in solitary confinement for six months. The abuse and humiliation she endured while incarcerated traumatized Mashinini and precipitated a nervous breakdown.

Upon release she continued her trade union work until 1985, contributing to the formation of the Congress of South African Trade Unions (COSATU). A year later she accepted a position as director of justice and reconciliation with the Anglican Church of South Africa, headed by Bishop Desmond TUTU (1931–).

Underlining the harshness of South African society, both Mashinini's daughter and her son-in-law met with violent deaths. Although not one of the most readily recognizable figures among South African women, Mashinini's life is illustrative of the hardship, discrimination, and tragedy routinely suffered by millions of women in South Africa because of their degraded status as both women and as blacks. Her autobiography, *Strikes Have Followed Me All My Life* (1991), chronicles Mashinini's sacrifice and highlights her spirited refusal to accept her inferior status.

Masire, Ketumile (Sir Quett Ketumile Joni Masire) (1925–) *Second president of Botswana*

Born into a minor headman's family in Kanye, southern BOTSWANA, Masire went to local schools before attending the well-known Tiger Kloof Institute, in SOUTH AFRICA. After earning a teaching certificate in 1949, he started the Seepapitso Secondary School, where he taught for six years until deciding to become a farmer. Changing careers again, in 1958 he became a journalist, editing the Botswana newspaper *Terisanyo,* which was devoted to promoting democracy.

In the 1960s Masire became actively involved in the country's politics as a member of the Democratic Party, which was led by Seretse KHAMA (1921–1980), a fellow graduate of Tiger Kloof. In 1965 the Democratic Party won 28 of the 31 contested seats in the country's new legislative assembly, giving it a mandate to lead Botswana to independence. Masire was elected the country's vice president the following year, and he served in this capacity until 1980.

He earned a reputation as a highly competent technocrat and was credited with directing the steady growth of Botswana's economy and INFRASTRUCTURE between 1966 and 1980. When Sir Seretse Khama died in 1980, Masire was the undisputed choice to succeed him. Under Masire's leadership, Botswana's annual economic growth of 10 percent was among the highest in the world. Diamonds continued to be the nation's most important source of earnings. Under Masire Botswana was seen as a model African country in terms of democratic politics and economic growth and management. He was knighted in 1991.

In 1998, after 17 years of service, Masire left the presidency amid factional infighting and accusations of CORRUPTION. Although he intended to return to farming, he was recruited by the United Nations to serve as facilitator of the peace process in the Democratic Republic of the CONGO, which was in the throes of the brutal civil war that destabilized the entire region. Masire was recognized for his efforts in negotiating a tenuous peace.

Masire's leadership style depended heavily on coalition building and cooperation through numerous regional and international organizations. He was the chairman of the SOUTHERN AFRICAN DEVELOPMENT COMMUNITY and served as vice chairman of the ORGANIZATION OF AFRICAN UNITY. He was also a member of the United Nations Group on African Development.

See also: BECHUANALAND (Vol. IV); DIAMOND MINING (Vol. IV).

Matanzima, Kaiser (Kaiser Daliwanga Matanzima) (1915–2003) *Former president of the Republic of the Transkei, in South Africa*

Matanzima was born in the Emigrant Tembuland region of the XHOSA-speaking Transkei, which at the time was one of the principal "Native Reserves" of SOUTH AFRICA. He and his brother George (1918–2000) were sons of a chief. By law and custom, Kaiser was also the nephew of future South African president, Nelson MANDELA (1918–). Both Matanzima and Mandela attended FORT HARE COLLEGE at the same time, with Matanzima earning his BA degree in 1939. Matanzima then returned to the Transkei, where he was soon appointed a chief and also became involved in the reserve's political system.

In the early 1950s Matanzima sided with the South African government and its APARTHEID plans by supporting the Bantu Authorities Act (1951). On the other hand, Mandela and the AFRICAN NATIONAL CONGRESS opposed that law, as well as the subsequent Promotion of Bantu Self-Government Act (1959), which Matanzima also supported. This second piece of legislation laid the foundation for transforming the Transkei and nine other "Native Reserves" into BANTUSTANS (later called homelands).

Upon learning of Matanzima's death Nelson Mandela stated, "We shall remember Daliwonga with great fondness. Although our political paths parted early on and we pursued political goals that were diametrically opposed, on family issues we remained friends throughout the years."

With the backing of the South African government, which took actions against his political opponents, Matanzima soon emerged as the central political figure in the Transkei. In 1963 he became the chief minister of the reserve, overseeing the transfer of limited self-government to the Transkei under the terms of the 1959 act. In 1976—the year of the SOWETO rebellion—the Transkei became the first homeland to become a supposedly "independent state" in South Africa's peculiar version of decolonization. Matanzima became the prime minister, and his brother was named attorney general. Three years later Kaiser became president and his brother prime minister. Kaiser Matanzima's hold on office depended on continued financial support from South Africa, which provided most of his government's budget and supplied key civil servants. When Matanzima retired in 1986, he was a wealthy man. His brother, George, continued as prime minister. In 1987, however, an army officer, Bantu Holomisa (1955–), ousted him in bloodless COUP D'ÉTAT, accusing him of CORRUPTION.

Matanzima continued to live in the Transkei and serve as the paramount chief, or king, of the Emigrant Tembu. The Republic of the Transkei disappeared as a separate political entity in 1994, as did the other so-called independent states. It became part of South Africa's newly formed Eastern Cape Province. At the time of his death Matanzima served in relative obscurity as a member of the Eastern Cape House of Traditional Leaders. With the exception of the ZULU leader, Mangosuthu Gatsha BUTHELEZI (1928–), virtually all of the Bantustan leaders were relegated to the political sidelines with the demise of apartheid.

Mauritania
Country located in northwestern Africa, bordered by WESTERN SAHARA and ALGERIA to the north, MALI to the east and south, SENEGAL to the south, and the Atlantic Ocean, to the west. It is approximately 398,000 square miles (1,030,800 sq km) in size, with almost 3 million inhabitants. The capital is NOUAKCHOTT, located on a coastal plateau. Mauritania's geographic location, straddling the Arab-Berber MAGHRIB and the largely black Sahelian region called the Sudan, predisposes the country to both internal and external ethnic and cultural tensions.

Not to be confused with the country, the Sudan is the region of central Africa below the Tropic of Cancer that the Arabs called *Bilad al-Sudan,* meaning "land of the blacks."

Mauritania at Independence In 1960 Mauritania became fully independent, ending a two-year period as an autonomous member of the French Community. Presidential elections the following year brought Moktar Ould Daddah (1924–) to power. Daddah formed a coalition government that resulted in the merging of the nation's major political parties into the Mauritanian People's Party (Parti du Peuple Mauritanienne, PPM). Daddah attempted to head off any potential conflicts and centralize his power by making the PPM the country's only legal political entity. He also made sure a significant minority of black Africans from the south were involved in the government. This was intended to ameliorate the bitterness felt by Mauritania's black citizens toward the politically dominant Maures, or northern Arab population. Further complicating ethnic and racial factors was the significant percentage of Mauritanians of combined Maure and black ancestry.

Any progress Daddah made, however, was undermined by a devastating drought in the Sahel region that spanned nearly two decades between the 1960s and 1980s. More than three-quarters of the country's livestock perished during this time, and much of the AGRICULTURE in the south was wiped out. Many of the country's nomadic people migrated to the cities, placing a great strain on a nation with little INFRASTRUCTURE to support the swelling urban population.

In 1966 Daddah made Arabic the official language for teaching in Mauritania's schools, leading to violent protests by the black African population.

Mauritania and Conflict in Western Sahara A Spanish possession since the late 1800s, Western Sahara became the central issue in Mauritanian politics during the 1970s. Early in the decade, with most African nations having attained independence, the indigenous SAHARAWI independence movement known as the POLISARIO Front attacked Spain's colonial holdings in Western Sahara. As a result, Spain prepared to withdraw from the region—although Spanish companies planned to retain their MINING rights to the region's profitable phosphate deposits.

In 1975, ignoring international opposition, Mauritanian and Moroccan officials met with the Spanish government in Madrid to establish an agreement for the three-way partition of Western Sahara. Mauritania claimed the territory's southern third, called the Tiris al Gharbiyya, with the rest falling under the control of MOROCCO. Spain dropped all claims to Western Sahara, in 1976, but retained rights to mining and fishing interests.

Mauritania's motivation for staking claims in Western Sahara belied its concerns about Moroccan expansionism. Morocco had for some time claimed territorial rights to Mauritania and recognized Mauritania as a legitimate independent country only as late as 1969. Elements within Mauritania also favored assimilation into Morocco, particularly Maure groups who wanted separation from the black African south. Because of this, Daddah's government initially called for total independence for Western Sahara, with the hopes that the territory would later decide to join with Mauritania due to the close ethnic ties between the Maures and the Saharawi. However, considering the clear Moroccan interest in the territory, Mauritania settled on the Tiris al Gharbiyya as a buffer against encroachment by their militarily superior Maghrib neighbor. This move was not popular among Mauritanians, however. Most Maures wanted either complete control of Western Sahara or full independence for the territory. The black African population in the south opposed any involvement in Western Sahara, which they considered to be an Arab concern unrelated to their own.

Ultimately the Mauritanian occupation of the Tiris al Gharbiyya proved to be a disaster. From Algeria, which supported the Saharawi cause, the Polisario immediately launched a broad offensive against Mauritanian troops. Despite aid from France, Saudi Arabia, and Morocco, Mauritania was unable to stamp out the Polisario resistance.

The ongoing conflict stunted Mauritania's post-independence DEVELOPMENT, and in 1978 Daddah was overthrown in a military COUP D'ÉTAT led by Colonel Mustapha Ould Salek, who became the new prime minister. Salek, too, was unable to solve the Western Sahara crisis, and in 1979 Colonel Mohammed Khouna Ould Haidalla (1940–) replaced Salek. By the end of the year Haidalla had negotiated a peace treaty with Polisario, and Mauritania withdrew its claims to the Tiris al-Gharbiyya.

Continuing Instability Haidalla named himself president and installed a civilian government, with Ahmed Ould Bneijara (1947–) as prime minister. However, in 1981 Haidalla responded to growing tensions by halting his nascent political reform efforts and reinstating military rule. Continuing aggression by Morocco and yet another failed coup supported by LIBYA underscored Haidalla's growing weakness. The president's decision in 1984 to recognize the Saharawi Arab Democratic Republic as the true government of Western Sahara caused an uproar within his own government and among Mauritanians who feared the move would instigate Moroccan attacks. Continuing drought conditions, CORRUPTION, and a failing economy all finally contributed to Haidalla's 1984 ouster, at the hands of the army chief of staff, Colonel Maaouya Ould Sid Ahmed TAYA (c. 1941–).

Internal ethnic problems continued under Taya, as black Africans in the south faced oppression at the hands of lighter-skinned Maures. In 1989 conflict erupted in Nouakchott and even spilled over into neighboring Senegal. Outbreaks of violence between Maures and black Senegalese in the Mauritanian capital ultimately led Taya to drive 100,000 Senegalese nationals from the country. In return, 240,000 Maures were expelled from Senegal. It was not until two years later that the two countries reestablished peaceful relations.

In 1992 Taya was officially elected to the presidency as head of the Social and Democratic Republican Party (Parti Républicain Démocratique et Social, PRDS). Though Mauritania's involvement in the Western Sahara conflict was largely over, President Taya still faced many of the same difficult issues as his predecessor. The country was poorly developed and relied heavily on foreign ECONOMIC ASSISTANCE. To combat the situation, Taya worked with the WORLD BANK and INTERNATIONAL MONETARY FUND to rebuild the economy. He also launched an effort to eliminate government corruption.

In spite of the nation's continuing problems, Taya and the PRDS maintained their control of Mauritania through both the 1997 and 2001 elections, though these victories were tainted by claims of electoral fraud. In 2002 Taya attempted to eliminate his opposition by reducing Mauritania to a single-party state. From Daddah to Taya, Mauritania came full circle in a cycle of political instability and autocratic rule.

See also: ETHNIC CONFLICT IN AFRICA (Vol. V); ETHNICITY AND IDENTITY (Vol. I); MAURITANIA (Vols. I, II, III, IV).

Mauritius Indian Ocean island nation that is 720 square miles (1,870 sq km) in size and is situated approximately 500 miles (805 km) east of MADAGASCAR. A coastal plain rings the island, backed by mountains that rise to an interior plateau.

Mauritius at Independence Mauritius, which became independent in 1968 and became a republic in 1992, was for a time the sugar capital of the British Empire. Companies imported LABOR from India to work in the sugar fields alongside the Africans who had been brought to the island in bondage before slavery was abolished in 1835. The result is that, today, the island's population is ethnically and linguistically quite diverse, though the majority of the people are Indo-Mauritian. French (reflecting the island's pre-British colonial heritage) and English are joint official languages. Creole and South Asian languages are spoken as well. In terms of RELIGION, most of the population is Hindu, although Christianity and Islam are also important.

In the 1960s the Mauritian economy was almost entirely dependent on a single cash crop, sugar. Although sugar continues to be an important export crop, political independence has allowed other activities, such as TOURISM, financial services, and manufacturing, to develop as strong elements within the economy. The manufacturing sector is particularly dependent on labor-intensive industries such as textiles. The economy relies on EXPORTS from the industrial sector, fueled by creating an island-wide "Export Processing Zone." The economic transformation of Mauritius has allowed it to take its place among the middle-income countries of the world.

Key to the economic growth of Mauritius has been its relative political stability. The Mauritian Labor Party (MLP), led by Seewoosagur Ramgoolam (1910–1985), was in power through 1982. That year, however, the rival Mauritian Militant Movement-Mauritian Socialist Party coalition won a parliamentary majority, and Anerood JUGNAUTH (1930–) became prime minister. His party base then became the Mauritian Socialist Movement (MSM), which lost the 1995 election to the MLP in alliance with the MMM. Navin Ramgoolam (1947–), the son of the country's first prime minister, assumed his father's old office. Although Jugnauth even lost his parliamentary seat in 1995, in 2000 the MSM swept back into power, and Jugnauth once again became the country's prime minister.

At the beginning of the 21st century, the government of Mauritius is attempting to diversify the economy further. In the same way that tourism and textile manufacturing replaced sugar, the government is now turning to information and communications technologies for the next stage in its economic DEVELOPMENT. Toward this end, the island has been helped by its high LITERACY rate (83 percent) and now universal schooling. It has developed its first cyber-city and is attracting major MULTINATIONAL CORPORATIONS, which are investing in software development, training, computer manufacturing, and call center facilities. Membership in the SOUTHERN AFRICAN DEVELOPMENT COMMUNITY, which it joined in the 1990s, positions Mauritius to provide much of the information and communications technology services for a large part of the African continent.

In 2000 ethnic, class, and religious tensions boiled over, and there were riots between the Creole and Hindu communities. In an effort to restore calm and political stability Jugnauth, a Hindu, relinquished the prime ministership to the deputy prime minister, Paul Raymond Berenger (1945–   ), who was a Creole Catholic. Jugnauth then became president of the republic.

See also: CASH CROPS (Vols. IV, V); ENGLAND AND AFRICA (Vols. III, IV, V); ETHNIC CONFLICT IN AFRICA (Vol. V); FRANCE AND AFRICA (Vols. III, IV, V); INDUSTRIALIZATION (Vols. IV, V); MAURITIUS (Vols. I, II, III, IV).

Further reading: Edward and Bridget Dommen, *Mauritius: An Island of Success: A Retrospective Study 1960–1993* (Oxford, U.K.: James Currey, 1999).

Mbabane Capital of SWAZILAND, located in the Mdimba Mountains in the northwestern part of the country. In the late 19th century, Mbabane developed as a settlement near the home of the then Swazi king, Mbadzeni (d. 1889). Because of its cool and pleasant highland location, the town became the administrative capital of British colonial Swaziland in 1902. (It retained its capital status when Swaziland became independent in 1968.) The city is mainly a center for government. However, in 1964 a railroad was built to MOZAMBIQUE, and this promoted the export of iron ore and tin, which are mined nearby. Iron

ore EXPORTS have declined in recent years, but the city has remained a commercial center for the surrounding agricultural region. With a population of approximately 70,000, Mbabane is second in size to Manzini, which, with 75,000 people, is both the largest city and a major industrial center of Swaziland.

Mbabane has recently started to promote its tourist potential in an attempt to compete with the booming tourist industry of SOUTH AFRICA. The city enjoys a temperate climate, scenic mountain landscapes, easy access to the culturally rich Ezulwini Valley, and a host of international hotels.

See also: ENGLAND AND AFRICA (Vols. III, IV, V); TOURISM (Vol. V); URBAN LIFE AND CULTURE (Vols. IV, V); URBANIZATION (Vols. IV, V).

Mbeki, Govan (Govan Archibald Mvunyelina Mbeki) (1910–2001) *South African political activist, intellectual, and journalist*

Govan Mbeki was born and raised in the Transkei region of the eastern Cape Province, SOUTH AFRICA. Coming from a prominent Christian family, he received an excellent EDUCATION, capped, in 1937, by a BA degree from FORT HARE COLLEGE. From the mid-1930s, Mbeki was an active opponent of the racist policies and system of government of South Africa and a leading member of the AFRICAN NATIONAL CONGRESS (ANC). In 1961 he joined the South African Communist Party, as well.

In the aftermath of the police shootings at SHARPEVILLE, in 1960, Mbeki was banned (which involved virtual house arrest and prevented an individual from being quoted in the media) and twice arrested. He went into hiding and in 1962 he became a member of the ANC's armed wing, UMKHONTO WE SIZWE (Spear of the Nation). The following year he was arrested along with other key ANC leaders in a home in Rivonia, a suburb outside JOHANNESBURG, and sentenced to life imprisonment for allegedly plotting to overthrow the government. Along with other ANC colleagues, among them Nelson MANDELA (1918–   ), Mbeki was sent to the fortress prison of ROBBEN ISLAND, located in False Bay off the beaches of CAPE TOWN.

In 1964 Mbeki's *South Africa: The Peasants' Revolt* was published in Great Britain, although it was banned in South Africa. The manuscript for the book was written while he was in prison and smuggled out on toilet paper.

After 25 years on Robben Island Mbeki was released in 1987, in large part because of his failing health. He chose to resume his political activism and was placed under house arrest in Port Elizabeth, an Eastern Cape city. In 1990 Mbeki published *Learning from Robben Island: The Prison Writings of Govan Mbeki*, followed by *Struggle for Liberation in South Africa; A Short History* (1991) and *Sunset at Midday: Latshon'ilang'emini!* (1996). In May 1994, when the ANC came to power in South Africa's first fully democratic elections, Mbeki was elected deputy president of the senate. He also served as a delegate to the National Council of Provinces. Having retired from political life in 1997, Mbeki died in 2001. His son Thabo MBEKI (1942–) succeeded Nelson Mandela as president of South Africa in 1999.

Mbeki, Thabo (1942–) *President of South Africa*

The successor to popular and universally respected South African president Nelson MANDELA (1918–), Mbeki has struggled to carry on the successes of Mandela's administration. Born in Idutywa, SOUTH AFRICA, and raised in the village of Mbewuleni, Mbeki is the son of the late anti-apartheid leader Govan MBEKI (1910–2001). Through the influence of his parents, both members of the South African Communist Party (SACP), Mbeki became interested in politics at an early age. Well schooled and precocious, Mbeki joined the Youth League of the AFRICAN NATIONAL CONGRESS (ANC), at age 14. He was expelled from secondary school in 1959 for organizing a student strike and only a few years later joined the SACP.

In 1963 Govan Mbeki, then one of the founders, along with Nelson Mandela, of the militant ANC wing known as UMKHONTO WE SIZWE, was arrested by the APARTHEID government and sentenced to life in prison on ROBBEN ISLAND. As a precaution the ANC sent Thabo Mbeki abroad to London, where he studied at the University of London and then the University of Sussex, earning a master's degree in economics. He also worked with the London ANC branch led by Oliver TAMBO (1917–1993). This experience led to Mbeki's significant role in organizing support for the ANC from exile. In 1970 he traveled to the Soviet Union for Marxist and military training, and then served the ANC in various African nations, including BOTSWANA, ZAMBIA, SWAZILAND, MOZAMBIQUE, and NIGERIA. His public relations efforts, particularly his attempts to encourage the involvement of anti-apartheid whites in the resistance, made him a prime diplomatic figure in the ANC.

In 1990 Mbeki returned to South Africa and played a major role in the negotiations leading to the end of the apartheid system. In 1994 Nelson Mandela was elected the country's first black president, and an era of extreme racism and oppression in South Africa finally move toward a close. Mbeki then became deputy president of Mandela's government.

Known for his political skills and unfailing work ethic, Mbeki was positioned by the ANC to succeed Mandela. By 1996 Mbeki was essentially acting as president for Mandela, whose age prevented him from enduring the full rigors of the office. The following year Mbeki became president of the ANC. This established him as Mandela's protegé and made his election to the national presidency inevitable. With Mandela's support, Mbeki became president after winning the 1999 elections.

The polar opposite of Mandela in terms of personality, the somber and reserved Mbeki has faced difficulties as president, despite his political prowess. Stepping from behind the scenes into the national and international limelight, Mbeki was greeted with skepticism by many who were not sure what to expect from the new president. Despite the fall of apartheid, South Africa still faced many pressing concerns, particularly high unemployment, rising crime rates, and the spread of HIV/AIDS.

In an effort to reverse the declining economy Mbeki broke from his Marxist background and promoted the privatization of many of South Africa's industries. He continued public works projects aimed at providing utilities to previously neglected rural areas. He also liberalized LABOR laws and decreased government spending. Under Mbeki, South Africa also began to take a larger role in southern Africa through the SOUTHERN AFRICAN DEVELOPMENT COMMUNITY. In connection with this he talked about "an African renaissance," which he saw South Africa as well positioned to lead. However, the country's economy continued to struggle, and the deepening crisis in neighboring ZIMBABWE diverted his attention from such an endeavor.

Mbeki garnered negative publicity in response to his peculiar position on the HIV/AIDS epidemic, to which he has seemed indifferent. He has gone as far as discounting the proven medical facts about the disease and refusing to support expensive efforts to provide needed drugs to AIDS victims. His position on this issue has led to great public outcry against the president, including criticism from Nelson Mandela, who has since publicly regretted his past support of Mbeki.

See also: HIV/AIDS AND AFRICA (Vol. V).

Mbikusita-Lewanika, Inonge (1943–) *Head of the Agenda for Zambia political party*

Inonge Mbikusita-Lewanika was born in Senanga, in the Western Province of ZAMBIA. Her father, Godwin

Mbikusita-Lewanika (c. 1907–1977), was a social welfare officer in the copper MINING town of Kitwe and was the first president of the Northern Rhodesia African National Congress. He later became the *litunga* (king) of the Lozi people from 1968 until 1977. Inonge Mbikusita-Lewanika was the fourth-born in a family of 13. She grew up in Kitwe's Busakile Township and attended Busakile Primary School. Upon graduation she went to Chipembi Girls Secondary School, located in Zambia's Central Province.

In 1960 Mbikusita-Lewanika went to Costa Mesa Junior College in California. There she earned a BS degree in home economics and a master's degree in EDUCATION and psychology. In 1979 she earned a doctorate from New York University. Mbikusita-Lewanika held a variety of teaching jobs, including positions at the Evelyn Hone College in LUSAKA, Mongu Teacher Training College in Western Province, and the University of Zambia. From 1980 to 1990 Mbikusita-Lewanika served in East and southern Africa as the UNICEF regional adviser and senior program officer.

In 1991 Mbikusita-Lewanika became actively involved in politics when she joined the opposition MOVEMENT FOR MULTIPARTY DEMOCRACY (MMD). That same year she was elected to parliament. Two years later Mbikusita-Lewanika was among 11 members of the MMD who resigned in protest against the party's direction. She remained in parliament, however, joining and becoming the leader of the National Party. Three years later, she left the National Party and joined the Agenda for Zambia party, which was led by her brother, Akashambatwa. In 2001 she took over the party's leadership and ran for the national presidency. The party finished tenth in the election, which included 11 major parties. In February 2003 Zambia's president, Levy MWANAWASA (1948–   ), appointed Mbikusita-Lewanika ambassador to the United States and special envoy responsible for 17 countries in the Americas and the Caribbean.

See also: LOZI (Vols. III, IV); POLITICAL PARTIES AND ORGANIZATIONS (Vols. IV, V); WOMEN IN INDEPENDENT AFRICA (Vol. V).

Mboya, Tom (Thomas Joseph Odhiambo Mboya) (1930–1969) *Kenyan labor union leader and politician*

A founding member of the dominant KENYAN AFRICAN NATIONAL UNION (KANU) and supporter of Kenya's first president, Jomo KENYATTA (c. 1891–1978), Mboya initially served as minister of justice when Kenya became independent in 1963. However, his LABOR UNION experience made him a natural choice for the position of labor minister as well. Mboya set about establishing a system of fair LABOR laws and practices for the new country. Within a short

time his role expanded to include the ministry for economic planning and DEVELOPMENT, and he was responsible for turning Kenya into a leader among new African nations in the areas of employment and economic growth.

Mboya, however, had his detractors. To some, especially to his long-time rival, vice president Oginga ODINGA (1912–1994), Mboya was not radical enough in the pursuit of the immediate redistribution of white-owned land to Africans. By the late 1960s Mboya also became increasingly critical of the authoritarianism and CORRUPTION that began to characterize Kenyatta's government. Mboya's break with Kenyatta was compounded by the fact that Mboya was a LUO, a minority ethnic group in a country dominated by Kenyatta's KIKUYU.

In 1969 Mboya was shot and killed by a Kikuyu reputed to have close ties to Kikuyu officials in Kenyatta's government. Although major investigations were carried out, nothing was ever proved, and suspicions of both ethnic and government involvement in Mboya's assassination linger to the present day.

See also: MBOYA, TOM (Vol. IV).

Further reading: Cherry Gertzel, *The Politics of Independent Kenya: 1963–1968* (Evanston, Ill.: Northwestern University Press, 1970); Tom Mboya, *Freedom and After* (Boston: Little, Brown, 1963).

medicine There has been a great variety of medical systems in Africa for centuries. During the colonial period Western biomedicine was introduced and became another widespread option for treatment. Despite decades of opposition from the biomedical community toward "traditional" medical systems, efforts have been made recently to establish a relationship of cooperation between biomedical and traditional systems.

From the patients' perspective, there are many options to choose from when illness occurs. Self-treatment is often the first action taken. Self-treatment is usually easier and cheaper than visiting one of many traditional healers or the nearest biomedical clinic. Often, over-the-counter drugs for common ailments are widely available at pharmacies or roadside kiosks, and many people have at least a limited knowledge of herbal remedies, which they can collect themselves.

With the widespread use of over-the-counter drugs, however, there is increasing concern regarding the evolution of drug-resistant illnesses. For example, patients may purchase a medication that does not specifically target their particular illness, or they may be able to afford only a partial dose of the correct medicine. In the long term, this can lead to drug-resistant illnesses. MALARIA, for example, has become resistant to treatment with chloroquine, a medicine used in many areas of Africa.

Although countries such as SOUTH AFRICA and KENYA have major medical treatment and research facilities that

By the middle of the 1960s, vast differences could be observed between the various practitioners of medicine. Compare, for example, the traditional healer on the left with the one dressed in Western-style clothing on the right. © *AP/Wide World Photos*

offer the latest in medical procedures, rural areas are largely underserved and have limited medical resources. Rural areas usually have higher patient-doctor ratios and, therefore, rural patients have longer waits. In addition, rural clinics often lack supplies, which leads patients to seek medicine on their own. This general lack of resources is usually the reason that rural Africans often choose to self-medicate first. Biomedical clinics are often far away, expensive, and have long lines for treatment. Some countries have policies that call for free public health care; however, others have had to implement user fees after making budget cutbacks or adopting STRUCTURAL ADJUSTMENT programs.

Government biomedical health care facilities have joined forces with international organizations, including the World Health Organization, to establish goals for treatment. In addition to treatment, many countries now offer preventative health care related to sexual education, sanitation, and neonatal care. Other international and NON-GOVERNMENTAL ORGANIZATIONS such as CARE, the

Centers for Disease Control, and the United Nations have implemented programs that provide biomedical services to remote and urban populations. In many areas of Africa, aggressive vaccination programs have substantially lowered the chances of contracting diseases such as measles, polio, and smallpox, which has been eradicated. A major effort, funded by the William H. Gates Foundation in 2003, is also underway to find a vaccine for malaria.

People can also seek treatment from one of the many types of traditional healers. Traditional healers can use a variety of tools when administering treatment including herbs, rituals, offerings, foods or food restrictions, charms, minerals, animal products, song and dance, or modern biomedicine.

In reality, many people exercise multiple health care options to treat a single illness. The growing cooperation between the biomedical system and traditional health care systems should increase options and improve treatment for people in Africa.

As a consequence of the cooperation between traditional and biomedical systems, pharmaceutical companies now collect information regarding medicinal plants that have been used for centuries in Africa. This information may be used to develop new treatments. The re-legitimization of traditional health care by African governments and international bodies has also resulted in the large-scale production and international trade of medicinal plants and substances. Some medicinal plant farmers now provide products for markets in Asia, Europe, and the United States.

Currently the access and availability of HIV/AIDS antiretroviral drugs is one of the more heated issues regarding Africa and medicine. Many of the people in countries with high HIV/AIDS prevalence rates do not have access to antiretroviral drugs due to their high costs. So far BOTSWANA is the only country to commit to making antiretroviral drugs available to all citizens at no cost. Discussions are ongoing regarding the legality of in-country pharmacies in Africa to produce antiretroviral drugs for lower prices.

See also: DISEASE IN MODERN AFRICA (Vol V); HEALTH AND HEALING IN MODERN AFRICA (Vol. V); HIV/AIDS AND AFRICA (Vol. V); MEDICINE (Vol. IV); UNITED NATIONS AND AFRICA (Vol. V).

Meles Zenawi (Ato Meles Zenawi) (1955–)
Prime minister of Ethiopia

Meles Legesse Zenawi was born May 9, 1955, in northern ETHIOPIA. His father belonged to the TIGRAY people and his mother came from a wealthy family in neighboring ERITREA. After attending secondary school in ADDIS ABABA, he continued his education studying medicine in the capital in the early 1970s. He left his studies to take part in the military COUP D'ÉTAT that deposed Emperor HAILE SELASSIE (1892–1975) in 1974.

Meles began his political career as a founder of the Marxist-Leninist League of Tigray. This organization provided the ideological base for the Soviet-supported Tigray People's Liberation Front (TPLF). During the mid-1980s the TPLF grew, with Meles eventually establishing supreme leadership. In 1989 he founded the ETHIOPIAN PEOPLE'S REVOLUTIONARY DEMOCRATIC FRONT (EPRDF) in order to broaden the base of support for the TPLF, which was seen as an exclusively Tigrayan party. Meles claimed victory in 1991 when his organization ousted Ethiopia's president, MENGISTU HAILE MARIAM (c. 1937–). In July 1991 Meles became the president of Ethiopia.

Meles soon won international support after instituting a movement away from the Marxist path that had failed the country up to that point. In August 1991, following a U.S.-brokered peace agreement, an unstable transitional government was appointed. In 1995 new elections led to the seating of the Council of People's Representatives, a new parliamentary body. Meles then stepped down as president, which was by then a largely ceremonial position, to become prime minister, a position that offered the leader more power.

As Ethiopia's leader Meles has struggled to bring Ethiopia's various ethnic groups together. An ethnic Tigray, he supported the right of self-determination for Eritrea, which has a large Tigrayan population. However, he has been unable to resolve the contentious issue of self-determination for Ethiopia's large OROMO population. For their part, the influential Amhara people opposed Meles's plans for ethnic decentralization and the potential break-up of Ethiopia, since they had long enjoyed the dominant position in the country's political life. Meles, however, largely ignored the public outcry.

Described as shy and soft-spoken, Meles has avoided publicity and media attention. Although he has played an integral role in liberalizing Ethiopia, at the same time his intentions of turning the country into a democratic state have been compromised by war with Eritrea and by his authoritarian tendencies.

See also: AMHARA (Vols. I, III, IV).

Mengistu Haile Mariam (c. 1937–) *Ethiopian dictator from 1977 to 1991*

Mengistu was born in ADDIS ABABA to an Amharan father and OROMO mother, both of whom were servants in the house of the nobleman Baron Dadkazmach Kbede Tasama. Baron Kbede financed Mengistu's primary education, and there is speculation that the baron, a regular visitor to the court of Ethiopian emperor HAILE SELASSIE (1892–1975), was Mengistu's father.

In 1957 Mengistu entered the army, later attending the Genet Military Academy in the city of Olatta. Upon graduation in 1966 he was commissioned as a lieutenant and went to work as a baggage handler and logistics coordinator for Haile Selassie. In the late 1960s Mengistu continued his military training at the Aberdeen Training Grounds, near Washington D.C. While in the United States, Mengistu witnessed racial prejudice first-hand, an experience that left him with anti-American sentiments.

Mengistu eventually rose to the rank of major and returned to the Genet Military Academy as a teacher in 1971. He later served in Ogaden, a disputed frontier region along the border between ETHIOPIA and SOMALIA. In June 1974 Mengistu became chairman of the Armed Forces Coordinating Committee, also called the Dergue.

Unable to abide the widespread CORRUPTION of Haile Selassie's government, Mengistu participated in the 1974 COUP D' ÉTAT that overthrew the emperor. Mengistu quickly became among the highest-ranking leaders in the new government. He served as one of the two vice chairmen of the Provisional Military Administrative Council (PMAC), a decision-making body made up of Dergue members that came to power after Selassie's fall. In the midst of internal struggles within the PMAC Mengistu rose to the fore. After a murderous period known as the "red terror," he purged his opposition from the government, gaining full control in 1977.

Mengistu introduced socialist reforms and allied his country with the Soviet Union during the Cold War, reversing Ethiopia's long-standing alliance with the United States. Mengistu initially attempted to empower the people of Ethiopia by nationalizing land ownership and organizing peasant associations, but his leadership quickly became brutal and dictatorial. As a result, he inspired fear among the diverse Ethiopian peoples and faced years of armed rebellion, especially in the northern region of TIGRAY and in Eritrea.

In the early 1990s with the withdrawal of Soviet aid after the fall of the Soviet Union, Mengistu's hold on power became even more tenuous. In 1991 the ETHIOPIAN PEOPLE'S REVOLUTIONARY DEMOCRATIC FRONT, a coalition of northern rebel groups led by the Tigray People's Liberation Front, captured Addis Ababa, causing Mengistu to flee to ZIMBABWE. Ethiopian attempts to get Zimbabwe to extradite the former dictator were unsuccessful.

See also: AMHARA (Vols. I, III, IV); COLD WAR AND AFRICA (Vol. IV); COMMUNISM AND SOCIALISM (Vol. V); FAMINE AND HUNGER (Vol. V); OGADEN (Vol. IV); SOVIET UNION AND AFRICA (Vol. V).

Messaoudi, Khalida (1958–) Algerian activist

Messaoudi was born in the Algerian village of Khabylia, south of ALGIERS. A math teacher as a young woman, she became politically active in her early twenties. In 1981 she joined a group of about 100 women that publicly protested the Family Code—proposed by Islamic fundamentalists—that called for the elimination of equal treatment of men and women. As the EDUCATION system became more influenced by fundamentalists, Messaoudi left teaching and entered politics.

In 1989 she helped found the Rally for Culture and Democracy (RCD), a political party that represents Berber interests and promotes modernization and secularization. Messaoudi's liberal political ideology made her a target of the fundamentalist Front for Islamic Salvation (FIS), a political party that desires an Islamic state in Algeria. Since 1993 Messaoudi has lived under a *fatwa*, or death sentence, handed down by the FIS. Despite living a clandestine and nomadic lifestyle to avoid assassination, the courageous Messaoudi won election to Algeria's Parliament in 1997.

See also: ISLAM, INFLUENCE OF (Vols. II, III, IV, V); WOMEN IN INDEPENDENT AFRICA (Vol. V).

Further reading: Khalida Messaoudi, *Unbowed: An Algerian Woman Confronts Islamic Fundamentalism* (Philadelphia: University of Pennsylvania Press, 1998).

Michel, James Alix See SEYCHELLES.

minerals and metals

Africa, which produces more than 50 types of minerals and metals, contributes greatly to the world's production of cobalt, diamonds, chromium, GOLD, manganese, and phosphates. Africa also produces a share of the world's output of bauxite, uranium, copper, coal, and platinum. The once-important metal resources of copper and iron have fallen in their level of production. At the same time the production of uranium and bauxite has risen in amount and importance.

The minerals Africa produces are used in a variety of activities and industries. Copper, for example, is used in the electronic industry and space exploration. Iron is used in manufacturing tools and constructing buildings. Uranium is used as an energy source as well as in the manufacturing of nuclear weapons.

In 2003 United States president George W. Bush (1946–) said in his State of the Union speech that one justification for the invasion of Iraq that year was an alleged attempt by Iraq to acquire uranium from NIGER for use in a nuclear arms program. The accuracy of this claim became the subject of contentious debate.

Although Africa, as a region, has enormous wealth in minerals and metals, these NATURAL RESOURCES are not distributed evenly throughout the continent. As a result only a handful of countries benefit from the MINING industry. For example, the two countries of SOUTH AFRICA and NIGERIA account for more than one-half of the total mineral production in Africa.

Still, the potential for greater benefits from the mining of minerals and metals is present, as many African countries possess these natural resources. For example, MAURITANIA, LIBERIA, and WESTERN SAHARA have rich deposits of iron ore, while the Copperbelt, stretching from ZAMBIA into the Democratic Republic of the CONGO, is rich in the mineral for which it is named. Major bauxite reserves are found in a band stretching across West Africa from GUINEA to TOGO.

Unfortunately, the countries that have major deposits of minerals and metals and also have developed the INFRASTRUCTURE to extract them remain heavily dependent on the export of these resources. Since most of these countries are not engaged in processing minerals for their own domestic markets or industries, they consequently lose out on much of the potential profit.

Zambia is an example of a mineral-rich country—in this case copper—that has not been able to turn its mineral resources into national wealth. A number of unrelated events contributed to the country's situation. Land-locked, Zambia was long dependent upon rail TRANSPORTATION through neighboring countries to export its copper. In 1965, when RHODESIA issued its UNILATERAL DECLARATION OF INDEPENDENCE, Zambia lost its rail connections to the south. Ten years later, the war in ANGOLA cut off its northern rail links to Benguela. Also in 1975 there was a sharp decline in world copper prices, which made the extraction of the metal unprofitable. By the time copper prices recovered in the late 1980s the country's mines, long deprived of adequate investment capital, faced rising production costs that cut deeply into the potential returns from increased world prices.

Geologists and speculators estimate that many of Africa's mineral and metal resources are yet to be discovered. Civil unrest and political instability have hindered the exploration process and many multinational mining companies have been hesitant to invest in some potentially mineral-rich areas.

Political Exploitation Because of the potential wealth that minerals and metals could provide to many African countries desperate for economic stimulus, their presence has frequently been used for political gain. In the middle of the political upheaval known as the CONGO CRISIS, for example, the Democratic Republic of the Congo's mineral-rich province of KATANGA seceded from the country under the leadership of the politically motivated Moïse TSHOMBE (1919–1969).

More recent manipulation of Africa's natural resources has been largely been linked to government opposition groups. In the 1990s rebel leader Jonas SAVIMBI (1934–2002) used money from diamonds to finance an armed rebellion against Angola's popularly elected government. Meanwhile, in SIERRA LEONE, the REVOLUTIONARY UNITED FRONT (RUF) has used the sale of illegal

diamonds to finance the purchase of arms during the country's civil war. In 2000 the United Nations (UN) issued a ban on diamonds from RUF-controlled areas in Sierra Leone in an effort to diminish their value. The UN ban was also extended to LIBERIA, a country that many of the diamonds passed through on their journey to the diamond centers of Antwerp and New York. In response, Sierra Leone set up a certification process for diamonds to distinguish those legally mined within the country. In 2003 the United Nations lifted its ban on Sierra Leone diamonds, though the ban on Liberia diamonds is still in effect.

See also: COLONIALISM, INFLUENCE OF (Vol. IV); COPPER (Vols. III, IV); COPPERBELT (Vol. IV); DIAMONDS (Vol. IV); MINERALS AND METALS (Vol. IV); MINERAL REVOLUTION (Vol. IV).

mining Process of extracting certain NATURAL RESOURCES from the ground, including coal, diamonds, GOLD, and copper. During the 1960s most African nations gained their independence, altering the dynamic of the mining industry in Africa. Many of the newly independent countries gained part ownership of mining developments, and with it an interest in ensuring their profitability. This often weakened the ability of miners' unions to gain wage increases or improvements in mining conditions.

African countries such as GHANA, ZAMBIA, and the Democratic Republic of the CONGO chose to nationalize the mining industries that had previously been dominated by private companies. The intention was to boost domestic economies; however, this proved to be ineffective. These countries lacked the expertise to manage the mines successfully, resulting in their continued dependence on foreign involvement in the industry. The slump in world metal prices during the 1970s also contributed to the problems these countries faced, as the lack of profits made it difficult for them to keep up with the maintenance of the mines and equipment.

In the 1980s the WORLD BANK and INTERNATIONAL MONETARY FUND implemented STRUCTURAL ADJUSTMENT programs that required African governments to begin privatizing their economies in order to increase competition, efficiency, and profits. As a result countries that had previously nationalized their mining industries began to reverse this policy and privatize their mines. This process further hindered the mining industry in these nations.

At the end of the 20th century the mining industry in Africa faced continued difficulties and was unable to provide a stable base for the continent's fledgling economies. Political instability has deterred DEVELOPMENT of potentially lucrative mineral deposits in many parts of Africa. At the same time what mining there is does little to support the local economy. Instead of being used to manufacture

Africa's Copperbelt region contains an estimated 30 percent of the world's copper reserves. Mining the copper is a costly process, in more ways than one. This operation in Katanga, shown in 1963, reveals the environmental damage done by open-pit copper mining. © United Nations

products, many of the mined minerals and metals are exported as raw materials. As a result most of the jobs created by mining are unskilled and the industry remains isolated from other business enterprises.

See also: COLONIALISM, INFLUENCE OF (Vol. IV); INTERNATIONAL MONETARY FUND (Vol. V); MINERALS AND METALS (Vols. IV, V).

missionaries Individuals who work in an organized institutional framework to convert others to their own RELIGION—non-Christians to Christianity, non-Muslims to Islam, and so on. In Africa, however, the term "missionary" has come to be associated with Christianity. During the colonial period the missionary system in Africa was largely a European-led undertaking. This, of course, followed the general rule of colonial administration, in which Europeans were in charge and gave orders to African subordinates. Africans responded to this by establishing autonomous churches that were independent from the mission churches, challenging them for adherents.

With the onset of African INDEPENDENCE MOVEMENTS in the 1950s and 1960s, European-run churches increasingly placed Africans in leadership positions. This occurred even in segregated SOUTH AFRICA, where, in 1986, Desmond TUTU (1931–) became the archbishop of Cape Town and the head of the country's Anglican Church. In recent decades, however, the fastest growing African Christian churches have been independent.

With the transition of church leadership to Africans, missionaries became far less important in evangelization and conversion. Their previous broad role in EDUCATION has largely disappeared as national governments assume larger responsibilities in the field. Missionaries have, however, continued to play important roles in Bible translation and health care, staffing mission hospitals that are sometimes the only medical providers in an area.

See also: CHRISTIANITY, INFLUENCE OF (Vols. II, III, IV, V); HEALTH AND HEALING IN MODERN AFRICA (Vol. V); MISSIONARIES (Vols. III, IV).

Further reading: Andrew F. Walls, *The Missionary Movement in Christian History: Studies in the Transmission of Faith* (Maryknoll, N.Y.: Orbis Books, 1996).

Mkapa, Benjamin (Benjamin William Mkapa)
(1938–) *President of Tanzania, elected in 1995*

Born in Ndanda, TANZANIA, Mkapa was educated at Kisongera Seminary, St. Francis College (Cambridge), and MAKERERE UNIVERSITY in UGANDA, where he earned a degree in English in 1962. Mkapa took positions in the civil and foreign service in mainland Tanganyika, which would soon join with ZANZIBAR to become the Republic of TANZANIA. Later he moved into media positions and served as managing editor of two national newspapers. In 1974 Tanzanian president Julius NYERERE (1922–1999) appointed Mkapa as his press secretary, and two years later Mkapa became the founding director of the Tanzanian press agency. In the years that followed, Mkapa also served in ministerial and ambassadorial positions in NIGERIA, Canada, and the United States.

Throughout the 1970s and 1980s Mkapa worked closely with Tanzania's first two presidents, Nyerere and Ali Hassan MWINYI (1925–). In 1995, with the endorsement of Nyerere, Mkapa was named the candidate for the ruling PARTY OF THE REVOLUTION (Chama Cha Mapinduzi, CCM). Mkapa won the 1995 election and was reelected to another five-year term in 2000.

Mkapa is widely seen as representing a new generation of African leadership that emphasizes economic DEVELOPMENT and market reform. After taking office Mkapa also appointed a presidential commission to study CORRUPTION in the country. This move helped lend credibility to his campaign promise to fix the governmental irregularities that plagued the Mwinyi government.

Despite economic reforms, however, Tanzania's dependence on foreign ECONOMIC ASSISTANCE has increased, which will likely have a negative impact on the country's long-term development prospects. Other than the economy, Mkapa's other challenges include establishing a lasting peace in the region and tackling the HIV/AIDS crisis that affects so many African nations.

See also: HIV/AIDS AND AFRICA (Vol. V).

Mobutu Sese Seko (Joseph-Désiré Mobutu)
(1930–1997) *Military dictator of the Democratic Republic of the Congo, which he renamed Zaïre*

Born Joseph-Désiré Mobutu in what was then the northern part of Belgian Congo, the future Congolese dictator was a member of the Bangala people, one of the country's more than 200 ethnic groups. He was educated at Roman Catholic mission schools before being drafted into the Congolese colonial army. He rose to the rank of sergeant-major, the highest rank attainable by an African under the Belgian colonial system.

After his army service, Mobutu became a journalist, eventually becoming editor-in-chief of the independence-oriented newspaper *Actualites Africaines*. There he became acquainted with two pro-independence leaders, Joseph KASAVUBU (c. 1913–1969) and Patrice LUMUMBA (1925–1961). His association with Lumumba eventually led to Mobutu taking an organizing role in Lumumba's Congolese National Movement (Mouvement National Congolais, MNC). This, in turn, led to positions in the government formed by Kasavubu and Lumumba when the Congo gained its independence in June 1960.

Seizing Power In the chaotic first days of Congolese independence, Mobutu initially proved himself a trustworthy lieutenant for Lumumba, helping to put down a mutiny among Congolese soldiers and taking on the duties of army chief of staff. However, with the arrival of United Nations peacekeeping troops, the secession of mineral-rich KATANGA province, and Lumumba's turning toward the former Soviet Union for assistance, Mobutu separated from Lumumba. In September 1960 he used his military strength to seize control of the government, which he held until turning power over to Kasavubu in January 1961.

During the early 1960s Mobutu concentrated his attention on the Congolese military, strengthening a force that was intensely loyal to him. In November 1965 he used this army to initiate a COUP D'ÉTAT, overthrowing Kasavubu and declaring himself head of state. Supported by major European powers and, because of his anti-Communist stance, the United States, Mobutu quickly managed to concentrate virtually all governing power in his own hands. Elections were cancelled, a government by decree was established, and the governors of the various Congolese regions were rendered powerless. Within a matter of months, Mobutu had complete control of the country, and the image of the dictator, wearing his trademark leopard-skin hat, became the dominant one in the country.

Since the early 1960s questions have consistently been raised about Mobutu's involvement in the death of Patrice Lumumba. While nothing has been proven, it is widely believed that Mobutu had at least some part in the one-time prime minister's death. The most likely scenario involves Mobutu ordering that Lumumba be taken from his jail cell, near Leopoldville, and transported to Katanga, where he eventually was murdered.

Economic Disaster The Congo is a vast region, rich in MINERALS AND METALS and other NATURAL RESOURCES. Although it was mismanaged and its people brutally repressed during the period of colonial rule, the Congo had the potential to become one of Africa's wealthiest independent nations. Under Mobutu, however, it quickly became an economic disaster. In the early years of his rule, in spite of nationalizing MINING and other industries, he encouraged FOREIGN INVESTMENT. He also brought in foreigners to replace the skilled workers who had fled during the chaotic first years of independence. This initially proved a successful strategy, and by 1970 the country seemed to be on the road to economic stability.

In 1973, however, Mobutu reversed policies, in effect encouraging citizens to claim the property and businesses of foreign investors. Foreign investment came to a grinding halt, the economy stumbled, and, within a few years, the country was virtually bankrupt. To make matters worse, Mobutu used whatever money was coming in—the majority of it being aid from European countries and the United States—for grandiose projects designed to further his own image. Little went to develop the potentially rich nation's economy or INFRASTRUCTURE. As a result, the standard of living fell, inflation soared, and unemployment rose rapidly. It was not long before the country was keeping afloat, economically, almost entirely on the basis of foreign aid and loans. By 1985, in fact, interest on foreign loans alone ate up more than 50 percent of the nation's budget.

Government Corruption under Mobutu Problems such as these, however, were only part of the country's economic and social woes. Government CORRUPTION

was another major element. In fact, 17 percent of the national budget was allotted as a "salary" for the head of state—Mobutu. But that was just the tip of the iceberg of the corruption. Estimates by various experts suggest that, during the 1970s, nearly 60 percent of all the money that the government took in ended up in the pockets of various officials. The government system of corruption and patronage was eventually labeled a *kleptocracy,* meaning "rule by thieves." Mobutu rewarded those who were loyal to him with both money and opportunities for graft. During this period Mobutu himself accumulated a fortune estimated at $5–$8 billion and maintained palaces in various parts of his own country as well as residences in Belgium, France, Switzerland, Italy, Portugal, and IVORY COAST.

Authenticity Programs The economy was not the only disaster area created by Mobutu. During the early 1970s, he also launched an "authenticity" campaign aimed at eliminating western-style behavior and returning the country and the people to a more African identity. In 1971 he renamed the country ZAÏRE, and embarked on an effort to have all citizens with Christian-style names change them to African names. With characteristic self-aggrandizement, he himself changed his name to Sese Seko Kuku Ngbendu Wazabanga, meaning "the warrior who knows no defeat because of his endurance and inflexible will and is all-powerful, leaving fire in his wake as he goes from conquest to conquest."

Mobutu's Fall from Power Although monuments and attempts at cultural revolution created a number of distractions, they could not hide the true effects of Mobutu's rule. Indeed, it was only through corruption and a menacing secret police force that the dictator was able to maintain his power in Zaïre. On the international level it was only through the economic support of democratic or capitalistic European and American governments—which considered Mobutu an ally in the Cold War—that he held on to power. During the 1980s, however, as the Cold War was coming to an end, the foreign support gradually diminished. By 1990, no longer able to justify their ties to Mobutu's corrupt and repressive regime, many countries ceased providing aid altogether. Left on his own Mobutu found his economy foundering. Troops mutinied because they were not paid, shopkeepers refused to accept the new, virtually worthless currency he created, and inflation soared.

Inflation reached staggering proportions in Mobutu's Zaïre. In 1989 one U.S. dollar was worth 250 zaïres (the nation's economic unit). In 1993, just four years later, one dollar was worth 2.6 million zaïres.

Opposition mounted, and, in the wake of political unrest, Mobutu was forced to legalize political parties once again. On top of this, he suffered from prostate cancer and required a great deal of medical attention, which he sought outside the country.

Mobutu's end came in the wake of horrific violence in RWANDA, Zaïre's neighbor to the east. In 1996 thousands of Rwandans—many of whom had long detested the Zaïrean dictator—fled that country and settled in Zaïre, creating an even more radical "anti-Mobutu" atmosphere. Led by Laurent KABILA (c. 1939–2001), rebel Rwandan forces organized and marched toward the Zaïrean capital of KINSHASA, where they found great popular support among Zaïreans. Mobutu fled from Kabila's advancing forces and sought political asylum in various countries, all of which turned him down. Finally MOROCCO gave him refuge. He died there in September 1997.

See also: ARMIES, COLONIAL (Vol. IV); BELGIAN CONGO (Vol. IV); COLD WAR AND AFRICA (Vols. IV, V); ECONOMIC ASSISTANCE (Vol. V); UNITED NATIONS AND AFRICA (Vols. IV, V); UNITED STATES AND AFRICA (Vols. IV, V).

Further reading: Michela Wrong, *In the Footsteps of Mr. Kurtz: Living on the Brink of Disaster in Mobutu's Congo* (New York: Perennial, 2002).

Mogadishu Capital and principal port of SOMALIA, located on the nation's southeastern Indian Ocean coast. This ancient port city, which dates back to the 10th century, served as an Italian colonial capital for the first half of the 20th century. In 1960 Mogadishu, then a city of some 86,000 people, became the capital of the independent nation of Somalia. During the 1960s the city invested in its port facilities, becoming a commercial and economic center in the process. Major EXPORTS included livestock, fruit, and hides. Major industries included processed foods, beverages, leather, cosmetics, wood products, and textiles. The Somali National University, located in the city, gained university status in 1959, and the city later became the site of several other schools of teaching, ART, health, and Islamic law.

Since the late 1980s Mogadishu's manufacturing and trading activities have declined severely due to the civil war that broke out between opposition forces and those loyal to then president Mohammed Siad BARRE (1910–1995). In 1991, before being forced out of office, Barre and his forces shelled portions of the city held by his opponents, causing massive destruction and killing perhaps 50,000 of the city's residents. Unrest and chaos continued, as soldiers supporting Mohammed Farah AIDEED (1934–1996), a longtime rival of Barre, fought with other rebelling factions in an attempt to maintain control of the city.

United Nations (UN) peacekeeping forces were stationed in the city at times during the 1990s. In 1993 a United States military intervention in support of the UN peacekeepers ended in disaster, with the deaths of a number of American soldiers and a subsequent withdrawal of U.S. forces. Although a Transitional National Government was set up in 2000, it has not been able to maintain peace in the city or the nation. The population of Mogadishu was estimated at 1,200,000 in 2003, but it is difficult to obtain a reliable figure due to the large number of temporary residents and war REFUGEES.

See also: ARAB COASTAL TRADE (Vols. I, II); BENADIR COAST (Vol. III); CIVIL WARS (Vol. V); ISLAM, INFLUENCE OF (Vols. II, III, IV, V); ITALY AND AFRICA (Vol. IV); MOGADISHU (Vols. II, III, IV); UNITED NATIONS AND AFRICA (Vols. IV, V); UNITED STATES AND AFRICA (Vols. IV, V); URBAN LIFE AND CULTURE (Vols. IV, V); URBANIZATION (Vols. IV, V).

Mogae, Festus (Festus Gontebanye Mogae) (1939–) *Third president of Botswana*

Born in Serowe, eastern BOTSWANA, Mogae went to school at Moeng College in his own country before going on to earn a bachelor's degree in economics from Oxford University and a master's degree in DEVELOPMENT economics from Sussex University, in the United Kingdom. Upon his return to Botswana, he served in the ministry of finance and development as a planning officer, director of economic affairs, and as permanent secretary. Between 1971 and 1976 Mogae also served on governing boards of the INTERNATIONAL MONETARY FUND, the African Development Bank, and the WORLD BANK.

In the early 1980s Mogae was appointed governor of the Bank of Botswana but left to serve as permanent secretary to President Ketumile MASIRE (1925–). Mogae supervised elections from 1982 to 1989, at which time he became minister of finance and development planning. In 1992 he was made Masire's vice president. When Masire decided to retire in 1998, Mogae was handpicked to be his successor, contingent upon elections to be held the following year.

Since Mogae took office following his easy victory in 1999, Botswana's economic and political situation has remained healthy. He has continued to support privatization of MINING and industry. His major challenge has been dealing with the country's HIV/AIDS epidemic. Recent United Nations reports classified Botswana as having the highest rate of infection in the world, with more than 30 percent of all adults infected with HIV, the virus that causes AIDS.

See also: HIV/AIDS AND AFRICA (Vol. V).

Mohammed VI (1963–) *King and head of state of Morocco*

Born Crown Prince Sidi Mohammed in the Moroccan capital of RABAT, Mohammed was groomed from an early age to eventually assume the throne. At the age of four he began Quranic studies, and he progressed through the Royal College and the College of Law at Rabat Mohammed V University. From there his studies took him to Belgium and France, where he completed his law degree in 1993.

As his father, King HASSAN II (1929–1999), became increasingly ill, Mohammed played a greater role in the governing of MOROCCO. In 1994 he became division general and second-in-command of the military. Five years later King Hassan died, and, in a matter of hours, Mohammed became King Mohammed VI. He was the eighteenth successive Alawite Muslim ruler of Morocco, part of a line that stretched back to the mid-17th century.

Though not as charismatic as his father, the new king has gained praise for assuming a less autocratic position than Hassan, allowing for more democratic practices, and promising to purge the government of CORRUPTION. He has also removed many of his father's friends from their holdover positions in the government and released a number of political prisoners. Though Mohammed came to power during a period of economic decline and rampant unemployment, Moroccans have looked to him as a welcome move away from elitist rule.

Moi, Daniel arap (Toroitich arap Moi) (1924–)
President of Kenya from 1978 to 2002

Moi was born Toroitich arap Moi in the Kenyan village of Kuriengwo. A member of the Kalenjin ethnic minority, he took the name Daniel upon his Christian baptism. As a youth Moi attended local mission schools before studying at Kapsabet Teacher Training College. He became a teacher after graduating in 1945, and he later advanced to the position of school administrator.

In 1955 the British colonial administration appointed Moi to fill a vacancy on the Kenyan Legislative Council. Two years later, when KENYA held its first elections in which Africans were allowed to vote, Moi was elected to the council. He was actively involved with the country's move toward independence. In 1960 he traveled as a delegate to London and participated in the Lancaster House Conference, a gathering that drafted Kenya's new constitution.

That same year Moi, along with Ronald Nagala (1948–1972), founded the Kenya African Democratic Union (KADU). The main goal of KADU was to protect the interests of Kenya's numerous minority peoples. After Kenya's independence in 1963, however, Moi struck a deal with the country's new president, Jomo KENYATTA (c. 1891–1978), and merged KADU with Kenyatta's party, the KENYAN AFRICAN NATIONAL UNION (KANU). As a result Kenya effectively became a one-party system controlled by KANU, and Kenyatta rewarded Moi by appointing him minister of home affairs, in 1964, and later vice president, in 1967.

Moi ascended to Kenya's presidency after Kenyatta's death in August 1978. The following year Moi was officially elected to the position. He ran unopposed in 1983 and 1988. During this time Moi went from a progressive reformist who ushered in an era of unprecedented freedoms to the repressive leader of an authoritarian regime. Moi increasingly consolidated his power, appointing fellow Kalenjin to positions of power, which in turn vexed Kenya's largest ethnic group, the KIKUYU. Despite his anti-majority policies, Moi maintained control thanks in large part to support from the United States for his pro-Western stance in the midst of the Cold War.

By the early 1990s however, Moi faced increasing pressure from the West to institute political and economic reforms. In 1992, under a U.S. threat to withdraw aid, Moi reintroduced multiparty elections. Despite increasing accusations of CORRUPTION, Moi won the presidency in 1992 and 1997. The legitimacy of these elections, however, was largely contested by opposition parties, leading to widespread riots. In addition, during Moi's last term in office, allegations of corruption increased. Term limits outlined in Kenya's constitution forced him to step down from the presidency in 2002. Moi endorsed Uhuru Kenyatta, Jomo Kenyatta's son, as his successor, but Kenyatta was defeated by a well-organized coalition of opposition parties that was led by his former political ally, Mwai KIBAKI (1931–). In the aftermath of KADU's defeat the new government launched an investigation into government corruption under Moi. However, in 2003 Moi obtained immunity from prosecution on corruption charges.

See also: DEMOCRATIZATION (Vol. V); ETHNICITY AND IDENTITY (Vol. I); KALENJIN (Vol. III).

Mombasa Major port city on the East African coast of present-day KENYA. Mombasa entered Kenya's post-independence era as the country's principal port and one of the major ports for Africa's entire Indian Ocean coastline. The DEVELOPMENT of the city's modern deepwater port facilities further entrenched its dominance. The major highway and railroad to the interior have Mombasa at their coastal terminus. Virtually all of the seaborne EXPORTS and imports for Kenya, UGANDA, RWANDA, and BURUNDI flow through Mombasa's docks. In addition to being a TRANSPORTATION center, the city also developed major industrial areas with the economic stimulus that accompanied independence. Among the major industries were OIL refineries, sugar processing, and the manufacturing of cement and fertilizer. Economic development meant jobs, and the availability of jobs drew KIKUYU and other Kenyans from the interior to the city.

In the process of economic and POPULATION GROWTH, Mombasa began to lose some of its original coastal character. The older Kiswahili- and Arabic-speaking population continued to predominate in the island quarters of the city, with mosques, houses with overhanging second stories, and narrow streets continuing to provide Mombasa with the characteristics of a long-established Swahili coastal city. However, more recently developed areas of the city, especially those on the mainland, became more national in character. Former Kenyan president Daniel arap MOI (1924–) also actively suppressed those elements of Mombasa's political life that sought to assert the coast's distinctiveness from the rest of the country.

The newest element in Mombasa's cultural and economic life is a booming TOURISM business. The initial tourism of the 1950s expanded very rapidly over the following decades. By the 1980s tourist-oriented hotels had sprung up along the beautiful beaches to the north and south of the city. The old Portuguese military post of Fort Jesus, which is now a museum, became a main tourist attraction, as did the city's old quarters. Furthermore, East Africa's game parks were readily accessible. More than a quarter-million tourists now arrive annually, providing employment for many of the city's 665,000 people.

See also: FORT JESUS (Vol. III); MOMBASA (Vols. II, III, IV); SWAHILI COAST (Vols. II, III, IV); URBANIZATION (Vol. V).

Mondlane, Eduardo (1920–1969) *Leader in Mozambique's drive for independence*

When he formed and assumed the leadership of the Front for the Liberation of Mozambique (Frente de Libertação de Moçambique, FRELIMO) in 1962, Eduardo Chivambo Mondlane was one of the best-educated nationalist leaders on the continent. He held a PhD in anthropology and had taught on the faculty of Syracuse University in New York State. He had accepted a faculty position in MOZAMBIQUE, but the pull of liberating his country from oppressive and stifling Portuguese colonial rule proved too compelling. Although Mondlane personally admired the nonviolence of Mohandas Gandhi (1869–1948) and Dr. Martin Luther King, Jr. (1929–1968), he ultimately concluded that armed resistance was the only way for Mozambique to achieve independence. The armed struggle began in 1964, and FRELIMO was soon making gains, achieving a military victory, for example, in the Cabo Delgado territory. However, a rift began to develop between the organization's hard-line Marxists and those who, like Mondlane, favored a more democratic organization. Ultimately FRELIMO grew increasingly radical, advocating not only independence but also major changes in the social order and government of Mozambique.

Mondlane was assassinated by a letter bomb in his office in DAR ES SALAAM, the capital of TANZANIA, in February 1969. Although those responsible for the murder have never definitely been identified, it was believed to be the work of either his Portuguese enemies or hostile elements within FRELIMO itself. FRELIMO's military commander, Samora MACHEL (1933–1986), succeeded Mondlane as the leader of the group. In 1975 Mozambique finally achieved its independence after years of armed struggle, with Machel becoming its first president.

In 1969, the same year of his death, Mondlane's book, *The Struggle for Mozambique*, appeared in a Penguin paperback edition as a title in its Penguin African Library series. Mondlane cites the economic exploitation, lack of EDUCATION, and cultural segregation of the Portuguese colonial rule as the reasons why he and others in FRELIMO launched a guerilla war of national liberation to create an independent Mozambique.

See also: COLONIAL RULE (Vol. IV); MONDLANE, EDUARDO (Vol. IV); NATIONALISM AND INDEPENDENCE MOVEMENTS (Vol. IV); PORTUGAL AND AFRICA (Vols. III, IV, V).

money and currency Prior to independence African countries utilized currencies based on those of the occupying colonial powers. Thus, the British colonies had pounds, shillings, and pence, while the French colonies utilized the franc. Independence brought considerable change. For example, the former French North African colonies of ALGERIA and TUNISIA replaced francs with dinars. However, 14 countries in sub-Saharan Africa continued to utilize the former colonial currency, the CFA franc.

Today the CFA franc is divided between the West African franc, which is the standard currency of the African Financial Community, and the Central African franc, which is the currency of Financial Cooperation in Central Africa. The French treasury has guaranteed the value of the CFA franc, which for a long time was exchanged at the rate of 1 CFA franc to .02 French francs. In 1994, however, the French government unilaterally devalued the CFA franc by half so that it was 1 CFA franc to .01 French franc. While this pegging of the African franc to the French franc ensures that the currency is readily convertible and stable, it also means that money exchange in 14 African countries is subject to continuing French control.

Other African countries gained control over their currencies at independence. While some continued to use the former colonial terms (e.g., the pound in EGYPT, shillings in KENYA, TANZANIA, and UGANDA, and francs in MADAGASCAR), the currencies were no longer linked to those of the former colonial power. The more usual practice, however, was to rename currencies as a way to demonstrate national independence. Thus, NIGERIA replaced the Nigerian pound with the naira, SOUTH AFRICA replaced the pound with the rand, and ZAMBIA and MALAWI each adopted the kwacha. LIBERIA, in West Africa, continues to use the U.S. dollar because of its long history of economic ties with that country.

Created in 1945, the CFA franc originally was the currency of the "Colonies Françaises d'Afrique" (French Colonies of Africa). The former colonies joined the French Community 13 years later, and CFA came to denote "Communauté Française d'Afrique" (French Community of Africa).

As African economies have slumped, however, national control of currencies and their worth led to drastic devaluation. The Nigerian naira is a prime example. In 1973 when Nigeria made the switch from the pound to the naira, 1 naira was worth $1.52 (U.S.). By 1990 it had fallen to 8 naira to $1, and, by 2003, it had sunk to 128 naira to $1.

See also: MONEY AND CURRENCY (Vols. I, II, III, IV).

Monrovia Capital and principal port of LIBERIA, located at the mouth of the St. Paul (Mesurado) River on the Atlantic Ocean. Monrovia was founded in 1822 by the American Colonization Society and therefore developed an American-oriented society that reflected its politically dominant Americo-Liberian population. American influence became even more pronounced during and after World War II (1939–45), when Liberia served as the major West African base for United States forces. After the United States expanded Monrovia's port facilities during the war, the city's economy subsequently thrived on export and import activities; major EXPORTS include iron ore and rubber. In addition, the city manufactures processed food, petroleum, pharmaceuticals, building materials, and furniture.

As the principal city of one of the two African members of the League of Nations (SOUTH AFRICA was the other), and capital of one of the founding member states of the United Nations, Monrovia has played an important international diplomatic role. In 1961, for example, it was the site of the conference that spawned the MONROVIA GROUP, a bloc of African countries united in their desire for a gradual unification of Africa's newly independent countries in a pan-African organization. Two years later the Monrovia group would come together with others to form the pan-African ORGANIZATION OF AFRICAN

UNITY with the stated purpose of eradicating all forms of colonialism from, and promoting peace and security throughout, the African continent.

The Liberian economy began to decline in the 1970s, and a high unemployment rate among Monrovia's growing population eventually led to widespread rioting in 1979. The following year Liberian army sergeant Samuel DOE (c. 1952–1990), an ethnic Krahn, led a bloody COUP D'ÉTAT that toppled President William R. TOLBERT (1913–1980), ending the Americo-Liberian political monopoly.

In 1990 the rebel forces led by Charles TAYLOR (1948–   ) besieged Monrovia, leading to the intervention of an ECONOMIC COMMUNITY OF WEST AFRICAN STATES (ECOWAS) peacekeeping force. Despite their efforts, Taylor's men still managed to capture and execute Doe, an action that sparked a devastating civil war that caused destruction and a mass exodus from the city. ECOWAS helped establish a tentative peace in the mid-1990s, but renewed fighting in other parts of Liberia forced large numbers of people to seek refuge in Monrovia. In 2003 the fighting spread once again into the city proper which, devastated by the fighting, saw its INFRASTRUCTURE and economy collapse. The population of the city was estimated at 543,000 in 2002, but the continuing warfare and disruption has made an accurate count impossible.

See also: CIVIL WARS (Vol. V); MONROVIA (Vol. IV); UNITED STATES AND AFRICA (Vols. IV, V); URBAN LIFE AND CULTURE (Vols. IV, V): URBANIZATION (Vols. IV, V).

Monrovia group (Monrovia bloc) Name given to a collection of African countries that, from 1961 to 1963, were united in their conservative, gradualist approach to pan-African unity. During the 1950s, as African nationalism and INDEPENDENCE MOVEMENTS gained momentum, some leaders began calling for the establishment of organizations whose purpose would be to encourage peace and cooperation in economic and social DEVELOPMENT on a continental scale. Although these groups all desired pan-African unity, they sometimes disagreed on how to achieve this goal.

In May 1961 leaders from NIGERIA, LIBERIA, TOGO, and GUINEA met in MONROVIA, the Liberian capital. Known as the Monrovia group, or Monrovian bloc, these countries were led by Nigerian prime minister Abubakar Tafawa BALEWA (1912–1966) and Liberian president William TUBMAN (1895–1971). One of the group's primary plans was to establish regional, as opposed to continental, alliances. These smaller alliances, they argued, could be the basis for gradual economic and social development. In addition, they believed that opportunities for direct FOREIGN INVESTMENT, especially from former colonizers, would be greater for countries within such alliances.

With this ideology, the Monrovia group defined itself in opposition to the CASABLANCA GROUP, which, in late 1960, had begun advocating the rejection of foreign influence and the immediate establishment of a "United States of Africa." Made up of mostly North African and some West African states, the Casablanca Group accused the Monrovia Group of being aristocratic and backward-looking. For its part, the Monrovia group felt that, in light of the instability that plagued the continent, a United States of Africa was doomed to failure.

During the early 1960s each bloc tried to convince newly independent African states to join its alliance. Countries that later aligned themselves with the Monrovia group included ETHIOPIA, SIERRA LEONE, Congo-Brazzaville (today's Republic of the CONGO), CAMEROON, SENEGAL, DAHOMEY (today's Republic of BENIN), the Malagasy Republic (today's MADAGASCAR), CHAD, UPPER VOLTA (today's BURKINA FASO), and NIGER.

Ultimately a conference planned by the Monrovia group evolved into a summit involving all 32 of the African countries that were independent at the time, from both the Monrovia and Casablanca groups. On May 25, 1963, in ADDIS ABABA, Ethiopia, 28 of the 32 countries adopted a pan-African unity charter, which was subsequently ratified by their governments. Thus the ORGANIZATION OF AFRICAN UNITY (OAU) was established. The OAU charter overrode the charters of the Monrovia and Casablanca groups, and the two alliances were dissolved.

See also: PAN-AFRICANISM (Vol. IV).

Moore, Bai T. (1920–1988) *Liberian civil servant and author*

Bai T. Moore was born in Dimeh, northwest of MONROVIA, LIBERIA. He attended elementary school in Liberia before going to the United States, where he studied first in Virginia public schools and then at Virginia Union University in Richmond. In 1941 Moore returned to Liberia, where he began his life-long career as a public servant. His literary career commenced in 1947 with the publication of his poetry in *Echoes from the Valley: Being Odes and other Poems,* a volume he coedited. Moore's main body of literary work was produced in the 1960s, beginning with a volume of poetry that appeared in 1962 under the title *Ebony Dust.* He also wrote a novella, *Murder in the Cassava Patch* (1963) and, in 1976, a popular novel called *The Money Doubler.* Moore's poems, noted for their innovative line structure, were written not only in English, but also in Vai and Gola, two local Liberian dialects. Through his poetry and his work in the public sector, Bai T. Moore promoted LITERACY and the rich Liberian cultural heritage.

See also: LITERATURE IN COLONIAL AFRICA (Vols. IV); LITERATURE IN MODERN AFRICA (Vol. V).

Morocco North African country measuring approximately 279,400 square miles (723,646 sq km), located in the MAGHRIB, bordering both the Mediterranean Sea and the Atlantic Ocean. In 1956, under the leadership of King Mohammed V (1909–1961), Morocco regained its independence from France. Upon King Mohammed's death in 1961, his son, King HASSAN II (1929–1999), ascended to the throne. At the beginning of his reign Morocco drafted its first democratic constitution, but political CORRUPTION and ineptitude led to government instability and popular dissatisfaction.

In 1965 King Hassan cemented his control by dissolving Parliament and implementing a form of direct rule. Similar to events in other North African states, the king nationalized all foreign-owned businesses and commercial AGRICULTURE, using the additional income to reward loyalty and win over the opposition.

In an effort to divert attention from his policies, Hassan chose to focus on nation building. This strategy included using nationalism to unify the Moroccan people against foreign targets. In 1975 he turned his attention to the WESTERN SAHARA, the southern Saharan provinces that were under Spanish occupation. At the time, Western Sahara was engulfed by war, with the indigenous SAHARAWI fighting for their independence from Spain. King Hassan, however, wanted to incorporate the area into Morocco, and he sent a contingent of 350,000 volunteers on the "Green March" to recapture the Sahara.

Named in honor of the holy color of Islam, the Green March was performed by unarmed marchers carrying pictures of the king, Moroccan flags, and copies of the Quran. In light of the marchers, the Spanish army withdrew, but the Saharawi felt as if they were under a foreign invasion. Morocco's seizure of the Saharan provinces fostered an armed national resistance movement by the POLISARIO Front, which represented some 100,000 Saharawi desiring independence.

The war with Polisario aided Hassan's domestic policy in that the Moroccan army was busy and content, but the invasion of Western Sahara caused conflict in the region and strained Morocco's relations with its neighbors as well as its weak economy. Despite the continued efforts of the United Nations to broker an end to the conflict, the status of Western Sahara governance was still still unresolved as late as the end of 2004.

In 1979 an economic crisis loomed over Morocco as its national debt grew, its economy stagnated, and its population increased. The INTERNATIONAL MONETARY FUND forced Morocco to cut its state subsidy on imported food, and the resultant increase in food prices led to a decline in the standard of living, which was accompanied by massive protests.

Throughout the 1980s and 1990s Morocco held multiple elections, but the vote was frequently split among various parties. King Hassan II used these inconclusive returns to exclude his opposition from government and solidify his direct rule.

During the late 1980s Morocco improved its relationships with neighboring African nations, resuming diplomatic relations with both ALGERIA and MAURITANIA. In 1989 Morocco signed a treaty that established the Arab Maghrib Union, a North African common market. In 1993 Morocco hosted the Economic Summit on the Middle East and North Africa as well as the Seventh Islamic Summit Conference, both in Casablanca.

In 1999, after 38 years of autocratic rule, King Hassan II died from a heart attack. He was quickly succeeded by his son, Crown Prince Sidi Mohammed (1963–), who was enthroned as King MOHAMMED VI. The young king has promised to purge CORRUPTION from the government, allow more freedom of the press, and encourage more democratic practices. Since his ascension to the throne, many of his father's friends have been removed from office and some political prisoners have been released. However, vestiges of his father's influence remain. The results of the 2002 election were similar to those in the past, with King Mohammed VI retaining direct control over major policy decisions.

See also: ARAB WORLD AND AFRICA (Vol. IV); MOROCCO (Vols. I, II, III, IV); UNITED NATIONS AND AFRICA (Vol. V); UNITED STATES AND AFRICA (Vols. IV, V).

Further reading: Stephen O. Hughes, *Morocco under King Hassan*, (Reading, U.K.: Ithaca, 2001); C. R. Pennell, *Morocco since 1830: A History* (New York: New York University Press, 2000).

Moroni (formerly Port-aux-Bountres) Capital and principal port city of the Federal Republic of COMOROS, located on the west coast of the island of Njazidja (known to the French as Grande Comore) in the Indian Ocean. At the time when the city was taken over by the French, in the late 19th century, it had already seen its original Polynesian and Malaysian settlers mix with more recently arrived Arab traders and merchants. Moroni replaced the city of Dzaoudzi as Comoros's administrative capital in 1958, and it remained the capital when President Ahmed Abdallah (1918–1989) declared the nation's independence in 1975.

The city's economy is based on the production of beverages, metal and wood products, and cement. It imports food products while exporting vanilla, cocoa, coffee, and ylang-ylang, a flower oil widely used in the perfume industry. The Arab history of Moroni is represented by the Arabic ARCHITECTURE visible in many of the buildings, the numerous mosques, and the Arab quarter of town with its narrow, winding streets. The city, which has a population of about 60,000, also has resorts and restaurants that are frequented by increasing numbers of foreign tourists.

While French is the official language and Arabic the religious language of Comoros, the people of Moroni, like the rest of the islands' inhabitants, speak variations of Comorian. Closely related to Kiswahili, Comorian is a Bantu language that, because of the people's long history of ocean trading, contains many words borrowed from Hindi, Persian, Portuguese, English, and French. Traditionally, Comorian has been written in Arabic script, but there have been recent attempts to use Roman script.

See also: ARABS (Vol. II); ARABS, INFLUENCE OF (Vols. II, III); FRANCE AND AFRICA (Vols. III, IV, V); INDIAN OCEAN TRADE (Vol. II); SWAHILI COAST (Vols. II, III, IV); TOURISM (Vol. V).

Mosisili, Pakalitha Bethuel (1945–) *Lesotho's prime minister, elected in 1998*

Mosisili was born in the town of Waterfall, in the Qacha's Nek district of LESOTHO. He attended local schools as a youth, then studied at the University of Botswana, Lesotho, and Swaziland, earning a bachelor's degree in 1970. Mosisili later studied in the United States, obtaining a master's degree in 1976 from the University of Wisconsin. Mosisili continued his education at the University of South Africa and in 1982 obtained a master of education degree in Canada from Simon Fraser University.

Mosisili's involvement in politics began in 1967, when he joined the Basutoland Congress Party (BCP). Actively involved in the BCP's Youth League, Mosisili was arrested during a state of emergency and was imprisoned for more than a year. Released in 1971, he remained active in the BCP, but strayed from the political arena until 1993, when he won election to Lesotho's Parliament as representative from Qacha's Nek. In 1995 Mosisili became deputy prime minister under Prime Minister Ntsa Mokhele (1918–1999). That same year Mosisili joined a mass exodus from the BCP to join Mokhele and his newly formed party—the Lesotho Congress for Democracy (LCD). Mosisili became deputy leader of the LCD, placing him in line to succeed the aging Mokhele as leader of the party. In 1998, when Mokhele retired, Mosisili assumed the LCD leadership, guiding the party to a landslide electoral victory later that year. With his party firmly in control of Parliament, Mosisili became Lesotho's prime minister.

However, opposition party leaders vigorously disputed the election results of 1998. Massive protests destabilized the country, and, worried that he was losing his grip on power, Mosisili asked for military assistance from SOUTH AFRICA. Although the South African forces met stiff resistance from Lesotho's coup-minded military, they eventually restored a semblance of order. In the aftermath of this unrest Lesotho founded the Interim Political Authority, a government agency that was to establish an Independent Electoral Commission and set the standards for new elections in 2002. Despite the previous protests, the LCD carried the 2002 elections as well, and Mosisili began a second term as Lesotho's prime minister.

Movement for Democratic Change (MDC)

Main opposition party in ZIMBABWE, founded in 1999 by LABOR leader Morgan TSVANGIRAI (1952–   ). During the 1990s large segments of Zimbabwe's population became increasingly concerned by the country's dire economic situation. However, Zimbabwe's president Robert MUGABE (1924–   ) and his ruling ZIMBABWE AFRICAN NATIONAL UNION-Patriotic Front (ZANU-PF) effectively silenced all political opposition through intimidation and violence. As a result, the 1996 presidential elections had the lowest voter turnout of any election since Zimbabwe became independent in 1980.

In an attempt to channel the nation's discontent with the Mugabe administration, Tsvangirai, the secretary general of the powerful Zimbabwe Congress of Trade Unions (ZCTU) joined together with leaders from other CIVIL SOCIETY organizations to form the Movement for Democratic Change (MDC). Besides the ZCTU, other organizations in the umbrella MDC coalition include the Zimbabwe Council of Churches, the Catholic Commission for Justice and Peace, the Legal Rights Foundation, and the Zimbabwe Human Rights Organization. Tsivangirai became MDC president.

In 2002 MDC representatives vied for parliamentary seats on a platform of economic discipline and government accountability. Although ZANU-PF won the elections by a narrow margin, the MDC had a strong showing that boded well for its future in Zimbabwe.

Following the 2002 elections Mugabe charged Tsvangirai with treason for allegedly plotting to assassinate him. The MDC claimed that the charges were nothing more than Mugabe's attempt to drain MDC resources and hinder its effectiveness as a viable opposition party.

See also: POLITICAL PARTIES AND ORGANIZATIONS (Vols. IV, V).

Further reading: Staffan Darnolf and Lisa Laakso, eds., *Twenty Years of Independence in Zimbabwe: From Liberation to Authoritarianism* (New York: Palgrave Macmillan, 2003).

Movement for Multiparty Democracy (MMD)

Zambian political party that challenged and defeated Kenneth KAUNDA (1924–   ) and his UNITED NATIONAL INDEPENDENCE PARTY (UNIP), which had been the only legal party within ZAMBIA for nearly 20 years. In 1972 Zambia's UNIP-controlled government adopted a one-party state system, forbidding the activity of other political parties. This lasted for nearly two decades, with Kaunda as both leader of UNIP and president of Zambia for all of those years. During his presidency the economy of Zambia gradually deteriorated, spurred by aggressive social spending and ill-conceived food subsidies. By the mid-1980s Zambia faced economic crisis, with inflation running rampant and riots erupting in response to government attempts to remove food subsidies.

In the years that followed, Zambia's problems only worsened. In 1990 Kaunda, pressured by the INTERNATIONAL MONETARY FUND and the WORLD BANK to implement further STRUCTURAL ADJUSTMENT, again cut subsidies for food. This time, however, he also implemented fees for hospital care and EDUCATION. Once more, Kaunda's moves caused violent riots. As a result, the call became more urgent for political change in the form of multiparty elections. In July 1990 a coalition of interest groups, led by Frederick CHILUBA (1943–   ), came together in LUSAKA to form a political party called the Movement for the Multiparty Democracy (MMD). That same year, conceding to increased domestic and international pressure for multiparty elections, Kaunda amended the constitution to allow for the formation of opposition political parties. At the same time, Kaunda called for free elections to be held in 1991.

The MMD was an alliance of various groups of Zambians including intellectuals, LABOR UNION leaders, politicians who had served in the UNIP government, entrepreneurs, and other business professionals. Chiluba, a former leader of the Zambia Congress of Trade Unions, was a powerful figure within Zambia's trade unions. Accusing the UNIP-controlled government of CORRUPTION and ineffectiveness, the MMD campaigned under the slogan "The Hour Has Come!," an allusion to the length of UNIP's uncontested governance.

The MMD campaign was popular, and MMD rallies were well attended. Though more than 20 political parties had registered by the time of the elections, the MMD held sway. In the October election Chiluba received three-fourths of the votes compared to Kaunda's one-fourth, making MMD the new majority party. The election set a precedent in Africa, marking a peaceful transition from one-party rule to a multiparty rule. Chiluba's pro-democracy pedigree was tarnished soon after, however. In 1996 he won reelection, but his victory was marred when he changed the constitution to bar Kaunda from running against him. In 2001 Chiluba proposed another constitutional change aimed at furthering his political ends. Wanting to run for a third term, he sought to eliminate the two-term limit for Zambian presidents. Domestic and international pressure against his proposal, however, eventually forced Chiluba to abandon his plans but only after his efforts had caused a rift in the MMD. Despite the exodus of some party members, the MMD candidate, Levy MWANAWASA (1948–   ), won the 2001 election, and the party maintained its hold on the presidency.

See also: DEMOCRATIZATION (Vol. V); POLITICAL PARTIES AND ORGANIZATIONS (Vols. IV, V).

Mozambican Liberation Front (Frente de Libertação de Moçambique, FRELIMO)

Anticolonial nationalist movement in MOZAMBIQUE that fought for the end of Portuguese colonial rule and upon assuming power became involved in a civil war. The Mozambican Liberation Front (FRELIMO) was founded in June 1962 in TANZANIA, to the north of MOZAMBIQUE. With the help of Julius NYERERE (1922–1999), then president of Tanzania, FRELIMO was created from the merger of the three existing nationalist groups within Mozambique. FRELIMO's main concern was realizing independence from Portugal. The founders of FRELIMO were exiles from Mozambique who demanded liberation from Portugal's harsh colonial rule. Despite the merger, however, FRELIMO remained internally divided as a result of ideological and ethnic differences, as well as personal rivalries within its leadership, headed by Eduardo MONDLANE (1920–1969).

FRELIMO received support from both the Soviet Union and the United States during the Cold War period. Under Mondlane FRELIMO created a resistance army of several thousand Africans and waged a guerrilla war against Portugal. In the early years of fighting, however, FRELIMO action was limited to remote parts of Mozambique. Despite the vast number of Portuguese troops sent to Mozambique, which reached a level of 70,000 during the middle of the 1960s, FRELIMO could not be deterred from its goal of independence.

After Mondlane was assassinated in 1969, Samora MACHEL (1933–1986) took over FRELIMO leadership. He extended the range of FRELIMO guerrilla activities. His success in expanding the zones of FRELIMO control in the country helped create a sense among Portuguese military leaders that they could not win the war. This in turn sparked the 1974 military COUP D'ÉTAT that brought down the Portuguese national government and opened the way for independence negotiations. After independence was declared in 1975, FRELIMO was made the only legal party in Mozambique. It then reorganized its ideology to follow a Marxist-Leninist path. Reform of the country's weakened economy was a main concern at this time.

Unfortunately for Mozambicans, civil war followed independence. Much-needed economic reform was foiled by the actions of the MOZAMBICAN NATIONAL RESISTANCE (RENAMO), which was supported by SOUTH AFRICA. Machel died in a mysterious plane crash, in 1986, and FRELIMO was taken over by Joaquim Alberto CHISSANO (1939–   ), who continued with earlier reforms and began peace talks with RENAMO.

In 1990, despite the raging civil war, a new constitution was created recognizing multiple political parties. After the civil war ended in 1992, general elections were held in 1994 and again in 1999, and Chissano's FRELIMO was victorious in both elections. As of the end of 2004, Chissano was president and head of the FRELIMO government of Mozambique.

See also: CIVIL WARS (Vol. V); COLD WAR AND AFRICA (Vols. IV, V); COLONIAL RULE (Vol. IV); INDEPENDENCE MOVEMENTS (Vol. V); NATIONALISM AND INDEPENDENCE MOVEMENTS (Vol. IV); POLITICAL PARTIES AND ORGANIZATIONS (Vols. IV, V); PORTUGAL AND AFRICA (Vols. III, IV, V).

Further reading: William Finnegan, *A Complicated War: The Harrowing of Mozambique* (Berkeley, Calif.: University of California Press, 1992); Colin Legum, *The Battlefronts of Southern Africa* (New York: Africana Publishing Co., 1988).

Mozambican National Resistance (Resistência Nacional Moçambicana, RENAMO)

Guerrilla opposition group and political party of MOZAMBIQUE. RENAMO, formed in 1976, was an invention of white army officers from RHODESIA (now ZIMBABWE). Its purpose was to destabilize Mozambique and make it difficult for that country to support the Rhodesian independence movement. Ironically, the Rhodesian officers filled RENAMO with disaffected members of the MOZAMBICAN LIBERATION FRONT (Front de Libertaçao de Moçambicana, FRELIMO), a political movement that had won independence for Mozambique in 1975. Initially used only to spy on guerrillas in neighboring Mozambique, RENAMO later expanded its activities to include destruction of INFRASTRUCTURE such as bridges and roads. It also began to terrorize Mozambique's rural population.

The first leader of RENAMO was André Matsangaíssa (d. 1979), a former FRELIMO soldier who had spent time in prison for car theft. Matsangaíssa was killed in battle and replaced by his deputy, Alfonso Dhlakama. By 1980 RENAMO had recruited between 1,000 and 2,000 men

The Mozambican Liberation Front (FRELIMO) fought for freedom from Portuguese colonial rule. FRELIMO rebels, like these shown training in neighboring Tanzania in 1965, finally achieved their goal in 1975. © AP/Wide World Photos

and operated mostly in the center of Mozambique, near the border of Rhodesia. When the white government of Rhodesia collapsed in 1980, RENAMO lost its greatest supporter. Soon after, however, SOUTH AFRICA increased its support, allowing RENAMO to continue its activities. South Africa's interest in RENAMO was related to Mozambique's government's support of UMKHONTO WE SIZWE, the military wing of the AFRICAN NATIONAL CONGRESS, which was seeking to overthrow South Africa's APARTHEID government.

In the early 1980s RENAMO opened multiple military fronts in Mozambique. This action expanded during the decade and caught FRELIMO largely unprepared. During this time the West offered RENAMO large amounts of international aid to help it counter the activities of FRELIMO, a pro-Marxist organization. This aid continued until the late 1980s, when several RENAMO massacres turned international opinion against the group.

Aid from the United States ended in 1988, after a State Department report claimed that RENAMO was responsible for the deaths of more than 100,000 civilians.

In the early 1990s FRELIMO's Joaquim Alberto CHISSANO (1939–), who became president of Mozambique in 1986, began peace talks with RENAMO. In 1992, in light of a new Mozambican constitution that instituted a multiparty political system, the two sides signed a peace agreement. RENAMO became an opposition political party, gradually increasing its political base and its share of seats in the Mozambican National Assembly.

See also: COLD WAR AND AFRICA (Vols. IV, V); COLONIAL RULE (Vol. IV); NATIONALISM AND INDEPENDENCE MOVEMENTS (Vol. IV); POLITICAL PARTIES AND ORGANIZATIONS (Vols. IV, V); PORTUGAL AND AFRICA (Vols. III, IV, V).

Further reading: William Finnegan, *A Complicated War: The Harrowing of Mozambique* (Berkeley, Calif.: University of California Press, 1992).

Mozambique Country located in southeast Africa that is bordered by MALAWI and TANZANIA to the north, the Indian Ocean to the east, SOUTH AFRICA and SWAZILAND to the south, and ZIMBABWE and ZAMBIA to the west. Mozambique has an area of about 297,800 square miles (771,300 sq km). While the coastal regions are generally low-lying, the central and northwestern areas of the interior rise to an elevation of 5,000 feet (1,524 m), with several higher points.

Mozambique at Independence In 1960 the responsibility for conducting the affairs of the Portuguese colony of Mozambique lay with a small but diverse group of Europeans, Asians, and African *assimilados*. (*Assimilados* was the term used to describe those Africans who were literate in Portuguese, had adopted European dress, and held mid-level jobs.) The disparity between this governing minority and the rest of Mozambique's population, and the harsh colonial rule that produced this gap formed the foundation for Mozambique's prolonged war of liberation and the troubled independence that followed.

The fight for national independence had its origins in the rebellion and resistance against Portuguese rule that continued into the early decades of the 20th century. By the 1940s the groundwork was being laid for the emergence of an organized nationalist movement focused on winning Mozambican independence.

From 1962 onward the drive for independence in Mozambique began to build, encouraged by successful rebellions in both ANGOLA and GUINEA-BISSAU, also Portuguese colonies at the time, as well as by the success of many of the former British and French colonies in gaining their independence. Portugal, however, refused to discuss independence for its colonies, leading many Mozambicans to take up armed struggle. Eventually several anticolonial political groups combined to form the MOZAMBICAN LIBERATION FRONT (Frente de Libertação de Moçambique, FRELIMO), in 1962. FRELIMO, led by Eduardo MONDLANE (1920–1969), soon began a violent insurgence campaign against Portuguese rule.

Under Mondlane and, later, under Samora MACHEL (1933–1986), FRELIMO used guerrilla military tactics to expand the territory under its control. Still the government of Portugal was determined to retain its colonial territory. However, in 1974 a disgruntled group within the Portuguese military, the Armed Forces Movement (AFM), led a successful COUP D'ÉTAT within Portugal itself. The AFM leaders were strongly against continuing colonial rule in Africa, and Portugal soon relinquished control of all its African possessions, including Mozambique. More than a decade after FRELIMO's war of resistance began, Mozambique finally gained independence on June 25, 1975.

At independence FRELIMO established a Marxist state and made other political parties illegal. FRELIMO aligned itself with the Soviet Union during the Cold War. Later FRELIMO supported the AFRICAN NATIONAL CONGRESS (ANC), which sought to overthrow the system of APARTHEID in neighboring SOUTH AFRICA. Both of these situations would greatly affect Mozambique's stability. Soon after independence a civil war began for control of the newly free Mozambique. This struggle was partially shaped by the international environment of the Cold War. With the Soviets backing FRELIMO, several other nations backed its rival the MOZAMBICAN NATIONAL RESISTANCE (Resistência Nacional Moçambicana, RENAMO). For example, until it became independent Zimbabwe in 1980, Rhodesia supported RENAMO. After 1980 South Africa, which saw the ANC as a common enemy, provided RENAMO with most of its support.

The vicious civil war plagued the first 10 years of Mozambican independence, which were also marked by economic turmoil. It is estimated that more than 1 million people died, with several million left as REFUGEES and internally displaced persons. At the same time, however, colonial modes of production and thinking were purged from the new state. For example, policies such as the forced cultivation of crops, forced LABOR, and racial discrimination were eliminated. Meanwhile a massive emigration of Portuguese colonists from Mozambique took place, weakening the INFRASTRUCTURE and economy, since many of those who fled were well trained and well paid.

In 1983 President Machel admitted that the socialist experiment in Mozambique was a failure and that Mozambique was in dire need of governmental reform. The prevailing FRELIMO commitment to communal farming and state-run AGRICULTURE had both alienated and angered farmers, some of whom called for the return of their land that had been appropriated by the state. In 1984 diplomatic talks were opened with South Africa; however, the talks were limited in their scope, resulting in agreements that were largely ignored. Machel's death in a mysterious plane crash, in 1986, only complicated matters.

Joaquim Alberto CHISSANO (1939–) succeeded Machel. Soon after, he began peace talks with RENAMO. In 1990 a new constitution was made, providing for a multiparty political system, a free-market economy, and unobstructed elections. The civil war finally ended in 1992, and by the middle of 1995 nearly 2 million refugees began returning to their homes. Facilitated by a successful United Nations peacekeeping mission, this massive return was the largest repatriation of people in the history of sub-Saharan Africa.

In 1994 Chissano retained the presidency by winning internationally supervised elections. His party, FRELIMO, also did well, winning the majority of seats contested for the national assembly. In 1998 Mozambique held its first local elections. However, RENAMO boycotted these elections, citing procedural flaws. Deciding to accommodate the opposition, the FRELIMO government agreed to international assistance in the elections. FRELIMO still dominated the elections for the National Assembly, and in 1998 Chissano was reelected. At the beginning of the 21st century, although it was beginning to show signs of economic growth, Mozambique was one of the world's least-developed nations.

See also: MOZAMBIQUE (Vols. I, II, III, IV); COLD WAR AND AFRICA (Vols. IV, V); CIVIL WARS (Vol. V); COLONIAL RULE (Vol. IV); INDEPENDENCE MOVEMENTS (Vol. V); PO-LITICAL PARTIES AND ORGANIZATIONS (Vol. V); PORTUGAL AND AFRICA (Vols. III, IV, V); SOVIET UNION AND AFRICA (Vols. IV, V).

Further reading: James Ciment, *Angola and Mozambique: Postcolonial Wars in Southern Africa* (New York: Facts on File, 1997); João M. Cabrita, *Mozambique: The Tortuous Road to Democracy* (New York: Palgrave, 2000).

On June 25, 1975, Mozambique's first president, Samora Machel, addressed a crowd assembled for Independence Day celebrations in Maputo. *© United Nations/Bob Van Lierop*

Mphahlele, Ezekiel (Es'kia Mphahlele, Bruno Eseki) (1919–) *South African writer, critic, and scholar of African literature*

Hailing from PRETORIA, SOUTH AFRICA, Mphahlele was a teacher—before being barred from the classroom for his anti-APARTHEID activism—and then a writer for JOHAN-NESBURG-based *Drum* magazine. In 1957 he went into self-imposed exile, going to the University of IBADAN, in NIGERIA, where he taught English literature. About the same time, he was writing his first major work, *Down Second Avenue,* which was published in 1959.

In Mphahlele's 1962 critical work, *The African Image,* he discusses both black and white African literature and calls on all African writers to shed their obsession with race relations to create characters with a more profound sense of humanity.

After the success of *Down Second Avenue,* Mphahlele worked as a staff writer, from 1961 to 1963, at the Paris-based *Présence Africaine,* a leading journal of the black consciousness movement called *négritude.* Throughout the 1960s Mphahlele traveled to universities in Africa, Europe, and the United States. He was a visiting scholar at the University of Denver, in the United States, from 1966 to 1968, during which time he earned a PhD in English literature. After lecturing for two years at the University of Nairobi, in KENYA, Mphahlele returned to teach in the United States, first at Denver, and then at the prestigious University of Pennsylvania. During this time, he wrote another autobiographical novel, *The Wanderers* (1971), which cemented his reputation as one of the foremost writers of African literature in English.

In 1977, tired of being a wanderer, Mphahlele returned to his native South Africa to teach at the University of the Witwatersrand, in Johannesburg, and to take part in the renaissance of black South African culture that was at hand. Into the 1980s he continued teaching and writing on literature and poetry before becoming professor emeritus at Witwatersrand in 1987.

See also: DRUM (Vol. IV); LITERATURE IN MODERN AFRICA (Vol. V); MPHAHLELE, EZEKIEL (Vol. IV); NÉGRI-TUDE (Vol. IV); URBAN LIFE AND CULTURE (Vols. IV, V).

Further reading: Es'kia Mphalele, et al., *Es'kia: Es-'kia Mphahlele on Education, African Humanism and Culture, Social Consciousness, Literary Appreciation* (Cape Town, South Africa: Kwela Books, 2003.)

MPLA See POPULAR MOVEMENT FOR THE LIBERATION OF ANGOLA.

Mswati III (1968–) *King and political head of Swaziland*

The son of King SOBHUZA II (1899–1982), Mswati was known as Prince Makhosetive before his coronation. The prince was educated in SWAZILAND and England, where he was living when he received news of the death of his father, who died, after 60 years of rule, in 1982. Swaziland was then ruled by a succession of regents until 1986, when Makhosetive was crowned as Mswati III.

In an effort to consolidate his power Mswati immediately disbanded the *liqoqo,* the traditional royal advisory group, and replaced a number of government officials. The king also publicly made the elimination of government CORRUPTION a priority of his administration. Despite his attempts, royal intrigue and conflict within the government remained characteristic of Mswati's rule.

In 2003 Mswati came under fire over his decision to choose an 18-year-old student as his tenth wife. The mother of the young woman accused Mswati of kidnapping her daughter.

Though Mswati's government has been troubled at times and often rendered ineffective by internal conflict, Swaziland continues to benefit from one of the stronger economies in Africa. In 1996, facing public pressure to make allowances for greater political freedom, Mswati established a constitutional commission to produce a revised constitution, replacing the one banned by Sobhuza II in 1973. Controversy and infighting prevailed, however, and as of 2003 the commission had yet to unveil a new constitution.

Mubarak, Hosni (1928–) *President of Egypt*

Mubarak was born in Kafr El-Meselha, EGYPT, in the same Nile Delta province as another Egyptian president, Anwar as-SADAT (1918–1981). After graduating from the National Military Academy in 1949, Mubarak began an illustrious military career in the Egyptian air force. He served first as a flight instructor, then as base commander, commander of the Air Force Academy, air force chief of staff, and, by 1972, commander in chief of the air force and deputy minister of war for Sadat's administration.

In 1973 Mubarak rose to international prominence by leading a victorious assault on Israeli forces on the east bank of the SUEZ CANAL, initiating another clash in the ongoing ARAB-ISRAELI WARS. Earning Sadat's trust and admiration, Mubarak was sent on diplomatic missions following an October cease-fire. Included in his itinerary were the direct negotiations with Israel that eventually led to the Camp David Peace Accords in 1978. During this time Sadat also named Mubarak vice president.

Mubarak's role in the government gradually increased until he virtually handled the day-to-day administration of the country. In 1980 he became vice chairman of the ruling National Democratic Party (NDP), a position that all but made him Sadat's successor to the presidency.

In 1981 Sadat was assassinated by Islamic fundamentalists. Slightly wounded in the attack, Mubarak was nominated by the NDP to assume the presidency. A week later, a voter referendum put Mubarak in office.

Mubarak moved immediately to crush the Islamic fundamentalist movement. An uprising in Asyut was put down and nearly 2,500 militant Islamists were imprisoned. Though Mubarak's actions were swift, radical Islamists who sought to undermine Egypt's secular government continued to be a threat. In 1995, while visiting the Ethiopian capital of ADDIS ABABA, Mubarak narrowly avoided an assassination attempt by Egyptian fundamentalists. The president responded with further arrests. By 1999 nearly 20,000 people had been imprisoned in an effort to extinguish the movement, and, the following year, the conflict was considered under control. TERRORISM, however, continues to be an issue for Mubarak's administration and a detriment to the Egyptian economy, which relies a great deal on TOURISM.

While struggling with Islamist opposition, Mubarak managed to make great strides both domestically and abroad. Through the 1980s and 1990s Mubarak initiated a number of economic reforms that resulted in consistent annual growth for the country. Mubarak also cracked down on CORRUPTION, purging the government of a number of officials from the Sadat administration.

In 1997, in what was termed Mubarak's "great pyramid" for Egypt, the president created the New Valley Canal project, an effort to transform portions of Egypt's large desert regions into farmland through the construction of a new canal.

In terms of foreign policy, Mubarak did much to reconnect Egypt with Arab neighbors alienated by Sadat's peace with Israel. He continued to foster strong relations with Western nations—including the United States—while also improving ties to the former Soviet Union. His decisive support of the Coalition forces in the first U.S.-Iraq conflict made Mubarak a prominent Arab leader in the eyes of the Western world.

Mubarak's reelection to the presidency in 1987, 1993, and 1999 attested to his success as president. In part, his longevity can be attributed to his ability to survive the ten assassination attempts that occurred during his time as president. However, Mubarak has clearly been a stabilizing force in Egypt and his administration has produced numerous beneficial results for the country. Of great concern for the Egyptian people is how much longer Mubarak will be able to serve in the role of the nation's leader. Seventy-six years old in 2004, and displaying some signs of infirmity, Mubarak had no clear successor.

See also: ISLAM, INFLUENCE OF (Vols. II, III, IV, V).

Mugabe, Robert (1924–) *First president of independent Zimbabwe*

Robert Gabriel Mugabe was born 1924 at the Roman Catholic Kutama Mission at Zvimba in what was then Southern Rhodesia (now ZIMBABWE). His mother was a teacher, and his father a carpenter at the mission. Educated initially in missionary schools, he completed his secondary and early college education through correspondence to qualify in 1941 as a secondary school teacher. After teaching for a few years he attended FORT HARE COLLEGE in SOUTH AFRICA, where he graduated with a BA in English and history in 1951. This was an eventful time in South Africa, for the National Party victory in 1948 led to APARTHEID. Fort Hare, which AFRICAN NATIONAL CONGRESS leaders such as Nelson MANDELA (1918–) and Oliver TAMBO (1917–1993) had attended, continued to educate leaders in the struggle for African rights in the face of the oppressive apartheid system.

Upon graduating from Fort Hare Mugabe returned to Southern Rhodesia to teach in government schools. Then in 1957 he went to GHANA to teach at a Catholic college. There he met Sally Heyfron (d. 1992), whom he later married. These were also the heady times of African independence. Ghana became independent that year under the leadership of the charismatic Kwame NKRUMAH (1909–1972), who had as a goal the liberation of the entire continent from colonial rule.

Mugabe was inspired by the socialist ideologies of Nkrumah and others in the first generation of African leaders at independence. He returned home in 1960 at a time when Rhodesia's white government was moving increasingly rightward and becoming ever more repressive. Ian SMITH (1919–) was soon to form the Rhodesian Front, and in 1965 he issued a UNILATERAL DECLARATION OF INDEPENDENCE that severed Rhodesia's ties with Britain.

Back home Mugabe became involved in politics. He worked as the publicity secretary and a youth organizer for the National Democratic Party (NDP), which demanded majority rule without sharing power with the white minorities. The government soon banned the NDP, but within a short time the ZIMBABWE AFRICAN PEOPLES' UNION (ZAPU), led by the moderate Joshua NKOMO (1917–1999), emerged in its place. Within a few months,

however, the government also banned ZAPU. Denied the right to engage publicly in politics, nationalist leaders such as Nkomo, Ndabaningi SITHOLE (1920–2000), and Mugabe moved to TANZANIA. Their political disagreements, however, led Mugabe and Sithole to break with Nkomo and establish the ZIMBABWE AFRICAN NATIONAL UNION (ZANU). Mugabe and other movement participants soon returned to Southern Rhodesia, where they were arrested. For the government the arrests signaled the end of the nationalist movement, especially its more militant elements.

For the next 10 years Mugabe was in detention. He used part of his time to earn two more degrees, both by correspondence. He also remained involved with leadership of ZANU. Soon after his release from prison, Mugabe became the chairman of ZANU.

Mugabe has had uneasy alliances with other nationalist leaders. Since the early years of struggle against the white-minority regime and continuing after independence, he and Nkomo formed several different alliances. In 1976 they created the PATRIOTIC FRONT to strengthen the political and military effort to end white-minority rule. Their alliance continued through the elections of 1980, which resulted in Mugabe becoming the first prime minister of independent ZIMBABWE. Eventually, however, Mugabe's ZANU co-opted and neutralized ZAPU, creating ZANU-PF.

Mugabe's early post-independence politics focused on strategic reconciliation, though within the rubric of a centralized one-party state. He reached out to the minority whites by guaranteeing them their property rights and shared political power with the minority Ndebele, who supported ZAPU. However, within a decade of independence Zimabwe's economy was declining, and it became embroiled in the regional conflict of the Democratic Republic of the CONGO.

In the midst of a growing crisis and Mugabe's declining popularity, the simmering controversy over land distribution came to the fore. In 2000, veterans of the Zimbabwean war for independence, with support from Mugabe, renewed their efforts at reclaiming land that was taken by the white minority under British colonization; more than one-third of Zimbabwe's arable land was owned by 4,000 whites. Despite losing a popular referendum that would have allowed land seizures without compensation, Mugabe has continued to support the land-taking. By August 2002 Mugabe had taken a hardline position, ordering all white commercial farmers to leave their land without compensation.

Mugabe's support for the squatters and his repressive rule led to foreign sanctions against Zimbabwe. Once heralded as a champion of the anticolonial movement, Mugabe became viewed by many in the international community as an authoritarian leader who was responsible for egregious HUMAN RIGHTS abuses and the continued decline of Zimbabwe's economy.

See also: COLONIAL RULE (Vol. IV); INDEPENDENCE MOVEMENTS (Vol. V); MISSIONARIES (Vols. IV, V); NATIONALISM AND INDEPENDENCE MOVEMENTS (Vol. IV); SOUTHERN RHODESIA (Vol. IV); STATE, ROLE OF (Vol. V).

Further reading: Stephen Chan, *Robert Mugabe: A Life of Power and Violence* (Ann Arbor, Mich.: University of Michigan Press, 2003); Martin Meredith, *Mugabe: Power and Plunder in Zimbabwe* (Oxford, U.K.: Public Affairs, 2002).

multinational corporations (MNCs) Firms that have direct investments and trade in two or more countries. Such companies can provide opportunities for economic growth. At the same time, however, they can distort local economies while ravaging the environment and ignoring HUMAN RIGHTS. Since MNCs are intended, first and foremost, to play an economic role, they commonly are viewed as a positive force in poor countries because they invest money from wealthy countries. Also, they can create jobs and improve terms of trade. New tax revenues from multinational corporations create economic opportunities for state expansion and investment. MNCs invest in the development of INFRASTRUCTURE, helping to improve roads, schools, electricity, and WATER RESOURCES in an effort to ensure a continued base of commerce. At their best they develop human capital and raise the quality of life for many. PepsiCo, for instance, has 142,000 employees and operates in virtually every country in the world. In 2002 it had more than $25 billion in sales. That is more than the total gross domestic product (the combined value of a nation's goods and services) of 38 of Africa's 54 countries. In SOUTH AFRICA alone the beverage company PepsiCo provides, directly or indirectly, tens of thousands of jobs. It also has programs for environmental protection, wastewater and effluent treatment, and pollution monitoring, as well as social programs such as those for combating HIV/AIDS.

Yet, despite the economic opportunities MNCs create, they are sharply criticized for their business practices. For instance, Ramatex, an Asian textile giant, insisted on pollution-control exemptions as a condition of doing business in NAMIBIA. The Namibian government chose to forego environmental standards in favor of job creation. The result has been alarmingly high levels of pollution and water use in a country where water is one of the scarcest NATURAL RESOURCES. In NIGERIA Shell Oil was accused of using its influence with the government to force the arrest of writer and activist Ken SARO-WIWA (1941–1995). After bringing attention to the environmental damage and human misery caused by Shell Oil operations, in 1995 Saro-Wiwa and a group of human rights activists were involved a clash with pro-government forces. Ultimately, he and eight colleagues were arrested and executed.

MNCs have entered into job creation agreements with host governments that lead to unconscionable human rights abuses verging on indentured servitude and child slavery. Other critics point out the disruptive influence MNCs have over the government and foreign policy of their home countries. The United States regularly works to ensure a market for U.S. goods. This has led to development projects for purchasing products that are not cost-effective, not price-competitive, or not most appropriate for the task at hand. The U.S. government, in particular, exerts its influence worldwide on behalf of its corporations. Indeed, the country stands accused of favoring the interests of American corporate lobbies at the expense of the economies of the countries involved.

At the heart of the criticism lies an imbalance of power that dates to the colonial era. The budgets of today's MNCs are often larger than the entire economy of their host countries. In these situations MNCs might be the largest employers and stand to provide the most economic opportunities. For countries in sub-Saharan Africa, they provide the most valuable, if not the only, significant link to the changing transnational world. Thus they wield tremendous power.

Yet, as argued by Nobel Prize-winning economist Milton Friedman (1912–　　), a company's only role is to maximize profits for shareholders, not to provide for the social good. At their worst MNCs can actually fuel conflict. MNC operations in Africa led critics to accuse corporations of complicity in unseemly activities, from human rights abuses to fueling CIVIL WARS. In an extreme case, the DeBeers MINING company purchased diamonds from LIBERIA even after it became clear they were actually "conflict diamonds" from rebels in SIERRA LEONE. DeBeers also purchased diamonds from ANGOLA, even when it was clear the profits from the sale supported Jonas SAVIMBI (1934–2002) in his efforts to destabilize the Angolan government. Indeed, these conflicts could not have continued if DeBeers had stopped providing a source of revenue. On the other side of the conflict the Angolan government received tax revenue from multinational British Petroleum. Clearly, in the globalized economy of the 21st century, MNCs are both bane and blessing.

See also: ECONOMIC ASSISTANCE (Vol. V), EXPORTS (Vol. V), INDUSTRIALIZATION (Vol. V), TRADE AND COMMERCE (Vol. V).

Further reading: Kenneth A. Rodman, *Sanctions Beyond Borders: Multinational Corporations and U.S. Economic Statecraft* (Lanham Md.: Rowman & Littlefield, 2001); Mark Casson, *Multinational Corporations* (Hants, U.K.: Edward Elgar Pub., 1990).

Muluzi, Bakili (1943–　　) *President of Malawi*

Born under British colonial rule in what was then Nyasaland, Elson Bakili Muluzi received his early education in the colony before traveling to Denmark and Britain for college. When Nyasaland became independent MALAWI in 1964, Muluzi became a court clerk and later received a parliamentary appointment. He quickly became an influential member of the Malawi Congress Party (MCP), led by President Hastings Kamuzu BANDA (c. 1898–1997). In 1982, however, Muluzi fell out of favor and withdrew from politics for a time. He resurfaced in 1993, leading the new UNITED DEMOCRATIC FRONT (UDF), which had formed after Banda's autocratic, one-party government had finally given way to pressure for a multiparty system. In the 1994 elections Muluzi and the UDF enjoyed strong support in the populous southern region of Malawi and beat out Banda and the MCP.

After some minor conflicts the UDF formed a coalition government with the Alliance for Democracy, which held sway in northern Malawi. As president, Muluzi focused on the dismal economy and health care situations in Malawi, one of the world's poorest nations. Roughly 65 percent of the population lived below the POVERTY line, and many died each month from complications arising from constant hunger. In addition about 15 percent of the adult population was infected with HIV/AIDS by 2003. Muluzi moved to privatize AGRICULTURE and encourage private investment to boost the economy, but the country still relies heavily on outside ECONOMIC ASSISTANCE.

Despite his announced commitment to improving Malawi's economy, in 1999, Muluzi married his second wife in an extravagant ceremony costing thousands of dollars of public money.

Muluzi was reelected in 1999 amid accusations of fraud. However, despite his efforts to revise the country's constitution, Muluzi was denied his attempt to run for a third term in 2004. At the end of Muluzi's administration Malawi still faced dramatic food shortages and government CORRUPTION, which has led some foreign donors to hold back much-needed aid.

See also: HIV/AIDS AND AFRICA (Vol. V).

Museveni, Yoweri (1944–   ) President of Uganda

An influential figure in the tumultuous history of post-independence UGANDA, Yoweri Kaguta Museveni was born to TUTSI parents in Ntungamo, in the southwestern region of the country. His education was superior to that of many Ugandans at the time, and he graduated from the University College in DAR ES SALAAM, TANZANIA, in 1970. He then found employment as a research assistant for the administration of then prime minister, Milton

OBOTE (1925–   ). The following year, however, Obote was overthrown in a COUP D'ÉTAT led by Major General Idi AMIN (c. 1925–2003), and Museveni was forced into exile in Tanzania.

There Museveni plotted a return to Uganda to unseat the new dictator, founding an army called the Front for National Salvation (FRONASA). In preparation for a campaign against Amin, FRONASA trained in MOZAMBIQUE along with the guerilla group known as the MOZAMBICAN LIBERATION FRONT. Museveni also drew inspiration from Tanzanian president Julius NYERERE (1922–1999), whose socialist ideals greatly influenced Museveni's later political career.

In 1978, in an ill-advised maneuver, Idi Amin ordered a surprise military incursion into Tanzania. FRONASA joined forces with rebel supporters of Milton Obote, forming the Uganda National Liberation Front (UNLF), and the UNLF joined Tanzanian troops in a counterassault, invading Uganda. By April 1979 the coalition troops had captured the capital of KAMPALA and sent Amin fleeing to LIBYA.

As a leader of the new Military Commission, Museveni served as defense minister for a succession of short-lived presidential administrations. In 1980 he formed a political party, the Uganda Patriotic Movement, but lost the presidential elections held that year to Milton Obote of the Uganda People's Congress. Convinced the results were fraudulent, Museveni separated from the government and formed his own personal militia, the National Resistance Army (NRA), which sought to overthrow the president. The Obote government gradually became as oppressive as Amin's, and in 1985 a military coup removed Obote and brought Basilio Okello (1929–1990) to power. Turmoil and violence continued to wrack Uganda as Museveni and Okello attempted to negotiate a peace. However, in 1986 the NRA captured Kampala and sent Okello into exile. Museveni then assumed the presidency.

Museveni immediately set about the task of closing the rifts that had divided Uganda since its independence from colonial rule, costing the lives of nearly 400,000 of its citizens. He eliminated all political parties save for the NRA, and formed a group of "resistance committees," which were responsible for security and for unmasking CORRUPTION. He made taming the military one of his priorities, though he has not been wholly successful in eliminating the random acts of violence that were characteristic of Ugandan military rule under Amin and Obote.

Convinced that Uganda's divisiveness was a result of forming political parties along religious, regional, and ethnic lines, in 1989 Museveni declared presidential elections would be conducted in a "no-party" format. Candidates ran as individuals, not sponsored by any political entity. Though this system was naturally advantageous to

Museveni, who won easily, the elections went smoothly and confirmed the wisdom of the president's idea. In 2001 the no-party system was used again, although amid great controversy, with Museveni again winning.

Uganda under Museveni improved dramatically, especially considering its war-torn early years. The economy grew steadily, aided by the general peace and Museveni's free-market policies. The expansion of the economy was also helped by the return of the Asian business owners who had been so integral to the nation's economy before Idi Amin drove them out in 1971. State-run EDUCATION also improved, and Uganda made significant strides in reducing the spread of HIV/AIDS.

However, the specter of Uganda's past still haunts the nation. Armed militias in northern and western Uganda have ties to other rebels in both RWANDA and the Democratic Republic of the CONGO, threatening Uganda's tenuous peace. Reports of kidnapping, torture, and abuse have been rising once again. The rebel threat has had a negative effect on TOURISM and other aspects of the economy.

In 1990 Tutsi rebels based in Uganda began incursions into Rwanda in an attempt to take down the government of Rwanda's HUTU president, Juvenal HABYARIMANA (1937–1994). Led by Museveni's longtime ally, Paul KAGAME (1957–), the Tutsi rebels called themselves the RWANDAN PATRIOTIC FRONT (Front Patriotique Rwandais, RPF). In 1994, as the rebels closed in on KIGALI, the capital, Habyarimana was assassinated, probably by RPF agents. His murder infuriated Rwanda's Hutu population, sparking what would become one of the most brutal genocides in history.

A 2000 amnesty bill for rebels who gave up their weapons failed to produce any results; a 2002 military offensive against the anti-government groups also failed. As Uganda's population grew at one of the world's fastest rates, Museveni faced the massive challenge of holding the nation together as he approached the end of his final term, in 2006.

See also: CIVIL WARS (Vol. V); HIV/AIDS AND AFRICA (Vol. V).

Further reading: Ondoga ori Amaza, *Museveni's Long March from Guerrilla to Statesman* (Kampala, Uganda: Fountain Publishers, 1998).

music Music continues to be an important facet of contemporary Africa. As many areas of the continent have become more urbanized and intimately linked to other regions of the world, Africa's music has evolved, reflecting these changes. The wide contact Africa enjoys with other continents and their cultures has facilitated a lively exchange of cultural expressions, particularly in the field of music. Just as African rhythms have exercised an enormous impact on musical forms all over the world, the influence of electric instruments from the West and popular music from the Middle East and the West have transformed both the shape of African music and the instruments on which it is played. The reciprocal nature of this process is evident: over the last three decades, the appeal of African popular music has extended well beyond the continent's shores.

Africa is host to many kinds of music, most of which are an admixture of different sources, across geographic regions and time. Music in Africa today represents a complicated and rich interplay between musical forms that are sometimes misleadingly conceptualized as overly polarized: traditional and modern, indigenous and foreign, religious and secular, etc. While, indeed, a clash of styles, approaches, values, and even world views is often discernible in the music of many countries, the boundaries that separate different styles are generally more porous and fluid than often recognized.

Raï music serves to illustrate some of these tendencies. *Raï*, which is popular among the youth of North Africa, mixes Arabic music with Western popular music. Initially, *raï* was a form of traditional Algerian music, sung by women. But since the late 1970s it has transformed its origins and appeal. It is popular with young people throughout North Africa, and commands a growing audience worldwide. Cheb Mami (1966–) and Cheb Khaled (1960–), both from ALGERIA, are its most widely known proponents. Khaled, who now is known by simply by his surname, electrified *raï* and served as its leading pioneer in its formative years. Because *raï*'s subject matter and lyrics often focus on secular issues, such as romance and alcohol consumption, Muslim authorities have sought to limit its appeal. The tensions between conservative Islamic forces and *raï* musicians, who detractors regard as purveyors of secularism, Western influence, and immorality, came to a head in 1994, when Cheb Hasni (1968–1994), a popular raï artist, was killed in Oran, Algeria by religious fundamentalists. Not surprisingly, Mami, Khaled, and other prominent *raï* musicians reside in the freer, more hospitable cultural climate that Paris affords.

In fact, many of Africa's most famous musicians live abroad in Western centers such as Paris, London, and New York. Sometimes, African musical artists who have large followings in their home countries are relatively unknown abroad, and those most celebrated in international musical circles do not enjoy the same elevated status at home. As well, such mainstays of Western popular music, such as Sade (born Helen Folasade Adu) (1959–) and

Dave Matthews (1967–), born in IBADAN, NIGERIA and JOHANNESBURG, SOUTH AFRICA respectively, although African by birth, are deeply rooted in the West, where they matured musically. Other musicians, such as Babatunde Olatunji (1927–2003) and Manu Dibango (1933–) have spent large portions of their productive careers abroad. In the case of Olatunji, despite growing up in Nigeria, he studied, lived, and worked in the United States beginning in 1950, collaborating with many important recording artists, including Carlos Santana (1947–), Mickey Hart (1943–), and the Grateful Dead.

Again, highlighting the reciprocity involved in the transfer of music and musicians between Africa and other continents and the resultant cross-fertilization, a number of Western artists have tapped into the vitality and innovation of African music, to their decided benefit. Paul Simon (1941–) rejuvenated his career as a result of his Grammy Award-winning *Graceland* album. In a controversial move at the time, he flouted the ban on recording with South African musicians, working with LADYSMITH BLACK MAMBAZO and other South African artists. In 1994 Ry Cooder (1947–) produced an album jointly with Malian Ali Farka Touré (1939–) entitled *Talking Timbuktu* and it too won a Grammy Award. Peter Gabriel (1950–) has done much to promote African and World Beat music, most notably his collaborative work with Youssou N'DOUR (1959–) of SENEGAL. In 2000 Sting (born Gordon Matthew Sumner) (1951–) scored a success with his song "Desert Rain," with the haunting chanting of Cheb Mami in the background.

Although a number of African recording artists have achieved mainstream commercial success both in Africa and in markets abroad, record sales and playing time on radio and music video programs are not necessarily the best barometer for measuring relative popularity or prestige. Record labels generally focus on African musicians who might appeal to the tastes of Western consumers, so that many of Africa's finest musicians remain unrecorded, or their music lacks adequate promotion. Included among the most widely recognized African artists of the last three or four decades would be: Ladysmith Black Mambazo and Miriam MAKEBA (1932–) of South Africa, FELA (1938–1997) and King Sunny ADE (1946–) of Nigeria, Manu Dibango of CAMEROON, Salif KEITA (1949–) of Mali, Youssou N'Dour of Senegal, Angelique Kidjo (1960–) of BENIN, Papa Wemba (1953–) and Tabu Ley Rochereau (1940–) of Democratic Republic of the CONGO, and Cesaria EVORA (1941–) of the Republic of CAPE VERDE.

Most of these musicians belong to one or more of Africa's many distinct musical genres, and are usually the most popular representatives of their respective genres. Ladysmith Black Mambazo has achieved worldwide fame as the preeminent *isicathamiya* vocal group. *Isicathamiya* (literally meaning "to step on one's toes lightly") is a

capella choral music from South Africa, common among the country's ZULU population. Miriam Makeba, Africa's most readily recognizable female singer over the last four and a half decades, sings in a variety of styles, but clearly draws upon her XHOSA heritage, most notably in her famous hit, "The Click Song." The Nigerian musician Fela developed a distinctive sound that fused West African rhythms with American jazz. He dubbed his energetic, at times hypnotic music, Afrobeat, a classification that today is applied to other Nigerian bands and musicians, including his son, Femi Kuti (1962–). By contrast, his fellow countryman King Sunny Ade produces a much more mellow, almost seductive sound. It lacks the hard edge or the political radicalism of Kuti's music, although both musicians emerged out of the highlife music tradition, which took shape in Nigeria and GHANA during the late 19th century and gained great popularity in the 1960s. Ade's musical style, combining complex, multilayered percussion with synchronized vocal harmonies and backed by synthesizers, electric keyboards, and electric and pedal steel guitars, is usually termed *juju*.

The popular dance music of Cameroon known as *makossa* has been honed by its main ambassador, Manu Dibango, a saxophonist, who has enjoyed an illustrious career in Africa, Europe, America, and the Caribbean. Salif Keita blends several musical styles together, including rock, jazz, Afro-Cuban rhythms, and Islamic music to produce what could be termed Afro-pop. Drawing on many of the same sources, Youssou N'Dour has popularized *mbalax,* a unique blend of Senegalese percussion music, mixed with Western pop and the rhythms of Cuba. Like Keita and N'Dour, Angelique Kidjo also borrows heavily from Western popular music, especially rock n' roll and funk. Her hard, driving music, sung in several languages, including her mother tongue of Fon, has proven particularly popular in France. Papa Wemba and Tabu Ley Rochereau are just two of the many musicians of central Africa associated with *soukous,* a style characterized by large guitar bands accompanied by Afro-Cuban rhythms, especially the rhumba. *Morna* is a style closely associated with Cesaria Evora, whose doleful songs, nostalgically lamenting failed relationships and homesickness have captured worldwide acclaim. She sings in Creole, Portuguese, and French, and is accompanied by guitar, clarinet, violin, and accordion.

It is instructive to note how many African musical styles have drawn upon traditions from various parts of the globe, where the impact of African peoples made itself felt centuries earlier as a result of the African diaspora. For instance reggae, which evolved as a musical genre in Jamaica among persons of African descent, has over time come to influence African musicians, owing in large part to the dynamism and genius of Bob Marley (1945–1981). Not only has reggae found its way into the African music scene, some African reggae artists have emerged in recent years, most notably South Africa's Lucky Dube (1964–   ). Similarly, American rhythm and blues, rock 'n' roll, and gospel, which all owe a large debt to their African origins, have profoundly altered African music. African musicians have also made significant contributions to the quintessentially African American genre of music known as jazz. Hugh MASEKELA (1931–   ), a South African-born trumpeter, left South Africa in the early 1960s to pursue a career abroad, achieving international recognition for his virtuosity. He succeeded in creating a distinctive sound, blending bebop jazz with African musical forms. Even before entering self-imposed exile, Masekela had gained fame within his homeland as a member of the Jazz Epistles, which included Kippie Moeketsi (1925–1983) and Abdullah IBRAHIM (1934–   ) (originally known as Dollar Brand). Ibrahim, a pianist and composer, has also built an international following. As with Masekela, although Ibrahim's music is classified within the idiom of American jazz, it is still rooted in a distinctively South African musical tradition.

Some critics warn that the crossover music many of Africa's most renowned musicians have embraced, bridging two or more different musical traditions, will lead to the westernization of African music and the eventual disappearance of authentic African musical genres.

See also: ENGLAND AND AFRICA (Vols. III, IV, V); FON (Vols. III, IV); FRANCE AND AFRICA (Vols. III, IV, V); MUSIC (Vols. I, II, III, IV); UNITED STATES AND AFRICA (Vols. IV, V); URBAN LIFE AND CULTURE (Vols. IV, V); URBANIZATION (Vols. IV, V).

Further reading: Sean Barlow & Banning Eyre, *Afropop!: An Illustrated Guide to Contemporary African Music* (Edison, N.J.: Chartwell Books, 1995); John Storm Roberts, *Black Music of Two Worlds: African, Caribbean, Latin, and African-American Traditions*, 2nd ed. (New York: Schirmer Books, 1998); Frank Tenaille, *Music is the Weapon of the Future: Fifty Years of African Popular Music* (Chicago: Lawrence Hill Books, 2002) Norman C. Weinstein, *A Night in Tunisia: Imaginings of Africa in Jazz* (Metuchen, N.J.: Scarecrow Press, 1992).

Mutharika, Bingu wa See MALAWI.

Mutombo, Dikembe (1966–   ) *Basketball player from the Democratic Republic of the Congo*

Dikembe Mutombo was born June 25, 1966, in KINSHASA, capital of the Democratic Republic of the CONGO. He went to the United States to pursue a degree in MEDICINE at Georgetown University on an academic scholarship, though he later switched his major from premed and received a bachelor's degree with a double major in linguistics and diplomacy. While at Georgetown he

came to the attention of the basketball coach and was convinced to join the team. He became Georgetown's all-time leader in field-goal percentage and second all-time leader in blocked shots.

In 1991 Mutombo was drafted by the Denver Nuggets of the National Basketball Association (NBA) and stayed with the team for five seasons. He has since played for other teams, including the Atlanta Hawks, the Philadelphia 76ers, the New Jersey Nets, and the New York Knicks. Standing 7' 2" (2.18 m) tall and weighing approximately 265 pounds (115 kg), his physique is ideally suited to the center position. His superb ability to rebound and block shots has prompted sportswriters to call him one of the best centers in the NBA. He has been named Defensive Player of the Year a record four times. He has also been chosen to play in eight NBA All-Star games.

Off the court, Mutombo has distinguished himself for his tireless humanitarian efforts. He established the Dikembe Mutombo Foundation to carry out various assistance projects, most notably donating $3 million toward the construction of a hospital in his homeland. In 1999 he received a President's Service Award in recognition of his extraordinary commitment to volunteer work. On tours of Africa, he has served as a spokesperson for CARE and otherwise uses his high-profile status to assist fellow Africans.

In addition to his own two children, Mutombo and his wife have adopted four others. He also provides financial support for approximately 50 relatives. Mutombo speaks several African languages as well as English, French, Portuguese, and Spanish.

See also: SPORTS AND ATHLETICS (Vol. V).

Muzorewa, Abel (Bishop Abel Tendekayi Muzorewa) (1925–   ) *Zimbabwean minister and political leader*

Born in Umtali (today's Mutare), in the eastern highlands of colonial Southern Rhodesia (present-day ZIMBABWE), Abel Tendekayi Muzorewa studied to become a minister in the American-based United Methodist Church (UMC). Following his ordination in 1953 he worked in the UMC for five years before going to the United States under UMC sponsorship. In 1963 he was awarded a master's degree in theology.

Muzorewa returned home (to what was then RHODESIA) to find the country in political turmoil. In 1965 Rhodesia's white-minority government issued a UNILATERAL DECLARATION OF INDEPENDENCE from Great Britain. Within a year a guerrilla war was being waged to overthrow Ian SMITH (1919–   ) and his white-minority government. In the midst of these developments, in 1968 Muzorewa was promoted to UMC bishop and then elected to head the church in Rhodesia. It was the first time in the country's history that a major church had selected an African as its head.

Muzorewa continued his strong links with the American Methodists. In 1980, Morningside College, a Methodist-affiliated college in Sioux City, Iowa, awarded him an honorary doctorate. At least four members of his family attended Morningside, with the most recent one graduating in 1995.

In 1971 Britain reached an agreement with the breakaway Rhodesian government to end sanctions in return for a commitment to a gradual transition to majority rule. Africans, however, were pressing for immediate majority rule. In light of the situation, Muzorewa co-founded the African National Council to mobilize opposition to the proposed British agreement with Smith. Though essentially a moderate nationalist movement, the African National Council for a short time became an umbrella organization for even the more activist Zimbabwean nationalist movements. Leaders of these movements included Ndabaningi SITHOLE (1920–2000), Robert MUGABE (1924–) of the ZIMBABWE AFRICAN NATIONAL UNION, and Joshua NKOMO (1917–1999) of the ZIMBABWE AFRICAN PEOPLE'S UNION.

The African National Council coalition soon broke down, however, with the guerrilla forces of Mugabe and Nkomo fully committed to a national war of liberation, which Muzorewa rejected. In 1978 Muzorewa, Sithole, and Smith signed an internal agreement that changed Rhodesia's name to "Zimbabwe Rhodesia" and provided for elections the following year. When the African National Council won the elections, Muzorewa became the prime minister. However, real power, including control over the army and the police, remained in the hands of Smith and the white minority.

Denounced by the guerrilla movements, Zimbabwe Rhodesia proved to be a short-lived experiment. The guerilla armies discredited Muzorewa as a nationalist leader and, with each victory on the battlefields, turned the tide in their favor. When the various warring factions signed the Lancaster House Agreement in September 1979, the independent state of Zimbabwe was created. Elections in 1980 essentially ended Muzorewa's political role in the country, though he was elected to Parliament. In 1996 Muzorewa challenged Mugabe for the presidency but received less than 5 percent of the vote.

See also: CHRISTIANITY, INFLUENCE OF (Vols. IV, V); INDEPENDENCE MOVEMENTS (Vol. V); NATIONALISM AND INDEPENDENCE MOVEMENTS (Vol. IV); SOUTHERN RHODESIA (Vol. IV).

Mwanawasa, Levy (Levy Patrick Mwanawasa)
(1948–) *Third president of Zambia, taking office in 2002*

Born in the MINING town of Mufulira, in Zambia's Copperbelt, Mwanawasa was one of 10 children. In a country where ethnicity plays an important role, he came from the Lenje ethnic group, one of the smaller groups in ZAMBIA. In 1973 Mwanawasa graduated from the University of Zambia with a law degree. After graduation he worked for private law firms until 1978, when he formed his own firm, Mwanawasa & Company. Mwanawasa served as Zambia's solicitor general from 1985 to 1986, but he returned to private practice the following year. In 1989 he became the first Zambian lawyer to be appointed an advocate and solicitor for the Supreme Court of England and Wales.

In March 1991 the Zambian president, Frederick CHILUBA (1943–), named Mwanawasa his vice president. That same year Mwanawasa was involved in a serious automobile accident that resulted in the death of his assistant. Opposition candidates used the accident against Mwanawasa, claiming that he had suffered brain damage and was unfit to hold political office. He resigned from the vice presidency in 1994 and accused Chiluba's government of CORRUPTION.

In 1996 Mwanawasa failed in a bid to gain the presidency of Zambia's ruling party, the MOVEMENT FOR MULTIPARTY DEMOCRACY (MMD). In 2001, however, the MMD national executive committee, led by Chiluba, nominated Mwanawasa as the its presidential candidate. Mwanawasa won a close election, defeating the runner-up, Anderson Mazoka (1945–), by less than 2 percent. Many objected to his inauguration, however, and opposition candidates, led by Mazoka, asked the Supreme Court to nullify the results and force a recount. Despite observers from the European Union having reported irregularities in the balloting, the Supreme Court rejected the petition by the opposition candidates. Mwanawasa was sworn in as president of Zambia on January 2, 2002. Because Chiluba had handpicked Mwanawasa, people expected Mwanawasa to be beholden to the former president. These critics were surprised when Mwanawasa allowed an inquiry into past indiscretions by Chiluba, who later lost his presidential immunity and was tried for embezzling public funds. The decision brought Mwanawasa new respect and his popularity increased as he vowed to continue his anti-corruption campaign, stating: "There will not be two sets of laws, one for the leadership and one for the citizens. If a leader transgresses the law, he will be punished."

See also: COPPERBELT (Vol. IV).

Mwinyi, Ali Hassan (1925–) *Former president of Tanzania*

Born in Kivure, Tanganyika, Ali Hassan Mwinyi moved to ZANZIBAR, where he trained as a teacher. Later he went to England where he earned a degree from the University of Durham in 1956. Mwinyi returned to Zanzibar and worked as a teacher and rose to the position of principal of the Zanzibar Teacher Training College. A devout Muslim, he was also a member of the AFRO-SHI-RAZI PARTY, the nationalist party that led Zanzibar to independence in 1963. He left the teaching profession in 1964 to become permanent secretary to the minister of EDUCATION in Zanzibar. He served in several political positions including minister of health, ambassador to EGYPT, and vice president. In April 1984 Mwinyi was elected president of Zanzibar. As such, according to the Tanzanian constitution, he also became Tanzania's vice president. As president of Zanzibar he introduced economic reforms that were more liberal than the socialist policies of President Julius NYERERE (1922–1999). He was viewed as a moderate, which made him a preferred candidate to be Nyerere's successor. Mwinyi also gained popularity in Zanzibar for bringing forth a new constitution there, strengthening the union with mainland Tanzania while affirming the autonomy of the islands.

Nyerere chose Mwinyi as the sole candidate the PARTY OF THE REVOLUTION (known by its Swahili name of Chama Cha Mapinduzi, CCM) to replace him. Although Mwinyi was the only candidate, both he and Nyerere campaigned vigorously to ensure the support of the majority of the people. As a result he received more than 90 percent of the vote. As the country's president, he inherited serious economic problems from Nyerere's socialist era including poor INFRASTRUCTURE, shortage of goods, and FOREIGN DEBT totaling approximately $3 billion.

In order to secure some debt relief Mwinyi agreed to abandon socialist principles and follow the conditions of the INTERNATIONAL MONETARY FUND. As a result, in 1986, Tanzanian's major donors rescheduled the bulk of the country's loans. In the same year, using a loan from the IMF, he introduced a three-year economic recovery plan. In 1989 he introduced the country's second national DEVELOPMENT plan. The following year, in October, Mwinyi was elected to a second term and also became chair of the ruling CCM when Nyerere relinquished the position. Two years into his second term Mwinyi initiated the transition to a multiparty state in response to internal and international pressure to reform the one-party system. Mwinyi served as president until 1995 and is credited with liberalizing the economy and reintroducing the multiparty system. His successor as president was Benjamin MKAPA (1938–   ), who came from the mainland.

See also: DEMOCRATIZATION (Vol. V).

Nairobi Capital city of KENYA and major urban center in the fertile central highlands of East Africa. Nairobi is located midway between MOMBASA, on the Indian Ocean, and Kisumu, on the shores of Lake VICTORIA. Founded in 1899 as a camp for railroad workers, Nairobi became the colonial capital in 1905, and it remained the capital when Kenya gained its independence, in 1963. It is home of the University of Nairobi, founded in 1956, and it came to host other institutions, including the Kenya Polytechnic (1961), the Kenya Institute of Administration (1961), Kenyatta University College (1972), the national museum, and the national theater.

By 1963 Nairobi already was the major commercial, industrial, and economic center for East Africa. Its role has since expanded, with industries producing cigarettes, processed foods, textiles, building materials, communication and TRANSPORTATION equipment, and beverages. It also ships agricultural products from the surrounding area to coastal Mombasa for export. As Nairobi is well connected by road, rail, and air to all major stops in East Africa—and within one day's drive from three of the most popular wild-game reserves—the city boasts a strong TOURISM industry.

With its temperate climate and cosmopolitan atmosphere, Nairobi continued to grow rapidly after independence. Soon, the POPULATION GROWTH overwhelmed the WATER RESOURCES and housing facilities, and shantytowns sprang up in the shadows of the city's modern skyscrapers. In 1962 the population was an estimated 266,800, but by 2002 the greater Nairobi area was home to more than 3 million residents. During this same time span, the Asian and European minority percentage of the population dropped from 40 percent to 4

percent, signaling Nairobi's transition from a colonial city to an African one.

The 45-square-mile (117-sq-km) Nairobi National Park is located about 4 miles (7 km) from the city's center and is thus easily accessible to visitors and locals alike. Much of East Africa's varied WILDLIFE, and nearly all of Kenya's major game animals except for elephants, can be seen in the park. Among its noteworthy features is a highly successful rhinoceros-breeding program.

See also: ASIAN COMMUNITIES (Vols. IV, V); BRITISH EAST AFRICA (Vol. IV); ENGLAND AND AFRICA (Vols. III, IV, V); NAIROBI (Vol. IV); URBAN LIFE AND CULTURE (Vols. IV, V); URBANIZATION (Vols. IV, V).

Namibia Mineral-rich, largely arid and semi-arid country located in southwest Africa, on the Atlantic Ocean. Namibia covers 318,300 square miles (824,400 sq km) and is bordered by ANGOLA, BOTSWANA, and SOUTH AFRICA. The most influential groups in Namibia include the Ovambo, who make up about 50 percent of the population, the HERERO, the Nama, and Afrikaner and German minorities. In 1990 Namibia became the last country in Africa to become independent.

Namibia as South West Africa Beginning 1915 Namibia—formerly German South West Africa—was

On March 21, 1990, Namibia finally achieved independence from South African rule. Following the hoisting of the Namibian flag, Sam Nujoma was sworn in as president by United Nations secretary-general Javier Perez de Cuellar. © *United Nations/J. Isaac*

ruled as a United Nations (UN) mandate by South Africa, whose established system of racial inequality slowed the progress toward independence. In the 1950s Namibians began organizing protests by any means possible, with African and mixed-race miners forming unions, holding strikes, and making vocal demands for civil rights.

In 1956 the Herero paramount chief, Hosea Kutako (1870–1970), succeeded in getting a representative to petition the United Nations for help. Although progress was still slowed by the bureaucratic foot-dragging of the South African government, INDEPENDENCE MOVE-MENTS were emerging all over the African continent, and it seemed that Namibian independence could not be far off.

In 1959 Namibians founded their own independence-minded political party, the South West Africa National Union (SWANU). It continued the UN petition process, called for better EDUCATION and health services for Africans, and demanded a more equitable distribution of the country's land and NATURAL RESOURCES. At the same time, SWANU began smuggling members across the border to British Bechuanaland (soon to be independent Botswana) to train as freedom fighters.

Despite the progress that SWANU was making toward independence, some Namibians felt that the organization was too accommodating to the South African government. Ovambo leader Sam NUJOMA (1929–   ) and members of his Ovamboland People's Organization broke from SWANU to create the SOUTH WEST AFRICAN PEOPLE'S ORGANIZATION (SWAPO), a more militant group that approached the independence movement with greater urgency. However, as they had done with SWANU, the South African government banned meetings and refused to recognize Nujoma's party.

In 1966, under mounting international pressure, the United Nations voted to revoke South Africa's mandate to govern SOUTH WEST AFRICA. South Africa, in turn, refused to recognize the UN action, and the movement toward independence lost momentum once again.

Having failed through peaceful, diplomatic means to meet their objectives, in 1966 SWAPO began an armed insurgency through their militant faction, the People's

Liberation Army of Namibia (PLAN). With the violence escalating in 1971, the UN Security Council took the reins in the negotiations for a peaceful transition to independence, officially recognizing SWAPO—which enjoyed broad support both in South West Africa and on the international stage—as the sole representative of the Namibian people. The United Nations then declared the South African occupation of South West Africa to be illegal and demanded that South Africa begin the dialogue for Namibian independence.

Throughout the late 1970s and into the 1980s the war for Namibian independence raged in both South West Africa and across the border, in Angola. PLAN, supported by both the MPLA and Cuban troops, continued its armed rebellion against white rule. The United Nations, meanwhile, continued to allow South Africa to defy its orders.

The war for liberation in Namibia was just one of many throughout southern Africa at the time. Inspired by the success of the POPULAR MOVEMENT FOR THE LIBERATION OF ANGOLA (Movimento Popular de Libertaçao de Angola, MPLA) large numbers of Namibian rebels began moving north to Angola, both to train and to launch offensives against South African troops posted along the border.

In 1986, after years of fraudulent negotiations and failed cease-fire agreements, South African troops from South West Africa moved into Angola. Over the next three years, the casualties on both sides continued to mount. By 1989 the futility of the situation finally became overwhelming for both sides. The United Nations brokered a cease-fire agreement and appointed a five-nation "Contact Group," which included the United States, to oversee independence negotiations between Namibian political parties and the South African government. Despite a few skirmishes, the cease-fire held, and elections were set for November. In voting that reflected Namibia's ethnic diversity, SWAPO emerged as the victorious party, with 57 percent of the votes, and Sam Nujoma became president of the Republic of Namibia. After creating a new constitution, Namibia declared its independence on March 21, 1990.

Since the first elections Nujoma's SWAPO, with its solid Ovambo electoral base, has increasingly dominated Namibian politics. Nujoma has proven to be a capable leader, directing a successful campaign of national reconciliation from his offices in WINDHOEK, Namibia's capital. The country still faces serious challenges, however, including an HIV/AIDS epidemic and long-standing disagreements regarding LAND USE and property rights.

See also: COLD WAR AND AFRICA (Vols. IV, V); CUBA AND AFRICA (Vol. V); HERERO (Vols. II, III, IV); INDEPENDENCE MOVEMENTS (Vol. V); NAMA (Vol. IV); OVAMBO (Vol. IV); UNITED NATIONS AND AFRICA (Vols. IV, V).

Nasser, Gamal Abdel (Gamal Abdul Nasser; Gamal Abdal Nasser) (1918–1970) *President of Egypt from 1954 to 1967*

Gamal Abdel Nasser's rise to the Egyptian presidency began with his participation in the 1952 military COUP D'É-TAT that removed the monarchy in EGYPT and set up a one-party, authoritarian state. Nasser became head of state in 1954 and began a sweeping program of land reform and economic and social DEVELOPMENT that Nasser called Arab Socialism. In addition, he nationalized heavy industry, giving oversight of production to a government ministry.

In the 1960s Nasser continued to implement his agenda of Arab socialism. In 1962 he nationalized the press, the CINEMA, THEATER, and BOOK PUBLISHING. He established a ministry of national guidance and a ministry of culture, which had authority over the media and controlled the public expression of ideas. Nasser even nationalized Cairo's influential al-Azhar University, Islam's oldest center of learning, and made it an arm of the government. This act infuriated many Muslims, especially those among the Muslim Brotherhood, which wanted an Islamic state to replace Nasser's secular regime.

Nasser's reforms often aimed at a redistribution of wealth. He made it illegal to own assets in excess of 10,000 Egyptian pounds. He returned rents to their 1944 level, benefiting small farmers. Further land reform measures broke up large corporate and individual estates, dividing them into smaller parcels of land that the government redistributed to the landless peasants. The government also established free EDUCATION programs and initiated health reform.

In terms of international affairs Nasser maintained a policy of nonalignment, or neutrality, even during the tensest moments of the Cold War between the Soviet and Western blocs. Nasser refused to take sides between the superpowers, often to the annoyance of the United States. When the United States refused Nasser's request to fund the construction of the ASWAN DAM, for example, he turned to the Soviet Union for financing. Built in the 1960s, the massive dam created additional farmland to be redistributed among the peasantry. Utilizing the electrical power generated by the dam, Nasser was able to build Egypt's industrial base. However, despite economic and social reform, inefficiency in the private and public sectors caused Egypt's economy to stagnate.

Nasser remained, like many Arab leaders, a vocal opponent of Israel and a strong supporter of Palestinian rights. However, Israel's quick defeat of Egyptian forces in the 1967 Six-Day War, one of a series of ARAB-ISRAELI

WARS, humiliated Egypt. As a result of this war Egypt lost the Gaza Strip and the Sinai Peninsula, which contained Egypt's richest OIL fields. Egypt also suffered a tremendous human loss, with 12,000 killed and 60,000 captured. Nasser took full responsibility for the defeat and offered to resign. However, Egyptians refused to accept Nasser's resignation. Nasser died of a heart attack in 1970. News of his death came as a shock to the Egyptian public, and millions turned out in CAIRO to view his funeral procession.

See also: ARAB WORLD AND AFRICA (Vol. V); COLD WAR AND AFRICA (Vol. IV); NASSER, GAMAL ABDEL (Vol. IV); NONALIGNED MOVEMENT (Vol. V).

Further reading: Dominique De Roux, *Gamal Abdel Nasser* (Lausanne, Switzerland: Age d'homme, 2000).

National Front for the Liberation of Angola (Frente Nacional de Libertação de Angola, FNLA)

Anticolonial movement founded in 1961 by Holden ROBERTO (1923–). The FNLA had its roots in the deep heritage and traditions of the Kongo people, who ruled the most important state in the region before the colonial era. As an organization, the FNLA emerged from the Union of Peoples of North Angola (UPNA), the political group that became the Union of Angolan People (União das Populações de Angola, UPA), in 1958. In 1961 a faction of the UPA led by Holden Roberto changed its name to the FNLA and began an armed insurrection against Portuguese colonial rule. Within a year of its founding the FNLA was sending rebels into ANGOLA from Kongo strongholds in what is now the Democratic Republic of the CONGO.

At times during the 1970s with the Cold War environment still shaping superpower decisions, both the United States Central Intelligence Agency and China supported the FNLA.

After Angola declared independence from Portugal in 1975, the FNLA soon faded away as a political and military force. Its leader, Roberto, went into exile, and its members joined the ranks of the remaining warring factions, which included the POPULAR MOVEMENT FOR THE LIBERATION OF ANGOLA and the NATIONAL UNION FOR THE TOTAL INDEPENDENCE OF ANGOLA. In the 1992 elections a reconstituted version of the FNLA attempted to regain power, but the movement received only a small percentage of the votes and dissolved once again.

See also: CHINA AND AFRICA (Vols. IV, V); COLD WAR AND AFRICA (Vol. V); COLONIAL RULE (Vol. IV); INDEPENDENCE MOVEMENTS (Vol. V); NATIONALISM AND INDEPENDENCE MOVEMENTS (Vol. IV); PORTUGAL AND AFRICA (Vols. III, IV, V); SOVIET UNION AND AFRICA (Vols. IV, V); UNITED STATES AND AFRICA (Vols. IV, V).

National Liberation Front (Front de Libération Nationale, FLN)

Long-time ruling party of ALGERIA that came to power after a prolonged armed struggle against French colonial rule. When Algeria achieved independence in 1962, the FLN faced the task of transforming itself from a liberation movement to a governing political party. There was considerable internal struggle and competition over the direction the party. Soon, however, Ahmed BEN BELLA (1916–), the country's prime minister emerged as the party's first leader. He had been the FLN's key political thinker during the war to oust the French. This made him a natural choice to head the party and the newly independent government it controlled. The following year Ben Bella became the country's president and instituted a one-party state with a political philosophy centered on socialism and pan-Arabism.

Although Ben Bella headed the party, he did not totally control it. In 1965 key FLN figures concluded that Ben Bella was seeking to garner too much power, and defense minister Houari BOUMEDIENNE (1927–1978) led a successful COUP D'ÉTAT to unseat Ben Bella. The FLN continued as Algeria's sole legal party, a position that was reaffirmed with the approval of a new national charter, or constitution. According to the charter, the FLN was the only legal political party, and Islam was the official religion.

By the late 1980s many young Algerians had grown disillusioned with the country's political leadership and their own uncertain future. When they started widespread riots in 1988, the FLN called for a national referendum in which voters approved a multiparty political system. As new political parties emerged, the FLN leadership was forced to revitalize. The major challenge to the FLN came from the fundamentalist Islamic Salvation Front (FIS), which won 55 percent of the seats in the 1989 local elections. In December 1991, in the first stage of the two-part election for the National Assembly, the FIS won more than 80 percent of the seats. The FLN won only 15 of the 231 contested seats. The army then stepped in, halted the second stage, declared the FIS to be illegal, and imprisoned its leadership.

In the aftermath of the elections, the sitting president, Chadli Benjedid (1929–), resigned, his successor, Mohammed Boudiaf (d. 1992), was assassinated, and an army general, Liamine Zeroual (1941–), became head of state. In 1995 Zeroual ran for president as the candidate of the newly founded National and Democratic Rally (Rassemblement National pour la Démocratie, RND). He won handily when the eight opposition parties boycotted the election.

The 1995 election marked the end of the FLN's hold on the presidency. In 1997 the FLN placed second in the National Assembly elections, winning 64 out of 380 seats. This total was fewer than the seats won by both the "moderate" Islamist Movement for a Peaceful Society (69 seats) and the RND (115 seats). The FLN and RND then formed a coalition majority in the assembly.

The FLN continues as a viable, though minority political party in Algeria. In 1999 both it and the RND supported the election of President Abdulaziz BOUTEFLIKA (1937–   ). Deprived of its former status as the ruling party in Algeria's one-party state, the future of the FLN now depends on how well its leaders can craft a message that will appeal to an electorate for whom the 1954–62 war for independence is increasingly a historical memory.

See also: BATTLE OF ALGIERS (Vol. IV); FRANCE AND AFRICA (Vols. III, IV, V); ISLAM, INFLUENCE OF (Vols. IV, V); NATIONAL LIBERATION FRONT (Vol. IV); POLITICAL PARTIES AND ORGANIZATIONS (Vols. IV, V).

Further reading: John Entelis, *Algeria: The Revolution Institutionalized* (Boulder, Colo.: Westview Press, 1986); Benjamin Stora, *Algeria, 1830–2000: A Short History*, Jane Marie Todd, trans. (Ithaca, N.Y.: Cornell University Press, 2001).

national parks One of the most familiar types of protected natural areas, national parks are important tools for CONSERVATION. In Africa the topic of conservation has led to conflict over a number of issues, including who gets to make decisions about NATURAL RESOURCES and how people view their relation to nature.

The International Union for the Conservation of Nature (IUCN) defines a protected area as "an area of land and/or sea especially dedicated to the protection and maintenance of biological diversity, and of natural and associated cultural resources, and managed through legal or other effective means." Besides national parks, the most common types of protected areas include *managed resource areas,* which try to encourage the use of natural resources in a sustainable, manageable way; *national monuments,* which protect culturally important sites; *nature reserves,* which are open only for scientific use; and *wilderness areas,* which forbid habitation and limit human impact in order to retain the wild characteristics of an area.

The world's first national park was Yellowstone National Park, in the United States. Established in 1872, it sought to both preserve one of the North American continent's great natural areas and, at the same time, to develop that area for recreational use. Its success led the United States to establish 14 other national parks, as well as 21 national monuments, by 1916. Since then establishing national parks has become one of the primary ways in which governments attempt to protect important natural areas. By limiting LAND USE and promoting activities that have minimal harmful impact on the environment, national parks serve as a major force in preserving nature for future generations.

Today Africa is the site of many spectacular national parks. South Africa's famous Kruger National Park, for example, provides a safe haven for some of the continent's most important WILDLIFE. Similarly, Mount Kenya National Park, which encompasses 276 square miles (715 sq km) and rises to altitudes over 17,000 feet (5,181 m), preserves a site that not only is of great physical beauty but that is of great cultural and religious importance. Parks like these represent an important investment in their countries' futures, not only in terms of preservation of their environments, but also in terms of the hard economics of TOURISM.

As of 2002 there were 109 national or international parks in North Africa, 136 in East Africa, 80 in Central Africa, 138 in West Africa, and 586 in southern Africa. The IUCN has established a target in which 10 percent of all land area in Africa should come under some form of environmental protection. So far, six African nations have achieved that goal: BOTSWANA, BURKINA FASO, NAMIBIA, RWANDA, SENEGAL, and TANZANIA. To a great extent, these efforts have been aided by outside donations, much of it from private, non-governmental agencies like the World Wildlife Fund, which provided nearly $10 million for African forest conservation in 2001.

The establishment of national parks, especially in Africa, has not been without problems. The idea of protected national parks arises from a particular "nature aesthetic," a view that holds that nature is of value in and of itself and that it should be "protected" by the government from human interference. Not all cultures, however, share this view, and, even if they "appreciate" nature, many cultures do not necessarily see a value to nature separate from its utility to humans. Indeed, for many cultures the loss of land to a national park represents a cultural as well as an economic hardship.

The conflict between the nature aesthetic and the view that the land has other uses has been particularly sharp in Africa. The first national park in Africa was Virunga National Park, which was originally known as Albert National Park. It was organized in 1925 in what was then the Belgian Congo (today's Democratic Republic of the CONGO). The effort, shared by both the Belgian and British governments, sought to protect the park's mountain gorillas.

When Virunga was proposed, however, a large human population had to be displaced in order to establish the 3,000-square-mile (7,770-sq-km) park. In doing this the authorities were attempting to save an endangered animal, but at the same time they were effectively establishing a vision of "what Africa should look like." Further, the decision was made by colonial administrations rather than by Africans. As a result a basic conflict arose. To the administrators, the land was being taken for the good of the area and of the world. To the local population, however, the land was simply being confiscated, like so much of the rest of Africa, by colonial imperialists.

Beyond this, from the African standpoint, establishing the park assumed a separation of human beings from a nature that can be dominated, controlled, or protected. This separation, as well as the whole nature aesthetic that went with it, was foreign to Africans. To the people who lived in and near the land that became Virunga National Park, human beings lived as a part of nature, and separating humans from their environment made no sense at all.

The conflict that marked the establishment of Africa's first national park still exists today. Nearly all African countries now have national parks systems. Most are modeled on either the U.S. system or one developed by SOUTH AFRICA during the 1920s. Not surprisingly, as the number of parks has increased, so has the number of problems.

The history of Virunga National Park once again provides a telling example. In 1979 Virunga was put on the World Heritage List, primarily to preserve the high level of BIODIVERSITY found within its borders and to continue protecting the diminishing mountain gorilla population. This designation, however, meant that the resources in the area were even less available than before. The situation became a crisis in 1994, when the war in neighboring Rwanda drove more than 40,000 REFUGEES into the park. These people collected great amounts of forest products each day for firewood and other necessities. Nearly 50,000 acres (20,234 hectares) were deforested in just a few months. In response the United Nations upgraded Virunga to a World Heritage Site in Danger, an ac-

Recently, the movement for the establishment of national parks has gained momentum from those who are making wildlife conservation a global concern. These rhinos are a protected species in South Africa's Kruger National Park. © Corbis

tion that, to refugees and local residents alike, seemed to blur the line between natural resource management and the right to survive.

Virunga provides an extreme example of the problems involved in creating national parks, but it is one that is becoming, in many ways, more common. In 1980 the IUCN created a new group, the World Conservation Strategy (WCS), for the purpose of finding ways to balance two critical requirements: the resident people's need for economic growth and the world's need for resource conservation. In actual practice, however, the WCS's concern with potential loss of biodiversity has outweighed any issues raised by resident peoples. As a result, throughout the 1980s and 1990s African governments set up new parks and reorganized and expanded old ones, all the while mimicking the actions of the one-time colonial powers by relocating large numbers of people.

Mkomazi Reserve, in Tanzania, Kibale Forest Reserve and Game Corridor, in UGANDA, and Central Kalahari Game Reserve, in Botswana, were set up with processes involving massive relocation of residents. Although the relocation of inhabitants in this way is less popular today, it remains a major part of government policy in many areas.

Relocation is not the only issue involved in the establishment and management of national parks. Of primary concern is the question of local land use. In northern Tanzania, for example, an intense debate developed between the MAASAI population and the government over the right to graze herds on pasture lands in national parks and protected areas. The conflict became so intense, in fact, that it led Tanzania's former president Julius NYERERE (1922–1999) to appoint a Maasai prime minister in 1980. Similar conflicts involving park-resident differences have taken place in Tsavo National Park, in KENYA, and around all of the borders of Great Limpopo Transfrontier Park, which covers parts of ZIMBABWE, MOZAMBIQUE, and South Africa.

Throughout Africa the benefits have been tremendous regarding the establishment of national parks and protected areas. The parks have helped reduce the loss of biodiversity and have lessened the pressures brought on by agricultural and industrial land use. Parks also have helped reduce pollution and limit the introduction of new plants and animals that often have disastrous effects on individual environments. Clearly, however, the existing parks cannot succeed and new ones cannot be created without the cooperation of resident populations. For this reason the IUCN has attempted to modify policies, advo-

cating a system that also recognizes the rights, concerns, and traditions of resident populations in all environmental protection projects. As a result, in the future, national parks and protected areas may not be the only way to reduce environmental change. Instead, there may be broader, more inclusive plans that will integrate conservation with development and local resource management.

See also: COLONIAL RULE (Vol. IV); COLONIALISM, INFLUENCE OF (Vol. IV); ECOLOGY AND ECOLOGICAL CHANGE (Vol. V); ENVIRONMENTAL ISSUES (Vol. V); NEOCOLONIALISM AND UNDERDEVELOPMENT (Vol. V).

Further reading: Roderick P. Neumann, *Imposing Wilderness: Struggles over Livelihood and Nation Preservation in Africa* (Berkeley, Calif.: University of California Press, 1998).

National Union for the Total Independence of Angola (União Nacional para a Independência Total de Angola, UNITA)

Anticolonial nationalist movement founded in 1966. After ANGOLA became independent in 1975, UNITA was one of the major factions that became embroiled in Angola's civil war. Jonas SAVIMBI (1934–2002) organized UNITA in 1966, combining elements that broke away from the NATIONAL FRONT FOR THE LIBERATION OF ANGOLA (Frente Nacional de Libertação de Angola, FNLA). Members of UNITA were drawn primarily from the Ovimbundu and Chokwe peoples of central and southern Angola. Originally UNITA was an organization sympathetic to the thought of Chinese Communist leader MAO ZEDONG (1893–1976). However, it evolved into an anti-Communist party after it accepted aid from Portugal in the armed conflict against the pro-Communist POPULAR MOVEMENT FOR THE LIBERATION OF ANGOLA (Movimento Popular de Libertação de Angola, MPLA).

When the MPLA declared independence from Portugal in 1975 UNITA, briefly aided by the FNLA, engaged the MPLA in what was to become Africa's most protracted civil war. Reflecting the political maneuvering of the Cold War, the United States backed UNITA to counter the support that the former Soviet Union and Cuba gave to the MPLA. At the height of hostilities UNITA also received support from the South African Defense Force, whose troops were fighting against both the MPLA in Angola and rebels in nearby NAMIBIA.

By 1988 the war in Angola was coming to a tentative close, and foreign troops began to withdraw. In 1992 this ultimately led to Angolan elections that resulted in a UNITA defeat. Although international observers judged the elections to be fair, Savimbi immediately declared the election a fraud, reigniting the civil war.

During the fighting that again enveloped the country, Savimbi's UNITA used proceeds from illegally smuggled Angolan diamonds to fund its insurrectionist campaign. As a result of the international condemnation of UNITA tactics, a splinter group, UNITA-R, suspended Savimbi and laid claim to the leadership of the party. UNITA soon split into three factions.

In the late 1980s Namibia, which lies between Angola and SOUTH AFRICA, had yet to achieve independence from South Africa. The fighting between South African troops and Namibia's rebel armies often spilled over into southern Angola.

Despite his professed desire to resolve the conflict, in 2002 Savimbi was assassinated by government troops, and within months UNITA signed an agreement to end hostilities. Although internal conflict persists in Angola, the reintegration of former UNITA combatants into the government is proving generally to be a success.

See also: CHINA AND AFRICA (Vol. V); COLD WAR AND AFRICA (Vol. IV); COLONIAL RULE (Vol. IV); CUBA AND AFRICA (Vol. V); INDEPENDENCE MOVEMENTS (Vol. V); NATIONALISM AND INDEPENDENCE MOVEMENTS (Vol. IV); OVIMBUNDU (Vol. IV); PORTUGAL AND AFRICA (Vols. III, IV, V); SOVIET UNION AND AFRICA (Vols. IV, V); UNITED STATES AND AFRICA (Vols. IV, V).

natural resources In Africa natural resources often have been the engine propelling DEVELOPMENT at the same time that their exploitation has contributed to social and environmental ills. The term *natural resources* has come to include any material goods existing in nature that can be exploited by human beings for economic gain.

The idea of natural resources became important in Africa early in the 20th century as Europe's colonial powers sought to profit from the continent's mineral riches. In the process, other African natural resources, including indigenous African FOOD CROPS, plants, and soil and WATER RESOURCES, were also exploited. After World War I (1914–18), the shift in the economics of colonialism forced European countries, the United Kingdom and France in particular, to mandate that colonial governments maintain greater levels of self-sufficiency. This, in turn, led to even greater exploitation of Africa's most precious commodities.

This pattern—generating wealth through the exploitation of natural resources—continued into the postcolonial era. African elites formed new businesses to trade GOLD, copper, iron, timber, and agricultural goods, as well as other products. As international markets grew and became more complex, uranium, diamonds, and, perhaps most critically, OIL became the engines for economic growth for African economies. Today, while the

United States and other advanced industrial economies rely on technology, industry, and service for the largest part of their economies, most African countries still survive by exploiting their natural resources.

There is no doubt that NIGERIA, for example, would suffer without the sale of oil, ZAMBIA without the sale of copper, NAMIBIA without the sale of uranium, GUINEA-BISSAU without the sale of groundnuts (peanuts), MAURITANIA without the sale of fish, and SIERRA LEONE without the sale of diamonds. However, exploitation of natural resources comes at a huge price. Costs frequently include permanent ecological change as well as long-term, and even irreversible, damage to the ecosystem.

The economy of GUINEA provides a telling example of how present-day needs are met at the expense of the future. Guinea's economy is dependent on a combination of the minerals bauxite, gold, iron ore, silver, lead, platinum, uranium, nickel, and cobalt. At the same time Mount Nimba, in Guinea, is a critical BIODIVERSITY resource that contains a large number of species found nowhere else. It is both a Reserve of the Biosphere and a UN World Heritage site. Yet even as the government has put in place CONSERVATION measures, MINING threatens the area's vitally important evergreen FORESTS and unique plant formations. Mining also has reduced the area that farmers can cultivate, forcing them to attempt to grow crops on marginal lands and use unsustainable agricultural practices.

Another challenge comes from global markets. The global marketplace often forces African exporters to consider short-term profits even if this means long-term environmental or market erosion. For instance, gemstone production in Zambia is focused predominantly in the informal market sector. This is because there are not adequate legal incentives or INFRASTRUCTURE to ensure that sellers abide by practices that benefit the country as a whole. As a result, the mining of Zambian emeralds, aquamarine, amethyst, and tourmaline is an important source of wealth, but it is not a sustainable pursuit. On its current path the resources will be exhausted, the environment will be destroyed, and only a few people will have ever gained any benefits.

Economic benefit and SUSTAINABLE DEVELOPMENT are major issues in regard to oil, which has provided some countries with the most valuable resource in their history. For example, oil exploitation in the NIGER DELTA, which became part of Nigeria under British colonialism, has become a mainstay of that country's economy. In fact, it totals 95 percent of the Nigerian national budget. Yet the Ijaw people of the region are among the country's poorest. Beyond this, in 1997–98 alone, oil spills amounted to 100,000 barrels (4.2 million gallons). Local AGRICULTURE has been poisoned and game animals have all but disappeared. More broadly, pollutants from the oil industry have contributed to ATMOSPHERIC CHANGE.

In recent years the mining of the mineral coltan (short for columbite-tantalite) has caused upheaval in Central Africa. Mined by hand from streambeds mainly in the Democratic Republic of the CONGO (DRC), coltan is used in mobile phones, beepers, and laptop computers to regulate voltage and store energy. The global technology boom that began in the 1990s increased demand for the mineral, causing its value to skyrocket to as much as $180 per pound ($400 per kg). To meet demand armed rebel factions from DRC, RWANDA, UGANDA, and BURUNDI have set up unregulated mining operations in Congo's NATIONAL PARKS. The rebels' mining activity—which can earn them as much as $20 million per month—threatens local human populations and endangers the parks' gorillas and elephants.

In Nigeria the effects of the oil industry are not confined to just the environment, however. Political CORRUPTION has resulted, leading to the degradation of water quality, electrification, EDUCATION, and medical care. On the social level, in 2000 alone, violence associated with the oil industry took as many as 5,000 lives.

Africa's vast natural resources are a double-edged sword. They are finite, non-renewable goods. As such, they are the primary engine contributing to economic growth in the short term. But they simultaneously represent one of the greatest threats to both the environment and sustained economic growth in the long term. Despite significant improvements in natural resource management in recent years, as long as irreplaceable natural goods are used as a means by which to generate wealth, they will pose hazards to the environment and threats to the long-term economic potential of Africa's most impoverished countries.

See also: COLONIALISM, INFLUENCE OF (Vol. IV); ECOLOGY AND ECOLOGICAL CHANGE (Vol. V); ENVIRONMENTAL ISSUES (Vol. V); MINERALS AND METALS (Vols. IV, V); MINING (Vol. IV); NATURAL RESOURCES (Vol. IV); PASTORALISM (Vol. IV).

Further reading: Peter Veit, *Africa's Valuable Assets: a Reader in Natural Resource Management* (Washington, D.C.: World Resources Institute, 1998).

Ndayizeye, Domitien See BURUNDI.

N'Djamena Capital of CHAD, located in the southwestern part of the country on the Chari River, the southern outlet of Lake Chad. The French founded the town as Fort-Lamy in 1900, after defeating the Sudanese merchant-warrior, Rabih bin Fadlallah (1845–1900), who, with his slave army, had established control of a large area east of Lake Chad. Fort-Lamy became an administrative center and military base of French Equatorial Africa before becoming the capital of Chad upon the country's independence, in 1960. Since then nearly continuous struggles for control of the country have created large-scale upheaval. The French name of the town, Fort-Lamy, was changed to the African name, N'Djamena, in 1973.

In 1990 the authoritarian government of Idriss DÉBY (1952–) took control. Eventually, democratic elections were held in 1996 and 1997, but an opposition group began fighting again in 2000. In 2002 a peace accord was signed, and Déby remained in power. Physically, N'Djamena reflects the country's tumultuous history, with many government buildings still bearing the scars of war. With a population estimated at slightly more than 600,000, N'Djamena serves as Chad's main commercial and economic center, as well as its political capital. It has a refrigerated slaughterhouse, and meat processing is the city's main industry. The city's markets trade in livestock, salt, dates, fish, cotton, and grains from the surrounding area. The city is also the site of the National School of Administration (founded in 1963) the University of Chad (1971), and the national museum, which specializes in prehistoric items.

See also: FRANCE AND AFRICA (Vols. III, IV, V); FRENCH EQUATORIAL AFRICA (Vol. IV); RABIH BIN FADLALLAH (Vol. IV); URBAN LIFE AND CULTURE (Vols. IV, V); URBANIZATION (Vols. IV, V).

N'Dour, Youssou (1959–) *Senegalese singer*
Born in DAKAR, the capital of SENEGAL, N'Dour was singing in public by the time he was 12 years old. He joined the Star Band in 1976, and three years later he formed his own band, the Etoile, which was renamed Super Etoile, in 1981. N'Dour quickly became the foremost proponent of the Senegalese musical style known as *mbalax,* a mix of West African, Cuban, and Western rhythms. He became known to a much broader audience in 1986, when he toured with English rock star Peter Gabriel (1950–) in support of the hit album "So," on which he sang. Since then, N'Dour's musical services have been requested by a great number of non-African recording artists, including Branford Marsalis (1960–) and Neneh Cherry (1964–).

N'Dour is recognized for his distinctive vocal inflections and his four- to five-octave vocal range. Reflecting his varied international audience, N'Dour records in French, English, Wolof, Pulaar (Fulfulde), and Serer. Over the years, he has used his fame to promote HUMAN RIGHTS and peace with such organizations as Amnesty International and the United Nations Children's Fund (UNICEF).

See also: MUSIC (Vol. V).

Negasso Gidada (1944–) *President of Ethiopia*

Born to OROMO parents in Dembi Dolo, ETHIOPIA, Negasso Gidada attended school in his home village and later in ADDIS ABABA, at Haile Selassie I University. From 1974 to 1991 he lived in Germany, where he became involved in Oromo causes, including the Union of Oromo Students in Europe and the Oromo Liberation Front. In 1989 Negasso Gidada came out in favor of the ETHIOPIAN PEOPLE'S REVOLUTIONARY DEMOCRATIC FRONT (EPRDF). By the time he returned to Ethiopia in 1991, the EPRDF controlled the country, having driven socialist dictator MENGISTU HAILE MARIAM (c. 1937–) from power.

Negasso joined the Oromo People's Democratic Organization (OPDO), eventually becoming part of its central committee. He then became minister of labor and social affairs and, later, minister of information under the transitional government headed by Prime Minister MELES ZENAWI (1955–), an ethnic TIGRAY. In 1995 Negasso Gidada was elected to the largely figurehead office of president of the Federal Democratic Republic of Ethiopia.

Meles and the EPRDF enacted a national government that favored the power of ethnically based regional governments, as opposed to centralized power in Addis Ababa. Rather than improving relations between Ethiopia's various ethnic groups, the plan exacerbated tensions and was decried particularly by the Amhara and the Oromo. The Tigray-led EPRDF thinly disguised its repression of these groups.

Caught between these sides, Negasso Gidada openly criticized elements in the EPRDF that repressed the Oromo. Ethnic tensions threatened to split the EPRDF coalition, which was made up of different ethnic organizations, including the OPDO. The situation came to a head when Negasso Gidada stormed out of a government meeting, officially severing his ties with Meles. In 2001 Negasso Gidada asked for political asylum in Italy. He held onto his claim to the presidency, however, until his term expired later that year. In his place, Girma Wolde-Giorgis (1917–), also an Oromo, was elected to the presidency. By the end of 2003 Ethiopia's "government by ethnicity" still appeared to be a shaky undertaking.

See also: AMHARA (Vols. I, III, IV); ETHNIC CONFLICT IN AFRICA (Vol. V); ETHNICITY AND IDENTITY (Vol. I); TIGRAY PEOPLE'S LIBERATION FRONT (Vol. V).

neocolonialism and underdevelopment Leaders and participants in the African INDEPENDENCE MOVEMENTS believed that ending colonial rule on the continent would free Africans to pursue a path of DEVELOPMENT of the continent's human and NATURAL RESOURCES for their own benefit rather than the benefit of their colonial rulers. However, within a few years of independence a number of African political leaders and intellectuals began to perceive the continuance of external indirect "neocolonial" control in the economic and cultural spheres, and even in the political sphere. Rather than developing, Africa seemed to be mired in underdevelopment. Dependency rather than true independence seemed to be Africa's situation.

It was Kwame NKRUMAH (1909–1972), the prime minister of GHANA at independence in 1957, who first coined the term "neocolonialism." As the central nationalist leader in his country's independence movement, he had believed that the achievement of political independence would almost inevitably lead to broad-based economic progress. By 1965, however, he had lost faith in such a formula, as indicated by the appearance of his book, *Neo-Colonialism: The Last State of Imperialism*. In it he argued that gaining national sovereignty did not in any substantial manner alter the fundamental economic, social, and cultural relationships of colonialism. Rather than the forces of African nationalism compelling the European colonial powers to withdraw from the continent, the colonial powers had engaged in their own process of decolonization. They bequeathed the appearance of sovereignty on the successor African states while retaining the real power for themselves. This neocolonialism expressed itself primarily through economic and monetary measures. African countries, for example, continued to export CASH CROPS and other raw materials to their former colonial rulers while importing manufactured goods from them. The currencies of the former French colonies remained pegged to the French franc. But, according to Nkrumah, there was also a new dimension to neocolonialism, that of the involvement of new actors in Africa's subjugation, including the United States.

Others soon picked up the concept of neocolonialism and began to utilize it to better understand the impasse that Africa had reached. In 1971 the Egyptian economist Samir Amin (1931–) published *L'Afrique de l'Ouest Bloquee: L'Economie Politique de la Colonisation, 1880–1970*, which was then translated and, in 1973, published as *Neo-Colonialism in West Africa*. At the time, Amin was the director of the UN African Institute for Economic Development and Planning, in DAKAR, SENEGAL. Previously he had been a senior government economist in EGYPT and a technical advisor for planning to the government of MALI as well as an economics professor in France and Senegal. The focus of Amin's work as an economist was, as he once said, on "the problems of unequal developments of capitalism on a world scale," whereby the developed capitalist countries had gradually arisen and come to dominate the underdeveloped countries of Africa and elsewhere. This process had taken place through the development of colonial TRADE AND COMMERCE, by which external firms came to dominate African markets. African participation in this colonial economy was oriented toward EXPORTS rather than internal development. This led to colonial economic enclaves such as the Copperbelt of ZAMBIA and the Democratic Republic of the CONGO or the cocoa-producing regions of West Africa. This type of economic development also worked against the emergence of a strong middle class that was vital for the development of the national economies of Africa. All of these dimensions of the colonial economy continued essentially unchanged after formal independence, thus creating the neocolonial situation.

NGUGI WA THIONG'O (1938–) waged a long campaign against the effects of colonialism. As a young lecturer in the Department of English at the newly established University of Nairobi, he was part of the successful effort in the late 1960s to replace it with the Department of African Languages and Literature. He next stopped using his English Christian name of James because of the links between the RELIGION of the MISSIONARIES and colonialism. In an interview after his decision to write his novels and plays only in Gikuyu (the Kikuyu language) or Kiswahili, he argued that "language is a carrier of a people's culture," which in turn transmits a people's values that are the basis for their identity. Thus, "when you destroy a people's language, you in essence destroy their identity."

African writers have also addressed the issues of neocolonialism, underdevelopment, and dependency. Indeed, these issues are central to much of the LITERATURE IN MODERN AFRICA. One of the central writers in this regard is Ngugi wa Thiong'o, of KENYA. As with most African authors of his or more recent generations, Thiong'o started out writing in the colonial language, which in his case was English. His 1977 novel, *Petals of Blood,* won him recognition. He soon concluded, however, that by continuing to write in a foreign language he was perpetuating neocolonialism and, furthermore, that he was producing Euro-African literature rather than genuine African literature. He thus wrote his next novel, *Caitaani mutharaba-ini* (1980; translated into English and appearing as *Devil on the Cross,* in 1983) in his own Gikuyu language. By this he sought to make explicit that an author's choice of language in the neocolonial context is inherently a political decision and that decolonizing African minds required writing in African and not European languages.

But by the 1970s many observers saw that rather than development African countries faced neocolonialism and underdevelopment. This was not limited to Africa, for scholars from Latin America, the Middle East, and parts of Asia also were concerned with the continued global dominance of the western world.

Neocolonialism, according to historians such as Walter RODNEY (1942–1980), has roots deep in the African past. In 1972 he published his highly influential *How Europe Underdeveloped Africa,* in which he argued that Europe's exploitation of Africa stretched back more than 500 years. It began with the maritime expansion of Europe that led to its dominance of global trade. This in turn led to the transatlantic slave trade, which became the basic factor in the continent's underdevelopment and its structural dependence on the West. With the end of the slave trade, Europe turned to promoting the export of Africa's raw materials as a means of extracting an economic surplus. Colonial rule intensified this process and also utilized Christianity, EDUCATION along Western lines, and promoting the use of European languages as means of political subordination. The colonial period thus locked Africa into a subordinate position of dependency that formal political independence alone was unequipped to end. Rodney concluded that Africa's subordination would continue as long as the Western, capitalist world remained dominant. In short, there was no ready escape for Africa from a world that was radically skewed in terms of developmental inequities.

More recently scholars have begun to examine Africa's neocolonial situation through "critical development theory." This approach moves beyond what have been largely economic explanations to include other dimensions of neocolonialism such as culture, gender, social structures, and POLITICAL SYSTEMS. At the heart of neocolonialism is determining to what extent the increasing involvement of the Western world has precluded future African development from progressing along African lines. Expanding globalization in the early 21st century makes this an even more complex and difficult question.

See also: CHRISTIANITY, INFLUENCE OF (Vols. IV, V); COLONIAL RULE (Vol. IV); COLONIALISM, INFLUENCE OF (Vol. IV); COPPERBELT (Vol. IV); LANGUAGE USAGE IN MODERN AFRICA (Vol. V); POSTCOLONIAL STATE (Vol. V); SLAVE TRADE (Vols. III, IV).

Further reading: Samir Amin and Chris Okechukwu Uroh, ed., *Africa and the Challenge of Development* (Ibadan, Nigeria: Hope Publications, 1998); Ngugi wa Thiong'o, *Decolonizing the Mind: The Politics of Language in African Literature* (Portsmouth, N.H.: Heinemann, 1986); Robert Young, *Postcolonialism: An Historical Introduction* (Oxford, U.K.: Blackwell Publishers, 2001).

Neto, Agostinho (António Agostinho Neto)
(1922–1979) *First president of Angola*

Neto, son of a Methodist pastor and a kindergarten teacher, was born near the town of Catete, ANGOLA, on September 17, 1922. A leading African intellectual and nationalist, Neto was also a doctor and poet, with his first volume published in 1948. However, it was as president of the POPULAR MOVEMENT FOR THE LIBERATION OF ANGOLA (Movimento Popular de Libertação de Angola, MPLA) and director of the armed struggle for independence from Portugal that he rose to international prominence.

In 1947 Neto received a scholarship from the Methodist church and traveled to study MEDICINE in Portugal, first at the University of Lisbon and, later, at Coimbra. In Portugal Neto was imprisoned several times for participating in demonstrations against the dictatorship of António de Oliveira Salazar (1889–1970) and for writing against the harsh conditions of life under Portuguese colonial rule in Africa. During this time, Neto became well known as an African intellectual and nationalist. When he was released from prison in 1958, Neto completed his medical studies, returning to Angola the following year with his wife, Maria Eugenia. In Angola Dr. Neto was afforded a life of peace and privilege that suited his inclination toward intellectual pursuits. However, he traded this lifestyle for one of hardship and political action when he chose to champion Angolan independence.

In 1960 Neto was arrested at his medical practice—which doubled as a meeting place for his political activities—and was again imprisoned. Two years later, while he was under house arrest, Neto, along with his wife and children, escaped to MOROCCO. Ultimately they moved to Léopoldville (now KINSHASA) in ZAÏRE (today's Democratic Republic of the CONGO).

In Léopoldville Neto was elected president of the MPLA, and over the next decade he directed the organization's armed struggle against Portuguese continued rule. Finally, in 1975, Angola won its independence, and Neto was sworn in as the first president of the People's Republic of Angola. As the leader of the country, Neto inherited a centuries-long legacy of colonial neglect and abuse, which included widespread POVERTY, illiteracy, and a general lack of basic health services. In addition to these internal difficulties, several belligerent outside forces, including the United States, refused to accept the legitimacy of Neto's government.

In 1977 Neto survived an attempted COUP D'ÉTAT by the Nitistas, a group of hard-line Communists in his government that was disenchanted with Neto's leadership. Neto proceeded to purge his government of Nitista influence, but he also tried to reorganize the Marxist-Leninist model of his government to address the shortcomings that the Nitistas had brought to light.

Upon his death of leukemia in the Soviet Union on September 10, 1979, Neto had yet to fulfill his hopes of an Angolan socialist state. Neto was succeeded as president by José Eduardo DOS SANTOS (1942–   ), who was to put Angola on a more Western-friendly course.

See also: COLD WAR AND AFRICA (Vols. IV, V); COLONIAL RULE (Vol. IV); INDEPENDENCE MOVEMENTS (Vol. V); NATIONALISM AND INDEPENDENCE MOVEMENTS (Vol. IV);

At midnight on November 10, 1975, Dr. Agostinho Neto, president of the Popular Movement for the Liberation of Angola, declared Angolan independence in Luanda, the capital. © *United Nations*

PORTUGAL AND AFRICA (Vols. III, IV, V); SOVIET UNION AND AFRICA (Vols. IV, V); UNITED STATES AND AFRICA (Vols. IV, V).

New Partnership for Africa's Development (NEPAD) Comprehensive strategic framework devised by African leaders to address the continent's major SUSTAINABLE DEVELOPMENT issues. To its critics NEPAD is not effective in economic terms because it does not address pre-existing inequities that are only made worse by market approaches.

POVERTY rates are high in Africa, where almost half its population of 400 million lives on less than $1 a day. Neoliberal economic reform and liberalization policies in the 1980s and 1990s have resulted in increased inequalities while undermining formal and informal social security programs and safety nets. NEPAD seeks Africa's DEVELOPMENT by calling for the end of its wars, the deepening of commitments to DEMOCRATIZATION and good governance, and the reduction of CORRUPTION. NEPAD relies on the invisible hand of the market. One of the main concerns of initiators of NEPAD has been to stave the trend of falling ECONOMIC ASSISTANCE to Africa for development purposes. Rich countries and international donors have been increasingly reluctant to support investment in Africa because of mismanagement and corrupt leaders.

NEPAD was conceived by African leaders of five major African countries: South Africa's Thabo MBEKI (1942–), Nigeria's Olusegun OBASANJO (c. 1937–), Algeria's Abdelaziz BOUTEFLIKA (1937–), Senegal's Abdoulaye WADE (1926–), and Egypt's Hosni MUBARAK (1928–). Their motivation was to gain from the benefits of free trade and EXPORTS. The framework for NEPAD, formally adopted in 2001 at the 37th Summit of the ORGANIZATION OF AFRICAN UNITY (recently transformed into the AFRICAN UNION), was presented as a blueprint for promoting the positive norms of international development: democracy, HUMAN RIGHTS, people-centered development, gender equality, and good governance.

NEPAD is different from many previous initiatives in Africa in that the framework is not imposed by outsiders but was drawn up by some of Africa's more respected leaders. Its supporters view NEPAD as a major step in the right direction for resolving Africa's economic "crisis." NEPAD seeks to attract foreign direct investment to Africa by proposing specific projects with measurable targets rather than relying on the historic handouts of overseas development assistance. For African leaders supporting NEPAD, the emphasis has been to figure out how to encourage exports and assuage doubts on the part of foreign investors, international donors, and wealthy Afri-cans about the stability of the African continent. This would potentially attract annual investments of $64 billion, which could lead to higher economic growth rates of up to 7 percent.

NEPAD is also unique in its use of a special "peer review mechanism." When operational, it would be in the form of a peer review forum comprised of African heads of state who monitor each other's performance on economic management, human rights, corruption, and democracy. A team of experts will provide regular monitoring through indicators of experts. Similar to other international regimes, the fear is that NEPAD will fall short in these internal reforms. By 2004 only 16 countries had pledge their support for the peer review mechanisms.

Critics of NEPAD point out that the initiative does not take into account Africa's unequal relations with the West in the last three centuries in terms of the slave trade, colonialism, and neocolonialism. It appears too docile in confronting some of the major negative aspects of contemporary globalization. Critics argue that rather than seeking an alternative development paradigm that builds on Africa's own history and culture, NEPAD simply extends the neoliberal, free-market development strategies that have repeatedly failed.

See also: COLONIALISM, INFLUENCE OF (Vol. IV); DISEASE IN MODERN AFRICA (Vol. V); HEALTH AND HEALING IN MODERN AFRICA (Vol. V); HIV/AIDS AND AFRICA (Vol. V); POPULATION GROWTH (Vol. V); STATE, ROLE OF (Vol. V).

Further reading: Thabo Mbeki, *Africa Define Yourself* (Cape Town: Tafelberg, 2002).

newspapers During the 1960s the press in Africa was deeply involved with the POLITICAL PARTIES AND ORGANIZATIONS seeking an end to colonial rule. To a large extent, when independence was achieved, the newspapers of many countries fell under government control. This was the case especially in countries ruled by single-party governments. During the widespread DEMOCRATIZATION that occurred in the 1990s, however, newspapers generally tended to become more independent and freer of government controls.

Many African countries have only a handful of newspapers. In some cases this is because of the small size of the country and its population; in other cases, factors such as low literacy or low per-capita income limit newspaper circulation. CHAD, for example is a relatively poor country with an adult literacy rate of under 48 percent. Not surprisingly, it has only one daily and one weekly newspaper, both published in French. KENYA, on the other hand, with four times the population of Chad, a per-capita income more than double that of Chad, and an adult literacy rate of 78 percent, has five dailies and several weekly newspapers.

The press is most developed in SOUTH AFRICA and in North African countries. Not surprisingly, these are the countries with the strongest economies and higher rates of literacy. South Africa has 19 dailies and 10 weekly papers. Most of them are published in English, though some are published in Afrikaans and other African languages. A couple of papers have been published for more than 150 years. During the APARTHEID era the Afrikaans papers supported the government, while the English-language newspapers opposed it. Consequently, the English papers were often under great pressure from the government.

The *Sunday Times,* with a readership of more than 3.5 million, is South Africa's best selling newspaper, while several dailies have readership in excess of 500,000 each. Ownership of South African newspapers is divided among five major newspaper groups, with one—the Independent Newspapers, run by an Irish tycoon—controlling more than half of the country's press. The newspaper with the highest circulation, *The Sowetan,* has a largely black readership and is owned by a black empowerment company formed in 1993.

In northeast Africa, a strong economy and the highly urbanized and literate population of EGYPT combine to support 11 dailies and 10 weekly newspapers. While the majority of daily papers are published in Arabic, some are in English or French, as are several of the weeklies. The paper with the largest circulation is the Arabic language daily *Al-Ahram,* with 1,160,000 readers. It has both English- and French-language weekly editions.

ALGERIA has 20 daily newspapers, although five of them account for 80 percent of the readership. Of these five, three are published in French and two in Arabic. The freedom of today's Algerian press, in contrast to the situation in the early years of Algerian independence, is illustrated by the fact that the five leading newspapers opposed the 2004 reelection of President Abdelaziz BOUTEFLIKA (1937–   ). The opposition had little effect, however, since he won with more than 80 percent of the votes.

Many African newspapers aspire to high standards. For example, *New Age,* in NIGERIA, strives to be one of the finest newspapers anywhere. The paper's statement of purpose says that it seeks to "occupy the high ground professionally and meet the needs of an informed and influential audience for news, analysis, comment and specialized features." For *New Age* quality means not only high journalism standards but also a modern full-color press.

See also: NEWSPAPERS (Vol. IV).

Nganga, Nakatindi Yeta (Princess Nakatindi Miriam Nganga) (1925–1972) *Zambian politician and prominent feminist*

Nakatindi Yeta Nganga was born in Barotseland in northwestern ZAMBIA, the daughter of the Lozi king Yeta III, (1871–1946), and the granddaughter of King Lubosi Lewanika (1845–1916). She attended primary school in the western province of Zambia and was the first princess to complete junior secondary school in Barotseland. Nganga then broke with tradition by being the first in the

royal family to study outside the country. She studied in SOUTH AFRICA where her classmates included Sir Seretse KHAMA (1921–1980), first president of BOTSWANA. Upon her return to Zambia she defied the royal establishment and became the first member of the royal family to enter the independence struggle, joining the UNITED NATIONAL INDEPENDENCE PARTY (UNIP).

Princess Nakatindi used her influence to help UNIP make an impact in the Western Province, where there was a strong resistance to the national struggle and the people preferred to remain as the kingdom of Barotseland. The colonial government had promoted the idea that if the Lozi people joined in the fight for national unity they would lose their rights and identity. Not surprisingly, this discouraged them from joining in the struggle. In 1962 Nganga became a UNIP candidate in a general election against a European, M. G. Rubb, a candidate of the United Federal Party led by Roy Welensky (1907–1991). Nganga lost the election, but, undeterred, she stood for election in Nalikwanda in 1964 and won. She was one of the first female members of Parliament and later held various top government positions. Remembered for fighting for women's rights long before the international declarations, Nganga spoke out in support of women's rights and advocated the creation of a national body to protect and promote them. Fittingly, Nakatindi became the first director of the Women's Brigade, the national body created for women's welfare.

See also: BAROTSELAND (Vol. IV); INDEPENDENCE MOVEMENTS (Vol. V); LEWANIKA, LUBOSI (Vol. IV); NATIONALISM AND INDEPENDENCE MOVEMENTS (Vol. IV); WELENSKY, ROY (Vol. IV); WOMEN IN MODERN AFRICA (Vol. V).

Ngugi wa Thiong'o (James Ngugi) (1938–   ) *Kenyan novelist and playwright*

Born James Thiong'o Ngugi in Limuru, KENYA, Ngugi is a member of the KIKUYU people, Kenya's largest ethnic group. Part of a large peasant family, he was educated at mission schools and then at Alliance High School, in Kikuyu town, near NAIROBI. In 1962, while studying at MAKERERE UNIVERSITY in KAMPALA, UGANDA, Ngugi produced his first major literary effort, a play called *The Black Hermit.* It was performed that year in the National Theater in Kampala. After graduating he traveled to England to study at the University of Leeds.

While in England Ngugi wrote his first novel, *Weep Not, Child* (1964), which was one of three works (the others being *The River Between* [1965] and *A Grain of Wheat* [1967]) that centered around the Mau Mau rebellion of the 1950s and its aftermath. As with many in Kenya, Ngugi's family was directly impacted by the Mau Mau rebellion. His brother was part of the movement, and he saw his stepbrother killed and his mother tortured during the violence.

With the publication of *A Grain of Wheat,* Ngugi's philosophy toward language and politics solidified into a firm anticolonial stance, mixed with bitterness against the new government of Kenya. Ngugi felt the government ignored the nation's peasants, who had played a vital role in winning independence from Britain. While working as a professor of English literature at the University of Nairobi, in 1967 Ngugi took part in a successful effort to change the department's name to African Languages and Literature. He also dropped his Christian name in favor of a Kikuyu version, and renounced Christianity, seeing it as a colonial influence.

In 1977 Ngugi publicly decided to abandon English and write only in Kikuyu or Kiswahili. He reasoned that language and culture were inseparable; therefore, English had the effect of a "cultural bomb," eradicating precolonial cultures and traditions even after independence. In that same year, Ngugi amplified his rhetoric against the Kenyan government in a novel, *Petals of Blood,* and a play, entitled *Ngaahika Ndena* (I Will Marry When I Want), which he wrote with Ngugi wa Mirii (1951–   ). The play, which scathingly addressed the inequalities of Kenyan society, was performed in Ngugi's hometown of Limuru, and it became so popular among the peasant population that the Kenyan government, then headed by President Daniel arap MOI (1924–   ), banned it and imprisoned Ngugi without a trial.

While in prison Ngugi took notes that later became the memoir *Detained: A Writer's Prison Diary* (1981), and he wrote the novel *Caitaani Mutharabaini* (Devil on the Cross) (1980). Ngugi was released a year later through the efforts of Amnesty International. Despite being banned from teaching positions, Ngugi remained a thorn in the government's side. In 1982 his theater group was banned, and Ngugi went into a self-imposed exile in London.

Matagari was extremely popular among Kenya's peasant population. Greatly concerned and under the impression that Matagari was a living person, the Kenyan police sought to arrest the fictional character. When they realized their mistake, the police instead "arrested" the book in 1986, barring its sale and confiscating all copies. It was not available again in Kenya until 10 years later.

Ngugi continued to write in exile, further defining his ideas of the importance of preserving native languages in *Decolonizing the Mind: The Politics of Language in African Literature* (1986). He also wrote the novel *Matigari* (1987), featuring a title character based on a Kikuyu folktale. He moved to the United States in 1989.

Unable to return to Kenya, he taught at a number of universities in the United States as well as in Australia and New Zealand.

See also: ALLIANCE HIGH SCHOOL (Vol. IV); AMNESTY INTERNATIONAL AND AFRICA (Vol. V); CHRISTIANITY, INFLUENCE OF (Vols. II, III, IV, V); COLONIALISM, INFLUENCE OF (Vol. IV); LANGUAGE USAGE IN MODERN AFRICA (Vol. V); LITERATURE IN MODERN AFRICA (Vol. V); MAU MAU (Vol. IV).

Further reading: James Ogude, *Ngugi's Novels and African History: Narrating the Nation* (Sterling, Va.: Pluto Press, 1999).

Niamey Capital of NIGER, located on the Niger River in the southwestern part of the country. Niamey was a small fishing village when, in 1902, the French arrived and established a military fort. From 1926 until 1956 the town served as the capital of the Niger Territory, within French West Africa. As late as 1940, however, it had only a few thousand inhabitants.

After World War II (1939–45), with greater African political autonomy looming, Niamey's population expanded as the town was viewed as a possible government center. When Niger became independent, in 1960, Niamey was named its capital. The city's international profile rose accordingly.

The construction of the Kennedy Bridge facilitated the expansion of Niamey to the south bank of the Niger River. Named after U.S. president John F. Kennedy (1917–1963), the bridge, finished in 1971, was funded by USAID, an American government organization that specializes in international DEVELOPMENT.

Attracting HAUSA and YORUBA merchants and traders from other parts of Niger—as well as from NIGERIA, the Republic of BENIN, and TOGO, to the south—Niamey steadily developed a bustling trade in agricultural products from the surrounding areas. Today the city's major EXPORTS include livestock, grain, vegetables, woven mats, and hides. The city also has a manufacturing sector, which produces bricks, leather products, textiles, shoes, charcoal, and building supplies. An economic downturn in the 1990s hampered Niamey's economic development, however.

Niamey is the site of Niger's National School of Administration (founded in 1963), the University of Niamey (1971), and several research institutes. It also hosts a national museum. In 2003 the population of the city was estimated at 748,000.

See also: FRANCE AND AFRICA (Vols. III, IV, V); FRENCH WEST AFRICA (Vol. IV); URBAN LIFE AND CULTURE (Vols. IV, V); URBANIZATION (Vols. IV, V).

Niger Landlocked West African country approximately 458,100 square miles (1,186,500 sq km) in size that is bordered to the north by ALGERIA and LIBYA, to the east by CHAD, to the south by NIGERIA and the Republic of BENIN, and to the west by BURKINA FASO and MALI. The capital is NIAMEY.

Niger at Independence Niger gained its independence from France on August 3, 1960, becoming a republic with Hamani DIORI (1916–1989) as president. The leader of the Nigerien People's Party (Parti Populaire Nigerien, PPN), President Diori served as Niger's leader from 1960 to 1974. On April 15, 1974, he was overthrown by a military COUP D'ÉTAT, and Lieutenant Colonel Seyni Kountche (1931–1987) took control of the government.

For nearly 13 years Kountche ruled Niger. He was considered a man of integrity, attempting to include all ethnic groups in his government. Kountche was succeeded by his army chief of staff, General Ali Saibou (1940–). Saibou adopted a new constitution in 1989 and formed the National Movement for a Development Society, which attempted to end the military dictatorship and return the country to a state of law. His administration was impaired by student and union protests calling for multiparty elections, and Kountche was eventually forced to hold a national conference to determine the fate of Niger's government. The first national conference was held on July 29, 1991, at which time the conference declared itself sovereign, suspended the constitution, and dissolved the government and the National Assembly. Amadou Cheiffou (1942–) assumed the task of overseeing the restructuring of legislative and presidential elections as well as running the country until the newly elected government was in place. On March 27, 1993, Mahamane Ousmane (1950–) was elected president of Niger for a five-year term, and the Alliance of the Forces of Change swept the legislative elections.

On January 27, 1996, with the country in the midst of a national crisis marked by a struggling economy and ethnic rebellions, the army staged another coup and assumed power. Colonel Ibrahim Baré Maïnassara (1949–1999) emerged as the leader, promising a return to democracy. But Maïnassara, a Muslim and member of the HAUSA ethnic group, supported the rise of Islamic fundamentalists within the country. He attempted to spark Niger's stagnant economy but met with little success. Increased opposition to Maïnassara's presidency culminated with his assassination, in 1999.

Prime Minister Ibrahim Assane Mayaki assumed leadership after Maïnassara's death, disbanding the National Assembly and temporarily suspending all political parties. In 1999 Mamadou TANDJA (1938–) was elected president of Niger's Fifth Republic with more than 59 percent of the vote. Real political power, however, remains in the hands of the military.

See also: NIGER (Vols. I, II, III, IV); FRANCE AND AFRICA (Vols. IV, V).

Further reading: Samuel Decalo, *Historical Dictionary of Niger* (Lanham, Md.: Scarecrow Press, 1997); Christian Lund, *Law, Power, and Politics in Niger: Land Struggles and the Rural Code* (New Brunswick, N.J.: Transaction Publishers, 1998).

Niger Delta Vast area measuring about 27,000 square miles (69,930 sq km) at the mouth of the Niger River, in southeastern NIGERIA. The discovery of OIL in this region a half-century ago sparked ethnic violence, as resident populations struggled with national and international forces to benefit from the profits.

The Niger Delta, with poorly drained soils that are high in clay content and not well suited for AGRICULTURE, contains a diverse COASTAL AND MARINE ECOSYSTEM replete with mangroves, swamp FORESTS, and lowland rain forests. It supports a high level of BIODIVERSITY. Its ecology is closely tied to the local population and to national and international interests. Seven million people, representing 20 ethnic groups, inhabit the delta region. The largest ethnic group, the Ijo, has inhabited the region for approximately 7,000 years and has established a strong cultural identity. There has been immense confusion and conflict between the diverse Ijo populations and the government of Nigeria over Ijo LAND USE and tenure systems. Consequently, the Nigerian government has effectively ignored and overridden local land governance in favor of its own system.

There is one main reason for the government's actions. With an estimated 25–30 billion barrels, the Niger Delta has one of the largest reserves of oil in Africa. The Nigerian National Petroleum Corporation, operated by the Royal Dutch Shell Company, retains a 55 percent share. The Shell Oil Company, a subsidiary of Royal Dutch Shell, holds another 30 percent share, while Chevron-Texaco, Elf, Agip, and several smaller companies hold or operate the remaining portion.

There are numerous threats to the delta's environment, including URBANIZATION, INDUSTRIALIZATION, waste discharges, and coastal erosion. Yet by far the greatest threat comes from the oil industry. Each well drilled produces 1,500 tons of a toxic mix of brine, WATER, and mud. There also is significant groundwater contamination. In addition, between 1987 and 1996 there were a reported 1,629 oil spills in the Niger Delta, with the numbers steadily increasing. Sabotage plays a major role in oil spills in Nigeria. The Ijo, OGONI, and other smaller ethnic groups inhabiting the delta region feel that they are at the margins of Nigerian society. Although their lands provide the engine for Nigeria's economic growth, the region's people are the poorest in the country. In 2000 the people of the Niger Delta region received $5.6 million in compensation for land lost, oil spills, tenement rates, and construction damage, while the state of Nigeria earned $18.9 billion in oil EXPORTS. During times of democracy in Nigeria, receipts returning to the region have increased slightly; however, they have nearly all gone to local leaders while the majority of the population remains starving and jobless. Even subsistence-level solutions are impossible. The water in the region is so polluted that fishing is virtually impossible, and the land, already poor, has been so degraded that it is entirely unsuitable for farming.

The disparity between the poverty of the delta's people and the richness of region's NATURAL RESOURCES has led to significant ethnic strife in the Niger Delta. This strife became steadily worse, moving from peaceful protest, in the 1970s, to armed resistance, at the turn of the millennium. Now thousands of people die each year and foreign oil industry workers have become regular targets for kidnapping.

Few options are left for the resident population. The design of the Nigerian state is such that elite classes, primarily in LAGOS, have benefited from oil extraction in much the same way that the British elite did in the era of colonial rule. In 1958, when oil was discovered in Nigeria in large quantities, the delta's resident populations argued that they could benefit more from their local resources if they were an independent country. This directly opposed Britain's plan of a single, united Nigeria.

During the colonial era the Royal Niger Company, which was responsible for oil extraction prior to Nigeria's independence in 1960, struck a contract with Shell D'Archy, now the Shell Petroleum and Development Company (SPDC) of Royal Dutch Shell. The SPCD is as embedded in Nigeria's current political and civilian elite circles as Shell D'Archy was in the colonial administration.

The ethnic strife and simmering Ogoni nationalism in the Niger Delta reached a crescendo in 1995 with the execution of playwright and activist Ken SARO-WIWA (1941–1995). His death produced an international backlash against Shell Oil and the Nigerian state. For their part, on December 11, 1998, the Ijo passed the Kaiama Declaration, which reiterated their claims on the rights to all natural resources in Ogoniland. The various Nigerian

governments in power since independence, democratic and dictatorial alike, cracked down on the rise of regional identity. Groups such as the Ijo Youth Council (IYC) and the Movement for the Survival of Ogoni People form a well-organized, collective front. While these movements are not new, their fervency, and the rise of extremist sub-groups such as the IYC's Egbesu Boys, is relatively recent.

Oil is a natural resource of high value in Nigeria, and it is critical for the country as a whole. But there are reasons for concern about local livelihoods, environmental change, SUSTAINABLE DEVELOPMENT, responsible governance, and respect for international law. To date, the Nigerian government and the oil companies have done little to address any of them.

See also: CIVIL WARS (Vol. V); COLONIAL RULE (Vol. IV); INDEPENDENCE MOVEMENTS (Vol. V); MULTINATIONAL CORPORATIONS (Vol. V); NATIONALISM AND INDEPENDENCE MOVEMENTS (Vol. IV); NIGER RIVER (Vols. I, III); NIGER DELTA (Vols. I, III).

Further reading: Martha G. Anderson and Philip M. Peek, *Ways of the Rivers: Arts and Environment of the Niger Delta.* (Seattle: University of Washington, 2002); Human Rights Watch, *The Price of Oil: Corporate Responsibility and Human Rights Violations in Nigeria's Oil Producing Communities* (New York: Human Rights Watch, 1999); T. A. Imobighe, et al., *Conflict and Instability in the Niger Delta* (Victoria, B.C., Canada: Spectrum 2002); Daniel A. Omoweh, *Shell Petroleum Development Company, the State and Underdevelopment of Nigeria's Niger Delta: A Study in Environmental Degradation* (Trenton, N.J.: Africa World Press, 2003).

Nigeria West African country located on the Gulf of Guinea and bounded by CHAD, CAMEROON, NIGER, and the Republic of BENIN. Covering some 356,700 square miles (923,900 sq km), Nigeria is not the largest country in Africa, but it is its most populous. In fact, Nigeria's 110 million people account for about one-seventh of the continent's population. The people of Nigeria have long shaped trends across the region and the continent, presenting the country with the opportunities and challenges that accompany a long historical legacy of political, ethnic, and religious complexity.

The territorial boundaries of modern-day Nigeria took shape in 1914, when Britain united the separate Colony of Nigeria and Protectorate of Nigeria, dividing the area into the north, south, and LAGOS colonies. The north was predominantly HAUSA-Fulani and Muslim; the south was largely YORUBA in the west and IGBO in the east, with a growing number of Christian converts. The resulting entity was large, diverse, and difficult to manage.

Nigeria gained its independence in October 1960 with a constitution that made it an ethnically based federation. Its three original regions—Northern, Western, and Eastern—reflected the three largest ethnic groups. The system of rule was parliamentary, with the central government's powers limited to defense and security, foreign relations, and commercial and fiscal policies. Regions retained most powers of domestic governance.

> Although Nigeria originally had three regions, the actual number of regions within the Nigerian federated system has fluctuated between four and 36, as the nation's leaders have experimented with various ways to maintain unity within the diverse nation.

The country that Nigerians inherited from the British was marked by ethnic, regional, and religious tensions. Large disparities in wealth existed between south and north, and the people who made up Nigeria's roughly 400 smaller ethnic groups were almost completely excluded from political and economic power.

Governmental Instability and Military Rule

After independence the new parliamentary democracy and the constitution that formed it were short-lived. On January 15, 1966, a group of Igbo army officers led by Major General Johnson Aguiyi-Ironsi (1924–1966) executed a successful COUP D'ÉTAT, assassinating the British-installed prime minister, Abubakar Tafawa BALEWA (1912–1966), and establishing a military government.

The new government was determined to centralize power, and it also was determined to maintain its hold on the OIL-rich Eastern Region. This worsened existing ethnic tensions, fomenting a strong anti-Igbo sentiment among Nigeria's other regions and ethnic groups. As a result, in July of the same year a second coup overthrew the government, assassinating Aguiyi-Ironsi and putting in power Gen. Yakubu GOWON (1934–), a leader from the northern Hausa ethnic group. Bloody ethnic violence ensued in which tens of thousands of Igbos were slaughtered. In addition thousands of Igbos who had migrated to the Northern Region were forced back to their southern homelands. Ultimately, Igbo nationalism grew, and Colonel Emeka Ojukwu (1933–) began an Igbo secessionist movement.

Gowon attempted to forge a federalist compromise through the creation of 12 semiautonomous states. Ojukwu saw this as a ploy, however, and in May 1967 he declared an independent Republic of BIAFRA in the eastern part of Nigeria. After three years of brutal civil war, the Biafra secessionists were defeated, and the central government once again had control of the east. Almost 100,000 Biafran soldiers and an estimated 500,000 to 2 million civilians died, primarily due to conflict-related starvation. The war also had social effects: a rise in ethnic animosities, a widening divide between northern and southern Nigerians, and increased tensions between the country's various religious groups. Minorities, who represented 20 to 25 percent of the population, were also victims of the conflict, and they began expressing their own discontent.

After the end of the civil war Nigeria's political life continued to be marked by ethnic and religious tensions and governmental turnovers. Gowon ruled until 1975, when a bloodless coup brought Murtala Muhammad (1938–1976) to power. A year later, when Murtala Muhammad was killed in a thwarted coup attempt, the Supreme Military Council turned to the army chief of staff, Lt. Gen. Olusegun OBASANJO (c. 1937–). Although he was a Yoruba, Obasanjo's military background and close ties to Murtala Muhammad gave him support in the north. In 1979 Obasanjo fulfilled a pledge to reestablish civilian rule, and Shehu Shegari (1924–) became the president of the Nigerian Second Republic. In 1983, however, Shagari was overthrown by Muhammadu Buhari (1942–), who ruled until he was overthrown by Maj.-Gen. Ibrahim BABANGIDA (1941–) in 1985.

Babangida ruled with an iron fist until 1993. At that time, even though he had allowed for a general election to be held on June 12, 1993, he annulled what international observers generally viewed as a free and fair voting process. Amid a storm of protest, Babangida appointed Ernest Shonekan (1936–) to run a transitional, or temporary, government, with Gen. Sani ABACHA (1943–1998) as vice chairman. This set off protests from supporters of Mashood ABIOLA (1937–1998), the reputed victor in the elections. On November 17, 1993, Abacha deposed Shonekan, dissolving the legislature and putting power once again in the hands of the military. Abiola's efforts to declare himself the legitimate ruler of Nigeria led Abacha to arrest him for treason. Ultimately, in June 1994 Abiola was put in prison, where he remained until his death in 1998.

The Abacha years were among the most brutal and corrupt in Nigeria's history. A Hausa and a Muslim, Abacha ruled with ultimate authority, continuing the domination of the northern groups over the rest of Nigeria. This had the effect of worsening the ever-present ethnic and religious divisions among the three major ethnic groups. It also increased tensions among Nigeria's myriad smaller ethnic groups, especially among the Ijo and OGONI in the NIGER DELTA, who were outraged at Abacha's tight control of the profits from the exploitation of oil and other NATURAL RESOURCES in their region.

Although Abacha promised the international community a transition to civilian rule, he had taken only token steps toward this when he died suddenly in June 1998. Gen. Abdulsalami Abubakar (1943–) took power, marshalling support for a democratic election in 1999. Obasanjo, a strong favorite in the Western Region, came to power once again, this time as a democratically elected, civilian leader. He was reelected in 2003, with 62 percent of the vote.

The Return of Democracy   With Obasanjo's new democracy came a new constitution. Based on an American model, it calls for a legislature with two separate houses as well as a strong executive branch. The judiciary branch is fairly independent, and the legislature is active, although Obasanjo's People's Democratic Party dominated it following his elections. Critically, Nigeria remains a federal system, but now with 36 states. The autonomy of the states is intended to reduce regionalized tensions.

Ethnic Conflicts and Oil   In spite of the presence of a democratically elected government since 1999, ethnicity in Nigeria remains as divisive an issue as ever. Obasanjo has the advantage of being a Yoruba who happens to have backing from the Northern Region. But he has been hard-pressed to win Igbo support. Even more important, his administration ultimately has heightened, rather than reduced, tensions with minority ethnic groups in the Niger Delta. In large part this is because the delta region—which is home to much of Nigeria's oil industry as well as to many of its ethnic minorities—has continued to remain mired in POVERTY, despite the fact that the region's oil wealth is primary in Nigeria's economy.

After the Nigerian civil war each of the country's political regions staked oil claims in the Niger Delta. In 1969 this led to a decree that gave the central government full control of the country's oil resources. The Nigerian National Oil Corporation was then set up, and in 1971 it began to regulate this centralized industry. One of the major effects of this was that the proceeds from the oil industry designated for the regional government dropped from 20 percent, in 1975, to 3 percent, in 1993.

The first oil pipeline in Nigeria was built by the Royal Dutch Shell Company in 1956. Stretched across the Delta region to Port Harcourt, it was built without local consultation. Nor was there any compensation for the loss of land or for the ongoing damage the pipeline caused to people's health or to the region's ecology. At independence the oil proceeds were to be divided 50 percent for the oil companies, 20 percent for the regional government, and 30 percent for the Nigerian population. As this allotment for the population was countrywide, its distribution was absorbed almost entirely in other, more populous, more politically entrenched regions than the delta.

These changes in the distribution of oil profits led to demands for local autonomy in the Niger Delta. This was especially true among the region's smaller ethnic groups. Previously, the Ijaw and Ogoni, like other kinship groups, were linked primarily by family, language, and culture. In response to the region's continued poverty and the loss of oil revenues, however, they became solidified ethnic groups with increasingly nationalistic feelings.

There are many reasons for the hostility between the delta region's ethnic groups and the government. These range from the lowering of the oil revenues received by the local communities to the lack of inclusion of delta leadership in decisions about the oil industry, and from the high poverty of the region to the lack of environmental safeguards. None of these causes is greater, however, than the lack of recognition of local identity. In their struggle for recognition, minority ethnic groups such as the Ijo and the Ogoni find themselves too few in number to wage an all-out war. But they find that they can successfully wage a battle of attrition, forcing shutdowns in oil production and taking a high cost in terms of investment and lives.

Religious Divisions   Historically, northern Nigeria is predominantly Muslim, and the south is predominantly Christian and/or animist. The long periods of military rule that marked independent Nigeria prevented the political rise of Islamic fundamentalism, even though those governments have been dominated by northerners. Ironically, the movements toward democracy and federalism have had the opposite effect, primarily because democracy brings with it freedom of RELIGION and federalism usually gives regional governments the right to exercise their own legislative desires. As a result, SHARIA, or Islamic law, has been rising as a state-level form of governance in Nigeria. The process began, in 1999, when one of Nigeria's northern states, Zamfara, adopted *sharia*. Soon other northern states followed suit. Although the drive to institute *sharia* drew hundreds of thousands of supporters to the streets in Zamfara, the move was not always greeted so enthusiastically. When the issue was raised in Kaduna state, in February 2000, as many as 400 people died in the public disturbances that followed.

Convinced that letting local governments rule by *sharia* would erode the democratic gains Nigeria had made, in July 2000 Obasanjo decreed that local governments did not have the right to govern by *sharia*. Governors countered that if *sharia* is the expressed will of the people, then denying it is anti-democratic. In the name of national stability Obasanjo looked the other way as state after state adopted *sharia*. By 2003 12 northern states—fully one-third of Nigeria—had adopted *sharia*.

Other Challenges   Obasanjo's political challenges are not limited to ethnic rivalry and religion, however. At the national level, CORRUPTION still abounds, HUMAN RIGHTS are regularly abused, and the economy shows little improvement. Indeed, despite Obasanjo's electoral campaign to clamp down on government corruption, according to Transparency International, Nigeria is second only to Bangladesh in the level of corruption. In fact, according to many observers, corruption is actually worse now than it was when Abacha was in power. Likewise, even though elections have increased the level of political rights, civil liberties continue to be eroded. Freedom House, a leading non-government organization measuring levels of democratic freedom, indicates that civil liberties continually declined from 1999 to 2002.

Regionally based ethnic and religious divides are the greatest problem Nigeria faces in terms of political stability. The economic divide between rich and poor, however, is the key issue Nigeria faces in terms of DEVELOPMENT. The country's economy is split into a modern, industrial oil economy and a subsistence AGRICULTURE economy. Oil accounts for more than 75 percent of the national economy and nearly 95 percent of the export economy. Yet gross domestic product remains at only $323 per capita. This indicates that Nigeria's huge oil revenues—approximately $19 billion each year—do little to improve the economic standing of the Nigerian people. To complicate matters further, even as oil has continued to be exploited, the quality of Nigeria's EDUCATION and health care has declined. Meanwhile, a high rate of inflation has degraded even the limited buying power of the average Nigerian. The country's oil is scarcely even used domestically and accounts for less than 15 percent of energy consumption.

Outside of the oil sector, natural gas, coal, tin, columbite, limestone, iron ore, lead, zinc, gypsum, barite, and kaolin are mined. Food products are manufactured, but poor soil in most areas limits the extent to which Nigeria's crops can be diversified. Cocoa remains the only major agricultural export. Cassava and yams, which are grown mostly for household consumption, dominate family farm production.

See also: ANIMISM (Vol. I); CHRISTIANITY, INFLUENCE OF (Vols. II, III, IV, V): ETHNIC CONFLICT IN AFRICA (Vol. V); ETHNIC GROUP (Vol. I); ETHNICITY AND IDENTITY (Vol. I); ISLAM, INFLUENCE OF (Vols. II, III, IV, V); NIGERIA (Vols. I, II, III, IV); NATIONALISM AND INDEPENDENCE MOVEMENTS (Vol. IV).

Further reading: Toyin Falola, *Violence in Nigeria: The Crisis of Religious Politics and Secular Ideologies* (Rochester, N.Y.: University of Rochester Press, 2001); Eghosa E. Osaghae, *Crippled Giant: Nigeria Since Independence* (Bloomington, Ind.: Indiana University Press, 1998); Rotimi T. Suberu, *Federalism and Ethnic Conflict in Nigeria* (Washington D.C.: United States Institute of Peace, 2001).

Nimeiri, Gaafar (Gaafar Mohamed El-Nimeiri)

(1930–   ) *Military leader and president of the Republic of the Sudan (1971–1985)*

A 1952 graduate of the Sudan Military College, Nimeiri underwent further military training in EGYPT. He admired President Gamal Abdel NASSER (1918–1970) of Egypt and soon organized a Free Officers' Association patterned after the organization that had brought Nasser to power. Returning to the Republic of the SUDAN, Nimeiri became a major figure in the political turmoil that engulfed the country in the years following independence from colonial rule.

Early on, Nimeiri commanded an army garrison in the southern Sudan, where he became convinced of the futility of the government's efforts to Arabicize and Islamize the region. Rebels were already contesting government control, thus initiating a lengthy civil war (1955–72). Frustrated by the lack of a competent government in Sudan, Nimeiri also participated in a number of attempted coups, finally succeeding in unseating President Ismail al-Azharj (1902–1969), in 1969. Following the COUP D'ÉTAT, Nimeiri became Sudan's prime minister. He outlawed political parties and disbanded Parliament before being driven from office, in 1971, by a Communist military uprising. Nimeiri was restored to power later that year and was handily elected to the presidency.

As president, Nimeiri took steps to end the civil war between the Sudan's northerners, who are primarily Arab and Muslim, and the southerners, who are mostly Africans and are Christians or followers of traditional religion. In 1972 he granted the south limited autonomy, temporarily ending hostilities. In 1976 Nimeiri survived a failed coup d'état by conservative Muslims led by future Sudanese president, Sadiq al-Mahdi (1935–   ).

Nimeiri attempted to address the country's failing economy by installing first a socialist plan and later a capitalist approach to AGRICULTURE. As part of his attempt to reform Sudanese agriculture, in 1981 Nimeiri launched the Kinanah sugar project, which became one of the world's largest sugar refineries. However, each attempt failed to produce significant results. Instead, Nimeiri found himself the target of a number of attempted coups.

Another source of conflict Nimeiri faced was southern resistance to his desire to establish a punitive version of Islamic law, or *SHARIA,* throughout the nation. Although he had approached resolving the civil war from the perspective of a military officer, he was now under growing pressure from Islamic fundamentalists. He thus concluded that his political survival was dependent on reversing his earlier position in favor of southern autonomy. Nimeiri declared a state of emergency in 1984 to help him impose his new judicial system, which employed punishments such as amputations and whippings for various crimes. Both Muslims and non-Muslims were subject to Nimeiri's "decisive justice courts." In contrast to his hard-line Islamist stance at home, Nimeiri joined Egyptian leader Anwar as-SADAT (1918–1981) as the first Muslim leaders to broach a peace with the Jewish state of Israel.

Ultimately Nimeiri accomplished little in terms of stabilizing Sudan. In 1985 deep-running frustrations over food shortages and another developing rebellion in southern Sudan combined to return the country to chaos. While Nimeiri was in Egypt, the minister of defense, General Siwar al-Dahab (1930–   ), led a coup that ended Nimeiri's administration. Nimeiri remained in Egypt for the next 14 years before returning home to Sudan in 1999.

See also: COMMUNISM AND SOCIALISM (Vol. V); ISLAM, INFLUENCE OF (Vols. II, III, IV, V).

Nkomo, Joshua (Joshua Mqabuko Nyongolo Nkomo) (1917–1999) *Nationalist leader and vice president of Zimbabwe*

Nkomo was widely known as "Father Zimbabwe" in recognition of his long struggle for independence from white rule in Southern Rhodesia (present-day ZIM-BABWE). Briefly forced into exile to avoid arrest, Nkomo was in London in 1960 when he was elected president in absentia of the newly formed Rhodesian National Democratic Party (NDP). He returned to Southern Rhodesia later in the year. When the white government banned NDP Nkomo founded the successor ZIMBABWE AFRICAN PEOPLE'S UNION (ZAPU), which was also banned. Dissident ZAPU members then formed the more militant ZIMBABWE AFRICAN NATIONAL UNION (ZANU), which emerged as ZAPU's principal rival among the country's African population.

Nkomo was a passionate advocate for international sanctions against Southern Rhodesia, and, as ZAPU president and the nation's most prominent African nationalist leader, he came under intense state scrutiny. The government of Ian SMITH (1919–   ) increasingly cracked down on its African opposition, and for almost a decade beginning in 1964 Nkomo was either in prison or under house arrest. Rather than diminishing Nkomo's political reputation, however, his detention enhanced his status as a martyr for the cause of national liberation. In 1974 Nkomo fled to ZAMBIA, from where he conducted a guerrilla war against Smith's white-minority regime. In 1976 Nkomo forged an alliance with ZANU, the other main opposition group, led by Robert MUGABE (1924–   ). Known as the PATRIOTIC FRONT, or ZANU-PF, this group forced Smith to negotiate a truce, which, in 1980, resulted in the creation of the independent, African-dominated Republic of Zimbabwe.

In the republic's first elections Mugabe and ZANU emerged victorious, largely because ZANU had support among the Shona people, Zimbabwe's majority ethnic group. ZAPU, on the other hand, was the party of the Ndebele, who constitute only 20 percent of the population. Nkomo was named minister of home affairs in Mugabe's government, but he was dismissed in 1982 for his alleged involvement in a plot to overthrow Mugabe.

During much of the 1980s Nkomo and ZAPU were engaged in factional fighting with ZANU. Both sides reportedly committed HUMAN RIGHTS atrocities, although Nkomo's ZAPU supporters took the worst abuse. In 1987 Nkomo and Mugabe finally reached an accord, merging their parties into ZANU-PF and thereby transforming Zimbabwe into a one-party state. For the duration of his political career, Nkomo remained extremely popular, especially in Matabeleland, his home region and where he was in charge of DEVELOPMENT. With his health in decline, he left politics in 1997 and died two years later.

See also: ETHNIC CONFLICT IN AFRICA (Vol. V); ETHNICITY AND IDENTITY (Vol. I); INDEPENDENCE MOVEMENTS (Vol. V); NDEBELE (Vol. IV); NKOMO, JOSHUA (Vol. IV); SHONA (Vol. I); SHONA KINGDOMS (Vols. III, IV); SOUTHERN RHODESIA (Vol. IV).

Nkrumah, Kwame (Francis Nwia Kofie Nkrumah) (1909–1972) *First president of Ghana*

After leading GHANA to independence, in 1957, and becoming president of the new republic, in 1960, Kwame Nkrumah focused on formulating domestic and African policy while responding to the pressures of the Cold War. Nkrumah centered his domestic policy on a rapid modernization of industries and communication, and the development of an educated African workforce. He believed that accomplishing these goals would be made easier by removing political opposition. To facilitate this, Nkrumah pushed through the passage of the Deportation Act of 1957 and the Detention Acts of 1958, 1959, and 1962, and he encouraged the intimidation of opposition party members. These tactics were hardly welcomed, and there were two assassination attempts against Nkrumah. In 1964 Nkrumah eliminated all opposition parties, establishing Ghana as a one-party state and appointing himself president for life.

Nkrumah's government improved Ghana's INFRASTRUCTURE, building new roads and constructing, in 1966, the AKOSOMBO DAM, which was to meet Ghana's expanding electrical needs. Nkrumah believed that these measures would allow Ghana to extricate itself from colonial and neocolonial exploitation and enable the country to be a leader of the PAN-AFRICANISM movement. In an attempt to lessen Ghana's dependence on cocoa EXPORTS, Nkrumah emulated Gamal Abdel NASSER (1918–1970), of EGYPT, and Ahmed Sékou TOURÉ (1922–1984), of GUINEA, by accepting aid from both the capitalist and the Communist blocs. In 1965, however, he published the book *Neocolonialism,* in which he explained how foreign companies and governments were becoming rich at the expense of African peoples. The United States took issue with the book and responded by withdrawing $35 million in economic aid. By 1966 Ghana was in serious economic trouble, due at least in part to the heavy debt incurred by Nkrumah's infrastructure programs.

Meanwhile, in foreign affairs Nkrumah focused on forming a United States of Africa, believing that the political unification of the continent would enable African countries to compete equally with industrialized nations in the global marketplace. He also believed that such a union would help African nations withstand the political pressures of the Cold War. In the 1930s Nkrumah had developed this concept of a United States of Africa while he was a college student in the United States of America. His beliefs were strengthened in 1945, when he participated in the fifth Pan-African Congress in Manchester, England. To that end, in 1958 Nkrumah joined Ghana with Guinea; MALI joined the union in 1961. Nkrumah planned to use this collaboration as a successful example of unification. He also wrote a book, *Why Africa Must Unite,* to promote his views. In 1963 he organized a conference at ADDIS ABABA, ETHIOPIA, for the heads of the 32 African states that had achieved independence by that time. The result of this conference was the founding of the ORGANIZATION OF AFRICAN UNITY (OAU), which pledged to work for African unity, freedom, and prosperity. The members, however, would remain individual African states rather than Nkrumah's desired United States of Africa.

Over time Nkrumah's spending on DEVELOPMENT projects and his concept of a united Africa overburdened Ghana's treasury. With the collapse of world cocoa prices during the early 1960s and the subsequent downturn in the country's economy, unemployment and inflation rose dramatically. Nkrumah responded with a socialist-based austerity program, which included higher taxes that brought protests from workers and farmers. In response to criticism, Nkrumah detained and imprisoned hundreds of opponents, bringing about allegations of HUMAN RIGHTS abuses. Ever more concerned about his hold on power, Nkrumah established a personal security service and presidential guard, both better equipped than the neglected army and police.

Despite Nkrumah's efforts, in 1966 a military COUP D'ÉTAT took place while he was traveling to Hanoi, North Vietnam. The government was taken over by the National Liberation Council, which dismissed Nkrumah as president and banned his Convention People's Party (CPP). Guinea's president Touré then invited Nkrumah to live in Guinea and preside with him as co-president. While living in Guinea Nkrumah wrote *Handbook for Revolutionary Warfare* (1968) and *Class Struggle in Africa* (1970). He died in 1972 in Romania, where he was receiving medical treatment for cancer. He was buried in Ghana.

Although controversial, Nkrumah is considered an authority on the political theory and practical application of PAN-AFRICANISM. A charismatic leader, Nkrumah believed that Ghana must lead the way to the total liberation of Africa from colonialism and its lingering effects, arguing that once political freedom was achieved, then economic freedom would follow.

See also: CASH CROPS (Vol. V); COCOA (Vol. IV); COLD WAR AND AFRICA (Vols. IV, V); NKRUMAH, KWAME (Vol. IV).

Further reading: Opoku Agyeman, *Nkrumah's Ghana and East Africa: Pan-Africanism and African Interstate Relations* (Cranbury, N.J.: Associated University Press, 1992); David Birmingham, *Kwame Nkrumah: The Father of African Nationalism* (Athens, Ohio: Ohio University Press, 1998); Charles Adom Boateng, *The Political Legacy of Kwame Nkrumah of Ghana* (Lewiston, N.Y.: Edwin Mellen Press, 2003); Trevor Jones, *Ghana's First Republic 1960–1966: The Pursuit of the Political Kingdom* (New York: Harper & Row, 1976); June Milne, compiler, *Kwame Nkrumah: The Conakry Years: His Life and Letters* (London: Panaf, 1990).

Nkumbula, Harry (1916–1983) *Zambian leader of African nationalism*

Nkumbula was born in the southern region of ZAMBIA (Northern Rhodesia, at the time), where his father was a chief of the Ila ethnic group. As a youth Nkumbula attended church-run schools before studying to become a teacher at Kafue Training College. In 1942 he moved to the city of Mufulira, where he became active in politics. Soon after, he went to the copper-MINING center of Kitwe and helped form the Kitwe African Society. Apprehensive about Nkumbula's growing political influence and hoping to divert his energies, colonial authorities gave him a scholarship to study at MAKERERE UNIVERSITY, in UGANDA. They later gave him a scholarship to study in England. There he became acquainted with other key African nationalist figures, including Hastings Kamuzu BANDA (c. 1898–1997), Jomo KENYATTA (c. 1891–1978), and Kwame NKRUMAH (1909–1972).

Nkumbula returned home to Northern Rhodesia in 1951 and joined the Northern Rhodesia African Congress, which, modeling itself after the AFRICAN NATIONAL CONGRESS of SOUTH AFRICA, reorganized and renamed itself the Northern Rhodesia African National Congress (NRANC). During this time Nkumbula also worked closely with the 20,000-member African Mineworkers Union, which was the colony's largest organized African group. At the time, African political activity in Northern Rhodesia centered around opposing the Central African Federation, the formation of which would have united Northern Rhodesia and Nyasaland (now MALAWI) with the white-dominant government of Southern Rhodesia. Nkumbula, along with fellow NRANC member Kenneth KAUNDA (1924–   ), organized African resistance to the federation, including boycotts and demonstrations. In 1955, however, their activities landed the pair in prison, where they both served two months time.

After their release Nkumbula and Kaunda gradually moved in different directions. In 1958 Kaunda and others left the NRANC to form what eventually became the UNITED NATIONAL INDEPENDENCE PARTY (UNIP). UNIP quickly ascended to the preeminent position among Northern Rhodesia's political parties, gaining the most parliamentary seats in the 1962 elections. The NRANC, however, won a sufficient number of seats to prevent a UNIP majority. As a result UNIP was compelled to form a coalition government, with Nkumbula as the education minister. The 1964 independence election, however, provided UNIP with a clear victory, leaving the NRANC as the opposition. In 1972, with the constitutional amendment that prohibited other political parties, the NRANC had to dissolve. Nkumbula, having lost his political base, joined UNIP.

In 1978 Nkumbula and Simon Kapwepwe (1922–1980), another veteran politician, challenged Kaunda for the UNIP presidency. In response Kaunda engineered the changing of the party rules, nullifying the candidacies of Nkumbula and Kapwepwe. Disillusioned, Nkumbula quit politics. He died five years later, leaving behind a political career that mirrored those of many other African leaders who had gained prominence during INDEPENDENCE MOVEMENTS, only to be excluded from leadership positions once independence became a reality.

See also: CENTRAL AFRICAN FEDERATION (Vol. IV); NATIONALISM AND INDEPENDENCE MOVEMENTS (Vol. IV); NORTHERN RHODESIA (Vol. IV); POLITICAL PARTIES AND ORGANIZATIONS (Vols. IV, V); SOUTHERN RHODESIA (Vol. IV).

Nonaligned Movement and Africa

During the Cold War, many states rejected strict alignment with either the Eastern bloc countries, led by the Soviet Union, or the Western bloc countries, led by the United States. Various African presidents and their states played important roles in the movement, which has continued since the end of the Cold War. The Nonaligned Movement (NAM) was created in September, 1961, when the leaders of 25 countries met in Belgrade, Yugoslavia. At the time, the threat of war between the former Soviet Union and the United States dominated international politics. The Nonaligned Movement was inspired by the Bandung Afro-Asian Conference of 1955. At that summit 29 African and Asian countries showed solidarity in distancing themselves from the Western and Soviet power blocs to avoid becoming pawns in Cold War power games.

Subsequent NAM conferences were usually held once every three years. As of 2003, five out of the 12 conferences were held in African countries: EGYPT (1964), ZAMBIA (1970), ALGERIA (1973), ZIMBABWE (1986), and SOUTH AFRICA (1998). The early conferences held in Africa featured widespread condemnation of Western colonialism and called for a rejection of the building of foreign military installations in Africa.

When Cold War tensions loosened in the 1990s, African countries used their membership in the NAM to campaign against the use of anti-personnel land mines, POVERTY, and disease. As of 2003, all African states except the embattled country of WESTERN SAHARA stood as member states of the NAM. The 116 NAM member states met in 2003, affirming the movement's relevance at its summit in Kuala Lumpur, Malaysia. There they outlined a plan of action to promote peace, security, justice, equality, democracy, and DEVELOPMENT in accordance with international law and the Charter of the United Nations.

See also: BANDUNG AFRO-ASIAN CONFERENCE (Vol. IV); COLD WAR AND AFRICA (Vols. IV, V); SOVIET UNION AND AFRICA (Vols. IV, V); UNITED NATIONS AND AFRICA (Vols. V); UNITED STATES AND AFRICA (Vols. IV, V).

non-government organizations

Independent associations, usually advocate groups, that have no governmental function or agenda. Today non-government organizations (NGOs) are a powerful third force along with governments and private enterprise. Until the early 1980s non-government organizations were generally thought of as independent organizations, such as churches, hospitals, and cultural organizations. They were not considered valuable as potential conduits for information or goods. Their role rapidly changed, however. In the late 1980s, international donors such as the UN Development Program, the WORLD BANK, the U.K. Department of International Development, and the U.S. Agency for International Development began looking at governments in the developing world with a more critical eye. High levels of government CORRUPTION and poor management of funds forced donors to look for alternative ways of providing funds for DEVELOPMENT, POVERTY relief, and other humanitarian efforts. Partnerships with private companies became more popular.

However, donors found that many project needs went unmet because private companies still operated under the pressure to maximize profits. Non-government organizations were singled out as a third path that could implement projects of interest to donors. As a result, between the late 1970s and 1992, donor funding for international NGOs rose from less than 2 percent to about 30 percent of income. For many local NGOs, donors were the sole source of funding.

The diversification of funding meant a rapid evolution in the makeup and function of many NGOs. Typical NGOs now have a formalized structure, are completely independent of government, operate as non-profit groups, and are objective in their quest to improve the lives of those in their project areas. With a broad array of responsibilities, the activities of NGOs now often overlap with those of various nonprofit, community-based, and volunteer organizations.

The explanation behind the recent explosion of NGO support was that, as new NGOs form, they could participate in the great DEMOCRATIZATION efforts that began in the early 1990s following the end of the Cold War era. NGO's did not intrinsically mandate a particular ideology, but instead focused on regular and active participation. In keeping with strategies of improved governance, donors could funnel funds without being challenged by the existing governments. Moreover, the structure of local NGOs integrated well with international NGOs, resulting in proliferation of international-local NGO partnerships with multiple revenue streams. These organizations, many soon realized, were far superior to state-run development agencies, which, in Africa, tended to exacerbate ethnic and class tensions between the ruling elite and the masses.

The changing role of NGOs has come with its own problems, however. For instance, when an NGO links to an international institution, such as the United Nations or the World Bank, it must conform to standards set by the international institution. Operating under the bureaucratic regulations of these larger institutions often causes the smaller NGO to lose the nimble and adaptive qualities that make it such a valuable mechanism. The NGOs end up unable to react to government actions or to cooperate fully with their international partners. In these cases, NGOs rapidly become irrelevant.

In the 21st century NGOs continue to provide valuable mediation between the private sector and government. In addition, the general consensus is that the effectiveness of NGOs is improving. For instance, the World Bank estimates that, between 1995 and 2003, 66 percent of projects that involved NGOs were successful, up from 48 percent in the five-year period 1990–95. In some places, such as SOMALIA, the number of NGOs increased rapidly in just a few years, as localized organizations began performing what are normally government functions.

Unfortunately, external donor funding of NGOs has led to opportunism and even fraud. An all too common situation is one in which so-called development brokers—often government bureaucrats laid off from STRUCTURAL ADJUSTMENT programs—create NGOs for the sole purpose of acquiring international funds for embezzlement or some other misappropriation.

However, enthusiasm for some NGOs is more modest, especially in cases where donors disagree on what it takes for NGOs to succeed. Current topics of discussion and debate for most NGOs include the role of the administrative environment, the experience of the particular NGO, the relationship between the NGO and its beneficiaries, the quality of the NGO monitoring, and the NGO leadership skills. They also take into consideration the fact that weak relationships with beneficiaries and low levels of community participation erode potential NGO success. Recently NGOs have been asked to improve their relationships with governments rather than simply replace government organs.

NGOs have also faced challenges from below. In KENYA, for instance, the formation of NGOs became popular among MAASAI groups seeking to improve pastoral development funding. NGOs coordinated land rights and linked them to international norms. In so doing, however, NGOs undermined Kenyan CIVIL SOCIETY at the community level. Rather than reflecting the views of the initial beneficiaries, these NGOs became proxies for doing the bidding of donors.

See also: STATE, ROLE OF (Vol. V).

Further reading: Roger C. Riddell and Mark Robinson, *Non-Government Organizations and Rural Poverty Alleviation* (Oxford, U.K.: Oxford University Press, 1995); Eve Sandberg, ed., *The Changing Politics of Non-Government Organizations in African States* (Westport, Conn.: Praeger Publishers, 1994).

Northern People's Congress (NPC) Political party of Northern Region of pre-independence NIGERIA. Formed in 1949, the Northern People's Congress (NPC) represented the interests of HAUSA-Fulani people in independence negotiations and in the drafting of a postcolonial constitution. When Nigeria did become independent, in 1960, NPC representatives in the coalition government were awarded positions of power. NPC president Abubakar Tafawa BALEWA (1912–1966), for example, exercised broad executive power as the nation's first prime minister.

At independence Nigeria had more than 80 political parties, symbolic of the ethnic, class, and regional divisions that made the country difficult to govern. Since the NPC was the main party of the Muslim-dominated Northern Region, it had to form alliances with other conservative parties to gain influence in national politics.

In 1966 Nigeria's ethnic tensions broke out in violence, with a group of IGBO army officers staging a COUP D'ÉTAT to remove northern Hausa-Fulani Muslims from the top of Nigeria's power structure. Balewa and fellow NPC leader, Ahmadu BELLO (1909–1966), were assassinated in the coup. As a result of the Eastern Region's secession to form BIAFRA, civil war soon engulfed the country, creating a power vacuum that was filled by a military government.

In 1979, when it seemed that Nigeria's civil strife was over, the military government approved a new constitution and made provisions for the election of a new civilian government. Old political parties were dissolved and reorganized into five new organizations for the election. The NPC, for its part, was folded into the National Party of Nigeria (NPN), which won the elections. The NPN founder, Shehu Shagari (1925–), formerly of the NPC, became Nigeria's new president. The NPN differed from the NPC, however, in that it garnered significant support in some non-Igbo states in southeastern Nigeria. Shagari won reelection in 1983 but was soon toppled in yet another military coup.

See also: CIVIL WARS (Vol. V); POLITICAL PARTIES AND ORGANIZATIONS (Vols. IV, V).

Further reading: Larry Diamond, *Class, Ethnicity, and Democracy in Nigeria: The Failure of the First Republic* (Syracuse, N.Y.: Syracuse University Press, 1988).

Nouakchott Capital and principal urban center of MAURITANIA, located on a plateau near the Atlantic coast. In 1957, three years prior to Mauritania's full independence, the small coastal village of Nouakchott was chosen to be the national capital. The following year a massive construction project was started to accommodate about 15,000 residents. Since that time, the population of the city has exploded, with an estimated 661,000 people living there today. The rapid growth can be attributed largely to the migration of REFUGEES from the Sahara during recurring periods of drought. Gated villas, luxurious by local standards, are visible from the slums located at the city's center. Islam is the state religion of Mauritania. Nouakchott's mosque, built with donations by a Saudi Arabian philanthropist, is a major feature of the urban landscape.

Although Nouakchott's industrial output is light, a nearby port, with its deepwater harbor built in the 1980s, provides the INFRASTRUCTURE to export OIL and copper. Small-scale commerce is active, and high-quality handicrafts can be purchased in the city's sprawling markets. In addition, Nouakchott is home to Mauritania's National Institute of Advanced Islamic Studies (founded in 1961) and the National School of Administration (1966).

See also: ARAB WORLD AND AFRICA (Vol. V); POPULATION GROWTH (Vol. V); SAHARA (Vols. I, II); URBAN LIFE AND CULTURE (Vols. IV, V); URBANIZATION (Vols. IV, V).

Ntaryamira, Cyprien (1956–1994) *President of Burundi*

Not much is known about Ntaryamira's early life. An agricultural engineer, he became involved in politics in the early 1970s, during the short civil war that was sparked by an attempted COUP D'ÉTAT against the dictator of BURUNDI, Michel Micombero (1940–1983). As many as 200,000 HUTU died in the conflict, and Ntaryamira, a Hutu, was forced into exile.

In 1983 Ntaryamira returned to his homeland. He found employment in the Foreign Ministry of TUTSI president Jean-Baptiste Bagaza (1946–). Ntaryamira became involved in underground movements to reform Bagaza's government, in particular a new political party, the FRONT FOR DEMOCRACY IN BURUNDI (FRODEBU). FRODEBU was led by Ntaryamira's close friend, the Hutu Melchior Ndadaye (1953–1993), and challenged the only legal party in Burundi, Bagaza's Union for National Progress.

In 1987 a coup d'état removed Bagaza from power and replaced him with the Tutsi Pierre BUYOYA (1949–). The following year ethnic violence between the Hutu and Tutsi erupted again in northern Burundi, and Buyoya sent the largely Tutsi army to reassert control. About 5,000 Hutu died as a result of the army's suppression, which Burundi's Hutu called a massacre.

This event eventually put great pressure on Buyoya to reform the government and allow for multiparty, democratic elections. The 1993 elections brought Ndadaye to the presidency, with Ntaryamira taking a ministerial position. Forming a government made up of both Hutu and Tutsi, Ndadaye seemed to be leading Burundi toward peace until a coup resulted in his assassination. After much controversy Ntaryamira was inaugurated as president.

Though Ntaryamira worked to ease ethnic tensions, his efforts proved fruitless. Two months after assuming power in 1994 Ntaryamira's plane crashed while returning to Burundi from a summit with other African leaders on Hutu-Tutsi violence. Ntaryamira was killed along with Juvenal HABYARIMANA (1937–1994), Rwanda's president. Though there were no eyewitnesses to the crash that killed Ntaryamira, it is commonly believed that the plane was shot down in an attempt to assassinate the Burundian president. The deaths of both leaders had far-reaching effects, particularly in RWANDA, where a horrific civil war ensued. In Burundi Ntaryamira's death actually had a pacifying effect, with the worst of the violence subsiding.

See also: ETHNIC CONFLICT IN AFRICA (Vol. V); ETHNICITY AND IDENTITY (Vol. I).

Nujoma, Sam (Samuel Daniel Shafiishuna Nujoma) (1929–) *First president of Namibia*

Born to a large family in Etunda, in the Omusati Region of SOUTH WEST AFRICA (present-day NAMIBIA), Nujoma studied at the Okahao Finnish Lutheran Mission School until 1945. He then moved to WALVIS BAY and, later, WINDHOEK, the country's capital. In Windhoek he worked as a dining-car waiter for South African Railways, gaining his first political experience while trying to organize a union for railway workers—an action that cost him his job. In 1959 Nujoma and fellow Ovambo Andimba (Herman) Toivo ja Toivo (1924–   ) founded the Ovamboland People's Organization (OPO), which Nujoma was elected to lead.

At the time, SOUTH AFRICA administered the former German colony, initially as a League of Nations mandate, and then from 1946 as a United Nations (UN) trust territory. Though it was supposed to be preparing Namibia for independence, South Africa essentially annexed the territory as its fifth province and brought it under the APARTHEID system.

In 1959 the OPO and the HERERO-led South West African National Union (SWANU) organized resistance against racially based relocation policies imposed by South Africa. The resistance led to a police massacre of 12 protesters, and Nujoma was arrested. He went into exile the following year.

While in exile Nujoma's OPO distanced itself from SWANU and formed the SOUTH WEST AFRICA PEOPLE'S ORGANIZATION (SWAPO). Despite his exile, as the leader of SWAPO, Nujoma made many international appearances, appealing for an end to South African rule in Namibia. When petitions to the United Nations failed, Nujoma turned to funneling weapons from ALGERIA to support SWAPO's guerrilla wing, the People's Liberation Army of Namibia (PLAN). They eventually launched an armed resistance in 1966. In 1978 the United Nations passed Resolution 435, which paved the way for Namibian independence. In 1989 Nujoma returned to Namibia after almost 30 years of exile and led SWAPO to victory in national elections. Nujoma became president, and the following year, after decades of South African delay and resistance, Namibia declared its independence.

As president, Nujoma benefited from Namibia's UN-organized transition toward DEMOCRATIZATION. Nujoma won reelection in 1994, and at the end of that term the Parliament's SWAPO majority amended the constitution to allow him to sit for a third term, which he began in 1998. This move caused alarm both in Namibia and abroad, as Nujoma has become increasingly authoritarian. He has been criticized for his Marxist ideals and his appreciation of Zimbabwe's increasingly autocratic president, Robert MUGABE (1924–   ). He has also made moves toward centralizing the government and he has lashed out against political opposition. He even banned all public demonstrations in 1997 after a hostage incident involving soldiers demanding jobs. In 2002 he assumed control of the Ministry of Information and Broadcasting, censoring all foreign television broadcasts. He has also come under fire from international organizations, such as Amnesty International, for his virulent anti-homosexual stance.

See also: AMNESTY INTERNATIONAL AND AFRICA (Vol. V); INDEPENDENCE MOVEMENTS (Vol. V); LEAGUE OF NATIONS AND AFRICA (Vol. IV); NATIONALISM AND INDEPEN-DENCE MOVEMENTS (Vol. IV); OVAMBO (Vols. II, IV); UNITED NATIONS AND AFRICA (Vols. IV, V).

Nwapa, Flora (Florence Nwanzuruahu Nkiru Nwapa) (1931–1993) *Nigerian author and publisher*

A child of IGBO parents who were both teachers, Flora Nwapa was born in Oguta, in eastern NIGERIA. She received her early education at schools in Nigeria and in 1957 graduated with a bachelor's degree from Nigeria's University College. The following year Nwapa traveled to study at the University of Edinburgh, in Scotland, where she received a teaching degree.

After Scotland Nwapa returned home to Nigeria, a country that was on the verge of independence, to work as a teacher and school administrator. With the encouragement of fellow Nigerian author Chinua ACHEBE (1930–   ), she also began writing a novel, *Efuru,* which was published in 1966. The story of an Igbo woman who finds a unique way of fitting in to her society, *Efuru* was one of the first English-language novels—if not the first—to be published by a Nigerian woman.

Following the publication of *Efuru,* Nigeria suffered through the BIAFRA rebellion, during which time Nwapa experienced first-hand the horrors of civil war. In 1967, the year the Biafran crisis began, Nwapa married Chief Gogo Nwakuche, with whom she eventually had three children.

After the war in 1971 Nwapa published *Idu,* another story of a Nigerian woman in crisis, as well as a collection of short stories called *This Is Lagos.* The latter book marked a change in setting from Nigeria's rural villages to the bustling former capital of the title, and exposed Nwapa to a new urban readership.

> When Flora Nwapa's novels were first published, literary critics, mostly males, failed to recognize their importance. As time went on, however, Nwapa's unique voice and her ability to capture the indomitable spirit of Igbo women made her a popular author among feminists in Africa and around the world.

In 1975 Nwapa published *Never Again,* an antiwar novella that recalled the fighting and starvation that she experienced first-hand during Nigeria's civil war. That same year, she quit her position as a government official to devote herself to writing. Frustrated with her publishers, Nwapa also started her own publishing company, Tana Press, and, in 1977, she founded the Flora Nwapa Book Company, both of which she used to publish her own works, including several children's books. Nwapa died in Nigeria after a brief illness in 1993.

See also: LITERATURE IN MODERN AFRICA (Vol. V); WOMEN IN INDEPENDENT AFRICA (Vol V).

Nyerere, Julius (Julius Kambarage Nyerere)
(1922–1999) *First president of Tanzania (1962–1985)*

Over the course of the 1950s Nyerere, a former teacher in Catholic mission schools, orchestrated the movement for Tanzanian independence. Central to this effort was the country's first political party, the Tanganyika African National Union (TANU). (Prior to 1964, mainland TANZANIA was known as Tanganyika.) Taking advantage of the international status of Tanganyika as a United Nations Trust Territory, Nyerere succeeded in getting elections scheduled. In 1960, following elections, the colonial power Britain granted Tanganyika limited self-government, and Nyerere became the nation's chief minister. Full independence came in 1961, with Nyerere becoming prime minister. When the country became a republic, in 1962, Nyerere was elected its first president.

In the 1960s and 1970s, Nyerere was recognized as one of Africa's most gifted and original political thinkers. He spoke and wrote extensively about his ideas for the continent's social, political, and economic DEVELOPMENT. Among his books are *Ujamaa: Essays on Socialism* (1968) and *Man and Development* (1974).

Political turmoil struck Tanganyika in 1963, when the African population of nearby ZANZIBAR staged a bloody revolution in the wake of its independence, overthrowing the government of the Busaidi sultan and forcing most of the island's Arab elite to flee. Not long after, the Tanganyika army attempted its own COUP D'ÉTAT, which Nyerere managed to suppress only with the backing of the British army. As a result of the political upheaval, in 1964 Nyerere led mainland Tanganyika to merge with Zanzibar to form the United Republic of Tanzania. With the establishment of a new constitution in 1965, Tanzania became a one-party state, and Nyerere's old party—still called TANU but now standing for the *Tanzanian* African National Union—governed the mainland. Zanzibar, for its part, continued to be run by the AFRO-SHIRAZI PARTY. The two parties finally merged in 1977 to form the PARTY OF THE REVOLUTION (in Kiswahili, Chama Cha Mapinduzi, CCM).

Nyerere had emerged as one of the key African leaders instrumental in the founding of the ORGANIZATION OF AFRICAN UNITY, in 1963, and he continued to be a firm believer in the unity of the continent as a whole—not just the two East African neighbors. He was also committed to the end of colonial rule throughout Africa and therefore offered sanctuary in Tanzania to members of African liberation movements from SOUTH AFRICA, ZIMBABWE, MOZAMBIQUE, and ANGOLA. In addition, in 1978, he sent 20,000 soldiers into UGANDA to depose its dictator, Idi AMIN (c. 1925–2003), after Amin had first invaded northwestern Tanzania. These activities, however, exacted a heavy toll on Nyerere's poor country.

Because he saw that Tanzania, and indeed most of Africa, was impoverished in the aftermath of colonialism, Nyerere advocated socialism based on African values. This led to the ARUSHA DECLARATION, in 1967. Its centerpiece was UJAMAA ("community" or "familyhood"), a cooperative state policy characterized by economic self-reliance, egalitarianism, and local rural development.

Nyerere's reforms reached all aspects of life within Tanzania. Nyerere fostered Kiswahili as the national and official language, and Kiswahili became the medium of instruction in schools at all levels. This, Nyerere felt, was a way of empowering those Tanzanians whose limited knowledge of English, previously the official language, would have excluded them from full participation in national life.

Nyerere's policies had a mixed record. The quality of life for Tanzanians improved dramatically, and the country soon became one of Africa's most stable, both politically and socially. And further, in an era when many African heads of state utilized their positions to enrich themselves and their families, Nyerere chose to live a modest lifestyle. Yet, Tanzania remained desperately poor, and even today its per-capita income is only $610. (In comparison, the per-capita income of KENYA is $1,000; of Uganda, $1,200; and of South Africa, $9,400. The per-capita income of the United States is about $36,300.) Much of the fault lies with the economic failure of *ujamaa*, which relied on an inefficient, socialistic system of AGRICULTURE.

Nyerere, the former school teacher, took an active hand in promoting the development of Kiswahili as a language of instruction. He translated two of Shakespeare's plays, *Julius Cesar* (1963) and *The Merchant of Venice* (1969), into Kiswahili as a way of expanding the literature books available for use in schools.

In 1985 Nyerere gained the respect of Tanzanians and of the world by being one of the first African presidents to retire voluntarily from office, although he remained chairman of CCM until 1990. His successor was the Zanzibari political leader, Ali Hassan MWINYI (1925–   ).

In 1999 Nyerere was in London for medical treatment when he died. Tanzanians genuinely mourned the passing of the man whom they all respectfully called *Mwalimu* (teacher).

See also: BUSAIDI (Vols. III, IV); COLONIAL RULE (Vol. IV); EDUCATION (Vols. IV, V); KISWAHILI (Vols. II, III, IV); LANGUAGE USAGE IN MODERN AFRICA (Vol. V); NYERERE, JULIUS (Vol. IV); TANGANYIKA (Vol. IV).

Further reading: William Edgett Smith, *We Must Run While They Walk; a Portrait of Africa's Julius Nyerere* (New York: Random House, 1971).

O

OAU See ORGANIZATION OF AFRICAN UNITY.

Obasanjo, Olusegun (Matthew Olusegun Fajinmi Aremu Obasanjo) (c. 1937–) *Nigerian military dictator elected president in 1999*

Born in YORUBA-dominated southwestern NIGERIA, Obasanjo dropped the English part of his name while he was in high school in rebellion against what was widely felt in Nigeria to be British cultural imperialism. In 1958, unable to afford college, he entered the military, quickly rising in the officer corps. After serving with UN peacekeeping forces in the long-running Congolese civil war, Obasanjo held several important commands during Nigeria's own civil war, also known as the Biafran War (1967–70). Extensive training at the Royal College of Military Engineering in England and with the Indian Army School of Engineering led to his posting as commander of Nigeria's army engineers.

In 1975 the Nigerian leader Yakubu GOWON (1934–) appointed Obasanjo federal commissioner of works and housing, and, following Gowon's ouster by General Murtala Muhammad (1938–1976), Obasanjo became army chief of staff. In the wake of Muhammad's assassination in 1976, Obasanjo assumed power, taking control of both the government and the army. Pledging to lead Nigeria into a new period of civilian rule, he vowed to hold democratic elections, led the nation in adopting a new constitution, and lifted the ban on political parties. In the promised democratic election of 1979, Obasanjo was defeated by Shehu Shagari (1925–), to whom he turned over the reins of government, initiating Nigeria's Second Republic.

> Although Obasanjo was widely praised for his DEMOCRATIZATION efforts during the 1970s, many found his policies to be repressive. In 1977, for example, Obasanjo's soldiers raided the home of musician FELA (1938–1997), an outspoken critic of the military regime. The soldiers burned down the house and threw the musician's aged mother from an upper-floor window. After his mother later died of the injuries she suffered, Fela composed a song, "Coffin for a Head of State," in which he describes trying to present his mother's coffin to the dictator.

After leaving the government Obasanjo started an agricultural company. He also became active in international affairs, at one point even being considered for secretary-general of the United Nations. Obasanjo remained on the sidelines of domestic politics during the 1980s, which was a turbulent decade in Nigeria. However, in 1995 the head of state, General Sani ABACHA (1943–1998), accused Obasanjo, along with scores of others, of treason, sending him to prison. In spite of numerous international protests, it was not until Abacha's death, in 1998, and the accession to power of General Abdulsalami Abubakar (1943–), that Obasanjo was finally released.

Obasanjo reentered politics, and in November 1998 he declared himself a candidate for president in the coming elections. In spite of charges and counter-charges of CORRUPTION and election rigging, international observers concluded that Obasanjo's victory over Chief Olu Falae

329

was legitimate, and Obasanjo was declared president in the spring of 1999. Since then he has struggled to solve the various economic, political, and social crises facing Nigeria. He supervised the creation of a new constitution, privatized and deregulated a number of businesses, and attempted to revitalize Nigeria's struggling agricultural sector. He also reorganized the Nigerian military, eliminating officers from political posts, and has made some inroads against governmental corruption.

Less successful, however, have been Obasanjo's efforts at dealing with Nigeria's infamous inter-ethnic conflicts. Hostility between the three main groups—the HAUSA of the north, the IGBO of the east, and the Yoruba of the west—continues. To make matters even more difficult, Nigeria's Muslim leaders have been advocating a return to the strict Islamic legal system of SHARIA. Caught in a debate over the extent of the central government's power to limit the authority of local governments—and unwilling to alienate completely Nigeria's large Muslim population—Obasanjo stood by as seemingly independent legal systems are established, often in direct conflict with the Nigerian constitution. As the 21st century began, this legal crisis was added to the others that challenged Nigeria's civilian government.

See also: BIAFRA (Vol. V); ETHNIC CONFLICT IN AFRICA (Vol. V).

Obiang, Teodoro (Teodoro Obiang Nguema Mbasogo) (1942–   ) President of Equatorial Guinea

Born in the continental region of EQUATORIAL GUINEA known as Río Muni, Obiang was schooled at Río Muni's administrative capital of Bata. He underwent military training in Spain, returning to Equatorial Guinea in 1965. The nephew of Equatoguinean dictator Francisco Macías Nguema (1922–1979), Obiang received special treatment and quickly rose through the military ranks, becoming military governor of the island of Fernando Po (now Bioko) and serving as director of the Black Beach prison. Enjoying Nguema's favor, Obiang became a lieutenant colonel in 1975.

The relationship between Obiang and the president quickly soured, however, when the dictator ordered the execution of Obiang's brother, in 1979. Later that year, Obiang launched a bloody COUP D'ÉTAT that ousted Nguema from power. Obiang assumed the presidency as head of a supreme military council. Nguema was tried, convicted on multiple charges, and executed.

Obiang led a country with no INFRASTRUCTURE, a completely devastated economy, and a population only one-third the size it had been when Nguema became the country's first president, in 1968. Conditions failed to improve under Obiang. He banned POLITICAL PARTIES AND ORGANIZATIONS, and despite promises of DEMOCRATIZATION he maintained supreme authority in Equatorial Guinea.

Obiang repeatedly ran unopposed in elections, as fraud and repression forced his opponents to withdraw. In 2001 the entire cabinet resigned in protest against Obiang's authoritarian rule. Running unopposed in 2003, the president was once again reelected.

Equatorial Guinea remains a dictatorial state where citizens lack political rights and suffer through miserable economic conditions. The discovery of OIL, which became the nation's prime export in 1999, has produced a significant enough economic boost to provide the country with sustained DEVELOPMENT, but nearly all of the profits have gone directly to Obiang and his supporters.

Obote, Milton (Apolo Milton Obote) (1924–   ) Ugandan political leader

Born in the village of Akokor, in northern UGANDA, Milton Obote rose to prominence during the pre-independence era of the 1950s. Successfully merging several once-independent political parties, he was able to defeat the dominant Democratic Party and become prime minister when Uganda emerged as an independent nation.

Although Obote won the election, he faced almost insurmountable problems as prime minister, the most important of which was trying to create a unified nation out of a divided population. The major obstacle to unity lay in the role traditionally played by Buganda, a kingdom that had a long history of autonomy and power under the British colonial administration of Uganda. The wealthiest and most powerful of all Ugandans, the Baganda, as people from Buganda are called, were not willing to relinquish their supremacy in the political, social, and economic arenas. By the mid-1960s the situation had erupted in violence. Obote responded by seizing the reins of power, suspending the constitution, and even ordering his army, under General Idi AMIN (c. 1925–2003), to attack Buganda's capital, KAMPALA.

Obote's one-party rule, which began to veer toward a more socialist state, was not well received by many Ugandans, and in 1971 Amin seized power in a COUP D'ÉTAT. Obote, who was out of the country at the time, fled to TANZANIA, where he remained throughout the eight years of murder and terror that followed.

In 1979 Obote, aided by an invasion from Tanzania, was back in Uganda. One year later, following an election that many people believe was rigged, Obote returned to power. By then, however, he was opposed by a wide range of forces, and he was able to keep office only by resorting to the same kind of terror that had been employed by Amin. Opposition to Obote came from the international community as well as from within, and it was not long before his tactics were denounced worldwide. Accused of being responsible for the murders of more than 100,000 of his people, Obote was finally overthrown in 1985. He eventually fled to ZAMBIA, where he was given political asylum.

See also: BUGANDA (Vols. III, IV); ENGLAND AND AFRICA (Vols. III, IV, V); OBOTE, MILTON (Vol. IV).

Further reading: Phares Mutibwa, *Uganda Since Independence: A Story of Unfulfilled Promise* (Trenton, N.J.: Africa World Press, 1992).

Odinga, Oginga (Jaramongi Oginga Odinga)
(1912–1994) *Luo political leader in Kenya*

Odinga was part of the powerful LUO political tradition that included Tom MBOYA (1930–1969). In 1960 the two were founding members of the KENYAN AFRICAN NATIONAL UNION (KANU), a political party that played a major role in securing Kenya's independence as well as the freedom of the party's imprisoned KIKUYU leader, Jomo KENYATTA (c. 1891–1978). In 1964 Kenyatta became the first president of independent Kenya, and Odinga was rewarded with the vice presidency.

Odinga's relationship with Kenyatta quickly soured, however. Kenyatta believed that the country needed a one-party political system in order to maintain national unity. To that end, Daniel arap MOI (1924–   ) agreed to merge his Kenyan African Democratic Union (KADU) with KANU, thereby further consolidating Kenyatta's power. Odinga strongly supported a multiparty system and believed KANU favored the Kikuyu minority. His opinions gradually led to his alienation from the party. In 1966 Mboya maneuvered to abolish the position of vice president, and Odinga was essentially removed from the government.

> The root of Odinga's opposition to Kenyatta was largely economic and ideological. He opposed the economic and political alliance that Kenyatta forged with the capitalist West during the era of the Cold War, preferring the ideology of African socialism. Odinga set forth his views in *Not Yet Uhuru*, published in 1967. In the book Odinga argued that true freedom *(uhuru)* for Kenya went beyond political independence to include economic independence as well.

Later in 1966 Odinga formed the Kenya People's Union (KPU) in an attempt to generate opposition to Kenyatta's government. Kenyatta cracked down on the KPU, however, imprisoning a number of its leaders and, in 1969, arresting Odinga on charges of staging a riot. Odinga served 15 months in prison, and the KPU was subsequently banned.

Kenyatta died in 1978, and Odinga was welcomed back into KANU by Moi, who had become Kenya's president. Odinga, however, continued his opposition stance, accusing both the old and the new governments of CORRUPTION. His vocal criticism once again led to his exile from the party, but this did little to quiet Odinga's call for a democratic, multiparty state. In 1991 he formed the National Democratic Party, which suffered a similar fate to the KPU. However, international protests against KANU, particularly in regard to HUMAN RIGHTS violations, gave Odinga's work added clout. His efforts sparked the formation of an alliance of opposition leaders called the Forum for the Restoration of Democracy (FORD). Bowing under pressure from FORD and abroad, Moi returned Kenya to a multiparty political system.

The multiparty elections of 1992 were a disappointment for Odinga. FORD suffered from internal dissension, with a faction of the party breaking away to support its own candidate for the presidency. This split the opposition's voter base and allowed for Moi to win the presidency again. Odinga finished fourth in the polls. He died in 1994 having earned the reputation as Kenya's "most persecuted politician," but also its strongest opposition voice. His son, Raila Odinga (1945–   ), currently is involved in Kenyan politics.

See also: NATIONALISM AND INDEPENDENCE MOVEMENTS (Vols. IV, V); ODINGA, OGINGA (Vol. IV); POLITICAL PARTIES AND ORGANIZATIONS (Vol. V).

Ogoni
Minority ethnic group living in the NIGER DELTA region of NIGERIA; their battle for recognition of their ethnic identity and civil rights has been linked to the distribution of OIL profits. The Ogoni people of southwest Nigeria are a minority under pressure. While under their land lies one of Africa's largest oil reserves, they remain among the poorest people in their country. This dichotomy has led to the rise of Ogoni unity and a strong nationalistic desire for a semiautonomous nation-state.

The Ogoni people live in a defined region in southwest Nigeria's Niger Delta. Numbering between 300,000 and 500,000, the Ogoni historically formed their ETHNICITY AND IDENTITY around linguistic and cultural norms, as opposed to a developed political state. This has sparked academic debate about whether the Ogoni were in fact an ethnic group before British colonialism or merely a loose conglomeration of kinships. There was some form of independent Ogoniland until the British incorporated the region into their colonial state, a move the Ogoni resisted until 1914.

In 1958 a significant amount of oil was found in the delta. The British government rapidly realigned the Royal Niger Company for oil extraction, and the company in turn contracted with Shell D'Archy (now the Shell Petroleum and Development Company—SPDC—of

Royal Dutch Shell) as a service provider. From the outset, the Ogoni people received only marginal amounts from the oil proceeds. When Nigeria became independent, in 1960, the new government took ownership of the oil. The Ogoni protested, and in 1968 Nigerian forces occupied the region. Many Ogoni were removed by force, and as many as 30,000 were killed. Their situation grew worse as the country descended into the Nigerian civil war, or Biafran War (1967–70). The IGBO, one of Nigeria's three major ethnic groups, seceded from the nation to form the Republic of BIAFRA. During the subsequent fighting between breakaway Biafra and the Nigerian government, both sides accused the Ogoni of collaborating with the enemy. In addition, as oil extraction continued, the environment was dramatically degraded, reducing agricultural and fishing potential, while new jobs were few and quality of life in the region declined. Today Nigeria earns between $18 billion and $20 billion per year in oil revenues with practically none of the proceeds going to the Ogoni.

Undoubtedly the sense of Ogoni identity crystallized around these political, social, and economic inequities. Ogoni ethnic mobilization simmered throughout the 1970s and 1980s, but in a relatively peaceful form. The character of this protest changed in October 1990, when youths in the village of Umuechem clashed with Shell Oil staff, and the Nigerian army came in to support the corporation at the expense of its citizens. Thousands of people were killed. In response to their worsening conditions and treatment at the hands of their own government, the Ogoni people formed the Movement for the Survival of the Ogoni People (MOSOP), led by activist and writer Ken SARO-WIWA (1941–1995). They passed an Ogoni Bill of Rights and demanded political autonomy and control over the NATURAL RESOURCES on Ogoni land.

Since the early 1990s thousands have died each year in the Niger Delta's clashes with the government. In 1993 Human Rights Watch, Amnesty International, and other international NON-GOVERNMENT ORGANIZATIONS started aiding the Ogoni. In the same year, then-president General Ibrahim BABANGIDA (1941–) passed the Treason and Treasonable Offences Decree, under which claims of "ethnic autonomy" were punishable by death. General Sani ABACHA (1943–1998), who overthrew the government of Ernest Shonekan (1936–) in 1993, subsequently used this decree to sentence to death and then execute Ken Saro-Wiwa, along with eight other activists, on November 10, 1995. During the resulting outcry, Nigeria became an international pariah and was suspended from the British Commonwealth of Nations until democratic elections were held, in 1999.

The international community largely believed that Nigeria's DEMOCRATIZATION under President Olusegun OBASANJO (c. 1937–) would improve Ogoni welfare, reduce Ogoni nationalism, and limit civil strife. But while there was a small increase in oil proceeds that were returned to the region, nearly all of the money has gone to local leaders to support the state, not the citizenry. The regime type may have changed, but the structure of the state has not. As much as 90 percent of state wealth is still generated by oil, and the oil industry forms a close bond with national leadership. The democratic government has shown just as high a propensity as the previous dictatorships for suppressing secessionism. As a result, strife in the Niger Delta has increased.

See also: ETHNIC CONFLICT IN AFRICA (Vol. V); INDEPENDENCE MOVEMENTS (Vol. V); MULTINATIONAL CORPORATIONS (Vol. V); NATIONALISM AND INDEPENDENCE MOVEMENTS (Vol. IV); ROYAL NIGER COMPANY (Vol. IV).

Further reading: Human Rights Watch, *The Price of Oil: Corporate Responsibility and Human Rights Violations in Nigeria's Oil Producing Communities* (New York: Human Rights Watch, 1999); Abdul Rasheed Na'Allah, ed., *Ogoni's Agonies: Ken Saro-Wiwa and the Crisis in Nigeria* (Trenton, N.J.: Africa World Press, 1998); Ken Saro-Wiwa, *Genocide in Nigeria: the Ogoni Tragedy* (Oxford, U.K.: African Books Collective, 1992).

oil Though only about 150 years in DEVELOPMENT, the oil industry is one of the largest and most lucrative in the world. Among the most valuable of all NATURAL RESOURCES, oil is principal to industrial production, cars and other TRANSPORTATION, heating, construction, cooking, even refinement of other energy sources. Oil is composed primarily of hydrocarbons, the combination of carbon and hydrogen. Hydrocarbons form deep under the earth's surface from the fossilized remains of sea organisms mixed with other organic material and subjected to intense pressure over millions of years. Plate tectonics, or the shifting of the earth's crust, is generally seen as a critical feature in oil formation, as the crust's movements help generate the necessary pressure. Some scientists hypothesize, however, that volcanic activity, rather than plate tectonics, has played the primary role in producing Africa's oil deposits.

Just as entire economies are dependent on oil consumption, some economies, particularly in Africa, South America, and the Middle East, are based almost entirely on oil production. In 1949 the world's largest oil producers, Venezuela, Iran, Iraq, Kuwait, and Saudi Arabia, met to form agreements to better manage the complex and rapidly growing international oil economy. In 1960 they formalized the ORGANIZATION OF PETROLEUM EXPORTING COUNTRIES (OPEC), which eventually expanded to number 13 countries. OPEC became a union of states designed to ensure pricing and the stability of the oil market. With oil accounting for a majority of export earnings in most of these countries, market stability is of great importance for fiscal planning. Today the world's seven largest oil producers are among the 11 current

OPEC countries, three of which are in Africa (ALGERIA, LIBYA, and NIGERIA). Combined, the seven countries account for nearly 80 percent of the more than 1 trillion barrels of known crude oil reserves.

Africa follows the Middle East and Latin America in both production and quantity of oil with nearly 100,000 million barrels of known reserves. In addition to the four OPEC nations, ANGOLA, the Republic of the CONGO, CAMEROON, the Democratic Republic of the CONGO, IVORY COAST, EGYPT, EQUATORIAL GUINEA, and TUNISIA all export oil. Oil exploration in MADAGASCAR, NAMIBIA, SOUTH AFRICA, and the Republic of the SUDAN indicates that these countries will also join the oil-exporting ranks.

The African oil industry has been growing substantially. Nigeria alone accounts for 39 percent of all sub-Saharan African oil production and stands to increase even further. Significant new finds in the Gulf of Guinea are expected to increase oil production in Angola, which generated 1.6 billion barrels in 2001, by as much as five-fold in the coming years. New finds in SÃO TOMÉ AND PRÍNCIPE and new opportunities for oil exploitation in CHAD are also expected to increase Africa's share of the oil market.

The growing oil economy represents simultaneously one of Africa's greatest opportunities and one of its greatest problems. Given low levels of development, INDUSTRIALIZATION, and automobile use, oil is not used at a high rate in Africa compared to Europe and the United States. The refining of oil in African countries is also limited compared to their Western counterparts. As a result oil used for transportation and industry is often imported African oil that was previously exported by large MULTINATIONAL CORPORATIONS for refinement overseas.

Oil is a large source of conflict in Africa. In Nigeria oil is found off the coast and in the NIGER DELTA. The latter, the largest single source of oil in sub-Saharan Africa, has become the site of ethnic and nationalist clashes fueled by controversy over the region's oil supply. The adverse environmental effects of oil drilling have degraded the land inhabited by Nigeria's Ijaw and OGONI peoples, among others. Worse, these groups receive virtually none of the financial benefits derived from the sale of oil taken from their lands. Thousands die each year from violent conflicts between these ethnic minorities and the Nigerian government, which has long collaborated with major oil companies such as Royal Dutch Shell and Chevron-Texaco to monopolize the delta's vast oil resources.

In Angola President José Eduardo DOS SANTOS (1942–) used oil revenues to stave off attacks from Jonas SAVIMBI (1934–2002) and his rebel army. Even after the death of Savimbi, in 2002, as much as $1 billion in oil revenue is still unaccounted for in the state budgets. International speculation is that the president used this money as patronage in an effort to maintain his office.

Indisputably, oil has driven a wedge in the Angolan economy, creating a small, wealthy business class atop a large, poor population trying to make a living in an economy ravaged by war. In Gabon, as in Angola, oil has proven to be an impediment, not a stimulant, to democracy, as it assists the privileged few in maintaining power. New oil states, such as Chad and São Tomé and Príncipe, will face similar dilemmas unless their resources are managed more equitably.

President dos Santos's patronage is both domestic and international. In fact, he is known to have given $100,000 to the presidential campaign of U.S. president George W. Bush (1948–) in the hopes of currying favor if Bush was elected. President Bush returned the donation.

In the late 1990s the WORLD BANK entered the African oil sector. In a new role for the international organization, it offered loan guarantees to stabilize an Exxon-Mobil-led consortium to build a 660-mile (1,062-km) pipeline from Chad to the coast of Cameroon, investing $180 million in the project. When it reaches full production this pipeline will deliver 250,000 barrels per day of crude oil to tankers waiting off the coast. The World Bank has put in place oversight mechanisms to help ensure economic accountability of the oil revenues in Chad and has mandated that the majority of the proceeds should go to development and not the creation of individual wealth. Critics argue that the World Bank has a poor record with extractive industries and improving governance and that it undermines democracy by holding the government accountable to the World Bank rather than the Chadian people for its fiscal decision-making. Some critics go so far as to argue that it is an effort to maximize the extraction of oil to the benefit of the prime users—Western countries—as opposed to Chad or Cameroon. Regardless, the World Bank, as well as countries such as the United States, which hold much of the power within the institution, will almost certainly play a larger role in Africa's oil industry in the coming years.

Oil provides unheard of economic opportunities in sub-Saharan Africa. The billions of dollars it produces cannot be matched by any other single source. Properly used, oil exports can provide the money necessary to jumpstart an economy, create new industries, and bring about national development. To date, however, oil production has tended to fuel CIVIL WARS, poor governance, and ethnic strife. At its current rate this nonrenewable natural resource will be exhausted before it can provide Africa with its potential economic benefits.

See also: INDEPENDENCE MOVEMENTS (Vol. V); UNITED STATES AND AFRICA (Vols. IV, V).

Further reading: Terry Karl, *The Paradox of Plenty: Oil Booms and Petro-States* (Berkeley, Calif.: University of California Press, 1997); Alan H. Gelb, *Oil Windfalls: Blessing or Curse?* (New York: Oxford University Press, 1988).

Olajuwon, Hakeem (1963–) *Basketball player from Nigeria*

Olajuwon, whose name translates as "always being on top," started playing basketball in his homeland of NIGERIA at age 15. In 1980 he was recruited by the University of Houston, and led the team to the National Collegiate Athletic Association (NCAA) basketball tournament in all three years he was on the team. In 1984 Olajuwon, nicknamed "The Dream," was the Houston Rockets' first-round draft choice (and the first pick of the entire draft), becoming a professional athlete in the National Basketball Association (NBA). He played for the Rockets until 2001, when he was traded to the Toronto Raptors. Hampered by a series of ailments and injuries, Olajuwan retired from professional basketball the next year.

Standing 7 feet tall (2.13 m) and weighing 255 pounds (115.7 kg), Olajuwon was a dominant defender, and he used his agility, exceptional footwork, and fade-away jump shot to excel on offense. He was particularly productive in playoff games and led the Rockets to back-to-back NBA championships in 1994 and 1995. In 1996 the NBA named him one of the league's 50 all-time greatest players. That same year Olajuwan, who became a U.S. citizen in 1993, was a member of the U.S. basketball team that won the gold medal at the Summer Olympics in Atlanta, Georgia. Among his many honors Olajuwan was chosen Most Valuable Player in 1993–94 and Defensive Player of the Year for the 1992–93 and 1993–94 seasons. In addition, he was selected to play in 12 All-Star games.

Olajuwon finished his playing days with a career average of 21.8 points per game. At the time of his retirement, he was the NBA's seventh all-time leading scorer, with 26,946 points, as well as the league's all-time leading shot blocker, with 3,830 blocked shots. He was also the first player in NBA history to register 2,000 blocked shots and 2,000 steals.

See also: SPORTS AND ATHLETICS (Vol. V).

Olympic Games See SPORTS AND ATHLETICS (Vol. V).

OPEC See ORGANIZATION OF PETROLEUM EXPORTING COUNTRIES.

Organization of African Unity (OAU) Continent-wide political body created to fight colonialism, promote unity and cooperation among African countries, and de-

Nigerian basketball player Hakeem Olajuwon, shown in action in 1988, won worldwide acclaim for his impressive skills. © *AP/Wide World Photos*

fend the sovereignty and territorial integrity of its members. Founded in 1963, the OAU was replaced by the AFRICAN UNION (AU) in 2001.

In the early 1960s there emerged two groups, each with its own idea on how to pursue African unity. One group, which supported a gradual approach to African unity, was called the MONROVIA GROUP. Originally made up of four African states that came together in 1961 in MONROVIA, LIBERIA, this group eventually came to include another bloc of states, the Brazzaville group. Made up of independent African states that were former French colonies, the Brazzaville group was especially concerned about the liberation war in ALGERIA (1954–62) and wanted to find a way of mediating the conflict without alienating France.

The other major bloc, called the CASABLANCA GROUP— it originally met in Casablanca, MOROCCO—was more radical. Made up mainly of socialist-leaning countries, the Casablanca group strongly advocated immediate political and economic unity among African states. This group was concerned about securing full independence for all African countries. Consequently the Casablanca group was more wary than the Monrovia group of the role that the colonial powers might play in opposing or compromising such independence.

During the early 1960s each group attempted to recruit newly independent African states. By 1963 leaders of the two groups sought reconciliation. Through the efforts of Ethiopia's Emperor HAILE SELASSIE (1892–1975), who represented the Monrovia group, and President Ahmed Sékou TOURÉ (1922–1984), of GUINEA, acting on behalf of the Casablanca group, the leaders of 32 independent African states met in ADDIS ABABA, ETHIOPIA, on May 25, 1963. At this summit they approved the charter creating the Organization of African Unity. Addis Ababa remained the OAU headquarters throughout the organization's existence. At its inception the OAU had three main governing bodies: the Assembly of the Heads of States and Governments, the Council of Ministers, and the General Secretariat. Each year a different African leader chaired the OAU.

The objectives of the OAU were to promote unity and solidarity among African states; to defend their sovereignty, territorial integrity, and independence; and to eradicate colonialism. Any independent African country could become a member of the organization. The OAU also welcomed the participation of African liberation movements that were not widely recognized as legitimate governments. These included the AFRICAN NATIONAL CONGRESS, in SOUTH AFRICA, the POPULAR MOVEMENT FOR THE LIBERATION OF ANGOLA, and the MOZAMBICAN LIBERATION FRONT.

In 1981 Morocco temporarily withdrew its OAU membership because some African countries recognized WESTERN SAHARA as an independent state. At the time, territory that presently belongs to Western Sahara was still claimed by Morocco.

After its creation in 1963 the OAU helped strengthen ties among African countries and raised the standing of the continent in international debates. Given the climate when the OAU was established, its initial actions were focused on providing both material resources and political backing for INDEPENDENCE MOVEMENTS in countries still under colonial rule. It also supported opposition to the APARTHEID regime in South Africa. In the year of its inception, the OAU formed the African Liberation Committee to provide financial support to liberation movements fighting Portuguese colonial rule in GUINEA-BISSAU, ANGOLA, and MOZAMBIQUE. The movements succeeded in 1974, when Portugal abandoned its

former African colonies. The OAU supported liberation movements against white-minority rule in ZIMBABWE and NAMIBIA, and it also successfully campaigned to bar South Africa from participating in the UN General Assembly. From 1974 until 1994, when white-minority rule and apartheid ended, South Africa was excluded from OAU membership.

The OAU also worked to preserve peace on the continent, although, in some cases, with limited success. It mediated a border dispute between Algeria and Morocco in 1964–65, and it also mediated the border conflicts of SOMALIA with Ethiopia and KENYA in 1968–70.

In 1986 the OAU established the African Commission on Human and People's Rights to monitor HUMAN RIGHTS practices in member nations.

During the 1990s the OAU was also concerned about strengthening the economies of member countries. To that end, it encouraged the creation of regional partnerships across the continent. In 1997 OAU members established the African Economic Community (AEC). Envisioned as an African common market, the AEC signed an agreement with regional African economic groupings including the SOUTHERN AFRICAN DEVELOPMENT COMMUNITY, the ECONOMIC COMMUNITY OF WEST AFRICAN STATES, the Maghrib Arab Union, and the Common Market for Eastern and Southern Africa.

While the OAU had some success, it faced problems that eventually undermined its ability to achieve its lofty goals. A primary subject of criticism was the clause in the OAU charter that guaranteed noninterference in the internal affairs of other member states. Because of this policy, the OAU could not act to help resolve CIVIL WARS in BIAFRA, Ethiopia, or Somalia. Unable to act in such situations, the OAU was criticized for condoning undemocratic leadership.

The OAU also lacked the capacity for effective peacekeeping. For example, troops sent to quell Chad's civil war in 1981—the first such action by the OAU—were forced to withdraw before completing their mission. To address this deficiency, in 1993 the OAU created the Mechanism for Conflict Prevention, Management and Resolution. The body enabled the OAU to intervene in conflicts in RWANDA, BURUNDI, the COMOROS, SIERRA LEONE, LIBERIA, Ethiopia, ERITREA, and the Democratic Republic of the CONGO. With its limited capacity, the OAU sometimes could do no more than send observers to document the conflicts. In other cases, OAU personnel worked closely with the UN observer missions or peacekeeping operations.

Throughout its existence the OAU was hampered by a lack of financial resources. It depended on member contributions for its operations, but, in many cases, members failed to pay their dues. To compound the situation, in the 1990s many OAU member states were unable to pay off mounting FOREIGN DEBT, making it even more difficult for them to meet their financial obligations. During this time the OAU was increasingly criticized for its inability to address Africa's major challenges, especially those related to economic DEVELOPMENT and the spread of HIV/AIDS. In response, the OAU redirected its energies to focus on developing the economies of member states. Citing the past failures of the OAU, Libya's leader, Muammar QADDAFI (1942–   ), proposed the creation of the African Union as a more effective institution for increasing prosperity in Africa. In the end, the AU was formally established in September 2001, in Sirte, LIBYA. In replacing the OAU, the AU sought to harmonize the economic and political policies of all African nations in order to improve pan-African welfare and provide Africans with a voice in international affairs. The AU member states believed that the new organization would have a stronger charter than the OAU and would be better funded. Future plans for the AU include an international court of justice, an African parliament, and a common African currency.

See also: COLONIAL RULE (Vol. IV); PAN-AFRICANISM (Vol. IV); UNITED NATIONS AND AFRICA (Vols. IV, V).

Further reading: Yassin El-Ayouty, *The Organization of African Unity After Thirty Years* (Westport, Conn.: Praeger, 1994); Gino J. Naldi, *The Organization of African Unity: An Analysis of its Role,* 2nd ed. (New York: Mansell, 1999).

Organization of Petroleum Exporting Countries (OPEC) and Africa

Association of countries that rely heavily on the production and sale of OIL for their national incomes. In 2003 the 11 member states of the Organization of Petroleum Exporting Countries produced an estimated 40 percent of the world's petroleum. As of 2004, OPEC's African member states were ALGERIA, LIBYA, and NIGERIA.

In 1960 oil ministers from the founding states of Iran, Iraq, Kuwait, Saudi Arabia, and Venezuela held the first OPEC conference, in Baghdad, Iraq. The first African state to join OPEC was Libya (1962), followed by Algeria (1969), and Nigeria (1971). The west-central African country of GABON joined OPEC in 1975, although it subsequently left the cartel in 1994.

During the 1960s OPEC had relatively little influence on international petroleum markets, which were dominated by huge Western oil companies. In the early 1970s, however, OPEC gained greater control of its production and pricing mechanisms. As a result it began to exert influence in crude-oil markets worldwide. In 1973, in light of United States support for Israel in the ARAB-ISRAELI WARS, Arab states imposed an oil embargo on both the United States and its European allies. Within months the OPEC price for a barrel of crude oil quadrupled. Although the embargo was largely the result of political posturing that had nothing to do with Africa, it greatly affected the civil war in Nigeria, where the country's warring factions sought to establish control of increasingly lucrative oilfields. Markets recovered after the embargo was called off in March 1974, but the power of the OPEC cartel could no longer be denied.

In 1986 OPEC states dealt with a crisis of a different nature when the market price of crude fell dramatically because of an international oil glut. Nigeria, which was still recovering from its civil war, was hit especially hard. During the 1990s, however, prices remained relatively stable, and the Nigerian oil industry recovered. Although operations in Nigeria remained riddled with CORRUPTION and inefficiency, by 2000 OPEC estimated the country's oil export revenues to be $17 billion. By comparison, Algeria's 2000 oil revenues were estimated at about $19 billion, and Libya's were about $10 billion.

Throughout OPEC's history, five Africans have served as the organization's secretary general. They are Omar el Badri (1970) and Abdallah Salem el Badri (1994), from Libya, Abderrahman Khene (1973–74), of Algeria, and Nigerians Chief M. O. Feyide (1975–76) and Dr. Rilwanu Lukman (1995–2000).

See also: ARAB WORLD AND AFRICA (Vol. V); NATURAL RESOURCES (Vol. V).

Oromo (Galla)

Largest ethnic group in ETHIOPIA, making up nearly one-half of the population. While this group has a presence in many areas of the Horn of Africa, most Oromo live in the central Ethiopian state of Oromia. They speak Oromiffa, which is an Eastern Cushitic language. Throughout their history the Oromo have had little political influence and have been marginalized by Ethiopia's dominant Amhara political leaders because of linguistic, cultural, and political differences.

The greater Oromo ethnic group is made up of several subgroups, including the Arsi and Borana. Despite notable differences among the subgroups, there is a pan-Oromo identity that has been forged by centuries of mistreatment and oppression by successive Ethiopian regimes. The Oromo were involved in the political upheaval of the 1970s and 1980s, following the fall of Emperor HAILE SELASSIE (1892–1975) in 1974. In later years, though, Oromo leaders worked to build coalitions with other ethnic minorities.

The Oromo gained political recognition through the Oromo Liberation Front (OLF), a rebel group formed in 1973. In 1990 the Tigray Peoples Liberation Front (TPLF) sponsored the founding of the Oromo People's Democratic Organization (OPDO) in an effort to broaden TPLF support throughout Ethiopia. In 1991, following a lengthy civil war, an umbrella opposition party replaced the Amhara-dominated government. This coalition party, called the ETHIOPIAN PEOPLE'S REVOLUTIONARY DEMO-CRATIC FRONT (EPRDF), was made up of several groups, including the TPLF, the OPDO, the Southern Ethiopia People's Democratic Organization, and the AMHARA NA-TIONAL DEMOCRATIC MOVEMENT.

The Oromo Liberation Front (OLF) states on its web page that its mission as a political organization is "to lead the national liberation struggle of the Oromo people against the Abyssinian (an older name for Ethiopian) colonial rule. The emergence of the OLF was a culmination of a century-old de-sire of the Oromo people to have a strong and uni-fied national organization to lead the struggle." Also, the OLF disparages the EPRDF-led govern-ment of Prime Minister MELES ZENAWI (1955–) as a "[Tigrayan] regime . . . that is merely a cosmetic change intended to affect the momentum of our just struggle."

Like other ethnic groups in Ethiopia, the Oromo people desire self-determination. This aspiration, among other political and economic problems, continues to cre-ate discord in Ethiopia. However, it has also inspired a federal system of government that seeks to balance ethnic rights and self-determination with maintaining the in-tegrity of the state of Ethiopia.

See also: AMHARA (Vols. I, III, IV); ETHNIC CONFLICT IN AFRICA (Vol. V); ETHNICITY AND IDENTITY (Vol. I); OROMO (Vols. I, II, III, IV).

Further reading: Asafa Jalata, ed., *Oromo National-ism and the Ethiopian Discourse: The Search for Freedom and Democracy* (Lawrenceville, N.J.: Red Sea Press, 1998).

Ouagadougou (Wagadugu) Capital of BURKINA FASO, located in the central part of that landlocked West African country. Ouagadougou is the former capital of the powerful Mossi state of the same name. Founded in the 11th century, by the 1750s Ouagadougou was an adminis-trative center for the Mossi people. In 1896 the city be-came the colonial administrative center for French UPPER VOLTA, part of French West Africa.

Ouagadougou is still the home of the traditional Mossi leader, *mogho naba*, but his power has di-minished since the colonial period. Because of its long history and ties with Mossi political authority, Ouagadougou appears less influenced by French colonialism than many other Francophone African states.

Although Ouagadougou is the administrative center of the nation, the city of Bobo-Dioulasso, located about 200 miles (322 km) to the southwest, remains its indus-trial center. Ouagadougou, with a population of approxi-mately 962,000, produces processed food, beverages, cotton goods, rugs, soap, matches, shoes, and handicrafts. It is connected by rail to the coastal city of ABIDJAN, in IVORY COAST, and by road to NIAMEY, in NIGER. The city has an international airport and is also the site of the na-tional University of Ouagadougou, founded in 1969.

See also: FRANCE AND AFRICA (Vols. III, IV, V); FRENCH WEST AFRICA (Vol. IV); MOSSI STATES (Vols. II, III, IV); OUA-GADOUGOU (Vols. II, III).

Ousmane Sembène (Sembene Ousmane, Ous-man Sembene) (1923–) *Senegalese writer and pio-neer in African cinema*

Born in 1923 in the Casamance region of French colonial SENEGAL, Ousmane Sembène was raised by an uncle who was a devout Muslim. Moving to DAKAR as a teenager he received limited education before taking a va-riety of jobs in the building trades. After serving with French forces in France and Germany during World War II (1939–45), he worked on the docks of Marseilles, France. It was at this time that Sembène began writing, and his experiences as an African laborer in France formed the background of his first novel, *Le Docker noir* (The black docker) in 1956. An active union member, Sembène eventually rose to a position of leadership among the longshoremen of the French docks before de-voting himself full-time to writing.

Sembène returned to SENEGAL not long before inde-pendence and he soon emerged as not only a writer of fic-tion but as an astute commentator on the life of the common people of the new nation. Always considering himself a Marxist-Leninist, he sought to depict the effects on ordinary working people of both colonialism and the self-serving, elitist officialdom that colonialism left in its wake. As a result his works from this period, including *Oh pays, mon beau peuple* (Oh, my beautiful people) and *Les Bouts de bois de Dieu* (God's bits of wood), reveal not only the people's struggle to achieve a sense of national consciousness but also the efforts of the elite to maintain power and control.

In 1961 Sembène's career changed dramatically when he went to the Soviet Union to study film. In CINEMA he found a medium even better suited than fiction for communicating with the masses of Senegal. Although he continued to write fiction, cinema soon became Sembène's primary means of artistic expression. Beginning in 1963 with *Borom Sarat*, a 20-minute movie that depicted a day in the life of a cart driver, Sembène's films became landmarks in the development of African cinema. Among his achievements were *Le Noire de . . .* (Black girl from . . .), the first sub-Saharan-produced feature film, and *Mandabi* (The money order), the first sub-Saharan film presented at the prestigious Cannes Film Festival, in France.

Sembène faced the dilemma of many African authors who wrote in a European language, which, in his case, was French. "I could have written in Wolof," he once stated, "but who would have read it?" Yet, by writing in French, only the educated elite and Westerners, and not the ordinary working people with whom he identified, could access his work. Film offered him a way out of this dilemma by letting him address directly the audience he most wanted to reach. Some of his films came out in both French and Wolof language versions.

From the first, Sembène's films found an audience, not only in Senegal but in the world beyond Africa as well. Indeed, audiences and critics in both Europe and North America lavishly praised *Black Girl from . . .* as well as *Mandabi*, a film that shows the postcolonial bureaucracy crushing a man who tries to cash a check from a relative in Paris. As his career developed Sembène became the most recognizable voice of African cinema on the international scene, winning prizes at film festivals at Cannes (1967), Venice (1969), and Atlanta (1970).

It was his audiences in his homeland, however, that were most important to Sembène, and throughout his career he would take films from village to village, showing his movies and discussing them with audiences. Although Sembène's films struck a responsive chord among the Senegalese people, the officials of his native country were not among his admirers. Films such as *Xala* (1974), which parodied the postcolonial Senegalese elite, and *Ceddo* (1976), a historical epic about the conflict between Islam and traditional African RELIGION, angered Senegalese officials so much that the films were banned by the government.

The government's efforts, however, failed to silence Sembène, and through the 1980s and 1990s his films continued to explore the life of simple African people at the same time that they portrayed the follies and evils of colonial and postcolonial oppression. As the years progressed Sembène persisted with his straightforward cinematic style, avoided using movie stars (or even polished actors), and rejected sophisticated camera work and effects. Instead Sembène relied on nonprofessional actors with whom his audiences could identify; he also maintained his use of elementary techniques that often made his films seem like home-movies—or even reality itself. These techniques helped his films achieve an artistry that transformed movies from elitist entertainment into something like traditional tales that could be shared among the common people he admired and hoped to serve.

See also: COMMUNISM AND SOCIALISM (Vol. V); FRANCE AND AFRICA (Vols. III, IV, V); FRENCH WEST AFRICA (Vol. IV); LABOR UNIONS (Vols. IV, V); LITERATURE IN COLONIAL AFRICA (Vol. IV); LITERATURE IN MODERN AFRICA (Vol. V).

Further reading: Roy Armes, *Third World Filmmaking and the West* (Berkeley, Calif.: University of California Press, 1987); C. D. Moore, *Evolution of an Artist: Social Realism in the Work of Ousmane Sembene* (Ann Arbor, Mich.: University of Michigan Press, 1984).

P

See AFRICAN PARTY FOR THE INDEPENDENCE OF GUINEA-BISSAU AND CAPE VERDE.

Pan-Africanist Congress (PAC) Militant black opposition organization in SOUTH AFRICA that emerged from the AFRICAN NATIONAL CONGRESS (ANC). Originating in 1959 as a breakaway faction of the African National Congress, the PAN-AFRICANIST CONGRESS (PAC) was geared to a more confrontational and populist brand of politics as a way to rid South Africa of APARTHEID. Consequently, it rejected the ANC's commitment to multiracialism in favor of an Africans-only policy, that became known as Africanism.

In March 1960, led by Robert SOBUKWE (1924–1978), the PAC organized a nationwide public demonstration against the hated identity documents, known as passes, that Africans were required to carry by South African law. The PAC encouraged followers to mobilize outside police stations without their passes and thus solicit arrest. On March 21, 1960, the first day of the antipass campaign, the police opened fire on the approximately 5,000 demonstrators that had congregated at a police station in SHARPEVILLE. As a result 69 protesters were killed and many more wounded.

In the state crackdown that followed, the PAC and ANC were both banned, and a state of emergency was declared. Sobukwe was imprisoned. Potlako Leballo (1924–) assumed leadership of the PAC in Sobukwe's absence. The PAC went into exile, setting up headquarters in various African states.

For much of its history in exile the PAC was troubled by factional disputes. In 1979 Leballo was displaced, and a succession of leaders followed. The PAC was unbanned in February 1990, but failed to gain widespread popularity in the lead-up to the 1994 elections. It refused to forsake violence and expressed reluctance to negotiate with the government toward some form of power sharing. Terrorist acts committed by its armed wing, the Azanian People's Liberation Army, and organizational weakness contributed to the PAC's failure to win broad-based support. It received less than 2 percent of the popular vote in the 1994 elections and remains a marginal political party.

Poqo (a word meaning "pure" in the XHOSA language) was the name of an armed underground offshoot of the PAC, formed to achieve PAC goals through the use of TERRORISM and other violent means. As a result of a 1963 raid on PAC headquarters in MASERU, capital of what was still the British colonial territory of Basutoland (present-day LESOTHO), police uncovered a list of Poqo members, thousands of whom were subsequently arrested in South Africa. By the mid-1960s Poqo was no longer a viable organization.

See also: BASUTOLAND (Vol. IV); PAN-AFRICANIST CONGRESS (Vol. IV).

Further reading: Gail M. Gerhart, *Black Power in South Africa: The Evolution of an Ideology* (Berkeley, Calif.: University of California Press, 1978); Tom Lodge, *Black Politics in South Africa since 1945* (New York: Longman,

1983); Tom Lodge, *South African Politics since 1994* (Cape Town, South Africa: David Philip Publishers, 1999).

pan-Africanism Ideology that emphasizes the commonality of all peoples of African heritage and calls for African unity to help combat the influence of colonialism in Africa. Toward the end of the 19th century a solidarity movement emerged among Africans and people of the African diaspora. Defining their goals through a series of congresses held between 1919 and 1945, subscribers to this "pan-Africanism" opposed European colonization of Africa and supported nationalism and INDEPENDENCE MOVEMENTS.

As independence spread across the continent in the mid-1900s, pan-Africanism became a guiding ideology in the building of relationships between the fledgling African governments. The most prominent leader of the movement at that time was Kwame NKRUMAH (1909–1972), the first president of GHANA. Various intergovernmental meetings and organizations began to emerge, beginning with the First Conference of Independent African States, held in ACCRA, Ghana. That meeting featured primarily North African countries, but subsequent pan-African groups, such as the Union of African States and the African and Malagasy Union, began to include more independent sub-Saharan states. The movement was especially influential in portions of Africa still without majority African rule, such as SOUTH AFRICA. There the PAN-AFRICANIST CONGRESS, a splinter group of the AFRICAN NATIONAL CONGRESS, formed in 1959, basing their opposition to the racist APARTHEID regime on pan-Africanist ideals. Pan-Africanism also spawned the BLACK CONSCIOUSNESS MOVEMENT, initiated in South Africa by anti-apartheid activist Steve BIKO (1946–1977).

Not every pan-Africanist group shared the same views. Clear differences were seen between the CASABLANCA GROUP (including Ghana, EGYPT, GUINEA, MALI, MOROCCO, ALGERIA, and LIBYA) and the MONROVIA GROUP (including LIBERIA, NIGERIA, TOGO, and CAMEROON and expanding later to include many more). The leaders of states in the Casablanca group desired the immediate establishment of a federated "United States of Africa," which they thought would be the best way to establish economic and political stability and exorcise lingering colonial influence. On the other hand, leaders of the Monrovia group took a more moderate stance, desiring a system of regional alliances prior to pursuing continental unification.

Eventually the various pan-Africanist groups gave way to two major entities, the ORGANIZATION FOR AFRICAN UNITY (OAU), founded in 1963, and the African-Malagasy-Mauritius Common Organization, founded in 1964. The OAU became the preeminent pan-African organization, with 53 member states in 1995. However, conflicts between and within member states often undermined the OAU's effectiveness. In 2001 the newest form of pan-Africanism took the form of the AFRICAN UNION (AU). Based on the European Union, the AU took the place of the OAU in 2002.

See also: DU BOIS, W. E. B. (Vol. IV); GARVEY, MARCUS (Vol. IV); *NÉGRITUDE* (Vol. IV); NKOMO, JOSHUA (Vols. IV, V); PAN-AFRICANISM (Vol. IV).

Party for Social Renewal (Partido para a Renovação Social, PRS) Political party in GUINEA-BISSAU.

See also: AFRICAN PARTY FOR THE INDEPENDENCE OF GUINEA AND CAPE VERDE (Vol. V); POLITICAL PARTIES AND ORGANIZATIONS (Vol. V); YALA, KOUMBA (Vol. V).

Party of the Revolutionary (Chama Cha Mapinduzi, in Kiswahili, CCM) Largest political party of TANZANIA. Known in Tanzania as Chama Cha Mapinduzi (CCM), the Party of the Revolutionary was established on February 5, 1977, as a result of a merger between the TANZANIAN AFRICAN NATIONAL UNION and the AFRO-SHIRAZI PARTY of ZANZIBAR. The first president of Tanzania, Julius NYERERE (1922–1999), proposed the merger to foster closer relations between mainland Tanzania and the island of Zanzibar.

Until 1992, when a multiparty system was introduced, CCM was the only political party in Tanzania. It remained the largest party even after Nyerere's successor, Ali Hassan MWINYI (1925–), ushered in a multiparty system. Attesting to the dominance of the party, all of Tanzania's presidents, including Nyerere, Mwinyi, and Benjamin MKAPA (1938–), belonged to the CCM party and were reelected to office.

See also: DEMOCRATIZATION (Vol. V); INDEPENDENCE MOVEMENTS (Vol. V); NATIONALISM AND INDEPENDENCE MOVEMENTS (Vol. IV); POLITICAL PARTIES AND ORGANIZATIONS (Vols. IV, V); POLITICAL SYSTEMS (Vol. V); TANGANYIKA (Vol. IV).

Further reading: Michael Okema, *Political Culture of Tanzania* (Lewiston, N.Y.: E. Mellen Press, 1996).

Patassé, Ange-Felix (1937–) *President of the Central African Republic*

Born in Ouham-Pendé, near the northwestern border of the CENTRAL AFRICAN REPUBLIC (CAR), Patassé had an improbable political career, considering he was a member of the Sara people, an ethnic group long under-represented politically in the CAR. He began a quick climb in the country's government during the regime of brutal dictator Jean-Bedel BOKASSA (1921–1996), who had assumed control of the CAR after overthrowing its first president, David DACKO (1930–). Patassé served as minister to a number of departments, including TRANSPORTATION and commerce, AGRICULTURE, health, environmental resources, and TOURISM.

In 1978, however, Patassé fell out of favor and was dismissed. The following year he went into exile in France, where he worked to develop opposition to Bokassa. After a French-led assault unseated Bokassa and restored Dacko to the presidency Patassé returned to the CAR. However, because of his ties to the Bokassa regime, he was arrested in 1979 and was held in the infamous Ngaragba prison, in BANGUI.

Upon his release Patassé remained in hiding, traveling in the CAR, LIBYA, CHAD, and France. While in exile he worked to rally opposition to Dacko's government and, later, to the government of General André Kolingba (1935–).

It wasn't until 1993 that Patassé found his opening. That year a failing economy and international pressure led Kolingba to reform his one-party government and allow for multiparty elections. Running as the candidate for the Movement for the Democratic Evolution of Central Africa (Mouvement pour la Libération du Peuple Centrafricaine, MLPC), Patassé won the presidency.

His position was not an enviable one. In financial ruin, the CAR was nearly without civil services and suffered from a decrease in support from its main benefactor, France. Patassé faced numerous coup attempts after his narrow victory over Kolingba and Dacko in 1999. In 2001–02 intervention by Libyan troops was all that saved Patassé from the opposition's attempts to unseat him. With a weak political base and only a minority of seats held by the MLPC in the legislature, Patassé found it difficult to make significant moves early in his presidency.

See also: FRANCE AND AFRICA (Vols. IV, V).

Patriotic Front (PF) See ZIMBABWE AFRICAN NATIONAL UNION.

P'Bitek, Okot (1931–1982) *Ugandan author*

Okot P'Bitek was born in the town of Gulu in the LUO-speaking Acholi region of northern UGANDA. His informal education provided him with a strong foundation in Luo oral literature and performance. After attending his local high school and the Church Missionary Society's elite King's College at Budo he went to Great Britain for further study. There he attended Bristol University, from which he received a certificate in education. He

then earned a law degree at University College of Wales at Aberystwyth. He subsequently attended Oxford University, studying social anthropology and writing a thesis on the traditional songs of his home area for his bachelor's degree in literature.

In 1964 P'Bitek returned to Uganda to teach at MAKERERE UNIVERSITY and become the director of the Uganda Cultural Center. While on a visit to ZAMBIA in 1966, he made comments that were critical of the Ugandan government, which earned him the enmity of President Milton OBOTE (1925–). This led him to emigrate to KENYA. During the years of dictatorial rule of Idi AMIN (c. 1925–2003) in Uganda, P'Bitek continued his exile and taught literature at the University of NAIROBI. After Amin's overthrow in 1979, P'Bitek returned to Uganda to resume teaching at Makerere University, where he stayed until his death in 1982.

In 1953 P'Bitek published his first novel, *Lak Tar Miyo Kinyero Wi Lobo (If Your Teeth are White, Laugh!)*, which was written in Luo. In 1956 he published his now classic long narrative poem, *Song of Lawino,* written in Luo in rhyming couplets. When he published an English version in 1966 it became a best-seller. His 1970 *Song of Ocol* also was in the form of a traditional Luo song. Both works reflected the ongoing cultural conflict between African and European values.

Through these and other works written in traditional Luo styles, P'Bitek sought to redefine the scope of African literature. He considered the genre of written narrative elitist and, as a poet and social critic, promoted performance as a more authentic expression of the African voice. In this he differed from many of his contemporary fellow authors who wrote in the colonial languages.

See also: CHURCH MISSIONARY SOCIETY (Vol. IV); LANGUAGE USAGE IN MODERN AFRICA (Vol. V); LITERACY (Vol. V); LITERATURE IN MODERN AFRICA (Vols. IV, V).

People's Rally for Progress (Rassemblement Populaire Pour le Progres, RPP) Political party of DJIBOUTI that was the country's only legal party for more than a decade. Djibouti, which was known as the FRENCH TERRITORY OF AFARS AND ISSAS from 1967 to 1977, is a country largely inhabited by these two ethnic groups. The Issas are the majority but, as the former name of the country indicates, the Afars are an influential minority. In 1977, when the country gained total independence from France, the Issas and the Afars were in a political struggle for control of Djibouti's government. Hassan GOULED APTIDON (1916–), an Issa, became president. As political conflict in the country continued in 1979 he formed the RPP in an attempt to unite both ethnic groups under one umbrella political party. This purpose was never served, however, as the RPP became dominated by the Issas. This was a precursor to the fate of Djibouti's government. In

1981 Gouled made Djibouti a one-party state, with the RPP as the country's only legal party. Gouled used the RPP's status to stifle political competition and strengthen Issa dominance of government.

After years of domestic and international pressure, in 1992 Gouled returned Djibouti to a multiparty system. The RPP maintained unchallenged control of government, however, leading to an uprising of Afar rebels organized under the Front for the Restoration of Unity and Democracy (FRUD). In 1994 a faction of FRUD signed a peace agreement with Gouled's government, but a more radical bloc within the organization continued to fight. In 1999, when Gouled stepped down from the presidency, he chose the head of Djibouti's secret police (and his nephew), Ismail Omar GUELLEH (1947–), to succeed him. Using the RPP's political strength, Guelleh easily defeated Moussa Ahmed Idriss later in 1999.

In 2002 the law limiting the number of political parties expired. As a result political parties proliferated, with all of them jockeying for an advantage in the 2003 parliamentary elections. Wary of a strong coalition of opposition parties, Guelleh united his RPP with four smaller parties to form the Union for the Presidential Majority. Despite the organized opposition, Guelleh's coalition party won all 65 contested seats for Parliament, solidifying Guelleh's and the RPP's hold on power.

See also: DEMOCRATIZATION (Vol. V); POLITICAL PARTIES AND ORGANIZATIONS (Vol. V).

Pereira, Aristides Maria (1923–) *President of the Republic of Cape Verde*

Aristides Pereira was the central figure in Cape Verdean politics for much of the late 20th century. Born in Boa Vista, in what was then the Portuguese colony of Cape Verde, Pereira began a career as a radio-telegraph technician. He eventually landed a job as head of the TELECOMMUNICATIONS department in GUINEA-BISSAU, where he worked up until 1960.

At the time, both Guinea-Bissau and Cape Verde were suffering under the colonial rule of fascist Portugal, led by António Salazar (1889–1970). In 1956 Pereira joined Amílcar CABRAL (1924–1973) and other nationalist leaders in forming the AFRICAN PARTY FOR THE INDEPENDENCE OF GUINEA AND CAPE VERDE (Partido Africano da Independência da Guiné e Cabo Verde, PAIGC). The party initially favored nonviolent means as a way of encouraging independence. However, in 1959 Pereira organized a dockworker strike in Guinea-Bissau that was met with a disproportionate response by the Portuguese colonial authorities. Fifty dockworkers were killed, causing PAIGC to abandon its peaceful protests in favor of guerilla warfare.

During PAIGC campaigns Pereira operated behind-the-scenes in neighboring GUINEA, where the PAIGC was headquartered. He worked to secure foreign aid for the struggle, receiving help from the former Soviet Union and the ORGANIZATION OF AFRICAN UNITY. He also arranged sabotage missions into Guinea-Bissau. By 1964 the PAIGC controlled two-thirds of Guinea-Bissau.

In 1968 Portuguese dictator Salazar had suffered a stroke and resigned, although the fascist regime continued in Portugal. By 1973 Pereira had become secretary general of PAIGC. That same year, however, Portuguese secret police assassinated Cabral, PAIGC's leader and inspirational head. Pereira was kidnapped but later rescued by the Guinean navy. He took control of PAIGC and led the movement to victory. In 1974 Portuguese military officers, disillusioned with the campaign in Africa, rose up and ended fascist rule in their country. Guinea-Bissau won its independence, and Cape Verde followed a year later. Pereira was elected president of the Republic of CAPE VERDE by a vast margin.

Pereira and PAIGC faced the very difficult task of transforming a nationalist political party into a functioning government. In 1981 the Cape Verdean PAIGC split from its Guinea-Bissau counterpart and formed the African Party for the Independence of Cape Verde (Partido Africano da Independência de Cabo Verde, PAICV).

During the struggle for independence PAIGC maintained the goal of uniting Guinea-Bissau and Cape Verde as a single autonomous nation. Following independence this ideal was still favored by Pereira and Guinea-Bissau president, Luis Cabral (1931–), Amílcar Cabral's brother. In 1980, however, Cabral's prime minister, João Bernardo Vieira, overthrew him, and the plan for unification was abandoned. The COUP D'ÉTAT also caused the Cape Verdean PAIGC to split and form the PAICV. Despite some tension, the two countries eventually signed a mutual cooperation treaty in 1988.

Beyond its political transition, Pereira and PAICV faced the task of promoting economic prosperity. The country's arid climate is frequently subject to devastating droughts, and its limited amount of land has led to an overflowing population and forced emigration for many Cape Verdeans. These factors, coupled with scant NATURAL RESOURCES, left Pereira little to work with. Pereira directed government efforts to reform agricultural practices and promote the CONSERVATION of WATER RESOURCES. Pereira succeeded in preventing economic collapse, largely due to foreign aid, but the nation's economy remained weak.

Cape Verde was essentially a one-party state until 1990, when new legislation provided for a multiparty election in 1991. The movement toward greater democracy proved detrimental to Pereira, however, as he and PAICV lost the election in a landslide to António Monteiro (1944–) and the Movement for Democracy. Pereira retired from politics, but in 2001 PAICV again became the dominant party, with Pereira's former prime minister, Pedro PIRES (1934–), winning the presidency.

See also: INDEPENDENCE MOVEMENTS (Vol. V); PORTUGAL AND AFRICA (Vols. III, IV, V).

photography Photography has been an important medium in Africa for more than 150 years. During the colonial period the camera conveyed images of Africa to the outside world, particularly to the western world. More specifically, photography during this period focused on Africa's landscapes, its WILDLIFE, and its people, with a particular emphasis on traditional cultures.

In the modern era, photography in Africa has continued this tradition of conveying impressions of the continent and its people to the outside world. However, the perspective of indigenous Africans—i.e., photography *by* Africans rather than *of* Africas—is increasingly valuable in conveying images of African life to the outside world. For example, Peter Magubane (1932–), a South African photographer, published *Vanishing Cultures of South Africa* in 1998 to record the traditional lifestyles of the various ethnic groups of SOUTH AFRICA. Over nearly 50 years as a photographer, Magubane has amassed a collection that is helping preserve the memory of that country's traditional cultures as seen from the inside

In contrast to the most common themes of colonial-era photography, recent efforts have tried to move beyond the emphasis on the exotic, instead portraying Africa in a more realistic way. One such effort resulted in the critically acclaimed *A Day in the Life of Africa,* a photo book project that collected images from around the continent taken by about 100 photographers during a 24-hour period in 2002. Proceeds of the book went to fund AIDS research and education.

Photography has effectively conveyed problems facing Africa, such as those stemming from CIVIL WARS and from FAMINE AND HUNGER. However, photojournalism that focuses on the challenges facing Africa sometimes creates an exaggerated sense of a continent gripped in crisis. On the other hand, during the APARTHEID era photojournalism helped expose the true harshness of the South African political system. Ian Berry (1934–), for example, was the only photographer present at SHARPEVILLE in 1960. By chance, he documented the tragedy that unfolded when South African police opened fire on a crowd of Africans, killing 69 of them.

As with people in other parts of the world, Africans also have an interest in photography for sharing pictures with family, friends, and the broader community. The

capital city of BAMAKO, MALI, was one of the places in Africa where self-taught photographers were well-established in the photography business by 1960. Seydou Keita (c. 1921–2001) was one of the most prominent of this group. Starting out at age 12 with a Kodak Brownie camera, he went on to a highly successful career as a studio portrait photographer before later working as a photographer for the Malian government. Across the continent there are individuals such as Keita who continue to earn their livelihood through photography. They do this primarily by catering to the high demand for family photographs and photos for identity documents such as passports and driver licenses. In recent years African art photography has become more popular both in Africa and abroad, especially in cosmopolitan cities such as Paris and New York.

See also: PHOTOGRAPHY (Vol. IV).

Pillar and Structure for the Salvation of Madagascar (Andry sy Riana Enti-Manavotra an'i Madagasikara, AREMA) Party of President Didier RATSIRAKA (1936–) that dominated MADAGASCAR politics from 1976 to 2002. Ratsiraka came to power by military coup in 1975 and quickly embarked on a socialist agenda. AREMA, an acronym of the party's name in Malagasy, Andry sy Riana Enti-Manavotra an'i Madagasikara, was formed in March 1976 as the means for implementing this program. In the years that followed Ratsiraka's strong hand assured AREMA's dominance despite Madagascar's competitive multiparty system. As a result, by 1983 AREMA held 85 percent of the seats in the National Assembly.

The party, however, never achieved institutional independence from Ratsiraka. Consequently, when the democracy movement forced Ratsiraka from power in 1993, the party was weakened. AREMA revived when Ratsiraka returned to power in 1997. However, the landslide victory of Ratsiraka's opponent, Marc RAVALOMANANA (1949–), in the 2002 elections, followed by Ratsiraka's self-imposed exile to Paris, once again diminished the party's importance.

See also: COMMUNISM AND SOCIALISM (Vol. IV); POLITICAL PARTIES AND ORGANIZATIONS (Vol. V).

Further reading: Philip M. Allen, *Madagascar: Conflicts of Authority in the Great Island* (Boulder, Colo.: Westview Press, 1995); Maureen Covell, *Madagascar: Politics, Economics, and Society* (London: F. Pinter, 1987).

Pires, Pedro (1934–) *President of the Republic of Cape Verde*

Pedro Pires was at the forefront of the struggle for independence in Cape Verde. Born on the island of Fogo, Pires was educated first in Cape Verde and later in Portugal, where he was forced into military service before he completed his studies. In 1961 he left the armed forces and joined the AFRICAN PARTY FOR THE INDEPENDENCE OF GUINEA AND CAPE VERDE (Partido Africano da Independência da Guiné e Cabo Verde, PAIGC), a nationalist organization founded by Amílcar CABRAL (1924–1973) and future Cape Verdean president Aristides PEREIRA (1923–). For the next three years Pires served the PAIGC in SENEGAL and France. In 1973 he was appointed president of the National Commission of PAIGC for Cape Verde. The following year he led the Cape Verdean arm of the PAIGC and headed the delegation to Portugal to negotiate for independence. When the island colony became the independent Republic of CAPE VERDE in 1975, Pires was elected prime minister under President Pereira.

In 1981 the African Party for Independence of Cape Verde (Partido Africano da Independência de Cabo Verde, PAICV) broke away from the PAIGC, and Pires became assistant secretary-general of the new party. During his terms as prime minister Pires was able to guide the economically struggling country to relatively significant levels of DEVELOPMENT, especially considering the nation's limited arable land and lack of NATURAL RESOURCES.

Pires spearheaded the nation's shift from a one-party system dominated by the PAIGC to a multiparty state. Ironically, this led to a temporary setback in Pires's political career, as the PAICV was defeated in the first open elections, in 1991, by António Monteiro (1944–) and his party, the Movement for Democracy. Throughout most of the late 1990s Pires continued to head the PAICV, and in 2001 he won the presidency, bringing the party back to prominence.

See also: INDEPENDENCE MOVEMENTS (Vol. V); PORTUGAL AND AFRICA (Vols. III, IV, V).

Further reading: Richard A. Lobban, Jr., *Cape Verde: Crioulo Colony to Independent Nation* (Boulder, Colo.: Westview Press, 1995).

Polisario (Frente Polisario)

Armed resistance movement of the SAHARAWI people of WESTERN SAHARA. Parts of today's Western Sahara were known as the coastal Spanish colonies of Saguia el Hamra and Río de Oro. *Polisario* is a shortened version of the Spanish name of the organization: Frente Popular para la Liberación de Saguia el Hamra y Río de Oro (Popular Front for the Liberation of Saguia el Hamra and Río de Oro).

During the colonial period, the Saharawi living in the western part of the Sahara suffered under both French and Spanish rule. In 1958, as nationalist movements swept across the African continent, a joint Spanish-French military operation defeated the Saharawi army. However, the resistance was reborn 10 years later as the Movement for the Liberation of the Sahara, led by Mohammed Sidi Brahim Bassiri (1942–1970).

In 1970 mass demonstrations led by the movement in LAAYOUNE, the Western Sahara capital, led to the massacre of protesters by Spanish forces. The Spanish also arrested Bassiri, who was never again heard from and presumably was killed soon after his arrest. Three years later Polisario was formed, and nonviolent methods of resistance were put aside. Ten days after its founding the rebel army carried out an attack on the Spanish outpost of El-Khanga. For the next two years Polisario harried Spanish forces and sabotaged the territory's European phosphate MINING operations, the lucrative reason that Spain wanted to remain in the territory. The Polisario movement received support from ALGERIA and Algerian president Houari BOUMEDIENNE (1927–1978), who became a champion of Saharawi self-rule. MOROCCO, however, led by King HASSAN II (1929–1999), and MAURITANIA, led by President Mokhtar Ould Daddah (1924–), had their own designs on the region.

In 1975, the same year that its long-ruling dictator Francisco Franco (1892–1975) died, Spain began to withdraw from the disputed region. With international pressure mounting to allow autonomy for the Saharawi, Morocco acted to lay claim on the territory. In October of that year, King Hassan launched the Green March, a mass migration of 350,000 Moroccan settlers into Western Sahara. At the end of the month Moroccan troops entered the territory, running into vigorous Polisario resistance. In November, despite UN condemnation and threats from Algeria, representatives from Spain, Morocco, and Mauritania met in Madrid and agreed to partition the Western Sahara among the African countries.

Although Spain officially ended its colonial rule in 1976, by then Moroccan troops, in the north, and Mauritanian troops, in the south, occupied the territory. Facing the aggression of the occupiers, the Polisario responded with more attacks on the phosphate industry, effectively ending mining operations. In early 1976 the movement declared a government-in-exile, the Saharawi Arab Democratic Republic (SADR), which was eventually recognized by 70 countries as well as the ORGANIZATION OF AFRICAN UNITY. Within the country, the Polisario acted not only as a military entity but it also organized food dispersal, medical care, and other civil services. The movement also coordinated the evacuation of a large portion of the Saharawi civilian population, with most seeking refuge in Algeria. By the middle of 1976 the Polisario initiated an all-out offensive, sending incursions into Mauritania and launching assaults on the Mauritanian capital of NOUAKCHOTT.

The Polisario then widened its offensive, attacking Spanish fishing boats and inflicting heavy losses on Moroccan forces. Despite French military assistance, the struggle took its toll on Mauritania, and in 1978 a COUP D'ÉTAT overthrew President Daddah. The subsequent government was quick to establish a peace with the Polisario.

By the end of 1979 the two sides had signed the Algiers Agreement, which stipulated a withdrawal of Mauritania's claims in Western Sahara.

Spain officially recognized the Polisario in 1978, ending hostilities and leaving Morocco as the Saharawis' only antagonist. With Morocco tenaciously maintaining its hold on the northern territory, the Polisario launched the Houari Boumedienne offensive in 1979 in honor of the late Algerian president. Vicious fighting and attempts by the Organization of African Unity and the United Nations to push a resolution did little to weaken the resolve of either side. Finally, in 1988, the Polisario and Morocco agreed to a UN-brokered peace plan. A tenuous cease-fire was established in 1991 pending a referendum on Western Saharan independence. However, Morocco used various tactics to delay the vote, and repeated attempts at negotiation have failed. As of 2004 the Polisario's goal of achieving self-rule for the Saharawi had yet to be reached.

See also: INDEPENDENCE MOVEMENTS (Vol. V); NATIONALISM AND INDEPENDENCE MOVEMENTS (Vol. IV); SPAIN AND AFRICA (Vol. IV); UNITED NATIONS AND AFRICA (Vol. V).

Further reading: Tony Hodges, *Western Sahara: The Roots of a Desert War* (Westport, Conn.: L. Hill, 1983); Yahia H. Zoubir and Daniel Volman, eds., *International Dimensions of the Western Sahara Conflict* (Westport, Conn.: Praeger, 1993).

political parties and organizations African political parties in the modern era fall roughly into four categories, two of which have their origin in the colonial period and two that have evolved in the era since African countries gained independence. The nationalism and INDEPENDENCE MOVEMENTS of the colonial period led to the emergence of two types of political parties. The first, which was common in the majority of African countries, were parties that organized in colonies where the colonial powers were overseeing a constitutional, and largely peaceful, transition from colonial rule to independence. One of the foremost examples of this type of party was the Convention People's Party (CPP) in GHANA, established in 1949. Through the CPP, its founder, Kwame NKRUMAH (1909–1972), challenged the dominant United Gold Coast Convention for leadership of the political process leading to independence. Similarly, in TUNISIA, the Neo-Destour Party, which had its roots in the older Destour Party, provided the vehicle for Habib BOURGUIBA (1903–2000) to lead his country to independence from France in 1956. Yet another example is the Tanganyikan African National Union, led by Julius NYERERE (1922–1999). That party, which evolved into the TANZANIAN AFRICAN NATIONAL UNION, negotiated Tanganyika's independence from Britain, helping Nyerere to become the country's prime minister and, eventually, president.

A second type of major modern political party emerged out of wars of liberation or otherwise bitterly contested independence struggles. In most such cases the colony was populated by significant numbers of European settlers who had gained considerable control over its government. For example, in SOUTH AFRICA, which had in effect been fully independent since 1910, a group of educated African leaders formed the AFRICAN NATIONAL CONGRESS (ANC), in 1912. The ANC pressured the white-controlled government to open the electoral process to Africans. Instead, white rule became even more oppressive and repressive, culminating with the advent of APARTHEID, in 1948. When, in 1960, the government outlawed African political parties and organizations, the ANC went underground and eventually established a military wing, UMKHONTO WE SIZWE. Fortunately, although the prolonged political struggle was punctuated by military activity, it ultimately ended not in open war but rather in a negotiated constitutional settlement that led, in 1994, to a democratic election. Successfully transforming itself from a liberation movement into a political party, the ANC won the election and went on to form the new South African government.

Other countries with large white-settler populations encountered much more warfare and bloodshed. This was especially true in ALGERIA, where, after a prolonged and costly struggle, the NATIONAL LIBERATION FRONT (Front de Libération Nationale, FLN) led the country to independence in 1962. The FLN then formed the new government. A similar process took place in the former Portuguese colonies of ANGOLA, MOZAMBIQUE, the Republic of CAPE VERDE, and GUINEA-BISSAU, as well as in the breakaway British colony of RHODESIA, which later became ZIMBABWE.

The fates of political parties based in the independence and liberation movements varied greatly. The expectation at independence had been that African countries would follow the example of the European countries that had ruled them and would have competitive elections and democratic governments. However, this often proved not to be the case. In Ghana, for example, Nkrumah established the CPP as the sole legal political party. When, in 1966, a COUP D'ÉTAT overthrew Nkrumah, the Convention People's Party also lost power. For decades Ghana remained in the political wilderness, struggling under a succession of mostly military governments. In 1996 the situation finally began to change when the CPP was one of two parties that supported John Agyekum KUFUOR (1938–) in democratic elections. Though Kufuor lost that year, he came back to win the 2000 election, restoring some power to the CPP.

A frequent occurrence elsewhere in Africa was the establishment of a single-party state not long after independence, followed by a military coup. The CENTRAL AFRICAN REPUBLIC is such an example. In other situations, however, ruling parties in one-party states managed to survive, although sometimes in a diminished capacity.

The FLN, in Algeria, and the Neo-Destour Party, in Tunisia, were secular in nature despite governing Muslim countries. In both countries, their failures to improve living conditions coincided with the rise of Islamic fundamentalism. The result was the formation of new Islamic fundamentalist political organizations. In 1986 in Tunisia, ZINE EL ABIDINE BEN-ALI (1936–), President Bourguiba's prime minister, ousted him from power, thereby opening up the political process. This revitalized the aging Neo-Destour Party, which became the Constitutional Democratic Assembly. In Algeria similar pressures also led to an opening of the political process. In 1995, the candidate of the new National and Democratic Rally (Rassemblement National pour la Démocratie, RND) won the presidential election, and the FLN was reduced to minority-party status after more than three decades in power.

The political history of Algeria illustrates the categories of political parties that have emerged in the years since Africa shed colonial rule. Internal and external pressures caused authoritarian political systems to loosen their grip on power, leading to the spread of DEMOCRATIZATION. Especially in the 1990s, new political parties formed to elect officials to office. The RND in Algeria and the recently formed Senegalese Democratic Party (Parti Democratique Sénégalais, PDS) are examples of this process. In 2000 the PDS ended the 40-year hold of the Senegalese Socialist Party on the country's government. Similar situations can be observed around the continent.

The other major type of political party that emerged after independence evolved out of political organizations that used force to replace an existing government. A leading example is the ETHIOPIAN PEOPLE'S REVOLUTIONARY DEMOCRATIC FRONT (EPRDF). The EPRDF, which now governs ETHIOPIA, began as an umbrella organization seeking to liberate the country from the despotic rule of MENGISTU HAILE MARIAM (c. 1937–). In UGANDA the National Resistance Movement (NRM) emerged during the chaos and political turmoil of the 1970s and early 1980s to challenge the government of Idi AMIN (c. 1925–2003) and then that of Milton OBOTE (1924–). Finally, in 1986 the NRM won out and its leader, Yoweri MUSEVENI (1944–), became the country's president. The NRM became the sole legal party, and in 2000 the country voted down a multiparty system.

Political parties and organizations have thus had a varied and checkered history since African countries gained their political independence. Military coups ended some parties. In other countries, where the state collapsed, they disappeared altogether. Others lost their vitality as the sole party in one-party states and could not compete effectively when democratic elections were restored. On the other hand, some continued to win elections when faced with new opposition.

See also: COLONIAL RULE (Vol. IV); CONVENTION PEOPLE'S PARTY (Vol. IV); DESTOUR PARTY (Vol. IV); NATIONALISM AND INDEPENDENCE MOVEMENTS (Vol. IV); POLITICAL PARTIES AND ORGANIZATIONS (Vol. IV); SETTLERS, EUROPEAN (Vol. IV); UNITED GOLD COAST CONVENTION (Vol. IV).

Further reading: Adebayo O. Olukoshi, ed., *The Politics of Opposition in Contemporary Africa* (Uppsala, Sweden: Nordiska Afrikainstitutet, 1998); M. A. Mohamed Salih, ed., *African Political Parties: Evolution, Institutionalism and Governance* (London: Pluto, 2003).

political systems A political system may be a dictatorship, democracy, monarchy, oligarchy, theocracy, plutocracy, aristocracy, meritocracy, or stratocracy. Since 1990 state governance in sub-Saharan Africa has been in significant transition. No longer are purely autocratic political systems tolerated; rather, some level of democracy is commonly sought.

Since independence most political systems in sub-Saharan Africa have been either dictatorships or democracies. Dictatorships, which can take many forms, are situations in which the power of rule is concentrated in the hands of one person. An *authoritarian* dictator is a leader who controls the political sphere without challenge. He—Africa's authoritarian dictators have all been males—stands above the law and is not accountable to the people. In this system there is generally very little popular political participation, if any, and the government controls the press. All of this is made possible through military force. MOZAMBIQUE, ANGOLA, GUINEA-BISSAU, and NIGERIA are among the many countries in Africa that have been governed this way at one point or another in recent history. Other countries, such as GHANA, under Kwame NKRUMAH (1909–1972), and ALGERIA, under Houari BOUMEDIENNE (1927–1978), were one-party states in which the military was under the tight control of the country's leadership.

A *totalitarian* dictator is one who exceeds authoritarian rule by seeking control of not just politics but society. Usually a totalitarian ruler justifies his actions by claiming to want to reform society. The late MOBUTU SESE SEKO (1930–1997) of the Democratic Republic of the CONGO (formerly ZAÏRE) and Idi AMIN (c. 1925–2003) of UGANDA are examples of totalitarian dictators.

Since the collapse of the Soviet Union, Africa's political systems have almost universally sought DEMOCRATIZATION. While the word democracy refers simply to rule by the people, in practice, democratic system types are diverse and complex. *Liberal democracies* generally have a representative government operating through the rule of law. In a healthy liberal democracy citizens enjoy significant personal freedoms, and political institutions such as the legislature, executive, and judiciary are in place and properly functioning. The United States is commonly named as an example of a liberal democracy. *Procedural democracies,* too, have democratic institutions. However, citizens in a procedural democracy may lack some personal freedoms, and a free press might be wanting. In *electoral democracies,* multiparty elections ensure that representatives reflect the will of the people, but democratic institutions might be in a state of continuous transformation, and personal freedoms might be more limited. Generally speaking, electoral democracies are only "semidemocratic" because authoritarian leaders can still retain significant power over the people.

The APARTHEID political system of SOUTH AFRICA was a variant of an authoritarian state. The country's non-whites had no voice in governing the country and were subject to arrest and imprisonment if they engaged in any form of vigorous protest over their exclusion from the political process. White South Africans, on the other hand, participated in multiparty elections to select their parliamentary representatives. Only with the 1994 elections was the political process opened to all adult South Africans.

In 1990 it appeared as if nearly all of Africa would make the transition from dictatorial political systems to democratic ones. However, more than a decade later only a few countries—among them Algeria, Ghana, MALI, Republic of BENIN, Guinea-Bissau, and NAMIBIA—have made significant progress. In some cases leaders of weak states have been unable to unify smaller, local political systems into a cohesive national system. Elsewhere, would-be autocrats have tried to usurp power and former autocrats have used the new political framework to reassert their power. Most African countries have stagnated in electoral or semi-democratic form. As a result they have regular multiparty elections but their political processes are highly flawed and there are significant limitations on personal freedoms. It nonetheless remains the professed goal of virtually every country in Africa to make the transition to a political system of consolidated liberal democracy.

See also: POLITICAL PARTIES (Vol. V).

Further reading: Michael Bratton and Nicolas van de Walle, *Democratic Experiments in Africa: Regime Transitions in Comparative Perspective* (Cambridge, U.K.: Cambridge University Press, 1997).

popular culture See CINEMA; LITERATURE IN MODERN AFRICA; MUSIC; RADIO AND TELEVISION; SPORTS AND ATHLETICS; TELECOMMUNICATIONS; THEATER.

Popular Movement for the Liberation of Angola (Movimento Popular de Libertação de Angola, MPLA)

Marxist anticolonial movement founded in 1956; in 1975 the MPLA formed the first government of independent ANGOLA. The MPLA officially was founded in 1956, with many of its members coming from the Communist Party of Angola. The organization arose because the disunity among the various nationalist movements in Angola called for a single, broad political party. Centered in the Angolan capital of LUANDA, the MPLA supported the Marxist-oriented social program favored by the nation's urban Mbundu population.

The MPLA movement faced much resistance, however. The Portuguese secret security force, known as PIDE, used its powers of arbitrary arrest and indefinite imprisonment to prevent the MPLA from garnering support throughout the Angolan countryside. Hounded by PIDE and unable to unite the country's urban elite with its rural population, the MPLA leadership went into exile. In 1960 they accepted the invitation of President Ahmed Sékou TOURÉ (1922–1984) of GUINEA and established headquarters in CONAKRY, Guinea's capital.

Ilidio Tomé Alves Machado (1915–), born to a slave mother in Luanda, was the MPLA's first president and one of those arrested by the PIDE. However, Machado was a man of ideas and not a leader of the masses. The organization's true leaders were Agostinho NETO (1922–1979), Mário Coelho Pinto de Andrade (1928–1990), and Viriato da Cruz (1928–1973). Neto was imprisoned for his writings against Portuguese colonialism and brutality, Pinto de Andrade was a prolific writer against Portuguese colonialism, and Viriato da Cruz was a former civil servant in the Department of Education who was fired in 1952 for his political activities.

Throughout the late 1960s and into the early 1970s the MPLA waged an armed struggle for independence against the Portuguese colonial army. Finally, in November 1975, the MPLA announced the People's Republic of Angola, with Neto as president. Unfortunately independence did not unify the disparate factions in Angola, and some foreign countries refused to recognize the MPLA as the nation's legitimate government. As a brutal civil war raged on, the pro-Communist MPLA received aid from Cuba and the Soviet Union. At the same time, the main opposition to the MPLA, the NATIONAL UNION FOR THE TOTAL INDEPENDENCE OF ANGOLA (União Nacional para a Independência Total de Angola, UNITA), received support from SOUTH AFRICA and the United States. In this way, the situation in Angola became a prime example of the political maneuvering and proxy wars that characterized the Cold War.

During the 1970s the MPLA became known as the MPLA-PT (Labor Party) and modeled itself as a Marxist-Leninist party. After Neto's death in 1979, however, José Eduardo DOS SANTOS (1942–) took over the leadership of the party and slowly established better relations with the West.

Under dos Santos the MPLA remained the only legal political organization in Angola until multiparty elections were held in 1992. Following its victory in those elections the MPLA was finally recognized internationally as the government of Angola, although the civil war between the MPLA and UNITA dragged on for another decade. As of 2004 the MPLA was the strongest party in Angola, holding a vast majority of seats in the National Assembly.

See also: COLD WAR AND AFRICA (Vols. IV, V); COLONIAL RULE (Vol. IV); CUBA AND AFRICA (Vol. V); INDEPENDENCE MOVEMENTS (Vol. V); NATIONALISM AND INDEPENDENCE MOVEMENTS (Vol. IV); PORTUGAL AND AFRICA (Vols. III, IV, V); SOVIET UNION AND AFRICA (Vols. IV, V); UNITED STATES AND AFRICA (Vols. IV, V).

population growth From 1900 until 1950 the annual population growth rate for the African continent overall was estimated at approximately 1.2 percent. The continent then underwent a dramatic population increase, with the annual growth rate rising to about 3.3 percent in the 1980s. This upward trend is attributed to a decrease in mortality rates and a concurrent increase in life expectancy.

The decrease in death rates was largely due to widespread vaccination programs, the increased availability of drugs, and the expansion of health care. These conditions resulted in a decline in many fatal diseases, such as smallpox.

Africa as a whole lowered its mortality rates with advances in social and economic DEVELOPMENT. At the same time, women's fertility rates remained relatively high. In 2001 the average fertility rate, which is the number of births per woman, was 5.2 for Africa. For other developing regions, the number stood at 2.8.

There is, of course, great variation in the population growth trends by country. For example, by 2001 MAURITIUS had undergone one of the most rapid declines in fertility rates in the world. This phenomenon is attributed to several changes, including delayed marriages, free EDUCATION, especially for women, and a greater tendency of community leaders—including religious leaders—to promote family planning practices. On the other hand, CAMEROON and NIGERIA both had a fertility rate of approximately 5.0 births per woman. This elevated rate is attributed to early marriages, absence of family planning, the cultural value placed on large families, and limited access to education and health care.

During the 1990s Africa's overall population growth rate declined to approximately 2.8 percent, and it is ex-

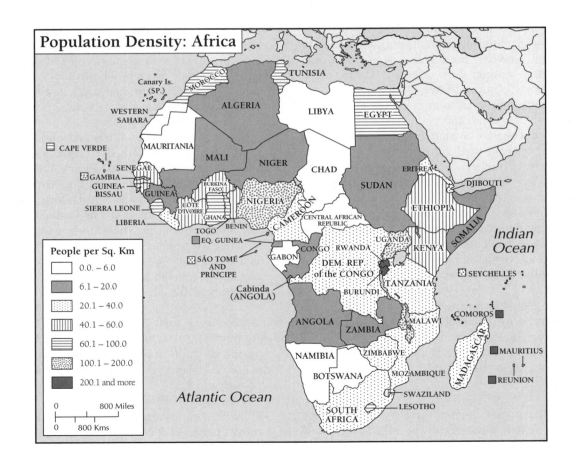

pected to continue to decline over the next 10 years. The continent's ongoing HIV/AIDS pandemic will have a great influence in this decline. In 2001 the average HIV-prevalence rate for adults in sub-Saharan Africa was 8.4 percent, though averages varied widely by region. Some countries of West Africa reported less than 2 percent HIV-prevalence, while certain countries in southern Africa reported a rate greater than 20 percent. The increase in mortality and decrease in life expectancy has resulted in projections of a 1 percent population growth rate in the near future for some countries.

While a declining growth rate helps to relieve the pressure of overpopulation, the nature of HIV/AIDS makes the issue of population growth much more complex. As a result of the disease, women feel the need to have more children to ensure the survival of some. The subsequent positive growth rates will require commensurate increases in agricultural production. But HIV/AIDS affects those who are sexually active, generally the young people who make up the most productive portion of the agricultural LABOR pool. In the 21st century, therefore, the countries in sub-Saharan Africa will have to find a balance between reducing the negative impacts of HIV/AIDS while encouraging a continued decline in population growth rates.

See also: DISEASE IN MODERN AFRICA (Vol. V); HEALTH AND HEALING IN MODERN AFRICA (Vol. V); HIV/AIDS IN AFRICA (Vol. V); MEDICINE (Vols. IV, V).

Further readings: James E. Rosen, *Africa's Population Challenge: Accelerating Progress in Reproductive Health* (Washington D.C.: Population Action International, 1998).

Port Louis Capital and principal port of MAURITIUS, located on the northwestern coast of the Indian Ocean island country. Port Louis dates from 1715, when a French sea captain visited the site and named it after King Louis XIV (1638–1715). The French imported large numbers of African slaves to work sugar plantations, but the British, who took control in 1814, abolished the practice of slavery in 1835. (They had outlawed the slave trade in 1807, but not slavery itself.) The British then brought laborers from India to work on the plantations. These developments largely determined the make-up of the population, language, and culture of Port Louis.

After independence in 1968 improvements were made to the Port Louis harbor. This facilitated the export of sugar, which was long the country's major source of income. By the 1980s, however, the economy began to diversify and Port Louis now has an active industrial sector that produces processed foods (including sugar), printed materials, wood products, and textiles. In fact, textiles now surpass sugar in terms of export earnings. The city also has become an offshore banking center. In recent years TOURISM has developed into another main-

stay of the economy and also has surpassed sugar in economic importance.

The city's historic structures, including the French Government House, built in 1738, and the Citadel, built in 1838, enhance the appeal of the city, as does its Chinese district, which has a casino, a horse track, and several markets. A museum of natural history houses an exhibit on the extinct dodo bird, and the nearby botanical gardens are another attraction. Port Louis is also the site of the national library, as well as numerous EDUCATION and research institutes. As of 2004 the population of Port Louis stood at approximately 140,000.

See also: CASH CROPS (Vols. IV, V); ENGLAND AND AFRICA (Vols. III, IV, V); FRANCE AND AFRICA (Vols. III, IV, V); SLAVERY (Vols. I, II, III, IV); URBAN LIFE AND CULTURE (Vols. IV, V); URBANIZATION (Vols. IV, V).

Portugal and Africa The longest-standing colonial presence in Africa, Portugal attempted to hold onto its African colonies after other European powers had granted those lands independence. After the end of World War II (1939–45) colonized people throughout the world increasingly began to challenge the legitimacy of their status as a colonial subjects. The rising tide of nationalism soon manifested itself as powerful INDEPENDENCE MOVEMENTS, all seeking to end colonial rule in Africa. For many one-time colonies, these movements culminated in the 1960s in the withdrawal of the colonizers and the achievement of national independence. For the colonies of Portugal, in contrast, it would take long and bloody wars in order to achieve independence, which did not come until the mid-1970s.

In ANGOLA the movements that fought against Portuguese control were the POPULAR MOVEMENT FOR THE LIBERATION OF ANGOLA, the NATIONAL FRONT FOR THE LIBERATION OF ANGOLA, and the NATIONAL UNION FOR THE TOTAL INDEPENDENCE OF ANGOLA. In MOZAMBIQUE the main liberation movement was the MOZAMBIQUE LIBERATION FRONT. The independence movement in GUINEA-BISSAU was spearheaded by the AFRICAN PARTY FOR THE INDEPENDENCE OF GUINEA AND CAPE VERDE.

In spite of the determination of the African freedom fighters in these lands, the achievement of independence was not entirely due to African resistance. The Portuguese government ultimately reached the point of wishing to shed its colonial baggage, which was placing enormous strain on the Portuguese economy, military, and citizenry. Ironically, while in other situations, such as France and ALGERIA, it was the colonial powers' military organizations that frequently demanded the maintenance of colonial power, in the case of Portugal, it was the military that ultimately forced the end of colonialism. The Portuguese Armed Forces Movement (AFM) was made up of disillusioned Portuguese military personnel who in 1974 overthrew the pro-colonial regime and replaced it with a government determined to withdraw from Portugal's colonies in Africa. This withdrawal took place soon afterward, with the Portuguese granting independence to their former colonial possessions in 1974 and 1975.

This independence was met with a feeling of triumph and hope for the independent states. However, not all of these states would have smooth sailing upon gaining their freedom. For one thing, with the end of Portuguese rule, the great majority of 200,000 Portuguese in Mozambique and 300,000 Portuguese in Angola left Africa. Along with them went many government officials and leaders in the private sector. These people had provided important skills and wherewithal that had kept the colonies functioning, since under colonial rule few Africans had access to EDUCATION and jobs above the level of menial LABOR. In their place were only people who were, deliberately, uneducated and untrained for these roles. Beyond this, skirmishes broke out among the many previously marginalized groups, all vying for power in the newly independent countries. In the case of Angola, the level of violence in the post-independence power struggles eventually dwarfed the violence that had led to independence.

Given the strained relations between Portugal and its former colonies, it took some time for new relationships to develop between the independent countries and Portugal. However, Portugal's former colonies continued to use Portuguese as their official language, a situation that provided a basis for resuming the ties that had once existed. Gradually relations were rebuilt, trade again began to take place, and Portuguese educators and technical specialists were sent to help with DEVELOPMENT projects. In time Portugal even served as an intermediary in the CIVIL WARS in Angola and Mozambique, allowing it to take a peace-making role in countries where it had, only shortly before, been a primary cause of bloodshed.

See also: COLD WAR AND AFRICA (Vols. IV, V); COLONIAL RULE (Vol. IV); NATIONALISM AND INDEPENDENCE MOVEMENTS (Vol. IV); PORTUGAL AND AFRICA (Vols. III, IV).

Further reading: David Birmingham, *Portugal and Africa* (New York: St. Martin's Press, 1999); Malyn Newitt, *Portugal in Africa: The Last Hundred Years* (London: Longman, 1981).

postcolonial state Alternative to the view that former colonial states in Africa require DEVELOPMENT, institutionalization, and improved governance. While in literal terms a *postcolonial state* is one that emerged from a state formed as an instrument of colonial rule, the term has in recent years taken on more particular normative connotations.

A state is the sum of the government, territory, and population of a country. However, states in Africa during the colonial era differed from other types of states. Rather than having as their fundamental responsibility the sovereignty of their borders and the protection of their people, the colonial states existed for the benefit of the colonial powers. The boundaries drawn during the Berlin Conference of 1884–85 were a reflection of the relationships of European states, not of African states. In fact, when it came to establishing colonial state boundaries, precolonial African political and ethnic divisions were generally ignored.

The dominant view is that postcolonial African states have been weak because of failures in African leadership. However, alternative views now challenge this notion. If African countries were supposed to move from undeveloped to developed, in a Western fashion, the system necessarily gives power to those states that are further along the path of development—namely, wealthy Western states.

Rather than adopting existing patterns of state formation, new African perspectives consider alternative modes of development. Such alternatives have been criticized for working against the forces of globalization. On the other hand, those who support the alternative modes of state building insist that their position is a legitimate response to the imbalances left from the colonial state system. They argue that mandates for "good government" in postcolonial states are a dysfunctional remnant of the colonial era. These mandates, it is said, succeeded in other contexts, but they are blind to the diverse histories and power structures of African countries.

These mandates also ignore potential institutional relationships that can actually improve governance. For instance, practices that might be negatively considered as "patronage" in the West may well end up building effective networks of kinship organization that contribute to good government. In other cases, what may be considered CORRUPTION in the West may actually prove to be a codified and historically valid system of payment for services rendered. This is especially true in cases in which the state either cannot afford or cannot support its civil service.

See also: BERLIN CONFERENCE (Vol. IV); COLONIAL RULE (Vol. IV); NEOCOLONIALISM AND UNDERDEVELOPMENT (Vol. V); STATE, ROLE OF (Vol. V).

Further reading: Jeffrey Herbst, *States and Power in Africa: Comparative Lessons in Authority and Control* (Princeton, N.J.: Princeton University Press, 2000); Mahmood Mamdani, *Citizen and Subject* (Princeton, N.J.: Princeton University Press, 1996).

poverty As the world moves toward reducing the number of people who suffer from the associated effects of food, water, and shelter deprivation, sub-Saharan Africa remains a stubborn exception. Definitions of poverty vary widely. What constitutes a basic necessity can vary by time and place, and a lifestyle that makes someone seem "poor" in one place can seem relatively affluent in another culture. For this reason, poverty is often defined as "relative" rather than "absolute."

Relative poverty usually indicates that though a person lacks what certain societies may deem "necessities," he or she is still able to satisfy his or her basic needs compared to those around him. For instance, a person in a Senegalese village might have shelter, food, and clothing—where many of his neighbors do not—but lacks electricity, which is almost a basic necessity by United States and European standards. Defining relative poverty is often very controversial, since what is "basic" may have cultural or social biases. It is controversial also because it is commonly seen as the job of government to address the problems faced by those below a changeable "poverty line"; the "poor" label, therefore, comes with ethical obligations or mandates for the state.

Absolute poverty, on the other hand, is less controversial. Under conditions of absolute poverty, a person cannot procure the basic needs for survival: food, water, and adequate housing. A worldwide "poverty line" of U.S. $1 (or the equivalent) per day is commonly used by international aid organizations, though the validity of that amount varies according to the cost of goods in a particular country or region. Often external factors, such as disease or local market collapse, can move someone from relative to absolute poverty.

Measuring Poverty Measuring poverty is a great challenge. For decades poverty was measured by the gross national product (GNP) or Gross Domestic Product (GDP), macroeconomic indicators that represent the sum monetary value of a country's goods and services for one fiscal year. GNP measures this value worldwide and GDP measures this value domestically. However, GNP and GDP are not ideal indicators of poverty. They measure income, not welfare. Furthermore, they are aggregate national statistics that do not address variations among

Under white minority rule in the mid-1970s, the black majority of Rhodesia (today's Zimbabwe) was greatly affected by poverty. Unable to afford child care, these women had to bring their children to work with them as they picked coffee beans on a white-owned plantation near the Mozambique border. © AP/Wide World Photos

smaller, regional populations. Also, these measures address only market activity, meaning that they do not measure other factors related to a person's ability to meet his or her needs. These other factors include housework, community service, time to spend with family, environmental degradation, and natural resource depletion.

In light of the limitations of GNP and GDP as poverty indicators, the UN Development Program uses the Human Development Index and Human Poverty Index. These indices take into consideration such microeconomic factors as individual EDUCATION and life expectancy. By these criteria, NIGER is commonly listed as the world's poorest country, with the next 21 countries on the list all in sub-Saharan Africa.

The Impact of Poverty on Living Standards

Poverty impacts many aspects of a person life and the country in which he or she lives. A persistent lack of food security leads to famine, a condition in which a person is unable to acquire safe, nutritionally adequate, and personally acceptable food. Sometimes the inability to meet basic food needs is tied to environmental factors such as poor soil conditions or severe drought; other times it is a political problem, such as territorial conflict or a lack of land-access rights. It can also be tied to an inability to purchase needed LABOR or fertilizer, or to lease land for farming purposes.

In Africa, poverty that affects AGRICULTURE also affects education. It is not uncommon in African countries for up to 80 percent of the population to rely on subsistence agriculture. In NAMIBIA, for example, 70 percent of the population survives on farming. In SWAZILAND the figure is 60 percent; in MADAGASCAR, 77 percent; in BURKINA FASO, 80 percent; and in RWANDA, more than 90 percent. Every birth is a new mouth to feed, so if a child is not working the field then he or she is a net drain on the family's ability to survive. As a result, in many countries children too young to farm go to school, but children old enough to farm do not. The percentage of enrolled students thus falls off precipitously in second and third grade. This mechanism turns poverty into a cycle: children don't obtain the basic LITERACY and education levels necessary to advance their ability to meet their own needs and, consequently, future generations will probably suffer the same fate.

The poverty cycle is also tied to employment. If literacy and education levels are low, then the skilled labor base is small, making it harder for countries to create jobs or attract foreign business. Yet, without salaried employment the majority of the population is forced to remain in subsistence agriculture, which too often precludes them and their families from obtaining the education level necessary for salaried employment.

Moreover, where poverty is high, health suffers. Water in poor households is often contaminated, leading to high incidences of MALARIA, worm parasites, and other diseases.

Poor parents can afford neither the primary health care to prevent these diseases nor the cost of treating them once they are contracted.

> **The negative effects of poverty have made it difficult to make progress in fighting one of the most dire health threats in contemporary Africa: HIV infection and AIDS. Already, more than 15 million Africans have died from the disease, and another 25 million people are HIV-positive. In rural Africa, once HIV is contracted, effective treatment is virtually impossible, since patented drugs cost approximately $1,500 per year. Even generic equivalents cost $600 per year, more than three times the per-capita income of most Africans and 60 times the per-capita health budget of many African countries. Even AIDS prevention is an economic problem, since the cost of condoms is prohibitive.**

The Impact of Poverty on the Environment

Over the past two decades the interaction between poverty and the environment has received tremendous attention. The "Green Revolution" in wealthy countries has increased the technology gap in agricultural practices to highlight the inefficiencies of many African agricultural systems. Also POPULATION GROWTH rates are higher where absolute poverty is common, putting a greater stress on the environment.

In the IVORY COAST, for instance, rice is a food staple. However, the soil is often rough, and 94 percent of rice paddies are rain fed (without irrigation). As a result, an acre of rice paddy in Ivory Coast produces less than one-sixth the amount produced by the equivalent paddy in the United States. According to the UN Human Settlements Program, the average household in Ivory Coast has 7.32 people, meaning that each household that relies on subsistence agriculture must produce about 1.2 tons of rice (1,219 kg) per year just to meet basic nutritional needs. Since normal cultivation techniques cannot produce this amount of rice, farmers must use dry rice cultivation and slash-and-burn techniques that, when implemented too frequently and extensively, take a toll on FORESTS. With the fastest-growing population of any region in the world (2.8 percent annual growth rate), there is little hope that Africa will lessen the stress on the natural resources in its poorer countries any time soon.

What Is Being Done About Poverty in Africa?

The classic view of alleviating poverty has been to increase DEVELOPMENT through modernization and INDUSTRIALIZATION. By adopting the technologies and market strategies of rich countries, the poor countries of the world hope to

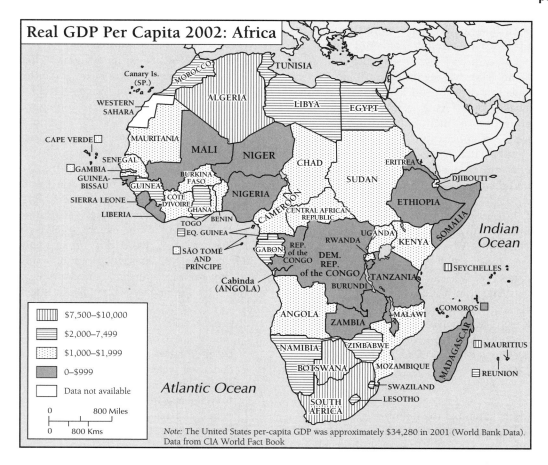

Real GDP Per Capita 2002: Africa

$7,500–$10,000

$2,000–7,499

$1,000–$1,999

0–$999

Data not available

0   800 Miles

0   800 Kms

Note: The United States per-capita GDP was approximately $34,280 in 2001 (World Bank Data). Data from CIA World Fact Book

progress at a rapid rate. Unfortunately this approach, popular in the 1960s and 1970s, has not proved successful. In the 1980s the WORLD BANK and the INTERNATIONAL MONETARY FUND offered loan packages related to macroeconomic incentives. The idea was that if African countries could get their financial policies and institutions functioning well, they would attract FOREIGN INVESTMENT and jobs, producing positive effects that would trickle down to the population. Instead, the net income of most African countries decreased in the 1980s and 1990s, the quality of life for most African people became worse, and the number of people in poverty increased.

Part of the problem has been the implementation of this approach. As part of STRUCTURAL ADJUSTMENT, African countries are required to reduce trade barriers, most notably import tariffs. Most wealthy countries, however, have high import tariffs on African goods, especially agricultural goods that compete with what their own farmers produce. This arrangement reduces the incentives for farmers to invest in agricultural technologies that can only be justified by high export earnings. It also discourages foreign investment by manufacturers, since importing African goods into overseas markets is not cost-effective.

On September 8, 2000, 150 countries, including the United States, signed the landmark United Nations Millen-

nium Declaration. In the declaration are eight Millennium Development goals and targets, the first of which is to halve the number of the world's poor and hungry by 2015. The second goal is to achieve universal education by 2015. The other stated goals call for improved gender equality and women's empowerment, a reduction in child mortality, improved maternal health care, a reduction in the spread of HIV/AIDS and malaria, and an increase in effective and environmentally sound development. It targets Africa specifically, stating that it will "take special measures to address the challenges of poverty eradication and sustainable development in Africa, including debt cancellation, improved market access, enhanced Official Development Assistance and increased flows of Foreign Direct Investment, as well as transfers of technology."

Unfortunately the trend has been in the opposite direction from the goals. Although the World Bank has made an effort to reduce debt, the reduction has not kept pace with newly created debt. Moreover, foreign direct investment in global stock decreased by more than half between 1980 and 1990, and that trend shows little sign of reversal. For the United States the percentage of its GNP devoted to African foreign aid (less than .15 percent) remained the lowest of all the industrialized countries.

The World Bank estimates that SENEGAL will be the only country in Africa to meet the Millennium poverty goals; the continent, as a whole, will see a net increase in poverty. By 2015 an estimated 600 million people, 70 percent of the population, will live on less than $2 per day, with more than half of those living on less than $1 per day.

The consequences of such failures are dire. The health, education, and ability of people to meet the most basic of food and shelter needs will decline. Life expectancy will continue to decline, diseases will continue to proliferate, and the quality of life will improve for only a scant few.

See also: COLONIALISM, INFLUENCE OF (Vol. IV); FAMINE AND HUNGER (Vol. V); FOOD CROPS (Vols. IV, V); HIV/AIDS AND AFRICA (Vol. V); HUMAN RIGHTS (Vol. V); NEO-COLONIALISM AND UNDERDEVELOPMENT (Vol. V); UNITED NATIONS AND AFRICA (Vol. V).

Further reading: John Iliffe, *The African Poor* (New York: Cambridge University Press, 2002); John Isbister, *Promises Not Kept: The Betrayal of Social Change in the Third World* (Bloomfield, Conn.: Kumarian Press, 2001); Amartya Sen, *Development as Freedom* (New York: First Anchor Books, 2000).

Praia Port city and capital of the Republic of CAPE VERDE, located on São Tiago (Santiago) Island, some 400 miles (644 km) off the coast SENEGAL. Praia was the capital of the Portuguese possession of Cape Verde. It maintained its status as capital when the nation gained independence in 1975. The city is the nation's largest urban area and its principal economic and commercial center. The coffee, sugarcane, and fruit produced on the islands pass through the port, and the city also has a strong fishing industry. TOURISM contributes to the local economy, as many of Cape Verde's visitors arrive at the Praia airport or docks before moving on to beach resorts in and near the city. The population of Praia was estimated at 99,400 in 2003.

See also: PORTUGAL AND AFRICA (Vols. III, IV, V); URBAN LIFE AND CULTURE (Vols. IV, V); URBANIZATION (Vols. IV, V).

Pretoria Administrative capital of SOUTH AFRICA, located in the northern part of the country in what is now the Gauteng Province. Founded in 1855, Pretoria became the capital of the Transvaal in 1860 and the administrative capital of the Union of South Africa in 1910. Today it continues to share its capital status with two other South African cities, CAPE TOWN, which is the legislative capital, and Bloemfontein, which is the judicial capital.

In sharp contrast to the APARTHEID era, when AFRIKANERS held a monopoly on government office and the civil service, present-day Pretoria reflects the democratic post-apartheid era, in which the administration of the state better represents the country's African majority. Nevertheless the city, with its 1,250,000 residents, continues to exhibit its earlier Afrikaner character, with numerous Afrikaner historic sites, including the house of Transvaal president Paul Kruger (1825–1904); Melrose House, where the Treaty of Vereeniging was signed to end the Anglo-Boer War (1899–1902); and the Voortrekker Monument, which honors the participants of the Great Boer Trek.

Pretoria is a center for higher EDUCATION institutions, including the University of Pretoria (founded 1908), the University of South Africa (founded 1873), and the famous Onderstepoort Veterinary Research Institute. There are numerous parks in the city, including the National Zoological Gardens, Venning Park, and the gardens of the Union Buildings, as well as several nature reserves. In October and November visitors and residents enjoy the plentiful blooming jacaranda trees that line the streets.

Except for areas such as Tshwane, which shows evidence of recent social change, the neighborhood settlement patterns of Pretoria tend to be holdovers from the apartheid years. Whites predominately occupy the areas close to the city center, and blacks live mainly in the outlying townships.

As the administrative capital for South Africa, Pretoria hosts numerous foreign embassies, giving the city an international flavor, especially since the end of apartheid (1994). There is also a strong industrial sector, emphasizing food processing, engineering, ceramics, chemicals and MINING. Good roads and rail networks leading to many other South African cities, including nearby JOHANNESBURG, make TRANSPORTATION relatively easy.

See also: AFRIKANER REPUBLICS (Vol. IV); BOER (Vol. III, IV); KRUGER, PAUL (Vol. IV); PRETORIA (Vol. IV); TRANSVAAL (Vol. IV); UNION OF SOUTH AFRICA (Vol. IV); URBAN LIFE AND CULTURE (Vols. IV, V); URBANIZATION (Vols. IV, V); VEREENIGING, TREATY OF (Vol. IV).

prophets and prophetic movements Present-day African societies are beset by a number of major ills, ranging from the HIV/AIDS pandemic to POVERTY to the overcrowding and lack of service associated with rapid URBANIZATION to the lack of sustained economic DEVELOPMENT. Prophets historically arise in times of crisis to try to put the social world into balance by applying new solutions to the problems rending society impotent. The crises confronting Africans today provide fertile grounds for prophetic movements.

Combining elements of Christianity, which had been introduced by European MISSIONARIES, and indigenous RELIGION, African prophetic movements attracted large numbers of people who no longer found the answers they were seeking in indigenous religious beliefs but also found that the Euro-centered Christian message of the missionaries did not meet the needs of African daily life. The churches they have founded fall within the broad category of African Initiated Churches (AICs).

The word *prophet* is commonly associated with a divinely inspired religious leader. In Africa, however, it more specifically refers to one whose belief in a direct communication with God allows him or her to make official judgments, moral pronouncements, and future predictions on the community's well-being. The charismatic African prophet interprets dreams and transmits messages from the spirit world. The word is communicated through indigenous methods that include MUSIC made with African instruments as well as lyrics and dance.

Indigenous African society is communal, working toward the good of the community, and African religious beliefs that include the idea of social renewal are a part of daily life. The concept of renewal is not for any one individual but for the entire group, a social reformation. Prophets arise in times of crisis, for example, an epidemic or governmental CORRUPTION, and they provide new solutions to problems that have arisen and that old approaches have failed to resolve.

Islam does not normally believe in prophets other than Mohammed, who is considered the last prophet. However, the tradition of belief in millenarianism, the return of the Mahdi, and the West African Sufi teachers indicate a Muslim hope for figures who can bring about social renewal. In northern NIGERIA, for example, the Islamic leader Alhajji Muhammadu Marwa (d. 1980) led the Maitatsine movement against corruption by the elites and against Christians in KANO in 1980–82.

The Maitatsine movement, supported by largely unemployed and poorly educated individuals who often had recently come to Kano from the rural areas, sparked a series of riots that led to a state of emergency in late 1980. After the police lost control of the situation, the Nigerian army and air force intervened. In the end, more than 4,000 people died, including Alhajji Muhammadu Marwa, and hundreds were arrested.

Christianity, in contrast to Islam, tends to legitimize prophecy, and it supports millenarianism and the idea of renewal similar to the African belief. In Africa prophets came into prominence and their churches have been accepted by local governments and entered the mainstream religious community. In West Africa the largest prophet-based movement is the Aladura movement, which represents a group of independent Pentecostal churches in Nigeria that emphasize healing prayer and visions. One of the key leaders was Joseph Babalola (c. 1906–1959), who in 1955 founded the Christ Apostolic Church. Today it has more than 500,000 members, runs two seminaries, and supports 26 high schools. Its mission activities extend elsewhere in West Africa and even to Houston, Texas, where it ministers to the sizeable expatriate Nigerian community. Other prophetic churches are more deeply rooted in the colonial era. The Christ Army Church of Nigeria, for example, was founded by Garrick Braide (c. 1882–1918), while the Harris Church of the IVORY COAST and the Church of the Twelve Apostles in GHANA originated with the Liberian-born evangelist William Wade Harris (1850–1929).

In East Africa the Holy Spirit Movement, which forms part of the wider movement of African-initiated churches, is illustrative of the ongoing emergence of new prophetic movements. In 1985 Alice Lakwena began a movement among the Acholi in northern UGANDA calling for the removal of evil forces and impurities in society. Speaking through a female Acholi spirit medium, the prophet said that God told her to bring the world back into balance by ridding Uganda of its corrupt government. Building an army based on retired Acholi soldiers who applied the tactics that they had learned as members of the King's East African Rifles during World War II (1939–45), the Holy Spirit Mobile Forces, as they were called, almost succeeded in toppling the country's government. In the end, though, they failed and Lakwena fled to neighboring KENYA, in 1987. Some of her followers, however, continued to fight in the CIVIL WARS that have plagued the region.

In 1955 Alice LENSHINA (1924–1978) founded the Lumpa Church, in ZAMBIA. With its opposition to secular authority, the church clashed first with the British colonial government and then came into conflict with Kenneth Kaunda's (1924–) UNITED NATIONAL INDEPENDENCE PARTY (UNIP) during the move for independence. After independence, a misunderstanding between the government and the church led to violence, with the main church building being burned. Many Lumpa church members moved to the Democratic Republic of the CONGO in self-imposed exile, and Lenshina and her husband were arrested, dying while in detention.

In southern Africa, prophetic movements and AICs took root in the late 19th and early 20th centuries. One of the earliest leaders was Isaiah Shembe (c. 1870–1935), who founded one of the earliest and most important AICs, the Church of Nazareth in SOUTH AFRICA. A son succeeded him as the leader of the church, which increased in size from about 100,000 members in 1960 to over a million in the 1980s. This expansion was part of the rapid expansion of AIC membership in southern Africa in general over the last several decades, with both small independent churches and large multi-congregational churches contributing to this growth.

See also: CHRISTIANITY, INFLUENCE OF (Vols. IV, V); HARRIS, WILLIAM WADE (Vol. IV); LUMPA CHURCH (Vol. IV); PROPHETS AND PROPHETIC MOVEMENTS (Vol. IV); RELIGION (Vols. III, IV, V).

Further reading: Heike Behrend, *Alice Lakwena and the Holy Spirits: War in Northern Uganda, 1985–97* (Athens, Ohio: Ohio University Press, 1999); James L. Cox and Gerrie ter Haar, eds., *Uniquely African?: African Christian Identity from Cultural and Historical Perspectives* (Trenton, N.J.: Africa World Press, 2003); Rosalind I. J. Hackett, ed., *New Religious Movements in Nigeria* (Lewiston, N.Y.: E. Mellen Press, 1987); J. N. K. Mugambi, *Christianity and African Culture* (Nairobi, Kenya: Acton Publishers, 2002); Isaac Phiri, *Proclaiming Political Pluralism: Churches and Political Transitions in Africa* (Westport, Conn.: Praeger, 2001); Bengt Sundkler and Christopher Steed, *A History of the Church in Africa* (New York: Cambridge University Press, 2000).

Provisional National Defense Council (PNDC)

Ruling party of GHANA under Jerry RAWLINGS (1947–) for more than 10 years. The PNDC took control of Ghana's government on December 31, 1981, after Rawlings led a successful COUP D'ÉTAT. Rawlings, a pilot in the country's air force and the leader of a prior successful coup, wanted the PNDC to be viewed as a different type of military-controlled government. Appointing civilians to many high-ranking posts, he stated that the PNDC was a populist government. Despite this stance, however, the PNDC was quick to ban other political parties.

At the time of the PNDC's inception Ghana faced severe economic troubles—its inflation rate stood at 200 percent and exports were at historic lows. To fix the struggling economy the PNDC introduced an Economic Recovery Plan (ERP). The ERP was marked by spending cuts and a request for aid from the WORLD BANK and the INTERNATIONAL MONETARY FUND. The ERP met with some initial success—lowering the inflation rate to 20 percent and expanding the economy at a healthy rate of 6 percent— but Ghana's economic problems continued, as unemployment remained extremely high.

Ghana's economy was not the only problem facing the PNDC. Many Ghanaians viewed Rawlings and his PNDC as authoritarian, accusing the regime of abusing HUMAN RIGHTS and intimidating opposition leaders. During the early 1980s, as the PNDC faced multiple coup attempts, proponents of a return to a civilian government continued to criticize the leadership's slow progress toward DEMOCRATIZATION. In response, in 1984, the PNDC formed the National Commission for Democracy (NCD), which called for public input in helping Ghana move toward representative democracy. The NCD eventually suggested the formation of district assemblies, and district elections were held in 1988. By 1992 the PNDC had removed the ban on political parties, and the country held multiparty presidential and parliamentary elections.

Rawlings and the National Democratic Congress Under Ghana's new multiparty system, political parties had to be new organizations—no reincarnations of previously active parties were allowed. So, when the PNDC was dissolved, Rawlings retired from the military. However, after months of wavering, he decided to reenter politics and run for president as a civilian. He became the candidate of the National Democratic Congress (NDC), which was, in spite of ostensible rules to the contrary, essentially a continuation of the PNDC. Despite questions about his human rights record and his mixed results with Ghana's economy, Rawlings won the presidency. In the elections of 1996 Rawlings and the NDC again won a majority of the vote and returned as Ghana's ruling government. During the NDC's eight years in power Ghana made some economic advances, but many of these gains deteriorated with the decline in international prices for the country's major EXPORTS. The NDC's reign ended in 2000, as constitutional term limits forced Rawlings to step down. In elections held that year John Agyekum KUFUOR (1938–), the leader of the opposition New Patriotic Party, defeated the NDC's presidential candidate, John Atta Mills (1944–). Kufuour's party also won a majority of the seats in Parliament, marking the first electoral transfer of control of the government since Ghana became independent in 1957.

See also: POLITICAL PARTIES AND ORGANIZATIONS (Vols. IV, V).

Further reading: Wisdom J. Tettey, Korbla P. Puplampu, and Bruce J. Berman, eds., *Critical Perspectives in Politics and Socio-economic Development in Ghana* (Boston: Brill, 2003).

Q

Qaddafi, Muammar (Gadaffi, Muammer el-; Khaddafi; Qadhdhafi) (1942–) *Libyan head of state*

The only son of an Arabized Berber family from the Hun Oasis near Sirte, Muammar Qaddafi received his Islamic and elementary EDUCATION from Egyptian teachers. His secondary education came from private tutors after his political activities—including demonstrations against the ruling monarch—led to his expulsion from the high school in Misurata, near TRIPOLI. Later Qaddafi studied at the University of Libya, the Libyan Military Academy at Benghazi, and the British Royal Signal Corps School before receiving his officer's commission in 1965.

Informing many of Qaddafi's actions and views, even at an early stage of his career, were his family experiences during the Italian colonial occupation and the speeches by Egyptian president Gamal Abdel NASSER (1918–1970) on Radio Cairo. Nasser had become the leader of the Arabic-speaking world and had won Qaddafi's admiration for his fight against the ways in which the superpowers—the United States and the former Soviet Union—were attempting to manipulate the people and countries of the Middle East and Africa. After Nasser's death, Qaddafi aspired to follow the Egyptian president's lead in implementing Pan-Arabism and African Islamic socialism. The lasting effects of Israel's victory in the 1948 Palestine War and Libya's apparent lack of support for the Arab cause also influenced Qaddafi.

Inspired by his long-standing political views—as well as by his disdain for the foreign control exercised over Libyan king Idris (1890–1983)—the 27-year-old Qaddafi, then an army captain, led a COUP D'ÉTAT in 1969. Qaddafi's "federation of the free officers" deposed King Idris, charging him with governmental CORRUPTION, nepotism, un-

even regulation of Islamic law, and failure to support EGYPT in the war against Israel.

Qaddafi led the new government as the prime minister of a 12-member Revolutionary Command Council (RCC). He closed the foreign military bases on Libyan soil, nationalized banks and insurance and OIL companies, confiscated the property of Libya's Italian and Jewish communities, outlawed political parties and LABOR UNIONS, and returned LIBYA to its Islamic roots by banning pork, outlawing alcohol and gambling, and returning the lettering of street signs and commercial advertisements to Arabic.

Qaddafi resigned as Libyan prime minister in 1972, although he did retain supreme governmental power as president of the RCC. Later in the 1970s Qaddafi took on the mantle of his hero, Nasser, promoting African Islamic socialism, pan-Arabism, and Arab nationalism as a means to foment a pan-Islamic revolution in Africa and the Middle East. At home he financed his socialist programs by reinvesting oil profits in the social INFRASTRUCTURE. After massive investment in the country's schools, hospitals, roads, and agricultural programs Qaddafi launched a cultural revolution in 1973. Calling Libya *Jamahiriya*, or "state of the masses," he set out to create a nation in which, in theory, the common citizen made decisions about the running of government through various levels of committees that channeled their ideas to the RCC. In practice, however, Qaddafi's policies created a nation that was a military dictatorship. Leaders of the revolution imprisoned and executed their political opponents, many of whom went into self-exile in Europe. By the late 1970s Qaddafi had consolidated his control over the government, the economy, and the religious life of the nation.

Qaddafi's approach to pan-Arabism represented a two-pronged attack on the industrialized nations. Feeling that the balkanization of the Arab world reduced its international clout, he sought to create a universal Islamic state. He started with neighboring states—first with Egypt and Syria, then with TUNISIA and ALGERIA, and then with CHAD and the Republic of the SUDAN. These unions, however, fell apart for various reasons, leaving Qaddafi with little to show for his massive investment of money.

Qaddafi's approach to spreading Islam on the African continent reportedly included a $2 million bribe to Jean-Bedel BOKASSA (1921–1996) of the CENTRAL AFRICAN REPUBLIC to become Muslim. Bokassa accepted the money, became a Muslim, and then immediately returned to his Christian roots.

The other prong of Qaddafi's attack on the industrialized powers was the support of liberation movements, including the Palestine Liberation Organization in its battles against Israel. Because he saw these liberation movements as helping his cause, Qaddafi often supported them without much investigation, satisfied that they would destabilize Western imperialism. This led him to become involved, in one way or another, with numerous groups labeled "terrorists" by the United States and its allies, a situation that brought him into direct conflict with the United States.

Following a chain of events that included maneuvers by the U.S. Sixth Fleet, a U.S. ban on Libyan oil imports, and the 1986 bombing of a disco in Berlin that was popular with U.S. soldiers, U.S. president Ronald Reagan (1911–2004) ordered an air strike against Libyan military and political targets. Qaddafi's personal compound was targeted, and, in the attack, he was wounded and his adopted daughter was killed. In 1988 terrorists bombed Pan-Am Flight 103 over Lockerbie, Scotland, apparently as Qaddafi's response to the attack on his personal quarters. Qaddafi refused to turn over the Libyans charged in the case, leading the United Nations to impose sanctions on his country. Eventually, however, the Libyan leader complied, allowing the suspects to stand trial in exchange for the lifting of UN sanctions.

At the beginning of the 21st century, Qaddafi tried to keep a low profile and improve relations with his oil customers in the European Union. He continues to support Islamic and pro-Palestinian causes, and he is reported to be active in African affairs, supplying weapons and military training to rebels in several sub-Saharan countries, including ZIMBABWE, IVORY COAST, SIERRA LEONE, and LIBERIA.

See also: ARAB WORLD AND AFRICA (Vol. V); ISLAM, INFLUENCE OF (Vols. II, III, IV, V).

Further reading: Henry M. Christman, ed., *Qaddafi's Green Book* (Buffalo, N.Y.: Prometheus Books, 1988); Brian L. Davis, *Qaddafi, Terrorism, and the Origins of the U. S. Attack on Libya* (New York: Praeger, 1990); Mansour El-Kikhia, *Libya's Qaddafi: the Politics of Contradiction* (Gainesville, Fla.: University Press of Florida, 1997); René Lemarchand, ed., *The Green and the Black: Qadhafi's Policies in Africa* (Bloomington, Ind.: Indiana University Press, 1988); George Tremlett, *Gadaffi: The Desert Mystic* (New York: Carroll & Graf, 1993).

R

Rabat Historic city and national capital of MOROCCO, located at the mouth of the Bou Regreg River, on the Atlantic coast in the northwestern part of the country. The urban settlement of Rabat dates as far back as the third century BCE. In the 12th century Rabat gained its initial importance when the Almohad sultans established a military base at the site. During the 17th century the city became the home of Andalusian Moors who had fled from Spain and made Rabat, and its twin city of Salé across the Bou Regreg, centers of corsair raiding. France, which established a protectorate over Morocco in 1912, made Rabat the capital of French Morocco, and it continued in that role when the country gained its independence in 1956.

Rabat's long history is evident in the numerous historical structures scattered throughout the city today. The tower of Hassan and the Almohad gateway date from the 12th century, while the corsair fortress of Casbah des Oudaia dates from the 17th century. A great wall, built by the third Almohad sultan, still encloses the ancient Muslim quarter (*medina*) and the Jewish quarter (*millah*).

The modern quarter, featuring substantial contributions by the French, is the site of the royal palace built in the 1950s. It also houses government offices and several educational facilities, including Muhammad V University, established in 1957, and the National Conservatory of Music, Dance and Dramatic Arts. In addition there are many museums that display Moroccan ART and artifacts.

Rabat's once active port has declined in importance primarily because deposits have clogged the mouth of the Bou Regreg. Today, aside from the national government, the city's economy is based mainly on the industries of textiles, processed foods, building materials, and TOURISM.

The combined population of the Rabat-Salé area was estimated at 1,636,000 in 2003.

See also: ALMOHADS (Vol. II); FRANCE AND AFRICA (Vols. III, IV, V); MUHAMMAD V, KING (Vol. IV); URBAN LIFE AND CULTURE (Vols. IV, V); URBANIZATION (Vols. IV, V).

radio and television Radio is still the most important mass medium in Africa, with ownership of radio sets being much higher than for any other broadcasting device. By 1997 UNESCO estimated radio ownership in Africa at about 170 million with a 4 percent annual growth rate. By 2002 it was estimated that there were more than 200 million radio sets, compared with only 62 million televisions.

Many people in African communities watch television or listen to the radio at the same time. More than 60 percent of the population in Africa is reached by existing radio transmitter networks while national television coverage is largely confined to major towns. Some countries still do not have their own national television broadcaster.

After many countries liberalized broadcasting in the 1980s, an increasing number of commercial stations have been established. However, in terms of the news that commercial stations air on their channels, there is a tendency simply to broadcast news from the government (which generally controls the news agencies) rather than from an international broadcaster or news agency. Unfortunately this type of news broadcast tends to focus on the government and ignores the news outside the urban areas. The exceptions to this are GHANA, MALI, NIGER, SOUTH AFRICA, and UGANDA, all of which have seen notable numbers of new community radio licensees. Radio is still a leading source of information and entertainment. Groups of people in many communities

In 1965 Rhodesians, both black and white, listened to a transistor radio as Prime Minister Ian Smith issued his unilateral declaration of independence from Britain. Radio is still the most important mass medium in Africa. © UPI

can be seen listening to the news, a popular sports event, or a talk show. African radio and television include a wide range of local and Western broadcasting including CNN, Voice of America, British Broadcasting Corporation (BBC), Radio Netherlands, and Deutche Welle.

As the Arabic-speaking world's cultural and informational hub, CAIRO, the capital of EGYPT, is a major center of broadcasting. Its first TV station began operations in 1960. Today government-controlled ETV has two nationwide channels plus additional regional channels. Al-Jazira and other networks are available to those with satellite reception. By 2000 there were nearly 8 million TV sets in Egypt, which was about one set for every nine people, and approximately 23 million radios.

In the last few decades radio and television in Africa have gone through many changes. From the time of independence many countries controlled the radio and television stations. From the late 1980s there was pressure on the government to liberalize the airwaves, and this government monopoly has gradually broken down. Radio and television are improving and are gradually becoming powerful instruments for public information and EDUCATION.

Despite the progress made, however, radio and television in Africa are still hampered by problems including shortage of funds, personnel, and material resources. African governments have always considered radio and television broadcasting vital elements which need to be controlled for information and for DEVELOPMENT. However, government control has gradually relaxed. In the 1990s private radio stations proliferated in almost every country in Africa, most broadcasting on frequency modulation (FM) channels with relatively low output and coverage area. This expanded coverage has expanded the diversity of information for both urban and rural areas. Similar developments, though not so pronounced, have taken place in television, with the privatization of ownership and the proliferation of cable and satellite broadcasting or relay stations.

Television in Africa began slowly. In late 1959 Southern Rhodesia (now ZIMBABWE) and NIGERIA initiated the process when they started their television services. In Zimbabwe this service was limited to the capital and broadcast black and white recorded series for around six hours per day. Television was only introduced in SOUTH AFRICA as late as 1977, a surprise considering the country's level of development. This was because some of the country's Calvinist theologians spoke critically of "the evils of television." By the end of the 1990s South African television broadcasts were seen in several neighboring countries. One of the last countries to receive television in Africa was MALAWI, whose television service only started in 1998. Most countries have one or two television stations. Some, like Uganda, have six television stations.

In recent years television has developed at a rapid rate throughout Africa. Television is improving and is gradually becoming a powerful instrument for public education, entertainment, and information. African governments are giving up their monopolistic control, and private stations are being established, forcing the government-owned stations to reassess their approach to broadcasting. Official television stations are under pressure to move their focus away from reporting the activities and official communiqués of the president and government ministers. A wide variety of television programs are aired on television including education campaigns, popular MUSIC shows, a variety of talk shows, plays, fashion shows, religious programs, and feature films.

While there has been a growth in the television industry, many of the new, private stations face major problems. Most tend to have insufficient budgets and are overly commercialized. Consequently, many have become retransmitters of programs from the powerful TV stations of the West. Many stations find themselves in a situation in which they are unable to produce their own programming due to a lack of equipment. Also, many radio and television stations tend to run for part of the day and close around midnight.

A popular medium of entertainment in many urban areas is the videocassette recorder, or VCR. Popular movies from the United States, China, Britain, and various African countries are rented and played in homes or public places. Due to the availability of video cameras, some operators make their own local videos based on popular themes. These have become especially popular in West Africa.

Satellite-based broadcasting has also gained in prominence in Africa since the 1990s. In 1995 the South African company M-Net launched the world's first digital direct-to-home subscriber satellite service. Known as DSTV, its subscribers have access to more than 30 video channels and 40 audio programs. These are available on C-band to the whole of Africa and on lower-cost KU-band to southern Africa, south of LUSAKA.

Last year South Africa's public broadcaster, the South African Broadcasting Corporation (SABC), launched Channel Africa, a new satellite-based news and entertainment channel aimed at providing programming content focused on the continent. It broadcasts news, current affairs, and informational programming on shortwave in English, French, Kiswahili, and Portuguese. Daily listenership in the sub-Saharan region is estimated at 7 to 9 million. The service also feeds programs in languages such as Chinyanya, Silozi, Ichibemba, and Shona to rebroadcasters via tapes and telephone links.

In 1998 North Africa started receiving direct-to-home (DTH) TV broadcasts from Nilesat, the continent's first locally owned geostationary satellite, capable of broadcasting up to 72 digital TV programs simultaneously. Operated by the Egyptian Radio and Television Union (ERTU), the country's national broadcaster, Nilesat's coverage extends as far south as northern parts of CHAD, the Republic of the SUDAN, ERITREA, and ETHIOPIA (as well as from MOROCCO in the west to the Arabian Gulf in the east). However, satellite broadcasts are expensive and very few people can afford to buy the equipment and pay the subscription fees.

The Union of National Radio & Television Organizations of Africa, a professional body with more than 48 active member organizations, is committed to the development of all aspects of broadcasting in Africa. It encourages the exchange of indigenous programming via satellite and videocassette and strives to obtain preferential satellite tariffs to facilitate news and program exchange.

See also: CINEMA (Vols. IV, V); TELECOMMUNICATIONS (Vol. V); RADIO (Vol. IV).

Further reading: Richard Fardon and Graham Furniss, eds., *African Broadcast Cultures: Radio in Transition.* (Oxford, U.K.: James Currey, 2000); Dhyana Zeigler and Molefi Asante, *Thunder and Silence: The Mass Media in Africa.* (Trenton, N.J.: Africa World Press, 1992); Graham Mytton, *Mass Communication in Africa* (London: Edward Arnold, 1983).

Ramaphosa, Cyril (1952–) *South African labor union organizer*

Ramaphosa grew up in SOWETO, SOUTH AFRICA, just outside of JOHANNESBURG. He began his political career as part of the BLACK CONSCIOUSNESS MOVEMENT while attending the University of the North. There he joined both the Student Christian Movement and the SOUTH AFRICAN

STUDENTS ORGANIZATION, the latter of which was founded in 1968 by Steve BIKO (1946–1977). In 1974 Ramaphosa organized a rally in support of the MOZAMBICAN LIBERATION FRONT (FRELIMO), a nationalist, liberation organization seeking to rid Mozambique of Portuguese rule. As a result of this anti-government activism, Ramaphosa was arrested and detained for 11 months under the provisions of the Terrorism Act.

Undeterred, Ramaphosa joined the Black Peoples' Convention after his release from jail. In 1976 he was again imprisoned, this time for six months. He then studied law and earned his degree from the University of South Africa in 1981. Continuing with his activism, Ramaphosa joined the Council of Unions of South Africa (CUSA) as a legal advisor. He gained national prominence in 1982 when he became general secretary of the newly formed National Union of Mineworkers (NUM). He withdrew the NUM from the all-black CUSA, in 1985, and joined it to the Council of South African Trade Unions (COSATU), multiracial labor-union federation. As head of the single largest union within COSATU, and a high-profile member of the UNITED DEMOCRATIC FRONT, an anti-APARTHEID opposition front, Ramaphosa assumed a political role on a national scale and forged important links with the exiled AFRICAN NATIONAL CONGRESS (ANC).

In 1987 Ramaphosa initiated a three-week miners' strike that involved the participation of 300,000 people. Under Ramaphosa's leadership, from 1982 to 1991, the NUM had become the largest South African workers' union, with membership growing from 6,000 at its inception to 300,000. Chosen by ANC president Nelson MANDELA (1918–) to serve as ANC secretary-general, Ramaphosa played a decisive role in spearheading talks with the ruling National Party about moving South Africa from minority-white rule to an inclusive, fully democratic political process. Ramaphosa's negotiating skills proved instrumental in bringing about this transition, securing free, one-person–one-vote national elections and helping to hammer out a new constitution.

Despite his remarkable abilities and exemplary contribution to both the anti-apartheid struggle and the coming to power of the ANC, Ramaphosa was, for the most part, passed over in the new ANC-led government. Instead of obtaining a high post in the new government, he became chairperson of the Constitutional Assembly. Some commentators have suggested that since Ramaphosa is not a XHOSA-speaker, as are many of the most prominent ANC leaders, he was excluded. In 1996 Ramaphosa, the former trade-union organizer, left politics for the world of business. He has become chairman of several large corporations and sits on the boards of others. Additionally, he was frequently mentioned as contender for the position of South African president.

See also: LABOR (Vol. V); POLITICAL PARTIES AND ORGANIZATIONS (Vol. V).

Rastafarianism (Ras Tafarianism) Religious movement started by black Jamaicans. Rastafarians, or Rastas, as they are commonly known, venerate former Ethiopian emperor, HAILE SELASSIE (1892–1975), whose name prior to becoming emperor was Ras Tafari Makonnen. Today there are an estimated 1 million Rastafarians worldwide.

Based on Biblical traditions, Rastafarianism emerged during the first half of the 20th century. In the 1920s Marcus Garvey (1887–1940), a prominent black Jamaican nationalist, exhorted the African diaspora to look to Africa for the coming of a black king who would deliver them from bondage. His prophecy coincided with the rise of Ras Tafari Makonnen, who in 1930 was crowned emperor of ETHIOPIA, taking the name Haile Selassie.

Garvey's message resonated with downtrodden black males in the urban slums of Jamaica who were concerned with throwing off the "slave mentality" that poisoned their community after centuries of white oppression. In 1935–36 the righteous indignation of the fledgling movement was heightened when, following the Italian invasion of Ethiopia, Haile Selassie was forced into exile. Although they preached nonviolence, early Rastas were virulently anticolonial and often took to the streets to protest the colonial power structure in Jamaica. Without an individual leader or organized hierarchy, however, the Rasta movement remained relatively small.

Haile Selassie himself had little regard for those who worshiped him. He did visit Jamaica once, calling for his followers to help liberate the people of Jamaica from white oppression. The date of his visit—April 25, 1966—along with the dates of his birth and coronation are among the most important in the Rasta religious calendar.

In the late 1960s and into the 1970s the politicized Rasta movement increasingly came under fire by the conservative establishment. During that time white leaders in Jamaica demonized Rastafarians, especially for their ritualistic smoking of marijuana, or *ganja*. (Claiming that they are supported by passages from the Bible, Rastas believe that the use of marijuana facilitates meditation and brings them closer to Jah, or God.) The leaders began portraying Rastafarians as rowdy, drug-fuelled bandits, finding them convenient scapegoats for the social violence that raged in the island's cities. In reality very few Rastas were involved in the violence, but the international reputation of the Rasta religion was sullied by the accusations.

In the 1970s a young Rasta named Bob Marley (1945–1981) gained international prominence through his lyrics over reggae MUSIC, which combined messages of racial harmony with black empowerment. With his regal bearing and positive message, Marley was widely regarded as a Rastafarian prophet. He visited KENYA and Ethiopia in 1978 and returned to Africa two years later at the official invitation of the new government of ZIMBABWE to play at that country's independence ceremony.

Today the Rastafarian religion is still relatively minor and lacks individual leadership. However, by continuing to promote a natural, peaceful, and meditative way of life, it is slowly gaining converts, both in Jamaica and around the world.

Rasta men let their hair grow into long, thick strands called dreadlocks. These "manes" identify them with Haile Selassie, who was also called the "Lion of Judah." However, as Bob Marley gained worldwide popularity in the 1970s, many people, both black and white, grew dreadlocks as a fashion statement that had nothing to do with the Rastafarian religion.

See also: AFRICAN DIASPORA (Vol. IV); ETHIOPIANISM (Vol. IV); PAN-AFRICANISM (Vols. IV, V).

Further reading: Barry Chavannes, *Rastafari: Roots and Ideology* (Syracuse, N.Y.: Syracuse University Press, 1994).

Ratsiraka, Didier (1936–) *Former president of Madagascar*

Ratsiraka was born in Vatomandry, near the provincial capital of Toamasina, on Madagascar's east coast. After completing primary school in his hometown he went on to secondary school in Paris. He later attended the French Naval Officers' School and was commissioned a captain. Of Betsimisaraka ethnicity, Ratsiraka served as Madagascar's military attaché to France from 1970 to 1972. In 1975 General Gabriel Ramanantsoa (1906–1979) took power in MADAGASCAR after a bloodless COUP D'ÉTAT, and Ratsiraka was named Ramanantsoa's minister of foreign affairs. When Ramanantsoa's leadership faltered Colonel Richard Ratsimandrava (1931–1975) took power in February 1975. Five days later elements within the military assassinated Ratsimandrava, with many believing that Ratsiraka was involved in the murder plot.

Ratsiraka was appointed president by a military directorate on June 15, 1975. In December of that year, after promoting himself to admiral, Ratsiraka won a popular election. However, he then doffed his military uniform and began espousing a "scientific socialist" platform driven by a plan for DEVELOPMENT through state investment. In March 1976 Ratsiraka founded the PILLAR AND STRUCTURE FOR THE SALVATION OF MADAGASCAR (Andry sy Riana Enti-manavotra an'i Madagasikara, AREMA) which became the lead party in a six-party governing coalition.

After Ratsiraka nationalized industry many foreign investors left Madagascar, and before long his economic plan caused the economy to collapse. From 1979 to 1991 he continued liberalizing the economy while maintaining tight control on military and political power.

After a 1991 civil-servants strike nearly forced him from power Ratsiraka agreed to a transitional government. He lost the 1993 election to Albert Zafy (1927–), only to win back the presidency in 1997. Following four more years of economic stagnation, in December 2001 Ratsiraka lost the general election to business owner and mayor of ANTANANARIVO, Marc RAVALOMANANA (1949–). Unwilling to accept his defeat, Ratsiraka contested the results and strong-armed the High Constitutional Court of Madagascar to call a run-off to determine the winner.

Ravalomanana, an ethnic Merina, responded by starting a broad popular insurrection. Ratsiraka attempted to rally support by playing on the ethnic tensions between Madagascar's coastal peoples, the *cotier,* and the Merina, a group from the central highlands that has long held a privileged position in Madagascar society. Ratsiraka shut down media outlets that supported Ravalomanana and he used his military to threaten those who criticized his leadership. However, after a few tense months Ratsiraka's methods failed. In late April the court announced that Ravalomanana had won the run-off with 51 percent of the ballots.

In July 2002, after Ravalomanana was declared the country's new president, Ratsiraka fled to France. In December 2003 he was sentenced in absentia to five years in prison for encouraging five Malagasy provinces to secede.

See also: ETHNICITY AND IDENTITY (Vol. V); FRANCE AND AFRICA (Vols. III, IV, V); MERINA (Vols. III, IV).

Ravalomanana, Marc (1949–) *President of Madagascar*

Born near the capital, ANTANANARIVO, Ravalomanana studied at a missionary school before leaving for a Protestant secondary school in Sweden. An ethnic Merina of a common caste, he came home to marry Lalao Rakotonirainy, have three children, and run his family's small yogurt company. With the help of the Roman Catholic Church, he won a small business loan from the WORLD BANK, building the company into Tiko, the largest agro-business interest in MADAGASCAR.

Ravalomanana successfully ran for mayor of Antananarivo in 1999. He quickly showed the ability to clean up both the city's politics and its streets, using this success as a platform to run for president in December 2001. The election results were highly contested by the sitting president, Didier RATSIRAKA (1936–), who claimed that Ravalomanana's victory fell short of the 50 percent necessary to avoid a run-off. Ravalomanana responded by calling hundreds of thousands of supporters to the streets. In February 2002 he declared himself president, leading to military conflict. After more than three months of violence Ravalomanana finally secured the office after a decision in his favor by the courts. He was officially inaugurated in May 2002, making him the country's first Merina president. He then acted to build his fledgling political party, Tiako-i-Madagasikara (meaning "I Love Madagascar," in Malagasy), which won a large majority in the December 2002 legislative elections.

Ravalomanana speaks Malagasy, the provincial language of Madagascar, and he is known to speak English better than the more common colonial language, French. This fact characterizes his leadership style and priorities—he is a man of the people with strong ties to the United States and a commitment to a capitalist path. To his detractors, he is a Christian zealot who is too eager to take hard-line positions when it favors his own merchant class. To his supporters, however, he is a self-made champion of the poor who is successfully rooting out CORRUPTION.

See also: MERINA (Vols. III, IV).

Rawlings, Jerry (Jeremiah John Rawlings)
(1947–) *Ghanaian army officer who ruled Ghana for more than 20 years*

Rawlings, the son of a Scottish father and a Ghanaian mother, was born in ACCRA, the capital of GHANA. His parents never married and he was raised by his mother. She managed to send him to the distinguished Achimota secondary school, from which Rawlings graduated in 1966. A year later he enlisted as a cadet in the air force. He eventually qualified as a pilot and earned a commission as a flight lieutenant.

During the 1970s Rawlings aligned himself with an anti-government movement within the army. In May 1979 he led an attempted COUP D'ÉTAT against the government that was quickly put down. Rawlings was jailed and then tried in public. In court Rawlings railed against the CORRUPTION within the military-led government, and his outspokenness gained him the admiration of low-level military personnel. In June Rawlings escaped from jail with help from the outside. Once freed he immediately went to a local radio station and broadcasted a call to overthrow the government of Lieutenant General Frederick W. K. Akuffo (1937– 1979). Within a day after overcoming resistance from pro-government forces, Rawlings' supporters had taken control of Ghana. In the aftermath of the coup the new government arrested many of the country's military leaders. Eight officers were executed, including three former leaders of Ghana—I. K. Acheampong (1931–1979), Akwasi Afrifa (1936–1979), and Akuffo.

Rawlings formed the Armed Forces Revolutionary Council (AFRC) to guide the new government, but he promised that elections would be held to return the country to civilian rule. In September 1979 Dr. Hilla Limann (1934–1998) won a narrow electoral victory and became Ghana's new president. Rawlings returned to the air force, but he remained in the political spotlight, criticizing the government for its lack of success in revitalizing Ghana's struggling economy.

In 1981 Rawlings led another coup and again took over Ghana's government. This time, however, there were no promises of relinquishing control. Rawlings immediately abolished the country's constitution, dismissed Parliament, and declared all political parties illegal, except for his newly created PROVISIONAL NATIONAL DEFENSE COUNCIL (PNDC). Rawlings made economic reform a priority, but like his predecessors, met with little success. The PNDC's failure to spark an economic turnaround combined with Rawlings's authoritative style of governing led to multiple coup attempts during the rest of the 1980s.

In 1990, facing increasing domestic and international pressure to move toward DEMOCRATIZATION, Rawlings formed the National Commission on Democracy (NCD) to organize debates on the subject of making Ghana a multiparty democracy. In 1991 the NCD recommended holding a national election for president, forming a national legislature, and creating the position of prime minister. The PNDC agreed with the suggestions and set an election date of November 3, 1992.

Rawlings, meanwhile, resigned from the military and announced his intention to run for president as a civilian. The candidate of the National Democratic Congress (NDC), a reincarnation of the PNDC, he won handily, receiving 58 percent of the vote. Though foreign observers said the election was fair, opposition leaders maintained that the results were corrupted by electoral abuse. To protest this perceived injustice, they encouraged their supporters to boycott the ensuing parliamentary elections. Without the participation of opposition parties the NDC won more than 90 percent of the 200 contested seats for Parliament.

In 1996 Rawlings again won election to Ghana's presidency. The NDC again gained a majority in Parliament, winning 130 of 200 seats. In 2000 Rawlings stated his intention to retire from politics. He nominated his vice president, John Atta Mills (1944–), as his successor, but Mills was defeated in a runoff election by John Agyekum KUFUOR (1938–). After leaving office Rawlings became involved in a campaign to fight HIV/AIDS in Africa, traveling across the continent to increase awareness of the disease and stress the need for health-care volunteers in combating the illness.

See also: HIV/AIDS AND AFRICA (Vol. V).

Further reading: Kevin Shillington, *Ghana and the Rawlings Factor* (New York: St. Martin's Press, 1992).

refugees The basic international definition of a refugee came from the 1951 convention of the United Nations High Commission on Refugees (UNHCR). According to the convention, a refugee was defined as a person who "owing to a well-founded fear of being persecuted for reasons of race, religion, nationality, membership of a particular social group, or political opinion, is outside the country of his nationality, and is unable to or, owing to such fear, is unwilling to avail himself of the protection of that country . . . ." Subsequently, this definition has been expanded to include those fleeing war or famine, and women who face persecution because of their refusal to comply with social constraints. Those who voluntarily leave their home countries for economic reasons, however, are not refugees under international law.

Modern Africa has faced wars of liberation, CIVIL WARS, and other types of violence associated with ethnic conflict, coups d'état, and war between states. These conflicts in turn have produced large numbers of both refugees and "internally displaced persons" (IDPs), who share many of the characteristics of refugees other than living outside their own countries. MOZAMBIQUE, for example, was a country long beset by armed conflict, first during its war of liberation, in the 1960s and early 1970s, and later during its civil war, in the 1980s and early 1990s. Neighboring MALAWI alone received several hundred thousand Mozambican refugees. By the time the United Nations brokered a cease-fire in 1993 there were more than 1.7 million Mozambican refugees in need of repatriation. An additional 3 million Mozambican citizens were classified as IDPs. By the end of 1996, however, the political and economic situation had stabilized, and few Mozambicans could still be classified as "refugees." The 100,000 or so who continued to stay in SOUTH AFRICA did so for the economic opportunities they had found there.

The case of Mozambique also illustrates another aspect of the refugee situation in Africa: It can improve. Indeed, by the mid-1990s, as long-standing regional conflicts were finally resolved, southern Africa ceased to be a principal source of refugees in Africa. ANGOLA was the one regional exception. There, and throughout the broad belt stretching across Central Africa to the Horn of Africa, both old and newer conflicts continued to produce large numbers of refugees and IDPs. In fact, Angola, BURUNDI, the Democratic Republic of the CONGO, ERITREA, SOMALIA, and the Republic of the SUDAN are six of the 10 countries in the world (the others being Afghanistan, Burma, Iraq, and the Palestinian territories) that, in 2001, accounted for 78 percent of refugees worldwide. In Sudan alone, a long-running civil war has led to an estimated 2 million deaths and 4 million displaced persons.

The 1990s also witnessed the outbreak of conflict and flow of refugees in the neighboring West African countries of GUINEA, GUINEA-BISSAU, IVORY COAST, LIBERIA,

and SIERRA LEONE. Conflict in Liberia was the source of the catastrophe, and that country's population suffered the worst consequences. At one point or another, over seven years of fighting, virtually every one of Liberia's approximately 3.3 million citizens was either a refugee or IDP. In 1998 the flood of 280,000 refugees from Sierra Leone was the largest single national exodus in the world that year. Refugees fleeing one country usually settle in a neighboring country. This is principally how the West Africa wars affected Guinea, which, in 2002, was hosting 182,000 refugees from Liberia. Ironically, some 220,000 people from war-torn Ivory Coast sought refuge across the border in Liberia by 2002.

Despite the terrible circumstances of the 1990s and the first years of the 21st century, the refugee situation in Africa has actually improved in comparative and absolute terms. In 1994 the UNHCR reported nearly 10 million African refugees, more than half of the world's total. By 2001 the figure had dropped to approximately 6.1 million, a little more than one-quarter of the world total. Still, this is a disproportionate number, since Africa has only 12 percent of the world's population. Furthermore, there has been a steady growth in IDPs over the same years, almost doubling from about 5 million to 9.5 million people. Until there are more resolutions of major conflicts, as was the case in Mozambique, the African continent will continue to witness great movements of both refugees and other displaced persons.

See also: ETHNIC CONFLICT IN AFRICA (Vol. V); UNITED NATIONS AND AFRICA (Vols. IV, V).

Further reading: Ebenezer Q. Blavo, *The Problems of Refugees in Africa: Boundaries and Borders* (Aldershot, U.K.: Ashgate, 1999).

religion Since independence, traditional African religions changed as universal religions exerted their influence over wider and wider regions. While this process had been taking place since the original spread of Christianity and Islam into Africa centuries ago, it took on new dimensions in the modern era.

Although universal religions have experienced success over many centuries in establishing themselves on the continent, African traditional religions (ATRs) continue to be widely distributed, and each ethnic group not affiliated with a universal religion has its own belief system. Typically, Christianity and Islam actively compete with one another for conversion of people who ascribe to African traditional religions. Many of the ATR practitioners who do convert to Islam or Christianity tend to blend their indigenous religious knowledge with that of the new religion, creating an entirely new syncretic belief system. The prophetic movements that emerged in Africa under colonial rule are an expression of this blending of indigenous and exogenous religious beliefs.

African Islam has assumed the status of an indigenous religion in much of the northern regions of the continent due to its long historical presence. In ETHIOPIA Christianity has the status of an indigenous religion. In sub-Saharan Africa Islam is second to Christianity in terms of the number of practitioners, including newcomers to the faith. However, on the whole Islam is growing faster than Christianity in Africa, and it is dominant in much of the savanna belt stretching across the continent from the Atlantic Ocean to the Red Sea and Indian Ocean. These are the regions where Islam was introduced early on. However, in much of this belt there remain those who adhere to traditional indigenous faiths.

Christianity is found in coastal areas of West Africa, across central Africa, in the interior of East Africa, and throughout southern Africa. Of the major world denominations of Christianity found in Africa, the Roman Catholic Church is the largest, while various Protestant denominations are also important. For example, the Anglican Church has more members in NIGERIA than does its American branch, the Episcopal Church. The largest growing segment of Christian churches are made up of the charismatic and Pentecostal churches.

As Christians and Muslims proselytize to Africans who practice ATRs, they come into competition with one another, a competition that can become deadly when mixed with politics. Nigeria demonstrates the problems presented by this type of competition. The geographical middle of that country, 10 states and the southern portion of two other states, make up the Middle Belt, which is populated by hundreds of ethnic groups. Muslims from the north and Christian MISSIONARIES from the south both sought converts in the region. In 1966 a military government abolished the regional system, allowing for a rapid spread of Christianity and Western-style EDUCATION into the region. Muslim northerners felt threatened by the expansion. In the 1970s Nigerian Muslims came under the influence of Muslim fundamentalists from Saudi Arabia, a fellow member of the ORGANIZATION OF PETROLEUM EXPORTING COUNTRIES. This association with Islamic fundamentalism encouraged Muslim Nigerians to press for making Nigeria an Islamic state or at the very least call for domestic Islamic law, or SHARIA. It was now the Christians' turn to feel threatened. In the 1980s minority ethnic groups spread charismatic Christian fundamentalism into the region, and so the cycle of religious conflict continued. As a result the region has been the site of numerous riots and massacres since the end of the 20th century.

Although embracing ATRs, Christianity, and Islam, the peoples of the African continent are contending with conflicts between these religions and various sub-sects. The frequent association of these competing religions with political power, particularly in states such as the Republic of the SUDAN and CHAD, continues to be a source of instability in Africa.

See also: CHRISTIANITY, INFLUENCE OF (Vols. II, III, IV, V), ISLAM, INFLUENCE OF (Vols. II, III, IV, V); PROPHETS AND PROPHETIC MOVEMENTS (Vols. IV, V); RELIGION (Vols. I, IV).

Further reading: Thomas D. Blakely, Walter E. A. van Beek, and Dennis L. Thomson, eds., *Religion in Africa: Experience and Expression* (Portsmouth, N.H.: Heinemann, 1994); Rosalind I. J. Hackett, *Art and Religion in Africa* (New York: Cassell, 1996); John S. Mbiti, *African Religions and Philosophy*, 2nd rev. ed. (Portsmouth, N.H.: Heinemann, 1990); Isaac Phiri, *Proclaiming Political Pluralism: Churches and Political Transitions in Africa* (Westport, Conn.: Praeger, 2001).

RENAMO See MOZAMBICAN NATIONAL RESISTANCE.

René, France-Albert (1935–) *President of the Seychelles*

A SEYCHELLES native, France-Albert René received his early education in the capital of Victoria before continuing his studies in Switzerland and England. Returning to the SEYCHELLES in 1957 he became involved with the British Labour Party (at the time the Seychelles were still a British colony) and thus began his long career in Seychellois politics. In 1964 he became a leading figure in the Seychelles burgeoning political scene by founding the Seychelles People's United Party (SPUP). The SPUP became one of the islands' two major parties, its opponent being the Seychelles Democratic Party (SDP), led by Sir James MANCHAM (c. 1939–). The parties differed on nearly every subject, particularly on the issue of relations with Britain. René and the SPUP favored complete independence from its colonizer; the SDP wanted to maintain close ties.

Ultimately, the Seychelles moved toward independence. Elections leading up to autonomy produced a controversial victory for the SDP, and in 1976 Mancham was awarded the presidency, with René as vice president.

René did not remain in Mancham's shadow for long, however. In 1977 the SPUP staged a COUP D'ÉTAT while Mancham was abroad in London, installing René as president. René immediately moved to centralize his power, establishing a new constitution that made the SPUP, now called the Seychelles People's Progressive Front, the nation's only legal political party.

René implemented a socialist economic strategy under which the Seychellois accrued the highest per capita income of any African peoples. However, with population constraints limiting the size of the workforce, the country's economy declined in the 1990s. René tried to counter the decline with a number of controversial economic initiatives, but these produced few results.

René's socialist policies made him the target of upper-class ire. Between 1978 and 1987 a number of coup attempts were made, including one by a group of mercenaries led by Irish colonel Michael "Mad Mike" Hoare. Mancham also tried unsuccessfully to agitate against René from exile in England. Military aid from TANZANIA helped René maintain power through these repeated threats.

Because the standard of living has increased for middle- and lower-class Seychellois under René's administration he has remained popular, winning elections in 1984 and in 1989. In 1993, under a new constitution that created a multiparty system, René easily defeated James Mancham's bid to reclaim the presidency. René also won elections in 1998 and in 2001, maintaining a remarkably long and relatively successful presidency in spite of economic troubles and constant threats of coup attempts.

In April 2004, however, René stepped down and hand-picked his vice president, James Michel (1944–   ), to succeed him. Despite giving up the presidency, René maintained his leadership position in the ruling Seychelles People's Progressive Front party.

Réunion Island   Longtime French possession and part of the Mascarene archipelago (which includes Rodrigues and MAURITIUS) in the western Indian Ocean. Officially settled by the French in the mid-1600s, the island has been under French rule ever since, save for a brief period during the Napoleonic Wars (1805–1815), when the British assumed control. A layover for ships on the Indian Ocean shipping routes, Réunion was also a major coffee producer until the British introduced sugarcane, which quickly became the island's essential industry. In economic decline after the 1869 opening of the SUEZ CANAL changed the major trade routes, Réunion continued to be a French colony until 1946, when it became a *département* (similar to a county or state) of France, with the city of Saint-Denis as its capital.

> **Réunion was formed through volcanic activity and is highly mountainous. Among the notable peaks on the island are Piton des Neiges, which is extinct, and Piton de la Fournaise, which still erupts regularly. For a small island, Réunion has a wide range of climates, with zones of heavy rainfall in the south and east and dry areas in the north and west. Though low elevations on the island tend to be tropical and humid, the peak of Piton des Neiges has been known to receive snow.**

As inhabitants of a French *département,* the Réunionese are full French citizens and have representation in the National Assembly. Sentiment among the Réu-

nionese has been increasingly for further, though not complete, autonomy. In 1991 riots against the French government left 10 dead in Saint-Denis. However, the benefits of French rule, as well as Réunion's economic reliance on France as the main destination for the island's EXPORTS, have kept much of the population from favoring total independence.

Economically, sugar and sugar products remain the island's main exports, and problems such as unemployment are still prevalent. TOURISM is also a major industry, but Réunion is routinely overshadowed by nearby MAURITIUS and the SEYCHELLES, which boast better beaches.

At the beginning of the 21st century, most of Réunion's population of approximately 744,000 was Creole, descended largely from the African slaves and Asian indentured laborers who worked the coffee and sugar plantations in the 1800s. Creole is also the island's main language, though French is the official tongue.

> **Réunion's high population density and low land area has led to high levels of emigration from the island. Many of the emigrants are males, who travel to France for further EDUCATION and often do not return. Because of this, Réunion has a skewed male-to-female ratio: approximately one man to every seven women.**

See also: FRANCE AND AFRICA (Vols. III, IV, V); MONO-CROP ECONOMIES (Vol. IV); RÉUNION ISLAND (Vols. III, IV).

Revolutionary United Front (RUF)   Rebel militia group that waged civil war against the SIERRA LEONE government between 1991 and 2001. Led by Foday SANKOH (1937–2003), the Revolutionary United Front (RUF) claimed to be a populist movement seeking to end government CORRUPTION in Sierra Leone. In 1991 the RUF launched its first offensive from LIBERIA, Sierra Leone's neighbor to the south. Although the rebels claimed to be fighting a war of liberation, they soon began violently plundering the villages they encountered.

Originally a small movement made up of an unruly collection of disenfranchised and marginalized individuals, the RUF quickly grew by using ruthless, forced-recruitment methods. These included supplying hallucinogenic drugs to child soldiers, who were often forced to kill or perform violent acts against family members as a rite of initiation. RUF rebels gained worldwide notoriety for their brutal acts, including torture, the abduction and rape of young girls, and the frequent burning of people and property.

Many believe that Charles TAYLOR (1948–), the former president of Liberia, played an instrumental role in funding the RUF attacks. He originally met Sankoh in the 1980s when they were both at a rebel training camp in LIBYA. Evidence indicates that Taylor resented Sierra Leone's support of ECOMOG forces, the military personnel sent by the ECONOMIC COMMUNITY OF WEST AFRICAN STATES to remove him from power in Liberia. Aided by willing buyers in Liberia, Sankoh and the RUF sold "conflict diamonds" that enabled them to purchase arms and drugs. Some RUF figures also amassed personal fortunes from the sale of illegal diamonds.

Despite peace agreements signed in 1999 and 2000, the war continued practically uninterrupted for 10 years. RUF rebels regularly violated the cease-fire terms. Ultimately, in May 2000, the RUF was subdued through a combined effort by British, UN, and ECOMOG forces. The rebels' principal leaders, including Foday Sankoh, were imprisoned. In May 2001, many former RUF rebels began returning to civilian life under a disarmament process sponsored by the Sierra Leone government. They were allowed to exchange their weapons for job training and compensation packages.

The end of hostilities was officially declared in January 2002. Later that year the RUF was one of about 20 parties that registered with Sierra Leone's national election commission to contest elections held that year. Sankoh fell ill soon after his arrest, and he died in UN custody in July 2003.

See also: UNITED NATIONS AND AFRICA (Vols. IV, V).

Rhodesia
Name given to the former British colony of Southern Rhodesia in the aftermath of the collapse of the Central African Federation, in 1963. Rhodesia became ZIMBABWE in 1980. In 1965 Rhodesia's prime minister, Ian SMITH (1919–), issued a UNILATERAL DECLARATION OF INDEPENDENCE from Britain. This was an effort to maintain the rule of the white minority, perhaps 5 percent of the country's population, over the African majority. Britain, however, refused to recognize Rhodesia's independence, and its African majority supported a long guerrilla war that ultimately forced the government in 1979 to acknowledge British sovereignty.

In 1980 Rhodesia became the independent, African-ruled country of Zimbabwe. This change in the country's name also erased the name of Cecil Rhodes (1853–1902), the leading builder of Britain's colonial African empire, from the map of the continent. At one time, Rhodes had two African countries named in his honor (Northern Rhodesia, now ZAMBIA, had changed its name upon independence, in 1964.) Further symbolizing the fundamental political shift that had taken place was the name change of the country's capital city from the English, Salisbury, to the African HARARE.

See also: CENTRAL AFRICAN FEDERATION (Vol. IV); ENGLAND AND AFRICA (Vols. III, IV, V); NORTHERN RHODESIA (Vol. IV); RHODES, CECIL (Vol. IV); SALISBURY (Vol. IV); SETTLERS, EUROPEAN (Vol. IV); SOUTHERN RHODESIA (Vol. IV).

Robben Island
Island near CAPE TOWN, SOUTH AFRICA, used as a prison for those deemed extremely "dangerous." Located in Table Bay, approximately 6 miles (10 km) from CAPE TOWN, Robben Island takes its name from the Dutch word for seals, which were once found there in large numbers. Beginning in the 16th century, passing Dutch and English ships frequently anchored at the island to pick up food from the mainland. During the 19th and 20th centuries various categories of people were sent to Robben Island to separate them from society: lepers, the insane, the medically quarantined, and African resistance leaders.

During World War II (1939–45) Robben Island was fortified to guard Cape Town against naval assault, and in the process its INFRASTRUCTURE was upgraded. Beginning in the early 1960s Robben Island served as a maximum-security prison for black criminals and, most notably, anti-APARTHEID activists. The government cracked down on black opposition groups, bringing many key members of the AFRICAN NATIONAL CONGRESS (ANC) and the PAN-AFRICANIST CONGRESS (PAC) to trial. Convicted ANC leaders such as Nelson MANDELA (1918–), Walter SISULU (1912–2003), and Govan MBEKI (1910–2001), and PAC president Robert SOBUKWE (1924–1978), were among the island's most notable prisoners.

Because of its physical isolation from the mainland, the island easily limited prisoners' contact with the outside world, adding to the hardship they endured. In addition to strict discipline and harsh treatment meted out by guards, prisoners also were required to perform hard labor in the island's lime mines or gather seaweed washed up on the shore.

When Nelson Mandela—arguably the world's most famous political prisoner—was held there, Robben Island came to symbolize the inhumanity and brutality of South Africa's apartheid regime. Despite long imprisonment on the bleak, windswept outcrop of rock that is Robben Island, he and his fellow inmates managed to keep alive a spirit of resistance. Upon his release from prison in 1989, Mandela seamlessly assumed the mantle of leadership of the ANC and the black opposition.

The detention of political prisoners on Robben Island was discontinued in 1991, but it still functioned

While imprisoned on Robben Island in the 1960s, Pan-Africanist Congress president Robert Sobukwe earned a degree in Economics from the University of London. © AP/Wide World Photos

as a medium-security prison until 1996. Since 1997 Robben Island has operated as a nature reserve and a museum of the apartheid era. It was declared a World Heritage site in 1999.

Further reading: Fran Lisa Buntman, *Robben Island and Prisoner Resistance to Apartheid* (New York: Cambridge University Press, 2003).

Roberto, Holden (Holden Roberto Alvaro)

(1923–) *Angolan nationalist*

Holden Carson Roberto was born on January 12, 1923, in Kongo-dominated São Salvadore, ANGOLA. His father worked for the Baptist mission, and his mother was the eldest child of the revolutionary Miguel Necaça. In 1925 Roberto was taken to Léopoldville (now KINSHASHA), in the Belgian Congo (present-day Democratic Republic of the CONGO), where he attended a Baptist mission school until 1940. He returned to Angola for a time and then went back to the Belgian Congo, where he worked for eight years as an accountant in the colonial administration.

In 1958 Roberto was elected to represent the Union of Angolan People (União das Populações de Angola, UPA) at the All-Africa People's Congress in ACCRA, the capital of newly independent GHANA. There Roberto met the elite of Africa's nationalist revolutionaries, including Patrice LUMUMBA (1925–1961) and Kenneth KAUNDA (1924–). The following year he returned to Léopoldville and took control of BaKongo efforts to overthrow the Portuguese colonial administration in Angola. Rejecting Marxism but supporting the ideas of China's MAO ZEDONG (1893–1976), Roberto believed that revolution was possible only through bloodshed. He also was sympathetic to the ideas of Angolan nationalist Agostinho NETO (1922–1979) regarding national independence, pan-African unity, and the elimination of colonial culture. By March 1961 Roberto had launched the first of many anti-Portuguese military offensives in Angola.

Roberto's UPA spawned the NATIONAL FRONT FOR THE LIBERATION OF ANGOLA (Frente Nacional de Libertação de Angola, FNLA), which by 1962 was acting as a government-in-exile for the Angolan people. During the 1970s the FNLA received support from China as well as the American Central Intelligence Agency. However, following Angolan independence, in 1975, the FNLA, once the strongest rival of the POPULAR MOVEMENT FOR THE LIBERATION OF ANGOLA (Movimento Popular de Libertação de Angola, MPLA) for the leadership of the anticolonial struggle, had ceased to be a serious fighting force. The Angolan power struggle continued, however, between the MPLA and the NATIONAL UNION FOR THE TOTAL INDEPENDENCE OF ANGOLA (União Nacional para a Independência Total de Angola, UNITA), both of which were backed by outside forces during the Cold War.

After the fall of the FNLA Roberto lived in exile in the Congo and later in France. Although some former FNLA troops were recruited by SOUTH AFRICA for its ongoing war with rebels in NAMIBIA, Roberto's main supporters reconciled with the MPLA and moved back to Angola. Roberto reconstituted the FNLA for the 1992 elections in Angola, but his party received an insignificant portion of the vote.

See also: COLD WAR AND AFRICA (Vols. IV, V); COLONIAL RULE (Vol. IV); INDEPENDENCE MOVEMENTS (Vol. V); NATIONALISM AND INDEPENDENCE MOVEMENTS (Vol. IV); PORTUGAL AND AFRICA (Vols. III, IV, V); SOVIET UNION AND AFRICA (Vols. IV, V); UNITED STATES AND AFRICA (Vols. IV, V).

Rodney, Walter (1942–1980) *Radical West Indian historian, educator, and political activist*

Born to a middle-class family in Georgetown, British Guiana (present-day Guyana), Walter George Rodney was an astute, politically engaged young student. After graduating with honors from the University of the West Indies, in Jamaica, Rodney attended London University, earning a

PhD in history in 1966. He then moved to DAR ES SALAAM, in TANZANIA, to teach. Two years later Rodney returned to the Caribbean, teaching at his alma mater and earning a reputation as an impassioned radical communist. In fact, he was ordered to leave Jamaica for his "subversive" writings and teachings.

In 1968 the Jamaican government—fearing Rodney's influence as a Marxist agitator—declared the popular professor a prohibited immigrant. Rodney left Jamaica and traveled to Montreal, Canada, returning later the same month. Upon his return the Jamaican government's refusal to allow him back into the country touched off student riots all over the Caribbean.

Denied access to Jamaican classrooms, Rodney went first to Cuba and then returned to Dar es Salaam, where he taught at the university from 1968 to 1974. It was during this period that he published his first major work, *A History of the Upper Guinea Coast: 1545–1800* (1970). Based on his doctoral dissertation, the book examined the historical development of the stretch of the upper West African coast that was a center of the transatlantic slave trade. Two years later he published his highly influential *How Europe Underdeveloped Africa* (1972). As the title indicates, it was an indictment of the European capitalist model that, Rodney asserted, kept Africa from developing strong indigenous economies. Highly popular in African universities, Rodney's text became perhaps the most influential African history book for a whole generation of scholars and leaders educated on the continent.

Rodney remained politically engaged while in Dar es Salaam, writing numerous articles and critical essays on such varied topics as forced labor, the African struggle for democracy, the policing of African societies, pan-Africanist theory, and the worldwide black power movement.

He returned to Guyana in 1974 to teach at the university. However, the Guyanese government, like the Jamaican government, viewed Rodney's radical thought as a serious threat and blocked his appointment. The following year he taught for a semester in the United States before returning to Guyana. Rodney had joined the communistic Working People's Alliance (WPA) in 1974 and began organizing the masses in Guyana, Grenada, and throughout the Caribbean region. By 1979 the WPA was an independent political party and Rodney was a marked man. When two government buildings were burned the Guyanese authorities had Rodney and seven others arrested for arson. In the months that followed the government often threatened and harassed Rodney until

June 13, 1980, when he was killed by a remote-controlled car bomb, not far from his birthplace in Georgetown. A soldier in Guyana's defense force was the primary suspect in the assassination. Rodney's third major history book, *A History of the Guyanese Working People: 1881–1905,* was published posthumously in 1981.

See also: HISTORICAL SCHOLARSHIP ON AFRICA (Vol. V); COMMUNISM AND SOCIALISM (Vol. V); NEOCOLONIALISM AND UNDERDEVELOPMENT (Vol. V).

Further reading: Walter Rodney, *How Europe Underdeveloped Africa* (Washington, D.C.: Howard University Press, 1981; Rupert Charles Lewis, *Walter Rodney's Intellectual and Political Thought* (Detroit, Mich.: Wayne State University Press, 1998).

Rosa, Henrique Pereira See GUINEA-BISSAU.

RUF See REVOLUTIONARY UNITED FRONT.

Russia and Africa See SOVIET UNION AND AFRICA.

Rwanda Landlocked country in Central Africa bordered by UGANDA to the north, TANZANIA to the east, BURUNDI to the south, and the Democratic Republic of the CONGO (DRC) to the west. Measuring approximately 9,600 square miles (24,900 sq km) and with a population of about 8 million people, Rwanda is one of Africa's smallest countries and its most densely populated.

Rwanda at Independence Rwanda received its independence from Belgium in 1962. Following a UN-monitored referendum, Gregoire KAYIBANDA (1924–1976) became the country's first president, and his party, the Bahutu Emancipation Movement (PARMEBAHUTU), won control of the new legislature. He proved to be a corrupt leader with a weak following. By 1973, when he was ousted in a military COUP D'ÉTAT led by Major General Juvenal HABYARIMANA (1937–1994), Kayibanda had very little popular support. Two years after taking over Habyarimana founded the National Revolutionary Movement for Development (MRND) and created a monolithic one-party state. He then reorganized the administration of the country along a French model of prefectures, which were broken down further into sub-prefectures, local communes, and then sectors of approximately 5,000 people. It would later become clear that this structure was an effective means for controlling the population from the top down.

The reorganization was part of the new constitution ratified by ballot in 1978. Habyarimana was elected president three times between 1978 and 1988, although each time he was the only candidate. In 1990, however, under significant pressure from both Rwandan CIVIL SOCIETY and international organizations, Habyarimana finally consented to a more open, multiparty democracy.

In 1994 Rwanda was the site of one of the most ferocious genocides in modern history when ethnic HUTU extremists systematically annihilated 10 percent of the population. Before the genocide approximately 84 percent of the Rwandan population was Hutu and 14 percent TUTSI. While some historians and social commentators have characterized Rwanda as being ethnically divided between Hutu and Tutsi, it is probably more accurate to characterize the division as an evolving relationship between two dynamic groups within a society. The division is also accurately characterized as being of caste or class. Unlike ethnic rivalries in other countries, the divide between Hutu and Tutsi is neither primordial nor static, as it has been possible for individuals to adopt one identity or the other depending on social standing or intermarriage. In particular, the period following the Rwandan revolution of 1959, which led to the overthrow of Tutsi leadership, was marked by significant intermingling of the two groups.

The distinction became important in postcolonial politics since the word *Tutsi* came to mean an elite person of status and *Hutu*, a commoner. Habyarimana was a Hutu and thus sought a populist base to counter elites, mostly Tutsi, who were favored under Belgian colonial rule. These ethnic and class differences were in place but remained dormant throughout the 1980s. It helped that Rwanda's economy was expanding through the growth in the coffee sector and substantial foreign ECONOMIC ASSISTANCE.

The Outbreak of Violence The good times would not last. One of the critical factors in the changing face of Rwanda was the estimated 600,000 Tutsi expatriates who began to take an interest in their home country. Most of these people had fled Rwanda either after the 1959 revolution or during Habyarimana's rule, but now they saw an opportunity to return. In 1986 Habyarimana declared that those who had been expelled in 1982 would not be allowed to repatriate. This led to rising militancy in the UGANDA-based refugee community. In 1988 the Tutsi REFUGEES declared their right to return.

Further complicating the situation, by 1989, the international coffee market had collapsed, and global prices dropped precipitously. Since some 80 percent of Rwanda's export earnings were based on coffee, the country's economy went into a tailspin. In the midst of this economic

When genocidal violence broke out in April 1994, hundreds of thousands of Rwandans fled the country. Although the violence had not entirely subsided, these refugees returned home in July of that year. © *United Nations/J. Isaac*

turmoil, Habyarimana's domestic support waned. Church groups that had long supported him began to question his ability to lead. Even foreign donors who had previously backed him now pushed for reforms. In the early 1990s, under this pressure, Habyarimana allowed for the growth of opposition political parties. At the same time though, he feared these new parties, knowing well that his MRND could not compete successfully in a large number of districts.

Abbé André Sibomana (1954–1998), the editor of Rwanda's principal newspaper, also served as vice president of the Association for the Defense of Human Rights and Civil Liberties. His continuing criticism of Habyarimana's government led to threats on his life and attempts to link him with involvement in the country's terrible genocide. The charges remained unsubstantiated.

In September 1990 the Tutsi-led RWANDAN PATRIOTIC FRONT (RPF) invaded from Uganda. The Habyarimana government used the occasion to define what he saw as his country's enemies: the Ugandan army, dissatisfied Hutu (mostly northerners who played a more moderate role in the 1959 revolution), the unemployed, criminals, foreigners married to Tutsi, and Tutsi still within the country. His former populism was clearly replaced by an effort to build a strong, oppressive state.

Habyarimana's forces successfully repelled the original RPF incursion, in 1990, but the attacks continued for the next two years. As a result Habyarimana was forced to consolidate his political base and use strong-arm tactics against his own population. In 1992 he and the RPF signed a cease-fire and power-sharing agreement. A UN mission arrived in Rwanda the following year.

Although he helped broker the peace agreement, Habyarimana was concurrently using the media and church groups to spread anti-Tutsi sentiments throughout the country. He argued that the "invaders" were attempting to install a new Tutsi regime that would enslave the majority Hutu population. Moreover, he argued, those who helped repel the Tutsi "devils" from their Christian country would be doing God's work. Following Habyarimana's rationale, the only way for Hutu to save themselves would be to kill the Tutsi before the Tutsi killed them. Habyarimana's rallying cry succeeded in fomenting hatred among the Hutu.

Rwanda's history took a sharp turn April 6, 1994. On that date Habyarimana and Cyprien NTARYAMIRA (1956–1994), the president of BURUNDI, were killed when their plane was shot down on its return from peace talks. This was the spark that lit the tinderbox. By July 1994, between 800,000 and 1 million people, mostly Tutsi and their Hutu "sympathizers," were dead, many hacked to death by their machete-wielding neighbors.

Rwanda since the Genocide With a fractured base the RPF seized power on July 4, 1994. A unity government was created with Pasteur Bizimungu (1951–), a Hutu, at the helm, and the United Nations was invited back to Rwanda. Late in 1994 the United Nations set up an International Criminal Tribunal for Rwanda in Arusha, TANZANIA. However, it became clear that RPF leader Paul KAGAME (1957–), a Tutsi who was both Rwanda's vice president and minister of defense, held the real power. Tutsi refugees were repatriated, and thousands of Hutu accused of genocide fled west, to the Congo. In the years that followed, few people in Rwanda dared to cross Kagame. One person who did challenge him, Hutu interior minister Seth Sendashonga (d. 1998), was assassinated under suspicious circumstances.

In 1998 Kagame ordered the United Nations out of Rwanda. A savvy propagandist himself, he convinced the population that UN inaction in 1994 meant that the organization lacked a purpose and was no longer wanted. He also convinced the international community, particularly the United States, that he was the best choice for stability in the country and the region. As a result of his lobbying tens of millions of dollars in foreign support followed the more than $100 million in reconstruction funds he had received in 1994. On March 24, 2000, President Bizimungu resigned, citing that he was tired of being a figurehead. Kagame then added *President* to his string of titles.

Throughout the late 1990s conflict between Rwanda and the Democratic Republic of Congo intensified, with Kagame targeting the DRC's president Laurent Kabila (c. 1939–2001). As payback for Kabila's support for the Interahamwe, a militant group seeking to overthrow the Tutsi-dominated government, Kagame provided military support to rebels seeking to overthrow Kabila. When Kabila was assassinated, in January 2001, many blamed Kagame, though no evidence has been uncovered to incriminate him. Within the month Kagame and Laurent Kabila's son, Joseph KABILA (1971–), the new Congolese president, met in Washington, D.C. to discuss a peace accord. Conflict continued for more than a year, but a peace treaty was signed between the two countries in 2002.

In August 2003 Rwanda held its first elections since the genocide. Running with no opposition from any viable candidates, Paul Kagame won in a landslide. It appeared that this solidified a stable Tutsi base of leadership in KIGALI. However, neither the elections nor the International Criminal Tribunal for Rwanda did much to heal the wounds created by more than a century of colonial rule and the decades of state-sponsored social division that followed.

See also: ETHNICITY AND IDENTITY (Vol. I); ETHNIC CONFLICT IN AFRICA (Vol. V); RWANDA (Vols. I, II, III, IV); UNITED NATIONS AND AFRICA (Vols. IV, V).

Further reading: Alison des Forges, *Leave None to Tell the Story: Genocide in Rwanda* (New York: Human Rights Watch, 1999); Peter Uvin, *Aiding Violence: The Development Enterprise in Rwanda* (West Hartford, Conn.: Kumarian Press, 1998); Gerard Prunier, *The Rwandan Crisis: History of a Genocide* (New York: Columbia University Press, 1995); Catharine Newbury, *The Cohesion of Oppression* (New York: Columbia University Press, 1993); Rene Lemarchand, *Rwanda and Burundi* (New York, Praeger Publishers, 1970).

Rwanda Patriotic Front (RPF)

Political party of Paul KAGAME (1957–   ), elected president of RWANDA in 2000. In the late 1980s Kagame and the former deputy commander of the UGANDA army, Major General Fred Rwigyema (c. 1955–1990), founded the Rwanda Patriotic Front (RPF). Made up of Rwandan political exiles and TUTSI citizens living in Uganda, the RPF supported an ethnic Tutsi army called the Rwanda Patriotic Army (RPA). In October 1990 the RPA launched its first armed incursion into Rwanda in an effort to unseat President Juvenal HABYARIMANA (1937–1994), an ethnic HUTU who had prevented Tutsi REFUGEES living in Uganda from returning home to Rwanda. These incursions escalated into a three-year civil war.

In August 1993 the RPF and the Habyarimana government reached a peace agreement that held until April 1994, when a plane carrying Habyarimana and Burundi's president, Cyprien NTARYAMIRA (1956–1994), crashed at the airport in KIGALI, Rwanda's capital. Though there were no eyewitnesses, it was believed that the plane was shot down by surface-to-air missiles. The incident sparked a period of extremely violent Hutu reprisals against the Tutsi. In July 1994 Kagame and the RPF responded to the Hutu-led violence by invading Rwanda and seizing control of Kigali. Five months later, in a move aimed at national unity, the RPF formed a transitional government with the Hutu Democratic Republican Movement and three other parties. Kagame was elected president by the RPF-controlled Rwandan National Assembly in 2000.

Further reading: Alison Des Forges, *Leave None to Tell the Story: Genocide in Rwanda* (New York: Human Rights Watch, 1999); Gérard Prunier. *The Rwanda Crisis: History of a Genocide* (London: C. Hurst, 1998).

S

Sadat, Anwar as- (1918–1981) *Egyptian president from 1970 to 1981*

Born in the delta region of EGYPT, Anwar as-Sadat was raised in CAIRO, where his father worked as a minor bureaucrat. He entered the Egyptian Military Academy in 1938, becoming, along with future president Gamal Abdel NASSER (1918–1970), one of the first generation of non-elites to attend the prestigious school. As a young military officer Sadat was greatly influenced by the examples of anticolonial world leaders. These included Mustafa Kemal Ataturk (1881–1938), the creator of the modern state of Turkey, and Mohandas Gandhi (1869–1948), who led the nonviolent resistance movement against Britain in India.

Sadat's participation in the 1948 Arab-Israeli War disillusioned him about the course of Egyptian politics under King Faruk (1920–1965). Sadat subsequently joined Nasser and other officers of the Free Officers Movement in the 1952 coup that overthrew Faruk and ultimately ushered Nasser into power. He remained in the background during Nasser's presidency (1954–70), seemingly content in his role as a journalist and government propagandist, writing about how nationalization, social mobilization, and pan-Arabism empowered the Egyptian people.

At Nasser's death, in 1970, Sadat was vice president, but he was a virtual unknown to the general public when he succeeded Egypt's long-time leader and became president. In 1971 Sadat moved to consolidate his power. Through a governmental purge known as the "Corrective Revolution," he eliminated potential competition from those in Nasser's former inner circle. Although Sadat publicly supported Nasser's socialist policies, he immediately began establishing his own distinct agenda.

In foreign policy Sadat shifted his perspective with regard to the Arab-Israeli conflict. In his attempt to maintain Egypt's leadership of the Arab world he insisted that 1971 was the year that Egypt and Israel would either make peace or go to war. When he was unable to manipulate the Cold War rivalry between the Soviet Union and the United States to get the Soviet Union to supply the weapons he wanted, Sadat expelled most of the Soviet advisers and technicians living in Egypt. Sadat also resisted the initiatives by the United States to attempt to mediate an Egyptian-Israeli settlement. His principal concern was that a separate peace with Israel would isolate Egypt from the rest of the Arab world and also alienate the Arab OIL-exporting countries upon which Egypt was now dependent for much of its oil.

In 1973 Sadat, dismayed by a fruitless peace process, led Egypt in the surprise attack on Israel known as the Yom Kippur War. Egypt was joined in the conflict by Syria and other Arab countries, their purpose to regain lands lost to Israel during the Six-Day War of 1967. A massive air and artillery assault initially caught Israel by surprise and allowed Egyptian forces to reoccupy the SUEZ CANAL. Though Israel quickly recovered and inflicted heavy losses upon the Egyptian army, Sadat's initiative pushed the two sides toward peace. On November 11, 1973, the United States helped conclude a cease-fire between the two nations. Through the subsequent Sinai I and II disengagement agreements, Egypt was able to reclaim a majority of the Sinai Peninsula that it had lost in 1967. In many ways, then, Sadat obtained his objectives through diplomacy. This ultimately led him to renounce war as a means of resolving the Arab-Israeli conflict.

Domestically Sadat made sweeping changes to his predecessor's governmental policies. He lifted censorship of the press. He dismantled Nasser's internal security apparatus and gave amnesty to political prisoners. In deference to Muslim activists he made religion compulsory in schools and rewrote the constitution to make Islamic law, or SHARIA, a "main source" (though not the only source) of law. Further distancing himself from Nasser, he changed the country's name to the Arab Republic of Egypt. In 1974 he launched *infitah,* an "open door policy" that encouraged foreign capitalists to invest in local enterprises.

In 1977 Sadat boldly challenged what was widely perceived as neocolonialism on the part of the INTERNATIONAL MONETARY FUND (IMF). The IMF had been pressuring Egypt to alter its economic policies in order to repay its debts. In particular, the IMF wanted Egypt to gradually phase out its government food subsidies, which the IMF claimed were draining the country's financial resources. In response Sadat removed all food subsidies in one day. The resulting price increase caused large-scale rioting and ultimately forced the IMF to back down and reschedule the repayment of Egypt's loans.

Sadat's daring politics, however, eventually began to turn on him. Sadat believed that peace with Israel was the first step to rebuilding the economy, which had suffered greatly following Egypt's multiple defeats in the ARAB–ISRAELI WARS. In 1977 Sadat accepted the invitation of Israel's Prime Minister Menachem Begin (1913–1992) to address the Israeli legislative body, the Knesset. In 1978 he participated along with Begin in the Camp David Summit, organized by U.S. president Jimmy Carter (1924–   ), which led to the 1979 Israeli-Egyptian Peace Accord. The peace process earned Sadat considerable acclaim in the West. *Time* magazine named him "Man of the Year" in 1977, and in 1979 he shared the Nobel Peace Prize with Begin.

However, Sadat's popularity at home and in the broader Arab world declined drastically. In spite of the United States expanding its economic and military aid, Egypt's economy was slow to recover. Sadat's *infitah* policy was contributing to inflation and a skewed distribution of wealth. Many in Egypt and other Arab countries had begun to view Sadat as being aligned with the West. When Islamic extremists assassinated Sadat in 1981 for making peace with Israel, few Egyptians mourned his death.

See also: GANDHI, MOHANDAS (Vol. IV); NEOCOLONIALISM AND UNDERDEVELOPMENT (Vol. V).

Further reading: Kirk J. Beattie, *Egypt during the Sadat Years* (New York: Palgrave, 2000); Raymond A. Hinnebusch, Jr., *Egyptian Politics under Sadat: The Post-Populist Development of an Authoritarian-modernizing State* (Boulder, Colo.: Lynne Rienner Publishers, 1988); Thomas W. Lippman, *Egypt after Nasser: Sadat, Peace, and the Mirage of Prosperity* (New York: Paragon House, 1989).

safari Swahili word, meaning "travel" or "journey," that has become associated with off-road trips in search of African WILDLIFE. For many years the image of the safari—complete with khaki-wearing tourists roaming in search of "big game"—dominated African TOURISM. Today, however, although foreign tourists still come in significant numbers to view lions, elephants, and other wild animals, the safari has changed dramatically. Indeed, Africans themselves now enjoy visiting the continent's NATIONAL PARKS and game reserves. In East and southern Africa, safaris have become well-organized, professional outings, often centered around accommodations at luxurious game lodges. Drivers and guides lead groups of camera-carrying tourists in sport utility vehicles or minivans, often using two-way radios to share information about wildlife observation opportunities, all in order to provide a truly satisfying experience for the tourists who frequent the lodges.

Accommodations offered in many of Africa's game lodges are like nothing else in the world. Tourists paying anywhere from $150 to more than $250 per night are greeted by the professionally dressed staff with an assortment of tropical fruit drinks. The staff, which lives in substantially more modest quarters, attends to the guests in their rooms, around the pool, and in the various common spaces of the lodge. Each day after an early drive in search of wildlife, food is arranged on buffet tables. Lunch and dinner are similarly served, and guests enjoy afternoon tea or evening cocktails on the veranda, enjoying views of herds of buffalo, gazelles, or elephants.

Although high-end tourism brings in the most money for the countries of East and southern Africa, mid-priced and even budget-priced alternatives are becoming more common. In some areas even camping accommodations are being provided for visitors. Indeed, in contrast to the conventional vehicle-driven safari, some tourists, especially in SOUTH AFRICA and BOTSWANA, choose to go on "walking safaris," where they hike through the nature preserve with a guide who is well educated in regard to animal behavior and the workings of a given ecosystem.

At the other extreme, safaris for hunting big game are once again appearing. Highly popular during the colonial period, hunting safaris tended to fade away with independence and the subsequent efforts at CON-SERVATION. Recently, however, owners—usually white—of large tracts of land have turned from cattle and sheep ranching to raising game. These farm-raised animals are then "hunted" by Americans and Europeans, who then can have their "trophies" mounted at conveniently located taxidermy shops.

Further reading: Kenneth M. Cameron, *Into Africa: The Story of the East African Safari* (London: Constable, 1990).

Saharawi People of WESTERN SAHARA who have been fighting for self-rule since the imposition of Spanish colonial rule, in 1884. The Saharawi are descended from Arabs who, in the 15th century, migrated from Yemen. By the 18th century the western Saharan region of Saguia el-Hamra had become known as the "Land of Saints," a center of Islamic culture. Before the Spanish colonial conquest toward the end of the 19th century, the Saharawi was a loose confederation of peoples. A governing body known as the Assembly of Forty featured representatives from each group, but the various Saharawi peoples were largely autonomous.

Determined to maintain its claims to the Canary Islands, Spain established a protectorate over the region between Cape Blanc and Cape Bojador, in 1884, and then established the colony of Spanish Sahara. By 1906 the Saharawi had mounted a strong resistance to the Spanish colonization effort. By 1912 France had entered the conflict after reaching an agreement with Spain to make MOROCCO a French protectorate. The Saharawi resisted the combined efforts of France and Spain until 1934, when they were temporarily pacified by the French army. In 1936 Spain finally gained full control of its colony.

In 1956 the Saharawi rose up again, and in 1958, with the support of now independent Morocco, a joint Spanish-French military effort called the Ecouvillon Operation annihilated the Saharawi army. Two years later Spain ceded some of the western Sahara to Morocco but maintained control over Saguia el-Hamra and the Río de Oro (now Dakhla) peninsula.

In 1967 the fiercely independent Saharawi once again began a resistance movement to Spanish rule, organizing the Movement for the Liberation of the Sahara. Mohammed Sidi Brahim Bassiri (1942–1970) led the renewed resistance effort. In 1970 a large, nonviolent demonstration in the colonial capital of LAAYOUNE (El Aaiun) led to a massacre of the demonstrators by Spanish forces. In response, in 1973, an organized armed resistance group named the Popular Front for the Liberation of Saguia el-Hamra and Río de Oro, or the POLISARIO Front, was formed. The Polisario launched campaigns against Span-

ish settlers until the European colonizer finally withdrew its claims to Western Sahara, in 1976. That year, the Saharawi declared the Saharawi Arab Democratic Republic. The victory for the Saharawi was short-lived, however, as Morocco and MAURITANIA entered into fray, laying claim to the north and south of the territory, respectively (See Western Sahara map, page 452.) The Polisario continued its battle for liberation, causing Mauritania to relinquish its claims, in 1979, and forcing a cease-fire with Morocco, in 1991.

The cease-fire was supposed to lead to a UN referendum that would decide Western Sahara's inde-pendence. However, Morocco rejected any appeals to withdraw claims to the region and attempted to influence the outcome of any potential referendum by sending thousands of Moroccan settlers into Western Sahara. The referendum has been repeatedly delayed as the United Nations attempts to identify eligible voters. As of 2004 the Saharawi had yet to throw off the yoke of Moroccan rule.

See also: UNITED NATIONS AND AFRICA (Vol. V).

Samba, Chéri (1956–) *Painter from the Democratic Republic of the Congo*

Born in 1956 in the colonial Belgian Congo, Chéri Samba dropped out of school at a young age to become a sign painter in his native KINSHASA. Without any formal ART training, he began painting and developed a vivid style that eventually combined bright, colorful graphics with political and social texts.

Although Samba's works have been compared to the political and historical paintings of such French artists as Edouard Manet (1832–1883) and Eugène Delacroix (1798–1863), his paintings also have been linked to the social realism of the Mexican artist Diego Rivera (1886–1957). In many ways, however, Samba, a self-taught artist, evolved his own style, one that is rooted in the direct communication of the advertising billboards he painted in his youth. Deeply committed to both social and political causes, Samba's art, like its creator, attempts to communicate, with both pictures and words, a demand for a more humanitarian world. In works such as his 1989 painting, *Le Sida (AIDS)*, for example, he depicts three women, two holding drug capsules and one grasping a globe, with all three objects covered with condoms; below are large letters spelling out the words "Aids is still incurable but preventable."

Samba's work has been widely exhibited in Africa, Europe, and North America, in group shows in such places as the Académie des Beaux-Arts, in Kinshasa, and the Centre George Pompidou-La-Villette, in Paris, and in individual exhibits in Paris, Barcelona, Berlin, Amsterdam, Chicago, and New York. There is a major collection of his work at the Institut des Musées Nationaux in his native Democratic Republic of the Congo.

Further reading: Bogumil Jewsiewicki, *Africa Explores: Twentieth Century African Art* (New York: Center for African Art, 1991).

Samkange, Stanlake (1922–1988) *Zimbabwean writer and activist*

Stanlake Samkange grew up in the family of a Methodist minister and became one of the best-known Zimbabwean intellectuals of his generation. A political activist in the 1950s, Samkange opposed the white settler monopoly of political power in the region and pushed for gradual civil reforms. He began planning for a school, Nyatsime College, in the early 1950s, and from 1957 to 1959 he studied at Syracuse University, in the United States.

In 1965 the Rhodesian government of Ian SMITH (1919–) issued its UNILATERAL DECLARATION OF INDEPENDENCE, which sparked an armed struggle for independence the following year. Samkange, opposed to militant methods of liberation, returned to the United States for further education. Already holding a master's degree from Syracuse, he enrolled at Indiana University, where he earned a doctorate in history. Between 1968 and 1976 he taught on the history faculties of Northeastern, Tennessee State, Fisk, and Harvard universities. During this period he wrote extensively, publishing both historical studies and fiction. Among his historical works were *Origins of Rhodesia* (1968) and *African Saga: A Brief Introduction to African History* (1971). One of his most popular works, a historical novel called *On Trial for My Country* (1966), is a fictional account of the intersecting lives of the Ndebele king, Lobengula (1836–1894), and Cecil John Rhodes (1853–1902). Samkange's 1968 historical study, *Origins of Rhodesia,* received the 1969 Herskovits Award of the U.S. African Studies Association as the best scholarly work published on Africa the previous year. Another book, *The Mourned One* (1975), dealt with African Christians and white MISSIONARIES.

In 1977 Samkange returned home to become a political advisor to Rhodesia's first African president, Bishop Abel MUZOREWA (1925–), and also to serve as secretary of education. African nationalists, however, regarded the Muzorewa government as a front for continued white power. When, in 1980, an independent ZIMBABWE emerged out of the political ashes of RHODESIA, Samkange left politics behind to become director of Harare Publishing House.

See also: LITERATURE IN MODERN AFRICA (Vol. V); LOBENGULA (Vol. IV); RHODES, CECIL (Vol. IV); SAMKANGE, STANLAKE (Vol. IV); SOUTHERN RHODESIA (Vol. IV).

Further reading: Terence Ranger, *Are We Not Also Men?: The Samkange Family and African Politics in Zimbabwe, 1920–64* (Portsmouth, N.H.: Heinemann, 1995); Stanlake Samkange, *On Trial for My Country* (Portsmouth, N.H.: Heinemann, 1967).

Sankoh, Foday (1937–2003) *Rebel leader in Sierra Leone*

A former photographer and television cameraman, Foday Sankoh was a student leader before joining the SIERRA LEONE army. He was imprisoned in 1971 for treason. Following his release from prison, in 1984, Sankoh trained at a camp for revolutionaries in LIBYA, where he met Charles TAYLOR (1948–), the future president of LIBERIA.

After returning to West Africa, Sankoh became the self-styled political leader of the REVOLUTIONARY UNITED FRONT (RUF), a rebel group that claimed to fight against government CORRUPTION in Sierra Leone. In March 1991, with Taylor's support, Sankoh and the RUF began launching attacks into Sierra Leone from LIBERIA.

Sankoh's stated purpose was to liberate Sierra Leone from the excesses of a corrupt elite. However, he and his rebel group quickly evolved into a band of pillagers. They used violent tactics including abduction, forced conscription of young boys, systematic raping of young girls, looting, and arson. They also profited from selling illegal diamonds to Liberian agents. During the war, which lasted from 1991 to 2001, as many as 50,000 people died. In addition, more than half the population fled Sierra Leone to seek refuge in neighboring countries.

With the nation in upheaval, in May 1997 Major Johnny Paul Koroma (1960–) led a COUP D'ÉTAT to overthrow Ahmad Tejan KABBAH (1932–), the democratically elected leader. Koroma then offered to share power with Sankoh and the RUF in the new military government called the Armed Forces Revolutionary Council (AFRC). However, in February 1998 troops from a peacekeeping force organized by the ECONOMIC COMMUNITY OF WEST AFRICAN STATES (ECOWAS) drove the AFRC from the capital at FREETOWN. Following the AFRC ouster, RUF rebels went back on the attack.

In January 1999 Sankoh was captured and sentenced to death for treason. In retaliation the RUF staged a bloody three-week occupation of Freetown. An estimated 5,000 civilians were burned or shot to death, 3,000 children were kidnapped, and hundreds of buildings were looted and burned by the rebels. Efforts to stop the violent conflict led, in July 1999, to an ECOWAS-brokered peace deal. The agreement, which was signed in LOMÉ, TOGO, gave Sankoh the vice presidency in a new coalition government. He also became the chairman of the Commission for the Management of Strategic Resources—the ministry responsible for running the diamond mines.

Frequent breaches of the peace accord stirred up popular unrest, and in May 2000 an estimated 20,000 people marched on Sankoh's villa in Freetown. Sankoh was eventually captured and sent to face war-crime charges in an international tribunal. In court appearances following his capture Sankoh was incoherent and sickly. In 2002 he suffered a stroke and was transferred from a prison cell to a prison hospital. Following repeated hospitalizations, he died in UN custody on July 31, 2003.

São Tomé (city)

São Tomé (city) Capital city and principal port of the tropical island country of SÃO TOMÉ AND PRÍNCIPE, which is located off the coast of GABON in western Central Africa. The city of São Tomé, located on the northeastern shore of the island of the same name, became the national capital at independence, in 1975. The island's economy, which in the colonial era was based on the production of sugar, has since changed over to the production of other CASH CROPS, especially cocoa and coffee. Today the port of São Tomé also exports copra (dried coconut meat) and bananas. The city's light industry includes the manufacture of soap, beverages, and tiles.

The 53,300 inhabitants of the city (2003 estimate) constitute about one-third of the entire population of the country. Most are descended from Portuguese colonists, African plantation workers, or a mix of the two. People in São Tomé speak Portuguese, the official language of the country, or a Portuguese-based Creole language.

Visitors to São Tomé enjoy the relaxed tropical climate and the city's numerous lush, beautifully kept parks and gardens. In addition, the city is the site of the National Museum of São Tomé and Príncipe, which is housed in an old Portuguese fort. São Tomé is characterized by its crumbling, yet charming, colonial buildings. These contrast sharply with the few Soviet-style buildings constructed after the postindependence government established ties with the Communist-bloc countries.

See also: PORTUGAL AND AFRICA (Vols. III, IV, V); SLAVERY (Vols. I, II, III, IV).

São Tomé and Príncipe

São Tomé and Príncipe Small nation made up of two islands, located just north of the equator off the coast of GABON, in western Central Africa. One-third of the country's 140,000 inhabitants (2003 estimate) live in the capital city of SÃO TOMÉ, located on the island of that name. Only one-fifth of the country's population lives on the smaller island of Príncipe.

Totaling some 390 square miles (1,010 sq km), the islands were first settled by the Portuguese in the late 15th century. Historically the islands' economic focus has been the production of CASH CROPS for export—first sugar, and later coffee and cocoa. From the beginning of their settlement, human captives were brought from the central African mainland to the islands to work on Portuguese-owned plantations.

São Tomé and Príncipe at Independence As a result of harsh working conditions, dissent among the laborers turned into an independence movement in the mid-20th century. When São Tomé and Príncipe gained independence, in 1975, the principal leader of the independence movement, Manuel Pinto da Costa (1937–), became the country's first president. At that time most of the Portuguese plantation owners and government officials left the country, leaving a population composed mostly of the descendants of freed slaves and people of mixed Portuguese and African ancestry.

After independence the nation was one of the first African countries to make substantial moves towards DEMOCRATIZATION. A strong commitment to civil liberties has led to an excellent HUMAN RIGHTS record and several peaceful national multiparty elections. In 2001 Fradique DE MENEZES (1942–) was elected president of the nation for a five-year term. However, in July 2003 a military junta led by Major Fernando Pereira briefly seized governmental power. Although de Menezes was soon reinstated, ongoing coup threats have cast a cloud over the country's future.

In addition to democratic reforms the nation has also instituted numerous economic reforms under STRUCTURAL ADJUSTMENT policies. Attempts to diversify the nation's economy, however, have met with mixed success. Although fertile volcanic soils and plentiful rainfall make the island nation well suited for AGRICULTURE, it is at the same time very isolated, making DEVELOPMENT difficult. Cocoa is the major export and is responsible for the majority of the country's foreign exchange earnings, but the islands still must rely on foreign ECONOMIC ASSISTANCE. Some fishing contributes to the economy. The recent discovery of offshore OIL reserves holds the potential for a rapid improvement in the economic situation of the islands' inhabitants.

The government of São Tomé and Príncipe recently has made efforts to invest in INFRASTRUCTURE related to TOURISM, hoping that the physical beauty of the tropical islands—with their dense FORESTS, dramatic volcanic peaks, and numerous endemic species—will attract many visitors.

See also: PORTUGAL AND AFRICA (Vols. III, IV, V); SÃO TOMÉ AND PRÍNCIPE (Vols. I, II, III, IV).

Saro-Wiwa, Ken (Kenule Beeson Saro-Wiwa)
(1941–1995) *Nigerian writer and political activist*

Born in the coastal town of Bori, in southern NIGERIA, Saro-Wiwa was a member of the OGONI, an ethnic minority living in the OIL-rich NIGER DELTA. Anticipating a career in academia, he attended the University of IBADAN and the Government College at Umuahia. He taught at Umuahia and then at the University of Lagos until the outbreak of the Biafran War (1967–70), at which time he became employed in civil administration. In 1968 he became administrator of the port of Bonny and afterwards took the position of minister of the Rivers State. Saro-Wiwa is most celebrated for his novels concerning the Biafran War. Beginning with *Sozaboy* (1985), he developed a large body of fiction, including *A Forest of Flowers* (1986), *Prisoners of Jebs* (1988), and *On a Darkling Plain* (1989). He also produced children's books, a book of poems, and a number of books based on the popular television series *Basi and Company*. Though his adult fiction dealt largely with the Biafran War and the upheaval in Nigeria, Saro-Wiwa's writing was sometimes humorous and often satirical.

Being part of an ethnic minority, Saro-Wiwa could not rely on his native tongue for his writing, as it would not reach a wide enough audience. Therefore, he wrote in English, distinguishing between "pure" English and "rotten" English, the latter being a pidgin Nigerian dialect. *Sozaboy* (Soldier Boy) won international recognition for its use of "rotten" English.

Saro-Wiwa is perhaps best remembered, however, for his political activism on behalf of his Ogoni people. The Ogoni homeland holds vast oil reserves, which are central to Nigeria's economy. The various military governments that ruled Nigeria since 1966 collaborated with MULTINATIONAL CORPORATIONS, such as the Shell Oil Company, to exploit the oil resources of Ogoniland. Oil extraction devastated the local environment, polluting the soil and water that the Ogoni had once thrived on. Being a minority in a country dominated by three major ethnic groups (the YORUBA, IGBO, and HAUSA-Fulani), the Ogoni could do little to voice their grievances.

Saro-Wiwa was horrified by the conditions his people were forced to live in and he formed the Movement for the Survival of the Ogoni People (MOSOP). The organization spoke out against dictator Sani ABACHA (1943–1998), accusing the government of conducting what amounted to genocide against the Ogoni. It also called for the even distribution of oil revenue, reparations from the oil companies, and the removal of oil company operations from Ogoni lands. Saro-Wiwa outlined these grievances in the essay collection *Nigeria: The Brink of Disaster* and *Similia: Essays on Anomic Nigeria*, both published in 1991.

Despite the fact that Saro-Wiwa and MOSOP advocated nonviolent protest, Abacha launched a campaign of retribution against the Ogoni. Nigerian soldiers rampaged through Ogoni villages in an effort to force the Ogoni back into submission. In 1993 Saro-Wiwa was imprisoned for four weeks on charges of treason but was released after an international outcry.

In 1994 a MOSOP meeting that Saro-Wiwa did not attend erupted into a clash between Saro-Wiwa's supporters and a pro-government faction, resulting in the deaths of four of the dissenting chiefs. The government seized the opportunity to imprison Saro-Wiwa again, along with eight other MOSOP leaders, on charges of inciting the murders. In 1995, after a trial that was, by all accounts, a mockery, the defendants were sentenced to death. Eight days later Saro-Wiwa and the other eight MOSOP members were executed.

The result of Saro-Wiwa's death was an international backlash against Abacha and the Shell Oil Company. Nigeria was suspended from the British Commonwealth, a number of nations ceased diplomatic relations with the country, and the WORLD BANK withdrew $100 million in aid. In spite of government propaganda aimed at defaming Saro-Wiwa, he has achieved the status of hero both among the Ogoni and worldwide.

Saro-Wiwa's *A Month and A Day: A Detention Diary* (1995), written while he was in prison and published after his death, expresses the universality of the Ogoni situation and argues that inequalities of power exist in every country.

See also: BIAFRA (Vol. V); CIVIL WARS (Vol. V); ENVIRONMENTAL ISSUES (Vol. V); LITERATURE IN MODERN AFRICA (Vol. V).

Sassou-Nguesso, Denis (1943–) *President of the Republic of the Congo*

The Republic of the CONGO, unstable and undermined by ethnic tensions since its independence from colonial rule in 1960, benefited little under the administration of Sassou-Nguesso. Born in Edou, in the north of the country, Sassou-Nguesso became involved in the nationalist movement against colonialism and left his teaching job to join the army. In 1962 he was made commander of the BRAZZAVILLE military zone. His career in the army became increasingly successful, culminating in his reaching the rank of colonel.

Sassou-Nguesso was close to the country's Marxist president, Marien Ngouabi (1938–1977), and became his minister of defense in 1975. Two years later he was appointed vice president of the military committee of Ngouabi's Congolese Worker's Party (Parti Congolais Du Travail, PCT). However, Nguouabi was assassinated that same year. Joachim Yhombi-Opango (1939–) assumed the presidency and moved away from Marxist ideals toward a more West-friendly government. Marxist elements in the PCT strongly opposed Yhombi-Opango and forced him from office in 1979. A provisional committee took over, with Sassou-Nguesso as its head. A month later he was officially appointed president.

However, Sassou-Nguesso continued to move the government away from a Marxist path. He initiated reforms designed to diminish government influence and privatize portions of the economy. In 1992 he allowed multiparty elections. Unfortunately, this led to disaster. The Panafrican Union for Social Democracy (Union Panafricaine pour la Démocratie Social, UPADS) won the elections, with Pascal Lissouba assuming the presidency. When a coalition government between UPADS and the PCT failed, the PCT allied with another party, the Union for Democratic Renewal (Union Pour le Renouveau Démocratique, URD). After a great deal of political controversy the PCT-URD coalition formed a separate gov- ernment and fomented a rebellion against Lissouba. Between 1993 and 1997 the conflict exploded into full civil war. The capital, Brazzaville, became a microcosm of the country as a whole. It was divided into three sections, with Sassou-Nguesso, Lissouba, and PCT-URD chairman Bernard Kolelas (1933–) each holding a section. The combatants laid the city to waste, forcing nearly all of its inhabitants to flee. It was not until late 1997 that Lissouba was forced into exile and Sassou-Nguesso declared victory.

After retaking the presidency, in 1998, Sassou-Nguesso was once again faced with war when Lissouba and Kolelas loyalists rebelled. In 1999 the intervention of GABON's president, Omar BONGO (1935–), eventually led to a peace with a majority of the rebels. Under international pressure Sassou-Nguesso reformed the constitution to democratize the government. In 2002 Sassou-Nguesso won the presidential elections, though there was significant evidence of fraud. Violence once again broke out following Sassou-Nguesso's election, as rebel activity escalated.

See also: CIVIL WARS (Vol. V); COMMUNISM AND SOCIALISM (Vol. V); ETHNIC CONFLICT IN AFRICA (Vol. V); STATE, ROLE OF (Vol. V).

Further reading: Amnesty International, *Republic of Congo: An Old Generation of Leaders in New Carnage* (New York: Amnesty International USA, 1999); Mbow M. Amphas, *Political Transformations of the Congo* (Durham, N.C.: Pentland Press, 2000).

Savimbi, Jonas (Savimbi Jonas Malheiro)
(1934–2002) *Angolan nationalist*

Jonas Savimbi was born in the Portuguese colony of ANGOLA. His father was an influential Ovimbundu chief who also worked on the Benguela railroad as a stationmaster. In addition his father was a preacher who promoted Protestant Christianity in opposition to the dominant Catholic Church. Savimbi was educated at Angolan missionary schools and ultimately earned a scholarship to study in Portugal. He studied MEDICINE in Lisbon, but his anti-Portuguese activism led him to move to Switzerland, where he continued his studies at the University of Lausanne.

Savimbi met Holden ROBERTO (1923–) in 1961 and soon joined Roberto's Popular Union of Angola (União das Populações de Angola, UPA), an independence movement aimed at toppling Portuguese colonial rule. Savimbi became the UPA secretary-general and played a key role in forming the NATIONAL FRONT FOR THE LIBERATION OF ANGOLA, a UPA splinter group. He soon broke with Roberto, however, believing in undertaking the independence struggle from within Angola rather than leading it from exile, as Roberto was doing. After spending time in guerrilla training camps in China, Savimbi returned to Angola, and in 1966 he formed the NATIONAL UNION FOR THE TOTAL INDEPENDENCE OF ANGOLA (União Nacional para a Independência Total de Angola, UNITA).

Although it claimed to oppose ethnic-based organizations, UNITA generally promoted the interests of the Ovimbundu peoples of southern and eastern Angola. Because of this, UNITA waged a guerrilla war against the Portuguese. After independence it also fought against the Mbundu-dominated, northern-based POPULAR MOVEMENT FOR THE LIBERATION OF ANGOLA (Movimento Popular de Libertação de Angola, MPLA), led by Agostinho NETO (1922–1979).

Neto became the president of Angola at independence, but civil war soon broke out. Other countries became deeply involved, and Angolan politics became enmeshed in the Cold War. Over the course of the civil war the United States, China, and SOUTH AFRICA backed UNITA and Savimbi, while Cuba and the former Soviet Union supported the MPLA government.

A peace agreement signed in 1991 led to UN-supervised elections two years later. UNITA lost the elections, but the party was offered positions in a government of national unity—including the vice presidency for Savimbi. Savimbi rejected the offer, and UNITA resumed its military struggle against the now-legitimate government of Angola.

In the 1990s UNITA's control of Angola's diamond-MINING region helped Savimbi illegally finance his ongoing armed rebellion. Although his opportunistic tactics brought international criticism, at the same time Savimbi was lauded by his supporters for being both a strong leader as well as a crusader for democracy. Ultimately Savimbi faced opposition both from within his own UNITA party and from the Angolan government. Savimbi was ambushed and assassinated by government troops on February 22, 2002.

See also: CHINA AND AFRICA (Vol. V); COLD WAR AND AFRICA (Vols. IV, V); COLONIAL RULE (Vol. IV); CUBA AND AFRICA (Vol. V); ETHNIC CONFLICT IN AFRICA (Vol. V); INDEPENDENCE MOVEMENTS (Vol. V); NATIONALISM AND INDEPENDENCE MOVEMENTS (Vol. IV); OVIMBUNDU (Vols. II, III, IV); PORTUGAL AND AFRICA (Vols. III, IV, V); SOVIET UNION AND AFRICA (Vols. IV, V); UNITED STATES AND AFRICA (Vols. IV, V).

Rebel leader Jonas Savimbi, shown here in 1989, used illegal diamond profits to fund UNITA, his opposition political group. Angola's civil war ended after Savimbi's assassination, in 2002. © AP/Wide World Photos

Further reading: Elaine Windrich, *The Cold War Guerrilla: Jonas Savimbi, the U.S. Media, and the Angolan War* (New York: Greenwood Press, 1992).

science Africa has a long history of scientific discovery and knowledge. However, scientific study by indigenous Africans stagnated during the colonial period, gaining momentum again only after independence. Prior to World War II (1939–45) it was common for African scientists to export objects of scientific importance to Europe to be studied by western scientists. After the war, however, scientific research centers and university science departments within Africa began training African scientists. By the 1960s and 1970s prestigious science departments had been established at many of Africa's major universities, including the University of LAGOS, in NIGERIA, and the University of DAR ES SALAAM, in TANZANIA. In addition science councils, such as the Scientific, Technical and Research Commission of the ORGANIZATION OF AFRICAN UNITY, were established to promote western science in Africa.

Unfortunately a widespread economic decline during the 1980s and 1990s forced states to decrease funding to their public university systems. As a result the quality of the scientific study at many of Africa's universities faltered. At the same time, however, scientific research performed by international agencies remained a strong component of foreign involvement in Africa. Today there are numerous NON-GOVERNMENTAL ORGANIZATIONS and government ministries that have teamed up to conduct research on the continent. The primary fields of study for these teams are the agricultural, biological, physical, and medical sciences.

An unwanted side effect of the international aspect of science training in Africa is the "brain drain" phenomenon. While some excellent African scientists received their advanced training from African universities, many others studied abroad in Europe or the United States. Because science studies in the West are better funded, the labs and science programs found there are generally superior to those in Africa. As a result some African scientists found it difficult to return to Africa to study, train, or teach, thereby draining the continent of some of its best and brightest scholars.

See also: SCIENCE (Vols. I, II, III, IV).

Senegal Country on West Africa's Atlantic coast that is defined to the north and northeast by the Senegal River. Senegal covers about 76,000 square miles (196,800 sq km) and is bordered to the north by MAURITANIA, to the east by the Republic of MALI, and to the south by GUINEA and GUINEA-BISSAU. In a unique feature of political geography, Senegal nearly surrounds the country of The GAMBIA, except for The Gambia's western, coastal border.

Senegal at Independence Upon gaining its independence from France, Senegal joined the Mali Federation in June 1960. The Mali Federation was short-lived, however, and in August Senegal pulled out. Senegal then became a republic, with Léopold SENGHOR (1906–2001) as the country's first president. By 1962 Senegal was politically unstable, and Senghor had to put down an attempted COUP D'ÉTAT. Consolidating his power, in 1966 Senghor replaced Senegal's multiparty democracy with a single-party state that was controlled by his SENEGALESE PROGRESSIVE UNION (Union Progressiste Sénégalaise, UPS).

At the time, Senegal's economy was, and still is, largely agricultural and dependent upon a single crop—groundnuts (peanuts). Under French rule the groundnut trade and other industries were controlled by private enterprises. This gradually changed, as Senghor promoted a form of African Socialism that placed control over much of the country's economic direction in the hands of the government.

However, Senghor moved away from economic socialism in the 1970s, and, in an effort to diversify the economy, he emphasized new industries beyond groundnut cultivation such as TOURISM and fishing. Still, the health of Senegal's economy remained greatly affected by factors outside of the country's control, including fluctuations in the international price of groundnuts and OIL.

In an effort to alleviate the dependent nature of its economy, in 1973 Senegal joined other West African nations to create the ECONOMIC COMMUNITY OF WEST AFRICAN STATES, which was organized to promote economic and political cooperation among its member nations.

In 1981 Senghor resigned, and his handpicked successor, Abdou DIOUF (1935–), assumed the presidency. Diouf continued Senghor's move toward privatization of industries formerly controlled by the government. He also continued Senegal's shift, begun by Senghor in 1978, from a single-party political system to a multiparty democracy. In the midst of these reforms Diouf faced a new threat, as armed separatists became active in Casamance, a southwestern region of Senegal isolated from the rest of the country by The Gambia. These separatists formed the Movement of Democratic Forces in the Casamance (Mouevement des Forces Démocratiques du le Casamance, MFDC) to organize their resistance.

Diouf continued to introduce further economic and political reforms, selling government-owned companies and allowing more political parties. In 1982, following an attempted coup d'état against The Gambia's president, Dawda Kairaba JAWARA (1924–), Senegal joined The Gambia in the SENEGAMBIA CONFEDERATION. The immediate purpose of the organization was to guarantee mutual security with a long-range plan for an economic and military union. However, in 1989 disputes over economic issues and the sharing of political power forced the dissolution of the organization.

Meanwhile Senegal faced new threats to its political and economic stability. From 1989 to 1991 it engaged Mauritania in a border war that began as a dispute over land and water access in the Senegal River plain. This conflict deteriorated into ethnic fighting between the Maures and a coalition of Fulani and Tukulors. At the same time, the MFDC continued its insurgency in the Casamance region, leading to a decline in the tourism industry and the movement of REFUGEES into neighboring Guinea-Bissau.

In 2000 an opposition party led by Abdoulaye WADE (1926–) defeated Diouf and his Socialist Party, which had evolved from the UPS. Despite the new leadership, Senegal continues to face diplomatic difficulties. Though the MFDC signed a peace accord with the government in 2001, die-hard secessionists remained active in the Casamance.

See also: FRANCE AND AFRICA (Vols. IV, V); SENEGAL (Vols. I, II, III, IV); SENEGAMBIA (Vol. III); SENEGAMBIA REGION (Vol. IV); SENEGAL RIVER (Vols. I, II).

Further reading: Adrian Adams and Jaabe So, *A Claim to Land by the River: A Household Senegal, 1720–1994* (New York: Oxford University Press, 1996); Elizabeth L. Berg, *Senegal* (New York: Marshall Cavendish, 1999).

Senegalese Progressive Union (Union Progressiste Sénégalaise, UPS)

Ruling Party of SENEGAL for more than 40 years. In 1976 it changed its name to the Socialist Party (Parti Socialiste, PS). Founded in 1958 by Senegal's first president, Léopold SENGHOR (1906–2001), the Senegalese Progressive Union (UPS) positioned itself as the ruling party by handily winning the national elections of 1959. In April 1960 Senegal gained its independence with Senghor as president. In 1966 Senghor declared Senegal a one-party state.

Even though the UPS was Senegal's only legal party, the country still held regular elections, and Senghor encouraged political opponents to join the UPS. Although Senghor easily won reelection for the third time, in 1973, Senegal's poor economy led to increasing dissatisfaction with his growing stranglehold on power. In 1976 Senghor pushed through changes to the constitution permitting the formation of competing parties, and the UPS changed its name to the Socialist Party.

Senghor and the Socialist Party Senghor and the PS handily won the national elections in 1978, and Senghor remained firmly in control of Senegal's government. When he retired in 1981 Senghor was able to handpick his successor, Abdou DIOUF (1935–).

Under Diouf, the PS organized youth and women's movements within the party, using the youth organizations as a feeder system for the national party. In 1991, in response to renewed pressure to increase political competition, Senegal's constitution was changed to allow for more political parties. Diouf lost the 2000 presidential election to Abdoulaye WADE (1926–), a defeat that marked an end to more than 40 years of PS political dominance. The party, however, still remained a strong force in Senegal's government.

See also: COMMUNISM AND SOCIALISM (Vol. V); DEMOCRATIZATION (Vol. V); FRANCE AND AFRICA (Vols. IV, V); POLITICAL PARTIES AND ORGANIZATIONS (Vols. IV, V).

Senegambia Confederation (1981–1989) Short-lived agreement between the Republic of SENEGAL and The GAMBIA that intended to integrate the military, trade, and governmental institutions of the two nations. Following the independence of Senegal (1960) and The Gambia (1965), several unsuccessful attempts were made to unite the two countries. Senegal completely surrounds The Gambia except along the coast, and the populations of both Senegal and The Gambia are mostly Wolof-speaking Muslims. They generally consider themselves a single people who were divided into two when France and Britain partitioned their territory during the colonial era. Furthermore, the territorial configuration of The Gambia as a political entity did not correlate well with the region's culture or economy.

In 1981 President Abdou DIOUF (1935–) of Senegal sent forces to help Gambian president Dawda Kairaba JAWARA (1924–) thwart an attempted COUP D'ÉTAT. The violent incident led the two presidents to draw up plans for confederation that would be put into effect the following year. According to the agreement, the individual states would maintain their independence and sovereignty, but the confederation would "strengthen the unity of their defense and their economies and the coordination of their policies in other fields."

Since Senegal was the larger of the two nations in both land area and population, Diouf was made the president and Jawara the vice president of the Senegambia Confederation. Two-thirds of the confederal parliament was selected from among the Senegalese Parliament, and the remaining one-third was selected from The Gambian House of Representatives. However, the union never lived up to its promise, for the most part because of The Gambia's reluctance to cede substantial governmental power to Senegal. In September 1989, eight years after its creation, The Gambia withdrew from the Senegambia Confederation and the union was dissolved.

See also: ENGLAND AND AFRICA (Vol. IV); FRANCE AND AFRICA (Vols. IV, V); SENEGAMBIA (Vol. III); SENEGAMBIA REGION (Vol. IV); WOLOF (Vols. II, IV).

Senghor, Léopold (Léopold Sédar Senghor) (1906–2001) *First president of Senegal*

Between the end of World War II, in 1945, and the independence of SENEGAL, in 1960, Léopold Senghor established himself as his country's leading political and cultural figure. He worked closely with French and African politicians, playing a critical role in Senegal's transition from colony to independent country. At the same time, he became a leading spokesperson for the pan-African literary and cultural movement known as *Négritude* and was a co-founder of *Présence Africaine,* which served as the movement's leading journal.

When Senegal achieved independence Senghor was in position to become the country's first president. Despite coming from a minority ethnic group, the Serer, and despite being a Christian in a country that was overwhelmingly Muslim, Senghor was widely recognized by the Senegalese people as the best candidate. His presidency was not an unqualified success, however, and he had to thwart an attempted COUP D'ÉTAT in 1962. Beyond this his steadfast alliance with France and the establishment of a one-party

Senegalese president Léopold Senghor, shown in 1972, was known as much for his literary and cultural achievements as he was for his political leadership. © *AP/Wide World Photos*

socialist state led to unrest and student riots. Yet he was an adroit politician, serving as president until 1980, when he voluntarily relinquished the office to his handpicked successor, Abdou DIOUF (1935–). Senghor was one of only a handful of African political leaders of his generation to retire willingly from presidential office, and by doing so he became a highly respected and influential elder African statesman.

Throughout his presidency Senghor continued with his literary and cultural activities. In 1966, for example, he sponsored the First World Festival of Negro Arts, in DAKAR. His French literary skills earned him the honor of being the first African elected to the French Academy, France's most distinguished intellectual institution. His election to the academy along with his sponsorship of the World Festival illustrate the complex Senghor—a man equal parts African and French.

See also: FRANCE AND AFRICA (Vols. IV, V); LITERATURE IN COLONIAL AFRICA (Vol. IV); LITERATURE IN MODERN AFRICA (Vol. V); NATIONALISM AND INDEPENDENCE MOVEMENTS (Vol. IV); NÉGRITUDE (Vol. IV); PAN-AFRICANISM (Vols. IV, V); *PRÉSENCE AFRICAINE* (Vol. IV); SENGHOR, LÉOPOLD (Vol. IV).

Further reading: Janet G. Vaillant, *Black, French, and African: A life of Léopold Sédar Senghor* (Cambridge, Mass.: Harvard University Press, 1990).

Seychelles Archipelago located in the western Indian Ocean. It is made up of two island clusters: the inhabited Mahé group of 40 islands, and the largely uninhabited coralline islands, numbering about 70. The Seychelles became an independent nation in the British Commonwealth in 1976.

The Seychelles were a French possession until 1814, when the Treaty of Paris turned control of the islands over to Britain. The Seychellois, as the islands' inhabitants are called, began moving toward independence in the 1960s. Britain allowed universal suffrage for the Seychellois, and an elected governing council was eventually set up to administer the colony. Increasing autonomy led to greater political activity, and a developing urban, professional middle class began to challenge the landed elite, who had dominated the islands' political scene since 1948.

This new middle class supported the development of two political parties: the Seychelles Democratic Party (SDP), led by Sir James MANCHAM (c. 1939–), and the Seychelles People's United Party (SPUP), led by France-Albert RENÉ (1935–). The parties differed in opinion on virtually every topic of importance to the Seychelles, particularly the issue of independence. Mancham's SDP favored continued ties with Britain, while René's SPUP wanted full autonomy. By the early 1970s, however, Britain's general lack of interest in the Seychelles, as well as burgeoning international criticism of colonialism, led the SDP, too, to change its tack and favor independence. In 1974 elections were held to establish a government in preparation for full autonomy. Mancham and the SDP won the elections amid great controversy and claims of rigged results. Regardless, a coalition government was formed, and in 1976 the Republic of the Seychelles became an independent nation within the British Commonwealth, with Mancham as president and René as vice president.

In 1971 an international airport opened on the Seychelles' main island of Mahé. The airport had an immediate impact, as travelers no longer had to endure long ocean voyages to reach the islands. TOURISM quickly became the Seychelles' dominant industry, and now accounts for three-quarters of the islands' economy.

Mancham held the presidency for only one year, however. While he was abroad a group of Tanzanian-trained SPUP members staged a COUP D'ÉTAT and placed René in power. René reorganized the government and SPUP, establishing a new constitution, in 1979, that allowed for only one legal political party, namely the SPUP's new incarnation, the Seychelles People's Progressive Front. Applying socialist policies, René won popular support among the Seychellois as the standard of living increased. René had enemies among the upper classes, however, and between 1978 and 1987 he had to survive a number of coup attempts.

In 1981 an attempt to overthrow René was made by a group of mercenaries led by the Irish colonel Michael "Mad Mike" Hoare, who was already famous for his exploits in the Democratic Republic of the CONGO. The mercenaries, posing as a rugby team, tried to enter the country but were discovered. They escaped by hijacking a passenger plane, eventually landing in SOUTH AFRICA, where the government imprisoned a number of the mercenaries for their crimes. Hoare claimed the attempted coup had been supported by South African intelligence.

The exiled Mancham also tried to undermine René's government, which responded by seizing lands owned by political opponents living outside of the Seychelles. In 1991 pressure from Britain and France led René to allow for a multiparty government. In spite of this René still won the presidential elections in 1993, 1998, and 2001. In April 2004, however, René stepped down and chose his vice president and long-time ally, James Alix Michel (1944–), to be his successor.

Today the Seychelles benefit from a strong tourist industry, drawing travelers from across the world to take in the islands' beaches and lush scenery. The islands also have a strong fishing industry, with main EXPORTS of coconuts, vanilla, and guano (bird droppings used for fertilizer). The Seychellois, largely a people of both African and Asian descent, live mostly in Victoria, the capital city on the main island of Mahé. Creole is the main spoken tongue, though English and French are also official languages.

See also: SEYCHELLES (Vols. I, II, III, IV).

sharia Islamic law, containing bodies of rules that govern Muslims. Although there are several schools of thought and law within Islam, the general notion of the strict application of *sharia* within pluralistic African countries has met with controversy. This has been true even when Muslim theologians and politicians have argued that any punishments meted out by the Islamic theological courts would apply only to Muslims.

The question of the imposition of *sharia* received a human face during the late 20th and early 21st centuries with the famous case of Safiyatu Huseini. An Islamic court found her guilty of adultery with a married man and condemned her to death by stoning. Her case, in which she claimed that her pregnancy was the result of rape, not adultery, is one of several that attracted international attention. Ultimately an appeals court overturned her conviction on the grounds of convincing evidence of rape.

The tenets of *sharia* are largely based on specific guidance laid down in the Quran and the way that Muslim Prophet Muhammad lived his life, known as the Sunna (the Way). Two other sources of authority are Qiyas, which is the application of *sharia* to new situations, and *ijma* (consensus). The practice of *sharia* is dependent on Islamic *ulema* (scholars), who study the laws and codify them through *maddhabs* (schools) where Islamic law, known as *fiqh*, is taught.

At the beginning of the 21st century, the widespread implementation of *sharia* was found in only a handful of countries, including Saudi Arabia, Iran, Sudan, LIBYA and Nigeria. Critics maintain that the *sharia* courts in Nigeria too often mete out harsh punishments without respecting *sharia* rules of evidence and testimony, which call for the requirement of four eyewitnesses and stipulate that a woman's testimony should be equal to a man's testimony.

See also: ISLAM, INFLUENCE OF (Vols. II, III, IV, V); LAW IN MODERN AFRICA (Vol. V).

Further reading: I. M. Lewis, *Islam in Tropical Africa* (Bloomington, Ind.: Indiana University Press 1966).

Sharpeville Black township located near JOHANNESBURG, SOUTH AFRICA, that was the site of the infamous Sharpeville Massacre, March 21, 1961. The tragic event brought international attention to this township located near Vereeniging. What sparked the massacre was a peaceful gathering, organized by the PAN-AFRICANIST CONGRESS (PAC), to protest the APARTHEID-era pass laws .

During the apartheid era, black South Africans were required to carry "passes," or identity cards that government officials used to monitor the movements of Africans within the country. The system of pass laws led to discrimination, harassment, and arbitrary arrests by the police. The attempt to eliminate the laws—and the government's obstinate determination to keep them in place—became a focal point of many protests during the anti-apartheid struggle.

In March 1961, in an attempt to call national attention to the government's unjust and racist pass laws, the PAC asked its followers to leave their pass books at home and march on police stations for voluntary arrest. Approximately 5,000 protesters gathered in the center of Sharpeville. Toward the end of the day the crowds had thinned and only about 300 protesters remained outside the station. At that time, despite the peaceful nature of the protest, nervous police officers opened fire on the crowd, killing 69 Africans and wounding 180 more. Most of the victims were shot in the back as they fled.

In response to the Sharpeville Massacre, the government declared a state of emergency, banned both the PAC and its rival, the AFRICAN NATIONAL CONGRESS (ANC), and arrested thousands of Africans. The events—including the way in which the South African government handled the situation—initiated international condemnation of the apartheid system. Within a few days, the United Nations Security Council passed a resolution that called for an end to apartheid.

The international and domestic reaction, however, did nothing to lessen support for apartheid among South Africa's white government leaders. Indeed, it seemed to make Prime Minister Hendrik VERWOERD (1901–1966) more determined than ever to enforce the country's racist laws. The administration's obstinacy in the face of international outrage sparked the formation of the ANC's military faction, UMKHONTO WE SIZWE, which launched a sabotage campaign against the government.

In 1966, in commemoration of the massacre, the United Nations declared March 21 the International Day for the Elimination of Racial Discrimination. Thirty years

later South African president Nelson MANDELA (1918–)
announced the signing of the new democratic constitution in Sharpeville. Today March 21 is celebrated in South
Africa as Human Rights Day.

See also: HUMAN RIGHTS (Vol. V); UNITED NATIONS
AND AFRICA (Vols. IV, V).

Further reading: Philip H. Frankel, *An Ordinary
Atrocity: Sharpeville and its Massacre* (Johannesburg: Witwatersrand University Press, 2001).

Sierra Leone   West African country measuring approximately 27,700 square miles (71,700 sq km). Sierra
Leone shares borders with GUINEA, to the north and east,
and LIBERIA, to the south. It also features about 250 miles
(402 km) of Atlantic Ocean coastline to the west. FREE-
TOWN, on the coast, is the capital.

Sierra Leone at Independence Sierra Leone received its independence from Britain in 1961, formally
bringing an end to a British colonial presence in the
Freetown area that dated back to 1808. Dr. Milton Margai
(1896–1964), who led the independence movement as
head of the SIERRA LEONE PEOPLE'S PARTY, remained prime
minister until his death, in 1964. He was succeeded by his
half brother, Sir Albert Margai (1910–1980). The party,
however, was perceived by many as favoring the Mende
ethnic group, and it was defeated in the 1967 general elections by the more inclusive All Peoples Congress, which
was led by Siaka Stevens (1905–1988). Following a COUP
D'ÉTAT early in his presidency, Stevens consolidated control
over the government, eventually declaring Sierra Leone a
one-party state in 1978.

Western observers characterized Stevens' leadership
as corrupt and repressive. Unwise public spending led
to economic inflation, pushing the cost of many basic
food items out of the reach of the average Sierra
Leonean. Purchasing power and the standard of living
declined, while unemployment and food prices soared,
leaving many people disillusioned with their leadership.

According to the National Bank of Sierra Leone,
prior to Steven's rule diamonds generated about
$200 million in profits in Sierra Leone's formal econ-
omy and provided 70 percent of foreign exchange
reserves. Under Stevens, however, the country's legitimate diamond industry quickly deteriorated. By
1987 diamonds passing through formal, taxable
channels were valued at only $100,000. Combined
with little economic diversification and insufficient
capital from FOREIGN INVESTMENT, the economy
quickly spiralled out of control.

The spread of CORRUPTION among figures in Stevens' government and throughout the civil service exacerbated Sierra Leone's socioeconomic and political
troubles. Popular unrest resulted in a number of attacks
by both civilian and army personnel. These included student riots as well as an assassination attempt on one of
Steven's vice presidents by a group of soldiers.

Political Instability Leads to Civil War In 1985
Stevens turned over the presidency to his handpicked successor, Joseph Momoh (1937–2003), who led the country
until 1992. That year, a group of disgruntled junior officers,
led by Valentine STRASSER (1965–), confronted Momoh
about the nonpayment of their salaries. Their protest escalated into a military coup d'état, and Strasser, merely 26
years old, ended up replacing Momoh as Sierra Leone's
leader. Beyond the nonpayment of their salaries, Strasser
and his fellow coup members were bitter about the situation that unfolded in 1991, when rebels attacked Sierra
Leone from Liberia. Led by Foday SANKOH (1937–2003),
the rebels, known as the REVOLUTIONARY UNITED FRONT
(RUF), claimed to want to end political corruption in Sierra
Leone. After they entered the country, however, they were
more interested in controlling the country's only sure
source of income, its diamond mines. In their efforts to take
control of the mines, RUF rebels killed, raped, maimed, and
otherwise terrorized thousands of Sierra Leoneans during a
brutal war that lasted 10 years.

In January 1996 Brigadier Julius Maada Bio (1964–)
overthrew Strasser, who was exiled to Guinea. In elections
held in March 1996, Ahmad Tejan KABBAH (1932–)
emerged victorious to become Sierra Leone's third president. Kabbah signed a peace accord with the RUF, in
November 1996, but the accord fell apart by the end of
the following year. Disenchanted by Kabbah's leadership,
Sankoh and an interim government called the Armed
Forces Revolutionary Council (AFRC), ousted Kabbah in
a coup. After fleeing to neighboring Guinea, Kabbah
began lobbying for international support to return him
to power. As a result of Kabbah's efforts, the United
Nations and neighboring West African states began applying sanctions to Sierra Leone. At the same time,
Britain also suspended the country's membership in the
British Commonwealth.

In February 1998 Nigerian-led ECOMOG forces—
the military arm of the ECONOMIC COMMUNITY OF WEST
AFRICAN STATES—drove the rebels and AFRC troops out of
Freetown, thus paving the way for Kabbah's return, in
1998. Peace was short-lived, however. The RUF attacked
the capital in January 1999, leaving an estimated 5,000
dead and thousands more maimed and injured. RUF
troops also looted and burned hundreds of homes before
ECOMOG forces finally drove them out. By July 1999,
when government and RUF leaders finally signed a peace
accord in LOMÉ, TOGO, Sierra Leone was one of the most
dangerous and least developed countries in the world.

> By signing the Lomé peace treaty, Foday Sankoh was given amnesty and allowed to live under house arrest, in Freetown. In May 2000, however, an angry mob of 20,000 civilians forced him from his home and captured him. Although he survived the ordeal, Sankoh was shot in the leg, beaten, and paraded naked through the streets of Freetown.

With both sides exhausted, the war was officially declared over in January 2002. In largely peaceful elections held in May 2002, Kabbah's Sierra Leone People's Party won a landslide victory. Although Sankoh died by what appeared to be natural causes while in UN custody, the other rebel leaders were tried by a special UN war-crimes court for crimes against humanity. This, along with a Truth and Reconciliation Commission, has led the way in uniting the war-torn country and mending rifts caused by decades of chronic social and economic instability.

See also: CIVIL WARS (Vol. V); SIERRA LEONE (Vols. I, II, III, IV); UNITED NATIONS AND AFRICA (Vols. IV, V).

Further reading: Earl Conteh-Morgan and Mac Dixon-Fyle, *Sierra Leone at the End of the Twentieth Century: History, Politics, and Society* (New York: P. Lang, 1999); Mariane C. Ferme, *The Underneath of Things: Violence, History, and the Everyday in Sierra Leone* (Berkeley, Calif.: University of California Press, 2001); Brett Sillinger, ed., *Sierra Leone: Current Issues and Background* (New York: Nova Science, 2003).

Sierra Leone People's Party (SLPP) Founded in 1951, the Sierra Leone People's Party governed SIERRA LEONE at independence, returning to power, following a COUP D'ÉTAT, in the 1990s. The party's symbol is the palm tree, its color is green, and its motto is "One Nation One People."

The SLPP brought together three political parties: the Peoples Party (PP), the Protectorate Education Progressive Union (PEPU), and the Sierra Leone Organization Society (SOS). The party led Sierra Leone to a peacefully negotiated independence, in April 1963, under the leadership of Sir Milton Margai (1896–1964). Margai became the first prime minister of Sierra Leone and served until his death, in 1964, when his half-brother, Sir Albert Margai (1910–1980), took over. The SLPP remained the governing party in Sierra Leone until 1967, when it was defeated by the All Peoples Congress (APC) headed by Siaka Stevens (1905–1988). Many of the SLPP members were ethnic Mende, and the organization was widely perceived as representing Mende interests. This view was reinforced by the fact that the primarily Mende southern

and eastern provinces, along with the western area around the capital FREETOWN, were relatively more developed than the northern province, which was mainly Temne. Additionally, economic mismanagement during Sir Albert's leadership contributed to the APC's rise in popularity. Ultimately, the SLPP went down in defeat to Siaka Stevens, who pledged extensive reform as part of his campaign platform.

Between 1967 and 1978 many members of SLPP were imprisoned, along with other opposition politicians. In 1978 Stevens instituted one-party rule, outlawing all other political parties, including the SLPP. The party was resurrected in 1995 following a referendum reinstating multiparty rule. Headed by Ahmad Tejan KABBAH (1932–   ), the SLPP emerged victorious in the March 1996 elections. The party has since governed through turbulent times, facilitating the transition to a peaceful Sierra Leone in the aftermath of the defeat of the REVOLUTIONARY UNITED FRONT. The original SLPP motto, "One Country, One People," was expanded in 1995, following the transition back to political pluralism, to include "The only way out, the only way forward, the only way through, and power to the people."

See also: ETHNICITY AND IDENTITY (Vol. V); MARGAI, MILTON (Vol. IV); MENDE (Vol. III); POLITICAL PARTIES AND ORGANIZATIONS (Vols. IV, V).

Sisulu, Albertina (Nontsikelelo Albertina Metetiwe Sisulu) (1918–   ) *South African antiapartheid activist*

The eldest of five orphaned children, Albertina Nontsikelelo was born in the Transkei, SOUTH AFRICA. After gaining certification as a nurse in JOHANNESBURG, she became politically involved as a result of her involvement with Walter SISULU (1912–2003), a pivotal member of the Youth League within the AFRICAN NATIONAL CONGRESS (ANC). They married in 1944. Walter's political activities and prolonged incarceration on ROBBEN ISLAND (1964–89) kept them apart for most of their marriage.

Albertina Sisulu joined the ANC Women's League, in 1948, and co-founded the Federation of South African Women, in 1954. During the 1950s she actively opposed the implementation of BANTU EDUCATION and the extension of the government's pass system to African women. For her defiance Sisulu was repeatedly subjected to state harassment, including detention, imprisonment, house arrest, and multiple banning orders, which prevented her from meeting with more than two people at any one time.

In 1983 she helped found the UNITED DEMOCRATIC FRONT (UDF), the leading organization dedicated to coordinating opposition groups in the struggle against APARTHEID. In 1984 she was sentenced to four years' imprisonment for her ANC-related activities, but the sentence was subsequently dismissed. Beginning in 1991 Sisulu served on the ANC's National Executive Committee, and when free democratic elections were introduced to South Africa, in 1994, she was elected to office as a member of Parliament representing the ANC.

Despite repeated detentions and the rigorous demands of her political activism, Albertina Sisulu raised five children. Because of her husband's political activities and extended absences, she also had to assume the role as the family's principal breadwinner and head. A number of her children and grandchildren played roles in the dismantling of the apartheid state, also suffering imprisonment and exile in the process. In addition to her parliamentary duties, she serves as president of the World Peace Council and is involved with numerous other organizations.

See also: WOMEN IN INDEPENDENT AFRICA (Vol. V).

Sisulu, Walter (Walter Max Ulyate Sisulu)

(1912–2003) *Leading figure of the African National Congress in South Africa*

A key leader of the AFRICAN NATIONAL CONGRESS (ANC) from the early 1940s, Walter Sisulu was committed to ending APARTHEID in SOUTH AFRICA. Because of his political activism he was frequently the target of government harassment and arrest. The tempo of repression against Sisulu and other anti-government activists greatly increased, beginning in 1960, when he was detained during the state of emergency that was imposed following the police massacre at SHARPEVILLE. After being arrested six times in 1962, Sisulu went underground. In 1963 he joined UMKHONTO WE SIZWE (Spear of the Nation), the ANC's armed wing, but he was arrested in July of the same year. At the Rivonia Trial in 1964 he served as the chief defense witness for his colleagues, who included Nelson MANDELA (1918–), Govan MBEKI (1910–2001), Raymond Mhlaba (1920–), Ahmad Kathrada (1920–), Lionel Bernstein (1920–2002), and Bob Hepple (1934–). The accused were found guilty but, against expectations, were not sentenced to death. Most of the defendants, including Sisulu, were sentenced to life imprisonment.

Named for the suburb of JOHANNESBURG where the accused were arrested in 1963, the Rivonia Trial did much to bring the injustices of apartheid to the attention of the international community. At the trial, held in PRETORIA, South African prosecutors brought treason and sabotage charges against Sisulu and his codefendants. All were found guilty.

From 1964 to 1984 Sisulu, along with Mandela, Mbeki, Kathrada, and Mhlaba, were imprisoned on ROBBEN ISLAND, which had become the principal prison for ANC and other black anti-government political activists. In 1984 he was transferred to Pollsmoor Prison, in CAPE TOWN. Finally, in 1989 Sisulu was released and reunited with his wife, Albertina SISULU (1918–).

Walter Sisulu went on to assume an active role in the ANC during the early 1990s, serving as deputy president from 1991 until 1994 and participating in negotiations between the ANC and the government of F. W. DE KLERK (1936–). Those negotiations culminated in the formation of South Africa's first multiparty, black-majority government. After 1994, well into his eighties, Sisulu continued to assist the ANC, working out of its headquarters in Johannesburg. In addition to his own direct political legacy, his son, Zwelakhe (1950–), a LABOR union leader and journalist, and his daughter, Lindiwe Nonceba (1954–), a member of Parliament, carry on the family tradition of political activism on behalf of the disadvantaged African majority.

See also: LABOR UNIONS (Vols. IV, V).

Sithole, Ndabaningi (1920–2000) *Zimbabwe politician*

A teacher by profession, Sithole made the leap into politics in 1960 when he joined the National Democratic Party (NDP), a nationalist movement headed by Joshua NKOMO (1917–1999) that was pushing for Southern Rhodesia's independence from Britain. Sithole became an executive member and rose to the position of treasurer. In 1962 the colonial government banned the NDP, leading to the immediate birth of the ZIMBABWE AFRICAN PEOPLE'S UNION (ZAPU). The following year dissension over Nkomo's leadership led to a split in the organization, with Sithole forming the ZIMBABWE AFRICAN NATIONAL UNION (ZANU).

At this time the political upheaval in Southern Rhodesia was increasing dramatically. Along with Northern Rhodesia and Nyasaland, the colony had been part of the Central African Federation beginning in 1953. However, that union collapsed in 1963, and Northern Rhodesia and Nyasaland achieved independence as ZAMBIA and MALAWI, respectively. Southern Rhodesia, now renamed simply RHODESIA, remained a colony of Britain.

In 1964 Ian SMITH (1919–), the Rhodesian prime minister banned ZAPU and ZANU and placed Sithole, Nkomo, and many others in detention. Then in 1965 Smith issued a UNILATERAL DECLARATION OF INDEPENDENCE from Britain. The former colonial power strenuously objected but did not send troops to reclaim the rebellious colony. This left Rhodesia in the control of a white-supremacist government that had no intentions of allowing Africans to participate in its country's political affairs.

As well as being a politician and clergyman, Sithole was also an author. In 1970 Oxford University Press published his *Obed Mutezo of Zimbabwe*, which Sithole had written while in prison, smuggling out the manuscript. The book is a biographical account of the events that led Obed Mutezo, a man from an ordinary, rural background, to join the nationalist movement. Oxford had also published Sithole's earlier *African Nationalism,* which stated the case for the African position within Southern Rhodesia.

Sithole was held in detention until 1969, when he was put on trial for an alleged assassination plot against Smith. He was sentenced to another six years imprisonment. Following his release in 1974 Sithole attempted to play a role in Zimbabwe's preparations for an African-led government, brought about by British pressure on Smith and continuing guerrilla warfare led by militant factions of both ZANU and ZAPU. In spite of Sithole's efforts, however, it was his rival, Robert MUGABE (1924–), who became prime minister of newly independent ZIMBABWE in 1980.

All told Sithole was arrested and put on trial three times for allegedly plotting assassinations. In 1969 he was convicted for plotting to take the life of Prime Minister Ian Smith. The next two times (1995 and 1996) he was accused of involvement in plots against ZANU leader and Zimbabwean president Robert Mugabe. Evidence against Sithole was weak in all three cases, and Sithole firmly declared each time that he had been falsely accused.

After independence Zimbabwe remained politically unstable. In the face of an intense—and frequently violent—political struggle, Sithole fled to the United States in 1987. He returned to Zimbabwe in 1991, however, and attempted to regain his political prominence. His efforts faltered and finally collapsed when the government levied charges against him accusing him of plotting to take Mugabe's life. Fearing the consequences of a guilty verdict, Sithole traveled back to the United States in 1997. He died after a heart operation in 2000.

See also: CENTRAL AFRICAN FEDERATION (Vol. IV); COLONIAL RULE (Vol. IV); ENGLAND AND AFRICA (Vols. III, IV, V); SITHOLE, NDABANINGI (Vol. IV).

Smith, Ian (1919–) *Prime minister of former Rhodesia (present-day Zimbabwe)*

Ian Smith was born in Selukwe, Southern Rhodesia. After completing high school he enrolled in Rhodes University in Grahamstown, SOUTH AFRICA. World War II (1939–45), however, interrupted his studies. He joined the British Royal Air Force and was a pilot in the North African and Italian theaters of war. On returning home Smith completed his commerce degree, married Janet Watt, with whom he had three children, and became a rancher. His political career began with a stint in the Legislative Assembly (1948–53) and continued with his election to the federal Parliament of the Central African Federation (CAF). In 1958 he became the chief government whip under Prime Minister Roy Welensky (1907–1991).

Smith came into the public eye during his time as prime minister of Rhodesia. A believer in white supremacy, he insisted that political control of Southern Rhodesia remain with whites, despite the position of blacks as the country's overwhelming majority. Resisting pressure from Britain for such changes he became one of the founders of the Rhodesian Front (RF) party. It became the majority party in the Southern Rhodesian Legislative Assembly and was in control of the government in 1964, when the dissolution of the CAF occurred and the country's name changed to RHODESIA. By this time, Smith was prime minister.

Ian Smith came to be referred to as "Iron Man Ian" or "Good Old Smithy" by his fellow white Rhodesians for his strong views regarding the racial supremacy of the white minority. His memoirs, *The Great Betrayal*, published in 1997, showed that he continued to persist in his views long after white-ruled Rhodesia was but a historical memory.

On November 11, 1965, Smith issued a UNILATERAL DECLARATION OF INDEPENDENCE (UDI) announcing Rhodesia's secession from the British Empire. Although he sought to evoke the ideals of the American Declaration of Independence to justify this move, the UDI was issued for the purpose of maintaining white-minority rule over the African majority. For several years Smith and his government negotiated with Britain in an effort to seek international legitimacy for Rhodesia, but internal African opposition prevented an agreement. In the meantime, a guerrilla war gradually escalated and put sufficient pressure on the government that Smith was forced to allow free elections. In 1979 Bishop Abel MUZOREWA (1925–) led his African National Council to electoral victory and replaced Smith as prime minister of what was now Zimbabwe-Rhodesia. Effective control of the military, police, and civil service, however, remained in white hands and Smith essentially remained the real head of state. This arrangement could not hold in the face of growing guerrilla and international pressure, however, and within a few months the Muzorewa government agreed to recognize Britain's sovereignty over the country. Britain in turn then granted the country independence under the name of ZIMBABWE, with Robert MUGABE (1924–   ) as the prime minister. The new constitutional arrangement granted whites 20 out of 100 seats in Parliament, and Smith remained a member until 1987, leading the RF opposition to Mugabe.

See also: CENTRAL AFRICAN FEDERATION (Vol. IV); ENGLAND AND AFRICA (Vols. IV, V); SOUTHERN RHODESIA (Vol. IV).

Sobhuza II (1899–1982) *King of Swaziland*

When Ngwane V (1876–1899) died in 1899, his infant son, Nkhotfotjeni, became the next monarch of SWAZILAND. The great-grandson of the first Swazi king, Sobhuza I (1785–1836), Nkhotfotjeni became Sobhuza II, though he did not actually assume power until some 20 years later. His grandmother, Ndlovukazi Labotsibeni, ruled as queen regent in the meantime.

Driven by her desire to regain Swazi lands lost to European encroachment, Labotsibeni groomed Sobhuza II to become a powerful leader. The young king was educated in Swaziland and at Lovedale College in SOUTH AFRICA. As Sobhuza II was preparing to take the throne, however, Britain established colonial rule over Swaziland. In 1907 Britain divided the nation among concessionaire companies, and the Swazis lost more than 60 percent of their lands.

In 1921 Sobhuza II became the official monarch of Swaziland, taking the title of Ngwenyama, or "the Lion." The following year he led a delegation to England demanding the return of his people's lands. Though this initial effort fell short, Sobhuza II continued to campaign over the next 15 years and ultimately succeeded in recouping an additional 13 percent of the Swazis' original lands.

Sobhuza II was a highly traditional leader, but he was also open to those western influences. When Swaziland finally gained independence in 1968, Sobhuza II continued to rule as an absolute monarch, preserving one of the few monarchies to survive colonialism.

Upon his country's independence Sobhuza II remarked, "As one of the last countries to achieve independence, we have had the opportunity of learning from nations which have won their independence before us. We have watched them crossing rivers [and] have seen [them] being swallowed by crocodiles. Now that we have seen the crocodile-infested drifts, we shall try to cross through crocodile-free drifts to a peaceful, independent Swaziland."

In 1973, facing political opposition, Sobhuza II further consolidated his power by suspending the constitution and abolishing both the Parliament and all political parties. His death in 1982 marked the end of a 60-year reign, the longest of any monarch of his time. After a lengthy interregnum, the Crown Prince Makhosetive (1968–   ), one of Sobhuza's 67 sons, became King MSWATI III.

Sobhuza, who was also known as "the Great Mountain," "the Bull," and "the Inexplicable," was greatly revered by the Swazi people. Upon his death all members of the Swazi kingdom shaved their heads as a symbol of their loss.

Sobukwe, Robert (1924–1978) *Leader of the Pan-Africanist Congress in South Africa*

A political activist from his student days at FORT HARE COLLEGE in the late 1950s, Robert Mangaliso Sobukwe broke with the AFRICAN NATIONAL CONGRESS (ANC) and co-founded the PAN-AFRICANIST CONGRESS (PAC). He believed that ANC's alliances with the anti-APARTHEID organizations representing other racial groups compromised the ANC's goals and undermined the self-confidence of black Africans. To signal its greater militancy and to increase its national stature, the PAC organized a campaign against pass books, the identity documents that Africans were legally compelled to carry at all times. Those who wished to participate in the protests were enjoined to report to police stations without their pass books and offer themselves up for arrest. On March 21, 1960, the first day of the campaign, nervous police opened fire on a peaceful crowd of African protesters outside a police station in SHARPEVILLE, resulting in 69 deaths. Sobukwe was arrested for incitement and imprisoned for three years.

When he was released he was rearrested by virtue of the so-called Sobukwe clause, which effectively meant that the government reserved the right to detain, without benefit of a trial, any person deemed to be a threat to the state. As a consequence, Sobukwe was sentenced to an additional six years, which he served on ROBBEN ISLAND. He was imprisoned in a small house, away from the other political prisoners, who included Nelson MANDELA (1918–   ). Upon Sobukwe's release from prison in 1969 he settled in Kimberley. However, he continued to be banned from meeting with more than one person at a time or from being quoted in the media. He was also forbidden to leave SOUTH AFRICA. While in prison Sobukwe received an economics degree from the University of London and also began studying law via correspondence. He ultimately established a law practice in Kimberley.

Sobukwe died of lung cancer in 1978. The Africanist philosophy he developed influenced the next generation of African political activists, particularly Steve BIKO (1946–1977), one of the most prominent anti-apartheid leaders during the 1970s, and others affiliated with the BLACK CONSCIOUSNESS MOVEMENT.

See also: KIMBERLEY (Vol. IV).

Further reading: Gail M. Gerhart, *Black Power in South Africa: The Evolution of an Ideology* (Berkeley, Calif.: University of California Press, 1978).

social capital Sociological concept that implies that trust among citizens, social networks, and community institutions has positive effects on democracy and economic growth. According to some social theorists, social capital is the assessed value of our social networks and the things we do for those we know. Like economic capital, social capital can be increased, spent, and depleted. For instance, as we exchange recipes with our neighbors, notes with our colleagues, and secrets with our friends, we build trust. This makes it more likely that we will share important information that we have, or impart our personal beliefs, such as whom we will vote for in an election. Churches, schools, civic associations, and even sports clubs can all be important venues for building social capital.

For most people, life is easier in communities where there is high social capital. Simply put, where there is a high level of social capital, people trust each other more so they help each other more. Whole networks of people emerge from such trust, making coordination and cooperation easier. This, in turn, leads to collective action and improved results. When people in positions of authority, such as politicians and powerful business interests, must live up to a collective, societal trust, the incentives for opportunism and CORRUPTION are reduced.

Those who believe in the idea of social capital maintain that it adds to a sense of civic identity. Therefore it is more likely that individuals will act in groups to express their views in a democratic fashion, achieving a more robust citizen rule. However, this is not always the case, particularly in Africa.

Social capital is not based on prescribed norms. It builds common views without particular attention to the "good" of any form of organization or rule. Instead of supporting democracy, it may build a common anger toward a government or business class that is exploiting the broader population. It may bring people together, in fact, to resist, rather than support, change. And it may actually help to undermine the growth of civic institutions that support a government that people do not like. This is a particular threat where economic liberalization, commonly thought of as the driving force behind economic DEVELOPMENT, leads to dramatically negative effects on key parts of the population of a country. For instance, in TANZANIA, President Julius NYERERE (1922–1999) created the UJAMAA policies of collective action. These policies significantly reduced ethnic, religious, and regional tensions in the country, but at the same time these policies undermined the nation's economic goals. Although a period of economic liberalization followed, *ujamaa* heightened the sense of individualism and eroded much of the newly established social unity. As a result, in recent years the overall economy has improved, but the average Tanzanian is both poorer and less likely to trust, or act in concert with, his or her neighbors.

Social capital is exceedingly important in Africa, where countries are trying simultaneously to change both political and economic institutions. More than 60 percent of sub-Saharan Africa lives a rural, agrarian lifestyle, precisely the population in which the forces of social capital are often weak. Indeed, contrary to the common myth, evidence shows that the majority of people in rural Africa prefer to solve problems on their own rather than in a group. As a result, among these populations there usually isn't the social capital necessary to form the networks that can support democratic civic change.

The growth of social capital in Africa is slow. Moreover the ability of African social capital to contribute to a desired political end is uncertain. Still there is evidence to suggest that a high level of social capital has a positive impact on household welfare in African communities. That is, an increase in social capital helps add to an increase in economic capital. For instance, when the government of SOUTH AFRICA entered into its Reconstruction and Development Program, it encouraged a social, political, and economic transformation that increased social capital. As trust and networks of trust grew, so did work opportunity and efficiency, which led to an increase in household expenditure among people participating in the program. Likewise, in SOMALIA the fall of the government in 1991 led to great upheaval. But in the Somali city of Boosaaso a high level of social capital encourage a flourishing of trade that led to a rapid increase in local incomes.

Further reading: Partha Dasgubta and Ismail Serageldin, eds., *Social Capital: a Multifaceted Perspective* (Washington D.C.: World Bank, 2000).

Somalia Country located in the Horn of Africa, bordered by DJIBOUTI to the northwest, the Gulf of Aden and the Indian Ocean to the north and east, and KENYA and ETHIOPIA to the west. The country covers approximately 246,000 square miles (637,100 sq km). Its nominal capital is MOGADISHU, though in recent years warring factions and various secessions have rendered any central government in Somalia ineffective.

Somalia at Independence In 1960 the former protectorate of British Somaliland and the trust territory of Italian Somaliland joined to become the United Republic of Somalia. Abdullah Osman Daar (1908–) of the dominant southern Somali Youth League (SYL) became president. Independence held great promise, as the ethnically uniform country experienced wide political freedom and participation. However, the fault lines were already drawn that would lead to a complete rupturing of the country in later years. Similar to countries such as CHAD and the Republic of the SUDAN, Somalia was deeply divided between its northern and southern populations. The economic and political dominance of the south, where Mogadishu is situated, created an imbalance of power in the country. In addition, although Somalia was almost entirely ethnically Somali, conflicts among various Somali clans, including the Majerteen, Mareehaan, Isaaq, and Hawiye, caused rifts not unlike those experienced in more ethnically divided nations like NIGERIA and RWANDA. Added to these conditions was the drive for a "Greater Somalia," a goal outlined in the national constitution that entailed the uniting of the Somali people in French Somaliland (now DJIBOUTI), in the Ogaden region of Ethiopia, and in the southern region, along the border with Kenya. Disorganized attempts to claim these regions ultimately destabilized all of Somalia.

Tensions between the north and the south boiled over for the first time in 1961 when, following political disputes over southern political dominance, northern military groups revolted against southern command. Also, in 1964 war broke out between Somalia and Ethiopia after four years of border skirmishes. The conflict only lasted a few months, but it was a harbinger of things to come.

Somalia under Barre In 1967 clan politics, arguments over the use of force to create "Greater Somalia," and party defections combined to destabilize the government. In 1969 President Abdirashid Ali Sharmarke was assassinated by a disgruntled member of a clan long powerless in the government. In the period of uncertainty that followed, a military group backed by the SYL seized power and brought Major General Mohammed Siad BARRE (1910–1995) in to serve as president. Barre immediately eliminated all threats to his power by disbanding the National Assembly, suspending the constitution, and outlawing political parties.

Somalia came under Barre's unique form of "scientific socialism," which combined Quranic teachings with Marxism and Barre's own cult of personality, which was evident in the appearance of multiple public portraits of the president in the company of such Communist figureheads as Karl Marx (1818–1883) and Vladimir Lenin (1870–1924). Barre's socialist position earned him the support of the Soviet Union, but in reality Barre's government was an autocratic regime kept in place through Barre's deft manipulation of clan politics and violent repression of opponents.

In 1977 Barre upset a temporary peace with Ethiopia by attempting once again to capture the Ogaden region. While an uprising at home sabotaged the effort, Ethiopian troops fended off the incursion and, in 1978, inflicted a humiliating defeat on the Somali military. Sporadic warfare continued in the region over the next 10 years. Ethiopian retribution forced Somalis living in the Ogaden back into Somalia, causing a massive wave of REFUGEES that the country was ill-equipped to handle. With the treasury dry, Barre became even more ruthless in his attempt to maintain power. He also tried to play the game of Cold War politics to secure funding, appealing to the United States, which had formerly supported Ethiopia. Employing increasingly brutal tactics, including letting his Red Beret soldiers unleash murderous campaigns against opposing clans, Barre held onto power until 1991, when guerrilla groups finally ousted the Somali strongman.

The 1990s: Descent into Chaos After Barre's fall from power, Somalia began to fracture. A region of northern Somalia declared itself independent of the rest of the country and named itself the Somaliland Republic, though the new country was never formally recognized by foreign nations. The national capital of Mogadishu became a battlefield between competing militias, led on one side by Mohammed Ali Mahdi and on the other by Mohammed AIDEED (1934–1996). Ultimately the fighting and a devastating drought combined to kill more than 300,000 Somalis. Troops from the United Nations and the United States attempted to establish a peace and bring in much-needed food supplies, but the continuing violence undermined both efforts. In particular, a 1993 U.S. attempt to capture Aideed turned into a debacle in which a number of U.S. soldiers died, leading the western power to end its military efforts in Somalia.

With no central government, Mogadishu and much of southern Somalia fell into chaos. Despite this, the Somaliland Republic, a semi-independent state in northern Somalia, basically remained stable and even saw its economy grow. In 1998 both Puntland, in northeastern Somalia, and Jubaland, in the south, also seceded from greater Somalia. A conference in 2000 established a new national government that was largely ignored, and in 2002 the region of Southwestern Somaliland declared independence. This final secession left Somalia at three-quarters the size it was at independence. In late 2002 a cease-fire was approved by all except the Somaliland Republic, but fragmented Somalia remains far from any real stability.

See also: CIVIL WARS (Vol. V); ETHNICITY AND IDENTITY (Vol. V); PUNT (Vol. I); SOMALIA (Vols. I, II, III, IV); UNITED NATIONS AND AFRICA (Vol. V); UNITED STATES AND AFRICA (Vols. IV, V).

South Africa Large, economically dominant nation at the southern tip of Africa, with an area of approximately 470,700 square miles (1,219,100 sq km), that contains several diverse ecosystems, many of them renowned for their unique beauty. South Africa completely surrounds the country of LESOTHO and is bordered by NAMIBIA to the northwest, by BOTSWANA and ZIMBABWE to the north, and by MOZAMBIQUE and SWAZILAND to the east.

With a large population of about 44,000,000 (in 2000) and an impressive array of mineral resources, South Africa towers above other nations in southern Africa as an economic and political colossus. It possesses the most industrialized economy on the continent, and the highest levels of managerial and technical expertise among its varied population. Yet it has had a turbulent history. In 1994 the map of South Africa was significantly redrawn. In place of its previous four provinces, which included the Cape, Natal, Orange Free State, and the Transvaal, and the so-called homelands, nine new provinces were created (Western Cape, Eastern Cape, Northern Cape, North-West, KwaZulu-Natal, Free State, Gauteng, Northern, and Mpumalanga). In addition, the new South Africa adopted fully 11 official languages (including also Ndebele, Northern Sotho, Southern Sotho, Swazi, Tsonga, Tswana, Venda, XHOSA, and ZULU), instead of only English and AFRIKAANS.

Further reflecting the emphasis given African culture, the popular "Nkosi sikelel' iAfrica" (God Bless Africa) joined "Die Stem van Suid Afrika" (The Call of South Africa) as the country's two official national anthems. Despite the new constitution (approved in December 1996 and implemented in stages over the following three years) and changed composition of government, South Africa continued to maintain three capitals: PRETORIA (administrative); CAPE TOWN (legislative), and Bloemfontein (judicial).

State Repression in the 1960s Following the political turbulence of the early 1960s, political quiescence characterized the remainder of the decade. Even though former colonies were achieving independence throughout Africa, South Africa moved in the opposite direction. Instead of relaxing settler control and moving toward a power-sharing arrangement with South Africa's majority black population, the government, led by the National Party (NP), intensified attacks on the African urban population. It attempted to separate the different racial groups within South Africa, in part by consigning Africans to nominally independent BANTUS-TANS or "homelands" that the government sought to develop in various parts of the country.

By and large, the government's repressive tactics aimed at crushing the opposition were successful for the duration of the decade and into the early 1970s. They did, however, transform South Africa into a police state, where basic civil liberties were abridged or altogether vio-lated on a routine basis. Economically, the country enjoyed a remarkable and sustained boom, which boosted the living standard of white South Africans to among the highest in the world, even while black South Africans lived in desperate POVERTY. The government's ability to maintain political stability resulted in confidence among foreign investors and a willingness of whites from other parts of the world to immigrate to South Africa.

At the same time, South Africa's standing in the international community progressively eroded. The criticism that the United Nations directed at South Africa became increasingly urgent beginning in the 1960s. In addition to its legally entrenched APARTHEID policies coming under intense scrutiny, the country's defiant refusal to surrender SOUTH WEST AFRICA (today's NAMIBIA), which it originally administered as a League of Nations mandate, also subjected South Africa to condemnation. In October 1966 the United Nations General Assembly voted to end South African administration. Five years later the International Court of Justice reaffirmed the illegal nature of South Africa's control of Namibia. In 1973 the UN General Assembly went so far as to declare apartheid "a crime against humanity." Four years later the UN Security Council authorized an arms embargo against the country.

Mounting Black Resistance The relative political calm that followed the neutralization of the African opposition in the first half of the 1960s was shattered, in 1973, by the outbreak of LABOR unrest among black workers. Faced with low wages, mounting inflation, and high unemployment, workers engaged in a series of illegal strikes. During the first three months of 1973 alone, more than 600 strikes were organized in DURBAN. Work stoppages and labor unrest soon spread to other industrial centers in the country. The government was slow to respond, with four years passing before it established the Wiehahn Commission of Inquiry to investigate the plight of black labor. In 1979, acting on the commission's recommendations, the state took the unprecedented step of offering legal recognition of LABOR UNIONS with African workers. But what appeared to be an important concession, was in fact a subtle attempt to impose greater control on black unionization by imposing a battery of restrictions on registered unions. In the meantime impatience with pervasive workplace exploitation and intolerable working conditions grew and fed the widespread discontent among black South Africans.

The founding of the BLACK CONSCIOUSNESS MOVEMENT (BCM) in the late 1960s fueled yet greater militancy among young black South Africans. Steve BIKO (1946–1977), a student activist from within the ranks of the multiracial National Union of South African Students (NUSAS), broke with NUSAS to found the SOUTH AFRICAN STUDENTS ORGANIZATION (SASO) in 1969. Biko was the BCM's most visible and gifted leader and proved instrumental in popularizing its appeal. The BCM ideology stressed black pride and the need for black independence from white assistance. Organizations under the BCM umbrella, like SASO and the Black Peoples Convention, exercised a profound impact on a new generation of black South Africans coming of age, instilling in them a heightened race consciousness and a fierce determination to end discrimination on the basis of race. Not coincidentally, in the years to follow, the greatest impetus toward overthrowing the apartheid regime, was spearheaded by African youth.

The full-scale struggle against apartheid was triggered on June 16, 1976, by the shooting of African students who were protesting against mandatory instruction in Afrikaans in their school curricula. Since Africans long associated AFRIKANERS and their language, Afrikaans, with apartheid and oppression, resentment ran high. The initial protest occurred in SOWETO, a township southwest of JOHANNESBURG, inhabited by black South Africans. In short order, however, riots and protests spread to other urban centers across the country. Black youth rose up in revolt, attacking symbols of state control. In particular, black policemen and black politicians cooperating with white authorities were singled out for attack and often killed.

In response, the government declared a state of emergency and carried on a campaign of repression against all forms of anti-government agitation. Thousands of protesters were arrested, and hundreds died. Most notably, Steve Biko was killed while in police custody. Other protesters carried on the liberation struggle abroad, often joining the ranks of the PAN-AFRICANIST CONGRESS or UMKHONTO WE SIZWE (Spear of the Nation, known simply as MK), the military arm of the AFRICAN NATIONAL CONGRESS (ANC), South Africa's preeminent black opposition organization. Beginning in the 1970s, these guerrilla groups stepped up acts of sabotage against government targets.

The Unraveling of Apartheid The government responded to the MK's acts of sabotage with a campaign of violent repression that catapulted South African politics into the international spotlight, where it became the target of intense condemnation. At the same time the economy stalled. Further contributing to the pressure applied to the state, several neighboring countries that had once been friendly to South Africa's white-minority government gained their independence, and power transferred to African nationalist movements. Beginning in the mid-1960s, Botswana, Lesotho, and Swaziland achieved their independence from British colonial rule. Then in 1975, Mozambique and ANGOLA finally overcame Portugal's armed attempts to maintain them as colonies. African pro-Marxist leaders gained power in both countries, and gave support to the enemies of the apartheid state. After 1980 when Zimbabwe's African majority wrested control from the white UNILATERAL DECLARATION OF INDEPENDENCE government of Ian SMITH (1919–),

South Africa could no longer count on the assistance or moral support of its neighbors. In fact, the new Zimbabwean president, Robert MUGABE (1924–), and his ZIMBABWE AFRICAN NATIONAL UNION were vehemently opposed to the racial policies of South Africa.

In the West numerous governments cut off trade with South Africa and otherwise imposed restrictions on investment. Some MULTINATIONAL CORPORATIONS cut back or altogether eliminated their operations in South Africa. Additionally, many public and private institutions divested themselves of any capital holdings in the South African economy.

Further complicating the attempts to shore up apartheid, many professional and skilled whites, particularly among the English-speaking community, fled South Africa, emigrating to Western countries. This exodus of entrepreneurs, managers, scientists, engineers, educators, and journalists ebbed and flowed, starting in the mid-1970s and continues to the present day.

Responding to this general economic crisis, Prime Minister P. W. BOTHA (1916–), who succeeded John Vorster (1917–1983), in 1978, responded aggressively to the changed domestic and international circumstances. He embarked on a series of reforms, which were more cosmetic than real, dismantling some of the features of apartheid. Africans became legally entitled to occupy skilled industrial positions for the first time since the 1920s, and the hated pass system, which profoundly limited the mobility of Africans, was eliminated in 1985. In an especially controversial move, Botha introduced a three-chamber parliament, one which gave representation to Coloured and Indian South Africans but, significantly, excluded South Africa's majority population group—black Africans. Spirited opposition to this initiative emerged from all sides, including Coloureds and Indians. Perhaps most importantly, in 1983 the multiracial UNITED DEMOCRATIC FRONT (UDF) was established to fight this development. The UDF represented more than 500 organizations from among trade unions, civic associations, and various philanthropic groups dedicated to ending the inequities of apartheid. Among anti-apartheid groups, both those under the UDF umbrella and those without, opposition escalated and became increasingly militant and violent. Public protests, although illegal, frequently were held, most notably at the funerals of slain anti-apartheid activists. Strikes, boycotts, and marches collectively demonstrated the strength and determination of the liberation movement.

Botha responded by concentrating power at the center, empowering the State Security Council with extraordinary powers which had been the traditional purview of the cabinet. Furthermore, with the new constitution of 1984, Botha acquired the newly created position of state president. Despite these consolidating measures undertaken to carry out a "total onslaught" policy against the opposition, Botha was buffeted by criticism on both the left and the right. Hard-liners committed to maintaining the superstructure of apartheid in all its integrity opposed concessions of any kind. Many AFRIKANERS believed that the Botha government was selling their birthright to the African majority, and turned to alternative POLITICAL PARTIES AND ORGANIZATIONS that were further to the right.

The extreme right wing Afrikaner Resistance Movement (founded in 1979) and the Conservative Party (1982) joined with the existing Reconstituted National Party to signal an important shift among the Afrikaner electorate, which had traditionally proffered its allegiance to the NP unfailingly. In particular, the Conservative Party garnered a significant portion of the NP's core base of supporters, and pushed it to adopt a less liberal approach or risk political suicide. Within the Afrikaner community, the relative unity it once enjoyed broke down at more than just the political level. Several key Afrikaner business leaders opened talks with the ANC in exile, recognizing the inevitability of having to negotiate with the black majority.

Other developments also gave indication of the government's inability to stem the rising tide of opposition. In 1984 a renewed wave of anti-government protests sparked more violence. To meet the crisis the government declared a state of emergency the following year and deployed the South African Defense Force and police on a wide-ranging scale in the ill-fated attempt to impose order. Despite the efforts of South Africa's formidable security forces, the country's black townships became ungovernable.

International condemnation mounted in the wake of this new South African crackdown. The awarding of the 1984 Noble Peace Prize to Desmond TUTU (1931–), the Anglican archbishop vociferous in his opposition to South Africa's racial policies, was intended to send a unambiguous political message. The U.S. Congress passed the Comprehensive Anti-Apartheid Act, over the veto of President Ronald Reagan (1911–2004). It imposed restrictions on American capital investment, the importation of South African goods, and direct airline access between the two countries. The Reagan administration generally pursued a conciliatory approach toward South Africa, opting to promote progress in racial relations through positive incentives instead of public criticism. However, this approach, known as CONSTRUCTIVE ENGAGEMENT, yielded little in the way of tangible results. In fact it effectively played into the hands of the NP and Botha, who sought to indefinitely defer power sharing with the African majority. Similarly, Margaret Thatcher (1925–), prime minister of Britain, adopted a soft stance with respect to South Africa. In spite of the restraint called for by Reagan and Thatcher, international pressure mounted, and economic and diplomatic sanctions against South Africa increased dramatically. These measures, especially the

suspension of foreign capital investment, severely undermined the health of the already struggling South African economy.

Despite attempts by neighboring countries to undermine South Africa's economy and capacity to govern, the white South African government appeared invincible. Ultimately the FRONTLINE STATES, as these neighboring countries were called, depended on access to South African goods, ports, and markets. In addition, many workers from the Frontline States sent the wages they earned in South Africa to their families back home, providing a major infusion of capital. This income came largely through employment in the GOLD, diamond, and coal MINING industries. South Africa offered clandestine assistance to rebel factions within Angola and Mozambique to destabilize their governments and thus undermine their ability to provide support to anti-government forces.

The Road to Reconciliation Although the hardline position of Botha and the NP government promised no sign of relaxation, Botha suffered a stroke in 1988, precipitating a rapid and unprecedented sequence of events. Botha surrendered leadership of the NP to the Transvaal provincial leader of the NP, F. W. DE KLERK (1936–), and months later he was replaced by de Klerk as president. De Klerk began implementing meaningful changes to better integrate black South Africans into mainstream political life. He entered into substantive talks with Nelson MANDELA (1918–), the former leader of the ANC who had been imprisoned since 1963. As a result of their lengthy discussions, de Klerk and Mandela reached an understanding that would form the basis of future negotiations aimed at arriving at some new, yet unspecified political arrangement that would include African political participation. On December 2, 1990, de Klerk announced that Mandela and other political prisoners would be unconditionally released from prison. Opposition political parties were no longer banned, and the government entered into earnest negotiations for some form of power sharing with the formerly disenfranchised members of South African society.

The Convention for a Democratic South Africa, which opened in December 1991, eventually led to a compromise reached on November 13, 1993 between the NP and the ANC. The negotiations between the government and opposition groups, the ANC being the most prominent among the latter, were protracted and frequently acrimonious. The early 1990s witnessed considerable violence among rival political factions courting South Africa's black constituency, with right-wing white political groups alternatively threatening violence or the establishment of a separate state for whites only. Especially violent were clashes between supporters of the ANC and the Zulu-dominated INKATHA FREEDOM PARTY (IFP), led by Mangosuthu Gatsha BUTHELEZI (1928–). Tensions had simmered between the ANC and the IFP since the 1970s when the Inkatha movement was formed. Because Inkatha appealed exclusively to Zulus, and because it was willing to cooperate with the white state, the ANC and Inkatha were at ideological odds.

These differences took on a violent character in the late 1980s and early 1990s, often reflecting not only political and ethnic divisions, but also the gulf between Inkatha members, who were often rural and engaged in migrant labor, and ANC supporters, who tended to be more urban. Despite the danger of these tensions spilling over into warring factions, the various groupings were able to agree to an interim constitution and the principle of fully democratic national elections. In 1994, in recognition of their efforts toward a peaceful transition to a new, more inclusive political arena, de Klerk and Mandela were jointly awarded the Nobel Peace Prize. In April of 1994 South Africa held its first national elections in which all South Africans of age could vote. Twenty different political parties participated, but the ANC won 63 percent of the votes and subsequently formed a coalition government. Mandela became South Africa's first black president, and during his one-term presidency he distinguished himself for his attempts to include South Africans of all races, ethnicities, and political backgrounds in the new "Rainbow Nation." On the international stage, his high-profile statesmanship won widespread praise and drew international focus to South Africa's unique situation.

Challenges Facing the New South Africa

Despite South Africa's positive changes, little foreign capital has been invested in South African markets. In general, an unstable workforce combined with extraordinarily high rates of crime and violence have hindered the country's economic growth.

After a single term Mandela stepped aside in favor of his handpicked successor, executive deputy president, Thabo MBEKI (1942–). Mbeki and the ANC again won a convincing victory in the election of 1999.

Even though apartheid has crumbled and been replaced by democratic rule, the high expectations held by South Africans have not entirely been fulfilled. Many lingering divisions between the various political parties, races, ethnic and language-speaking groups, still are present in South Africa. Its future is also somewhat clouded by the horrific loss of lives as a result of exceptionally high rates of HIV/AIDS infection.

As a result of decades of apartheid a culture of violence is ingrained in South African society. The situation is made worse by high rates of gun ownership and the enormous gulf that separates rich from poor. The division often corresponds to the color line, with whites having a disproportionate share of the country's wealth. Despite nearly a decade of democratic rule and a controversial government program of affirmative action, formerly dispossessed South Africans still lack access to land, and their levels of training and EDUCATION continue to lag be-

hind those of whites. A large percentage of black South Africans still lack even basic services such as electricity, running water, and sewers. Eager to court FOREIGN INVESTMENT, the ANC-led government has charted a moderate fiscal policy with an approach that has largely been pro-business. This is surprising, given the ANC's past alliances with the South African Communist Party (SACP) and the labor movement, and in light of its own platform, embodied in the 1955 Freedom Charter, which called for a commitment to socialist policies. Not surprisingly, this fiscally conservative approach has hurt the ANC's relationship with organized labor and the SACP.

In the attempt to heal the many and deep wounds of the apartheid era, the TRUTH AND RECONCILIATION COMMISSION, a 17-member body that included Archbishop Tutu, was formed in April 1996 to hold hearings throughout the entire country. It sought to bring to light the atrocities and immeasurable suffering of the previous five decades, so that the nation could move forward. The commission partly succeeded in bringing a sense of closure to many victims of apartheid by exposing the gross injustices and inequities of the system.

See also: HIV/AIDS AND AFRICA (Vol. V); POLITICAL PARTIES AND ORGANIZATIONS (Vols. IV, V); SOUTH AFRICA (Vols. I, II, III, IV).

Further reading: Heather Deegan, *The Politics of the New South Africa: Apartheid and After* (New York: Longman, 2001); Tom Lodge, *Politics in South Africa: From Mandela to Mbeki*, 2nd ed. (Oxford, U.K.: James Currey, 2003); Robert Ross, *A Concise History of South Africa* (New York: Cambridge University Press, 1999); Leonard Thompson, *A History of South Africa,* 3rd ed. (New Haven, Conn.: Yale University Press, 2001).

South African Students Organization (SASO)

Anti-apartheid student group active in SOUTH AFRICA in the 1970s. During the mid-1960s the multiracial National Union of South African Students (NUSAS) gained support among black students looking for an outlet to express anti-government sentiments. NUSAS membership, however, was mostly white, and the organization gradually became ineffective. Unable to persuade NUSAS leadership to take a bolder stance in the fight against APARTHEID, the group's black members became increasingly disillusioned with the organization.

At the NUSAS 1967 Congress a group of black delegates led by Steve BIKO (1946–1977) initiated a debate on the lack of power given to blacks within NUSAS. Later that year Biko proposed the idea of an all-black student movement, and by year's end plans were made for the first conference of the South African Students Organization (SASO). At the first meeting, held in 1978, Biko was elected the organization's president. Initially SASO was amicable toward NUSAS. However, by 1970 SASO discredited NUSAS for not representing all South African students. Led by Biko, SASO became synonymous with the BLACK CONSCIOUSNESS MOVEMENT (BCM), which promoted black pride and black self-determination in regard to changing the South African government.

Initially the South African government did not interfere with SASO and other BCM groups, due to its split with NUSAS. By 1973, however, the government's stance changed, and Biko and other SASO members were banned from further political activity. In 1974 SASO and its sister organization, the Black People's Convention (BPC), organized rallies to support the nationalist MOZAMBICAN LIBERATION FRONT, which was engaged in a war to free MOZAMBIQUE from Portuguese colonial rule. Later that year the South African government arrested a group of SASO leaders, later known as the "SASO Nine," for their role in the rallies. Biko testified for the defense, using their trial to highlight the injustices of the apartheid government and to promote the tenets of the BCM. Despite his efforts, in 1976 the SASO Nine were sentenced to prison on ROBBEN ISLAND. This was also the year of the SOWETO rebellion, which was launched by African high school students influenced by SASO and its black consciousness ideology.

In 1977 Biko was arrested while returning home from a political meeting. While in the custody of the South African Security Police, he was beaten and later died from brain injuries. Later that year the government banned SASO and all other organizations associated with the BCM. The BCM did not end, however, and in 1978 the former BCM groups formed the Azanian People's Organization to carry on the fight against apartheid.

Southern African Development Community (SADC) Regional community of states that seeks economic cooperation and DEVELOPMENT. The Southern African Development Coordination Conference (SADCC) was the forerunner to the Southern African Development Community (SADC). During the late 1970s leaders of nine southern African nations realized that in order to advance their political struggles, they also needed to cooperate in social and economic development. This realization was facilitated by the positive experiences of many members working together as the FRONTLINE STATES (ANGOLA, BOTSWANA, MOZAMBIQUE, TANZANIA, ZAMBIA, and ZIMBABWE), all of which were cooperating among themselves to ward off the aggression and pressure emanating from the APARTHEID government of SOUTH AFRICA. This relationship established a constructive precedent for the formation of a new regional community. The first of many SADCC annual meetings was convened in 1979 in Arusha, Tanzania, with the six Frontline States as well as LESOTHO, MALAWI, and SWAZILAND in attendance.

By the early 1990s member states felt that it was time for the conference to have a more formal status. Thus, in 1992 the SADCC broadened its goals and became the SADC. It set high standards for the region, emphasizing peace, solidarity, security, HUMAN RIGHTS, DEMOCRATIZATION, and the rule of law. From the beginning the objectives of the community were concrete, focusing on economic development and political growth. Among its many objectives, the SADC sought economic interdependence among member states. It also promoted the development of common political systems and values and sought to maximize productive employment. Sustainable use of the region's NATURAL RESOURCES was a stated goal as well. The end of apartheid rule in South Africa and the democratic election of 1994 led to that country's admission into the SADC as its eleventh member state. Given the size and importance of the South African economy, the organization's prospects for success greatly improved.

Structurally, the SADC is a decentralized institution whose member states formulate and implement policy decisions. The organization has more than a dozen commissions and councils, including the Summit, which is the policy-making body, and the Integrated Committee of Ministers, which is responsible for ensuring the coordination and harmonization of policies and activities that cross various states and economic sectors.

The SADC has demonstrated a range of possibilities in regional cooperation. Although there have been some problems, which is the case in any regional project of this scope, the SADC has been very successful. One of its main achievements was the focus on the region's INFRASTRUCTURE. The SADC prioritized the rehabilitation of roads, railways, and harbors, all of which are essential to economic development and cooperation.

The SADC currently has 14 member countries including Angola, Botswana, the Democratic Republic of the CONGO, Lesotho, Malawi, MAURITIUS, Mozambique, NAMIBIA, SEYCHELLES, South Africa, Swaziland, Tanzania, Zambia, and Zimbabwe. As of 2004 the organization headquarters were located in GABORONE, Botswana, and Angola's president, Jose Eduardo DOS SANTOS (1942–   ), was serving as chairperson.

Further reading: York Bradshaw and Stephen N. Ndegwa, eds., *The Uncertain Promise of Southern Africa* (Bloomington, Ind.: Indiana University Press, 2000); Peter Vale, *Security and Politics in South Africa: The Regional Dimension* (Boulder, Colo.: Lynne Rienner Publishers, 2003).

South West Africa Name of the territory that became independent NAMIBIA. The former German colony of South West Africa was a mandate territory of the League of Nations, which assigned it to be administered by SOUTH AFRICA following World War I (1914–18). After World War II (1939–45) the League of Nations was dissolved and its role in South Africa was assumed by the United Nations (UN). In 1946 the status of South West Africa was changed from mandate to United Nations trust territory, and the United Nations then reassigned the territory to the South African government. Before long the South African administration was ruling South West Africa as if it were an integral part of South Africa itself, with that country's increasingly repressive, racist policies.

The German and AFRIKAANS-speaking whites of South West Africa participated in an elective form of government, based in WINDHOEK, the capital. They worked in concert with the South African government to exclude Africans and mixed-race people from the political system. The exclusionary government, a version of the official APARTHEID government in South Africa, remained in place for more than 40 years.

Finally in 1990, following a protracted struggle that claimed many lives, the African people of South West Africa gained their independence under a UN-supervised transition and renamed their country Namibia.

See also: SOUTH WEST AFRICA (Vol. IV); UNITED NATIONS AND AFRICA (Vols. IV, V).

South West African People's Organization (SWAPO) Nationalist party at the forefront of the struggle for independence of NAMIBIA from SOUTH AFRICA. It became Namibia's dominant political party after independence was achieved in 1990. SWAPO came into being in 1960 when Namibia was still known as SOUTH WEST AFRICA. The party evolved out of the Ovambo People's Organization, the resistance party established by Andimba (Herman) Toivo ja Toivo (1924–   ) and future Namibian president Sam NUJOMA (1929–   ). At the time of SWAPO's founding Nujoma was in exile, attempting to rally international support for Namibia's independence from South Africa, which had controlled the country since World War I (1914–18). When Nujoma's efforts proved futile SWAPO formed a guerrilla wing, the People's Liberation Army of Namibia (PLAN). In 1966 PLAN launched an armed resistance that was based in ANGOLA and backed by both the POPULAR MOVEMENT FOR THE LIBERATION OF ANGOLA (Movimento Popular de Libertação de Angola, MPLA) and the former Soviet Union. PLAN's operations led to Toivo ja Toivo's arrest in 1968. Toivo ja Toivo was sentenced to a 20-year prison term but was released in 1984. He was imprisoned on ROBBEN ISLAND, with other political prisoners, including Nelson MANDELA (1918–   ), the future president of South Africa.

Although PLAN made little headway in terms of territorial gain, its actions did attract international attention, and in 1978 the United Nations declared SWAPO the only legitimate representative of Namibia. Nujoma and SWAPO negotiated with the United Nations Security Council, securing the passage of Resolution 435, which outlined the course of Namibia's independence. South Africa managed to delay the resolution through diplomatic means, finally yielding in 1988. A cease-fire agreement was signed, and in 1989 SWAPO swept the elections, with Nujoma becoming president. Namibia declared independence the following year. With its strong Ovambo electoral base, SWAPO continued as the governing party into the 21st century.

See also: INDEPENDENCE MOVEMENTS (Vol. V); NATIONALISM AND INDEPENDENCE MOVEMENTS (Vol. IV); OVAMBO (Vols. II, IV); POLITICAL PARTIES (Vol. V); UNITED NATIONS AND AFRICA (Vols. IV, V).

Soviet Union and Africa In the second half of the 20th century the Soviet Union's influence in Africa was largely confined within the framework of the Cold War. As African nations began to achieve independence, they were faced with pressure to cast their lots with either the communist Soviet Union or the capitalist United States of America. The effort to avoid getting embroiled in Cold War intrigue led to the birth of the NONALIGNED MOVEMENT, which allowed nations to maintain a neutral stance.

Many newly autonomous African states favored the support of the Soviet Union over that of the United States, a country they associated with Europe and colonialism. The Soviet Union was in turn willing to support African governments that espoused communist or socialist ideals. Like the support from the Unites States, Soviet support typically came in the form of military and financial aid. However, in cases like the ASWAN DAM, in EGYPT, the Soviet Union also provided engineers, advisors, and workers to complete significant public works projects.

During this period the Soviet Union's alliances with various African nations frequently were subject to changes and full reversals. One clear example was in the Horn of Africa, where, in the 1970s, the Soviet Union supported the socialist regime of Mohammed Siad BARRE (1910–1995) in SOMALIA. Somalia's conflict with ETHIOPIA over the Ogaden region mirrored the conflict between the Soviet Union and the United States, which backed Ethiopia. When the socialist government of MENGISTU HAILE MARIAM (1937–   ) assumed control in Ethiopia, the Soviet Union chose to back Ethiopia, the more influential country in the region. Consequently the United States withdrew support from Mengistu's country and began supporting Somalia. In such cases the Soviet Union's involvement in Africa and its attempts to support nascent socialist governments often served to increase the scale and intensity of conflicts. This was true in the Democratic Republic of the CONGO and ANGOLA as well as in the Horn of Africa.

The Russian Federation and Africa In 1991 the collapse of the Soviet Union and the sudden absence of Soviet support was disastrous for many African states, burdened as they were by heavy internal opposition and failing economies. In many cases, these states chose to move toward DEMOCRATIZATION. In Somalia's case, however, Barre's form of socialism as a choice of government ideology began to fall from favor, and he was driven from power.

Since the fall of the Soviet Union, the subsequent Russian Federation has continued to pursue an active role in Africa's affairs. As a permanent member of the UN Security Council, Russia has been involved in international peacekeeping missions in WESTERN SAHARA, ERITREA, Ethiopia, and the Democratic Republic of the Congo. In his *Concept of the Russian Federation's Foreign Policy*, Russian president Vladimir Putin (1952–) stated that "Russia will expand its interaction with African countries and promote the soonest possible settlement of regional military conflicts in Africa." Russia has also supported economic measures in Africa, including the NEW PARTNERSHIP FOR AFRICA'S DEVELOPMENT and the Plan of Actions on Africa, a debt-relief initiative for which Russia plans to write off $26 billion of debt it is owed by African countries. Russia also enjoys particularly good relations with South Africa, which was the first African country to recognize the Russian Federation after the end of the Soviet era.

See also: COLD WAR AND AFRICA (Vols. IV, V); COMMUNISM AND SOCIALISM (Vol. V); CUBA AND AFRICA (Vol. V); UNITED STATES AND AFRICA (Vols. IV, V); SOVIET UNION AND AFRICA (Vol. IV).

Soweto Abbreviation for the South Western Township, the largest township in SOUTH AFRICA. In the 1940s the APARTHEID government of South Africa created Soweto as an agglomeration of 26 smaller townships. The plan was for Soweto to become home to black Africans working in the neighboring JOHANNESBURG area. Between the two world wars the area had developed into slums of poorly constructed shacks. In 1948 the slums were cleared and permanent housing was constructed.

Life in Soweto was difficult. Low income levels combined with repressive government restrictions that were in place during the apartheid era created an atmosphere of fear and anger. The ever-present danger of urban youth gangs called TSOTSIS exacerbated the situation. In the 1970s Soweto emerged at the forefront of protests in South Africa. On June 16, 1976, anti-apartheid sentiments boiled over in an uprising that garnered international attention.

It began with schoolchildren assembling to protest the required use of AFRIKAANS as a language of instruction in Soweto high schools. Without provocation, white police shot at the children, killing one student and injuring several others. A violent rampage followed in the wake of the killing, and protests spread throughout the country.

Tin-roof shacks like these were typical of the housing for blacks living in Soweto. In 1976, four years after this photo was taken, Soweto's residents rioted, unable to endure substandard living conditions and government oppression. © AP/Wide World Photos

Hundreds died in clashes with the police during the months that followed. The post-apartheid government subsequently designated June 16 as a national day of remembrance, known as Youth Day.

Kliptown, one of the earlier residential areas of Soweto, contains Freedom Square. In 1952 this was the site at which the Freedom Charter was drafted. One of the most famous documents in modern African history, the charter became a cornerstone of the AFRICAN NATIONAL CONGRESS (ANC). The site has recently been renamed Sisulu Square in honor of the late ANC leader, Walter SISULU (1912–2003).

Soweto's population (estimated at 1,243,000 in 2003) remains mostly African. Housing ranges from shacks, which are common in African shantytowns, to mansions. Although the majority of Soweto residents commute to Johannesburg to work, local residents have established several tour companies designed to give visitors the "Soweto experience." The homes of Nelson MANDELA (1918–) and his his former wife, Winnie MANDELA (1934–), are major attractions on the tours.

See also: FREEDOM CHARTER (Vol. IV); URBAN LIFE AND CULTURE (Vols. IV, V); URBANIZATION (Vols. IV, V).

Soyinka, Wole (Akinwande Oluwole Soyinka)
(1934–) *Nigerian writer and Nobel Prize laureate*

One of the best known and most respected contemporary African writers, Soyinka fuses traditional African motifs with modern, European literary forms. His creative combining of disparate elements is as striking in its presentation as it is deep in its intellectual questioning of the problems of contemporary African identity.

In 1960 Soyinka returned to NIGERIA from England, where he had studied drama at Leeds University and then worked for two years with London's Royal Court Theater. His 1960 play, *Trials of Brother Jero,* about a fraudulent African preacher, had already earned him a reputation as an emerging literary figure. Upon his return he took up the study of Nigerian folklore at the University of IBADAN, and he also founded Masks, a theater group that was instrumental in the creation of contemporary Nigerian theater. During this period Soyinka wrote *Dance of the Forests,* an early work that brought him fame. The play utilizes traditional drumming, dancing, and music to celebrate Nigeria's independence, while also issuing a warning about the pitfalls that might lie before the new nation.

Soyinka spent the 1960s and 1970s intensely involved in both literature and politics. He traveled much, but he also produced some of his most noteworthy works, including *The Road* (1965), a play that succeeds in integrating YORUBA religious mythology into a clearly modern drama, and *The Interpreters,* a novel in which he explores themes related to contrasting Western and indigenous beliefs.

The Road is considered by many critics to be Soyinka's best play. In it the Yoruba god Ogun—the traditional deity of the forge, creation, and destruction—is transformed into the controller of electricity and automotive travel, with car accidents becoming a symbol of the god's destructive power.

Soyinka's strong political views brought him into conflicts with the Nigerian government. In 1964 he was arrested—apparently without any cause—on a charge of forcing a radio newscaster to announce invalid election results. Jailed for three months, he was eventually released amid an outpouring of protest from the international community of writers. This incarceration, however, was just a prelude to the long imprisonment Soyinka endured during Nigeria's bloody civil war (1967–70) in which the Nigerian federal government ultimately defeated and reincorporated the secessionist nation of BIAFRA. Most Yoruba sided with the government, but Soyinka became an outspoken critic of the war, adamantly opposing the international sale of armaments to either side. Angered by Soyinka's activities, the Nigerian government arrested him in 1967. Soyinka spent the next two years in prison, enduring a long list of torments, from solitary confinement to the refusal of prison officials to give him books or writing materials. The authorities even denied him basic medical treatment.

Soyinka managed not only to survive his imprisonment but also to produce poems and letters, which he wrote using homemade ink on anything he could find, from cigarette packs to toilet paper. Finally released in 1969, Soyinka left Nigeria, living in England and then GHANA before finally returning home in 1975, when a new, more democratic government was in power.

Following his long period in prison Soyinka's art took on tones that were at once darker and more lyrical. *The Man Died: Prison Notes of Wole Soyinka* (1972) and his second novel, *Season of Anomy* (1973), for example, deal in astonishing detail in the day-to-day experiences of prison. The graphic scenes of torture and murder left many readers with a sense of hopelessness about the future of Africa—or virtually anywhere else. A play from the same period, *Madmen and Specialists* (1970), is equally dark, dealing with a doctor who returns home from war, now fully trained in the "art" of torture, to practice his new-found "speciality" on his own father. In contrast, however, in 1988 Soyinka published a biography of his own father, *Isara: A Voyage around Essay* that is considered one of his most beautiful books. Based on a collection of papers left behind when his father died, the book brings to life a man who faced the cultural divisions of the colonial era. As he yearned for his traditional world, the book's hero also understood the need to adapt to the world brought to Nigeria by the European powers.

During the 1980s Soyinka's opposition to dictatorship and his pessimism about Africa's political future intensified. Typical of his work from this period is his play, *A Play of Giants,* in which four African leaders meet at the United Nations, in New York, and casually discuss the brutality and criminality of their governments. Soyinka's political estrangement culminated in another period of exile during the 1990s, when the military regime of

General Sani ABACHA (1943–1998) gave the writer, in effect, a choice between a death sentence and voluntary exile. When Abacha died in 1998, Soyinka returned to Nigeria.

From his earliest works, Soyinka has been a challenging, even difficult writer, especially for non-African audiences. His novels are complex and dense, and his plays use dance, MUSIC, and choral techniques that are unfamiliar to non-African actors and directors. In spite of this, however, readers both in Africa and in the world beyond have found him to be a modern master, a writer whose vision at once is clearly and accurately fixed on the immediate world around him and on universal truths beyond. His 1986 Nobel Prize in Literature, the first awarded to a sub-Saharan African author, testifies to the scope, quality, and impact of his literary art.

See also: COLONIALISM, INFLUENCE OF (Vol. IV); ENGLAND AND AFRICA (Vols. III, IV, V); LITERATURE IN COLONIAL AFRICA (Vol. IV); LITERATURE IN MODERN AFRICA (Vol. V); SOYINKA, WOLE (Vol. IV).

Further reading: James Gibbs, ed., *Critical Perspectives on Wole Soyinka* (Colorado Springs, Colo.: Three Continents, 1980); David E. Herdeck, *Three Dynamite Authors: Derek Walcott, Naguib Mafouz, Wole Soyinka* (Colorado Springs, Colo.: Three Continents, 1995); Margaret Laurence, *Long Drums and Cannons: Nigerian Dramatists and Novelists* (Portsmouth, N.H.: Praeger, 1968).

sports and athletics Organized athletic competitions and feats of physical skill and prowess have long been a part of African social life and culture. Modern competitive sports and athletics first entered Africa in the colonial period and achieved growing visibility and significance after independence.

Sports organized along western lines emerged in Africa in connection with schools run by MISSIONARIES. By the 1890s the dual English-XHOSA language newspaper *Imvo zabaNtsundu*, for example, was carrying the results of cricket matches between African boarding schools in SOUTH AFRICA. Soccer, which is called football in Africa (as it is in Europe), captured the imagination of young men on ZANZIBAR in the years following World War I (1914–18), and Zanzibaris began to organize leagues for their teams. Throughout colonial Africa, sports clubs and organizations became increasingly popular, so that by the 1950s and 1960s many Africans, especially urbanites, were either participating in or following sports, both amateur and professional.

The real boom in African sports came with national independence for African countries. Participation in international sports competition such as the Olympics and the Commonwealth Games became just as important in its own right as membership in international organizations. At the continental level sports helped promote PAN-AFRICANISM. African athletes first gathered for the All-African Games in BRAZZAVILLE, Republic of the CONGO, in 1965. The eighth All-African Games took place in NIGERIA in 2003. At the national level sports provided a unifying force and national focus as part of the nation-building process. Sports events within countries serve as an important leisure time activity for both participants and fans who support their favorite teams or athletes. As in Europe and the United States RADIO AND TELEVISION have served to popularize sports as a whole and also serve as a venue for their commercialization.

The Olympics The Olympic Games provide the most visible measure of achievement for individual African athletes and for countries as well. Since it is a competition for the athletes of sovereign nations, only a few African athletes participated before 1960. South Africans took part in the Games beginning in 1904, but their participation was limited to whites. One of them, Reginald Walker, was the first person from Africa to win a gold medal, in the 100 meters, in 1908. The 1960 Games were the turning point. Ike Quartey of GHANA won the light-welterweight boxing silver medal, thus making him the first black African to win an Olympic medal. A few days later Abebe BIKILA (1932–1973) of ETHIOPIA created a sensation by running the marathon barefoot and besting Rhadi Ben Abdesselem of MOROCCO to become the first sub-Saharan African athlete to win a gold medal, a feat that he repeated in 1964.

Bikila's marathon victory was the start of African dominance in the long distance events. Ethiopians also won the marathon in 1968 and in 2000. In 1996, an Ethiopian, Fatuma Roba (1973–), was the first African to win the women's marathon. She also won the Boston Marathon from 1997 to 1999, with Kenyan women winning from 2000 to 2002. Kenyan men won the Boston Marathon in 1988, 1991–2000, and 2002–03, with an Ethiopian winning in 1989. In 2004, the top two women finishers were from Africa, with Kenyan Catherine Ndereba (1972–).

The 1968 Olympics were a breakthrough for Africans. Medalists included Tunisia's Mohammed Gammoudi (c. 1940–), who won the 5,000-meter gold, and Kipchoge KEINO (1940–), of KENYA, who won the 1,500-meter gold and the 5,000-meter silver. Two other Kenyans also took home gold medals: Naftuli Temu, who won the 10,000-meter race, and Amos Biwott (1947–), winner in the 3,000-meter steeplechase. In addition, the Kenyan men's team won the silver in the 4x400-meter race.

The first African woman medalist in track and field not from South Africa was Nawal el Moutawakil (1962–) from MOROCCO who won the 400-meter hurdles in 1984. In 1992 African women won the gold in the 1,500 and 10,000 meters and silver in the 10,000 meters and 4x100 meter. That same year African men won 15 track and field medals, including three gold medals. Eight years later there were 17 African men medalists (5 gold) and eight women (3 gold).

The other Olympic event that has had significant African participation is boxing, with ALGERIA, Morocco, Ghana, and Nigeria providing most of the medalists. Beginning with Quartey's 1960 silver, African boxers have won an additional 16 bronze medals and one gold.

African teams have also been successful in the Olympics, beginning with Ghana's bronze medal in soccer in 1992. In 1996 Nigeria won the gold in soccer, as did CAMEROON in 2000.

In all Africans have won 237 gold medals. South Africa, which participated in the Olympics from 1904 to 1960 and then was suspended due to its APARTHEID policies until 1992, has the most medals at 63, including seven in 2000. Kenya is next with 54, placing it thirty-first among all nations, followed by Ethiopia with 24, Nigeria with 17, Egypt and Morocco with 16, and Algeria with 12. Other African countries have also won medals.

Team Sports Soccer's greatest competition, the World Cup, is another major international venue for showcasing African athletic talent. In 1970 Morocco was the first African team to qualify for the World Cup, with ZAÏRE (present-day Democratic Republic of the CONGO) doing so in 1974 and TUNISIA in 1978. In the 1982 World Cup there were at least two teams from Africa, and by 2002 teams from SENEGAL, South Africa, Cameroon, Nigeria, and Tunisia all qualified. Senegal reached the quarterfinals before losing. The only other African team to reach that level was Cameroon in 1990. South Africa's bid to host the 2006 World Cup, and thus be the first African nation to do so, lost by one vote, but it is expected to be successful in its bid for the 2010 World Cup.

South Africa did host the 1995 Rugby Union World Cup. Rugby is predominantly a game of the British Isles and former dominions such as South Africa, New Zealand, and Australia. For the most part it is not popular in Africa outside the southern part of the continent, although IVORY COAST was represented in 1995. ZIMBABWE had its national teams play in the first and second Cups (1987 and 1991), while South Africa was in the 1995 Cup, which it hosted and won, and the 1999 Cup, where it placed third. NAMIBIA participated in the 2003 Cup.

Cricket is another sport associated with the former British Empire and is especially popular in the West Indies, India, and Pakistan, as well as England and Australia. In Africa it is mostly played in South Africa and Zimbabwe. South Africa is the only team from the conti-

nent to have participated in the Cricket World Cup, having done so in 1992 and again in 1999.

Individual Athletic Accomplishments Individual athletes Africa have made their mark internationally in a number of different sports, ranging from boxing to track and field to basketball. As noted above, Kenyan and Ethiopian men and women runners have come to dominate the marathon internationally, first rising to prominence in the 1960s and then to dominance in the 1990s. Individual African players are found on many professional soccer teams in Europe after first playing on their national teams or professional teams in Africa. Occasionally a boxer from Africa, such as Ghana's Azumah Nelson (1958–), has held world titles in his weight class. Even though basketball is not a major team sport in Africa, some of the continent's most prominent international star athletes are basketball players. Two of the pioneers in this regard are the Nigerian Hakeem OLAJUWON (1963–), who was the National Basketball Association's MVP in 1994, and Dikembe MUTOMBO (1966–), from the Democratic Republic of the Congo. With their success and that of others, the college basketball ranks now have a number of players from Africa.

Further reading: William J. Baker and James A. Mangan, eds., *Sport in Africa: Essays in Social History* (New York: Africana Publishing Co., 1987); Paul Darby, *Africa, Football and FIFA: Politics, Colonialism and Resistance* (Portland, Ore.: Frank Cass, 2002).

state, role of The world is largely governed by a system in which states are the most important political units. They are often confused with governments, but in fact they are much more. States are the sum of the government, territory, and population of a country. Weak or "soft" states of sub-Saharan Africa have created economic challenges, problems of governance, and fierce conflicts.

It is the fundamental responsibility of the state to defend its borders and protect its people. In an ideal state this means that the military and police represent legitimate power. In sub-Saharan Africa a recurrent problem is a lack of state capacity. The soft state is incapable of upholding the laws the government creates. Lack of funds, training, and INFRASTRUCTURE mean that the state cannot adequately protect its citizens. Moreover, leaders at all levels of government can act in their own self-interest at the expense of their constituents without fear of being caught or even impugned. Soft states cannot ensure that governmental affairs are carried out in an efficient manner, which can threaten DEMOCRATIZATION. Also these states cannot efficiently collect and utilize taxes, leaving the government without a revenue base to make the investments necessary for DEVELOPMENT.

Where states are incapable of carrying out their primary functions, it is common for rival interests to challenge the existing authority. For example, in TANZANIA during the 1970s the state directives of President Julius NYERERE (1922–1999) were challenged by existing local networks of economic cooperation. As a result the nationalized collective farming policy known as *UJAMAA* failed.

In such countries as the Democratic Republic of the CONGO, LIBERIA, SIERRA LEONE, and ANGOLA, rival political factions have challenged the authority of soft states. Typically, the upstarts have been able to use wealth obtained by controlling a state's NATURAL RESOURCES—especially diamonds—to build armies. The result has been long, violent CIVIL WARS that are essentially rooted in a challenge to supremacy of state leadership and organization.

In some cases, a weak but functioning state fails. It might be recognized internationally as the legal authority in a particular country, but it does not effectively control the territory. The root of this failure is commonly identified as the creation of African states by colonial fiat rather than through a process that would have taken into consideration population distributions and historic trends.

Other states actually collapse. According to some political scientists, "state collapse" refers to a situation in which authority, law, and political order no longer exist. State collapse contrasts with "change in government," whereby the leaders are replaced, or "regime change," whereby a country might overhaul its type of governance. In state collapse, primary institutions such as state banks or courts cease to function, and order and power are contested. The country of SOMALIA, in the Horn of Africa, is an example of a state that collapsed. After a decade of civil war and the absence of a cohesive state authority, alternative local political structures emerged to take over primary functions normally carried out by the state. CHAD, UGANDA, LIBERIA, MOZAMBIQUE, and ETHIOPIA are other states that have collapsed.

See also: CIVIL SOCIETY (Vol. V).

Further reading: Jeffrey Herbst, *States and Power in Africa: Comparative Lessons in Authority and Control* (Princeton, N.J.: Princeton University Press, 2000); William Reno, *Warlord Politics and African States* (Boulder, Colo.: Lynne Rienner Publishers, 1999).

Strasser, Valentine (Valentine Esegrabo Melvin Strasser) (1967–) *Military head of state in Sierra Leone from 1992 to 1996*

Born into a Krio family in SIERRA LEONE, Strasser attended the prestigious Sierra Leone Grammar School, the oldest secondary school in the nation. After high school he joined the military, becoming a second lieutenant in 1987.

His experiences fighting against the REVOLUTIONARY UNITED FRONT motivated his rise to power. After being injured in battle Strasser became disillusioned with the low pay, outdated weaponry, and poor conditions that charac-

terized the Sierra Leone Army. In April 1992 he spearheaded a protest by disgruntled junior and middle-ranking soldiers. The group marched into FREETOWN, ostensibly to voice their grievances to President Joseph Momoh (1937–2003), who had governed the country since 1985. Soon, however, the march escalated into a COUP D'ÉTAT. When it was over Strasser, at 25 years old, found himself Sierra Leone's youngest ever head of state—and the first of Krio descent.

To justify their actions the dissident soldiers cited the inability of the government to reverse the country's deteriorating economic situation. They also noted the extensive government CORRUPTION and the general indifference of the country's leadership to the poor living conditions of the populace. The coup leaders also cited the fact that they had not been paid their salaries for an extended period of time yet were expected to defend Momoh's government against rebel attacks.

During his four years in power Strasser led the National Provisional Ruling Council in making some positive strides in improving the economy, rebuilding ruined INFRASTRUCTURE, and safeguarding the security of average Sierra Leoneans. He mounted a massive clean-up campaign in Freetown and reduced inflation. His government also imposed STRUCTURAL ADJUSTMENT policies that were required by the INTERNATIONAL MONETARY FUND as a condition of receiving ECONOMIC ASSISTANCE. Further decentralizing the government he privatized some state corporations and reduced the civil service workforce. Strasser promised a return to civilian rule in five years, scheduling elections for February 1996.

However, although it experienced some success, Strasser's government was also marked by instability. An attempted coup on December 29, 1992, led Strasser to execute 26 political opponents, an act that provoked international condemnation of his regime. In light of the clampdown that followed, the world's leading HUMAN RIGHTS organization, Amnesty International, accused Strasser of various atrocities. Nevertheless, he pressed on, curtailing freedom of the press and turning a blind eye to accusations of corruption within his own government.

On January 16, 1996, prior to elections, Strasser's second-in-command, Brigadier Julius Maada Bio (1964–), overthrew him. After a brief exile in neighboring GUINEA Strasser attended law school in England on a United Nations scholarship. He dropped out after one year, claiming a lack of funds, and lived in Britain under an assumed name until his student visa ran out. When Britain rejected his application for asylum, Strasser was deported back to Sierra Leone, in December 2000. Although heads of state are entitled to a pension under Sierra Leone's constitution, the government contended that, since Strasser was not democratically elected, he was ineligible for this benefit.

See also: AMNESTY INTERNATIONAL AND AFRICA (Vol. V).

structural adjustment Economic belt-tightening policies that countries are encouraged to adopt in order to receive ECONOMIC ASSISTANCE. Amid the economic turmoil of the 1980s many African nations looked to international organizations such as the WORLD BANK and the INTERNATIONAL MONETARY FUND for economic help. As a means of protecting their investments these lending organizations demanded certain conditions from the states that desired their help. Collectively these conditions became known as structural adjustment programs.

The main objectives of structural adjustment programs include removing government controls on economic structures, reducing government spending on social services, and expanding commerce and industry in the private sector. Economists in favor of structural adjustment programs believe that free markets increase efficiency and thus are conducive to DEVELOPMENT. They argue that the lack of competition in many African nations has contributed to high levels of government CORRUPTION and waste.

In order to support a free-market system, African governments were asked to remove subsidies for AGRICULTURE, which are commonly implemented to keep food prices artificially low for urban populations. Supporters of the proposed changes argued that food prices would rise and food producers would benefit. This, in turn, would provide incentive for increased agricultural production, a necessary increase in light of Africa's rapid POPULATION GROWTH. The privatization of WATER RESOURCES, communications, TRANSPORTATION, and energy industries was another key element of structural adjustment programs.

Under structural adjustment reforms governments were also required to devalue their currencies and allow them to fluctuate freely on the international market. This often made imports cheaper. In some places the devaluation undermined the local market of consumer goods. However, pro-structural development economists claimed that, eventually, individuals and companies would learn to produce only those goods and items that were in demand and which they could sell at a profit.

In some areas the devaluation of currency decreased wages, increasing POVERTY levels for wage LABOR. Among other negative effects of structural adjustment, the policy of decreasing government services resulted in reduced government spending on EDUCATION, health care, and other social safety net systems. This resulted in the implementation of user fees for public health-care systems and also increased the cost of education. Theoretically, the gap in social services would be filled by investments from the private sector. However, in Africa, this private investment has been slow to materialize.

Recently there has been sharp criticism of structural adjustment programs in Africa. While supporters of the changes point to GHANA as a success story, opponents argue that Ghana's economy would have improved regardless of whether these programs were adopted or not. In 1996 a group of NON-GOVERNMENT ORGANIZATIONS formed the Structural Adjustment Participatory Review Initiative to study the impact of these programs. Ghana, UGANDA, and ZIMBABWE were chosen as the focal points of the analysis in Africa. The initiative's final report, published in 2002, found that, although they were implemented with good intentions, many of the structural adjustment policies have backfired. The impact of these programs varied tremendously depending on the livelihood activities of the individuals they were meant to help and whether they were urban or rural dwellers.

However, there are numerous case studies that have found evidence of positive change, including the rooting out of government CORRUPTION, participation in global markets, and the implementation of tighter budgets that greatly improve a country's financial outlook.

Further reading: Christina H. Gladwin, *Structural Adjustment and African Women Farmers* (Gainesville, Fla.: University of Florida Press, 1991); Kwadwo Konadu-Agyemang, ed., *IMF and World Bank Sponsored Structural Adjustment Programs in Africa: Ghana's Experience, 1983–1999* (Burlington, Vt.: Ashgate, 2002); Thandika Mkandawire and Charles C. Soludo, eds., *African Voices on Structural Adjustment: A Companion to Our Continent, Our Future* (Trenton, N.J.: Africa World Press, 2003).

Sudan, Republic of the Northeast African country bordered by EGYPT to the north, the Red Sea to the northeast, ERITREA and ETHIOPIA to the east, KENYA, UGANDA, and the Democratic Republic of the CONGO to the south, and the CENTRAL AFRICAN REPUBLIC, CHAD, and LIBYA to the west. Covering approximately 966,800 square miles (2,504,000 sq km), the Sudan is Africa's largest country. Its capital is KHARTOUM.

The Republic of the Sudan at Independence The movement of the Sudan toward independence was sparked by the 1952 revolution in Egypt that brought Colonel Muhammad Naguib (1901–1984) to power, ending the Egyptian monarchy. Naguib supported Sudanese autonomy, and in 1953 he signed an agreement with the British to end the joint rule of the Sudan as established under the Anglo-Egyptian Condominium.

The colonial administration of the Sudan had favored the country's largely Arab and Muslim northerners. So, as independence approached, many non-Muslim southerners feared the north would end up with a disproportionate amount of political authority. The declaration of Arabic as the national language and a growing number of northern Sudanese who were given government positions bore out the validity of this fear. In 1955 southern soldiers mutinied against their northern officers initiating the first conflict of a civil war that contin-

In addition to ongoing civil war, the Republic of the Sudan has been wracked by devastating drought. In 1998 this mother brought her starving son to a famine relief center in Ajiep, southern Sudan. © UN/DPI photo/Eskender Debebe

ued through the early years of Sudan's history as a sovereign state.

In 1956, with the north-south conflict already raging, the Sudan became an independent republic under Prime Minister Ismail al Azhari (1902–1969). Azhari was soon replaced by Abd Allah Khalil (1888–1970), who struggled to establish a government in the face of rampant CORRUPTION and widespread political dissension. Ultimately, however, it was Khalil's mismanagement of Sudan's production of cotton, the country's prime economic commodity and its leading export, that led to his demise. In 1958 General Ibrahim Abboud (1900–1983) led a military COUP D'ÉTAT. Incapable of improving the Sudan's dire situation and threatened by ongoing violence perpetrated by southern guerrilla troops known as the Anya Nya, Abboud gave way, in 1964, to a short-lived civilian government. Colonel Gafaar NIMEIRI (1930–) seized power in 1969.

Nimeiri consolidated his power by outlawing all political parties and dissolving Parliament. He did, however, manage to negotiate an end to the civil war that had ravaged the country since independence. The 1972 agreement between Nimeiri's government and the main rebel

group, the Southern Sudan Liberation Front, to which the Anya Nya belonged, was brokered by HAILE SELASSIE (1892–1975) of Ethiopia and resulted in general autonomy for southern Sudan. A year later the Sudan's first permanent constitution was approved.

Peace did not last, however, as Nimeiri followed policies that once again raised the ire of southern Sudanese. In 1983 he established Islamic law, or SHARIA, as the country's supreme law. This, coupled with a collapsing economy and food shortages, resulted in a renewal of hostilities in the south led by the Sudan People's Liberation Army (SPLA). In 1985 Nimeiri was overthrown by the Sudanese military. In the end, Nimeiri's regime left the Sudan with a shattered economy and $9 billion of debt. Elections held the following year established the civilian Sadiq al-Mahdi (1935–) as the country's leader. By 1989, he, too, had been overthrown.

The Sudan under al-Bashir and al-Turabi After Sadiq al-Mahdi, the Sudan's ruler was Lieutenant General Omar Hasan Ahmad al-BASHIR (1945–). Al-Bashir openly favored the Muslim north, strengthening *sharia* and establishing closer ties with Arab nations. He extended the nation's civil war and attempted to starve the southern region by directing international food aid to the north. Upon his official election to the presidency in 1993, however, it became apparent that the real power in the Sudan lay not with al-Bashir but with Hassan Abd Allah al-TURABI (1932–), the speaker of the Sudanese Parliament.

The lengthy civil war has wreaked havoc on the Sudan's population. Combined with DROUGHT AND DESERTIFICATION, by the late 1980s it had turned nearly a third of the country's population into REFUGEES. The actions of the militant Islamic government cut off the country from much potential international relief assistance, especially after the United States listed the Sudan as a major supporter of international TERRORISM. The United States also launched missile attacks on suspected chemical weapons manufacturing facilities in Sudan in the aftermath of the 1998 bombing of the U.S. embassies in NAIROBI and DAR ES SALAAM.

Known worldwide as an outspoken supporter of Islam and *sharia,* al-Turabi had long worked to make Sudan a country that was fullly Islamic. Essentially governing from behind the scenes, al-Turabi tried to have Parliament increase his powers even further, but al-Bashir balked and disbanded the legislative body. The following year al-Turabi was forced from al-Bashir's National Congress party to form his own Popular National Congress party.

When al-Turabi made conciliatory moves toward southern rebels, apparently in an effort to undermine al-Bashir, he was placed under house arrest. The civil war seemed headed for a conclusion when al-Bashir and the SPLA negotiated a six-year peace plan. However, fighting continued throughout the country.

In the western region of DARFUR, the ongoing war has been especially devastating. There the al-Bashir government has looked the other way as horse-mounted Arab raiders—called *janjaweed* by the Darfurians—pillaged southern villages. Toward the end of 2004, tens of thousands of Darfurians had died in the *janjaweed* attacks, and more than a million people were left homeless, creating a severe humanitarian crisis that affected both Sudan and neighboring Chad. The inability to reconcile the differences of its northern and southern regions, a problem mirrored in such countries as MALI, Chad, and NIGERIA, threatens any hope for stability in the Sudan.

See also: ANGLO-EGYPTIAN CONDOMINIUM (Vol. IV); CASH CROPS (Vols. IV, V); CIVIL WARS (Vol. V); GEZIRA SCHEME (Vol. IV); ISLAM, INFLUENCE OF (Vols. II, III, IV, V); SUDAN, REPUBLIC OF THE (Vols. I, II, III, IV).

Further reading: J. Millard Burr and Robert O. Collins, *Revolutionary Sudan: Hasan al-Turabi and the Islamist State, 1989–2000* (Boston: Brill, 2003); P. M. Holt and M. W. Daly, *The History of the Sudan, From the Coming of Islam to the Present Day*, 4th ed. (New York: Longman, 1988); Donald Petterson, *Inside Sudan: Political Islam, Conflict, and Catastrophe* (Boulder, Colo.: Westview Press, 1999).

Suez Canal Waterway in EGYPT linking the Mediterranean Sea and the Red Sea. At its completion in 1868 the Suez Canal was considered an engineering marvel as well as a commercial success. However, during the 20th century it has been the focus of intense national and international crises. Beginning with the anti-British riots of the 1950s and the nationalization of the canal by the government of Gamal Abdel NASSER (1918–1970), the Suez Canal has been the focus of contention between the forces of Egyptian nationalism and pan-Arabism and the remnants of British and French colonial power. The appearance of the new state of Israel served to exacerbate the situation, and, from the 1960s to the 1980s the canal became, in many ways, a pawn in the larger game of Arab-Israeli relations.

After the 1956 Suez Crisis, the canal operated under Egyptian authority for more than a decade. The Six-Day War of 1967, however, changed that dramatically. With Israel taking possession of the Sinai Peninsula and the eastern banks of the canal, Egypt closed down the canal in protest, obtaining financial aid from other Arab countries to compensate for lost revenue.

After the Yom Kippur War of 1973 between Israel and the Arab states, Egypt regained control of the eastern bank of the canal. Aided by the U.S. Navy, Egypt cleared the canal of sunken ships, mines, and other impediments to shipping, and the canal was finally reopened in 1975, after an eight-year closure.

Since then it has operated continuously, although traffic significantly declined during the 1980s and 1990s. The development of OIL reserves outside the Middle East and the increased size of oil tankers too big to negotiate the canal have led to its decreased importance. In response, plans were announced in 1997 to lower fees and to deepen the canal enough to handle the larger ships. Currently 14 percent of all of the world's shipping passes through the Suez Canal, as does 26 percent of all oil exports.

See also: ARAB-ISRAELI WARS (Vols. IV, V); COLD WAR AND AFRICA (Vols. IV, V); ENGLAND AND AFRICA (Vols. IV, V); FRANCE AND AFRICA (Vol. IV); MEDITERRANEAN SEA (Vol. I); NILE RIVER (Vol. I); RED SEA (Vol. I); SUEZ CANAL (Vol. IV).

Further reading: D. A. Farnie, *East and West of Suez: The Suez Canal in History, 1854–1956* (Oxford, U.K.: Oxford University Press, 1969); Muhammad H. Heikal, *Cutting the Lion's Tail: Suez through Egyptian Eyes* (New York: Arbor House, 1987).

sustainable development Concept used to describe a process of economic and social improvement that does not deplete NATURAL RESOURCES or do irreparable harm to the environment. ENVIRONMENTAL ISSUES became internationalized in 1972, when leaders of most countries of the world gathered in Stockholm, Sweden, to discuss for the first time the growing concerns of global environmental damage. They especially focused on the challenges of pollution and the threat of overpopulation. Since that time, national and international DEVELOPMENT policies have reflected a greater attention to sustainability with respect to both human development and ecological processes. Understanding the environmental sustainability of development is important, if only because the livelihood of more than half the world's population are based on AGRICULTURE, forestry, and fishing. The term *sustainable development* entered the lexicon of international relations following the publication of "Our Common Future," a UN report issued in 1987.

In 1992 representatives at the Earth Summit held in Rio De Janeiro, Brazil, launched Agenda 21. This comprehensive proposal laid out the actions to be taken by the United Nations system, national governments, and CIVIL SOCIETY groups in all countries where human activity impacted the environment. Following Agenda 21, 178 countries adopted international conventions pertaining to deforestation, BIODIVERSITY loss, and climate change. More recently, the World Summit for Sustainable Development, or the JOHANNESBURG Summit, was held in SOUTH AFRICA in 2002. It concluded that both environmental protection and the well-being of future generations are closely linked with issues of POVERTY reduction. This new focus on the social dimensions of sustainable development has a particular relevance for present-day Africa, where many states have launched development programs that show little regard for environmental protection.

See also: CONSERVATION (Vol. V); ECOLOGY AND ECOLOGICAL CHANGE (Vol. V); FORESTS (Vol. V); POPULATION GROWTH (Vol. V); UNITED NATIONS AND AFRICA (Vols. IV, V).

Further reading: Michael Darkoh and Apollo Rwomire, eds., *Human Impact on Environment and Sustainable Development in Africa* (Burlington, Vt.: Ashgate, 2003).

SWAPO See SOUTH WEST AFRICAN PEOPLE'S ORGANIZATION.

Swaziland Small land-locked southeastern African country, about 6,700 square miles (17,400 sq km) in size, surrounded mostly by SOUTH AFRICA but sharing a short border with MOZAMBIQUE. A monarchy, Swaziland's administrative and judicial capital is MBABANE; the legislative capital and royal residence is located at Lobamba.

Lobamba is traditionally held as the residence of the Queen Mother, known as the Ndlovukazi (She-Elephant). The geographic and spiritual center of Swaziland, Lobamba is also the site of many of the Swazis' most important cultural ceremonies.

Swaziland at Independence At the start of the 1960s Swaziland began to move toward independence from British colonial rule with a flurry of political activity. SOBHUZA II (1899–1982), the Swazi king or Ngwenyama (The Lion), formed the Imbokodvo National Movement (INM), which promoted traditional Swazi government and culture. In the 1964 legislative elections the INM won a sweeping victory and became the country's dominant party. In 1968 Swaziland achieved full independence with a monarchical form of government. It was to be the only monarchy in Africa that successfully survived the transition from the indirect rule of the colonial era to modern statehood.

In 1972 the INM once again won a majority in national elections, but there was enough of an opposition showing to lead Sobhuza to act radically, abolishing the constitution and the parliament and seizing all political power for himself. He also banned all political parties and LABOR UNIONS, saying that his act was a necessary measure to rid Swaziland of the remnants of colonialism. Sobhuza did, however, install a version of a cabinet system, headed by a prime minister.

Ultimately Sobhuza's reign in Swaziland lasted longer than the reign of any other contemporary monarch. During his reign Swaziland enjoyed strong economic DEVELOPMENT, especially in its agricultural sector, and political consistency, luxuries few other post-independence African nations could claim. This development, however, took place in the shadow of APARTHEID in neighboring South Africa, and much of the country's economic growth depended on TOURISM by South Africans who flocked to the country's gambling casinos.

Following the death of Sobhuza's, in 1982, political controversy erupted in the royal family. It continued until his son, Prince Makhosetive (1968–   ), was crowned as King MSWATI III. In an effort to centralize his power, Mswati III dissolved the traditional royal advisory council, the Liqoqo, which had become highly influential during Sobhuza's reign. The new king also purged the government of a number of officials in an effort to combat CORRUPTION.

Under Mswati III, Swaziland continued to enjoy relative prosperity, though political infighting at times upset the stability of Mswati's administration. In addition the Swazi public began to demand greater DEMOCRATIZATION of the government. As a result, in 1993, Mswati allowed

for legislative elections. In 1996 the king began the process to establish a new constitution for Swaziland, but as of 2003 no results had been achieved.

See also: COLONIAL RULE (Vol. IV); SWAZILAND (Vols. I, II, III, IV).

Further reading: D. Hugh Gillis, *The Kingdom of Swaziland: Studies in Political History* (Westport, Conn. Greenwood Press, 1999).

T

Tambo, Oliver (1917–1993) *Leader of the African National Congress in South Africa*

After joining the AFRICAN NATIONAL CONGRESS, in the early 1940s, Oliver Reginald Tambo rose through the ranks to become one of the organization's most important leaders. In 1960, when the government of SOUTH AFRICA cracked down in earnest on all forms of black political dissent, Tambo was chosen by ANC's executive leadership to go into exile to lead the organization from abroad. The decision proved prescient, as the ANC was banned in April 1960, and it became increasingly difficult to coordinate activities from within South Africa.

With the arrest of many leading ANC members at a farm in Rivonia, outside JOHANNESBURG, in 1963, Tambo emerged as the highest-ranking member still free and beyond the government's reach. From 1958 to 1969 he was ANC deputy president. He also served as acting president from 1967 to 1969, following the death of ANC president Chief Albert John Lutuli (1889–1967). Tambo was elected president in 1969 and reelected in 1985.

Tambo's efforts from abroad helped the ANC gain legitimacy and widespread recognition as a government-in-exile. Under his direction ANC bases were established in many countries surrounding South Africa, most notably in ZAMBIA and TANZANIA. He traveled widely, conducting diplomatic negotiations on behalf of the ANC with heads of state, UN representatives, the ORGANIZATION OF AFRICAN UNITY, and, in the 1980s, with influential white South African business leaders. By 1990 the ANC had established missions in 27 different countries.

After more than 30 years in exile Tambo returned to South Africa in December 1990. Due to his poor health, Tambo transferred the ANC presidency to Nelson MAN-DELA (1918–), his longtime friend and fellow anti-apartheid crusader, after Mandela was released from prison in 1990. Tambo then assumed the honorary position of national chairman of the ANC.

Tambo died shortly before South Africa's first fully democratic elections, which brought the ANC into power, in 1994. Although not the symbol of the anti-apartheid struggle that Mandela became during his long years in prison, Tambo was equally important in making possible the elections that ended APARTHEID.

See also: INDEPENDENCE MOVEMENTS (Vol. V); POLITICAL PARTIES AND ORGANIZATIONS (Vol. V).

Tandja, Mamadou (1938–) *President of Niger*

Born in Maine-Soroa, NIGER to the Kanouri ethnic group, Tandja was educated in a military school and joined the national army. Through years of service he rose to the rank of colonel. In 1974 he played a vital role in organizing the COUP D'ÉTAT that overthrew Niger's president, Hamani DIORI (1916–1989). Tandja's associate and fellow military leader, Senyi Kountché (1931–1987), assumed the presidency. Over the next several years Tandja served in high-ranking government positions until he retired from the military early in the 1990s.

In 1993 Mamadou Tandja was an unsuccessful candidate for president in the first democratic elections held in Niger in more than 20 years. The victor, Mahamane Ousmane (1950–), eventually was undermined by civil unrest, violence, and mounting economic crises. He was ousted by another military coup, in 1996, when Colonel Ibrahim Bare Mainassara (d. 1999) placed himself at the head of the new government by means of rigged elections.

As public dissatisfaction and unrest grew, Tandja and other political rivals joined together to fight for free elections, forming the Front for the Restoration and Defense of the Democracy. In 1996 Tandja turned himself in and was arrested as a political dissident. In 1999, however, Mainassara was assassinated, making way for a free, democratic election. Later that year Tandja was elected president of Niger with approximately 59 percent of the vote. As president, Tandja forged a coalition majority with supporters of former president Ousmane. In terms of economics, however, he faced a mounting national debt and extreme crises related to POVERTY, unemployment, poor health care, and social and economic instability.

Further reading: Robert B. Charlick, *Niger: Personal Rule and Survival in the Sahel* (Boulder, Colo.: Westview Press, 1991; Christian Lund, *Law, Power, and Politics in Niger: Land Struggles and the Rural Code* (New Brunswick, N.J.: Transaction Publishers, 1998).

Tansi, Sony Labou (1947–1995) *Congolese novelist*

Born in Kimwanza, Belgian Congo (present-day Democratic Republic of the CONGO), Tansi was educated at the École Normale Supérieure, the French high school in BRAZZAVILLE, Republic of the CONGO, where he was to continue to reside and work. He began writing seriously in 1971, and devoted himself to writing full-time after teaching for a brief period.

In 1978 Tansi published a satirical play, *La parenthése de sang* (Parentheses of blood), and, the following year, founded the Rocado Zulu Théâtre troupe. At that time he also published his first novel, *La Vie et demie* (published in English as *The Tortuous Path of the Fable*).

Although Tansi was a vocal proponent of the Kongo people, his theatrical productions were dedicated to all Africans and the challenges they faced in postcolonial Africa. Tansi once said of his theater, ". . . people come to the Rocado from all over the place, there is a superposition of multiple cultures. Thus theater simultaneously allows them to discover very different universes, the discovery of African diversity."

Tansi's novels include *L'antipeuple* (The antipeople, 1983), *Les septs solitides de Lorsa Lopez* (The seven solitudes of Lorsa Lopez, 1985), and *Les yeux du volcan* (Eyes of the volcano, 1988). In these works Tansi often chronicles the experiences of a sympathetic character in a cruel and unforgiving world. To its chagrin, Congo's one-party government proved unable to silence Tansi, whose popular novels and dramatic productions gave average Congolese people a voice in the face of inept leadership. Tansi died of an AIDS-related illness in 1995.

See also: BELGIAN CONGO (Vol. IV); LITERATURE IN MODERN AFRICA (Vol. IV).

Tanzania Country in East Africa covering approximately 342,100 square miles (886,000 sq km) and made up of mainland Tanganyika and the offshore Indian Ocean islands of ZANZIBAR, Pemba, and Mafia. Tanzania is bordered by UGANDA and KENYA to the north, the Indian Ocean to the east, MOZAMBIQUE, MALAWI, and ZAMBIA to the south, and RWANDA and BURUNDI to the west. It also shares Lake Tanganyika in the west with the Democratic Republic of the CONGO and borders on Lake VICTORIA to the north. The capital has been the coastal city of DAR ES SALAAM, but it is being shifted in stages to the more centrally located DODOMA.

Tanzania at Independence Tanganyika became independent, in 1961, as a result of a sustained lobbying effort before the United Nations (UN); before independence it was officially ruled as a TRUST TERRITORY by Britain under the auspices of the United Nations. Julius NYERERE (1922–1999), the country's central nationalist figure, became its first prime minister and then its first president when Tanganyika became a republic, in 1962. Three years later Tanganyika united with ZANZIBAR and formed the United Republic of Tanganyika and Zanzibar, which was renamed the United Republic of Tanzania. The mainland portion dominated the major issues between the two political units especially in foreign affairs and defense. Led by Nyerere, Tanzania participated actively in many regional, continental, and international affairs. The country became a member of the Commonwealth of Nations and joined with Kenya and Uganda to form the East African Common Services Organization in 1961, which from 1967 to 1977 was called the EAST AFRICAN COMMUNITY (EAC). In 1966 Kenya, Uganda, and Tanzania each established its own national currency based on the shilling, but all three national shillings remained legal tender across the region, and all remained convertible into British pounds.

Tanzania also played an important role in assisting INDEPENDENCE MOVEMENTS fighting for liberation in other African countries. An active member of the FRONTLINE STATES, Tanzania suffered economically for its support of liberation movements in Mozambique, ANGOLA, GUINEA-BISSAU, SOUTH AFRICA, and ZIMBABWE. Tanzania also played a leading role in the Nonaligned Movement and the ORGANIZATION OF AFRICAN UNITY. President Nyerere, who became known internationally as a leading statesman, was one of the founding members of Nonaligned Movement and the Frontline States. In 1979 Tanzanian troops helped to overthrow Ugandan dictator, Idi AMIN (c. 1925–2003). After Amin attempted to seize part of Tanzania its troops quickly moved into Uganda and forced Amin from power. They helped install a new government and withdrew as soon as their task was accomplished. Due to Nyerere's leadership Tanzania gained fame as a supporter of Africa's values and liberation. Tanzania was seen as a progressive African nation and a political base for revolutionary activists from around the world, including African-Americans.

In 1967 President Nyerere established a national policy that had a lasting impact on the society and economy of the country. Outlined in the ARUSHA DECLARATION, named after the town in which he made the proclamation, the policy sought to transform the country. Nyerere declared that Tanzania would pursue socialist policies. The major tenet of his philosophy was a brand of African Socialism, or collectivism, called UJAMAA. It was centered on community and was characterized by economic self-reliance, egalitarianism, and local rural DEVELOPMENT. In this regard villages were intended to be socialist organizations created by the people and governed by the people. Villages were grouped for effective development and sharing of resources. Nyerere's socialist objective was to build a society in which the community's material welfare took precedence over an individual's and in which all members would have equal rights and opportunities and live in peace with their neighbors without suffering, injustice, or exploitation.

In order to meet his objective of having a sole political party mobilizing and controlling the population, Nyerere merged his Tanganyika African Union (TANU) and Zanzibar's AFRO-SHIRAZI PARTY (ASP) into a single party, Chama Cha Mapinduzi (CCM), which translates as PARTY OF THE REVOLUTION. Nyerere's objective was for the party to be a vehicle for the flow of ideas and policy directives between the village level and the government. To pursue his objective of building an egalitarian society, Nyerere nationalized the economy and increased taxes. He made it illegal for government ministers and party officials to have shares or directorships in companies or to receive more than one salary in an attempt to prevent the development of an exploitative class. The result is that Tanzania did not develop great economic disparities within its population.

Nyerere, who had trained as a teacher, set forth his views about socialism in books such as *Freedom and Socialism: A Selection from Writings & Speeches, 1965–1967,* which appeared from the Dar es Salaam office of Oxford University Press in 1968.

While Nyerere was moving ahead with his socialist ideology, the country's economy plummeted. The *ujamaa* policy, the OIL crisis of the 1970s, and the falling world market prices for the country's principal CASH CROPS negatively affected the country's economy. In addition, Tanzania's commitment to liberation movements and its invasion of Uganda added to the country's economic difficulties. As a result the country was near bankruptcy. Tanzania remained one of the world's poorest countries with a per-capita income at the time of $270 (it is currently $610) and dependent mainly on agricultural production of sisal and cloves, since it lacked significant mineral resources. AGRICULTURE accounts for 85 percent of its export earnings.

In 1985 Nyerere stepped down from the presidency and was succeeded by Ali Hassan MWINYI (1925–   ), who was from Zanzibar. Nyerere retained his position as chair of the ruling CCM party and continued to influence the country's politics until his death, in October 1999. Mwinyi introduced new policy directions and belt-tightening STRUCTURAL ADJUSTMENT programs to help integrate the parallel economies of Tanzania and Zanzibar and stimulate economic growth. From 1986 Tanzania embarked on an adjustment program to eliminate government control of the economy and encourage participation of the private sector. Under compulsion from the INTERNATIONAL MONETARY FUND, Tanzania initiated economic recovery measures that generated increases in agricultural production and financial support from donor nations. At this time national and international pressure forced President Mwinyi, in 1992, to introduce a more inclusive election system. In 1995, for the first time in 30 years, multiparty elections were held, contested by 13 political parties. Benjamin MKAPA (1938–   ) of the CCM party won the election and was reelected to a second five-year term in 2000. From 1996 onward Tanzania's economy continued to grow due to improvements in production and increased EXPORTS. In 1993 the WORLD BANK classified Tanzania as the second-poorest country in the world. By 2000, however, it had risen by two positions.

While his socialist economic policies were less than fully successful, Nyerere must be credited with the expansion of the use of one national language, a major feat for a country with more than 120 ethnic groups, of which the largest groups (the Sukuma and Nyamwezi) together represent only one-fifth of the population. Tanzania, however, has maintained the use of Kiswahili and English as the main languages, with English being the official language and Kiswahili the common national language. In 2002 the population of Tanzania was about 35 million, which reflects a significant POPULATION GROWTH since independence.

See also: COMMUNISM AND SOCIALISM (Vol. V); NON-ALIGNED MOVEMENT AND AFRICA (Vol. V); TANZANIA (Vols.

I, II, III, IV); TRUST TERRITORY (Vol. IV); UNITED NATIONS AND AFRICA (Vols. IV, V).

Further reading: C. Legum and G. Mmari, eds., *Mwalimu: The Influence of Nyerere* (London: Africa World Press, 1995); Kelly Askew, *Performing the Nation: Swahili Music and Cultural Politics in Tanzania* (Chicago: University of Chicago, 2002).

Tanzanian African National Union (TANU)

First political party of independent TANZANIA. The Tanzanian African National Union emerged out of the *Tanganyika* African National Union (the original TANU), which was formed in 1954. It in turn had grown out of the Tanganyika African Association (TAA), which was founded by the British colonialists in 1929 for Africans but was inadequate to further African nationalism. Julius NYERERE (1922–1999), who became the first president of the country, and other leaders transformed the TAA into the Tanganyika African National Union (TANU) in order to spearhead the fight against colonialism. TANU adopted three main strategies at its formation: to pressure the British government, to pressure the Trusteeship Council of the United Nations, and to rally general African and international support for Tanganyika's independence. TANU's efforts resulted in its winning a large number of seats on the Tanganyika Legislative Council in elections held in 1958. Two years later TANU won 70 of 71 seats in the country's new Legislative Assembly.

Tanganyika became independent on December 9, 1961, and Nyerere was elected prime minister, modeling Britain's parliamentary system. The following year Tanganyika changed to become a republic with Nyerere as its president. Nyerere appointed a presidential commission, in 1964, to investigate the formation of a one-party state in Tanganyika. This was the same year that ZANZIBAR and Tanganyika merged to form Tanzania. The commission's report led to the adoption of TANU (now the *Tanzanian* African National Union) as the sole political party, in 1965. On February 5, 1977, TANU and the AFRO-SHIRAZI PARTY, the sole Zanzibari political party, merged to form Chama Cha Mapinduzi (CCM, called the PARTY OF THE REVOLUTION in English) with Nyerere as its leader until his retirement from direct party politics, in 1990.

See also: ARUSHA DECLARATION (Vol. V); INDEPENDENCE MOVEMENTS (Vol. V); NATIONALISM AND INDEPENDENCE MOVEMENTS (Vol. IV); POLITICAL PARTIES AND ORGANIZATIONS (Vols. IV, V); POLITICAL SYSTEMS (Vol. V); TANGANYIKA (Vol. IV).

Further reading: Susan Geiger, *TANU Women: Gender and Culture in the Making of Tanganyikan Nationalism, 1955–1965* (Portsmouth, N.H.: Heinemann, 1997); Cranford Pratt, *The Critical Phase in Tanzania, 1945–1968: Nyerere and the Emergence of a Socialist Strategy* (New York: Cambridge University Press, 1976).

Tati-Loutard, Jean-Baptiste (1938–) *Congolese statesman and poet*

Tati-Loutard was born in the Belgian Congo (present-day Democratic Republic of the CONGO) and received his higher education at the University of Bordeaux, in France. In 1966 he returned to the Congolese capital, BRAZZAVILLE, to teach at the Center for Higher Education. In the late 1970s Tati-Loutard was recognized as a leader in the cultural movement of his country and other French-speaking African states, becoming minister of culture, arts, and sport and acting minister of foreign affairs. Tati-Loutard is best known internationally for his poetry, which features classical styles. A student of the black literary movement known as Négritude, Tati-Loutard used his poetry as a platform for exploring the black literary voice and the human condition in general. In the late 1990s Tati-Loutard became Congo's OIL minister on the strength of his ability to write about and disseminate the government's policies.

See also: LITERATURE IN MODERN AFRICA (Vol. V); NÉGRITUDE (Vol. IV).

Taya, Maaouya Ould Sid Ahmed (c. 1941–) *President of Mauritania*

Born in the Atar region of MAURITANIA, Taya became deeply involved in the turbulent politics of his country. He joined the army early on, serving as an assistant to President Moktar Ould Daddah (1924–) before leading troops against POLISARIO guerrillas in the Mauritania-occupied region of WESTERN SAHARA. At the time Mauritania had divided the disputed region with MOROCCO, with both countries facing strong resistance from the indigenous SAHARAWI people. Controversy over the struggle in Western Sahara led to a COUP D'ÉTAT, unseating Daddah and bringing Mustapha Salek to power. Taya served as minister of defense until Salek resigned, in 1979.

In 1980 Mohamed Khouna Ould Haidalla (1940–) became president and attempted to reform the government from a single-party to a multiparty system. Taya became army chief of staff, essentially serving as Haidalla's prime minister. Haidalla's administration gradually became more oppressive as he defended himself against a number of attempted coups. Measures to stimulate the economy were instituted with little effect. In 1982 Taya led a military coup and assumed the presidency.

Under Taya, Mauritania's government remained a multiparty system, but the new constitution broadened the president's powers and allowed for unlimited terms. In 1992 Taya was officially elected president as the leader of the Social and Democratic Republican Party (Parti Républicain Démocratique et Social, PRDS). He won again in 1997 amid electoral controversy. Both Taya and the PRDS continued to dominate Mauritanian politics through the 2001 elections as well.

As president Taya has been dogged by a number of troubling issues. The country has suffered from inconsistent DEVELOPMENT and a fragile economy, relying heavily on foreign ECONOMIC ASSISTANCE. Though the Western Sahara conflict ended under President Haidalla, Mauritania itself still struggles with ethnic tensions and racism, as dark-skinned Mauritanians have often faced extreme prejudice from lighter-skinned Arabic Mauritanians. Also, despite having officially abolished slavery four times, most recently in 1981, HUMAN RIGHTS groups have repeatedly uncovered evidence that the heinous practice continues in Mauritania under Taya's leadership.

In addition, Taya has continued to face hostility against his administration, leading him to ban a number of opposition parties, including, in 2002, the antiracism Action for Change (AC) party. The outlawing of the AC party left Mauritania once again a one-party state.

Taylor, Charles (1948–) *Former head of state of Liberia*

Charles McArthur Taylor was the son of an American father and a mother from the Americo-Liberian elite. After attending college in the United States and earning a degree in economics Taylor worked as a mechanic in Boston, Massachusetts. There he became active in organizations seeking to end the long-standing domination of LIBERIA by the Americo-Liberians' True Whig Party.

Taylor returned to Liberia when a COUP D'ÉTAT brought Sergeant Samuel DOE (c. 1952–1990) to power in 1980. Taylor eventually headed the country's General Services Agency, but, accused of embezzling almost a million dollars from the government, he fled to the United States in 1983. There he was arrested, but he escaped from jail and fled, spending the next five years in hiding. It is rumored that Taylor spent much of that time in LIBYA as a guest of Colonel Muammar QADDAFI (1942–).

Beginning in 1985 Taylor devoted four years to organizing his National Patriotic Front of Liberia (NPFL), an anti-Doe group that became increasingly militant. Eventually he put together a rebel force that he led in an invasion of Liberia on Dec. 24, 1990. For a while Taylor enjoyed the support of the United States as well as a large number of Liberians, who saw hope in his announced plans to democratize Liberia, return it to civilian rule, and to redistribute the power and wealth of the Americo-Liberians among the nation's other ethnic groups. By July 1990, however, many people had grown disenchanted with Taylor, and he was losing support. Indeed, when he and some of his armed force entered MONROVIA, the Liberian capital, factional disputes within his own NPFL made it impossible for him to take control of the city.

Civil war and ethnic hostilities dominated Liberian life for the next half-decade, but, when forthcoming elections were announced, Taylor was able to launch an effective campaign and win the election. Unfortunately, once in office he proved unable to do much of anything to solve the political, economic, and ethnic crises facing the country. At the same time he became caught up in fomenting unrest in other countries, supporting rebel groups in places such as SIERRA LEONE.

In 2003 accusations of corruption forced Liberian president Charles Taylor (right) to leave the country. Nigerian president Olusegun Obasanjo (left) offered Taylor refuge in Nigeria. *© AP/Wide World Photos*

In the early years of the 21st century Taylor proved unable to hold his country together. By 2003 Liberia had descended into virtual anarchy, and international pressure forced Taylor to flee to NIGERIA. In 2004, with the help of a United Nations mission, an interim government began restoring order to the ravaged land.

See also: CIVIL WARS (Vol. V); ETHNIC CONFLICT IN AFRICA (Vol. V); UNITED STATES AND AFRICA (Vols. IV, V).

telecommunications Although Africa still lags behind other regions of the world, the continent has witnessed the rapid DEVELOPMENT of telecommunications over the last two decades. A substantial increase in the rate of expansion and modernization of fixed networks has taken place along with the explosion of mobile networks. Mobile networks have spread rapidly, and subscribers have now surpassed fixed-line users in most countries, underscoring the latent demand for basic voice services. Due to the low cost and long range of the cellular base stations, many rural areas are also covered. But the high cost of mobile usage, which in 2002 was approximately 20–40 U.S. cents per minute, makes it too expensive for most local calls or wireless Internet access.

The number of fixed telephone lines also steadily increased. Between 1995 and 2001 the number of fixed lines jumped from 12.5 million to 21 million across Africa. Northern Africa had 11.4 million of the lines, while southern Africa had another 5 million lines, leaving 4.6 million for rest of the continent.

In general, African governments left the responsibility for maintaining public telephones to the private sector. In many countries this resulted in an increase in the number of public telephone places and telecenters. In SENEGAL, for example, there are now more than 10,000 commercial public phone bureaus that employ more than 15,000 people. While most of these phone service centers are in urban areas, a growing number are being established in rural locations. Some are even able to provide Internet access and other advanced services to the public.

At the beginning of the 1990s cellular operators were present in only six African countries. By 2002, however, there were more than 100 cellular networks in 48 countries serving more than 14 million customers. Operators provide access mainly in the capital cities, but they also are beginning to be found in some secondary towns and along major truck routes.

Some cellular operators are providing extra services including data transmission, short message sending, and even financial transactions. Calling cards and PIN-based public and cellular phones are becoming popular across the continent. This is creating a new revenue stream in the sale of telephone airtime by small shops and telecenters. This development can also form the basis for more advanced telephone-based services, including electronic commerce. This is already the case in ZAMBIA and SOUTH AFRICA, where mobile-phone-based bill-payment systems have been launched.

The use of the Internet has grown relatively rapidly in most urban areas in Africa in much the same pattern as the adoption of the mobile phone. In 1997 only a handful of African countries had local Internet access, but by 2000 it was available in every capital city.

According to statistics compiled in 2001 it was estimated that 24 million Africans had mobile phones. It also was estimated that 20 million people had fixed-line telephones and 5.9 million had personal computers. The growth rate in users that was seen in the 1990s has slowed down in most countries, primarily because most of the users who can afford a computer and telephone have already obtained connections. As of mid 2002 the number of dial-up Internet subscribers was close to 1.7 million, up 20 percent from the previous year. This was mainly due to growth in a few of the larger countries such as EGYPT, South Africa, MOROCCO, and NIGERIA. Of the total subscribers, northern Africa and southern Africa are responsible for about 1.2 million, leaving about 500,000 for the remaining 49 sub-Saharan countries.

In Africa each computer with an Internet or e-mail connection usually supports three to five users. This puts current estimates of the total number of African Internet users at around 5 million. In response to the high cost of Internet services and the slow speed of connections, lower-cost e-mail-only services attract subscribers. Similarly, because of the relatively high cost of local electronic mailbox services from African Internet service providers, a large proportion of African e-mail users make use of the free Web-based services such as Hotmail, Yahoo, or Excite, most of which are in the United States.

The use of fiber-optic cable for international traffic is still in the beginning stages in Africa, and most international telecom connections are carried via satellite. Currently five submarine cables provide some international fiber connectivity to Africa. These cables connect most of North and West Africa's coastal countries to networks in Europe. All remaining international bandwidth is provided by satellite providers. The high costs and limited service are attributed to the monopoly environment in which most of the communications companies operate, but this is slowly changing with increased privatization.

Some of the factors hampering the development of telecommunication in Africa include irregular or nonexistent electricity supplies, tax regimes that regard computers and cell phones as luxury items, and limited business environments characterized by inflation, currency instability, and exchange controls.

See also: RADIO AND TELEVISION (Vol. V).

Further reading: Eli M. Noam, ed., *Telecommunications in Africa* (New York: Oxford University Press, 1999).

terrorism   The word *terrorism* dates to the Reign of Terror (1793–94) of the French Revolution. During this period Robespierre (1758–1794) and the Jacobins violently purged French society of 12,000 so-called enemies of the revolution in hopes of making a better society. As a concept and a practice, though, terrorism existed in deed if not name long before this. Many scholars trace its beginnings to Phineas, a Jewish high priest. Historian Flavius Josephus (37 CE–100 CE) described how Phineas and his Sicarii (militant Zealots) killed a number of Jewish priests in an effort to frighten the remaining priests into opposing Rome. "The panic," Josephus wrote, "was more alarming than the calamity itself; everyone, as on the battlefield, hourly expected death."

While today's terrorism may differ from that of the ancient past in scope and execution, the roots remain the same. As characterized by the United Nations, terrorism is distinguished from other violence in that its motivation is to generate, increase, or spread fear in an effort to change the social order. It is not killing for killing's sake. It is an "act intended to cause death or serious bodily injury to a civilian . . . when the purpose of such act, by its nature or context, is to intimidate a population, or to compel a government or an international organization to do or to abstain from doing any act." Those who employ it believe that they are using the most effective tool of revolt or war to fight against those who oppress them.

The root causes of terrorism are complex. For instance, Nobel laureate Kim Dae Jung (1925–) stated that "at the bottom of terrorism is POVERTY." Those who are poor, advocates of this view believe, have little to lose and everything to gain. They are at the bottom of the social or economic order, and only by upending this order can they move ahead. Some leaders, including Tony Blair, former president of SOUTH AFRICA Nelson MANDELA (1918–), and President Robert MUGABE (1924–) of ZIMBABWE, have called for significant investment by wealthy countries in poverty alleviation, declaring that this will help dissuade would-be terrorists. The very real fear is that an African variant of terrorism can rise. Little economic opportunity, social deprivation, and loss of cultural identity—all rampant in Africa—provide the seeds of terrorist growth and mutation.

Another cause of terrorism is political motivation. Where the problem with the social order is ideology rather than economic oppression, modern day zealots of all religions and creeds feel isolated from the political structure. This explanation has been used most fervently in recent years to explain the actions of radical Muslims who oppose secular Muslim governments. According to this argument, these radical Muslims see no opportunity for participation in the current system since the religious law under which they wish to live is excluded from the political system. In this sense, terrorism becomes a highly violent form of political participation. Perhaps the best example of this in Africa is in NIGERIA. Throughout the oppressive regimes of Ibrahim BABANGIDA (1941–), Sani ABACHA (1943–1998), and Abdulsalami Abubakar (1943–1998) the government maintained a monopoly on violence. Terrorism, while it existed, was uncommon. With DEMOCRATIZATION and the presidency of Olusegun OBASANJO (c. 1937–) in 1999, the state became less oppressive and more open to the freedom of association, RELIGION, and expression. Rules were more formalized, primarily at the regional level. The new secular government accepted mass participation but only in a secular manner. Those who wanted to see the rise of SHARIA, Islamic law, could not participate in a fashion that would bring it about. For them, resorting to terrorist acts became a way of trying to change the new political system. They gained enough legitimacy to bring about a constitutional crisis in which the central government had to bar states from electing leaders that would bring about a shift to *sharia*. In recent years there has been a radicalization of *sharia* not only in Nigeria but in ALGERIA, SOMALIA, and even SOUTH AFRICA.

In Africa, a strong state has tended to be a deterrent to terrorism. State violence can keep the peace or oppress but it is not, by definition, terrorism. This has been the case, for instance, in KENYA, TANZANIA, MALI, ZAMBIA, CAMEROON, and MALAWI. In reverse, one of the greatest contributors to the rise in terrorism has been the weakness of states. A collapsed state is one that can no longer perform the functions expected of it. This means that it cannot secure its population or its borders. Nor can it provide police, banks, a financial system, or any of the other elements of a functioning contemporary society. LIBERIA, SIERRA LEONE, and the Democratic Republic of the CONGO all serve as examples, while GUINEA, CHAD, the CENTRAL AFRICAN REPUBLIC, the Republic of the CONGO, the Republic of the SUDAN, and ANGOLA have significantly deteriorated in this direction.

The quintessential example, however, is Somalia. When the former dictator Mohammed Siad BARRE (1919–1995) was ousted, in January 1991, what remained of his soft, autocratic state collapsed. After a brief period of anarchy, local leadership—religious and ethnic—filled the void, as the country became a violent and dangerous place. Since 2000 President ABDIKASSIM SALAD HASSAN (1941–) has unsuccessfully tried to recentralize authority in the hands of the state. He has been powerless in stopping secessionist movements in Somaliland and Puntland, both of which have set up quasi states. Perhaps more importantly, his government has not been strong enough to ensure that local leaders will follow national laws instead of their own. Important INFRASTRUCTURE has collapsed, schools are not functioning, hospitals are closed, civil services have not resumed, and jobs are virtually nonexistent. Many groups are unhappy with the status quo and have little to lose by trying to do something about it, particularly since the police and military are too weak to stop them. Warlords have taken the place of politicians. Moreover, where these local leaders want to see the rise of a radical Islamic state in Somalia or empathize with groups in other countries trying to do the same, the state lacks the ability to stop them. Al-Ittihad al-Islami, an organization that did not even make the U.S. Foreign Terrorist Organization list until after September 11, 2001, is now strong enough to be considered one of the greatest terrorist threats in Africa. Their influence has crossed the border to ETHIOPIA, and the United States has pointed to their connections with Al Qaeda, the organization responsible for the September 11 attacks. What Somalia has taught the world is that failed states provide a fertile ground for terrorist groups to grow.

Terrorist acts escalated in Africa in the 1990s. Violent attacks were stepped up against the government in Algeria, against Egyptian president Hosni MUBARAK (1928–) while he was in Ethiopia, and Western tourists in EGYPT. The biggest event came on August 8, 1998, when two bombs, believed planted by Al Qaeda, destroyed the U.S. embassies in NAIROBI, Kenya and DAR ES SALAAM, Tanzania. Hundreds of Kenyan, Tanzanian, and American nationals were killed. This began a new era in the role of Africa in global terrorism, and U.S. policy changed. In Somalia, in particular, the United States set out a policy, still in place, that seeks to remove the terrorist threat, ensure against Somalia as a base of terrorist operations, prevent terrorists from destabilizing the region, and overcome the challenges of governance in Somalia. However, even as the United States has realized the rising global terrorist threat stemming from Africa, organizations have proliferated in East Africa in particular, providing training grounds and bases that have been used to launch attacks against the United States and its allies.

African leaders have made significant attempts to quell the rising terrorist tide, with successive antiterrorist statements and pacts on the part of the ORGANIZATION OF AFRICAN UNITY (OAU). These culminated in 1999 with the Convention on the Prevention and Combating of Terrorism. Signed in ALGIERS, Algeria, this acknowledged the link between countering terrorism and recognizing civil rights while reinforcing continent-wide efforts to cooperate against the rise of extremism.

Despite the great efforts of the United States, its allies, the OAU, and its successor, the AFRICAN UNION, the nature of terrorism in Africa and around the world appears to be becoming more global. Affordable TELECOMMUNICATIONS and technologies—such as cell phones and the Internet—have facilitated its growth. This has blurred the line between terrorist organization and supporter. Indeed, while the United States chased Al-Ittihad al-Islami, Al Qaeda, and other organizations in Africa, the National Islamic Front of Sudan has simultaneously served as government, government backer of terrorist groups, and a non-state terrorist group. It is situations like this that have made scholars and political leaders alike realize that they have a long way to go before they can effectively determine how to recognize terrorism, let alone how to confront its globalization from an Africa base.

See also: STATE, ROLE OF (Vol. V).

Further reading: Douglas Farah, *Blood From Stones: the Secret Financial Network of Terror* (New York: Broadway Books, 2004); Sherene Razack, *Dark Threats and White Knights, the Somalia Affair, Peacekeeping, and the New Imperialism* (Toronto: University of Toronto Press, 2004); Rahul Mahajan, *The New Crusade: America's War on Terrorism* (New York: Monthly Review Press, 2002).

theater Used to disseminate foreign and indigenous literature and to teach those who are not literate, the staged play became very important as an African literary genre after independence. Many African cultural traditions, masquerades, festivals, and story telling in which costume and dance were a part of communication were used for instruction and information. MISSIONARIES taught Africans about theater and used it for instructional purposes. European-style educational institutions such as the William Ponty Teacher Training School, Achimota College, and MAKERERE UNIVERSITY helped to contribute European expression to an African theater rooted in African values.

Many of the first African playwrights used their colonial training to produce European-style plays, sometimes providing an anticolonial message. Those playwrights who were educated under colonialism and came into prominence after independence often used the genre to provide a political critique of fledgling African governments. Other playwrights used the genre of popular theater for popular EDUCATION, providing people with the facts on the medical issues surrounding the HIV/AIDS epidemic and the hazards inherent in the cultural practice of female circumcision.

In West Africa the best-known dramatist is Nigerian writer Wole SOYINKA (1934–), who won the Nobel Prize in Literature in 1986. Writing in English, he used myths to provide a means of indirectly criticizing the government, and because his plays focused on a YORUBA cultural setting, he educated non-Yoruba audiences about Yoruba culture. As the early years of independence unfolded Soyinka used social and religious themes to debunk the prevailing ideas of a glorious African past and to deflate the enthusiasm about the future in his play *A Dance of the Forests* (1963). Like Chinua ACHEBE (1930–) did for the IGBO in his novel *Things Fall Apart* (1958), Soyinka portrays the consequences of the intrusion of British colonialism among the Yoruba in his *Death and the King's Horseman* (1975), his most successful play internationally.

During the 1960s and 1970s many playwrights were Yoruba, a people that easily translated ideas from their culture to the stage. Nigerian Femi Osofisan (1946–   ) emerged in the 1970s, writing plays about the Biafran civil war (1967–70). In his play *Sons and Daughters* (1964), Ghanaian Joe de Graft (1924–1978) dramatized the generational and cultural conflicts between parents with an indigenous education and children with a colonial education. *The Dilemma of a Ghost* (1965), a dramatic work by Ama Ata AIDOO (1942–   ), demonstrates the problems of intercultural marriages. A pioneer in developing Ghanaian national theater, Efua Sutherland (1924–1996) used radio as the first stage for which she wrote plays such as *The Marriage of Anansew* (1975).

In East Africa playwrights wrote about colonial events. These writers included NGUGI WA THIONG'O (1938–   ) of KENYA, who collaborated with Micere Mugo (1942–   ) in writing *The Trial of Dedn Kimathi* (1976), and Ebrahim Hussein (1943–   ), who wrote *Kinjeketile* (1969) and *Kwenye Ukingo wa Thim* (1988). These writers also dealt in contemporary political critiques. The direct criticism of the Kenyan government conveyed in the 1977 performance of *Nagaahika Ndeenda* by Ngugi wa Thiong'o and Ngugi wa Mirii resulted in the imprisonment of Ngugi wa Thiong'o, the exiling of Ngugi wa Mirii, and the destruction of the Kamiriithu Community Educational and Cultural Center, where the play was performed. Despite these attempts at censorship, the play continued to be staged in other locations.

In SOUTH AFRICA the history of theater began in 1947 with the establishment of the National Theatre Organization, a group that performed for white audiences only. In the 1950s the Union Artists joined with the African Music and Drama Association and the Rehearsal Room at Dorkay House in JOHANNESBURG for the production of urban English-speaking performances. In 1972 the multiracial Spaced Theater was opened in CAPE TOWN by Brian Astubury, Yvonne Bryceland, and Athol FUGARD (1932–   ), who is South Africa's most popular English-speaking playwright. Fugard's early work focuses on anti-APARTHEID themes in his Sophiatown "Township" plays, political violence in *My Children, My Africa* (1989), and the need for reconciliation in a democratized South Africa in *Playland* (1992).

In North Africa the 1960s were theatrically dynamic in EGYPT, which was known for its role as the cultural leader of the Arab world. The government of Gamal Abdel NASSER (1918–1970) sponsored theater companies through the Ministry of Culture, and many playwrights and directors applied the knowledge they gained in their study abroad to the Egyptian genre. While playwrights contested over language usage, they merged local, Arab, and European themes in their plays. Ali Salim (1936–   )

used satire in comedies, including *Bir al-qamh* (The wheat-pit, 1968), a play that addressed the world's myopic archaeological interest in Egypt's past. Alfred Faraj (1929–   ) wrote for the wider Arab audience, focusing on classical topics of the universal Islamic state in his *Hallaq Baghdad* (The barber of Baghdad, 1963). In his two-act play, *al-Farafir* (The Farfurs, 1964), Yusuf Idris (1927–   ) merged indigenous genres with popular comedies. One of the most important playwrights of the 1960s and 1970s was Najib Surur (1932–1978), who used Arabic verse in drama.

African theater continues to merge indigenous culture with foreign cultural elements experienced in African life into a hybrid literary genre for the literate and a popular theater for the nonliterate. The products of African playwrights are essential to the understanding of the tremendous upheaval experienced in Africa during the age of colonialism and in the turbulent times of independence that followed.

See also: ACHIMOTA COLLEGE (Vol. IV); BIAFRA (Vol. V); COLONIALISM, INFLUENCE OF (Vol. IV); COLONIAL RULE (Vol. IV); ÉCOLE WILLIAM PONTY (Vol. IV); LITERATURE IN MODERN AFRICA (Vol. V); *THINGS FALL APART* (Vol. IV).

Further reading: Martin Banham, James Gibbs, and Femi Osofisan, eds., *African Theatre: Playwrights & Politics* (Bloomington, Ind.: Indiana University Press, 2001); Martin Banham, James Gibbs, and Femi Osofisan, eds., *African Theatre Women* (Bloomington, Ind.: Indiana University Press, 2002); Biodun Jeyifo, ed., *Modern African Drama: Backgrounds and Criticism* (New York: W. W. Norton, 2002); Lokangaka Losambe and Devi Sarinjeive, eds., *Precolonial and Post-colonial Drama and Theatre in Africa* (Trenton, N.J.: Africa World Press, 2001).

Tigray Large ethnic group concentrated in ERITREA and ETHIOPIA. The northern province in which the majority of Ethiopia's Tigray live is also called Tigray. The Tigray people speak the Semitic language of Tigrinya. Today they make up about one-third of Eritrea's population and about 6 percent of Ethiopia's population.

Most Tigrayans are members of the Coptic ETHIOPIAN ORTHODOX CHURCH, although some have converted from Coptic Christianity to Islam. The Tigray are primarily agricultural, but they also raise livestock for important EXPORTS.

Over the years the Tigray have resisted attempts at cultural assimilation by the Amhara, the dominant group in Ethiopia. At the same time they are in competition with other ethnic groups in the region, including the OROMO. Ethnic relations in Ethiopia have been extremely contentious in recent years, with the Tigray occupying a central role in determining the face of Ethiopian politics, most notably through the Tigray People's Liberation Front (TPLF).

Beginning in the 1960s the Tigray fought back against the poor treatment they received from the regime of former Emperor HAILE SELASSIE (1892–1975). After Selassie was deposed, in 1974, the Tigray, through the TPLF, launched a protracted fight against the military government of MENGISTU HAILE MARIAM (c. 1937–   ). The battle against the Amhara-dominated government in Ethiopia included efforts to establish an independent Tigrayan republic. Eventually, in 1991, the TPLF allied with other oppressed groups, including the Oromo People's Democratic Organization, to take control of the government. The new coalition governing party, called the ETHIOPIAN PEOPLE'S REVOLUTIONARY DEMOCRATIC FRONT, ousted Mengistu Haile Mariam, replacing him with MELES ZENAWI (1955–   ), from Tigray. However, Tigray control of Ethi-opia has not alleviated contentious ethnic politics and conflict continues in the region.

See also: AMHARA (Vols. I, III, IV); ETHNIC CONFLICT IN AFRICA (Vol. V); ETHNICITY AND IDENTITY (Vol. V); TIGRAY (Vols. I, IV); TIGRINYA (Vol. I).

Further reading: Alemseged Abbay, *Identity Jilted, or, Reimagining Identity?: The Divergent Paths of the Eritrean and Tigrayan Nationalist Struggles* (Lawrenceville, N.J.: Red Sea Press, 1998); John Young, *Peasant Revolution in Ethiopia: The Tigray People's Liberation Front, 1975–1991* (Cambridge, U.K.: Cambridge University Press, 1997).

Todd, Garfield (1908–2002) *Prime minister of Southern Rhodesia from 1953 to 1958*

Garfield Todd was born in 1908 in New Zealand and came to Southern Rhodesia (present-day ZIMBABWE) with his wife, Jean Grace Wilson, as a missionary in 1934. He entered politics in Southern Rhodesia, which was then a self-governing colony within the British Empire. In 1946 Todd became a Legislative Assembly member representing Salisbury, the capital that later became HARARE. A charismatic public speaker, he became Southern Rhodesia's prime minister in 1953, leading the United Rhodesia Party.

As a moderate politician Todd introduced and supported various laws that extended voting, home ownership, and land ownership rights to Southern Rhodesia's African majority. In the country's racially charged political climate, the white minority came to view Todd as too liberal. The African majority, however, considered him not progressive enough. When his cabinet resigned over his policies, in 1958, Todd was removed from office.

He remained outspoken and sympathetic to the rights of black Africans following the UNILATERAL DECLARATION OF INDEPENDENCE issued in 1965 by Ian SMITH (1919–   ). The Smith government of the newly named RHODESIA restricted Todd to his farm and even imprisoned him briefly. After the African majority gained independence as Zimbabwe in 1980 Todd reentered politics as

a member of the Senate before leaving public life for good, in 1985. He died on October 13, 2002, in Bulawayo, Zimbabwe, at the age of 93.

See also: ENGLAND AND AFRICA (Vols. III, IV, V); MISSIONARIES (Vols. III, IV, V); SOUTHERN RHODESIA (Vol. IV).

Further reading: Dickson A. Mungazi, *The Last British Liberals in Africa: Michael Blundell and Garfield Todd* (Westport, Conn.: Praeger, 1999); Ruth Weiss with Jane L. Parpart, *Sir Garfield Todd and the Making of Zimbabwe* (London: British Academic Press, 1999).

Togo Small West African country about 22,000 square miles (57,000 sq km) in size located on the Gulf of Guinea and sharing borders with GHANA to the west, the Republic of BENIN to the east, and BURKINA FASO to the north.

Togo at Independence Togo received its independence from France in 1960, with Sylvanus Olympio (1902–1963) becoming president the following year. Conservative and authoritarian in his leadership, Olympio strove to achieve economic independence from France through tax policies and trade restrictions. However, his failure to take care of his military personnel led to his death following a COUP D'ÉTAT in 1963.

Led by Sergeant Étienne EYADEMA (1935–2005), the new government invited former Togolese prime minister Nicolas Grunitzkey (1913–1969), to become the new leader of government. However, this arrangement lasted only four years, and in 1967 Eyadema, now a general, led another coup and installed himself as president of Togo.

In 1969 Eyadema created the Togolese People's Rally (Rassemblement du Peuple Togolais, RPT) and turned Togo into a one-party state. In an effort to create political unity, in 1974 he launched a cultural revolution that called for the rejection of foreign personnel and place names. In addition he encouraged Togo's 20 to 30 ethnic groups (depending upon classification) to assert their individual cultures, a divisive measure. He changed his first name from the French Étienne to Gnassingbe, a name of the northern Kabye ethnic group to which he belongs.

With the support of Togo's army, which Eyadema staffed mostly with men from his native region, he was able to maintain political stability during the 1970s and early 1980s. However, fraudulent tactics during elections, a weak economy, and government CORRUPTION led to bomb attacks in LOMÉ, the capital, during the 1980s. This overt challenge to his government led Eyadema to arrest and detain dissidents. Later reports of torture and disappearances have led Amnesty International and other organizations to charge the Eyadema regime with numerous HUMAN RIGHTS violations.

Togo Since 1990 In the 1990s Togo's domestic policy focused on the challenge of creating a multiparty, democratic state. In 1991 Eyadema suspended the conference to establish a transition government to democracy, leading to more political unrest. To appease his opponents Eyadema named Joseph Kokou Koffigoh (1948–), the leader of the strongest opposition group, as prime minister.

From 1991 until the elections of 1993 general strikes and violence threatened Togo's political and social stability. The resulting government repression forced thousands of Togolese to flee to Benin, Burkina Faso, and Ghana. The exodus embroiled the region in a foreign policy crisis, with Eyadema accusing these countries of harboring the "dissidents," who were branded as criminals. In the 1993 elections a fragmented opposition and low voter turnout allowed Eyadema to win. In legislative elections held the following year, opposition parties won by a small margin. Eyadema was able to limit the opposition's threat, however, by naming Edem Kodjo (1938–), who led a small opposition party, as prime minister. In 2002 Eyadema dismissed Kodjo and the RPT subsequently won another landslide electoral victory. In 2005 Eyadema died while in transit to Paris for emergency medical treatment. After a special parliamentary session, Eyadema's son, Faure, was named the new president of Togo.

See also: AMNESTY INTERNATIONAL AND AFRICA (Vol. V); FRANCE AND AFRICA (Vol. IV); GERMANY AND AFRICA (Vol. IV); TOGO (Vols. I, II, III, IV); TOGOLAND (Vol. IV).

Further reading: A. A. Curkeet, *Togo: Portrait of a West African Francophone Republic in the 1980s* (Jefferson, N.C.: McFarland & Co., 1993).

Tolbert, William (William Richard Tolbert, Jr.)
(1913–1980) *Former president of Liberia*

Born to a prominent Americo-Liberian farming family in Bensonville, near the national capital of MONROVIA, Tolbert received an EDUCATION that prepared him for national leadership. He entered government employment soon after his graduation from Liberia College, in 1934, and within a decade had won a seat in the House of Representatives. In 1951 William TUBMAN (1895–1971), who was elected Liberia's president in 1944, selected Tolbert as his vice presidential running mate. Following Tubman's victory Tolbert held the office of vice president until Tubman's death, in 1971, at which time he assumed the presidency. In 1975 Tolbert won election on his own.

The Liberian economy, which had been relatively strong during the Tubman era, began to decline during Tolbert's presidency. Worsening economic conditions, the country's long-standing social and economic inequalities, and the long-simmering resentment on the part of the indigenous population against the Americo-Liberian elite finally brought down the government. Riots in Monrovia in 1979—sparked by a steep rise in the price of rice, which was the basic food staple—brought about a COUP D'ÉTAT led by army sergeant Samuel DOE (1952–1990) in

1980. The army mutineers murdered Tolbert in his bed and took control of the government.

Tolbert's death marked the end of 133 years of constitutional government in Liberia, and also heralded a period of unprecedented upheaval in the decades that followed.

See also: CIVIL WARS (Vol. V).

Tombalbaye, François (N'Garta Tombalbaye)
(1918–1975) *Former president of Chad*

Born in southern CHAD during French colonial rule, Tombalbaye had little education. His involvement in LABOR UNIONS led to a role in creating the Chadian Progressive Party (Parti Progressiste Tchadian, PPT), led by Gabriel Lisette (1919–2001). Lisette, who was originally from the French Caribbean island of Guadeloupe, was named prime minister when Chad became autono-mous, in 1957. Upon independence Chad was already an ethnically divided country, and Tombalbaye took advantage of Lisette's inability to bring the country together. In 1959 Tombalbaye effectively carried out a "coup by telegram," stripping Lisette of his Chadian citizenship while the prime minister was abroad and then assuming control of the government.

Tombalbaye immediately banned all political parties other than his PPT and attempted to quash the opposition. Faced with riots in 1963, he announced a state of emergency and began a massive roundup of any and all political adversaries. By the middle of the following year Tombalbaye had consolidated his power.

The president next turned to removing French influence from the country, the first of his efforts to Africanize Chad. However, because there were few trained Chadian replacements for the expelled French officials, government services declined drastically, with CORRUPTION running rampant. The Africanization process alienated the Arabic and Berber peoples living in the northern regions of the country.

Tombalbaye made little effort to reach out to the north, and his discrimination led to Muslim riots. In 1965 civil war erupted between the north and south, and Tombalbaye was forced to call on France for military intervention. In 1971 Tombalbaye used a supposed coup attempt funded by LIBYA, Chad's neighbor to the north, as an excuse to sever relations with that country. This led Libyan leader Muammar QADDAFI (1942–) to sponsor the Chad National Liberation Front (Front du Libération Nationale du Tchad, FROLINAT), a Muslim-dominated rebel army in northern Chad.

Conditions in Chad continued to worsen at an alarming rate. Financially the country was in ruins, and a drought had devastated AGRICULTURE. In 1972 students launched a strike in the capital city of Fort Lamy, a clear demonstration of how Tombalbaye's popularity was waning, even in the south. Tombalbaye reacted with increasing paranoia, arresting another 1,000 supposed conspirators, including southerners. He also severed ties with Israel in an attempt to gain favor with Muslims and to secure aid from Arab countries. The ploy worked to temporarily limit FROLINAT's advance, which by then had won control of a large portion of northern Chad.

In 1973 Tombalbaye had his military chief of staff, Colonel Félix Malloum (1932–), and a group of other government officials arrested, accusing them of carrying out animal sacrifices in an effort to undermine his administration. The official charge was "political sorcery."

To reduce the threat to his regime, Tombalbaye made a number of misguided efforts at reviving the country. To help combat the drought he initiated Operation Agriculture, a so-called volunteer effort in which the military rounded up civilians and forced them to plant cotton on unused lands. To boost morale the president once again turned to Africanization, or, as he termed it, "Chaditude." He renamed various locations in the country, including Fort Lamy, which became N'DJAMENA. Government officials were forced to use African names, and Tombalbaye himself took the first name N'Garta. He also used fiery oratory against France to stir up national pride.

Ultimately Tombalbaye was able to unite the country; however, it was united *against* him. By 1975 southerners and the military had joined the northerners in wanting Tombalbaye gone, and he was killed in a military mutiny.

See also: CIVIL WARS (Vol. V); FRANCE AND AFRICA (Vols. III, IV, V); ISLAM, INFLUENCE OF (Vols. II, III, IV).

Touré, Ahmed Sékou (1922–1984) *First president of Guinea*

Although he received limited formal EDUCATION, Ahmed Sékou Touré dominated the political scene of GUINEA by using his innate ability to consolidate and rally the country's diverse population, which was divided by language, RELIGION, and region. As president he adopted African socialism as his domestic policy and favored the PAN-AFRICANISM espoused by Kwame NKRUMAH (1909–1972) as his "continental policy." In other foreign policy matters, Sékou Touré imitated Egypt's Gamal Abdel NASSER (1918–1970) and his nonalignment in the context of the Cold War between the capitalist and Communist worlds.

Sékou Touré learned the extent of Guinea's reliance on French economic support when France cut virtually all ECONOMIC ASSISTANCE to the former colony. He immediately sought to diversify the country's economy, which was overwhelmingly oriented toward AGRICULTURE, allocating almost half of his budget to the industrial sector. Soon, however, Guinea faced a serious trade deficit, and Touré was forced to denationalize industry. He then tried to encourage FOREIGN INVESTMENT by relaxing restrictions on Guinea's MARKETS, by making guarantees against nationalization, and by instituting favorable tax incentives.

Under Touré's Three-Year Plan, farmers worked in cooperatives to qualify for government credits, services, supplies, and rental tractors. However, of the 500 cooperatives that the Plan projected, by 1963 only 291 were formed. Agricultural production declined even though farming occupied 75 percent of the country's workforce. Although Guinea enjoyed a good climate and relatively fertile soil and its level of mechanization increased, many agricultural producers rejected Touré's reforms. By the mid-1960s the program failed, and by the late 1960s Guinea had to rely on expensive, imported food.

When Sékou Touré had assumed control in 1958, he tolerated a multiparty system of government. By 1962, however, he was stressing political organization based on a one-party state, which, in Guinea's case, became his Democratic Party of Guinea (PDG). Increasingly paranoid of a COUP D'ÉTAT, he surrounded himself with a loyal cadre, appointing many Maninka speakers from his hometown, Faranah, to positions in the government and to the leadership of the military. Touré expelled foreigners, arrested and executed political opponents, and purged the army and the governmental elite. Many who were brought to Camp Boiro, a military base in CONAKRY, were never heard from again.

In 1975–76 the failure of Guinea's agricultural economy led to a famine that caused many farmers to migrate to neighboring countries. Most of those who remained reverted to subsistence farming and augmented their incomes through bartering and smuggling. By 1978, in light of Guinea's widespread economic failures, Sékou Touré attempted, with mixed success, to bring Guinea back into the economy of the capitalist world.

As part of his Guinean "Cultural Revolution," Sékou Touré also instituted reforms in education. At independence nearly all of Guinea's population was illiterate in French, the official language, and only 2 percent of Guinea's children were attending school. He nationalized all schools—with the exception of Muslim Quranic schools—so that more students had access to education from primary school to the university level. Sékou Touré's educational revolution attempted to reclaim indigenous cultural independence by using indigenous languages for education. Funded by the United Nations Economic, Social, and Cultural Organization, Guinea implemented the Maternal Language Program, by which students learned in and became literate in indigenous languages in addition to the colonial language. Sékou Touré's ultimate aim was uni-

Ahmed Sékou Touré assumed the leadership of Guinea in 1958 and led the country until his death. Here he is seen addressing the Organization of African States in 1982. © AP/Wide World Photos

versal compulsory education, but he never had enough funding to achieve that goal.

In 1982 Sékou Touré was reelected Guinea's president. However, his term was cut short when he died during emergency heart surgery while at the Cleveland Clinic Foundation in Cleveland, Ohio. His death left a void in Guinean politics that was later filled by Lansana CONTÉ (1934–   ), who came to power following a bloodless coup.

See also: COLD WAR AND AFRICA (Vols. IV, V); COMMUNISM AND SOCIALISM (Vol. V); DEVELOPMENT (Vol. V); FRANCE AND AFRICA (Vols. III, IV, V); NONALIGNED MOVEMENT AND AFRICA (Vol. V); SÉKOU TOURÉ, AHMED (Vol. IV).

Touré, Amadou Toumani (1948–   ) *President of Mali*

Now known as a staunch advocate for peace, ironically Touré began his career in the Malian military. Born in 1948 in Mopti, MALI, Touré attended military school in his home country before receiving further training in the former Soviet Union and France. Touré had risen to the rank of lieutenant colonel when Lieutenant Moussa Traoré (1936–   ) deposed Mali's first president, Modibo KEITA

(1915–1977), in a COUP D'ÉTAT in 1968. Traoré, a highly autocratic ruler, frustrated Touré's military aspirations, putting him at odds with the Traoré government.

Throughout the 1980s Malians cried out for democratic reforms with little success. Finally, popular dissatisfaction reached a boiling point. In 1991, in what became known as the Malian Revolution, demonstrators in the capital of BAMAKO and throughout Mali rioted after police fired on the crowds, killing 300. Horrified by the violence Touré rallied the army to overthrow Traoré. Following the coup d'état Touré headed a committee that drafted a new constitution and established the structure for a new government. Elections were held fourteen months later, and Alpha Oumar KONARÉ (1946–   ) became president.

Touré then put politics aside in favor of humanitarian work. In collaboration with former U.S. president Jimmy Carter (1924–   ), Touré created the Children's Foundation in defense of children's rights and launched a campaign to eradicate the guinea worm parasite, a major health threat in Mali and elsewhere in Africa. As a result of his efforts, Touré was asked by Kofi ANNAN (1938–   ) of the United Nations to head a delegation for peace in the CENTRAL AFRICAN REPUBLIC. This led to a greater role for

Touré in terms of peacekeeping, particularly for the Great Lakes region, where countries such as RWANDA, BURUNDI, UGANDA, and the Democratic Republic of the CONGO have been frequently plagued by violence and HUMAN RIGHTS violations. For his success in conflict resolution, Touré was awarded the Africa Prize for Leadership in 1996.

Concerned about the state of his home country, in 2002 Touré reentered politics as a candidate in the Malian presidential elections. He won the election, and, for the first time in the nation's history, one democratically elected administration gave way to another. A peaceful transition of power such as the one from Touré to Konaré is a rare occurrence in Africa. Touré was only the second African military leader to willingly surrender power, the first being Olusegun OBASANJO (c. 1937–) of NIGERIA.

Known affectionately as "A-T-T," Touré is very popular with the Malian people, who cherish his optimistic outlook and emphasis on traditional beliefs and values as a foundation for a successful future. One of his well known sayings is "When the night is darkest, the dawn is at hand."

See also: DEMOCRATIZATION (Vol. V).

tourism   With the advent of commercial jet airliners, international tourism evolved from being the privilege of a wealthy few into a market for the broad middle class. Several countries in Africa have discovered and successfully exploited the international tourism market in recent decades. Africa is well endowed with potential tourist attractions, and countries in East and southern Africa have invested in the INFRASTRUCTURE necessary to attract billions of tourist dollars every year. The countries of West Africa have also begun to promote tourism with events such as the All Africa Games and the West Africa Travel Show, both held in NIGERIA in 2003.

One of the most successful types of tourism is ecotourism. The continent is ideal for ecotourism, with its variety of ecological zones ranging from deserts to rain forests. Ecotourism in Africa includes safaris in rugged open-topped land cruisers in naturally preserved NATIONAL PARKS, river rafting on the Zambezi or the Nile, scuba diving and deep-sea fishing off the coast of East Africa, and camel rides in the Kalahari or Sahara deserts. Hundreds of private and national organization now promote sustainable ecotourism in Africa.

The unique ecology and wildlife that is readily on display in the large national parks, especially in East and southern Africa, attract many of the tourists who come to Africa. Some governments and private tourism companies have tapped into tourists' concern for environmental CONSERVATION by implementing policies that reduce impact on WILDLIFE and natural areas. African governments that rely upon tourism have implemented regulations that limit the total number of people who can visit particular preserves on a daily basis and ecotourism companies are quick to advertise these ecologically friendly policies. Research facilities, such as the cheetah or chimpanzee rescue centers in SOUTH AFRICA, have also tapped into the tourism market. These research centers offer daily or weekly paid tours of the facilities and combine this with wildlife and nature education.

Aside from the large and well-known wildlife species, such as the lion, buffalo, and leopard, Africa is a wonderland for ornithologists. Thousands of colorful birds are the subject of bird-watching tours in East and southern Africa. Africa's waters also offer a host of ecotourist activities. Recently, international concern for Africa's coral reefs has brought about new conservation efforts and has increased tourism to these areas. For example, the coral reefs of KENYA, the SEYCHELLES, and MADAGASCAR have been targeted for tourism DEVELOPMENT as well as preservation.

Africa has many other attractions, aside from ecotourism destinations, which bring tourists from all over the world. Some of the most well-known cultures are from Africa, such as the MAASAI. Visitors come to see the vibrant reenactments of cultural ceremonies that they have read about in publications such as *National Geographic* magazine or have seen on television and movies. The bright ceremonial attire of the Maasai or some West African ethnic groups have been so well publicized that tourists incorrectly assume they will find all Africans dressed in this manner. Tourism hotels and lodges often offer ethnic dance and MUSIC shows catered to foreign tourists.

The colorful and bustling markets are also popular among tourists. Open-air markets have existed in Africa for centuries, providing a venue to sell agricultural goods, clothing, household furnishings, and livestock. The spread of tourism has resulted in the addition of markets that cater solely to tourists, offering indigenous ART, cloth, and jewelry, all of which are popular souvenirs.

Africa also offers numerous historical sites for those interested in its long and rich past. Archaeological research such as that in ETHIOPIA—where the human ancestor, "Lucy," dating back more than 3 million years was discovered—has demonstrated that Africa was home to humans and their ancestors from an early time. The Rift Valley in East Africa, especially Olduvai Gorge, has become a popular tourist destination due to its link with our ancient ancestors. The fossil and DNA evidence also suggests that *Homo sapiens* originated in Africa between 150,000 and 100,000 years ago.

With its ancient pyramids along the Nile, the Egyptian Museum in CAIRO and its magnificent collection of more than 120,000 objects, and a a multitude of good hotels and TRANSPORTATION facilities, Egypt has long been an important tourist destination. One of the most important attractions has been the Great Pyramid of Giza, which dates back to 5,000 years ago. Many tourists are interested in seeing the ruins of Great Zimbabwe, whose first walls were built in the 12th century. Some tourists enjoy participating in activities that are as old as many African civilizations, such as camel rides through deserts. West African countries, such as GHANA and SENEGAL, that do not have the attraction of big game animals and nature preserves are promoting historical sites associated with the former slave trade.

South Africa offers a unique tourist experience in its wine country. The rolling hills near CAPE TOWN attract many tourists every year. South African wine has become well known throughout the world and is exported to many countries. Along with the culture of wine, South Africa has developed a reputation for excellent cuisine.

Visitors to Cape Town have a choice of a wide variety of accommodations, from modestly priced bed-and-breakfast inns to five-star hotels. In 2000 *Conde Nast Travelers'* Readers Choice Award for the best hotel in the world went to the Cape Grace Hotel, which is located on the Cape Town waterfront. In the 2002 poll the nearby Table Bay Hotel was named the fourth-best hotel in the world.

Although Africa is rich in tourist attractions, the economic benefit of this sector of the economy has not been realized equally throughout the continent. Southern Africa (including South Africa, NAMIBIA, LESOTHO, BOTSWANA, and SWAZILAND) receives the greatest percentage (20–30 percent) of tourists to Africa. Political instability and poor infrastructure have been the biggest roadblocks to tourism development in countries in West and Central Africa. Africa as a whole has only 2 percent (approximately $6.6 billion) of the world's tour-ism market. This means there is great potential to increase its share of tourism. Since 1995, growth in the tourism industry in Africa has been consistently above the world average.

See also: ARCHAEOLOGY IN AFRICA (Vols. IV, V); GOREÉ ISLAND (Vol. III); GREAT PYRAMID (Vol. I); GREAT ZIMBABWE (Vol. II); *HOMO SAPIENS* (Vol. I); KALAHARI DESERT (Vols. I, II); OLDUVAI GORGE (Vol. I); RIFT VALLEY (Vol. I); SAFARI (Vol. V); SAHARA (Vols. I, II); SUSTAINABLE DEVELOPMENT (Vol. V).

Further reading: *Travel and Tourism in Africa* (London: Mintel International Group Ltd., 2002); Sue Derwent, *Guide to Cultural Tourism in South Africa* (Cape Town, South Africa: Struik Publishers, 1999); Peter U. C. Dieke, *The Political Economy of Tourism Development in Africa* (New York: Cognizant Communication Corp., 2000); Isaac Sindiga, *Tourism and African Development: Change and Challenge of Tourism in Kenya* (Aldershot, U.K.: Ashgate, 1999).

trade and commerce   One of the main goals of many postcolonial African leaders has been to develop their countries' economies by diversifying trade and finding a profitable advantage in a particular industrial or technological sector. Unfortunately these efforts have not been successful enough to counteract Africa's long-term economic reliance on the export of low-profit raw goods. As a result CASH CROPS grown for export and products from the continent's vast NATURAL RESOURCES are still the mainstay of the economies of most African nations.

This problematic economic situation is not new to Africa. For centuries trade routes lined Africa's northern and coastal areas to Europe, Asia, the Middle East, and the Indian subcontinent. For many hundreds of years a number of different products moved back and forth across these routes. But for many years the most visible form of commerce was the slave trade. Then during the colonial era the emphasis shifted to the extraction of African resources for the benefit of European markets. For the most part this was undertaken by European colonial governments and private companies such as the Royal Niger Company, the United Africa Company, and the British East Africa Company.

Both of these forms of trade—the slave trade and the commerce in natural resources—still exist in postcolonial Africa. Indeed, trade in raw goods remains the dominant element in African commerce.

Although slavery has been officially outlawed by most countries for some time, some sociologists estimate that there still are almost 27 million slaves in the world today and that the trade in humans continues in many parts of Africa.

As some analysts argue, poor countries with good soil and a relatively uneducated LABOR force have, ironically, a comparative advantage when it comes to prices on the international market. This, in turn, can lead these countries to ultimately generate the wealth and DEVELOP-

MENT they need for the private sector to surge into new arenas. In MAURITIUS, for example, the surge in the sugar market led, first, to the growth of an important CLOTH AND TEXTILES industry and, in more recent years, to new high-tech businesses. Similarly, SOUTH AFRICA, BOTSWANA, and UGANDA have successfully diversified their economies to include both industrial and technological bases.

Not everyone agrees with this strategy or even with this analysis. Some analyses maintain that development that begins with the exporting of raw materials ultimately maintains the system of exploitation typified by the colonial era. The only difference, they argue, is that now African elites rather than colonial elites benefit from this exploitation of the poor and the natural bounty of the continent. To support their argument, these analysts point to the many countries of Africa, including MOROCCO, EGYPT, KENYA, IVORY COAST, and others, in which the economic base is too dependent upon agriculture and the extraction of minerals and other resources.

Regardless of which position analysts take, however, it is clear that, for their long term development and prosperity, it will be important for African nations to develop beyond both agricultural or resource-exploiting economies. Not surprisingly many countries—and their leaders—have come to see this as one of the main challenges of the 21st century.

See also: CONSTRUCTIVE ENGAGEMENT (Vol. V); EAST AFRICAN COMMUNITY (Vol. V); ECONOMIC COMMUNITY FOR WEST AFRICAN STATES (Vol. V); EXPORTS (Vol. V); GLOBAL ECONOMY, AFRICA AND THE (Vol. V); MONEY AND CURRENCY (Vols. I, II, III, IV); MINERALS AND METALS (Vol. V); MULTINATIONAL CORPORATIONS (Vol. V); ORGANIZATION OF PETROLEUM EXPORTING COUNTRIES (Vol. V); SLAVE TRADE (Vol. IV); TOURISM (Vol. V); TRADE AND COMMERCE (Vols. I, II, III, IV).

Further reading: Kevin Bales, *Disposable People: New Slavery in the Global Economy* (Berkeley, Calif.: University of California Press, 2000).

transportation Primarily because of little public investment, transportation in postcolonial Africa remains largely made up of modest rail networks, barely emerging private aviation, and private buses and trucks running on modest networks of roads. The INFRASTRUCTURE needed for effective public transportation is, for the most part, lacking throughout sub-Saharan Africa. To a great extent this is a legacy of the colonial era. During the colonial period, for example, Britain and France made only minimal transportation investments. In contrast, Portugal's DEVELOPMENT of transportation systems within LUANDA, the capital of ANGOLA, was significant. Portugal also developed a rail link between MAPUTO, the capital of MOZAMBIQUE, and PRETORIA, SOUTH AFRICA, as well as other rail networks along Mozambique's coastal areas. Since independence much of Africa has seen the decay of what limited infrastructure had developed.

In spite of the fact that Africa represents more than six times the land area of Europe, according to the WORLD BANK, as of 2000 there were only 994,194 miles (1.6 million km) of roads in sub-Saharan Africa compared to 1,677,700 miles (2.7 million km) in Europe. In general, North African countries are much better served. For example, ALGERIA has nearly 44,739 miles (72,000 km) of paved highways and 398 miles (640 km) of expressway. Many of Africa's roads are in significantly ill repair, requiring four-wheel drive vehicles or else reducing the life of cars. KENYA, with one of the best road and rail systems in the subcontinent, has only 41,423 miles (63,663 km) of roads and 1,625 miles (2,615 km) of rail line. Even TANZANIA, with a rail system traced to the African socialism of Julius NYERERE (1922–1999) in the 1970s, suffers from this plight. Despite massive investment by the Tanzanian government and China, the country has only 54,681 miles (88,000 km) of roads, and 1,330 miles (2,141 km) of rail lines. Only the regional superpower, SOUTH AFRICA, stands ahead with 113,294 miles (182,329 km) of roads, including 1,263 miles (2,032 km) of expressways, and nearly 13,670 miles (22,000 km) of rail lines.

Getting around on these road and rail lines can be challenging. In some parts of the country the portion of the population that can afford to purchase private cars outstrips the ability of the government to invest in road construction. LAGOS, NIGERIA is thought to have worse traffic congestion on its highways than Los Angeles, California.

Yet the high levels of POVERTY throughout the continent mean that relatively few suffer the ills of traffic congestion. Rather, the majority of people must fight for public transportation. Some cities have public buses. The dearth of public investment in this sector has led entrepreneurs to form private bus cooperatives. Every country in sub-Saharan Africa has them, albeit by different names. *Matatus* in Kenya, Tanzania, and UGANDA, *carrapides* in SENEGAL, *danfos* and *molues* in Nigiera, *tro tros* in GHANA, *poda podas* in SIERRA LEONE, and *taxi brousse* in MADAGASCAR, all are essentially the same thing. They are minibuses owned by middle-class and elite businesspeople and operated by a team of a driver and a tout. This is the most important form of transportation throughout the continent. The private minibus has long been under attack for packing too many people in each vehicle and for driving at speeds that are too high, resulting in high numbers of fatalities each year. In 2003 Kenya became the first country to attempt to regulate significantly this private system, but the economic consequences have led to many challenges.

Where private buses often bring individuals to market with their goods, private trucking industries have

Despite assistance from abroad, airline transportation in sub-Saharan Africa has not flourished. Zambia's national airline, Zambia Airways, survived for 30 years before going bankrupt in 1995, four years after this photo was taken. © *United Nations/M. Grant*

flourished in the place of scant rail services. They have been cardinal to the African intra-country and cross-border shipping industry.

Most countries in Africa have their own airlines. Virtually all were started as a public carrier and have since privatized. The share Africa holds of the global airline market is small—about 3.7 percent. The Yamoussoukro Decision on African aviation in 1999, sponsored by the United Nations, led to continent-wide liberalization that has brought about significant growth in Africa air transport. Given its high cost, it will nonetheless continue to serve only a modest few of sub-Saharan Africa's nearly 800 million citizens.

See also: COLONIALISM, INFLUENCE OF (Vol. IV); INDUSTRIALIZATION (Vol. V); TRADE AND COMMERCE (Vol. V); TRANSPORTATION (Vol. IV).

tribes and tribalism The terms "tribe" and "tribalism" were popularized by Europeans who applied them to non-European, nonwhite societies to imply that these societies were disorganized, inferior, and uncivilized.

Prior to European contact Africans did not use words equivalent to "tribe" to describe their own social groups. The word is a European construct that conceptualizes the relationships within non-state societies that hold them together. Europeans theorize that the structure of these societies is largely based on kinship, shared culture, and relations among kinship groups. However, many groups that have long been identified as tribes are made up of peoples who speak different languages, practice different rituals, and follow different leaders. As a consequence of this misunderstanding, the European concept of African ETHNICITY AND IDENTITY was, and in many cases still is, skewed.

During the late 19th century the prevailing European concepts of social evolution were greatly affected by the landmark study, *Origin of the Species* (1859), written by Charles Darwin (1808–1882). This study, which originally was narrowly applied to some biological systems, was subsequently juxtaposed onto social structures around the world. Under this concept of "Social Darwinism," social inequalities are natural, and African forms of social organization were marked as "unfit for survival." At the same time, Europeans' desires to control the wealth of the African continent led them to try to remove legitimate African governments from power. In order to justify their actions, they devised specious rationalizations based on a profound misunderstanding of African society. These arguments were typified by the colonial claim that it was an ethical imperative—the so-called white man's burden—to raise African social organization to the level of the "superior" European model.

During the 20th century the media often referred to any conflict between two groups of Africans as an outgrowth of "tribalism." This bred the misconception that African groups could not get along with one another. It also obscured the nature of many conflicts, demonstrating contempt for the issues that actually cause it. In RWANDA and BURUNDI, for example, conflict between the HUTU and the TUTSI was characterized in the world press as "tribalism," when, in fact, the roots of the conflict were in the economics of LAND USE and the divisive European colonial policies that empowered one group, the Tutsi, to rule over the other.

In ZIMBABWE, the government has used the "tribal" term to disparage local liberation movements, such as the ZIMBABWE AFRICAN PEOPLE'S UNION (ZAPU). The government tries to dismiss the political opposition by reporting to the press that the group is based on frivolous "tribal" interests when, in fact, the group has broad, multiethnic support and a proper grievance against the government.

See also: ETHNIC GROUP (Vol. IV); KINSHIP (Vol. IV).

Further reading: Kenneth Christie, ed., *Ethnic Conflict, Tribal Politics: A Global Perspective* (Richmond, Surrey, U.K.: Curzon, 1998); Harold R. Isaacs, *Power and Identity: Tribalism in World Politics* (New York: Foreign Policy Association, 1979); Roger Sandall, *The Culture Cult: Designer Tribalism and other Essays* (Boulder, Colo.: Westview Press, 2001); Leroy Vail, ed., *The Creation of Tribalism in Southern Africa* (Berkeley, Calif.: University of California Press, 1989).

Tripoli (Tarablus al-Gharb) Capital of LIBYA, located in the northwestern part of the country along the Mediterranean coast. Once a quiet former colonial town, Tripoli began a radical transformation in 1958 following the discovery of OIL reserves in Libya. Large numbers of foreigners came to live and work in the emerging oil industry, and western-style dress became the norm for men in the urban areas. Money brought in by oil production financed new housing projects, schools, water delivery systems, and roads. There were so many cars that driving in downtown Tripoli became difficult and the city's first parking meters had to be installed. The downtown commercial sector catered to foreign businesspeople, and one hotel even had its own movie theater and casino.

Attracted by the employment opportunities, many rural Libyans moved into the city as well. Tripoli's suburbs became populated by members of a growing Libyan middle class of shopkeepers, whose goods were bought by the Western shoppers who flooded Tripoli's shopping district every day.

During the 1970s and 1980s, however, the pattern of DEVELOPMENT changed drastically. Tripoli's streets emptied as Muammar QADDAFI (1942–), who came to power in 1969, made it known that foreigners were no longer welcome. The city soon lost a significant part of its European population, especially when the government expelled those Italians who had remained from the colonial era. Others left when the government confiscated their property. The absence of foreigners had an adverse effect on many parts of Tripoli's economy, including the hotels and restaurants that lost patrons, the taxi drivers who lost fares, and the emerging middle class, which lost its clientele. A subtle government action that made it clear that foreigners were unwelcome in Tripoli was the removal of all foreign-language signs and advertisements and a new emphasis on Arabic words, which began to appear on everything down to hotel monograms.

In 1986 the United States accused Qaddafi of sponsoring international TERRORISM, and American president Ronald Reagan (1911–2004) ordered the bombing of government offices and military installations in Tripoli and Benghazi, another Libyan Mediterranean port. The bombing destroyed parts of Tripoli, causing as many as 31 deaths and leaving hundreds injured. Toward the end of the 20th century, however, the volatile situation between the two countries improved. Today Tripoli is Libya's largest city, home to an estimated 1.5 million people.

> Tripoli attracts a growing number of tourists, who come to see its Roman walls, the arch of Marcus Aurelius, the Karamanli Mosque, and the former royal palace. Also, visitors can go to the city's traditional markets to bargain for beautiful handicrafts, including GOLD and silver jewelry, leather goods, pottery, clothing, and carpets.

See also: ITALY AND AFRICA (Vol. IV); TOURISM (Vol. V); TRIPOLI (Vol. IV); TRIPOLITANIA (Vol. IV); UNITED STATES AND AFRICA (Vols. IV, V).

Truth and Reconciliation Commission (TRC) Council established by South African president Nelson MANDELA (1918–) to investigate the crimes committed by the government during the APARTHEID era in SOUTH AFRICA (1948–94). Headed by Archbishop Desmond TUTU (1931–), one of the most prominent leaders of the anti-apartheid movement, the TRC is composed of the Amnesty Committee, the Reparation and Rehabilitation Committee, and the Human Rights Violations Committee. The commission was envisioned as an alternative to the war-crimes-tribunal model advocated by many black Africans seeking justice for the atrocities committed by the white apartheid government.

Still operative as of 2004, the TRC gathers the testimony of both those who supported apartheid and those who suffered under it. It offers amnesty to those who fully confess to racial crimes committed during the apartheid era as long as the offending party can demonstrate that their actions were motivated by political expediency rather than racial hatred. The desired result of this method is to expose the truth, allow the airing of grievances, and lay blame on those responsible. Ideally this will allow the country to vent its anger, forgive, and move on to a racially unified future. Though welcomed by many, this approach also has its critics, most of whom believe amnesty should not be an option for those who participated in one of the most brutal reigns of racial oppression in world history.

See also: CHRISTIANITY, INFLUENCE OF (Vol. V); ETHNIC CONFLICT IN AFRICA (Vol. V); HUMAN RIGHTS (Vol. V); RACE AND RACISM (Vol. IV).

Tshombe, Moïse (Moïse Kapenda Tshombe)
(1919–1969) *Political leader in Katanga, Democratic Republic of the Congo*

Born at Sandoa, in southwestern KATANGA in the present-day Democratic Republic of the CONGO, Moïse Tshombe was a life-long advocate of autonomy for the mineral-rich province. He also had close ties with European, especially Belgian, interests and made extensive use of Belgian technicians and military mercenaries during his tenure as head of the breakaway Katangan government.

The son of a successful businessman, Tshombe was educated by Methodist MISSIONARIES. He entered politics in the mid-1950s, serving in the Katanga Provincial Council and as the head of a local Katangan business group. In 1958 he helped form CONAKAT, the Confederation of Tribal Associations of Katanga, which quickly became his political power base. Through CONAKAT Tshombe sought autonomy for Katanga, even within the Belgian Congo, as well as close ties to Belgium. This placed Tshombe in direct conflict with future prime minister Patrice LUMUMBA (1925–1961), who advocated an independent, but united Congo. The May 1960 elections that preceded Congolese independence saw Tshombe's CONAKAT party winning only eight legislative seats. Despite their poor showing, CONKAT retained control of Katanga.

Within two weeks of independence Tshombe announced that Katanga was seceding to become an independent country. Supported by massive financial, political, technical, and military aid from Belgium, he was able to hold off both the national forces and UN peacekeepers, who were fighting to reunify the country. In the course of events, Lumumba was handed over to the Katanga government and was subsequently murdered under uncertain circumstances. Ultimately, in 1963, Tshombe was forced to admit defeat and seek safe haven in Spain.

The next year, however, President Joseph KASAVUBU (c. 1913–1969) invited Tshombe to return to the Congo as the prime minister of a government of reconciliation. Calling on European assistance, Tshombe was able to put down the rebellions that were endangering Kasavubu's government. He then set his sights on ousting Kasavubu, who ultimately dismissed Tshombe. Tshombe, for his part, refused to recognize Kasavubu's authority and, in the chaos that was developing, Joseph-Désiré Mobutu (1930–1997), later known as MOBUTU SESE SEKO, seized power in a COUP D'ÉTAT.

Tshombe went into exile but was kidnapped while on a flight from Spain and taken to ALGERIA. Algerian authorities refused to extradite him to the Congo, where he had been charged with treason and sentenced to death in absentia. Instead they held him under house arrest, where he remained until his death, apparently from a stroke, in June 1969.

See also: BELGIAN CONGO (Vol. IV); BELGIUM AND AFRICA (Vol. IV); CONGO CRISIS (Vol. V).

Tsiranana, Philibert (c. 1912–1978) *First president of Madagascar*

Born into a Tsimhety peasant family living in northeastern MADAGASCAR, Tsiranana completed a secondary education and later studied in France, where he earned a technical-education certificate.

Tsiranana entered Madagascar politics in the early 1950s, which was a tumultuous time in the island's history. A nationalist rebellion against French colonial rule had left about 100,000 people dead. The violence and repression that followed produced a split in the nationalist movement, with a more militant faction professing support for communism and a more moderate element willing to retain ties with France. Tsiranana headed the moderate faction and, with the backing of the Catholic Church, founded the Social Democratic Party. He won election to the French National Assembly, in 1956, and in 1958 became prime minister of the Madagascar National Assembly.

When Madagascar became an independent republic, in 1960, Tsiranana became president. He ruled the country for the next dozen years, following a pro-West foreign policy. He even retained ties with SOUTH AFRICA because of its importance as a trading partner. However, increased disapproval of ties with South Africa and its APARTHEID policies led to discontent with Tsiranana's leadership.

Deteriorating economic conditions over the late 1960s proved to be the last straw, and in 1971 a peasant rebellion broke out.

A rigged 1972 election, in which Tsiranana garnered 99.9 percent of the vote, led to urban demonstrations and a military COUP D'ÉTAT that ended Tsiranana's political career. In 1975 he was charged and tried for conspiracy connected with the assassination of President Richard Ratsimandrava (1931–1975), but he was acquitted. Tsiranana died three years later.

See also: COMMUNISM AND SOCIALISM (Vol. V); FRANCE AND AFRICA (Vols. III, IV, V); NATIONALISM AND INDEPENDENCE MOVEMENTS (Vol. IV).

Further reading: Mervyn Brown, *A History of Madagascar* (Princeton, N.J.: Markus Wiener Publishers, 2000).

tsotsis (comtotsis, comrage totsis) Youth gangs of SOUTH AFRICA. The *tsotsis* had their origins in the growing URBANIZATION of the inter-war period, became a fixture of black urban life in the APARTHEID era, and remain prevalent in the post-apartheid era. A single member is called a *tsotsi*.

The term *tsotsi* first came into usage in the early 1940s. Possibly derived from the Nguni word *tsotsa*, meaning "flashily dressed." Another possible derivation involves a pronunciation shift of the words *zoot suit*, which was a preferred outfit of the *tsotsis*. It remains an apt term to describe many *tsotsis*, who today sport thick gold chains, sunglasses (even at night), and stylish clothing in an attempt to emulate the wealthy and the criminals depicted in their favorite American and European films. *Tsotsis* are also associated with their own language. Called *tsotsitaal*, it is derived from a mixture of AFRIKAANS and English interspersed with African slang.

The first township gangs emerged among African youth in DURBAN and JOHANNESBURG as early as the 1920s. By the 1940s they were a staple feature of URBAN LIFE AND CULTURE in these cities, as well as in PRETORIA and CAPE TOWN. During the apartheid era *tsotsis* served multiple purposes, from providing a structure for organizing militant resistance, to protecting neighborhoods from the violent tactics of the police, to increasing the strength of criminal organizations that preyed largely on their fellow township inhabitants.

Under apartheid, black South Africans were relegated to segregated areas such as SOWETO and the barren Cape Flats. The police had little interest in protecting the township populations from the *tsotsis,* so their crimes went largely unreported outside of these areas. Over time the *tsotsis* consolidated, forming ever larger gangs that came to dominate certain townships. Complicating matters, the insurgent AFRICAN NATIONAL CONGRESS (ANC) encouraged the boycotting of schools and disobedience toward the government.

By the 1990s this strategy of induced anarchy had left behind a generation of uneducated youth with little respect for authority. These youth provided a fertile pool of potential *tsotsis*. As black Africans gained access to areas outside the townships after the fall of the apartheid government, many *tsotsis* took advantage of their new freedoms and ventured into the previously segregated white suburbs to commit crimes. These ventures carried less risk than crimes committed within the black townships, as people there began taking matters into their own hands, beating or killing captured gangsters.

Many black South Africans believed the end of apartheid would lead to a life of economic security. The reality of the post-apartheid era, however, was marked by continued POVERTY and the absence of job prospects. The bleak economy proved a useful tool for *tsotsi* recruitment, as many unemployed youths joined the roving gangs of criminals that continued to wreak havoc. The activities of the *tsotsis* remained an issue into the 21st century, presenting the ANC and the government it controls with a problem they, in part, encouraged.

See also: BANTUSTANS (Vol. V); CAPE COLOURED PEOPLE (Vol. IV); RESISTANCE AND REBELLION (Vol. IV); UMKHONTO WE SIZWE (Vol. V).

Further reading: Clive Glaser, *Bo-tsotsi: The Youth Gangs of Soweto, 1935–1976* (Portsmouth, N.H.: Heinemann, 2000).

Tsvangirai, Morgan (1952–) *Zimbabwean labor-union leader*

Born in eastern ZIMBABWE (Southern Rhodesia, at the time), Morgan Tsvangirai left school and subsequently became the foreman at a nickel mine. This was during the era of the African nationalist struggle against the white-minority government of RHODESIA, led by Ian SMITH (1919–). Tsvangirai rose through the ranks of LABOR UNION leadership to become head of the mine-workers union, and in 1988 he was elected secretary-general of the Zimbabwe Congress of Trade Unions (ZCTU). ZCTU unions represented 700,000 workers, providing Tsvangirai with a strong political base.

During the early 1990s the ZCTU leadership found itself increasingly at odds with the ZIMBABWE AFRICAN NATIONAL UNION-PATRIOTIC FRONT (ZANU-PF), the ruling party of Zimbabwean president Robert MUGABE (1924–). By 1997 the union coalition was organizing "stay-aways," or strikes, to protest Mugabe's proposed tax increases, which would be especially burdensome to Zimbabwe's largely urban, working-class people. Mugabe wanted increased tax revenue to provide pensions for war veterans, who formed one of his important support bases. The stay-away strikes brought the country's economy to a halt, forcing the government to cancel the tax increases.

The strikes also propelled Tsvangirai to the forefront of Zimbabwean politics. Rising discontent with the failing economy, as well as Mugabe's increasingly despotic rule, helped fuel the emergence of political opposition groups. In 1999 these groups came together to form the MOVEMENT FOR DEMOCRATIC CHANGE (MDC). Tsvangirai played a key leadership role, becoming the movement's president. The core MDC support came from the LABOR movement and younger, better-educated urban Zimbabweans.

For the first time in its 20 years of governing the country, the ruling ZANU-PF party faced strong and credible political opposition. In 2000 the MDC spearheaded opposition to Mugabe's attempt to change the national constitution to allow the seizing of farms from whites without compensating them. Such a step probably would have led to food shortages and higher prices, a development that would be detrimental to the MDC's urban base.

In the 2002 elections Tsvangirai led the MDC to win 57 parliamentary seats (to 62 for ZANU-PF). As a candidate, however, Tsvangirai lost the parliamentary seat he contested. In light of the MDC's success Mugabe's government, which had employed intimidation tactics in the election, moved to stifle further political opposition. Its tactics included bringing charges of high treason against Tsvangirai for participating in an alleged plot to assassinate Mugabe.

See also: MINING (Vols. IV, V); SOUTHERN RHODESIA (Vol. IV); URBANIZATION (Vols. IV, V).

Tuaregs Berber-speaking peoples of the Sahara region of North Africa. With a present-day population slightly less than 1 million, Tuaregs live in relatively isolated communities, or confederations, throughout ALGERIA, LIBYA, BURKINA FASO, CHAD, NIGER, and the Republic of MALI.

For centuries Tuaregs lived as nomadic pastoralists and desert traders. Since independence, however, increasing DEVELOPMENT and URBANIZATION in North Africa have altered the traditional lifestyle of many Tuaregs. As a result, in the early 1990s Tuareg rebels rose up in an armed rebellion to protest government policies that forced them to establish more permanent settlements. Since that time, peace agreements have largely curtailed the violence. However, rebels in traditional Tuareg strongholds such as Agades, Niger, continue to agitate for less government interference.

See also: AGADES (Vol. III); BERBERS (Vols. I, II, III, IV, V); TUAREGS (Vols. I, II, III, IV).

Tubman, William (William Vacanarat Shadrach Tubman) (1895–1971) *Former president of Liberia*

Coming from a family long devoted to public service, William Tubman chose to enter the military in 1910. After several civil-service positions he eventually studied law and went into politics, serving in the national legislature and on the Supreme Court. In 1951, as leader of the True Whig Party, he began the first of seven consecutive terms as president of LIBERIA. The linchpins of his programs were attracting FOREIGN INVESTMENT as a way to foster DEVELOPMENT for his country and providing the neglected interior of the country with the economic stimuli and INFRASTRUCTURE needed to integrate it into the national life. He died on July 23, 1971, while in London for surgery. His vice president, William R. TOLBERT (1913–1980), succeeded him as president.

See also: TUBMAN, WILLIAM (Vol. IV).

Further reading: Tuan Weh, *Love of Liberty: The Rule of President William V. S. Tubman in Liberia 1944–1971* (New York: Universe, 1976).

Tunis Capital of TUNISIA located on the edge of the Lake of Tunis, an inlet of the Gulf of Tunis on the Mediterranean Sea. Founded before the ninth century BCE by the Libyans, Tunis is the oldest city of Tunisia. Its long history has been overshadowed by the fame of nearby Carthage. After coming under the control of numerous different groups it was part of the French protectorate (1881–1956), during which time much of the modern portion of the city was built. In 1956 the city became the capital of the newly independent nation of Tunisia.

The region around Tunis is suited for AGRICULTURE and produces olives and cereal, which are processed in the city. Other industries include textiles, carpets, cement, metal products, fertilizer, and electronics. In addition to these businesses, there is an important TOURISM industry.

Visitors to the city enjoy the international theater, the thermal baths modeled after the ancient Roman baths, ruins of the Roman aqueducts, nearby Carthage, bustling markets, and the annual Festival of Carthage. A five-star hotel at Gammarth, The Residence, is located on the city's beachfront. Tunis is also the site of the mosque of Az-Aaytunah (the Mosque of the Olive Tree), which was built in the eighth century. This mosque and many others are housed within the Muslim quarter, called the *medina*. This section of the city is enclosed by a wall, and winding alleyways lead people past the markets (called *souks*), houses, and a museum of arts and artifacts. There is also the newer European quarter, which, with its French street names and overhanging balconies, serves as a strong reminder of the colonial period. Living conditions in the city improved greatly after independence, and in 2003 the population of the city stood at approximately 700,000.

See also: CARTHAGE (Vol. I); FRANCE AND AFRICA (Vols. III, IV, V); ISLAM, INFLUENCE OF (Vols. II, III, IV, V); URBAN LIFE AND CULTURE (Vols. IV, V); URBANIZATION (Vols. IV, V).

Tunisia Country in North Africa on the Mediterranean Sea bordered by LIBYA to the east and by ALGERIA to the west. It covers approximately 60,000 square miles (155,400 sq km). The capital is TUNIS.

Tunisia at Independence Tunisia gained its independence from France in 1957, and by 1960 President Habib BOURGUIBA (1903–2000) was ruling the country with enormous executive powers. Based on a largely personal interpretation of the doctrine of African Socialism, Bourguiba's domestic policies focused on planned economic growth and modernization. As a consequence, Bourguiba's Neo-Destour Party changed its name to the Socialist Destourian Party.

Bourguiba's first five-year plan tried to create new industries and diversify the country's urban areas. He also set in motion a major land reform effort, nationalizing the large former European land holdings in 1964 and enabling the ministry of AGRICULTURE to redistribute 400,000 acres of farmland. By the end of the 1960s, however, Bourguiba was meeting strong opposition to his agrarian reform plan and to the nationalization of Tunisian-owned farms and olive orchards, with Tunisians rebelling against what they viewed as widespread government CORRUPTION. Bourguiba's foreign policy during this period emphasized support for struggles for African independence. In contrast to his stance on African independence, however, Bourguiba was a moderate member of the Arab League, supporting a negotiated settlement in the Arab-Israeli conflict.

Because Bourguiba supported Algerian independence, Tunisia's relationship with France was problematic, and Tunisian and French troops frequently clashed along the Tunisian-Algerian border. This led Bourguiba to insist that the remaining French military installations be removed from Tunisian soil. As a result, by 1963 France had evacuated its naval installation at Bizerte. Tensions between Tunisia and France eased, however, once Algeria received its independence, in 1962. For the rest of the decade Tunisia enjoyed favored-nation trade status with France.

The position of strength that Bourguiba had enjoyed in the 1960s eroded during the 1970s and 1980s, as Tunisians became increasingly restive with the government's domestic policies. The ruling party split into conservatives and liberals, and in 1981, despite the fact that Bourguiba authorized the formation of opposition political parties, there were demonstrations against the government.

The situation was equally bleak in the area of foreign policy. In 1974 Bourguiba reversed himself and created a union with Libya, joining the parliaments, militaries, and governments of the two countries and giving Libya the role of the dominant partner. Because Bourguiba had done this without consulting his advisors, the union was dissolved before it began. This, in turn, led for a search for someone to replace the president, who was deemed to have become unstable. In 1987 General ZINE EL ABIDINE BEN ALI (1936–) assumed the presidency while the hero of the revolution, Bourguiba, retired.

Ben Ali's domestic policies moved toward liberal reforms, and he changed the name of the government party to the Constitutional Democratic Rally. However, after he met fierce political opposition from Islamic fundamentalists in the elections of 1989 and 1994, Ben Ali returned to his predecessor's tactics of political repression, imprisoning the leaders of the opposition and restricting the Islamic political parties. Ben Ali's foreign policy focused on regional cooperation. In 1987 he signed a treaty of economic cooperation with other states in the MAGHRIB, including Algeria, Libya, MAURITANIA, and MOROCCO. Ben Ali was reelected in 1999.

See also: ARAB WORLD AND AFRICA (Vols. IV, V); ARAB-ISRAEL WARS (Vols. IV, V); FRANCE AND AFRICA (Vols. III, IV, V); DESTOUR PARTY (Vol. IV); TUNISIA (Vols. I, II, III, IV).

Further reading: Mira Fromer Zussman, *Development and Disenchantment in Rural Tunisia: the Bourguiba Years* (Boulder, Colo.: Westview Press, 1992).

Turabi, Hassan Abd Allah al- (1932–) *Islamic fundamentalist leader in the Republic of the Sudan*

A controversial figure, al-Turabi has become one of the world's most prominent supporters of Islam and Islamic law, or SHARIA. Born in Wad al-Turabi, Sudan, during the period of British colonial rule, al-Turabi later moved to KHARTOUM, the capital. After earning his law degree at the University of Khartoum he continued his studies in London and Paris before returning to the Sudan.

Following independence, in 1956, the Sudan was beset by political instability. Constant tension marred relations between the north and south. In the north, where Khartoum and much of the nation's political authority was located, the people were primarily Arabic speakers and Islamic. In the south the population spoke other languages and practiced Christianity or indigenous religions. In 1964 the revolution began, and in 1969 Gaafar NIMEIRI (1930–), a northerner, overthrew the military government and assumed the presidency.

Al-Turabi took part in the revolution and became head of the Muslim Brotherhood, or Islamic Charter. He molded the group into a powerful organization known as the National Islamic Front (NIF) assuming the position as the chief opposition leader against Nimeiri's government. As the organization's leader, al-Turabi became a hard-line advocate of *sharia,* insisting that a secular Islamic state was untenable for devout Muslims.

By this time al-Turabi's position and extensive education had made him an international spokesperson for Islam. Although Nimeiri imprisoned al-Turabi multiple times for his outspoken criticism of the government, ultimately al-Turabi's influence proved so great that the president was forced to work with the Islamic leader. As a result Nimeiri appointed al-Turabi attorney general in 1979. This position was highly advantageous for al-Turabi, who immediately began to alter the legal system to follow Quranic imperatives. However, as Nimeiri lost his grip on the presidency, he once again imprisoned al-Turabi, who regained his freedom only after Nimeiri's government fell.

Al-Turabi is relatively unique among fundamentalist Muslim leaders in that he is concerned with public image. He has been known to speak freely to Western journalists and even to his harshest critics. His skills in public relations have earned him the facetious title of the "Madison Avenue Ayatollah."

Upon his release al-Turabi once again began agitating for the Sudan to become a fully Islamic state. In the 1986 elections, he and the NIF made significant strides. In 1988 al-Turabi once again became attorney general, this time in the elected government of Prime Minister Sadiq al-Mahdi (1935–   ). Al-Turabi's desire for the full Islamization of Sudan heightened tensions between the north and the south, and his unwillingness to compromise finally led to his dismissal from the government.

Briefly out of Sudanese politics, al-Turabi toured the world, speaking on the subject of *sharia* in the Islamic state. However, in 1989, Omar Hassan Ahmad al-BASHIR (1945–   ) led a coup that ousted the Mahdi government, and al-Turabi quickly rose to become the actual power behind al-Bashir's administration. As head of the Popular Arab and Islamic Congress, al-Turabi essentially ran the Sudanese government. Still unfailing in his desire to see Sudan become a religious Islamic state, al-Turabi and the al-Bashir government continued the ongoing civil war with the south. Western critics harshly criticized the government for its fundamentalist position and supposed support of international TERRORISM.

In support of his beliefs, al-Turabi has argued that "in the absence of *sharia* in poor, largely illiterate societies like Sudan, corruption ruled because there was also no accountability or moral checks on government . . . Only when all subscribe to the moral code of Islam in public affairs can corruption be eliminated."

See also: CIVIL WARS (Vol. V); ISLAM, INFLUENCE OF (Vols. II, III, IV, V); RELIGION (Vols. IV, V).

Tutsi Minority ethnic group of RWANDA and BURUNDI. Since the end of the colonial era, the Tutsi, who form roughly 14 percent of the populations of Rwanda and Burundi, have been locked in an excessively violent struggle for dominance with the HUTU, the majority ethnic group of both nations. The Tutsi share the Hutu language and religious beliefs. They are largely pastoralist, valuing cattle as a sign of prestige and wealth. The agricultural Hutu have taken on this characteristic as well. With much intermingling and blurring of the ethnic lines between Tutsi and Hutu, the ongoing struggle between the two groups is in reality fueled less by ethnicity than by political power and class distinctions. Though greatly outnumbered by the Hutu, the Tutsi have historically enjoyed superior status, with Tutsi monarchies ruling over the Hutu who made up the lower class. Class tensions between the two groups were heightened during Belgian colonial rule, during which the Tutsi were the beneficiaries of Belgian favoritism.

Upon Rwandan independence, in 1962, the Hutu had assumed power after overthrowing the Tutsi monarchy the previous year. Hutu president Juvenal HABYARIMANA (1937–1994) dominated the country's politics. Strongly opposed to a recurrence of Tutsi rule, Habyarimana refused to allow Tutsi exiles in UGANDA to reenter the country. These exiles then formed the RWANDAN PATRIOTIC FRONT (RPF). Invasions by the RPF in 1990 and subsequent years were repelled by the Rwandan army.

In 1992 a peace agreement was reached, but the tenuous agreement fell apart in 1994. That year the plane in which Habyarimana and Burundian president Cyprien NTARYAMIRA (1956–1994) were traveling crashed—probably shot down—killing both leaders. The resulting upheaval led to a campaign of genocide, with as many as 1 million people, mostly Tutsi, killed by Hutu death squads. Later that year the RPF, led by Paul KAGAME (1957–   ) invaded again and took control of Rwanda. Though a joint Tutsi-Hutu government was established, Kagame and the Tutsi clearly commanded the power.

In Burundi independence began with Tutsi rule. When the Hutu rose up against Tutsi prime minister Michel Micombero (1940–1972) in 1972, the Tutsi retaliated, systematically killing about 150,000 Hutu. In 1988 a military COUP D'ÉTAT led by Tutsi Pierre BUYOYA (1949–   ) caused another Hutu uprising and another brutal Tutsi campaign of ethnic cleansing, resulting in an estimated 20,000 more deaths.

The Tutsi lost control of Burundi following multiparty elections in 1993. They were themselves victims of genocidal attacks that year, after the assassination of the elected Hutu president Melchior Ndadaye (1953–1993). An estimated 150,000 Tutsi were killed during the violence that followed Ndadaye's murder. However, in 1996 Buyoya once again seized power. The Tutsi-Hutu conflict in Burundi raged until 1995, when peace talks seemed to make progress toward reconciliation.

See also: ETHNIC CONFLICT IN AFRICA (Vol. V); TUTSI (Vols. II, III, IV).

Further reading: Aimable Twagilimana, *Hutu and Tutsi* (New York: Rosen Publishing Group, 1998).

Tutu, Desmond (Archbishop Desmond Mpilo Tutu) (1931–) *Archbishop of Cape Town, South Africa*

The son of a Methodist school headmaster in Klerksdorp, SOUTH AFRICA, Desmond Tutu eventually became the champion of the peaceful resistance to APARTHEID. He lived in black townships for most of his youth. When Tutu was hospitalized with tuberculosis, in 1945, he met Trevor Huddleston (1913–), a British priest. Huddleston had a profound influence on Tutu and inspired the young man to become an Anglican priest himself. Tutu recovered his health just prior to the official institutionalization of apartheid as government policy, in 1948.

Having missed nearly two years of school because of his sickness, Tutu worked hard to catch up. He eventually graduated from the University of South Africa in 1954 and taught for a time before being ordained as a priest in 1961. The following year Tutu won a scholarship to study theology in London, an opportunity that allowed his family to escape horrible living conditions in JOHANNESBURG. The time spent in London resulted in a master's degree and a taste of a life in which he was treated with respect by white counterparts. This experience played a large role in Tutu's emergence as an antiapartheid leader.

In the early 1970s Tutu lectured at universities in LESOTHO, BOTSWANA, and SWAZILAND. In 1976 he became bishop of Lesotho, and within a few years he became the general secretary of the South African Council of Churches. About that time the struggle between the apartheid government and the oppressed black population was nearing its peak, with hundreds of black African protesters having already died as a result of the repression of demonstrations by South African police. In this environment Tutu took a leading role in protesting the racism and violent mistreatment he and his fellow black Africans faced on a daily basis.

In 1985 Tutu became bishop of Johannesburg. At the same time he became the first black archbishop of CAPE TOWN. From this position Tutu fully came to the forefront of the struggle against apartheid, which continued unabated. In 1986, with violence sweeping the country, the South African government declared a state of emergency.

Tutu desired the same government reforms that were the aim of other black African leaders, such as Nelson MANDELA (1918–). However, he did not agree with the violent means that Mandela and other members of the AFRICAN NATIONAL CONGRESS had turned to in the battle against apartheid. In impassioned speeches, sermons, and official statements, Tutu unequivocally supported nonviolent protest as the way to end racist rule in South Africa. He promoted economic sanctions, in particular, as the best means to undermine South Africa's affluent, white ruling class. For his efforts, in 1984 Tutu won the Nobel Peace Prize. Fortunately for Tutu, his nonviolent stance and international recognition protected him from a backlash from the South African government.

In 1989, with the rise of F. W. DE KLERK (1936–) to the presidency, the efforts of Tutu and others finally began bearing fruit. In 1993 de Klerk announced the country's first multiracial elections. The following year Nelson Mandela became president, and apartheid was at an end.

> Tutu scorned the U.S. government for its reluctance to impose economic sanctions against South Africa. He called President Ronald Reagan's policy of CONSTRUCTIVE ENGAGEMENT and "friendly persuasion" a failure. In 1986 Tutu won a partial victory when the U.S. Congress overrode Reagan's veto to pass a number of economic sanctions.

In an effort to heal the country torn by years of racism and ethnic strife, in 1995 Mandela selected Tutu to head the newly created TRUTH AND RECONCILIATION COMMISSION. The commission was designed to study the countless cases of racial crimes committed by the apartheid government. Hearing the testimony of both victims and perpetrators, the commission offered amnesty to those who fully confessed to their crimes and could offer clear political motivations. Though some criticized the commission as being too merciful to those who had once supported apartheid, Tutu was widely considered the perfect person to lead the healing process. Though Tutu battled cancer in the late 1990s, as of 2004 he remained an enormously popular and respected leader of the people of South Africa.

See also: CHRISTIANITY, INFLUENCE OF (Vol. V).

Tutuola, Amos (1920–1997) *Yoruba writer from Nigeria*

With only a limited formal education, Amos Tutuola emerged in the 1960s as one of the foremost authors from NIGERIA, a country that was producing other great writers, including Chinua ACHEBE (1930–) and Wole SOYINKA (1934–). His first novel, *The Palm-Wine Drinkard and His Dead Palm-Wine Tapster in Deads' Town* (1952), was rife with magical elements drawn from YORUBA folklore and was written in the English of the ordinary people, which made it more accessible. The novel became a sensation abroad, both for its use of oral tradition and its fresh language. Many well-educated Nigerians, however, held it in disdain as the product of a poorly educated writer who had an insufficient command of English to utilize the language properly.

The Palm-Wine Drinkard was followed by a number of other novels, including *My Life in the Bush of Ghosts* (1954), *Simbi and the Satyr of the Dark Jungle* (1955), *Ajaiyi and His Inherited Poverty* (1967), and *The Witch-Herbalist of the Remote Town* (1981), though none of these approached the success of Tutuola's first effort. All of these novels draw from traditional Yoruba stories, but they also include the influences of colonialism and Christianity. Though critically acclaimed outside of Nigeria, Tutuola's novels were unpopular with members of the Nigerian elite, who criticized them as unpolished. Tutuola essentially ignored his critics and continued to write novels that were in an idiom that the general Nigerian—and particularly Yoruba—public could understand. Tutuola also adapted a number of his works for the stage. His success earned him teaching positions at the University of Ife and at the University of Iowa, in the United States. He died in 1997 in IBADAN, Nigeria.

See also: FOLKLORE (Vol. I); LANGUAGE USAGE IN MODERN AFRICA (Vol. V); LITERATURE IN COLONIAL AFRICA (Vol. IV); LITERATURE IN MODERN AFRICA (Vol. V).

U

Uganda

Uganda East African country approximately 91,100 square miles (236,000 sq km) in size and bordered by (clockwise from the north) the Republic of the SUDAN, KENYA, TANZANIA, RWANDA, and the Democratic Republic of the CONGO. Lake VICTORIA dominates the geography of the southeastern part of the country. The capital is KAMPALA.

Uganda at Independence Under British colonial rule Uganda was a composite of disparate ethnic groups and once-proud kingdoms. Among the most important of these was the kingdom of BUGANDA, which was populated primarily by the Ganda people. During the colonial period, the British authorities tended to favor Buganda, giving it greater autonomy than other kingdoms and fostering a wealthy and influential Ganda elite. Over the years this produced a volatile mix of jealousy and political intrigue that caused major problems upon Uganda's independence in 1962. As full autonomy approached the British authorities also granted self-government to the kingdom of Buganda, whose first prime minister was Benedicto Kiwanuka (1922–1972).

During the elections of 1962, however, Kiwanuka was defeated by Milton OBOTE (1925–   ), the leader of the Uganda People's Congress (UPC). Obote, of the Langi people, initially accepted Buganda as a federated part of the greater nation. He formed a coalition government with the conservative Ganda party known as the Kabaka Yekka (meaning "King Alone"). Obote became prime minister, and the Ganda *kabaka,* or king, Mutesa II (1924–1969) became Uganda's first president. However, the coalition became increasingly frayed by internal friction between the UPC and the Ganda, who were dissatisfied with playing a secondary role in the government. Mutesa's presidency was largely a figurehead position.

Obote clashed with the Baganda over territory and struggled to balance Buganda's autonomy with a centralized national government.

Facing mounting criticism and opposition from all parts of his government, in 1966, Obote reacted by suspending the constitution and arresting a number of opposition officials. The new constitution that was instituted abolished all kingdoms within Uganda and gave the prime minister presidential powers. When the Ganda protested and demanded the withdrawal of the Ugandan government presence from Buganda. Obote responded by sending Ugandan troops, led by future Ugandan president Idi AMIN (1925–2003), to arrest the *kabaka.* The royal palace was burned down, but Mutesa escaped and fled into exile.

Obote began to rely more heavily on the military to maintain his now dictatorial power. However, the ethnic divisiveness that plagued the countryside was also a prominent feature of the Ugandan military. Rifts began to divide Obote's Langi and the Acholi people on one side, and the Kakwa of Idi Amin on the other. Obote began to see Amin as a threat to his power and planned to have him arrested. However, Amin acted first, launching a COUP D'ÉTAT, in 1971, while Obote was abroad.

Uganda under Amin Although Ugandans (and the Ganda) were initially supportive of Amin's coup, their approval quickly disappeared as the country found itself under a brutal military regime. Almost immediately Amin launched a reign of terror that would eventually earn him the nickname "Butcher of Africa." He began to purge the military of Acholi and Langi troops, staging mass executions of any Ugandans he presumed to be supporters of the former president. Spending extensively on the military, Amin let the rest of Uganda's economy decline. In 1972 he banished Uganda's Asian population, who owned much of Uganda's business and industry. Amin then handed the seized businesses to army officials with little business experience. Before long the country's economy collapsed.

As Uganda dissolved into general chaos, Amin reacted more and more violently to perceived threats to his power. In 1978, in an attempt to distract and unite the country, Amin ordered an invasion of Tanzania. Tanzania struck back with the help Ugandan exiles and their Uganda National Liberation Army (UNLA). Future Ugandan president Yoweri MUSEVENI (1944–) was among the UNLA forces that captured Kampala, in 1979, sending Amin fleeing into exile. Approximately 300,000 Ugandans had been killed during Amin's regime.

The Return of Obote The political arm of the UNLA, called the Uganda National Liberation Front, assumed control of the country. In 1980, after the chosen UNLA leaders failed to make headway in settling the country's crisis, a cadre of UNLA members, including Museveni, led a military coup. Museveni, who by this time had built his own private militia, sat on the military council that governed until elections were held later that year. Running for the UPC, Milton Obote won the elections, once again assuming control of Uganda.

Obote immediately faced resistance from Museveni, who formed the National Resistance Army (NRA) and launched a civil war to unseat the president. Obote responded with brutal tactics reminiscent of Idi Amin's. Unable to defeat the NRA, Obote fell victim to ethnic tensions within his own army. Obote, a Langi, was overthrown by the Acholi commander, Basilio Okello (1929–1990). General Tito Okello (1914–1996; no relation to Basilio Okello) assumed the presidency.

Uganda under Museveni Like Obote, however, Okello failed to hold off the NRA. In 1986 the NRA captured Kampala, and Museveni assumed the presidency of a nation ravaged by years of military atrocities and economic neglect. He set about reforming the government and taming the highly militaristic atmosphere that pervaded Uganda following years of conflict and dictatorial rule. Believing that political parties formed along ethnic and regional lines had fueled the conflicts in Uganda, Museveni established the NRA as the sole legal party. In 1989 he decreed that presidential candidates could only run as individuals, not sponsored by any party. Elections held that year went smoothly, with Museveni winning. Voters approved of the "no-party" system, which was used again in 2001 with the same victorious results for Museveni.

That conditions in Uganda improved dramatically under Museveni is undeniable. The economy underwent consistent DEVELOPMENT, and Asian business owners were encouraged to return and resume their essential roles. Uganda has also made remarkable progress against the spread of HIV/AIDS, the disease that has spread wildly throughout the African continent. In addition, cases of violence and HUMAN RIGHTS violations diminished. In 2003, however, Museveni still struggled to subdue armed rebel movements in the north and west of the country.

See also: CIVIL WARS (Vol. V); ETHNIC CONFLICT IN AFRICA (Vol. V); HIV/AIDS AND AFRICA (Vol. V); UGANDA (Vols. I, II, III, IV).

ujamaa Economic and social policy proposed by Tanzanian president Julius NYERERE (1922–1999) that advocated collective, grassroots DEVELOPMENT. Developed during the late 1960s, *ujamaa* was a policy that Nyerere hoped would provide TANZANIA with a stable, socially responsible path towards development. Drawing on African social traditions, *ujamaa,* in the spirit of the root of the word, *jamaa,* which translates as "family," based its economic policy on mutual help and respect.

Nyerere's vision of *ujamaa* entailed good will and assistance among the people and communal ownership of many goods. With *ujamaa,* hard work and sharing both the means and the fruits of the people's LABOR were the best path for bettering the lives of the majority of the Tanzanian people.

In practice, however, *ujamaa* had mixed results. Its economic goals often were undermined by poor planning and mismanagement, causing decreased agricultural production and economic hardship. As a result, in the years since Nyerere's death, in 1999, Tanzania's leadership has been providing for more private sector involvement in the economy. In contrast, *ujamaa* proved successful in other areas, fostering EDUCATION and DEMOCRATIZATION to such an extent that Tanzania now boasts one of the region's lowest rates of illiteracy as well as a notable political stability.

See also: ARUSHA DECLARATION (Vol. V); SOCIAL CAPITAL (Vol. V).

Umkhonto we Sizwe Armed guerrilla wing of the AFRICAN NATIONAL CONGRESS, which sought the overthrow of APARTHEID from 1961 to 1990. In the wake of the SHARPEVILLE Massacre of 1960, which involved the shooting of 249 unarmed anti-apartheid protestors (69 of them fatally), the government of SOUTH AFRICA declared a state of emergency and banned the African National Congress (ANC) and other black opposition groups. As a result the ANC went underground and embarked upon an armed struggle with the goal of toppling the apartheid state. After nearly 50 years of being committed to nonviolence, the ANC leadership recognized the futility of this approach and in December 1961 formed an armed wing known as Umkhonto we Sizwe (Spear of the Nation), or for short, MK. It targeted public facilities like police stations, post offices, and power pylons, initially attempting to avoid the loss of human life. Nelson MANDELA (1918–) became head of the new guerilla organization and traveled abroad for military training, mainly in ALGERIA and ETHIOPIA.

In 1963 state security forces captured MK's high command at a farm in Rivonia, outside JOHANNESBURG. During the ensuing high-profile Rivonia Trial, ANC stalwarts such as Govan MBEKI (1910–2001) and Walter SISULU (1912–2003) were arrested. They and Mandela—who was already in prison—were sentenced to life terms and imprisoned on ROBBEN ISLAND for their involvement in MK activities. Remaining at large members of MK left South Africa, renewing operations in various states in southern Africa.

In exile the MK fighters participated in the liberation struggles of African peoples against colonial regimes in ZIMBABWE, MOZAMBIQUE, and ANGOLA. They also benefited from financial support and insurgency training provided by the Soviet Union and the Eastern Bloc countries. In the 1970s MK rebuilt its organization within South Africa and by 1976 began targeting public installations. This fresh wave of attacks drew upon the new militancy among South Africa's black youth following the police shootings of children in SOWETO, a sprawling township outside Johannesburg that housed the city's black population. Among its most daring acts of sabotage, MK attacked a massive state-owned OIL-refinery complex in 1980 and the Koeberg nuclear plant in CAPE TOWN in 1983. As the 1980s wore on, the tempo of attacks intensified, with an ever-increasing toll in fatalities, particularly as a result of car bombs aimed at the South African military, police, and justice system.

Umkhonto we Sizwe was officially disbanded in August 1990, after the ban on black opposition groups including MK had been lifted, and the ANC embarked upon meaningful negotiations with the ruling white-minority government toward a new political dispensation that would involve power sharing with the black opposition. During hearings convened by the TRUTH AND RECONCILIATION COMMISSION, revelations came to light of HUMAN RIGHTS abuses in MK camps outside South Africa during the years of exile, somewhat tarnishing the MK legacy in the liberation struggle. With the ANC's capture of political power, in 1994, began the awkward process of integrating MK guerrilla fighters into the very organizations dedicated to suppressing, harassing, and even killing them—the South African National Defense Force and national police service.

See also: RESISTANCE AND REBELLION (Vol. IV).

unilateral declaration of independence (UDI)
Assertion of independence by the white-minority government of RHODESIA from Britain. The declaration by Rhodesia's prime minister, Ian SMITH (1919–), took place on November 11, 1965.

By 1965 talks between Britain and the Smith government had broken down. Smith and his radical, white-supremacist political party, the Rhodesian Front (RF), worried that the success of INDEPENDENCE MOVEMENTS in neighboring Nyasaland (which became MALAWI) and Northern Rhodesia (which became ZAMBIA) would lead to similar results in Rhodesia if the white-minority community did not take full control. After easily winning the elections in 1965, Smith had the backing of the white electorate for declaring independence.

Britain refused to recognize the new state and considered Smith's UDI as an act of rebellion. As a result Rhodesia was unable to secure international recognition as an independent republic. Britain applied minimal but continuous diplomatic, military, and economic pressure on the white Rhodesian government to negotiate a settlement regarding the future of the country's black majority. They also imposed sanctions to limited effect. Ultimately UDI failed not because of British actions but due to the opposition of the country's African majority and the long struggle they waged to gain control. In 1979 the Rhodesian government recognized Britain's constitutional authority. Britain then oversaw the settlement that led to the emergence of independent ZIMBABWE.

See also: DECOLONIZATION (Vol. IV); ENGLAND AND AFRICA (Vols. III, IV, V); SETTLERS, EUROPEAN (Vol. IV); SOUTHERN RHODESIA (Vol. IV).

UNIP See UNITED NATIONAL INDEPENDENCE PARTY.

UNITA See NATIONAL UNION FOR THE TOTAL INDEPENDENCE OF ANGOLA.

United Democratic Front (UDF, South Africa)
Broad-based alliance of groups in SOUTH AFRICA dedicated to ending APARTHEID. The United Democratic Front (UDF) is made up of more than 500 grassroots organizations, including community and professional associations, women's and youth groups, LABOR UNIONS, and a broad range of anti-government activists. The UDF fought to dismantle apartheid and create a color-blind, socially just South Africa. As part of this the organization embraced the guiding principles of the Freedom Charter, which had been formulated in 1955 by the AFRICAN NATIONAL CONGRESS (ANC) and other liberation organizations. The UDF was formed in August 1983 in direct response to the government's move to introduce a new constitution. The centerpiece of that constitution was a tricameral parliament involving separate chambers for whites, Coloureds, and Asians (but none for the majority African population). This initiative, engineered by Prime Minister P. W. BOTHA (1916–), was a transparent at-

tempt to foster an image of reform for the benefit of an increasing critical international community, while retaining the underlying edifice of apartheid. Instead of deflecting international condemnation and placating domestic opposition, however, the new constitution ultimately intensified hostility toward the government's refusal to implement real change.

The UDF was multiracial and, originally, middle-class in orientation. As its national profile grew it rapidly emerged as the most powerful vehicle of anti-government opposition. As a result it increasingly drew on a working-class membership. Much of its momentum came from the renewed wave of protest among urban Africans that began in 1984. Its strongest support came from the regions known for their militancy, the Transvaal and the Eastern Cape. As an umbrella organization, the UDF coordinated bus boycotts, rent boycotts, worker strikes, and protests. UDF supporters also worked to render large areas of South Africa ungovernable and, in the place of government structures, to substitute new local institutions representing the interests of the masses. Perhaps its greatest contribution to the anti-apartheid struggle was its ability to provide a national apparatus so that the various opposition groups around the country could achieve common goals. It also served as a front organization for the ANC, which had been banned since 1960, and most of whose leaders were either abroad in exile or in South African prisons. Not only did UDF members adopt the ANC's Freedom Charter as their blueprint for a new post-apartheid South Africa, but they also acknowledged the ANC as South Africa's only legitimate political party. It regarded the ANC's former president, Nelson MANDELA (1918–), who had been sentenced to life in prison on ROBBEN ISLAND, as the country's moral leader.

During the state of emergency, which was in place from 1985 to 1990, many UDF members were harassed, banned, and jailed. In the wake of the comprehensive restrictions that the government imposed upon the UDF in February 1988, many members drifted to the Mass Democratic Movement, which also functioned as an alliance of anti-apartheid groups. Shortly after replacing Botha as prime minister, F. W. DE KLERK (1936–) removed the banning orders for the UDF, ANC, and other opposition groups. The following year, in August 1991, as the country was progressing toward a more inclusive and democratic political dispensation, the UDF dissolved itself after having achieved its main goals.

See also: ASIAN COMMUNITIES (Vols. IV, V); CAPE COLOURED PEOPLE (Vol. IV); FREEDOM CHARTER (Vol. IV); TRANSVAAL (Vol. IV)

Further reading: Gregory F. Houston, *The National Liberation Struggle in South Africa: A Case Study of the United Democratic Front, 1983–1987* (Aldershot, U.K.: Ashgate, 1999); Ineke van Kessel, *"Beyond Our Wildest Dreams": The United Democratic Front and the Transforma-* tion of South Africa (Charlottesville, Va.: University Press of Virginia, 2000); Jeremy Seekings, *The UDF: A History of the United Democratic Front in South Africa, 1983–1991* (Athens, Ohio: Ohio University Press, 2000).

United National Independence Party (UNIP)

Political party of ZAMBIA that controlled the government through the first 27 years of independence. In 1959 Mathias Mainza CHONA (1930–2001) founded UNIP as a successor party to the banned Northern Rhodesia African National Congress (NRANC), a more militant offshoot of the AFRICAN NATIONAL CONGRESS (ANC). Chona was the party's first president, but only because Kenneth KAUNDA (1924–), UNIP's de facto leader, was in prison. Upon his release, in 1960, Kaunda assumed his role as president of the party. He then went about positioning the party at the forefront of the African nationalist movement in Northern Rhodesia (now Zambia). The objectives of the party were to fight British colonial rule and to bring about independence.

In 1962 UNIP urged civil disobedience to initiate changes in Northern Rhodesia's constitution. The campaign was effective, and the constitution was altered to ensure that the Africans were fairly enfranchised. Later that year, elections for the legislature ended in a stalemate between UNIP and the white-supremacist United Federal Party. UNIP, however, joined with the NRANC, which was led by Harry NKUMBULA (1916–1983), to form an African-led coalition government.

The party fared better in the elections of 1964, handily winning a legislative majority and naming Kaunda prime minister. In October of that year Northern Rhodesia gained its independence and was renamed Zambia. Kaunda became president, and UNIP began its long reign as the controlling party of the country.

Widespread political violence marked the elections of 1968. In 1972 Kaunda, alarmed by the political gains of his opponents, made UNIP the only legal party of Zambia. The country thus joined the widespread movement on the continent toward one-party states. Over the next 20 years the party's political dominance became increasingly untenable as economic difficulties and failed social programs led to popular dissatisfaction.

In 1991 the National Assembly, under pressure from the MOVEMENT FOR MULTIPARTY DEMOCRACY (MMD), abolished the country's one-party system of government. Later that year, Zambia held multiparty elections in which Frederick CHILUBA (1943–) and the MMD ended Kaunda's and UNIP's control of the government. Though the party remains active, it has yet to regain its position as the majority party of Zambia.

See also: NORTHERN RHODESIA (Vol. IV); UNITED NATIONAL INDEPENDENCE PARTY (Vol. IV); POLITICAL PARTIES AND ORGANIZATIONS (Vol. IV, V).

United Nations and Africa The United Nations (UN) is the preeminent world body, comprising 191 countries, of which more than two-thirds are developing countries. At its creation the organization had 51 members. African countries, including LIBERIA, ETHIOPIA, EGYPT, and APARTHEID-era SOUTH AFRICA, were among the original members. The organization now includes most African countries, many of which were under colonial rule when the United Nations was created.

The UN General Assembly is made up of representatives from all the member states and meets once a year. The most powerful organ of the United Nations is the Security Council. Its role is to maintain peace and security between nations. Since it is one of the most important organs, membership on the council is a significant matter. The Security Council has five permanent members: the United States, the United Kingdom, France, China, and Russia. The permanent members exert the major influence on the council. A negative vote or veto by any of the permanent members can stop a proposal. However, there are 10 representatives for other areas of the world. The African, Latin American, and Western European blocs choose two members each, and the Arab, Asian, and Eastern European blocs choose one member each. The final seat alternates between Asian and African selections. As a result of this arrangement, Africa always has two representatives on the Security Council and at times three. In 2004, for instance, there were three African members—ALGERIA, ANGOLA and The Republic of BENIN. The Security Council, unlike other organs of the United Nations, which can only make recommendations to member governments, has the power to make decisions that member governments must carry out under the UN Charter.

The chief executive of the United Nations, the secretary general, is important with regard to highlighting global issues and bringing sensitivity of the issues. Since 1992 the secretary general has come from Africa, which may have helped bring African issues higher on the agenda. From 1992 to 1996 an Egyptian, Boutros Boutros-Ghali (1922–   ), served as secretary general. In 1996 an American veto prevented him from having a second term. From 1997 Kofi ANNAN (1938–   ) of GHANA has served as the secretary general and was reappointed to serve for a second term to last until 2006.

From the 1960s Africa has had a major impact on the United Nations, primarily through the ORGANIZATION OF AFRICAN UNITY (OAU). The OAU, which was transformed into the AFRICAN UNION (AU) in 2002, maintained observer status at the United Nations since its creation in 1963. During this time the OAU coordinated collective action among African nations at the United Nations, a process that proved crucial during the 1960s, when many African countries had liberation movements and were not independent.

In 1974 African countries succeeded in having the United Nations take action against SOUTH AFRICA, which was a founding member of the organization but which maintained the much-hated policy of racial segregation known as apartheid. Because of its racist policies, South Africa was barred from participating in the UN General Assembly.

The United Nations has played a major role in encouraging countries under colonial rule to attain their independence. The UN participation was most evident in supervising elections that led to independence in the African countries of TOGO, in 1960, and in NAMIBIA, in 1989. Still concerned with the question of colonialism, which affects countries such as WESTERN SAHARA, in 2000 the General Assembly declared 2001–10 as the second International Decade for the Eradication of Colonialism.

One of the major areas in which the United Nations has had an impact in Africa is in peacekeeping. Between 1960 and 2000 the African continent saw 13 major conflicts, many of them CIVIL WARS, to which the United Nations sent military personnel. Some interventions were outright successes, some had questionable outcomes, and others had mixed results based on the measurement of their objectives and their outcomes. Still others were outright failures. Nonetheless, the role of the United Nations in conflict resolution has been vital.

In Africa UN peacekeeping efforts started with the CONGO CRISIS, in which the United Nations intervened from 1960 to 1964. In 1959 anticolonial rioting broke out in the Congo. Belgium, the colonial power, attempted to pacify the situation by offering a gradual path to independence. The demand for independence was so strong, however, that Belgium abandoned its original approach and instead announced that the country would become independent within a few months. Joseph KASAVUBU (c. 1913–1969) was elected president, and Patrice LUMUMBA (1925–1961) became the prime minister. Immediately after the declaration of independence, mutinies broke out. Another complication arose as Moïse TSHOMBE (1919–1969) proclaimed independence for mineral-rich KATANGA province. This was further aggravated by the presence of Belgian troops. Kasavubu and Lumumba asked for UN intervention.

While the UN efforts prevented the secession of Katanga, its success in the Congo was limited. Indeed, little was done to improve the conditions and the future of the Congolese people. This was similar to what happened during the 1990s in LIBERIA, where UN forces only served to delay the victory for one political party rather than prevent it.

In addition to its humanitarian causes, one of the great responsibilities of the United Nations is to monitor elections worldwide. In 1994, two years after Mozambique's civil war ended, Mozambicans like this woman in Catembe voted under the watchful eye of United Nations officials. © *United Nations/P. Sudhakaran*

UN intervention in SOMALIA in 1992–93 proved even more problematic. There, UN forces led by the United States were drawn into confrontations with the local people with the objective of forcing peace. The result was that the peacekeepers were seen as being involved in the situation rather than objectively pursuing a peaceful outcome. Not surprisingly, UN intervention in Somalia has been seen as an example of peacekeeping failure in Africa.

Given the failure in Somalia, there was reluctance for the United Nations to be involved in similar conflicts. Shortly afterwards, for example, the members of the Security Council initially refused to authorize UN intervention in the genocide that was taking place in RWANDA. In the end, the UN force of 5,500 that was sent was insufficient to halt the killing, and many Africans felt betrayed, thinking that the United Nations failed to prevent the deaths of hundreds of thousands of people.

In contrast UN peacekeeping efforts proved more successful in Namibia, where all three countries involved—South Africa, Cuba, and ANGOLA—were interested in achieving a peaceful outcome. The United Nations supervised the withdrawal of Cuban forces from Angola, which represented a clear success for the United Nations. The Cuban withdrawal was linked to decolonization, and the United Nations ultimately supervised the plebiscite that led to the independence of Namibia from South Africa.

Although the United Nations is mostly known for its role in maintaining peace and security, a large proportion of its resources is devoted to economic development, social development, and SUSTAINABLE DEVELOPMENT. Africa has been a recipient of substantial UN resources and programs, many of which have had important impacts on Africa's population. In each African country, for example, the UN Development Program maintains an office through which the organization connects to governments and other development partners to bring knowledge, experience, and resources from across the region and around the world.

See also: BELGIAN CONGO (Vol. IV); COLONIAL RULE (Vol. IV); CUBA AND AFRICA (Vol. V); DECOLONIZATION (Vol. IV); ECONOMIC ASSISTANCE (Vol. V); UNITED NATIONS AND AFRICA (Vol. IV).

Further reading: Norrie Maqueen, *United Nations Peacekeeping in Africa since 1960* (New York: Longman, 2002).

United States and Africa The relationship between the United States (U.S.) and the African continent, which underwent dramatic changes in the 1950s, has become increasingly complex in the years since. Today there are multiple and diverse sets of relationships between them.

Prior to the era of African independence U.S. interests in Africa were limited, in large part due to Europe's colonial control of most of the continent. To a great extent U.S. involvement was limited to activities like those of American MISSIONARIES, who were at work in many parts of the continent. Other activities came from the African-American community within the United States, where African-Americans such as W. E. B. Du Bois (1868–1963) and Marcus Garvey (1887–1940) were enthusiastically espousing PAN-AFRICANISM and where there had long been supporters of a Back-to-Africa Movement. Beyond this, some Africans who later were to become prominent political leaders of their countries studied in the United States, often at historically black universities such as Lincoln University in Pennsylvania. Economic relations between the United States and Africa were minimal, with the Firestone Rubber Plantation in LIBERIA as one of the few major American economic undertakings in Africa.

In the early 1960s, as the Cold War developed, the United States used humanitarian aid to establish ties to emerging African states. This U.S. Air Force plane dropped bags of corn to flood victims in Tanzania. © *U.S. Air Force*

World War II (1939–45) drew American attention to Africa, especially to North Africa, where many Americans fought and died. After the war, with decolonization clearly in the offing, American interest began to grow. In the late 1940s, for example, AFRICAN STUDIES began to arise as an scholarly field of study. In the following decade, the Cold War also began to take shape. When African countries gained their independence from their former colonial rulers (LIBYA, in 1951, the Republic of the SUDAN, in 1954, MOROCCO and TUNISIA, in 1956, and GHANA, in 1957), the United States began to compete actively with the Soviet Union for influence with their leaders and citizens. In 1958 the U.S. Department of State created the Bureau of African Affairs to oversee its relations with the emerging sub-Saharan African countries (the North African countries were under the Bureau of Near Eastern Affairs). Especially under the assistant secretary of state for African affairs, G. Mennen Williams (1911–1988), who served

under President John F. Kennedy (1917–1963), the bureau actively promoted and encouraged political independence for Africa. President Kennedy also launched the Peace Corps, which sent thousands of young Americans to serve in Africa as volunteers. The U.S. Agency for International Development (USAID) also began to provide ECONOMIC ASSISTANCE for African DEVELOPMENT, especially to countries such as EGYPT, Ethiopia and SOMALIA, the Republic of the Sudan, and the Democratic Republic of the CONGO. Support for African independence and development also was politically important in the United States, especially among the growing black electorate coming out of the civil rights era.

The optimism of the early years of successful INDE-PENDENCE MOVEMENTS, however, did not last. The CONGO CRISIS of the early 1960s was a harbinger of the political instability that was to become characteristic of much of the continent. Also, a number of more radical leaders came to power, and, like Libya's Muammar QADDAFI (1942–), they were suspicious of U.S. motives and policies. The situation was further complicated in the 1960s by the outbreak of wars of liberation in the Portuguese colonies of ANGOLA, MOZAMBIQUE, and GUINEA-BISSAU. Since Portugal was an important ally in the North Atlantic Treaty Organization (NATO), the United States was unwilling to openly oppose Portugal's efforts to retain its colonies. A similar situation emerged in southern Africa. There, in the context of Cold War politics, the APARTHEID government of South Africa became an important, if not overt, ally of the United States in what it perceived as the struggle against Communism in southern Africa.

During this period apartheid became a flash point in American politics, for unlike any other country on the continent, the racially politicized politics of South Africa bore considerable resemblance to the situation in the United States. Eventually, it became increasingly difficult for a country that had lived through the civil rights era to sanction South Africa's racially oppressive political system. In 1986 anti-apartheid sentiment in the United States led to the passage of the Comprehensive Anti-Apartheid Act, with Congress overriding a presidential veto by President Ronald Reagan (1911–2004) to enact the legislation. By this time, however, the Cold War was nearing its end, and the collapse of the Berlin Wall, in 1989, signaled the beginning of the end of the international influence of the Soviet Union.

Freed from the constraints of the Cold War, relations between the United States and Africa underwent yet another major change. The United States could now openly support and encourage the forces of DEMOCRATIZATION in South Africa and other parts of the continent. It no longer needed to support autocratic, tyrannical leaders such as the Congo's MOBUTU SESE SEKO (1930–1997) out of concern that pro-Soviet leaders might replace them. The United States also no longer needed to try and outbid the Soviet Union in the provision of economic assistance, which led to a decline in overall foreign aid to Africa and other parts of the so-called Third World. However, since much of the earlier aid had ended up in the private bank accounts of tyrants like Mobutu, declining dollar amounts of aid did not necessarily equate with a decline in effective aid.

The type of political instability, warfare, and ethnic conflict that has gripped LIBERIA, RWANDA, and BURUNDI continue to command the attention of Americans. More recently, new concerns have come to characterize American-African relations. The emergence of the HIV/AIDS crisis in Africa has led to sharp debates within the United States regarding how best to respond to the pandemic. In 2003 U.S. president George W. Bush (1946–) announced that the United States would contribute $15 billion to the fight against HIV/AIDS, resulting in a major shift in the flow of aid to Africa. The African Growth and Opportunity Act, first passed in 2000 and amended in 2002, focuses on opening up economies and building free markets as the most effective means for promoting African development. Countries that meet certain requirements are eligible for tariff preferences in their trade with the United States. In 2003 as many as 37 countries met the criteria.

Security concerns have also come to the forefront of American dealings with Africa. Several African countries hold vast deposits of OIL, and the United States is looking to them as potential source of oil imports in the increasingly probable event that the flow of oil from the Middle East is disrupted. Even before the terrorist attacks of September 11, 2001, TERRORISM became another security concern. The 1998 bombings of the U.S. embassies in NAIROBI, KENYA and DAR ES SALAAM, TANZANIA were one of the major precursors of the 9/11 attack. In the aftermath of 9/11, the United States became increasingly concerned with the absence of a functioning state in SOMALIA, a situation that made the country a haven for international terrorists, especially those associated with radical Islam. In response, the United States stationed 1,500 troops in neighboring DJIBOUTI. In this way, the Horn of Africa once again became an important arena for American strategic planning, just as it was prior to the overthrow of Emperor HAILE SELASSIE (1892–1975) in 1974.

See also: BACK-TO-AFRICA MOVEMENT (Vol. IV); COLD WAR AND AFRICA (Vols. IV, V); DU BOIS, W. E. B. (Vol. IV); GARVEY, MARCUS (Vol. IV); SOVIET UNION AND AFRICA (Vols. IV, V); UNITED STATES OF AMERICA AND AFRICA (Vol. IV).

Further reading: Asgede Hagos, *Hardened Images: The Western Media and the Marginalization of Africa* (Trenton, N.J.: Africa World Press, 2000); Zaki Laïdi, *The Superpowers and Africa: The Constraints of a Rivalry, 1960–1990*, Patricia Baudoin, trans. (Chicago: University of Chicago Press, 1990); Peter J. Schraeder, *United States Foreign Policy Toward Africa: Incrementalism, Crisis, and Change* (New York: Cambridge University Press, 1994).

Upper Volta Name given to the present-day country of BURKINA FASO during French colonial rule and also for the first 24 years after gaining independence. Upper Volta was renamed Burkina Faso (roughly translated as "the Land of Incorruptible Men") in 1984 by then president Thomas Sankara (1949–1987).

See also: UPPER VOLTA (Vol. IV).

urbanization The population of Africa historically has been predominantly rural, but the initial change in the rate of urbanization that occurred during the colonial period has accelerated during the post-colonial era. In the postcolonial era, Africa, like other more developed continents, saw the rise of modern metropolises, such as JO-

HANNESBURG and CAIRO, cities with strong industry, commerce, and tall skyscrapers.

Rural-to-Urban Migration The principal reason for increased urbanization in Africa is rural-to-urban migration. Due to this pattern the urban population in sub-Saharan Africa rose from less than 15 percent in 1950 to more than 30 percent in 2000. The percentages, however, vary greatly among individual countries. For example, in 2000 the WORLD BANK estimated that RWANDA had 6 percent and UGANDA had 14 percent of their respective populations living in urban areas. In contrast, the figures for the Republic of the CONGO and IVORY COAST, respectively, were 63 and 46 percent. Reasons for rural-to-urban migration include ethnic conflicts, natural disasters, land scarcity, and the desire to escape rural POVERTY. Widespread ETHNIC CONFLICT IN AFRICA has caused people to flee from violence in rural areas. (The opposite is common, too, with urban violence causing a mass exodus from the cities to the rural outskirts).

Typically people who find limited resources for survival in the countryside move to the city in hopes of finding a wage job or some other way to make a living. In certain cities in central, eastern, and southern Africa, rural-to-urban migration has increased dramatically since the independence era (c. 1960), when Africans were finally allowed to live in cities legally. Although urbanization is occurring rapidly, there are still strong links between urban and rural residents in much of Africa; it is common for urban immigrants to send a portion of their earnings home to their families and to return to the countryside during holidays or between jobs.

The Challenging Urban Environment With the massive migration of people to the cities, unemployment rates there are high, and people who arrive poor typically continue to suffer from poverty in the city as well. For these individuals jobs in the formal economic sector are especially difficult to come by. An informal economy, however, has served to absorb many of the otherwise unemployed migrants over the last several decades. In fact, the informal market is considered the most active and fastest growing part of many national economies in Africa.

Even if an urban migrant is able to find a job in the informal economy, however, living conditions usually are poor at best. The great influx of migrants has resulted in severe urban housing shortages, forcing people to gather in slums or squatter settlements. Due to the housing shortages rents are high and consume a substantial portion of income. Squatter settlements, frequently built on marginal lands, lack appropriate WATER sources, waste disposal, health-care facilities, schools, and electricity. One squatter settlement outside of NAIROBI has been built up on "black cotton" soil—a clay soil that does not absorb water—and flooding is a problem every time it rains. The policy of some governments has been to bulldoze squatter settlements like these, claiming that they are illegal and that they constitute unsightly health hazards. Other governments have allowed such settlements to develop into more substantial communities.

Women in Cities Despite the poverty and unemployment faced by urban migrants, life in many cities represents a marked improvement in the status of WOMEN IN INDEPENDENT AFRICA. Women have better access to information and EDUCATION when they move to cities, thereby giving them more control over their own fertility and, hence, more control over the size of their families. In addition, throughout the 1970s and 1980s urban women benefited from an unforeseen effect of a declining African economy: men became more likely to establish stable unions with them in order to make enough money to live.

Efforts at Improvement Some African countries have not yet recovered from economic recession. After independence the INTERNATIONAL MONETARY FUND and the World Bank loaned money to African countries with a number of conditions, including a commitment to limit government spending on social services. Known as STRUCTURAL ADJUSTMENT programs, these conditions are designed to build a healthy economy. Positive results, however, have been slow in coming, and the policies have greatly impacted the poor in both urban and rural areas by reducing health-care services. They also have allowed the INFRASTRUCTURE to go unimproved, and have limited housing, water, electricity, and waste disposal projects. By cutting back civil service jobs, these structural adjustment programs have also increased unemployment.

The Rise of African Super-Cities One of the most obvious changes to the urban landscape in Africa has been the increasing magnitude of Africa's large cities. In the 1960s Johannesburg, SOUTH AFRICA, was the only city outside North Africa with more than 1 million inhabitants. Today there are 27 cities with a population greater than 1 million. This phenomenon has largely been caused by the concentration of commerce and industry in only one large city within each country. Recently, however, some secondary cities have begun to grow very rapidly, sometimes surpassing the rate of growth found in the most highly populated cities.

Character of Africa's Urban Centers As cities grew during the postcolonial period they responded in different ways to this growth, and today there are differences in the character of various cities in Africa. Some cities, such as DAKAR, in SENEGAL, and KINSHASA, in the Democratic Republic of the CONGO, have a colonial legacy evident in their layouts and ARCHITECTURE. These types of cities often served as capitals during colonial times and maintained that status upon independence. They already had the industrial infrastructure established by colonial interests, making them the best location for further industrial development after independence.

Other cities, such as Lamu, in Kenya, and Timbuktu, in the Republic of MALI, maintain a more "indigenous" feel, while still others have developed with a combination of colonial and African characteristics. The city of KHARTOUM, in the Republic of the SUDAN, still seems to be structured to cater predominantly to its European residents. This is the case in Nairobi, Kenya, and PRETORIA, South Africa, as well. Districts in these cities are still home to many Westerners, and they are characterized by a cosmopolitan, international flavor.

A unique type of postcolonial African urban center is the planned city. The inland city of ABUJA, for example, was built from the ground up as the new federal capital of NIGERIA when LAGOS, the former capital, became too densely populated to serve as an effective administrative center. Under slightly different circumstances, the more easily accessible city of DODOMA, located near the center of TANZANIA, became the new federal capital replacing DAR ES SALAAM, an old and densely settled city located on the coast.

Even in 1964 Johannesburg was a booming urban center, with high rise apartments and traffic-choked streets. © *Library of Congress*

> Nearly all African urban centers share one common feature—a bustling mass-TRANSPORTATION system. Many governments have allowed for privatization of some mass transportation, leading to the dominance of overcrowded *matatus,* or small minibuses.

See also: COLONIALISM, INFLUENCE OF (Vol. IV); ECONOMIC ASSISTANCE (Vol. V); INDUSTRIALIZATION (Vol. V); POPULATION GROWTH (Vol. V); TIMBUKTU (Vols. II, III, IV); URBAN LIFE AND CULTURE (Vols. IV, V).

Further reading: Salah El-Shakhs, *Future Urban Development in Emerging Mega-Cities in Africa* (New Brunswick, N.J.: Rutgers Center for Urban Policy Research, 1995); Karen A. Foote, Kenneth H. Hill, and Linda G. Martin, eds., *Demographic Change in Sub-Saharan Africa* (Washington D.C.: National Academy Press, 1993); Margaret Peil and Pius O. Sada *African Urban Society* (Chichester, N.Y.: Wiley, 1984); David Simon, *Cities, Capital and Development: African Cities in the World Economy* (New York: Halstead Press, 1992); Richard E. Stren and Rodney R. White, eds., *African Cities in Crisis: Managing Rapid Urban Growth* (Boulder, Colo.: Westview Press, 1989).

urban life and culture   African cities range from modern centers of international commerce scattered with skyscrapers, to smaller urban centers with historic structures and local markets. Regardless of the type of city, however, urban centers in Africa tend to be bustling and vibrant.

After much of Africa gained national independence, many rural Africans saw the cities as the land of opportunity. The rural-to-urban migration that began under colonialism intensified during this period. The new wave of migrants included many women, who had been discouraged from relocating to the cities during the colonial era. Migrants expected to find more employment opportunities and a better quality of life in the cities. While some did find employment, many did not and were forced to be creative about making a living. Their entrepreneurial spirit resulted in a well-developed, informal economic sector. Critical to the exchange of consumer goods in the economies of African nations, the street vendors and open-air markets of the informal sector have contributed greatly to the vibrant nature of urban landscapes. The informal sector is a major source of employment for urban women. Selling used clothing sent by aid organizations in the West is a major informal economic industry. Many urban dwellers wear formal modern office attire from the West. The used clothing vendors offer these articles at much lower prices than the formal shops in the cities.

Another area in which the informal market thrives is TRANSPORTATION. The widespread lack of public transportation in many African cities has resulted in extensive networks of private minibuses offering transportation to urban dwellers. The overcrowded minibuses, adorned with popular artwork and blasting local radio stations, take people back and forth between work, school, home, markets, and stores.

Urban neighborhoods are often segregated. The elite, both foreign and local, live in guarded neighborhoods with large gated houses. Expatriates and embassy personnel dominate some neighborhoods. On the other side of the spectrum, the lack of affordable urban housing has forced many of the poorer city dwellers to live in squatter settlements known as "shantytowns." Houses in shantytowns are often made from iron, wood, plastic, or whatever materials can be found locally. These settlements are usually not officially recognized municipalities, and therefore they often lack running water, electricity, waste disposal, and health-care facilities. However, some governments and NON-GOVERNMENTAL ORGANIZATIONS have implemented projects to bring these facilities to shantytowns.

In addition to the daytime chaos of pedestrians and vehicles navigating busy streets, urban nightlife is also vibrant. African young people frequent the many bars and discos that have opened in recent years, which play popular Western and African MUSIC. Most major cities also have theaters for drama or musical performances. Colorfully lighted signs advertising local and Western products add to the energy of the urban landscape during the day and night.

Unfortunately, with the massive influx of migrants and the shortages of jobs and housing, crime also has become a problem for many African cities. In addition, it is not unusual to see homeless people begging for food or money. These factors add to the chaotic feel of the urban areas in Africa.

See also: COLONIALISM, INFLUENCE OF (Vol. V); THEATER (Vol. V); URBANIZATION (Vols. IV, V); URBAN LIFE AND CULTURE (Vol. IV).

Further reading: Paul Tiyambe Zeleza and Cassandra Rachel Veney (eds.), *Leisure in Urban Africa* (Trenton, N.J.: Africa World Press, 2003); Margaret Peil, *Cities and Suburbs: Urban Life in West Africa* (New York: Africana Publishing Company, 1981).

V

Verwoerd, Hendrik (Hendrik Frensch Verwoerd; H. F. Verwoerd) (1901–1966) *Prime minister of South Africa*

A rigid ideologue and fierce believer in white supremacy throughout his career, Verwoerd was a leading architect of the racial policy of APARTHEID in SOUTH AFRICA. After becoming prime minister, in 1958, Verwoerd was at the height of his political power in 1960. At that time, South Africa faced increasing criticism for its racial policies from fellow members of the British Commonwealth. Verwoerd responded defiantly, setting out on a course to free South Africa from the influence of Britain and other commonwealth members.

In May 1961 a Verwoerd-backed popular referendum was passed—with only whites voting—approving the creation of a South African republic. With the new government in place, a month later Verwoerd forced a confrontation with the commonwealth. South Africa unilaterally withdrew from the organization, severing relations with Britain that dated back to 1795.

Verwoerd then pressed on with a policy, eventually known as "separate development," that continued apartheid and sought to relegate nonwhites to 10 separate homelands. Ostensibly encouraging the development of these homelands into independent nations, Verwoerd's policy was, in effect, a means of depriving blacks of South African citizenship. Although the program met with protest and resistance on the part of black South Africans—as well as the international community—Verwoerd's government managed to keep protests in check for many years. It could not, however, stop the international outcry that increasingly drove South Africa into political and economic isolation.

Verwoerd himself survived an assassination attempt that took place in JOHANNESBURG in April 1960. A second attempt on his life on September 6, 1966, proved successful. A mentally unbalanced parliamentary messenger stabbed Verwoerd to death in CAPE TOWN. Succeeded by John Vorster (1915–1983), another ardent supporter of apartheid, Verwoerd left behind a legacy of a bitterly divided country whose repressive government had become an international outcast.

See also: VERWOERD, HENDRIK FRENCSH (Vol. IV).

Further reading: Henry Kenney, *Architect of Apartheid: H. F. Verwoerd, an Appraisal* (Johannesburg: J. Ball, 1980).

Victoria Capital and lone port of the Republic of SEYCHELLES, located on the northeastern coast of Mahé Island in the Indian Ocean. Britain assumed colonial control of the Seychelles from France in 1814, but it administered the territory as part of MAURITIUS, another Indian Ocean island colony, until 1903. When the Seychelles became a separate crown colony that year, Victoria—named in honor of Britain's queen—served as the colonial capital. The city's subsequent development reflected its British colonial character. Victoria's locally famous Clock Tower, built in 1902, served to represent the islands' status as an independent British colony.

Victoria continued as the capital of the Republic of the Seychelles upon its independence, in 1976. Some of the government buildings have not changed from the time of their construction earlier in the 20th century and serve as a reminder of the colonial past. However, many of the roads have been restored and the city, one of the smallest capitals in the world with only 23,000 inhabitants, has a quiet and clean atmosphere. All of the other settlements on the islands are villages, and most of the people who live on the island of Mahé live in the city of Victoria. While English and French are the official languages, most of the people speak a French-based Creole language.

The economy depends on industries associated with copra (dried coconut meat), vanilla, guano (bird dropping fertilizer), and cinnamon. Recently TOURISM, mostly focusing on the natural history and physical beauty of the surroundings, has become increasingly important. Victoria's international airport, built with British funds in 1971, is the main point of entry for tourists visiting the Seychelles. The town offers a host of small hotels, a botanical garden, and a natural history museum.

See also: ENGLAND AND AFRICA (Vols. III, IV, V); FRANCE AND AFRICA (Vols. III, IV, V).

Victoria, Lake Large body of water located near East Africa's Great Rift Valley. Lake Victoria was called *Ukerewe* prior to European exploration in the 18th century. Today it is called *Victoria Nyanza* by many Africans. At once a biological wonder and a critical natural resource, Africa's largest freshwater lake teems with life while providing a livelihood for millions of people from East Africa through EGYPT. Today the lake is dying, and one of the world's most concerted scientific efforts is trying to save it.

At 26,830 square miles (69,490 sq km), Lake Victoria is second in surface area only to Lake Superior in North America among the world's freshwater lakes. The lake measures 270 feet (82 m) at its deepest. Lake Victoria is historically among the most species-diverse lakes on earth, making its continued BIODIVERSITY a great concern to scientists. As a principal source of the Nile River, it is a critical resource not only for the 30 million inhabitants who live near it but also for the people of Republic of the SUDAN and Egypt, countries through which the river runs on its way north to the Nile Delta before emptying into the Mediterranean Sea.

Significant changes to Lake Victoria began under colonial rule. The British cleared the vegetation around the lake, felled forests, and drained wetlands in order to create plantations for tea, coffee, and sugar to be exported to European markets. Runoff from the plantations severely polluted the lake and the surrounding ecosystems, reducing their biological functions. Local AGRICULTURE also attracted migrant workers, who ultimately became permanent residents, thus increasing the consumption of lake fish. Fishing for export further reduced fish numbers and even caused the extinction of some fish species.

In 1956 the British colonial administration introduced into the lake the Nile perch (*lates nilotica*), a nonnative fish species. It had the intended effect of increasing fish catches for export, but, while the Nile perch accounted for about 1 percent of the fish catch in the 1960s, today it makes up more than 80 percent. It is thought that this predatory fish has caused the extinction of hundreds of fish species found nowhere else. In particular, Lake Victoria was once host to an unknown number, probably between 400 and 800, of small cichlid fish species. Now, as a direct result of the introduction of the Nile perch, less than half of those species remain.

The changing fish life has had a critical impact on local economies. Smaller cichlids, now hard to catch in sufficient numbers, have long been food staples for local communities. The Nile perch lives in deeper waters that cannot be reached by small boats and, thus, the fish benefits only the bigger commercial FISHING operations, which generally service foreign markets. In this sense the shift in fish species has been a great benefit to large businesses but a significant blow to local fishing markets. Further, related industries such as fish processing have also been significantly affected. A Kenyan research group, Friends of Lake Victoria, and other local organizations have been working with local communities to try to mitigate some of these negative economic impacts through aquaculture development.

Further compounding damage to the lake's ecology, industrial companies dumped untreated pollutants into the water—a practice that continues today—causing a proliferation of algae. TANZANIA alone is responsible for dumping more than a half-million gallons of untreated sewage and industrial waste into the lake daily, which leads to diseases such as typhoid, cholera, and diarrhea. The ongoing destruction of the lake's wetlands reduces the water-purifying function of such ecosystems.

Another great change in the Lake Victoria ecosystem is the growth of water hyacinth (*Eichhorina crassipes*), which was first observed in 1989. Originally from the Amazon basin, water hyacinth grows at an alarming rate, clogging water channels, changing hydrological cycles, causing flooding, strangling other flora, and blocking sunlight in the water, all of which can lead to massive fish kills. The weed weaves itself into such a dense matt that boats cannot pass. Water hyacinth also makes an ideal home for snails, which can proliferate diseases such as bilharzias, and mosquitoes, which spread malaria and other diseases. Further, when hyacinth dies, it releases toxins that kill other flora and fauna.

Service at Uganda's Owen Falls Hydroelectric facility, the most important hydroelectric source in the region, is regularly interrupted because of problems related to water hyacinth, the weed has become the largest single problem facing Lake Victoria. The Lake Victoria Environmental Management Plan, managed by the Global Environment Facility of the UN Environment Program, has allocated $76 million to alleviate the problem, but efforts to control water hyacinth growth have met with only modest success.

Beginning in the colonial era, pollution combined with the introduction of non-native species to the Lake Victoria ecosystem greatly reduced the catches of local fishers like these. © *Corbis*

In 1994 a genocidal war in RWANDA led to many thousands of human corpses being thrown into the Kagera River, which flows into Lake Victoria. Many of the bodies became so tangled in the thick water hyacinth that they could not be recovered. The decay of the bodies caused such health hazards that the government of UGANDA considered parts of the lake a disaster area.

The combined impact of the Nile perch and the water hyacinth has exacted a terrible cost to indigenous communities. Ecologically, there is a consensus among scientists that unless something is done to halt its destruction, Lake Victoria soon will cease to sustain life. With so many millions of lives—human and otherwise—in the balance, local communities have been collaborating with international agencies to develop lake-management strategies. It remains to be seen, however, if these economic and environmental efforts will be sufficient or if the damage is irreversible.

See also: COLONIAL RULE (Vol. IV); ECOLOGY AND ECOLOGICAL CHANGE (Vol. V); NILE RIVER (Vol. I); SPEKE, JOHN HANNING (Vol. IV); VICTORIA, LAKE (Vols. I, II).

Further reading: Tijs Goldschmidt, *Darwin's Dreampond: Drama in Lake Victoria* (Boston, Mass.: MIT Press, 1996).

Volta Lake   World's largest man-made lake, located in east-central GHANA. Volta Lake was the result of the construction of the AKOSOMBO DAM across the lower Volta River in the mid-1960s. With a surface area of about 3,274 square miles (8,480 sq km), the lake now covers some 45 percent of Ghana's land area.

The main purpose of the Akosombo Dam was to generate hydroelectricity, which it does in large quantities (up to 768,000-kilowatts). Over time, however, the lake has become a prime recreation area and tourist attraction, as well. It also provides the country with WATER RESOURCES for irrigation and is an important TRANSPORTATION link. Ferry service across the lake was initiated in 1989, at first with rehabilitated craft, and then, in 2001, with new, 150-passenger ferries. The Volta River Authority, which is responsible for the administration of the hydroelectric dam, also oversees the DEVELOPMENT of the areas adjoining the lake.

See also: INDUSTRIALIZATION (Vol. V); LAKES AND RIVERS (Vol. I); TOURISM (Vol. V); VOLTA RIVER (Vol. II); VOLTA BASIN (Vol. III).

Wade, Abdoulaye (1926–) *President of Senegal*

Wade received his primary education in SENEGAL before studying in France. Returning to Senegal with doctorate degrees in both law and economics, he taught at the University of Dakar and opened his own law firm. In the early 1970s he turned to politics, founding Senegal's second political party, the Senegalese Democratic Party. An outspoken opponent of the dominant SENEGALESE SOCIALIST PARTY (Parti Socialiste, PS), he ran unsuccessfully for president four times between 1978 and 1993. After serving as minister of state under President Abdou DIOUF (1935–), he finally won the presidency, in 2000, ending the PS's 40-year rule over Senegal.

Wade's opposition to the PS led to charges against him of everything from treason to complicity in murder. But he steadfastly maintained his innocence, remaining determined to make substantive changes in Senegal's government. Elected at a time when the country faced severe economic crises, as well as increasingly loud demands for a more democratic political system, Wade offered few specific programs during his campaign for office. Instead he promised only to work hard and to build a revitalized, more democratic nation.

Wade's election was greeted with approval around the country, where people had long been eager for economic, political, and social reform. International observers also saw his victory as advancing DEMOCRATIZATION on the continent. Since taking office, he has faced criticism for the continued weak economy, as well as charges of nepotism and CORRUPTION. Still, Wade's government has managed to make slow progress, with minor increases in economic growth and hopes for a decrease in the rate of inflation.

Walvis Bay

City on the Atlantic coast of NAMIBIA (formerly SOUTH WEST AFRICA) and important deepwater port. Located about 250 miles (402 km) west of WINDHOEK, the country's capital, Walvis Bay is a city of approximately 50,000 inhabitants. It is situated at the mouth of the Kuiseb River on the Atlantic Ocean and is surrounded on three sides by the Namib Desert. It is one of only two ocean harbors in Namibia, the other being Lüderitz, farther to the south.

Britain annexed Walvis Bay in 1878 as part of the Cape Colony, to keep it out of the hands of Germany, at the time Britain's imperial rival. The surrounding region became the German colony of South West Africa. Upon the unification of SOUTH AFRICA, in 1910, Walvis Bay became part of its Cape Province. From 1922 to 1977 Walvis Bay and all of Namibia were administered by South Africa, originally as a League of Nations mandate and then, subsequent to 1948, as a UN trust territory.

In 1977 the United Nations passed a resolution declaring null and void the South African claim to Walvis Bay. Nevertheless, and despite Namibia's achieving independence in 1990, South Africa governed it directly from 1978 to 1992. Negotiations between Namibia and South Africa led to joint administration from 1992 to 1994, at which time South Africa relinquished sovereignty. Due to its historical connections with the Cape Colony, Walvis Bay lacks the German characteristics of nearby coastal Swakopmund, which the Germans had founded in the colonial era.

In addition to being the country's main port Walvis Bay is also the only one that accommodates deepwater anchorage. Walvis Bay handles 85 percent of the country's foreign trade, which includes EXPORTS of uranium, copper, and lead. Fishing is an important facet of the city's ECONOMY, with rich harvests of anchovies, pilchards, and mackerel. The bay is also renowned for its varied bird life south of the port, including pelicans, cormorants, and pink flamingoes. The pleasant climate, coastal setting, fishing, and bird life make Walvis Bay a popular tourist destination.

See also: GERMANY AND AFRICA (Vol. IV); LEAGUE OF NATIONS AND AFRICA (Vol. IV); TOURISM (Vol. V); TRUST TERRITORY (Vol. IV); UNITED NATIONS AND AFRICA (Vols. IV, V).

warfare and weapons Since 1960 Africa has been the site of some of the longest-running and most devastating wars in the world. In general these wars have been of three different types: struggles for independence, CIVIL WARS, and border disputes. During the COLD WAR (1945–91), global powers including the United States, the Soviet Union, and China insinuated themselves into African conflicts. In their attempts to gain allies, they exported equipment, such as tanks and anti-aircraft machine guns, and offered military expertise to help African forces achieve their goals. As a result combat across the continent became increasingly lethal.

In addition to killing millions of combatants, warfare in Africa also has created large numbers of REFUGEES, people who have fled their homes because of the threat of violence. Living in makeshift camps or as exiles in foreign countries, these people have been subject to exposure, hunger, violence, and disease, all of which have claimed many more lives.

Wars of Independence By the late 1950s European colonialism on the continent seemed to be coming to an end, and Britain, France, and Belgium began to hand their colonial governments back over to African-led political organizations. In many cases the transfer of power was peaceful. In other cases—France in ALGERIA and Portugal in its colonies—independence came only with violence. Portugal, in particular, tenaciously maintained its hold on colonial authority. As a result, from 1961 until 1974 independence movements in the Portuguese colonies of ANGOLA, CAPE VERDE, GUINEA-BISSAU, and MOZAMBIQUE all waged wars against the Portuguese colonial government.

The insurgents had weapons such as machine guns, mines, and grenades, but they were poorly armed in comparison to the Portuguese forces. Because of this, African forces did not engage in conventional battleground warfare but instead resorted to guerilla tactics. These included attacking individuals and launching raids on police barracks, government offices, and other installations crucial to the colonial power infrastructure.

In Angola and Mozambique the rebels usually avoided the urban colonial strongholds and instead operated from rural areas. Local populations often showed their support by offering water, food, and shelter. Since close combat in the rural areas favored the rebels, the Portuguese regularly attacked enemy positions using World War II–era bombers mounted with forward-firing machine guns before sending in ground troops.

Leaders of independence movements such as the POPULAR MOVEMENT FOR THE LIBERATION OF ANGOLA and the MOZAMBICAN LIBERATION FRONT followed a Marxist ideology. Believing that gender equality was an important aspect of the state, these organizations encouraged able-bodied women to become soldiers in the guerrilla armies.

By 1974 Portugal had undergone a change of leadership and began its withdrawal from the continent. However, in both Angola and Mozambique, the ethnically driven independence movements that had fought Portugal then clashed with each other, vying for control of the postindependence national governments. In both countries the postindependence civil wars were also proxy wars within the larger Cold War, and the support of powerful foreign nations contributed to the continuation of these civil wars until the 1990s.

In southern Africa, too, guerrilla warfare was the norm. The difference, though, was that instead of fighting for the overthrow of a colonial occupier, the insurgents wanted to oust a white minority government and make the change to black majority rule. This was the case in RHODESIA (today's ZIMBABWE) and SOUTH WEST AFRICA (today's NAMIBIA), as well as in SOUTH AFRICA. In general, the white minority governments of these countries supported each other. Rebel forces, on the other hand, received support from the African governments in the FRONTLINE STATES, as the neighboring countries became known collectively. Centrally located ZAMBIA played a leading role in the activities of the Frontline States.

Civil Wars Religious differences also caused civil strife in several African countries. In CHAD and the Republic of the SUDAN, devastating wars between Muslims and Christians have been ongoing since the end of colonialism. In the Sudan conflict alone, it is estimated that more than 2 million people have died. Since 1990, conflicts between Nigeria's Muslim and Christian populations have resulted in thousands of deaths. In the early 1990s Algeria, too, was the site of religion-based civil war. There, Muslim fundamentalists clashed with the more secular Muslims in the government, sparking a 12-year civil war in which up to 100,000 people died.

Besides ideology and religion, ethnic and regional differences also emerged as common causes of civil war in Africa. In an unfortunate pattern that was seen all over the continent, the jubilance of independence quickly gave way to internal ethnic strife. Such conflicts were particularly violent in, among other places, BURUNDI, the Democratic Republic of the CONGO, the Republic of the CONGO, DJIBOUTI, ERITREA, ETHIOPIA, GUINEA, LIBERIA, NIGERIA, SIERRA LEONE, SENEGAL, SOMALIA, RWANDA, TANZANIA, and UGANDA.

Border Wars Since 1960 several conflicts in Africa have been fought over disputed borders. These include the ongoing conflicts between ERITREA and ETHIOPIA, in the Horn of Africa, and the struggle of the SAHARAWI people against the Moroccan government in present-day WESTERN SAHARA. In the 1980s CHAD and LIBYA were engaged in three separate conflicts for control of the Aouzou Strip, an area in the Sahara desert along the Chad-Libya border that was thought to have uranium deposits.

Clearly, wars in Africa are fought for a variety of reasons, and there are no easy solutions for avoiding them in the future. International organizations such as the African Union and the United Nations make efforts to bring warring sides to the negotiating table, but very often this occurs only after great losses already have been incurred.

The Cold War (1945–91) between the United States and the Soviet Union had repercussions that spread around the globe. The war was considered "cold" because the two combatants never actually engaged in direct military conflict. This was because, if used, the overwhelmingly destructive nuclear weapons that both countries possessed could conceivably put an end to the human race. Fortunately, warfare among Africans has not included the threat of nuclear weapons, since no African nation has nuclear capability. In the early 1990s, however, South Africa did possess six uranium bombs it had constructed. When power was transferred to the black majority after 1994, the outgoing government voluntarily dismantled the bombs.

See also: ARAB-ISRAELI WARS (Vols. IV, V); BIAFRA (Vol. V); ETHNIC CONFLICT IN AFRICA (Vol. V); WARFARE AND WEAPONS (Vols. I, II, III, IV).

water resources Africa possesses some of the most noteworthy water resources on the planet. Yet for thousands of years a lack of access to clean water has remained one of the primary problems on the continent.

Africa's rivers range from the famous, like the Nile, Niger, and Congo, to the not so famous, including the Cuanza, Rufiji, and Shabeelle. These rivers not only are invaluable waterways, but, in many regions, they are critical sources of water for everything from irrigation to drinking. Africa also is a continent of lakes, with some of the largest and deepest lakes in the world. These lakes are vital ecosystems that provide food and other essentials to millions of people.

How big are Africa's rivers? The continent's longest river, the Nile, is the longest in the world. Africa's third largest river, the NIGER, which is the principal river of western Africa, is 2,500 miles (4,023 km) in length. The odd, boomerang-shaped course of the Niger is the result of the fact that it once was two rivers that changed course and linked together when the Sahara desert dried up, around 4000 to 1000 BCE.

Unfortunately Africa's rivers and lakes cannot provide the continent with all the water it needs for nourishing its people and irrigating its crops. For this reason rainfall always has been critical to food production—and therefore survival—in Africa, a continent with land features that vary from the deserts of the Sahara to the rain forests of the equatorial regions. Beyond the great ranges of rainfall in Africa's various regions, which can make the land both too arid and too wet to farm, Africa also has endured long periods of great climatic change during which rainfall increased or decreased dramatically. In East Africa, for example, the Warm Period, which lasted from approximately 1000 to 1270 CE, saw a marked decrease in rainfall. In contrast the years between 1270 and 1850 CE, which have become known as the Little Ice Age, were significantly wetter than others.

In spite of the apparent wealth of water on the continent, Africa has faced—and currently still faces—what amounts to a water crisis. With the most rapid growth rate of any area in the developing world, Africa has repeatedly found that its systems of water and food production cannot keep pace with its constant population increase. As a result only about 62 percent of the people of Africa currently have access to safe drinking water, the lowest percentage of any continent. Equally problematic, only about 60 percent of all Africans have adequate sanitation, a situation that is responsible for the waterborne diarrheal illnesses that kill approximately 2,500 African children each day.

The problem of drinking water and sanitation is compounded, of course, by the food shortages that are in themselves a crisis for Africa. Much of Africa's land must be irrigated in order to produce enough food to support the people. The situation is critical, therefore, with AGRI-CULTURE, industry, and individuals all competing for scarce water resources.

The pressing problem, then, is how to deal with the current water crisis in Africa—now and in the future. One plan that has emerged in recent years has been to rely on privatization, letting independent, private corporations take the job of providing water to Africa's people, farms, and industries. In theory this should make an excellent solution, since private corporations, in contrast to the governments of developing countries, frequently have both the financial and scientific resources to find and exploit new supplies of water.

In practice, however, privatization has not always worked well. In KENYA, for example, privatization of water production has had to take place alongside a general localization of government. As a result the private corporations engaged in supplying water must work with small, local governments rather than larger regional or even national agencies. Having less power than larger governments to leverage the corporations, these small, local agencies frequently have had to make crippling concessions—sometimes even guaranteeing price levels that are too high for them to support. In addition, the prospect of dealing with many individual bureaucracies—and with the inevitable additional costs involved—often scares off investors and corporate executives alike.

The southwestern country of GABON provides an interesting case in the problem of privatization. In 1997 the Vivendi organization took over management of water and electricity production in that country, promising major improvements to the nation's INFRASTRUCTURE. The corporation not only carried out those improvements but by 2002 it also turned the debt-ridden public corporation into a profit-making business. However, 40 percent of Gabon's people still remained without safe drinking water—a level as poor as many other parts of Africa.

Scientists and politicians alike have argued that water is fast becoming the next great resource challenge for our planet's population. In Africa some policy makers and government leaders have chosen to focus on generating water through engineering and scientific efforts. Others have tried to make water a public item free of economic considerations, arguing that no person or government should be denied water for lack of funds.

See also: POPULATION GROWTH (Vol. V); ECOLOGY AND ECOLOGICAL CHANGE (Vol. V); ENVIRONMENTAL ISSUES (Vol. V); NATURAL RESOURCES (Vol. V).

Further reading: Mikiyasu Nakayame, ed., *International Waters in Southern Africa* (New York: United Nations University Press, 2003); Thomas J. Crisman, ed., *Conservation, Ecology, and Management of African Fresh Waters* (Gainesville, Fla.: University of Florida Press, 2003).

Western Sahara   Disputed territory in northwestern Africa, bordered by MOROCCO to the north, ALGERIA to the east, MAURITANIA to the south, and the Atlantic Ocean to the west. The indigenous SAHARAWI of Western Sahara have been locked in a continuous struggle for independence since the imposition of Spanish colonial rule, in 1884.

The modern history of Western Sahara is characterized by outside rule and internal resistance. Since Spain declared a protectorate over the region from Cape Blanc to Cape Bojador, in 1884, and established the colony of Spanish Sahara, the Saharawi have engaged in an unending effort to reclaim their indepedence. In 1958 it took the Ecouvillon Operation, a joint Spanish-French military maneuver, to finally, if temporarily, subdue Saharawi resistance.

The territory remained "pacified" for nearly a full decade. The region of the western Sahara was declared a Spanish province in 1961. In 1963 and again in 1965 the United Nations (UN) asserted the Saharawis' right to self-rule and encouraged Spain to decolonize the territory.

In 1967 the Saharawi began to agitate once again for independence. The Movement for the Liberation of the Sahara was organized under Mohammed Sidi Brahim Bassiri (1942–1970). By this time Spain had ceded a portion of the region to Morocco but retained control of the areas of Saguia el-Hamra and Río de Oro (now Dakhla). The Spanish were particularly interested in the large mineral wealth of the region, especially phosphates, of which the world's largest reserves were discovered in Boukra in 1963. The discovery of the Boukra phosphate deposits led to the construction of a massive, 18-mile-long conveyor belt to carry the phosphate to the coast for export.

In 1970 massive demonstrations were held in the capital of LAAYOUNE. The Spanish colonial authority responded with a civilian massacre and hundreds of arrests. Turning away from nonviolent protest, the Saharawi organized the Popular Front for the Liberation of Saguia el-Hamra and Río de Oro, or POLISARIO, in 1973. That same year the Polisario launched its first assault on the Spanish. With aid from ALGERIA, the armed resistance clashed with Spanish forces repeatedly, capturing the commander of the Spanish troops in May 1975. At a meeting in September between the two sides the Spanish agreed to turn over power gradually to the Polisario in exchange for continuing Spanish control over mineral and fishing resources. In the wake of the agreement Spain began withdrawing some of its occupying forces. The United Nations officially named the territory Western Sahara that same year.

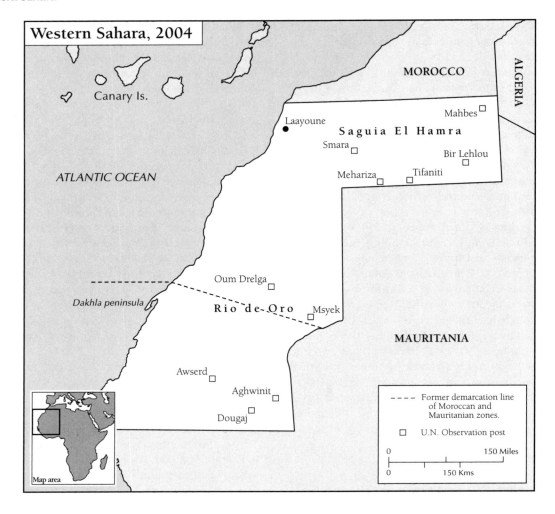

Western Sahara, 2004

MOROCCO

ALGERIA

Canary Is.

Mahbes □

Laayoune ●

S a g u i a   E l   H a m r a

Smara □

Bir Lehlou □

ATLANTIC OCEAN

Mehariza □   Tifaniti □

Oum Drelga □

Dakhla peninsula

R i o   d e   O r o   Msyek □

MAURITANIA

Awserd □

Aghwinit □

Dougaj □

- - - - Former demarcation line
of Moroccan and
Mauritanian zones.

□   U.N. Observation post

0   150 Miles

0   150 Kms

Map area

This victory, however, proved to be a moot one for the peoples of Western Sahara. Both Morocco and Mauritania were poised to take advantage of the withdrawl of the Spanish military and claim the territory for themselves. In October 1975, King HASSAN II (1929– 1999) of Morocco ordered the Green March, a massive migration of 350,000 Moroccan settlers into Western Sahara, a move designed to give Morocco a firm claim to the territory. Before the Green March crossed the border, Moroccan troops entered, meeting fierce Polisario opposition. The United Nations condemned the march, and Algeria warned the encroaching countries against interfering with Western Saharan independence. Nevertheless, in November Spain, Morocco, and Mauritania reached an agreement that partitioned the territory between the two Morocco and Mauritania (Morroco claiming the northern two-thirds and Mauritania claiming the remainder) while allowing Spain to maintain its MINING and fishing interests.

In anticipation of a drawn-out conflict the Polisario dissolved the traditional Djemaa, or governing body, and formed the Polisario Provisional Saharawi National Coun-

cil. It also facilitated the evacuation of Saharawi civilians, with most becoming REFUGEES in Algeria.

By the end of 1975 Moroccan and Mauritanian troops had entered their respective regions of control. In 1976 Spain officially ended its colonial rule over Western Sahara, and the Polisario officially began another campaign against new occupiers. It declared a government-in-exile, the Saharawi Arab Democratic Republic, which was subsequently recognized as legitimate by 70 countries as well as the ORGANIZATION FOR AFRICAN UNITY. The Polisario then launched a widespread offensive, focusing primarily on Mauritania but also waging devastating battles against Moroccan troops and capturing Spanish fishing vessels. Assaults by the Polisario on the Boukra conveyor belt essentially shut down the phosphate industry in Western Sahara. By 1978, with its capital of NOUAKCHOTT twice bombarded by Polisario forces, the Mauritanian government fell in a COUP D'ÉTAT brought on in part by the ongoing conflict in Western Sahara. The new government quickly acted to end hostilities, and in 1979 Mauritania agreed to relinquish their claims to the disputed territory.

This left Morocco as the last obstacle in the way of Western Saharan independence. Bitter fighting continued to rage between the two sides until 1988, when a UN peace plan was finally accepted. A cease-fire was established in 1991 in anticipation of a referendum on Western Saharan independence the following year. However, the referendum has been repeatedly delayed due to conflict over voter eligibility, as Morocco has continued to send settlers into the territory to skew any referendum results. Various negotiation attempts have failed, and in 2001 Morocco placed limits on UN workers trying to identify true Saharawi voters, making the task virtually impossible. The following year King MOHAMMED VI (1963–) of Morocco declared his country would "not renounce an inch" of Western Sahara, indicating that independence for the embattled territory is not on the immediate horizon.

See also: SPAIN AND AFRICA (Vol. IV); SPANISH SAHARA (Vol. IV); UNITED NATIONS AND AFRICA (Vol. V); WESTERN SAHARA (Vols. I, II, III, IV).

wildlife Africa is home to some of the most exotic wildlife species on the planet, including mammals such as lions, leopards, cheetahs, elephants, giraffes, and hippopotamuses, as well as an astonishing array of bird, reptile, and insect life. Wildlife has long represented an important resource for Africans, and, in the past, hunting was a sustainable activity that provided an important part of Africans' livelihood. With the coming of colonialism, however, this changed. Increases in population, the shifting of populations to towns and urban centers, and the international demand for African wildlife as commodities all contributed to diminishing animal populations and near extinction for many creatures. Recently, however, important changes have been made to preserve Africa's fauna. African wildlife, for example, has been recognized for its role in an important economic activity—ecotourism. At the same time ecologists, wildlife biologists, and nature advocates have succeeded in convincing people of the ecological value of Africa's unique and diverse wildlife. This has helped bring about important efforts to save— and, in some cases, even increase the numbers of—Africa's wild creatures.

The cheetah is a prime example of a species that has benefited from recent preservation efforts. Just a few years ago the cheetah was seriously threatened, with only approximately 12,000 of them remaining in 30 African countries. Today cheetahs are the subject of extensive research projects aimed at their breeding and reintroduction into the wild. Such CONSERVATION efforts are, in many areas, combined with public EDUCATION and cooperation, the goal of which is to prevent farmers and herders from killing cheetahs and other wildlife. Similar efforts are being made on behalf of wild dogs,

another species facing near extinction. Rampant outbreaks of canine distemper, as well as habitat reduction, have contributed to such a rapid loss of population that only 3,500 to 5,000 of these creatures are left in the wild. Research and reintroduction efforts have helped, but still more work must be done before the wild-dog population is safe.

Large numbers of ecotourists visit Africa each year. Many of them stay in luxury lodges, while others utilize simpler, less expensive facilities. Regardless of precisely where these ecotourists stay or exactly how much they spend, these people represent millions of dollars worth of TOURISM for countries such as KENYA, SOUTH AFRICA, TANZANIA, and BOTSWANA. Because of this, concern for endangered and threatened species has risen dramatically within these countries. As a result many are extending more and more protection to their wildlife through the establishment of NATIONAL PARKS and, most recently, the creation of transnational parks that aim to protect wildlife and habitats.

Wildebeests represent an even more successful story, one that bears directly on the area of ecotourism. From its low point during the 1970s the wildebeest population has increased dramatically. The prime reason for this lies in the number of tourists who come to Tanzania's Serengeti and Kenya's Masai Mara parks specifically to see the annual wildebeest migration. Each July as many as 500,000 wildebeests cross the Serengeti into the Masai Mara, fording crocodile-infested rivers and bringing with them a host of other creatures, from zebras and gazelles to predatory lions and hyenas. Four months later they reverse their journey, traveling back to the Serengeti. By establishing connecting natural preserves in Tanzania and Kenya, the annual migration—and the income from ecotourism—have been preserved.

One of the most important aspects of African wildlife is the fact that the continent has such great BIODIVERSITY, being home to a large number of species found nowhere else on the planet. In MADAGASCAR, for example, the lemur has been brought to the brink of extinction. The same is true of many types of chameleons. Madagascar, however, recently has committed itself to tripling the size of its nature preserves in order to protect these and other creatures.

Elsewhere, however, efforts have not been as successful. In spite of years of publicity and major efforts by a diverse array of groups, elephants and gorillas continue to face peril in the Democratic Republic of the CONGO (DRC).

Civil war in the eastern Congo continues to threaten the endangered gorilla population. But even in the war-torn Congo preservation efforts have made headway. The DRC contains the world's largest nesting area for marine turtles, an area that is now protected by the Conkouati-Douli National Park.

In the Transmara district of Kenya, farmers and aid organizations have come up with innovative techniques for dealing with elephants that raid farmers' maize fields. Farmers man tall watchtowers and take turns standing guard throughout the night, scaring off elephants that come to the fields. In addition, farmers have surrounded their maize fields with hot chili pepper plants, which have proved effective in warding off grazing elephants.

Ecotourism, of course, is not the only wildlife story in Africa. Because of the continent's diverse and unique wildlife, there are numerous research organizations operating there. Their work involves everything from exploring hunting strategies to investigating the social interactions of various creatures. This research has provided knowledge of the complex, social network of elephants, the matriarchal social hierarchy of hyenas, and countless other fascinating aspects of the animal world.

See also: ENVIRONMENTAL ISSUES (Vol. V).

Further readings: Luke Hunter, Susan Rhind, and David Andrew, *Watching Wildlife: Southern Africa* (London: Lonely Planet, 2002); Martin B. Withers and David Hosking, *Wildlife of East Africa* (Princeton, N.J.: Princeton University Press, 2002).

Windhoek National capital of NAMIBIA, located in the center of the country in a valley that protects it from the dry winds of the surrounding area. The region around Windhoek has been occupied since the 18th century by HERERO and Damara peoples, and, by the middle of that century, a European Christian missionary community had been established there. The origins of the present-day city, however, date to 1890, when Germany made Windhoek

Ecotourists travel to southern Africa from around the world to view wildlife that live nowhere else, such as this giraffe. © *Corbis*

the headquarters of its colony of South West Africa. In 1915, during the course of World War I (1914–18), SOUTH AFRICA occupied the German colony and its capital of Windhoek, maintaining control until Namibia gained independence in 1990. During this period Windhoek served as the territorial capital for what was, in effect, South Africa's fifth province. It remained the capital city upon independence

Despite the predominance of African ethnic groups within Windhoek's population—and despite the long occupation of the city by historically Dutch and British South Africa—German culture is still prominent in the city. Descendants of German settlers have built numerous German Style buildings, and many of Windhoek's restaurants feature German cuisine.

The South African influence also is seen today, especially in the residential patterns of the city. Reflecting the APARTHEID laws imposed by the South African government, the city is functionally divided, to some degree, into three sectors, one each for Africans, whites, and Coloureds. The fastest growing area of the modern city is the largely African area known as Katutura.

In addition to government and educational institutions, the processing of cattle and sheep from the surrounding area serves as the basis for Windhoek's economy. In recent years TOURISM also has become an increasingly important economic activity, with visitors enjoying the relaxed environment, the annual Oktoberfest, and the nation's game reserves, including the nearby Daan Viljoen Reserve. Extensive road and rail systems connect the city to the rest of the country and to SOUTH AFRICA, and the city is home to the country's major international airport. Although Windhoek has grown recently due to the migration of workers from Namibia's rural regions, with only 221,000 people, it remains a fairly small city, especially for a national capital.

See also: GERMANY AND AFRICA (Vol. IV); URBAN LIFE AND CULTURE (Vols. IV, V).

women in independent Africa
The lives of women, which had in many areas remained virtually unchanged for decades or even centuries, changed dramatically with the coming of colonialism, as their male partners headed off to work in towns, mines, and on plantations. Today in postcolonial Africa, although many of these patterns persist, in other ways women's lives are changing rapidly. Women who became de facto household heads when their husbands moved to wage-LABOR positions may still find themselves in this position now. However, women are no longer prohibited or discouraged from migrating to cities. Indeed, women have become an important part of the informal economy in African urban areas. In addition women themselves are finding opportunities in wage-labor positions, most notably as secretaries but also in more prestigious pro-

fessions, including research and EDUCATION. As the Western gender movement penetrates Africa, women and men are increasingly provided equal access to resources such as land, credit, equipment, and employment. This movement is new and, in most situations, women are still at a disadvantage in most regards.

One of the consequences of the increased awareness of women's issues in Africa is a recent movement against the traditional female-circumcision ceremonies that many ethnic groups have carried out for generations. The procedure, which many African women who have experienced it describe as female genital mutilation, is considered by many in Africa and on the international scene as a severe HUMAN RIGHTS abuse. As a result of this attention, many African nations have passed laws against female circumcision. Enforcement, however, has not been able to prevent this deeply engrained tradition from being performed.

The postcolonial period also has seen a dramatic increase in female enrollment in primary, secondary, and post-secondary education. Across Africa many parents have made the commitment to educate their daughters, even though the male-to-female ratio is still quite disparate at the post-secondary level. The increase in female education also has had effects in terms of women demanding control over their reproductive rights. Increased formal education of girls and women is correlated with the increase in the average age for a woman's marriage and first pregnancy.

In general, although there are some similarities, there are marked differences between the lives of women in rural and urban settings. Rural women usually find themselves busy with AGRICULTURE-related tasks, child rearing, and household activities. Women in urban areas are also responsible for child rearing and household activities, which they combine with a small business or wage labor. Women in rural areas tend to depend on their children to assist in household chores and farming activities. Women in urban settings either rely on their children or on hired household help. which can be paid for because of the greater access to cash.

African urban areas also face the problem of female prostitution. In most urban areas there are any number of women who find work as prostitutes. Prostitution became a widespread phenomenon during colonial times, when men migrated without their families to the cities. Today it persists as a profession, and in the current HIV/AIDS environment prostitutes have become the focus of research focusing on finding a cure or vaccine for the virus.

In terms of appearance, women in rural areas are still mostly seen in dresses or skirts, either made of traditional African fabrics or in modern Western styles. Women in the cities are often seen wearing modern Western business attire, although slacks are still rarely worn by African women. In both rural and urban Muslim areas women are often seen wearing traditional Muslim attire, with their

East Africa's dual cultures, traditional and modern, are exemplified by these two young women from Kenya, photographed in 1964. Women who adopted Western styles were often criticized by their elders for valuing money above true happiness. © *AP/Wide World Photos*

heads and sometimes their faces covered. In most places in Africa it is not uncommon to see women carrying large loads of firewood or produce on their heads as they travel home or to the market. Women with children nestled close to their backs in a piece of African cloth are also commonly seen.

See also: COLONIALISM, INFLUENCE OF (Vol. IV); GENDER IN MODERN AFRICA (Vol. V); HIV/AIDS AND AFRICA (Vol. V); ISLAM, INFLUENCE OF (Vols. II, III, IV, V); LITERATURE IN MODERN AFRICA (Vol. V); WOMEN IN COLONIAL AFRICA (Vol. IV).

Further reading: Margaret Jean Hay and Sharon Stichter, eds., *African Women South of the Sahara* (London: Longman Group Limited, 1984); Claire Robertson and Iris Berger, eds., *Women and Class in Africa* (New York: Holmes and Meier Publishers, Inc., 1986); Patricia W.

Romero, *Life Histories of African Women* (London: Ashfield Press Ltd., 1988); Joya Uraizee, *This is No Place for a Woman: Nadine Gordimer, Buchi Emecheta, Nayanatara Saghal, and the Politics of Gender* (Trenton, N.J.: Africa World Press, 2000).

World Bank   Giving more money and wielding more influence than any other international donor organization in Africa, the World Bank has responded to failures, criticisms, and its own internal challenges over the past half century by reinventing itself and shifting the emphasis of its programs. The need for the creation of the World Bank and its sister organization, the INTERNATIONAL MONETARY FUND (IMF), was realized at a meeting at a UN Monetary and Financial Conference, held in Bretton Woods, New

Hampshire, in July 1944. The Bretton Woods Agreement, which was reached in July of that year, led to the inauguration of the World Bank, on June 25, 1946.

In its first decade of existence the World Bank committed $9.6 billion ($53.24 billion in 2002 dollars) in loans. By the early 1960s it became clear that four shifts in policy were necessary. First, the World Bank had to start considering DEVELOPMENT "programs" as opposed to just individualized projects. Second, certain lending conditions needed to be placed on these projects. Specifically, certain procedures had to be consistent with the World Bank's economically liberal philosophy, including appropriate accounting and dispersing, as well as economic policies such as tax administration and structure, monetary policy, and foreign exchange rates. Third, the policy of promoting constant lending requirements regardless of a country's credit qualifications or economic standing needed to be redressed. Fourth, more funds were needed for the developing world. While funds increased, there was little support for lending increases in Africa. As of June 1968 the World Bank, combined with its International Development Association, had committed only about $1.16 billion ($6 billion in 2002 dollars), or 8.7 percent of its worldwide commitments to Africa.

Throughout this period the World Bank's mission continued to be refocused on "development." Industrial development, agricultural production, and mineral EXPORTS were all seen as engines for economic growth. To facilitate this, the largest funding sectors included, in order, TRANSPORTATION, electrical power, industrial development, and agricultural development projects. So-called soft development lagged behind. Funding for EDUCATION, for instance, began only in 1966, and in the first two years it accounted for only $82 million of loans to Africa.

By the early 1970s it became clear that Africa's development plans were ineffective and that changes were necessary at the operational level. The organization itself needed decentralization. It also needed to give a stronger role to developing countries in policymaking, as well as increased flexibility in the terms and conditions of lending. World Bank president Robert McNamara obliged, and the institution itself went through significant changes.

By the end of the 1970s, however, evidence suggested that the revised World Bank policies actually decreased performance and that, combined with the global oil shock of 1973 (and again in 1979), development in Africa was stymied. In 1979 the African governors of the World Bank wrote to President McNamara to request a new assessment of economic development in Africa and the direction of World Bank funding for it. This resulted in the 1981 report, "Accelerated Development in Sub-Saharan Africa: An Agenda for Action, " commonly called the "Berg Report" after its principal author Elliot Berg. The Berg Report ostensibly followed on the heels of a re-

port adopted by the ORGANIZATION OF AFRICAN UNITY (OAU) called "The Lagos Plan of Action for the Implementation of the Monrovia Strategy for the Economic Development of Africa." Far from agreeing with the OAU plan, the Berg Report outlined 13 points on which African polities must change. These changes were all along the lines of reforming monetary and fiscal policies, decreasing the role of the public sector, and opening up markets to MULTINATIONAL CORPORATIONS. With funding in the hands of the World Bank, and decision making within the World Bank primarily vested in U.S. and British leadership, nearly all of the Lagos Plan, save the goal of creating an African Economic Union by 2000, was set aside.

Officially, the rate of growth for the continent slowed in the 1970s to 0.8 percent. But, in truth, growth actually decreased once certain factors were considered. For example, once the growth of the oil sector in NIGERIA was taken out of the equation, continent-wide growth actually was -0.3 percent.

What emerged from all this were World Bank–funded STRUCTURAL ADJUSTMENT programs (SAPs). Far more ambitious than the development projects of the 1960s and 1970s, these programs sought to fundamentally change the way governments function. Conditions were placed on lending, and while many African leaders saw this as a violation of sovereignty, given the high levels of debt already accrued by most African countries, there was little practical dissent.

The changes brought about included lifting price controls, devaluing inflated currencies, cutting government expenditure on social services, reducing the size of bureaucracy and civil service, and privatizing state-owned corporations. In exchange for making these changes, governments would receive significant multiyear investments at favorable terms and, in some cases, a reorganization or partial reduction of existing debt. The short-term effect of structural adjustment was that life became much harder for the common person, who had to pay much more for food, transportation, and other basic needs and now had to start paying school fees—and possibly lose his or her job as well.

By 1987 it was clear that the early structural adjustment programs in countries such as KENYA, TANZANIA, and GHANA required austerity measures that were too painful for these nations to bear. Enhanced Structural Adjustment Facilities (ESAF) were undertaken in cooperation with the IMF. Under these ESAFs, short-term financial assistance was given to help with fiscal consolidation while reducing inflation, creating nutrition schemes for children, and providing micro-credit lending for the poor.

As a result of SAPs and ESAFs, Africa's debt burden increased from $55 billion, in 1980 ($120 billion in 2002 dollars), to $150 billion, in 1990 ($206.49 billion in 2002 dollars). Meanwhile, economic growth slowed to negative 2.2 percent. In other words, life in 1990 was worse for the average person living in sub-Saharan Africa than it was at independence.

Structural adjustment was quickly blamed for rising food prices as well as the decreased public investment in health and education that led to the decay of already ailing health sectors. It was also blamed for educational system deterioration, high unemployment, increased debt, and dependence on capital transfers from wealthy countries in the form of aid.

In 1989 the World Bank released a report called "Sub-Saharan Africa: From Crisis to Sustainable Growth." This report discussed how the World Bank had learned from past mistakes but believed that structural adjustment was the proper course for it to take. Most important, this report introduced three important concepts for development. First, it considered the conditions for creating an "enabling environment" for the private sector to grow African economies. Second, it introduced the idea that development was not possible without also considering the environment and the management of NATURAL RESOURCES. Finally, it clearly articulated the belief that the fundamental obstacle to development in Africa had been the crisis of African leadership and the absence of sound governance. This last element, which is a pillar of World Bank thought still today, was immediately controversial, since it overlooked the widely held belief that many of Africa's problems stemmed from a combination of the colonial legacy and unsound mandates from the World Bank and its partners during the postcolonial era.

The early and mid-1990s saw the DEMOCRATIZATION of the majority of African countries and the birth of new opportunities. It did not, however, see significant new development. Indeed, by the early 1990s scholars and internal World Bank evaluations alike began criticizing structural adjustment programming. Yet in 1994 the World Bank put out another report, this one entitled "Adjustment in Africa: Reform, Results, and the Road Ahead." While this report praised efforts to date, it also contained analyses that noted how SAPs were having disastrous effects on Africa.

A sea change in World Bank thinking came a year later when James D. Wolfensohn became the World Bank's president. What emerged in the place of new SAPs in 1999 were country-specific Poverty Reduction Strategy Papers (PRSP). By 2003 there were 46 countries with PRSPs or Interim PRSPs. This is a marked shift in strategy, aimed at "democratizing development" by encouraging local participation in development. A significant debt-reduction initiative—Highly Indebted Poor Countries (HIPC)—was concurrently undertaken. If a country met the stringent HIPC requirements for change, then it would see a significant debt reduction and a "new start" down the World Bank's neo-liberal path.

PRSPs have come under significant scrutiny on several themes. Most notably, half a decade later there are still only a small handful of African countries—TANZANIA, The Republic of BENIN, CHAD, MALI, UGANDA, CAPE VERDE, ETHIOPIA, BOTSWANA, ANGOLA, RWANDA, the Republic of the SUDAN, and LIBERIA—that have achieved the minimum 5 percent growth rates necessary to avoid economic backsliding, and Angola, Rwanda, and Sudan can attribute their growth more to war recovery than fundamental change. In addition, many critics have questioned the wisdom of opening Africa's new industries—many of which are in a new, fragile state—to the buffeting of the global economy.

As of 2003 the World Bank had $15.2 billion in ongoing investments in Africa—adjusting for inflation that is more than double its investment in 1968. Yet African countries have yet to reap the benefits of such investment. A fundamental shift took place with the change of millennium, and it continues. Between 2000 and 2003 World Bank lending to Africa increased more than 50 percent. At the same time, investment in social protection and risk management, rural development, urban development and human development, and natural resource management came at the expense of public-sector governance and financial-sector development. As has become the nature of the World Bank in Africa, it is responding to criticisms and shifting international tides. The question is whether the policies of this new decade will succeed where the policies of previous decades have failed.

See also: GLOBAL ECCONOMY, AFRICA AND (Vol. V); NEOCOLONIALISM AND UNDERDEVELOPMENT (Vol. V); ECONOMIC ASSISTANCE (Vol. V).

Further reading: Catherine Caufield, *Masters of Illusion: The World Bank and the Poverty of Nations* (New York: Henry Holt and Co., 1997); Graham Harrison, *The World Bank and Africa: The Construction of Governance States,* (New York: Routledge, 2004).

X

Xhosa Bantu-speaking people of SOUTH AFRICA who belong to the Nguni cluster of Southern Bantu. The Xhosa population surpassed 7 million at the beginning of the 21st century.

Historically, the Xhosa were cattle-herding agriculturists. However, with the encroachment of European settlers on their lands in the 19th century and the ensuing URBANIZATION during the 20th and 21st centuries, many Xhosa worked on white-owned farms or in the GOLD mines, or migrated to the cities to find work.

> The etymology of the word *Xhosa* is uncertain. Some believe that the name derives from the Khoikhoi word *kosa,* which means "angry men" or "destroyers." Others believe that the Xhosa are named after an ancient chief by the same appellation. The present-day Xhosa are made up of people from different chiefdoms, and many within the Xhosa community identify themselves with these chiefdoms. Nelson MANDELA (1918–), for instance, is Thembu, while Winnie Nomzamo MANDELA (1936–), his former wife, is Pondo.

After the 1948 elections, South Africa fell under the system of APARTHEID, which greatly affected the Xhosa. Most importantly, the Xhosa were the largest group of people within the nationalist AFRICAN NATIONAL CONGRESS (ANC), which became the most visible and influential anti-apartheid group. In 1959 a BANTUSTAN, or "black homeland," was created for the Xhosa in the Transkei. (See map on page 44 of this volume.) Under the leadership of Kaiser MATANZIMA (1915–2003), the Xhosa homeland became self-governing, in 1963, and was granted so-called independence, in 1976. Unlike most of the other Bantustans, the Transkei contained a large contiguous area and only two other, smaller fragments. The other Bantustan for the Xhosa, the Ciskei, which was set up in 1961, fell into the general pattern for the Bantustans, containing only fragmented portions of the historic Xhosa homeland. Furthermore, these fragments were sited in remote rural areas, heavily overcrowded, and with largely infertile soils that were unable to support even their existing populations, let alone the millions the apartheid government forcibly moved into these areas.

As the era of apartheid continued, many anti-apartheid leaders arose from the Xhosa. In the 1970s, for example, Steve BIKO (1946–1977), a Xhosa from the Ciskei Bantustan, helped found the SOUTH AFRICAN STUDENTS ORGANIZAITON and became a leader of the BLACK CONCIOUSNESS MOVEMENT. Oliver TAMBO (1917–1993), who led the ANC from exile, came from Pondoland.

With the South African government's spurious granting of independence to the Transkei, in 1976, and the Ciskei, in 1981, the Xhosa officially were no longer citizens of South Africa. This independence, however, was largely a political illusion that was not recognized by the international community. Except for a few opportunistic individuals, the Xhosa themselves also rejected the independent Bantustans. Both homelands eventually fell with the collapse of apartheid and became reintegrated with South Africa.

The era of apartheid entered its final stages in the early 1990s. As free elections neared, different factions attempted to jockey for positions of political relevance. The INKATHA FREEDOM PARTY (IFP), a ZULU-dominated political party from the KwaZulu Bantustan and led by Mangosuthu Gatsha BUTHELEZI (1928–), targeted the ANC as its political adversary. As a result, violent clashes erupted in Natal between the Zulu adherents of the two organizations and in JOHANNESBURG between the Zulu who supported the IFP and the Xhosa and others who supported the ANC. Though the IFP claimed that the ANC favored Xhosa interests, other ethnic groups, including many Zulu, supported the ANC, and the violence between the two ethnic groups eventually subsided.

In 1994 Nelson Mandela became South Africa's first black president, and the ANC gained control of Parliament. With the ANC's victory, many Xhosa ascended to positions of political power. In 1999 Thabo MBEKI (1942–), also a Xhosa, succeeded Mandela as South Africa's second president. However, some Xhosa, including Transkei leader Bantu Holomisa (1955–), broke with the ANC to found the rival United Democratic Movement. Such developments illustrated that while the Xhosa have a clear, historically based ethnic identity, this identity also contains deeply rooted sub-identities and rivalries.

See also: ETHNICITY AND IDENTITY (Vol. V): POLITICAL PARTIES AND ORGANIZATIONS (Vols. IV, V); XHOSA (Vols. II, III, IV).

Y

Yala, Koumba (Koumba Iala, Kumba Yalla) (c. 1953–) *Former president of Guinea-Bissau*

Born into a peasant family of the majority Balanta ethnic group, Koumba Yala received a graduate degree in law and philosophy from Lisbon Classic University, in Portugal. Upon graduating he taught philosophy and eventually headed some of Guinea-Bissau's top educational institutions. He joined the AFRICAN PARTY FOR THE INDEPENDENCE OF GUINEA AND CAPE VERDE (PAIGC) and was sent to Communist Germany and Russia to be trained as a future leader of the group. In 1989, however, PAIGC leadership expelled him from the ranks, citing his frequent divergence from party teaching. Yala then went on to co-found the Democratic Social Front. In 1993 he split with that group to form the PARTY FOR SOCIAL RENEWAL (Partido para a Renovaçao Social, PRS). In the country's first multiparty elections, which were held in 1994, Yala and others vied to unseat President João Bernardo Vieira (1939–), who represented the PAIGC. According to independent observers Yala certainly received more votes than Vieira. However, Vieira maneuvered to remain in power.

> **Yala was rarely seen without a bright red hat, a symbol of authority among members of his Balanta ethnic group.**

In 1998–99, civil war in GUINEA-BISSAU eventually drove President Vieira into exile, after which an interim government was installed. This interim government called for new multiparty elections to be held in 1999 for both the National Assembly and presidency. In the elections, with 12 parties competing, Yala received 38 percent of the vote. In the runoff election, which took place in 2000, he captured 72 percent of the vote to become Guinea-Bissau's new president. Yala's PRS took roughly one-third of the seats in the National Assembly.

Once in power, Yala soon alienated his constituency by becoming increasingly authoritarian. His pledges to fight CORRUPTION were ridiculed when several million dollars in ECONOMIC ASSISTANCE disappeared and nobody was charged with wrongdoing. In addition, Yala's promises to revitalize AGRICULTURE and improve both the health and EDUCATION systems went unrealized. In September 2003 Yala and most of his PRS cohorts were ousted in a COUP D'ÉTAT led by General Verissimo Correia Seabra, the head of the armed forces. The military then chose Henrique Rosa (1946–) to serve as interim president until new presidential elections, scheduled for 2005, could be held.

See also: COMMUNISM AND SOCIALISM (Vol. V); PORTUGAL AND AFRICA (Vols. III, IV, V).

Yamoussoukro

Official capital of IVORY COAST, located in the south-central part of the nation, 170 miles (274 km) northwest of the former capital, ABIDJAN. Originally a small village, Yamoussoukro came under French control during the colonial period. By 1935 future president Félix HOUPHOUËT-BOIGNY (1905–1993) had become Yamoussoukro's leader. After the nation gained its independence, in 1960, Houphouët-Boigny was named Ivory Coast's president. (He served as president until 1993.) Under his leadership the government initiated large-scale investment in the city, constructing buildings and a major highway linking Yamoussoukro with Abidjan, which was the national capital. In 1983 Yamoussoukro replaced Abidjan as the national capital, but most of the financial and government offices remained in the former capital.

Yamoussoukro's Our Lady of Peace Basilica, modeled after St. Peter's in Rome, was built between 1986 and 1989. Considered the largest Christian place of worship in the world, the enormous structure stands 489 feet (149 m) at its highest point. Félix Houphouët-Boigny, the former president of Ivory Coast, sponsored the $150 million project and offered it as a gift to the Vatican. Pope John Paul II consecrated the church in 1990.

In 2001 the Ivorian government began its move to the new capital. However, despite heavy investments in Yamoussoukro's industrial sector, the DEVELOPMENT of the capital has lagged. Although the 2003 population was estimated at 185,600—revealing an eight-fold growth since 1970—the city still lacked the familiar vibrancy of West African cities.

See also: FRANCE AND AFRICA (Vols. III, IV, V); URBAN LIFE AND CULTURE (Vols. IV, V); URBANIZATION (Vols. IV, V).

Yaoundé Capital city of CAMEROON, located on the south-central plateau, inland from the Gulf of Guinea. Founded by German explorers in the late 19th century, Yaoundé became the headquarters for the German colony of Kamerun in 1909. After World War I (1914–18) the city fell within the French-controlled zone of Kamerun (Britain controlled the other part of the colony), and it became a French mandate, held under the auspices of the League of Nations. Yaoundé continued to be a modest-sized town of under 10,000 people throughout the inter-war years, remaining largely Beti in ethnic composition but with a resident European population as well. By the early 1960s the population had risen to about 90,000, and when the British and French areas were united to form the CAMEROON Federal Republic, in 1961, Yaoundé became the capital. In 1972 Yaoundé remained the capital when the country became the united Republic of Cameroon.

While the city has developed as an administrative and TRANSPORTATION center, its industrial sector is small, producing mostly cigarettes, timber products, printed materials, palm products, construction materials, soap, and handicrafts. There are numerous government offices and educational institutions, including the University of Yaoundé (founded in 1962), the Pasteur Institute of Cameroon, which conducts biomedical research, as well as other schools focused on health, EDUCATION, AGRICULTURE, journalism, and international relations. The national museum offers an impressive collection of Cameroonian sculpture. Yaoundé is well connected to other major urban areas of the country by rail, road, and air.

The population of the city was estimated at 1,400,000 in 2003, and the Beti, while still the largest ethnic group, are no longer a majority. A bustling capital city, Yaoundé attracts residents from throughout Camer-oon and retains a significant European population. Visitors and residents alike continue to enjoy the pleasant atmosphere of the tree-lined streets and the spectacular views of the surrounding tropical forests.

See also: FRANCE AND AFRICA (Vols. III, IV, V); GERMANY AND AFRICA (Vol. IV); LEAGUE OF NATIONS AND AFRICA (Vol. IV); URBAN LIFE AND CULTURE (Vols. IV, V); URBANIZATION (Vols. IV, V).

Yoruba General term used to describe the language, peoples, and kingdoms of southwestern NIGERIA, Republic of BENIN, and TOGO. Not long after Nigerian independence, in 1960, the various ethnic, cultural, and religious threads that had been woven into a single state by British colonial powers began to unravel. Within months wrangling over the boundaries of Nigeria's federal regions—the Northern Region, dominated by the HAUSA-Fulani, the Western Region, dominated by the Yoruba, and the Eastern Region, dominated by the IGBO—escalated into political conflict. The feelings of divisiveness were exacerbated by the fact that Nigeria's central government was clearly dominated by northern Muslims, in spite of the large numbers of educated Yoruba and Igbo serving in both the government and the military.

By 1966 the situation had deteriorated, and the Nigerian central government suffered from a series of coups as various ethnic groups vied for control. Civil war broke out the following year, with the federal government, led by General Yakubu GOWON (1934–), attempting to put down the Igbo secessionist state of BIAFRA. This period saw the Yoruba, as a group, attempt to find a middle ground in which to survive the conflict between the central government, which was dominated by northerners, and the secessionist Igbo.

The end of civil war, in 1970, brought peace but not stability. Indeed, Nigeria endured the rule of a number of brutal dictators before the establishment of a fragile democracy in the late 1990s. Ethnic and religious dissension, too, became increasingly intense. All this tended to give the Yoruba, among whom Christianity and Islam coexist, a fairly prominent role in the Nigerian central government. Indicative of this fact, in 1999 the Yoruba-speaking Olusegun OBASANJO (c. 1937–) swept into power as a democratically elected president with the strong support of northerners. As a result, in spite of the fact that Obasanjo promised some of the first, substantive democratic reforms in years, he was seen as a traitor to the Christian southerners because of his support from, and moderate stance toward, northern Muslims.

See also: CHRISTIANITY, INFLUENCE OF (Vols. IV, V); ETHNICITY AND IDENTITY (Vol. V); ILORIN (Vol. IV); ISLAM, INFLUENCE OF (Vols. IV, V); YORUBA (Vols. I, II, IV) YORUBALAND (Vol. II, III).

Further reading: Ruth Watson, *"Civil Disorder is the Disease of Ibadan": Chieftaincy & Civic Culture in a Yoruba City* (Athens, Ohio: Ohio University Press, 2003).

Z

Zambia Landlocked country in southern Africa. Zambia, which was the former British colony of Northern Rhodesia, covers an area of approximately 290,600 square miles (752,700 sq km) and is surrounded by ANGOLA, the Democratic Republic of the CONGO, TANZANIA, MALAWI, MOZAMBIQUE, ZIMBABWE, BOTSWANA, and NAMIBIA. Most of the country lies on a plateau that rises to 8,000 feet (2,434 m) in the east.

Zambia is one of the most urbanized countries in Africa, with about 50 percent of the nation's population living in cities. LUSAKA, the capital, is the largest. Other major urban areas are the Copperbelt cities of Kitwe and Ndola and the major tourist city of Livingstone, in the south. In 2001 the country's population was about 9.8 million. Zambia has nine provinces, each headed by a provincial minister.

Zambia at Independence In 1964 Zambia, with vast NATURAL RESOURCES of copper, cobalt, zinc, and emeralds, had a fairly prosperous colonial economy. It had a well-established private sector dominated by expatriate business interests, MULTINATIONAL CORPORATIONS, and commercial farmers. It also was the world's third-largest copper producer. In spite of all this there was minimum DEVELOPMENT in the INFRASTRUCTURE, and the country lacked qualified Zambian personnel.

> **At the time of Zambia's independence there were only 107 Zambian university graduates, and only four of these were female.**

The new government started developing the country almost from scratch. The government drew up four national development plans between 1964 and 1991. The objectives were to develop the country's industry and create new jobs. The government also sought to improve the country's infrastructure, building major roads as well as the Lusaka International Airport, which opened in 1967. Improving the health and EDUCATION systems were other key objectives. The first university in the country, the University of Zambia, was built in 1966 and had an initial enrolment of 312 students. The development plans included diversifying the economy to promote balanced economic development and rural development. The plans also included nationalizing positions and ownership to reduce expatriate domination.

In the first decade after independence Zambia experienced economic growth that supported the development of social services, health facilities, housing, and schools. A large portion of the population moved from rural to urban areas. The government introduced a system of free education and health care. Also, the government established a hospital system made up of general hospitals in the main cities with smaller health centers in outlying regions. At least 12 general hospitals were built, including the University Teaching Hospital in Lusaka. The first doctors trained in Zambia graduated in 1972. In addition, missionary hospitals continued to provide services mostly in the rural areas.

In 1968 President Kenneth KAUNDA (1924–) announced the state control of privately owned companies. The government took over control of a wide range of commercial activities ranging from retail shops to meat-packing plants and quarrying operations. A total of 28 companies were placed under government-control. In 1969 the state created the Industrial Development Corporation to spearhead INDUSTRIALIZATION. In that same year, economic reforms led the government to buy 51 percent of the shares from the two MINING companies, Anglo-American Corporation and Roan Selection Trust, giving the state majority ownership of Zambia's copper-mining industry. In the end the state controlled 80 percent of the economy in various sectors including mining, energy, TRANSPORTATION, TOURISM, finance, AGRICULTURE, trade, manufacturing, and construction.

From the very beginning Zambia supported African liberation movements and vowed to help other African countries attain independence. Zambia played a leading role as one of the FRONTLINE STATES. Because of its commitment Lusaka became the headquarters of 15 African liberation movements from other countries including Zimbabwe, SOUTH AFRICA, Mozambique, and Angola. As a result of its stand Zambia suffered economically, as the ruling governments from these countries attacked and destroyed the country's infrastructure. Zambia also became a haven for REFUGEES, who later weighed heavily on its economy.

Zambia supported economic sanctions against the white-minority government in RHODESIA, leading the Rhodesian army to retaliate by destroying parts of Zambia's transportation network. Zambia stopped transporting its goods via rail through Rhodesia to the seaport of Beira in Mozambique, which posed a major problem for the landlocked country. Its overseas EXPORTS and imports were transported through the port of DAR ES SALAAM, Tanzania by plane, and by truck through the Great North Road, which was an expensive route. In 1975 the Chinese government assisted in building the Tanzania-Zambia Railways (Tazara), a rail line that connected Dar es Salaam and Zambia, which helped ease the country's transportation problem.

In the 1960s and early 1970s the country's economy grew, primarily because of high copper production and increased maize and manufacturing output. In the mid-1970s, however, the economic situation deteriorated. The price of copper on the international market fell, and copper production decreased. Also, food production decreased, making agricultural commodities more expensive. The situation was worsened by the economic sanctions against Rhodesia, formerly a major trading partner.

In addition, government-controlled firms failed to perform for a number of reasons, including a lack of appropriate technology, a dependence on imported raw materials, and inexperienced managers, who in many cases were political appointees rather than experts in the field. Also, government control led to a lack of a competitive environment, which created stagnation in the industries.

The situation was made worse by the creation of a one-party state, in 1973. Kaunda's UNITED NATIONAL INDE-PENDENCE PARTY became the only legal political party. By the 1980s people were unhappy with the economic and political climate. At the same time the INTERNATIONAL MONETARY FUND and the WORLD BANK, as a condition for future aid, advised the government to introduce tough economic measures under its STRUCTURAL ADJUSTMENT program. Shortages of basic goods, unemployment, and removal of food subsidies led to rioting and strikes. At this time people called for multiparty rule and a change in government. To make the situation even worse, in 1986 South Africa launched attacks against Zambia and other neighboring countries, targeting camps that were suspected of being used by the liberation forces of the AFRICAN NATIONAL CONGRESS.

Multiparty Politics under Kaunda Kaunda was forced to legalize rival political parties in 1990. Afterward, a new party, the MOVEMENT FOR MULTIPARTY DEMOCRACY (MMD), emerged. The MMD was led by Frederick CHILUBA (1943–), a LABOR-UNION leader who won the 1991 election. The peaceful transition was hailed as one of the best in Africa. Chiluba introduced market-oriented economic policies that favored privatization. Initially Chiluba's economic and political plans were seen as progressive. However, privatization led to thousands of workers being laid off, and many were forced to take early retirement. All of this added to the already high unemployment. Zambia's foreign debt also continued to drag down the economy. By the late 1990s Zambia was classified as a low-income country. It has been classified with 40 other developing countries as "heavily indebted poor countries."

Chiluba changed the constitution to block Kaunda from having another bid at the presidency and was re-elected president in 1996. In 2001 he attempted to find a way to bypass the constitutional two-term limit but failed. Chiluba then selected and campaigned for Levy MWANAWASA (1948–), who won the election despite charges of rigging. Although handpicked by Chiluba, Mwanawasa turned out to be independent and open, permitting the trial of his predecessor for misappropriation of public funds in 2003.

Zambia has continued to play significant political and economic roles in the region and on the continent. Since 1998 the state has worked to find a peaceful solution in the Democratic Republic of the Congo (DRC). In 1999 Chiluba's mediation efforts resulted in the signing of the Lusaka Ceasefire Agreement, which set the stage for the peace process. One of the leading members of the SOUTHERN AFRICAN DEVELOPMENT COMMUNITY, Zambia has played leading roles in various organizations and has hosted meetings of the former ORGANIZATION FOR AFRICAN UNITY, which recently has evolved into the AFRICAN UNION.

See also: CHINA AND AFRICA (Vol. V); COPPERBELT (Vol. IV); NORTHERN RHODESIA (Vol. IV); ZAMBIA (Vols. I, II, III, IV).

Further reading: Robert I. Rotberg, *Ending Autocracy, Enabling Democracy: The Tribulations of Southern Africa, 1960–2000* (Washington, D.C.: Brookings Institution Press, 2002); Jennifer A. Widner, ed., *Economic Change and Political Liberalization in Sub-Saharan Africa* (Baltimore: Johns Hopkins University Press, 1994).

Zanzibar African state made up of the two main islands of Unguja (Zanzibar) and Pemba with a number of adjacent islets about 30 miles (48 km) off the coast of mainland TANZANIA in the Indian Ocean. A part of Tanzania since 1964, Zanzibar covers an area of approximately 640 square miles (1,660 sq km). Its mixed Arab and African population was estimated at 750,000 in 2000. The island's capital is ZANZIBAR CITY.

Zanzibar at Independence Zanzibar gained its independence from Britain on December 10, 1963, with the Busaidi sultan, Jamshid ibn Abdullah (1929–), as the first head of state and another member of the ruling oligarchy, Muhammad Shamte Hamadi, as prime minister. At independence there were three contesting political parties. The Zanzibar Nationalist Party (ZNP) and the Zanzibar and Pemba People's Party (ZPPP) represented Zanzibari Arab interests, and the AFRO-SHIRAZI PARTY (ASP) represented African interests. Even before the first elections the two Arab parties formed a coalition, which led to their victory in the elections and their central role in the government that took power in 1963.

The election was marred by racial and religious differences and was followed by a week of civil unrest in which many died. On January 12, 1964, John Okello, a Ugandan who had been living on Pemba, took charge of a group of 300 followers who armed themselves by seizing the police barracks. Reacting to years of Arab dominance and oppression, the African populace rallied to Okello's side. Thousands of Arabs and Indians died in the resulting violence, and thousands of others fled for safety, often in unseaworthy boats. The sultan went into exile, and Abeid Amani KARUME (1905–1972), the ASP leader, became president and head of the ruling Revolutionary Council.

In October 1964 Zanzibar united with mainland Tanganyika to become the United Republic of Tanzania; Julius NYERERE (1922–1999) became the president. Under this arrangement, the president of Zanzibar served as the first vice president of Tanzania if the president was from the mainland and as the second vice president if the country's president was from Zanzibar. Nyerere merged his TANZANIA AFRICAN NATIONAL UNION (TANU) and Zanzibar's ASP into a single party, Chama Cha Mapinduzi (CCM), meaning PARTY OF THE REVOLUTION in Kiswahili. Under the terms of the union, Zanzibar continued to exercise a degree of independence in most of its affairs, except defense and foreign affairs, which were to be the responsibility of the central government. This arrangement enabled Karume to chart an independent course for the island's domestic affairs. He received ECONOMIC ASSISTANCE from the Soviet Union, Cuba, and China, which in turn isolated Zanzibar from the West in the context of the Cold War.

In 1972 Karume was assassinated and was succeeded by Sheikh Aboud JUMBE (1920–) as Zanzibar's president and the first vice president of Tanzania. Jumbe held office until 1984, when growing Zanzibari resentment against the union with the mainland led to his resignation. Ali Hassan MWINYI (1925–) became the president, and in 1985 Mwinyi became the first Zanzibari to serve as the president of the union. In the 2000 election, Amani Karume (1948–), son of the late Abeid Karume, led the CCM to victory and became the island's president.

Zanzibar's economy is largely dependent on AGRICULTURE. Its main products are cassava, sweet potatoes, rice, maize, plantains, citrus fruit, and coconuts. Cloves and cacao are major CASH CROPS that, along with coconuts, are exported. There is a sizable fishing industry, and TOURISM has become an important part of the economy. Lime is the country's sole mineral resource. Beginning in the 1990s the government of Zanzibar has been aggressively implementing economic reforms and has legalized foreign exchange bureaus on the islands.

> Zanzibar is at the heart of the distinctive *taraab*, or sung poetry, tradition. The diva of this haunting style is Siti binti Saad (c. 1885–1950), who in 1928 became the first East African singer to make commercial recordings.

The main languages spoken in Zanzibar are Kiswahili and English, with the latter serving as the official language but the former being the everyday language of the people. The Kiswahili spoken in Zanzibar is said to be the most standard form of the language, which makes the island an ideal place to learn it.

See also: BUSAIDI (Vol. IV); INDIAN OCEAN TRADE (Vol. II); SITI BINTI SAAD (Vol. IV); SWAHILI COAST (Vol. II); ZANZIBAR (Vols. II, III, IV),

Zanzibar City East African port city located on the Zanzibar Channel, which separates the island of ZANZIBAR from the African mainland. Originally a Swahili settlement, Zanzibar City became the capital of the Omani Arab sultanate in the 1830s. In the 1890s Britain made the island part of a protectorate that lasted until 1963.

At that time Zanzibar island was granted independence, with the British turning the island back over to the sultanate. A year later a violent revolution led by non-Arab Africans swept the sultan and his government from power, and Zanzibar was declared a republic. The island then joined with Tanganyika to form the nation of TANZANIA. As the primary urban center, Zanzibar City served as the island's administrative headquarters, operating somewhat independently from the federal Tanzanian government based in the mainland cities of DAR ES SALAAM and DODOMA.

Zanzibar's economy has long been based on the cultivation of cloves, which are still important export items today. The manufacturing of clove oil—used mainly in health and beauty products—is the major industry in the city.

Also, TOURISM has become an economic mainstay in recent decades, thanks to the beautiful beaches and the island's ambience. Another attraction is the city's unique mix of Arab, South Asian, and Swahili ARCHITECTURE, a style that is evident in many of the houses and mosques that are adorned with elaborate wood and stone carvings on the doors and facades. The modern area of Zanzibar City, on the other hand, is filled with drab apartment buildings built by East Germans in the aftermath of the 1964 revolution.

See also: BUSAIDI (Vol. IV); ENGLAND AND AFRICA (Vols. III, IV, V); ISLAM, INFLUENCE OF (Vols. II, III, IV, V); SLAVE TRADE ON THE SWAHILI COAST (Vol. III); SWAHILI COAST (Vols. II, III, IV); URBAN LIFE AND CULTURE (Vols. IV, V); URBANIZATION (Vols. IV, V); ZANZIBAR CITY (Vol. IV).

Zimbabwe Present-day country in southeastern Africa 150,900 square miles (390,800 sq km) in size and marked by a large central plateau. Zimbabwe is bordered to the east by MOZAMBIQUE, to the south by SOUTH AFRICA, to the west by BOTSWANA, and to the north by ZAMBIA. Zimbabwe has remained under the international spotlight, initially for being a white-minority-ruled nation until 1980 and more recently due to its steady political and economic decline.

In the early 1960s independent African governments were replacing those of the colonial rulers throughout most of the continent. Fearing that they too might face a situation of majority rule in the aftermath of the collapse of the Central African Federation, in 1963, the white-settler minority of Southern Rhodesia issued a UNILATERAL DECLARATION OF INDEPENDENCE from Britain in 1965. Coalescing behind Ian SMITH (1919–) and his Rhodesia Front (RF), they also changed the country's name to RHODESIA. Britain refused to recognize the new state, and there was continuous but minimal diplomatic, military, and economic pressure to convince the white majority for a settlement. The sanctions had limited effect. In the

meantime the country's African population also became more politically organized and increasingly militant.

By the 1970s two major African nationalist INDEPENDENCE MOVEMENTS—the ZIMBABWE AFRICAN NATIONAL UNION (ZANU) and the ZIMBABWE AFRICAN PEOPLE'S UNION (ZAPU)—had reached the point where they could stage an increasingly effective guerrilla campaign to overthrow the white-minority regime. This struggle became regarded as the second CHIMURENGA, or Chimurenga Chechipiri. Mozambique, which after a long struggle had rid itself of Portuguese colonial rule in 1975, and Zambia supported the two organizations. ZAPU primarily represented the Ndebele, who lived in the western portions of the country, while ZANU became the bearer of the majority Shona aspirations. In 1976 the two groups entered an informal pact to create the PATRIOTIC FRONT. By joining forces, they were able to inflict increasing losses on the Rhodesian Security forces, which in turn led to exodus of many whites from Rhodesia. By 1979 pressures from the international community, a unified African majority, and a relentless guerrilla movement provided the way for an "internal settlement." This was an effort to preserve the major elements of white privilege in the country while providing the semblance of African rule through Bishop Abel MUZOREWA (1925–). ZAPU leader Joshua NKOMO (1917–1999) and ZANU head Robert MUGABE (1924–) agreed on a joint position and boycotted elections that led to Muzorewa's election.

Rejected by the black majority, the internal settlement did little to abate the fighting. Muzorewa's government lasted barely six months. The war finally ended in 1979 with a peace agreement negotiated in Lancaster House, London. This led to an agreement on a new constitution, transitional arrangements, and a cease-fire.

Zimbabwe at Independence In the 1980 elections that followed the Lancaster House agreement ZANU candidates won comfortably. Robert Mugabe thus became the first prime minister of the Republic of Zimbabwe. ZANU promoted reconciliation, agreeing to share power with ZAPU, though with an eye toward co-opting the opposition within a one-party state that had the appearance of a multiparty system However, the alleged discovery of secret arms of ZAPU cadres, which it was claimed were to be used in overthrowing the new government, led to severe reprisals. Thousands, mostly from the Ndebele areas, were killed by the Zimbabwean army and paramilitary brigades that functioned outside formal military command structures. The Mugabe-led ZANU-PF party has completely dominated the government since this event and has not tolerated dissent or opposition.

Mugabe inherited a segregated nation, which had seen years of domination by the white minority. For the first seven years after independence, whites elected 20 members to 20 reserved seats in Parliament, out of the

In 1976 people took to the streets of Bulawayo to show their jubilant support for Joshua Nkomo, the leader of the African National Council. The transfer to black-majority rule in Rhodesia was still four years away. © AP/Wide World Photos

total 100 seats. At independence approximately 4,000 white farmers held more than a third of the total land and a majority of the most productive land. The Lancaster House agreement precluded a takeover of private property by the state without compensation. The large commercial farms were profitable and contributed the bulk of agricultural growth through maize and tobacco. During the first few years after independence the economy boomed partly because of elimination of the sanctions imposed on Rhodesia and the opening up of export markets. The first decade of independence witnessed years of brisk economic growth interspersed with years that saw drops in the growth rate due to drought and declines in demand for Zimbabwe's mineral EXPORTS. By the end of the decade economic decline, marked by zero growth rates, a foreign exchange crisis, and further drought, had set in.

Zimbabwe since 1990 Throughout the 1990s there has been a steady decline in the living standards of people

in Zimbabwe, costing the regime support and galvanized civic groups and the country's LABOR UNION movement. A third period of opposition politics started with civic organization for constitutional reform in 1997. During the 1990s there were a number of strikes as unemployment and inflation soared. In 1997, to challenge the proposed constitutional amendment that would have further strengthened the powers of the president, CIVIL SOCIETY organizations and the Zimbabwe Confederation of Trade Unions (ZCTU) formed the National Constitutional Assembly (NCA). In response to this opposition, the government established its own commission to draft a new constitution. The NCA boycotted the government's commission and ZCTU organized mass demonstrations. Growing resentment among the urban masses provided the opening for the emergence of an opposition party. The MOVEMENT FOR DEMOCRATIC CHANGE (MDC) was founded as a wide coalition of interest groups, including trade unions, civic groups, white farmers, and the business community. These groups were united in their aim to defeat ZANU-PF politically and transform the structures of power in the state. Morgan TSVANGIRAI (1952–), the head of the trade-union movement, beame the principal MDC leader.

The MDC emerged in the context of Zimbabwe's deteriorating national economy and the eroding popularity of the ruling party, especially in urban areas. With the 2002 elections in sight, Mugabe expanded the land-seizure program. Thousands of black workers and white farm owners were evicted, MDC supporters were intimidated, and journalists were attacked. In the presidential elections Mugabe was declared the winner, while international observers declared the vote neither free nor fair. To retain power, Mugabe reignited the land-ownership issue. The most fertile land in Zimbabwe had been under the control of the white minority, and redistribution became a key issue for Zimbabweans, especially for those without land living in the rural areas.

Throughout its first two decades of independence Zimbabwe, though supposedly having a multiparty political system, became increasingly a one-party state. Robert Mugabe and his ZANU-PF won its first parliamentary majority in the initial 1980 election and continued to do so in 1985, 1990, and 1995. ZAPU had initially constituted a strong regional party, but it was then transformed into a partner and later repressed as a dissident. Responding to the growing CORRUPTION in the ruling party and in defense of multiparty democracy, there briefly emerged the Zimbabwe United Movement (ZUM), which contested the 1990 election and then collapsed under heavy pressure. Electoral apathy marked the 1995 election.

By adopting land redistribution as an electoral tactic Mugabe was able to appeal to his key constituency and cling to power, but his hold on power continued to be tenuous, and Zimbabwe remained on the brink of collapse. Industrial and agricultural growth shrank by double digits. With unemployment soaring over 50 percent and inflation approaching 300 percent, Zimbabwean society became increasingly unstable. In 2003 more than 6.7 million people were estimated to be at risk of starvation. In just a few years Zimbabwe moved from being one of southern Africa's success stories to being a source of unending problems.

At independence a policy that was expected to redress the historical patterns of racial and class inequalities has instead degenerated into oppression, leading to society-wide chaos and the possibility of state collapse. The land question and the current governance crisis in Zimbabwe are intimately linked and exacerbated by the intransigence of an octogenarian president, Robert Mugabe. It will probably take decades for Zimbabwe to regain its stature in the region.

One of the more unusual contributing factors to Zimbabwe's economic difficulties was the Mugabe government's intervention in the civil war in the Democratic Republic of the CONGO (DRC) to prop up the shaky government of Laurent KABILA (c. 1939–2001) and then that of his son, Joseph KABILA (1971–). More than 11,000 Zimbabwean troops have been in the Congo, at huge expense to the Zimbabwean government. Without a common border or a shared history of cooperation, the question is why Zimbabwe continues this expensive involvement. The answer seems to lie with the benefits that may accrue to Zimbabwe's ruling elite through joint business ventures, particularly in the MINING sector. According to one outspoken Zimbabwean critic of Mugabe, his government "seems intent on raiding the DRC and making it an economic colony."

See also: CENTRAL AFRICAN FEDERATION (Vol. IV); ENGLAND AND AFRICA (Vols. III, IV, V); SOUTHERN RHODESIA (Vol. IV); NDEBELE (Vol. IV); SHONA (Vols. I, IV); ZIMBABWE (Vols. I, II, III, IV).

Further reading: Horace Campbell, *Reclaiming Zimbabwe: The Exhaustion of the Patriarchal Model of Liberation* (Trenton, N.J. : Africa World Press, 2003); Staffan Darnolf and Lisa Laakso, eds., *Twenty Years of Independence in Zimbabwe: From Liberation to Authoritarianism* (New York: Palgrave Macmillan, 2003); Martin Meredith, *Mugabe: Power and Plunder in Zimbabwe* (Oxford, U.K.: Public Affairs, 2002).

Zimbabwe African National Union (ZANU) Nationalist movement and political party in power for the first 22 years of independent ZIMBABWE. ZANU-PF is the political party that emerged after the unification of the ZIMBABWE AFRICAN PEOPLE'S UNION (ZAPU), led by Joshua NKOMO (1917–1999), and the Zimbabwe African National Union (ZANU), led by Robert MUGABE (1924–). Both ZANU and ZAPU were anticolonial movements that originated in the liberation struggle in former RHODESIA. Throughout the 1970s both movements carried out guerrilla campaigns against the white-minority government.

ZANU was the most radical ideologically. It sought no compromise with the white Rhodesian majority and emphasized its struggle for total independence. During the guerrilla war, the military wings of ZANU and ZAPU—the Zimbabwe African National Liberation Army (ZANLA) and Zimbabwe African People's Liberation

Army (ZIPRA) respectively—controlled most of the country. ZAPU largely represented the Ndebele people, while ZANU drew its sympathies from among the majority Shona people.

At independence, in 1980, ZANU promoted reconciliation. It agreed to share power but with the goal of es-

In 1979 in Salisbury, Rhodesia, Africans rallied in support of ZANU leader Robert Mugabe, who became independent Zimbabwe's first president. © *UPI*

tablishing a one-party socialist state. ZANU-PF emerged by dismantling and co-opting key members of ZAPU. The parliamentary majority of ZANU allowed it to pass constitutional amendments further consolidating Robert Mugabe's powers by making him the first executive president. The relationship between the party and state organs merged, thus concentrating power in the hands of few.

During the mid-1990s there was some degree of internal party DEMOCRATIZATION. With the fall of socialist regimes around the world and the rise of liberal multiparty democracy, many ZANU members openly questioned the ideological goals of Marxist-Leninism, the one-party state, and the use of violence. ZANU's primary elections were often closely contested, with factional divisions and personal rivalries spilling over into the public discourse. However, until the late 1990s political challenges to ZANU were disorganized and organizationally weak. This was evident in the growing voter apathy in urban areas and higher turnout and support for the ruling party in rural areas.

Opposition to the ruling ZANU-PF government coalesced around the LABOR movement and civic groups. The growing economic malaise severely affected the livelihoods of urban workers, eventually triggering demonstrations. The strong response of the ZANU-PF government in banning demonstrations and the mass firing of government workers paved the way for the creation of the MOVEMENT FOR DEMOCRATIC CHANGE (MDC), a coalition of Zimbabwe's major LABOR UNIONS and CIVIL SOCIETY organizations.

During the parliamentary elections in 2000 the MDC won 57 of the 120 open seats with strong support from urban voters. ZANU-PF won 62 seats. The electoral setback reduced the ability of ZANU-PF to amend the Zimbabwean constitution unilaterally. The party yet again tried intimidating the opposition, controlling the media, and mobilizing rural voters around the issue of land reform. The ruling party since 2000 has rallied around the slogan, "The economy is the land," suggesting the redistribution of land held by a white minority to the black majority will improve their living standards and create the basis for future growth in the economy.

After Robert Mugabe, ZANU-PF faces an uncertain future. There are many among its current leadership who could replace the 80-year-old leader. However, ZANU-PF is like many other single-party regimes in Africa, existing mainly due to the charisma of its leader and relying on its ability to neutralize competing factions.

See also: INDEPENDENCE MOVEMENTS (Vol. IV); NDEBELE (Vols. III, IV); POLITICAL PARTIES AND ORGANIZATIONS (Vols. IV, V); SHONA (Vols. II, III).

Further reading: Horace Campbell, *Reclaiming Zimbabwe: The Exhaustion of the Patriarchal Model of Liberation* (Trenton, N.J.: Africa World Press, 2003); Stephen Chan, *Robert Mugabe: A Life of Power and Violence* (Ann Arbor, Mich.: University of Michigan Press, 2003); Ruth Weiss, *Zimbabwe and the New Elite* (New York: British Academic Press, 1994).

Zimbabwe African People's Union (ZAPU)

Opposition party that fought for Zimbabwean independence. In 1961 the white-minority government of Southern Rhodesia banned the National Democratic Party. In response, Joshua NKOMO (1917–1999) established the Zimbabwe African People's Union (ZAPU). The government quickly banned ZAPU, too, and Nkomo was forced to establish a government-in-exile. ZAPU soon split. The original core group retained Ndebele support, and a breakaway group, the ZIMBABWE AFRICAN NATIONAL UNION (ZANU), drew support from Zimbabwe's majority Shona people. ZANU was led by Ndabaningi SITHOLE (1920–2000) and Robert MUGABE (1924–).

In 1964 the Southern Rhodesian government issued a UNILATERAL DECLARATION OF INDEPENDENCE from the United Kingdom and renamed the country RHODESIA. Despite being banned, both ZAPU and ZANU took up separate armed struggles against the increasingly oppressive white-minority rule—and occasionally against each other. As the independence struggle intensified in 1976, the two rebel groups came together to form the PATRIOTIC FRONT, although they each kept their own organizational structures.

When Rhodesia became independent ZIMBABWE, in 1980, ZAPU was labeled as a dissident organization concerned mostly with issues related to Zimbabwe's Ndebele minority population. During the first post-independence elections ZAPU won only 20 parliamentary seats, mostly in its stronghold, Matabeland. ZANU, on the other hand, won 57 parliamentary seats. ZAPU received five cabinet positions, including Joshua Nkomo's appointment as minister of home affairs. However, this veneer of ZANU-ZAPU collaboration was short-lived.

Soon after independence the goal of the ZANU leaders was to dismantle the opposition within the Patriotic Front and establish a monolithic, single-party socialist state. ZANU even sent the Zimbabwean army's Fifth Brigade to intimidate ZAPU dissidents in Matabeland. ZANU's message to the Ndebele was clear—reconsider your support for ZAPU or face the consequences.

Nkomo left Zimbabwe in 1982 but he returned to participate in the 1985 election. Violence was again part of the electoral process, as ZANU cadres used strong-arm tactics to intimidate opposition members. ZANU once again swept the elections while ZAPU's support declined further. This time ZANU did not offer ZAPU any cabinet seats. Firmly in control of Zimbabwe, Mugabe and ZANU set about negotiating a Unity Accord to create the coalition Zimbabwe African National Union-Patriotic Front (ZANU-PF) ruling party. Under the provisions of the accord the ZANU government released ZAPU prisoners. The political implications of the accord, however, reduced ZAPU to a minor political party within ZANU-PF.

See also: INDEPENDENCE MOVEMENTS (Vol. V); NATIONALISM AND INDEPENDENCE MOVEMENTS (Vol. IV); POLITICAL PARTIES AND ORGANIZATIONS (Vols. IV, V); SOUTHERN RHODESIA (Vol. IV).

Further reading: Norma J. Kriger, *Guerrilla Veterans in Post-War Zimbabwe: Symbolic and Violent Politics, 1980–1987* (New York: Cambridge University Press, 2003).

Zine El Abidine Ben-Ali (1936–) *President of Tunisia*

Born in Hammam Sousse, in the Sahel region of TUNISIA, Ben-Ali received military training in France and the United States. A member of the Neo-Destour Party, he served in a number of government positions, including director general of national security, secretary of state, and minister of the interior. In 1987 Ben-Ali became prime minister under President Habib BOURGUIBA (1903–2000). Facing popular unrest and debilitating illness, Bourguiba ruled in an increasingly authoritarian manner. Finally citing a constitutional provision, Ben-Ali deposed Bourguiba, in November 1987, on the grounds of the president's poor health. The move was widely supported by the Tunisian population.

Ben-Ali quickly turned his attention to democratizing the country, working to establish a multiparty system and releasing hundreds of political prisoners. However, Ben-Ali and the Neo-Destour Party (renamed the Constitutional Democratic Rally) largely controlled the government and banned any party with religious affliations in an effort to limit the influence of Islamic fundamentalists. In 1992 Ben-Ali launched a massive domestic project called the National Solidarity Fund (NSF). The NSF provided assistance to more than 1,000 of Tunisia's most underdeveloped villages, constructing houses, schools, roads, and health centers and creating thousands of jobs. The United Nations used the NSF as the basis for the World Solidarity Fund, which was also devised by Ben-Ali.

In terms of foreign policy, Ben-Ali continued his predecessor's policy of nonalignment in regard to the Cold War conflict between the United States and the Soviet Union. However, his support for the Iraqi people during the Gulf War (1991) led the United States, Saudi Arabia, and Kuwait to pull back much-needed investments, which Ben-Ali won back only after years of hard lobbying.

Ben Ali won reelection in a landslide, in 1994, and again in 1999. In 2001 he initiated a reform bill designed to create the "Republic of the Future." The bill made advances in terms of civil liberties and HUMAN RIGHTS and established new governmental branches in an effort to further democratize the country.

See also: DEMOCRATIZATION (Vol. V); DESTOUR PARTY (Vol. IV).

Further reading: Andrew Borowiec, *Modern Tunisia: A Democratic Apprenticeship* (Westport, Conn.: Praeger, 1998); Sadok Chaabane, *Ben Ali on the Road to Pluralism in Tunisia* (Washington, D.C.: American Educational Trust, 1997).

Zulu

Bantu-speaking people of SOUTH AFRICA who belong to the Nguni cluster of Southern Bantu, many of whom live in the KwaZulu-Natal Province. The Zulu resisted the colonial advances of Britain in South Africa into the early 20th century. By the 1950s, however, the once-mighty Zulu monarchy had long been subjugated to the authority of the white South African government. With the introduction of APARTHEID and the Bantu Self-Government Act of 1959 came the BANTUSTANS, land set aside as "homelands" for the country's black African peoples. In 1970 the Zulu homeland, KwaZulu, was established from parts of the historical Zulu stronghold of Zululand. (See map on page 44 of this volume.)

The idea of a single Zulu homeland was in many ways a modern concept. Though Zulu royalty had existed since the 18th century, many Zulu did not view the monarchy as representing all of the Zulu people. Furthermore, only about half of the South African Zulu population lived in KwaZulu. During the 1970s, however, the controlling faction of KwaZulu, led by the Bantustan's chief minister, Mangosuthu Gatsha BUTHELEZI (1928–), initiated a campaign to unite the Zulu people. Viewed largely as an effort to strengthen Buthelezi and his cultural movement, Inkatha, at the expense of his main opponent, the AFRICAN NATIONAL CONGRESS (ANC), the promotion of Zulu nationalism met with mixed results. Uninspired by Buthelezi's glorification of past Zulu rulers, many Zulu eschewed Inkatha and remained loyal to the ANC. During the 1980s thousands of people died as a result of conflict between the two Zulu factions. The conflict spread to JOHANNESBURG in the 1990s, as Inkatha transformed into the INKATHA FREEDOM PARTY (IFP), a political party created to compete in South Africa's first racially-inclusive elections. In the early 1990s the IFP's Zulu members fought with the XHOSA, who were viewed as the principal ethnic group within the ANC.

With the end of apartheid, in 1994, KwaZulu rejoined the Natal province, forming a new province named KwaZulu-Natal. In the elections of 1994 the IFP gained control of that province's government, marking their only significant electoral victory. In the following years, however, the ANC continued to garner support from a large segment of the Zulu population. At the beginning of the 21st century the ANC, which controlled the national government, moved closer to gaining power over the province named after the Zulu.

See also: ETHNICITY AND IDENTITY (Vol. I); HIV/AIDS IN AFRICA (Vol. V); POLITICAL PARTIES AND ORGANIZATIONS (Vols. IV, V); SHAKA (Vol. III); ZULU (Vols. III, IV).

Further reading: Daphna Golan, *Inventing Shaka: Using History in the Construction of Zulu Nationalism* (Boulder, Colo.: Lynne Rienner Publishers, 1994).

GLOSSARY

agriculturalists Sociological term for "farmers."

agro-pastoralists People who practice both farming and animal husbandry.

alafin Yoruba word for "ruler" or "king."

Allah Arabic for "God" or "Supreme Being."

Americo-Liberian Liberians of African-American ancestry.

ancestor worship Misnomer for the traditional practice of honoring and recognizing the memory and spirits of deceased family members.

al-Andalus Arabic term for Muslim Spain.

animism Belief that inanimate objects have a soul or life force.

anglophone English speaking.

apartheid Afrikaans word that means "separateness"; a formal system and policy of racial segregation and political and economic discrimination against South Africa's nonwhite majority.

aphrodesiac Food or other agent thought to arouse or increase sexual desire.

askia Arabic word meaning "general" that was applied to the Songhai kings. Capitalized, the word refers to a dynasty of Songhai rulers.

assimilados Portuguese word for Africans who had assimilated into the colonial culture.

Australopithicus africanus Hominid species that branched off into *Homo habilis* and *A. robustus*.

Australopithicus anamensis Second-oldest species of the hominid *Australopithicus*.

Australopithicus ramadus Oldest of the apelike, hominid species of *Australopithicus*.

Australopithicus robustus A sturdy species of *Australopithicus* that came after *A. africanus* and appears to have been an evolutionary dead end. *Australopithecus robustus* roamed the Earth at the same time as *Homo habilis*.

balkanization The breaking apart of regions or units into smaller groups.

barter Trading system in which goods are exchanged for items of equal value.

bey Governor in the Ottoman Empire.

Bilad al-Sudan Arabic for "Land of the Blacks."

bride price The payment made by a groom and his family to compensate the bride's father for the loss of her services because of marriage.

British Commonwealth Organization of sovereign states that were former colonies under the British Empire.

caliph Title for Muslim rulers who claim to be the secular and religious successors of the Prophet Muhammad.

caliphate Muslim state ruled by a caliph.

caravel A small, maneuverable ship used by the Portuguese during the Age of Discovery.

caste A division of society based on wealth, privilege, rank, or occupation.

circumcision The cutting of the clitoris (also called clitorectomy or clitoridectomy) or the prepuce of the penis; a rite of passage in many African societies.

cire perdu French for "lost wax," a technique used to cast metals.

clan A group that traces its descent from a common ancestor.

conflict diamonds Gems that are sold or traded extra-legally in order to fund wars.

conquistadores Spanish for "conquerors"; term used to describe the Spanish leaders of the conquest of the Americas during the 1500s.

constitutional monarchy State with a constitution that is ruled by a king or queen.

customary law Established traditions, customs, or practices that govern daily life and interaction.

degredados Portuguese criminals who were sent to Africa by the Portuguese king to perform hazardous duties related to exploration and colonization.

dhow Arabic word for a wooden sailing vessel with a triangular sail that was commonly used to transport trade goods.

diaspora Word used to describe a large, readily distinguishable group of people settled far from their ancestral homelands.

divination The interpretation of supernatural signs, usually done by a medicine man or priest.

djembe African drum, often called "the healing drum" because of its use in healing ceremonies.

emir A Muslim ruler or commander.

emirate A state ruled by an emir.

endogamy Marriage within one's ethnic group, as required by custom or law.

enset Another name for the "false banana" plant common in Africa.

ethnic group Term used to signify people who share a common culture.

ethno-linguistic Word used to describe a group whose individuals share racial characteristics and a common language.

eunuch A man who has been castrated (had his testicles removed), generally so that he might be trusted to watch over a ruler's wife or wives.

francophone French speaking.

government transparency Feature of an open society in which the decisions and the policy-making process of leaders are open to public scrutiny.

griot Storyteller, common in West African cultures, who preserves and relates the oral history of his people, often with musical accompaniment.

gross domestic product (GDP) Total value of goods and services produced by a nation's economy, within that nation. GDP is measured within a certain time frame, usually a year.

gross national product (GNP) Total value of goods and services produced by the residents of a nation, both within the nation as well as beyond its borders. Like GDP, GNP is measured within a certain time frame, usually a year.

hajj In Islam, a pilgrimage to Mecca.

hajjiyy "Pilgrim" in Arabic.

hegira Arabic for "flight" or "exodus"; generally used to describe the move of the Muslim prophet Muhammad from Mecca to Medina.

hominid Biological term used to describe the various branches of the Hominidae, the family from which modern humans descend according to evolutionary theory.

ideology A coherent or systematic way of looking at human life and culture.

imam A spiritual and political leader of a Muslim state.

imamate The region or state ruled by an imam.

indigénat Separate legal code used by France in its judicial dealings with the indigenous African population of its colonies.

infidel Term used as an epithet to describe one who is unfaithful or an unbeliever with respect to a particular religion .

infrastructure Basic physical, economic, and social facilities and institutions of a community or country .

Janissary From the Turkish for "new soldier," a member of an elite Ottoman military corps.

jebel "Mountain" in Arabic.

kabaka The word for "king" in Babito and Buganda cultures.

kemet Egyptian for "black earth."

kora Small percussion instrument played by some griots.

kraal Enclosure for cattle or a group of houses surrounding such an enclosure.

lineage A group whose individuals trace their descent from a common ancestor; usually a subgroup of a larger clan.

lingua franca Common language used by speakers of different languages.

Luso-African Word that describes the combined Portuguese and African cultures, especially the offspring of Portuguese settlers and indigenous African women. (The Latin name for the area of the Iberian Peninsula occupied by modern Portugal was Lusitania.)

madrasa Theological school for the interpretation of Islamic law.

Mahdi Arabic word for "enlightened one," or "righteous leader"; specifically, the Muslim savior who, in Islamic belief, is to arrive shortly before the end of time.

mamluk Arabic for "one who is owned"; capitalized, it is a member of an elite military unit made up of captives enslaved and used by Islamic rulers to serve in Middle Eastern and North African armies.

mansa Mande term for "king" or "emperor."

marabout A mystical Muslim spiritual leader.

massif A mountainous geological feature.

mastaba Arabic for an inscribed stone tomb.

matrilineal Relating to descent on the maternal, or mother's, side.

medina Arabic word for the old section of a city.

megaliths Archaeological term meaning "large rocks"; used to describe stelae and such features as cairns and tumuli that mark important places or events for many ancient cultures.

mestizo Adjective meaning "of mixed blood."

mfecane Zulu word meaning "the crushing." When capitalized, the word refers to the nineteenth-century Zulu conquests that caused the mass migration of peoples in southern Africa.

microliths Archaeological term meaning "small rocks"; used to describe sharpened stone blade tools of Stone Age cultures.

Monophysite Related to the Christian tradition that holds that Jesus Christ had only one (divine) nature.

Moor An Arab or Berber conqueror of al-Andalus (Muslim Spain).

mulatto The offspring of a Negroid (black) person and a Caucasoid (white) person.

mwami Head of the Tutsi political structure, believed to be of divine lineage.

negusa negast "King of kings" in Ethiopic; traditional title given to the ruler of Ethiopia.

neocolonialism Political or economic policies by which former colonial powers maintain their control of former colonies.

Nilotic Relating to peoples of the Nile, or Nile River basin, used especially to describe the languages spoken by these peoples.

Nsibidi Secret script of the Ekoi people of Nigeria.

oba Yoruba king or chieftain.

pasha A high-ranking official in the Ottoman Empire.

pashalik Territory or province of the Ottoman Empire governed by a pasha.

pass book A feature of apartheid-era South Africa, pass books were identification documents that black Africans, but not whites, were required by law to carry at all times.

pastoralists People whose livelihood and society center on raising livestock.

patriarch Male head of a family, organization, or society.

patrilineal Relating to descent through the paternal, or father's, side.

poll tax A tax of a fixed amount per person levied on adults.

polygyny The practice of having more than one wife or female mate at one time.

prazeros Portuguese settlers in Africa who held prazos.

prazos Similar to feudal estates, parcels of land in Africa that were leased to Portuguese settlers by the Portuguese king.

primogeniture A hereditary system common in Africa by which the eldest child, or more commonly, the eldest son, receives all of a family's inheritance.

proverb A short popular expression or adage. Proverbs are tools for passing on traditional wisdom orally.

pygmy Greek for "fist," a unit of measurement; used to describe the short-statured Mbuti people.

qadi Arabic for "judge."

Quran (also spelled Koran) Arabic for "recitation," and the name of the book of Muslim sacred writings.

ras A title meaning "regional ruler" in Ethiopia.

rondavel Small, round homes common in southern Africa.

salaam Arabic for "peace."

sarki Hausa word for "king."

scarification Symbolic markings made by pricking, scraping, or cutting the skin.

secret society Formal organizations united by an oath of secrecy and constituted for political or religious purposes.

shantytowns A town or part of a town consisting mostly of crudely built dwellings.

sharia Muslim law, which governs the civil and religious behavior of believers.

sharif In Islamic culture, one of noble ancestry.

sheikh (shaykh, sheik) Arabic word for patrilineal clan leaders.

sirocco Name given to a certain type of strong wind in the Sahara Desert.

souk Arabic word for "market."

stelae Large stone objects, usually phallus-shaped, whose markings generally contain information important to those who produced them.

stratified Arranged into sharply defined classes.

stratigraphy The study of sequences of sediments, soils, and rocks; used by archaeologists to determine the approximate age of a region.

sultan The king or sovereign of a Muslim state.

sultanate The lands or territory ruled by a sultan.

syncretism The combining of religious beliefs to form a new religion.

taboo (adj.) forbidden by custom, usually because of the fear of retribution by supernatural forces; (n.) a prohibition based on morality or social custom.

tafsir Arabic for "interpretation," especially as regards the Quran.

taqwa In Islam, the internal ability to determine right from wrong.

taro Another name for the cocoyam, an edible tuber common throughout Africa.

tauf Puddled mud that, when dried, serves as the foundation for some homes in sub-Saharan Africa.

teff A grass native to Africa that can be threshed to produce flour.

theocracy Government of a state by officials who are thought to be guided by God.

ulamaa Islamic learned men, the inheritors of the tradition of the prophet Muhammad.

vizier A high-ranking official in a Muslim state, esp. within the Ottoman Empire.

SUGGESTED READINGS FOR INDEPENDENT AFRICA

Abbott, George C. *Debt Relief and Sustainable Development in Sub-Saharan Africa.* Brookfield, Vt.: E. Elgar, 1993.

Ajayi, J. F. A. and Crowder, Michael, eds. *History of West Africa.* 2 vols. Vol 2. 2nd ed. Burnt Mill, Harlow, Essex, England: Longman, 1987.

Barber, James. *Mandela's World: The International Dimension of South Africa's Political Revolution, 1990–1999.* Athens, Oh.: Ohio University Press, 2004.

Bargat, François, and William Dowell. *The Islamic Movement in North Africa.* 2nd ed.; Austin, Tex.: University of Texas Press, 1997.

Beck, Roger B. *The History of South Africa.* Westport, Conn.: Greenwood Press, 2000.

Berry, Sara. *No Condition is Permanent: The Social Dynamics of Agrarian Change in Sub-Saharan Africa.* Madison, Wisc: University of Wisconsin Press, 1993.

Birmingham, David. *Portugal and Africa.* Athens: Ohio University Press, 2004.

—————— and Martin, Phyllis M., eds. *History of Central Africa.* 2 vols. New York: Longman, 1983.

Bledsoe, Caroline H. *Contingent Lives: Fertility, Time, and Aging in West Africa.* Chicago: University of Chicago Press, 2002.

Bonner, Raymond. *At the Hand of Man: Peril and Hope for Africa's Wildlife.* New York: Random House, 1994.

Booth, Karen M. *Local Women, Global Science: Fighting AIDS in Kenya.* Bloomington: Indiana University Press, 2003.

Brett, Michael, and Fentress, Elizabeth. *The Berbers.* Malden, Mass.: Blackwell Publishing, 1997.

Brockington, Dan. *Fortress Conservation: The Preservation of the Mkomazi Game Reserve, Tanzania.* Bloomington: Indiana University Press, 2002.

Cabrit, Joao M. *Mozambique: The Tortuous Road to Democracy.* New York: Palgrave Macmillan, 2001.

Carmody, Padráig. *Tearing the Social Fabric: Neoliberalism, Deindustrialization, and the Crisis of Governance in Zimbabwe.* Westport, Conn: Heinemann, 2001.

Chafer, Tony. *The End of Empire in French West Africa: France's Successful Decolonization?* New York: Berg Publishers, 2002.

Charry, Eric. *Mande Music: Traditional and Modern Music of the Maninka and Mandinka of Western Africa.* Chicago: University of Chicago Press, 2000.

Ciment, James. *Algeria: The Fundamentalist Challenge.* New York: Facts on File, 1997.

Covell, Maureen. *Madagascar: Politics, Economy, and Society.* New York: F. Pinter, 1987.

Crisman, Thomas L., et al., eds. *Conservation, Ecology, and Management of African Freshwaters.* Gainesville: University Press of Florida, 2003.

Davis, R. Hunt Jr., ed. *Apartheid Unravels.* Gainesville: University of Florida Press, 1991.

Englebert, Pierre. *State Legitimacy and Development in Africa.* Boulder, Colo.: Lynne Rienner, 2002.

Entelis, John P. *Islam, Democracy and the State in North Africa.* Bloomington: Indiana University Press, 1997.

Erlich, Hoggai and Gershoni, Israel, eds. *The Nile: Histories, Cultures, Myths.* Boulder, Colo.: Lynne Rienner, 2000.

Falola, Toyin. *The History of Nigeria*. Westport, Conn.: Greenwood Press, 1999.

Feierman, Steven. Peasant *Intellectuals: Anthropology and History in Tanzania*. Madison: University of Wisconsin Press, 1990.

Forrest, Joshua B. *Lineages of State Fragility: Rural Civil Society in Guinea-Bissau*. Athens: Ohio University Press, 2004.

Gifford, Paul. *African Christianity: Its Public Role*. Bloomington: Indiana University Press, 1998.

Gondola, Didier. *The History of Congo*. Westport, Conn.: Greenwood Press, 2002.

Gordon, Jacob U. *African Leadership in the Twentieth Century*. Lanham, Md.: University Press of America, 2002.

Hale, Sondra. *Gender Politics in Sudan: Islamism, Socialism and the State*. Boulder, Colo.: Westview Press, 1996.

Hansen, Karen Tranberg. *Salaula: The World of Secondhand Clothing in Zambia*. Chicago: University of Chicago Press, 2000.

Harvey, Robert. *The Fall of Apartheid: The Inside Story from Smuts to Mbeki*. New York: Palgrave, 2003.

Haugerud, Angelique. *The Culture of Politics in Modern Kenya*. New York: Cambridge University Press, 1997.

Hodges, Tony. *Angola: The Anatomy of an Oil State*. 2nd ed. Bloomington, Ind.: Indiana University Press, 2003.

Holt, Peter Malcolm, and Daly, M. W. *The History of the Sudan, from the Coming of Islam to the Present Day*. 4th ed. New York: Longman, 1988.

Hopwood, Derek. *Habib Bourguiba of Tunisia: The Tragedy of Longevity*. New York: St. Martin's Press, 1992.

Hulme, David, and Marshall Murphree, eds. *African Wildlife and Livelihoods: The Promise and Performance of Community Conservation*. Westport, Conn: Heinemann, 2001.

Hyden, Goran, Hastings W. O. Okoth-Ogendo, and Bamidele Olowu, eds. *African Perspectives on Governance*. Trenton, N.J.: Africa World Press, 2000.

Hyden, Goran, Michael Leslie, and Folu F. Ogundimu, eds. *Media and Democracy in Africa*. New Brunswick, N.J.: Transaction Publishers, 2002.

Ihedru, Obioma M., ed. *Contendng Issue in African Development*. Westport, Conn.: Greenwood Press, 2001.

Iliffe, John. *The African Poor: A History*. New York: Cambridge University Press, 1987.

_____. *East African Doctors: A History of the Modern Profession*. New York: Cambridge University Press, 1998.

Isichei, Elizabeth Allo. *A History of Nigeria*. London: Longmans, 1983.

Iyob, Ruth. *The Eritrean Struggle for Independence: Domination, Resistance, Nationalism, 1941–1993*. New York: Cambridge University Press, 1995.

Jalloh, Alusine and Toyin Falola, eds. *Black Business and Economic Power in Africa*. Rochester, N.Y.: University of Rochester Press, 2002.

Janzen, John M. *Ngoma: Discourses of Healing in Central and Southern Africa*. Berkeley: Univ. of Calif. Press, 1992.

Johnson, Douglas H. *The Root Causes of Sudan's Civil Wars*. Bloomington, Ind.: Indiana University Press, 2003.

Jones, Bruce D. *Peacemaking in Rwanda: The Dynamics of Failure*. Boulder, Colo.: Lynne Rienner, 2001.

Kassem, Maye. *Egyptian Politics: The Dynamics of Authoritarian Rule*. Boulder, Colo.: Lynne Rienner, 2004.

Laremont, Ricardo René, ed. *The Cause of War and the Consequence of Peacekeeping in Africa*. Westport, Conn: Heinemann, 2001.

La Fontaine, J. S. *City Politics: A Study of Leopoldville, 1962–63*. New York: Cambridge University Press, 1970.

Lancaster, Carol. *Aid to Africa: So Much to Do, So Little Done*. Chicago: University of Chicago Press, 1999.

Lazreg, Marnia. *The Eloquence of Silence: Algerian Women in Question*. New York: Routledge, 1994.

Lemarchand, René, ed. *The Green and the Black: Qadhafi's Policies in Africa*. Bloomington: Indiana Univ. Press, 1988.

Leonard, David K. and Straus, Scott. *Africa's Stalled Development: International Causes and Cures*. Boulder, Colo.: Lynne Rienner, 2002.

Little, Peter D. *The Elusive Granary: Herder, Farmer, and State in Northern Kenya*. New York: Cambridge University Press, 1992.

_____. *Somalia: Economy Without State.* Bloomington: Indiana University Press, 2003.

Lodge, Tom. *Politics in South Africa: From Mandela to Mbeki.* Bloomington: Indiana University Press, 2003.

McMillan, Della E. *Sahel Visions: Planned Settlement and River Blindness Control in Burkina Faso.* Tucson: University of Arizona Press, 1995.

Manning, Patrick. *Francophone Sub-Saharan Africa, 1880–1995.* 2nd ed. New York: Cambridge University Press, 1998.

Marcus, Harold G. *A History of Ethiopia.* Berkeley: University of California Press, 1994.

Mazrui, Ali A. and Alamin M. Mazrui. *The Power of Babel: Language and Governance in the African Experience.* Chicago: University of Chicago Press, 1998.

Miller, James, and Jerome Bookin-Weiner. *Morocco: The Arab West* (Boulder, Ciolo.: Westview Press, 1998).

Mshomba, Richard E. *Africa in the Global Economy.* Boulder, Colo.: Lynne Rienner, 2000.

Nugent, Paul and A. I. Asiwaju, eds. *African Boundaries: Barriers, Conduits, and Opportunities.* New York: Pinter, 1996.

Nzongola-Ntalaja. *The Congo: From Leopold to Kabila: A People's History.* New York: Palgrave, 2002.

Osaghae, Eghosa E. *Crippled Giant: Nigeria Since Independence.* Bloomington: Indiana University Press, 1998.

Osei, Akwasi P. *Ghana: Recurrence and Change in a Post-independence African State.* New York: P. Lang, 1999.

O'Toole, Thomas. *The Central African Republic: The Continent's Hidden Heart.* Boulder: Westview Press, 1986.

Pankhurst, Richard. *The Ethiopians: A History.* London: Blackwell, 2001.

Peel, J. D. Y. *Religious Encounter and the Making of the Yoruba.* Bloomington: Indiana University Press, 2002.

Pennell, C. R., *Morocco since 1830: A History.* New York: New York University Press, 2000.

Petterson, Donald. *Inside Sudan: Political Islam, Conflict, and Catastrophe.* Boulder, Colo.: Westview Press, 1999.

Phiri, Isaac. *Proclaiming Political Pluralism: Churches and Political Transitions in Africa.* Westport, Conn: Praeger Publishers, 2001.

Pitcher, M. Anne. *Transforming Mozambique: The Politics of Privatization, 1975–2000.* New York: Cambridge University Press, 2002.

Quinn, John James. *The Road Oft Traveled: Developmental Policies and State Ownership of Industry in Africa.* Westport, Conn: Praeger Publishers, 2002.

Ruedy, John Douglas. *Modern Algeria: The Origins and Development of a Nation.* Bloomington: Indiana University Press, 1992.

Scherrer, Christian P. *Genocide and Crisis in Central Africa: Conflict Roots, Mass Violence, and Regional War.* Westport, Conn: Praeger Publishers, 2001.

Schmidt, Peter R. and Roderick J. McIntosh, eds. *Plundering Africa's Past.* Bloomington: Indiana University Press, 1996.

Sidahmed, Abdel Salam. *Politics and Islam in Contemporary Sudan.* New York: St. Martin's Press, 1996.

Singhal, Arvind and W. Stephen Howard. *The Children of Africa Confront AIDS.* Athens, Oh.: Ohio University Press, 2004.

Sparks, Alistair. *Beyond the Miracle: Inside the New South Africa.* Chicago: University of Chicago Press, 2003.

Spring, Anita and Barbara E. McDade, eds. *African Entrepreneurship: Theory and Reality.* Gainesville: University Press of Florida, 1998.

Stone, Martin. *The Agony of Algeria.* New York: Columbia University Press, 1997.

Tettey, Wisdom J., Korbla P. Puplampu, and Bruce J. Berman, eds. *Critical Perspectives in Politics and Socio-economic Development in Ghana.* Boston: Brill Academic Publishers, 2003.

Thomas, Linda E. *Under the Canopy: Ritual Process and Spiritual Resilience in South Africa.* Columbia: University of South Carolina Press, 1999.

Thomas-Emeagwali, Gloria, ed. *Science and Technology in African History with Case Studies from Nigeria, Sierra Leone, Zimbabwe and Zambia.* Lewiston, N.Y.: The Edwin Mellen Press, 1992.

Thompson, Leonard Monteath. *A History of South Africa.* 3rd ed. New Haven, Conn.: Yale University Press, 2001.

Turino, T. *Nationalists, Cosmopolitans, and Popular Music in Zimbabwe.* Chicago: Univ. of Chicago Press, 2000.

Vandewalle, Dirk. *Libya since Independence: Oil and State Building.* Ithaca, N.Y.: Cornell University Press, 1998.

Vaughan, Olufemi. *Nigerian Chiefs: Traditional Power in Modern Politics, 1890s–1990s.* Rochester, N.Y.: University of Rochester Press, 2000.

Villalón, Leonardo A., and Phillip A. Huxtable, eds. *The African State at a Critical Juncture: Between Disintegration and Reconfiguration.* Boulder, Colo.: Lynne Rienner, 1998.

Villalón, Leonardo A. *Islamic Society and State Power in Senegal.* New York: Cambridge University Press, 1995.

Waterman, Christopher Alan. *Jùjú: A social History and Ethnography of an African Popular Music.* Chicago: University of Chicago Press, 1990.

Weaver, Mary Anne. *A Portrait of Egypt.* New York: Farrar, Strauss & Giroux, 1999.

White, Luise. *The Assassination of Herbert Chitepo: Texts and Politics in Zimbabwe.* Bloomington: Indiana University Press, 2003.

Wright, Donald R. *The World and a Very Small Place in Africa: A History of Globalization in Niumi, the Gambia.* Armonk, N.Y.: M.E. Sharpe, 2004.

Wright, John. *Libya, a Modern History* Baltimore, Md.: Johns Hopkins University Press, 1982.

SUGGESTED READINGS FOR GENERAL STUDIES

Atlases

Ajayi, J. F. Ade, and Michael Crowder, eds. *Historical Atlas of Africa*. Harlow, Essex, England: Longman, 1985.

Freeman-Grenville, G. S. P. *The New Atlas of African History*. New York: Simon & Schuster, 1991.

Griffiths, Ieuan Ll. *The Atlas of African Affairs*. 2nd ed. New York: Routledge, 1994.

Kasule, Samuel. *The History Atlas of Africa*. New York: Macmillan, 1998.

McEvedy, Colin. *The Penguin Atlas of African History*. Rev. ed. London and New York: Penguin Books, 1995.

Murray, Jocelyn, ed. *Cultural Atlas of Africa*. New York: Checkmark Books, 1998.

Culture, Society, and Peoples

Allman, Jean, ed. *Fashioning Africa: Power and the Politics of Dress*. Bloomington: Indiana University Press, 2004.

Anderson, Martha G., and Mullen Kreamer, Christine. *Wild Spirits, Strong Medicine: African Art and the Wilderness*. New York: Basic Civitas Books, 1999.

Banham, Martin, James Gibbs, and Femi Osofisan, eds. *African Theatre: Playwrights and Politics*. Bloomington: Indiana University Press, 2001.

Barber, Karin, ed. *Readings in African Popular Culture*. Bloomington: Indiana University Press, 1997.

Bates, Daniel G. *Cultural Anthropology*. New York: Simon & Schuster, 1996.

Baur, John. *2000 Years of Christianity in Africa: An African History, 62–1992*. Nairobi, Kenya: Paulines, 1994.

Berger, Iris and White, E. Francis, eds. *Women in Sub-Saharan Africa*. Bloomington: Indiana Univ. Press, 1999.

Bodman, Herbert L. and Nayereh Tohidi, eds. *Women in Muslim Societies: Diversity Within Unity*. Boulder, Colo.: Lynne Rienner, 1998.

Diagram Group, The. *Encyclopedia of African Peoples*. New York: Facts On File, 2000.

Diawara, Manthia. *African Cinema: Politics and Culture*. Bloomington: Indiana University Press, 1992.

Elleh, Nnamdi. *African Architecture: Evolution and Transformation*. New York: McGraw-Hill, 1996.

Ephirim-Donkor, Anthony. *African Spirituality*. Trenton, N.J.: Africa World Press, 1998.

Feierman, Steven and John M. Janzen, eds. *The Social Basis of Health and Healing in Africa*. Berkeley: University of California Press, 1992.

Fisher, Robert B. *West African Religious Traditions*. Maryknoll, New York: Orbis Books, 1998.

Floyd, Samuel A., Jr. *The Power of Black Music*. New York: Oxford University Press, 1995.

Frobenius, Leo, and Fox, Douglas C. *African Genesis: Folk Tales and Myths of Africa*. New York: Dover Publications, 1999.

Hackett, Rosalind J. *Art and Religion in Africa*. London: Cassell, 1996.

Hiskett, Mervyn. *The Course of Islam in Africa*. Edinburgh: Edinburgh University Press, 1994.

Keita, J. H. Kwabena. *The Music of Africa.* New York: Norton, 1974.

Kubik, Gerhard. *Africa and the Blues.* Jackson: University Press of Mississippi, 1999.

Mbiti, John. *African Religions and Philosophy.* 2d ed. Oxford: Heinemann Educational Publishers, 1990.

Meyer, Laurie. *Art and Craft in Africa.* Paris: Terrail, 1995.

Peters, F. E. *The Hajj.* Princeton, N. J.: Princeton University Press, 1994.

Ray, Benjamin C. *African Religions: Symbol, Ritual, and Community,* 2d ed. Upper Saddle River, N.J.: Prentice Hall, 2000.

Rosen, Lawrence. *The Culture of Islam: Changing Aspects of Contemporary African Life.* Chicago: University of Chicago Press, 2002.

Sindima, Harvey J. *Drums of Redemption: An Introduction to African Christianity.* Westport, Conn.: Greenwood Press, 1994.

Thompson, Robert Farris. *Flash of the Spirit: African and Afro-American Art and Philosophy.* New York: Random House, 1984.

Vansina, Jan. *Art History in Africa: An Introduction to Method.* New York: Longman, 1984.

Verran, Helen. *Science and an African Logic.* Chicago: University of Chicago Press, 2001.

Willett, Frank. *African Art: An Introduction.* Rev. ed. New York: Thames and Hudson, 1993.

Zaslavsky, Claudia. *Africa Counts: Number and Pattern in African Cultures,* 3d ed. Chicago: Lawrence Hill Books, 1999.

History

Austen, Ralph A. *Africa in Economic History.* London: James Currey, 1996.

Azevedo, Mario Joaquim, Gerald W. Hartwig and K. David Patterson, eds. *Disease in African History: An Introductory Survey and Case Studies.* Durham, North Carolina: Duke University Press, 1978.

Berger, Iris and E. Frances White. *Women in Sub-Saharan Africa: Restoring Women to History.* Bloomington: Indiana University Press, 1999.

Curtin, Philip D., Steven Feierman, Leonard Thompson, and Jan Vansina. *African History: From Earliest Times to Independence.* 2nd ed. London and New York: Longman, 1995.

Davidson, Basil. *Africa in History.* New York: Touchstone, 1991.

_____. *African Civilization Revisited.* Trenton, New Jersey: Africa World Press, 1998.

Esposito, John L., ed. *The Oxford History of Islam.* New York, Oxford University Press, 2000.

Fage, John D., with William Tordoff. *A History of Africa.* 4th ed. London: Routledge, 2002.

Falola, Toyin, ed. *Africa. 5 vols. Vol. 5. Contemporary Africa.* Durham, N.C.: Carolina Academic Press, 2000.

Freund, Bill. *The Making of Contemporary Africa: The Development of African society since 1800.* 2nd ed. Boulder, Colo.: Lynne Rienner, 1998.

Harris, Joseph E. *Africans and Their History.* 2nd rev. ed. New York: Meridian Books, 1998

Iliffe, John. *Africans: The History of a Continent.* Cambridge, U.K.: Cambridge University Press, 1995.

Isichei, Elizabeth A. *A History of Christianity in Africa: From Antiquity to the Present.* Lawrenceville, N.J.: Africa World Press,1995.

July, Robert. *A History of the African People.* 5th ed. Prospect Heights, Ill.: Waveland Press, Inc., 1997.

Levtzion, Nehemia and Randall L. Pouwels, eds. *The History of Islam in Africa.* Athens: Ohio University Press, 2000.

McCann, James. *Green Land, Brown Land, Black Land: An Environmental History of Africa, 1800–1990.* Westport, Conn.: Heinemann, 1999.

Olaniyan, Richard, ed. *African History and Culture.* Harlow, Essex, U.K.: Longman, 1982.

Oliver, Roland, and Atmore, Anthony. *Africa since 1800.* New York: Cambridge University Press, 1994.

Ransford, Oliver. *Bid the Sickness Cease: Disease in the History of Black Africa*. London : J. Murray, 1983.

Reader, John. *Africa: A Biography of the Continent*. New York: Alfred A. Knopf, 1998.

Rodney, Walter. *How Europe Underdeveloped Africa*. Rev. ed. Washington, D.C.: Howard University Press, 1981.

Shillington, Kevin. *History of Africa*. New York: St. Martins Press, 1995.

Sweetman, David. *Women Leaders in African History*. Exeter, N.H.: Heinemann, 1984.

Geography

Adams, William M., Andrew S. Goudi, and Antony R. Orme. *The Physcial Geography of Africa*. New York: Oxford University Press, 1996.

Binns, Tony. *People and Environment in Africa*. New York: Wiley, 1995.

Grove, A. T. *The Changing Geography of Africa*. New York: Oxford University Press, 1993.

Newman, James L. *The Peopling of Africa: A Geographic Interpretation*. New Haven, Conn.: Yale Univ. Press, 1995.

Smith, Anthony. *The Great Rift: Africa's Changing Valley*. London: BBC Books, 1988.

Other Works

Azevedo, Mario, ed. *Africana Studies: A Survey of Africa and the African Diaspora*. 2nd ed. Durham, N.C.: Carolina Academic Press, 2004.

Bates, Robert H., V. Y. Mudimbe, and Jean O'Barr. *Africa and the Disciplines*. Chicago: University of Chicago Press, 1993.

Booker, M. Keith. *The African Novel in English: An Introduction*. Portsmouth, N.H.: Heinemann, 1998.

Falola, Toyin, and Jennings, Christian, eds. *Africanizing Knowledge: African Studies Across the Disciplines*. New Brunswick, N.J.: Transaction Publishers, 2002.

Falola, Toyin and Steven J. Salm. *Globalization and Urbanization in Africa*. Trenton, N.J. : Africa World Press, 2004.

Gordon, April A., and Donald L. Gordon. *Understanding Contemporary Africa*. 3rd ed. Boulder, Colo.: Lynne Rienner Publishers, 1996.

Griffiths, Ieuan Ll. *The African Inheritance*. New York: Routledge, 1995.

Hallen, Barry. *A Short History of African Philosophy*. Bloomington: Indiana University Press, 2002.

Hansen, Art, and Della E. McMillan, eds. *Food in Sub-Saharan Africa*. Boulder, Colo.: Lynne Rienner Publishers, 1986.

Isichei, Elizabeth. *Voices of the Poor in Africa*. Rochester, N.Y.: University of Rochester Press, 2002.

Khapoya, Vincent B. *The African Experience: An Introduction*. 2d ed. Upper Saddle River, N.J.: Prentice Hall, 1994.

Killam, Douglas and Ruth Rowe, eds., *The Companion to African Literatures*. Bloomington: Indiana University Press, 2000.

Legum, Colin. *Africa Since Independence*. Bloomington: Indiana University Press, 1999.

Martin, Phyllis M. and Patrick O'Meara. *Africa*. 3d ed. Bloomington, Ind., 1995.

Mazrui, Ali A. *The Africans: A Triple Heritage*. London: BBC Publications, 1986.

Middleton, John, ed. *Encyclopedia of Africa South of the Sahara*. 4 Vols. New Haven, Conn.: Yale University Press, 1998.

Nurse, Derek, and Heine, Bernd. *African Languages: An Introduction*. New York: Cambridge University Press, 2000.

Phillipson, David W. *African Archaeology*. 2nd ed. New York: Cambridge University Press, 1994.

Rake, Alan. *African Leaders: Guiding the New Millennium*. Lanham, Md.: Scarecrow Press, 2001.

Rwomire, Apollo. *Social Problems in Africa: New Visions*. Westport, Conn: Praeger Publishers, 2001.

Teferra, Damtew, and Philip G. Altbach. *African Higher Education: An International Reference Handbook.* Bloomington: Indiana University Press, 2003.

Tordoff, William. *Government and Politics in Africa.* 4th ed. Bloomington, Ind.: Indiana University Press, 2002.

Country Studies

There are three series of specific country studies which readers can consult for more detailed studies of individual African countries.

The on-going African Historical Dictionaries series published by Scarecrow Press, with 53 volumes in the African series to date. An example of the volumes available is:

Bobb, F. Scott. *Historical Dictionary of Democratic Republic of the Congo (Zaire).* Lanham, Md.: Scarecrow Press, 1999.

The World Bibliographic Series published by ABC-Clio Press, with 53 volumes. The series has ceased publication. An example of the volumes available is:

Lawless, Richard I., compiler, *Algeria.* Revised ed. Santa Barbara, Calif.: Clio Press, 1995.

The Federal Research Division of the Library of Congress has published individual handbooks for 22 African countries under the Country Studies/Area Handbook Program sponsored by the U.S. Department of Army. An example of the volumes available is:

Metz, Helen C., ed. *Nigeria, A Country Study.* 5th ed. Washington, D.C.: Federal Research Division, Library of Congress, 1992.

INDEX FOR THIS VOLUME

Bold page numbers indicate main entries. Page numbers followed by the letter *c* refer to a timeline; the letter *f* refers to illustrations; and the letter *m* indicates a map.

CUMULATIVE INDEX

Bold roman numerals and page numbers indicate main entries. Page numbers followed by the letter *c* refer to a timeline; the letter *f* refers to illustrations; the letter *m* indicates a map; and the letter *t* indicates a table.